An Introduction to
Management Science

Quantitative Approaches to Decision Making

SIXTH EDITION

An Introduction to Management Science

Quantitative Approaches to Decision Making

SIXTH EDITION

David R. Anderson
University of Cincinnati

Dennis J. Sweeney
University of Cincinnati

Thomas A. Williams
Rochester Institute of Technology

WEST PUBLISHING COMPANY
St. Paul ▼ New York ▼ Los Angeles ▼ San Francisco

COPYRIGHT © 1976, 1979, 1982, 1985, 1988, 1991 by WEST PUBLISHING CO.
50 West Kellogg Boulevard
P.O. Box 64526
St. Paul, Minnesota 55164–0526

98 97 96 95 94 93 92 91   8 7 6 5 4 3 2 1

Library of Congress Cataloging in Publication Data

Anderson, David Ray, 1941–
    An introduction to management science: quantitative
    approaches to decision making/David R. Anderson, Dennis
    J. Sweeney, Thomas A. Williams.—6th ed.
    p.   cm

    Includes bibliographical references (p.   ) and index.
    ISBN 0-314-79321-6
    1. Management Science. I. Sweeney, Dennis J. II. Williams,
Thomas Arthur, 1944- . III. Title.
HD30.25.A53 1991
658.4′03—dc20

                                    90-19477
                                  CIP ∞

To Our Parents

Contents

Preface

The purpose of this sixth edition, as with previous editions, is to provide students with a sound conceptual understanding of the role that management science plays in the decision-making process. The focus is on the part of management science referred to as quantitative approaches to decision making. The text describes the many quantitative methods that have been developed over the years, explains how they work, and shows how they can be applied and interpreted by the decision maker.

We have written this book with the needs of the nonmathematician in mind; it is applications oriented. In each chapter a problem is described in conjunction with the quantitative procedure being introduced. The development of the quantitative technique or model includes applying it to the problem in order to generate a solution or recommendation. We have found that this approach helps to motivate the student by demonstrating not only how the procedure works, but also how it can contribute to the decision-making process.

Changes in the Sixth Edition

In preparing the sixth edition we have been careful to maintain the overall format and approach of the previous editions. However, based upon our own classroom experience and suggestions from users of previous editions, a number of significant changes have been made to enhance the content, managerial orientation, and readability of the text.

Notes and Comments Notes and comments have been added at the end of many sections of the text. In an introductory treatment of a subject such as management science it is not possible to provide a complete coverage of all managerial issues and technical details. The purpose of the notes and comments feature is to mention additional issues we think students should be aware of and/or to note a technical detail that could cause some difficulty in applying the material.

Linear Programming Applications A new section on data envelopment analysis has been added to Chapter 4. Data envelopment analysis is a linear programming based techique that is rapidly gaining in popularity for evaluating the efficiency of comparable organizations. It has been used extensively in franchise operations and in the not-for-profit sector. We believe the number of applications have reached the point where students can benefit from being exposed to data envelopment analysis in an introductory course. A new case and new problems have also been added to this chapter.

Multicriteria Decision Making   A new Chapter 15 on multicriteria decision making has been added. In recent years we have seen a growing recognition that methods for dealing with multiple, often noncommensurable, criteria are needed. An expanded treatment of goal programming is included in this chapter. We show that the philosophy of preemptive priorities is consistent with many decision making processes and how linear programming methodology can be employed to solve goal programming problems with preemptive priorities. The chapter also includes an introduction to the analytic hierarchy process and expert choice.

Waiting Line Models   The material on waiting line models has been expanded considerably. Also, at the request of several users, we now treat waiting lines before computer simulation. The major change to the waiting lines chapter has been to extend coverage to additional situations that occur in practice. Even though the mathematics are sometimes difficult, the situations being modeled are easily understood by students. The Management Scientist software package has also been extended to handle the new models.

Transportation, Assignment, and Transshipment Problems   The treatments of the transportation, assignment, and transshipment problems have been unified around the notion of a network flow model. In the first three sections of Chapter 7, we show the network flow models of these problems and how easy it is to develop a linear programming model from the graphical network representation. The fourth section shows the use of the transshipment model for a production and inventory scheduling problem. This emphasizes the fact that applications do not always involve shipment of goods from one point to another.

The last two sections of the chapter detail special purpose solution procedures for the transportation and assignment problems. The material on the transportation simplex algorithm has been completely rewritten to provide a more unified treatment. A phase I, phase II approach is employed. Phase I is described as the phase where heuristics are used to find a feasible solution; the minimum-cost method is demonstrated. Phase II is explained as an interative procedure for moving from the initial feasible solution to the optimal solution. The MODI method is used to find a route to bring into solution and the stepping-stone method is used to find the route leaving the solution and to adjust the flow over the transportation network.

The Management Scientist Software Package Revised   Version 2.0 of The Management Scientist is available to adopters. It is also available shrinkwrapped with the text at a small additional charge. Version 2.0 includes a number of improvements. The most notable improvements are increased solution speed for transportation and assignment problems, the addition of several new waiting line models, and redesign of menus to enhance the user friendliness of all modules.

Other Changes   A variety of other changes have been made throughout the text. All of them cannot be listed here, but we will mention a few.

1. The introduction provides a more in depth discussion of the problem solving and decision making processes.
2. The inventory chapter now includes a section on periodic review models. The chapter ending application details how SuperX, Inc. uses this approach. A new section on just-in-time is also included.

3. The Management Scientist computer printouts are used in the linear programming chapters. An appendix to Chapter 3 also shows how LINDO/PC is used. LINDO/PC continues to be used in the integer programming chapter.

Prerequisite

The mathematical prerequisite for this text is a course in algebra. An introductory knowledge of probability and statistics would be desirable, but not necessary, for Chapters 10–14 and 16, 17. Only Chapter 19, which discusses calculus-based solution procedures and which we consider optional, requires a knowledge of differential calculus.

Throughout the text we have utilized generally accepted notation for the topic being covered. Thus students who pursue study beyond the level of this text should find the difficulties of reading more advanced material minimized. To assist in further study, a bibliography is included in the backmatter of the book.

Course Outline Flexibility

The text has been designed to enhance the instructor's flexibility in selecting topics to meet specific course needs. The single-quarter and single-semester outlines that follow are a sampling of the many options available.

One-quarter outline stressing linear programming, model development, and applications.

Introduction (Chapter 1)
Introduction to Linear Programming (Chapters 2 and 3)
Linear Programming Applications (selected portions of Chapters 4 and 7)
Project Management: PERT/CPM (Chapter 10)
Waiting Lines (Chapter 12)
Computer Simulation (Chapter 13)
Decision Analysis (Chapter 14)

The instructor in a one-semester course who wants to focus on model development and other applications could either spend more time on the applications in Chapter 4 or cover additional topics. One possible outline, stressing linear programming, model development, and applications, would be

Introduction (Chapter 1)
Introduction to Linear Programming (Chapters 2 and 3)
Linear Programming Applications (Chapter 4)
Simplex Method (Chapters 5 and 6)
Transportation, Assignment, and Transshipment Models (Chapter 7)
Project Management: PERT/CPM (Chapter 10)
Inventory Models (Chapter 11)
Waiting Lines (Chapter 12)
Computer Simulation (Chapter 13)
Decision Analysis (Chapter 14)
Multicriteria Decision Making (Chapter 15)

Ancillaries

A complete package of support materials accompanies the text: a Solutions Manual; a Study Guide, coauthored by John A. Lawrence and Barry Alan Pasternack, California State University at Fullerton; a Test Bank, prepared by Constance McLaren, Indiana State University; transparency masters; and *The Management Scientist*™ Version 2.0, an IBM-compatible software package capable of solving a variety of management science problems. This menu-driven software package has been revised for the sixth edition and has been designed to provide a high degree of user flexibility, including the ability to easily save and modify problems. We believe that the applications orientation of the text, combined with this package of support materials, provides a solid framework for introducing students to management science.

Acknowledgments

We owe a debt to many of our colleagues and friends for their helpful comments and suggestions during the development of this and previous editions. Among these are Robert L. Armacost, E. Leonard Arnoff, Uttarayan Bagchi, Edward Baker, Norman Baker, James Bartos, Richard Beckwith, Stanley Brooking, Jeffrey Camm, Thomas Case, John Eatman, Ron Ebert, Don Edwards, Peter Ellis, Lawrence Ettkin, Jim Evans, Robert Garfinkel, Damodar Golhar, Stephen Goodman, Jack Goodwin, Richard Gunther, Nicholas G. Hall, David Hott, Raymond Jackson, Muhannad Khawaja, Bharat Kolluri, Darlene Lanier, John Lawrence, Jr., Phillip Lowery, Prem Mann, Kamlesh Mathur, Joseph Mazzola, Richard McCready, Patrick McKeown, Constance McLaren, Edward Minieka, Richard C. Morey, Alan Neebe, Brian F. O'Neil, David Pentico, Gary Pickett, B. Madhusudan Rao, Handanhal V. Ravinder, Douglas V. Rippy, Richard Rosenthal, Carol Stamm, Willban Terpening, William Truscott, James Vigen, Ed Winkofsky, Bruce Woodworth, M. Zafer Yakin, and Cathleen Zucco.

Our associates from organizations who supplied the Management Science in Practice applications made a major contribution to the text. These individuals are cited in a credit line on the first page of each application.

We are also indebted to our editor, Mary Schiller, production editor, Tad Bornhoft, and others at West Publishing Company for their editorial counsel and support during the preparation of this text.

David R. Anderson
Dennis J. Sweeney
Thomas A. Williams

An Introduction to Management Science

Quantitative Approaches to Decision Making

SIXTH EDITION

Introduction

Management science (MS), an approach to managerial decision making that is based on scientific method, makes extensive use of quantitative analysis. A variety of names exists for the body of knowledge involving quantitative approaches to decision making; in addition to management science, another widely known and accepted name is *operations research* (OR). Today many use the terms *operations research* and *management science* interchangeably. We shall treat them as synonyms throughout the text.

The scientific management revolution of the early 1900s, initiated by Frederic W. Taylor, provided the foundation for MS/OR. But modern management science/operations research is generally considered to have originated during the World War II period, when operations research teams were formed to deal with strategic and tactical problems faced by the military. These teams, which often consisted of people with diverse specialties (e.g., mathematicians, engineers, behavioral scientists, etc.), were joined together to solve a common problem through the utilization of the scientific method. After the war many of these team members continued their research on quantitative approaches to decision making.

Two developments, which occurred during the post–World War II period, led to the growth and use of management science in nonmilitary organizations. First, continued research on quantitative approaches to decision making resulted in numerous methodological developments. Probably the most significant development was the discovery by George Dantzig, in 1947, of the simplex method for solving linear programming problems. Many more methodological developments followed, and, in 1957, the first book on operations research was published by Churchman, Ackoff, and Arnoff.[1]

Concurrently with these methodological developments there was a virtual explosion in computing power made available through digital computers. Computers enabled practitioners to implement the methodological advances successfully to solve a large variety of industrial problems. The computer technology explosion continues; microcomputers are now more powerful than the mainframe computers of the 1960s. Today variants of the

---

[1]C. W. Churchman, R. L. Ackoff, and E. L. Arnoff, *Introduction to Operations Research* (New York: John Wiley & Sons, 1957).

post–World War II methodological developments are being used on microcomputers to solve problems larger than those solved on mainframe computers in the 1970s.

1.1 ▼ PROBLEM SOLVING AND DECISION MAKING

Problem solving can be defined as the process of identifying a difference between some actual and some desired state of affairs and then taking action to resolve the difference. For problems important enough to justify the time and effort of careful analysis, the problem-solving process involves the following seven steps:

1. Identify and define the problem.
2. Determine the set of alternative solutions.
3. Determine the criterion or criteria that will be used to evaluate the alternatives.
4. Evaluate the alternatives.
5. Choose an alternative.
6. Implement the selected alternative.
7. Evaluate the results, and determine if a satisfactory solution has been obtained.

Decision making is the term generally associated with the first five steps of the problem-solving process. Thus, the first step of decision making is to identify and define the problem. Decision making ends with the choosing of an alternative, which is the act of making the decision.

Let us consider the following example of a decision-making process. For the moment assume that you will be graduating from college in the next few months, that you have completed the interviewing process, and that you have been lucky enough to receive job offers from four companies. Your problem is that you are currently unemployed and that you would like a position that will lead to a satisfying career.

Once the problem of obtaining a position that will lead to a satisfying career has been defined, the next step in the decision-making process is to identify the set of alternatives available. Assume that the alternatives available to you are these four job offers: one from a company located in Rochester, New York; one from a company located in Dallas, Texas; one from a company located in Greensboro, North Carolina; and one from a company located in Pittsburgh, Pennsylvania. Thus, the alternatives for your decision problem can be stated as follows:

1. Accept the position offered by the company located in Rochester, New York.
2. Accept the position offered by the company located in Dallas, Texas.
3. Accept the position offered by the company located in Greensboro, North Carolina.
4. Accept the position offered by the company located in Pittsburgh, Pennsylvania.

The next phase of the problem-solving process involves determining the criterion or criteria that will be used to evaluate the four alternatives. Obviously the starting salary is going to be a factor of some importance. If this were the only criterion of importance to you, the alternative selected as ''best'' would be the one with the highest starting salary. Problems in which the objective is to find the best solution with respect to one criterion are referred to as *single-criterion* decision problems.

For the current problem suppose that you have also concluded that the potential for advancement and the location of the job are two other criteria of major importance. Thus, the three criteria in your decision problem are starting salary, potential for advancement, and location. Problems that involve more than one criterion are referred to as *multicriteria* decision problems.

TABLE 1.1
Data for the Job Evaluation Decision-Making Problem

Alternative	Starting Salary	Potential for Advancement	Job Location
Rochester	$28,500	Average	Fair
Dallas	$26,000	Excellent	Average
Greensboro	$26,000	Good	Excellent
Pittsburgh	$27,000	Average	Good

The next step of the decision-making process is to evaluate each of the alternatives with respect to each criterion. For example, evaluating each alternative relative to the starting salary criterion is done simply by recording the starting salary for each job alternative. Evaluating each alternative with respect to the potential for advancement and the location of the job is more difficult to do, however, since these evaluations are based primarily on subjective factors that are oftentimes difficult to quantify. Assume for now that you have decided to measure potential for advancement and job location by rating each of these criteria as poor, fair, average, good, or excellent. The data that you have compiled are shown in Table 1.1.

You are now ready to make a choice from the available alternatives. What makes this choice phase so difficult is that the criteria are probably not all equally important, and no one alternative is "best" with regard to all criteria. Although we will present a method for dealing with situations like this later in the text, for now let us suppose that after a careful evaluation of the data in Table 1.1, you have decided to select alternative 3; thus, alternative 3 is referred to as the *decision*.

At this point in time, the decision-making process is complete. In summary, we see that this process involves five steps:

1. Define the problem.
2. Identify the alternatives.
3. Determine the criteria.
4. Evaluate the alternatives.
5. Choose an alternative.

Note that missing from this list are the last two issues in the problem solving process: implementing the selected alternative and evaluating the results in order to determine if a satisfactory solution has been obtained. This is meant not to diminish the importance of each of these activities, but to emphasize the more limited scope of the term *decision making* as compared to the term *problem solving*. Figure 1.1 summarizes the relationship between these two concepts.

Although decision making can take place in any setting, management science is an approach that is applicable primarily to decision making in a managerial context. Experts in decision making such as Herbert Simon indicate that in order "to understand what is involved in decision making that term has to be interpreted broadly—so broadly as to become almost synonymous with managing."[2] As we begin to look more carefully at the

[2]H.A. Simon, *The New Science of Decision Making,* rev. ed. (Englewood Cliffs, N.J.: Prentice-Hall, 1977), p. 39.

FIGURE 1.1
The Relationship Between Problem Solving and Decision Making

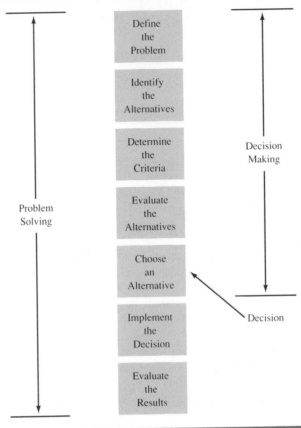

role of management science in decision making, we will concentrate our attention on problems that practicing managers might encounter in their roles as decision makers.

1.2 ▼ QUANTITATIVE ANALYSIS AND THE DECISION-MAKING PROCESS

Consider the flowchart presented in Figure 1.2. Note that we have combined the first three phases of the decision-making process under the heading of "Structuring the Problem" and the latter two phases under the heading "Analyzing the Problem." Let us now consider in more detail how to carry out the set of activities that make up the decision-making process.

Figure 1.3 shows that the analysis phase of the decision-making process may take on two basic forms: qualitative and quantitative. Qualitative analysis is based primarily on the manager's judgment and experience; it includes the manager's intuitive "feel" for the problem and is more an art than a science. If the manager has had experience with similar problems, or if the problem is relatively simple, heavy emphasis may be placed upon a qualitative analysis. However, if the manager has had little experience with similar prob-

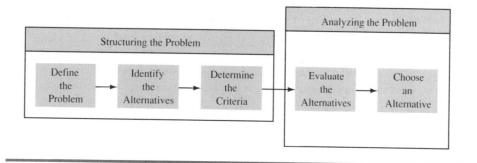

FIGURE 1.2
An Alternate Classification of the Decision-Making Process

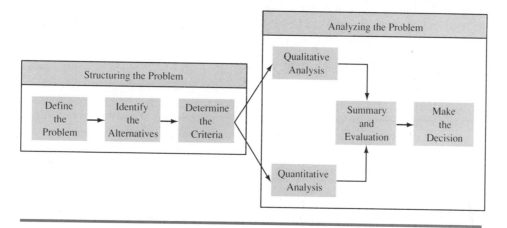

FIGURE 1.3
The Role of Qualitative and Quantitative Analysis

lems, or if the problem is sufficiently complex, then a quantitative analysis of the problem can be a very important consideration in the manager's final decision.

When using the quantitative approach, an analyst will concentrate on the quantitative facts or data associated with the problem and develop mathematical expressions that describe the objectives, constraints, and relationships that exist in the problem. Then, by using one or more quantitative methods, the analyst will provide a recommendation based on the quantitative aspects of the problem.

While skills in the qualitative approach are inherent in the manager and usually increase with experience, the skills of the quantitative approach can be learned only by studying the assumptions and methods of management science. A manager can increase decision-making effectiveness by learning more about quantitative methodology and by better understanding its contribution to the decision-making process. The manager who is knowledgeable in quantitative decision-making procedures is in a much better position to compare and evaluate the qualitative and quantitative sources of recommendations and ultimately to combine the two sources in order to make the best possible decision.

The box in Figure 1.3 entitled "Quantitative Analysis" encompasses most of the subject matter of this text. We will consider a managerial problem, introduce the appropriate quantitative methodology, and then develop the recommended decision.

In closing this section, let us briefly state some of the reasons why a quantitative approach might be used in the decision-making process:

1. The problem is complex, and the manager cannot develop a good solution without the aid of quantitative analysis.
2. The problem is very important (for example, a great deal of money is involved), and the manager desires a thorough analysis before attempting to make a decision.
3. The problem is new, and the manager has no previous experience to draw on.
4. The problem is repetitive, and the manager saves time and effort by relying on quantitative procedures to make the routine decision recommendations.

1.3 ▼ THE QUANTITATIVE ANALYSIS PROCESS

The problem definition step of the decision-making process is the most critical component in determining the success or failure of any quantitative approach to decision making. It usually takes imagination, teamwork, and considerable effort to transform a rather general problem description into a well-defined problem that can be approached quantitatively. For example, a broadly described excessive inventory problem must be clearly defined in terms of specific objectives and operating constraints before an analyst can begin the quantitative analysis process.

To be successful in applying the quantitative approach to decision making, the management scientist must work closely with the manager or user of the results. When both the management scientist and the manager agree that the problem has been adequately defined, the management scientist will begin work on developing a model that can be used to represent the problem mathematically. Solution procedures can then be developed for the model in order to select the decision that "best" solves the problem.

Model Development

Models are representations of real objects or situations. These representations, or models, can be presented in various forms. For example, a scale model of an airplane is a representation of a real airplane. Similarly, a child's toy truck is a model of a real truck. The model airplane and toy truck are examples of models that are physical replicas of real objects. In modeling terminology, physical replicas are referred to as *iconic* models.

A second classification of models includes those that are physical in form, but that do not have the same physical appearance as the object being modeled. Such models are referred to as *analog* models. The speedometer of an automobile is an analog model; the position of the needle on the dial represents the speed of the automobile. A thermometer is another analog model representing temperature.

A third classification of models—the primary type of model we will be studying—includes those that represent a problem by a system of symbols and mathematical relationships or expressions. Such models are referred to as *mathematical* models and are a critical part of any quantitative approach to decision making. For example, the total profit from the sale of a product can be determined by multiplying the profit per unit by the quantity sold. If we let x represent the number of units sold and P the total profit, then, with a profit of $10 per unit, the following mathematical model defines the total profit earned by selling x units:

$$P = 10x \tag{1.1}$$

The purpose, or value, of any model is that it enables us to draw conclusions about the real situation by studying and analyzing the model. For example, an airplane designer might test an iconic model of a new airplane in a wind tunnel in order to learn about the potential flying characteristics of the full-size airplane. Similarly, a mathematical model may be used to draw conclusions about how much profit will be earned if a specified quantity of a particular product is sold. According to the mathematical model of equation (1.1), we would expect to obtain a $30 profit by selling three units of the product.

In general, experimenting with models requires less time and is less expensive than experimenting with the real object or situation. Certainly, a model airplane is quicker and less expensive to build and study than the full-size airplane. Similarly, the above mathematical model allows a quick identification of profit expectations without requiring the manager actually to produce and sell x units. Models also have the advantage of reducing the risk associated with experimenting with the real situation. In particular, bad designs or bad decisions that cause the model airplane to crash or a mathematical model to project a $10,000 loss can be avoided in the real situation.

The accuracy of the conclusions and decisions based on a model are dependent on how well the model represents the real situation. The more closely the model of the airplane represents the real airplane, the more accurate the conclusions and predictions about the airplane's flight characteristics will be. Similarly, the closer the mathematical model represents the company's true profit–volume relationship, the more accurate the profit projections will be.

Since this text deals with mathematical models, let us look more closely at the mathematical modeling process. When initially considering a managerial problem, we usually find that the problem definition phase leads to a specific objective, such as maximization of profit or minimization of cost, and possibly a set of restrictions or constraints, such as production capacities. The success of the mathematical model and quantitative approach will depend heavily on how accurately the objective and constraints can be expressed in terms of mathematical equations or relationships.

A mathematical expression that describes the problem's objective is referred to as the *objective function*. For example, the profit equation $P = 10x$ would be an objective function for a firm attempting to maximize profit. A production capacity constraint would be necessary if, for instance, 5 hours are required to produce each unit and there are only 40 hours available per week. Let x indicate the number of units produced each week. The production time constraint is given by

$$5x \le 40 \tag{1.2}$$

The value of $5x$ is the total time required to produce the x units; the symbol $\le$ indicates that the production time required must be less than or equal to the 40 hours available.

The question or decision problem is the following: How many units of the product should be scheduled each week in order to maximize profit? A complete mathematical model for this simple production problem is

$$\begin{array}{ll} \text{maximize} & P = 10x \qquad \text{objective function} \\ \text{subject to (s.t.)} & \\ & \left. \begin{array}{l} 5x \le 40 \\ x \ge 0 \end{array} \right\} \quad \text{constraints} \end{array}$$

The $x \ge 0$ constraint requires the production quantity x to be greater than or equal to zero, which simply recognizes the fact that it is not possible to manufacture a negative number of units. The optimal solution to this model can be easily calculated and is given by $x = 8$, with an associated profit of $80. This model is an example of a linear programming model. In subsequent chapters we will discuss more complicated mathematical models and learn how to solve them in situations where the answers are not nearly so obvious.

In the above mathematical model the profit per unit ($10), the production time per unit (5 hours), and the production capacity (40 hours) are environmental factors that are not under the control of the manager or decision maker. Such environmental factors, which can affect both the objective function and the constraints, are referred to as the *uncontrollable inputs* to the model. The inputs that are controlled or determined by the decision maker are referred to as the *controllable inputs* to the model. In the above example, the production quantity x is the controllable input to the model. The controllable inputs are the decision alternatives specified by the manager and thus are also referred to as the *decision variables* of the model.

Once all controllable and uncontrollable inputs are specified, the objective function and constraints can be evaluated and the output of the model determined. In this sense, the output of the model is simply the projection of what would happen if those particular environmental factors and decisions occurred in the real situation. A flowchart of how controllable and uncontrollable inputs are transformed by the mathematical model into output is shown in Figure 1.4. A similar flowchart showing the specific details of the production model is shown in Figure 1.5.

As stated earlier, the uncontrollable inputs are those the decision maker cannot influence. The specific controllable and uncontrollable inputs of a model depend on the particular problem or decision-making situation. In the production problem the production time available, 40, is an uncontrollable input. However, if it were possible to hire more employees or use overtime, the number of hours of production time would become a controllable input and therefore a decision variable in the model.

Uncontrollable inputs either can be known exactly or can be uncertain and subject to variation. If all uncontrollable inputs to a model are known and cannot vary, the model is referred to as a *deterministic* model. Corporate income tax rates are not under the influence of the manager and thus constitute an uncontrollable input in many decision models. Since these rates are known and fixed (at least in the short run), a mathematical model with corporate income tax rates as the only uncontrollable input would be a deterministic model. The distinguishing feature of a deterministic model is that the uncontrollable input values are known in advance.

If any of the uncontrollable inputs are uncertain and subject to variation, the model is referred to as a *stochastic* or *probabilistic* model. An uncontrollable input to many

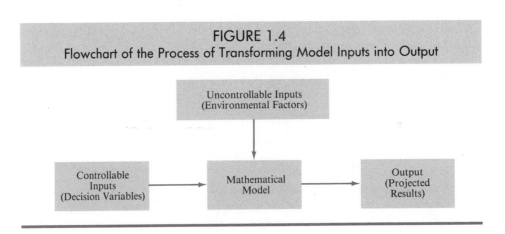

FIGURE 1.4
Flowchart of the Process of Transforming Model Inputs into Output

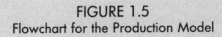

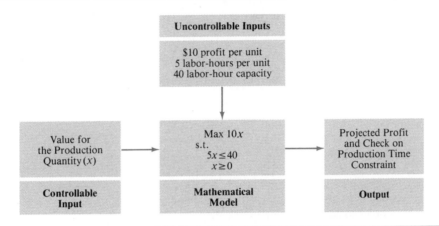

FIGURE 1.5
Flowchart for the Production Model

production planning models is demand for the product. Since future demand may be any of a range of values, a mathematical model that treats demand with uncertainty would be called a stochastic model. In the production model the number of hours of production time required per unit, the total hours available, and the unit profit were all uncontrollable inputs. Since the uncontrollable inputs were all known to take on fixed values, the model is deterministic. If, however, the number of hours of production time per unit could vary from 3 to 6 hours depending on the quality of the raw material, the model would be stochastic. The distinguishing feature of a stochastic model is that the value of the output cannot be determined even if the value of the controllable input is known because the specific values of the uncontrollable inputs are unknown. In this respect, stochastic models are often more difficult to analyze.

Data Preparation

The next step in the process of quantitative analysis is the preparation of the data required by the model. Data in this sense refer to the values of the uncontrollable inputs to the model. All uncontrollable inputs or data must be specified before we can analyze the model and select a recommended decision or solution for the problem.

In the production model the values of the uncontrollable inputs or data were $10 per unit for profit, 5 hours per unit for production time, and 40 hours for production capacity. In the development of the model these data values were known and were incorporated into the model as it was being developed. If the model is relatively small and the uncontrollable input values or data required are few, the quantitative analyst will probably combine model development and data preparation into one step. That is, in these situations the data values are inserted as the equations of the mathematical model are developed.

However, in many mathematical modeling situations the data, or uncontrollable input values, are not readily available. In these situations the management scientist may know that the model will need profit per unit, production time, and production capacity data, but the values are not known until the accounting, production, and engineering departments can be consulted. Rather than attempting to collect the required data as the model is being developed, the analyst will usually adopt a general notation for the model development step and then perform a separate data preparation step to obtain the uncontrollable input values required by the model.

Using the general notation

$$c = \text{profit per unit}$$
$$a = \text{production time in hours per unit}$$
$$b = \text{production capacity in hours}$$

the model development step of the production problem would result in the following general model:

$$\max cx$$
$$\text{s.t.}$$
$$ax \leq b$$
$$x \geq 0$$

Then a separate data preparation step to identify the values for c, a, and b would be necessary in order to complete the model.

Many inexperienced quantitative analysts assume that once the problem has been defined and a general model developed, the problem is essentially solved. These individuals tend to believe that data preparation is a trivial step in the process and can be easily handled by clerical staff. Actually, especially with large-scale models that have numerous data input values, this assumption could not be farther from the truth. For example, a moderate-size linear programming model with 50 decision variables and 25 constraints will have over 1300 data elements that must be identified in the data preparation step. The time required to prepare these data and the possibility of data collection errors will make the data preparation step a critical part of the quantitative analysis process. Often a fairly large database is needed to support a mathematical model, and information systems specialists become involved in the data preparation step.

Model Solution

Once the model development and data preparation steps have been completed, we can proceed to the model solution step. In this step the analyst will attempt to identify the values of the decision variables that provide the "best" output for the model. The specific decision-variable value or values providing the "best" output will be referred to as the *optimal solution* for the model. For the production problem the model solution step involves finding the value of the production quantity decision variable x that maximizes profit while not causing a violation of the production capacity constraint.

One procedure that might be used in the model solution step involves a trial-and-error approach, where the model is used to test and evaluate various decision alternatives. In the production model this would mean testing and evaluating the model under various production quantities or values of x. Referring to Figure 1.5, note that we could input trial values for x and check the corresponding output for projected profit and satisfaction of the production capacity constraint. If a particular decision alternative does not satisfy one or more of the model constraints, the decision alternative is rejected as being *infeasible*, regardless of the objective function value. If all constraints are satisfied, the decision alternative is *feasible* and is a candidate for the "best" solution or recommended decision. Through this trial-and-error process of evaluating selected decision alternatives, a decision maker can identify a good—and possibly the best—feasible solution to the problem. This solution would then be the recommended decision for the problem.

Table 1.2 shows the results of a trial-and-error approach to solving the production model of Figure 1.5. The recommended decision is a production quantity of 8 since the feasible solution with the highest projected profit occurs at $x = 8$.

While the trial-and-error solution process is often acceptable and can provide valuable information for the manager, it has the drawbacks of not necessarily providing the best solution and of being inefficient in terms of requiring numerous calculations if many decision alternatives are tried. Thus, quantitative analysts have developed special solution procedures for many models that are much more efficient than the trial-and-error approach. Throughout this text you will be introduced to solution procedures that are applicable to the specific mathematical models that will be formulated. While some relatively small models or problems can be solved by hand computations, most practical applications require the use of a computer.

It is important to realize that the model development and model solution steps are not completely separable. While an analyst will want to develop an accurate model or representation of the actual problem situation, the analyst will also want to be able to find a solution to the model. If we approach the model development step by attempting to find the most accurate and realistic mathematical model, we may find the model so large and complex that it is impossible to obtain a solution. In this case a simpler and perhaps more easily understood model with a readily available solution procedure is preferred even if the recommended solution is only a rough approximation of the best decision. As you learn more about quantitative solution procedures, you will have a better idea of the types of mathematical models that can be developed and solved.

After a model solution has been obtained, both the management scientist and the manager will be interested in determining how good the solution really is. While the analyst has undoubtedly taken many precautions to develop a realistic model, often the goodness or accuracy of the model cannot be assessed until model solutions are generated. Model testing and validation are frequently conducted with relatively small "test" problems that have known or at least expected solutions. If the model generates the expected solutions, and if other output information appears correct, the go-ahead may be given to use the model on the full-scale problem. However, if the model test and validation identify potential problems or inaccuracies inherent in the model, corrective action, such as model modification and/or collection of more accurate input data, may be taken. Whatever the corrective action, the model solution will not be used in practice until the model has satisfactorily passed testing and validation.

TABLE 1.2
Trial-and-Error Solution for the Production Model of Figure 1.5

Decision Alternative (Production Quantity) x	Projected Profit	Total Hours of Production	Feasible Solution? (capacity = 40)
0	0	0	Yes
2	20	10	Yes
4	40	20	Yes
6	60	30	Yes
8	80	40	Yes
10	100	50	No
12	120	60	No

Report Generation

The final step in the quantitative analysis process is the preparation of managerial reports based on the model's solution. Referring to Figure 1.3, we see that the solution based on the quantitative analysis of a problem is one of the inputs that is considered by the manager before making a final decision. Thus, it is essential that the results of the model appear in a managerial report that can be easily understood by the decision maker. The report will include the recommended decision and other pertinent information about the model results that may be helpful to the decision maker.

A Note Regarding Implementation

Although the generation of a managerial report is the final step in the quantitative analysis process, the implementation of the information contained in the report is a final action that remains to be taken by the manager or decision maker. As discussed in Section 1.2, it is the responsibility of the manager to integrate the quantitative solution with qualitative considerations in order to make the best possible decision. After doing this, the manager must oversee the implementation and follow-up evaluation of the decision. During the implementation and follow-up the manager should continue to monitor the contribution of the model. At times, this process may lead to requests for model expansion or refinement that will cause the management scientist to return to one of the earlier steps of the quantitative analysis process.

Successful implementation of results is of critical importance to the management scientist as well as the manager. If the results of the quantitative analysis process are not implemented, the entire effort may be of no value. It doesn't take too many unsuccessful implementations before the management scientist is out of work. Because implementation often requires people to do things differently (and more effectively, one hopes), it often meets with resistance. People want to know, ''What's wrong with the way I've been doing it?'' and so on. One of the most effective ways to ensure a successful implementation is to secure as much user involvement as possible throughout the modeling process. If the user feels he/she has been involved in identifying the problem and developing the solutions, he/she is much more likely to enthusiastically implement the results. The success rate for implementing the results of a management science project is much greater for those projects in which there has been extensive user involvement.

1.4 ▼ MANAGEMENT SCIENCE IN PRACTICE

In this section we present a brief overview of the management science techniques covered in this text. We will then present the results of surveys that show which techniques have been used most frequently in practice and what needs to be done to enable you to successfully utilize quantitative approaches throughout your career.

Management Science Techniques

The following management science techniques are covered in this text.

Linear Programming Linear programming is a problem-solving approach that has been developed for situations involving maximizing or minimizing a linear function subject to linear constraints that limit the degree to which the objective can be pursued. The production model developed in the previous section (see Figure 1.5) is an example of a simple linear programming model.

Integer Linear Programming Integer linear programming is an approach used for problems that can be set up as linear programs with the additional requirement that some or all of the decision recommendations be integer values.

Network Models A network is a graphical description of a problem consisting of circles called nodes that are interconnected by lines called arcs. Specialized solution procedures exist for these types of problems, enabling us to quickly solve many managerial problems in such areas as transportation system design, information system design, and project scheduling.

Project Management: PERT/CPM In many situations managers assume the responsibility for planning, scheduling, and controlling projects that consist of numerous separate jobs or tasks performed by a variety of departments, individuals, etc. PERT and CPM are techniques for helping managers carry out their project management responsibilities.

Inventory Models Inventory models are used to help managers faced with the dual problems of maintaining sufficient inventories to meet demand for goods and, at the same time, incurring the lowest possible inventory holding costs.

Waiting Line or Queueing Models Waiting line or queueing models have been developed to help managers understand and make better decisions concerning the operation of systems involving waiting lines.

Computer Simulation Computer simulation is a technique used to model the operation of a system over time. This technique employs a computer program to model the operation and perform simulation computations.

Decision Analysis Decision analysis can be used to determine optimal strategies in situations involving several decision alternatives and an uncertain or risk-filled pattern of events.

Goal Programming Goal programming is a technique for solving multicriteria decision problems, usually within the framework of linear programming.

Analytic Hierarchy Process A multicriteria decision-making technique that permits the inclusion of subjective factors in arriving at a recommended decision.

Forecasting Forecasting methods are techniques that can be used to help predict future aspects of a business operation.

Markov Process Models Markov process models are useful in studying the evolution of certain systems over repeated trials. For example, Markov processes have been used to describe the probability that a machine that is functioning in one period will continue to function or break down in another period.

Dynamic Programming Dynamic programming is an approach that allows us to break up a large problem in such a fashion that once all the smaller problems have been solved, we are left with an optimal solution to the large problem.

TABLE 1.3
The Utilization of Management Science and Operations Research Methodologies

| | Frequency of Use (% of respondents) | | |
	Never	Moderate	Frequent
Statistical	1.6	38.7	59.7
Computer simulation	12.9	53.2	33.9
PERT/CPM	25.8	53.2	21.0
Linear programming	25.8	59.7	14.5
Queueing theory	40.3	50.0	9.7
Nonlinear programming	53.2	38.7	8.1
Dynamic programming	61.3	33.9	4.8
Game theory	69.4	27.4	3.2

Methods Used Most Frequently

A survey of corporate executives conducted by Forgionne[3] indicated how often a variety of management science techniques are used. As Table 1.3 shows, the most frequently used techniques are statistical methods, computer simulation, PERT/CPM, linear programming, and queueing theory. A survey by Ledbetter and Cox[4] lends further support to these findings by ranking regression (statistical analysis), linear programming, simulation, network models (PERT/CPM), queuing, dynamic programming, and game theory in order of usage.

A survey by Thomas and DaCosta[5] showed that 88 percent of all large corporations use forecasting and over 50 percent use quantitative approaches to production scheduling, inventory control, capital budgeting, and transportation. A study conducted by Gaither[6] of the applications of management science in manufacturing firms also supports the high frequency of utilization for statistical analysis, simulation, and linear programming. However, PERT/CPM is identified as the method most frequently used in the manufacturing firms surveyed. The manufacturing firms also report a higher than average usage of queueing theory, nonlinear programming, and integer programming.

As part of a survey of practitioners in government, industry, and academia, Shannon, Long, and Buckles[7] asked practitioners to indicate whether or not they were familiar with the various quantitative methods and whether or not they had actually used the methods in specific applications. The results, which are shown in Table 1.4, provide further support that linear programming, simulation, network analysis, and queueing theory are perhaps the most frequently known and utilized management science techniques.

[3]G.A. Forgionne, "Corporate Management Science Activities," *Interfaces* 13, n. 3 (1983):20–23.
[4]W. Ledbetter and J. Cox, "Are OR Techniques Being Used?" *Industrial Engineering* 9, no. 2 (1977):19–21.
[5]G. Thomas and J. DaCosta, "A Sample Survey of Corporate Operations Research," *Interfaces* 9, no. 4 (1979):102–11.
[6]N. Gaither, "The Adoption of Operations Research Techniques by Manufacturing Organizations," *Decision Sciences* 6, no. 4 (1975):797–813.
[7]R. E. Shannon, S. S. Long, and B. P. Buckles, "Operations Research Methodologies in Industrial Engineering: A Survey," *AIIE Transactions* 12, no. 4 (1980):364–67.

TABLE 1.4
Familiarity with and Use of Various Quantitative Methods by
Management Science Practitioners

Method	Familiarity Rank	Usage (%)
Linear programming	1	83.8
Simulation	2	80.3
Network analysis	3	58.1
Queueing theory	4	54.7
Decision trees	5	54.7
Integer programming	6	38.5
Dynamic programming	7	32.5
Nonlinear programming	8	30.7
Markov processes	9	31.6
Replacement analysis	10	38.5
Game theory	11	13.7
Goal programming	12	20.5

Implications for the Use of Management Science

Recently, Morgan[8] reviewed 12 company surveys and 3 practitioner surveys that have been conducted in the last 30 years, including each of the studies referred to above. Her analysis provided further support that PERT/CPM, linear programming, and simulation are among the most frequently used methods. More importantly, however, after critical examination of all the survey results, she concluded that (1) any firm just beginning to use management science techniques should locate analysts in the functional areas, not in centralized units; (2) the initial use of management science should focus on the more frequently used and more useful techniques; and (3) the barriers to the use of management science can best be removed by increasing the manager's understanding of management science techniques. Furthermore, in order to gain the confidence and support of top management, MS/OR analysts must learn to sell their approaches and solutions, with particular emphasis placed on improving communications with managers.

Helping to bridge the gap between the manager and the MS/OR analyst is a major focus of this text. As authors, and MS/OR practitioners, we want to help develop an understanding of what the management science techniques are, how they are used, and, most importantly, how they can assist managers throughout their careers in making better decisions.

1.5 ▼ A MICROCOMPUTER SOFTWARE PACKAGE

As stated earlier, developments in computer technology have been a major factor in making quantitative methods available to decision makers. Currently microcomputer soft-

[8]C. L. Morgan, "A Survey of MS/OR Surveys," *Interfaces* 19, no. 6 (1989):95–103.

ware packages of quantitative methods are making many techniques easier to use. A software package called *The Management Scientist* has been prepared to accompany this text. It can be used to solve problems in the text as well as small-scale problems encountered in practice. Working with this software package will give you an understanding of the role of the computer in applying quantitative methods to decision problems.

The Management Scientist software package contains modules, or programs, that will enable you to solve problems in the following chapters and topical areas:

Chapters 2–6	Linear programming
Chapter 7	Transportation and assignment problems
Chapter 8	Integer linear programming
Chapter 9	Shortest route and minimal spanning tree
Chapter 10	PERT/CPM
Chapter 11	Inventory models
Chapter 12	Waiting-line models
Chapter 14	Decision analysis
Chapter 16	Forecasting
Chapter 17	Markov processes

Use of The Management Scientist with this text is optional. Occasionally we will insert a figure in the text that will show the output The Management Scientist would have provided for the problem being solved. But, familiarity with the software is not necessary to understand the figure. If you decide to use The Management Scientist software package, it will come with directions for installing the package on your microcomputer. The remainder of this section provides an introductory description of the software package.

Top Level Menu

After installing and starting to run The Management Scientist software, you will encounter the Top Level Menu shown in Figure 1.6. The choices on the menu provide access to the corresponding modules, or programs. Simply enter the number of your selection, press "Return," and the requested module will be loaded into the computer's memory.

FIGURE 1.6
Top-Level Menu of The Management Scientist Software Package

```
                    THE MANAGEMENT SCIENTIST

                        Top Level Menu

    1   Linear Programming              7   PERT/CPM

    2   Transportation                  8   Inventory Models

    3   Assignment                      9   Waiting Lines

    4   Integer Linear Programming     10   Decision Analysis

    5   Shortest Route                 11   Forecasting

    6   Minimal Spanning Tree          12   Markov Processes

                    13   EXIT PROGRAM
```

When you have obtained the solution information from the module selected, the program will return you to the Top Level Menu. At this point you may select another module or select menu choice 13, which will let you exit the package.

All of the programs in The Management Scientist are menu-driven. At various steps of all modules, menus will appear on the screen. By entering the number corresponding to your choice, you will be able to proceed as desired with the analysis and solution.

Problem Selection Menu

After you select a module from the Top Level Menu, the module will load into the computer's memory and a title screen for the module will be displayed. The title screen contains a brief description of the types of problems the module can be used to solve.

After the title screen appears, you may press "Return," to obtain the problem selection menu, such as the one shown for the assignment problem in Figure 1.7. From the problem selection menu you may choose to create a new problem, retrieve a previously saved problem from a data disk, continue with the current problem, delete a previously saved problem on a data disk, or exit the module by returning to the Top Level Menu.

Data Input

Anytime a problem is being considered for the first time, you must select the option to create a new problem from the problem selection menu (see Figure 1.7). The module will then guide you through the data input process by displaying prompts that indicate the information or data to be entered. By first studying the quantitative method in the text, you should easily understand the information or data prompts displayed by the module.

Problem Disposition Menu

Once a problem has been created, The Management Scientist will display the problem disposition menu. From this menu you may choose to solve the problem, display/edit the problem, or return to the problem selection menu. If you choose to solve the problem, The Management Scientist will solve the problem and display the solution on the screen.

FIGURE 1.7
Opening Menu for the Assignment Problem Module of
The Management Scientist Software Package

```
            PROBLEM SELECTION MENU

        Choices

            1    Create a New Problem

            2    Retrieve a Previously Saved Problem

            3    Continue with the Current Problem

            4    Delete a Previously Saved Problem

            5    Return to the Top Level Menu
```

Solution and Output Information

The type of information provided and its interpretation varies with the module selected. By reading the corresponding chapter in the text, you should be able to interpret the output information. After the solution and other output information have been displayed on the screen, you will be provided with the option of deciding whether or not to send the information to the printer. If you choose to obtain printed output, input data as well as the solution information will be printed.

Data Editing

Occasionally during the data input process you may strike the wrong key or numerical value and then press "Return." This will enter the incorrect value into the program. However, by selecting the display/edit option from the problem disposition menu you will be given the opportunity to modify or change any of the original input data.

Saving, Retrieving, and/or Deleting Problems

The Management Scientist allows you to save problems for future use on a data disk. You will be given the opportunity to specify the disk drive to be used for problem saving when you initially start up the software package. Thereafter, the problem saving option on the problem disposition menu can be used to save a problem on the selected disk drive. If this option is selected you will be provided with instructions for naming the problem. The problem will be saved automatically, using the name specified.

When reentering the module at a later date, the Retrieve option from the problem selection menu will let you recall a previously saved problem. Simply enter the name of the saved problem, and it will be loaded and become active in the module. When you no longer need access to a particular problem, the Delete option from the problem selection menu can be used to erase the problem from your data disk.

Further Advice about Data Input

When using The Management Scientist, you may find the following data input suggestions helpful.

1. Do not enter commas (,) with your input data. For example, to enter the numerical value of 104,000, simply type the six digits 104000.
2. Do not enter the dollar sign ($) for profit or cost data. For example, a cost of $20.00 should be entered as 20.
3. Do not enter the percent sign (%) if percentage input is requested. For a percentage of 25%, simply enter 25. Do not enter 25% or 0.25.
4. If the computer did not interpret your input correctly (for example, you tried to input a comma), the message "Redo from start" may appear. This message refers to the input question or prompt you are currently responding to. The message means to respond to the same question or prompt again.
5. For data values containing the digit zero, be sure to enter the numeric 0 rather than the letter O.
6. Occasionally a quantitative model will be formulated with fractional values such as $1/4$, $2/3$, $5/6$, and so on. The data input for the computer must be in decimal form. The fraction of $1/4$ can be entered as .25. However, the fractions $2/3$ and $5/6$ have repeating

decimal forms. In cases such as these we recommend the convention of rounding to five places. Thus, the corresponding decimal values of .66667 and .83333 should be entered.

7. Finally, we recommend that in general you attempt to scale extremely large input data so that smaller numbers may be input and operated on by the computer. For example, a cost of $2,500,000 may be scaled to 2.5 with the understanding that the data used in the problem reflect millions of dollars.

▼ SUMMARY

This is a book about how management science may be used to help managers make better decisions. The focus of the text is on the decision-making process and on the role of management science in that process. We have discussed the problem orientation of this process and in an overview have shown how mathematical models can be used in this type of analysis.

The difference between the model and the situation or managerial problem it represents is an important point. Mathematical models are abstractions of real-world situations and, as such, cannot capture all the aspects of the real situation. However, if a model can capture the major relevant aspects of the problem and provide a solution recommendation, it can be a valuable aid to decision making.

One of the characteristics of management science that will become increasingly apparent as we proceed through the text is the search for a best solution to the problem. In carrying out the quantitative analysis, we shall be attempting to develop procedures for finding the ''best'' or optimal solution.

▼ GLOSSARY

Problem solving   The process of identifying a difference between some actual and some desired state of affairs and then taking action to resolve the difference.

Decision making   The process of defining the problem, identifying the alternatives, determining the criteria, evaluating the alternatives, and choosing an alternative.

Decision   The alternative selected.

Single criterion decision problem   A problem in which the objective is to find the ''best'' solution with respect to just one criterion.

Multicriteria decision problem   A problem that involves more than one criterion; the objective is to find the ''best'' solution, taking into account all the criteria.

Model   A representation of a real object or situation.

Iconic model   A physical replica or representation of a real object.

Analog model   While physical in form, an analog model does not have a physical appearance similar to the real object or situation it represents.

Mathematical model   Mathematical symbols and expressions used to represent a real situation.

Objective function   A mathematical expression used to represent the criterion for evaluating solutions to a problem.

Constraints   Restrictions or limitations imposed on a problem.

Controllable input   The decision alternatives or inputs that can be specified by the decision maker.

Uncontrollable input   The environmental factors or inputs that cannot be controlled by the decision maker.

Deterministic model   A model in which all uncontrollable inputs are known and cannot vary.

Stochastic model   A model in which at least one uncontrollable input is uncertain and subject to variation; stochastic models are also referred to as **probabilistic models.**

Feasible solution   A decision alternative or solution that satisfies all constraints.

Infeasible solution   A decision alternative or solution that violates one or more constraints.

▼ PROBLEMS

1. Define the terms *management science* and *operations research*.
2. Describe the major reasons for the growth in the use of management science since World War II.
3. Discuss the different roles played by the qualitative and quantitative approaches to managerial decision making. Why is it important for a manager or decision maker to have a good understanding of both of these approaches to decision making?
4. A firm has just completed a new plant that will produce over 500 different products, using over 50 different production lines and machines. The product scheduling decisions are critical in that sales will be lost if customer demands are not met on time. If no individual in the firm has had experience with this production operation, and if new production schedules must be generated each week, why should the firm consider a quantitative approach to the production scheduling problem?
5. List and discuss the steps of the quantitative analysis process.
6. Give an example of each of the three types of models discussed in this chapter: iconic, analog, and mathematical.
7. What are the advantages of analyzing and experimenting with a model as opposed to a real object or situation?
8. Recall the production model from Figure 1.5:

$$\max\ 10x$$
$$\text{s.t.}$$
$$5x \leq 40$$
$$x \geq 0$$

Suppose the firm in this example considers a second product that has a unit profit of $5 and requires 2 hours for each unit produced. Use y as the number of units of product 2 produced.

   a. Show the mathematical model when both products are considered simultaneously.
   b. Identify the controllable and uncontrollable inputs for this model.
   c. Draw the flowchart of the input–output process for this model (see Figure 1.5).
   d. What are the optimal solution values of x and y?
9. Is the model developed in problem 8 a deterministic or a stochastic model? Explain.
10. Suppose we modify the model in Figure 1.5 to obtain the following mathematical model:

$$\max\ 10x$$
$$\text{s.t.}$$
$$ax \leq 40$$
$$x \geq 0$$

where a is the number of hours required for each unit produced. With $a = 5$, the optimal solution is $x = 8$. If we have a stochastic model with $a = 3, a = 4, a = 5$, or $a = 6$ as the possible values for the number of hours required per unit, what is the optimal value for x? What problems does this stochastic model cause?

11. A retail store in Des Moines, Iowa, receives shipments of a particular product from Kansas City and Minneapolis. Let

$$x = \text{units of product received from Kansas City}$$
$$y = \text{units of product received from Minneapolis}$$

  a. Write an expression for the total units of product received by the retail store in Des Moines.
  b. Shipments from Kansas City cost $.20 per unit, and shipments from Minneapolis cost $.25 per unit. Develop an objective function representing the total cost of shipments to Des Moines.
  c. Assuming the monthly demand at the retail store is 5000 units, develop a constraint that requires 5000 units to be shipped to Des Moines.
  d. No more than 4000 units can be shipped from Kansas City, and no more than 3000 units can be shipped from Minneapolis in a month. Develop constraints to model this situation.
  e. Of course, negative amounts cannot be shipped. Combine the objective function and constraints developed to state a mathematical model for satisfying the demand at the Des Moines retail store at minimum cost.

12. Suppose you are going on a weekend trip to a city that is d miles away. Develop a model that determines your round-trip gasoline costs. What assumptions or approximations do you have to make in order to treat this model as a deterministic model? Are these assumptions or approximations acceptable to you?

13. For most products, higher prices result in a decreased demand, whereas lower product prices result in an increased demand. Let

$$d = \text{annual demand for a product in units}$$
$$p = \text{price per unit}$$

Assume that a firm accepts the following price–demand relationship as being realistic:

$$d = 800 - 10p$$

where the price p must be between $20 and $70.
  a. How many units can the firm sell at the $20 per-unit price? At the $70 per-unit price?
  b. Show the mathematical model for the total revenue (TR), which is the annual demand multiplied by the unit price.
  c. Based on other considerations, the firm's management will only consider price alternatives of $30, $40, and $50. Use your model from part (b) to determine the price alternative that will maximize the total revenue.
  d. What are the expected annual demand and the total revenue according to your recommended price?

14. Suppose that a manager has a choice between the following two mathematical models of a given situation: (a) a relatively simple model that is a reasonable approximation

of the real situation and (b) a thorough and complex model that is the most accurate mathematical representation of the real situation possible. Why might the model described in (a) be preferred by the manager?

 15. The O'Neill Shoe Manufacturing Company will produce a special-style shoe if the order size is large enough to provide a reasonable profit. For each special-style order the company incurs a fixed cost of $1000 for the production setup. The variable cost is $30 per pair, and each pair sells for $40.

   a. Let x indicate the number of pairs of shoes produced. Develop a mathematical model for the total cost of producing x pairs of shoes.

   b. Let P indicate the total profit. Develop a mathematical model for the total profit realized from an order for x pairs of shoes.

   c. How large must the shoe order be before O'Neill will break even?

16. Financial Analysts, Inc., is an investment firm that manages stock portfolios for a number of clients. A new client has just requested that the firm handle an $80,000 portfolio. As an initial investment strategy the client would like to restrict the portfolio to a mix of the following two stocks:

Stock	Price/ Share	Estimated Annual Return/Share	Maximum Possible Investment
Oil Alaska	$50	$6	$50,000
Southwest Petroleum	$30	$4	$45,000

Let

$$x = \text{number of shares of Oil Alaska}$$

$$y = \text{number of shares of Southwest Petroleum}$$

   a. Develop the objective function, assuming that the client desires to maximize the total annual return.

   b. Show the mathematical expression for each of the following three constraints:

     (1) Total investment funds available are $80,000.

     (2) Maximum Oil Alaska investment is $50,000.

     (3) Maximum Southwest Petroleum investment is $45,000.

Note: Adding the $x \geq 0$ and $y \geq 0$ constraints provides a linear programming model for the investment problem. A solution procedure for this model will be discussed in Chapter 2.

17. Models of inventory systems frequently consider the relationships among a beginning inventory, a production quantity, a demand or sales, and an ending inventory. For a given production period j, let

$$s_{j-1} = \text{ending inventory from the previous period}$$
$$\text{(beginning inventory for period } j)$$
$$x_j = \text{production quantity in period } j$$
$$d_j = \text{demand in period } j$$
$$s_j = \text{ending inventory for period } j$$

a. Write the mathematical relationship or model that describes how the above four variables are related.

b. What constraint should be added if production capacity for period j is given by C_j?

c. What constraint should be added if safety stock requirements for period j mandate an ending inventory of at least I_j?

INTRODUCTION TO CHAPTER ENDING MANAGEMENT SCIENCE IN PRACTICE

Management Science in Practice write-ups prepared by practitioners are presented at the end of 15 chapters. We feel these provide a meaningful extension to the text material. The purpose of these application write-ups is to provide the reader with a better appreciation for the types of companies that use management science and the types of problems these companies are able to solve.

Each Management Science in Practice write-up begins with a description of the company involved and continues with a discussion of the areas where the company has successfully applied quantitative methods. The remainder of the write-up deals with an application that is closely related to the preceding chapter and/or part of the book. An effort has been made to avoid unnecessary technical detail and to focus on the managerial aspects and the value of the results to the company.

Since Chapter 1 is designed to provide an introduction to management science, we have not emphasized any particular solution methodology. Thus, we have placed the Mead Corporation write-up at the end of this first chapter because it provides an overview of several areas in which management science can be used effectively. It is evidence of the impact quantitative approaches to decision making are having at some companies.

Mead Corporation*
Dayton, Ohio

Mead Corporation is basically a forest products company that manufactures paper, pulp, and lumber; converts paperboard into shipping containers and beverage carriers; and distributes paper, school supplies, and stationery. Mead is also a major distributor of pipe, valves, and other industrial materials to refineries, petrochemical and power plants, and oil-well drillers. Mead is the nation's leading independent producer of ductile iron castings for automobiles and construction equipment. The company also makes rubber products for the exploration and production of gas and oil. Mead's Advanced Systems Group develops businesses for the future, including storing, retrieving, printing, and reproducing data through the innovative application of digital technology.

MANAGEMENT SCIENCE AT MEAD CORPORATION

Management science applications at Mead are developed and implemented by the company's Operations Research (OR) Department. The OR Department provides timely, efficient internal consulting services to the operating groups and corporate staff in the functional areas of operations, finance, marketing, and human resources. The department assists decision makers by providing them with analytical tools of management science as well as personal analysis and recommendations. Through conversations and observations, the department recognizes needs where management science techniques are applicable and recommends appropriate projects. In addition, the department provides a resource reservoir for information and assistance on quantitative methodology and assumes responsibility for keeping current in management science techniques that could produce efficiencies at Mead. This charter results in a variety of projects and applications that span the corporation. Four examples of management science applications at Mead are described below.

A CORPORATE PLANNING SYSTEM

The OR Department built and maintains a corporate planning system. This system allows business units to create and evaluate their five-year plans in an interactive computer environment.

Once the individual business units have finished their planning, the system consolidates the information at a group level. The assumptions of the units and the group are evaluated and reconciled. The use of this computer model facilitates this process by ensuring uniformity of calculations and reporting by all the

*The authors are indebted to Dr. Edward P. Winkofsky, Mead Corporation, Dayton, Ohio, for providing this application.

planning units. Ultimately, the information is consolidated and evaluated at a corporate level.

A TIMBERLAND-FINANCING MODEL

Another example of a management science application involves the development of a timberland-financing model. Working directly with financial management, analysts assisted in the creation of a deterministic model that considered the major factors in a timberland-financing arrangement. The model was used to examine the liability and profitability of timberland acquisition under various assumptions concerning forest growth rates, the inflation rate, and other financial considerations. By using the model, management was able to examine fully the acquisition and modify the financial arrangement as operating conditions warranted. The model is currently operated and modified by financial management and is considered a major tool in the examination of timberland financing.

INVENTORY ANALYSIS

Inventory analysis is an area in which more sophisticated tools of management science have been used. Simulation models have been used to describe the major factors (e.g., demand or usage rates, lead times, production rates, etc.) in an inventory system. Typical costs included in an inventory model are purchase, storage, ordering, stockout, and degradation costs. The simulation model is used to evaluate reorder points, safety stocks, customer service levels, review periods, and the response time of the inventory system to extraordinary events.

Once developed and in place, the model can be updated as economic and operating conditions change. Thus, the model can be used by management to evaluate its inventory system on an ongoing basis and to ensure that it is operating in a cost-efficient manner. These inventory simulation models are user friendly and can be operated and maintained by management with little formal computer training.

A TIMBER-HARVESTING MODEL

Mead has also used models to assist with the long-range management of the company's timberland. Through the use of large-scale linear programs, timber-harvesting plans have been developed to cover a substantial time horizon. These models consider wood market conditions, mill pulpwood requirements, harvesting capacities, and general forest management principles. Within these constraints the model develops an optimal harvesting and purchasing schedule based on discounted cash flow. Alternative schedules are developed to reflect various assumptions concerning forest growth, wood availability, and general economic conditions.

Quantitative methods are also used in the development of the inputs for the linear programming models described above. Timber prices and supplies as well as mill requirements must be forecast over the time horizon. Advanced sampling techniques are used to evaluate land holdings and to project forest growth. The harvest schedule is developed through the use of a number of management science techniques.

SUMMARY

The applications briefly described above—although only a few of the many management science projects at Mead—convey the breadth of the activities currently in use within the company. The management scientist at Mead must be able to work in a number of different environments and be proficient in a wide range of quantitative methods. In addition, the analyst must possess exceptional oral and written communication skills. Only with this background will the analyst be able to achieve the major objective of management science at Mead—the development and implementation of user-friendly quantitative models that will support and enhance management decision making throughout the organization.

Questions

1. Which techniques listed in Table 1.3 are being used in the four management science applications described at the Mead Corporation?
2. Which of the Mead applications use a deterministic model, and which use a stochastic model? What conditions in the applications indicate a stochastic model is necessary?
3. Discuss how the four steps of the quantitative analysis process described in Section 1.3 occur in Mead's inventory analysis application.
4. Discuss the benefits associated with the management science applications at Mead.

2

Linear Programming: The Graphical Method

Linear programming is a problem-solving approach that has been developed to help managers make decisions. Some typical applications of linear programming are described below:

1. A manufacturer wants to develop a production schedule and an inventory policy that will satisfy sales demand in future periods. Ideally the schedule and policy will enable the company to satisfy demand and at the same time *minimize* the total production and inventory costs.
2. A financial analyst must select an investment portfolio from a variety of stock and bond investment alternatives. The analyst would like to establish the portfolio that *maximizes* the return on investment.
3. A marketing manager wants to determine how best to allocate a fixed advertising budget among alternative advertising media such as radio, television, newspaper, and magazine. The manager would like to determine the media mix that *maximizes* the advertising effectiveness.
4. A company has warehouses in a number of locations throughout the United States. Given a set of customer demands for its products, the company would like to determine which warehouse should ship how much product to which customers so that the total transportation costs are *minimized*.

These are only a few examples of situations where linear programming has been used successfully, but the examples illustrate the diversity of linear programming applications. A close scrutiny reveals one basic property that all of these examples have in common. In each example we were concerned with *maximizing* or *minimizing* some quantity. In example 1 we wanted to minimize costs, in example 2 we wanted to maximize return on investment, in example 3 we wanted to maximize advertising effectiveness, and in example 4 we wanted to minimize total transportation costs. *In all linear programming problems, the maximization or minimization of some quantity is the objective.*

A second property of all linear programming problems is that there are restrictions or *constraints* that limit the degree to which the objective can be pursued. In example 1 the manufacturer is restricted by constraints requiring product demand to be satisfied and by the constraints limiting production capacity. The financial analyst's portfolio problem is constrained by the total amount of investment funds available and the maximum amounts that can be invested in each stock or bond. The marketing manager's media selection decision is constrained by a fixed advertising budget and the availability of the various media. In the transportation problem the minimum cost shipping schedule is constrained by the supply of product available at each warehouse. *Thus, constraints are another general feature of every linear programming problem.*

2.1 ▼ A SIMPLE MAXIMIZATION PROBLEM

Par, Inc., is a small manufacturer of golf equipment and supplies whose management has decided to move into the market for medium- and high-priced golf bags. Par's distributor is enthusiastic about the new product line and has agreed to buy all the golf bags Par produces over the next 3 months.

After a thorough investigation of the steps involved in manufacturing a golf bag, management has determined that each golf bag produced will require the following operations:

1. Cutting and dyeing the material
2. Sewing
3. Finishing (inserting umbrella holder, club separators, etc.)
4. Inspection and packaging

The director of manufacturing has analyzed each of the operations and concluded that if the company produces a medium-priced, standard model, each bag will require $7/10$ hour in the cutting and dyeing department, $1/2$ hour in the sewing department, 1 hour in the finishing department, and $1/10$ hour in the inspection and packaging department. The more expensive deluxe model will require 1 hour of cutting and dyeing time, $5/6$ hour of sewing time, $2/3$ hour of finishing time, and $1/4$ hour of inspection and packaging time. This production information is summarized in Table 2.1.

The accounting department has analyzed these production figures, assigned all relevant variable costs, and arrived at prices for both bags that will result in a profit[1] contribution of $10 for every standard bag and $9 for every deluxe bag produced.

In addition, after studying departmental workload projections, the director of manufacturing estimates that 630 hours of cutting and dyeing time, 600 hours of sewing time,

TABLE 2.1
Production Operations and Production Requirements per Bag

Product	Production Time (hours)			
	Cutting and Dyeing	*Sewing*	*Finishing*	*Inspection and Packaging*
Standard bag	$7/10$	$1/2$	1	$1/10$
Deluxe bag	1	$5/6$	$2/3$	$1/4$

[1]From an accounting perspective, this is more correctly described as the contribution margin per bag; for example, overhead has not been allocated.

708 hours of finishing time, and 135 hours of inspection and packaging time will be available for the production of golf bags during the next 3 months.

Par's problem is to determine how many standard and how many deluxe bags it should produce in order to maximize profit contribution. If you were in charge of production scheduling for Par, Inc., what decision would you make? That is, how many standard bags and how many deluxe bags would you produce in the next 3 months? Write your decision below. Later you can check and see how well you did.

Number of Standard Bags	**Number of Deluxe Bags**	**Total Profit**

2.2 ▼ THE OBJECTIVE FUNCTION

As pointed out earlier, every linear programming problem has a maximization or minimization objective. For the Par problem the objective is to maximize profit. We can write this objective in mathematical form with the introduction of some simple notation. Let

$$x_1 = \text{number of standard bags Par, Inc., produces}$$

$$x_2 = \text{number of deluxe bags Par, Inc., produces}$$

Par's profit contribution will come from two sources: (1) the profit contribution made by producing x_1 standard bags and (2) the profit contribution made by producing x_2 deluxe bags. Since Par makes \$10 for every standard bag produced, the company will make $\$10x_1$ if x_1 standard bags are produced. Also, since Par makes \$9 for every deluxe bag produced, the company will make $\$9x_2$ if x_2 deluxe bags are produced. Denoting the total profit contribution by z, we have

$$\text{Total profit contribution} = z = \$10x_1 + \$9x_2$$

From now on we will assume that the profit contribution is measured in dollars and write the total profit contribution expression without the dollar signs. That is,

$$\text{Total profit contribution} = z = 10x_1 + 9x_2 \qquad (2.1)$$

Par's problem can now be stated as one of choosing values for the variables x_1 and x_2 that will yield the highest possible value of z. In linear programming terminology we refer to x_1 and x_2 as the *decision variables*. Since the objective—maximize total profit contribution—is a function of these decision variables, we refer to $10x_1 + 9x_2$ as the *objective function*. Using max as an abbreviation for maximize, Par's objective is written as follows:

$$\text{max } z = \text{max } 10x_1 + 9x_2 \qquad (2.2)$$

In the Par, Inc., problem, any particular production combination of standard and deluxe bags is referred to as a *solution* to the problem. However, only those solutions that satisfy *all* the constraints are referred to as *feasible solutions*. The particular feasible production combination (feasible solution) that results in the largest profit contribution will be referred to as the *optimal* production combination or, equivalently, the *optimal solution.* At this point, however, we have no idea what the optimal solution will be. Indeed, we have not even developed a procedure for identifying feasible solutions. The procedure for determining feasible solutions requires us first to identify all the constraints of the problem.

2.3 ▼ THE CONSTRAINTS

Every standard and deluxe bag produced must go through four manufacturing operations. Since there is a limited amount of production time available for each of these operations, we can expect that four constraints will limit the total number of golf bags Par can produce.

From the production information (see Table 2.1) we know that every standard bag Par manufactures will use $7/10$ hour of cutting and dyeing time. Hence, the total number of hours of cutting and dyeing time used in the manufacture of x_1 standard bags will be $7/10 x_1$. On the other hand, every deluxe bag Par produces will use 1 hour of cutting and dyeing time; thus, x_2 deluxe bags will use $1x_2$ hours of cutting and dyeing time. The total cutting and dyeing time required for the production of x_1 standard bags and x_2 deluxe bags is given by

$$\text{Total cutting and dyeing time required} = 7/10 x_1 + 1x_2$$

Since the director of manufacturing has stated that Par has at most 630 hours of cutting and dyeing time available, it follows that the product combination we select must satisfy the requirement

$$7/10 x_1 + 1x_2 \leq 630 \qquad (2.3)$$

where the symbol $\leq$ means *less than or equal to*. Relationship (2.3) is referred to as an inequality and denotes the fact that the total number of hours used for the cutting and dyeing operation in the production of x_1 standard bags and x_2 deluxe bags must be less than or equal to the maximum amount of cutting and dyeing time Par, Inc., has available.

From Table 2.1 we also see that every standard bag manufactured will require $1/2$ hour of sewing time and that every deluxe bag manufactured will require $5/6$ hour of sewing time. Since there are 600 hours of sewing time available, it follows that

$$1/2 x_1 + 5/6 x_2 \leq 600 \qquad (2.4)$$

is the mathematical representation of the sewing constraint. Verify for yourself that the constraint for finishing capacity is

$$1x_1 + 2/3 x_2 \leq 708 \qquad (2.5)$$

and that the constraint for inspection and packaging capacity is

$$1/10 x_1 + 1/4 x_2 \leq 135 \qquad (2.6)$$

We now have specified the mathematical relationships for the constraints associated with the four production operations. Are there any other constraints we have forgotten?

Can Par produce a negative number of standard or deluxe bags? Clearly, the answer is no. Thus, in order to prevent the decision variables x_1 and x_2 from having negative values, two constraints

$$x_1 \geq 0 \quad \text{and} \quad x_2 \geq 0 \qquad (2.7)$$

must be added. The symbol $\geq$ means *greater than or equal to*. These constraints ensure that the solution to the problem will contain nonnegative values for the decision variables and are thus referred to as the *nonnegativity constraints*. Nonnegativity constraints are a general feature of all linear programming problems and will be written in the following abbreviated form:

$$x_1, x_2 \geq 0$$

2.4 ▼ THE MATHEMATICAL STATEMENT OF THE PAR, INC., PROBLEM

The mathematical statement or mathematical formulation of the Par, Inc., problem is now complete. We have succeeded in translating the objective and constraints of the "real-world" problem into a set of mathematical relationships referred to as a *mathematical model*. The complete mathematical model for the Par problem is as follows:

$$\max \quad 10x_1 + 9x_2$$

subject to (s.t.)

$$
\begin{aligned}
\tfrac{7}{10}x_1 + 1x_2 &\leq 630 && \text{Cutting and dyeing} \\
\tfrac{1}{2}x_1 + \tfrac{5}{6}x_2 &\leq 600 && \text{Sewing} \\
1x_1 + \tfrac{2}{3}x_2 &\leq 708 && \text{Finishing} \\
\tfrac{1}{10}x_1 + \tfrac{1}{4}x_2 &\leq 135 && \text{Inspection and packaging} \\
x_1, x_2 &\geq 0
\end{aligned}
$$

Our job now is to find the product mix (that is, the combination of x_1 and x_2) that satisfies all the constraints and, at the same time, yields a value for the objective function that is greater than or equal to the value given by any other feasible solution. Once this is done, we will have found the optimal solution to the problem.

The above mathematical model of the Par problem is a *linear program*. The problem has the objective and constraints that we said earlier were common properties of all linear programs. But what is the special feature of this mathematical model that makes it a linear program? The special feature that makes it a linear program is that the objective function and all constraint functions (the left-hand sides of the constraint inequalities) are linear functions of the decision variables.

Mathematical functions in which each variable appears in a separate term and is raised to the first power are called *linear functions*. The objective function ($10x_1 + 9x_2$) is linear since each decision variable appears in a separate term and has an exponent of 1. If the objective function had appeared as $10x_1^2 + 9\sqrt{x_2}$, it would not have been a linear function, and we would not have a linear program. The amount of production time required in the cutting and dyeing department ($\tfrac{7}{10}x_1 + 1x_2$) is also a linear function of the decision variables for the same reason. Similarly, the functions of the left-hand side of all the constraint inequalities (the constraint functions) are linear functions. Thus, the mathematical formulation of the Par problem is referred to as a linear program.

We can now note that linear *programming* has nothing to do with computer programming. The use of the word *programming* here means "choosing a course of action." Linear programming involves choosing a course of action when the mathematical model of the problem contains only linear functions.

▼ NOTES AND COMMENTS ▼

1. The three assumptions necessary for a linear programming model to be appropriate are proportionality, additivity, and divisibility. *Proportionality* means that the contribution to the objective function and the amount of resources used are proportional to the value of each decision variable. *Additivity* means that the value of the objective function and the total resources used can be found by summing the objective function contribution and the resources used for all decision variables. *Divisibility* means that the decision variables are continuous. The divisibility assumption plus the nonnegativity constraints means that decision variables can take on any value greater than or equal to zero.

2. Management scientists formulate and solve a variety of mathematical models that contain an objective function and a set of constraints. Models of this type are referred to as *mathematical programming models*. Linear programming models are a special type of mathematical programming models in that the objective function and all constraint functions are linear.

2.5 ▼ GRAPHICAL SOLUTION

A linear programming problem involving only two decision variables can be solved using a graphical solution procedure. Let us begin the graphical solution procedure by developing a graph that displays the possible solutions (x_1 and x_2 values) for the Par problem. The graph (Figure 2.1) will have values of x_1 on the horizontal axis and values of x_2 on the vertical axis. Any point on the graph can be identified by the x_1 and x_2 values, which indicate the position of the point along the x_1 and x_2 axes, respectively. Since every point (x_1, x_2) corresponds to a possible solution, every point on the graph is called a *solution point*. The solution point where $x_1 = 0$ and $x_2 = 0$ is referred to as the origin.

The next step is to determine which of the solution points correspond to feasible solutions for the linear program. Both x_1 and x_2 are required to be nonnegative, so we need only consider that portion of the graph where $x_1 \geq 0$ and $x_2 \geq 0$. In Figure 2.2 the arrows point to the portion of the solution region where these nonnegativity requirements are satisfied. Since linear programming decision variables are always required to be nonnegative, all future graphs will show only the portion of the solution region corresponding to nonnegative values for the decision variables.

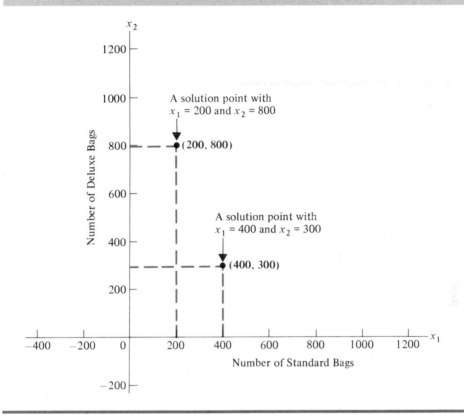

FIGURE 2.1
Graph of Solution Points for the Two-Variable Par, Inc., Problem

Earlier we saw that the inequality representing the cutting and dyeing constraint is

$$\tfrac{7}{10}x_1 + 1x_2 \leq 630$$

To show all solution points that satisfy this relationship, we start by graphing the solution points satisfying the constraint as an equality. That is, the points where $\tfrac{7}{10}x_1 + 1x_2 = 630$. Since the graph of this equation is a line, it can be obtained by identifying two points that satisfy the equation and then drawing a line through the points. Setting $x_1 = 0$ and solving for x_2, we see that the point ($x_1 = 0$, $x_2 = 630$) satisfies the above equation. To find a second point satisfying this equation, we set $x_2 = 0$ and solve for x_1. By doing this, we obtain $\tfrac{7}{10}x_1 + 1(0) = 630$, or $x_1 = 900$. Thus, a second point satisfying the equation is ($x_1 = 900$, $x_2 = 0$). Given these two points, we can now graph the line corresponding to the equation

$$\tfrac{7}{10}x_1 + 1x_2 = 630$$

This line, which will be called the cutting and dyeing *constraint line,* is shown in Figure 2.3. We label this line "C & D" to indicate that it represents the cutting and dyeing constraint.

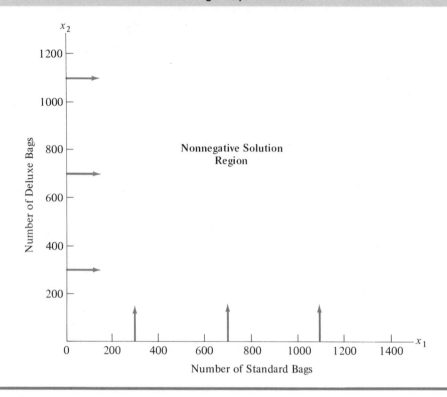

FIGURE 2.2
The Nonnegativity Constraints

Recall that the inequality representing the cutting and dyeing constraint is

$$\tfrac{7}{10}x_1 + 1x_2 \leq 630$$

Can you identify all of the solution points that satisfy this constraint? Since all points on the line satisfy $\tfrac{7}{10}x_1 + 1x_2 = 630$, we know any point on this line must satisfy the constraint. But where are the solution points satisfying $\tfrac{7}{10}x_1 + 1x_2 < 630$? Consider two solution points: $(x_1 = 200, x_2 = 200)$ and $(x_1 = 600, x_2 = 500)$. You can see from Figure 2.3 that the first solution point is below the constraint line and the second is above the constraint line. Which of these solutions will satisfy the cutting and dyeing constraint? For the point $(x_1 = 200, x_2 = 200)$ we see that

$$\tfrac{7}{10}x_1 + 1x_2 = \tfrac{7}{10}(200) + 1(200) = 340$$

Since the 340 hours is less than the 630 hours available, the $(x_1 = 200, x_2 = 200)$ production combination, or solution point, satisfies the constraint. For the point $(x_1 = 600, x_2 = 500)$ we have

$$\tfrac{7}{10}x_1 + 1x_2 = \tfrac{7}{10}(600) + 1(500) = 920$$

The 920 hours is greater than the 630 hours available, so the $(x_1 = 600, x_2 = 500)$ solution point does not satisfy the constraint and is thus not feasible.

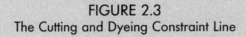

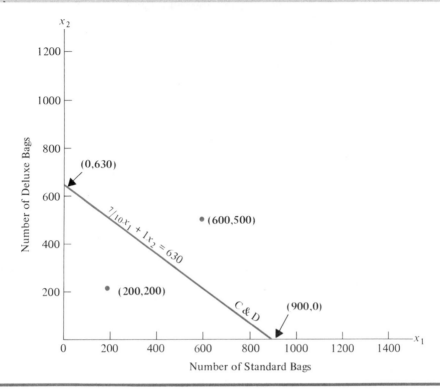

FIGURE 2.3
The Cutting and Dyeing Constraint Line

It turns out that if a particular solution point is not feasible, then all other solution points on the same side of the constraint line are not feasible. If a particular solution point is feasible, then all other solution points on the same side of the constraint line are feasible. Thus, one needs to evaluate the constraint function for only one solution point to determine which side of a constraint line is in the feasible region. In Figure 2.4, we indicate all points satisfying the cutting and dyeing constraint by the shaded region.

We continue by identifying the solution points satisfying each of the other three constraints. The solutions that are feasible for each of these constraints are shown in Figure 2.5.

We now have four separate graphs showing the feasible solution points for each of the four constraints. In a linear programming problem we need to identify the solution points that satisfy *all* the constraints *simultaneously*. To find these solution points, we can draw all four constraints on one graph and observe the region containing the points that do in fact satisfy all the constraints simultaneously.

The graphs in Figures 2.4 and 2.5 can be superimposed to obtain one graph with all four constraints. This combined-constraint graph is shown in Figure 2.6. The shaded region in this figure includes every solution point that satisfies all the constraints simultaneously. Since solutions that satisfy all the constraints are termed *feasible solutions,* the shaded region is called the feasible solution region, or simply the *feasible region.* Any point on the boundary of the feasible region or within the feasible region is a *feasible solution point.*

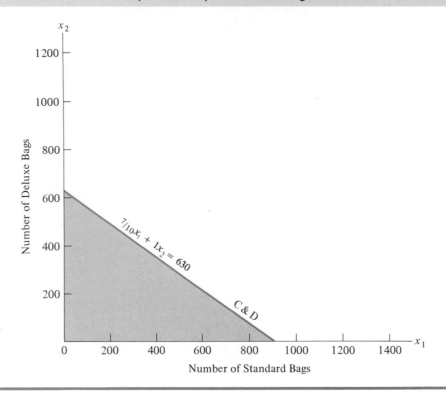

FIGURE 2.4
Feasible Solutions for the Cutting and Dyeing Constraint Are
Represented by the Shaded Region

Now that we have identified the feasible region, we are ready to proceed with the graphical solution method and find the optimal solution to the Par, Inc., problem. Recall that the optimal solution for a linear programming problem is the feasible solution that provides the best possible value of the objective function. Let us start the optimizing step of the graphical solution procedure by redrawing the feasible region on a separate graph. The graph is shown in Figure 2.7.

One approach to finding the optimal solution would be to evaluate the objective function for each feasible solution; the optimal solution would then be the one yielding the largest value. The difficulty with this approach is that there are too many feasible solutions (actually an infinite number), and, thus, it would not be possible to evaluate all feasible solutions. Hence, this trial-and-error procedure cannot be used to identify the optimal solution.

Rather than trying to compute the profit contribution for each feasible solution, we select an arbitrary value for profit contribution and identify all the feasible solutions (x_1, x_2) that yield the selected value. For example, what feasible solutions provide a profit contribution of $1800? These solutions are given by the values of x_1 and x_2 in the feasible region that will make the objective function

$$10x_1 + 9x_2 = 1800$$

FIGURE 2.5
Feasible Solutions for the Sewing, Finishing, and Inspection and Packaging Constraints Are Represented by the Shaded Regions

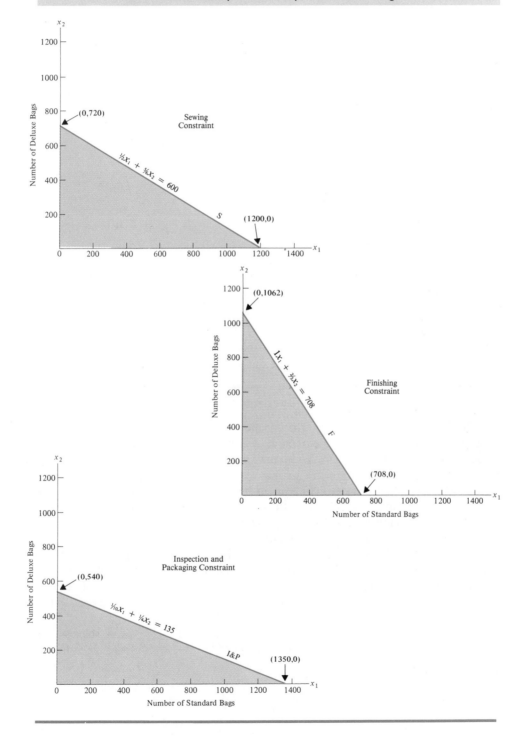

FIGURE 2.6
Combined-Constraint Graph Showing the Feasible Solution Region for the Par, Inc., Problem

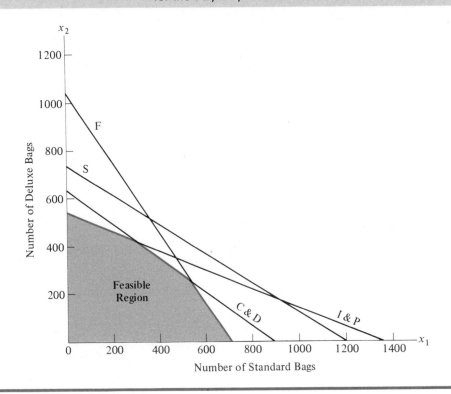

The above expression is simply the equation of a line. Thus, all feasible solution points (x_1, x_2) yielding a profit contribution of $1800 must be on the line. We learned earlier in this section how to graph a constraint line. The procedure for graphing the profit or objective function line is the same. Letting $x_1 = 0$, we see that x_2 must be 200; thus, the solution point $(x_1 = 0, x_2 = 200)$ is on the line. Similarly, by letting $x_2 = 0$, we see that the solution point $(x_1 = 180, x_2 = 0)$ is also on the line. Drawing the line through these two points identifies all the solutions that have a profit contribution of $1800. A graph of this profit line is presented in Figure 2.8.

Since the objective is to find the feasible solution yielding the largest profit contribution, let us proceed by selecting higher profit contributions and finding the solutions yielding the selected values. For instance, let us find all solutions yielding profit contributions of $3600 and $5400. To do so, we must find the x_1 and x_2 values that are on the following lines:

$$10x_1 + 9x_2 = 3600$$

and

$$10x_1 + 9x_2 = 5400$$

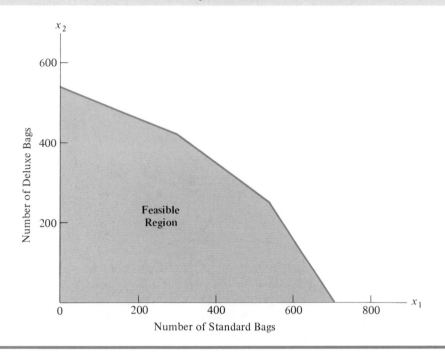

FIGURE 2.7
Feasible Solution Region for the Par, Inc., Problem

Number of Deluxe Bags (x_2)

Feasible Region

Number of Standard Bags (x_1)

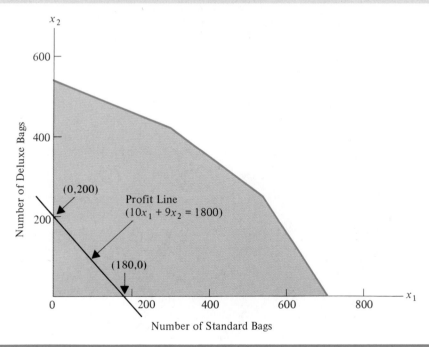

FIGURE 2.8
$1800 Profit Line for the Par, Inc., Problem

Number of Deluxe Bags (x_2)

(0,200)

Profit Line
($10x_1 + 9x_2 = 1800$)

(180,0)

Number of Standard Bags (x_1)

Using the previous procedure for graphing profit and constraint lines, we have drawn the $3600 and $5400 profit lines on the graph in Figure 2.9. While not all solution points on the $5400 profit line are in the feasible region, at least some points on the line are, and, thus, it is possible to obtain a feasible solution that provides a $5400 profit contribution.

Can we find a feasible solution yielding an even higher profit contribution? Look at Figure 2.9 and see what general observations you can make about the profit lines already drawn. Note the following: (1) the profit lines are *parallel* to each other, and (2) higher profit lines are obtained as we move farther from the origin. This can also be seen algebraically. Let z represent total profit. The objective function is

$$z = 10x_1 + 9x_2$$

Solving for x_2 in terms of x_1 and z, we obtain

$$9x_2 = -10x_1 + z$$
$$x_2 = -{}^{10}\!/_9 x_1 + {}^1\!/_9 z \tag{2.8}$$

Equation (2.8) is the *slope-intercept form* of the linear equation relating x_1 and x_2. The coefficient of x_1, $-{}^{10}\!/_9$, is the slope of the line, and the term ${}^1\!/_9 z$ is the x_2 intercept (that is, the value of x_2 where the graph of equation (2.8) crosses the x_2 axis). Substituting the profit contributions of $z = 1800$, $z = 3600$, and $z = 5400$ into equation (2.8) yields the following slope-intercept equations for the profit lines shown in Figure 2.9:

For $z = 1800$,

$$x_2 = -{}^{10}\!/_9 x_1 + 200$$

FIGURE 2.9
Selected Profit Lines for the Par, Inc., Problem

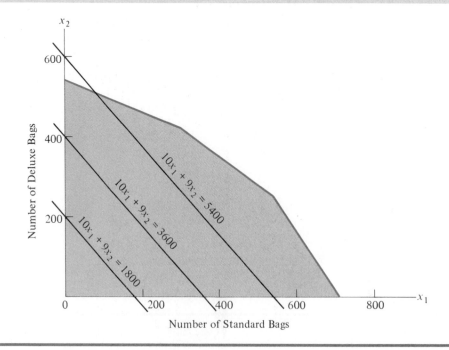

Number of Standard Bags

For $z = 3600$,

$$x_2 = -\tfrac{10}{9}x_1 + 400$$

For $z = 5400$,

$$x_2 = -\tfrac{10}{9}x_1 + 600$$

The slope $(-\tfrac{10}{9})$ is the same for each profit line since the profit lines are parallel. Further, we see that the x_2 intercept increases with larger profit contributions. Thus, higher profit lines are farther from the origin.

Because the profit lines are parallel and higher profit lines are farther from the origin, we can obtain solutions that yield increasingly larger values for the objective function by continuing to move the profit line farther from the origin in such a fashion that it remains parallel to the other profit lines. However, at some point we will find that any further outward movement will place the profit line completely outside the feasible region. Since solutions outside the feasible region are unacceptable, the point in the feasible region that lies on the highest profit line is the optimal solution to the linear program.

You should now be able to identify the optimal solution point for the Par, Inc., problem. Use a ruler or the edge of a piece of paper, and move the profit line as far from the origin as you can. What is the last point in the feasible region that you reach? This point, which is the optimal solution, is shown graphically in Figure 2.10.

The optimal values of the decision variables are the x_1 and x_2 values at the optimal solution. Depending on the accuracy of the graph, you may or may not be able to determine the *exact* x_1 and x_2 values. Referring to the graph in Figure 2.10, the best we can do is conclude that the optimal production combination consists of approximately 550 standard bags (x_1) and approximately 250 deluxe bags (x_2).

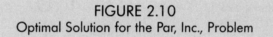

FIGURE 2.10
Optimal Solution for the Par, Inc., Problem

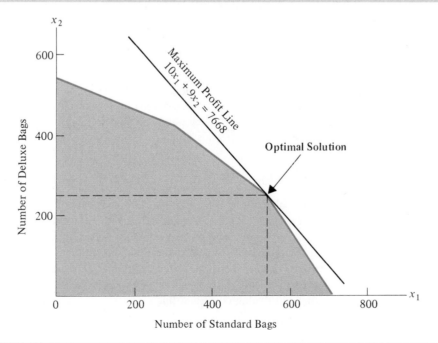

A closer inspection of Figures 2.6 and 2.10 shows that the optimal solution point is at the intersection of the cutting and dyeing and the finishing constraint lines. That is, the optimal solution point is on both the cutting and dyeing constraint line

$$\tfrac{7}{10}x_1 + 1x_2 = 630 \tag{2.9}$$

and the finishing constraint line

$$1x_1 + \tfrac{2}{3}x_2 = 708 \tag{2.10}$$

Thus, the optimal values of the decision variables x_1 and x_2 must satisfy both equations (2.9) and (2.10) simultaneously. Using equation (2.9) and solving for x_1 gives

$$\tfrac{7}{10}x_1 = 630 - 1x_2$$

or

$$x_1 = 900 - \tfrac{10}{7}x_2 \tag{2.11}$$

Substituting this expression for x_1 into equation (2.10) and solving for x_2 provide the following:

$$1(900 - \tfrac{10}{7}x_2) + \tfrac{2}{3}x_2 = 708$$
$$900 - \tfrac{10}{7}x_2 + \tfrac{2}{3}x_2 = 708$$
$$900 - \tfrac{30}{21}x_2 + \tfrac{14}{21}x_2 = 708$$
$$- \tfrac{16}{21}x_2 = -192$$
$$x_2 = \frac{192}{\tfrac{16}{21}} = 252$$

Using $x_2 = 252$ in equation (2.11) and solving for x_1 we obtain

$$x_1 = 900 - \tfrac{10}{7}(252)$$
$$= 900 - 360 = 540$$

The exact location of the optimal solution point is $x_1 = 540$ and $x_2 = 252$. Hence, the optimal production quantities for Par, Inc., are 540 standard bags and 252 deluxe bags, with a resulting profit contribution of $10(540) + 9(252) = \$7668$.

For a two-decision variable linear programming problem the exact values of the decision variables at the optimal solution can be determined by first using the graphical solution procedure to identify the optimal solution point and then solving the two simultaneous constraint equations associated with this point.

A Note on Graphing Lines

As can be seen from the graphical solution of the Par, Inc., problem, an important aspect of the graphical method is the ability to graph lines showing the constraints and the objective function of the linear program. The procedure we have used for graphing the equation of a line is to find any two points satisfying the equation and then draw the line through the two points. For the Par, Inc., constraints, the two points were easily found by first setting $x_1 = 0$ and solving the constraint equation for x_2. Then we set $x_2 = 0$ and solved for x_1. For the cutting and dyeing constraint line

$$\tfrac{7}{10}x_1 + 1x_2 = 630$$

this procedure identified the two points ($x_1 = 0$, $x_2 = 630$) and ($x_1 = 900$, $x_2 = 0$). The cutting and dyeing constraint line was then graphed by drawing a line through these two points.

All constraint and objective function lines in two-variable linear programs can be graphed if two points on the line can be identified. However, finding the two points on the line is not always as easy as shown in the Par, Inc., problem. For example, consider the following constraint:

$$2x_1 - 1x_2 \leq 100$$

Using the equality form and setting $x_1 = 0$, we find the point ($x_1 = 0$, $x_2 = -100$) is on the constraint line. Setting $x_2 = 0$, we find a second point ($x_1 = 50$, $x_2 = 0$) on the constraint line. If we have drawn only the nonnegative ($x_1 \geq 0$, $x_2 \geq 0$) portion of the graph, the first point ($x_1 = 0$, $x_2 = -100$) cannot be plotted because $x_2 = -100$ is not on the graph. Whenever we have two points on the line, but one or both of the points cannot be plotted in the nonnegative portion of the graph, the simplest approach is to enlarge the graph to include the negative x_1 and/or x_2 axes. In this example the point ($x_1 = 0$, $x_2 = -100$) can be plotted by extending the graph to include the negative x_2 axis. Once both points satisfying the constraint equation have been located, the line can be drawn. The constraint line and the feasible solutions for the constraint $2x_1 - 1x_2 \leq 100$ are shown in Figure 2.11.

As another example, let us consider a constraint of the form

$$1x_1 - 1x_2 \geq 0$$

To find all solutions satisfying the constraint as an equality, we first set $x_1 = 0$ and solve for x_2. This shows that the origin ($x_1 = 0$, $x_2 = 0$) is on the constraint line. Setting $x_2 = 0$ and solving for x_1 provides the same point. However, we can obtain a second point on the line by setting x_2 equal to any value other than zero and then solving for x_1. For instance, setting $x_2 = 100$ and solving for x_1, we find that the point ($x_1 = 100$, $x_2 = 100$) is on the line. With the two points ($x_1 = 0$, $x_2 = 0$) and ($x_1 = 100$, $x_2 = 100$), the constraint line $1x_1 - 1x_2 = 0$ and the feasible solutions for $1x_1 - 1x_2 \geq 0$ can be plotted as shown in Figure 2.12.

Summary of the Graphical Solution Procedure for Maximization Problems

As we have seen, the graphical solution procedure is a method for solving two-variable linear programming problems such as the Par, Inc., problem. The steps of the graphical solution procedure for a maximization problem are summarized below.

1. Prepare a graph of the feasible solution points for each of the constraints.
2. Determine the feasible region by identifying the solution points that satisfy all the constraints simultaneously.
3. Draw an objective function line showing the values of the x_1 and x_2 variables that yield a specified value of the objective function.
4. Move parallel objective function lines toward larger objective function values until further movement would take the line completely outside the feasible region.
5. A feasible solution point on the objective function line with the largest value is an optimal solution.

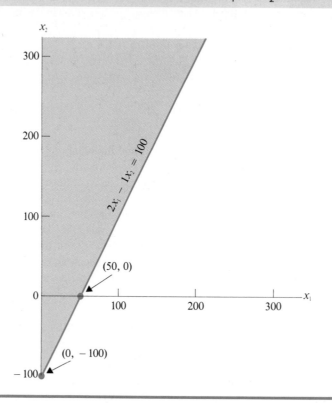

FIGURE 2.11
Feasible Solutions for the Constraint $2x_1 - 1x_2 \leq 100$

$2x_1 - 1x_2 = 100$

(50, 0)

(0, -100)

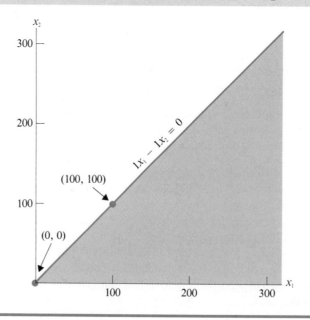

FIGURE 2.12
Feasible Solutions for the Constraint $1x_1 - 1x_2 \geq 0$

$1x_1 - 1x_2 = 0$

(100, 100)

(0, 0)

Slack Variables

In addition to the optimal solution of $x_1 = 540$ standard bags and $x_2 = 252$ deluxe bags and the expected profit of $7668, management of Par, Inc., will probably want information about the production time requirements for each production operation. We can obtain this information by substituting the optimal x_1 and x_2 values into the constraint functions for the linear program. For the Par, Inc., problem the production time requirements are as follows:

$$\frac{7}{10}(540) + 1(252) = 630 \text{ hours of cutting and dyeing time}$$
$$\frac{1}{2}(540) + \frac{5}{6}(252) = 480 \text{ hours of sewing time}$$
$$1(540) + \frac{2}{3}(252) = 708 \text{ hours of finishing time}$$
$$\frac{1}{10}(540) + \frac{1}{4}(252) = 117 \text{ hours of inspection and packaging time}$$

The above results show management that the production of 540 standard bags and 252 deluxe bags will require all available cutting and dyeing time (630 hours) and all available finishing time (708 hours), while 120 hours of sewing time $(600 - 480)$ and 18 hours of inspection and packaging time $(135 - 117)$ will remain idle. The 120 hours of unused sewing time and 18 hours of unused inspection and packaging time are referred to as *slack* for the two departments. In linear programming terminology any unused or idle capacity for a $\leq$ constraint is referred to as the *slack* associated with the constraint.

Often variables are added to the formulation of a linear programming problem to represent the slack, or idle capacity. Such variables are called *slack variables,* and since the unused capacity makes no contribution to profit, they have coefficients of zero in the objective function. After the addition of slack variables to the mathematical statement of the Par, Inc., problem, the mathematical model appears as follows:

$$\max \quad 10x_1 + 9x_2 + 0s_1 + 0s_2 + 0s_3 + 0s_4$$

s.t.

$$\frac{7}{10}x_1 + 1x_2 + 1s_1 \qquad\qquad\qquad = 630$$
$$\frac{1}{2}x_1 + \frac{5}{6}x_2 \qquad + 1s_2 \qquad\qquad = 600$$
$$1x_1 + \frac{2}{3}x_2 \qquad\qquad + 1s_3 \qquad = 708$$
$$\frac{1}{10}x_1 + \frac{1}{4}x_2 \qquad\qquad\qquad + 1s_4 = 135$$

$$x_1, x_2, s_1, s_2, s_3, s_4 \geq 0$$

Whenever a linear program is written in a form with all constraints expressed as equalities, it is said to be written in *standard form.*

At the optimal solution, $x_1 = 540$ and $x_2 = 252$, the values for the slack variables are as follows:

Constraint	Value of Slack Variable
Cutting and dyeing	$s_1 = 0$
Sewing	$s_2 = 120$
Finishing	$s_3 = 0$
Inspection and packaging	$s_4 = 18$

Could we have used the graphical solution to provide some of this information? The answer is yes. By finding the optimal solution point on Figure 2.6, we can see that the cutting and dyeing and the finishing constraints restrict, or *bind,* the feasible region at this point. Thus, this solution requires the use of all available time for these two operations. In other words, the graph shows us that the cutting and dyeing and the finishing departments will have zero slack. On the other hand, since the sewing and the inspection and packaging constraints are not binding the feasible region at the optimal solution, we can expect some unused time or slack for these two operations.

As a final comment on the graphical analysis of the Par, Inc., problem, we call your attention to the sewing capacity constraint as shown in Figure 2.6. Note, in particular, that this constraint did not affect the feasible region. That is, the feasible region would be the same whether the sewing capacity constraint were included or not. This tells us that there is enough sewing time available to accommodate any production level that can be achieved by the other three departments. Since the sewing constraint does not affect the feasible region and thus cannot affect the optimal solution, it is called a *redundant constraint.*

▼ NOTES AND COMMENTS ▼

1. In the standard form representation of a linear programming model the objective function coefficients for slack variables are zero. This implies that slack variables that represent unused resources do not affect the value of the objective function. However, in some applications, unused resources can be sold and contribute to profit. In such cases the ordinary slack variable becomes a decision variable representing the amount of resources to be sold. A nonzero coefficient in the objective function would reflect the profit associated with selling a unit of the resource.

2. Redundant constraints do not affect the feasible region and as a result can be removed from a linear programming model without affecting the optimal solution. However, if the linear programming model is to be solved later, changes in some of the data might change a previously redundant constraint into a critical binding constraint. Thus, we recommend keeping all constraints in the linear programming model even though at some point in time one or more of the constraints may be redundant.

2.6 ▼ EXTREME POINTS AND THE OPTIMAL SOLUTION

Suppose that the profit contribution for the Par, Inc., standard bag is reduced from $10 to $5 per bag, while the profit contribution for the deluxe bag and all the constraints remain unchanged. The complete linear programming model of this new problem is identical to the mathematical model in Section 2.4, except for the revised objective function:

$$\max z = 5x_1 + 9x_2$$

How does this change in the objective function affect the optimal solution to the Par, Inc., problem? Figure 2.13 shows the graphical solution of the Par, Inc., problem with the revised objective function. Note that since the constraints have not changed, the feasible region has not changed. However, the profit lines have been altered to reflect the new objective function.

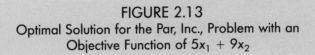

FIGURE 2.13
Optimal Solution for the Par, Inc., Problem with an Objective Function of $5x_1 + 9x_2$

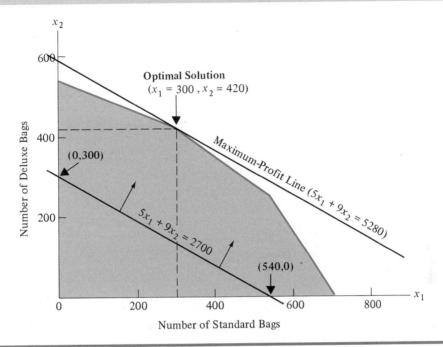

By moving the profit line in a parallel manner toward higher profit values, we find the optimal solution as shown in Figure 2.13. The values of the decision variables at this point are $x_1 = 300$ and $x_2 = 420$. The reduced profit contribution for the standard bag has caused a change in the optimal solution. In fact, as you may have suspected, we are cutting back the production of the lower-profit standard bags and increasing the production of the higher-profit deluxe bags.

What have you noticed about the location of the optimal solutions in the two linear programming problems that we have solved thus far? Look closely at the graphical solutions in Figures 2.10 and 2.13. An important observation that you should be able to make is that the optimal solutions occur at one of the vertices or ''corners'' of the feasible region. In linear programming terminology these vertices are referred to as the *extreme points* of the feasible region. The Par, Inc., problem has five vertices, or five extreme points, for its feasible region (see Figure 2.14). We can now formally state our observation about the location of optimal solutions as follows:[2]

> An optimal solution to a linear programming problem can be found at an extreme point of the feasible region for the problem.

---

[2]We will see in Section 2.8 that there are two special cases (infeasibility and unboundedness) in linear programming where there is no optimal solution. Thus, the above statement does not apply to these cases.

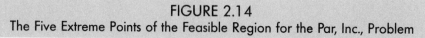

FIGURE 2.14
The Five Extreme Points of the Feasible Region for the Par, Inc., Problem

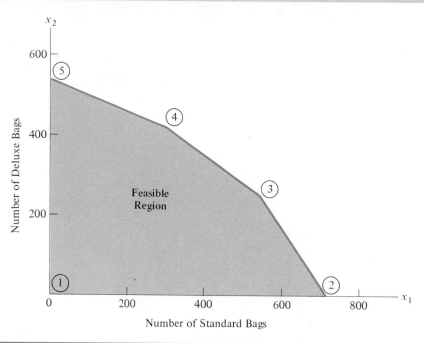

This property means that if you are looking for the optimal solution to a linear programming problem, you do not have to evaluate all feasible solution points. In fact, you have to consider *only* the feasible solutions that occur at the extreme points of the feasible region. Thus, for the Par, Inc., problem, instead of computing and comparing the profit contributions for all feasible solutions, we can find the optimal solution by evaluating the five extreme-point solutions and selecting the one that provides the largest profit contribution. Actually the graphical solution procedure is nothing more than a convenient way of identifying an optimal extreme point for two-variable problems.

2.7 ▼ A SIMPLE MINIMIZATION PROBLEM

The Par, Inc., problem involved maximization; however, many linear programming problems involve minimization. For example, consider the case of M&D Chemicals. M&D Chemicals produces two products that are sold as raw materials to companies manufacturing bath soaps, laundry detergents, and other soap products.

Based on an analysis of current inventory levels and potential demand for the coming month, M&D's management has specified that the total production for products 1 and 2 combined must be at least 350 gallons. Separately, a major customer's order for 125 gallons of product 1 must also be satisfied. Product 1 requires 2 hours of processing time per gallon while product 2 requires 1 hour of processing time per gallon, and for the coming month 600 hours of processing time are available. M&D's objective is to satisfy the above requirements at a minimum total production cost. Production costs are $2 per gallon for product 1 and $3 per gallon for product 2.

To find the minimum cost production schedule, let us write the M&D Chemicals problem as a linear program. Following a procedure similar to the one used for the Par, Inc., problem, we first define the decision variables and the objective function for the problem. Let

$$x_1 = \text{number of gallons of product 1 produced}$$
$$x_2 = \text{number of gallons of product 2 produced}$$

Since the production costs are \$2 per gallon for product 1 and \$3 per gallon for product 2, the minimization of the total cost objective function can be written as

$$\min 2x_1 + 3x_2$$

Next consider the constraints placed on the M&D Chemicals problem. To satisfy the major customer's demand for 125 gallons of product 1, we know x_1 must be at least 125. Thus, we write the constraint

$$1x_1 \geq 125$$

Since the total combined production of both products must be at least 350 gallons, we can write the constraint

$$1x_1 + 1x_2 \geq 350$$

Finally, since the limitation on available processing time is 600 hours, we add the constraint

$$2x_1 + 1x_2 \leq 600$$

After adding the nonnegativity constraints ($x_1, x_2 \geq 0$), we have the following linear program for the M&D Chemicals problem:

$$\min \quad 2x_1 + 3x_2$$

s.t.

$$
\begin{aligned}
1x_1 \qquad\ &\geq 125 \quad \text{Demand for product 1} \\
1x_1 + 1x_2 &\geq 350 \quad \text{Total production} \\
2x_1 + 1x_2 &\leq 600 \quad \text{Processing time} \\
x_1, x_2 &\geq 0
\end{aligned}
$$

Since the linear programming model has only two decision variables, the graphical solution procedure can be used to find the optimal production quantities. The graphical method for this problem, just as in the Par problem, requires us first to graph the constraint lines in order to find the feasible region. By graphing each constraint line separately and then checking points on either side of the constraint line, the feasible solutions for each constraint can be identified. By combining the feasible solutions for each constraint on the same graph, we obtain the feasible region shown in Figure 2.15.

To find the minimum cost solution, we now draw the objective function line corresponding to a particular total cost value. For example, we might start by drawing the line $2x_1 + 3x_2 = 1200$. This line is shown in Figure 2.16. Clearly there are points in the feasible region that would provide a total cost of \$1200. To find the values of x_1 and x_2 that provide smaller total cost values, we move the objective function line in a lower left

FIGURE 2.15
The Feasible Region for the M&D Chemicals Problem

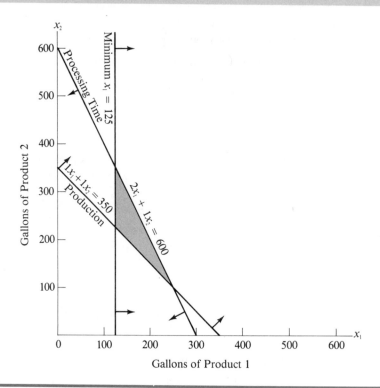

direction until, if we moved it any farther, it would be entirely outside the feasible region. Note that the objective function line $2x_1 + 3x_2 = 800$ intersects the feasible region at the extreme point $x_1 = 250$ and $x_2 = 100$. This extreme point provides the minimum cost solution with an objective function value of 800. From Figures 2.15 and 2.16 we can see that the total production volume constraint and the processing time constraint are binding. Just as in every linear programming problem, the optimal solution occurs at an extreme point of the feasible region.

Summary of the Graphical Solution Procedure for Minimization Problems

The steps of the graphical solution procedure for a minimization problem are summarized below:

1. Prepare a graph of the feasible solution points for each of the constraints.
2. Determine the feasible region by identifying the solution points that satisfy all the constraints simultaneously.
3. Draw an objective function line showing the values of the x_1 and x_2 variables that yield a specified value of the objective function.

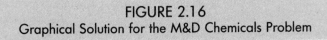

FIGURE 2.16
Graphical Solution for the M&D Chemicals Problem

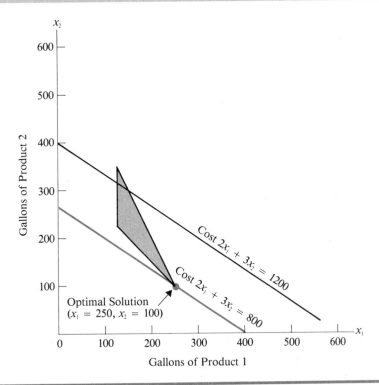

4. Move parallel objective function lines toward smaller objective function values until further movement would take the line completely outside the feasible region.
5. A feasible solution point on the objective function line with the smallest value is an optimal solution.

Surplus Variables

A complete analysis of the minimum cost solution to the M&D Chemicals problem shows that the desired total production of $1x_1 + 1x_2 = 350$ gallons has been achieved by using all available processing time of $2x_1 + 1x_2 = 2(250) + 1(100) = 600$ hours. In addition, note that the constraint requiring meeting product 1 demand has been satisfied with $x_1 = 250$ gallons. In fact, the production of product 1 exceeds its minimum level by $250 - 125 = 125$ gallons. This excess production for product 1 is referred to as *surplus*. In linear programming terminology any excess quantity corresponding to a $\geq$ constraint is referred to as surplus.

Recall that with a $\leq$ constraint, a slack variable can be added to the left-hand side of the inequality to convert the constraint to equality form. With a $\geq$ constraint a *surplus variable* can be subtracted from the left-hand side of the inequality to convert the constraint to equality form. Just as with slack variables, surplus variables are given a coefficient of zero in the objective function because they have no effect on its value. After including two surplus variables for the $\geq$ constraints and one slack variable for the $\leq$

constraint, the linear programming model of the M&D Chemicals problem appears as follows:

$$\min \quad 2x_1 + 3x_2 + 0s_1 + 0s_2 + 0s_3$$

s.t.

$$
\begin{array}{rcl}
1x_1 - 1s_1 &=& 125 \\
1x_1 + 1x_2 - 1s_2 &=& 350 \\
2x_1 + 1x_2 + 1s_3 &=& 600 \\
\end{array}
$$

$$x_1, x_2, s_1, s_2, s_3 \geq 0$$

All the constraints are now equalities. Hence, the above formulation is the standard form representation of the M&D Chemicals problem. At the optimal solution of $x_1 = 250$ and $x_2 = 100$, the values of the surplus and slack variables are as follows:

Constraint	Value of Surplus or Slack Variables
Demand for product 1	$s_1 = 125$
Total production	$s_2 = 0$
Processing time	$s_3 = 0$

Refer to Figures 2.15 and 2.16. Note that the zero surplus and slack variables are associated with the constraints that are binding at the optimal solution: that is, the total production and processing time constraints. The surplus of 125 units is associated with the nonbinding constraint on the demand for product 1.

Note that in the Par, Inc., problem all the constraints were of the $\leq$ type and that in the M&D Chemicals problem the constraints were a mixture of $\geq$ and $\leq$ types. The number and types of constraints encountered in a particular linear programming problem will depend on the specific conditions existing in the problem. Linear programming problems may have some $\leq$ constraints, some $\geq$ constraints, and some $=$ constraints. For an equality constraint, feasible solutions must lie directly on the constraint line.

An example of a linear program with all three constraint forms is given below (problem 35 at the end of the chapter will ask you to solve this problem using the graphical procedure):

$$\min \quad 2x_1 + 2x_2$$

s.t.

$$
\begin{array}{rcl}
1x_1 + 3x_2 &\leq& 12 \\
3x_1 + 1x_2 &\geq& 13 \\
1x_1 - 1x_2 &=& 3 \\
\end{array}
$$

$$x_1, x_2 \geq 0$$

The standard form representation of this problem is

$$\min \quad 2x_1 + 2x_2 + 0s_1 + 0s_2$$

s.t.

$$1x_1 + 3x_2 + 1s_1 \qquad = 12$$
$$3x_1 + 1x_2 \qquad - 1s_2 = 13$$
$$1x_1 - 1x_2 \qquad = 3$$
$$x_1, x_2, s_1, s_2 \geq 0$$

This formulation requires a slack variable for the $\leq$ constraint and a surplus variable for the $\geq$ constraint. However, neither a slack nor a surplus variable is required for the third constraint since it is already in equality form.

The graphical solution procedure is a convenient way to find optimal extreme point solutions for two-variable linear programming problems. When solving linear programs graphically, it is not necessary to write the problem in its standard form. Nevertheless, we should be able to compute the values of the slack and surplus variables and understand what they mean. In Chapter 3 we shall see that the values of slack and surplus variables are included in the computer solution of linear programs. In Chapter 5 we will introduce an algebraic solution procedure, the simplex method, which can be used to find optimal extreme-point solutions for linear programming problems having as many as several thousand decision variables. The mathematical steps of the simplex method involve solving simultaneous equations that represent the constraints of the linear program. Thus, in setting up a linear program for solution by the simplex method we must have one linear equation for each constraint in the problem; therefore, the problem must be in its standard form.

As a final point, it is important to realize that the standard form of the linear programming problem is equivalent to the original formulation of the problem. That is, the optimal solution to any linear programming problem is the same as the optimal solution to the standard form of the problem. The standard form has not changed the basic problem; it has only changed how we write the constraints for the problem.

2.8 ▼ SPECIAL CASES

In this section we discuss three special situations that can arise when we attempt to solve linear programming problems.

Alternate Optimal Solutions

From our discussion of the graphical solution procedure, we know that optimal solutions can be found at the extreme points of the feasible region. Now let us consider the special case where the optimal objective function line coincides with one of the binding constraint lines on the boundary of the feasible region. We will see that this can lead to the case of *alternate optimal solutions;* in such cases more than one solution provides the optimal value for the objective function.

As an example of the case of alternate optimal solutions, let us return to the Par, Inc., problem with the four constraints and feasible region as previously defined. However, let us assume that the profit for the standard bag (x_1) has been decreased to $6.30. The revised objective function becomes $6.3x_1 + 9x_2$. The graphical solution of this problem is shown in Figure 2.17. Note that the optimal solution still occurs at an extreme point. In fact, it occurs at two extreme points: extreme point ④ ($x_1 = 300$, $x_2 = 420$) and extreme point ③ ($x_1 = 540$, $x_2 = 252$).

The objective function values at these two extreme points are identical; that is,

$$6.3x_1 + 9x_2 = 6.3(300) + 9(420) = 5670$$

and

$$6.3x_1 + 9x_2 = 6.3(540) + 9(252) = 5670$$

Furthermore, any point on the line connecting the two optimal extreme points also provides an optimal solution. For example, the solution point ($x_1 = 420$, $x_2 = 336$), which is halfway between the two extreme points, also provides the optimal objective function value of

$$6.3x_1 + 9x_2 = 6.3(420) + 9(336) = 5670$$

A linear programming problem with alternate optima is generally a good situation for the manager or decision maker. It means that several combinations of the decision vari-

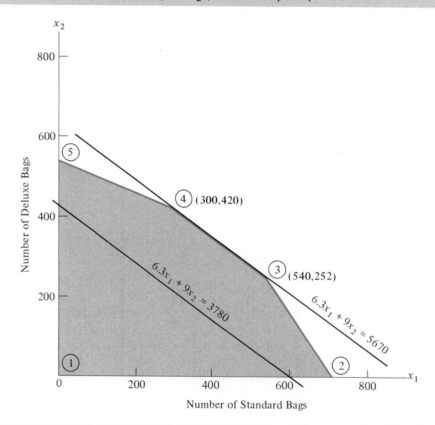

FIGURE 2.17
Par, Inc., Problem with an Objective Function of
$6.3x_1 + 9x_2$ (Alternate Optima)

ables are optimal and that the manager can select the specific optimal solution that is the most desirable.

Infeasibility

Infeasibility occurs when there is no solution to the linear programming problem that satisfies all the constraints, including the nonnegativity conditions $x_1, x_2 \geq 0$. Graphically, infeasibility means that a feasible region does not exist; that is, there are no points that satisfy all of the constraints and the nonnegativity conditions simultaneously. To illustrate this situation, let us look again at the problem faced by Par, Inc.

Suppose that management had specified that at least 500 of the standard bags and at least 360 of the deluxe bags must be manufactured. The graph of the solution region may now be constructed to reflect these new requirements (see Figure 2.18). The shaded area in the lower left-hand portion of the graph depicts those points satisfying the departmental constraints on the availability of time. The shaded area in the upper right-hand portion depicts those points satisfying the minimum production requirements of 500 standard and 360 deluxe bags. But there are no points satisfying both sets of constraints. Thus, we see

FIGURE 2.18
No Feasible Region for the Par, Inc., Problem with Minimum Production Requirements of 500 Standard and 360 Deluxe Bags

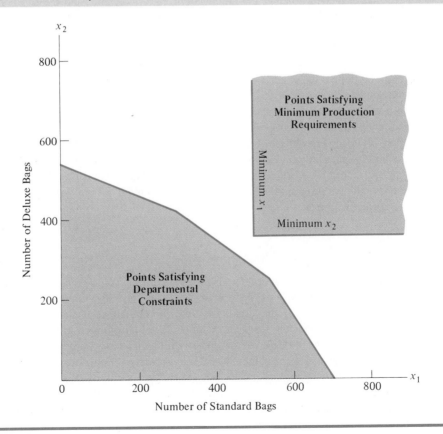

TABLE 2.2
Resources Needed to Manufacture 500 Standard Bags and 360 Deluxe Bags

Operation	Minimum Required Resources (hours)	Available Resources (hours)	Additional Resources Needed (hours)
Cutting and dyeing	$\frac{7}{10}(500) + 1(360) = 710$	630	80
Sewing	$\frac{1}{2}(500) + \frac{5}{6}(360) = 550$	600	None
Finishing	$1(500) + \frac{2}{3}(360) = 740$	708	32
Inspection and packaging	$\frac{1}{10}(500) + \frac{1}{4}(360) = 140$	135	5

that if management imposes these minimum production requirements, there will be no feasible solution to the linear programming model.

How should we interpret infeasibility in terms of this current problem? First, we should tell management that given the resources available (that is, cutting and dyeing time, sewing time, finishing time, and inspection and packaging time), it is not possible to make 500 standard bags and 360 deluxe bags. Moreover, we can tell management exactly how much of each resource must be expended in order to make it possible to manufacture 500 standard and 360 deluxe bags. Table 2.2 shows the minimum amounts of resources that must be available, the amounts currently available, and the additional amounts that are required. Thus, we need 80 more hours of cutting and dyeing time, 32 more hours of finishing time, and 5 more hours of inspection and packaging time in order to meet management's minimum production requirements.

If, after seeing the above information, management still wants to manufacture 500 standard and 360 deluxe bags, additional resources must be provided. Perhaps this will mean hiring another person to work in the cutting and dyeing department, transferring a person from elsewhere in the plant to work part time in the finishing department, or having the sewing people help out periodically with the inspection and packaging. As you can see, there are many possibilities for corrective management action, once we discover that there is no feasible solution. The important thing to realize is that linear programming analysis can help determine whether or not management's plans are feasible. By analyzing the problem using linear programming, we are often able to point out infeasible conditions and initiate corrective action.

Unboundedness

A solution to a linear programming problem is *unbounded* if the value of the solution may be made infinitely large without violating any of the constraints. This condition might be termed "managerial utopia." If this condition were to occur in a profit maximization problem, it would be true that the manager could achieve an unlimited profit.

In linear programming models of real-world problems the occurrence of an unbounded solution means that the problem has been improperly formulated. We know that it is not possible to increase profits indefinitely. Therefore, we must conclude that if a profit maximization problem results in an unbounded solution, the mathematical model is not a sufficiently accurate representation of the real-world problem. Usually what has happened is that a constraint has been inadvertently omitted in the problem formulation.

As an illustration, consider the simple numerical example:

$$\max \quad 20x_1 + 10x_2$$

s.t.

$$1x_1 \qquad \geq 2$$
$$1x_2 \leq 5$$
$$x_1, x_2 \geq 0$$

In Figure 2.19 we have graphed the feasible region associated with this problem. Note that we can only indicate part of the feasible region since the feasible region extends indefinitely in the direction of the x_1 axis. Looking at the objective function lines in Figure 2.19, we see that the solution to this problem may be made as large as we desire. That is, no matter what solution we pick, there will always be some feasible solution with a larger value. Thus, we say that the solution to this linear program is *unbounded*.

FIGURE 2.19
Example of an Unbounded Problem

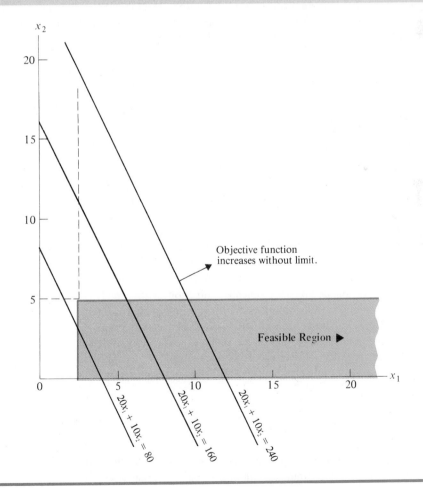

▼ NOTES AND COMMENTS ▼

1. Infeasibility is independent of the objective function. It exists because the constraints are so restrictive that there is no feasible region for the linear programming model. Thus, when you encounter infeasibility, making changes in the coefficients of the objective function will not help; the problem will remain infeasible.
2. Unboundedness is often the result of a missing constraint. However, a change in the objective function may cause a previously unbounded problem to become bounded with an optimal solution. For example, the graph in Figure 2.19 shows an unbounded solution for the objective function max $20x_1 + 10x_2$. However, changing the objective function to max $-20x_1 -10x_2$ will provide the optimal solution $x_1 = 2$ and $x_2 = 0$ even though no changes have been made in the constraints.

▼ SUMMARY

Two problems, Par, Inc., and M&D Chemicals, were formulated as linear programs and solved by a graphical solution procedure. In studying the graphical solution procedure we noted that if an optimal solution to a linear programming problem exists, it can be found at an extreme point of the feasible region.

In the process of formulating mathematical models of the problems presented in this chapter the following general definition of a linear program was developed. A linear program is a mathematical model that has the following properties:

1. A linear objective function that is to be maximized or minimized
2. A set of linear constraints
3. Variables that are all restricted to nonnegative values

We have seen how slack variables can be used to write less-than-or-equal-to constraints in equality form and how surplus variables can be used to write greater-than-or-equal-to constraints in equality form. The value of a slack variable can usually be interpreted as the amount of unused resource, while the value of a surplus variable indicates the amount over and above some stated minimum requirement. When all constraints have been written as equalities, the linear program has been written in its standard form. In the special cases of infeasibility and unboundedness we showed that there is no optimal solution to the problem. In the case of infeasibility there are no feasible solutions, while in the case of unboundedness the objective function can be made infinitely large for a maximization problem and infinitely small for a minimization problem. In addition, a third special case, alternate optima, was discussed. In this case we have two optimal extreme points, and all the points on the line segment connecting them are also optimal.

While the graphical solution procedure is not used to solve larger linear programs, the intuition developed in this chapter is helpful in understanding the solution of any linear program.

▼ GLOSSARY

Objective function   All linear programs have a linear objective function that is to be either maximized or minimized. In many linear programming problems the objective function will be used to measure the profit or cost of a particular solution.

Constraint   An equation or inequality that rules out certain combinations of decision variables as feasible solutions.

Constraint function   The left-hand side of a constraint (that is, the portion of the constraint containing the variables).

Solution   Any set of values for the variables.

Optimal solution   A feasible solution that maximizes or minimizes the value of the objective function.

Nonnegativity constraints   A set of constraints that requires all variables to be non-negative.

Mathematical model   A representation of a problem where the objective and all constraint conditions are described by mathematical expressions.

Linear program   A mathematical model with a linear objective function, a set of linear constraints, and nonnegative variables.

Linear equations or functions   Mathematical expressions in which the variables appear in separate terms and are raised to the first power.

Feasible solution   A solution that satisfies all the constraints.

Feasible region   The set of all feasible solutions.

Redundant constraint   A constraint that does not affect the feasible region. If a constraint is redundant, it can be removed from the problem without affecting the feasible region.

Extreme point   Graphically speaking, extreme points are the feasible solution points occurring at the vertices or "corners" of the feasible region. With two-variable problems, extreme points are determined by the intersection of the constraint lines.

Slack variable   A variable added to the left-hand side of a less-than-or-equal-to constraint to convert the constraint into an equality. The value of this variable can usually be interpreted as the amount of unused resource.

Surplus variable   A variable subtracted from the left-hand side of a greater-than-or-equal-to constraint to convert the constraint into an equality. The value of this variable can usually be interpreted as the amount over and above some required minimum level.

Standard form   A linear program in which all the constraints are written as equalities. The optimal solution of the standard form of a linear program is the same as the optimal solution of the original formulation of the linear program.

Alternate optima   The situation in which a linear program has two or more optimal solutions.

Infeasibility   The situation in which there is no solution to the linear programming problem that satisfies all the constraints.

Unboundedness   A maximization linear programming problem is said to be unbounded if the value of the solution may be made infinitely large without violating any of the constraints. A minimization problem is unbounded if the value of the solution may be made infinitely small.

▼ PROBLEMS

1. Which of the following mathematical relationships could be found in a linear programming model, and which could not? For the relationships that are unacceptable for linear programs, state your reasons.

   a. $-1x_1 + 2x_2 - 1x_3 \leq 70$

   b. $2x_1 - 2x_3 = 50$

   c. $1x_1 - 2x_2^2 + 4x_3 \leq 10$

    d. $3\sqrt{x_1} + 2x_2 - 1x_3 \geq 15$
    e. $1x_1 + 1x_2 + 1x_3 = 6$
    f. $2x_1 + 5x_2 + 1x_1x_2 \leq 25$

2. Find the feasible solution points for the following constraints:
    a. $4x_1 + 2x_2 \leq 16$
    b. $4x_1 + 2x_2 \geq 16$
    c. $4x_1 + 2x_2 = 16$

3. Graphing constraint lines is an essential step in the graphical method. Show a separate graph of the constraint lines and feasible solutions for each of the following constraints:
    a. $3x_1 + 2x_2 \leq 18$
    b. $12x_1 + 8x_2 \geq 480$
    c. $5x_1 + 10x_2 = 200$

4. Show a separate graph of the constraint lines and feasible solutions for each of the following constraints:
    a. $3x_1 - 4x_2 \geq 60$
    b. $-6x_1 + 5x_2 \leq 60$
    c. $5x_1 - 2x_2 \leq 0$

5. Given below are three objective functions for linear programming problems:

$$z = 7x_1 + 10x_2$$

$$z = 6x_1 + 4x_2$$

$$z = -4x_1 + 7x_2$$

Determine the slope of each objective function. Show the graph of each of the three objective functions for $z = 420$.

6. Solve the following linear program:

$$\max \quad 5x_1 + 5x_2$$

$$\text{s.t.}$$

$$1x_1 \qquad\qquad \leq 100$$

$$1x_2 \leq \quad 80$$

$$2x_1 + 4x_2 \leq 400$$

$$x_1, x_2 \geq 0$$

7. Identify the feasible region for the following set of constraints:

$$\tfrac{1}{2}x_1 + \tfrac{1}{4}x_2 \geq \quad 30$$

$$1x_1 + \quad 5x_2 \geq 250$$

$$\tfrac{1}{4}x_1 + \tfrac{1}{2}x_2 \leq \quad 50$$

$$x_1, x_2 \geq 0$$

8. Identify the feasible region for the following set of constraints:

$$2x_1 - \quad 1x_2 \leq \quad 0$$

$$-1x_1 + 1.5x_2 \leq 200$$

$$x_1, x_2 \geq 0$$

9. Identify the feasible region for the following set of constraints:

$$3x_1 - 2x_2 \geq 0$$
$$2x_1 - 1x_2 \leq 200$$
$$1x_1 \qquad \leq 150$$
$$x_1, x_2 \geq 0$$

10. Consider the following linear programming problem:

$$\max \quad 2x_1 + 3x_2$$
s.t.
$$1x_1 + 2x_2 \leq 6$$
$$5x_1 + 3x_2 \leq 15$$
$$x_1, x_2 \geq 0$$

Find the optimal solution. What is the value of the objective function at the optimal solution?

11. Consider the following linear programming problem:

$$\max \quad 3x_1 + 3x_2$$
s.t.
$$2x_1 + 4x_2 \leq 12$$
$$6x_1 + 4x_2 \leq 24$$
$$x_1, x_2 \geq 0$$

a. Find the optimal solution.
b. If the objective function is changed to $2x_1 + 6x_2$, what will the optimal solution be?
c. How many extreme points are there? What are the values of x_1 and x_2 at each extreme point?

12. Consider the following linear programming problem:

$$\max \quad 3x_1 + 2x_2$$
s.t.
$$2x_1 + 2x_2 \leq 8$$
$$3x_1 + 2x_2 \leq 12$$
$$1x_1 + .5x_2 \leq 3$$
$$x_1, x_2 \geq 0$$

a. Find the optimal solution. What is the value of the objective function?
b. Does this problem have a redundant constraint? If so, what is it? Does the solution change if the redundant constraint is removed from the problem? Explain.

13. Consider the following linear programming problem:

$$\min \quad x_1 + 2x_2$$

s.t.

$$x_1 + 4x_2 \leq 21$$
$$2x_1 + x_2 \geq 7$$
$$3x_1 + 1.5x_2 \leq 21$$
$$2x_1 + 6x_2 \geq 0$$
$$x_1, x_2 \geq 0$$

a. Find the optimal solution and the value of the objective function.

b. Determine the amount of slack or surplus for each constraint.

c. Suppose the objective function is changed to max $5x_1 + 2x_2$. Find the optimal solution and the value of the objective function.

14. What constraint lines combine to form extreme point ④ of the Par, Inc., problem (see Figures 2.6 and 2.14)? Solve the simultaneous linear equations to show that the exact values of x_1 and x_2 at this extreme point are $x_1 = 300$ and $x_2 = 420$.

15. Suppose that the management of Par, Inc., encounters each of the following situations:

a. The accounting department revises its estimate of profit contribution on the deluxe bag to $18 per bag.

b. A new low-cost material is available for the standard bag, and the profit contribution per standard bag can be increased to $20 per bag. (Assume the profit contribution of the deluxe bag is the original $9 value.)

c. New sewing equipment is available that would increase the sewing operation capacity to 750 hours. (Assume $10x_1 + 9x_2$ is the appropriate objective function.)

If each of the above conditions is encountered separately, what are the optimal solution and the profit contribution for each situation?

16. Refer to the feasible region for the Par, Inc., problem in Figure 2.14.

a. Develop an objective function that will make extreme point ⑤ the optimal extreme point.

b. What is the optimal solution using the objective function you selected in part (a)?

c. What are the values of the slack variables associated with this solution?

17. Kelson Sporting Equipment, Inc., makes two different types of baseball gloves: a regular model and a catcher's model. The firm has 900 hours of production time available in its cutting and sewing department, 300 hours of production time available in its finishing department, and 100 hours of production time available in its packaging and shipping department. The production time requirements and the profit per glove are given below:

| Model | Production Time (hours) | | | Profit/Glove |
	Cutting and Sewing	Finishing	Packaging and Shipping	
Regular model	1	½	⅛	$5
Catcher's model	³⁄₂	⅓	¼	$8

a. Assuming that the company wants to maximize profit, how many gloves of each model should Kelson manufacture?

b. What is the profit Kelson can earn with the above production quantities?

c. How many hours of production time will be scheduled in each department?

d. What is the slack time in each department?

18. The Erlanger Manufacturing Company makes two products. The profit estimates are $25 for each unit of product 1 sold and $30 for each unit of product 2 sold. The labor-hour requirements for the products in each of three production departments are summarized below:

	Product 1	Product 2
Department *A*	1.50	3.00
Department *B*	2.00	1.00
Department *C*	.25	.25

The production supervisors in the departments have estimated that the following number of labor-hours will be available during the next month: 450 hours in department *A*, 350 hours in department *B*, and 50 hours in department *C*. Assuming that the company is interested in maximizing profits, answer the following:

a. What is the linear programming model for this problem?

b. Find the optimal solution. How much of each product should be produced, and what is the projected profit?

c. What are the scheduled production time and the slack time in each department?

19. Yard Care, Inc., manufactures a variety of lawn care products, including two well-known lawn fertilizers. Each fertilizer product is a blend of two raw materials known as K40 and K50. During the current production period 900 pounds of K40 and 400 pounds of K50 are available. Each pound of the product known as "Green Lawn" uses $\frac{3}{5}$ pound of K40 and $\frac{2}{5}$ pound of K50. Each pound of the product known as "Lawn Care" uses $\frac{3}{4}$ pound of K40 and $\frac{1}{4}$ pound of K50. In addition, a current limit on the availability of packaging materials restricts the production of Lawn Care to a maximum of 500 pounds.

a. If the profit contribution for both products is $3 per pound, how many pounds of each product should the company manufacture?

b. Should it be a concern to the company that the availability of packaging materials is restricting the production of Lawn Care? What would happen to the production quantities and the projected profit if the firm were able to remove the restriction on the amount of Lawn Care that could be produced?

20. Investment Advisors, Inc., is a brokerage firm that manages stock portfolios for a number of clients. A new client has requested that the firm handle an $80,000 investment portfolio. As an initial investment strategy the client would like to restrict the portfolio to a mix of the following stocks:

Stock	Price/Share	Estimated Annual Return/Share	Risk Index/Share
U.S. Oil	$25	$3	.50
Hub Properties	$50	$5	.25

The risk index for the stock is a rating of the relative risk of the two investment alternatives. For the data given, U.S. Oil is judged to be the riskier investment. By constraining the total risk for the portfolio, the investment firm avoids placing excessive amounts of the portfolio in potentially high-return, but also high-risk investments. For the current portfolio an upper limit of 700 has been set for the total risk index of all investments. In addition, the firm has set an upper limit of 1000 shares for the more risky U.S. Oil stock. How many shares of each stock should be purchased in order to maximize the total annual return?

21. Consider the following linear program:

$$\min \quad 3x_1 + 4x_2$$

$$\text{s.t.}$$

$$1x_1 + 3x_2 \geq 6$$

$$1x_1 + 1x_2 \geq 4$$

$$x_1, x_2 \geq 0$$

Identify the feasible region and find the optimal solution. What is the value of the objective function?

22. Identify the three extreme point solutions for the M&D Chemicals problem (see Section 2.7). Identify the value of the objective function and the values of the slack and surplus variables at each extreme point.

23. Greentree Kennels, Inc., provides overnight lodging for a variety of pets. A particular feature at Greentree is the quality of care the pets receive, including excellent food. The kennel's dog food is made by mixing two brand-name dog food products to obtain what the kennel calls the "well-balanced dog diet." The data for the two dog foods are as follows:

Dog Food	Cost/ Ounce	Protein (%)	Fat (%)
Bark Bits	$.06	30	15
Canine Chow	$.05	20	30

If Greentree wants to be sure that the dogs receive at least 5 ounces of protein and at least 3 ounces of fat per day, what is the minimum cost mix of the two dog food products?

24. Jack Kammer has been trying to figure out the correct amount of fertilizer that should be applied to his lawn. After getting his soil analyzed at the local agricultural agency, he was advised to put at least 60 pounds of nitrogen, 24 pounds of phosphorous compounds, and 40 pounds of potassium compounds on the lawn this season. One-third of the mixture is to be applied in May, one-third in July, and one-third in late September. After checking the local discount stores, Jack finds that one store is currently having a sale on packaged fertilizer. One type on sale is the 20-5-20 mixture containing 20% nitrogen, 5% phosphorous compounds, and 20% potassium compounds and selling at $4 for a 20-pound bag. The other type on sale is a 10-10-5 mixture selling for $5 for a 40-pound bag. Jack would like to know how many bags

of each type he should purchase so he can combine the ingredients to form a mixture that will meet the minimum agricultural agency requirements. Like all homeowners plagued by large lawns, Jack would like to spend as little as possible to keep his lawn healthy. What should Jack do?

25. Car Phones, Inc., sells two models of car telephones: model x and model y. Records show that 3 hours of sales time are used for each model x phone that is sold and 5 hours of sales time for each model y phone. A total of 600 hours of sales time is available for the next 4-week period. In addition, management planning policies call for minimum sales goals of 25 units for both model x and model y.

   a. Show the feasible region for the Car Phones, Inc., problem.

   b. Assuming the company makes a $40 profit contribution for each model x sold and a $50 profit contribution for each model y sold, what is the optimal sales goal for the company for the next 4-week period?

   c. Develop a constraint and show the feasible region if management adds the restriction that Car Phones must sell at least as many model y phones as model x phones.

   d. What is the new optimal solution if the constraint in part (c) is added to the problem?

26. Kats is a new pet-food product. Each 16-ounce can of Kats consists of a blend, or mixture, of two pet-food ingredients. Let

$$x_1 = \text{the number of ounces of ingredient } A \text{ in a 16-ounce can}$$

$$x_2 = \text{the number of ounces of ingredient } B \text{ in a 16-ounce can}$$

Each ounce of ingredient A contains $\frac{1}{2}$ ounce of protein and $\frac{1}{8}$ ounce of fat. Each ounce of ingredient B contains $\frac{1}{10}$ ounce of protein and $\frac{1}{3}$ ounce of fat. Restrictions are that a 16-ounce can of Kats must have at least 4 ounces of protein and 2.5 ounces of fat. If ingredient A costs $.04 per ounce and ingredient B costs $.03 per ounce, what is the minimum cost blend of ingredients A and B in each 16-ounce can of Kats? Identify and interpret the values of the surplus variables for the problem.

27. Innis Investments manages funds for a number of companies and wealthy clients. The investment strategy is tailored to each client's needs. For a new client, Innis has been authorized to invest up to $1.2 million in two investment funds: a stock fund and a money market fund. Each unit of the stock fund costs $50 and provides an annual rate of return of 10%; each unit of the money market fund costs $100 and provides an annual rate of return of 4%.

   The client wants to minimize risk subject to the requirement that the annual income from the investment be at least $60,000. According to Innis's risk measurement system, each unit invested in the stock fund has a risk index of 8, and each unit invested in the money market fund has a risk index of 3; the higher risk index associated with the stock fund simply indicates that it is the riskier investment. Innis's client has also specified that at least $300,000 be invested in the money market fund.

   a. Determine how many units of each fund Innis should purchase for the client in order to minimize the total risk index for the portfolio.

   b. How much annual income will this investment strategy generate?

   c. Suppose the client desires to maximize annual return. How should the funds be invested?

28. Bryant's Pizza, Inc., is a producer of frozen pizza products. The company makes a profit of $1.00 for each regular pizza it produces and $1.50 for each deluxe pizza produced. Each pizza includes a combination of dough mix and topping mix. Currently the firm has 150 pounds of dough mix and 50 pounds of topping mix. Each regular pizza uses 1 pound of dough mix and 4 ounces of topping mix. Each deluxe pizza uses 1 pound of dough mix and 8 ounces of topping mix. Based on past demand Bryant can sell at least 50 regular pizzas and at least 25 deluxe pizzas. How many regular and deluxe pizzas should the company make in order to maximize profits?
   a. Show the above problem in standard form.
   b. What are the values and interpretations of all slack and surplus variables?
   c. Which constraints are binding the optimal solution?

29. Wilkinson Motors, Inc., sells standard automobiles and station wagons. The firm makes $400 profit for each automobile it sells and $500 profit for each station wagon it sells. The company is planning next quarter's order, which the manufacturer says cannot exceed 300 automobiles and 150 station wagons. Dealer preparation requires 2 hours for each automobile and 3 hours for each station wagon. Next quarter the company has 900 hours of shop time available for new car preparation. How many automobiles and station wagons should be ordered so that profit is maximized?
   a. Show the linear programming model of the above problem.
   b. Show the standard form and identify the slack variables.
   c. Identify the extreme points of the feasible region.
   d. Find the optimal solution.
   e. Which constraints are binding?

30. Ryland Farms in northwestern Indiana grows soybeans and corn on its 500 acres of land. An acre of soybeans brings a $100 profit and an acre of corn brings a $200 profit. Because of a government program no more than 200 acres may be planted in soybeans. During the planting season 1200 hours of planting time will be available. Each acre of soybeans requires 2 hours, while each acre of corn requires 6 hours. How many acres of soybeans and how many acres of corn should be planted in order to maximize profits?
   a. Show the linear programming model of the above problem.
   b. Show the standard form and identify all slack variables.
   c. Find the optimal solution.
   d. Identify all the extreme points of the feasible region.
   e. If the farm could get either more hours of labor for planting or additional land, which should it attempt to obtain? Why?

31. RMC is a small firm that produces a variety of chemical products. In a particular production process, three raw materials are blended (mixed together) to produce two products: a fuel additive and a solvent base. Each ton of fuel additive is a mixture of $2/5$ ton of material 1 and $3/5$ ton of material 3. A ton of solvent base is a mixture of $1/2$ ton of material 1, $1/5$ ton of material 2, and $3/10$ ton of material 3. After deducting relevant costs, the company makes $40 for every ton of fuel additive produced and $30 for every ton of solvent base produced.

   RMC's production is constrained by a limited availability of the three raw materials. For the current production period RMC has available the following quantities of each raw material:

Raw Material	Amount Available for Production
Material 1	20 tons
Material 2	5 tons
Material 3	21 tons

a. Given the limited availability of raw materials, how many tons of each product should RMC produce in order to maximize profits? What is the maximum profit?

b. Is there any unused material? If so, how much?

c. Are there any redundant constraints? If so, which ones?

32. Reconsider the RMC situation in problem 31.

a. Identify all the extreme points of the feasible region.

b. Suppose RMC discovers a way to increase the profit of solvent base to $60 per ton. Does this change the optimal solution? If so, how?

c. Suppose the profit for the solvent base is $50 per ton. What is the optimal solution now? Comment on any special characteristics that may exist with this profit for the solvent base.

33. Reconsider the RMC situation in problem 31. Suppose that management adds the requirements that at least 30 tons of fuel additive and at least 15 tons of solvent base must be produced.

a. Graph the constraints for this revised RMC problem. What happens to the feasible region? Explain.

b. If there are no feasible solutions, explain what is needed to produce 30 tons of fuel additive and 15 tons of solvent base.

34. Consider the following linear program:

$$\max \quad 1x_1 + 2x_2$$

s.t.

$$1x_1 \qquad\quad \leq 5$$
$$\qquad 1x_2 \leq 4$$
$$2x_1 + 2x_2 = 12$$
$$x_1, x_2 \geq 0$$

a. Show the feasible region.

b. What are the extreme points of the feasible region?

c. Find the optimal solution using the graphical procedure.

35. Consider the following linear program:

$$\min \quad 2x_1 + 2x_2$$

s.t.

$$1x_1 + 3x_2 \leq 12$$
$$3x_1 + 1x_2 \geq 13$$
$$1x_1 - 1x_2 = 3$$
$$x_1, x_2 \geq 0$$

a. Show the feasible region.

b. What are the extreme points of the feasible region?

c. Find the optimal solution using the graphical procedure.

36. Write the following linear program in standard form:

$$\max \quad 5x_1 + 2x_2 + 8x_3$$

s.t.

$$1x_1 - 2x_2 + \tfrac{1}{2}x_3 \leq 420$$
$$2x_1 + 3x_2 - 1x_3 \leq 610$$
$$6x_1 - 1x_2 + 3x_3 \leq 125$$
$$x_1, x_2, x_3 \geq 0$$

37. For the linear program

$$\max \quad 4x_1 + 1x_2$$

s.t.

$$10x_1 + 2x_2 \leq 30$$
$$3x_1 + 2x_2 \leq 12$$
$$2x_1 + 2x_2 \leq 10$$
$$x_1, x_2 \geq 0$$

a. Write this problem in standard form.

b. Solve the problem.

c. What are the values of the three slack variables at the optimal solution?

38. Given the linear program

$$\max \quad 3x_1 + 4x_2$$

s.t.

$$-1x_1 + 2x_2 \leq 8$$
$$1x_1 + 2x_2 \leq 12$$
$$2x_1 + 1x_2 \leq 16$$
$$x_1, x_2 \geq 0$$

a. Write the problem in standard form.

b. Solve the problem.

c. What are the values of the three slack variables at the optimal solution?

39. For the linear program

$$\min \quad 6x_1 + 4x_2$$

s.t.

$$2x_1 + 1x_2 \geq 12$$
$$1x_1 + 1x_2 \geq 10$$
$$1x_2 \leq 4$$
$$x_1, x_2 \geq 0$$

a. Write the problem in standard form.
b. Solve the problem using the graphical solution procedure.
c. What are the values of the slack and surplus variables?

40. Does the following linear program involve infeasibility, unboundedness, and/or alternate optimal solutions? Explain.

$$\max \quad 4x_1 + 8x_2$$

s.t.

$$2x_1 + 2x_2 \le 10$$
$$-1x_1 + 1x_2 \ge 8$$
$$x_1, x_2 \ge 0$$

41. Does the following linear program involve infeasibility, unboundedness, and/or alternate optimal solutions? Explain.

$$\max \quad 1x_1 + 1x_2$$

s.t.

$$8x_1 + 6x_2 \ge 24$$
$$4x_1 + 6x_2 \ge -12$$
$$2x_2 \ge 4$$
$$x_1, x_2 \ge 0$$

42. Consider the following linear program:

$$\max \quad 1x_1 + 1x_2$$

s.t.

$$5x_1 + 3x_2 \le 15$$
$$3x_1 + 5x_2 \le 15$$
$$x_1, x_2 \ge 0$$

a. What is the optimal solution for this problem?
b. Suppose that the objective function is changed to $1x_1 + 2x_2$. Find the new optimal solution.
c. By adjusting the coefficient of x_2 in the objective function, develop a new objective function that will make the solutions found in parts (a) and (b) above alternate optimal solutions.

43. Consider the following linear program:

$$\max \quad 1x_1 - 2x_2$$

s.t.

$$-4x_1 + 3x_2 \le 3$$
$$1x_1 - 1x_2 \le 3$$
$$x_1, x_2 \ge 0$$

a. Graph the feasible region for the problem.
b. Is the feasible region unbounded? Explain.

c. Find the optimal solution.

d. Does an unbounded feasible region imply that the optimal solution to the linear program will be unbounded?

44. Discuss what happens to the M&D Chemicals problem (see Section 2.7) if the cost per gallon for product 1 is increased to $3.00 per gallon. What would you recommend? Explain.

45. For the M&D Chemicals problem in Section 2.7, discuss the effect of management's requiring total production of 500 gallons for the two products. List two or three actions M&D should consider to correct the situation you encounter.

46. Reconsider the Kelson Sporting Equipment, Inc., production example (problem 17). Discuss the concepts of infeasibility, unboundedness, and alternate optima as they occur in each of the following situations:

a. Management has requested that the production of baseball gloves (regular model plus catcher's model) be such that the total number of gloves produced is at least 750. That is, $1x_1 + 1x_2 \geq 750$.

b. The original problem has to be solved again because the profit for the regular model is adjusted downward to $4 per glove.

c. What would have to happen for this problem to be unbounded?

47. Management of High Tech Services (HTS) would like to develop a model that will help allocate technician's time between service calls to regular contract customers and new customers. A maximum of 80 hours of technician time is available over the 2-week planning period. In order to satisfy cash flow requirements, at least $800 in revenue (per technician) must be generated during the 2-week period. Technician time for regular customers generates $25 per hour. However, technician time for new customers only generates an average of $8 per hour because in many cases a new customer contact does not provide billable services. To ensure that new customer contacts are being maintained, the time technicians spend on new customer contacts must be at least 60% of the time technicians spend on regular customer contacts. Given the above revenue and policy requirements, HTS would like to determine how to allocate technician's time between regular customers and new customers so that the total number of customers contacted during the 2-week period will be maximized. Technicians require an average of 50 minutes for each regular customer contact and 1 hour for each new customer contact.

a. Develop a linear programming model that will enable HTS to determine how to allocate technician's time between regular customers and new customers.

b. Graph the feasible region.

c. Solve the appropriate simultaneous linear equations to determine the values of x_1 and x_2 at each extreme point of the feasible region.

d. Find the optimal solution.

▼ CASE PROBLEM

ADVERTISING STRATEGY

Midtown Motors, Inc., has hired a marketing services firm to develop an advertising strategy for promoting Midtown's used-car sales. The marketing firm has recommended that Midtown use spot announcements on both television and radio as the advertising media for the proposed promotional campaign. Advertising strategy guidelines are expressed as follows:

1. Use at least 30 announcements for combined television and radio coverage.
2. Do not use more than 25 radio announcements.
3. The number of radio announcements cannot be less than the number of television announcements.

The television station has quoted a cost of $1200 per spot announcement, and the radio station has quoted a cost of $300 per spot announcement. Midtown's advertising budget has been set at $25,500. The marketing services firm has rated the various advertising media in terms of audience coverage and recall power of the advertisement. For Midtown's media alternatives, the television announcement is rated at 600, and the radio announcement is rated at 200. Midtown's president would like to know how many television and how many radio spot announcements should be used in order to maximize the overall rating of the advertising campaign.

Midtown's president believes the television station will consider running the Midtown spot announcement on its highly rated evening news program (at the same cost) if Midtown will consider using additional television announcements.

MANAGERIAL REPORT

Perform an analysis of advertising strategy for Midtown Motors, and prepare a report to Midtown's president presenting your findings and recommendations. Include (but do not limit your discussion to) a consideration of the following:

a. The recommended number of television and radio spot announcements
b. The relative merits of each advertising medium
c. The rating that would be necessary for the news program before it would make sense to increase the number of television spots
d. The number of television spots that should be purchased if the news program is rated highly enough to make increasing the number of television spots advisable
e. The restrictions placed on the advertising strategy that Midtown might want to consider relaxing or altering
f. The best use of any possible increase in the advertising budget
g. Any other information that may help Midtown's president make the advertising strategy decision

Include a copy of your linear programming model and graphical solution in the appendix to your report.

3

Linear Programming: Sensitivity Analysis and Computer Solution

In this chapter we provide an introduction to sensitivity analysis and the use of computers for solving linear programming problems. Sensitivity analysis associated with the optimal solution provides valuable supplementary information for the decision maker. After showing how sensitivity analysis can be conducted using a graphical approach, we demonstrate how The Management Scientist, a microcomputer software package for solving linear programming problems, can be used to solve the Par, Inc., and M&D Chemicals problems presented in Chapter 2. In discussing the computer solution for these problems we will focus on the interpretation of the computer output, which includes the optimal solution and sensitivity analysis information. The chapter concludes with a discussion of the formulation, computer solution, and sensitivity analysis of a linear programming problem involving more than two decision variables. A chapter appendix describes how LINDO/PC, a popular microcomputer package developed by Linus Schrage at the University of Chicago, can be used to solve linear programs.

3.1 ▼ INTRODUCTION TO SENSITIVITY ANALYSIS

Sensitivity analysis is the study of how changes in the coefficients of a linear program affect the optimal solution. Using sensitivity analysis we can answer questions such as the following:

1. How will a *change in a coefficient of the objective function* affect the optimal solution?
2. How will a *change in the right-hand-side value for a constraint* affect the optimal solution?

Since sensitivity analysis is concerned with how the above changes affect the optimal solution, the analysis does not begin until the optimal solution to the original linear programming problem has been obtained. For this reason sensitivity analysis is often referred to as *postoptimality analysis*.

The primary reason that sensitivity analysis is important to decision makers is that real-world problems exist in a dynamic environment. Prices of raw materials change, demand fluctuates, companies purchase new machinery to replace old, global labor markets cause changes in production costs, employee turnover occurs, and so on. If a linear programming model has been used in such an environment, we can expect some of the coefficients to change over time. A manager will want to determine how such changes affect the optimal solution to the original linear programming problem. Sensitivity analysis provides the information needed to respond to such changes without requiring the complete solution of a revised linear program.

Recall the Par, Inc., problem introduced in Chapter 2.

$$\max \quad 10x_1 + 9x_2$$

subject to (s.t.)

$$\frac{7}{10}x_1 + 1x_2 \leq 630 \quad \text{Cutting and dyeing}$$

$$\frac{1}{2}x_1 + \frac{5}{6}x_2 \leq 600 \quad \text{Sewing}$$

$$1x_1 + \frac{2}{3}x_2 \leq 708 \quad \text{Finishing}$$

$$\frac{1}{10}x_1 + \frac{1}{4}x_2 \leq 135 \quad \text{Inspection and packaging}$$

$$x_1, x_2 \geq 0$$

The optimal solution, $x_1 = 540$ standard bags and $x_2 = 252$ deluxe bags, is based on profit figures of \$10 per standard bag and \$9 per deluxe bag. However, suppose we later learn that because of a price reduction the profit contribution per standard bag has been reduced to \$7. Sensitivity analysis can be used to determine whether or not the production schedule calling for 540 standard bags and 252 deluxe bags is still the best solution. If it is, there will be no need to solve a modified linear program with $7x_1 + 9x_2$ as the objective function.

Sensitivity analysis can also be used to determine which coefficients in a linear programming model are most critical. For instance, suppose Par, Inc.'s management believes that the \$9 profit contribution per deluxe bag is only a rough estimate of the profit contribution that will actually be obtained. If sensitivity analysis shows that 540 standard bags and 252 deluxe bags will be the optimal solution as long as the profit contribution for the deluxe bag is between \$5 and \$13, management should feel comfortable with the rough estimate of \$9 per bag and the recommended production quantities. However, if sensitivity analysis shows that 540 standard bags and 252 deluxe bags will be the optimal solution only if the profit contribution for the deluxe bag is between \$8.90 and \$9.25, management may want to review the accuracy of the \$9-per-bag profit estimate.

Another aspect of sensitivity analysis is concerned with changes in the right-hand sides of the constraints. Recall that in the Par, Inc., problem the optimal solution used all the cutting and dyeing time and all the finishing time. How would the optimal solution and the total profit change if Par, Inc., could obtain additional time for either of these operations? Sensitivity analysis can help determine how much each added hour is worth and how many hours can be added before diminishing returns set in.

3.2 ▼ GRAPHICAL SENSITIVITY ANALYSIS

For linear programming problems with two decision variables, graphical solution methods can be used to perform sensitivity analysis on the objective function coefficients and the right-hand side values for the constraints.

Objective Function Coefficients

Let us consider how changes in the objective function coefficients might affect the optimal solution to the Par, Inc., problem. The current contribution to profit is $10 per unit for the standard bag and $9 per unit for the deluxe bag. It seems obvious that an increase in the profit contribution for one of the bags might lead management to increase production of that bag and a decrease in the profit contribution for one of the bags might lead management of decrease production of that bag. But it is not as obvious how much the profit contribution would have to change before management would want to change the production quantities.

The current optimal solution to the Par, Inc., problem calls for producing 540 standard bags and 252 deluxe bags. The *range of optimality* for each objective function coefficient provides the range of values over which the current solution will remain optimal. Managerial attention should be focused on those objective function coefficients that have a narrow range of optimality and coefficients near the endpoints of the range. These are the coefficients where a small change can necessitate modifying the optimal solution. Let us now compute the ranges of optimality for the Par, Inc., problem.

Figure 3.1 shows the graphical solution to the Par, Inc., problem. A careful inspection of this graph shows that as long as the slope of the objective function is between the

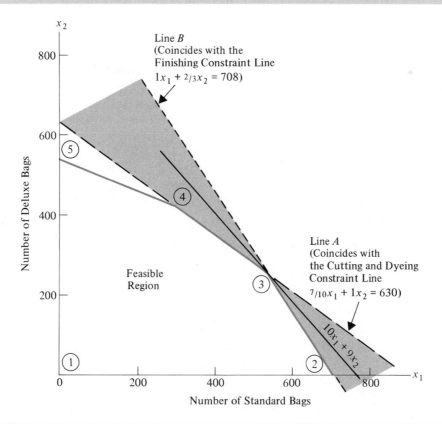

FIGURE 3.1
Graphical Solution of Par, Inc., Problem with Slope of Objective Function Between Slopes of Lines A and B; Extreme Point ③ Is Optimal

slope of line A (which coincides with the cutting and dyeing constraint line) and the slope of line B (which coincides with the finishing constraint line), extreme point ③ with $x_1 = 540$ and $x_2 = 252$ will be optimal. Changing an objective function coefficient for x_1 or x_2 will cause the slope of the objective function to change. In Figure 3.1 we see that such changes cause the objective function line to rotate around extreme point ③. However, as long as the objective function line stays within the shaded region, extreme point ③ will remain optimal.

Rotating the objective function line *counterclockwise* causes the slope to become less negative and hence the slope increases. When the objective function line has been rotated counterclockwise (slope increased) enough to coincide with line A, we obtain alternate optima between extreme points ③ and ④. Any further counterclockwise rotation of the objective function line will cause extreme point ③ to be nonoptimal. Hence, the slope of line A provides an upper limit for the slope of the objective function line.

Rotating the objective function line *clockwise* causes the slope to become more negative, and hence the slope decreases. When the objective function line has been rotated clockwise (slope decreased) enough to coincide with line B, we obtain alternate optima between extreme points ③ and ②. Any further clockwise rotation of the objective function line will cause extreme point ③ to be nonoptimal. Hence, the slope of line B provides a lower limit for the slope of the objective function line.

From the above discussion it should be clear that extreme point ③ will be the optimal solution as long as

Slope of line $B \leq$ slope of objective function line $\leq$ slope of line A

In Figure 3.1 we see that the equation for line A, the cutting and dyeing constraint line, is as follows:

$$\tfrac{7}{10}x_1 + 1x_2 = 630$$

By solving the above equation for x_2, we can write the equation for line A in its slope-intercept form. This yields

$$x_2 = -\tfrac{7}{10}x_1 + 630$$

$$\uparrow \qquad\qquad \uparrow$$

Slope of   Intercept of
line A line A on
           x_2 axis

Thus, the slope for line A is $-\tfrac{7}{10}$, and its intercept on the x_2 axis is 630.

The equation for line B in Figure 3.1 is

$$1x_1 + \tfrac{2}{3}x_2 = 708$$

Solving for x_2 provides the slope-intercept form for line B. Doing so yields

$$\tfrac{2}{3}x_2 = -1x_1 + 708$$
$$x_2 = -\tfrac{3}{2}x_1 + 1062$$

Thus, the slope of line B is $-\tfrac{3}{2}$, and its intercept on the x_2 axis is 1062.

Now that the slopes of lines A and B have been computed, we see that in order for extreme point ③ to remain optimal we must have

$$-\tfrac{3}{2} \leq \text{slope of objective function} \leq -\tfrac{7}{10} \qquad (3.1)$$

Let us now consider the general form of the slope of the objective function. Let c_1 denote the profit of a standard bag, c_2 denote the profit of a deluxe bag, and z denote the value of the objective function. Using this notation, the objective function can be written as

$$z = c_1 x_1 + c_2 x_2$$

Writing this equation in slope-intercept form, we obtain

$$c_2 x_2 = -c_1 x_1 + z$$

and

$$x_2 = -\frac{c_1}{c_2} x_1 + \frac{z}{c_2}$$

Thus, we see that the slope of the objective function is given by $-c_1/c_2$. Substituting $-c_1/c_2$ into expression (3.1), we see that extreme point ③ will be optimal as long as the following expression is satisfied:

$$-\tfrac{3}{2} \le -\frac{c_1}{c_2} \le -\tfrac{7}{10} \tag{3.2}$$

To compute the range of optimality for the standard-bag profit contribution, we hold the profit contribution for the deluxe bag fixed at its initial value $c_2 = 9$. Doing so in (3.2), we obtain

$$-\tfrac{3}{2} \le -\frac{c_1}{9} \le -\tfrac{7}{10}$$

Using the left-hand inequality, we have

$$-\tfrac{3}{2} \le -\frac{c_1}{9} \qquad \text{or} \qquad \tfrac{3}{2} \ge \frac{c_1}{9}$$

Thus,

$$\tfrac{27}{2} \ge c_1 \qquad \text{or} \qquad c_1 \le \tfrac{27}{2} = 13.5$$

Using the right-hand inequality, we have

$$-\frac{c_1}{9} \le -\tfrac{7}{10} \qquad \text{or} \qquad \frac{c_1}{9} \ge \tfrac{7}{10}$$

Thus,

$$c_1 \ge \tfrac{63}{10} \qquad \text{or} \qquad c_1 \ge 6.3$$

Combining the above limits for c_1 provides the following range of optimality for the standard-bag profit contribution:

$$6.3 \le c_1 \le 13.5$$

In the original Par, Inc., problem the standard bag had a profit contribution of $10. The resulting optimal solution was 540 standard bags and 252 deluxe bags. The range of optimality for c_1 tells Par, Inc.'s management that, with other coefficients unchanged, the profit contribution for the standard bag can be anywhere between $6.30 and $13.50 and the production quantities of 540 standard bags and 252 deluxe bags will remain optimal.

Note, however, that while the production quantities will not change, the total profit contribution (value of objective function) will change due to the change in profit contribution per standard bag.

The above computations can be repeated, holding the profit contribution for standard bags constant at $c_1 = 10$. In this case the range of optimality for the profit contribution of deluxe bags, c_2, can be determined. Check to see that this range is $6.67 \leq c_2 \leq 14.29$.

In cases where the rotation of the objective function line about an optimal extreme point causes the objective function line to become *vertical,* there will be either no upper limit or no lower limit for the slope as it appears in the form of expression (3.2). To see how this special situation can happen in graphical sensitivity analysis, assume that the objective function for the Par, Inc., problem had been $18x_1 + 9x_2$; in this case, extreme point ② in Figure 3.2 provides the optimal solution. Rotating the objective function line counterclockwise around extreme point ② provides an upper limit for the slope when the objective function line coincides with line B. Since we have previously seen that the slope of line B is $-\frac{3}{2}$, the upper limit for the slope of the objective function line must be $-\frac{3}{2}$. However, rotating the objective function line clockwise results in the slope becoming more and more negative, approaching a value of minus infinity as the objective function line becomes vertical; in this case there is no lower limit for the slope of the objective function. Using the upper limit of $-\frac{3}{2}$, we can write

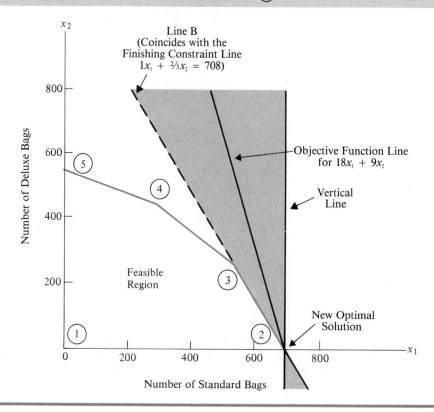

FIGURE 3.2
Graphical Solution of Par, Inc., Problem with Optimal Solution at Extreme Point ②

$$-\frac{c_1}{c_2} \leq -\frac{3}{2}$$

Slope of the
objective function line

Following our previous procedure of holding c_2 constant at its original value, $c_2 = 9$, we have

$$-\frac{c_1}{9} \leq -\frac{3}{2} \qquad \text{or} \qquad \frac{c_1}{9} \geq \frac{3}{2}$$

Solving for c_1 provides the following result:

$$c_1 \geq \frac{27}{2} = 13.5$$

In reviewing Figure 3.2 we note that extreme point ② remains optimal for all values of c_1 above 13.5. Thus, we obtain the following range of optimality for c_1 at extreme point ②:

$$13.5 \leq c_1 < \infty$$

Simultaneous Changes The range of optimality for objective function coefficients is only applicable for changes made to one coefficient at a time. All other coefficients are assumed fixed at their initial values. If two or more objective function coefficients are changed simultaneously, further analysis is necessary to determine whether the optimal solution will change. However, when solving two variable problems graphically, inequality (3.2) suggests an easy way to determine whether simultaneous changes in both objective function coefficients will cause a change in the optimal solution. Simply compute the slope of the objective function ($-c_1/c_2$) for the new coefficient values. If this ratio is greater than or equal to the lower limit on the slope of the objective function and less than or equal to the upper limit, then the changes made will not cause a change in the optimal solution.

Let us illustrate this approach by considering changes in both of the objective function coefficients for the Par, Inc., problem. Suppose the profit contribution per standard bag is increased to $13 and simultaneously the profit contribution per deluxe bag is reduced to $8. Recall that the ranges of optimality for c_1 and c_2 (both computed in a one-at-a-time manner) are

$$6.3 \leq c_1 \leq 13.5 \tag{3.3}$$

$$6.67 \leq c_2 \leq 14.29 \tag{3.4}$$

Given these ranges of optimality, we can conclude that changing either c_1 to $13 or c_2 to $8 (but not both) would not cause a change in the optimal solution of $x_1 = 540$ and $x_2 = 252$. But we cannot conclude from the ranges of optimality that changing both coefficients simultaneously would not result in a change in the optimal solution.

In expression (3.2) we showed that extreme point ③ remains optimal as long as

$$-\frac{3}{2} \leq -\frac{c_1}{c_2} \leq -\frac{7}{10}$$

If c_1 is changed to 13 and simultaneously c_2 is changed to 8, the new objective function slope will be given by

$$-\frac{c_1}{c_2} = -\frac{13}{8} = -1.625$$

Since this value is less than the lower limit of $-\frac{3}{2}$, the current solution of $x_1 = 540$ and $x_2 = 252$ will no longer be optimal. By resolving the problem with $c_1 = 13$ and $c_2 = 8$ we will find that extreme point ② is the new optimal solution.

Looking at the ranges of optimality, we concluded that changing either c_1 to \$13 or c_2 to \$8 (but not both) would not cause a change in the optimal solution. But in recomputing the slope of the objective function with simultaneous changes for both c_1 and c_2, we saw that the optimal solution did change. This emphasizes the fact that a range of optimality, by itself, can only be used to draw a conclusion about changes made to *one objective function coefficient at a time*.

Right-Hand Sides

Let us now consider how a change in the right-hand side for a constraint may affect the feasible region and perhaps cause a change in the optimal solution to the problem. For example, suppose an additional 10 hours of production time is made available in the cutting and dyeing department of Par, Inc. The right-hand side of the cutting and dyeing constraint is changed from 630 to 640, and the constraint is rewritten as

$$\tfrac{7}{10}x_1 + x_2 \le 640$$

By obtaining an additional 10 hours of cutting and dyeing time, we have expanded the feasible region for the problem, as shown in Figure 3.3. Since the feasible region has been enlarged, we know that the current solution remains feasible. But it may no longer be optimal. We must determine whether or not one of the new feasible solutions provides an improvement in the value of the objective function. Applying the graphical solution procedure to the problem with the enlarged feasible region shows that the extreme point at $x_1 = 527.5$ and $x_2 = 270.75$ now provides the optimal solution. The new value for the objective function is $10(527.5) + 9(270.75) = \$7711.75$; this provides an increase in profit of $\$7711.75 - \$7668.00 = \$43.75$. Thus, the increased profit occurs at a rate of \$43.75/10 hours = \$4.375 per hour added.

The change in the value of the objective function per unit increase in the value of the right-hand side is called the *shadow price*. Thus, the shadow price for cutting and dyeing production time is \$4.375 per hour. The shadow price of a particular constraint is considered important because it may be possible to purchase or obtain additional units of the resource. If the cost of cutting and dyeing time has not been deducted in computing the profit coefficients, it can be shown that management should be willing to pay up to \$4.375 per hour for additional hours of this resource.

We caution here that the value of the shadow price may be applicable only for small changes in the right-hand side. As more and more resources are obtained and the right-hand side continues to increase, other constraints will become binding and reduce the rate of change in the value of the objective function. For example, in the Par, Inc., problem at some point enough hours can be added to the cutting and dyeing department so that the constraint will no longer be binding. The optimal solution will then be found at the intersection of the inspection and packaging constraint line and the finishing constraint line. At this point additional hours for the cutting and dyeing department will be of no value. The topic of how much one can change a right-hand side before it is no longer desirable to do so will be discussed further in the next section.

The shadow price is defined as the per unit change in value of the objective function per unit increase in the right-hand side. A nonbinding constraint is one that has a positive

FIGURE 3.3
Effect of a 10-Unit Change in the Right-Hand Side of the Cutting and Dyeing Constraint

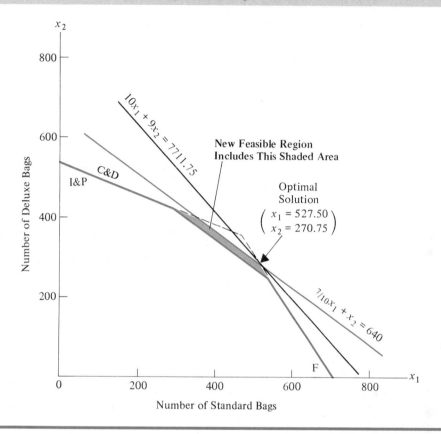

amount of slack or surplus. Clearly, then, a small increase in the right-hand side of such a constraint will only change the amount of slack or surplus and will not affect the value of the objective function. Thus, the shadow price for any nonbinding constraint will always be zero.

Cautionary Note on the Interpretation of Shadow Prices

As stated previously, the shadow price is the change in the value of the objective function per unit increase in the right-hand side of a constraint. When the right-hand side of the constraint represents the amount of a resource available, the associated shadow price is often interpreted as the amount one should be willing to pay for one additional unit of the resource. However, such an interpretation is not always correct. To see why, we need to understand the difference between sunk and relevant costs. A sunk cost is one that is not affected by the decision made. It will be incurred no matter what values the decision variables assume. A relevant cost is one that depends on the decision made. The amount of a relevant cost will vary depending on the values of the decision variables.

Let us reconsider the Par, Inc., problem. The amount of cutting and dyeing time available is 630 hours. The cost of the time available is a sunk cost if it must be paid regardless of the number of standard and deluxe golf bags produced. It would be a relevant cost if Par only had to pay for the number of hours of cutting and dyeing time actually used to produce golf bags. All relevant costs should be deducted in the objective function of a linear program. Sunk costs should not be reflected in the objective function. For Par, Inc., we have been assuming that the company must pay its employees for labor time whether or not it is used. Therefore, the cost of the labor hours resource for Par, Inc., is a sunk cost and has not been reflected in the objective function.

When the cost of a resource is *sunk,* the shadow price can be interpreted as the value of an additional unit of the resource. It is the amount the company should be willing to pay for one additional unit of the resource. When the cost of a resource used is relevant, the shadow price can be interpreted as the amount by which the value of the resource exceeds its cost. Thus, when the resource cost is relevant, the shadow price can be interpreted as the maximum premium over the normal cost that the company should be willing to pay for one unit of the resource.

▼ NOTES AND COMMENTS ▼

1. If two objective function coefficients change simultaneously, it is possible for both to move outside their respective ranges of optimality and not affect the optimal solution. For instance, in a two-variable linear program, both coefficients can double in value without changing the slope of the objective function.
2. The shadow price gives the change in value of the objective function per unit increase in the right-hand side of a constraint. A positive shadow price means *increasing* the right-hand side will *increase* the value of the objective function. Conversely, a negative shadow price means *decreasing* the right-hand side will *increase* the value of the objective function.
3. Managers are frequently called on to provide an economic justification for new technology. Often the new technology is developed, or purchased, in order to conserve resources. The shadow price can be helpful in such cases because it can be used to determine the savings attributable to the new technology by showing the savings per unit of resource conserved.

3.3 ▼ COMPUTER SOLUTION OF LINEAR PROGRAMS

Computer programs designed to solve linear programming problems are now widely available. Most large companies, as well as most universities, have access to these computer programs. The developmental effort for large-scale "software packages" has come primarily from computer manufacturers and/or software service companies such as IBM, Control Data, and Ketron. Usually after a short period of familiarization with the specific features of the package, users can solve linear programming problems with few difficulties. Problems involving thousands of variables and thousands of constraints can now be solved routinely through the use of computer packages. Most large linear programs can be solved with just a few minutes of computer time; small linear programs usually require only a few seconds.

More recently there has been a virtual explosion of software for microcomputers. A large number of "user-friendly" computer programs that can be used to solve linear programs on microcomputers are now available. These programs, developed by academicians and small software companies, are almost all easy to use. Most of these programs are designed to solve smaller linear programs (a few hundred variables at most). To solve large-scale linear programs involving several thousand variables and constraints, software packages designed for mainframe computers are usually needed.

The Management Scientist, a microcomputer software package developed by the authors of this text, contains a linear programming module. Let us demonstrate how the linear programming module can be used to solve the Par, Inc., problem. Since computer input must utilize decimal rather than fractional data values, the Par, Inc., problem is restated below with decimal coefficients:

$$\max \quad 10x_1 + \quad 9x_2$$

$$\text{s.t.}$$

$$0.7x_1 + \quad 1x_2 \leq 630 \quad \text{Cutting and dyeing}$$

$$0.5x_1 + .83333x_2 \leq 600 \quad \text{Sewing}$$

$$1.0x_1 + .66667x_2 \leq 708 \quad \text{Finishing}$$

$$0.1x_1 + \quad 0.25x_2 \leq 135 \quad \text{Inspection and packaging}$$

$$x_1, x_2 \geq 0$$

Note that in the above form the coefficient of x_2 in the sewing constraint is written as .83333, which is the closest five-place decimal value to the fraction $5/6$. A similar rounding occurs for the x_2 coefficient in the finishing constraint, where the decimal .66667 is used as the closest five-place decimal value to the fraction $2/3$. When this rounding of the input data is required, we may expect the computer solution to be slightly different than the hand-calculated solution based on the exact fraction values. However, as you will see, the two solutions are extremely close, and the slight rounding of the input data causes no serious problem.

After the user selects the linear programming module of The Management Scientist, the problem selection menu appears as shown in Figure 3.4. In the following figures, user responses are shown in color; the information printed by the computer is shown in

FIGURE 3.4
Linear Programming Menu from The Management Scientist
(User Response Shown in Color)

```
                    PROBLEM SELECTION MENU

          Choices

              1    Create a New Problem

              2    Retrieve a Previously Saved Problem

              3    Continue with the Current Problem

              4    Delete a Previously Saved Problem

              5    Return to the Top Level Menu

     PLEASE MAKE YOUR SELECTION AND PRESS RETURN    1
```

black. Note that the user has made choice 1, "Create a New Problem." After making this choice, the user is requested to type in the objective function and constraints.

Figure 3.5 shows the computer prompts and how the user types in the problem. The computer prints "OBJECTIVE FUNCTION:." The user then types the objective function as shown. After the user presses the return or enter key, the computer prints "CON-STRAINT 1:." The user then types in the constraint and again presses the return key. Note that the symbol < is interpreted as ≤ by The Management Scientist. The computer will continue to ask for constraints until the user types END. Figure 3.5 shows that the user has typed in the 4 constraints and then typed END when asked for constraint 5.

Typing END tells The Management Scientist that the complete problem has been entered. The computer then prints the problem disposition menu as shown in Figure 3.6. At this point the user can make choice 1 to solve the problem; choice 2 to save the problem for future use; choice 3 to display/edit the problem; or choice 4 to return to the problem

FIGURE 3.5
User Input of Par, Inc., Problem with The Management Scientist

```
OBJECTIVE FUNCTION:  MAX 10X1 + 9X2

CONSTRAINT  1:  .7X1 + 1X2 < 630

CONSTRAINT  2:  .5X1 + .83333X2 < 600

CONSTRAINT  3:  1X1 + .66667X2 < 708

CONSTRAINT  4:  1X1 + .25X2 < 135

CONSTRAINT  5:  END
```

FIGURE 3.6
User Makes Choice 1 Directing The Management Scientist to Solve the Par, Inc., Problem

```
                    PROBLEM DISPOSITION MENU

        Choices

              1    Solve the Problem

              2    Save the Problem

              3    Display/Edit the Problem

              4    Return to the Problem Selection Menu


    PLEASE MAKE YOUR SELECTION AND PRESS RETURN   1
```

FIGURE 3.7
Par, Inc., Solution Using The Management Scientist

```
Objective Function Value =        7667.994100
```

Variable	Value	Reduced Costs
X1	539.998410	0.000000
X2	252.001099	0.000000

Constraint	Slack/Surplus	Dual Prices
1	0.000000	4.374956
2	120.000702	0.000000
3	0.000000	6.937531
4	17.999870	0.000000

OBJECTIVE COEFFICIENT RANGES

Variable	Lower Limit	Current Value	Upper Limit
X1	6.300000	10.000000	13.499931
X2	6.666700	9.000000	14.285715

RIGHT HAND SIDE RANGES

Constraint	Lower Limit	Current Value	Upper Limit
1	495.600010	630.000000	682.363160
2	479.999300	600.000000	No Upper Limit
3	580.001460	708.000000	900.000000
4	117.000130	135.000000	No Upper Limit

selection menu. Choice 1 was selected, and the solution generated by The Management Scientist is shown in Figure 3.7.

Interpretation of Computer Output

Let us look more closely at The Management Scientist output in Figure 3.7 and interpret the computer solution provided for the Par, Inc., problem. First, note the number 7667.994100 which appears to the right of "Objective Function Value." Rounding this value, we can conclude that the optimal solution to the Par problem will provide a profit of $7668. Directly below the objective function value we find the values of the decision variables at the optimal solution. Thus, after rounding we have $x_1 = 540$ standard bags and $x_2 = 252$ deluxe bags as the optimal production quantities.

The information in the column labeled "Reduced Costs" indicates how much the objective function coefficient of each decision variable would have to improve[1] before it would be possible for that variable to assume a positive value in the optimal solution. If a decision variable is already positive in the optimal solution, its reduced cost is zero. For the Par, Inc., problem the optimal solution is $x_1 = 540$ and $x_2 = 252$. With both variables

---

[1]For a maximization problem, improve means get bigger; for a minimization problem, improve means get smaller.

already having positive values, their corresponding reduced costs are zero. In Section 3.4 we will interpret the reduced cost for a decision variable that does not have a positive value in the optimal solution.

Immediately following the optimal x_1 and x_2 values and the reduced cost information, the computer output provides information about the status of the constraints. Recall that the Par, Inc., problem had four less-than-or-equal-to constraints corresponding to the hours available in each of four production departments. The information shown in the column labeled "Slack/Surplus" provides the value of the slack variable for each of the departments. This information is summarized below:

Constraint Number	Constraint Name	Slack
1	Cutting and dyeing	0
2	Sewing	120
3	Finishing	0
4	Inspection and packaging	18

From the above information we see that the binding constraints (the cutting and dyeing and the finishing constraints) have zero slack at the optimal solution. The sewing department has 120 hours of slack, or unused capacity, and the inspection and packaging department has 18 hours of slack or unused capacity.

The column labeled "Dual Prices" contains information about the value of each of the four resources at the optimal solution. The dual price is defined as follows:

> The dual price associated with a constraint is the *improvement* in the optimal value of the objective function per unit increase in the right-hand side of the constraint.

Thus, we see that the nonzero dual prices of 4.374956 for constraint 1 (cutting and dyeing constraint) and 6.937531 for constraint 3 (finishing constraint) tell us that an additional hour of cutting and dyeing time improves (increases) the value of the objective function by $4.37 and an additional hour of finishing time improves (increases) the value of the objective function by $6.94. Thus, if the cutting and dyeing time were increased from 630 to 631 hours, with all other coefficients in the problem remaining the same, Par's profit would be increased by $4.37 from $7668 to $7668 + $4.37 = $7672.37. A similar interpretation for the finishing constraint implies that an increase in available finishing time from 708 to 709 hours, with all other coefficients in the problem remaining the same, would increase Par's profit to $7668 + $6.94 = $7674.94. Since the sewing and the inspection and packaging constraints both have slack or unused capacity available, the dual prices of zero show that additional hours of these two resources will not improve the value of the objective function.

As you may recall from the discussion of shadow prices in Section 3.2, the information in the "Dual Prices" column provides the shadow prices for Par's four resources. In fact, in the case of a *maximization* linear program, the dual price is the *same* as the shadow price. However, as we shall discuss later, in a minimization linear program the dual price is the *negative* of the corresponding shadow price.

Referring again to the computer output in Figure 3.7, we see that after providing the constraint information on slack/surplus variables and dual prices, The Management Scientist prints the ranges on the objective function coefficients and the right-hand sides of the constraints.

Considering the information provided under the computer output heading labeled "OBJECTIVE COEFFICIENT RANGES," we see that variable x_1, which has a current profit coefficient of 10, has the following range of optimality for c_1:

$$6.30 \leq c_1 \leq 13.50$$

This tells us that as long as the profit contribution associated with the standard bag is between \$6.30 and \$13.50, the production of $x_1 = 540$ standard bags and $x_2 = 252$ deluxe bags will remain the optimal solution. Note that this is the range of optimality that we obtained by performing graphical sensitivity analysis for c_1 in Section 3.2.

Using the objective function coefficient range information for deluxe bags, we see that The Management Scientist has computed the following range of optimality:

$$6.67 \leq c_2 \leq 14.29$$

This tells us that as long as the profit contribution associated with the deluxe bag is between \$6.67 and \$14.29, the production of $x_1 = 540$ standard bags and $x_2 = 252$ deluxe bags will remain the optimal solution.

The final section of the computer printout ("RIGHT HAND SIDE RANGES") contains ranging information for the constraint right-hand sides. As long as the constraint right-hand side stays within this range, the associated dual price gives the improvement in value of the objective function per unit increase in the right-hand side. For example, let us consider the cutting and dyeing constraint with a current right-hand side of 630. Since the dual price for this constraint is \$4.37, we can conclude that additional hours will increase the objective function by \$4.37 per hour. It is also true that a reduction in the hours available will reduce the value of the objective function by \$4.37 per hour. From the range information given we see that the dual price of \$4.37 is valid for increases up to 682.363160 and decreases down to 495.600010. A similar interpretation for the finishing constraint's right-hand side (constraint 3) shows that the dual price of \$6.94 is applicable for increases up to 900 hours and decreases down to 580.001460 hours.

As mentioned, the right-hand-side ranges provide limits within which the dual prices are applicable. For changes outside the range the problem must be resolved to find the new optimal solution and the new dual price. We shall call the range over which the dual price is applicable the *range of feasibility*. The ranges of feasibility for the Par, Inc., problem are summarized below.

Constraint	Min RHS	Max RHS
Cutting and dyeing	495.6	682.4
Sewing	480.0	No upper limit
Finishing	580.0	900.0
Inspection and packaging	117.0	No upper limit

As long as the values of the right-hand sides are within the above ranges, the dual prices shown on the computer output will not change. Values of the right-hand sides outside these limits will result in changes in the dual price information.

At this point it is important to note that the sensitivity analysis presented in computer output is based on the assumption that coefficients are changed *one at a time,* with all other coefficients of the problem remaining as stated in the original problem. The sensitivity analysis information provided in computer output does not apply to two or more simultaneous changes in the problem.

Simultaneous Changes As stated above, the ranges for objective function coefficients and constraint right-hand sides are only applicable for changes in a single coefficient. However, with the help of the *100 percent rule,*[2] some analysis of simultaneous changes is possible. If simultaneous changes in two or more objective function coefficients are made, the optimal solution will not change as long as the 100 percent rule is satisfied. Similarly, if simultaneous changes are made in two or more right-hand sides, the dual prices will not change as long as the 100 percent rule is satisfied.

To apply the 100 percent rule, for each coefficient changed we must compute the percentage of the allowable increase or allowable decrease represented by the change. For an objective function coefficient the allowable increase is the maximum amount the coefficient may be increased without exceeding the upper limit of the range of optimality. Similarly, the allowable decrease is the maximum amount the coefficient may be decreased without dropping below the lower limit of the range of optimality. For a constraint right-hand side the allowable increase is the maximum amount the right-hand side value may be increased without exceeding the upper limit of the range of feasibility, and the allowable decrease is the maximum amount the right-hand side value may be decreased without violating the lower limit of the range of feasibility. We now state the 100 percent rule as it applies to simultaneous changes in objective function coefficients and to simultaneous changes in constraint right-hand sides.

100 Percent Rule for Objective Function Coefficients

For all objective function coefficients changed, sum the percentages of allowable increases and allowable decreases. If the sum of percentages does not exceed 100 percent, then the optimal solution will not change.

100 Percent Rule for Constraint Right-Hand Sides

For all right-hand sides changed, sum the percentages of allowable increases and allowable decreases. If the sum of percentages does not exceed 100 percent, then the dual prices will not change.

Let us illustrate the 100 percent rule by considering simultaneous changes in the right-hand sides for the Par, Inc., problem. Suppose, for instance, that in the Par, Inc., problem we could obtain 20 additional hours of cutting and dyeing time and 100 additional hours of finishing time. The allowable increase for cutting and dyeing time is $52.36316 = 682.36316 - 630.0$, and the allowable increase for finishing time is $192.0 = 900.0 - 708.0$ (see Figure 3.7). The 20 additional hours of cutting and dyeing time are $(20/52.363130)(100) = 38.19\%$ of the allowable increase in the constraint's

---

[2]See S. P. Bradley, A. C. Hax, and T. L. Magnanti, (Reading, Mass.: Addison-Wesley, 1977).

right-hand side. The 100 additional hours of finishing time are $(100/192)(100) = 52.08\%$ of the allowable increase in the finishing time constraint's right-hand side. The accumulated percentage of change is $38.19\% + 52.08\% = 90.27\%$. Since the accumulative percentage of change does not exceed 100%, we can conclude that the dual prices are applicable and that the objective function will improve by $(20)(4.37) + (100)(6.94) = 781.40$.

Interpretation of Computer Output—A Second Example

As another example of interpreting computer output, let us reconsider the M&D Chemicals minimization problem introduced in Section 2.7. The linear programming model for this problem is restated below, where x_1 = number of gallons of product 1 and x_2 = number of gallons of product 2 and it is desired to minimize production cost.

$$\min \quad 2x_1 + 3x_2$$

s.t.

$$
\begin{array}{lll}
1x_1 & \geq 125 & \text{Demand for product 1} \\
1x_1 + 1x_2 & \geq 350 & \text{Total production requirement} \\
2x_1 + 1x_2 & \leq 600 & \text{Processing time limitation} \\
x_1, x_2 & \geq 0
\end{array}
$$

The solution obtained using The Management Scientist is presented in Figure 3.8. The computer output shows that the minimum cost solution yields an objective function value of $800. The values of the decision variables show that 250 gallons of product 1 (x_1 = 250) and 100 gallons of product 2 (x_2 = 100) provide the minimum-cost solution.

The "Slack/Surplus" information shows that the $\geq$ constraint for the demand of product 1 (see constraint 1) has a surplus of 125 units. This tells us that production of product 1 in the optimal solution exceeds demand by 125 gallons. The "Slack/Surplus" values are zero for the total production requirement (constraint 2) and the processing time limitation (constraint 3); this indicates that these constraints are binding at the optimal solution.

The "Dual Prices" column again shows us the *improvement* in the objective function per unit increase in the right-hand side of the constraint. Focusing first on the dual price of 1.00 for the processing time constraint (constraint 3), we see that if we can increase the processing time from 600 hours to 601 hours, the objective function value will *improve* by $1. Since the objective is to minimize costs, improvement in this case means a lowering of costs. Thus, if 601 hours of processing time are available, the value of the optimal solution will improve to $800 - $1 = $799. The "RIGHT HAND SIDE RANGES" section of the output shows that the upper limit for the processing time constraint (constraint 3) is 700 hours. Thus, the dual price of $1 per unit would be applicable for every additional hour of processing time up to a total of 700 hours.

Let us again return to the "Dual Prices" section of the output and consider the dual price for the total production constraint (constraint 2). The *negative dual price* tells us that the objective function *will not improve* if the value of the right-hand side is increased by one unit. In fact, the dual price of -4.00 tells us that if the right-hand side of the total production constraint is increased from 350 to 351 units, the value of the objective function will get worse by the amount of $4. Since becoming worse means an increase in

FIGURE 3.8
Solution of the M&D Chemicals Problem Provided
by The Management Scientist

Objective Function Value =   800.000000

Variable	Value	Reduced Costs
X1	250.000000	0.000000
X2	100.000000	0.000000

Constraint	Slack/Surplus	Dual Prices
1	125.000000	0.000000
2	0.000000	-4.000000
3	0.000000	1.000000

OBJECTIVE COEFFICIENT RANGES

Variable	Lower Limit	Current Value	Upper Limit
X1	No Lower Limit	2.000000	3.000000
X2	2.000000	3.000000	No Upper Limit

RIGHT HAND SIDE RANGES

Constraint	Lower Limit	Current Value	Upper Limit
1	No Lower Limit	125.000000	250.000000
2	300.000000	350.000000	475.000000
3	475.000000	600.000000	700.000000

cost, the value of the objective function will become $800 + $4 = $804 if the one-unit increase in the total production requirement is made.

Since the dual price refers to improvement in the value of the objective function per unit increase in the right-hand side, a constraint with a negative dual price should not have its right-hand side increased. In fact, if the dual price is negative, efforts should be made to reduce the right-hand side of the constraint. If the right-hand side of the total production constraint were decreased from 350 units to 349 units, the dual price tells us the total cost could be lowered by $4 to $800 − $4 = $796.

The interpretation of the dual price is the improvement in the value of the objective function per unit increase in the right-hand side of a constraint. However, as we have seen, the interpretation of an *improvement* in the value of an objective function depends on whether we are solving a maximization or a minimization problem. The dual price for a ≤ constraint will always be greater than or equal to 0 because increasing the right-hand side cannot make the value of the objective function worse. Similarly, the dual price for a ≥ constraint will always be less than or equal to 0 because increasing the right-hand side cannot improve the value of the objective function.

We caution that the interpretation of dual prices means that for maximization problems, dual prices and shadow prices are the same; for minimization problems, they have opposite signs. If you are using a different software package, you should check to see what convention and terminology are being used for this type of sensitivity analysis information.

Finally, consider the right-hand-side ranges provided in Figure 3.8. The *ranges of feasibility* for the M&D Chemicals problem are summarized below.

Constraint	Min RHS	Max RHS
Product 1 demand	None	250
Total production requirement	300	475
Processing time limitation	475	700

As long as the right-hand sides are within the above ranges, the dual prices shown on the computer printout are applicable. We now turn to the computer solution and the interpretation of computer output for a linear program involving more than two decision variables.

▼ NOTES AND COMMENTS ▼

1. Computer software packages for solving linear programs are readily available. Most of these provide the optimal solution, dual or shadow price information, the range of optimality for the objective function coefficients, and the range of feasibility for the right-hand sides. The labels used for the ranges of optimality and feasibility may vary, but the meaning is the same as what we have described here.
2. Whenever one of the right-hand sides is at an end point of its range of feasibility, the dual and shadow prices only provide one-sided information. In this case, they only predict the change in the optimal value of the objective function for changes toward the interior of the range.
3. A condition called *degeneracy* can cause a subtle difference in how we interpret changes in the objective function coefficients beyond the end points of the range of optimality. Degeneracy occurs when the dual price equals zero for one of the binding constraints. Degeneracy does not affect the interpretation of changes toward the interior of the range of optimality. However, when degeneracy is present, changes beyond the end points of the range do not necessarily mean a different solution will be optimal. From a practical point of view, changes beyond the end points of the range of optimality necessitate resolving the problem.
4. The 100 percent rule permits an analysis of multiple changes in the right-hand sides or multiple changes in the objective function coefficients. But the 100 percent rule cannot be applied to changes in both objective function coefficients *and* right-hand sides at the same time. In order to consider simultaneous changes for *both* right-hand-side values and objective function coefficients, the problem must be resolved.

3.4 ▼ MORE THAN TWO DECISION VARIABLES

The graphical solution procedure is useful only for linear programs involving two decision variables. Computer software packages are designed to handle linear programs involving large numbers of variables and constraints. In this section we discuss the formulation and computer solution of a linear program involving four decision variables. As we shall see, the approach to problem formulation and computer solution is essentially the same as for problems with two decision variables. After obtaining a verbal statement of the problem, we define the decision variables that will enable us to write the objective function and constraints associated with the problem as a linear program. Once the problem has been formulated, we can use a computer software package to obtain the optimal solution.

The Electronic Communications, Inc., Problem

Electronic Communications, Inc., manufactures portable radio systems that can be used for two-way communications. The company's new product, which has a range of up to 25 miles, is particularly suitable for use in a variety of business and personal applications. The distribution channels for the new radio are as follows:

1. Marine equipment distributors
2. Business equipment distributors
3. National chain of retail stores
4. Mail order

Because of differing distribution and promotional costs, the profitability of the product will vary with the distribution channel. In addition, the advertising cost and the personal sales effort required will vary with the distribution channels. Table 3.1 summarizes the profit, advertising cost, and personal sales effort data pertaining to the Electronic Communications problem. Additional facts are that the firm has set the advertising budget at $5000 and that there is a maximum of 1800 hours of sales force time available for allocation to the sales effort. Management has also decided to produce exactly 600 units for the current production period. Finally, an ongoing contract with the national chain of retail stores requires that at least 150 units be distributed through this distribution channel.

Electronic Communications, Inc., is now faced with the problem of establishing a strategy that will provide for the distribution of the radios in such a way that overall profitability of the new radio production will be maximized. Decisions must be made as to how many units should be allocated to each of the four distribution channels, as well as how to allocate the advertising budget and sales force effort to each of the four distribution channels.

TABLE 3.1
Profit, Advertising Cost, and Personal Sales Time Data for the Electronic Communications, Inc., Problem

Distribution Channel	Profit per Unit Sold	Advertising Cost per Unit Sold	Personal Sales Effort per Unit Sold
Marine distributors	$90	$10	2 hours
Business distributors	$84	$ 8	3 hours
National retail stores	$70	$ 9	3 hours
Mail order	$60	$15	None

Formulation of the Electronic Communications, Inc., Problem

To formulate a linear programming model for the Electronic Communications, Inc., problem, we introduce the following four decision variables:

x_1 = the number of units produced for the marine equipment distribution channel

x_2 = the number of units produced for the business equipment distribution channel

x_3 = the number of units produced for the national retail chain distribution channel

x_4 = the number of units produced for the mail order distribution channel

Using the data in Table 3.1, the objective function for maximizing the profit associated with the radios can be written as follows:

$$\max 90x_1 + 84x_2 + 70x_3 + 60x_4$$

Let us now proceed to formulate the constraints for the problem. Since the advertising budget has been set at $5000, the constraint that limits the amount of advertising expenditure can be written as follows:

$$10x_1 + 8x_2 + 9x_3 + 15x_4 \leq 5000$$

Similarly, since the sales time is limited to 1800 hours, we obtain the constraint

$$2x_1 + 3x_2 + 3x_3 \leq 1800$$

Management's decision to produce exactly 600 units during the current production period is expressed as

$$1x_1 + 1x_2 + 1x_3 + 1x_4 = 600$$

Finally, to account for the fact that the number of units distributed by the national chain of retail stores must be at least 150, we add the constraint

$$1x_3 \geq 150$$

Combining all of the constraints with the nonnegativity requirements enables us to write the complete linear programming model for the Electronic Communications, Inc., problem as follows:

$$\max \quad 90x_1 + 84x_2 + 70x_3 + 60x_4$$

s.t.

$$
\begin{aligned}
10x_1 + \; 8x_2 + \; 9x_3 + 15x_4 &\leq 5000 \quad \text{Advertising budget} \\
2x_1 + \; 3x_2 + \; 3x_3 \qquad\quad\; &\leq 1800 \quad \text{Sales force availability} \\
1x_1 + \; 1x_2 + \; 1x_3 + \; 1x_4 &= \;\; 600 \quad \text{Production level} \\
1x_3 \qquad\qquad &\geq \;\; 150 \quad \text{Retail stores requirement}
\end{aligned}
$$

$$x_1, x_2, x_3, x_4 \geq 0$$

Computer Solution and Interpretation for the Electronic Communications, Inc., Problem

A portion of the output obtained using The Management Scientist to solve the Electronic Communications problem is shown in Figure 3.9. The "Objective Function Value" section shows that the optimal solution to the problem will provide a maximum profit of $48,450. The optimal values of the decision variables are given by $x_1 = 25$, $x_2 = 425$, $x_3 = 150$, and $x_4 = 0$. Thus, the optimal strategy for Electronic Communications is to concentrate on the business equipment distribution channel with $x_2 = 425$ units. In addition, the firm should allocate 25 units to the marine distribution channel ($x_1 = 25$) and meet its 150-unit commitment to the national retail chain store distribution channel ($x_3 = 150$). With $x_4 = 0$, the optimal solution indicates that the firm should not use the mail order distribution channel.

Let us now look at the information contained in the column labeled "Reduced Costs." Recall that the reduced costs indicate how much each objective function coefficient would have to improve before the corresponding decision variable could assume a positive value in the optimal solution. As the computer output shows, the first three reduced costs are zero since the corresponding decision variables already have positive values in the optimal solution. However, the reduced cost of 45 for decision variable x_4 tells us that the profit for the new radios distributed via the mail order channel would have to increase from its current value of $60 per unit to at least $60 + $45 = $105 per unit before it would be profitable to begin using the mail order distribution channel.

The computer output information for the slack/surplus variables and the dual prices is restated below.

Constraint Number	Constraint Name	Type of Constraint	Slack or Surplus	Dual Price
1	Advertising budget	≤	0	3
2	Sales force availability	≤	25	0
3	Production level	=	0	60
4	Retail stores requirement	≥	0	−17

We see that the advertising budget constraint has a slack of zero, indicating that the entire budget of $5000 has been used. The corresponding dual price of 3 tells us that an additional dollar added to the advertising budget will improve the objective function (increase the profit) by $3. Thus, the possibility of increasing the advertising budget should be seriously considered by the firm. The slack of 25 hours for the sales force availability constraint shows that the allocated 1800 hours of sales time are adequate to distribute the radios produced and that 25 hours of sales force time will remain unused. Since the production level constraint is an equality, the zero slack/surplus shown on the output is expected. However, the dual price of 60 associated with this constraint shows that if the firm will consider increasing the production level for the radios, the value of the objective function, or profit, will improve at the rate of $60 per radio produced. Finally, the surplus of zero associated with the retail store distribution channel commitment is a result of this constraint being binding. The negative dual price indicates that increasing the commitment from 150 to 151 units will actually decrease the profit by $17. Thus, Electronic Communications may want to consider reducing its commitment to the retail store distribution channel. A *decrease* in the commitment will actually improve profit at the rate of $17 per unit.

FIGURE 3.9
A Portion of the Computer Output Provided by The Management Scientist for the Electronic Communications, Inc., Problem

```
Objective Function Value =         48450.000000

        Variable              Value            Reduced Costs
    --------------------  --------------------  ----------------------
          X1                25.000031              0.000000
          X2               424.999970              0.000000
          X3               150.000000              0.000000
          X4                 0.000000             45.000000

        Constraint         Slack/Surplus          Dual Prices
    --------------------  --------------------  ----------------------
           1                 0.000000              3.000000
           2                24.999542              0.000000
           3                 0.000000             60.000000
           4                 0.000000            -17.000000
```

Let us now consider the additional sensitivity analysis information provided by the computer output shown in Figure 3.10. The ranges of optimality for the objective function coefficients are

$$84 \leq c_1 < \text{No upper limit}$$

$$50 \leq c_2 \leq 90$$

$$\text{No lower limit} < c_3 \leq 87$$

$$\text{No lower limit} < c_4 \leq 105$$

FIGURE 3.10
Objective Coefficient and Right-Hand Side Ranges Provided by the Management Scientist for the Electronic Communications, Inc., Problem

OBJECTIVE COEFFICIENT RANGES

Variable	Lower Limit	Current Value	Upper Limit
X1	84.000000	90.000000	No Upper Limit
X2	50.000011	84.000000	90.000000
X3	No Lower Limit	70.000000	87.000000
X4	No Lower Limit	60.000000	105.000000

RIGHT HAND SIDE RANGES

Constraint	Lower Limit	Current Value	Upper Limit
1	4950.001000	5000.000000	5850.000000
2	1775.000490	1800.000000	No Upper Limit
3	515.000000	600.000000	603.571350
4	0.000000	150.000000	199.999100

The current solution, or strategy, remains optimal, provided that the objective function coefficients remain in the above ranges of optimality. Note in particular the range of optimality associated with the mail order distribution channel coefficient, c_4. This information is consistent with the earlier observation for the "Reduced Costs" portion of the output. In both instances we see that the per-unit profit would have to increase to $105 before the mail order distribution channel could be in the optimal solution with a positive value.

Finally, the sensitivity analysis information on "RIGHT HAND SIDE RANGES," as shown in Figure 3.10, provides the ranges of feasibility for the right-hand-side values.

Constraint	Min RHS	Current Value	Max RHS
Advertising budget	4950	5000	5850
Sales force	1775	1800	No upper limit
Production level	515	600	603.57
Retail stores requirement	0	150	200

Several interpretations of the above ranges are possible. In particular, recall that the dual price for advertising budget enabled us to conclude that each $1 increase in the budget would improve the profit by $3. The above range for the advertising budget shows that this statement about the value of increasing the budget is appropriate up to an advertising budget of $5850. Increases above this level would not necessarily be beneficial. Also note that the dual price of -17 for the retail stores requirement suggested the desirability of reducing this commitment. The above range of feasibility for this constraint shows that the commitment could be reduced to zero and the value of the reduction would be at the rate of $17 per unit.

Let us again point out that the sensitivity analysis or postoptimality analysis provided by computer software packages for linear programming problems considers only *one change at a time*, with all other coefficients of the problem remaining as originally specified. As mentioned earlier, simultaneous changes can sometimes be analyzed without resolving the problem, provided that the cumulative changes are not large enough to violate the 100 percent rule.

Finally, recall that the complete solution to the Electronic Communications problem requested information not only on the number of units to be distributed over each channel, but also on the allocation of the advertising budget and the sales force effort to each distribution channel. Since the optimal solution is $x_1 = 25$, $x_2 = 425$, $x_3 = 150$, and $x_4 = 0$, we can simply evaluate each term in a given constraint to determine how much of the constraint resource is allocated to each distribution channel. For example, the advertising budget constraint of

$$10x_1 + 8x_2 + 9x_3 + 15x_4 \leq 5000$$

shows $10x_1 = 10(25) = \$250$, $8x_2 = 8(425) = \$3400$, $9x_3 = 9(150) = \$1350$, and $15x_4 = 15(0) = \$0$. Thus, the advertising budget allocations are, respectively, $250, $3400, $1350, and $0 for each of the four distribution channels. Making similar calculations for the sales force constraint results in the managerial summary of the Electronic Communications optimal solution as shown in Table 3.2.

TABLE 3.2
Profit Maximizing Strategy for the Electronic Communications, Inc., Problem

Distribution Channel	Volume	Advertising Allocation	Sales Force Allocation (hours)
Marine distributors	25	$ 250	50
Business distributors	425	3400	1275
National retail stores	150	1350	450
Mail order	0	0	0
Totals	600	$5000	1775
Projected total profit = $48,450			

▼ SUMMARY

In this chapter we have presented the important concepts of sensitivity analysis and shown how computer software packages can be used to solve linear programming problems. We first developed graphical sensitivity analysis in order to demonstrate how a change in a coefficient of the objective function or in the right-hand-side of a constraint can affect the optimal solution to the problem. Methods were introduced for finding the ranges of optimality for the objective function coefficients and the ranges of feasibility for the right-hand sides of the constraints. The concept of a shadow price was introduced as a measure of the change in the value of the objective function for a one-unit increase in the right-hand side of a constraint. In cases where the constraint involves a limit on an available resource, the shadow price provides important information that helps to determine the desirability of obtaining additional units of the resource. The dual price provides essentially the same information; it provides the improvement in the optimal value of the objective function per unit increase in the right-hand side of a constraint. For maximization problems the shadow and dual prices are equal; for minimization problems they are equal in absolute value but have opposite signs.

Sensitivity analysis is conducted after the optimal solution to the original linear programming problem has been obtained. For this reason, sensitivity analysis is often referred to as postoptimality analysis. The standard sensitivity analysis procedures are based on the assumption that only one of the coefficients of the problem changes; all other coefficients are assumed to be held constant at their initial values. It is possible to do some limited sensitivity analysis on the effect of changing more than one coefficient at a time. For two variable problems the effect of changing both objective function coefficients can be determined by recomputing the slope $(-c_1/c_2)$. For larger problems the effect of simultaneous changes can be determined by using the 100 percent rule.

Since the graphical method and graphical sensitivity analysis are limited to linear programs with two decision variables, a computer solution procedure was presented as a practical method of solving linear programming problems with any number of decision variables. Although many software packages are available for computer solution, we used The Management Scientist to illustrate linear programming solutions on a microcomputer. We demonstrated the "user-friendly" aspect of the data input. Then we showed the computer output for three example problems in order to demonstrate the use and interpretation of the results. In addition to the value of the objective function and the optimal values of the decision variables, the computer output provides a variety of additional information concerning slack, surplus, and dual prices, as well as objective function coefficient and right-hand-side ranges. In the chapter appendix we show how LINDO/PC, a popular software package developed by Linus E. Schrage at the University of Chicago, is used.

▼ GLOSSARY

Sensitivity analysis   The evaluation of how changes in the coefficients of a linear programming problem affect the optimal solution to the problem.

Postoptimality analysis   Another name for sensitivity analysis, indicating that the analysis is performed after the optimal solution to the original linear programming problem has been obtained.

Range of optimality   The range of values over which an objective function coefficient may vary without causing any change in the values of the decision variables in the optimal solution.

Shadow price   The change in the value of the objective function per unit increase in the right-hand side associated with a constraint.

Reduced cost   The amount by which an objective function coefficient would have to improve (increase for a maximization problem, decrease for a minimization problem), before it would be possible for the corresponding variable to assume a positive value in the optimal solution.

Dual price   The improvement in the value of the objective function per unit increase in a constraint right-hand side. In a maximization problem the dual price is the same as the shadow price. In a minimization problem the dual price is the negative of the shadow price.

Range of feasibility   The range of values over which a right-hand side may vary without changing the value and interpretation of the dual or shadow price.

100 percent rule   A rule indicating when simultaneous changes in two or more objective function coefficients will not cause a change in the optimal values for the decision variables. It can also be applied to indicate when two or more right-hand-side changes will not cause a change in any of the dual prices.

▼ PROBLEMS

1. Recall the RMC problem (Chapter 2, problem 31). Letting

$$x_1 = \text{tons of fuel additive produced}$$

$$x_2 = \text{tons of solvent base produced}$$

leads to the following formulation of the RMC problem:

$$\max \quad 40x_1 + 30x_2$$

s.t.

$$\frac{2}{5}x_1 + \frac{1}{2}x_2 \leq 20 \quad \text{Material 1}$$

$$\frac{1}{5}x_2 \leq 5 \quad \text{Material 2}$$

$$\frac{3}{5}x_1 + \frac{3}{10}x_2 \leq 21 \quad \text{Material 3}$$

$$x_1, x_2 \geq 0$$

Use the graphical sensitivity analysis approach to determine what ranges of values for the profit per ton of the fuel additive and solvent base can exist without causing RMC to change from the current optimal solution of 25 tons of fuel additive and 20 tons of solvent base.

2. For the RMC situation (problem 1) use the graphical sensitivity analysis approach to determine what happens if an additional 3 tons of material 3 become available. What is the corresponding shadow price?

3. Consider the linear program given below.

$$\max \quad 2x_1 + 3x_2$$

s.t.

$$x_1 + x_2 \leq 10$$
$$2x_1 + x_2 \geq 4$$
$$x_1 + 3x_2 \leq 24$$
$$2x_1 + x_2 \leq 16$$
$$x_1, x_2 \geq 0$$

  a. Solve this problem using the graphical solution procedure.
  b. Compute the range of optimality for c_1.
  c. Compute the range of optimality for c_2.
  d. Suppose c_1 is increased from 2 to 2.5. What is the new optimal solution?
  e. Suppose c_2 is decreased from 3 to 1. What is the new optimal solution?

4. Refer again to problem 3.
  a. Compute the shadow prices for constraints 1 and 2 and interpret them.
  b. What are the dual prices for constraints 1 and 2? Interpret them.

5. Consider the linear program given below.

$$\min \quad x_1 + x_2$$

s.t.

$$x_1 + 2x_2 \geq 7$$
$$2x_1 + x_2 \geq 5$$
$$x_1 + 6x_2 \geq 11$$
$$x_1, x_2 \geq 0$$

  a. Solve this problem using the graphical solution procedure.
  b. Compute the range of optimality for c_1.
  c. Compute the range of optimality for c_2.
  d. Suppose c_1 is increased to 1.5. Find the new optimal solution.
  e. Suppose c_2 is decreased to $\frac{1}{3}$. Find the new optimal solution.

6. Refer again to problem 5.
  a. Compute and interpret the shadow prices for the constraints.
  b. What are the dual prices? Interpret them.

7. Consider the linear program given below.

$$\max \quad 5x_1 + 7x_2$$

s.t.

$$2x_1 + x_2 \geq 3$$
$$-x_1 + 5x_2 \geq 4$$
$$2x_1 - 3x_2 \leq 6$$
$$3x_1 + 2x_2 \leq 35$$
$$\tfrac{3}{7}x_1 + x_2 \leq 10$$
$$x_1, x_2 \geq 0$$

a. Solve this problem using the graphical solution procedure.
b. Compute the range of optimality for c_1.
c. Compute the range of optimality for c_2.
d. Suppose c_1 is decreased to 2. What is the new optimal solution?
e. Suppose c_2 is increased to 10. What is the new optimal solution?

8. Refer again to problem 7 and suppose the objective function coefficient for c_2 is reduced to 3.
a. Resolve using the graphical solution procedure.
b. Compute the dual prices for constraints 2 and 3.

9. Refer again to problem 3.
a. Suppose c_1 is increased to 3 and c_2 is increased to 4. Find the new optimal solution.
b. Suppose c_1 is increased to 3 and c_2 is decreased to 2. Find the new optimal solution.

10. Refer again to problem 7.
a. Suppose c_1 is decreased to 4 and c_2 is increased to 10. Find the new optimal solution.
b. Suppose c_1 is decreased to 4 and c_2 is increased to 8. Find the new optimal solution.
c. Suppose c_1 is increased to 20 and c_2 is increased to 28. Find the new optimal solution.

11. Recall the Kelson Sporting Equipment problem (Chapter 2, problem 17). Letting

$$x_1 = \text{number of regular gloves}$$

$$x_2 = \text{number of catcher's mitts}$$

leads to the following formulation:

$$\max \quad 5x_1 + 8x_2$$

s.t.

$$x_1 + \tfrac{3}{2}x_2 \leq 900 \quad \text{Cutting and sewing}$$
$$\tfrac{1}{2}x_1 + \tfrac{1}{3}x_2 \leq 300 \quad \text{Finishing}$$
$$\tfrac{1}{8}x_1 + \tfrac{1}{4}x_2 \leq 100 \quad \text{Packaging and shipping}$$
$$x_1, x_2 \geq 0$$

The computer solution obtained using The Management Scientist is shown in Figure 3.11.

a. What is the optimal solution, and what is the value of the profit contribution?

b. Which constraints are binding?

c. What are the dual prices for the resources? Interpret each.

d. If overtime can be scheduled in one of the departments, where would you recommend doing so?

12. Refer again to the computer solution of the Kelson Sporting Equipment problem in Figure 3.11 (see problem 11 above).

a. Compute the ranges of optimality for the objective function coefficients.

b. Interpret the ranges in part (a) for the Kelson problem.

c. Interpret the range of feasibility for the right-hand sides.

d. How much will the value of the optimal solution improve if 20 extra hours of packaging and shipping time are made available?

13. Recall the Investment Advisors problem (Chapter 2, problem 20). Letting

$$x_1 = \text{shares of U.S. Oil}$$

$$x_2 = \text{shares of Hub Properties}$$

FIGURE 3.11
The Management Scientist Solution of the Kelson Sporting Equipment Problem

Objective Function Value =   3700.001500

Variable	Value	Reduced Costs
X1	500.001500	0.000000
X2	149.999298	0.000000

Constraint	Slack/Surplus	Dual Prices
1	174.999634	0.000000
2	0.000000	2.999985
3	0.000000	28.000061

OBJECTIVE COEFFICIENT RANGES

Variable	Lower Limit	Current Value	Upper Limit
X1	4.000000	5.000000	12.000120
X2	3.333300	8.000000	10.000000

RIGHT HAND SIDE RANGES

Constraint	Lower Limit	Current Value	Upper Limit
1	725.000370	900.000000	No Upper Limit
2	133.332016	300.000000	400.000000
3	74.999992	100.000000	134.999817

leads to the following formulation:

$$\max \quad 3x_1 + 5x_2 \qquad \text{Maximum annual return}$$

s.t.

$$25x_1 + 50x_2 \leq 80{,}000 \quad \text{Funds available}$$
$$0.50x_1 + 0.25x_2 \leq \quad 700 \quad \text{Risk maximum}$$
$$1x_1 \qquad\qquad \leq \quad 1000 \quad \text{U.S. Oil maximum}$$
$$x_1, x_2 \geq 0$$

The computer solution of this problem is shown in Figure 3.12.

a. What is the optimal solution, and what is the value of the total estimated annual return?

b. Which constraints are binding? What is your interpretation of this in terms of the problem?

c. What are the dual prices for the constraints? Interpret each.

d. Would it be beneficial to relax the constraint on the amount invested in U.S. Oil? Why or why not?

14. Refer again to Figure 3.12, which shows the computer solution of problem 13.

a. How much would the estimated per-share return for U.S. Oil have to increase before it would be beneficial to increase the investment in this stock?

FIGURE 3.12
The Management Scientist Solution of the Investment Advisors Problem

```
Objective Function Value =    8399.999000

     Variable              Value              Reduced Costs
---------------------  -------------------  ---------------------
        X1               800.000120             0.000000
        X2              1199.999880             0.000000


    Constraint          Slack/Surplus            Dual Prices
---------------------  -------------------  ---------------------
        1                 0.000000               0.093333
        2                 0.000000               1.333333
        3               199.999878               0.000000


OBJECTIVE COEFFICIENT RANGES

  Variable      Lower Limit      Current Value      Upper Limit
------------  ---------------  ---------------  ---------------
     X1          2.500000         3.000000        10.000000
     X2          1.500000         5.000000         6.000000


RIGHT HAND SIDE RANGES

  Constraint     Lower Limit      Current Value      Upper Limit
------------  ---------------  ---------------  ---------------
      1        65000.008000     80000.000000    140000.016000
      2          399.999970       700.000000       774.999940
      3          800.000120      1000.000000    No Upper Limit
```

b. How much would the estimated per-share return for Hub Properties have to decrease before it would be beneficial to reduce the investment in this stock?

c. How much would the total annual return be reduced if the U.S. Oil maximum were reduced to 900 shares?

15. Recall the Wilkinson Motors problem (Chapter 2, problem 29). Letting

$$x_1 = \text{number of automobiles}$$

$$x_2 = \text{number of station wagons}$$

leads to the following formulation:

$$\max \quad 400x_1 + 500x_2 \qquad \text{Maximum profit contribution}$$

s.t.

$$2x_1 + 3x_2 \leq 900 \quad \text{Dealer preparation time}$$

$$1x_1 \qquad \leq 300 \quad \text{Auto limit}$$

$$1x_2 \leq 150 \quad \text{Wagon limit}$$

$$x_1, x_2 \geq 0$$

The computer solution of this problem is shown in Figure 3.13.

a. How many regular automobiles and station wagons should Wilkinson order? What will the profit contribution be if all the units ordered are sold?

FIGURE 3.13
The Management Scientist Solution of the Wilkinson Motors Problem

```
Objective Function Value =    170000.000000

        Variable              Value              Reduced Costs
   -----------------    -----------------    -----------------------
        X1                300.000000              0.000000
        X2                100.000000              0.000000


        Constraint         Slack/Surplus            Dual Prices
   -----------------    -----------------    -----------------------
        1                   0.000000              166.666672
        2                   0.000000               66.666656
        3                  50.000000                0.000000


OBJECTIVE COEFFICIENT RANGES

    Variable       Lower Limit      Current Value      Upper Limit
   -----------   ---------------   ---------------   ---------------
        X1         333.333340        400.000000       No Upper Limit
        X2           0.000000        500.000000        600.000000


RIGHT HAND SIDE RANGES

   Constraint      Lower Limit      Current Value      Upper Limit
   -----------   ---------------   ---------------   ---------------
        1          600.000000        900.000000       1050.000000
        2          225.000000        300.000000        450.000000
        3          100.000000        150.000000       No Upper Limit
```

b. How much would the profit contribution of the regular automobiles have to decrease before Wilkinson would consider modifying its optimal solution?

c. Should Wilkinson consider raising the limit on the number of station wagons ordered beyond 150?

d. If the profit contribution for regular automobiles is reduced by $30 and the profit contribution for station wagons is increased by $50, should Wilkinson consider changing the order? Explain.

16. Recall the Innis Investments problem (Chapter 2, problem 27). Letting

$$x_1 = \text{units purchased in the stock fund}$$

$$x_2 = \text{units purchased in the money market fund}$$

leads to the following formulation:

$$\text{min} \quad 8x_1 + 3x_2$$

s.t.

$$50x_1 + 100x_2 \leq 1{,}200{,}000 \quad \text{Funds available}$$
$$5x_1 + 4x_2 \geq 60{,}000 \quad \text{Annual income}$$
$$x_2 \geq 3{,}000 \quad \text{Min. Units in Money Market}$$
$$x_1, x_2 \geq 0$$

The computer solution is shown in Figure 3.14.

a. What is the optimal solution, and what is the minimum total risk?

b. Specify the range of optimality for the objective function coefficients.

c. How much annual income will be earned by the portfolio?

d. What is the rate of return for the portfolio?

e. What is the dual price for the funds available constraint?

f. What is the marginal rate of return on extra funds added to the portfolio?

17. Refer again to problem 16 and the computer solution shown in Figure 3.14.

a. Suppose the risk index for the stock fund (the value of c_1) increases from its current value of 8 to 12. How does the optimal solution change, if at all?

b. Suppose the risk index for the money market fund (the value of c_2) increases from its current value of 3 to 3.5. How does the optimal solution change, if at all?

c. Suppose c_1 increases to 12 and c_2 increases to 3.3. How does the optimal solution change, if at all?

18. Suppose that in a product-mix problem x_1, x_2, x_3, and x_4 indicate the units of products 1, 2, 3, and 4, respectively, and the linear program is

$$\text{max} \quad 4x_1 + 6x_2 + 3x_3 + 1x_4$$

s.t.

$$1.5x_1 + 2x_2 + 4x_3 + 3x_4 \leq 550 \quad \text{Machine } A \text{ hours}$$
$$4x_1 + 1x_2 + 2x_3 + 1x_4 \leq 700 \quad \text{Machine } B \text{ hours}$$
$$2x_1 + 3x_2 + 1x_3 + 2x_4 \leq 200 \quad \text{Machine } C \text{ hours}$$
$$x_1, x_2, x_3, x_4 \geq 0$$

The computer solution developed using The Management Scientist is shown in Figure 3.15.

FIGURE 3.14
The Management Scientist Solution of the Innis Investments Problem

```
Objective Function Value =    62000.000000

        Variable              Value              Reduced Costs
   -----------------    -----------------    ---------------------
         X1                3999.998000            0.000000
         X2               10000.002000            0.000000


        Constraint         Slack/Surplus           Dual Prices
   -----------------    -----------------    ---------------------
          1                  0.000000              0.056667
          2                  0.000000             -2.166667
          3               7000.002000              0.000000


OBJECTIVE COEFFICIENT RANGES

     Variable        Lower Limit       Current Value       Upper Limit
   -------------    -------------    -----------------    -------------
        X1              3.750000          8.000000        No Upper Limit
        X2          No Lower Limit        3.000000            6.400000


RIGHT HAND SIDE RANGES

    Constraint       Lower Limit        Current Value        Upper Limit
   -------------    -------------    -----------------    ----------------
         1          779999.880000    1200000.000000       1499999.750000
         2           48000.008000      60000.000000        102000.016000
         3          No Lower Limit      3000.000000         10000.002000
```

a. What is the optimal solution, and what is the value of the objective function?
b. Which constraints are binding?
c. Which machines have excess capacity available? How much?
d. If the objective function coefficient of x_1 is increased by 0.50, will the optimal solution change?

19. Refer again to the computer solution of problem 18 in Figure 3.15.
   a. Identify the range of optimality for each objective function coefficient.
   b. Suppose the objective function coefficient for x_1 is decreased by 3, the objective function coefficient of x_2 is increased by 1.5, and the objective function coefficient for x_4 is increased by 1. What will the new optimal solution be?
   c. Identify the range of feasibility for the right-hand side values.
   d. If the number of hours available on machine A is increased by 300, will the dual price for that constraint change?

20. Consider the following linear program and computer solution shown in Figure 3.16.

$$\min \quad 15x_1 + 15x_2 + 16x_3$$

$$\text{s.t.}$$

$$1x_1 \qquad + \quad 1x_3 \leq 30$$

$$0.5x_1 - 1x_2 + 6x_3 \geq 15$$

$$3x_1 + 4x_2 - 1x_3 \geq 20$$

$$x_1, x_2, x_3 \geq 0$$

FIGURE 3.15
Solution of Problem 18 Provided by The Management Scientist

```
Objective Function Value =    525.000000
```

Variable	Value	Reduced Costs
X1	0.000000	0.050000
X2	25.000004	0.000000
X3	125.000000	0.000000
X4	0.000000	3.500000

Constraint	Slack/Surplus	Dual Prices
1	0.000000	0.300000
2	425.000000	0.000000
3	0.000000	1.800000

OBJECTIVE COEFFICIENT RANGES

Variable	Lower Limit	Current Value	Upper Limit
X1	No Lower Limit	4.000000	4.050000
X2	5.923077	6.000000	9.000000
X3	2.000000	3.000000	12.000000
X4	No Lower Limit	1.000000	4.500000

RIGHT HAND SIDE RANGES

Constraint	Lower Limit	Current Value	Upper Limit
1	133.333344	550.000000	800.000000
2	275.000000	700.000000	No Upper Limit
3	137.500000	200.000000	824.999940

  a. What is the optimal solution, and what is the optimal value for the objective function?
  b. Which constraints are binding?
  c. What are the dual prices? Interpret each.
  d. What are the shadow prices?
  e. If you could change the right-hand side of one constraint by one unit, which one would you choose? What would be the new value of the right-hand side?
21. Refer again to the computer solution of problem 20 in Figure 3.16.
  a. Interpret the ranges of optimality for the objective function coefficients.
  b. Suppose c_1 is increased by 0.25. What is the new optimal solution?
  c. Suppose c_1 is increased by 0.25 and c_2 is decreased by 0.25. What is the new optimal solution?
22. Supersport Footballs, Inc., has the problem of determining the best number of All-Pro (x_1), College (x_2), and High-School (x_3) models of footballs to produce in order to maximize profits. Constraints include production capacity limitations (minutes of time available) in each of three departments (cutting and dyeing, sewing, and inspection and packaging) as well as a constraint that requires production of at least

FIGURE 3.16
Solution of Problem 20 Provided by The Management Scientist

Objective Function Value =   139.729736

Variable	Value	Reduced Costs
X1	7.297298	0.000001
X2	0.000000	0.675674
X3	1.891892	0.000001

Constraint	Slack/Surplus	Dual Prices
1	20.810810	0.000000
2	0.000000	-3.405406
3	0.000000	-4.432433

OBJECTIVE COEFFICIENT RANGES

Variable	Lower Limit	Current Value	Upper Limit
X1	1.333333	15.000000	15.543477
X2	14.324326	15.000000	No Upper Limit
X3	13.500005	16.000000	180.000000

RIGHT HAND SIDE RANGES

Constraint	Lower Limit	Current Value	Upper Limit
1	9.189190	30.000000	No Upper Limit
2	3.333333	15.000000	111.249992
3	-2.500000	20.000000	89.999992

1000 All-Pro footballs. The linear programming model of Supersport's problem is shown below:

$$\max \quad 3x_1 + 5x_2 + 4x_3$$

s.t.

$$12x_1 + 10x_2 + 8x_3 \leq 18{,}000 \quad \text{Cutting and dyeing}$$
$$15x_1 + 15x_2 + 12x_3 \leq 18{,}000 \quad \text{Sewing}$$
$$3x_1 + 4x_2 + 2x_3 \leq 9{,}000 \quad \text{Inspection and packaging}$$
$$1x_1 \qquad\qquad\qquad \geq 1{,}000 \quad \text{All-Pro model}$$
$$x_1, x_2, x_3 \geq 0$$

The computer printout of the solution to the Supersport problem is shown in Figure 3.17.

a. How many footballs of each type should Supersport produce in order to maximize the profit contribution?

b. Which constraints are binding?

FIGURE 3.17
Solution of the Supersport Footballs Problem Provided by The Management Scientist

Objective Function Value =   4000.000000

Variable	Value	Reduced Costs
X1	1000.000000	0.000000
X2	200.000122	0.000000
X3	0.000000	0.000000

Constraint	Slack/Surplus	Dual Prices
1	4000.000000	0.000000
2	0.000000	0.333333
3	5199.999500	0.000000
4	0.000000	-2.000000

OBJECTIVE COEFFICIENT RANGES

Variable	Lower Limit	Current Value	Upper Limit
X1	No Lower Limit	3.000000	5.000000
X2	5.000000	5.000000	No Upper Limit
X3	No Lower Limit	4.000000	4.000000

RIGHT HAND SIDE RANGES

Constraint	Lower Limit	Current Value	Upper Limit
1	14000.000000	18000.000000	No Upper Limit
2	14999.998000	18000.000000	24000.000000
3	3800.000500	9000.000000	No Upper Limit
4	0.000000	1000.000000	1200.000120

   c. Interpret the slack and/or surplus in each constraint.
   d. Interpret the range of optimality for the profit contribution of the three footballs.
23. Refer again to the computer solution of problem 22 (see Figure 3.17).
   a. Overtime rates in the sewing department are $12 per hour. Would you recommend that the company consider using overtime in that department? Explain.
   b. What is the shadow price for the fourth constraint? Interpret its value for management.
   c. Note that the reduced cost for x_3 is zero, but x_3 is not in the solution at a positive value. What is your interpretation of this?
   d. Suppose that the profit contribution of the College ball is increased by $1. How do you expect the solution to change?
   Note: Problems 24 and 25 and the case problem require computer solution and interpretation of the results.
24. A manufacturer makes three components for sale to refrigeration companies. The components are processed on two machines: a shaper and a grinder. The times (in minutes) required on each machine are given below.

| Component | Machine | |
	Shaper	Grinder
1	6	4
2	4	5
3	4	2

The shaper is available for 120 hours, and the grinder is available for 110 hours. No more than 200 units of component 3 can be sold, but up to 1000 units of each of the other components can be sold. In fact, the company already has orders for 600 units of component 1 that must be satisfied. The profit contributions for components 1, 2, and 3 are $8, $6, and $9, respectively.

a. Formulate and solve for the recommended production quantities. Use any computer code available.

b. What are the ranges of optimality for the profit contributions of the three components? Interpret these ranges for company management.

c. What are the ranges of feasibility for the right-hand sides? Interpret these ranges for company management.

d. If more time could be made available on the grinder, how much would it be worth?

e. If more units of component 3 can be sold by reducing the sales price by $4, should the company reduce the price?

25. The Pfeiffer Company manages approximately $15 million for clients. For each client, Pfeiffer chooses a mix of three investment vehicles: a growth stock fund, an income fund, and a money market fund. Each client has different investment objectives and tolerance for risk. In order to accommodate these differences, Pfeiffer places limits on the percentage of each portfolio that may be invested in the three funds and assigns a portfolio risk index to each client.

Here's how the system works for Dennis Hartmann, one of Pfeiffer's clients. Based on an evaluation of Hartmann's risk tolerance, Pfeiffer has assigned Hartmann's portfolio a risk index of .05. Furthermore, to maintain diversity, the fraction of Hartmann's portfolio invested in the growth and income funds must be at least 10% for each, and at least 20% must be in the money market fund.

The risk ratings for the growth, income, and money market funds are 0.10, 0.05, and 0.01, respectively. A portfolio risk index is computed as a weighted average of the risk ratings for the three funds where the weights are the fraction of the portfolio invested in each of the funds. Hartmann has given Pfeiffer $300,000 to manage. Pfeiffer is currently forecasting a yield of 20% on the growth fund, 10% on the income fund, and 6% on the money market fund.

a. Develop a linear programming model to select the best mix of investments for Hartmann's portfolio.

b. Use any linear programming computer code to solve the model you developed in part (a).

c. How much may the yields on the three funds vary before it will be necessary for Pfeiffer to modify Hartmann's portfolio?

d. If Hartmann were more risk tolerant, how much of a yield increase could he expect? For instance, what if his portfolio risk index is increased to 0.06?

e. If Pfeiffer revised his yield estimate for the growth fund downward to 0.10, how would you recommend modifying Hartmann's portfolio?

f. What information must Pfeiffer maintain on each client in order to use this system to manage client portfolios?

g. On a weekly basis Pfeiffer revises the yield estimates for the three funds. Suppose Pfeiffer has 50 clients. Describe how you would envision Pfeiffer making weekly modifications in each client's portfolio and deciding how to allocate the total funds managed among the three investment funds.

▼ CASE PROBLEM

PRODUCT MIX

TJ's, Inc., makes three nut mixes for sale to grocery chains located in the Southeast. The three mixes, referred to as the Regular Mix, the Deluxe Mix, and the Holiday Mix, are made by mixing together different percentages of five types of nuts.

In preparation for the fall season, TJ's has just purchased the following shipments of nuts at the prices shown:

Type of Nut	Shipment Amount (pounds)	Cost per Shipment
Almonds	6000	$7500
Brazil	7500	$7125
Filberts	7500	$6750
Pecans	6000	$7200
Walnuts	7500	$7875

The Regular Mix consists of 15% almonds, 25% Brazil nuts, 25% filberts, 10% pecans, and 25% walnuts. The Deluxe Mix consists of 20% of each type of nut, and the Holiday Mix consists of 25% almonds, 15% Brazil nuts, 15% filberts, 25% pecans, and 20% walnuts.

TJ's accountant has analyzed the cost of packaging materials, sales price per pound, etc., and determined that the contribution to profit is $1.65 per pound for the Regular Mix, $2.00 per pound for the Deluxe Mix, and $2.25 per pound for the Holiday Mix. These figures do not include the cost of the nuts included in the different mixes because that cost can vary greatly in the commodity markets.

Customer orders already received are summarized below:

Type of Mix	Orders (pounds)
Regular	10,000
Deluxe	3,000
Holiday	5,000

Because demand is running high, it is expected that TJ's will receive many more orders than can be satisfied.

TJ's is committed to using the nuts available to maximize profit over the fall season; nuts not used will be given to the Free Store. But even if it is not profitable to do so, TJ's president has indicated that the orders already received must be satisfied.

MANAGERIAL REPORT

Perform an analysis of TJ's product mix problem, and prepare a report for TJ's president that summarizes your findings. Be sure to include information and analysis on the following:

1. The cost per pound of the nuts included in the Regular, Deluxe, and Holiday mixes
2. The optimal product mix and profit contribution
3. Recommendations regarding how profit contribution can be increased if additional quantities of nuts can be purchased
4. A recommendation as to whether TJ's should purchase an additional 1000 pounds of almonds for $1000 from a supplier who overbought
5. Recommendations regarding how profit contribution could be increased (if at all) if TJ's does not satisfy all existing orders

APPENDIX

Solving Linear Programs with LINDO/PC

LINDO/PC, developed by Linus E. Schrage at the University of Chicago, is a microcomputer version of the popular LINDO computer package that is widely available on mainframe computers. LINDO/PC allows the user to interact with the computer in a conversational mode. By this we mean that once the program has been loaded in the microcomputer, the user inputs the objective function and constraints as requested by the computer program. When satisfied that all data have been entered correctly, the user enters the command GO, and the LINDO/PC system solves the problem. The optimal solution and its related information are available at the user's computer monitor.

We will use the Par, Inc., problem to demonstrate the use of LINDO/PC. The data input portion of a LINDO/PC computer session on an IBM Personal Computer is shown in Figure 3.18. The information keyed in by the user is shown in color, and the response from the computer package is shown in black. Note in particular the interactive nature of the system, with the alternating user input and LINDO/PC response. Specific commands and symbols shown in Figure 3.18 are described as follows:

1. The "A>" is the user prompt for the IBM Personal Computer. The user command "LINDO" causes the LINDO/PC program to be loaded.
2. LINDO/PC begins by sending the symbol ":" to indicate that it is waiting for an instruction from the user.
3. The user keys in the objective function as it appears in the mathematical statement of the problem.
4. LINDO/PC then sends the symbol "?" to indicate it is waiting for additional input concerning the linear program being solved.
5. The user input ST stands for "subject to," notifying the program that information about the constraints is to follow.
6. After inputting each of the constraints with the symbol<, which is interpreted as $\leq$ by LINDO/PC, the user inputs END to signal that the data input is complete.
7. LINDO/PC again responds with ":" to indicate that it is waiting for an instruction.
8. The user inputs the optional instruction LOOK ALL, which results in the computer's printing the linear programming problem that LINDO/PC is ready to solve. LOOK ALL is not a required instruction, but using it provides an easy check on the accuracy of the input data. With LINDO/PC the objective function is identified as row 1. Thus, under the "SUBJECT TO" heading we see the cutting and dyeing constraint identified as row 2, the sewing constraint as row 3, the finishing constraint as row 4, and the inspection and packaging constraint as row 5.

With the input data complete, the LINDO/PC package proceeds to develop the solution of the problem when given the command GO. The output from LINDO/PC is shown in Figure 3.19.

FIGURE 3.18
Data Input Session with LINDO/PC (User Response Shown in Color)

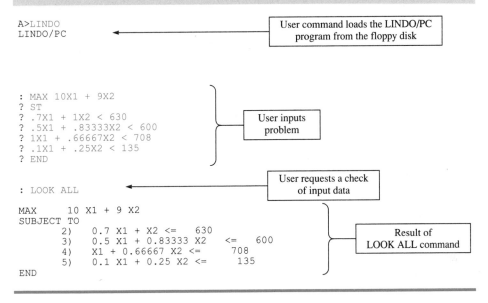

The first section of the output is self-explanatory. After printing the values of the slack variables and dual prices, LINDO/PC asks the user the following question: "DO RANGE (SENSITIVITY) ANALYSIS?" The user response of YES requests ranges on the objective function coefficients and the right-hand sides of the constraints.

Considering the information provided under the computer output heading labeled "OBJ COEFFICIENT RANGES," we see that variable x_1, which has a current profit coefficient of 10, has an allowable increase of 3.5 and an allowable decrease of 3.7. Adding 3.5 to and subtracting 3.7 from the current coefficient of 10 provides the following range of optimality for c_1:

$$6.3 \leq c_1 \leq 13.5$$

Similarly, the range of optimality for c_2 is found to be

$$6.67 \leq c_2 \leq 14.29$$

The information under the heading labeled "RIGHT HAND SIDE RANGES" permits computing the range of feasibility for each right-hand side. Simply subtract the allowable decrease from the current value to get the lower limit, and add the allowable increase to the current value to get the upper limit. Doing so we obtain

Constraint	Min RHS	Max RHS
Cutting & Dyeing	495.6	682.4
Sewing	480.0	No upper limit
Finishing	580.0	900.0
Inspecting & Packaging	117.0	No upper limit

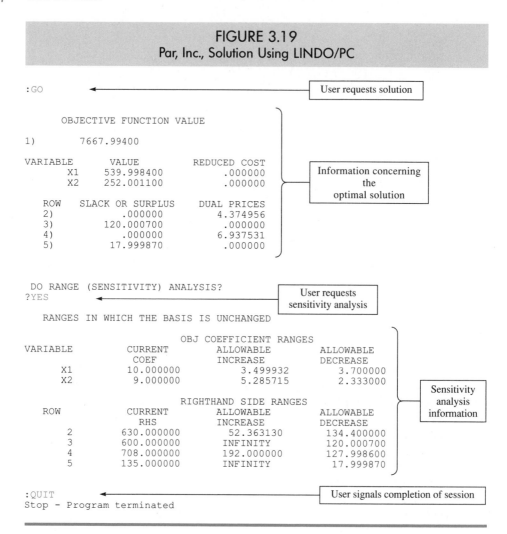

FIGURE 3.19
Par, Inc., Solution Using LINDO/PC

Note in Figure 3.19 that at the completion of the sensitivity analysis LINDO/PC sends ":" and waits for another instruction. In this case the user selected QUIT to signal the end of the LINDO/PC session. An optional instruction at this point would be ALT, which would have enabled the user to alter or modify one or more aspects of the problem and seek additional solution information.

Linear Programming Applications

Our study thus far has been directed at understanding linear programming in terms of the graphical solution method, sensitivity analysis, and the interpretation of computer solutions to linear programming problems. This background is essential for knowing when linear programming is an appropriate problem-solving tool and for interpreting the results of a linear programming solution to a problem.

In practice, linear programming has proven to be one of the most successful quantitative approaches to managerial decision making. Numerous applications have been reported in the chemical, airline, steel, paper, petroleum, and other industries. The specific problems that have been studied are diverse and have included production scheduling, media selection, financial planning, capital budgeting, transportation, plant location, product-mix, staffing, blending, and many others.

As the variety of applications mentioned above would suggest, linear programming is a flexible problem-solving tool with applications in many disciplines. In this chapter we present applications from the areas of marketing, finance, and production management. In the final section an application from the relatively new field of data envelopment analysis is presented. Computer solutions obtained using The Management Scientist software package are presented for many of the examples.

4.1 ▼ SOME GUIDELINES FOR MODEL FORMULATION

In the applications that follow, you will see how a variety of problems can be formulated as linear programs. While the linear programming model formulation process is an art that is learned with practice and experience, the following general guidelines or steps may be helpful as you begin to formulate your own linear programming models.

1. Understand the problem thoroughly.
2. State the problem as concisely as possible, making verbal statements of the following:
   a. *The objective*—the goal of the problem, such as to maximize profit, minimize cost, minimize time, and so on

b. *The decision variables*—the aspects of the problem you can control or determine that will help achieve the stated objective

c. *The constraints*—the restrictions or conditions that must be satisfied for the solution to be feasible

3. Using the decision variables as the unknowns (for example, x_1, x_2, and so on), develop mathematical expressions that describe the objective and each of the constraints. Remember that since the method is linear programming, the expressions used for the objective and the constraints must be *linear relationships*[1].

4. Add the nonnegativity requirements ($x_i \geq 0$) for each of the decision variables.

At this point you should have a linear programming model that represents the problem or application under study. The solution of the model will provide the optimal values for the decision variables and sensitivity analysis information. Proper interpretation can provide valuable decision-making information for the manager.

4.2 ▼ MARKETING APPLICATIONS
Media Selection

Media selection applications of linear programming are designed to help marketing managers allocate a fixed advertising budget across various advertising media. Potential media include newspapers, magazines, radio, television, and direct mail. In most of these applications the objective is to maximize audience exposure. Restrictions on the allowable allocation usually arise through considerations such as company policy, contract requirements, and availability of media. In the application that follows we illustrate how a media selection problem might be formulated and solved using a linear programming model.

Consider the case of the Relax-and-Enjoy Lake Development Corporation. Relax-and-Enjoy is developing a lakeside community at a privately owned lake and is in the business of selling property for vacation and/or retreat cottages. The primary market for these lakeside lots includes all middle- and upper-income families within approximately 100 miles of the development. Relax-and-Enjoy has employed the advertising firm of Boone, Phillips and Jackson to design the promotional campaign for the project.

After considering possible advertising media and the market to be covered, Boone has made the preliminary recommendation to restrict the first month's advertising to five sources. At the end of the month, Boone will then reevaluate its strategy based on the month's results. Boone has collected data on the number of potential purchase families reached, the cost per advertisement, the maximum number of times each medium is available, and the expected exposure for each of the five media. The expected exposure is measured in terms of an exposure unit, a measure of the relative value of one advertisement in each of the media. These measures, based on Boone's experience in the advertising business, take into account such factors as audience profile (age, income, and education of the audience reached), image presented, and quality of the advertisement. The information collected is presented in Table 4.1.

Relax-and-Enjoy has provided Boone with an advertising budget of $30,000 for the first month's campaign. In addition, Relax-and-Enjoy has imposed the following restrictions on how Boone may allocate these funds: at least 10 television commercials must be used, and at least 50,000 potential purchasers must be reached during the month. In

---

[1]Linear relationships, as described in Chapter 2, are mathematical expressions in which the variables appear in separate terms and appear only to the first power. For example, $3x_1 + 2x_2 \leq 50$ is a linear relationship.

TABLE 4.1
Advertising Media Alternatives for the Relax-and-Enjoy Lake Development Corporation

Advertising Media	Number of Potential Purchase Families Reached	Cost per Advertisement	Maximum Times Available per Month*	Expected Exposure Units
1. Daytime TV (1 min), station WKLA	1000	$1500	15	65
2. Evening TV (30 sec), station WKLA	2000	$3000	10	90
3. Daily newspaper (full page), *The Morning Journal*	1500	$400	25	40
4. Sunday newspaper magazine (½ page color), *The Sunday Press*	2500	$1000	4	60
5. Radio, 8:00 A.M. or 5:00 P.M. news (30 sec), station KNOP	300	$100	30	20

*The maximum number of times the medium is available is either the maximum number of times the advertising medium occurs (e.g., four Sundays for medium 4) or the maximum number of times Boone will allow the medium to be used.

addition, no more than $18,000 may be spent on television advertisements. What advertising media selection plan should the advertising firm recommend?

We begin by defining the decision variables as follows:

$$x_1 = \text{number of times daytime TV is used}$$

$$x_2 = \text{number of times evening TV is used}$$

$$x_3 = \text{number of times daily newspaper is used}$$

$$x_4 = \text{number of times Sunday newspaper is used}$$

$$x_5 = \text{number of times radio is used}$$

With the objective of maximizing the expected exposure, the objective function becomes

$$\max 65x_1 + 90x_2 + 40x_3 + 60x_4 + 20x_5$$

The constraints for the model can now be formulated from the information given:

$$
\left.
\begin{aligned}
x_1 &\leq 15 \\
x_2 &\leq 10 \\
x_3 &\leq 25 \\
x_4 &\leq 4 \\
x_5 &\leq 30
\end{aligned}
\right\}
\begin{aligned}
&\text{Availability} \\
&\text{of media}
\end{aligned}
$$

TABLE 4.2
Advertising Plan for the Relax-and-Enjoy Lake Development Corporation

Media	Frequency	Budget
Daytime TV	10	$15,000
Daily newspaper	25	10,000
Sunday newspaper	2	2,000
Radio	30	3,000
		$30,000

Total audience contacted = 61,500

Expected exposure = 2370

$$1500x_1 + 3000x_2 + 400x_3 + 1000x_4 + 100x_5 \leq 30{,}000 \quad \text{Budget}$$

$$x_1 + x_2 \geq 10$$
$$1500x_1 + 3000x_2 \leq 18{,}000$$
$$\left. \right\} \quad \begin{array}{l}\text{Television}\\ \text{restrictions}\end{array}$$

$$1000x_1 + 2000x_2 + 1500x_3 + 2500x_4 + 300x_5 \geq 50{,}000 \quad \begin{array}{l}\text{Audience}\\ \text{coverage}\end{array}$$

$$x_1, x_2, x_3, x_4, x_5 \geq 0$$

The solution to this five-variable, nine-constraint linear programming model is presented in Table 4.2.

A possible shortcoming of this model is that even if the expected exposure measure were not subject to error, there is no guarantee that maximization of total expected exposure will lead to a maximization of profit or of sales (a common surrogate for profit). However, this is not a shortcoming of linear programming; rather, it is a shortcoming of the use of exposure as a criterion. Certainly if we were able to measure directly the effect of an advertisement on profit, we would use total profit as the objective to be maximized.

In addition, you should be aware that the media selection model as formulated in this section does not include considerations such as the following:

1. Reduced exposure value for repeat media usage
2. Cost discounts for repeat media usage
3. Audience overlap by different media
4. Timing recommendations for the advertisements

A more complex formulation—more variables and constraints—can often be used to overcome some of these limitations, but it will not always be possible to overcome all of them with a linear programming model. However, even in these cases a linear programming model can often be used to arrive at an approximation of the best decision. Management evaluation combined with the linear programming solution should then make possible the selection of an overall effective advertising strategy.

▼ NOTES AND COMMENTS ▼

1. In general, we use x_1, x_2, and so on to denote the decision variables in a linear programming model. At the beginning of the model formulation we carefully present the notation used and the definition of each decision variable. While the

notation x_1, x_2, and so on can be used in any linear programming model, some management scientists prefer to use a notation scheme that is more descriptive of each decision variable. For example, the media selection model could have been formulated with *DTV* denoting the daytime TV, *ETV* denoting the evening TV, *DN* denoting the daily newspaper, and so on. In this case the objective function would have been written as

$$\max 65DTV + 90ETV + 40DN + 60SN + 20R$$

The constraints would be restated in terms of the *DTV, ETV, DN, SN* and *R* notation. In any case realize that the model can be formulated with any notation or combination of notations for the decision variables. Regardless of the choice, it is always a good idea to carefully define the decision variables and the notation used at the beginning of the model formulation.

2. Note that the media selection model, perhaps more than most other linear programming models, required crucial subjective evaluations of the exposure ratings for the media alternatives. While marketing managers may have substantial data concerning advertising exposure, the final coefficients used in the objective function include considerations based primarily on managerial judgment. However, judgment input is an acceptable way of obtaining data for a linear programming model.

Marketing Research

Marketing research is conducted by a variety of organizations in order to learn about consumer characteristics, attitudes, and preferences toward products and/or services offered by an organization. Often the actual research is performed by a marketing research firm that specializes in providing client organizations with the desired market information. Typical services offered by a marketing research firm include designing the study, conducting market surveys, analyzing the data collected, and providing summary reports and recommendations for the client. In the research design phase, targets or quotas may be established for the number and types of respondents to be reached by a survey. With quota guidelines established, the objective of the marketing research firm is to conduct the survey so as to meet the client's needs at a minimum cost.

Market Survey, Inc. (MSI), is a marketing research firm that specializes in evaluating consumer reaction to new products, services, and advertising campaigns. A client firm has requested assistance from MSI in ascertaining consumer reaction to a recently marketed product for household use. During meetings with the client it was agreed that door-to-door personal interviews would be used to obtain information from both households with children and households without children. In addition, it was agreed that both day and evening interviews would be necessary in order to allow for a variety of household work schedules. Specifically, the client's contract called for MSI to conduct 1000 interviews with the following quota guidelines:

1. At least 400 households with children would be interviewed.
2. At least 400 households without children would be interviewed.
3. The total number of households interviewed during the evening would be at least as great as the number of households interviewed during the day.
4. At least 40% of the interviews for households with children would be conducted during the evening.
5. At least 60% of the interviews for households without children would be conducted during the evening.

Since the interviews of households with children take additional interviewer time, and since evening interviewers are paid more than daytime interviewers, the cost of an interview varies with the type of interview. Based on previous research studies, estimates of the interview costs are as follows:

	Interview Cost	
Household	*Day*	*Evening*
Children	$20	$25
No children	$18	$20

What is the household, time-of-day interview plan that will satisfy the contract requirements at a minimum total interviewing cost?

The formulation of a linear programming model for the Market Survey problem is a good opportunity to introduce the use of double-subscripted decision variables. Using x to represent the decision variables, we will use two subscripts for x, with the first subscript indicating whether the interview involves children or not and the second subscript indicating whether the interview is in the day or evening. Using 1 for children and 2 for no children, and 1 for day and 2 for evening, double subscripts can be used to identify the following four decision variables:

x_{11} = the number of interviews for households with children to be conducted during the day

x_{12} = the number of interviews for households with children to be conducted during the evening

x_{21} = the number of interviews for households without children to be conducted during the day

x_{22} = the number of interviews for households without children to be conducted during the evening

We begin the linear programming model formulation by using the cost-per-interview data to develop the following objective function:

$$\min 20x_{11} + 25x_{12} + 18x_{21} + 20x_{22}$$

The constraint requiring a total of 1000 interviews is written as

$$x_{11} + x_{12} + x_{21} + x_{22} = 1000$$

The five specifications concerning the types of interviews are as follows:

1. Households with children:

$$x_{11} + x_{12} \geq 400$$

2. Households without children:

$$x_{21} + x_{22} \geq 400$$

3. At least as many evening interviews as day interviews:

$$x_{12} + x_{22} \geq x_{11} + x_{21}$$

The usual format for linear programming model formulation and computer input places all decision variables on the left-hand side of the inequality and a constant (possibly zero) on the right-hand side. Thus, we will rewrite this constraint as

$$-x_{11} + x_{12} - x_{21} + x_{22} \geq 0$$

4. At least 40% of interviews for households with children during the evening:

$$x_{12} \geq .4(x_{11} + x_{12})$$

or

$$-.4x_{11} + .6x_{12} \geq 0$$

5. At least 60% of interviews for households without children during the evening:

$$x_{22} \geq .6(x_{21} + x_{22})$$

or

$$-.6x_{21} + .4x_{22} \geq 0$$

By adding the nonnegativity requirements, the four-variable, six-constraint linear programming model becomes

$$\min \quad 20x_{11} + 25x_{12} + 18x_{21} + 20x_{22}$$

s.t.

$x_{11} +$	$x_{12} +$	$x_{21} +$	x_{22}	$= 1000$	Total interviews
$x_{11} +$	x_{12}			≥ 400	Households with children
		$x_{21} +$	$x_{22} \geq$	400	Households without children
$-x_{11} +$	$x_{12} -$	$x_{21} +$	$x_{22} \geq$	0	More evening interviews
$-.4x_{11} +$	$.6x_{12}$			≥ 0	Evening households with children
		$-.6x_{21} +$	$.4x_{22} \geq$	0	Evening households without children

$$x_{11}, x_{12}, x_{21}, x_{22} \geq 0$$

The computer solution to the above linear program is shown in Figure 4.1. Using the results of the computer solution, we see that the minimum cost of $20,320 occurs with the following interview schedule:

Household	Number of Interviews		Totals
	Day	Evening	
Children	240	160	400
No children	240	360	600
Totals	480	520	1000

As can be seen, 480 interviews will be scheduled during the day and 520 during the evening. Households with children will be covered by 400 interviews and households without children will be covered by 600 interviews.

Selected sensitivity analysis information from Figure 4.1 shows a dual price of -19.2 for constraint 1. This tells us that the objective function will get worse (the cost

FIGURE 4.1
Computer Solution of the Market Survey Problem
Using The Management Scientist

```
Objective Function Value =    20320.000000

        Variable              Value                Reduced Costs
   -----------------    -----------------    ---------------------
         X11              240.000015              0.000001
         X12              159.999985              0.000001
         X21              240.000000              0.000002
         X22              360.000000              0.000000


        Constraint         Slack/Surplus            Dual Prices
   -----------------    -----------------    ---------------------
            1               0.000000              -19.200001
            2               0.000000               -2.799999
            3             200.000000                0.000000
            4              40.000000                0.000000
            5               0.000000               -4.999998
            6               0.000000               -1.999998
```

will increase) by \$19.20 if the number of interviews is increased from 1000 to 1001. Thus, \$19.20 is the incremental cost of obtaining additional interviews. It is also the savings that could be realized by reducing the number of interviews from 1000 to 999. The dual price for the requirement of 400 households with children (constraint 2) indicates that requesting additional interviews of households with children will not improve the objective function. In fact, additional interviews of households with children will add to the total cost at a rate of approximately \$2.80 per interview.

The surplus variable with a value of 200 for constraint 3 shows that 200 more households without children will be interviewed than required. Similarly, the surplus variable with a value of 40 for constraint 4 shows that the number of evening interviews exceeds the number of daytime interviews by 40. The zero values for the surplus variables in constraints 5 and 6 indicate that the more expensive evening interviews are being held at a minimum.

4.3 ▼ FINANCIAL APPLICATIONS
Portfolio Selection

Portfolio selection problems involve situations in which a financial manager must select specific investments—for example, stocks, bonds—from a variety of investment alternatives. This type of problem is frequently encountered by managers of mutual funds, credit unions, insurance companies, and banks. The objective function for portfolio selection problems is usually maximization of expected return or minimization of risk. The constraints usually take the form of restrictions on the type of permissible investments, state laws, company policy, maximum permissible risk, and so on.

Problems of this type have been formulated and solved using a variety of mathematical programming techniques. However, if in a particular portfolio selection problem it is possible to formulate a linear objective function and linear constraints, then linear programming can be used to solve the problem. In this section we show how a portfolio selection problem can be formulated and solved as a linear program.

Consider the case of Welte Mutual Funds, Inc., located in New York City. Welte has just obtained $100,000 by converting industrial bonds to cash and is now looking for other investment opportunities for these funds. Considering Welte's current investments, the firm's top financial analyst recommends that all new investments should be made in the oil industry, steel industry, or government bonds. Specifically, the analyst has identified five investment opportunities and projected their annual rates of return. The investments and rates of return are shown in Table 4.3.

Management of Welte has imposed the following investment guidelines:

1. Neither industry (oil or steel) should receive more than 50% of the total new investment.
2. Government bonds should be at least 25% of the steel industry investments.
3. The investment in Pacific Oil, the high-return but high-risk investment, cannot be more than 60% of the total oil industry investment.

What portfolio recommendations—investments and amounts—should be made for the available $100,000? Given the objective of maximizing projected return subject to the budgetary and managerially imposed constraints, we can answer this question by formulating a linear programming model of the problem. The solution to this linear programming model will then provide investment recommendations for the management of Welte Mutual Funds.

Let

$$x_1 = \text{dollars invested in Atlantic Oil}$$

$$x_2 = \text{dollars invested in Pacific Oil}$$

$$x_3 = \text{dollars invested in Midwest Steel}$$

$$x_4 = \text{dollars invested in Huber Steel}$$

$$x_5 = \text{dollars invested in government bonds}$$

Using the projected rates of return shown in Table 4.3, the objective function for maximizing the total return for the portfolio can be written as

$$\max 0.073x_1 + 0.103x_2 + 0.064x_3 + 0.075x_4 + 0.045x_5$$

TABLE 4.3
Investment Opportunities for Welte Mutual Funds

Investment	Projected Rate of Return (%)
Atlantic Oil	7.3
Pacific Oil	10.3
Midwest Steel	6.4
Huber Steel	7.5
Government bonds	4.5

The constraint specifying the investment of $100,000 is written as

$$x_1 + x_2 + x_3 + x_4 + x_5 = 100,000$$

The requirements that neither the oil nor the steel industry should receive more than 50% of the $100,000 investment are as follows:

$$x_1 + x_2 \leq 50,000 \quad \text{Oil industry}$$
$$x_3 + x_4 \leq 50,000 \quad \text{Steel industry}$$

The requirement that government bonds be at least 25% of the steel industry investment is expressed as follows:

$$x_5 \geq 0.25 \ (x_3 + x_4)$$

or

$$-0.25x_3 - 0.25x_4 + x_5 \geq 0$$

Finally, the constraint that Pacific Oil cannot be more than 60% of the total oil industry investment becomes

$$x_2 \leq 0.60(x_1 + x_2)$$

or

$$-0.60x_1 + 0.40x_2 \leq 0$$

By adding the nonnegativity restrictions, the complete linear programming model for the Welte Mutual Fund investment problem is as follows:

max $0.073x_1 + 0.103x_2 + 0.064x_3 + 0.075x_4 + 0.045x_5$

s.t.

$x_1 +$	$x_2 +$	$x_3 +$	$x_4 +$	$x_5 =$	100,000	Available funds
$x_1 +$	x_2			$\leq$	50,000	Oil industry maximum
		$x_3 +$	x_4	$\leq$	50,000	Steel industry maximum
	$-$	$0.25x_3 -$	$0.25x_4 +$	$x_5 \geq$	0	Government bonds minimum
$-0.6x_1 +$	$0.4x_2$			$\leq$	0	Pacific Oil restriction

$$x_1, x_2, x_3, x_4, x_5 \geq 0$$

This problem was solved using The Management Scientist. The output is shown in Figure 4.2. In Table 4.4 we show how the funds are divided among the securities. Note that the optimal solution indicates that the portfolio should be diversified among all the investment opportunities except Midwest Steel. The projected annual return for this portfolio is $8,000, which is an overall return rate of 8%.

FIGURE 4.2
Computer Solution of Welte Mutual Funds Problem Using The Management Scientist

```
Objective Function Value =        8000.000000

         Variable              Value            Reduced Costs
    -----------------    -----------------    -----------------
           X1             19999.998000            0.000000
           X2             30000.002000            0.000000
           X3                 0.000000            0.011000
           X4             40000.000000            0.000000
           X5             10000.000000            0.000000


        Constraint          Slack/Surplus         Dual Prices
    -----------------    -----------------    -----------------
            1                 0.000000            0.069000
            2                 0.000000            0.022000
            3             10000.000000            0.000000
            4                 0.000000           -0.024000
            5                 0.000000            0.030000
```

TABLE 4.4
Optimal Portfolio Selection for Welte Mutual Funds

Investment	Amount	Expected Annual Return
Atlantic Oil	$ 20,000	$1460
Pacific Oil	30,000	3090
Huber Steel	40,000	3000
Government bonds	10,000	450
	$100,000	$8000

Expected annual return of $8000 = 8%

Using the computer printout for the Welte investment problem as shown in Figure 4.2, we see that the dual price for constraint 3 is zero. This is because the steel industry maximum is not a binding constraint; increases in the steel industry limit of $50,000 will not improve the value of the objective function. Indeed, the slack variable for this constraint shows that the current steel industry investment is $10,000 below its limit of $50,000. The dual prices for the other constraints are nonzero, indicating that they are binding constraints at the optimal solution.

The dual price of 0.069 for constraint 1 shows that the objective function can be increased by 0.069 if one more dollar can be made available for the portfolio investment. If more funds can be obtained at a cost of less than 6.9%, management should consider obtaining them. On the other hand, if a return in excess of 6.9% can be obtained by investing funds elsewhere (other than in these five securities), management should question the wisdom of investing the entire $100,000 in this portfolio.

Similar interpretations can be given to the other dual prices. Note, however, that the dual price for constraint 4 is negative; its value is −0.024. This indicates that increasing the value on the right-hand side of the constraint by one unit can be expected to cause a change in the objective function of -0.024. In terms of the optimal portfolio, this means that if Welte invests one more dollar in government bonds, the total return will decrease by 2.4 cents. To see why this is so, note again from the dual price for constraint 1 that the marginal return on the funds invested in the portfolio is 6.9% (the average return is 8%). The rate of return on government bonds is 4.5%. Thus, the cost of investing one more dollar in government bonds is the difference between the marginal return on the portfolio and the marginal return on government bonds: $6.9\% - 4.5\% = 2.4\%$.

Note that the optimal solution with $x_3 = 0$ shows that Midwest Steel should not be included in the portfolio. The associated reduced cost for x_3 of .011 tells us that the objective function coefficient for Midwest Steel would have to increase by .011 before it would be desirable to consider the Midwest Steel investment alternative. With this increase the Midwest Steel return would be $0.064 + 0.011 = 0.075$, making this investment just as desirable as the currently used Huber Steel investment alternative.

Finally, a simple modification of the Welte linear programming model permits determining the fraction of available funds invested in each security. That is, we divide each of the right-hand-side values by 100,000. Then the optimal values for the variables will give the fraction of funds that should be invested in each security for a portfolio of any size.

▼ NOTES AND COMMENTS ▼

The optimal solution to the Welte Mutual Funds problem indicated that $20,000 is to be spent on the Atlantic Oil stock. If Atlantic Oil sells for $75 per share, we would have to purchase exactly 266⅔ shares in order to spend exactly $20,000. The difficulty of purchasing fractional shares is usually handled by purchasing the largest possible integer number of shares with the allotted funds (for example, 266 shares of Atlantic Oil). This approach guarantees that the budget constraint will not be violated. This, of course, introduces the possibility that the solution will no longer be optimal, but the danger is slight if a large number of securities are involved. In cases where the analyst believes it is critical for the decision variables to have integer values, the problem must be formulated as an integer linear programming model. Integer linear programming is the topic of Chapter 8.

Financial-Mix Strategy

Financial-mix strategies involve the selection of means for financing company projects, inventories, production operations, and various other activities. In this section we illustrate how linear programming can be used to solve problems of this type by formulating and solving a problem involving the financing of production operations. In this particular application a financial decision must be made with regard to how much production is to be supported by internally generated funds and how much is to be supported by external funds.

The Jefferson Adding Machine Company will begin production of two new models of electronic calculators during the next 3 months. Since these models require an expansion of the current production operation, the company will need operating funds to cover material, labor, and other expenses during the initial production period. Revenue from this initial production period will not be available until after the end of the period. Thus, the company must arrange financing for these operating expenses before production can begin.

Jefferson has set aside $3000 in internal funds to cover expenses of this operation. If additional funds are needed, they will have to be generated externally. A local bank has offered a line of short-term credit in an amount not to exceed $10,000. The interest rate over the life of the loan will be 12% per year on the average amount borrowed. One stipulation set by the bank requires that the remainder of the company cash set aside for this operation plus the accounts receivable for this product line be at least twice as great as the outstanding loan plus interest at the end of the initial production period.

In addition to the financial restrictions placed on this operation, labor capacity is also a factor for Jefferson to consider. Only 2500 hours of assembly time and 150 hours of packaging and shipping time are available for the new product line during the initial 3-month production period. Relevant cost, price, and production time requirements for the two models, referred to as models Y and Z, are shown in Table 4.5.

Additional restrictions have been imposed by company management in order to guarantee that the market reaction to both products can be tested; that is, at least 50 units of model Y and at least 25 units of model Z must be produced in this first production period.

Since the cost of the units produced using borrowed funds will in effect experience an interest charge, the profit contributions for the units of models Y and Z produced on borrowed funds will be reduced. Hence, we adopt the following notation for the decision variables in this problem:

x_1 = units of model Y produced with company funds

x_2 = units of model Y produced with borrowed funds

x_3 = units of model Z produced with company funds

x_4 = units of model Z produced with borrowed funds

How much will the profit contribution be reduced for units produced on borrowed funds? To answer this question, one must know for how long the loan will be outstanding. We assume that all units of each model are sold as they are produced to independent distributors and that the average rate of turnover of accounts receivable is 3 months. Since company management has specified that the loan is to be repaid by funds generated by the units produced on borrowed funds, the funds borrowed to produce one unit of model Y or Z will be repaid approximately 3 months later. Hence, the profit contribution for each unit

TABLE 4.5
Cost, Price, and Labor Data for the Jefferson Adding Machine Company

Model	Unit Cost (Materials and Other Variable Expenses)	Selling Price	Profit Margin	Labor Hours Required Assembly	Packaging and Shipping
Y	$ 50	$ 58	$ 8	12	1
Z	$100	$120	$20	25	2

of model Y produced on borrowed funds is reduced from \$8 to \$8 $-$ (\$50 $\times$ 0.12 $\times$ ¼ yr) = \$6.50, and the profit contribution for each unit of model Z produced on borrowed funds is reduced from \$20 to \$20 $-$ (\$100 $\times$ 0.12 $\times$ ¼ yr) = \$17. With this information we can now formulate the objective function for Jefferson's financial mix problem:

$$\max\ 8x_1 + 6.5x_2 + 20x_3 + 17x_4$$

We can also specify the following constraints for the model:

$$12x_1 + 12x_2 + 25x_3 + 25x_4 \leq 2{,}500 \quad \text{Assembly capacity}$$
$$x_1 + x_2 + 2x_3 + 2x_4 \leq 150 \quad \text{Packaging and shipping capacity}$$
$$50x_1 + 100x_3 \leq 3{,}000 \quad \text{Internal funds available}$$
$$50x_2 + 100x_4 \leq 10{,}000 \quad \text{External funds available}$$
$$x_1 + x_2 \geq 50 \quad \text{Model } Y \text{ requirement}$$
$$x_3 + x_4 \geq 25 \quad \text{Model } Z \text{ requirement}$$

In addition, the following constraint must be included to satisfy the bank loan requirement:

$$\text{Cash} + \text{accounts receivable} \geq 2(\text{loan} + \text{interest})$$

This restriction must be satisfied at the end of the period. Recalling that accounts receivable are outstanding for an average of 3 months, the following relationships can be used to derive a mathematical expression for the above inequality at the end of the period:

$$\text{Cash} = 3000 - 50x_1 - 100x_3$$
$$\text{Accounts receivable} = 58x_1 + 58x_2 + 120x_3 + 120x_4$$
$$\text{Loan} = 50x_2 + 100x_4$$
$$\text{Interest} = (0.12 \times \text{¼ yr})(50x_2 + 100x_4) = 1.5x_2 + 3x_4$$

Therefore, the constraint resulting from the bank restriction can be written as

$$3000 - 50x_1 - 100x_3 + 58x_1 + 58x_2 + 120x_3 + 120x_4 \geq 2(51.5x_2 + 103x_4)$$

or

$$3000 \geq -8x_1 + 45x_2 - 20x_3$$

which is equivalent to

$$-8x_1 + 45x_2 - 20x_3 + 86x_4 \leq 3000$$

Adding the nonnegativity constraints, the complete linear programming model for the Jefferson Adding Machine Company can now be stated:

$$\max\quad 8x_1 + 6.5x_2 + 20x_3 + 17x_4$$

s.t.

$$12x_1 + 12x_2 + 25x_3 + 25x_4 \leq 2{,}500$$
$$x_1 + x_2 + 2x_3 + 2x_4 \leq 150$$
$$50x_1 + 100x_3 \leq 3{,}000$$
$$50x_2 + 100x_4 \leq 10{,}000$$

$$x_1 + x_2 \geq 50$$
$$x_3 + x_4 \geq 25$$
$$-8x_1 + 45x_2 - 20x_3 + 86x_4 \leq 3{,}000$$
$$x_1, x_2, x_3, x_4 \geq 0$$

The computer solution to this four-variable, seven-constraint financial-mix problem is shown in Figure 4.3. The profit of $1191.86 is realized with the optimal solution of $x_1 = 50$, $x_2 = 0$, $x_3 = 5$, and $x_4 = 40.7$. Note that the reduced cost of zero for x_2 tells us that the objective function coefficient *does not have to increase* in order to consider bringing x_2 into the optimal solution. This is an indication that an alternate optimal solution exists for the problem. Figure 4.4 shows a computer solution yielding an alternate optimal solution. The profit of $1191.86 is now associated with the solution $x_1 = 0$, $x_2 = 50$, $x_3 = 30$, and $x_4 = 15.7$.

Obviously management could implement either of the solutions shown in the figures and maximize profit. The solution in Figure 4.4 is summarized in Table 4.6 along with the expected profit and borrowed funds for each model of calculator. This solution requires the company to use all its internal funds ($3000), but only slightly more than $4000 of the available $10,000 line of credit.

Some additional interpretations from the computer printout in Figure 4.4 show that assembly capacity (constraint 1, slack = 757.6 hours) and packaging and shipping capacity (constraint 2, slack = 8.6 hours) are adequate to meet the production requirements. Additional hours of these resources will not improve the value of the optimal solution. The dual price associated with the internal funds constraint (constraint 3) shows that a profit improvement of approximately $0.24 can be made from an additional dollar of internal funds. With this high return on the internal funds investment, Jefferson may want to seriously consider allocating additional internal funds to this project. The negative dual price for constraint 5 tells us that increases in the model Y production requirement

FIGURE 4.3
Computer Solution of Jefferson Adding Machine Problem Using The Management Scientist

Objective Function Value =   1191.860350

Variable	Value	Reduced Costs
X1	50.000000	0.000001
X2	0.000000	0.000000
X3	5.000000	0.000001
X4	40.697674	0.000000

Constraint	Slack/Surplus	Dual Prices
1	757.558230	0.000000
2	8.604660	0.000000
3	0.000000	0.239535
4	5930.232400	0.000000
5	0.000000	-2.395349
6	20.697670	0.000000
7	0.000000	0.197674

FIGURE 4.4
Alternate Optimal Solution of Jefferson Adding Machine Problem Using The Management Scientist

```
Objective Function Value =    1191.860350

        Variable            Value             Reduced Costs
   -----------------  -------------------  ----------------------
          X1              0.000000              0.000001
          X2             50.000000              0.000000
          X3             30.000000              0.000001
          X4             15.697672              0.000000


       Constraint       Slack/Surplus          Dual Prices
   -----------------  -------------------  ----------------------
           1             757.558230            0.000000
           2               8.604660            0.000000
           3               0.000000            0.239535
           4            5930.232400            0.000000
           5               0.000000           -2.395350
           6              20.697670            0.000000
           7               0.000000            0.197674
```

TABLE 4.6
Optimal Financial Mix for the Production of Jefferson Adding Machines

Model	Units	Expected Profit	Amount of Borrowed Funds
Model Y			
Borrowed funds (x_2)	50	$ 325	$2500
Model Z			
Company funds (x_3)	30	600	—
Borrowed funds (x_4)	15.7	267	1570
Totals		$1192	$4070

will reduce the profit margin. In fact, the negative dual price shows that reducing the current 50-unit requirement for model Y will actually increase profits at the rate of approximately $2.40 per unit reduction in the requirement.

▼ NOTES AND COMMENTS ▼

The profit contributions for the two Jefferson Adding Machine products were based on the difference between the selling price per unit and the "cost" per unit. An important consideration in the determination of the cost per unit is the difference between sunk costs and relevant costs. *Sunk costs* are costs already incurred, such as for previously purchased materials, overhead, indirect labor, and so on. Since they have already been incurred or will be incurred regardless of the decisions being made, these costs are not relevant or affected by the values of the decision variables.

Sunk costs *should not be considered* when developing the objective function for a linear programming model. Note that Table 4.5 shows that the unit costs are based on the relevant variable costs of the materials as well as on other variable expenses. The environmental protection case at the end of the chapter will give you a chance to identify relevant costs in the development of a linear programming model.

4.4 ▼ PRODUCTION MANAGEMENT APPLICATIONS
Production Scheduling

One of the most important areas of linear programming deals with multi-period planning applications such as production scheduling. The solution to a production scheduling problem enables the manager to establish an efficient low-cost production schedule for one or more products over several time periods, such as weeks, months, and so on. Essentially, a production scheduling problem can be viewed as a product-mix problem for each of several periods in the future. The manager must determine the production levels that will allow the company to meet product demand requirements, given limitations on production capacity, labor capacity, and storage space. At the same time, it is desired to minimize the total cost of carrying out this task.

One major reason for the widespread application of linear programming to production scheduling problems is that these problems are of a recurring nature. A production schedule must be established for the current month, then again for the next month, for the month after that, and so on. When the production manager looks at the problem each month, he/she will find that while demands for the products have changed, production times, production capacities, storage space limitations, and so on are roughly the same. Thus, the production manager is basically resolving the same problem handled in previous months. Hence, a general linear programming model of the production scheduling procedure may be frequently applied. Once the model has been formulated, the manager can simply supply the data—demands, capacities, and so on—for the given production period, and the linear programming model can then be used to develop the production schedule. Thus, one linear programming formulation may have many repeat applications.

Let us consider the case of the Bollinger Electronics Company, which produces two different electronic components for a major airplane engine manufacturer. The airplane engine manufacturer notifies the Bollinger sales office each quarter as to what the monthly requirements for components will be during each of the next 3 months. The monthly requirements for the components may vary considerably depending on the type of engine the airplane engine manufacturer is producing. The order shown in Table 4.7 has just been received for the next 3-month period.

TABLE 4.7
Three-Month Demand Schedule for Bollinger Electronics Company

	April	May	June
Component 322A	1000	3000	5000
Component 802B	1000	500	3000

After the order is processed, a demand statement is sent to the production control department. The production control department must then develop a 3-month production plan for the components. Knowing the preference of the production department manager for constant demand levels that result in balanced workloads and constant machine and labor utilization, the production scheduler might consider the alternative of producing at a constant rate for all 3 months. This would set monthly production quotas at 3000 units per month for component 322A and 1500 units per month for component 802B. Why not adopt this schedule?

While this schedule would be quite appealing to the production department, it may be undesirable from a total-cost point of view. In particular, this schedule ignores inventory costs. Consider the projected inventory levels that would result from this schedule calling for constant production (Figure 4.5). We see that this production schedule would lead to high inventory levels. When we consider the cost of tied-up capital and storage space, a schedule that provides lower inventory levels might be economically more desirable.

At the other extreme of the constant rate production schedule is the produce-to-meet-demand approach. While this schedule eliminates the inventory holding cost problem, the wide monthly fluctuations in production levels may cause some serious production problems and costs. For example, production capacity would have to be available to meet the total 8000-unit peak demand in June. Also, unless other components could be scheduled on the same production equipment in April and May, there would be significant unused capacity and thus low machine utilization in those months. These large production variations might also require substantial labor adjustments which in turn could lead to increased employee turnover and training problems. Thus, it appears that the best production schedule will be one that is a compromise between the two alternatives.

The production manager will want to identify and consider the following costs:

1. Production costs
2. Storage costs
3. Change-in-production-level costs

In the remainder of this section we show how a linear programming model of the production and inventory process for Bollinger Electronics can be formulated to account for these costs in such a fashion that the total cost is minimized.

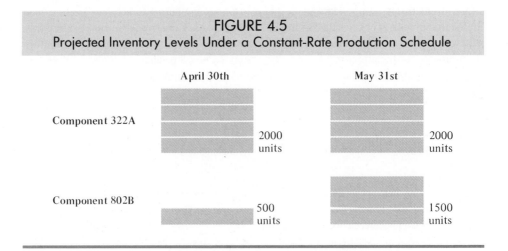

FIGURE 4.5
Projected Inventory Levels Under a Constant-Rate Production Schedule

In order to develop the model, we will use a double-subscript notation for the decision variables. The first subscript will indicate the product number and the second subscript the month. Thus, in general we let x_{im} denote the production volume in units for product i in month m. Here $i = 1, 2$, and $m = 1, 2, 3$; $i = 1$ refers to component 322A, $i = 2$ refers to component 802B, $m = 1$ refers to April, $m = 2$ refers to May, and $m = 3$ refers to June. The purpose of the double subscript is to provide a more descriptive notation. We could simply use x_6 to represent the number of units of product 2 produced in month 3, but x_{23} is more descriptive in that we know directly the product and month the variable represents.

If component 322A costs $20 per unit produced and component 802B costs $10 per unit produced, the production cost part of the objective function becomes

$$\text{Production cost} = 20x_{11} + 20x_{12} + 20x_{13} + 10x_{21} + 10x_{22} + 10x_{23}$$

You should note that in this problem the production cost per unit is the same each month. Thus, we need not include production costs in the objective function; that is, no matter what production schedule is selected, the total production costs will remain the same. In other words, the production costs are not relevant costs for the production scheduling decision under consideration. In cases where the cost per unit is expected to change each month, the variable production costs per unit per month must be included in the objective function. Since the solution for the Bollinger Electronics problem will be the same whether or not these costs are included, we have elected to include them so that the value of the linear programming objective function will include all the costs associated with the problem.

To incorporate the relevant inventory costs into the model, we introduce a double-subscripted decision variable to indicate the number of units of inventory for each product for each month. We let s_{im} be the inventory level for product i at the end of month m.

Bollinger has determined that on a monthly basis, inventory holding costs are 1.5% of the cost of the product; that is, $(0.015)(\$20) = \$0.30$ per unit for component 322A and $(0.015)(\$10) = \$0.15$ per unit for component 802B. A common assumption made in using the linear programming approach to production scheduling is now invoked. We assume that monthly ending inventories are an acceptable approximation to the average inventory levels throughout the month. Given this assumption, the inventory holding cost portion of the objective function can be written as follows:

$$\text{Inventory holding cost} = 0.30s_{11} + 0.30s_{12} + 0.30s_{13} + 0.15s_{21} + 0.15s_{22}$$
$$+ 0.15s_{23}$$

In order to incorporate the costs due to fluctuations in production levels from month to month, we need to define the following additional decision variables:

$$I_m = \text{increase in the total production level during}$$
$$\text{month } m \text{ compared with month } m - 1$$

$$D_m = \text{decrease in the total production level during}$$
$$\text{month } m \text{ compared with month } m - 1$$

After estimating the effects of employee layoffs, turnovers, reassignment training costs, and other costs associated with fluctuating production levels, Bollinger estimates that the cost associated with increasing the production level for any given month is $0.50 per unit increase. A similar cost associated with decreasing the production level for any given month is $0.20 per unit. Thus, the third portion of the objective function can be written as follows:

$$\text{Production fluctuation costs} = 0.50I_1 + 0.50I_2 + 0.50I_3 + 0.20D_1 + 0.20D_2$$
$$+ 0.20D_3$$

You should note here that Bollinger has elected to measure the cost associated with production fluctuations as a function of the change in the total number of units produced in month m compared with the total number of units produced in month $m - 1$. In other production scheduling applications the production fluctuations might be measured in terms of machine hours or labor hours required rather than in terms of the total number of units produced.

Combining all three costs, the complete objective function becomes

$$\min 20x_{11} + 20x_{12} + 20x_{13} + 10x_{21} + 10x_{22} + 10x_{23} + 0.30s_{11}$$
$$+ 0.30s_{12} + 0.30s_{13} + 0.15s_{21} + 0.15s_{22} + 0.15s_{23} + 0.50I_1$$
$$+ 0.50I_2 + 0.50I_3 + 0.20D_1 + 0.20D_2 + 0.20D_3$$

Now let us consider the constraints. First, we must guarantee that the schedule meets customer demand. Since the units shipped can come from the current month's production or from inventory carried over from previous periods, we have the following basic requirements:

$$\begin{pmatrix} \text{Ending} \\ \text{inventory} \\ \text{from previous} \\ \text{month} \end{pmatrix} + \begin{pmatrix} \text{current} \\ \text{production} \end{pmatrix} \geq \begin{pmatrix} \text{this month's} \\ \text{demand} \end{pmatrix}$$

The difference between the left-hand side and the right-hand side will be the amount of ending inventory at the end of this month. Thus, the demand requirement takes the form

$$\begin{pmatrix} \text{Ending} \\ \text{inventory} \\ \text{from previous} \\ \text{month} \end{pmatrix} + \begin{pmatrix} \text{current} \\ \text{production} \end{pmatrix} - \begin{pmatrix} \text{ending} \\ \text{inventory} \\ \text{for this} \\ \text{month} \end{pmatrix} = \begin{pmatrix} \text{this} \\ \text{month's} \\ \text{demand} \end{pmatrix}$$

Suppose that the inventories at the beginning of the 3-month scheduling period were 500 units for component 322A and 200 units for component 802B. Recalling that the demand for both products in the first month (April) was 1000 units, the constraints for meeting demand in the first month become

$$500 + x_{11} - s_{11} = 1000$$
$$200 + x_{21} - s_{21} = 1000$$

Moving the constants to the right-hand side, we have

$$x_{11} - s_{11} = 500$$
$$x_{21} - s_{21} = 800$$

Similarly, we need demand constraints for both products in the second and third months. These can be written as follows:

$$\text{Month 2: } s_{11} + x_{12} - s_{12} = 3000$$
$$s_{21} + x_{22} - s_{22} = 500$$

$$\text{Month 3: } s_{12} + x_{13} - s_{13} = 5000$$

$$s_{22} + x_{23} - s_{23} = 3000$$

If the company specifies a minimum inventory level at the end of the 3-month period of at least 400 units of component 322A and at least 200 units of component 802B, we can add the constraints

$$s_{13} \geq 400$$

$$s_{23} \geq 200$$

Let us suppose that we have the additional information available on production, labor, and storage capacity given in Table 4.8. Machine, labor, and storage space requirements are given in Table 4.9. To reflect these limitations, the following constraints are necessary:
Machine capacity:

$$0.10x_{11} + 0.08x_{21} \leq 400 \qquad \text{Month 1}$$

$$0.10x_{12} + 0.08x_{22} \leq 500 \qquad \text{Month 2}$$

$$0.10x_{13} + 0.08x_{23} \leq 600 \qquad \text{Month 3}$$

Labor capacity:

$$0.05x_{11} + 0.07x_{21} \leq 300 \qquad \text{Month 1}$$

$$0.05x_{12} + 0.07x_{22} \leq 300 \qquad \text{Month 2}$$

$$0.05x_{13} + 0.07x_{23} \leq 300 \qquad \text{Month 3}$$

Storage capacity:

$$2s_{11} + 3s_{21} \leq 10,000 \qquad \text{Month 1}$$

$$2s_{12} + 3s_{22} \leq 10,000 \qquad \text{Month 2}$$

$$2s_{13} + 3s_{23} \leq 10,000 \qquad \text{Month 3}$$

One final set of constraints must be added. These are necessary in order to guarantee that I_m and D_m will reflect the increase or decrease in the total production level for month m. Suppose that the production levels for March, the month before the start of the current production scheduling problem, had been 1500 units of component 322A and 1000 units of component 802B for a total production level of $1500 + 1000 = 2500$ units. We can find the amount of the change in production for April from the relationship

TABLE 4.8
Machine, Labor, and Storage Capacities for Bollinger Electronics

	Machine Capacity (hours)	Labor Capacity (hours)	Storage Capacity (square feet)
April	400	300	10,000
May	500	300	10,000
June	600	300	10,000

TABLE 4.9
Machine, Labor, and Storage Requirements for Components 322A and 802B

	Machine (hours/unit)	Labor (hours/unit)	Storage (sq. ft./unit)
Component 322A	0.10	0.05	2
Component 802B	0.08	0.07	3

$$\text{April production} - \text{March production} = \text{change}$$

Using the April production decision variables, x_{11} and x_{21}, and the March production of 2500 units, the above relationship can be rewritten as

$$x_{11} + x_{21} - 2500 = \text{change}$$

Note that the change can be positive or negative. A positive change reflects an increase in the total production level, and a negative change reflects a decrease in the total production level. Using the above relationship, the increase in production variable for April, I_1, and the decrease in production variable for April, D_1, can be used to specify the following constraint for the change in total production for the month of April:

$$x_{11} + x_{21} - 2500 = I_1 - D_1$$

Of course, we cannot have an increase in production and a decrease in production during the same 1-month period; thus, either I_1 or D_1 will be zero. If April requires 3000 units of production, we will have $I_1 = 500$ and $D_1 = 0$. If April requires 2200 units of production, we will have $I_1 = 0$ and $D_1 = 300$. This approach of denoting the change in production level as the difference between two nonnegative variables, I_1 and D_1, permits both positive and negative changes in the total production level. If a single variable, say c_m, had been used to represent the change in production level, then because of the nonnegativity requirement, only positive changes would be possible.

Using the same approach in May and June (always subtracting the previous month's total production from the current month's total production), we have the following constraints for the second and third months of the production scheduling period:

$$(x_{12} + x_{22}) - (x_{11} + x_{21}) = I_2 - D_2$$
$$(x_{13} + x_{23}) - (x_{12} + x_{22}) = I_3 - D_3$$

Placing the variables on the left-hand side and the constants on the right-hand side, the complete set of what are commonly referred to as production-smoothing constraints can be written as

$$
\begin{aligned}
x_{11} + x_{21} \qquad\qquad\qquad\qquad\quad - I_1 + D_1 &= 2500 \\
-x_{11} - x_{21} + x_{12} + x_{22} \qquad\qquad - I_2 + D_2 &= 0 \\
- x_{12} - x_{22} + x_{13} + x_{23} - I_3 + D_3 &= 0
\end{aligned}
$$

The initially rather small, 2-product, 3-month scheduling problem has now developed into an 18-variable, 20-constraint linear programming problem. Note that in the problem we were concerned only with one type of machine process, one type of labor, and one type of storage area. In actual production scheduling problems you may encounter several machine types, several labor grades, and/or several storage areas. Thus, you are probably beginning to realize how large-scale linear programs of production systems come about. A typical application might involve developing a production schedule for 100 products over a 12-month horizon. Such a problem could have over 1000 variables and constraints.

The computer solution to the Bollinger Electronics production scheduling problem is shown in Figure 4.6. A portion of the managerial report based on the computer solution is shown in Table 4.10.

FIGURE 4.6
Computer Solution of the Bollinger Electronics Production Scheduling Problem Using The Management Scientist

```
Objective Function Value =    225294.953000

        Variable            Value            Reduced Costs
      ---------------    ---------------    ---------------
          X11             500.000000           0.000002
          X12            3199.999000           0.000003
          X13            5199.999500           0.000004
          X21            2499.999500           0.000002
          X22            2000.000980           0.000001
          X23               0.000000           0.060719
          S11               0.000000           0.192860
          S12             200.000977           0.000000
          S13             400.000000           0.000000
          S21            1699.999510           0.000000
          S22            3200.000000           0.000003
          S23             200.000000           0.000000
          I1              500.001460           0.000000
          I2             2199.998800           0.000000
          I3                0.000000           0.000000
          D1                0.000000           0.700000
          D2                0.000000           0.700000
          D3                0.000000           0.700000


        Constraint       Slack/Surplus         Dual Prices
      ---------------    ---------------    ---------------
            1               0.000000          -20.000002
            2               0.000000          -10.000002
            3               0.000000          -20.107142
            4               0.000000          -10.150002
            5               0.000000          -20.499996
            6               0.000000          -10.439282
            7               0.000000          -20.799995
            8               0.000000          -10.589281
            9             149.999939            0.000000
           10              20.000015            0.000000
           11              80.000000            0.000000
           12             100.000061            0.000000
           13               0.000000            2.142897
           14              39.999985            0.000000
           15            4899.997100            0.000000
           16               0.000000            0.046428
           17            8600.000000            0.000000
           18               0.000000            0.500000
           19               0.000000            0.500000
           20               0.000000            0.500000
```

TABLE 4.10
Minimum-Cost Production Schedule Information for Bollinger Electronics

Activity	April	May	June
Production			
Component 322A	500	3,200	5,200
Component 802B	2,500	2,000	0
Totals	3,000	5,200	5,200
Ending inventory			
Component 322A	0	200	400
Component 802B	1,700	3,200	200
Machine usage			
Scheduled hours	250	480	520
Slack capacity hours	150	20	80
Labor usage			
Scheduled hours	200	300	260
Slack capacity hours	100	0	40
Storage usage			
Scheduled storage	5,100	10,000	1,400
Slack capacity	4,900	0	8,600

Total schedule cost (including production, inventory, and production smoothing) = $225,295

Let us now consider the monthly variation in the production and inventory schedule shown in Table 4.10. Recall that the inventory cost for component 802B is one-half the inventory cost for component 322A. Therefore, as might be expected, component 802B is produced heavily in the first month (April) and then held in inventory for the demand that will occur in future months. Component 322A tends to be produced when needed, and only small amounts are carried in inventory.

The costs of increasing and decreasing the total production volume tend to smooth the monthly variations. In fact, the minimum cost schedule calls for a 500-unit increase in total production in April and a 2200-unit increase in total production in May. The May production level of 5200 units is then maintained during June.

The machine usage section of the report shows ample machine capacity available in all 3 months. However, labor and storage capacity both show full utilization (slack = 0 for constraint 13 and constraint 16 in Figure 4.6) in the month of May. The dual price shows that an additional hour of labor capacity in May will improve the objective function (lower cost) by approximately $2.14. This information may help the production manager decide whether to add labor overtime during the month of May. A similar interpretation for the dual price for constraint 16 shows that each additional square foot of storage space made available during May will improve the objective function by slightly less than 5 cents per square foot.

We have seen in this illustration that a linear programming model of a 2-product, 3-month production system has provided some valuable information in terms of identifying a minimum-cost production schedule. In larger production systems, where the number of variables and constraints is too large to track manually, linear programming models can provide a significant advantage in developing cost-saving production schedules.

In checking the appropriateness of a linear programming model, it is always a good idea to review the units of measurement for the objective function and the constraints. For example, the machine capacities for Bollinger Electronics problem were stated in units of *hours*. With component 322A requiring 0.10 hours (6 minutes) per unit and component 802B requiring 0.08 (4.8 minutes) per unit, the constraint for the 400 hours available in month one was correctly stated as

$$0.10x_{11} + 0.08x_{12} \leq 400$$

The unit of measurement is consistent in that hours is used for both the left-hand side and the right-hand side. The constraint

$$6x_{11} + 4.8x_{12} \leq 400$$

would be incorrectly stated because the use of minutes on the left-hand side would be inconsistent with the use of hours on the right-hand side. This inconsistency could be corrected by converting the right-hand side capacity to 400 hours × (60 minutes/hour) = 24,000 minutes. Thus, while there is flexibility in selecting the unit of measurement to use, it is necessary to check for consistency.

Labor Planning

Labor planning or scheduling problems frequently occur when managers must make decisions involving departmental staffing requirements for a given period of time. This is particularly true when labor assignments have some flexibility and at least some labor effort can be assigned to more than one department or work center. This is often the case when employees have been cross-trained on two or more jobs. In the following example we show how linear programming can be used to determine not only an optimal product mix but also an optimal labor allocation for the various departments.

McCarthy's Everyday Glass Company is planning to produce two styles of drinking glasses during the next month. The glasses are processed in four separate departments. Excess equipment capacity is available and will not be a constraining factor. However, the company's labor resources are limited and will probably limit the production volume for the two products. The labor requirements per case produced (one dozen glasses) are shown in Table 4.11.

TABLE 4.11
Hours of Labor per Case of Product

Department	Product 1	Product 2
1	0.070	0.100
2	0.050	0.084
3	0.100	0.067
4	0.010	0.025

The company makes a profit of $1.00 per case of product 1 and $0.90 per case of product 2. If the number of hours available in each department is fixed, we can formulate McCarthy's problem as a standard product-mix linear program. We use the usual notation:

$$x_1 = \text{cases of product 1 manufactured}$$

$$x_2 = \text{cases of product 2 manufactured}$$

$$b_i = \text{hours of labor available in department } i, i = 1, 2, 3, 4$$

The linear program can be written as

$$\max \quad 1.00x_1 + 0.90x_2$$

s.t.

$$0.070x_1 + 0.100x_2 \leq b_1$$

$$0.050x_1 + 0.084x_2 \leq b_2$$

$$0.100x_1 + 0.067x_2 \leq b_3$$

$$0.010x_1 + 0.025x_2 \leq b_4$$

$$x_1, x_2 \geq 0$$

To solve this product-mix problem, we would ask the production manager to specify the hours available in each department (b_1, b_2, b_3, and b_4); then we could solve for the profit-maximizing product mix. However, in this case we assume that the manager has some flexibility in allocating labor resources, and we would like to make a recommendation for this allocation as well as determining the optimal product mix.

Suppose that after consideration of the training and experience qualifications of the workers, we find this additional information:

Possible Labor Assignments	Hours of Labor Available
Department 1 only	430
Department 2 only	400
Department 3 only	500
Department 4 only	135
Departments 1 or 2	570
Departments 3 or 4	300
Total Available	2335

Of the 2335 hours available for the month's production, we see that 870 hours can be allocated with some management discretion. The constraints for the hours available per department are as follows:

$$b_1 \leq 430 + 570 = 1000$$

$$b_2 \leq 400 + 570 = 970$$

$$b_3 \leq 500 + 300 = 800$$

$$b_4 \leq 135 + 300 = 435$$

Since the 570 hours that have a flexible assignment between departments 1 and 2 cannot be assigned to both departments simultaneously, we need the following additional constraint:

$$b_1 + b_2 \leq 430 + 400 + 570 = 1400$$

Similarly, for the 300 hours that can be allocated between departments 3 and 4, we need the constraint

$$b_3 + b_4 \leq 500 + 135 + 300 = 935$$

In this formulation we are now treating the hours of labor assigned to the departments as variables. The objective function coefficients for these variables will be zero, since the b_i variables do not directly affect profit. After placing all variables on the left-hand side of the constraints, we obtain the following linear program:

$$\max \quad 1.00x_1 + 0.90x_2 + 0b_1 + 0b_2 + 0b_3 + 0b_4$$

s.t.

$$
\begin{aligned}
0.070x_1 + 0.100x_2 - b_1 & & & & & \leq & 0 \\
0.050x_1 + 0.084x_2 & - b_2 & & & & \leq & 0 \\
0.100x_1 + 0.067x_2 & & - b_3 & & & \leq & 0 \\
0.010x_1 + 0.025x_2 & & & - b_4 & & \leq & 0 \\
b_1 & & & & & \leq & 1000 \\
& b_2 & & & & \leq & 970 \\
& & b_3 & & & \leq & 800 \\
& & & b_4 & & \leq & 435 \\
b_1 + & b_2 & & & & \leq & 1400 \\
& & b_3 + & b_4 & & \leq & 935
\end{aligned}
$$

$$x_1, x_2, b_1, b_2, b_3, b_4 \geq 0$$

This linear programming model will actually solve two problems: (1) it will find the optimal product mix for the planning period, and (2) it will allocate the hours of available labor to the departments in such a fashion that profits will be maximized. The solution to this 6-variable, 10-constraint model is shown in Table 4.12.

Note that the optimal labor plan utilizes all 2335 hours of labor. In this solution there is no idle time in any of the departments. This will not always be the case in problems of this type; however, if the manager does have the freedom to assign certain employees to different departments, the effect will probably be a reduction in the overall idle time. The linear programming model automatically assigns employees to the departments in the most profitable manner. If the manager had used judgment to allocate the hours to the departments, and if we had then solved the product-mix problem with fixed b_i, we would in all probability have found slack in some departments while other departments represented bottlenecks because of insufficient resources.

Variations in the basic formulation of this section might be used in situations such as allocating raw material resources to products, allocating machine time to products, and allocating sales force time to product lines or sales territories.

TABLE 4.12
Optimal Production Plan and Labor Allocation for
McCarthy's Everyday Glass Company

Production plan:
Product 1 = 4700 cases
Product 2 = 4543 cases

Labor allocation:
Department 1   783 hours
Department 2   617 hours
Department 3   774 hours
Department 4   161 hours
Total   2335 hours

Profit = $8789

4.5 ▼ BLENDING PROBLEMS

Blending problems arise whenever a manager must decide how to blend two or more resources in order to produce one or more products. In these situations the resources contain one or more essential ingredients that must be blended in such a manner that the final products will contain specific percentages of the essential ingredients. In most of these applications, then, management must decide how much of each resource to purchase in order to satisfy product specifications and product demands at minimum cost.

Blending problems occur frequently in the petroleum industry (such as blending crude oil to produce different-octane gasolines), chemical industry (such as blending chemicals to produce fertilizers, weed killers, and so on), and food industry (such as blending input ingredients to produce soft drinks, soups, and so on). Because of the widespread application of blending problems, the objective in this section is to illustrate how linear programming can be applied to solve these types of problems.

The Grand Strand Oil Company produces regular-grade and premium-grade gasoline products, which are sold to independent service stations in the southeastern United States. The Grand Strand refinery manufactures the gasoline products by blending three petroleum components. The gasolines are sold at different prices, and the petroleum components have different costs. The firm would like to determine how to mix or blend the three components into the two gasoline products in such a way as to maximize profits.

Data available show that the regular-grade gasoline can be sold for $0.50 per gallon and the premium-grade gasoline for $0.54 per gallon. For the current production planning period, Grand Strand can obtain the three petroleum components at the cost per gallon and in the quantities shown in Table 4.13.

The product specifications for the regular and premium gasolines restrict the amounts of each component that can be used in each gasoline product. The product specifications are listed in Table 4.14. Current commitments to distributors require Grand Strand to produce at least 10,000 gallons of regular-grade gasoline.

The Grand Strand blending problem is to determine how many gallons of each component should be used in the regular-grade gasoline blend and how many gallons of each component should be used in the premium-grade gasoline blend. The optimal blending solution should maximize the firm's profit, subject to the constraints on the available

TABLE 4.13
Petroleum Cost and Supply for the Grand Strand Blending Problem

Petroleum Component	Cost/Gallon	Maximum Available
Component 1	$0.25	5,000 gallons
Component 2	$0.30	10,000 gallons
Component 3	$0.42	10,000 gallons

TABLE 4.14
Product Specifications for the Grand Strand Blending Problem

Product	Specifications
Regular gasoline	At most 30% component 1
	At least 40% component 2
	At most 20% component 3
Premium gasoline	At least 25% component 1
	At most 40% component 2
	At least 30% component 3

petroleum supplies shown in Table 4.13, the product specifications shown in Table 4.14, and the required 10,000 gallons of regular-grade gasoline.

We can use the following notation to define the decision variables:
Let

$$x_{ij} = \text{gallons of component } i \text{ used in gasoline } j,$$

where $i = 1$, 2, or 3 for components 1, 2, or 3,

and $j = r$ if regular or $j = p$ if premium

The six decision variables become

x_{1r} = gallons of component 1 in regular gasoline

x_{2r} = gallons of component 2 in regular gasoline

x_{3r} = gallons of component 3 in regular gasoline

x_{1p} = gallons of component 1 in premium gasoline

x_{2p} = gallons of component 2 in premium gasoline

x_{3p} = gallons of component 3 in premium gasoline

Note that previously we have always used numbers as the subscripts for decision variables. Continuing to use numerical subscripts, we could have let $j = 1$ for regular gasoline and $j = 2$ for premium gasoline. However, the use of the r and p subscripts is descriptive and will enable us easily to identify the gasoline product being referred to by the decision variable.

Using the six decision variables, the total number of gallons of each type of gasoline produced can be expressed by summing the number of gallons produced using each of the 3 petroleum components. That is,

Total Gallons Produced

$$\text{Regular gasoline} = x_{1r} + x_{2r} + x_{3r}$$

$$\text{Premium gasoline} = x_{1p} + x_{2p} + x_{3p}$$

Similarly, the total gallons of each petroleum component used can be expressed by the following sums:

Total Petroleum Component Usage

$$\text{Component 1} = x_{1r} + x_{1p}$$

$$\text{Component 2} = x_{2r} + x_{2p}$$

$$\text{Component 3} = x_{3r} + x_{3p}$$

The objective function of maximizing the profit contribution can be developed by identifying the difference between the total revenue from the two types of gasoline and the total cost of the three petroleum components. By multiplying the $0.50 per gallon price by the total gallons of regular gasoline, the $0.54 per gallon price by the total gallons of premium gasoline, and the component cost per gallon figures in Table 4.13 by the total gallons of each component used, the objective function can be written as follows:

$$\max \quad 0.50(x_{1r} + x_{2r} + x_{3r}) + 0.54(x_{1p} + x_{2p} + x_{3p})$$
$$-0.25(x_{1r} + x_{1p}) - 0.30(x_{2r} + x_{2p}) - 0.42(x_{3r} + x_{3p})$$

By combining terms, the objective function can be written as

$$\max \quad 0.25x_{1r} + 0.20x_{2r} + 0.08x_{3r} + 0.29x_{1p} + 0.24x_{2p} + 0.12x_{3p}$$

The limitations on the availability of the three petroleum components can be expressed by the following three constraints:

$$x_{1r} + x_{1p} \leq 5000 \quad \text{Component 1}$$

$$x_{2r} + x_{2p} \leq 10,000 \quad \text{Component 2}$$

$$x_{3r} + x_{3p} \leq 10,000 \quad \text{Component 3}$$

Six constraints are now required to meet the product specifications stated in Table 4.14. The first specification states that component 1 can account for at most 30% of the total gallons of regular gasoline produced. That is,

$$\frac{x_{1r}}{x_{1r} + x_{2r} + x_{3r}} \leq 0.30$$

or

$$x_{1r} \leq 0.30(x_{1r} + x_{2r} + x_{3r})$$

Rewriting this constraint with the variables on the left-hand side and a constant on the right-hand side, the first product specification constraint becomes

$$0.70x_{1r} - 0.30x_{2r} - 0.30x_{3r} \leq 0$$

The second product specification listed in Table 4.14 can be written as

$$\frac{x_{2r}}{x_{1r} + x_{2r} + x_{3r}} \geq 0.40$$

or

$$x_{2r} \geq 0.40(x_{1r} + x_{2r} + x_{3r})$$

and thus

$$-0.40x_{1r} + 0.60x_{2r} - 0.40x_{3r} \geq 0$$

Similarly, the four additional blending specifications shown in Table 4.14 can be written as

$$-0.20x_{1r} - 0.20x_{2r} + 0.80x_{3r} \leq 0$$
$$0.75x_{1p} - 0.25x_{2p} - 0.25x_{3p} \geq 0$$
$$-0.40x_{1p} + 0.60x_{2p} - 0.40x_{3p} \leq 0$$
$$-0.30x_{1p} - 0.30x_{2p} + 0.70x_{3p} \geq 0$$

The constraint for at least 10,000 gallons of the regular-grade gasoline is written

$$x_{1r} + x_{2r} + x_{3r} \geq 10,000$$

Thus the complete linear programming model with 6 decision variables and 10 constraints can be written as follows:

$$\max \quad 0.25x_{1r} + 0.20x_{2r} + 0.08x_{3r} + 0.29x_{1p} + 0.24x_{2p} + 0.12x_{3p}$$

s.t.

$$
\begin{aligned}
x_{1r} \phantom{+ 0.00x_{2r} + 0.00x_{3r}} + x_{1p} \phantom{+ x_{2p} + x_{3p}} &\leq 5{,}000 \\
x_{2r} \phantom{+ 0.00x_{3r}} + x_{2p} \phantom{+ x_{3p}} &\leq 10{,}000 \\
x_{3r} + x_{3p} &\leq 10{,}000 \\
0.70x_{1r} - 0.30x_{2r} - 0.30x_{3r} &\leq 0 \\
-0.40x_{1r} + 0.60x_{2r} - 0.40x_{3r} &\geq 0 \\
-0.20x_{1r} - 0.20x_{2r} + 0.80x_{3r} &\leq 0 \\
0.75x_{1p} - 0.25x_{2p} - 0.25x_{3p} &\geq 0 \\
-0.40x_{1p} + 0.60x_{2p} - 0.40x_{3p} &\leq 0 \\
-0.30x_{1p} - 0.30x_{2p} + 0.70x_{3p} &\geq 0 \\
x_{1r} + x_{2r} + x_{3r} &\geq 10{,}000 \\
x_{1r}, x_{2r}, x_{3r}, x_{1p}, x_{2p}, x_{3p} &\geq 0
\end{aligned}
$$

The computer solution to the Grand Strand blending problem is shown in Figure 4.7. The blending solution that provides a profit of $4650 is summarized in Table 4.15. The optimal blending strategy shows that 10,000 gallons of regular gasoline should be produced. Regular gasoline will consist of a blend of component 1 (1250 gallons) and component 2 (8750 gallons). The 15,000 gallons of premium gasoline are to be manu-

FIGURE 4.7
Computer Solution of the Grand Strand Blending Problem Using The Management Scientist

Objective Function Value =   4650.000500

Variable	Value	Reduced Costs
X1R	1249.999020	0.000000
X2R	8749.997100	0.000000
X3R	0.000000	0.000000
X1P	3750.001000	0.000000
X2P	1250.005860	0.000000
X3P	10000.000000	0.000000

Constraint	Slack/Surplus	Dual Prices
1	0.000000	0.290000
2	0.000000	0.240000
3	0.000000	0.120000
4	1750.000490	0.000000
5	4749.999000	0.000000
6	1999.999390	0.000000
7	0.000000	0.000000
8	4749.998000	0.000000
9	5499.997100	0.000000
10	0.000000	-0.040000

TABLE 4.15
Grand Strand Gasoline Blending Strategy

| Gasoline | Gallons of Component (Percentage) | | | Total |
	Component 1	Component 2	Component 3	
Regular	1250 (12.5%)	8750 (87.5%)	—	10,000
Premium	3750 (25.0%)	1250 (8.3%)	10,000 (66.7%)	15,000

factured from a blend of all three petroleum components: 3750 gallons of component 1, 1250 gallons of component 2, and 10,000 gallons of component 3.

The interpretation of the slack and surplus variables associated with the product specification constraints (constraints 4 to 9) in Figure 4.7 needs some clarification. If the constraint is a ≤ constraint, the value of the slack can be interpreted as the gallons of component usage below the maximum amount of the component usage specified by the constraint. For example, the slack of 1750 for constraint 4 shows that component 1 usage is 1750 gallons below the maximum amount of component 1 that could have been used in the production of 10,000 gallons of regular gasoline. If the product specification constraint is a ≥ constraint, a surplus variable shows the gallons of component usage above the minimum amount of component usage specified by the blending constraint. For example, the surplus of 4750 for constraint 5 shows that component 2 usage is 4750 gallons above the minimum amount of component 2 that could have to be used in the production of 10,000 gallons of regular gasoline.

▼ NOTES AND COMMENTS ▼

A convenient way to define the decision variables in a blending problem is to use a matrix in which the rows correspond to the raw materials and the columns correspond to the final products. For example, in the Grand Strand blending problem we could define the decision variables as follows:

		Final Products	
		Regular Gasoline	*Premium Gasoline*
Raw Materials	*Component 1*	x_{1r}	x_{1p}
	Component 2	x_{2r}	x_{2p}
	Component 3	x_{3r}	x_{3p}

There are two advantages to this approach: (1) it provides a systematic way to define the decision variables for any blending problem; (2) it provides a visual image of the decision variables in terms of how they are related to the raw materials, products, and each other.

4.6 ▼ DATA ENVELOPMENT ANALYSIS

Data envelopment analysis (DEA) is a new application of linear programming that has been used to measure the relative efficiency of operating units with the same goals and objectives. For example, DEA has been used to measure the relative efficiency of individual fast-food outlets in the same chain. In this case the goal of DEA was to identify the inefficient outlets which should be targeted for further study and, if necessary, corrective action. Other applications of DEA have measured the relative efficiencies of hospitals, banks, courts, schools, and so on. In these applications the performance of each hospital, bank, court, or school was measured relative to the performance of all operating units in the same system.

The operating units of most organizations have multiple inputs, such as staff size, salaries, hours of operation, and advertising budget, as well as multiple outputs, such as profit, market share, and growth rate. In these situations it is often difficult for a manager to determine which operating units are inefficient in converting their multiple inputs into multiple outputs. This is where data envelopment analysis has proven to be a helpful managerial tool.

The DEA approach uses a linear programming model to construct a hypothetical composite operating unit based on all units in the reference group. The output of the composite unit is determined by computing a weighted average of the outputs of all units in the reference group. The input for the composite unit is determined by using the same weights to compute a weighted average of the inputs for all units in the reference group. Constraints in the linear programming model require all outputs of the composite unit to be *greater than or equal* to the outputs of the unit being evaluated. If the inputs for the composite unit can be shown to be *less than* the inputs for the unit being evaluated, the composite unit will be shown to have the same, or more, output for *less input*. In this case, the model will show that the composite unit is more efficient than the unit being evaluated. In other words, the unit being evaluated is *less efficient* than the composite unit. Since the composite unit is based on all units in the reference group, the unit being evaluated can be judged *relatively inefficient* when compared to the other units in the group.

Evaluating the Performance of Hospitals

Let us illustrate the application of data envelopment analysis by evaluating the performance of a group of four hospitals. In the example we will consider three measures of input and four measures of output. These measures are as follows:

Input measures:

1. The number of full-time equivalent (FTE) nonphysician personnel
2. The amount spent on supplies
3. The number of bed-days available

Output measures:

1. Patient-days of service under Medicare
2. Patient-days of service not under Medicare
3. Number of nurses trained
4. Number of interns trained

Summaries of the input and output measures for a one-year period at each of the four hospitals are shown in Tables 4.16 and 4.17. Let us show how DEA can use these data to identify any relatively inefficient hospitals.

In applying DEA a linear programming model will have to be developed for each hospital whose efficiency is to be evaluated. In the following discussion we will develop a model that can be used to assess the relative efficiency of County Hospital. (Problem 26 at the end of the chapter will ask you to develop a model to assess the relative efficiency of General Hospital.) In developing the linear programming model for County Hospital, the weights used to construct the composite hospital are the variables. They are defined as follows:

$$wg = \text{weight applied to inputs and outputs for General Hospital}$$
$$wu = \text{weight applied to inputs and outputs for University Hospital}$$
$$wc = \text{weight applied to inputs and outputs for County Hospital}$$
$$ws = \text{weight applied to inputs and outputs for State Hospital}$$

As noted, the weights will be used to determine the inputs and outputs for the hypothetical composite hospital. The input/output relationships that will be included in the model will have the following general form:

TABLE 4.16
Annual Resources Consumed (Inputs) for Four Hospitals

Input Measure	Hospital			
	General	*University*	*County*	*State*
Full-time equivalent nonphysicians	285.20	162.30	275.70	210.40
Supply expense (000's)	123.80	128.70	348.50	154.10
Bed-days available (000's)	106.72	64.21	104.10	104.04

TABLE 4.17
Annual Services Provided (Outputs) for Four Hospitals

Output Measure	Hospital			
	General	*University*	*County*	*State*
Medicare patient-days (000's)	48.14	34.62	36.72	33.16
Non-medicare patient-days (000's)	43.10	27.11	45.98	56.46
Nurses trained	253	148	175	160
Interns trained	41	27	23	84

$$\begin{pmatrix} \text{Input/output} \\ \text{of the} \\ \text{composite} \\ \text{hospital} \end{pmatrix} = \begin{pmatrix} \text{input/output} \\ \text{at} \\ \text{General} \\ \text{Hospital} \end{pmatrix} wg + \begin{pmatrix} \text{input/output} \\ \text{at} \\ \text{University} \\ \text{Hospital} \end{pmatrix} wu$$

$$+ \begin{pmatrix} \text{input/output} \\ \text{at} \\ \text{County} \\ \text{Hospital} \end{pmatrix} wc + \begin{pmatrix} \text{input/output} \\ \text{at} \\ \text{State} \\ \text{Hospital} \end{pmatrix} ws$$

In formulating the DEA linear programming model, we will use the above expression to develop a constraint for each input measure and each output measure. In computing the weights for the four hospitals forming the composite hospital, the DEA linear programming model will require the sum of the weights to equal 1. Thus, for the four-hospital example, the first constraint will be as follows:

$$wg + wu + wc + ws = 1$$

Using the general input/output relationship for each of the four output measures, the four output constraints for the DEA model are written as follows:

$$48.14wg + 34.62wu + 36.72wc + 33.16ws \geq 36.72 \quad \text{Medicare}$$
$$43.10wg + 27.11wu + 45.98wc + 56.46ws \geq 45.98 \quad \text{Non-Medicare}$$
$$253wg + 148wu + 175wc + 160ws \geq 175 \quad \text{Nurses}$$
$$41wg + 27wu + 23wc + 84ws \geq 23 \quad \text{Interns}$$

Output for the composite hospital

Output for County Hospital

The above four constraints require the linear programming solution to provide weights such that all four outputs for the composite hospital will be greater than or equal to the four outputs of County Hospital. If a solution satisfying the output constraints can be found, then the composite hospital produces at least as much of each output as County Hospital.

Next, we need to consider the three input measures. The DEA linear programming model contains the variable E, which determines the fraction of County Hospital's input required by the composite hospital. The use of E, which is referred to as the efficiency index, is shown on the next page.

| | Input Resources | |
Input Measure	Used By County Hospital	Available to Composite Hospital
FTE nonphysicians	275.70	275.70E
Supplies (000's)	348.50	348.50E
Bed-days (000's)	104.10	104.10E

As shown above, the resources available to the composite hospital are simply a multiple of the resources used at County Hospital. If $E = 1$, the resources available to the composite hospital are the same as those used by County Hospital. If E is greater than 1, the composite hospital would have available proportionally more resources, while if E is less than 1, the composite hospital would have available proportionally less resources. The linear programming constraints for the three input measures are written as follows:

$$285.20wg + 162.30wu + 275.70wc + 210.40ws \leq 275.70E \text{ FTE nonphysicians}$$

$$123.80wg + 128.70wu + 348.50wc + 154.10ws \leq 348.50E \text{ Supplies}$$

$$106.72wg + 64.21wu + 104.10wc + 104.04ws \leq 104.10E \text{ Bed-days}$$

Input for the composite hospital

Input capacities for the composite hospital

If a solution with $E < 1$ can be found, the composite hospital does not need as many resources as County Hospital needs.

The objective function for the DEA model is to minimize the value of E, which is equivalent to minimizing the input resources available to the composite hospital. Thus, the objective function is written as

$$\min \quad E$$

The DEA efficiency conclusion is based on the optimal objective function value for E. The decision rule is as follows:

If $E = 1$, the composite hospital requires *as much input* as County Hospital does. There is no evidence that County Hospital is inefficient.

If $E < 1$, the composite hospital requires *less input* to obtain the output achieved by County Hospital. The composite hospital is more efficient; thus, County Hospital can be judged relatively inefficient.

The DEA linear programming model for the efficiency evaluation of County Hospital has five decision variables and eight constraints. The complete model is rewritten below:

Min $\quad E$

s.t.

$$wg + wu + wc + ws = 1$$
$$48.14wg + 34.62wu + 36.72wc + 33.16ws \geq 36.72$$
$$43.10wg + 27.11wu + 45.98wc + 56.46ws \geq 45.98$$
$$253wg + 148wu + 175wc + 160ws \geq 175$$

$$41wg + 27wu + 23wc + 84ws \geq 23$$
$$-275.50E + 285.20wg + 162.30wu + 275.70wc + 210.40ws \leq 0$$
$$-348.50E + 123.80wg + 128.70wu + 348.50wc + 154.10ws \leq 0$$
$$-104.10E + 106.72wg + 64.21wu + 104.10wc + 104.04ws \leq 0$$
$$wg, wu, wc, ws \geq 0$$

Note that in the above formulation of the model, we have moved the terms involving E to the left-hand side of the three input constraints because E is a decision variable. The above linear program was solved using The Management Scientist software package. The computer printout of the solution is shown in Figure 4.8.

We first note that the objective function shows that the efficiency score for County Hospital is 0.905. This tells us that the composite hospital can obtain at least the level of each output that County Hospital obtains by having available no more than 90.5% of the input resources required by County Hospital. Thus, the composite hospital is more efficient, and the DEA analysis has identified County Hospital as being relatively inefficient.

From the solution in Figure 4.8, we see that the composite hospital is formed from the weighted average of General Hospital (wg = .212), University Hospital (wu = .260), and State Hospital (ws = .527). Each input and output of the composite hospital is determined by the same weighted average of the inputs and outputs of these three hospitals.

The "Slack/Surplus" column provides some additional information about the efficiency of County Hospital compared to the composite hospital. Specifically, the composite hospital has at least as much of each output as County Hospital has (constraints 2–5) and provides 1.6 more nurses trained (surplus for constraint 4) and 37 more interns trained (surplus for constraint 5). The slack of 0 from constraint 8 shows that the composite

FIGURE 4.8
Computer Solution of the Data Envelopment Analysis County Hospital Model for Problem Using The Management Scientist

```
OPTIMAL SOLUTION

Objective Function Value =    0.905238

        Variable              Value            Reduced Costs
    ----------------    -----------------    -------------------
          E                0.905238             0.000000
          WG               0.212266             0.000000
          WU               0.260447             0.000000
          WC               0.000000             0.094762
          WS               0.527286             0.000000


      Constraint         Slack/Surplus          Dual Prices
    ----------------    -----------------    -------------------
          1                0.000000             0.238886
          2                0.000000            -0.000014
          3                0.000000            -0.000014
          4                1.615387             0.000000
          5               37.027027             0.000000
          6               35.642986             0.000000
          7           174422.297000             0.000000
          8                0.000000             0.000010
```

hospital uses approximately 90.5% of the bed-days used by County Hospital. The slack values for constraints 6 and 7 show that less than 90.5% of the FTE nonphysician and the supplies expense resources used at County Hospital are used by the composite hospital.

It is clear that the composite hospital is more efficient than County Hospital and that we are justified in concluding that County Hospital is relatively inefficient compared to the hospitals in the group. Given the results of the DEA analysis, hospital administrators should examine operations to determine how County Hospital resources can be more effectively utilized.

▼ NOTES AND COMMENTS ▼

1. Remember that the goal of data envelopment analysis is to identify operating units that are relatively inefficient. The method *does not* necessarily identify the operating units that are *relatively efficient*. Just because the efficiency index is $E = 1$, we cannot conclude that the unit being analyzed is relatively efficient. Indeed, any unit that has the largest output on any one of the output measures cannot be judged relatively inefficient. Thus, units that are not relatively inefficient may still be able to improve their absolute efficiency.
2. If there is one unit that is superefficient, DEA will show all other units to be relatively inefficient. Such would be the case if a unit producing the most of every output also consumes the least of every input. Such cases are extremely rare in practice.
3. In applying data envelopment analysis to problems involving a large group of operating units, practitioners have found that roughly 50% of the operating units can be identified as inefficient. Comparing each relatively inefficient unit to the units contributing to the composite unit may be helpful in understanding how the operation of each relatively inefficient unit can be improved.

▼ SUMMARY

In this chapter we have presented a broad range of applications that illustrate how linear programming can be used to assist in the decision-making process. Using a variety of situations, we have formulated and solved problems from the areas of marketing, finance, and production management. In addition, we have shown how linear programming can be applied to blending problems and the relatively new area of data envelopment analysis.

Many of the illustrations presented in this chapter are scaled-down versions of actual situations where linear programming has been applied. In real-world applications, the problem may not be so concisely stated, the data for the problem may not be as readily available, and the problem will most likely involve more decision variables and/or constraints. However, a thorough study of the applications in this chapter is a good place to begin for an individual who eventually hopes to be able to apply linear programming to real-world problems.

We included a printout from the Management Scientist software package for many of the applications presented in the chapter. The computer results provided an opportunity to discuss the information contained in the computer output and make interpretations based on sensitivity analysis.

▼ PROBLEMS

Note to student. The following problems have been designed to give you an understanding and appreciation of the broad range of problems that can be formulated as linear programs. You should be able to formulate a linear programming model for each of the problems. However, you will need access to a linear programming computer package in order to develop the solution and make the requested interpretations.

1. *Product mix.* Better Products, Inc., manufactures three products on two machines. In a typical week, 40 hours of time are available on each machine. The profit contribution and production time in hours per unit are as follows:

	Product 1	Product 2	Product 3
Profit/unit	$30	$50	$20
Machine 1 time/unit	0.5	2.0	0.75
Machine 2 time/unit	1.0	1.0	0.5

Two operators are required for machine 1. Thus, 2 hours of labor must be scheduled for each hour of machine 1 time. Only one operator is required for machine 2. A maximum of 100 labor hours is available for assignment to the machine during the coming week. Other production requirements are that product 1 cannot account for more than 50% of the units produced and that product 3 must account for at least 20% of the units produced.

   a. How many units of each product should be produced in order to maximize the profit contribution? What is the projected weekly profit associated with your solution?
   b. How many hours of production time will be scheduled on each machine?
   c. What is the value of an additional hour of labor?
   d. Assume that labor capacity can be increased to 120 hours. Would you be interested in using the additional 20 hours available for this resource? Develop the optimal product mix assuming the extra hours are made available.

2. *Media selection.* The Westchester Chamber of Commerce periodically sponsors public service seminars and programs. Currently, promotional plans are under way for this year's program. Advertising alternatives include television, radio, and newspaper. Audience estimates, costs, and maximum media usage limitations are shown below:

	Television	Radio	Newspaper
Audience per advertisement	100,000	18,000	40,000
Cost per advertisement	$2,000	$300	$600
Maximum media usage	10	20	10

To ensure a balanced usage of advertising media, radio advertisements must not exceed 50% of the total number of advertisements authorized. In addition, it has been

requested that television account for at least 10% of the total number of advertisements authorized.

a. If the promotional budget is limited to $18,200, how many commercial messages
should be run on each medium in order to maximize total audience contact? What
is the allocation of the budget among the three media, and what is the total
audience reached?

b. What is the estimated audience contact that would result from an extra $100
allocated to the advertising budget?

3. *Diet problem.* Bluegrass Farms, Inc., in Lexington, Kentucky, is experimenting with
a special diet for its racehorses. The feed components available for the diet are a
standard horse feed product, a vitamin-enriched oat product, and a new vitamin and
mineral feed additive. The nutritional values in units per pound and the costs for the
three feed components are as follows:

	Standard	Enriched Oat	Additive
Ingredient A	0.8	0.2	0
Ingredient B	1.0	1.5	3.0
Ingredient C	0.1	0.6	2.0
Cost per pound	$0.25	$0.50	$3.00

a. Suppose that the horse trainer sets the minimum daily diet requirements at three
units of ingredient A, six units of ingredient B, and four units of ingredient C.
Also suppose that for weight control the trainer does not want the total daily feed
for a horse to exceed 6 pounds. What is the optimal daily mix of the three feed
components?

b. What is the cost per pound for the daily mix?

c. Using the dual price, determine what would happen to the total cost if the total
daily feed allowance were increased from 6 to 7 pounds? Explain why this occurs.

4. *Overtime planning.* Hartman Company is trying to determine how much of each of
two products should be produced over the coming planning period. Shown below is
information concerning labor availability, labor utilization, and product profitability.

	Product 1	Product 2	Labor Available
Profit/unit	$30.00	$15.00	—
Dept. A hours/unit	1.00	0.35	100 hours
Dept. B hours/unit	0.30	0.20	36 hours
Dept. C hours/unit	0.20	0.50	50 hours

a. Develop a linear programming model of the Hartman Company problem. Solve
the model to determine the optimal production quantities of products 1 and 2.

b. In computing the per-unit profit, Hartman does not deduct labor costs because
they are considered fixed for the upcoming planning period. However, suppose
overtime can be scheduled in some of the departments. Which departments would

you recommend scheduling for overtime? How much would you be willing to pay per hour of overtime in each department?

c. Suppose that 10, 6, and 8 hours of overtime may be scheduled in departments A, B, and C, respectively. The cost per hour of overtime is $18 in department A, $22.50 in department B, and $12 in department C. Formulate a linear programming model that can be used to determine the optimal production quantities if overtime is made available. What are the optimal production quantities, and what is the revised profit? How much overtime do you recommend using in each department? What is the increase in profit if overtime is used?

5. *Investment and loan planning.* The employee credit union at State University is planning the usage of funds for the coming year. The credit union makes four types of loans to its members. In addition, the credit union invests in risk-free securities in order to stabilize income. The various revenue-producing investments together with annual rates of return are as follows:

Type of Loan/Investment	Annual Rate of Return (%)
Automobile loans	8
Furniture loans	10
Other secured loans	11
Signature loans	12
Risk-free securities	9

The firm will have $2,000,000 available for investment during the coming year. State laws and credit union policies impose the following restrictions on the composition of the credit union's loans and investments:

(1) Risk-free securities may not exceed 30% of the total funds available for investment.

(2) Signature loans may not exceed 10% of the funds invested in all loans (automobile, furniture, other secured and signature loans).

(3) Furniture loans plus other secured loans may not exceed the automobile loans.

(4) Other secured loans plus signature loans may not exceed the funds invested in risk-free securities.

How should the $2,000,000 be allocated to each of the loan/investment alternatives in order to maximize total annual return? What is the projected annual return?

6. *Quality assurance.* Hilltop Coffee manufactures a coffee product by blending three types of coffee beans. The cost per pound and the available pounds of each bean are as follows:

Bean	Cost/Pound	Available Pounds
1	$0.50	500
2	0.70	600
3	0.45	400

Consumer tests with coffee products were used to provide ratings on a 0-to-100 scale, with higher ratings indicating higher quality. Product quality standards for the blended coffee require a consumer rating for aroma to be at least 75 and a consumer rating for taste to be at least 80. The individual ratings of the aroma and taste for coffee made from 100% of each bean are as follows:

Bean	Aroma Rating	Taste Rating
1	75	86
2	85	88
3	60	75

It can be assumed that the aroma and taste attributes of the coffee blend will be a weighted average of the attributes of the beans used in the blend.

  a. What is the minimum cost blend that will meet the quality standards and provide 1000 pounds of the blended coffee product?

  b. What is the cost per pound for the coffee blend?

  c. Use the surplus variables to determine the aroma and taste ratings for the coffee blend.

  d. If additional coffee were to be produced, what would be the expected cost per pound?

7. *Blending problem.* Ajax Fuels, Inc., is developing a new additive for airplane fuels. The additive is a mixture of three ingredients: A, B, and C. For proper performance, the total amount of additive (amount of A + amount of B + amount of C) must be at least 10 ounces per gallon of fuel. However, because of safety reasons, the amount of additive must not exceed 15 ounces per gallon of fuel. The mix or blend of the three ingredients is critical. At least 1 ounce of ingredient A must be used for every ounce of ingredient B. The amount of ingredient C must be greater than one-half the amount of ingredient A. If the cost per ounce for ingredients A, B, and C is $0.10, $0.03, and $0.09, respectively, find the minimum cost mixture of A, B, and C for each gallon of airplane fuel.

8. *Labor planning.* G. Kunz and Sons, Inc., manufactures two products used in the heavy equipment industry. Both products require manufacturing operations in two departments. Production time in hours and profit figures for the two products are as follows:

	Product 1	Product 2
Profit/unit	$25	$20
Dept. A hours	6	8
Dept. B hours	12	10

For the coming production period, Kunz has a total of 900 hours of labor available, which can be allocated to either of the two departments. Find the production plan and labor allocation (hours assigned in each department) that will maximize profits.

9. *Transportation.* The C&P Company has two manufacturing plants, one located in Kansas City and another in Louisville. Each month's production is shipped to regional warehouses, which store the products until orders are received from customers. The production capacities and the warehouse demands for the coming month are as follows:

Plant	Capacity	Warehouse	Demand
Kansas City	500	Region 1	200
Louisville	400	Region 2	250
		Region 3	300

Transportation costs in dollars per unit shipped are as follows:

		Warehouses	
Plant	Region 1	Region 2	Region 3
Kansas City	2.10	2.25	3.00
Louisville	2.00	2.40	2.80

a. Develop a transportation schedule that will determine the number of units shipped from each plant to each warehouse so that warehouse demands are satisfied at a minimum total transportation cost. (*Note:* The problem is referred to as a transportation problem; transportation problems will be treated further in Chapter 7.)

b. If the production costs are 2.00 per unit at the Kansas City plant and 2.25 per unit at the Louisville plant, how would you revise your transportation schedule to minimize the total production and transportation costs?

10. *Staff scheduling.* The Clark County Sheriff's Department schedules police officers for 8-hour shifts. The beginning times for the shifts are 8:00 A.M., noon, 4:00 P.M., 8:00 P.M., midnight, and 4:00 A.M.. An officer beginning a shift at one of the above times works for the next 8 hours. During normal weekday operations, the number of officers needed varies depending on the time of day. The department staffing guidelines require the following minimum number of officers on duty:

Time of Day	Minimum Number of Officers
8:00 A.M.–noon	5
Noon–4:00 P.M.	6
4:00 P.M.–8:00 P.M.	10
8:00 P.M.–midnight	7
Midnight–4:00 A.M.	4
4:00 A.M.–8:00 A.M.	6

Determine the number of police officers that should be scheduled to begin the 8-hour shifts at each of the six times (8:00 A.M., noon, 4:00 P.M., 8:00 P.M., midnight, and 4:00 A.M.) such that the total number of officers required is minimized. (*Hint:* Let x_1 = the number of officers beginning work at 8:00 A.M., x_2 = the number of officers beginning work at noon, and so on.)

11. *Portfolio selection.* National Insurance Associates carries an investment portfolio of a variety of stocks, bonds, and other investment alternatives. Currently $200,000 of funds have become available and must be considered for new investment opportunities. The four stock options National is considering and the relevant financial data are as follows:

| | Investment Alternative | | | |
	A	B	C	D
Price per share	$100	$50	$80	$40
Annual rate of return	0.12	0.08	0.06	0.10
Risk measure per dollar invested (higher values indicate greater risk)	0.10	0.07	0.05	0.08

The risk measure indicates the relative uncertainty associated with the stock in terms of its realizing the projected annual return. The risk measures are provided by the firm's top financial advisor.

National's top management has stipulated the following investment guidelines:
(1) The annual rate of return for the portfolio must be at least 9%.
(2) No one stock can account for more than 50% of the total dollar investment

a. Use linear programming to develop an investment portfolio that minimizes risk.
b. If the firm ignores risk and uses a maximum return-on-investment strategy, what is the investment portfolio?
c. What is the dollar difference between the portfolios recommended in parts (a) and (b)? Why might the company prefer the model development in part (a)?

12. *Production routing.* Lurix Electronics manufactures two products that can be produced on two different production lines. Both products have their lowest production costs when produced on the more modern of the two production lines. However, the modern production line does not have the capacity to handle the total production. As a result, some production will have to be routed to the older production line. Shown below are the data for total production requirements, production line capacities, and production costs:

| | Production Cost/Unit | | Minimum Production |
	Modern Line	*Old Line*	*Requirements*
Product 1	$3.00	$5.00	500 units
Product 2	$2.50	$4.00	700 units
Production line capacities	800	600	

Formulate a linear programming model that can be used to make the production routing decision. What are the recommended decision and the total cost?

13. *Purchasing.* Edwards Manufacturing Company purchases two component parts from three different suppliers. The suppliers have limited capacity, and no one supplier can meet all of Edwards' needs. In addition, the supplies differ in the prices charged for the components. Component price data are as follows:

| | Supplier | | |
	1	2	3
Price/unit—component 1	$12	$13	$14
Price/unit—component 2	$10	$11	$10

Each supplier has a limited capacity in terms of the total number of components it can supply. However, as long as Edwards provides sufficient advance orders, each supplier can devote its capacity to component 1, component 2, or any combination of the two components, as long as the total number of units ordered is within its capacity. Supplier capacities are as follows:

Supplier	Total Components Capacity
Supplier 1	600
Supplier 2	1000
Supplier 3	800

If the Edwards production plan for the next production period includes 1000 units of component 1 and 800 units of component 2, what purchases do you recommend? That is, how many units of each component should be ordered from each supplier? What is the total purchase cost for the components?

 14. *Make or buy.* The Carson Stapler Manufacturing Company forecasts a 5000-unit demand for its Sure-Hold model during the next quarter. This stapler is assembled from three major components: base, staple cartridge, and handle. Until now Carson has manufactured all three components. However, the forecast of 5000 units is a new high in sales volume, and it is doubtful that the firm will have sufficient production capacity to make all the components. The company is considering contracting a local firm to produce at least some of the components. The production time requirements per unit are as follows:

	Production Time (hours)			Total Department Time Available (hours)
Department	Base	Cartridge	Handle	
A	0.03	0.02	0.05	400
B	0.04	0.02	0.04	400
C	0.02	0.03	0.01	400

After considering the firm's overhead, material, and labor costs, the accounting department has determined the unit manufacturing cost for each component. These data, along with the purchase price quotations by the contracting firm, are as follows:

Component	Manufacturing Cost	Purchase Cost
Base	$0.75	$0.95
Cartridge	$0.40	$0.55
Handle	$1.10	$1.40

a. Determine the make-or-buy decision for Carson that will meet the 5000-unit demand at a minimum total cost. How many units of each component should be made, and how many purchased?

b. Which departments are limiting the manufacturing volume? If overtime could be considered at the additional cost of $3 per hour, which department(s) should be allocated the overtime? Explain.

c. Suppose that up to 80 hours of overtime can be scheduled in department A. What do you recommend?

15. *Blending probelm.* Seastrand Oil Company produces two grades of gasoline: regular and high octane. Both types of gasoline are produced by blending two types of crude oil. Although both types of crude oil contain the two important ingredients required to produce both gasolines, the percentage of important ingredients in each type of crude oil differs, as does the cost per gallon. The percentage of ingredients A and B in each type of crude oil and the cost per gallon are shown below:

Type of Crude Oil	Cost	Ingredient A	Ingredient B	
1	$0.10	20%	60%	⎯Crude 1 is 60% ingredient B
2	$0.15	50%	30%	

Each gallon of regular must contain at least 40% of A, whereas each gallon of high octane can contain at most 50% of B. Daily demand for regular octane gasoline is 800,000 gallons and daily demand for high octane is 500,000 gallons. How many gallons of each type of crude oil should be used in regular and in high octane gasoline in order to satisfy daily demand at a minimum cost?

16. *Cutting stock.* The Ferguson Paper Company produces rolls of paper for use in adding machines, desk calculators, and cash registers. The rolls, which are 200 feet long, are produced in widths of $1\frac{1}{2}$, $2\frac{1}{2}$, and $3\frac{1}{2}$ inches. The production process provides 200-foot rolls in 10-inch widths only. The firm must therefore cut the rolls to the desired final product sizes. The seven cutting alternatives and the amount of waste generated by each are as follows:

| Cutting | Number of Rolls | | | Waste |
Alternative	1½ in	2½ in	3½ in	(inches)
1	6	0	0	1
2	0	4	0	0
3	2	0	2	0
4	0	1	2	½
5	1	3	0	1
6	1	2	1	0
7	4	0	1	½

The minimum requirements for the three products are as follows:

Roll Width (inches)	Units
1½	1000
2½	2000
3½	4000

a. If the company wants to minimize the number of units of the 10-inch rolls that must be manufactured, how many 10-inch rolls will be processed on each cutting alternative? How many rolls are required, and what is the total waste (inches)?

b. If the company wants to minimize the waste generated, how many 10-inch units will be processed on each cutting alternative? How many rolls are required, and what is the total waste (inches)?

c. What are the differences in approaches (a) and (b) to this trim problem? In this case which objective do you prefer? Explain. What are the types of situations that would make the other objective more desirable?

17. *Inspection.* The Get-Well Pill Company inspects capsule medicine products by passing the capsules over a special lighting table where inspectors visually check for cracked or partially filled capsules. Currently any of three inspectors can be assigned to the visual inspection task. The inspectors, however, differ in accuracy and speed abilities and are paid at slightly different wage rates. The differences are as follows:

Inspector	Speed (units per hour)	Accuracy (%)	Hourly Wage
Davis	300	98	$5.90
Wilson	200	99	$5.20
Lawson	350	96	$5.50

Operating on a full 8-hour shift, the company needs at least 2000 capsules inspected with no more than 2% of these capsules having inspection errors. In addition, because of the fatigue factor of this inspection process, no one inspector can be assigned this task for more than 4 hours per day. How many hours should each inspector be assigned to the capsule inspection process during an 8-hour day if it is desired to minimize the cost of inspection? What volume will be inspected per day, and what is the daily capsule inspection cost?

18. *Equipment Acquisition.* The Two-Rivers Oil Company near Pittsburgh transports gasoline to its distributors by trucks. The company has recently received a contract to begin supplying gasoline distributors in southern Ohio and has $600,000 available to spend on the necessary expansion of its fleet of gasoline tank trucks. Three models of gasoline tank truck are available:

Truck Model	Capacity (gallons)	Purchase Cost	Monthly Operating Cost, Including Depreciation
Super Tanker	5000	$67,000	$550
Regular Line	2500	$55,000	$425
Econo-Tanker	1000	$46,000	$350

The company estimates that the monthly demand for the region will be 550,000 gallons of gasoline. Due to the size and speed differences of the trucks, the different truck models will vary in terms of the number of deliveries or round trips possible per month. Trip capacities are estimated at 15 trips per month for the Super Tanker, 20 trips per month for the Regular Line, and 25 trips per month for the Econo-Tanker. Based on maintenance and driver availability, the firm does not want to add more than 15 new vehicles to its fleet. In addition, the company has decided to purchase at least three of the new Econo-Tankers to use on the short-run low-demand routes. As a final constraint, the company does not want more than half of the new models to be Super Tankers.

a. If the company wishes to satisfy the gasoline demand with a minimum monthly operating expense, how many models of each truck should be purchased?

b. If the company did not require at least three Econo-Tankers and did not limit the number of Super Tankers to at most half of the new models, how many models of each truck should be purchased?

19. *Multiperiod planning.* The Silver Star Bicycle Company will be manufacturing both men's and women's models for their Easy-Pedal 10-speed bicycles during the next 2 months. The company would like to develop a production schedule indicating how many bicycles of each model should be produced in each month. Current demand forecasts call for 150 men's and 125 women's models to be shipped during the first month and 200 men's and 150 women's models to be shipped during the second month. Additional data are shown below:

Model	Production Costs	Labor Required for Manufacturing (hours)	Labor Required for Assembly (hours)	Current Inventory
Men's	$40	10	3	20
Women's	$30	8	2	30

Last month the company used a total of 4000 hours of labor. The company's labor relations policy will not allow the combined total hours of labor (manufacturing plus assembly) to increase or decrease by more than 500 hours from month to month. In addition, the company charges monthly inventory at the rate of 2% of the production cost based on the inventory levels at the end of the month. The company would like to have at least 25 units of each model in inventory at the end of the 2 months.

a. Establish a production schedule that minimizes production and inventory costs and satisfies the labor-smoothing, demand, and inventory requirements. What inventories will be maintained, and what are the monthly labor requirements?

b. If the company changed the constraints so that monthly labor increases and decreases could not exceed 250 hours, what would happen to the production schedule? How much will the cost increase? What would you recommend?

20. *Labor balancing.* The Williams Calculator Company manufactures two kinds of calculators: the TW100 and the TW200. The assembly process requires three people. The assembly times are as follows:

	Assembler 1	Assembler 2	Assembler 3
TW100	4 min	2 min	3½ min
TW200	3 min	4 min	3 min
Maximum hours available per day	8	8	8

The company policy is to balance workloads on all assembly jobs. In fact, management wants to schedule work so that no assembler will have more than 30 minutes more work per day than other assemblers. This means that in a regular 8-hour shift, all assemblers will be assigned at least 7½ hours of work. If the firm makes a $2.50 profit for each TW100 and a $3.50 profit for each TW200, how many units of each calculator should be produced per day? How much time will each assembler be assigned per day?

21. *Multiperiod production and inventory planning.* Multiperiod production and inventory planning models determine a production schedule and an ending inventory schedule for each of several periods that will achieve a goal of maximizing profit or minimizing cost. Considering selling price, regular production costs, overtime costs, inventory carrying costs, and lost sales costs, develop a 3-period production and inventory planning model for Allen Manufacturing Company. Relevant information is as follows:

Period	Selling Price ($/unit)	Production Cost ($/unit)	Demand	Ending Inventory Cost ($/unit)
1	$5.00	$2.80	500	$0.50
2	$5.00	$2.90	300	$0.50
3	$5.50	$3.00	400	$0.55

Period	Regular Production Capacity (units)	Overtime Production Capacity (units)
1	250	100
2	300	100
3	300	125

The overtime cost per unit in each period is 20% greater than the production cost per unit shown above. The lost sales cost, which is $4 per unit in any period, accounts for lost customer goodwill, but does not account for the cost associated with the lost revenue. The beginning inventory for period 1 is 100 units. In addition, the firm would like to have at least 50 units in ending inventory for period 3 in order to prepare for product needs in period 4.

To account for the multiperiod aspects of the problem, each period, t, will require balance equations or constraints based on the following relationships:

$$\text{Lost sales } (t) = \text{demand } (t) - \text{sales } (t)$$

$$\text{Ending inventory } (t) = \text{beginning inventory } (t) + \text{production } (t) - \text{sales } (t)$$

Develop a linear program that can be used to determine the optimal production and inventory schedule for Allen Manufacturing. Determine the sales, regular production, overtime production, ending inventory, and lost sales for each of the three periods. What is the net profit associated with your solution?

22. *Multiperiod Financial Planning.* The Morton Financial Instituion must decide what percentage of available funds to commit to each of two investments, referred to as A and B, over the next four periods. The following table shows the amount of new funds available for each of the four periods, as well as the cash expenditure required for each investment (negative values) or the cash income from the investment (positive values). Data shown are in thousands of dollars, and reflect the amount of expenditure or income if 100% are invested in either A or B. For example, if Morton elects to invest 100% in investment A, they will incur cash expenditures of $1,000 in month 1, $800 in month 2, $200 in month 3, and income of $200 in month 4. Note, however, if Morton made the decision to invest 80% in investment A, the cash expenditures or income would be 80% of the values shown.

	Period			
	1	*2*	*3*	*4*
New funds available for investment	1500	400	500	100
Investment A	−1000	−800	−200	200
Investment B	−800	−500	−300	300

The amount of funds available in any period is the sum of the new investment funds for the period, the new loan funds, the savings from the previous period, the cash income from investment A, and the cash income from investment B. The funds available in any period can be used to pay the loan and interest from the previous period, placed in savings, used to pay the cash expenditures for investment A, or used to pay the cash expenditures for investment B.

Assume an interest rate of 10% per period for savings and an interest rate of 18% per period on borrowed funds. Let

$$S(t-1) \text{ denote the savings for period } t-1$$

and

$$L(t-1) \text{ denote the new loan funds for period } t-1$$

Then, in any period, the savings income from the previous period is $1.1S(t-1)$ and the loan and interest expenditure from the previous period is $1.18L(t-1)$.

At the end of period 4, investment A is expected to have a cash value of $3,200 (assuming a 100% investment in A), while investment B is expected to have a cash value of $2,500 (assuming a 100% investment in B). Additional income and expenses at the end of period 4 will be income from savings in period 4 less the repayment of the period 4 loan plus interest.

Let the decision variables be as follows:

$$x_1 = \text{the porportion of investment } A \text{ undertaken}$$

$$x_2 = \text{the porportion of investment } B \text{ undertaken}$$

For example, if $x_1 = .5$, we would invest $500 in investment A during the first period, and all remaining cash flows and ending investment A values would be multiplied by .5. The same holds for investment B. The model must include constraints $x_1 \le$ and $x_2 \le 1$ to make sure that at most 100% of the investments can be undertaken.

If at most $200 can be borrowed in any period, determine the proportion of investment A, the proportion of investment B, and the amount of savings and borrowing in each period that will maximize the cash value for the firm at the end of the four periods.

23. *Staff scheduling.* Western Family Steakhouse offers a variety of low-cost meals and quick service. Other than management, the steakhouse operates with two full-time employees who work 8 hours per day. The rest of the employees are part-time employees who are scheduled for 4-hour shifts during meal times. On Saturdays the steakhouse is open from 11:00 A.M. to 10:00 P.M. Management would like to develop a schedule for part-time employees that will minimize labor costs and still provide excellent customer service. The average wage rate for the part-time employees is $3.60 per hour. The total number of full-time and part-time employees needed varies with the time of the day as follows:

Time	Total Number of Employees
11:00 A.M.–noon	9
Noon–1:00 P.M.	9
1:00 P.M.–2:00 P.M.	9
2:00 P.M.–3:00 P.M.	3
3:00 P.M.–4:00 P.M.	3
4:00 P.M.–5:00 P.M.	3
5:00 P.M.–6:00 P.M.	6
6:00 P.M.–7:00 P.M.	12
7:00 P.M.–8:00 P.M	12
8:00 P.M.–9:00 P.M.	7
9:00 P.M.–10:00 P.M.	7

One of the full-time employees comes on duty at 11:00 A.M., works 4 hours, takes an hour off, and returns for another 4 hours. The other full-time employee comes to work at 1:00 P.M. and works the same 4-hour-on, 1-hour-off, 4-hour-on work pattern.

    a. Develop a minimum-cost schedule for the part-time employees.

    b. What is the total payroll for the part-time employees? How many part-time shifts are needed? Use the surplus variables to comment on the desirability of scheduling at least some of the part-time employees for 3-hour shifts.

    c. Assume part-time employees can be assigned either a 4-hour shift or a 3-hour shift. Develop a minimum-cost schedule for the part-time employees. How many part-time shifts are needed, and what is the cost savings compared with the previous schedule?

24. *Interpretation of computer output.* Shown below is a portion of the computer output when The Management Scientist is used to solve the media selection problem for the Relax-and-Enjoy Lake Development Corporation (see Section 4.2).

```
Objective Function Value =   2369.999500

     Variable          Value          Reduced Costs
     --------      ------------      ---------------
        X1          10.000000            0.000023
        X2           0.000000           64.999969
        X3          25.000000            0.000004
        X4           1.999994            0.000004
        X5          30.000000            0.000002

    Constraint     Slack/Surplus       Dual Prices
     --------      ------------      ---------------
        1             5.000000            0.000000
        2            10.000000            0.000000
        3             0.000000           15.999998
        4             2.000006            0.000000
        5             0.000000           13.999998
        6             0.000000            0.060000
        7             0.000000          -25.000015
        8          2999.999000            0.000000
        9         11500.015600            0.000000
```

Media availability — Budget — Television restrictions — Audience coverage

    a. How much would the expected exposure increase per dollar added to the budget? Given the current budget, what is the average exposure per advertising dollar? Does the marginal return from enlarging the budget seem to make enlarging the budget a good investment?

    b. From an analysis of the dual prices, comment on whether or not the television commercials are a good idea.

25. *Hospital efficiency analysis.* In Section 4.6 data envelopment analysis was used to evaluate the relative efficiencies of four hospitals. Data for three input measures and four output measures were provided in Tables 4.16 and 4.17.

    a. Use these data to develop a linear programming model that could be used to evaluate the performance of General Hospital.

    b. The computer solution obtained using The Management Scientist is shown on the next page. Does the solution indicate that General Hospital is relatively inefficient?

    c. Which hospital or hospitals make up the composite unit used to evaluated General Hospital? State why this is true.

```
Objective Function Value =    1.000000

        Variable              Value              Reduced Costs
     --------------------  --------------------  -----------------------
            E              1.000000                0.000000
            WG             1.000000                0.000000
            WU             0.000000                0.000000
            WC             0.000000                0.330682
            WS             0.000000                0.215189
```

26. *Hospital efficiency analysis.* Data envelopment analysis has been used to measure the relative efficiency of a group of hospitals [H. David Sherman, "Hospital Efficiency Measurement and Evaluation," *Medical Care* (October 1984):] Sherman's study involved seven teaching hospitals; data on three input measures are contained in Table 4.18, and data on four output measures are contained in Table 4.19.

   a. Formulate a linear programming model so that data envelopment analysis can be used to evaluate the performance of hospital *D*.

   b. Solve the model using a computer software package.

TABLE 4.18
Annual Resources Consumed (Inputs) for Seven Hospitals

Hospital	Full-Time Equivalent Nonphysicians	Supply Expense (000's)	Bed-Days Available (000's)
A	310.0	134.60	116.00
B	278.5	114.30	106.80
C	165.6	131.30	65.52
D	250.0	316.00	94.40
E	206.4	151.20	102.10
F	384.0	217.00	153.70
G	530.1	770.80	215.00

TABLE 4.19
Annual Services Provided (Outputs) for Seven Hospitals

Hospital	Patient Days (65 or older) (000's)	Patient Days (under 65) (000's)	Nurses Trained	Interns Trained
A	55.31	49.52	291	47
B	37.64	55.63	156	3
C	32.91	25.77	141	26
D	33.53	41.99	160	21
E	32.48	55.30	157	82
F	48.78	81.92	285	92
G	58.41	119.70	111	89

c. Is hospital D relatively inefficient? What is the interpretation of the value of the objective function?

d. How many patient days of each type are produced by the composite hospital?

e. Which hospitals would you recommend hospital D consider emulating in order to improve the efficiency of its operation?

27. *Hospital efficiency analysis.* Refer again to the data presented in problem 26.

   a. Formulate a linear programming model that can be used to perform data envelopment analysis for hospital E.

   b. Solve the model using a computer software package.

   c. Is hospital E relatively inefficient? What is the interpretation of the value of the objective function?

   d. Which hospitals are involved in making up the composite hospital? Can you make a general statement about which hospitals will make up the composite unit associated with a unit that is not inefficient?

28. *Efficiency of fast-food restaurants.* The Ranch House, Inc., operates five fast-food restaurants. Input measures for the restaurants include weekly hours of operation, full-time equivalent staff, and weekly supply expenses. Output measures of performance include average weekly profit, market share, and annual growth rate. Data for the input and output measures are shown in Tables 4.20 and 4.21.

   a. Develop a linear programming model that can be used to evaluate the performance of the Clarksville Ranch House restaurant.

   b. Solve the model using a computer software package.

   c. Is the Clarksville Ranch House restaurant relatively inefficient? Discuss.

TABLE 4.20
Input Data for Five Fast-Food Restaurants

Restaurant	Hours of Operation	FTE Staff	Supplies
Bardstown	96	16	850
Clarksville	110	22	1400
Jeffersonville	100	18	1200
New Albany	125	25	1500
St. Matthews	120	24	1600

TABLE 4.21
Output Data for Five Fast-Food Restaurants

Restaurant	Weekly Profit	Market Share	Growth Rate
Bardstown	$3800	25%	8.0%
Clarksville	$4600	32%	8.5%
Jeffersonville	$4400	35%	8.0%
New Albany	$6500	30%	10.0%
St. Matthews	$6000	28%	9.0%

d. Where does the composite restaurant have more output than the Clarksville restaurant? How much less of each input resource does the composite restaurant require when compared to the Clarksville restaurant?

e. What other restaurants should be studied in order to find suggested ways for the Clarksville restaurant to improve its efficiency?

▼ CASE PROBLEM

Environmental Protection

Skillings Industrial Chemicals, Inc., operates a refinery in southwestern Ohio near the Ohio River. The company's primary product is manufactured from a chemical process that requires the use of two raw materials denoted as material A and material B. The production of 1 pound of the finished product requires the use of 1 pound of material A and 2 pounds of material B. The output of the chemical process is 1 pound of finished product, 1 pound of liquid waste material, and 1 pound of solid waste by-product. The solid waste by-product is given to a local fertilizer plant as payment for picking it up and disposing of it. Since the liquid waste material has no market value, the refinery has been dumping it directly into the Ohio River. Skillings' manufacturing process is shown schematically in Figure 4.9.

Recently imposed governmental pollution guidelines established by the Environmental Protection Agency will not permit disposal of the liquid waste directly into the river. The refinery's research group has developed the following set of alternative uses for the liquid waste material:

1. Produce a secondary product K by adding 1 pound of raw material A to every pound of liquid waste.

2. Produce a secondary product M by adding 1 pound of raw material B to every pound of liquid waste.

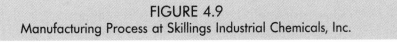

FIGURE 4.9
Manufacturing Process at Skillings Industrial Chemicals, Inc.

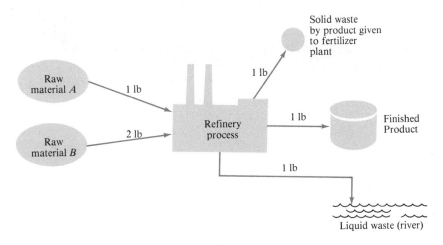

3. Specially treat the liquid waste so that it meets pollution standards before dumping it directly into the river.

These three alternatives are depicted in Figure 4.10.

The company's management knows that the secondary products will be low in quality and may not be very profitable. However, management is also aware of the fact that the special treatment alternative will be a relatively expensive operation. The company's problem is to determine how to satisfy the pollution regulations and still maintain the highest possible profit. How should the liquid waste material be handled? Should Skillings produce product *K*, produce product *M*, use the special treatment, or employ some combination of the three alternatives?

Last month 10,000 pounds of the company's primary product were produced. The accounting department has prepared a cost report showing the breakdown of fixed and variable expenses that were incurred during the month.

Cost Analysis for 10,000 Pounds of Primary Product

Fixed cost allocation	
Administrative expenses	$12,000
Refinery overhead	4,000
Variable costs	
Raw material *A*	15,000
Raw material *B*	16,000
Direct labor	5,000
Total	$52,000

In the above cost analysis, the fixed cost portion of the expenses is the same every month regardless of production level. Direct labor costs are expected to run $0.20 per pound for product *K* and $0.10 per pound for product *M*.

The company's primary product sells for $5.70 per pound. Secondary products *K* and *M* sell for $0.85 per pound and $0.65 per pound, respectively. The special treatment of the liquid waste will cost $0.25 per pound.

FIGURE 4.10
Alternatives for Handling the Refinery Liquid Waste

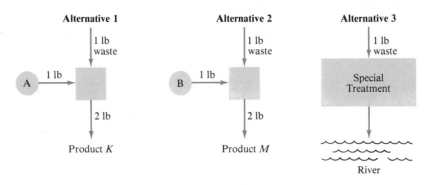

One of the company's accountants feels that product K is too expensive to manufacture and cannot be sold at a price that recovers its material and labor cost. The accountant's recommendation is to eliminate product K as an alternative.

For the upcoming production period 5000 pounds of raw material A and 7000 pounds of raw material B will be available. Develop a production and waste disposal plan for the production period.

MANAGERIAL REPORT

Develop an approach to the problem that will allow the company to determine how much primary product to produce, given the limitations on the amounts of the raw material available. Include recommendations as to how the company should dispose of the liquid waste to satisfy the environmental protection guidelines. How many pounds of product K should be produced? How many pounds of product M should be produced? How many pounds of liquid waste should be specially treated and dumped directly into the river? Include a discussion and analysis of the following in your report:

1. A cost analysis showing the profit contribution per pound for the primary product, product K, and product M.
2. The optimal production quantities and waste disposal plan, including the projected profit.
3. A discussion of the value of additional pounds of each raw material.
4. A discussion of the sensitivity analysis of the objective function coefficients.
5. Comments on the accountant's recommendation to eliminate product K as an alternative. Does the recommendation appear reasonable? What is your reaction to the recommendation? How would the optimal solution change if product K were eliminated?

▼ CASE PROBLEM

Textile Mill Scheduling

The Scottsville Textile Mill[1] produces five different fabrics. Each fabric can be woven on one or more of the mill's 38 looms. The sales department has forecast demand for the next month. The demand data are shown in Table 4.22 along with data on the selling price per yard and the variable cost per yard. The mill operates 24 hours per day and is scheduled for 30 days during the coming month.

The mill has two types of looms: dobbie and regular. The dobbie looms are more versatile and can be used for all five fabrics. The regular looms can produce only three of the fabrics. There are a total of 38 looms—8 dobbie and 30 regular. The rate of production for each fabric on each type of loom is given in Table 4.23. The time required to change over from producing one fabric to another is negligible and does not have to be considered.

The Scottsville Textile Mill satisfies all demand with either its own woven fabric or fabric purchased from another mill. That is, fabrics that cannot be woven at the Scottsville

[1]This case is based on the Calhoun Textile Mill Case by Jeffrey D. Camm, P. M. Dearing, and Suresh K. Tadisina, 1987.

TABLE 4.22
Monthly Demand, Price, Variable Cost, and Purchase Price Data for Scottsville Fabrics

Fabric	Demand (yds)	Selling Price ($/Yd)	Variable Cost ($/Yd)	Purchase Price ($/Yd)
1	16,500	0.99	0.66	0.80
2	22,000	0.86	0.55	0.70
3	62,000	1.10	0.49	0.60
4	7,500	1.24	0.51	0.70
5	62,000	0.70	0.50	0.70

TABLE 4.23
Loom Production Rates

Fabric	Dobbie Rate (yd/hr)	Regular Rate (yd/hr)
1	4.63	*
2	4.63	*
3	5.23	5.23
4	5.23	5.23
5	4.17	4.17

*Fabrics 1 and 2 can be manufactured only on the dobbie loom.

Mill because of limited loom capacity will be purchased from another mill. The purchase price of each fabric is also shown in Table 4.22.

MANAGERIAL REPORT

Develop a model that can be used to schedule production for the Scottsville Textile Mill, and, at the same time, determine how many yards of each fabric must be purchased from another mill. Include a discussion and analysis of the following in your report:

1. The final production schedule and loom assignments for each fabric.
2. The projected profit.
3. A discussion of the value of additional loom time. The mill is considering purchasing a ninth dobbie loom. What is your estimate of the monthly profit contribution of this additional loom?
4. A discussion of the ranges for the objective function coefficients.
5. A discussion of how the objective of minimizing total costs would provide a different model than the objective of maximizing profit. How would the interpretation of the ranges for the objective function coefficients differ for these two models?

Marathon Oil Company*
Findlay, Ohio

Marathon Oil Company was founded in 1887 when 14 oilmen pooled their properties to organize an oil-producing company in the Trenton Rock oil fields of Ohio. In 1924 Marathon entered the refining and marketing phase of the petroleum industry. Today Marathon is a fully integrated oil company with significant international operations. It employs over 18,000 people, and company activities extend to six continents. In the United States the company markets petroleum products in 21 states, primarily in the Midwest and Southeast.

MANAGEMENT SCIENCE AT MARATHON OIL COMPANY

Most of the management science applications at Marathon Oil involve the firm's Operations Research Department. This department was formed in 1963 in order to aid problem solving and decision making in all areas of the company. Approximately 50% of the applications involve linear programming. Typical problems include refinery models, distribution models, gasoline and fuel oil blending models, and crude oil evaluation studies. Another 30% of the applications involve complex chemical engineering simulation models of process operations. The remainder of the management science applications involves solution techniques using nonlinear programming, network flow algorithms, and statistical techniques such as regression analysis.

A Marketing Planning Model

Marathon Oil Company has four refineries within the United States, operates 50 light products terminals, and has product demand at over 100 locations. The Marketing Operations Division is faced with the problem of determining which refinery should supply which terminal and, at the same time, determining which products should be transported via which pipeline, barge, or tanker in order to achieve a minimum cost. Product demand must be satisfied, and the supply capability of each refinery must not be exceeded. To help solve this difficult problem, Marathon's Operations Research Department developed a marketing planning model for the Marketing Operation Division.

The marketing planning model is a large-scale linear programming model that takes into account sales not only at Marathon product terminals but also at all exchange locations. An exchange contract is an agreement with other oil product marketers that involves exchanging or trading Marathon's products for theirs at different locations. Thus, some geographic imbalance between supply and demand

*The authors are indebted to Jerry T. Ranney and Keith R. Weiss of Marathon Oil Company, Findlay, Ohio, for providing this application.

can be reduced. Both sides of the exchanges are represented since this not only affects the net requirements at a demand location, but in addition has important financial implications. All pipelines, barges, and tankers within Marathon's marketing area are also represented in the linear programming model.

The optimization of gasoline blending for each refinery, based on blendstock availabilities and the gasoline demand structure, is accomplished in the model by the inclusion of gasoline blending submodels. Thus, the linear programming model is a combination of a blending model and a transportation model.

The objective of the linear programming model is to minimize the cost of meeting a given demand structure, taking into account sales price, pipeline tariffs, exchange contract costs, product demand, terminal operating costs, refining costs, and product purchases. The current linear programming matrix size is approximately 1800 rows by 6000 columns.

The marketing planning model is used to solve a wide variety of planning problems. These vary from evaluating gasoline blending economics to analyzing the economics of a new terminal or pipeline. Although the types of problems that can be solved are almost unlimited, the model is most effective in handling the following:

1. Evaluating additional product demand locations, pipelines, refinery units, and exchange contracts
2. Determining profitability of shifting sales from one product demand location to another
3. Showing effects on refinery gasoline blending when octane requirements are increased, blendstock availabilities are decreased, or there is a major shift in the demand pattern
4. Determining the effects on supply and distribution when a pipeline increases its tariff
5. Optimizing production of the three grades of gasoline at the four refineries

The linear programming model not only solves these problems, but also gives the financial impact of each solution.

Benefits

With daily sales of about 10 million gallons of refined light product, a saving of even one-thousandth of a cent per gallon can result in significant long-term savings. At the same time, what may appear to be a savings in one area, such as refining or transportation, may actually add to overall costs when the effects are fully realized throughout the system. The marketing planning model allows a simultaneous examination of this total effect.

Questions

1. What is the primary objective of Marathon's marketing planning model?
2. Describe the types of problems the marketing planning model is most effective in handling.
3. If daily savings using the model are one-tenth of a cent per gallon sold, what is the projected daily savings?

5

Linear Programming: The Simplex Method

In Chapter 2 we showed how the graphical solution procedure can be used to solve linear programming problems involving two decision variables. However, most linear programming problems are too large to be solved graphically, and, thus, an algebraic solution procedure must be employed. The most widely used algebraic procedure for solving linear programming problems is called the *simplex method*.[1] Computer programs based on this method can routinely solve linear programming problems having as many as several thousand variables and several thousand constraints.

5.1 ▼ AN ALGEBRAIC OVERVIEW OF THE SIMPLEX METHOD

Let us begin our discussion by introducing a problem that will be used to demonstrate the simplex method. HighTech Industries imports electronic components that are used to assemble two different models of personal computers. One model is called the HT Deskpro Computer, and the other model is called the HT Portable Computer. HighTech's management is currently interested in developing a weekly production schedule for both of these products.

The Deskpro generates a profit contribution of $50 per unit and the Portable generates a profit contribution of $40 per unit. For the next week's production a maximum of 150 hours of assembly time can be made available. Each unit of the Deskpro requires 3 hours of assembly time, and each unit of the Portable requires 5 hours of assembly time. In addition, HighTech currently has in inventory only 20 of the display units used in the Portable; thus, no more than 20 units of the Portable may be assembled. Finally, only 300 square feet of warehouse space can be made available for new production of these products. Each unit of the Deskpro requires 8 square feet of warehouse space, and each unit of the Portable requires 5 square feet of warehouse space.

---

[1]N. Karmarkar, at Bell Labs, has developed a linear programming solution procedure that may eventually supersede the simplex method. At this time the simplex method is by far the most widely used.

In order to develop a linear programming model for the HighTech problem, we will use the following decision variables:

$$x_1 = \text{number of units of the Deskpro assembled}$$

$$x_2 = \text{number of units of the Portable assembled}$$

The complete mathematical model for the HighTech Industries problem is presented below.

$$\max \quad 50x_1 + 40x_2$$

s.t.

$$3x_1 + 5x_2 \le 150 \quad \text{Assembly time}$$
$$1x_2 \le 20 \quad \text{Portable display}$$
$$8x_1 + 5x_2 \le 300 \quad \text{Warehouse space}$$
$$x_1, x_2 \ge 0$$

Adding a slack variable to each of the constraints permits us to write the problem in standard form.

$$\max \quad 50x_1 + 40x_2 + 0s_1 + 0s_2 + 0s_3 \tag{5.1}$$

s.t.

$$3x_1 + 5x_2 + 1s_1 \qquad\qquad = 150 \tag{5.2}$$
$$1x_2 \quad + 1s_2 \qquad = 20 \tag{5.3}$$
$$8x_1 + 5x_2 \qquad\qquad + 1s_3 = 300 \tag{5.4}$$
$$x_1, x_2, s_1, s_2, s_3 \ge 0 \tag{5.5}$$

Algebraic Properties of the Simplex Method

Constraint equations (5.2) to (5.4) form a system of three simultaneous linear equations with five variables. When a set of simultaneous linear equations has more variables than constraints, one can expect an infinite number of solutions. The simplex method is an algebraic procedure that can be used to solve a system of simultaneous linear equations involving more variables than equations. In addition, the simplex method will identify a solution that provides the best possible value for the objective function.

We cannot expect that every solution to equations (5.2)–(5.4) will satisfy the non-negativity conditions $x_1, x_2, s_1, s_2, s_3 \ge 0$. Consequently, not every solution to equations (5.2)–(5.4) will be a feasible solution. Thus, when solving a set of simultaneous linear equations, the simplex method eliminates from consideration those solutions that do not also satisfy the nonnegativity requirements.

Determining a Basic Solution

Since the HighTech Industries constraint equations have more variables (five) than equations (three), the simplex method finds solutions for these equations by assigning zero values to two of the variables and then solving for the values of the remaining three variables. For example, if we set $x_2 = 0$ and $s_1 = 0$, the system of constraint equations becomes

$$3x_1 \qquad\qquad = 150 \qquad\qquad (5.6)$$

$$1s_2 \qquad = 20 \qquad\qquad (5.7)$$

$$8x_1 \qquad + 1s_3 = 300 \qquad\qquad (5.8)$$

By setting $x_2 = 0$ and $s_1 = 0$ we have reduced the system of three simultaneous linear equations with five variables to a system of three simultaneous linear equations with three variables (x_1, s_2, and s_3).

Using equation (5.6) to solve for x_1, we have

$$3x_1 = 150$$

and hence $x_1 = 150/3 = 50$. Equation (5.7) provides $s_2 = 20$. Finally, substituting $x_1 = 50$ into equation (5.8) results in

$$8(50) + 1s_3 = 300$$

Solving for s_3, we obtain $s_3 = -100$.

Thus, we have obtained the following solution to the three-equation, five-variable set of linear equations determined by the HighTech constraints:

$$x_1 = 50$$
$$x_2 = 0$$
$$s_1 = 0$$
$$s_2 = 20$$
$$s_3 = -100$$

The above solution is referred to as a *basic solution* for the HighTech linear programming problem. In order to provide a general procedure for determining a basic solution, consider a standard form linear programming problem consisting of n variables (including decision variables, slack variables, and surplus variables) and m linear equations, where n is greater than m.

A Basic Solution.

To determine a basic solution, set $n - m$ of the variables equal to zero, and solve the m linear constraint equations for the remaining m variables.[2]

In terms of the HighTech problem, a basic solution can be obtained by setting any two variables equal to zero and then solving the system of three linear equations for the remaining three variables. We shall refer to the $n - m$ variables set equal to zero as the *nonbasic variables* and the remaining m variables (allowed to be nonzero) as the *basic variables*. Thus, in the example above, x_2 and s_1 are the nonbasic variables, and x_1, s_2, and s_3 are the basic variables.

[2]There are cases where a unique solution cannot be found for the resulting system of m equations in m variables. However, these cases will never be encountered when using the simplex method.

Basic Feasible Solutions

A basic solution can be either feasible or infeasible. A *basic feasible solution* is a basic solution that also satisfies the nonnegativity conditions. The basic solution found by setting x_2 and s_1 equal to 0 and then solving for x_1, s_2, and s_3 is not a feasible solution because $s_3 = -100$. However, suppose that we had chosen to make x_1 and x_2 nonbasic variables (i.e., $x_1 = 0$ and $x_2 = 0$). Solving for the corresponding basic solution is easy because the three constraint equations reduce to

$$1s_1 \quad = 150$$
$$1s_2 \quad = \quad 20$$
$$1s_3 = 300$$

The complete solution (including the nonbasic variables) corresponding to $x_1 = 0$ and $x_2 = 0$ is

$$x_1 = \quad 0$$
$$x_2 = \quad 0$$
$$s_1 = 150$$
$$s_2 = \quad 20$$
$$s_3 = 300$$

This solution is a basic solution since it was obtained by setting two of the variables equal to zero and solving for the other three variables. Moreover, it is a basic *feasible* solution since all of the variables are greater than or equal to zero.

In Figure 5.1 we show a graph of the feasible region for the HighTech problem. We see that the basic feasible solution obtained by setting $x_1 = 0$ and $x_2 = 0$ corresponds to extreme point 1 of the feasible region. This is not just a coincidence; all basic feasible solutions correspond to extreme points of the feasible region. Thus, for every extreme point of the feasible region of a linear programming problem there is a corresponding basic feasible solution.

In Chapter 2 we showed that the optimal solution to a linear programming problem can be found at an extreme point. Since for every extreme point there is a corresponding basic feasible solution, we can now conclude that there is an optimal basic feasible solution.[3] The simplex method is an iterative procedure for moving from one basic feasible solution (extreme point) to another until the optimal solution is reached.

5.2 ▼ TABLEAU FORM

A basic feasible solution to the system of m linear constraint equations and n variables is required as a starting point for the simplex method. From this starting point the simplex method successively generates better basic feasible solutions to the system of linear equations. When the objective function can no longer be improved in this fashion, the optimal solution has been reached. The purpose of tableau form is to provide an initial basic feasible solution that is required to get the simplex method started.

[3] We are only considering cases where there is an optimal solution. That is, in the cases of infeasibility and unboundedness there is no optimal solution, so there cannot be an optimal basic feasible solution.

FIGURE 5.1
Feasible Region and Extreme Points for the HighTech Industries Problem

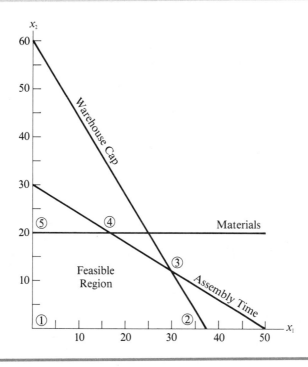

Recall that for the HighTech problem the standard form representation of the problem is

$$\max \quad 50x_1 + 40x_2 + 0s_1 + 0s_2 + 0s_3$$

s.t.

$$3x_1 + 5x_2 + 1s_1 \qquad\qquad = 150$$
$$1x_2 \qquad + 1s_2 \qquad = 20$$
$$8x_1 + 5x_2 \qquad\qquad + 1s_3 = 300$$

$$x_1, x_2, s_1, s_2, s_3 \geq 0$$

When a linear programming problem with all less-than-or-equal-to constraints is written in standard form, it is easy to find a basic feasible solution. We simply set the decision variables equal to zero and solve for the values of the slack variables. Note that doing this results in the values of the slack variables being set equal to the right-hand-side values of the constraint equations. For the HighTech problem this yields $x_1 = 0$, $x_2 = 0$, $s_1 = 150$, $s_2 = 20$, and $s_3 = 300$ as the initial basic feasible solution. This solution corresponds to using the origin, extreme point ① in Figure 5.1, as the initial basic feasible solution.

If we study the standard form representation of the HighTech constraint equations closely, we can identify two properties that make it possible to find an initial basic feasible solution. The first property, which enables us to find a basic solution, requires that the following conditions be satisfied:

a. For each constraint equation the coefficient of one of the m basic variables in that equation must be 1, and the coefficients for all the remaining basic variables in that equation must be 0.

b. The coefficient for each basic variable may be 1 in only one constraint equation.

When these conditions are satisfied, there is exactly one basic variable associated with each equation, and for each of the m equations it is a different basic variable. Thus, if the $n - m$ nonbasic variables are set equal to zero, the values of the basic variables can be read from the right-hand side to the constraint equations.

The second property that enables us to find a basic feasible solution requires that the values on the right-hand sides of the constraint equations be nonnegative. This ensures that the basic solution obtained by setting the basic variables equal to the right-hand-side values is feasible.

If a linear programming problem satisfies the two properties above, it is said to be in tableau form. Thus, we see that the standard form representation of the HighTech problem is already in tableau form. In fact, the standard form and tableau form for linear programs that have all less-than-or-equal-to constraints and nonnegative right-hand-side values are the same. Later in this chapter we will show how to set up tableau form for problems involving equality and greater-than-or-equal-to constraints; in these cases the standard form representation of the problem and the tableau form representation are not the same.

To summarize, the following three steps are necessary in order to prepare a linear programming problem for solution using the simplex method:

Step 1 Formulate the problem.

Step 2 Set up the standard form representation of the problem by adding slack and/or subtracting surplus variables.

Step 3 Set up the tableau form representation of the problem.

5.3 ▼ SETTING UP THE INITIAL SIMPLEX TABLEAU

After a linear programming problem has been converted to tableau form, we have an initial basic feasible solution that can be used to begin the simplex method. To provide a convenient means for performing the calculations required by the simplex solution procedure, we will first develop what is referred to as the initial *simplex tableau*.

Part of the initial simplex tableau is a table containing all the coefficients shown in the tableau form representation of a linear program. If we adopt the general notation

$$c_j = \text{objective function coefficient for variable } j$$

$$b_i = \text{right-hand-side value for constraint } i$$

$$a_{ij} = \text{coefficient associated with variable } j \text{ in constraint } i$$

we can show this portion of the simplex tableau as follows:

c_1	c_2	$\ldots c_n$	
a_{11}	a_{12}	$\ldots a_{1n}$	b_1
a_{21}	a_{22}	$\ldots a_{2n}$	b_2
.	.	$\ldots$.	.
.	.	$\ldots$.	.
a_{m1}	a_{m2}	$\ldots a_{mn}$	b_m

Thus, for the HighTech problem we obtain the following partial initial simplex tableau:

50	40	0	0	0	
3	5	1	0	0	150
0	1	0	1	0	20
8	5	0	0	1	300

Note that the row above the first horizontal line contains the coefficients of the objective function in the tableau form representation of the problem. The elements appearing between the horizontal lines and to the left of the vertical line are the coefficients of the constraint equations, and the elements to the right of the vertical line are the corresponding right-hand-side values.

Later we may want to refer to the objective function coefficients, all the right-hand-side values, or all the coefficients in the constraints as a group. To do this we will find the following general notation helpful:

c row $=$ row of objective function coefficients

b column $=$ column of right-hand-side values of the constraint equations

A matrix $=$ m rows and n columns of coefficients of the variables in the constraint equations

Using this notation we can show the above portion of the initial simplex tableau as follows:

c row	
A matrix	b column

To help us recall that each of the columns contains the coefficients of one variable, we will write the variable associated with each column directly above the column. Doing this, we obtain

x_1	x_2	s_1	s_2	s_3	
50	40	0	0	0	
3	5	1	0	0	150
0	1	0	1	0	20
8	5	0	0	1	300

The initial simplex tableau contains the tableau form of the problem; thus, it is easy to identify the initial basic feasible solution. First, we note that for each basic variable there is a corresponding column that has a 1 in the only nonzero position. Such columns are known as unit columns or unit vectors. Second, there is a row of the tableau associated with each basic variable. This row has a 1 in the unit column corresponding to the basic variable. The value of each basic variable is then given by the b_i value in the row associated with the basic variable. For example, in the HighTech problem, row 3 of the simplex tableau is associated with basic variable s_3 since this row has a 1 in the unit column corresponding to s_3; therefore, the value of this basic variable is given by $s_3 = b_3 = 300$. Table 5.1 shows the column corresponding to basic variable s_2, the row associated with s_2, and its value, $s_2 = 20$.

TABLE 5.1
Illustration of Procedure for Identifying Values of Basic Variables from the Simplex Tableau

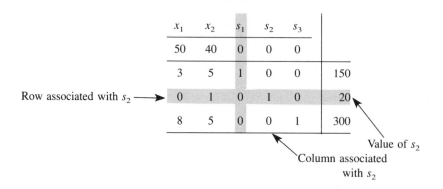

	x_1	x_2	s_1	s_2	s_3	
	50	40	0	0	0	
	3	5	1	0	0	150
Row associated with s_2 →	0	1	0	1	0	20
	8	5	0	0	1	300

Value of s_2

Column associated with s_2

5.4 ▼ IMPROVING THE SOLUTION

In order to improve the initial basic feasible solution, the simplex method must generate a new basic feasible solution (extreme point) that yields a better value for the objective function. To do so requires changing the set of basic variables; this is accomplished by selecting one of the current nonbasic variables to make basic and one of the current basic variables to make nonbasic in such a fashion that the new basic feasible solution yields an improved value for the objective function. The simplex method provides an easy way to carry out this change of variables in the basic feasible solution.

For computational convenience we will add two new columns to the present form of the simplex tableau. One column is labeled "*Basis*" and the other column is labeled "c_B." In the *Basis* column we list the current basic variables, and in the c_B column we list the corresponding objective function coefficient for each of these basic variables. For the HighTech problem this results in the following initial simplex tableau:

Basis	c_B	x_1	x_2	s_1	s_2	s_3	
		50	40	0	0	0	
s_1	0	3	5	1	0	0	150
s_2	0	0	1	0	1	0	20
s_3	0	8	5	0	0	1	300

Note that in the column labeled *Basis*, s_1 is listed as the first basic variable since its value is given by the right-hand-side value for the first equation (that is, $s_1 = b_1 = 150$); s_2 is listed second since its value is given by $s_2 = b_2 = 20$; and $s_3 = b_3 = 300$ is listed last.

Can we improve the value of the objective function by moving to a new basic feasible solution? To help find out if this is possible, we add two rows to the bottom of the tableau. The first row, labeled z_j, represents the decrease in the value of the objective function that will result if one unit of the variable corresponding to the *j*th column of the *A* matrix is brought into the basis—that is, if this variable is made a basic variable with a value of 1. The term *basis* is used here to refer to the set of basic variables. The second row, labeled $c_j - z_j$, represents the net change in the value of the objective function if one unit of the variable corresponding to the jth column of the A matrix is brought into solution. We refer to $c_j - z_j$ as the *net evaluation row*.

Let us first see how the entries in the z_j row are computed. Suppose that we consider increasing the value of the nonbasic variable x_1 by one unit—that is, from $x_1 = 0$ to $x_1 = 1$. In order to make this change and at the same time continue to satisfy the constraint equations, the values of some of the other variables will have to be changed. As we will show, the simplex method requires that the necessary changes be made to basic variables only. For example, in the first constraint we have

$$3x_1 + 5x_2 + 1s_1 = 150$$

The current basic variable in this constraint equation is s_1. Assuming that x_2 remains a nonbasic variable with a value of 0, if x_1 is increased in value by 1, then s_1 must be decreased by 3 for the constraint to be satisfied. Similarly, if we were to increase the value of x_1 by 1 (and keep $x_2 = 0$), we can see from the second and third equations that although s_2 would not decrease, s_3 would decrease by 8.

From analyzing all the constraint equations, we see that making x_1 a basic variable with a value of 1 will result in a decrease of 3 units in s_1, a decrease of 0 units in s_2, and a decrease of 8 units in s_3. Thus, we see that the coefficients in the x_1 column indicate the amount of decrease in the current basic variables when the nonbasic variable x_1 is increased from 0 to 1. In general, all the column coefficients can be interpreted this way. For instance, if we make x_2 a basic variable at a value of 1 (while keeping x_1 a nonbasic variable at a value of 0), s_1 will decrease by 5, s_2 will decrease by 1, and s_3 will decrease by 5.

Recall that the values in the c_B column of the simplex tableau are the objective function coefficients for the current basic variables. Hence, to compute the values in the z_j row we form the sum of the products obtained by multiplying the elements in the c_B column by the corresponding elements in the jth column of the A matrix. Doing this, we obtain

$$z_1 = 0(3) + 0(0) + 0(8) = 0$$

$$z_2 = 0(5) + 0(1) + 0(5) = 0$$

$$z_3 = 0(1) + 0(0) + 0(0) = 0$$

$$z_4 = 0(0) + 0(1) + 0(0) = 0$$

$$z_5 = 0(0) + 0(0) + 0(1) = 0$$

Since the objective function coefficient of x_1 is 50, the value of $c_1 - z_1$ is $50 - 0 = 50$. This indicates that the net result of bringing one unit of x_1 into the current basis will be an increase in profit of \$50. Hence, in the net evaluation row corresponding to x_1 we enter 50. In the same manner we can calculate the $c_j - z_j$ values for the remaining variables. The result is the following initial simplex tableau:

Basis	c_B	x_1 50	x_2 40	s_1 0	s_2 0	s_3 0	
s_1	0	3	5	1	0	0	150
s_2	0	0	1	0	1	0	20
s_3	0	8	5	0	0	1	300
z_j		0	0	0	0	0	0
$c_j - z_j$		50	40	0	0	0	↑

Profit

In this tableau we also see a 0 in the z_j row in the last column. This zero represents the profit associated with the current basic feasible solution. It was computed by multiplying the values of the basic variables, which are given in the last column of the simplex tableau, by their corresponding contribution to profit as given in the c_B column. That is, profit $= 150(0) + 20(0) + 300(0) = 0$.

From the net evaluation row we see that each unit of the Deskpro (x_1) increases the value of the objective function by 50 and each unit of the Portable (x_2) increases the value of the objective function by 40. Since x_1 causes the largest per-unit increase, we choose it as the variable to bring into the basis. We must next determine which of the current basic variables to make nonbasic. In doing so we first note that since each unit of x_1 that is brought into the solution increases the objective function by \$50, we would like to make x_1 as large as possible.

In discussing how to compute the z_j values, we noted that each of the coefficients in the x_1 column indicates the amount of decrease in the corresponding basic variable that would result from increasing x_1 by one unit. Hence, only the positive coefficients need to be considered in determining the current basic variable that will become nonbasic at a value of zero. Considering the first row, we see that every unit of the Deskpro produced will cause us to use 3 hours of assembly time (i.e., reduce s_1 by 3). In the current solution $s_1 = 150$ and $x_1 = 0$. Thus—considering this row only—the maximum possible value of x_1 can be calculated by solving

$$3x_1 = 150$$

which provides

$$x_1 = 50$$

If x_1 is 50 (and x_2 remains a nonbasic variable with a value of 0), s_1 will have to be reduced to zero in order to satisfy the first constraint:

$$3x_1 + 5x_2 + 1s_1 = 150$$

Considering the second row, $0x_1 + 1x_2 + 1s_2 = 20$, we see that the coefficient of x_1 is 0. Thus, increasing x_1 will not have any effect on s_2; that is, increasing x_1 cannot drive the basic variable in the second row (s_2) to zero. Indeed, increases in x_1 will leave s_2 unchanged.

Finally, since the coefficient of x_1 is 8 in the third row, every unit that we increase x_1 will cause a decrease of 8 units in s_3. Since the value of s_3 is currently 300, we can solve

$$8x_1 = 300$$

to find the maximum possible increase in x_1 before s_3 will become nonbasic at a value of 0. Solving, we see that x_1 cannot be any larger than $300/8 = 37.5$.

Considering the three rows (constraints) simultaneously, we see that row 3 is the most restrictive. That is, producing 37.5 units of the Deskpro will use all of the warehouse space and force the corresponding slack variable to become nonbasic at a value of $s_3 = 0$.

In making the decision to produce as many Deskpro units as possible, we must change the set of variables in the basic feasible solution (i.e., obtain a new basis). The nonbasic variable x_1 will now become a basic variable while the previous basic variable, s_3, will become a nonbasic variable with $s_3 = 0$. This interchange of roles between two variables is the essence of the simplex method. The way the simplex method moves from one basic feasible solution to another is by selecting a nonbasic variable to replace one of the current basic variables. This process of moving from one basic feasible solution to another is called an *iteration*. We now summarize the rules for selecting a nonbasic variable to make basic and selecting a current basic variable to make nonbasic.

Criterion for Entering a New Variable into the Basis. Look at the net evaluation row $(c_j - z_j)$, and select the variable to enter the basis that will cause the largest per-unit improvement in the value of the objective function. In the case of a tie we follow the convention of selecting the variable to enter the basis that corresponds to the leftmost of the columns.

Criterion for Removing a Variable from the Current Basis. Suppose the incoming basic variable corresponds to column j in the A portion of the simplex tableau. For each row i compute the ratio b_i/a_{ij} for each a_{ij} greater than 0. The basic variable to remove from the basis corresponds to the minimum of these ratios. In case of a tie we follow the convention of selecting the variable to leave the basis that corresponds to the uppermost of the tied rows.

Let us illustrate the above procedure by applying it to the HighTech problem. To illustrate the computations involved, we add an extra column to the right of the tableau showing the b_i/a_{ij} ratios.

Basis	c_B	x_1 50	x_2 40	s_1 0	s_2 0	s_3 0		$\dfrac{b_i}{a_{i1}}$
s_1	0	3	5	1	0	0	150	$\dfrac{150}{3} = 50$
s_2	0	0	1	0	1	0	20	—
s_3	0	⑧	5	0	0	1	300	$\dfrac{300}{8} = 37.5$
	z_j	0	0	0	0	0	0	
	$c_j - z_j$	50	40	0	0	0		

We see that $c_1 - z_1 = 50$ is the largest positive value in the $c_j - z_j$ row. Hence, x_1 is selected to become the new basic variable. Checking the ratios b_i/a_{i1} for values of a_{i1} greater than 0, we see that $b_3/a_{31} = 300/8 = 37.5$ is the minimum of these ratios Thus, the current basic variable associated with row 3 (s_3) is the variable selected to leave the basis. In the tableau we have circled $a_{31} = 8$ to indicate that the variable corresponding to the first column is to enter the basis and that the basic variable corresponding to the third row is to leave the basis. Adopting the usual linear programming terminology, we refer to this circled element as the *pivot element*. The column and the row containing the pivot element are called the *pivot column* and the *pivot row*, respectively.

To improve the current solution of $x_1 = 0$, $x_2 = 0$, $s_1 = 150$, $s_2 = 20$, and $s_3 = 300$, we should increase x_1 to 37.5. The production of 37.5 units of the Deskpro results in a profit of $50(37.5) = 1875$. In producing 37.5 units of the Deskpro we will use all the available warehouse space, and, thus, s_3 will be reduced to zero. Hence, x_1 will become the new basic variable, replacing s_3 in the previous basis.

5.5 ▼ CALCULATING THE NEXT TABLEAU

In the previous section we concluded that the initial basic feasible solution obtained by setting $x_1 = 0$ and $x_2 = 0$ could be improved by introducing x_1 into the basis to replace

s_3. To determine the new basic feasible solution corresponding to making x_1 a basic variable, it will be necessary to update the simplex tableau.

Recall that the initial simplex tableau contains the coefficients of the tableau form representation of the linear program. Because of the special properties of the tableau form, the initial simplex tableau contains a unit column corresponding to each basic variable.

We now want to update the simplex tableau in such a fashion that the column associated with the new basic variable is a unit column; in this way its value will be given by the right-hand-side value of the corresponding row. Thus, we would like the column in the new tableau corresponding to x_1 to look just like the column corresponding to s_3 in the original tableau. Hence, our goal is to make the column in the A matrix corresponding to x_1 appear as

$$0$$
$$0$$
$$1$$

The way in which we transform the simplex tableau so that it still represents an equivalent system of constraint equations with the above properties is to use elementary row operations.

Elementary Row Operations

1. Multiply any row (equation) by a nonzero number.
2. Replace any row (equation) by the result of adding or subtracting a multiple of another row (equation) to it.

The application of these elementary row operations to a system of simultaneous linear equations will not change the solution to the system of equations; however, the elementary row operations will change the coefficients of the variables and the values of the right-hand sides.

The objective in performing elementary row operations is to transform the system of constraint equations into a form that makes it easy to identify the new basic feasible solution. Consequently, we must perform the elementary row operations in such a manner that we transform the column for the variable entering the basis into a unit column. We emphasize that the feasible solutions to the original constraint equations are the same as the feasible solutions to the modified constraint equations obtained by performing elementary row operations. However, many of the numerical values in the simplex tableau will change as the result of performing these row operations. Thus, the present method of referring to elements in the simplex tableau may lead to confusion.

Up to now we have made no distinction between the A matrix and b column coefficients in the tableau form representation of the problem and the corresponding coefficients in the simplex tableau. Indeed, we showed that the initial simplex tableau is formed by properly placing the a_{ij}, c_j, and b_i elements as given in the tableau form representation of the problem into the simplex tableau. We will refer to the portion of the simplex tableau that initially contained the a_{ij} values with the symbol $\bar{A}$, and the portion of the tableau that initially contained the b_i values with the symbol $\bar{b}$. In terms of the simplex tableau, elements in $\bar{A}$ will be denoted by $\bar{a}_{ij}$, and elements in b will be denoted by $\bar{b}_i$. We recognize that $\bar{A} = A$ and $\bar{b} = b$ in the initial simplex tableau. However, in subsequent simplex tableaus this relationship will not hold. The overbar notation should avoid any confusion when we wish to distinguish between (1) the original constraint coefficient values a_{ij} and right-hand-side values b_i of the tableau form, and (2) the simplex tableau elements $\bar{a}_{ij}$ and $\bar{b}_i$.

Now let us see how elementary row operations are used to create the next simplex tableau for the HighTech problem. Recall that the goal is to transform the column in the $\bar{A}$ portion of the simplex tableau corresponding to x_1 to a unit column; that is,

$$\begin{bmatrix} \bar{a}_{11} \\ \bar{a}_{21} \\ \bar{a}_{31} \end{bmatrix} = \begin{bmatrix} 0 \\ 0 \\ 1 \end{bmatrix}$$

In order to set $\bar{a}_{31} = 1$, we perform the first elementary row operation by multiplying the pivot row (row 3) by $\frac{1}{8}$ to obtain the equivalent equation

$$\tfrac{1}{8}(8x_1 + 5x_2 + 0s_1 + 0s_2 + 1s_3) = \tfrac{1}{8}(300)$$

or

$$1x_1 + \tfrac{5}{8}x_2 + 0s_1 + 0s_2 + \tfrac{1}{8}s_3 = \tfrac{75}{2} \qquad (5.9)$$

We refer to (5.9) in the updated simplex tableau as the new pivot row.

In order to set $\bar{a}_{11} = 0$ we perform the second elementary row operation by first multiplying the new pivot row by 3 to obtain the equivalent equation

$$3(1x_1 + \tfrac{5}{8}x_2 + 0s_1 + 0s_2 + \tfrac{1}{8}s_3) = 3(\tfrac{75}{2})$$

or

$$3x_1 + \tfrac{15}{8}x_2 + 0s_1 + 0s_2 + \tfrac{3}{8}s_3 = \tfrac{225}{2} \qquad (5.10)$$

Subtracting equation (5.10) from row 1 of the simplex tableau completes the application of the second elementary row operation; thus, after dropping the terms with zero coefficients, we obtain

$$(3x_1 + 5x_2 + 1s_1) - (3x_1 + \tfrac{15}{8}x_2 + \tfrac{3}{8}s_3) = 150 - \tfrac{225}{2}$$

or

$$0x_1 + \tfrac{25}{8}x_2 + 1s_1 - \tfrac{3}{8}s_3 = \tfrac{75}{2} \qquad (5.11)$$

Since $\bar{a}_{21} = 0$, no row operations need be performed on the second row of the simplex tableau. Replacing rows 1 and 3 with the coefficients in equations (5.11) and (5.9), respectively, we obtain the new simplex tableau

		x_1	x_2	s_1	s_2	s_3	
Basis	c_B	50	40	0	0	0	
s_1	0	0	$\tfrac{25}{8}$	1	0	$-\tfrac{3}{8}$	$\tfrac{75}{2}$
s_2	0	0	1	0	1	0	20
x_1	50	1	$\tfrac{5}{8}$	0	0	$\tfrac{1}{8}$	$\tfrac{75}{2}$
	z_j						1875
	$c_j - z_j$						

Dropping terms having zero coefficients, the corresponding system of equations is

$$\begin{aligned} \tfrac{25}{8}x_2 + 1s_1 \quad\quad - \tfrac{3}{8}s_3 &= \tfrac{75}{2} \\ 1x_2 \quad\quad + 1s_2 \quad\quad\quad &= 20 \\ 1x_1 + \tfrac{5}{8}x_2 \quad\quad\quad + \tfrac{1}{8}s_3 &= \tfrac{75}{2} \end{aligned}$$

Assigning zero values to the nonbasic variables x_2 and s_3 permits us to identify the following new basic feasible solution:

$$s_1 = \tfrac{75}{2}$$
$$s_2 = 20$$
$$x_1 = \tfrac{75}{2}$$

This solution is also provided by the last column in the new simplex tableau. The profit associated with this solution is obtained by multiplying the solution values for the basic variables as given in the $\bar{b}$ column by their corresponding objective function coefficients as given in the c_B column; that is,

$$0(\tfrac{75}{2}) + 0(20) + 50(\tfrac{75}{2}) = 1875$$

Interpreting the Results of an Iteration

Starting with the initial simplex tableau, elementary row operations are used to change the elements in the simplex tableau in such a manner that we are able to identify a new basic feasible solution that improves the value of the objective function. Carrying out the process of determining a new simplex tableau is referred to as an iteration of the simplex method. In our example the initial basic feasible solution was

$$x_1 = 0$$
$$x_2 = 0$$
$$s_1 = 150$$
$$s_2 = 20$$
$$s_3 = 300$$

with a corresponding profit of $0. One iteration of the simplex method moved us to another basic feasible solution with an objective function value of $1875. This new basic feasible solution is

$$x_1 = \tfrac{75}{2}$$
$$x_2 = 0$$
$$s_1 = \tfrac{75}{2}$$
$$s_2 = 20$$
$$s_3 = 0$$

In Figure 5.2 we see that the initial basic feasible solution corresponds to extreme point ①. The first iteration moved us in the direction of the greatest increase per unit in profit—that is, along the x_1 axis. We moved away from extreme point ① in the x_1 direction until we could not move farther without violating one of the constraints. The

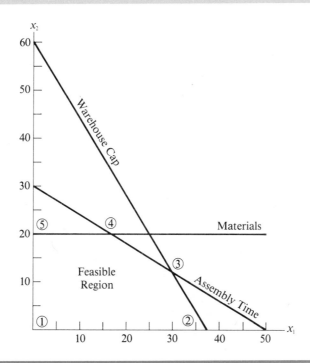

FIGURE 5.2
Feasible Region and Extreme Points for the HighTech Industries Problem

tableau we calculated after one iteration is the basic feasible solution corresponding to extreme point ②.

We note from Figure 5.2 that at extreme point ② the warehouse space constraint is binding and that there is slack in the other two constraints. From the simplex tableau we see that the amount of slack for these two constraints is given by $s_1 = 75/2$ and $s_2 = 20$.

Moving Toward a Better Solution

To see if a new better basic feasible solution can be found, we need to calculate the z_j and $c_j - z_j$ rows for the new simplex tableau. Recall that the elements in the z_j row are the sum of the products obtained by multiplying the elements in the c_B column of the simplex tableau by the corresponding elements in the columns of the $\bar{A}$ matrix. Thus, we obtain

$$z_1 = 0(0) \quad\; + 0(0) + 50(1) \; = 50$$
$$z_2 = 0(25/8) \quad + 0(1) + 50(5/8) = 250/8$$
$$z_3 = 0(1) \quad\; + 0(0) + 50(0) \; = 0$$
$$z_4 = 0(0) \quad\; + 0(1) + 50(0) \; = 0$$
$$z_5 = 0(-3/8) + 0(0) + 50(1/8) = 50/8$$

Subtracting z_j from c_j to compute the net evaluation row, we obtain the following simplex tableau:

		x_1	x_2	s_1	s_2	s_3	
Basis	c_B	50	40	0	0	0	
s_1	0	0	25/8	1	0	-3/8	75/2
s_2	0	0	1	0	1	0	20
x_1	50	1	5/8	0	0	1/8	75/2
z_j		50	250/8	0	0	50/8	1875
$c_j - z_j$		0	70/8	0	0	-50/8	

Let us now analyze the $c_j - z_j$ row to see if we can introduce a new variable into the basis and continue to improve the objective function. Using the rule for determining which variable should enter the basis next, we select x_2 since it has the highest positive coefficient in the $c_j - z_j$ row.

To determine which variable will be removed from the basis when x_2 enters, we must compute for each row i the ratio $\bar{b}_i / \bar{a}_{i2}$ (remember, though, that we should compute this ratio only if $\bar{a}_{i2}$ is greater than zero); then we select the variable to leave the basis that corresponds to the minimum ratio. As before, we will show these ratios in an extra column of the simplex tableau:

		x_1	x_2	s_1	s_2	s_3		$\dfrac{\bar{b}_i}{\bar{a}_{i2}}$
Basis	c_B	50	40	0	0	0		
s_1	0	0	(25/8)	1	0	-3/8	75/2	$\dfrac{75/2}{25/8} = 12$
s_2	0	0	1	0	1	0	20	$\dfrac{20}{1} = 20$
x_1	50	1	5/8	0	0	1/8	75/2	$\dfrac{75/2}{5/8} = 60$
z_j		50	250/8	0	0	50/8	1875	
$c_j - z_j$		0	70/8	0	0	-50/8		

Since 12 is the minimum ratio, s_1 will leave the basis. The pivot element is $\bar{a}_{12} = 25/8$, which is circled in the above tableau. The nonbasic variable x_2 must now be made a basic variable. This means that we must perform the elementary row operations that will convert the x_2 column into a unit column; that is, we will have to transform the second column in the tableau to the form

$$\begin{array}{c} 1 \\ 0 \\ 0 \end{array}$$

We can do this by performing the following elementary row operations:

Step 1 Multiply every element in row 1 (the pivot row) by 8/25 in order to make $\bar{a}_{12} = 1$.
Step 2 Subtract the new row 1 (that is, the new pivot row) from row 2 in order to make $\bar{a}_{22} = 0$.
Step 3 Multiply the new pivot row by 5/8, and subtract the result from row 3 in order to make $\bar{a}_{32} = 0$.

Although the above elementary row operations again change the appearance of the simplex tableau, they do not alter the solutions to the system of equations contained in the tableau. The only difference is that now we have x_2, s_2, and x_1 as the basic variables and s_1 and s_3 as the nonbasic variables. The new tableau resulting from these row operations is as follows:

Basis	c_B	x_1 50	x_2 40	s_1 0	s_2 0	s_3 0	
x_2	40	0	1	$8/25$	0	$-3/25$	12
s_2	0	0	0	$-8/25$	1	$3/25$	8
x_1	50	1	0	$-5/25$	0	$5/25$	30
z_j		50	40	$14/5$	0	$26/5$	1980
$c_j - z_j$		0	0	$-14/5$	0	$-26/5$	

Note that the values of the basic variables are $x_2 = 12$, $s_2 = 8$, and $x_1 = 30$, and the corresponding profit is $40(12) + 0(8) + 50(30) = 1980$.

We must now determine whether or not to bring any other variable into the basis and thereby move to another basic feasible solution. Looking at the net evaluation row, we see that every element is zero or negative. Since $c_j - z_j$ is less than or equal to zero for both of the nonbasic variables s_1 and s_3, any attempt to bring a nonbasic variable into the basis at this point will result in lowering the current value of the objective function. Hence, the above tableau represents the optimal solution. In general, the simplex method uses the following criterion to determine if the optimal solution has been obtained.

Stopping Criterion.

The optimal solution to a linear programming problem has been reached when all of the entries in the net evaluation row ($c_j - z_j$) are zero or negative. In such cases the optimal solution is the current basic feasible solution.

Interpreting the Optimal Solution

The optimal solution to the HighTech problem, consisting of the basic variables x_1, x_2, and s_2 and nonbasic variables s_1 and s_3, is written as follows:

$$x_1 = 30$$
$$x_2 = 12$$
$$s_1 = 0$$
$$s_2 = 8$$
$$s_3 = 0$$

The value of the objective function is $1980. Thus, if the management of HighTech Industries wants to maximize profit, HighTech should produce 30 units of the Deskpro and 12 units of the Portable. In addition, since $s_2 = 8$, management should note that there will be a slack of 8 Portable display units left at the optimal solution. Moreover, since

$s_1 = 0$ and $s_3 = 0$, there is no slack associated with the assembly time constraint and the warehouse space constraint; in other words, these constraints are both binding. Consequently, if it is possible to obtain additional assembly time and/or additional warehouse space, management should consider doing so.

Referring to Figure 5.2, we can see graphically the process that the simplex method used to determine an optimal solution. The initial basic feasible solution corresponds to the origin ($x_1 = 0$, $x_2 = 0$, $s_1 = 150$, $s_2 = 20$, $s_3 = 300$). The first iteration caused x_1 to enter the basis and s_3 to leave. The new basic feasible solution corresponds to extreme point ② ($x_1 = 75/2$, $x_2 = 0$, $s_1 = 20$, $s_2 = 75/2$, $s_3 = 0$). At the next iteration x_2 entered the basis, and s_1 left. This brought us to extreme point ③, the optimal solution ($x_1 = 30$, $x_2 = 12$, $s_1 = 0$, $s_2 = 8$, $s_3 = 0$).

For the HighTech problem, with only two decision variables, we had a choice of using the graphical or simplex method. For problems with more than two variables, we shall always use the simplex method.

5.6 ▼ SOLUTION OF A SAMPLE PROBLEM

In this section we illustrate the use of the simplex method for a linear programming problem involving four decision variables. To check your understanding of the previous sections, you should attempt to solve the problem before studying the solution presented.

Solve the following linear program using the simplex method:

$$\max \quad 4x_1 + 6x_2 + 3x_3 + 1x_4$$

s.t.

$$\tfrac{3}{2}x_1 + 2x_2 + 4x_3 + 3x_4 \leq 550$$
$$4x_1 + 1x_2 + 2x_3 + 1x_4 \leq 700$$
$$2x_1 + 3x_2 + 1x_3 + 2x_4 \leq 200$$
$$x_1, x_2, x_3, x_4 \geq 0$$

First, we add slack variables to convert the problem to standard form:

$$\max \quad 4x_1 + 6x_2 + 3x_3 + 1x_4 + 0s_1 + 0s_2 + 0s_3$$

s.t.

$$\tfrac{3}{2}x_1 + 2x_2 + 4x_3 + 3x_4 + 1s_1 \qquad\qquad = 550$$
$$4x_1 + 1x_2 + 2x_3 + 1x_4 \qquad + 1s_2 \qquad = 700$$
$$2x_1 + 3x_2 + 1x_3 + 2x_4 \qquad\qquad + 1s_3 = 200$$
$$x_1, x_2, x_3, x_4, s_1, s_2, s_3 \geq 0$$

The next step is to write the problem in tableau form. Since all the constraints are less-than-or-equal-to constraints, and since the right-hand-side values for the constraints are all nonnegative, the standard form and tableau form are the same. Thus, we can set up the initial simplex tableau and begin the simplex method.

Basis	c_B	x_1 4	x_2 6	x_3 3	x_4 1	s_1 0	s_2 0	s_3 0		$\bar{b}_i$ $\overline{\bar{a}_{i2}}$
s_1	0	$3/2$	2	4	3	1	0	0	550	$550/2 = 275$
s_2	0	4	1	2	1	0	1	0	700	$700/1 = 700$
s_3	0	2	③	1	2	0	0	1	200	$200/3 = 66\,2/3$
	z_j	0	0	0	0	0	0	0	0	
	$c_j - z_j$	4	6	3	1	0	0	0		

Two iterations of the simplex method are required to reach the optimal solution.
Result of iteration 1:

Basis	c_B	x_1 4	x_2 6	x_3 3	x_4 1	s_1 0	s_2 0	s_3 0		$\bar{b}_i$ $\overline{\bar{a}_{i3}}$
s_1	0	$1/6$	0	⑩$/3$	$5/3$	1	0	$-2/3$	$416\,2/3$	125
s_2	0	$10/3$	0	$5/3$	$1/3$	0	1	$-1/3$	$633\,1/3$	380
x_2	6	$2/3$	1	$1/3$	$2/3$	0	0	$1/3$	$66\,2/3$	200
	z_j	4	6	2	4	0	0	2	400	
	$c_j - z_j$	0	0	1	-3	0	0	-2		

Result of iteration 2:

Basis	c_B	x_1 4	x_2 6	x_3 3	x_4 1	s_1 0	s_2 0	s_3 0	
x_3	3	$3/60$	0	1	$15/30$	$3/10$	0	$-6/30$	125
s_2	0	$195/60$	0	0	$-15/30$	$-5/10$	1	0	425
x_2	6	$39/60$	1	0	$15/30$	$-1/10$	0	$12/30$	25
	z_j	$81/20$	6	3	$9/2$	$3/10$	0	$54/30$	525
	$c_j - z_j$	$-1/20$	0	0	$-7/2$	$-3/10$	0	$-54/30$	

Since the $c_j - z_j$ elements are all less than or equal to zero, there is no nonbasic variable that we can introduce into solution and obtain an increase in the value of the objective function. Therefore, the current solution is optimal. The complete optimal solution is given by

$$x_1 = 0$$
$$x_2 = 25$$
$$x_3 = 125$$
$$x_4 = 0$$
$$s_1 = 0$$
$$s_2 = 425$$
$$s_3 = 0$$

The value of the objective function is 525.

5.7 ▼ TABLEAU FORM: THE GENERAL CASE

When a linear program contains all less-than-or-equal-to constraints with nonnegative right-hand-side values, it is easy to set up a tableau form. In this case we simply add a slack variable to each constraint. However, obtaining tableau form is somewhat more complex if the linear program contains greater-than-or-equal-to constraints, equality constraints, and/or negative right-hand-side values. In this section we describe how to develop tableau form for each of these situations.

Greater-Than-or-Equal-to Constraints

Suppose that in the HighTech Industries problem, management wanted to ensure that the combined total production for both models would be at least 25 units. This requirement means that the following constraint must be added to the current linear program:

$$1x_1 + 1x_2 \geq 25$$

Adding this constraint results in the following modified HighTech Industries problem:

$$\max \quad 50x_1 + 40x_2$$

s.t.

$$
\begin{aligned}
3x_1 + 5x_2 &\leq 150 \quad \text{Assembly time} \\
1x_2 &\leq 20 \quad \text{Portable display} \\
8x_1 + 5x_2 &\leq 300 \quad \text{Warehouse space} \\
1x_1 + 1x_2 &\geq 25 \quad \text{Minimum total production} \\
x_1, x_2 &\geq 0
\end{aligned}
$$

A graph of the feasible region for this modified problem is shown in Figure 5.3. Extreme points ②, ③, and ④ have not changed, but the extreme points we have labeled ① and ⑤ are in different locations than they were in the original problem. The origin ($x_1 = 0$ and $x_2 = 0$) is no longer feasible. We note, however, that extreme point ③ remains feasible. Thus, even though part of the original feasible region has been cut off, we should expect to obtain the same optimal solution. To use the simplex method to solve this modified HighTech problem, we need to describe how to set up the tableau form for a linear programming problem that contains greater-than-or-equal-to constraints.

First, we use three slack variables and one surplus variable to write the problem in standard form. This provides the following:

$$\max \quad 50x_1 + 40x_2 + 0s_1 + 0s_2 + 0s_3 + 0s_4$$

s.t.

$$
\begin{aligned}
3x_1 + 5x_2 + 1s_1 &= 150 && (5.12) \\
1x_2 + 1s_2 &= 20 && (5.13) \\
8x_1 + 5x_2 + 1s_3 &= 300 && (5.14) \\
1x_1 + 1x_2 - 1s_4 &= 25 && (5.15) \\
x_1, x_2, s_1, s_2, s_3, s_4 &\geq 0
\end{aligned}
$$

FIGURE 5.3
Feasible Region and Extreme Points for Modified HighTech Industries Problem

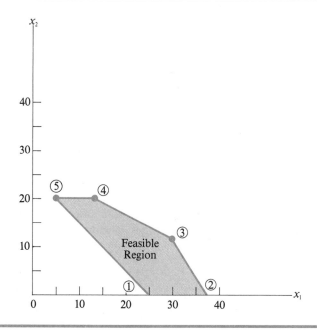

Now let us consider how we obtain an initial basic feasible solution in order to start the simplex method. Previously we set $x_1 = 0$ and $x_2 = 0$ and selected the slack variables as the initial basic variables. The extension of this notion to the modified HighTech problem would suggest setting $x_1 = 0$ and $x_2 = 0$ and selecting the slack and surplus variables as the initial basic variables. However, in looking at the graph in Figure 5.3 we can see that the solution corresponding to $x_1 = 0$ and $x_2 = 0$, which is the origin, is no longer a feasible solution. The inclusion of the greater-than-or-equal-to constraint has eliminated the origin from the feasible region.

To see this another way, refer to equation (5.15) in the standard form representation of the problem. When x_1 and x_2 are set equal to zero, equation (5.15) reduces to $-1s_4 = 25$, and, hence, $s_4 = -25$. Thus, setting x_1 and x_2 to zero results in the basic solution

$$x_1 = 0$$
$$x_2 = 0$$
$$s_1 = 150$$
$$s_2 = 20$$
$$s_3 = 300$$
$$s_4 = -25$$

Here s_4 represents the amount by which this solution falls short of the newly specified minimum total production constraint. Clearly this is not a basic feasible solution since s_4 violates the nonnegativity requirement. The difficulty is that the standard form representation of the problem and the tableau form representation of the problem are not equivalent when the problem contains greater-than-or-equal-to constraints.

In order to set up the tableau form for this problem, we shall resort to a mathematical "trick" that will enable us to find an initial basic feasible solution in terms of the slack variables s_1, s_2, and s_3 and a new variable we shall denote a_4. The new variable constitutes the mathematical "trick." Variable a_4 really has nothing to do with the HighTech problem; it merely serves to enable us to set up the tableau form and thus obtain an initial basic feasible solution. Since this new variable has been artificially created in order to start the simplex method, we will refer to it as an *artificial variable*.

The notation for artificial variables is similar to the notation used to refer to the elements of the A matrix. To avoid any confusion between the two, the elements of the A matrix (constraint coefficients) always have two subscripts, whereas artificial variables always have only one subscript.

With the addition of an artificial variable, we can convert the standard form representation of the modified HighTech problem into tableau form. We add artificial variable a_4 to constraint (5.15) to obtain the following representation of the system of equations in tableau form:

$$
\begin{aligned}
3x_1 + 5x_2 + 1s_1 & & & = 150 \\
1x_2 & + 1s_2 & & = 20 \\
8x_1 + 5x_2 & + 1s_3 & & = 300 \\
1x_1 + 1x_2 & & - 1s_4 + 1a_4 & = 25
\end{aligned}
$$

Note that the subscript on the artificial variable identifies the constraint with which it is associated. This is also the convention we have followed for slack and surplus variables; s_1 is associated with the first constraint, s_2 is associated with the second constraint, and so on. Thus, a_4 is the artificial variable associated with the fourth constraint.

Since the variables s_1, s_2, s_3, and a_4 each appear in a different constraint with a coefficient of 1, and since the right-hand sides are nonnegative, both requirements of the tableau form have been satisfied. We can now obtain an initial basic feasible solution by setting $x_1 = x_2 = s_4 = 0$. The complete solution is

$$
\begin{aligned}
x_1 &= 0 \\
x_2 &= 0 \\
s_1 &= 150 \\
s_2 &= 20 \\
s_3 &= 300 \\
s_4 &= 0 \\
a_4 &= 25
\end{aligned}
$$

Is this solution feasible in terms of our real-world problem? No, it is not. It does not satisfy the combined total production requirement of 25 units. We must make an important distinction between a basic feasible solution for the tableau form of our problem and a feasible solution for the real-world problem. A basic feasible solution for the tableau form of a linear programming problem is not always a feasible solution for the real-world problem.

The reason for creating the tableau form is to obtain an initial basic feasible solution that is required to start the simplex method. Thus, we see that whenever it is necessary to introduce artificial variables, the initial simplex solution will not in general be feasible for the real-world problem. This situation is not as difficult as it might seem, however, since the only time we must have a feasible solution for the real-world problem is at the last iteration of the simplex method. Thus, if we could devise a way to guarantee that any artificial variable would be eliminated from the basic feasible solution before the optimal solution is reached, there would be no difficulty.

The way in which we guarantee that artificial variables will be eliminated before the optimal solution is reached is to assign each artificial variable a very large cost in the objective function. For example, in the modified HighTech problem we could assign a very large negative number as the profit coefficient for artificial variable a_4. Hence, if this variable is in the basis, it will substantially reduce profits. As a result, this variable will be eliminated from the basis as soon as possible, and this is precisely what we want to happen.

As an alternative to picking a large negative number like $-100,000$ for the profit coefficient, we will denote the profit coefficient of each artificial variable by $-M$. Here it is assumed that M represents a very large number—in other words, a number of very large magnitude, and hence the letter M. This notation will make it easier to keep track of the elements of the simplex tableau that depend on the profit coefficients of the artificial variables. Using $-M$ as the profit coefficient for artificial variable a_4 for the HighTech problem, we can write the objective function for the tableau form of the problem as follows:

$$\max 50x_1 + 40x_2 + 0s_1 + 0s_2 + 0s_3 + 0s_4 - Ma_4$$

The initial simplex tableau for the modified HighTech Industries problem is shown below.

Basis	c_B	x_1 50	x_2 40	s_1 0	s_2 0	s_3 0	s_4 0	a_4 $-M$	
s_1	0	3	5	1	0	0	0	0	150
s_2	0	0	1	0	1	0	0	0	20
s_3	0	8	5	0	0	1	0	0	300
a_4	$-M$	1	1	0	0	0	-1	1	25
z_j		$-M$	$-M$	0	0	0	M	$-M$	$-25M$
$c_j - z_j$		$50+M$	$40+M$	0	0	0	$-M$	0	

The above tableau corresponds to the solution $s_1 = 150$, $s_2 = 20$, $s_3 = 300$, $a_4 = 25$, and $x_1 = x_2 = s_4 = 0$. In terms of the simplex tableau this is a basic feasible solution since all the variables are greater than or equal to zero and $n - m = 7 - 4 = 3$ of the variables are equal to zero. However, in terms of the modified HighTech problem, $x_1 = x_2 = 0$ is clearly not feasible. This situation is caused by the fact that the artificial variable is in the current basic solution at a positive value. Let us complete the simplex solution to this problem and see if the artificial variable is driven out of solution, as we hope it will be.

Since $c_1 - z_1 = 50 + M$ is the largest value in the net evaluation row, we see that x_1 will become a basic variable during the first iteration of the simplex method. Further calculations with the simplex method show that x_1 will replace a_4 in the basic solution. The simplex tableau after the first iteration is presented below.

Result of iteration 1:

Basis	c_B	x_1	x_2	s_1	s_2	s_3	s_4	a_4	
		50	40	0	0	0	0	$-M$	
s_1	0	0	2	1	0	0	3	-3	75
s_2	0	0	1	0	1	0	0	0	20
s_3	0	0	-3	0	0	1	8	-8	100
x_1	50	1	1	0	0	0	-1	1	25
z_j		50	50	0	0	0	-50	50	1250
$c_j - z_j$		0	-10	0	0	0	50	$-M-50$	

Graphically, we see in Figure 5.4 that this iteration has moved us from the origin (labeled A) to extreme point ①. The current solution is now feasible since there are no artificial variables in solution. We now have the situation where the basic feasible solution contained in the simplex tableau is also a feasible solution to the real-world problem.

Since a_4 is an artificial variable that was added simply to obtain an initial basic feasible solution, we can now drop its associated column from the simplex tableau. Indeed, whenever artificial variables are used, they can be dropped from the simplex tableau as soon as they have been eliminated from the basic feasible solution.

FIGURE 5.4
Sequence of Simplex Solutions for the Modified HighTech Industries Problem

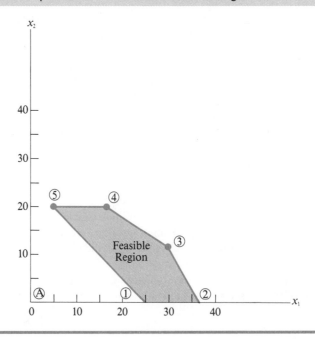

When artificial variables are required to obtain an initial basic feasible solution, the iterations required to eliminate the artificial variables are referred to as *phase I* of the simplex method. When all the artificial variables have been eliminated from the basis, phase I is complete, and a basic feasible solution to the real-world problem has been obtained. Thus, by dropping the column associated with a_4 from the current tableau, we obtain the following simplex tableau at the end of phase I.

		x_1	x_2	s_1	s_2	s_3	s_4	
Basis	c_B	50	40	0	0	0	0	
s_1	0	0	2	1	0	0	3	75
s_2	0	0	1	0	1	0	0	20
s_3	0	0	−3	0	0	1	8	100
x_1	50	1	1	0	0	0	−1	25
	z_j	50	50	0	0	0	−50	1250
	$c_j - z_j$	0	−10	0	0	0	50	

We are now ready to begin phase II of the simplex method. This phase simply continues the simplex method computations after all artificial variables have been removed. At the next iteration, variable s_4 with $c_j - z_j = 50$ is entered into the solution, and variable s_3 is eliminated. The simplex tableau after this iteration is

		x_1	x_2	s_1	s_2	s_3	s_4	
Basis	c_B	50	40	0	0	0	0	
s_1	0	0	$25/8$	1	0	$-3/8$	0	$75/2$
s_2	0	0	1	0	1	0	0	20
s_4	0	0	$-3/8$	0	0	$1/8$	1	$25/2$
x_1	50	1	$5/8$	0	0	$1/8$	0	$75/2$
	z_j	50	$250/8$	0	0	$50/8$	0	1875
	$c_j - z_j$	0	$70/8$	0	0	$-50/8$	0	

In Figure 5.4 we see that this solution corresponds to extreme point ②. One more iteration is required. This time x_2 comes into solution, and s_1 is eliminated. After performing this iteration, the following simplex tableau shows that the optimal solution has been reached.

		x_1	x_2	s_1	s_2	s_3	s_4	
Basis	c_B	50	40	0	0	0	0	
x_2	40	0	1	$8/25$	0	$-3/25$	0	12
s_2	0	0	0	$-8/25$	1	$3/25$	0	8
s_4	0	0	0	$3/25$	0	$2/25$	1	17
x_1	50	1	0	$-5/25$	0	$5/25$	0	30
	z_j	50	40	$14/5$	0	$26/5$	0	1980
	$c_j - z_j$	0	0	$-14/5$	0	$-26/5$	0	

From Figure 5.4 we see that this optimal solution corresponds to extreme point ③. Thus, the optimal solution to the revised problem is the same as the solution for the original problem. However, the simplex method required more iterations to reach this extreme point. This was so because it required an extra iteration to eliminate the artificial variable (a_4) in phase I in order to obtain a basic feasible solution for the real-world problem.

Fortunately, once we obtain an initial simplex tableau using artificial variables, we need not concern ourselves with whether or not the basic solution at a particular iteration is feasible for the real-world problem. We need only follow the rules for the simplex method. If we reach the stopping criterion (that is, all $c_j - z_j \leq 0$) and all the artificial variables have been eliminated from the solution, then we have found the optimal solution. On the other hand, if we reach the stopping criterion and one or more of the artificial variables remain in solution at a positive value, then there is no feasible solution to the problem. This special case will be discussed further in Section 5.9.

Equality Constraints

When an equality constraint occurs in a linear programming problem, we need to add an artificial variable to obtain tableau form and an initial basic feasible solution. For example, if the equality constraint is

$$6x_1 + 4x_2 - 5x_3 = 30$$

we would simply add an artificial variable—say, a_1—to create a basic feasible solution in the initial simplex tableau. With the artificial variable the above equation becomes

$$6x_1 + 4x_2 - 5x_3 + 1a_1 = 30$$

Now a_1 can be selected as the basic variable for this row, and its value is given by the right-hand side. Once we have created tableau form by adding an artificial variable to each equality constraint, the simplex method proceeds exactly as before.

Eliminating Negative Right-Hand-Side Values

One of the properties of tableau form of a linear program is that the values on the right-hand sides of the constraints have to be nonnegative. In formulating a linear programming problem, we may find one or more of the constraints have negative right-hand-side values. To see how this might happen, suppose that the management of HighTech has specified that the number of units of the Portable model, x_2, has to be less than or equal to the number of units of the Deskpro model, x_1, after setting aside five units of the Deskpro for internal company use. We could formulate this constraint as

$$x_2 \leq x_1 - 5 \tag{5.16}$$

Subtracting x_1 from both sides of the inequality places both variables on the left-hand side of the inequality. Thus,

$$-x_1 + x_2 \leq -5 \tag{5.17}$$

Since this is a constraint with a negative right-hand-side value, we can develop an equivalent constraint with a nonnegative right-hand side by multiplying both sides of the constraint by -1. In doing so, we recognize that multiplying an inequality constraint by -1 changes the direction of the inequality.

Thus, to convert (5.17) to an equivalent constraint with a nonnegative right-hand-side value, we multiply by -1 to obtain

$$x_1 - x_2 \geq 5 \qquad\qquad (5.18)$$

We now have an acceptable nonnegative right-hand-side value. Tableau form for this constraint can now be obtained by subtracting a surplus variable and adding an artificial variable.

For a greater-than-or-equal-to constraint, multiplying by -1 creates an equivalent less-than-or-equal-to constraint. For example, suppose we had the following greater-than-or-equal-to constraint:

$$6x_1 + 3x_2 - 4x_3 \geq -20$$

Multiplying by -1 to obtain an equivalent constraint with a nonnegative right-hand-side value leads to the following less-than-or-equal-to constraint

$$-6x_1 - 3x_2 + 4x_3 \leq 20$$

Tableau form can be created for this constraint by adding a slack variable.

For an equality constraint with a negative right-hand-side value, we simply multiply by -1 to obtain an equivalent constraint with a nonnegative right-hand-side value. An artificial variable can then be added to create the tableau form.

Summary of the Steps to Create Tableau Form

Step 1 If the original formulation of the linear programming problem contains one or more constraints with negative right-hand-side values, multiply each of these constraints by -1. Doing this will change the direction of the inequalities. This step will provide an equivalent linear program with nonnegative right-hand-side values.

Step 2 For $\leq$ constraints add a slack variable to obtain an equality constraint. The coefficient of the slack variable in the objective function is assigned a value of zero. This provides the tableau form for the constraint, and the slack variable becomes one of the basic variables in the initial basic feasible solution.

Step 3 For $\geq$ constraints subtract a surplus variable to obtain an equality constraint, and then add an artificial variable to obtain the tableau form. The coefficient of the surplus variable in the objective function is assigned a value of zero. The coefficient of the artificial variable in the objective function is assigned a value of $-M$. The artificial variable becomes one of the basic variables in the initial basic feasible solution.

Step 4 For equality constraints add an artificial variable to obtain the tableau form. The coefficient of the artificial variable in the objective function is assigned a value of $-M$. The artificial variable becomes one of the basic variables in the initial basic feasible solution.

To obtain some practice in applying the above steps, convert the following example problem into tableau form, and then set up the initial simplex tableau:

$$\max \quad 6x_1 + 3x_2 + 4x_3 + 1x_4$$

s.t.

$$-2x_1 - \tfrac{1}{2}x_2 + 1x_3 - 6x_4 = -60$$
$$1x_1 \qquad\quad + 1x_3 + \tfrac{2}{3}x_4 \le 20$$
$$-1x_2 - 5x_3 \qquad\quad \le -50$$
$$x_1, x_2, x_3, x_4 \ge 0$$

To eliminate the negative right-hand-side values in constraints 1 and 3, we apply step 1. Multiplying both constraints by -1, we obtain the following equivalent linear program:

$$\max \quad 6x_1 + 3x_2 + 4x_3 + 1x_4$$

s.t.

$$2x_1 + \tfrac{1}{2}x_2 - 1x_3 + 6x_4 = 60$$
$$1x_1 \qquad\quad + 1x_3 + \tfrac{2}{3}x_4 \le 20$$
$$1x_2 + 5x_3 \qquad\quad \ge 50$$
$$x_1, x_2, x_3, x_4 \ge 0$$

Note that the direction of the $\le$ inequality in constraint 3 has been reversed as a result of multiplying the constraint by -1. By applying step 4 for constraint 1, step 2 for constraint 2, and step 3 for constraint 3, we obtain the following tableau form:

$$\max \quad 6x_1 + 3x_2 + 4x_3 + 1x_4 + 0s_2 + 0s_3 - Ma_1 - Ma_3$$

s.t.

$$2x_1 + \tfrac{1}{2}x_2 - 1x_3 + 6x_4 \qquad\qquad\quad + 1a_1 \qquad\quad = 60$$
$$1x_1 \qquad\quad + 1x_3 + \tfrac{2}{3}x_4 + 1s_2 \qquad\qquad\qquad = 20$$
$$1x_2 + 5x_3 \qquad\qquad\qquad - 1s_3 \qquad + 1a_3 = 50$$
$$x_1, x_2, x_3, x_4, s_2, s_3, a_1, a_3 \ge 0$$

The initial simplex tableau corresponding to this tableau form is

Basis	c_B	x_1	x_2	x_3	x_4	s_2	s_3	a_1	a_3	
		6	3	4	1	0	0	$-M$	$-M$	
a_1	$-M$	2	$\tfrac{1}{2}$	-1	6	0	0	1	0	60
s_2	0	1	0	1	$\tfrac{2}{3}$	1	0	0	0	20
a_3	$-M$	0	1	5	0	0	-1	0	1	50
	z_j	$-2M$	$-\tfrac{3}{2}M$	$-4M$	$-6M$	0	M	$-M$	$-M$	$-110M$
	$c_j - z_j$	$6 + 2M$	$3 + \tfrac{3}{2}M$	$4 + 4M$	$1 + 6M$	0	$-M$	0	0	

▼ NOTES AND COMMENTS ▼

We have shown how to convert constraints with negative right-hand sides to equivalent constraints with positive right-hand sides. Actually there is nothing wrong with formulating a linear program and including negative right-hand sides. But if you want to use the ordinary simplex method to solve the linear program, you must first eliminate the negative right-hand sides. Some computer codes, including The Management Scientist, have procedures which accommodate negative right-hand sides.

5.8 ▼ SOLVING A MINIMIZATION PROBLEM USING THE SIMPLEX METHOD

There are two ways in which we can use the simplex method to solve a minimization problem. The first approach requires that we change the rule used to introduce a variable into the basis. Recall that in the maximization case we select the variable with the largest positive $c_j - z_j$ as the variable to introduce next into the basis. This is because the value of $c_j - z_j$ tells us the amount the objective function will increase if one unit of the variable in column j is brought into solution. To solve the minimization problem, we can simply reverse this rule. That is, we can select the variable with the most negative $c_j - z_j$ as the one to introduce next. Of course, this approach means the stopping rule for the optimal solution will also have to be changed. Using this approach to solve a minimization problem, we would stop when every value in the net evaluation row is zero or positive.

The second approach to solving the minimization problem is the one we shall employ in this book. It is based on the fact that any minimization problem can be converted to an equivalent maximization problem by multiplying the objective function by -1. Solving the resulting maximization problem will provide the optimal solution to the minimization problem.

Let us illustrate this second approach by using the simplex method to solve the M&D Chemicals problem introduced in Chapter 2. Recall that in this problem, management wanted to minimize the cost of producing two products subject to a demand constraint for product 1, a minimum total production quantity requirement, and a constraint on available processing time. The mathematical statement of the M&D Chemicals problem is shown below.

$$\min \quad 2x_1 + 3x_2$$

s.t.

$$1x_1 \qquad \geq 125 \quad \text{Demand for product 1}$$
$$1x_1 + 1x_2 \geq 350 \quad \text{Total production}$$
$$2x_1 + 1x_2 \leq 600 \quad \text{Processing time}$$
$$x_1, x_2 \geq 0$$

To solve this problem using the simplex method, we first multiply the objective function by -1 to convert the minimization problem into the following equivalent maximization problem:

$$\max \quad -2x_1 - 3x_2$$

s.t.

$$
\begin{aligned}
1x_1 & & \geq 125 & \quad \text{Demand for product 1} \\
1x_1 + 1x_2 & & \geq 350 & \quad \text{Total production} \\
2x_1 + 1x_2 & & \leq 600 & \quad \text{Processing time} \\
x_1, x_2 & \geq 0 &
\end{aligned}
$$

The tableau form for this problem is as follows:

$$\max \quad -2x_1 - 3x_2 + 0s_1 + 0s_2 + 0s_3 - Ma_1 - Ma_2$$

s.t.

$$
\begin{aligned}
1x_1 & & - 1s_1 & & & + 1a_1 & & = 125 \\
1x_1 + 1x_2 & & & - 1s_2 & & & + 1a_2 & = 350 \\
2x_1 + 1x_2 & & & & + 1s_3 & & & = 600 \\
x_1, x_2, s_1, s_2, s_3, a_1, a_2 & \geq 0
\end{aligned}
$$

The initial simplex tableau is shown below:

Basis	c_B	x_1	x_2	s_1	s_2	s_3	a_1	a_2	
		-2	-3	0	0	0	$-M$	$-M$	
a_1	$-M$	①	0	-1	0	0	1	0	125
a_2	$-M$	1	1	0	-1	0	0	1	350
s_3	0	2	1	0	0	1	0	0	600
z_j		$-2M$	$-M$	M	M	0	$-M$	$-M$	$-475M$
$c_j - z_j$		$-2 + 2M$	$-3 + M$	$-M$	$-M$	0	0	0	

At the first iteration, x_1 is brought into the basis, and a_1 is eliminated. After dropping the a_1 column from the tableau, the result of the first iteration is shown below.

Basis	c_B	x_1	x_2	s_1	s_2	s_3	a_2	
		-2	-3	0	0	0	$-M$	
x_1	-2	1	0	-1	0	0	0	125
a_2	$-M$	0	①	1	-1	0	1	225
s_3	0	0	1	2	0	1	0	350
z_j		-2	$-M$	$2 - M$	M	0	$-M$	$-250 - 225M$
$c_j - z_j$		0	$-3 + M$	$-2 + M$	$-M$	0	0	

Continuing with additional iterations of the simplex method provides the final simplex tableau shown below.

Basis	c_B	x_1	x_2	s_1	s_2	s_3	
		-2	-3	0	0	0	
x_1	-2	1	0	0	1	1	250
x_2	-3	0	1	0	-2	-1	100
s_1	0	0	0	1	1	1	125
	z_j	-2	-3	0	4	1	-800
	$c_j - z_j$	0	0	0	-4	-1	

In Chapter 2 we used the graphical solution procedure to determine the optimal solution to this problem. The feasible region and solution are shown again in Figure 5.5. The simplex method has provided the same optimal solution with $x_1 = 250$, $x_2 = 100$, $s_1 = 125$, $s_2 = 0$, and $s_3 = 0$. Note, however, that the value of the objective function is -800 in the final simplex tableau. We must now multiply this value by -1 to

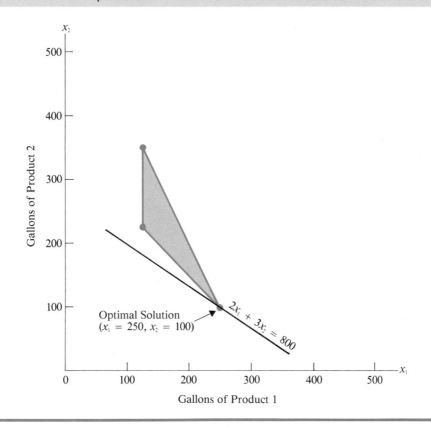

FIGURE 5.5
Graphical Solution for the M & D Chemicals Problem

obtain the value of the objective function to the original minimization problem (total cost = 800).

In the next section we shall concentrate on discussing some important special cases that may occur when trying to solve any linear programming problem. We will only consider the case for maximization problems, recognizing that all minimization problems may be placed into this form by multiplying the objective function by -1.

5.9 ▼ SPECIAL CASES

In Chapter 2 we discussed how infeasibility, unboundedness, and alternate optima could occur when solving linear programming problems using the graphical solution procedure. These special cases can also arise when using the simplex method. In addition, a special case referred to as *degeneracy* can theoretically cause difficulties for the simplex method. In this section we show how these special cases can be recognized and handled when the simplex method is used.

Infeasibility

Infeasibility occurs whenever there is no solution to the linear program that satisfies all the constraints, including the nonnegativity constraints. From the perspective of the graphical solution procedure, this means that there is no feasible region. Let us now see how infeasibility is recognized when the simplex method is used.

In Section 5.7, when discussing artificial variables, we mentioned that infeasibility can be recognized when the stopping criterion indicates that an optimal solution has been obtained and one or more of the artificial variables remain in the solution at a positive value. As an illustration of this situation, let us consider another modification of the HighTech Industries problem. Suppose management had imposed a minimum combined total production requirement of 50 units. The revised problem formulation is shown below.

$$\max \quad 50x_1 + 40x_2$$

s.t.

$$3x_1 + 5x_2 \leq 150 \quad \text{Assembly time}$$
$$1x_2 \leq 20 \quad \text{Portable display}$$
$$8x_1 + 5x_2 \leq 300 \quad \text{Warehouse space}$$
$$1x_1 + 1x_2 \geq 50 \quad \text{Minimum total production}$$
$$x_1, x_2 \geq 0$$

A graph of the feasible region for the problem is shown in Figure 5.6. From the graph we can see that there are no solutions that satisfy both the original HighTech problem constraints and the minimum combined total production constraint ($1x_1 + 1x_2 \geq 50$). Let

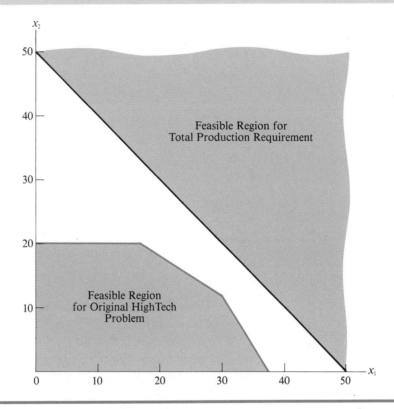

FIGURE 5.6
Graph of Solution Region for Modified HighTech Industries Problem

us solve this modified HighTech problem using the simplex method. The simplex tableaus are shown below.

Initial tableau:

Basis	c_B	x_1 50	x_2 40	s_1 0	s_2 0	s_3 0	s_4 0	a_4 $-M$	
s_1	0	3	5	1	0	0	0	0	150
s_2	0	0	1	0	1	0	0	0	20
s_3	0	8	5	0	0	1	0	0	300
a_4	$-M$	1	1	0	0	0	-1	1	50
	z_j	$-M$	$-M$	0	0	0	M	$-M$	$-50M$
	$c_j - z_j$	$50+M$	$40+M$	0	0	0	$-M$	0	

Result of the first iteration:

Basis	c_B	x_1 50	x_2 40	s_1 0	s_2 0	s_3 0	s_4 0	a_4 $-M$	
s_1	0	0	$25/8$	1	0	$-3/8$	0	0	$75/2$
s_2	0	0	1	0	1	0	0	0	20
x_1	50	1	$5/8$	0	0	$1/8$	0	0	$75/2$
a_4	$-M$	0	$3/8$	0	0	$-1/8$	-1	1	$25/2$
z_j		50	$\dfrac{250-3M}{8}$	0	0	$\dfrac{50+M}{8}$	M	$-M$	$1875 - \dfrac{25M}{2}$
$c_j - z_j$		0	$\dfrac{70+3M}{8}$	0	0	$\dfrac{-50-M}{8}$	$-M$	0	

Final tableau:

Basis	c_B	x_1 50	x_2 40	s_1 0	s_2 0	s_3 0	s_4 0	a_4 $-M$	
x_2	40	0	1	$8/25$	0	$-3/25$	0	0	12
s_2	0	0	0	$-8/25$	1	$3/25$	0	0	8
x_1	50	1	0	$-5/25$	0	$5/25$	0	0	30
a_4	$-M$	0	0	$-3/25$	0	$-2/25$	-1	1	8
z_j		50	40	$\dfrac{70+3M}{25}$	0	$\dfrac{130+2M}{25}$	M	$-M$	$1980 - 8M$
$c_j - z_j$		0	0	$\dfrac{-70-3M}{25}$	0	$\dfrac{-130-2M}{25}$	$-M$	0	

In the final tableau, just as you might have suspected, the artificial variable a_4 is in solution at a positive value; thus, phase I has not been completed. Note that $c_j - z_j \leq 0$ for all the variables; therefore, according to the stopping criterion, this should be the optimal solution. But this solution is not feasible for the modified HighTech Industries problem since $x_1 = 30$ and $x_2 = 12$ results in a combined total production of 42 units instead of at least 50 units. The fact that the artificial variable is in solution at a value of $a_4 = 8$ tells us that the final solution violates the fourth constraint ($1x_1 + 1x_2 \geq 50$) by 8 units.

If management is interested in knowing which of the first three constraints is preventing us from satisfying the total production requirement, a partial answer can be obtained from the final simplex tableau. Note that $s_2 = 8$, but that s_1 and s_3 are nonbasic variables at values of zero. This tells us that the assembly time and warehouse space constraints are binding. Since there are not enough assembly time and warehouse space available, we cannot satisfy the minimum combined total production requirement.

The management implications here are that additional assembly time and/or warehouse space must be made available in order to satisfy the total production requirement. If more time and/or space cannot be made available, management will have to relax the total production requirement by at least 8 units.

In summary, a linear program is infeasible if there is no solution that satisfies all the constraints simultaneously. Graphically, we recognize this situation as the case where there is no feasible region. *In terms of the simplex method we recognize infeasibility as the case where one or more of the artificial variables remains in the final solution at a positive value.* In closing, we note that for linear programming problems with all $\leq$ constraints and nonnegative right-hand sides, there will always be a feasible solution. That is, since it is not necessary to introduce artificial variables to set up the initial simplex tableau for these types of problems, there could not possibly be an artificial variable in the final solution.

Unboundedness

For maximization problems we say that a linear program is unbounded if the value of the solution may be made infinitely large without violating any constraints. While discussing unboundedness for graphical method in Section 2.8, we mentioned that unbounded profit maximization problems do not occur in practice. Thus, when unboundedness occurs, we can generally look for an error in the formulation of the problem.

The simplex method will automatically identify any unboundedness that exists before the final simplex tableau is reached. What will happen is that the rule for determining the variable to be removed from the basis will not work. Recall that in order to determine which variable to remove from the current basis, we calculate the ratio $\bar{b}_i / \bar{a}_{ij}$ for each $\bar{a}_{ij}$ greater than 0. Then we pick the smallest ratio to tell us which variable to remove from the current basic feasible solution.

The coefficients in a particular column of the $\bar{A}$ matrix indicate how much each of the current basic variables will decrease if one unit of the variable associated with that particular column is brought into solution. Suppose, then, that for a particular linear programming problem we reach a point where the rule for determining which variable to enter the basis results in the decision to enter variable x_2. Assume that for this variable $c_2 - z_2 = 5$, and that all $\bar{a}_{i2}$ in column 2 are ≤ 0. Thus, each unit of x_2 brought into solution increases the objective function by five units. Furthermore, since $\bar{a}_{i2} \leq 0$ for all i, this means that none of the current basic variables will be driven to zero, no matter how many units of x_2 we introduce. Thus, we can introduce an infinite amount of x_2 into solution and still maintain feasibility. Since each unit of x_2 increases the objective function by 5, we will have an unbounded solution. Hence *the way we recognize the unbounded situation is that all the $\bar{a}_{ij}$ are less than or equal to 0 in column j, and the simplex method indicates that variable x_j is to be introduced into solution.*

To illustrate this concept, let us consider the example of an unbounded problem we introduced in Section 2.8:

$$\max \quad 20x_1 + 10x_2$$

$$\text{s.t.}$$

$$1x_1 \qquad \geq 2$$

$$1x_2 \leq 5$$

$$x_1, x_2 \geq 0$$

We subtract a surplus variable, s_1, from the first constraint equation and add a slack variable, s_2, to the second constraint equation to obtain the standard form representation of the problem. We then add an artificial variable, a_1, to the first constraint equation in order to obtain the tableau form and set up the initial simplex tableau in terms of the basic variables a_1 and s_2. After bringing in x_1 at the first iteration, our simplex tableau is as follows:

Basis	c_B	x_1 20	x_2 10	s_1 0	s_2 0	a_1 $-M$	
x_1	20	1	0	-1	0	1	2
s_2	0	0	1	0	1	0	5
	z_j	20	0	-20	0	20	40
	$c_j - z_j$	0	10	20	0	$-M-20$	

Since s_1 has the largest positive $c_j - z_j$, we know we can increase the value of the objective function most rapidly by bringing s_1 into the basis. But $\bar{a}_{13} = -1$ and $\bar{a}_{23} = 0$; hence, we cannot form the ratio $\bar{b}_i/\bar{a}_{i3}$ for any $\bar{a}_{i3} > 0$ since there are no values of $\bar{a}_{i3}$ that are greater than zero. This is our indication that the solution to the linear program is unbounded. The reason the solution is unbounded is that each unit of s_1 that is brought into solution drives zero units of s_2 out of solution (since $\bar{a}_{23} = 0$) and provides one extra unit of x_1 (since $\bar{a}_{13} = -1$). The reason for this is that s_1 is a surplus variable and can be interpreted as the amount of product 1 we produce over the minimum amount required. Since the simplex tableau indicates that we can introduce as much of s_1 as we desire without violating any constraints, this tells us that we can make as much as we want above the minimum amount of x_1 required. Thus, there will be no upper bound on the value of the objective function since the objective function coefficient associated with x_1 is positive.

In summary, a maximization linear program is unbounded if it is possible to make the value of the optimal solution as large as desired without violating any of the constraints. We can recognize this condition graphically as the case where the feasible region extends to infinity in a direction in which the objective function increases. When employing the simplex solution procedure, an unbounded linear program is easy to recognize. *If, at some iteration, the simplex method tells us to introduce variable j into the solution and all the $\bar{a}_{ij}$ are less than or equal to zero in the jth column, the linear program has an unbounded solution.*

We emphasize that the case of an unbounded solution will never occur in real-world cost minimization or profit maximization problems because it is not possible to reduce costs to minus infinity or to increase profits to plus infinity. Thus, if we encounter an unbounded solution to a linear programming problem, we should carefully reexamine the formulation of the problem to determine if there has been a formulation error.

Alternate Optimal Solutions

A linear program with two or more optimal solutions is said to have alternate optima. In Section 2.8 we saw that alternate optima are recognized when using the graphical solution procedure when the objective function line is parallel to one of the binding constraint lines. When using the simplex method, we cannot recognize that a linear program has alternate optima until the final simplex tableau is reached. Then if the liner program has alternate optima, $c_j - z_j$ will equal zero for one or more of the *nonbasic* variables.

To illustrate the case of alternate optima when using the simplex method, consider changing the objective function for the HighTech problem from $50x_1 + 40x_2$ to $30x_1 + 50x_2$; in doing so, we obtain the revised linear program:

$$\max \quad 30x_1 + 50x_2$$

s.t.

$$3x_1 + 5x_2 \leq 150$$
$$1x_2 \leq 20$$
$$8x_1 + 5x_2 \leq 300$$
$$x_1, x_2, \geq 0$$

The graphical solution to this problem is shown in Figure 5.7. Clearly extreme points ③ and ④ are alternate optimal solutions. The final simplex tableau for this problem is shown below.

		x_1	x_2	s_1	s_2	s_3	
Basis	c_B	30	50	0	0	0	
x_2	50	0	1	0	1	0	20
s_3	0	0	0	$-8/3$	$25/3$	1	$200/3$
x_1	30	1	0	$1/3$	$-5/3$	0	$50/3$
	z_j	30	50	10	0	0	1500
	$c_j - z_j$	0	0	-10	0	0	

FIGURE 5.7
Graphical Solution to HighTech Industries Problem with Alternate Optimal Solutions

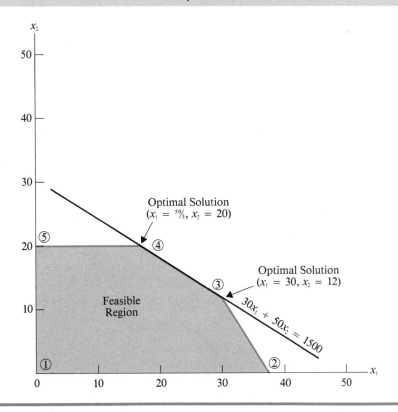

All values in the net evaluation row are less than or equal to zero, indicating that an optimal solution has been found. This solution is given by $x_1 = 50/3$, $x_2 = 20$, $s_1 = 0$, $s_2 = 0$, and $s_3 = 200/3$ and corresponds to extreme point ④ in Figure 5.7. The value of the objective function is 1500.

In looking at the net evaluation row in the optimal simplex tableau, we see that the $c_j - z_j$ value for nonbasic variable s_2 is equal to zero. This indicates that the linear program has alternate optima. In other words, since the net evaluation row entry for s_2 is zero, we can introduce s_2 into the basis without changing the value of the solution. The tableau obtained after introducing s_2 is given below.

Basis	c_B	x_1 30	x_2 50	s_1 0	s_2 0	s_3 0	
x_2	50	0	1	$8/25$	0	$-3/25$	12
s_2	0	0	0	$-8/25$	1	$3/25$	8
x_1	30	1	0	$-5/25$	0	$5/25$	30
z_j		30	50	10	0	0	1500
$c_j - z_j$		0	0	-10	0	0	

After introducing s_2 we have a different basic feasible solution: $x_1 = 30$, $x_2 = 12$, $s_1 = 0$, $s_2 = 8$, and $s_3 = 0$. However, this new solution is also optimal since $c_j - z_j \leq 0$ for all j. Another way to confirm that this solution is still optimal is to note that the value of the solution has remained equal to 1500. This solution corresponds to extreme point ③ in Figure 5.7.

In summary, we can recognize that a linear programming problem has alternate optima when using the graphical approach by observing that the objective function is parallel to one of the binding constraints. *When using the simplex method, we can recognize alternate optima if $c_j - z_j$ equals zero for one or more of the nonbasic variables in the final simplex tableau.*

Degeneracy

A linear program is said to be *degenerate* if one or more of the basic variables have a value of zero. Degeneracy does not cause any particular difficulties for the graphical solution procedure; however, degeneracy can theoretically cause difficulties when the simplex method is used to solve a linear programming problem.

To see how a degenerate linear program could occur, consider a change in the right-hand-side value of the assembly time constraint for the HighTech problem. For example, what if the number of hours available had been 175 instead of 150? The modified linear program is shown below.

$$\max \quad 50x_1 + 40x_2$$

s.t.

$$3x_1 + 5x_2 \leq 175 \quad \text{Assembly time increased to 175 hours}$$
$$1x_2 \leq 20 \quad \text{Portable display}$$
$$8x_1 + 5x_2 \leq 300 \quad \text{Warehouse space}$$
$$x_1, x_2 \geq 0$$

The simplex tableau after one iteration is presented below.

Basis	c_B	x_1 50	x_2 40	s_1 0	s_2 0	s_3 0	
s_1	0	0	$25/8$	1	0	$-3/8$	$125/2$
s_2	0	0	1	0	1	0	20
x_1	50	1	$5/8$	0	0	$1/8$	$75/2$
	z_j	50	$250/8$	0	0	$50/8$	1875
	$c_j - z_j$	0	$70/8$	0	0	$-50/8$	

The entries in the net evaluation row indicate that x_2 should enter the basis. By calculating the appropriate ratios to determine the pivot element, we obtain

$$\frac{\bar{b}_1}{\bar{a}_{12}} = \frac{125/2}{25/8} = 20$$

$$\frac{\bar{b}_2}{\bar{a}_{22}} = \frac{20}{1} = 20$$

$$\frac{\bar{b}_3}{\bar{a}_{32}} = \frac{75/2}{5/8} = 60$$

We see that there is a tie between the first and second rows. This is an indication that we will have a degenerate basic feasible solution at the next iteration. Recall that when there is a tie, we follow the convention of selecting the uppermost row as the pivot row. This means that s_1 will leave the basis. But from the tie for the minimum ratio we see that the basic variable in row 2, s_2, will also be driven to zero. Since it does not leave the basis, we will have a basic variable with a value of zero after performing this iteration. The simplex tableau after this iteration is as follows:

Basis	c_B	x_1 50	x_2 40	s_1 0	s_2 0	s_3 0	
x_2	40	0	1	$8/25$	0	$-3/25$	20
s_2	0	0	0	$-8/25$	1	$3/25$	0
x_1	50	1	0	$-5/25$	0	$5/25$	25
	z_j	50	40	$70/25$	0	$130/25$	2050
	$c_j - z_j$	0	0	$-70/25$	0	$-130/25$	

As expected, we have a basic feasible solution with one of the basic variables, s_2, equal to zero. Whenever we have a tie in the minimum $\bar{b}_i/\bar{a}_{ij}$ ratio, there will always be a basic variable equal to zero in the next tableau. Since we are at the optimal solution in the above case, we do not care that s_2 is in solution at a zero value. However, if degeneracy occurs at some iteration prior to reaching the optimal solution, it is theoretically possible for the simplex method to cycle; that is, the procedure could possibly alternate between the same set of nonoptimal basic feasible solutions and never reach the optimal solution. Cycling has not proved to be a significant difficulty in practice. Therefore, we do not recommend introducing any special steps into the simplex method to eliminate the possibility that degeneracy will occur. If while performing the iterations of the simplex algorithm a tie occurs for the minimum $\bar{b}_i/\bar{a}_{ij}$ ratio, then we recommend simply selecting the upper row as the pivot row.

▼ NOTES AND COMMENTS ▼

We have stated that infeasibility is recognized when the stopping rule is encountered but one or more artificial variables are in solution at a positive value. We note here that this does not necessarily mean that all artificial variables must be nonbasic to have a feasible solution. An artificial variable could be in solution at a zero value.

▼ SUMMARY

In Chapter 2 we showed how linear programming problems with two decision variables can be solved using the graphical method. In this chapter the simplex method was introduced as an algebraic procedure for solving linear programming problems. Although the simplex method can be used to solve small linear programs by hand calculations, as problems get larger, even the simplex method becomes too cumbersome for efficient hand computation. As a result we must utilize a computer if we want to solve large linear programs in any reasonable length of time. The computational procedures of most computer software packages are based on the simplex method.

We described how developing the tableau form of a linear program is a necessary step in the simplex solution procedure. This required learning how to convert greater-than-or-equal-to constraints, equality constraints, and constraints with negative right-hand-side values into the form necessary to write a linear program in tableau form.

For linear programs with greater-than-or-equal-to constraints and/or equality constraints, artificial variables are used in order to obtain tableau form. An objective function coefficient of $-M$, where M is a very large number, is assigned to each artificial variable. If there is a feasible solution to the real-world problem, all artificial variables will be driven out of solution (or to zero) before the simplex method reaches its stopping criterion. The iterations required to remove the artificial variables from solution constitute what is called phase I of the simplex method.

Two techniques were mentioned for solving minimization problems. The first approach involved changing the rule for introducing a variable into solution and changing the stopping criterion. The second approach involved multiplying the objective function by -1 to obtain an equivalent maximization problem. With this change, any minimization problem can be solved using the steps required for a maximization problem.

As a review of the material in this chapter we now present a detailed step-by-step procedure for solving linear programs using the simplex method.

Step 1 Formulate a linear programming model of the problem.
Step 2 Define an equivalent linear program by performing the following operations.
    a. Multiply each constraint with a negative right-hand-side value by -1, and change the direction of the constraint inequality;
    b. For a minimization problem, convert the problem to an equivalent maximization problem by multiplying the objective function by -1.

Step 3 Set up the standard form representation of the linear program by adding appropriate slack and surplus variables.

Step 4 Set up the tableau form representation of the linear program in order to obtain an initial basic feasible solution. All linear programs must be put in this form before the initial simplex tableau can be obtained.

Step 5 Set up the initial simplex tableau to keep track of the calculations required by the simplex method.

Step 6 Choose the nonbasic variable with the largest $c_j - z_j$ to bring into the basis.

Step 7 Choose as the pivot row that row with the smallest ratio of $\bar{b}_i/\bar{a}_{ij}$ for $\bar{a}_{ij} > 0$. This ratio is used to determine which variable will leave the basis when variable j enters the basis. This ratio also indicates how many units of variable j can be introduced into solution before the basic variable in the ith row equals zero.

Step 8 Perform the necessary elementary row operations to convert the column for the incoming variable to a unit column. Once these row operations have been performed, read the values of the basic variables from the b column of the tableau.

Step 9 Test for optimality. If $c_j - z_j \leq 0$ for all columns, we have the optimal solution. If not, return to step 6.

In Section 5.9 we discussed how the special cases of infeasibility, unboundedness, alternate optima, and degeneracy can occur when solving linear programming problems with the simplex method.

▼ GLOSSARY

Simplex method An algebraic procedure for solving linear programming problems. The simplex method uses elementary row operations to iterate from one basic feasible solution (extreme point) to another until the optimal solution is reached.

Basic solution Given a linear program in standard form, with n variables and m constraints, a basic solution is obtained by setting $n - m$ of the variables equal to zero and solving the constraint equations for the values of the other m variables. If a unique solution exists, it is a basic solution.

Basic feasible solution A basic solution that is also feasible; that is, it satisfies the nonnegativity constraints. A basic feasible solution corresponds to an extreme point.

Elementary row operations Operations that may be performed on a system of simultaneous equations without changing the solution to the system of equations.

Tableau form The form in which a linear program must be written before setting up the initial simplex tableau. When a linear program is written in this form, its A matrix contains m unit columns corresponding to the basic variables, and the values of these basic variables are given by the values in the b column. A further requirement is that the entries in the b column be greater than or equal to zero.

Simplex tableau A table used to keep track of the calculations made when the simplex method is employed.

Unit vector or unit column A vector or column of a matrix, which has a zero in every position except one. In the nonzero position there is a 1. There is a unit column in the simplex tableau for each basic variable.

Net evaluation row The row in the simplex tableau that contains the value of $c_j - z_j$ for every variable (column).

Current solution When carrying out the simplex method, the current solution refers to the current basic feasible solution (extreme point).

Basis   The set of variables that is not restricted to equal zero in the current basic solution. The variables that make up the basis are termed basic variables, and the remaining variables are called nonbasic variables.

Iteration   An iteration of the simplex method consists of the sequence of steps (row operations) performed in moving from one basic feasible solution to another.

Pivot column   The column in the simplex tableau corresponding to the nonbasic variable that is about to be introduced into solution.

Pivot row   The row in the simplex tableau corresponding to the basic variable that will leave the solution.

Pivot element   The element of the simplex tableau that is in both the pivot row and the pivot column.

Artificial variable   A variable that has no physical meaning in terms of the original linear programming problem, but serves merely to enable a basic feasible solution to be created for starting the simplex method. Artificial variables are assigned an objective function coefficient of $-M$, where M is a very large number.

Phase I   When artificial variables are present in the initial simplex tableau, phase I refers to the iterations of the simplex method that are used to drive the artificial variables out of solution. At the end of phase I the basic feasible solution in the simplex tableau is also feasible for the real-world problem.

Degeneracy   When one or more of the basic variables has a value of zero.

▼ PROBLEMS

1. Use elementary row operations to solve the following system of linear equations; that is, find the values of x_1 and x_2 that satisfy both equations.

$$6x_1 + 3x_2 = 33$$
$$10x_1 - 2x_2 = 6$$

2. Use elementary row operations to solve the following system of linear equations; that is, find the values of x_1, x_2, and x_3 that satisfy all three equations.

$$1x_1 + 3x_2 - 1x_3 = 4$$
$$2x_1 + 4x_2 + 2x_3 = 22$$
$$5x_1 - 2x_2 + 1x_3 = 27$$

3. Consider the following linear program:

$$\max \quad 5x_1 + 9x_2$$

s.t.

$$\tfrac{1}{2}x_1 + 1x_2 \le 8$$
$$1x_1 + 1x_2 \ge 10$$
$$\tfrac{1}{4}x_1 + \tfrac{3}{2}x_2 \ge 6$$
$$x_1, x_2 \ge 0$$

a. Write the problem in standard form.

b. How many variables will be set equal to zero in a basic solution for this problem? Explain.

c. Use elementary row operations to find the basic solution that corresponds to s_1 and s_2 equal to zero.

d. Use elementary row operations to find the basic solution that corresponds to x_1 and s_3 equal to zero.

e. Are your solutions for part (c) and/or (d) basic feasible solutions? Extreme-point solutions? Explain.

f. Use the graphical approach to identify the solutions found in parts (c) and (d). Do the graphical results agree with your answer to part (e)? Explain.

4. The following partial initial simplex tableau is given:

Basis	c_B	x_1	x_2	x_3	s_1	s_2	s_3	
		5	20	25	0	0	0	
		2	1	0	1	0	0	40
		0	2	1	0	1	0	30
		3	0	$-\frac{1}{2}$	0	0	1	15
z_j								
$c_j - z_j$								

a. Complete the initial tableau.

b. Write the problem in its tableau form.

c. What is the initial basis? Does this correspond to the origin? Explain.

d. What is the value of the objective function at this initial solution?

e. For the next iteration, what variable should enter the basis, and what variable should leave the basis?

f. How many units of the entering variable will be in the next solution? Before making this first iteration, what should be the value of the objective function after the first iteration?

g. Find the optimal solution using the simplex method.

5. Solve the following linear program using the graphical approach:

$$\max\ 4x_1 + 5x_2$$

s.t.

$$2x_1 + 2x_2 \le 20$$
$$3x_1 + 7x_2 \le 42$$
$$x_1, x_2 \ge 0$$

Put the linear program in tableau form, and solve using the simplex method. Show the sequence of extreme points generated by the simplex method on your graph.

6. Explain in your own words why the tableau form and the standard form are the same for problems with less-than-or-equal-to constraints and nonnegative b_i's.

7. Solve the Ryland Farm problem (Chapter 2, problem 30) using the simplex method. Locate the solution found at each iteration on the graph of the feasible region.

8. Recall the Par, Inc., problem introduced in Section 2.1. The complete mathematical model for this problem, originally presented in Section 2.4, is restated below:

$$\max \quad 10x_1 + 9x_2$$

s.t.

$$\begin{array}{ll} \frac{7}{10}x_1 + 1x_2 \le 630 & \text{Cutting and dyeing} \\ \frac{1}{2}x_1 + \frac{5}{6}x_2 \le 600 & \text{Sewing} \\ 1x_1 + \frac{2}{3}x_2 \le 708 & \text{Finishing} \\ \frac{1}{10}x_1 + \frac{1}{4}x_2 \le 135 & \text{Inspecting and packaging} \\ x_1, x_2 \ge 0 \end{array}$$

where

$$x_1 = \text{number of standard bags produced}$$
$$x_2 = \text{number of deluxe bags produced}$$

a. Use the simplex method to determine how many bags of each model Par should manufacture?
b. What is the profit Par can earn with the above production quantities?
c. How many hours of production time will be scheduled for each operation?
d. What is the slack time in each operation?

9. Solve the RMC problem (Chapter 2, problem 31) using the simplex method. At each iteration, locate the basic feasible solution found by the simplex method on the graph of the feasible region.

10. Solve the following linear program:

$$\max \quad 2.5x_1 + 5x_2 + 1x_3 + 1x_4$$

s.t.

$$\begin{array}{l} 1x_1 + 1.4x_2 + 0.2x_3 + 0.8x_4 \le 1600 \\ 2x_1 + 2x_2 + 1.6x_3 + 1x_4 \le 1300 \\ 1.2x_1 + 1x_2 + 1x_3 + 1.2x_4 \le 960 \\ x_1, x_2, x_3, x_4 \ge 0 \end{array}$$

11. Solve the following linear program using both the graphical and the simplex methods:

$$\max \quad 2x_1 + 8x_2$$

s.t.

$$\begin{array}{l} 3x_1 + 9x_2 \le 45 \\ 2x_1 + 1x_2 \ge 12 \\ x_1, x_2 \ge 0 \end{array}$$

Show graphically how the simplex method moves from one basic feasible solution to another. Find the coordinates of all extreme points of the feasible region.

12. How many basic solutions are there to a linear program that has seven variables and four constraints when written in standard form?

13. Explain in your own words why, when we are trying to determine which basic variable to eliminate at a particular iteration, we consider only the $\bar{a}_{ij}$ that are strictly greater than zero.

14. Referring to problem 8, suppose that instead of introducing x_1 into the solution at the first iteration of the simplex method for the Par, Inc., problem, you had mistakenly introduced x_2.
   a. Conduct the simplex calculations for the Par, Inc., problem, and introduce x_2 into the basis at the first iteration. Then continue with the simplex method until an optimal solution has been reached.
   b. Do we always have to introduce the variable into the solution that has the largest $c_j - z_j$ value?
   c. Why does the criterion for introducing the variable into the solution use the largest $c_j - z_j$ value?
15. Suppose that we did not remove the basic variable with the smallest ratio of $\bar{b}_i/\bar{a}_{ij}$ at a particular iteration. What effect would this have on the simplex tableau for our next solution?
16. Suppose a company manufactures three products from two raw materials where

	Product A	Product B	Product C
Raw material I	7 lb	6 lb	3 lb
Raw material II	5 lb	4 lb	2 lb

If the company has available 100 pounds of material I and 200 pounds of material II, and if the profits for the three products are $20, $20, and $15, how much of each product should be produced in order to maximize profits?

17. Liva's Lumber, Inc., manufactures three types of plywood. The data below summarize the production hours per unit in each of three production operations and other data for the problem.

| | Operations (hours) | | | Profit/ |
Plywood	I	II	III	Unit
Grade A	2	2	4	$40
Grade B	5	5	2	$30
Grade X	10	3	2	$20
Maximum time available	900	400	600	

How many units of each grade of lumber should be produced?

18. Ye Olde Cording Winery in Peoria, Illinois, makes three kinds of authentic German wine: Heidelberg Sweet, Heidelberg Regular, and Deutschland Extra Dry. The raw materials, labor, and profit for a gallon of each of these wines are summarized below.

Wine	Grapes Grade A (bushels)	Grapes Grade B (bushels)	Sugar (pounds)	Labor (hours)	Profit/ Gallon
Heidelberg Sweet	1	1	2	2	$1.00
Heidelberg Regular	2	0	1	3	$1.20
Deutschland Extra Dry	0	2	0	1	$2.00

If the winery has 150 bushels of grade A grapes, 150 bushels of grade B grapes, 80 pounds of sugar, and 225 labor-hours available during the next week, what product mix of wines will maximize the company's profit?

a. Solve by the simplex method.

b. Interpret all slack variables.

c. An increase in what resources could improve the company's profit?

19. Set up the tableau form for the following linear program (do not attempt to solve):

$$\max \quad 4x_1 + 2x_2 - 3x_3 + 5x_4$$

s.t.

$$2x_1 - 1x_2 + 1x_3 + 2x_4 \geq 50$$
$$3x_1 \qquad - 1x_3 + 2x_4 \leq 80$$
$$1x_1 + 1x_2 \qquad + 1x_4 = 60$$
$$x_1, x_2, x_3, x_4 \geq 0$$

20. Set up the tableau form for the following linear program (do not attempt to solve):

$$\min \quad 4x_1 + 5x_2 + 3x_3$$

s.t.

$$4x_1 \qquad + 2x_3 \geq \quad 20$$
$$1x_2 - 1x_3 \leq -8$$
$$1x_1 - 2x_2 \qquad = -5$$
$$2x_1 + 1x_2 + 1x_3 \leq \quad 12$$
$$x_1, x_2, x_3 \geq 0$$

21. Solve the following linear program:

$$\min \quad 3x_1 + 4x_2 + 8x_3$$

s.t.

$$4x_1 + 2x_2 \qquad \geq 12$$
$$4x_2 + 8x_3 \geq 16$$
$$x_1, x_2, x_3 \geq 0$$

22. Solve the following linear program:

$$\min \quad 4x_1 + 2x_2 + 3x_3$$

s.t.

$$1x_1 + 3x_2 \qquad \geq 15$$
$$1x_1 \qquad + 2x_3 \geq 10$$
$$2x_1 + 1x_2 \qquad \geq 20$$
$$x_1, x_2, x_3 \geq 0$$

23. Captain John's Yachts, Inc., located in Fort Lauderdale, Florida, rents three types of ocean-going boats: sailboats, cabin cruisers, and Captain John's favorite, the luxury yachts. Captain John advertises his boats with his famous "you rent—we pilot" slogan, which means that the company supplies the captain and crew for each rented

boat. Each rented boat, of course, has one captain, but the crew sizes (that is, deck hands, galley hands, and so on) differ. The crew requirements, in addition to a captain, are one for sailboats, two for cabin cruisers, and three for yachts. Ten employees are captains, and an additional 18 employees qualify for the crew positions. Currently Captain John has rental requests for all of his boats: four sailboats, eight cabin cruisers, and three luxury yachts. If Captain John's daily profit is $50 for sailboats, $70 for cruisers, and $100 for luxury yachts, how many boats of each type should he rent?

24. The Our-Bags-Don't-Break (OBDB) plastic bag company manufactures three plastic refuse bags for home use: a 20-gallon garbage bag, a 30-gallon garbage bag, and a 33-gallon leaf and grass bag. Using purchased plastic material, three operations are required to produce each end product: cutting, sealing, and packaging. The production time required to process each type of bag in every operation and the maximum production time available for each operation are shown below (note that the production time figures in this table are per box of each type of bag)

	Production Time (seconds/box)		
Type of Bag	*Cutting*	*Sealing*	*Packaging*
20 gallons	2	2	3
30 gallons	3	2	4
33 gallons	3	3	5
Time available	2 hours	3 hours	4 hours

If OBDB makes a profit of $0.10 for each box of 20-gallon bags produced, $0.15 for each box of 30-gallon bags, and $0.20 for each box of 33-gallon bags, what is the optimal product mix?

25. Kirkman Brothers ice cream parlors sell three different flavors of Dairy Sweet ice milk: chocolate, vanilla, and banana. Due to extremely hot weather and a high demand for its products, Kirkman has run short of its supply of ingredients: milk, sugar, and cream. Hence, Kirkman will not be able to fill all the orders received from its retail outlets, the ice cream parlors. Due to these circumstances, Kirkman has decided to make the best amounts of the three flavors, given the constraints on supply of the basic ingredients. The company will then ration the ice milk to the retail outlets.

   Kirkman has collected the following data on profitability of the various flavors, availability of supplies, and amounts required for each flavor.

		Usage/Gallon		
Flavor	**Profit/ Gallon**	*Milk (gallons)*	*Sugar (pounds)*	*Cream (gallons)*
Chocolate	$1.00	0.45	0.50	0.10
Vanilla	$0.90	0.50	0.40	0.15
Banana	$0.95	0.40	0.40	0.20
Maximum available		200	150	60

Determine the optimal product mix for Kirkman Brothers. What additional resources could be used profitably?

26. Uforia Corporation sells two different brands of perfume: Incentive and Temptation No. 1. Uforia sells exclusively through department stores and employs a three-person sales staff to call on its customers. The amount of sales time necessary for each sales representative to sell one case of each product varies with experience and ability. Data on the average time for each of Uforia's three sales reps is presented below.

	Average Sales Time per Case (minutes)	
Salesperson	Incentive	Temptation No.1
John	10	15
Brenda	15	10
Red	12	6

Each sales representative spends approximately 80 hours per month in the actual selling of these two products. Cases of Incentive and Temptation No. 1 sell at profits of $30 and $25, respectively. How many cases of each perfume should each person sell during the next month in order to maximize the firm's profits? (*Hint:* Let x_1 = number of cases of Incentive sold by John, x_2 = number of cases of Temptation No. 1 sold by John, x_3 = number of cases of Incentive sold by Brenda, and so on.)

27. Recall the RMC problem (Chapter 2, problem 31). Letting

$$x_1 = \text{tons of fuel additive produced}$$

$$x_2 = \text{tons of solvent base produced}$$

leads to the following formulation of the RMC problem:

$$\max \quad 40x_1 + 30x_2$$

s.t.

$$\frac{2}{5}x_1 + \frac{1}{2}x_2 \leq 20 \quad \text{Material 1}$$
$$\frac{1}{5}x_2 \leq 5 \quad \text{Material 2}$$
$$\frac{3}{5}x_1 + \frac{3}{10}x_2 \leq 21 \quad \text{Material 3}$$
$$x_1, x_2 \geq 0$$

Suppose management required that at least 10 tons of each product be produced. Modify the above formulation, as appropriate, and solve using the simplex method.

28. Catalina Yachts, Inc., is a builder of cruising sailboats. It manufactures three models of sailboats: the C-32, the C-40, and the C-48. The company, because of its excellent reputation, is in the position of being able to sell all the boats it manufactures. Catalina is currently in the process of taking orders for the coming year. How many orders for each model should be accepted in order to maximize profits?

The manufacture of each model requires different amounts of time spent on each of three operations: molding, carpentry, and finishing. The number of days required to perform each of these activities on the three models is given below.

	Production Time (person-days)		
Model	Molding	Carpentry	Finishing
C-32	3	5	4
C-40	5	12	5
C-48	10	18	8

Based on past experience, management expects the profit per boat to be $5000 on the C-32, $10,000 on the C-40, and $20,000 on the C-48.

Catalina currently has 40 people employed in manufacturing these sailboats: 10 in molding, 20 in carpentry, and 10 in finishing. On the average each employee works 240 days per year. The only other constraint is a management-imposed restriction on the number of C-48 models that may be sold. Because Catalina does not want the C-48 to become commonplace, it will not take orders for more than 20 of this model.

Note: In problems 29 to 34, we provide examples of linear programs that result in one or more of the following situations:

(1) Optimal solution
(2) Infeasible solution
(3) Unbounded solution
(4) Alternate optimal solution
(5) Degenerate solution

For each linear program, determine the solution situation that exists, and indicate how you identified each situation using the simplex method. For the problems with alternate optimal solutions, calculate at least two optimal solutions.

29. max $\quad 4x_1 + 8x_2$

s.t.

$$2x_1 + 2x_2 \leq 10$$
$$-1x_1 + 1x_2 \geq 8$$
$$x_1, x_2 \geq 0$$

30. min $\quad 3x_1 + 3x_2$

s.t.

$$2x_1 + 0.5x_2 \geq 10$$
$$2x_1 \qquad\quad \geq 4$$
$$4x_1 + 4x_2 \geq 32$$
$$x_1, x_2 \geq 0$$

31. max $\quad 1x_1 + 1x_2$

s.t.

$$8x_1 + 6x_2 \geq 24$$
$$4x_1 + 6x_2 \geq -12$$
$$2x_2 \geq 4$$
$$x_1, x_2 \geq 0$$

32. max $\quad 2x_1 + 1x_2 + 1x_3$

s.t.

$$4x_1 + 2x_2 + 2x_3 \geq 4$$
$$2x_1 + 4x_2 \qquad \leq 20$$
$$4x_1 + 8x_2 + 2x_3 \leq 16$$
$$x_1, x_2, x_3 \geq 0$$

33. max $\quad 2x_1 + 4x_2$

s.t.

$$1x_1 + \tfrac{1}{2}x_2 \leq 10$$
$$1x_1 + 1x_2 = 12$$
$$1x_1 + \tfrac{3}{2}x_2 \leq 18$$
$$x_1, x_2 \geq 0$$

34. min $\quad -4x_1 + 5x_2 + 5x_3$

s.t.

$$-1x_2 + 1x_3 \geq 2$$
$$-1x_1 + 1x_2 + 1x_3 \geq 1$$
$$1x_3 \leq -1$$
$$x_1, x_2, x_3 \geq 0$$

35. Supersport Footballs, Inc., manufactures three kinds of football: an All-Pro model, a College model, and a High School model. All three footballs require operations in the following departments: cutting and dyeing, sewing, and inspecting and packaging. The production times and maximum production availabilities are shown below.

	Production Time (minutes)		
Model	*Cutting and Dyeing*	*Sewing*	*Inspecting and Packaging*
All-Pro	12	15	3
College	10	15	4
High School	8	12	2
Time available	300 hours	200 hours	100 hours

Current orders indicate that at least 1000 All-Pro footballs must be manufactured.

a. If Supersport realizes a profit of $3 for each All-Pro model, $5 for each College model, and $4 for each High School model, how many footballs of each type should be produced? What occurs in the solution of this problem? Why?

b. If Supersport can increase sewing time to 300 hours and inspecting and packaging time to 150 hours by using overtime, what is your recommendation?

6

Simplex-Based Sensitivity Analysis and Duality

In Chapter 3 we defined sensitivity analysis as the study of how the optimal solution and the value of the optimal solution to a linear program change, given changes in the various coefficients of the problem. First, we showed how graphical sensitivity analysis can be performed for linear programs involving two decision variables; then, as part of the discussion of the computer solution of linear programs, we showed how sensitivity analysis can be performed with the help of computer output. In this chapter we discuss how the sensitivity analysis information contained in the computer solution of linear programs is developed. As we will show, the final simplex tableau contains the information that is used to compute the shadow and/or dual prices, as well as ranges for the objective function coefficients and ranges for the right-hand-side values. The topic of duality is also introduced. We will see that associated with every linear programming problem is a dual problem that has an interesting economic interpretation.

6.1 ▼ SENSITIVITY ANALYSIS WITH THE SIMPLEX TABLEAU

The usual sensitivity analysis for linear programs involves computing ranges for the objective function coefficients and the right-hand-side values, as well as shadow and/or dual prices.

Objective Function Coefficients

Sensitivity analysis for an objective function coefficient involves placing a range on the coefficient's value. We call this range the *range of optimality*. As long as the actual value of the objective function coefficient is within the range of optimality, *the current basic feasible solution will remain optimal*. Thus, for a nonbasic variable the range of optimality defines the possible objective function coefficient values for which that variable will remain nonbasic. In contrast, the range of optimality for a basic variable defines the objective function coefficient values for which that variable will remain basic, and hence part of the current optimal basic feasible solution.

In computing the range of optimality for an objective function coefficient, all other coefficients in the problem are assumed to remain at their original values; in other words, *only one coefficient is allowed to change at a time*. To illustrate the process of computing ranges for objective function coefficients, recall the HighTech linear programming problem introduced in Chapter 5. The linear program that we developed for this problem is restated below.

$$\max \quad 50x_1 + 40x_2$$

s.t.

$$3x_1 + 5x_2 \leq 150 \quad \text{Assembly time}$$
$$1x_2 \leq 20 \quad \text{Portable display}$$
$$8x_1 + 5x_2 \leq 300 \quad \text{Warehouse space}$$
$$x_1, x_2 \geq 0$$

where

$$x_1 = \text{number of units of the Deskpro assembled}$$
$$x_2 = \text{number of units of the Portable assembled}$$

The final simplex tableau for the HighTech problem is reproduced below.

Basis	c_B	x_1	x_2	s_1	s_2	s_3	
		50	40	0	0	0	
x_2	40	0	1	$8/25$	0	$-3/25$	12
s_2	0	0	0	$-8/25$	1	$3/25$	8
x_1	50	1	0	$-5/25$	0	$5/25$	30
z_j		50	40	$14/5$	0	$26/5$	1980
$c_j - z_j$		0	0	$-14/5$	0	$-26/5$	

Recall that when the simplex method is used to solve a linear program, an optimal solution is recognized when all entries in the net evaluation row ($c_j - z_j$) are ≤ 0. Since the above simplex tableau satisfies this criterion, the solution shown is optimal. However, if a change in one of the objective function coefficients were to cause one or more of the $c_j - z_j$ values to become positive, then the current solution would no longer be optimal; in such a case one or more additional simplex iterations would be necessary to find the new optimal solution. *Thus, we conclude that the range of optimality for an objective function coefficient is determined by those coefficient values that maintain*

$$c_j - z_j \leq 0 \tag{6.1}$$

for all values of j.

To illustrate how the range of optimality is determined, we will compute the range of optimality for c_1, the profit per unit of the Deskpro. Using c_1 (instead of 50) as the objective function coefficient of x_1, the revised final simplex tableau is as follows:

Basis	c_B	x_1 c_1	x_2 40	s_1 0	s_2 0	s_3 0	
x_2	40	0	1	$8/25$	0	$-3/25$	12
s_2	0	0	0	$-8/25$	1	$3/25$	8
x_1	c_1	1	0	$-5/25$	0	$5/25$	30
z_j		c_1	40	$\dfrac{64 - c_1}{5}$	0	$\dfrac{c_1 - 24}{5}$	$480 + 30c_1$
$c_j - z_j$		0	0	$\dfrac{c_1 - 64}{5}$	0	$\dfrac{24 - c_1}{5}$	

Since the $c_j - z_j$ entries for the basic variables are all still zero, the current solution will remain optimal as long as the value of c_1 results in $c_j - z_j \leq 0$ for the two nonbasic variables s_1 and s_3. Hence, we must have

$$\frac{c_1 - 64}{5} \leq 0$$

and

$$\frac{24 - c_1}{5} \leq 0$$

Using the first inequality, we obtain

$$c_1 - 64 \leq 0$$

or

$$c_1 \leq 64 \tag{6.2}$$

Similarly, from the second inequality we see that

$$24 - c_1 \leq 0$$

or

$$24 \leq c_1 \tag{6.3}$$

Since c_1 must satisfy both (6.2) and (6.3), the range of optimality for c_1 is as given by

$$24 \leq c_1 \leq 64 \tag{6.4}$$

To see how management of HighTech can make use of the above sensitivity analysis information, suppose an increase in material costs reduces the profit contribution per unit for the Deskpro to \$30. The range of optimality indicates that the current solution ($x_1 = 30$, $x_2 = 12$, $s_1 = 0$, $s_2 = 8$, $s_3 = 0$) is still optimal. To verify this, let us recompute the final simplex tableau after reducing the value of c_1 to 30.

		x_1	x_2	s_1	s_2	s_3	
Basis	c_B	30	40	0	0	0	
x_2	40	0	1	$8/25$	0	$-3/25$	12
s_2	0	0	0	$-8/25$	1	$3/25$	8
x_1	30	1	0	$-5/25$	0	$5/25$	30
z_j		30	40	$34/5$	0	$6/5$	1380
$c_j - z_j$		0	0	$-34/5$	0	$-6/5$	

Since $c_j - z_j \leq 0$ for all variables, the original solution is still optimal. That is, the optimal solution with $c_1 = 30$ is the same as the optimal solution with $c_1 = 50$. Note, however, that the decrease in profit contribution per unit of the Deskpro has caused a reduction in total profit from \$1980 to \$1380.

What if the profit contribution per unit were reduced even further—say, to \$20? Referring to the range of optimality for c_1 given by (6.4), we see that $c_1 = 20$ is outside the range; thus, we know that a change this large will cause a new basis to be optimal. To verify this, consider modifying the above final simplex tableau by replacing c_1 by 20 (instead of 30).

		x_1	x_2	s_1	s_2	s_3	
Basis	c_B	20	40	0	0	0	
x_2	40	0	1	$8/25$	0	$-3/25$	12
s_2	0	0	0	$-8/25$	1	$3/25$	8
x_1	20	1	0	$-5/25$	0	$5/25$	30
z_j		20	40	$44/5$	0	$-4/5$	1080
$c_j - z_j$		0	0	$-44/5$	0	$4/5$	

As expected, the current solution ($x_1 = 30$, $x_2 = 12$, $s_1 = 0$, $s_2 = 8$, and $s_3 = 0$) is no longer optimal since the entry in the s_3 column of the net evaluation row is greater than zero. This implies that at least one more simplex iteration must be performed to reach the optimal solution. You should continue to perform the simplex iterations (by introducing s_3) on the above tableau to verify that the new optimal solution will require the production of $16\frac{2}{3}$ units of the Deskpro and 20 units of the Portable.

The procedure we used to compute the range of optimality for c_1 is the general procedure used for any basic variable. Compute inequality (6.1) for each nonbasic variable; the smallest upper bound is the upper limit, and the largest lower bound is the lower limit of the range. The procedure for computing the range of optimality for nonbasic variables is even easier since a change in the objective function coefficient for a nonbasic variable causes only one $c_j - z_j$ entry to change in the final simplex tableau. To illustrate the approach, we show below the final simplex tableau for the original HighTech problem after replacing 0, the objective function coefficient for s_1, with the coefficient c_{s_1}.

Basis	c_B	x_1 50	x_2 40	s_1 c_{s_1}	s_2 0	s_3 0	
x_2	40	0	1	$8/25$	0	$-3/25$	12
s_2	0	0	0	$-8/25$	1	$3/25$	8
x_1	50	1	0	$-5/25$	0	$5/25$	30
	z_j	50	40	$14/5$	0	$26/5$	1980
	$c_j - z_j$	0	0	$c_{s_1} - 14/5$	0	$-26/5$	

Note that the only changes in the tableau are in the s_1 column. In applying inequality (6.1) to compute the range of optimality, we get

$$c_{s_1} - 14/5 \leq 0$$

and hence

$$c_{s_1} \leq 14/5$$

Therefore, as long as the objective function coefficient for s_1 is less than or equal to $14/5$, the current solution will be optimal. Since there is no lower bound on how much the coefficient may be decreased, we write the range of optimality for c_{s_1} as

$$-\infty < c_{s_1} \leq 14/5$$

The same approach works for all nonbasic variables. In a maximization problem there is no lower limit on the range of optimality, and the upper limit is given by z_j. Thus, the range of optimality for the objective function coefficient of any nonbasic variable is given by

$$-\infty < c_j \leq z_j \tag{6.5}$$

Since s_1 is a slack variable in the HighTech problem, its objective function coefficient is not subject to variability. That is, the objective function coefficient for s_1 will always be zero, and hence s_1 would never be brought into the solution. But, as we will see in the next section, the upper limit on the range for a nonbasic slack variable provides the shadow price for the corresponding constraint.

Let us summarize the steps necessary to compute the range of optimality for objective function coefficients. In stating the steps we assume that it is desired to compute the range of optimality for c_k, the coefficient of x_k, in a maximization problem. Keep in mind that x_k in this context may refer to one of the original decision variables, a slack variable, or a surplus variable.

Steps to Compute the Range of Optimality

Step 1 Replace the numerical value of the objective function coefficient for x_k with c_k everywhere it appears in the final simplex tableau.

Step 2 If variable x_k is a basic variable, recompute $c_j - z_j$ for each nonbasic variable; if x_k is a nonbasic variable, it is only necessary to recompute $c_k - z_k$.

Step 3 Requiring that $c_j - z_j \leq 0$, solve each inequality for any upper or lower bounds on c_k. If there are two or more upper bounds on c_k, the smaller of these is the upper bound on the range of optimality. If there are two or more lower bounds, the largest of these is the lower bound on the range of optimality.

Step 4 If the original problem is a minimization problem that was converted to a maximization problem in order to apply the simplex method, multiply the inequalities obtained in step 3 by -1, and change the direction of the inequalities to obtain the ranges of optimality for the original minimization problem.

By using the range of optimality to determine whether a change in an objective function coefficient is large enough to cause a change in the optimal solution, we can often avoid the process of formulating and solving a modified linear programming problem.

Right-Hand-Side Values

In many linear programming problems we can interpret the right-hand-side values (the b_i's) as the resources available. For instance, in the HighTech Industries problem the right-hand side of constraint 1 represents the available assembly time, the right-hand side of constraint 2 represents the number of Portable display units available, and the right-hand side of constraint 3 represents the available warehouse space. Shadow prices provide information on the value of additional resources; the ranges over which these shadow prices are valid are given by the ranges for the right-hand-side values.

Shadow Prices. In Chapter 3 we stated that the change in value of the objective function per-unit increase in a constraint's right-hand-side value is called a *shadow price*.[1] When the simplex method is used to solve a linear programming problem, the values of the shadow prices are easy to obtain. They are found in the z_j row of the final simplex tableau. To illustrate this point, the final simplex tableau for the HighTech problem is again reproduced.

Basis	c_B	x_1 50	x_2 40	s_1 0	s_2 0	s_3 0	
x_2	40	0	1	$8/25$	0	$-3/25$	12
s_2	0	0	0	$-8/25$	1	$3/25$	8
x_1	50	1	0	$-5/25$	0	$5/25$	30
z_j		50	40	$14/5$	0	$26/5$	1980
$c_j - z_j$		0	0	$-14/5$	0	$-26/5$	

The z_j values for the three slack variables are $14/5$, 0, and $26/5$, respectively. Thus, the shadow price for the assembly time constraint is $14/5 = 2.80$, the shadow price for the Portable display constraint is 0.00, and the shadow price for the warehouse space constraint is $26/5 = 5.20$. We see that obtaining more warehouse space will have the biggest positive impact on HighTech's profit.

To see why the z_j values for the slack variables in the final simplex tableau are the shadow prices, let us first consider the case for slack variables that are part of the optimal basic feasible solution. Each of these slack variables will have a z_j value of zero, implying

---

[1]The dual prices provided by LINDO/PC and The Management Scientist are closely related (see Chapter 3). The dual price gives the improvement in the objective function per-unit increase in the right-hand side. For maximization problems the shadow and dual prices are the same; for minimization problems the dual price is the negative of the shadow price.

a shadow price of zero for the corresponding constraint. For example, consider slack variable s_2, a basic variable in the HighTech problem. This variable was added to the constraint $1x_2 \leq 20$ (Portable display) in order to set up the standard form representation of the problem. With s_2 added to the left-hand side, we obtained

$$1x_2 + 1s_2 = 20$$

Algebraically we see that s_2 is the difference between the number of Portable display units available and the number of those actually used in the optimal solution.

Since $s_2 = 8$ in the optimal solution, HighTech will have 8 Portable display units unused. Consequently, how much would management of HighTech Industries be willing to pay to obtain additional Portable display units? Clearly the answer is nothing since at the optimal solution HighTech has an excess of this particular component. Additional amounts of this resource are of no value to the company, and, consequently, the shadow price for this constraint is zero. In general, if a slack variable is a basic variable in the optimal solution, the value of z_j—and hence the shadow price of the corresponding resource—is zero.

Consider the nonbasic slack variables—for example, s_1. In the previous subsection we determined that the current solution will remain optimal as long as the objective function coefficient for s_1 (denoted c_{s_1}) stays in the following range:

$$-\infty < c_{s_1} \leq {14}/_5$$

That is, $s_1 = 0$ as long as the objective function coefficient for s_1 is less than or equal to 14/5. Thus, HighTech would not allow any slack to occur in the first constraint unless it is worth more than $14/5 = 2.80$ per hour to do so. In other words, HighTech should use all of its assembly time unless it is paid more than \$2.80 per hour not to use it. We can conclude then that \$2.80 is the value to HighTech of 1 hour of assembly time used in the production of Deskpro and Portable computers. Thus, if additional time can be obtained, HighTech should be willing to pay up to \$2.80 per hour for it.

A similar interpretation can be given to the z_j value for each of the nonbasic slack variables. That is, z_j is the value of one additional unit of the resource in the row corresponding to that slack variable.

With a greater-than-or-equal-to constraint, the value of the shadow price for a maximization problem will be less than or equal to zero because a one-unit increase in the value of the right-hand side cannot be helpful; it makes it more difficult to satisfy the constraint. As a result, for a maximization problem the optimal value of the objective function can be expected to decrease when the right-hand side of a greater-than-or-equal-to constraint is increased. The shadow price gives the amount of the expected change—a negative number, since we expect a decrease. As a result, the shadow price for a greater-than-or-equal-to constraint is given by the negative of the z_j entry for the corresponding surplus variable in the optimal simplex tableau.

Finally, it is possible to compute shadow prices for equality constraints. They are given by the z_j values for the corresponding artificial variables. We will not develop this case in detail here since we have recommended dropping each artificial variable column from the simplex tableau as soon as the corresponding artificial variable leaves the basis.

To summarize, when the simplex method is used to solve a linear programming problem, the shadow prices for the constraints are contained in the final simplex tableau. The following table summarizes the method for determining the shadow prices for the various constraint types in a maximization problem solved by the simplex method.

Constraint Type	Shadow Price Given by
$\leq$	z_j value for the slack variable associated with the constraint
$\geq$	Negative of the z_j value for the surplus variable associated with the constraint
$=$	z_j value for the artificial variable associated with the constraint

Recall that we convert a minimization problem to a maximization problem by multiplying the objective function by -1 before using the simplex method. Therefore, for minimization problems we need to multiply the shadow prices computed from the simplex tableau for the equivalent maximization problem by -1 in order to determine the effect of a right-hand-side change on the original minimization problem.

Range of Feasibility. As we have just seen, the z_j row in the final simplex tableau can be used to determine the shadow price and as a result predict the change in the value of the objective function corresponding to a unit change in a b_i. This interpretation is only valid, however, as long as the change in b_i is not large enough to make the current basic solution infeasible. Thus, we will be interested in calculating a range of values over which a particular b_i can vary without any of the current basic variables becoming infeasible (i.e., less than zero). This range of values will be referred to as the *range of feasibility*.

To demonstrate the effect of changing a b_i, consider increasing the amount of assembly time available in the HighTech problem from 150 to 160 hours. Will the current basis still yield a feasible solution? If so, given the shadow price of $2.80 for the assembly time constraint, we can expect an increase in the value of the objective function of $10(2.80) = 28$. Shown below is the final simplex tableau corresponding to an increase in the assembly time of 10 hours.

		x_1	x_2	s_1	s_2	s_3	
Basis	c_B	50	40	0	0	0	
x_2	40	0	1	$8/25$	0	$-3/25$	15.2
s_2	0	0	0	$-8/25$	1	$3/25$	4.8
x_1	50	1	0	$-5/25$	0	$5/25$	28.0
	z_j	50	40	$14/5$	0	$26/5$	2008
	$c_j - z_j$	0	0	$-14/5$	0	$-26/5$	

The same basis, consisting of the basic variables x_2, s_2, and x_1, is feasible since all the basic variables are nonnegative. Note also that, just as we predicted, the value of the optimal solution has increased by 28 (from 1980 to 2008).

You may wonder whether we had to resolve the problem completely to find this new solution. The answer is no! The only changes in the final simplex tableau (as compared with the final simplex tableau with $b_1 = 150$) are the differences in the values of the basic variables and the value of the objective function. That is, only the last column of the simplex tableau has changed. The entries in this new last column of the simplex tableau were obtained by merely adding 10 times the first four entries in the s_1 column to the last column in the previous tableau:

$$
\begin{array}{c}
\text{New} \\
\text{solution}
\end{array}
=
\underset{\substack{\text{Old} \\ \text{solution}}}{\begin{bmatrix} 12 \\ 8 \\ \underline{30} \\ 1980 \end{bmatrix}}
+ \underset{\substack{\text{Change} \\ \text{in } b_1}}{10}
\underset{s_1 \text{ column}}{\begin{bmatrix} 8/25 \\ -8/25 \\ \underline{-5/25} \\ 14/5 \end{bmatrix}}
=
\underset{\substack{\text{New} \\ \text{solution}}}{\begin{bmatrix} 15.2 \\ 4.8 \\ \underline{28.0} \\ 2008 \end{bmatrix}}
$$

Let us now consider why this procedure can be used to find the new solution. First, recall that each of the coefficients in the s_1 column indicates the amount of decrease in the corresponding basic variable that would result from increasing s_1 by one unit. In other words, these coefficients tell us how many units of each of the corresponding current basic variables will be driven out of solution if one unit of variable s_1 is brought into solution. Bringing one unit of s_1 into solution, however, is the same as reducing the availability of assembly time (decreasing b_1) by one unit; increasing b_1, the available assembly time, by one unit has just the opposite effect. Therefore, the entries in the s_1 column can also be interpreted as the changes in the values of the current basic variables corresponding to a one-unit increase in b_1.

The change in the value of the objective function corresponding to a one-unit increase in b_1 is given by the value of z_j in that column (the shadow price). In the foregoing case the availability of assembly time increased by 10 units; thus, we multiplied the first four entries in the s_1 column by 10 to obtain the change in value of the solution.

How do we know when a change in b_1 is so large that the current basis will become infeasible? We shall first answer this question specifically for the HighTech Industries problem and then state the general procedure for less-than-or-equal-to constraints. The approach taken with greater-than-or-equal-to and equality constraints will then be discussed.

We begin by showing how to compute upper and lower bounds for the maximum amount that b_1 can be changed before the current optimal basis becomes infeasible. We have seen how to find the new basic feasible solution values, given a 10-unit increase in b_1. In general, given a change in b_1 of Δb_1, the new values for the basic variables in the HighTech problem are given by

$$
\begin{bmatrix} x_2 \\ s_2 \\ x_1 \end{bmatrix}
=
\begin{bmatrix} 12 \\ 8 \\ 30 \end{bmatrix}
+ \Delta b_1
\begin{bmatrix} 8/25 \\ -8/25 \\ -5/25 \end{bmatrix}
=
\begin{bmatrix} 12 + 8/25\,\Delta b_1 \\ 8 - 8/25\,\Delta b_1 \\ 30 - 5/25\,\Delta b_1 \end{bmatrix}
\tag{6.6}
$$

As long as the new value of each basic variable remains nonnegative, the current basis will remain feasible and therefore optimal. We can keep the basic variables nonnegative by limiting the change in b_1 (that is, Δb_1) so that we satisfy each of the following conditions:

$$
12 + 8/25\Delta b_1 \geq 0 \tag{6.7}
$$

$$
8 - 8/25\Delta b_1 \geq 0 \tag{6.8}
$$

$$
30 - 5/25\Delta b_1 \geq 0 \tag{6.9}
$$

Note that the left-hand sides of the above inequalities represent the new values of the basic variables after b_1 has been changed by Δb_1.

Solving for Δb_1 in inequalities (6.7), (6.8), and (6.9), we obtain

$$\Delta b_1 \geq (25/8)(-12) = -37.5$$

$$\Delta b_1 \leq (-25/8)(-8) = 25$$

$$\Delta b_1 \leq (-25/5)(-30) = 150$$

Since all three inequalities must be satisfied, the most restrictive limits on b_1 must be satisfied in order for all the current basic variables to remain nonnegative. Therefore, Δb_1 must satisfy

$$-37.5 \leq \Delta b_1 \leq 25 \tag{6.10}$$

The initial amount of assembly time available was 150 hours. Therefore, $b_1 = 150 + \Delta b_1$, where b_1 is the amount of assembly time available. We add 150 to each of the three terms in expression (6.10) to obtain

$$112.5 \leq 150 + \Delta b_1 \leq 175 \tag{6.11}$$

Replacing $150 + \Delta b_1$ with b_1, we obtain the range of feasibility for b_1:

$$112.5 \leq b_1 \leq 175$$

This range of feasibility for b_1 indicates that as long as the available assembly time is between 112.5 and 175 hours, the current optimal basis will remain feasible. This is why we call this range the range of feasibility.

Since the shadow price for b_1 (assembly time) is $14/5$, we know profit can be increased by \$2.80 by obtaining an additional hour of assembly time. Suppose then that we increase b_1 by 25; that is, we increase b_1 to the upper limit of its range of feasibility, 175. The profit will increase to $\$1980 + (\$2.80)25 = \$2050$, and the values of the optimal basic variables become

$$x_2 = 12 + 25(8/25) = 20$$

$$s_2 = 8 + 25(-8/25) = 0$$

$$x_1 = 30 + 25(-5/25) = 25$$

What has happened to the solution? The increased assembly time has caused a revision in the optimal production plan. HighTech should produce more of the Portable and less of the Deskpro. Overall the profit will be increased by $(\$2.80)(25) = \$70$. Note that although the optimal solution has changed, the basic variables that were optimal before are still optimal.

The procedure for determining the range of feasibility has been illustrated with the assembly time constraint. The procedure for calculating the range of feasibility for the right-hand side of any less-than-or-equal-to constraint is the same. The first step [paralleling equation (6.6)] for a general constraint i is to calculate the range of values for b_i that satisfy the inequalities shown below.

$$
\begin{bmatrix} \bar{b}_1 \\ \bar{b}_2 \\ \cdot \\ \cdot \\ \cdot \\ \bar{b}_m \end{bmatrix} + \Delta b_i \begin{bmatrix} \bar{a}_{1j} \\ \bar{a}_{2j} \\ \cdot \\ \cdot \\ \cdot \\ \bar{a}_{mj} \end{bmatrix} \geq \begin{bmatrix} 0 \\ 0 \\ \cdot \\ \cdot \\ \cdot \\ 0 \end{bmatrix} \qquad (6.12)
$$

Current solution   Column of the final simplex
(last column of   tableau corresponding to the
the final simplex   slack variable associated
tableau)   with constraint i

The inequalities are used to identify lower and upper limits on Δb_i. The range of feasibility can then be established by the maximum of the lower limits and the minimum of the upper limits.

Similar arguments presented can be used to develop a procedure for determining the range of feasibility for the right-hand-side value of a greater-than-or-equal-to constraint. Essentially the procedure is the same, with the column corresponding to the surplus variable associated with the constraint playing the central role. For a general greater-than-or-equal-to constraint i, we first calculate the range of values for Δb_i that satisfy the inequalities shown in equation (6.13).

$$
\begin{bmatrix} \bar{b}_1 \\ \bar{b}_2 \\ \cdot \\ \cdot \\ \cdot \\ \bar{b}_m \end{bmatrix} - \Delta b_i \begin{bmatrix} \bar{a}_{1j} \\ \bar{a}_{2j} \\ \cdot \\ \cdot \\ \cdot \\ \bar{a}_{mj} \end{bmatrix} \geq \begin{bmatrix} 0 \\ 0 \\ \cdot \\ \cdot \\ \cdot \\ 0 \end{bmatrix} \qquad (6.13)
$$

Current solution   Column of the final simplex
(last column of   tableau corresponding to the
the final simplex   surplus variable associated
tableau)   with constraint i

Once again, these inequalities establish lower and upper limits on Δb_i. Given these limits, the range of feasibility is easily determined.

A range of feasibility for the right-hand side of an equality constraint can also be computed. To do so for equality constraint i one could use the column of the final simplex tableau corresponding to the artificial variable associated with constraint i in equation (6.12). Since we have suggested dropping the artificial variable columns from the simplex tableau as soon as the artificial variable becomes nonbasic, these columns will not be available in the final tableau. Thus, more involved calculations are required to compute a range of feasibility for equality constraints. Details may be found in more advanced texts.

As long as the change in a right-hand-side value is such that b_i stays within its range of feasibility, the same basis will remain feasible and optimal. Changes that force b_i outside its range of feasibility will force us to perform additional simplex iterations to find the new optimal solution consisting of a different set of basic variables. More advanced linear programming texts show how this can be done without completely resolving the problem. In any case the calculation of the range of feasibility for each b_i is valuable management information and should be included as part of the management report on any linear programming project. The range of feasibility is typically made available as part of the computer solution to the problem.

Simultaneous Changes

By reviewing the procedures for developing the range of optimality and the range of feasibility, we note that only one coefficient at a time was permitted to vary. That is why our statements concerning changes within these ranges were made with the understanding that no other coefficients are permitted to change. However, sometimes we can make the same statements when either two or more objective function coefficients or two or more right-hand sides are varied simultaneously. When the simultaneous changes satisfy the 100 percent rule, the same statements are applicable. The 100 percent rule was explained in Chapter 3, but we will briefly review it here.

Let us call the amount a coefficient can be increased before reaching the upper limit of its range the allowable increase, and the amount a coefficient can be decreased before reaching the lower limit of its range the allowable decrease. Now suppose simultaneous changes are made in two, or more, objective function coefficients. For each coefficient changed, we compute the percentage of the allowable increase, or decrease, represented by the change. If the sum of the percentages for all changes does not exceed 100%, we say that the 100 percent rule is satisfied and that the simultaneous changes will not cause a change in the optimal solution. However, just as with a single objective function coefficient change, the value of the solution will change because of the change in the coefficients.

Similarly, if two or more changes in constraint right-hand-side values are made, we again compute the percentage of allowable increase or decrease represented by each change. If the sum of the percentages for all changes does not exceed 100%, we say that the 100 percent rule is satisfied. The shadow prices are then valid for determining the change in value of the objective function associated with the right-hand-side changes.

▼ NOTES AND COMMENTS ▼

The notes and comments in Chapter 3 concerning sensitivity analysis are also applicable here. In particular, recall that the 100 percent rule cannot be applied to simultaneous changes in the objective function *and* the right-hand sides; it applies only to simultaneous changes in one or the other. Also note that this rule *does not* mean that simultaneous changes that do not satisfy the rule will necessarily cause a change in the solution. For instance, any proportional change in *all* the objective function coefficients will leave the optimal solution unchanged, and any proportional change in *all* the right-hand sides will leave the shadow prices unchanged.

6.2 ▼ DUALITY

Every linear programming problem has an associated linear programming problem called the *dual*. Referring to the original formulation of the linear programming problem as the *primal*, we will see how the primal can be converted into its corresponding dual. Then we will solve the dual linear programming problem and interpret the results. A fundamental property of the primal–dual relationship is that the optimal solution to either the primal or the dual problem also provides the optimal solution to the other. In cases where the primal and the dual problems differ in terms of computational difficulty, we can choose the easier problem to solve.

Let us return to the HighTech Industries problem. The original formulation—the primal—is as follows:

$$\max \quad 50x_1 + 40x_2$$

s.t.

$$3x_1 + 5x_2 \leq 150 \quad \text{Assembly time}$$
$$1x_2 \leq 20 \quad \text{Portable display}$$
$$8x_1 + 5x_2 \leq 300 \quad \text{Warehouse space}$$
$$x_1, x_2 \geq 0$$

A maximization problem with all less-than-or-equal-to constraints and nonnegativity requirements for the decision variables is said to be in *canonical form*. For a maximization problem in canonical form, such as the HighTech Industries problem, the conversion to the associated dual linear program is relatively easy. Let us state the dual of the HighTech problem and then identify the steps taken to make the primal–dual conversion. The HighTech dual problem is as follows:

$$\min \quad 150u_1 + 20u_2 + 300u_3$$

s.t.

$$3u_1 \quad\quad\quad + \quad 8u_3 \geq 50$$
$$5u_1 + 1u_2 + 5u_3 \geq 40$$
$$u_1, u_2, u_3 \geq 0$$

The variables u_1, u_2, and u_3 are referred to as dual variables.

With the above example in mind, we make the following general statements about the *dual of a maximization problem in canonical form.*

1. The dual is a minimization problem.
2. The dual has all greater-than-or-equal-to constraints.
3. When the primal has n decision variables ($n = 2$ in the HighTech problem), the dual will have n constraints. The first constraint of the dual is associated with variable x_1 in the primal, the second constraint in the dual is associated with variable x_2 in the primal, and so on.
4. When the primal has m constraints ($m = 3$ in the HighTech problem), the dual will have m decision variables. Dual variable u_1 is associated with the first primal constraint, dual variable u_2 is associated with the second primal constraint, and so on.
5. The right-hand sides of the primal constraints become the objective function coefficients in the dual.
6. The objective function coefficients of the primal become the right-hand sides of the dual constraints.
7. The constraint coefficients of the ith primal variable become the coefficients in the ith constraint of the dual.
8. Both the primal and the dual have nonnegativity restrictions for the variables.

The above eight statements are the general requirements that must be satisfied when converting a maximization problem in canonical form to its associated dual. While these requirements may seem cumbersome at first, practice with a few simple problems will show that the primal–dual conversion process is relatively easy to implement.

Since we have formulated the HighTech dual linear programming problem, let us now proceed to solve it. With three variables in the dual, we will use the simplex method. After subtracting surplus variables s_1 and s_2 to obtain the standard form, adding artificial variables a_1 and a_2 to obtain the tableau form, and multiplying the objective function by -1 in order to convert the dual problem to an equivalent maximization problem, we arrive at the following initial simplex tableau.

		u_1	u_2	u_3	s_1	s_2	a_1	a_2	
Basis	c_B	-150	-20	-300	0	0	$-M$	$-M$	
a_1	$-M$	3	0	8	-1	0	1	0	50
a_2	$-M$	5	1	5	0	-1	0	1	40
	z_j	$-8M$	$-M$	$-13M$	M	M	$-M$	$-M$	$-90M$
	$c_j - z_j$	$-150 + 8M$	$-20 + M$	$-300 + 13M$	$-M$	$-M$	0	0	

At the first iteration u_3 is brought into the basis, and a_1 is removed. The second tableau, with the a_1 column dropped, is shown below.

		u_1	u_2	u_3	s_1	s_2	a_2	
Basis	c_B	-150	-20	-300	0	0	$-M$	
u_3	-300	$3/8$	0	1	$-1/8$	0	0	$50/8$
a_2	$-M$	$25/8$	1	0	$5/8$	-1	1	$70/8$
	z_j	$\dfrac{-900 - 25M}{8}$	$-M$	-300	$\dfrac{300 - 5M}{8}$	M	$-M$	$\dfrac{-15{,}000 - 70M}{8}$
	$c_j - z_j$	$\dfrac{-300 + 25M}{8}$	$-20 + M$	0	$\dfrac{-300 + 5M}{8}$	$-M$	0	

At the second iteration, u_1 is brought into the basis, and a_2 is removed. The third tableau, with the a_2 column removed, is

		u_1	u_2	u_3	s_1	s_2	
Basis	c_B	-150	-20	-300	0	0	
u_3	-300	0	$-3/25$	1	$-5/25$	$3/25$	$26/5$
u_1	-150	1	$8/25$	0	$5/25$	$-8/25$	$14/5$
	z_j	-150	-12	-300	30	12	-1980
	$c_j - z_j$	0	-8	0	-30	-12	

Note that all of the artificial variables have now been driven out of the basis and that all the entries in the net evaluation row are less than or equal to zero. The optimal solution has been reached; it is $u_1 = 14/5$, $u_2 = 0$, $u_3 = 26/5$, $s_1 = 0$, and $s_2 = 0$. Since we have been maximizing the negative of the dual objective function, the value of the objective function for the optimal dual solution must be $-(-1980) = 1980$.

Shown below is the final simplex tableau for the original HighTech Industries problem.

Basis	c_B	x_1 50	x_2 40	s_1 0	s_2 0	s_3 0	
x_2	40	0	1	$8/25$	0	$-3/25$	12
s_2	0	0	0	$-8/25$	1	$3/25$	8
x_1	50	1	0	$-5/25$	0	$5/25$	30
	z_j	50	40	$14/5$	0	$26/5$	1980
	$c_j - z_j$	0	0	$-14/5$	0	$-26/5$	

The optimal solution to the primal problem is $x_1 = 30$, $x_2 = 12$, $s_1 = 0$, $s_2 = 8$, and $s_3 = 0$. The optimal value of the objective function is 1980.

What observation can we make about the relationship between the optimal value of the objective function in the primal and the optimal value in the dual for the HighTech problem? The optimal value of the objective function is the same (1980) for both. This relationship is true for all primal and dual linear programming problems and is stated as property 1.

Property 1

If the dual problem has an optimal solution, the primal problem has an optimal solution, and vice versa. Furthermore, the values of the optimal solutions to the dual and primal problems are equal.

This property tells us that if we had solved only the dual problem, we would have known that HighTech could make a maximum of $1980.

Economic Interpretation of the Dual Variables

Before making further observations about the relationship between the primal and the dual solutions, let us consider the meaning or interpretation of the dual variables u_1, u_2, and u_3. Remember that in setting up the dual problem, each dual variable is associated with one of the constraints in the primal. Specifically, u_1 is associated with the assembly time constraint, u_2 with the Portable display constraint, and u_3 with the warehouse space constraint.

To understand and interpret these dual variables better, let us return to property 1 of the primal–dual relationship, which stated that the objective function values for the primal and dual problems must be equal. At the optimal solution the primal objective function results in

$$50x_1 + 40x_2 = 1980 \qquad (6.14)$$

while the dual objective function is

$$150u_1 + 20u_2 + 300u_3 = 1980 \qquad (6.15)$$

Using equation (6.14), let us restrict our interest to the interpretation of the primal objective function. Since x_1 and x_2 are the number of units of the Deskpro and the Portable that are assembled respectively, we have

$$\begin{pmatrix} \text{Dollar value} \\ \text{per unit of} \\ \text{Deskpro} \end{pmatrix} \begin{pmatrix} \text{number of} \\ \text{units of} \\ \text{Deskpro} \end{pmatrix} + \begin{pmatrix} \text{dollar value} \\ \text{per unit of} \\ \text{Portable} \end{pmatrix} \begin{pmatrix} \text{number of} \\ \text{units of} \\ \text{Portable} \end{pmatrix} = \begin{array}{l} \text{total dollar} \\ \text{value or} \\ \text{profit} \end{array}$$

Performing a similar interpretation of the dual objective function, equation (6.15), we see that the coefficients 150, 20, and 300 can be interpreted as the number of units of resources available. Thus, we have

$$\begin{pmatrix} \text{Units of} \\ \text{resource} \\ 1 \end{pmatrix} u_1 + \begin{pmatrix} \text{units of} \\ \text{resource} \\ 2 \end{pmatrix} u_2 + \begin{pmatrix} \text{units of} \\ \text{resource} \\ 3 \end{pmatrix} u_3 = \begin{array}{l} \text{total dollar value} \\ \text{or resource} \\ \text{cost} \end{array}$$

In order to be consistent in our units, and noting that, at optimality, the values of the primal and dual objective functions are equal, we see that the dual variables must carry the interpretation of being the value per unit of resource. Thus, for the HighTech problem,

$$u_1 = \text{dollar value per hour of assembly time}$$

$$u_2 = \text{dollar value per unit of the Portable display}$$

$$u_3 = \text{dollar value per square foot of warehouse space}$$

Did we ever attempt to identify the value of these resources previously? Recall that in Section 6.1, when we considered sensitivity analysis of the right-hand sides, we identified the value of an additional unit of each resource. These values were called shadow prices and are helpful to the decision maker in determining whether additional units of the resources should be made available.

The analysis in Section 6.1 led to the following shadow prices for the resources in the HighTech problem.

Resource	Value per Additional Unit (Shadow Price)
Assembly time	$2.80
Portable display	$0.00
Warehouse space	$5.20

Let us now return to the optimal solution for the HighTech dual problem. The values of the dual variables at the optimal solution are $u_1 = \frac{14}{5} = 2.80$, $u_2 = 0$, and $u_3 = \frac{26}{5} = 5.20$. This observation leads to the important economic interpretation that the values of the dual variable and the shadow price are one and the same. Thus, the optimal values of the dual variables identify the shadow price of each additional resource or input unit at the optimal solution.

In light of the above discussion, the following interpretation of the primal and dual problems can be made.

Primal Problem. Given a value per unit of each product or output unit, determine how much of each output should be produced in order to maximize the value of the total output. Constraints require the amount of each resource used to be less than or equal to the amount available.

Dual Problem. Given the availability of each resource or input, determine the value for each unit of input such that the value of the total input (that is, the resource cost) is minimized. Constraints require the resource value per unit of input to be greater than or equal to the value of each unit of output.

Using the Dual to Identify the Primal Solution

At the beginning of this section we mentioned that an important feature of the primal–dual relationship is that when an optimal solution is reached, the value of the optimal solution for the primal problem is the same as the value of the optimal solution for the dual problem. However, the question remains: If we solve only the dual problem, how can we identify the optimal values for the primal variables?

Recall that in Section 6.1 we showed that when a primal problem is solved by the simplex method, the optimal values of the primal variables appear in the rightmost column of the final tableau, and the shadow prices (values of the dual variables) are found in the z_j row. Since the final simplex tableau of the dual problem provides the optimal values of the dual variables, the values of the primal variables should be found in the z_j row of the optimal dual tableau. This is, in fact, the case and is formally stated as property 2.

Property 2

Given the simplex tableau corresponding to the optimal dual solution, the optimal values of the primal decision variables are given by the z_j entries for the surplus variables; furthermore, the optimal values of the primal slack variables are given by the negative of the $c_j - z_j$ entries for the u_j variables.

This property enables us to use the final simplex tableau for the dual of the HighTech problem to determine the optimal primal solution of $x_1 = 30$ units of the Deskpro and $x_2 = 12$ units of the Portable. These optimal values of x_1 and x_2, as well as the values for all primal slack variables, are given in the z_j and $c_j - z_j$ rows of the final simplex tableau of the dual problem, which is shown again below.

Basis	c_B	u_1	u_2	u_3	s_1	s_2	
		-150	-20	-300	0	0	
u_3	-300	0	$-3/25$	1	$-5/25$	$3/25$	$26/5$
u_1	-150	1	$8/25$	0	$5/25$	$-8/25$	$14/5$
z_j		-150	-12	-300	30	12	-1980
$c_j - z_j$		0	-8	0	-30	-12	

Primal solution: $s_1 = 0$ $s_2 = 8$ $s_3 = 0$ $x_1 = 30$ $x_2 = 12$ Profit $= 1980$

Finding the Dual of Any Primal Problem

The HighTech Industries primal problem provided a good introductory problem to illustrate the concept of duality as it was formulated as a maximization problem in canonical form. For this form of primal problem we have seen that conversion to the dual problem is rather easy. However, what if the primal is a minimization problem and/or some of the constraints are not of the $\leq$ form? While we could state a special set of rules for converting each variety of primal problem into its associated dual, we tend to believe it is easier first to convert any primal problem to an equivalent maximization problem in canonical form. Once this has been accomplished, we can find the dual problem by following the procedure used to convert the HighTech Industries primal problem into its dual.

We will show the steps necessary for converting any primal linear program into a maximization problem in canonical form by considering the following primal linear programming problem.

$$\min 2x_1 - 3x_2$$

s.t.

$$1x_1 + 2x_2 \leq 12$$
$$4x_1 - 2x_2 \geq 3$$
$$6x_1 - 1x_2 = 10$$
$$x_1, x_2 \geq 0$$

The appropriate steps are stated in general and then are applied to the example problem.

1. If the problem involves a minimization objective function, convert the problem to an equivalent maximization problem by multiplying the objective function by -1.

Thus, the objective function for the example becomes

$$\max \quad -2x_1 + 3x_2$$

2. Convert any $\geq$ constraint to an equivalent $\leq$ constraint by multiplying both sides of the constraint by -1.

Thus, constraint 2 for the example becomes

$$-4x_1 + 2x_2 \leq -3$$

3. For each equality constraint, form two inequality constraints, one with a $\leq$ form and one with a $\geq$ form; then use rule 2 above to convert the $\geq$ constraint to a $\leq$ form.

Thus, constraint 3 for the example is rewritten as two inequality constraints:

$$6x_1 - 1x_2 \leq 10$$
$$6x_1 - 1x_2 \geq 10$$

Using rule 2 for the greater-than-or-equal-to constraint, these constraints can be rewritten as

$$6x_1 - 1x_2 \leq \quad 10$$
$$-6x_1 + 1x_2 \leq -10$$

Thus, the initial primal problem has been restated in the following equivalent form:

$$\max \quad -2x_1 + 3x_2$$

s.t.

$$1x_1 + 2x_2 \leq 12$$
$$-4x_1 + 2x_2 \leq -3$$
$$6x_1 - 1x_2 \leq 10$$
$$-6x_1 + 1x_2 \leq -10$$
$$x_1, x_2 \geq 0$$

With the primal problem in canonical form for a maximization problem, we can easily convert to the dual linear programming problem by the primal–dual procedure presented earlier in this section. The dual becomes[2]

$$\min \quad 12u_1 - 3u_2 + 10u_3' - 10u_3''$$

s.t.

$$1u_1 - 4u_2 + 6u_3' - 6u_3'' \geq -2$$
$$2u_1 + 2u_2 - 1u_3' + 1u_3'' \geq 3$$
$$u_1, u_2, u_3', u_3'' \geq 0$$

Since the equality primal constraint required two $\leq$ constraints, we denoted the dual variables associated with these constraints as u_3' and u_3''. This reminds us that u_3' and u_3'' both refer to the third constraint in the initial primal problem. Since there are two dual variables associated with an equality constraint, the interpretation of the dual variable as the shadow price of the right-hand-side resource must be modified slightly. The shadow price is given by the difference between the two dual variables. Thus, the shadow price for the equality constraint $6x_1 - x_2 = 10$ is given by the value of $u_3' - u_3''$ in the optimal solution to the dual. Hence, the shadow price for an equality constraint can be negative.

Computational Considerations

We have shown that solving either the primal or the dual problem provides the solution to the other as well. Thus, whenever computation time and effort are important considerations in solving linear programs, practitioners have the option of solving either the primal or the dual, depending on which is easier to solve.

Recall that if the primal problem has m constraints and n variables, the dual problem will have n constraints and m variables. Also recall that the basic solution identified at each iteration of the simplex method contains as many basic variables as constraints in the problem. For most computer implementations of the simplex method, the number of computations performed at each iteration and the total number of iterations are proportional to the number of basic variables in the problem. Thus, in general, we expect linear programs with a larger number of constraints, and therefore a larger number of basic variables, to require greater computational time and effort. As a result, when there is a substantial difference in the number of constraints in the primal and dual problems,

---

[2]Note that the right-hand side of the first constraint is negative. Thus, we must multiply both sides of the constraint by -1 to obtain a positive value for the right-hand side before attempting to solve the problem with the simplex method.

practitioners often recommend solving the form of the problem (primal or dual) with fewer constraints.

▼ NOTES AND COMMENTS ▼

1. Care must be exercised when performing sensitivity analysis when a degenerate solution exists. When the solution to the primal problem is degenerate, the shadow prices are not unique.

2. With today's high-speed computers and linear programming software packages, converting to the dual to gain a computational advantage is usually not necessary.

▼ SUMMARY

In this chapter we showed how sensitivity analysis can be performed using the information in the final simplex tableau. This included computing the range of optimality for objective function coefficients, shadow prices, and the range of feasibility for the right-hand sides. This sensitivity information is routinely made available as part of the solution report provided by most linear programming computer packages.

We stress here that the sensitivity analysis is based on the assumption that only one coefficient is allowed to change at a time; all other coefficients are assumed to remain at their original values. It is possible to do some limited sensitivity analysis on the effect of changing more than one coefficient at a time; the 100 percent rule was mentioned as being useful in this context.

In studying duality we saw how the original linear programming problem, called the primal, can be converted into its associated dual linear programming problem. Solving either the primal or the dual provides the solution to the other. In cases where the primal has relatively few variables, but many constraints, the dual often possesses computational advantages. Finally, we learned that the value of the dual variable (shadow price) identifies the economic contribution or value of additional resources in the primal problem.

▼ GLOSSARY

Range of optimality The range of values over which an objective function coefficient may vary without causing any change in the optimal solution (that is, the values of all the variables will remain the same, but the value of the objective function will change).

Shadow price The change in value of the objective function per-unit increase in the value of the right-hand side associated with a linear programming constraint.

Range of feasibility The range of values over which a b_i may vary without causing the current basic solution to become infeasible. The values of the variables in solution will change, but the same variables will remain basic.

Primal problem The original formulation of a linear programming problem.

Canonical form for a maximization problem A maximization problem with all less-than-or-equal-to constraints and nonnegativity requirements for the decision variables.

Dual problem A linear programming problem associated with the primal problem. Solution of the dual also provides the solution to the primal.

Dual variable The variable in a dual linear programming problem. Its optimal value is the shadow price for the associated primal resource.

▼ PROBLEMS

1. For the HighTech problem we found the range of optimality for c_1, the profit contribution per unit of the Deskpro. Find
   a. The range of optimality for c_2.
   b. The range of optimality for c_{s_2}.
   c. The range of optimality for c_{s_3}.
   d. Suppose the per-unit profit contribution of the Portable (c_2) dropped to \$35. How would the optimal solution change? What is the new value for total profit?

2. For the HighTech problem we found the range of feasibility for b_1, the assembly time available. Find
   a. The range of feasibility for b_2.
   b. The range of feasibility for b_3.
   c. How much will HighTech's profit increase if there is a 20-square-foot increase in the amount of warehouse space available (b_3)?

3. Consider the linear program

$$\max \quad 7.5x_1 + 15x_2 + 10x_3$$

$$\text{s.t.}$$

$$
\begin{aligned}
2x_1 \qquad\quad + 2x_3 &\le 8 \\
\tfrac{1}{2}x_1 + 2x_2 + 1x_3 &\le 3 \\
1x_1 + 1x_2 + 2x_3 &\le 6 \\
x_1, x_2, x_3 &\ge 0
\end{aligned}
$$

   a. Find the optimal solution.
   b. Calculate the range of optimality for c_1.
   c. What would be the effect of a 2.5-unit increase in c_1 (from 7.5 to 10) on the optimal solution and the value of that solution?
   d. Calculate the range of optimality for c_3.
   e. What would be the effect of a five-unit increase in c_3 (from 10 to 15) on the optimal solution and the value of that solution?

4. Consider again the linear programming problem presented in problem 3.
   a. Compute the ranges of feasibility for b_1, b_2, and b_3.
   b. How much will the value of the objective function change if b_1 is increased from 8 to 9?
   c. How much will the value of the objective function change if b_2 is increased from 3 to 4?
   d. How much will the value of the objective function change if b_3 is increased from 6 to 7?

5. Recall the Par, Inc., problem introduced in Chapter 2. The linear program for this problem is

$$\max \quad 10x_1 + 9x_2$$

$$\text{s.t.}$$

$$
\begin{aligned}
\tfrac{7}{10}x_1 + 1x_2 &\le 630 && \text{Cutting and dyeing time} \\
\tfrac{1}{2}x_1 + \tfrac{5}{6}x_2 &\le 600 && \text{Sewing time} \\
1x_1 + \tfrac{2}{3}x_2 &\le 708 && \text{Finishing time} \\
\tfrac{1}{10}x_1 + \tfrac{1}{4}x_2 &\le 135 && \text{Inspecting and packaging time} \\
x_1, x_2 &\ge 0
\end{aligned}
$$

where

$$x_1 = \text{number of standard bags produced}$$

$$x_2 = \text{number of deluxe bags produced}$$

The final simplex tableau is

		x_1	x_2	s_1	s_2	s_3	s_4	
Basis	c_B	10	9	0	0	0	0	
x_2	9	0	1	$30/16$	0	$-21/16$	0	252
s_2	0	0	0	$-15/16$	1	$5/32$	0	120
x_1	10	1	0	$-20/16$	0	$30/16$	0	540
s_4	0	0	0	$-11/32$	0	$9/64$	1	18
	z_j	10	9	$70/16$	0	$111/16$	0	7668
	$c_j - z_j$	0	0	$-70/16$	0	$-111/16$	0	

a. Calculate the range of optimality for the profit contribution, c_1, of the standard bag.

b. Calculate the range of optimality for the profit contribution, c_2, of the deluxe bag.

c. If the profit contribution per deluxe bag drops to $7 per unit, how will the optimal solution be affected?

d. What unit profit contribution would be necessary for the deluxe bag before Par, Inc., would consider changing its current production plan?

e. If the profit contribution of the deluxe bags can be increased to $15 per unit, what is the optimal production plan? State what you think will happen before you compute the new optimal solution.

6. For the Par, Inc., problem (problem 5):

a. Calculate the range of feasibility for b_1 (cutting and dyeing time capacity).

b. Calculate the range of feasibility for b_2 (sewing capacity).

c. Calculate the range of feasibility for b_3 (finishing capacity).

d. Calculate the range of feasibility for b_4 (inspection and packaging capacity).

e. Which of these four departments are you interested in scheduling for overtime? Explain.

7. a. Calculate the final simplex tableau for the Par, Inc., problem (problem 5) after increasing b_1 from 630 to $682\frac{4}{11}$.

b. Would the current basis be optimal if b_1 were increased further? If not, what would be the new optimal basis?

8. Also for the Par, Inc., problem (problem 5):

a. How much would profit increase if an additional 30 hours became available in the cutting and dyeing department (that is, if b_1 were increased from 630 to 660)?

b. How much would profit decrease if 40 hours were removed from the sewing department?

c. How much would profit decrease if because of an employee accident there were only 570 hours instead of 630 available in the cutting and dyeing department?

9. Below are additional conditions encountered by Par, Inc. (problem 5).

a. Suppose because of some new machinery Par, Inc. was able to make a small reduction in the amount of time it took to do the cutting and dyeing (constraint 1) for a standard bag. What effect would this have on the objective function?

b. Management believes that by buying a new sewing machine the sewing time for standard bags can be reduced from $\frac{1}{2}$ hour to $\frac{1}{3}$ hour. Do you think this machine would be a good investment? Why?

10. Recall the RMC problem (Chapter 2, problem 31). Letting

$$x_1 = \text{tons of fuel additive produced}$$

$$x_2 = \text{tons of solvent base produced}$$

leads to the following formulation of the RMC problem:

$$\max \quad 40x_1 + 30x_2$$

s.t.

$$\frac{2}{5}x_1 + \frac{1}{2}x_2 \leq 20 \quad \text{Material 1}$$

$$\frac{1}{5}x_2 \leq 5 \quad \text{Material 2}$$

$$\frac{3}{5}x_1 + \frac{3}{10}x_2 \leq 21 \quad \text{Material 3}$$

$$x_1, x_2 \geq 0$$

The final simplex tableau is shown below.

Basis	c_B	x_1 40	x_2 30	s_1 0	s_2 0	s_3 0	
x_2	30	0	1	$\frac{10}{3}$	0	$-\frac{20}{9}$	20
s_2	0	0	0	$-\frac{2}{3}$	1	$\frac{4}{9}$	1
x_1	40	1	0	$-\frac{5}{3}$	0	$\frac{25}{9}$	25
z_j		40	30	$\frac{100}{3}$	0	$\frac{400}{9}$	1600
$c_j - z_j$		0	0	$-\frac{100}{3}$	0	$-\frac{400}{9}$	

a. Compute the ranges of optimality for c_1 and c_2.

b. Suppose that because of an increase in production costs the profit per ton on the fuel additive is reduced to \$30 per ton. What effect will this have on the optimal solution?

c. What is the shadow price for the material 1 constraint? What is the interpretation?

d. If RMC had an opportunity to purchase additional materials, which material would be the most valuable? How much should the company be willing to pay for this material?

11. Refer again to problem 10.

a. Compute the range of feasibility for b_1 (Material 1 availability).

b. Compute the range of feasibility for b_2 (Material 2 availability).

c. Compute the range of feasibility for b_3 (Material 3 availability).

d. What is the shadow price for material 3? Over what range of values for b_3 is this shadow price valid?

12. Consider the following linear program:

$$\max \quad 3x_1 + 1x_2 + 5x_3 + 3x_4$$

s.t.

$$3x_1 + 1x_2 + 2x_3 \qquad = 30$$
$$2x_1 + 1x_2 + 3x_3 + 1x_4 \geq 15$$
$$2x_2 \qquad + 3x_4 \leq 25$$

$$x_1, x_2, x_3, x_4 \geq 0$$

a. Find the optimal solution.
b. Calculate the range of optimality for c_3.
c. What would be the effect of a four-unit decrease in c_3 (from 5 to 1) on the optimal solution and the value of that solution?
d. Calculate the range of optimality for c_2.
e. What would be the effect of a three-unit increase in c_2 (from 1 to 4) on the optimal solution and the value of that solution?

13. Consider the final simplex tableau shown below.

Basis	c_B	x_1	x_2	x_3	x_4	s_1	s_2	s_3	
		4	6	3	1	0	0	0	
x_3	3	3/60	0	1	1/2	3/10	0	-6/30	125
s_2	0	195/60	0	0	-1/2	-5/10	1	-1	425
x_2	6	39/60	1	0	1/2	-1/10	0	12/30	25
z_j		81/20	6	3	9/2	3/10	0	54/30	525
$c_j - z_j$		-1/20	0	0	-7/2	-3/10	0	-54/30	

The original right-hand-side values were $b_1 = 550$, $b_2 = 700$, and $b_3 = 200$.
a. Calculate the range of feasibility for b_1.
b. Calculate the range of feasibility for b_2.
c. Calculate the range of feasibility for b_3.

14. Suppose that in a product-mix problem x_1, x_2, x_3, and x_4 indicate the units of products 1, 2, 3, and 4, respectively, and we have

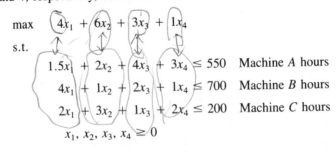

$$\max \quad 4x_1 + 6x_2 + 3x_3 + 1x_4$$

s.t.

$$1.5x_1 + 2x_2 + 4x_3 + 3x_4 \leq 550 \quad \text{Machine } A \text{ hours}$$
$$4x_1 + 1x_2 + 2x_3 + 1x_4 \leq 700 \quad \text{Machine } B \text{ hours}$$
$$2x_1 + 3x_2 + 1x_3 + 2x_4 \leq 200 \quad \text{Machine } C \text{ hours}$$

$$x_1, x_2, x_3, x_4 \geq 0$$

a. Formulate the dual to this problem.
b. Solve the dual. Use the dual solution to show that the profit-maximizing product mix is $x_1 = 0$, $x_2 = 25$, $x_3 = 125$, and $x_4 = 0$.
c. Use the dual variables to identify the machine or machines that are producing at maximum capacity. If the manager can select one machine for additional production capacity, which machine should have priority? Why?

15. Find the dual problem for the linear program given below.

$$\max \quad 10x_1 + 9x_2 + 4x_3 + 6x_4$$

s.t.

$$3x_1 + 2x_2 + 4x_3 + 2x_4 \leq 70$$
$$5x_1 + 5x_2 + 1x_3 + 3x_4 \leq 60$$
$$5x_1 + 6x_2 + 3x_3 + 1x_4 \leq 25$$
$$x_1, x_2, x_3, x_4 \geq 0$$

16. Write the following primal linear program in canonical form:

$$\max \quad 5x_1 + 1x_2 + 3x_3$$

s.t.

$$1x_1 + 1x_2 \qquad \geq 40$$
$$2x_1 + 3x_2 + 1x_3 \leq 50$$
$$3x_1 + 2x_2 + 2x_3 \leq 25$$
$$1x_2 + 1x_3 \geq 10$$
$$x_1, x_2, x_3 \geq 0$$

From a computational point of view, would you rather solve the above linear programming problem or its dual?

17. Write the following primal problem in canonical form:

$$\max \quad 3x_1 + 1x_2 + 5x_3 + 3x_4$$

s.t.

$$3x_1 + 1x_2 + 2x_3 \qquad = 30$$
$$2x_1 + 1x_2 + 3x_3 + 1x_4 \geq 15$$
$$2x_2 \qquad + 3x_4 \leq 25$$
$$x_1, x_2, x_3, x_4 \geq 0$$

18. Write the dual of problem 17.
19. Consider the following linear program:

$$\max \quad 2x_1 + 3x_2$$

s.t.

$$1x_1 + 2x_2 \leq 8$$
$$3x_1 + 2x_2 \leq 12$$
$$x_1, x_2 \geq 0$$

a. Write the dual of this problem.
b. Solve both the primal and the dual problems using the graphical procedure.
c. Solve both the primal and the dual problems using the simplex method.
d. Using your results from parts (b) and (c), identify where and how you can observe properties 1 and 2 of the primal–dual relationship.

20. Photo Chemicals produces two types of photograph-developing fluids at a cost of $1.00 per gallon. Let

$$x_1 = \text{gallons of product 1}$$

$$x_2 = \text{gallons of product 2}$$

Photo Chemicals management has required that at least 30 gallons of product 1 and at least 20 gallons of product 2 be produced. It is also required that at least 80 pounds of a perishable raw material be used in production. A linear programming formulation of the problem follows:

$$\min \quad 1x_1 + 1x_2$$

s.t.

$$1x_1 \qquad \geq 30 \quad \text{Minimum product 1}$$

$$1x_2 \geq 20 \quad \text{Minimum product 2}$$

$$1x_1 + 2x_2 \geq 80 \quad \text{Minimum raw material}$$

$$x_1, x_2 \geq 0$$

a. Write this primal linear program in canonical form for a maximization problem.
b. Show the dual problem.
c. Solve the dual problem, and show that the optimal production plan is $x_1 = 30$ and $x_2 = 25$.
d. Recall that the third constraint involved a management request that the current 80 pounds of a perishable raw material be used as soon as possible. However, after learning that the optimal solution calls for an excess production of five units of product 2, management is reconsidering the raw material requirement. Specifically, you have been asked to identify the cost effect if this constraint were relaxed. Use the dual variable to indicate the change in the cost if only 79 pounds of raw material had to be used.

21. Write the dual problem for the following linear program:

$$\min \quad 3x_1 + 1x_2 + 2x_3$$

s.t.

$$2x_1 + 1x_2 + 3x_3 = 5$$

$$4x_1 + 1x_2 + 1x_3 = 4$$

$$2x_1 \qquad + 1x_3 \leq 7$$

$$1x_1 + 2x_2 \qquad \geq 4$$

$$x_1, x_2, x_3 \geq 0$$

22. Find the dual problem for the following linear programming problem:

$$\min \quad 4x_1 + 3x_2 + 6x_3$$

s.t.

$$1x_1 + 0.5x_2 + 1x_3 \geq 15$$

$$2x_2 + 1x_3 \geq 30$$

$$1x_1 + 1x_2 + 2x_3 \geq 20$$

$$x_1, x_2, x_3 \geq 0$$

23. A sales representative who sells two products is trying to determine the number of calls that should be made during the next month to promote each product. Based on

past experience, there is an average $10 commission for every call for product 1 and a $5 commission for every call for product 2. The company requires at least 20 calls per month for each product and not more than 100 calls per month on any one product. In addition, the sales representative spends about 3 hours for each call for product 1 and 1 hour for each call for product 2. If there are a total of 175 selling hours available next month, how many calls should be made for each of the two products in order to maximize the commission?

a. Formulate a linear program for this problem.

b. Formulate and solve the dual problem.

c. Use the final simplex tableau for the dual to determine the optimal number of calls for the products. What is the maximum commission?

d. Interpret the values of the dual variables.

24. Consider the linear program

$$\max \quad 3x_1 + 2x_2$$

$$\text{s.t.}$$

$$1x_1 + 2x_2 \leq 8$$

$$2x_1 + 1x_2 \leq 10$$

$$x_1, x_2 \geq 0$$

a. Solve this problem using the simplex method. Keep a record of the value of the objective function at each extreme point.

b. Formulate and solve the dual of this problem using the graphical procedure.

c. Compute the value of the dual objective function for each extreme-point solution of the dual problem.

d. Compare the values of the objective functions for each primal and dual extreme-point solution.

e. Can a dual feasible solution yield a value less than a primal feasible solution? Can you state a result concerning bounds on the value of the primal solution provided by any feasible solution to the dual problem?

25. Consider the following linear program:

$$\max \quad 15x_1 + 30x_2 + 20x_3$$

$$\text{s.t.}$$

$$1x_1 \qquad + \quad 1x_3 \leq 4$$

$$0.5x_1 + \quad 2x_2 + \quad 1x_3 \leq 3$$

$$1x_1 + \quad 1x_2 + \quad 2x_3 \leq 6$$

$$x_1, x_2, x_3 \geq 0$$

Solve using the simplex method, and answer the following questions:

a. What is the optimal solution?

b. What is the value of the objective function?

c. Which constraints are the binding constraints?

d. How much slack is available in the nonbinding constraints?

e. What are the shadow prices associated with the three constraints? Which right-hand-side value would have the greatest effect on the value of the objective function if it could be changed?

f. Develop the appropriate ranges for the coefficients of the objective function. What is your interpretation of these ranges?

g. Develop and interpret the ranges of feasibility for the right-hand-side values.

Performance Analysis Corporation*

Chapel Hill, North Carolina

Performance Analysis Corporation, founded in 1979, is a management consulting company that specializes in the use of management science to design more efficient and effective operations for a wide variety of chain stores. Performance Analysis Corporation has evaluated the operation of banks, savings and loans, grocery chains, etc. Recently the company has become involved in evaluating the efficiency of fast-food outlets. In the following application we describe how linear programming methodology has been used to provide an evaluation model for a chain of fast-food restaurants.

FAST-FOOD BUSINESS

The fast-food business for a chain such as McDonalds, Kentucky Fried Chicken, etc., is characterized by hundreds, or even thousands, of individual restaurants, some of which are company owned and some of which are franchised. A typical restaurant may gross close to a million dollars annually; thus, the impact of relatively minor improvements at a large proportion of the restaurants can have a substantial effect on a chain's profitability and market share.

Although each individual restaurant in a given chain usually offers the same type of menu (with some minor geographical variations), they often must deal with vastly different environments and competition. In addition, the age of the restaurant, facade used, ease of access and egress, hours of operation, scale of operation, etc., can vary substantially from restaurant to restaurant.

A major objective of company management in the fast-food industry involves the performance evaluations of managers of individual restaurants in the chain. These evaluations are the basis for awarding year-end bonuses and for personal advancement purposes. Unfortunately, there is not a single measure of performance such as profit that can be used as the basis for the evaluation since other measures such as market share and rate of growth are also important.

A LINEAR PROGRAMMING EVALUATION MODEL

One approach to the store evaluation problem utilizes the concept of Pareto optimality. According to this concept, a restaurant in a given chain is *relatively* inefficient if there are other restaurants in the same chain that have the following characteristics:

*The authors are indebted to Richard C. Morey of Performance Analysis Corp., Chapel Hill, N.C., for providing this application.

1. Have the same or worse environment.
2. Produce at least the same levels of *all* outputs.
3. Utilize no more of *any* resource and *less* of at least one of the resources.

The mechanism for discovering which of the restaurants are Pareto inefficient involves the development and solution of a linear programming model. Constraints on the problem involve requirements concerning the minimum acceptable levels of output (e.g., profit, market share, etc.) and conditions imposed by uncontrollable elements in the environment. The objective function calls for the minimization of the resources necessary to produce the output. Solution of the model produces the following output for each restaurant:

1. A score that assesses the level of so-called relative technical efficiency achieved by the particular restaurant over the time period in question.
2. The reduction in controllable resources and/or the augmentation of outputs over the time period in question for an inefficient restaurant to have been rated as efficient.
3. A peer group of other restaurants with which each restaurant can be compared in the future.

Sensitivity analysis, especially that concerning the shadow prices, provides important managerial information. For each constraint concerning a minimum acceptable output level, the shadow price tells the manager how much one more unit of output would increase his/her efficiency measure. Analysis of the ranges for each of the constraint coefficients (the a_{ij}'s) provides information concerning how much outputs could be reduced or inputs increased before the restaurant would become inefficient.

TYPES OF FACTORS UTILIZED

The approach is capable of handling three types of factors: quantitative controllable factors such as salaries paid, local advertising expenditures, etc.; noncontrollable quantitative factors such as the median income in the geographic area served by the restaurant, the unemployment rate, etc.; and qualitative factors such as the degree of competition, appearance of restaurant, etc. The outputs include total sales of various types (e.g., by time of day), profits, market share, rate of growth of sales, etc.

BENEFITS

The analysis typically identifies 40%–50% of the restaurants as underperforming, given the previously stated conditions concerning the inputs available and outputs produced. We have found that if all of the relative inefficiencies identified are eliminated simultaneously, the resulting increase in corporate profits is typically in the neighborhood of 5%–10%. This is truly a substantial increase given the large scale of operations involved.

The district manager has an objective score card for each restaurant manager that indicates areas (e.g., overtime salary) where improvements may be in order.

The efficient restaurants can be used to generate a set of best practices that can be models for other restaurants. Of primary benefit are the reactions of restaurant managers who appreciate that the evaluation process that they are subject to recognizes the environment they are forced to operate within, deals with noncommensurability of outputs involved, is theory based and nonpolitical, and is defensible, understandable, and equitable.

Questions

1. State in your own words what it means for one restaurant in a chain to be relatively inefficient relative to another restaurant in the same chain.
2. Suppose the evaluation model showed that for a particular restaurant the resource mix necessary to produce a given output mix was 90% of what another restaurant was using to produce that same mix of output. Would you conclude that the restaurant was relatively efficient or inefficient? Why?

7

Transportation, Assignment, and Transshipment Problems

Transportation, assignment, and transshipment problems belong to a special class of linear programming problems called *network flow problems*. A separate chapter is devoted to these problems for two reasons. First, a wide variety of applications can be modeled as transportation, assignment, or transshipment problems. Second, these problems have a mathematical structure that has enabled management scientists to develop efficient specialized solution procedures for solving them; as a result, very large problems can be solved with just a few seconds of computer time.

The approach we take in this chapter is to introduce each problem with an illustrative application. We first develop a graphical representation, called a network, of the problem, then show how a linear programming model of the problem can be formulated. The network representation makes it easy to see the close relationship among the three types of problems. After showing how the three types of problems can be formulated and solved as linear programs, we present special-purpose solution procedures for the transportation and assignment problems in the last two sections of the chapter.

7.1 ▼ THE TRANSPORTATION PROBLEM: THE NETWORK MODEL AND A LINEAR PROGRAMMING FORMULATION

The transportation problem arises frequently in planning for the distribution of goods and services from several supply locations to several demand locations. Usually the quantity of goods available at each supply location (origin) is limited, and the goods are needed at each of the several demand locations (destinations). The objective in a transportation problem is to minimize the cost of shipping goods from the origins to the destinations.

Let us illustrate by considering the transportation problem faced by Foster Generators, Inc. This problem involves the transportation of a product from three plants to four distribution centers. Foster Generators, Inc., has production operations in Cleveland, Ohio; Bedford, Ind.; and York, Pa. Production capacities for these plants over the next 3-month planning period for one particular type of generator are as follows:

Origin	Plant	3-Month Production Capacity (units)
1	Cleveland	5,000
2	Bedford	6,000
3	York	2,500
		Total 13,500

The firm distributes its generators through four regional distribution centers located in Boston, Chicago, St. Louis, and Lexington (Ky.); the 3-month forecast of demand for the distribution centers is as follows:

Destination	Distribution Center	3-Month Demand Forecast (units)
1	Boston	6,000
2	Chicago	4,000
3	St. Louis	2,000
4	Lexington	1,500
		Total 13,500

Management would like to determine how much of its production should be shipped from each plant to each distribution center. Figure 7.1 shows graphically the 12 distribution routes Foster can use. Such a graph is called a *network;* the circles are referred to as *nodes* and the lines connecting the nodes as *arcs*. Each origin and destination is represented by a node, and each possible shipping route is represented by an arc. The amount of the supply is written next to each origin node, and the amount of the demand is written next to each destination node. The goods shipped from the origins to the destinations represent the flow in the network. Note that the direction of flow (from origin to destination) is indicated by the arrows.

For the Foster Generators transportation problem, the objective is to determine the routes to be used and the quantity to be shipped via each route that will provide the minimum total transportation cost associated with meeting all distribution center demands. The cost for each unit shipped on each route is given in Table 7.1 and is shown on each arc in Figure 7.1.

A linear programming model can be used to solve the Foster Generators transportation problem. We shall use double-subscripted decision variables, with x_{11} denoting the number of units shipped from origin 1 (Cleveland) to destination 1 (Boston), x_{12} denoting the number of units shipped from origin 1 (Cleveland) to destination 2 (Chicago), and so on. In general, the decision variables for a transportation problem having m origins and n destinations are written as follows:

$$x_{ij} = \text{number of units shipped from origin } i \text{ to destination } j,$$
$$\text{where } i = 1, 2, \ldots , m \text{ and } j = 1, 2, \ldots , n$$

Note that there is one decision variable for each arc in Figure 7.1. Using this notation, $x_{24} = 500$ would correspond to shipping 500 units from Bedford (origin 2) to Lexington (destination 4).

FIGURE 7.1
The Network Representation of the Foster Generators Transportation Problem

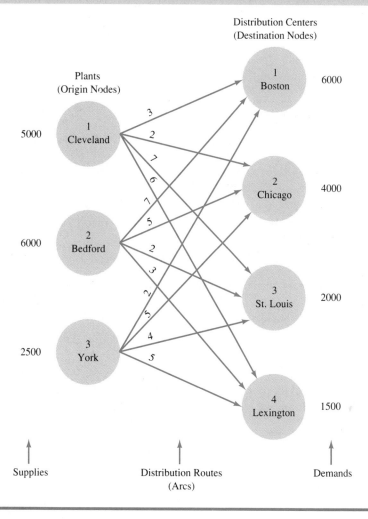

TABLE 7.1
Transportation Cost per Unit for the Foster Generators Transportation Problem

Origin	Destination			
	Boston	*Chicago*	*St. Louis*	*Lexington*
Cleveland	3	2	7	6
Bedford	7	5	2	3
York	2	5	4	5

Since the objective of the transportation problem is to minimize the total transportation costs, we can use the cost data in Table 7.1, or on the arcs in Figure 7.1, to develop the following cost expressions:

Transportation costs for
units shipped from Cleveland $= 3x_{11} + 2x_{12} + 7x_{13} + 6x_{14}$

Transportation costs for
units shipped from Bedford $= 7x_{21} + 5x_{22} + 2x_{23} + 3x_{24}$

Transportation costs for
units shipped from York $= 2x_{31} + 5x_{32} + 4x_{33} + 5x_{34}$

The sum of the above expressions provides the objective function showing the total transportation costs for Foster Generators, Inc.

Constraints are needed for a transportation problem because each origin has a limited supply and each destination has a specific demand. Consider the supply constraints first. The capacity at the Cleveland plant is 5000 units. With the total number of units shipped from the Cleveland plant expressed as $x_{11} + x_{12} + x_{13} + x_{14}$, the supply constraint for the Cleveland plant can be written as

$$x_{11} + x_{12} + x_{13} + x_{14} \le 5000 \quad \text{Cleveland supply}$$

With three origins (plants), the Foster Generators transportation problem has three supply constraints. Given the capacity of 6000 units at the Bedford plant and 2500 units at the York plant, the two additional supply constraints are as follows:

$$x_{21} + x_{22} + x_{23} + x_{24} \le 6000 \quad \text{Bedford supply}$$

$$x_{31} + x_{32} + x_{33} + x_{34} \le 2500 \quad \text{York supply}$$

With the four distribution centers as the destinations, the following four demand constraints are needed to ensure that destination demands will be satisfied:

$$x_{11} + x_{21} + x_{31} = 6000 \quad \text{Boston demand}$$

$$x_{12} + x_{22} + x_{32} = 4000 \quad \text{Chicago demand}$$

$$x_{13} + x_{23} + x_{33} = 2000 \quad \text{St. Louis demand}$$

$$x_{14} + x_{24} + x_{34} = 1500 \quad \text{Lexington demand}$$

Combining the objective function and constraints into one model provides the following 12-variable, 7-constraint linear programming formulation of the Foster Generators transportation problem:

$$\min \quad 3x_{11} + 2x_{12} + 7x_{13} + 6x_{14} + 7x_{21} + 5x_{22} + 2x_{23} + 3x_{24} + 2x_{31} + 5x_{32} + 4x_{33} + 5x_{34}$$

s.t.

$$
\begin{aligned}
x_{11} + x_{12} + x_{13} + x_{14} & & & \le 5000 \\
x_{21} + x_{22} + x_{23} + x_{24} & & & \le 6000 \\
x_{31} + x_{32} + x_{33} + x_{34} & & & \le 2500 \\
x_{11} \quad\quad + x_{21} \quad\quad + x_{31} & & & = 6000 \\
x_{12} \quad\quad + x_{22} \quad\quad + x_{32} & & & = 4000 \\
x_{13} \quad\quad + x_{23} \quad\quad + x_{33} & & & = 2000 \\
x_{14} \quad\quad + x_{24} \quad\quad + x_{34} & & & = 1500
\end{aligned}
$$

$$x_{ij} \ge 0 \quad \text{for } i = 1, 2, 3 \text{ and } j = 1, 2, 3, 4$$

Comparing the linear programming formulation to the network in Figure 7.1, some observations can be made. All the information needed for the linear programming formulation is on the network. There is one constraint for each node and one variable for each arc. The sum of the variables corresponding to arcs out of an origin node must be less than or equal to the supply, and the sum of the variables corresponding to the arcs into a destination node must be equal to the demand.

The computer solution to the Foster Generators problem (see Figure 7.2) shows that the minimum total transportation cost is $39,500. The values for the decision variables show the optimal amounts to ship over each route. For example, with $x_{11} = 3500$, we see that 3500 units should be shipped over the Cleveland–Boston route, and with $x_{12} = 1500$, 1500 units should be shipped from Cleveland to Chicago. Other values of the decision variables indicate the remaining shipping quantities and routes. The minimum cost transportation schedule is shown in Table 7.2. Figure 7.3 provides a graphical summary of the optimal solution on the network.

FIGURE 7.2
Computer Solution of the Foster Generators Transportation Problem Using The Management Scientist

```
Objective Function Value =      39500.000000

        Variable              Value              Reduced Costs
    ------------------  ------------------  ------------------------
          X11              3500.000000              0.000000
          X12              1500.000000              0.000000
          X13                 0.000000              8.000000
          X14                 0.000000              6.000000
          X21                 0.000000              1.000000
          X22              2500.000000              0.000000
          X23              2000.000000              0.000000
          X24              1500.000000              0.000000
          X31              2500.000000              0.000000
          X32                 0.000000              4.000000
          X33                 0.000000              6.000000
          X34                 0.000000              6.000000
```

TABLE 7.2
Optimal Solution to the Foster Generators Transportation Problem

Route		Units	Per-Unit	Total
From	To	Shipped	Cost	Cost
Cleveland	Boston	3500	$3	$10,500
Cleveland	Chicago	1500	$2	3,000
Bedford	Chicago	2500	$5	12,500
Bedford	St. Louis	2000	$2	4,000
Bedford	Lexington	1500	$3	4,500
York	Boston	2500	$2	5,000
				$39,500

FIGURE 7.3
Optimal Solution to the Foster Generators Transportation Problem

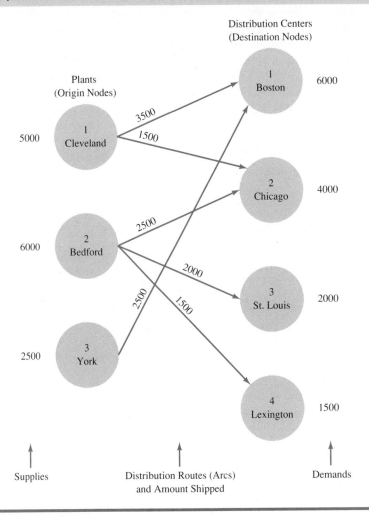

Distribution Centers
(Destination Nodes)

Plants
(Origin Nodes)

Supplies

Distribution Routes (Arcs)
and Amount Shipped

Demands

Problem Variations

The Foster Generators problem is an illustration of the basic transportation model. Additional variations of the basic transportation problem may involve one or more of the following situations:

1. Total supply not equal to total demand
2. Maximization objective function rather than minimization
3. Route capacities or route minimums
4. Unacceptable routes

With slight modifications in the linear programming model, these situations can be easily accommodated.

Often *the total supply is not equal to the total demand.* If total supply exceeds total demand, no modification in the linear programming formulation is necessary. Excess supply will appear as slack in the linear programming solution. Slack for any particular origin can be interpreted as the unused supply or amount not shipped from the origin.

If total supply is less than total demand, the linear programming model of a transportation problem will not have a feasible solution. In this case it is often desirable to provide a minimum-cost shipping schedule for the available supply and also to indicate which destinations will have unsatisfied demand. To obtain such a solution, we modify the network representation by adding a dummy origin with a supply equal to the difference between the total demand and the total supply. With the addition of the dummy origin, and an arc from the dummy origin to each destination, the linear programming model will have a feasible solution. A zero per-unit cost is assigned to each arc leaving the dummy origin so that the value of the optimal solution for the revised problem will represent the shipping cost for the units actually shipped (no shipments will actually be made from the dummy origin). When the optimal solution is implemented, the destinations showing shipments being received from the dummy origin will be the destinations experiencing a shortfall or unsatisfied demand.

In some transportation problems the objective is to find a solution that maximizes profit or revenue. Using the profit- or revenue-per-unit values as coefficients in the objective function, we simply solve a maximization rather than a minimization linear program. The constraints are not affected by this change.

The linear programming formulation of the transportation problem can also accommodate *capacities on one or more of the arcs*. For example, suppose that in the Foster Generators problem the York-to-Boston route (origin 3 to destination 1) was found to have a capacity of 1000 units because of limited space availability on its normal mode of transportation. This route capacity can be accommodated by adding a constraint to the linear programming model that provides an upper limit on the corresponding decision variable. With x_{31} denoting the amount shipped from York to Boston in the Foster Generators problem, the route capacity constraint for the York-to-Boston route would appear as

$$x_{31} \leq 1000$$

Similarly, route minimums can be specified. For example,

$$x_{22} \geq 2000$$

would guarantee that a previously committed order for a Bedford-to-Chicago delivery of 2000 units would be maintained in the optimal solution.

As a final special situation, we note that in transportation problems it may not be possible to establish a route from every origin to every destination. That is, *some routes may be unacceptable*. To handle this situation, we simply drop the corresponding arc from the network and remove the corresponding variable from the linear programming formulation. For example, if the Cleveland-to-St. Louis route were determined to be unacceptable or unusable, the arc from Cleveland to St. Louis could be dropped in Figure 7.1, and x_{13} could be removed from the linear programming formulation. Solving the resulting 11-variable, 7-constraint model would provide the optimal solution while guaranteeing that the Cleveland-to-St. Louis route is not used.

A General Linear Programming Model of the Transportation Problem

In order to show the general linear programming model of the transportation problem, we use the following notation:

i = index for origins, $i = 1, 2, \ldots, m$

j = index for destinations, $j = 1, 2, \ldots, n$

x_{ij} = number of units shipped from origin i to destination j

c_{ij} = cost per unit of shipping from origin i to destination j

s_i = supply or capacity in units at origin i

d_j = demand in units at destination j

The general linear programming model of the m-origin, n-destination transportation problem is

$$\min \quad \sum_{i=1}^{m} \sum_{j=1}^{n} c_{ij} x_{ij}$$

s.t.

$$\sum_{j=1}^{n} x_{ij} \leq s_i \qquad i = 1, 2, \ldots, m \quad \text{Supply}$$

$$\sum_{i=1}^{m} x_{ij} = d_j \qquad j = 1, 2, \ldots, n \quad \text{Demand}$$

$$x_{ij} \geq 0 \qquad \text{for all } i \text{ and } j$$

As mentioned above, additional constraints of the form $x_{ij} < L_{ij}$ can be added if the route from origin i to destination j has capacity L_{ij}. A transportation problem that includes constraints of this type is called a *capacitated transportation problem*.

▼ NOTES AND COMMENTS ▼

1. Many practitioners believe that the first step in formulating a transportation problem should be to construct a network model for the problem. Nodes are drawn to represent the origins and destinations, and arcs connecting them are drawn to represent the feasible shipping routes. It is then easy to translate the network model into a linear programming model. Just develop a constraint for each node and include a variable for each arc.

2. Transportation problems encountered in practice usually lead to very large linear programs. It is not unusual to encounter a transportation problem with 100 origins and 100 destinations. Such a problem would involve $10,000 = (100)(100)$ variables. For such a problem, special-purpose solution procedures (see Section 7.5) are much more efficient than general-purpose linear programming codes. But if speed is not an issue, a general-purpose linear programming code that has the capability to solve large problems will solve most transportation problems.

3. To handle a situation in which some routes may be unacceptable, we stated that you should drop the corresponding arc from the network and remove the corresponding variable from the linear programming formulation. In using a general linear programming computer package to handle this type of situation, it is often easier to add a constraint to the formulation that sets the variable we want to remove equal to 0.

4. The optimal solution to a transportation model will consist of integer values for the decision variables as long as all supply and demand values are integers. This is because of the special mathematical structure of the linear programming model. Each variable appears in exactly one supply and one demand constraint, and all coefficients in the constraint equations are 1's and 0's.

7.2 ▼ THE ASSIGNMENT PROBLEM: THE NETWORK MODEL AND A LINEAR PROGRAMMING FORMULATION

The assignment problem arises in a variety of decision-making situations. For example, typical assignment problems involve assigning jobs to machines, assigning workers to tasks or projects, assigning sales personnel to sales territories, assigning contracts to bidders, and so on. A distinguishing feature of the assignment problem is that *one* job, worker, etc., is assigned to *one and only one* machine, project, etc. Specifically, we look for the set of assignments that will optimize a stated objective, such as minimize cost, minimize time, or maximize profits.

As an illustration of the assignment problem, let us consider the case of Fowle Marketing Research, Inc., which has just received requests for market research studies from three new clients. The company is faced with the task of assigning project leaders to each of these three new research studies. Currently three individuals are relatively free from other major commitments and are available for the project leader assignments. Fowle's management realizes, however, that the time required to complete each study will depend on the experience and ability of the project leader assigned to the study. Since the three projects have been judged to have approximately the same priority, the company would like to assign project leaders such that the total number of days required to complete all three projects is minimized. If a project leader is to be assigned to one and only one client, what assignments should be made?

In order to answer the assignment question, Fowle's management must first consider all possible project leader–client assignments and then estimate the corresponding project completion times. With three project leaders and three clients, there is a total of nine possible assignment alternatives. The alternatives and the estimated project completion times in days are summarized in Table 7.3. Using these data, we see that Terry would require 10 days to complete client 1's project, while Carle would require 9 days for the same project. Similar completion time statements can be made about any of the other possible assignments.

TABLE 7.3
Estimated Project Completion Times (Days) for the Fowle, Inc., Assignment Problem

Project Leader	Client 1	Client 2	Client 3
1. Terry	10	15	9
2. Carle	9	18	5
3. McClymonds	6	14	3

In Figure 7.4, we show the network representation of the Fowle, Inc., assignment problem. The nodes correspond to the project leaders and clients, and the arcs represent the possible assignments of project leaders to the clients. The supply at each origin node and the demand at each destination node are one; the cost of assigning a project leader to a client is the time it takes that project leader to complete the client's task. Note the similarity between the network model of the assignment problem (Figure 7.4) and the network model of the transportation problem (Figure 7.1). The assignment problem is a special case of the transportation problem in which the amount shipped over each arc is zero or one.

Since the assignment problem is a special case of the transportation problem, the linear programming formulation can be developed quickly from the graphical model provided by the network. Again, we need a constraint for each node and a variable for each arc. As in the transportation problem, we shall find it helpful to use double-subscripted decision variables, with x_{11} denoting the assignment of project leader 1 (Terry) to client 1, x_{12} denoting the assignment of project leader 1 (Terry) to client 2, and so on. Thus, the decision variables for the Fowle, Inc., assignment problem are defined as follows:

$$x_{ij} = \begin{cases} 1 \text{ if project leader } i \text{ is assigned to client } j \\ 0 \text{ otherwise} \end{cases}$$

$$\text{where } i = 1, 2, 3, \text{ and } j = 1, 2, 3$$

FIGURE 7.4
A Network Model of the Fowle, Inc., Assignment Problem

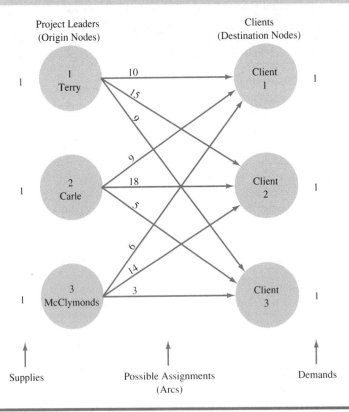

Using this notation, $x_{21} = 1$ and $x_{31} = 0$ would tell us that project leader 2 (Carle) is assigned to client 1, and project leader 3 (McClymonds) is not assigned to client 1.

Following this notation and using the completion time data in Table 7.3, we can develop the following completion time expressions:

$$\text{Days required for Terry's assignment} = 10x_{11} + 15x_{12} + 9x_{13}$$

$$\text{Days required for Carle's assignment} = 9x_{21} + 18x_{22} + 5x_{23}$$

$$\text{Days required for McClymonds' assignment} = 6x_{31} + 14x_{32} + 3x_{33}.$$

The sum of the completion times for the three project leaders will provide the total days required to complete the three assignments. Thus, the objective function is min $10x_{11} + 15x_{12} + 9x_{13} + 9x_{21} + 18x_{22} + 5x_{23} + 6x_{31} + 14x_{32} + 3x_{33}$.

The constraints for the assignment problem reflect the conditions that each project leader can be assigned to at most one client and that each client must have one assigned project leader. These constraints are written as follows:

$$
\begin{aligned}
x_{11} + x_{12} + x_{13} &\leq 1 \quad \text{Terry's assignment} \\
x_{21} + x_{22} + x_{23} &\leq 1 \quad \text{Carle's assignment} \\
x_{31} + x_{32} + x_{33} &\leq 1 \quad \text{McClymonds' assignment} \\
x_{11} + x_{21} + x_{31} &= 1 \quad \text{Client 1} \\
x_{12} + x_{22} + x_{32} &= 1 \quad \text{Client 2} \\
x_{13} + x_{23} + x_{33} &= 1 \quad \text{Client 3}
\end{aligned}
$$

Note that there is one constraint for each node in Figure 7.4.

Combining the objective function and constraints into one model provides the following nine-variable, six-constraint linear programming model of the Fowle, Inc., assignment problem:

$$\min \quad 10x_{11} + 15x_{12} + 9x_{13} + 9x_{21} + 18x_{22} + 5x_{23} + 6x_{31} + 14x_{32} + 3x_{33}$$

s.t.

$$
\begin{aligned}
x_{11} + x_{12} + x_{13} & & & \leq 1 \\
& x_{21} + x_{22} + x_{23} & & \leq 1 \\
& & x_{31} + x_{32} + x_{33} & \leq 1 \\
x_{11} & + x_{21} & + x_{31} & = 1 \\
x_{12} & + x_{22} & + x_{32} & = 1 \\
x_{13} & + x_{23} & + x_{33} & = 1
\end{aligned}
$$

$$x_{ij} \geq 0 \quad \text{for } i = 1, 2, 3, \text{ and } j = 1, 2, 3$$

Figure 7.5 shows the computer solution of the Fowle, Inc., assignment problem. Terry is assigned to client 2 ($x_{12} = 1$), Carle is assigned to client 3 ($x_{23} = 1$), and McClymonds is assigned to client 1 ($x_{31} = 1$). The total completion time required is 26 days. This solution is summarized in Table 7.4.

FIGURE 7.5
Computer Solution of the Fowle, Inc., Assignment Problem Using The Management Scientist

```
Objective Function Value =      26.000000

        Variable              Value              Reduced Costs
   -----------------    -----------------    ---------------------
          X11              0.000000                1.000000
          X12              1.000000                0.000000
          X13              0.000000                4.000000
          X21              0.000000                0.000000
          X22              0.000000                3.000000
          X23              1.000000                0.000000
          X31              1.000000                0.000000
          X32              0.000000                2.000000
          X33              0.000000                1.000000
```

TABLE 7.4
Optimal Project Leader Assignments for the Fowle, Inc., Problem

Project Leader	Assigned Client	Days
Terry	2	15
Carle	3	5
McClymonds	1	6
Total days		26

Problem Variations

Since the assignment problem can be viewed as a special case of the transportation problem, the problem variations that may arise in an assignment problem parallel those for the transportation problem. Specifically, we can handle the following:

1. The number of agents not equal to the number of tasks
2. A maximization objective function
3. Unacceptable assignments

The situation in which the number of agents is not equal to the number of tasks is analogous to total supply not equaling total demand in a transportation problem. If the number of agents exceeds the number of tasks there is no difficulty in the linear programming model; the extra agents simply remain unassigned. For instance, if there were four project leaders in the Fowle Marketing Research problem, one would remain unassigned in the optimal solution. If the number of tasks exceeds the number of agents, the linear programming model will have no feasible solution. In this situation a simple modification is to add enough dummy agents to make the number of agents equal to the number of tasks. For instance, in the Fowle Marketing Research problem we might have had five clients and only three project leaders. By adding two dummy project leaders, we can create a new assignment problem with the number of project leaders equal to the number of clients. The objective function coefficients for the assignment of dummy project leaders would be set equal to zero so that the value of the optimal solution would represent the total number of days required by the assignments actually made (no assignments will actually be made to the clients receiving dummy project leaders). The optimal solution would then call for assigning project leaders to three of the five clients; the other two clients would not receive project leaders at this time.

If the assignment alternatives are evaluated in terms of revenue or profit rather than time or cost, the linear programming formulation can be solved as a maximization rather than a minimization problem. In addition, if one or more assignments are unacceptable, the corresponding decision variable can be removed from the linear programming formulation. This could happen, for example, if a project leader did not have the experience necessary for one or more of the client assignments.

A General Linear Programming Model of the Assignment Problem

The general assignment problem involves m agents and n tasks. If we let $x_{ij} = 1$ or 0 according to whether agent i is assigned to task j or not, and if c_{ij} denotes the cost of assigning agent i to task j, then we can write the general assignment model as follows:

$$\min \ \sum_{i=1}^{m} \sum_{j=1}^{n} c_{ij}x_{ij}$$

s.t.

$$\sum_{j=1}^{n} x_{ij} \leq 1 \qquad i = 1, 2, \ldots, m \ \text{Agents}$$

$$\sum_{i=1}^{m} x_{ij} = 1 \qquad j = 1, 2, \ldots, n \quad \text{Tasks}$$

$$x_{ij} \geq 0 \qquad \text{for all } i \text{ and } j$$

If the number of tasks, n, exceeds the number of agents, m (that is, if demand exceeds supply), $n - m$ dummy agents must be included in order for us to obtain a feasible solution.

Multiple Assignments

At the beginning of this section we indicated that a distinguishing feature of the assignment problem is that *one* agent is assigned to *one and only one* task. In situations where one agent can be assigned to two or more tasks, the linear programming formulation of the problem can be easily modified to account for such cases. For example, let us assume that in the Fowle Marketing Research problem Terry was permitted to be assigned to up to two clients; in this case the constraint representing Terry's assignment would be rewritten as $x_{11} + x_{12} + x_{13} \leq 2$. In general, if a_i denotes the upper limit for the number of tasks to which agent i can be assigned, we can write the agent constraints as

$$\sum_{j=1}^{n} x_{ij} \leq a_i \qquad i = 1, 2, \ldots, m$$

Thus, we see that one advantage of formulating and solving assignment problems as linear programs is that special cases such as the situation involving multiple assignments can be easily handled.

▼ NOTES AND COMMENTS ▼

1. As noted, the assignment model is a special case of the transportation model. We stated in the notes and comments at the end of the previous section that the optimal solution to the transportation problem will consist of integer values for the decision variables as long as the supplies and demands are integer valued. For the assignment problem, all supplies and demands equal 1; thus, the optimal solution must be integer valued.
2. Combining the method for handling multiple assignments with the notion of a dummy agent provides another means of dealing with situations when the number of tasks exceeds the number of agents. That is, we add one dummy agent, but provide the dummy agent with the capability to handle multiple tasks. The number of tasks the dummy agent can handle is equal to the difference between the number of tasks and the number of agents.

7.3 ▼ THE TRANSSHIPMENT PROBLEM: THE NETWORK MODEL AND A LINEAR PROGRAMMING FORMULATION

The transshipment problem is an extension of the transportation problem in which intermediate nodes, referred to as *transshipment nodes,* are added to account for locations such as warehouses. In this more general type of distribution problem, shipments are permitted to occur between any pair of the three general types of nodes: origin nodes, transshipment nodes, and destination nodes. For example, the transshipment problem permits shipments of goods from one supply location (origin) to another supply location, from one transshipment location to another, from one destination location to another, and directly from origins to destinations.

As was true for the transportation problem, the supply available at each origin is limited, and the demand at each destination is known. The objective in the transshipment problem is to determine how many units should be shipped over each arc in the network so that all destination demands are satisfied with the minimum possible transportation cost.

Let us consider the transshipment problem faced by Ryan Electronics. Ryan is an electronics company with production facilities located in Denver and Atlanta. Components produced at either facility may be shipped to either of the firm's regional warehouses which are located in Kansas City and Louisville. From the regional warehouses the firm supplies retail outlets in Detroit, Miami, Dallas, and New Orleans. The key features of the problem are shown in the network model depicted in Figure 7.6. Note that the supply at each plant and the demand at each retail outlet are shown in the left and right margins, respectively. Nodes 1 and 2 are the origin nodes, nodes 3 and 4 are the transshipment nodes, and nodes 5, 6, 7, and 8 are the destination nodes. The transportation cost per unit for each distribution route is shown in Table 7.5 and on the arcs of the network model.

FIGURE 7.6
Network Representation of the Ryan Electronics Transshipment Problem

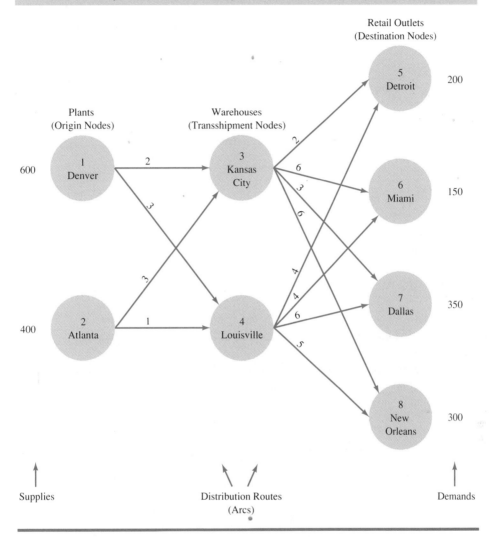

As with the transportation and assignment problems, it is easy to formulate a linear programming model of the transshipment problem, given the network representation. Again, we need a constraint for each node and a variable for each arc. Let x_{ij} denote the number of units shipped from node i to node j. For example, x_{13} denotes the number of units shipped from the Denver plant to the Kansas City warehouse, x_{14} denotes the number of units shipped from the Denver plant to the Louisville warehouse, and so on. Since the supply at the Denver plant is 600 units, the amount shipped out of the Denver plant must be less than or equal to 600. Mathematically this supply constraint is written

$$x_{13} + x_{14} \leq 600$$

Similarly, for the Atlanta plant we have

$$x_{23} + x_{24} \leq 400$$

TABLE 7.5
Unit Transportation Costs for the Ryan Electronics Transshipment Problem

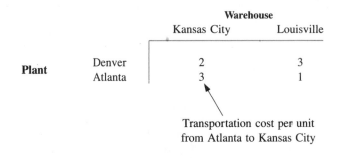

		Warehouse	
		Kansas City	Louisville
Plant	Denver	2	3
	Atlanta	3	1

Transportation cost per unit
from Atlanta to Kansas City

		Retail Outlet			
		Detroit	Miami	Dallas	New Orleans
Warehouse	Kansas City	2	6	3	6
	Louisville	4	4	6	5

Transportation cost per unit
from Louisville to Detroit

Let us now consider how we must write the constraints corresponding to the two transshipment nodes. For node 3 (the Kansas City warehouse) we must guarantee that the number of units shipped out must equal the number of units shipped into the warehouse. Since

Number of units
shipped out of node 3 $= x_{35} + x_{36} + x_{37} + x_{38}$

and

Number of units
shipped into node 3 $= x_{13} + x_{23}$

we obtain

$$x_{35} + x_{36} + x_{37} + x_{38} = x_{13} + x_{23}$$

Placing all the variables on the left-hand side of the expression enables us to write the constraint corresponding to node 3 as

$$-x_{13} - x_{23} + x_{35} + x_{36} + x_{37} + x_{38} = 0$$

In a similar manner, the constraint corresponding to node 4 is

$$-x_{14} - x_{24} + x_{45} + x_{46} + x_{47} + x_{48} = 0$$

In order to develop the constraints associated with the destination nodes, we recognize that for each node the amount shipped to the destination must equal the demand. For example, to satisfy the demand for 200 units at node 5 (the Detroit retail outlet), we can write

$$x_{35} + x_{45} = 200$$

Similarly, for nodes 6, 7, and 8, we have the following constraints:

$$x_{36} + x_{46} = 150$$

$$x_{37} + x_{47} = 350$$

$$x_{38} + x_{48} = 300$$

As usual the objective function reflects the total shipping cost over the 12 shipping routes. Combining the objective function and constraints leads to a 12-variable, 8-constraint linear programming model of the Ryan Electronics transshipment problem (see Figure 7.7).

The optimal solution was obtained using the linear programming module of The Management Scientist. Figure 7.8 shows the computer output, and Table 7.6 summarizes the optimal solution.

FIGURE 7.7
Linear Programming Formulation of the Ryan Electronics Transshipment Problem

$$\min\ 2x_{13} + 3x_{14} + 3x_{23} + 1x_{24} + 2x_{35} + 6x_{36} + 3x_{37} + 6x_{38} + 4x_{45} + 4x_{46} + 6x_{47} + 5x_{48}$$

s.t.

$x_{13} + x_{14}$ ≤ 600	Origin node	
$x_{23} + x_{24}$ ≤ 400	constraints	
$-x_{13} - x_{23} + x_{35} + x_{36} + x_{37} + x_{38}$ = 0	Transshipment node	
$-x_{14} - x_{24} + x_{45} + x_{46} + x_{47} + x_{48}$ = 0	constraints	
$x_{35} + x_{45}$ = 200		
$x_{36} + x_{46}$ = 150	Destination node	
$x_{37} + x_{47}$ = 350	constraints	
$x_{38} + x_{48}$ = 300		

$$x_{ij} \geq 0 \quad \text{for all } i \text{ and } j$$

FIGURE 7.8
Computer Solution to Ryan Electronics Transshipment Problem Using the Linear Programming Module of The Management Scientist.

```
Objective Function Value =       5200.000000

        Variable              Value              Reduced Costs
    --------------------  --------------------  --------------------
          X13               600.000000              0.000000
          X14                 0.000000              0.000000
          X23                 0.000000              3.000000
          X24               400.000000              0.000000
          X35               200.000000              0.000000
          X36                 0.000000              1.000000
          X37               350.000000              0.000000
          X38                50.000000              0.000000
          X45                 0.000000              3.000000
          X46               150.000000              0.000000
          X47                 0.000000              4.000000
          X48               250.000000              0.000000
```

TABLE 7.6
Optimal Solution to the Ryan Electronics Transshipment Problem

Route From	To	Units Shipped	Per-Unit Cost	Total Cost
Denver	Kansas City	600	$2	$1200
Atlanta	Louisville	400	$1	400
Kansas City	Detroit	200	$2	400
Kansas City	Dallas	350	$3	1050
Kansas City	New Orleans	50	$6	300
Louisville	Miami	150	$4	600
Louisville	New Orleans	250	$5	1250
				$5200

As mentioned at the beginning of this section, in the transshipment problem it is possible to have arcs between any pair of nodes. All such shipping patterns are possible in a transshipment problem. We still only require one constraint per node, but the constraint must include a variable for every arc entering or leaving the node. For origin nodes we require that the sum of the shipments out minus the sum of the shipments in be less than or equal to the origin supply. For destination nodes the sum of the shipments in minus the sum of the shipments out must equal demand. For transshipment nodes we require that the sum of the shipments out equal the sum of the shipments in, just as before.

A General Linear Programming Model of the Transshipment Problem

The general linear programming model of the transshipment problem is

$$\min \sum_{\text{all arcs}} c_{ij} x_{ij}$$

s.t.

$$\sum_{\text{arcs out}} x_{ij} - \sum_{\text{arcs in}} x_{ij} \le s_i \qquad \text{Origin nodes } i$$

$$\sum_{\text{arcs out}} x_{ij} - \sum_{\text{arcs in}} x_{ij} = 0 \qquad \text{Transshipment nodes}$$

$$\sum_{\text{arcs in}} x_{ij} - \sum_{\text{arcs out}} x_{ij} = d_j \qquad \text{Destination nodes } j$$

$$x_{ij} \ge 0 \quad \text{for all } i \text{ and } j$$

where

$$c_{ij} = \text{per-unit cost of shipping from node } i \text{ to node } j$$
$$s_i = \text{supply at node } i$$
$$d_j = \text{demand at node } j$$

One final case deserves mention. Sometimes there are capacities on arcs. In this case we simply add an upper bound constraint on the variable representing the amount shipped over the capacitated route. This is the same way route capacities are handled for the transportation problem. This more general type of transshipment problem is called the *capacitated transshipment problem.*

▼ NOTES AND COMMENTS ▼

1. In more advanced treatments of linear programming and network flow problems, the capacitated transshipment problem is called the pure network problem. Very efficient special-purpose solution procedures are available for network problems and their special cases. In Sections 7.5 and 7.6 we present special-purpose solution procedures for the transportation and assignment problems.
2. In the general linear programming formulation of the transshipment problem the constraints for the destination nodes are often written as

$$\sum_{\text{arcs out}} x_{ij} - \sum_{\text{arcs in}} x_{ij} = -d_j$$

The advantage of writing the constraints this way is that the left-hand side of each constraint then represents the flow out of the node minus the flow in. But such a constraint would then have to be multiplied by -1 to obtain a nonnegative right-hand side before solving the problem by many linear programming codes.

7.4 ▼ A PRODUCTION AND INVENTORY APPLICATION

Some applications of the transportation and transshipment models have nothing to do with the transportation of goods. For instance, in Section 7.2 we saw that the assignment problem can be viewed as a transportation problem involving the assignment of agents to tasks. Another type of problem that can be formulated and solved as a transportation or transshipment problem involves production and inventory scheduling. Let us illustrate this type of application by considering the problem faced by Contois Carpets.

When Contois Carpets installs new carpeting, one of the services offered is free removal of the existing carpet. Steve Contois, the owner, has observed that much of the carpeting removed is in good shape; he feels that if the carpet were cleaned and sanitized, it could be resold. As a result, Contois has invested in equipment that can be used to clean and sanitize the carpet prior to reselling it.

Contois would now like to develop a production and inventory schedule for the cleaning and sanitizing operation that will minimize the total production and inventory costs for the next 4 quarters. Table 7.7 shows the production capacity, demand, and cost estimates for each of the 4 quarters. Note that the production capacity, the demand, and the production cost vary by quarter; however, the cost to carry inventory from one quarter to the next is a constant $0.25 per yard. Let us now see how Contois' production and inventory scheduling problem can be formulated and solved as a transshipment problem.

We begin by developing a network representation of the problem. First, we create 4 nodes corresponding to the production center in each quarter and 4 nodes corresponding

TABLE 7.7
Production, Demand, and Cost Estimates for Contois Carpets

Quarter	Production Capacity (square yards)	Demand (square yards)	Production Cost ($ per square yard)	Inventory Cost ($ per square yard)
1	600	400	2	.25
2	300	500	5	.25
3	500	400	3	.25
4	400	400	3	.25

to the demand center in each quarter. Each production center node is connected by an outgoing arc to the demand center node for the same period. The flow on the arc represents the number of square yards of carpet cleaned and sanitized in that period. For each demand center node, an outgoing arc is used to represent the amount of inventory (square yards of carpet) carried over to the demand center node for the next period. Figure 7.9 shows the network model. Note that nodes 1 through 4 represent the production facility for each quarter and nodes 5 through 8 represent the demand center for each quarter. The quarterly production capacities are shown in the left margin and the quarterly demands are shown in the right margin.

The objective is to determine a production and inventory schedule that will minimize the total production and inventory cost over all periods. Constraints involve production capacity in each quarter and demand that must be satisfied in each quarter. As usual, a linear programming model can be developed from the network model by establishing a constraint for each node and a variable for each arc. Let us begin by showing how the constraint corresponding to node 1 is developed.

Let x_{15} denote the number of square yards of carpet cleaned and sanitized in quarter 1. Since the capacity of the facility is at most 600 square yards in quarter 1, the production capacity constraint for quarter 1 can be written as

$$x_{15} \leq 600$$

Using similar decision variables for the other 3 quarters allows us to write the production capacities for quarters 2 through 4 as shown below.

$$x_{26} \leq 300$$
$$x_{37} \leq 500$$
$$x_{48} \leq 400$$

Note that there is only 1 variable in each production capacity constraint; this is because there is only one arc out of the production node for each period.

Let us now consider the development of the constraints for each of the demand nodes. For node 5 we have one arc entering the node, which represents the number of square yards of carpet that were cleaned and sanitized in quarter 1, and one arc leaving the node, which represents the number of square yards of carpet that were not sold in quarter 1 and are carried over for possible sale in quarter 2. In general, for each quarter the beginning inventory plus the production minus the ending inventory must equal demand. However,

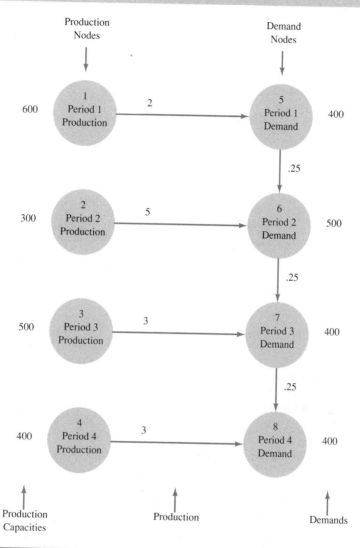

FIGURE 7.9
Network Representation of Contois Carpets Problem

for quarter 1, there is no beginning inventory; thus, the constraint for node 5 can be written as

$$x_{15} - x_{56} = 400$$

The constraints associated with the demand nodes in periods 2, 3, and 4 are written as

$$x_{56} + x_{26} - x_{67} = 500$$
$$x_{67} + x_{37} - x_{78} = 400$$
$$x_{78} + x_{48} = 400$$

Note that the constraint for node 8 (4th period demand) only involves two variables since there is no provision for ending inventory.

Since the objective is to minimize total production and inventory cost, the objective function can be written as

$$\min \quad 2x_{15} + 5x_{26} + 3x_{37} + 3x_{48} + .25x_{56} + .25x_{67} + .25x_{78}$$

The complete linear programming formulation of the Contois Carpets problem can now be written as shown below.

$$\min \quad 2x_{15} + 5x_{26} + 3x_{37} + 3x_{48} + .25x_{56} + .25x_{67} + .25x_{78}$$

s.t.

$$
\begin{array}{rcl}
x_{15} & \leq & 600 \\
x_{26} & \leq & 300 \\
x_{37} & \leq & 500 \\
x_{48} & \leq & 400 \\
x_{15} - x_{56} & = & 400 \\
x_{26} + x_{56} - x_{67} & = & 500 \\
x_{37} + x_{67} - x_{78} & = & 400 \\
x_{48} + x_{78} & = & 400 \\
\end{array}
$$

$$x_{ij} \geq 0 \quad \text{for all } i \text{ and } j$$

The Contois Carpets problem was solved using the linear programming module of The Management Scientist. The results are shown in Figure 7.10. We see that Contois Carpets should clean and sanitize 600 square yards of carpet in quarter 1, 300 square yards in quarter 2, 400 square yards in quarter 3, and 400 square yards in quarter 4. Note also that 200 square yards will be carried over from quarter 1 to quarter 2. The total production and inventory cost for this production and inventory schedule is $5150.

FIGURE 7.10
Computer Solution of the Contois Carpets Problem Using The Management Scientist

```
OPTIMAL SOLUTION

Objective Function Value =   5150.000000

        Variable              Value              Reduced Costs
    -----------------    -----------------    -----------------
          X15              600.000000              0.000000
          X26              300.000000              0.000000
          X37              400.000000              0.000000
          X48              400.000000              0.000000
          X56              200.000000              0.000000
          X67                0.000000              2.250000
          X78                0.000000              0.000000
```

▼ NOTES AND COMMENTS ▼

1. Oftentimes the same problem can be modeled in different ways. In this section we modeled the Contois Carpets problem as a transshipment problem. It can also be modeled as a transportation problem. (In problem 16 at the end of the chapter we ask you to develop such a model.)

2. In the network models we have developed for the transshipment problem, the amount leaving the starting node for an arc was always equal to the amount entering the ending node for that arc. An extension of the network model is the case where there is a gain as an arc is traversed. The amount entering the destination node may be greater or smaller than the amount leaving the origin node. For instance, if cash is the commodity flowing across an arc, then as one moves from one period to the next, the cash earns interest. Thus, the amount of cash entering the next period is greater than the amount leaving the previous period by the amount of interest earned. Networks with gains are treated in more advanced texts on network flow programming.

7.5 ▼ THE TRANSPORTATION SIMPLEX METHOD: A SPECIAL-PURPOSE SOLUTION PROCEDURE

Solving transportation problems using a general-purpose linear programming code is fine for small- to medium-sized problems. However, often these problems grow very large (a problem with 100 origins and 1000 destinations would have 100,000 variables), and, thus, more efficient solution procedures are needed. The special network structure of the transportation problem has enabled management scientists to develop special-purpose solution procedures that greatly simplify the computations.

In Section 7.1 we introduced the Foster Generators, Inc., transportation problem and showed how it could be formulated and solved as a linear program. The linear programming formulation involved 12 variables and 7 constraints. It would certainly be time consuming to attempt to solve such a problem by hand using the simplex method; however, in this section we show a special-purpose solution procedure, called the *transportation simplex method,* that takes advantage of the network structure of the transportation problem and makes it possible to solve large transportation problems efficiently on a computer and small transportation problems by hand.

Let us see how the transportation simplex method works by applying it to the Foster Generators problem. The transportation simplex method, like the simplex method for linear programs, is a two-phase procedure; it involves first finding an initial feasible solution and then proceeding iteratively to make improvements in the solution until an optimal solution is reached. In order to summarize the data conveniently and to keep track of the calculations, a *transportation tableau* is usually employed. The transportation tableau for the Foster Generators problem is presented in Table 7.8.

Note that the 12 *cells* in the tableau correspond to the 12 arcs shown in Figure 7.1; that is, each cell corresponds to the route from one plant to one distribution center. The entries in the right-hand margin of the tableau represent the supply available at each plant, and the entries in the bottom margin represent the demand at each distribution center. The

TABLE 7.8
Transportation Tableau for the Foster Generators Transportation Problem

	Boston	Chicago	St. Louis	Lexington	Origin Supply
			Destination		
Cleveland	3	2	7	6	5000
Origin Bedford	7	5	2	3	6000
York	2	5	4	5	2500
Destination Demand	6000	4000	2000	1500	13,500

Cell corresponding to
shipments from
Bedford to Boston

Total supply
and total demand

entries in the upper right-hand corner of each cell represent the per-unit cost of shipping over the corresponding route. Note also that total supply equals total demand. The transportation simplex method can be applied only to a balanced (total supply = total demand) problem; if a problem is not balanced, a dummy origin or dummy destination must be added.

Phase I: Finding an Initial Feasible Solution

The first phase of the transportation simplex method involves finding an initial feasible solution. An initial feasible solution is a set of arc flows that satisfies each demand requirement without shipping more from any origin node than the supply available. The procedures most often used to find an initial feasible solution to a transportation problem are called heuristics. A _heuristic_ is a common-sense procedure for quickly finding a solution to a problem.

There are several heuristics that have been developed to find an initial feasible solution to a transportation problem. Although some heuristics can find an initial feasible solution very quickly, oftentimes the solution they find is not very good in terms of minimizing total cost. On the other hand, some heuristics may not find an initial solution as quickly, but the solution they find is often very good in terms of minimizing total cost.

The heuristic we describe for finding an initial feasible solution to a transportation problem is called *the minimum cost method*. This heuristic strikes a compromise between finding a feasible solution quickly and finding a feasible solution that is close to the optimal solution.

The minimum cost method for identifying an initial feasible solution requires that we begin by allocating as much flow as possible to the minimum cost arc. In Table 7.8 we see that the Cleveland–Chicago, Bedford–St. Louis, and York–Boston routes each qualify as the minimum cost arc since they each have a per-unit transportation cost of 2. When ties such as this occur, we follow the convention of selecting the arc to which the most flow can be allocated. Since this corresponds to shipping 4000 units from Cleveland to Chicago, we write 4000 in the Cleveland–Chicago cell of the transportation tableau. This reduces the supply at Cleveland from 5000 to 1000; hence, we cross out the 5000 supply value and replace it with the reduced value of 1000. In addition, since allocating 4000 units to this arc satisfies the demand at Chicago, we reduce the Chicago demand to zero and eliminate the corresponding column from further consideration by drawing a line through it. The transportation tableau now appears as shown in Table 7.9

Now we look at the reduced tableau consisting of all unlined cells in order to identify the next minimum cost arc. There is a tie between the Bedford–St. Louis and York–Boston routes. More units of flow can be allocated to the York–Boston route so we choose it for the next allocation. This results in an allocation of 2500 units over the York–Boston route. To update the tableau, the York supply is reduced to zero, and we eliminate this row from further consideration by lining through it. Continuing the process results in an

TABLE 7.9
Transportation Tableau After One Iteration of the Minimum Cost Method

	Boston	Chicago	St. Louis	Lexington	Supply
Cleveland	3	2 4000	7	6	1000 ~~5000~~
Bedford	7	5	2	3	6000
York	2	5	4	5	2500
Demand	6000	~~4000~~ 0	2000	1500	

allocation of 2000 units over the Bedford–St. Louis route and the elimination of the St. Louis column since its demand goes to zero. The transportation tableau obtained after carrying out the second and third iterations is shown in Table 7.10.

We now have two arcs that qualify for the minimum cost arc with a value of 3: Cleveland–Boston and Bedford–Lexington. A flow of 1000 units can be allocated to the Cleveland–Boston route and a flow of 1500 to the Bedford–Lexington route, so we allocate 1500 units to the Bedford–Lexington route. Doing so results in a demand of zero at Lexington, and, hence, this column is eliminated. The next minimum cost allocation is 1000 over the Cleveland–Boston route. After making these two allocations, the transportation tableau appears as shown in Table 7.11.

The only remaining unlined cell is now Bedford–Boston. Allocating 2500 units to the corresponding arc uses up the remaining supply at Bedford and satisfies all the demand at Boston. The resulting tableau is shown in Table 7.12.

This solution is feasible since all the demand is satisfied and all the supply is used. The total transportation cost resulting from this initial feasible solution is calculated in Table 7.13. Phase I of the transportation simplex method is now complete; we have an initial feasible solution.

Summary of the Minimum Cost Method Before applying phase II of the transportation simplex method, let us summarize the steps of the minimum cost method for obtaining an initial feasible solution to the transportation problem.

Step 1 Identify the cell in the transportation tableau with the lowest cost, and allocate as much flow as possible to this cell. In case of a tie, choose the cell corresponding

TABLE 7.10
Transportation Tableau After Three Iterations of the Minimum Cost Method

	Boston	Chicago	St. Louis	Lexington	Supply
Cleveland	3	2 / 4000	7	6	1000 / ~~5000~~
Bedford	7	5	2 / 2000	3	4000 / ~~6000~~
~~York~~	2 / ~~2500~~	5	4	5	0 / ~~2500~~
Demand	~~6000~~ / 3500	~~4000~~ / 0	~~2000~~ / 0	1500	

TABLE 7.11
Transportation Tableau After Five Iterations of the Minimum Cost Method

	Boston	Chicago	St. Louis	Lexington	Supply
~~Cleveland~~	3 ~~1000~~	2 ~~4000~~	7	6	0 ~~1000~~ ~~5000~~
Bedford	7	5	2 2000	3 1500	2500 ~~4000~~ ~~6000~~
~~York~~	2 ~~2500~~	5	4	5	0 ~~2500~~
Demand	~~6000~~ ~~3500~~ 2500	~~4000~~ 0	~~2000~~ 0	~~1500~~ 0	

to the arc over which the most units can be shipped. If ties still exist, choose any of the tied cells.

Step 2 Reduce the row supply and the column demand by the amount of flow allocated to the cell identified in step 1.

Step 3 If *all* row supplies and column demands have been exhausted, then stop; the allocations made will provide an initial feasible solution. Otherwise, continue with step 4.

Step 4 If the row supply is now zero, eliminate the row from further consideration by drawing a line through it. If the column demand is now zero, eliminate the column by drawing a line through it.

Step 5 Continue with step 1 for all unlined rows and columns.

Phase II: Iterating to the Optimal Solution

Phase II of the transportation simplex method is a procedure for iterating from the initial feasible solution identified in phase I to the optimal solution. Recall that each cell in the transportation tableau corresponds to an arc (route) in the network model of the transportation problem. The first step at each iteration of phase II is to identify an incoming arc. The *incoming arc* is the currently unused route (unoccupied cell) where making a flow allocation will cause the largest per-unit reduction in total cost. Flow is then assigned to the incoming arc, and the amounts being shipped over all other arcs to which flow has been assigned (occupied cells) are adjusted as necessary to maintain a feasible solution.

TABLE 7.12
Final Tableau Showing the Initial Feasible Solution Obtained Using the Minimum Cost Method

	Boston	Chicago	St. Louis	Lexington	Supply
Cleveland	3 1000	2 4000	7	6	0 ~~1000~~ ~~5000~~
~~Bedford~~	7 ~~2500~~	5	2 ~~2000~~	3 ~~1500~~	0 ~~2500~~ ~~4000~~ ~~6000~~
~~York~~	2 ~~2500~~	5	4	5	0 ~~2500~~
Demand	~~6000~~ ~~3500~~ ~~2500~~ 0	~~4000~~ 0	~~2000~~ 0	~~1500~~ 0	

TABLE 7.13
Total Cost of the Initial Feasible Solution Obtained Using the Minimum Cost Method

From	Route To	Units Shipped	Per-Unit Cost	Total Cost
Cleveland	Boston	1000	$3	$ 3,000
Cleveland	Chicago	4000	$2	8,000
Bedford	Boston	2500	$7	17,500
Bedford	St. Louis	2000	$2	4,000
Bedford	Lexington	1500	$3	4,500
York	Boston	2500	$2	5,000
				Total $42,000

In the process of adjusting the flow assigned to the occupied cells, an *outgoing arc* is identified and dropped from the solution. Thus, at each iteration in phase II a currently unused arc (unoccupied cell) is brought into solution, and an arc to which flow is currently assigned (occupied cell) is removed from solution.

To show how phase II of the transportation simplex method works, we must explain how the incoming arc (cell) is identified, how the adjustments are made to the other occupied cells when flow is allocated to the incoming arc, and how the outgoing arc (cell) is identified. Let us first turn to the issue of identifying the incoming arc.

As mentioned, the incoming arc is the one that will cause the largest per-unit reduction in the total cost of the current solution. In order to identify this arc, for each unused arc we must compute the amount by which total cost will be reduced by shipping one unit over that arc. An approach referred to as the MODI method provides a simple method for making this computation.

The MODI method requires that we define an index, u_i, for each row of the tableau and an index, v_j, for each column of the tableau. These row and column indices are computed by requiring that the cost coefficient for each occupied cell equal $u_i + v_j$. If c_{ij} is the per-unit shipping cost from origin i to destination j, then we require that $u_i + v_j = c_{ij}$ for each occupied cell. Let us return to the initial feasible solution for the Foster Generators problem, which we found using the minimum cost method (see Table 7.14), and use the MODI method to identify the incoming arc.

Requiring that $u_i + v_j = c_{ij}$ for all the occupied cells in the initial feasible solution leads to a system of six equations and seven indices or variables:

Occupied cell	$u_i + v_j = c_{ij}$
Cleveland–Boston	$u_1 + v_1 = 3$
Cleveland–Chicago	$u_1 + v_2 = 2$
Bedford–Boston	$u_2 + v_1 = 7$
Bedford–St. Louis	$u_2 + v_3 = 2$
Bedford–Lexington	$u_2 + v_4 = 3$
York–Boston	$u_3 + v_1 = 2$

TABLE 7.14
Initial Feasible Solution to the Foster Generators Problem

	Boston	Chicago	St. Louis	Lexington	Supply
	3	2	7	6	
Cleveland	1000	4000			5000
	7	5	2	3	
Bedford	2500		2000	1500	6000
	2	5	4	5	
York	2500				2500
Demand	6000	4000	2000	1500	

Since there is one more index than equation in the above system, we can freely pick a value for one of the indices and then solve for the others. We shall always choose $u_1 = 0$ and then solve for the values of the other indices. Setting $u_1 = 0$, we get the following system of equations:

$$0 + v_1 = 3$$
$$0 + v_2 = 2$$
$$u_2 + v_1 = 7$$
$$u_2 + v_3 = 2$$
$$u_2 + v_4 = 3$$
$$u_3 + v_1 = 2$$

Solving these equations leads to the following values for $u_1, u_2, u_3, v_1, v_2, v_3$, and v_4:

$$u_1 = 0 \qquad v_1 = 3$$
$$u_2 = 4 \qquad v_2 = 2$$
$$u_3 = -1 \qquad v_3 = -2$$
$$v_4 = -1$$

Management scientists have shown that for each *unoccupied* cell, $e_{ij} = c_{ij} - u_i - v_j$ provides the per-unit change in total cost that will be obtained by allocating one unit of flow to the corresponding arc. Rewriting the tableau containing the initial feasible solution for the Foster Generators problem, and replacing the previous marginal information with the values of u_i and v_j, we obtain Table 7.15. In Table 7.15, the value of e_{ij} has been computed for each unoccupied cell; it is the circled number in the cell. Thus, we see that shipping one unit over the route from origin 1 to destination 3 (Cleveland–St. Louis) will increase total cost by $9; shipping one unit from origin 1 to destination 4 (Cleveland–Lexington) will increase total cost by $7; shipping one from origin 2 to destination 2 (Bedford–Chicago) will decrease total cost by $1; and so on.

On the basis of the calculated per-unit changes, we see that the best arc in terms of cost reduction is associated with the Bedford–Chicago route (origin 2–destination 2); thus, the cell in row 2 and column 2 is chosen as the incoming cell. There will be a $1 decrease in total cost for every unit of flow assigned to this arc. The question now is this: How much flow should we assign to this arc? Since the total cost decreases by $1 per unit assigned, we would like to allocate the maximum possible flow. To find that maximum, we must recognize that in order to maintain feasibility each unit of flow assigned to this arc will require adjustments in the flow over the other currently used arcs. The *stepping-stone method* can be used to determine what adjustments are necessary and to identify an outgoing arc.

The Stepping-Stone Method for Adjusting Flow and Identifying the Outgoing Arc

Suppose we allocate 1 unit of flow to the incoming arc (the Bedford–Chicago route). In order to not exceed the number of units to be shipped to Chicago, and thus maintain feasibility, we would have to reduce the flow assigned to the Cleveland–Chicago arc to 3999. But then we would have to increase the flow on the Cleveland–Boston arc to 1001 so that the total Cleveland supply of 5000 units could be shipped. Finally, we would have to reduce the flow on the Bedford–Boston arc by 1 in order to exactly satisfy the Boston demand. Table 7.16 summarizes the cycle of adjustments just described.

TABLE 7.15
Result of Using the MODI Method to Compute Per-Unit Cost Changes for the Initial Feasible Solution to the Foster Generators Problem

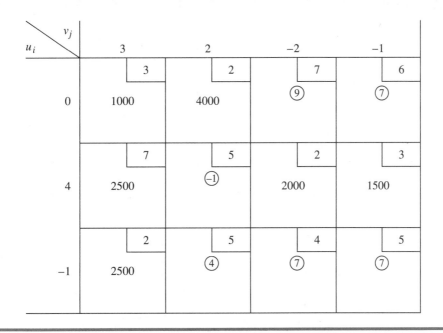

TABLE 7.16
Cycle of Adjustments in Occupied Cells Necessary to Maintain Feasibility When Shipping One Unit from Bedford to Chicago

	Boston	Chicago	St. Louis	Lexington	Supply
	3	2	7	6	
Cleveland	1001 ← 50	3999			5000
	1000	4000			
	7	5	2	3	
Bedford	2499	1	2000	1500	6000
	2500				
	2	5	4	5	
York	2500				2500
Demand	6000	4000	2000	1500	

We have seen that the cycle of adjustments necessary when an allocation is made to the Bedford–Chicago arc required changes in four cells: the incoming cell (Bedford–Chicago) and three currently occupied cells. We can view these four cells as forming a stepping-stone path in the tableau, where the corners of the path are currently occupied cells. The idea behind the stepping-stone path name is to view the tableau as a pond with the occupied cells as stones sticking up in the pond. To identify the stepping-stone path for an incoming cell, we start at the incoming cell and move in horizontal and vertical directions, using occupied cells as the stones at the corners of the path; the objective is to step from stone to stone and return to the incoming cell where we started. To help focus attention on which occupied cells are part of the stepping-stone path, we draw each occupied cell in the stepping-stone path as a cylinder; this should help to reinforce the image of these cells as stones sticking up in the pond. Table 7.17 depicts the stepping-stone path associated with the incoming arc associated with the Bedford–Chicago route.

In the above stepping-stone path we have depicted the cycle of adjustments as proceeding in a counterclockwise fashion from the incoming arc. We could also have proceeded in a clockwise fashion, and exactly the same cycle of adjustments would be obtained. Thus, moving either way is equivalent.

In Table 7.17 we have placed a plus sign ($+$) or a minus sign ($-$) in each occupied cell on the stepping-stone path. A "$+$" indicates that the allocation to that cell will increase by the same amount that we allocate to the incoming cell. A "$-$" indicates that the allocation to that cell will decrease by the amount allocated to the incoming cell. Thus,

TABLE 7.17
Stepping-Stone Path with the Bedford–Chicago Route as Incoming Arc

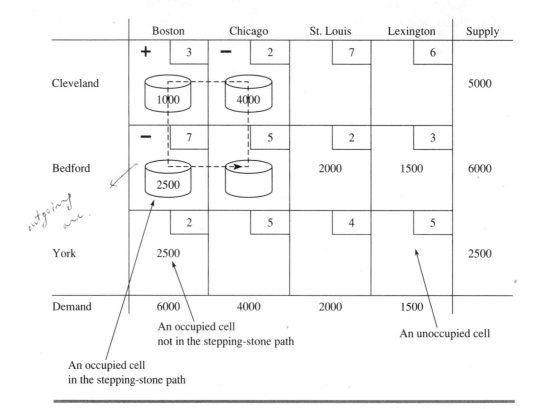

An occupied cell not in the stepping-stone path

An unoccupied cell

An occupied cell in the stepping-stone path

to determine the maximum amount that may be allocated to the incoming cell, we simply look to the cells on the stepping-stone path identified with a "$-$". Since no arc can have a negative flow allocated to it, the "$-$" cell with the smallest amount allocated to it will determine the maximum amount that can be allocated to the incoming cell. After allocating this maximum amount to the incoming cell, we then make all the adjustments necessary on the stepping-stone path to maintain feasibility. The incoming cell becomes an occupied cell, and the outgoing cell is dropped from the current solution.

In the Foster Generators problem, the Bedford–Boston and Cleveland–Chicago cells are the ones where the allocation will decrease (the ones with a "$-$") as flow is allocated to the incoming arc (Bedford–Chicago). Since the 2500 units assigned to Bedford–Boston is smaller than the 4000 units assigned to Cleveland–Chicago, we identify Bedford–Boston as the outgoing arc. The new solution is then obtained by allocating 2500 units to the Bedford–Chicago arc, making the appropriate adjustments on the stepping-stone path, and dropping Bedford–Boston from the solution. Table 7.18 shows the tableau associated with this new solution.

Note that the only changes from the previous tableau are located on the stepping-stone path originating in the Bedford–Chicago cell. We are now ready to see if further improvement in the current solution can be made. Again, the first step is to apply the MODI method to find the best incoming arc.

To apply the MODI method, we compute the row and column indices by requiring that $u_i + v_j = c_{ij}$ for all occupied cells. The values of u_i and v_j can easily be computed directly on the tableau. To illustrate how this is done, recall that we begin the MODI method by setting $u_1 = 0$. Thus, for the two occupied cells in row 1 of the table, $v_j = c_{ij}$; as a result, $v_1 = 3$ and $v_2 = 2$. Moving down the column associated with each newly

TABLE 7.18
New Solution After One Iteration in Phase II of the Transportation Simplex Method

	Boston	Chicago	St. Louis	Lexington	Supply
Cleveland	3 3500	2 1500	7	6	5000
Bedford	7	5 2500	2 2000	3 1500	6000
York	2 2500	5	4	5	2500
Demand	6000	4000	2000	1500	

computed column index, we can compute the row index associated with each occupied cell in that column by subtracting v_j from c_{ij}. Doing so for the newly found column indices, v_1 and v_2, we find that $u_3 = 2 - 3 = -1$ and $u_2 = 5 - 2 = 3$. Next, we use these newly found row indices to compute the column indices wherever there are occupied cells in the associated rows. Doing so allows us to compute $v_3 = 2 - 3 = -1$ and $v_4 = 3 - 3 = 0$. Table 7.19 shows these new row and column indices.

Also shown in Table 7.19 are the net changes (the circled numbers) in the value of the solution that will result from allocating one unit to each unoccupied cell. Recall that these net changes are given by $e_{ij} = c_{ij} - u_i - v_j$. Reviewing the tableau in Table 7.19, we see that the per-unit change for every unoccupied cell is now greater than or equal to zero. Since there is no arc to which flow can be assigned to decrease the total cost, we have reached the optimal solution. The optimal solution, together with its total cost, is summarized in Table 7.20. As expected, this solution is exactly the same as the one obtained using the linear programming solution approach (Figure 7.2).

Maintaining $m + n - 1$ Occupied Cells Recall that m represents the number of origins and n represents the number of destinations. A solution to a transportation problem that does not have a $m + n - 1$ cells with positive allocations is said to be degenerate. The solution to the Foster Generators problem is not degenerate; there are 6 occupied cells and $m + n - 1 = 3 + 4 - 1 = 6$. The problem with degeneracy is that there must be $m + n - 1$ occupied cells in order to use the MODI method to compute all the row and column indices. When degeneracy occurs, we must artificially create an occupied cell in order to compute the row and column indices. Let us illustrate how degeneracy could occur and how to deal with it.

TABLE 7.19
MODI Evaluation of Each Cell in Solution

TABLE 7.20
Optimal Solution to the Foster Generators Transportation Problem

From	Route To	Units Shipped	Per-Unit Cost	Total Cost
Cleveland	Boston	3500	$3	$10,500
Cleveland	Chicago	1500	$2	3,000
Bedford	Chicago	2500	$5	12,500
Bedford	St. Louis	2000	$2	4,000
Bedford	Lexington	1500	$3	4,500
York	Boston	2500	$2	5,000
				$39,500

TABLE 7.21
Transportation Tableau with a Degenerate Initial Feasible Solution

u_i \ v_j	3	6		Supply
0	3 35	6 25	7	60
−1	8	5 30	7	30
	4	9	11 30	30
Demand	35	55	30	

Table 7.21 shows the initial feasible solution obtained using the minimum cost method for a transportation problem involving $m = 3$ origins and $n = 3$ destinations. To use the MODI method for this problem, we must have $m + n - 1 = 3 + 3 - 1 = 5$ occupied cells. Since the initial feasible solution has only 4 occupied cells, the solution is degenerate.

Suppose we try to use the MODI method to compute row and column indices to begin phase II for this problem. Setting $u_1 = 0$, and computing the column indices for each occupied cell in row 1, we obtain $v_1 = 3$ and $v_2 = 6$ (see Table 7.21). Continuing, we would then compute the row indices for all occupied cells in columns 1 and 2. Doing so yields $u_2 = 5 - 6 = -1$. At this point, we would be unable to compute any more row and column indices because there are no occupied cells in rows 1 or 2 of column 3.

In order to compute all the row and column indices when there are less than $m + n - 1$ occupied cells, we must create 1 or more ''artificially'' occupied cells with a flow of 0. For the tableau in Table 7.21, one artificially occupied cell must be created in order to make the number of occupied cells equal to 5. Any currently unoccupied cell can be made an artificially occupied cell if doing so makes it possible to compute the remaining row and column indices. For instance, treating the cell in row 2 and column 3 of the tableau in Table 7.21 as an artificially occupied cell will enable us to compute u_3 and v_3, but placing it in row 2 and column 1 will not.

As we previously stated, whenever an artificially occupied cell is created, we assign a flow of 0 to the corresponding arc. Table 7.22 shows the tableau resulting from creating an artificially occupied cell in row 2 and column 3 of the tableau in Table 7.21. Since the creation of the artificially occupied cell results in 5 occupied cells, we can now compute the remaining row and column indices. Using the row 2 index ($u_2 = -1$) and the artificially occupied cell in row 2, we compute the column index for column 3; thus, $v_3 = c_{23} - u_2 = 7 - (-1) = 8$. Then, using the column 3 index ($v_3 = 8$) and the occupied cell in row 3 and column 3 of the tableau, we can compute the row 3 index; thus, $u_3 = c_{33} - v_3 = 11 - 8 = 3$. Table 7.22 shows the complete set of row and column indices as well as the net change per unit for each unoccupied cell.

Reviewing the net changes in Table 7.22, we identify the cell in row 3 and column 1 (net change $= -2$) as the incoming cell. The stepping-stone path showing the cycle of adjustments necessary to maintain feasibility is shown in Table 7.23. From Table 7.23 we

TABLE 7.22
Transportation Tableau with an Artificial Cell in Row 2 and Column 3

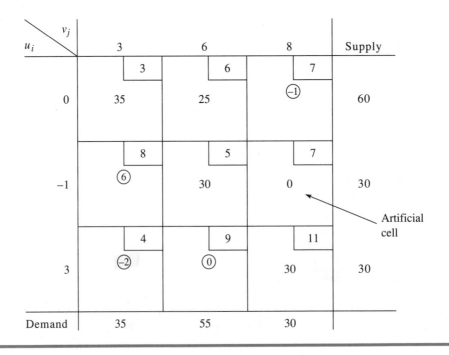

TABLE 7.23
Stepping-stone Path for the Incoming Cell in Row 3 and Column 1

u_i \ v_j	3	6	8	Supply
0	**−** 3 35	**+** 6 25	7	60
−1	8	**−** 5 30	**+** 7 0	30
3	4	9	**−** 11 30	30
Demand	35	55	30	

see that the stepping-stone path can be more complex than the simple one that was obtained for the incoming cell in the Foster Generators problem. The one in Table 7.23 requires adjustments in all 5 occupied cells in order to maintain feasibility. Again, the "+" and "−" labels simply show where increases and decreases in the allocation will occur as units of flow are added to the incoming cell. The smallest flow in a decreasing cell is a tie between the cell in row 2 and column 2 and the cell in row 3 and column 3.

Since the smallest amount in a decreasing cell is 30, the allocation we make to the incoming cell is 30 units. However, when 30 units are allocated to the incoming cell and the appropriate adjustments are made to the occupied cells on the stepping-stone path, the allocations to 2 cells go to 0 (row 2, column 2 and row 3, column 3). We may choose either one as the outgoing cell, but not both. One will be treated as unoccupied; the other will become an artificially occupied cell with a flow of 0 allocated to it. The reason we cannot let both become unoccupied cells is that doing so would lead to a degenerate solution, and, as before, we could not use the MODI method to compute the row and column indices for the next iteration. When ties occur in choosing the outgoing cell, any one of the tied cells can be chosen as the artificially occupied cell, and the MODI method can then be used to recompute the row and column indices. As long as no more than 1 cell is dropped at each iteration, the MODI method will work.

The solution obtained after allocating 30 units to the incoming cell in row 3 and column 1 and making the appropriate adjustments on the stepping-stone path leads to the tableau shown in Table 7.24. Note that we have chosen to treat the cell in row 2 and column 2 as the artificially occupied cell. The new row and column indices have been computed, and we see that the cell in row 1 and column 3 will be the next incoming cell. Each unit allocated to this cell will further decrease the value of the solution by 1. The

[handwritten margin note: decreasing cell 로에 the smallest one을 선택!]

TABLE 7.24
New Row and Column Indicies Obtained After
Allocating 30 Units to the Incoming Cell

u_i \\ v_j	3	6	8	Supply
0	3 5	6 55	7 (−1)	60
−1	8 (6)	5 0	7 30	30
1	4 30	9 (2)	11 (2)	30
Demand	35	55	30	

stepping-stone path associated with this incoming cell is shown in Table 7.25. The cell in row 2 and column 3 is the outgoing cell; the tableau after this iteration is shown in Table 7.26. Note that the optimal solution has been found and that, even though several solutions at earlier iterations were degenerate, it is not degenerate.

Summary of the Transportation Simplex Method

The transportation simplex method is a special-purpose solution procedure applicable to any network model having the special structure of the transportation problem. It is actually a clever implementation of the general simplex method for linear programming that takes advantage of the special mathematical structure of the transportation problem; but because of the special structure, the transportation simplex method is hundreds of times faster than the general simplex method.

In order to apply the transportation simplex method, we must have a transportation problem with total supply equal to total demand; thus, for some problems we may need to add a dummy origin or dummy destination to put the problem in this form. The transportation simplex method takes the problem in this form and applies a two-phase solution procedure. In phase I, the minimum cost method is applied to find an initial feasible solution. Phase II starts with the initial feasible solution and iterates until an optimal solution is reached. The steps of the transportation simplex method for a minimization problem are summarized below.

TABLE 7.25
Stepping-Stone Path Associated with the Incoming Cell in Row 1 and Column 3

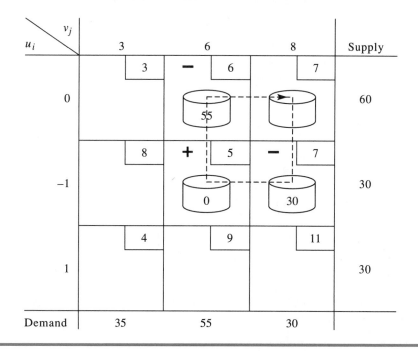

$u_i \diagdown v_j$	3	6	8	Supply
0	3	— 6 55	→ 7	60
−1	8	+ 5 0	— 7 30	30
1	4	9	11	30
Demand	35	55	30	

TABLE 7.26
Optimal Solution to a Problem with a Degenerate Initial Feasible Solution

$u_i \diagdown v_j$	3	6	7	Supply
0	3 5	6 25	7 30	60
−1	8 ④	5 30	7 ①	30
1	4 30	9 ②	11 ③	30
Demand	35	55	30	

PHASE I

Step 1. Find an initial feasible solution using the minimum cost method.

PHASE II

Step 1. If the initial feasible solution is degenerate, add an artificially occupied cell wherever necessary. Then use the MODI method to identify the incoming cell. The incoming cell is the one with the smallest value for $c_{ij} - u_i - v_j$. If $c_{ij} - u_i - v_j > 0$ for all unoccupied cells, stop; in this case the optimal solution has been found. Otherwise, go to step 2.

Step 2. Find the stepping-stone path associated with the incoming cell. Label each cell on the stepping-stone path whose flow will increase with a "+" and each cell whose flow will decrease with a "−".

Step 3. Choose as the outgoing cell the "−" cell on the stepping-stone path with the smallest flow. If there is a tie, choose any one of the tied cells. The tied cells that are not chosen will be artificially occupied with a flow of 0 at the next iteration.

Step 4. Allocate to the incoming cell the amount of flow currently allocated to the outgoing cell; make the appropriate adjustments to all cells on the stepping-stone path, and continue with step 1.

Problem Variations Let us see how the following problem variations are handled with the transportation simplex method:

1. Total supply not equal to total demand
2. Maximization objective
3. Unacceptable transportation routes (arcs)

The case where the total supply is not equal to the total demand can be handled easily by the transportation simplex method if we first introduce a dummy origin or dummy destination. If total supply is greater than total demand, we introduce a *dummy destination* with demand exactly equal to the excess of supply over demand. Similarly, if total demand is greater than total supply, we introduce a *dummy origin* with supply exactly equal to the excess of demand over supply. In either the excess demand or the excess supply case, we assign cost coefficients of zero to every arc into a dummy destination and to every arc out of a dummy origin. This is because no shipments will actually be made from a dummy origin or to a dummy destination when the solution is implemented.

The transportation simplex method can also be used to solve maximization problems. The only modification necessary involves the selection of an incoming cell. Instead of picking the cell with the most negative e_{ij} value, we pick that cell for which e_{ij} is largest. That is, we pick the cell that will cause the largest per-unit increase in the objective function.

To handle unacceptable transportation routes, we require that infeasible arcs carry an extremely high cost, denoted M, in order to keep them out of solution. Thus, if we have a transportation route (arc) from an origin to a destination that for some reason cannot be used, we simply assign this arc a per-unit cost of M, and, thus, it will not enter the solution. Unacceptable arcs would be assigned a per-unit cost of $-M$ in a maximization problem.

Let us now consider another example to show how the above difficulties can be resolved. In the process we will also show how production costs can be taken into account in a transportation problem. Suppose we have three plants (origins) with production capacities as follows:

Plants	Production Capacity
P_1	50
P_2	40
P_3	30
	Total 120

We also have demand for the product at three retail outlets (destinations). The demand forecasts for the current planning period are presented below.

Retail Outlets	Forecasted Demand
R_1	45
R_2	15
R_3	30
	Total 90

over supply

The production cost at each plant is different, and the sales prices at the retail outlets vary. Taking prices, production costs, and shipping costs into consideration, the profits for producing one unit at plant i, shipping it to retail outlet j, and selling it at retail outlet j are presented in Table 7.27.

We note first that the total production capacity exceeds the total demand at the retail outlets. Thus, we must introduce a dummy retail outlet with demand exactly equal to the excess production capacity. We therefore add retail outlet R_4 with a demand of 30 units. The per-unit profit for shipping from each plant to retail outlet R_4 is set to zero since these units will not actually be shipped. To obtain an initial feasible solution, we use the minimum cost method. However, since this is a maximization problem, the minimum cost method must be changed to a corresponding maximum profit method. That is, we select the shipping route that will maximize profit instead of minimizing cost. The initial feasible solution obtained using this approach is shown in Table 7.28.

Now let us compute the value of $e_{ij} = c_{ij} - u_i - v_j$, where the value of e_{ij} represents the per-unit change in total profit resulting from allocating one unit to the unoccupied cell in row i and column j. Table 7.29 shows the values of u_i, v_j, and e_{ij} obtained.

Since this is a maximization problem, the cell with the largest positive value for e_{ij} is the incoming cell. This is the cell in row 3 and column 3 (the route between P_3 and R_3).

TABLE 7.27
Profit per Unit for Producing at Plant i and Selling at Retail Outlet j

		Retail Outlets		
		R_1	R_2	R_3
	P_1	10	8	7
Plants	P_2	6	11	6
	P_3	12	7	11

TABLE 7.28
Initial Feasible Solution to the Maximization Transportation Problem with a Dummy Destination

8 ?

	R_1	R_2	R_3	R_4	
P_1	10 15	⑥	7 30	0 5	~~35~~ 5 50
P_2	6	11 15	6	0 25	~~25~~ 40
P_3	12 30	7	11	0	30
	45 / ~~15~~ / 0	15 / 0	30 / 0	⟨30⟩ dummy	

TABLE 7.29
MODI Method Identifies Cell in Row 3, Column 3 as Incoming Cell

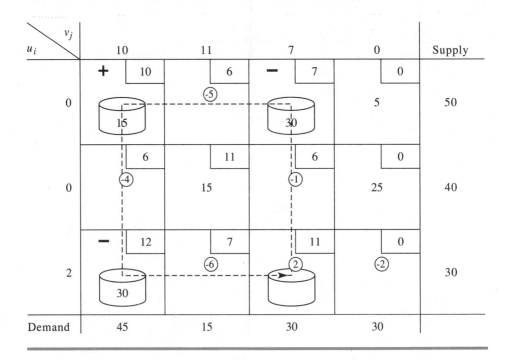

u_i \ v_j	10	11	7	0	Supply
0	+ 10 15	6 (-5)	− 7 30	0 5	50
0	6 (-4)	11 15	6 (-1)	0 25	40
2	− 12 30	7 (-6)	11 2	0 (-2)	30
Demand	45	15	30	30	

The stepping-stone path includes two "$-$" cells ($P_1 - R_3$ and $P_3 - R_1$), and there is a tie between them for the outgoing cell. Either may be chosen; we have chosen to treat the cell in row 1 and column 3 as being artificially occupied. After allocating 30 units of flow to the incoming cell and making the appropriate adjustments on the stepping-stone path, we obtain the solution shown in Table 7.30.

The MODI method has been used in Table 7.30 to obtain new values for u_i, v_j and e_{ij}. All values of e_{ij} are negative, indicating that making an allocation to any unoccupied cell will decrease the value of the solution. Since this is a maximization problem, we conclude that the current solution is optimal. When implementing this solution, we would ship 45 units from plant P_1 to retail outlet R_1, 15 units from P_2 to R_2, and 30 units from P_3 to R_3. We are left with an excess supply of 5 units at P_1 and 25 units at P_2. Note that nothing is shipped over the artificially occupied cell in row 1, column 3.

▼ NOTES AND COMMENTS ▼

1. Much research in the 1970s and 1980s has been devoted to developing efficient special-purpose solution procedures for network problems. The transportation simplex method is generally recognized as one of the best; it is used in The Management Scientist software package. A simple extension of this method can also be used to solve transshipment problems.

TABLE 7.30
Optimal Solution to the Maximization Problem

u_i \ v_j	10	11	7	0	Supply
0	10 45	6 (−5)	7 0	0 5	50
0	6 (−4)	11 15	6 (−1)	0 25	40
4	12 (−2)	7 (−8)	11 30	0 (−4)	30
Demand	45	15	30	30	

2. As we have previously noted, each cell in the transportation tableau corresponds to an arc (route) in the network model of the problem and a variable in the linear programming formulation. Phase II of the transportation simplex method is thus the same as phase II of the simplex method for linear programming. At each iteration one variable is brought into solution, and another variable is dropped from solution. The reason the method works so much better for transportation problems is that the special mathematical structure of the constraint equations means that only addition and subtraction operations are necessary. We can implement the entire procedure in a transportation tableau that has one row for each origin and one column for each destination. A simplex tableau for such a problem would require a row for each origin, a row for each destination, and a column for each arc; thus, the simplex tableau would be much larger.

7.6 ▼ THE ASSIGNMENT PROBLEM: A SPECIAL-PURPOSE SOLUTION PROCEDURE

As mentioned previously, the assignment problem is a special case of the transportation problem. Thus, the transportation simplex method can be used to solve the assignment problem. However, the assignment problem has an even more special structure; all supplies and demands equal 1. Because of this additional special structure, special-purpose solution procedures have been designed specifically to solve the assignment problem; one such procedure is called the *Hungarian method*. In this section we will show how the Hungarian method can be used to solve the Fowle Marketing Research, Inc., problem.

Recall that the Fowle, Inc., problem involved assigning project leaders to research projects; there were three project leaders available and three research projects to be completed. Fowle's assignment alternatives and estimated project completion times in days are restated in Table 7.31. A table or matrix such as this will be associated with every assignment problem.

The Hungarian method involves what is called *matrix reduction*. By subtracting and adding appropriate values in the matrix, the method determines an optimal solution to the assignment problem. There are three major steps associated with the procedure. Step 1 provides the initial matrix reduction.

TABLE 7.31
Estimated Project Completion Times (Days) for the Fowle, Inc., Assignment Problem

	Client		
Project Leader	*1*	*2*	*3*
Terry	10	15	9
Carle	9	18	5
McClymonds	6	14	3

Step 1 Reduce the initial matrix by subtracting the smallest element in each row from every element in that row. Then, using the row-reduced matrix, subtract the smallest element in each column from every element in that column.

Thus, we first reduce the matrix in Table 7.31 by subtracting the minimum value in each row from each element in the row. With the minimum values of 9 for row 1, 5 for row 2, and 3 for row 3, our row-reduced matrix becomes

	1	2	3
Terry	1	6	0
Carle	4	13	0
McClymonds	3	11	0

The assignment problem represented by this reduced matrix is equivalent to our original assignment problem in the sense that the same solution will be optimal. To understand why, first note that the row 1 minimum element, 9, has been subtracted from every element in the first row. Since Terry must still be assigned to one of the clients, the only change is that in this revised problem the time for any assignment will be nine days less. Similarly, Carle and McClymonds are shown with completion times requiring 5 and 3 fewer days, respectively.

Continuing with step 1 in the matrix reduction process, we now subtract the minimum element in each column of the row-reduced matrix from every element in the column. This also leads to an equivalent assignment problem; that is, the same solution will still be optimal, but the times required to complete each project are reduced. With the minimum values of 1 for column 1, 6 for column 2, and 0 for column 3, the reduced matrix becomes

	1	2	3
Terry	0	0	0
Carle	3	7	0
McClymonds	2	5	0

The goal of the Hungarian method is to continue reducing the matrix until the value of one of the solutions is zero—that is, until an assignment of project leaders to clients can be made that, in terms of the reduced matrix, requires a total time expenditure of zero days. Then, as long as there are no negative elements in the matrix, the zero-valued solution will be optimal. The way in which we perform this further reduction and recognize when we have reached an optimal solution is described in the following two steps.

Step 2 Find the minimum number of straight lines that must be drawn through the rows and the columns of the current matrix so that all the zeros in the matrix will be covered. If the minimum number of straight lines is the same as the number of rows (or equivalently, columns) in the matrix, an optimal assignment with value zero can be made. If the minimum number of lines is less than the number of rows, go to step 3.

Applying step 2 as shown below, we see that the minimum number of lines required to cover all the zeros is 2. Thus, we must continue to step 3.

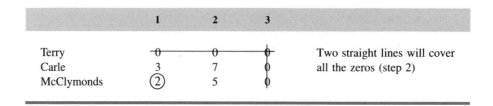

	1	2	3
Terry	0	0	0
Carle	3	7	0
McClymonds	②	5	0

Two straight lines will cover all the zeros (step 2)

Step 3 Subtract the value of the smallest unlined element from every unlined element, and add this same value to every element at the intersection of two lines. All other elements remain unchanged. Return to step 2 and continue until the minimum number of lines necessary to cover all the zeros in the matrix is equal to the number of rows.

The minimum unlined element is 2. In the matrix above we have circled this element. Subtracting 2 from all unlined elements and adding 2 to the intersection element for Terry and client 3 produces the new matrix shown below.

	1	2	3
Terry	0	0	2
Carle	1	5	0
McClymonds	0	3	0

Returning to step 2, we find that the minimum number of straight lines required to cover all the zeros in the current matrix is 3. The following matrix illustrates the step 2 calculations:

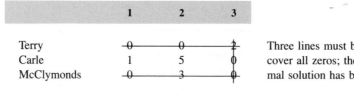

	1	2	3
Terry	0	0	2
Carle	1	5	0
McClymonds	0	3	0

Three lines must be drawn to cover all zeros; therefore, the optimal solution has been reached

According to step 2, then, it must be possible to find an assignment with a value of zero. Such an assignment can be found by first locating any row or column which contains only one zero. (If all have more than one, choose the one with the fewest or any tied with it.) We draw a square around the zero, indicating an assignment, and eliminate that row and column from further consideration. Since row 2 has only one zero in the Fowle, Inc., problem, we assign Carle to 3 and eliminate row 2 and column 3 from further consideration. McClymonds must then be assigned to 1 (the only remaining zero in row 3), and finally Terry to 2. The solution to the Fowle, Inc., problem is shown below; in terms of the reduced matrix, it requires a time expenditure of zero days.

	1	2	3
Terry	0	[0]	0
Carle	1	5	[0]
McClymonds	[0]	3	0

The value of the optimal assignment can be found by referring to the original assignment problem and summing the solution times associated with the optimal assignment—in this case, Terry to 2, Carle to 3, and McClymonds to 1. Thus, we obtain the solution time of $15 + 5 + 6 = 26$ days.

Finding the Minimum Number of Lines

Sometimes it is not obvious how the lines should be drawn through rows and columns of the matrix in order to cover all the zeros with the smallest number of lines. In these cases the following heuristic works well. Choose any row or column with a single zero. If it is a row, draw a line through the column the zero is in; if it is a column, draw a line through the row the zero is in. Continue in this fashion until all the zeros are covered.

If you make the mistake of drawing too many lines to cover the zeros in the reduced matrix and thus conclude an optimal solution has been reached when it has not, you will find you cannot identify a zero-value assignment. Thus, if you think you have reached the optimal solution, but the zero-value assignments cannot be found, go back to the previous step, and check to see if you have actually determined the minimum number of lines necessary to cover the zero elements.

Problem Variations

We now discuss how to handle the following problem variations when using the Hungarian method:

1. Number of agents not the same as the number of tasks
2. Maximization objective
3. Unacceptable assignments

The Hungarian method requires that the number of rows (people, objects, and so on) equal the number of columns (tasks, clients, and so on). Suppose that in the Fowle, Inc., example four project leaders had been available for assignment to the three new clients. Fowle still faces the same basic problem—namely, which project leaders should be assigned to which clients in order to minimize the total days required. The project completion time estimates with a fourth project leader are shown in Table 7.32.

We have seen how to apply the Hungarian method when the number of rows and the number of columns are equal. Therefore, we can apply the same procedure if we can add a new client. Since we do not have another client, we simply add a dummy column, or a dummy client. This dummy client is nonexistent, so the project leader assigned to the dummy client in the optimal assignment solution will in effect be the unassigned project leader.

What project completion time estimates should we show in this new dummy column? Actually any arbitrary value is acceptable as long as all project leaders are given the same completion time. However, since the dummy client assignment will not actually take

TABLE 7.32
Estimated Project Completion Time (Days) for the Fowle, Inc., Assignment Problem with Four Project Leaders

Project Leader	Client 1	2	3
Terry	10	15	9
Carle	9	18	5
McClymonds	6	14	3
Higley	8	16	6

place, a zero project completion time for all project leaders seems logical. The Fowle, Inc., assignment problem with a dummy client, labeled *D*, is shown in Table 7.33. (Problem 22 at the end of the chapter asks you to use the Hungarian method to determine the optimal solution to this problem.)

Note that if we had considered the case of four new clients and only three project leaders, we would have had to add a dummy row (dummy project leader) in order to apply the Hungarian method. The client receiving the dummy leader would not actually be assigned an immediate project leader and would have to wait until one becomes available. In order to obtain a problem form compatible with the solution algorithm, it may be necessary to add several dummy rows or dummy columns, but never both.

To illustrate how maximization assignment problems can be handled, let us consider the problem facing management of Salsbury Discounts, Inc. Suppose that Salsbury Discounts, Inc., has just leased a new store and is attempting to determine where various departments should be located within the store. The store manager has four locations that have not yet been assigned a department and is considering five departments that might occupy the four locations. The departments under consideration are a shoe, a toy, an auto parts, a housewares, and a record department. The store manager would like to determine the optimal assignment of departments to locations in order to maximize profits. After a careful study of the layout of the remainder of the store, and based on his experience with similar stores, the store manager has made estimates of the expected annual profit for each department in each location. These are presented in Table 7.34.

We now have an assignment problem that requires a maximization objective. However, we have a problem involving more rows than columns. Thus, we must first add a

TABLE 7.33
Estimated Project Completion Time (Days) for the Fowle, Inc., Assignment Problem with a Dummy Client

Project Leader	Client 1	2	3	D ← Dummy Client
Terry	10	15	9	0
Carle	9	18	5	0
McClymonds	6	14	3	0
Higley	8	16	6	0

TABLE 7.34
Estimated Annual Profit (Thousands of Dollars) for Each Department–Location Combination

Department	Location 1	2	3	4
Shoe	10	6	12	8
Toy	15	18	5	11
Auto parts	17	10	13	16
Housewares	14	12	13	10
Record	14	16	6	12

dummy column, corresponding to a dummy or fictitious location, in order to apply the Hungarian method. After adding a dummy column, we obtain the 5 × 5 Salsbury Discount, Inc., assignment problem shown in Table 7.35.

We can obtain an equivalent minimization assignment problem by converting all the elements in the matrix to opportunity losses. This conversion is accomplished by subtracting every element in each column from the largest element in the column.

It turns out that finding the assignment that minimizes opportunity loss leads to the same solution that maximizes the value of the assignment in the original problem. Thus, any maximization assignment problem can be converted to a minimization problem by converting the assignment matrix to one in which the elements represent opportunity losses. Hence, we begin our solution to this maximization assignment problem by developing an assignment matrix where each element represents the opportunity loss from not making the "best" assignment. The opportunity losses are presented in Table 7.36.

The opportunity loss from putting the shoe department in location 1 is $7000. That is, if we put the shoe department, instead of the best department (auto parts), in that location, we forgo the opportunity to make an additional $7000 in profit. The opportunity loss associated with putting the toy department in location 2 is zero since it yields the highest profit in that location. What about the opportunity losses associated with the dummy column? Well, the assignment of a department to this "dummy" location means that the department will not be assigned a store location in the optimal solution. Since all

TABLE 7.35
Estimated Annual Profit (Thousands of Dollars) for Each Department–Location Combination, Including a Dummy Location

Department	Location 1	2	3	4	5 (Dummy Location)
Shoe	10	6	12	8	0
Toy	15	18	5	11	0
Auto parts	17	10	13	16	0
Housewares	14	12	13	10	0
Record	14	16	6	12	0

TABLE 7.36
Opportunity Loss (Thousands of Dollars) for Each Department–Location Combination

Department	Location 1	2	3	4	5 (Dummy Location)
Shoe	7	12	1	8	0
Toy	2	0	8	5	0
Auto parts	0	8	0	0	0
Housewares	3	6	0	6	0
Record	3	2	7	4	0

departments earn the same amount from this dummy location, zero, the opportunity loss for each department is zero.

Following steps 1, 2, and 3 of the Hungarian method, we can proceed to determine the maximum profit assignment. (Problem 24 at the end of this chapter asks you to use the Hungarian method to determine the optimal solution to this problem.)

As an illustration of how we can handle unacceptable assignments, suppose that in the Salsbury Discounts, Inc., assignment problem the store manager believed that the toy department should not be considered for location 2 and the auto parts department should not be considered for location 4. Essentially the store manager is saying that, based on other considerations, such as size of area, adjacent departments, and so on, these two assignments are unacceptable alternatives.

Using the same approach for the assignment problem that we did for the transportation problem, we define a value of M for unacceptable minimization assignments and a value of $-M$ for unacceptable maximization assignments, where M is an arbitrarily large value. In fact, M is assumed so large that M plus or minus any value is still extremely large. Thus, an M-valued cell in an assignment matrix retains its M value throughout the matrix reduction calculations. An M-valued cell can never be zero, so it can never be an assignment in the final solution.

The Salsbury Discounts, Inc., assignment problem with the two unacceptable assignments is shown in Table 7.37.

TABLE 7.37
Estimated Profit for the Salsbury Department–Location Combinations

Department	Location 1	2	3	4	5
Shoe	10	6	12	8	0
Toy	15	$-M$	5	11	0
Auto parts	17	10	13	$-M$	0
Housewares	14	12	13	10	0
Record	14	16	6	12	0

When this assignment matrix is converted to an opportunity loss matrix, the $-M$ profit value will be changed to M. (Problem 26 at the end of this chapter asks you to solve this assignment problem.)

▼ SUMMARY

In this chapter we introduced transportation, assignment, and transshipment problems. All three types of problems belong to the special category of linear programs called *network flow problems*. The network model of a transportation problem consists of nodes representing a set of origins and a set of destinations. In the basic model an arc is used to represent the route from each origin to each destination. Each origin has a supply and each destination has a demand. The problem is to determine the optimal amount to ship from each origin to each destination.

The assignment model is a special case of the transportation model in which all supply and all demand values are equal to 1. We represent each agent as an origin node and each task as a destination node. The transshipment model is an extension of the transportation model to distribution problems involving transfer points referred to as transshipment nodes. In this more general model we allow for arcs between any pair of nodes. A variation of the transshipment problem allows for placing capacities on the arcs. This variation, called the *capacitated transshipment problem,* is also known in the network flow literature as the pure network problem.

We showed how each of these network flow problems could be modeled as a linear program and solved each using a general-purpose linear programming computer package. However, many practical applications of network flow models lead to very large problems for which general-purpose linear programming codes are not very efficient. The transportation simplex method was presented as an efficient special-purpose solution procedure for solving transportation problems. The procedure, and its extension to the transshipment problem, has been shown to be hundreds of times faster than the general-purpose simplex method for large transportation and transshipment problems.

An important feature to keep in mind when solving network flow problems is that the optimal solution will be integral as long as all supplies and demands are integral. Therefore, when solving any transportation, assignment, or transshipment problem in which the supplies and demands are integral, we can expect to obtain an integer-valued solution.

▼ GLOSSARY

Network   A graphical representation of a problem consisting of numbered circles (nodes) interconnected by a series of lines (arcs); arrowheads on the arcs show the direction of flow. Transportation, assignment, and transshipment problems are network flow problems.

Nodes   The intersection or junction points of a network (shown as circles).

Arcs   The lines connecting the nodes in a network.

Transportation problem   A network flow problem that often involves minimizing the cost of shipping goods from a set of origins to a set of destinations; it can be formulated and solved as a linear program by including a variable for each arc and a constraint for each node.

Capacitated transportation problem   A variation of the basic transportation problem in which there are capacities on some or all of the arcs.

Assignment problem   A network flow problem that often involves the assignment of agents to tasks; it can be formulated as a linear program and is a special case of the transportation problem.

Transshipment problem   An extension of the transportation problem to distribution problems involving transfer points and possible shipments between any pair of nodes.

Capacitated transshipment problem   A variation of the transshipment problem in which there are capacities on some or all of the arcs.

Transportation simplex method   A special-purpose solution procedure for the transportation problem.

Heuristic   A common-sense procedure for quickly finding a solution to a problem. Heuristics are used to find initial feasible solutions for the transportation simplex method.

Minimum cost method   A heuristic used to find an initial feasible solution to a transportation problem; it is easy to use and usually provides a good (but not optimal) solution.

MODI method   A procedure for determining the per-unit cost change associated with assigning flow to an unused arc in the transportation simplex method.

Stepping-stone path   The sequence of occupied cells that receive flow adjustments when flow is assigned to an unused arc in the transportation simplex method.

Incoming arc   The unused arc (represented by an unoccupied cell in the transportation tableau) to which flow is assigned during an iteration of the transportation simplex method

Degenerate solution   A solution to a transportation problem in which fewer than $m + n - 1$ arcs (cells) have positive flow; m is the number of origins, and n is the number of destinations.

Dummy origin   An origin added to a transportation problem in order to make the total supply equal to the total demand. The supply assigned to the dummy origin is the difference between the total demand and the total supply.

Dummy destination   A destination added to a transportation problem in order to make the total supply equal to the total demand. The demand assigned to the dummy destination is the difference between the total supply and the total demand.

Hungarian method   A special-purpose solution procedure for solving the assignment problem.

Dummy row(s)   Extra row(s) added to an assignment problem to provide the equal number of rows and columns required by the Hungarian solution procedure.

Dummy column(s)   Extra column(s) added to an assignment problem to provide the equal number of rows and columns required by the Hungarian method.

Opportunity loss   For each cell in an assignment matrix the opportunity loss is the difference between the largest value in the column and the value in the cell. The entries in the cells of an assignment matrix must be converted to opportunity losses to solve maximization problems using the Hungarian method.

▼ PROBLEMS

1. Consider the following network representation of a transportation problem:

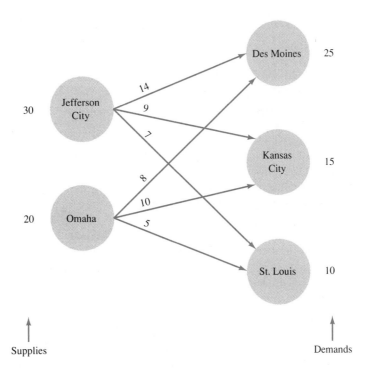

The supplies, demands, and per-unit transportation costs are shown on the network.

a. Develop a linear programming model for this problem; be sure to define the variables in your model.

b. Solve the linear program in order to determine the optimal solution.

2. A product is produced at three plants and shipped to three warehouses (the transportation costs per unit are shown in the table below).

Plant	Warehouse W_1	Warehouse W_2	Warehouse W_3	Plant Capacity
P_1	20	16	24	300
P_2	10	10	8	500
P_3	12	18	10	100
Warehouse demand	200	400	300	

a. Show a network representation of the problem.

b. Develop a linear programming model for minimizing transportation costs; solve this model to determine the minimum cost solution.

c. Suppose the entries in the table above represent profit per unit from producing at plant i and selling to warehouse j. How does the model formulation change from that in part (b)?

3. Consider the following information concerning a transportation problem:

		Destination			Supply
		Boston	*Atlanta*	*Houston*	**Supply**
Origin	Detroit	5	2	3	100
	St. Louis	8	4	3	300
	Denver	9	7	5	300
	Demand	300	200	200	

Cost/unit

a. Develop a network representation of this problem.
b. Develop a linear programming model for this transportation problem.
c. Solve the linear program formulated in part (b). What is the minimum cost solution? How many units are shipped over each transportation route?
d. Assume that a requirement is that 100 units must be shipped over the Detroit–Boston route. How would the linear programming model have to be modified to reflect this change?
e. Suppose that a labor dispute temporarily eliminates the Denver–Boston and the St. Louis–Atlanta routes. How would the linear programming model have to be revised to reflect these changes?
f. First, solve the transportation problem with the modification in part (d), and then resolve with the modification in part (e). What effect will each of these changes have on the total transportation costs and the specific transportation schedule?

4. Arnoff Enterprises manufactures the central processing unit (CPU) for a line of personal computers. The CPUs are manufactured in Seattle, Columbus, and New York and shipped to warehouses in Pittsburgh, Mobile, Denver, Los Angeles, and

	Warehouse					Units
	Pittsburgh	Mobile	Denver	Los Angeles	Washington	Available
Seattle	10	20	5	9	10	9000
Plant Columbus	2	10	8	30	6	4000
New York	1	20	7	10	4	8000
Units Required	3000	5000	4000	6000	3000	21,000

Washington, D.C., for further distribution. The transportation tableau (page 308) shows the number of CPUs available at each plant and the number of CPUs required by each warehouse. The shipping costs (dollars per unit) are also shown.

a. Develop a network representation of this problem.

b. Determine the amount that should be shipped from each plant to each warehouse in order to minimize the total shipping cost.

c. The Pittsburgh warehouse has just increased its order by 1000 units, and Arnoff has authorized the Columbus plant to increase its production by 1000 units. Do you expect this development to lead to an increase or a decrease in total shipping costs? Solve for the new optimal solution.

5. Refer again to problem 1.

  a. Set up the transportation tableau for the problem.

  b. Use the minimum cost method to find an initial feasible solution.

6. Refer again to problem 2. Use the transportation simplex method to find an optimal solution.

7. Consider the following minimum cost transportation problem:

		Destination			
		Los Angeles	San Francisco	San Diego	Supply
Origin	San Jose	4	10	6	100
	Las Vegas	8	16	6	300
	Tucson	14	18	10	300
	Demand	200	300	200	700

  a. Use the minimum cost method to find an initial solution.

  b. Use the transportation simplex method to find an optimal solution.

  c. How would the optimal solution change if we must ship 100 units on the Tucson–San Diego route?

  d. Because of road construction, the Las Vegas–San Diego route is now unacceptable. Resolve the initial problem.

8. Consider the minimum cost transportation problem shown at the top of page 310.

  a. Use the minimum cost method to find an initial feasible solution.

  b. Use the transportation simplex method to find an optimal solution.

  c. Using your solution to part (b), identify an alternate optimal solution.

	D_1	D_2	D_3	
O_1	6	8	8	250
O_2	18	12	14	150
O_3	8	12	10	100
	150	200	150	

9. Solve the following minimum cost transportation problem:

		Destination		
	D_1	D_2	D_3	Supply
O_1	1	3	4	200
Origin O_2	2	6	8	500
O_3	2	5	7	300
Demand	200	100	400	

Since total supply (1000 units) exceeds total demand (700 units), which origins may consider alternate uses for their excess supply and still maintain a minimum total transportation cost solution?

10. Klein Chemicals, Inc., produces a special oil-base material that is currently in short supply. Four of Klein's customers have already placed orders which in total exceed the combined capacity of Klein's two plants. Klein's management faces the problem of deciding how many units it should supply to each customer. Since the four customers are in different industries, the pricing structure enables different prices to

be charged to different customers. However, slightly different production costs at the two plants and varying transportation costs between the plants and customers make a "sell to the highest bidder" strategy unacceptable. After considering price, production costs, and transportation costs, Klein has established the following profit per unit for each plant–customer alternative.

profits per unit.

		Customer			
		D_1	D_2	D_3	D_4
Plant	Clifton Springs	$32	$34	$32	$40
	Danville	$34	$30	$28	$38

The plant capacities and customer orders are as follows:

Plant Capacity (units)	Distributor Orders (units)
Clifton Springs 5000	D_1 2000
	D_2 5000
Danville 3000	D_3 3000
	D_4 2000
8,000	*12,000*

How many units should each plant produce for each customer in order to *maximize* profits? Which customer demands will not be met?

11. Sound Electronics, Inc., produces a battery-operated tape recorder at plants located in Martinsville, N.C.; Plymouth, N.Y.; and Franklin, Mo. The unit transportation cost for shipments from the three plants to distribution centers in Chicago, Dallas, and New York are as follows:

From	Chicago	To Dallas	New York
Martinsville	1.45	1.60	1.40
Plymouth	1.10	2.25	0.60
Franklin	1.20	1.20	1.80

After considering transportation costs, management has decided that under no circumstances will it use the Plymouth–Dallas route. The plant capacities and distributor orders for the next month are as follows:

Plant	Capacity (units)	Distributor	Orders (units)
Martinsville	400	Chicago	400
Plymouth	600	Dallas	400
Franklin	300	New York	400

Because of different wage scales at the three plants, the unit production cost varies from plant to plant. Assuming the costs are $29.50 per unit at Martinsville, $31.20 per unit at Plymouth, and $30.35 per unit at Franklin, find the production and distribution plan that minimizes production and transportation costs.

12. The Ace Manufacturing Company has orders for three similar products:

Product	Orders (units)
A	2000
B	500
C	1200

Three machines are available for the manufacturing operations. All three machines can produce all the products at the same production rate. However, due to varying defect percentages of each product on each machine, the unit costs of the products vary depending on the machine used. Machine capacities for the next week, and the unit costs, are as follows:

Machine	Capacity (units)
I	1500
II	1500
III	1000

		Product		
		A	B	C
Machine	I	$1.00	$1.20	$0.90
	II	$1.30	$1.40	$1.20
	III	$1.10	$1.00	$1.20

a. Use the transportation model to develop the minimum cost production schedule for the products and machines.

b. Do alternate optimal production schedules exist? If the production manager would like the minimum cost schedule to have the smallest possible number of change-overs of products on machines, which solution would you recommend?

13. Forbelt Corporation has a 1-year contract to supply motors for all refrigerators produced by the Ice Age Corporation. Ice Age manufactures the refrigerators at four locations around the country: Boston, Dallas, Los Angeles, and St. Paul. Plans call for the following number (in thousands) of refrigerators to be produced at each location:

Boston	50
Dallas	70
Los Angeles	60
St. Paul	80

Forbelt has three plants that are capable of producing the motors. The plants and production capacities (in thousands) are as follows:

Denver	100
Atlanta	100
Chicago	150

Because of varying production and transportation costs, the profit Forbelt earns on each lot of 1000 units depends on which plant it was produced at and which destination it was shipped to. The following table gives the accounting department estimates of the profit per unit (shipments will be made in lots of 1000 units):

	Shipped To			
Produced At	Boston	Dallas	Los Angeles	St. Paul
Denver	7	11	8	13
Atlanta	20	17	12	10
Chicago	8	18	13	16

Given profit maximization as a criterion, Forbelt would like to determine how many motors should be produced at each plant and how many motors should be shipped from each plant to each destination.

a. Develop a network representation of this problem.

b. Find the optimal solution.

14. In Table 7.15 the per-unit cost changes for each unoccupied cell are shown.

a. Consider the arc connecting Bedford and Chicago as a candidate for the incoming arc. Allocate 1 unit of flow, and make the necessary adjustments on the stepping-stone path to maintain feasibility. Compute the value of the new solution, and show that the change in value is exactly what had been indicated by the per-unit cost change obtained using the MODI method.

b. Repeat part (a) for the arc connecting York and Lexington.

15. Refer again to the Contois Carpets problem for which the network representation is shown in Figure 7.9. Suppose Contois has a beginning inventory of 50 yards of carpet and requires an inventory of 100 yards at the end of period 4.

a. Develop a network representation of this modified problem.

b. Develop a linear programming model, and solve for the optimal solution.

16. Refer again to the Contois Carpets problem for which the network representation is shown in Figure 7.9. This problem can also be formulated and solved as a transportation problem.

a. Develop a network representation of this as a transportation problem. (*Hint:* Eliminate the inventory arcs, and add arcs showing that production in a period can be used to satisfy demand in the current period and all future periods.)

b. Solve the problem using the transportation simplex method.

17. Scott and Associates, Inc., is an accounting firm that has three new clients. Three project leaders will be assigned to the three clients. Based on the different backgrounds and experiences of the leaders, the various leader–client assignments differ in terms of projected completion times. The possible assignments and the estimated completion times in days are shown below.

Project Leader	Client 1	2	3
Jackson	10	16	32
Ellis	14	22	40
Smith	22	24	34

a. Develop a network representation of this problem.
b. Formulate the problem as a linear program, and solve. What is the total time required?

18. Consider again problem 17. Use the Hungarian method to obtain the optimal solution.
19. In problem 17 assume that an additional employee is available for possible assignment. The following table shows the assignment alternatives and the estimated completion times:

Project Leader	Client 1	2	3
Jackson	10	16	32
Ellis	14	22	40
Smith	22	24	34
Burton	14	18	36

a. What is the optimal assignment?
b. How did the assignment change compared to the best assignment possible in problem 17? Was there any savings associated with considering Burton as one of the possible project leaders?
c. Which project leader remains unassigned?

20. Wilson Distributors, Inc., is opening two new sales territories in the western states. Three individuals currently selling in the Midwest and the East are being considered for promotion to regional sales manager positions in the two new sales territories. Management has estimated total annual sales (in thousands of dollars) for the assignment of each individual to each sales territory. The management sales projections are as follows:

Regional Managers	Sales Region Northwest	Southwest
Bostock	$100	$95
McMahon	$85	$80
Miller	$90	$75

a. Develop a network representation of the problem.

b. Formulate and solve a linear programming model to obtain the optimal solution to this problem.

21. Refer again to problem 20. Use the Hungarian method to obtain the optimal solution.

22. Solve the Fowle Marketing Research, Inc., assignment problem (Section 7.6) with four project leaders available for assignment to the three clients. The estimated project completion times in days are as follows:

Project Leader	Client 1	Client 2	Client 3
Terry	10	15	9
Carle	9	18	5
McClymonds	6	14	3
Higley	8	16	6

23. **a.** Develop a network representation of the Salsbury Discount, Inc., department–location assignment problem using the estimated annual profit data provided in Table 7.34.

b. Formulate a linear programming model, and solve for the department–location assignment that maximizes profit.

24. Use the Hungarian method to solve the Salsbury Discount, Inc., problem using the profit data in Table 7.34.

25. Consider the Salsbury Discount, Inc., assignment problem with two unacceptable assignments (see Table 7.37).

a. Develop a network representation of the problem.

b. Formulate and solve a linear programming model.

26. Use the Hungarian method to solve the Salsbury Discount, Inc., problem as described in problem 25.

27. In a job shop operation, four jobs may be performed on any of four machines. The numbers of hours required for each job on each machine are summarized below. What is the minimum total time job–machine assignment?

Job	Machine A	Machine B	Machine C	Machine D
1	32	18	32	26
2	22	24	12	16
3	24	30	26	24
4	26	30	28	20

28. Mayfax Distributors, Inc., has four sales territories, each of which must be assigned a sales representative. From past experience the firm's sales manager has estimated the sales volume for each sales representative in each sales territory. Find the sales representative–territory assignments that will maximize sales (data given in thousands).

Sales Representative	Sales Territory A	B	C	D
Washington	44	80	52	60
Benson	60	56	40	72
Fredricks	36	60	48	48
Hodson	52	76	36	40

29. Four secretaries are available to type any of three company reports. Given the typing times in hours, what is the minimum total time secretary–report assignment?

Secretary	Report A	B	C
Phyllis	24	12	10
Linda	19	11	11
Dave	25	16	16
Marlene	25	14	13

30. Four trucks must be dispatched to each of four customer locations. The assignments and the distances traveled by each truck in making the trips are shown below. What truck–customer assignments minimize the total distance traveled by the four trucks? Note that two unacceptable assignments are indicated because the specific truck involved is not equipped to carry the type of shipment involved. The unacceptable assignments show M as the distance traveled.

Truck	Customer A	B	C	D
1	130	125	120	135
2	120	110	100	120
3	125	120	M	140
4	150	150	140	M

31. A market research firm has three clients who have each requested that the firm conduct a sample survey. Four statisticians are available to assign to these three projects; however, all four statisticians are busy, and therefore each can handle at most one of the clients. The following data show the number of hours it would take for each statistician to complete each job; the differences in time are due to differences in experience and ability among the statisticians.

Statistician	Client A	Client B	Client C
1	150	210	270
2	170	230	220
3	180	230	225
4	160	240	230

a. Formulate and solve a linear programming model for this problem.
b. Suppose that the time it takes statistician 4 to complete the job for client *A* is increased from 160 to 165 hours. What effect will this have on the solution?
c. Suppose that the time it takes statistician 4 to complete the job for client *A* is decreased to 140 hours. What effect will this have on the solution?
d. Suppose that the time it takes statistician 3 to complete the job for client *B* increases to 250 hours. What effect will this have on the solution?

32. Hatcher Enterprises uses a chemical called Rbase in production operations at 5 divisions. There are only 6 suppliers of Rbase that meet Hatcher's quality control standards. All 6 of the suppliers can produce Rbase in sufficient quantities to accommodate the needs of each division. The quantity of Rbase needed by each of Hatcher's divisions and the price per gallon charged by each supplier are given below.

Division	Demand (thousands of gallons)	Supplier	Price per gallon
1	40	1	$12.60
2	45	2	$14.00
3	50	3	$10.20
4	35	4	$14.20
5	45	5	$12.00
		6	$13.00

The cost per gallon for shipping from each supplier to each division is provided in the following table:

Division	1	2	3	4	5	6
1	2.75	2.50	3.15	2.80	2.75	2.75
2	.80	.20	5.40	1.20	3.40	1.00
3	4.70	2.60	5.30	2.80	6.00	5.60
4	2.60	1.80	4.40	2.40	5.00	2.80
5	3.40	.40	5.00	1.20	2.60	3.60

Hatcher believes it is important to spread business among suppliers so that the company will be less affected by supplier problems (e.g., labor strikes, resource availability, etc.). Company policy is that each division should have a separate supplier.

a. For each supplier–division combination, compute the total cost of supplying the division's demand.

b. Determine the optimal assignment of suppliers to divisions.

33. A company has two plants (P_1 and P_2), one regional warehouse (W), and two retail outlets (R_1 and R_2). The plant capacities, retail outlet demands, and per-unit shipping costs are shown in the following network:

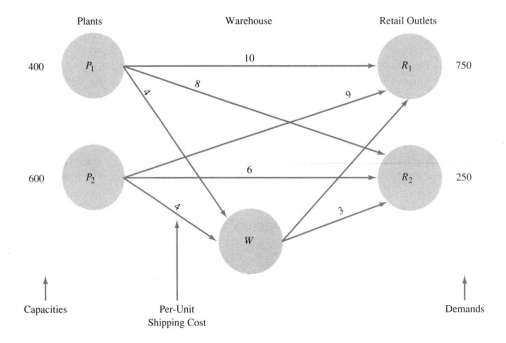

a. Formulate a linear programming model to minimize shipping costs for this problem.

b. If you have access to a linear programming computer code, determine the optimal solution for the model formulated in part (a).

c. What change would have to be made in the linear programming model if the maximum amount of goods that can be shipped from W to R_1 is 500? How would this change the optimal solution?

34. Adirondack Paper Mills, Inc., has paper plants located in Augusta, Me., and Tupper Lake, N.Y. Warehouse facilities are located in Albany, N.Y., and Portsmouth, N.H. Distributors are located in Boston, New York, and Philadelphia. The plant capacities and distributor demands for the next month are as follows:

Plant	Capacity (units)	Distributor	Demand (units)
Augusta	300	Boston	150
Tupper Lake	100	New York	100
		Philadelphia	150

The unit transportation costs for shipments from the two plants to the two warehouses and from the two warehouses to the three distributors are shown below.

		Warehouse	
		Albany	*Portsmouth*
Plant	Augusta	7	5
	Tupper Lake	3	4

		Distributor		
		Boston	*New York*	*Philadelphia*
Warehouse	Albany	8	5	7
	Portsmouth	5	6	10

a. Draw the network representation of the Adirondack Paper Mills problem.

b. Formulate the Adirondack Paper Mills problem as a linear programming problem.

c. If you have access to a linear programming computer code, determine the minimum cost shipping schedule for the problem.

35. Consider a transshipment problem consisting of three origin nodes, two transshipment nodes, and four destination nodes. The supplies at the origin nodes and the demands at the destination nodes are as follows:

Origin	**Supply**
1	400
2	450
3	350

Destination	**Demand**
1	200
2	500
3	300
4	200

The per-unit shipping costs are provided in the following table:

			To					
			Transshipment		*Destination*			
			1	2	1	2	3	4
From	*Origin*	1	6	8	—	—	—	—
		2	8	12	—	—	—	—
		3	10	5	—	—	—	—
	Transshipment	1	—	—	9	7	6	10
		2	—	—	7	9	6	8

a. Draw the network representation of this problem.

b. Formulate this as a linear programming problem.

c. Solve for the optimal solution.

36. Moore and Harman Company is in the business of buying and selling grain. An important aspect of the company's business is arranging for the purchased grain to be shipped to customers. If the company can keep freight costs low, profitability will be improved.

Currently the company has purchased three rail cars of grain at Muncie, Ind.; six rail cars at Brazil, Ind.; and five rail cars at Xenia, Ohio. Twelve carloads of grain have been sold. The locations and the amount sold at each location are as follows:

Location	Number of Rail Car Loads
Macon, Ga.	2
Greenwood, S.C.	4
Concord, S.C.	3
Chatham, N.C.	3

All shipments must be routed through either Louisville or Cincinnati. Given below are the shipping costs per bushel (in cents) from the origins to Louisville and Cincinnati as well as the costs per bushel to ship from Louisville and Cincinnati to the destinations.

From \ To	Louisville	Cincinnati
Muncie	8	6
Brazil	3	8
Xenia	9	3

Cost per bushel from Muncie to Cincinnati is 6¢

From \ To	Macon	Greenwood	Concord	Chatham
Louisville	44	34	34	32
Cincinnati	57	35	28	24

Cost per bushel from Cincinnati to Greenwood is 35¢

Determine a shipping schedule that will minimize the freight costs necessary to satisfy demand. Which (if any) rail cars of grain must be held at the origin until buyers can be found?

37. A rental car company has an imbalance of cars at 7 of its locations. The network below shows the locations of concern (the nodes) and the cost to move a car between locations. A positive number by a node indicates an excess supply at the node, and a negative number indicates an excess demand.

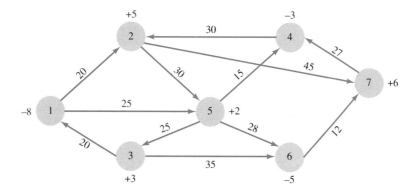

a. Develop a linear programming model of this problem.

b. Solve the model formulated in part (a) to determine how the cars should be redistributed among the locations.

38. Shown below is the linear programming formulation of a transshipment problem.

$$\min \quad 11x_{13} + 12x_{14} + 10x_{21} + 8x_{34} + 10x_{35} + 11x_{42} + 9x_{45} + 12x_{52}$$

s.t.

$$
\begin{aligned}
x_{13} + \quad x_{14} - \quad x_{21} &\qquad\qquad\qquad\qquad\qquad \le 5 \\
x_{21} \qquad\qquad\qquad - \quad x_{42} \qquad - \quad x_{52} &\le 3 \\
x_{13} \qquad\qquad - x_{34} - \quad x_{35} \qquad\qquad\qquad &= 6 \\
- \quad x_{14} \qquad\qquad - x_{34} \qquad + \quad x_{42} + \quad x_{45} \qquad\qquad &\le 2 \\
x_{35} \qquad\qquad\quad + \quad x_{45} - \quad x_{52} &= 4
\end{aligned}
$$

$$x_{ij} \ge 0 \quad \text{for all } i, j$$

Show the network representation of this problem.

▼ CASE PROBLEM

ASSIGNING UMPIRE CREWS*

The American Baseball League consists of 14 professional baseball teams organized into two divisions: the Western Division, with Seattle, Oakland, California, Texas, Kansas City, Minnesota, and Chicago, and the Eastern Division, with Milwaukee, Detroit, Cleveland, Toronto, Baltimore, New York, and Boston.

In addition to the schedules for each team, the American League must determine the best way to assign the umpire crews to the various games played throughout the league. Umpire crews are assigned to specific home-team cities for the two-, three-, or four-game series in that city, but are not assigned on an individual-game basis. Since there are 14

*The authors are indebted to James R. Evans, consultant to the American League, New York, N.Y., for providing this case problem.

American League teams, there can be as many as 7 ''games'' (double-headers count as one ''game'' in assigning crews); hence, 7 umpire crews must be assigned.

Several considerations are important in making the umpire crew assignments. Because of the amount of travel required, airline costs can be substantial. Thus, from a cost point of view, umpire crew assignments with minimum travel distances are desired. However, a second consideration in the assignment of the umpire crews is that there should be a balance such that each crew works approximately the same number of games with each team and in each city. The considerations of minimizing travel distances and, at the same time, balancing the crew assignments among the teams and cities are in conflict.

In addition to the above considerations, a number of requirements must be satisfied. The most important of these are

1. A crew cannot travel from city A to city B if the last game in city A is a night game and the first game in city B is an afternoon game on the next day.
2. A crew cannot travel from a West Coast location (Seattle, Oakland, or California) to Chicago or any Eastern Division city without a day off.
3. Because of flight scheduling difficulties, a crew traveling into or out of Toronto must have a day off unless coming from or going to New York, Boston, Detroit, or Cleveland.
4. Any crew traveling from a night game in Seattle, Oakland, or California cannot be assigned to Kansas City or Texas for a game on the next day.
5. No crew should be assigned to the same team for more than two series in a row.

The umpire crews have already been scheduled for the first four series of the five-series schedule shown in Table 7.38. Table 7.39 summarizes the crew assignments for the first four series in the schedule and shows the pairings for the fifth series. The number next to each team identification indicates the umpire crew assigned for that pairing. For example, for the fourth series, crew 1 is assigned to the Boston–Toronto games, crew 2 is assigned to the Detroit–California games, and so on.

Table 7.40 shows the distances from the cities where the fourth series is being played to the cities where the fifth series is being played. There are some other issues league management would like considered in assigning crews to the next series. Over the past nine series, crew 4 has umpired three series with Kansas City and three series with Milwaukee. Also, crew 5 has not been assigned to any games with New York, Toronto, or Detroit over the past month.

Required

Prepare a written recommendation to league management concerning the assignment of umpire crews to the fifth series that will minimize the distance traveled.

TABLE 7.38
Segment of the American League Schedule Showing Five Series

Series	Date	SEA	OAK	CAL	TEX	KC	MIN	CHI	MKE	DET	CLE	TOR	BAL	NY	BOS
									Home Team						
1	Mon.		CAL*		BOS*		SEA		TOR*	NY*	KC*		CHI*		
	Tues.		CAL*		BOS*		SEA		TOR*	NY*	KC*		CHI*		
	Wed.		CAL		BOS*		SEA		TOR*	NY	KC*		CHI*		
2	Thurs.	DET*		MKE*	KC*						CHI*		TOR*		MIN*
	Fri.	DET*	NY*	MKE*	KC*						CHI*		TOR*		MIN*
	Sat.	DET*	NY	MKE*	KC*						CHI		TOR*		MIN*
	Sun.	DET	NY(2)	MKE	KC*						CHI		TOR		MIN*
3	Mon.	MKE*		NY*		BOS*							MIN*		
	Tues.	MKE*	DET*	NY*	CHI*	BOS*						CLE*	MIN*		
	Wed.	MKE*	DET*	NY*	CHI*	BOS*						CLE*	MIN*		
	Thurs.	MKE*	DET	NY*	CHI*							CLE*			
4	Fri.	NY*	MKE*	DET*	BAL*		CLE*	KC*				BOS*			
	Sat.	NY*	MKE	DET*	BAL*		CLE*	KC*				BOS			
	Sun.	NY*	MKE	DET	BAL*		CLE	KC				BOS			
5	Mon.					TEX*		CLE*				BOS*			
	Tues.					TEX*	BOS*	CLE*	CAL*	SEA*		BAL*		OAK*	
	Wed.					TEX*	BOS*	CLE*	CAL*	SEA*		BAL*		OAK*	
	Thurs.					TEX*	BOS		CAL	SEA*		BAL*		OAK*	

*Denotes night game or early-evening start.
(2)Denotes doubleheader (two games in one day).

TABLE 7.39
Umpire Crew Assignments for the First Four Series

Series	Home Team													
	SEA	OAK	CAL	TEX	KC	MIN	CHI	MKE	DET	CLE	TOR	BAL	NY	BOS
1		CAL^5		BOS^3		SEA^7		TOR^4	NY^1	KC^6		CHI^2		MIN^1
2	DET^3	NY^2	MKE^7	KC^5						CHI^6	CLE^1	TOR^4		
3	MKE^2	DET^7	NY^3	CHI^6	BOS^5							MIN^4		
4	NY^7	MKE^3	DET^2	BAL^6		CLE^5	KC^4				BOS^1			
5					TEX	BOS	CLE	CAL	SEA		BAL		OAK	

Example: For the fourth series, umpire crew 1 is assigned to the Boston at Toronto series

TABLE 7.40
A Cost Matrix for Umpire Crew Assignments (Series 5)

Crew From	KC	MIN	CHI	To MKE	DET	TOR	NY
SEA(7)	1825	1399	2007	1694	1939	2124	2421
OAK(3)	1498	1589	2125	1845	2079	2286	2586
CAL(2)	1363	1536	2035	1756	1979	2175	2475
TEX(6)	506	853	798	843	982	1186	1383
MIN(5)	394	0	334	297	528	780	1028
CHI(4)	403	334	0	74	235	430	740
TOR(1)	968	897	497	583	206	0	366

▽
M A N A G E M E N T   S C I E N C E   I N   P R A C T I C E
▽

Optimal Decision Systems, Inc.*
Cincinnati, Ohio

Optimal Decision Systems, Inc. (ODS), is a management consulting firm that specializes in the development and implementation of decision support systems for manufacturing, transportation, and distribution applications. ODS was formed in 1978 and has a clientele that includes many Fortune 500 companies.

Systems developed by ODS use computerized models to provide managers with a menu of "good" alternatives from which the "best" alternative can be selected. Several examples of the types of problems for which ODS has developed decision support systems are listed below.

1. Locating manufacturing and distribution facilities
2. Designing sales territories, including how various distribution centers should supply the territories
3. Routing and scheduling truck fleets
4. Scheduling production systems to minimize inventory costs while maintaining desired service levels
5. Allocating capital to various investment opportunities

The majority of these applications (80%) have involved the development and implementation of large-scale mathematical programming models (linear programming, network, or mixed-integer linear programming models). Probability models and simulation have been the primary quantitative methodologies employed in the remaining applications. In addition, in almost every application, statistical analysis has played a heavy support role, particularly in the estimation of the parameters of the models.

TRUCK FLEET MANAGEMENT

The Fleet Management System (FMS) was developed by ODS for the management of private truck fleets. The heart of this system is a transshipment model that schedules and routes the company fleet over a user-specified time horizon (usually 1 to 7 days) in a way that optimizes one of the following measures of performance:

1. Savings over the use of common carrier truck fleets
2. Minimum total cost
3. Maximum total net revenue
4. Maximum load ratio (ratio of loaded miles to total miles driven by the fleet)
5. Some weighted combination of the above

In determining the optimal solution, all user-specified constraints on the operation of the truck fleet are simultaneously satisfied. Examples of such constraints are

*The authors are indebted to Richard A. Murphy and Thomas E. Thompson, Optimal Decision Systems, Inc., for providing this application.

1. Specified load movement, pickup, and delivery times
2. Minimum or maximum levels of utilization of the fleet
3. Operating hours at pickup points and delivery points
4. Restrictions on driver work hours

The Fleet Management System (FMS) accurately models the operation of a fleet, and, thus, the results of the optimization are extremely useful input to strategic (long-term), tactical (intermediate-term), and operational (short-term) planning. Some of the strategic issues that can be addressed by FMS are fleet sizing, the location of driver domiciles, equipment selection and mix, alternative operating practices (one-shift versus two-shift operation, use of double teams and/or trailer pools), and location of maintenance and refueling facilities. Tactical issues might include the timing and level of seasonal capacity such as leased drivers and equipment, the determination of which freight should be handled by common carrier and which should be handled by the private fleet, the determination of appropriate internal pricing mechanisms, the timing of the increase or decrease of capacity by driver domicile, and/or the determination of scheduling rules and procedures that yield efficient driver tours. The primary issue of operational planning is the determination of an efficient work tour for each driver.

A TRANSSHIPMENT MODEL FOR TRUCK FLEET MANAGEMENT

The primary function of the Fleet Management System is to determine an optimal schedule and route for each driver over the appropriate time horizon. For illustrative purposes, assume that all drivers (each with tractor and trailer) are located at a single domicile and that the objective is to maximize the savings that can be obtained over using common carriers for the same shipments. The system assumes the structure of a transshipment model. Capacity nodes represent the location of a driver at a particular point in time. Demand nodes represent the origin of a load movement which requires a truck to be made available for a load pickup. A driver at a capacity node is assigned to an arc connecting to a demand node. For each unit of flow on this arc (each driver assigned) cost is incurred which is the sum of the cost to travel to the location of the load movement plus any holding or delay costs that will be incurred if the driver experiences idle time. Arcs in the transshipment network are then used to assign the picked-up load to delivery locations. The net contribution on these delivery arcs is a savings the company realizes by using its own fleet of trucks rather than employing common carriers. This savings is the common carrier cost less the fuel, labor, idle time, and any other costs incurred by the company in making its own deliveries. Note that on completion of the delivery, the driver's location is defined as a capacity node, and, thus, the driver becomes available for reassignment at another point in time. Through the use of this transshipment model, the flow of the company's fleet of trucks can be scheduled over the time period of interest.

AN APPLICATION AND RESULTS

The Fleet Management System was used to develop schedules for a Fortune 500 manufacturing company that operates a private fleet of over 100 drivers and tractors. The fleet is used primarily to move raw materials into and out of the company's manufacturing facilities located in over 40 locations throughout the United States and Canada. The fleet is also used to deliver finished goods to high-priority customer accounts where service levels are critical for continued business with the customer. Prior to implementation of the Fleet Management System, the fleet had been dispatched and managed on a purely manual basis, and the company was concerned about the high cost of the truck fleet operation.

The company's objective was to use the Fleet Management System to identify a set of short-range and long-range changes in the operation that could yield significant improvements in cost and efficiency. In this case an annual saving of $1.9 million was possible by improving freight selection and by scheduling the trucks more efficiently (with fewer empty miles). In addition, specific recommendations were made to alter the size, location, and equipment mix of the truck fleet.

Questions

1. Draw a network that shows the transshipment model for truck fleet management.
2. What are the units of supply and demand at the nodes in your network? What are the units of flow over the shipping routes?

8

Integer Linear Programming

In this chapter we turn our attention to a class of problems that are modeled as linear programs with the additional requirement that some or all of the decision variables must be integer. Such problems are called *integer* linear programming problems. The use of integer variables provides additional modeling flexibility. As a result, the number of practical applications that can be addressed with linear programming methodology is enlarged. The cost of the added flexibility is that problems involving integer variables are usually much more difficult to solve. In fact, although linear programming problems involving several thousand continuous variables can be routinely solved with commercial linear programming codes, the solution of integer linear programming problems involving less than 100 variables can cause great difficulty. However, experienced management scientists can usually identify the types of integer linear programs that are easiest to solve; in such cases problems with hundreds (and sometimes thousands) of integer variables can be solved with available computer codes such as IBM's MPSX-MIP and LINDO.

The plan of this chapter is to provide an applications-oriented introduction to integer linear programming. After a short section describing the different types of integer linear programming models, we show how a graphical procedure can be used to solve problems involving two decision variables. We then discuss, in some detail, two common integer linear programming applications: capital budgeting and distribution system design. Next, we have included a section detailing the branch-and-bound solution procedure for integer linear programs with more than two variables. This solution procedure is employed by almost all commercial integer linear programming computer codes available today and is regarded as the most efficient general-purpose solution procedure. The concluding section concerns the computer solution of integer linear programs. A new application involving bank location is introduced, formulated, and solved using LINDO/PC.

8.1 ▼ TYPES OF INTEGER LINEAR PROGRAMMING MODELS

The only difference between the problems studied in this chapter and the ones studied in the earlier chapters on linear programming is that some of the variables are required to be

329

integer. If all of the variables are required to be integer, we say we have an *all-integer linear program*. Stated below is a two-variable, all-integer linear programming model.

$$\text{max} \quad 2x_1 + 3x_2$$

s.t.

$$3x_1 + 3x_2 \leq 12$$

$$\tfrac{2}{3}x_1 + 1x_2 \leq 4$$

$$1x_1 + 2x_2 \leq 6$$

$$x_1, x_2 \geq 0 \text{ and integer}$$

You will note that if the phrase "and integer" is dropped from the above model, we are left with the familiar two-variable linear program. The linear program that results from dropping the integer requirements for the decision variables is referred to as the *LP* (linear programming) *Relaxation* of the integer linear program.

If some, but not necessarily all, of the decision variables in a problem are required to be integer, we say we have a *mixed-integer linear program*. The following is a two-variable, mixed-integer linear program:

$$\text{max} \quad 3x_1 + 4x_2$$

s.t.

$$-1x_1 + 2x_2 \leq 8$$

$$1x_1 + 2x_2 \leq 12$$

$$2x_1 + 1x_2 \leq 16$$

$$x_1, x_2 \geq 0 \text{ and } x_2 \text{ integer}$$

The LP Relaxation of the above mixed-integer linear program is obtained by dropping the requirement that x_2 be integer.

In most practical applications the integer variables are only permitted to assume the values zero or one. In such cases we say we have a *binary* or a *0–1 integer linear program*. Zero–one problems may be of either the all-integer or the mixed-integer type. The capital budgeting, distribution system design, and bank location problems discussed in later sections of this chapter all make use of *0–1* variables.

8.2 ▼ GRAPHICAL SOLUTION

Security Realty Investors currently has $1,365,000 that is available for new rental property investments. After an initial screening, Security has reduced the investment alternatives to a series of townhouses and a group of apartment buildings in a large apartment complex. The townhouses can be purchased in blocks of three for the price of $195,000 per block, but there are only four blocks of townhouses available for purchase at this time. Each building in the apartment complex contains 12 dwelling units and sells for $273,000. The individual apartment buildings can be purchased separately, and the complex developer has agreed to build as many 12-unit buildings as Security would like to purchase.

Security's property manager is free to devote 140 hours per month to these investments. Each block of townhouses will require 4 hours of the property manager's time each month, while each apartment building will require 40 hours per month. The yearly cash flow (after deducting mortgage payments and operating expenses, is estimated at $2000 per block of townhouses and $3000 per apartment building. Security would like to allocate its investment funds to apartment buildings and townhouses in order to maximize the yearly cash flow.

In order to develop an appropriate mathematical model for this problem, let us introduce the following definitions for the decision variables:

$$x_1 = \text{number of blocks of townhouses purchased}$$

$$x_2 = \text{number of apartment buildings purchased}$$

The objective function, measuring cash flow in thousands of dollars, can be written as

$$\text{max} \quad 2x_1 + 3x_2$$

There are three constraints that must be satisfied:

$$195x_1 + 273x_2 \leq 1365 \quad \text{Funds available in thousands of dollars}$$

$$4x_1 + 40x_2 \leq 140 \quad \text{Manager's time in hours}$$

$$x_1 \leq 4 \quad \text{Townhouse availability in blocks}$$

In addition, the variables must be restricted to nonnegative values. Also, since fractional values for the blocks of townhouses and/or number of apartment buildings are unacceptable, the decision variables x_1 and x_2 must be integer. Thus, we see that the proper model for the Security Realty problem is the following all-integer linear program:

$$\text{max} \quad 2x_1 + 3x_2$$
s.t.
$$195x_1 + 273x_2 \leq 1365$$
$$4x_1 + 40x_2 \leq 140$$
$$x_1 \leq 4$$
$$x_1, x_2 \geq 0 \text{ and integer}$$

A first approach to solving such a problem might be to drop the integer requirements and solve the resulting LP Relaxation. You might then round off the decision variables in an attempt to find the optimal solution to the integer linear program. However, as we shall see, such an approach may not yield the optimal solution. In fact, rounding off values of the decision variables can sometimes result in an infeasible solution.

The linear program resulting from dropping the integer requirements for the decision variables (the LP Relaxation) is written as follows:

$$\text{max} \quad 2x_1 + 3x_2$$
s.t.
$$195x_1 + 273x_2 \leq 1365$$
$$4x_1 + 40x_2 \leq 140$$
$$x_1 \leq 4$$
$$x_1, x_2 \geq 0$$

The optimal solution to the LP Relaxation (see Figure 8.1) is given by $x_1 = 2.44$ and $x_2 = 3.26$. The objective function value for this solution is 14.66, corresponding to a cash

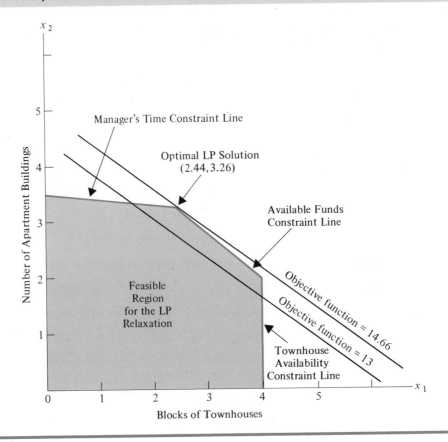

FIGURE 8.1
Graphical Solution to the LP Relaxation of the Security Realty Problem

flow of $14,660. However, this solution is not feasible for the integer linear programming problem since the decision variables assume fractional values.

Rounding the decision variables to the nearest integer value yields a solution of $x_1 = 2$ and $x_2 = 3$ for an objective function value of 13, or a $13,000 annual cash flow. In Figure 8.2 we show the feasible solution points that provide integer values for x_1 and x_2. Is the rounded solution of $x_1 = 2$ and $x_2 = 3$ the optimal integer solution? The answer is no! As can be seen in Figure 8.2, the optimal integer solution is $x_1 = 4$ and $x_2 = 2$, with an objective function value of 14.00, or a $14,000 annual cash flow. For Security Realty, the approach of rounding the linear programming solution to the nearest integer solution was not a good strategy. The rounded solution of $x_1 = 2$ and $x_2 = 3$ would have cost Security Realty $1000 a year in cash flow.

As can be seen from the Security Realty problem, the graphical procedure for solving two-variable integer linear programs is quite similar to the graphical procedure for solving linear programs. First, a graph of the feasible region for the LP Relaxation is constructed. Then the feasible integer points are denoted by heavy dots. The integer solution point on the best objective function line can then be located; this point is the optimal solution to the integer linear programming program.

FIGURE 8.2
The Integer Solution to the Security Realty Problem

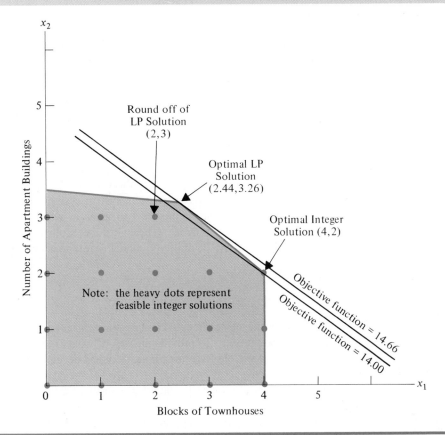

Also from our analysis of the Security Realty Investors problem, an important observation can be made about the relationship between the value of the optimal integer solution and the value of the optimal LP Relaxation solution. This observation is stated for *maximization problems*[1] as property 1.

Property 1.
The value of the optimal solution to any integer or mixed-integer linear program involving maximization yields a value *less than* or *equal to* the value of the optimal solution to its LP Relaxation.

The above property means that an *upper bound* on the value of any maximization integer or mixed-integer linear program can be found by solving its associated LP Relaxa-

[1]For minimization problems, property 1 would be stated with greater than or equal to substituted for less than or equal to.

tion. This property can be seen in Figure 8.2. The optimal LP solution is on the highest objective function line and has a value of $14.66. The optimal integer solution is on a lower objective function line and has a smaller value, $14.00. As we shall see, property 1 is used in the branch-and-bound solution procedure for solving integer linear programs.

We note in closing this section that mixed-integer linear programs with two-decision variables can be solved by a simple modification of the graphical procedure outlined above. (Problem 5 at the end of the chapter requires the graphical solution of a mixed-integer linear program.)

8.3 ▼ APPLICATIONS OF INTEGER LINEAR PROGRAMMING

In the previous section we saw an illustration of an all-integer linear program: the Security Realty Investors problem. In this section we discuss two applications involving *0–1* or binary integer variables: the capital budgeting and distribution system design problems. We have chosen these applications because they represent two areas in which integer linear programming has been used widely in practice. Through these applications you should begin to develop an appreciation of the flexibility in model development provided by *0–1* variables.

Capital Budgeting

Capital budgeting is an area where the management science approach has often led to considerable savings and/or increased profits. To provide an idea of what is involved in capital budgeting, let us consider the Ice-Cold Refrigerator problem and develop its linear programming formulation.

The Ice-Cold Refrigerator Company can invest capital funds in a variety of company projects that have varying capital requirements over the next 4 years. Faced with limited capital resources, the company must select the most profitable projects and budgets for the capital expenditures. The estimated present values of the projects, the capital requirements, and the available capital projections[2] are shown in Table 8.1.

TABLE 8.1
Project Present Values, Capital Requirements, and Available Capital Projections for the Ice-Cold Refrigerator Company

Project	Estimated Present Value ($)	Capital Requirements ($)			
		Year 1	*Year 2*	*Year 3*	*Year 4*
Plant expansion	90,000	15,000	20,000	20,000	15,000
Warehouse expansion	40,000	10,000	15,000	20,000	5,000
New machinery	10,000	10,000	0	0	4,000
New product research	37,000	15,000	10,000	10,000	10,000
Available capital funds		40,000	50,000	40,000	35,000

[2]The estimated present value is the net return for the project discounted back to the beginning of year 1.

The following definitions are chosen for the decision variables:

x_1 = 1 if the plant expansion project is accepted; 0 if rejected

x_2 = 1 if the warehouse expansion project is accepted; 0 if rejected

x_3 = 1 if the new machinery project is accepted; 0 if rejected

x_4 = 1 if the new product research project is accepted; 0 if rejected

The linear programming formulation of this capital budgeting problem has a separate constraint for each year's available funds and a separate constraint requiring each variable to be less than or equal to 1. The linear programming formulation is given below (monetary units are expressed in thousands of dollars).

$$\max \quad 90x_1 + 40x_2 + 10x_3 + 37x_4$$

s.t.

$$
\begin{aligned}
15x_1 + 10x_2 + 10x_3 + 15x_4 &\le 40 \\
20x_1 + 15x_2 \quad\quad\quad + 10x_4 &\le 50 \\
20x_1 + 20x_2 \quad\quad\quad + 10x_4 &\le 40 \\
15x_1 + 5x_2 + 4x_3 + 10x_4 &\le 35 \\
x_1 &\le 1 \\
x_2 &\le 1 \\
x_3 &\le 1 \\
x_4 &\le 1 \\
x_1, x_2, x_3, x_4 &\ge 0
\end{aligned}
$$

The optimal solution to this linear program is $x_1 = 1$, $x_2 = 0.5$, $x_3 = 0.5$, and $x_4 = 1$, with a total estimated present value of $152,000. The difficulty with a linear programming approach to the capital budgeting problem is now readily apparent. Unless it is possible to implement the warehouse expansion and new machinery projects in 50% increments, the current solution is not feasible. Thus, some adjustment in the linear programming solution, such as rounding x_2 and x_3 (possibly leading to a nonoptimal solution), must be made prior to implementation.

A preferable approach is to reformulate the Ice-Cold Refrigerator Company problem as a *0–1* integer linear program. The *0–1* integer linear programming formulation is shown below:

$$\max \quad 90x_1 + 40x_2 + 10x_3 + 37x_4$$

s.t.

$$
\begin{aligned}
15x_1 + 10x_2 + 10x_3 + 15x_4 &\le 40 \\
20x_1 + 15x_2 \quad\quad\quad + 10x_4 &\le 50 \\
20x_1 + 20x_2 \quad\quad\quad + 10x_4 &\le 40 \\
15x_1 + 5x_2 + 4x_3 + 10x_4 &\le 35 \\
x_1, x_2, x_3, x_4 &= 0, 1
\end{aligned}
$$

The LP Relaxation of the *0–1* integer program is given by the linear programming formulation above.

The optimal integer solution[3] is given by $x_1 = 1$, $x_2 = 1$, $x_3 = 1$, and $x_4 = 0$, with a total estimated present value of $140,000. We note that this optimal solution could not have been discovered by simply rounding the linear programming solution. In fact, the best feasible solution that can be found by considering all possible roundings of the fractional variables in the linear programming solution is $x_1 = 1$, $x_2 = 0$, $x_3 = 0$, $x_4 = 1$, with a total estimated present value of $127,000. This is substantially less than the value of the optimal integer solution to the capital budgeting problem.

The ability to avoid fractional values is one of two main reasons that an integer programming formulation is usually preferred for capital budgeting problems. The second reason most management scientists prefer a *0–1* integer programming model for the capital budgeting problem is the flexibility provided in developing certain nonbudgetary constraints. These constraints are often important in capital budgeting problems and can be formulated only through the use of *0–1*—sometimes called logical—variables.

Multiple-Choice and Mutually Exclusive Constraints

Suppose that instead of one warehouse expansion project, the Ice-Cold Refrigerator Company actually has three warehouse expansion projects under consideration. One of the warehouses must be expanded because of increasing product demand, but there is not sufficient new demand to make expansion of more than one warehouse profitable. The following variable definitions and *multiple-choice constraint* could be incorporated into the previous *0–1* integer linear programming model to reflect this situation. Let

$x_2 = 1$ if the original warehouse expansion project is accepted; 0 if rejected

$x_5 = 1$ if the second warehouse expansion project is accepted; 0 if rejected

$x_6 = 1$ if the third warehouse expansion project is accepted; 0 if rejected

The multiple-choice constraint reflecting the requirement that one and only one of these projects may be selected is written as follows:

$$x_2 + x_5 + x_6 = 1$$

It is easy to see why this is called a multiple-choice constraint. Since x_2, x_5, and x_6 are allowed to assume only the values 0 or 1, one and only one of these projects must be selected from among the three choices. Note that if fractional values (as in linear programming) were allowed for the decision variables, we could not enforce the requirement of selecting one and only one project (e.g., $x_2 = 1/3$, $x_5 = 1/3$, $x_6 = 1/3$ would satisfy the constraint).

If it had not been required that one warehouse be expanded, then our multiple-choice constraint could be modified as follows:

$$x_2 + x_5 + x_6 \leq 1$$

This modification allows for the case of no warehouse expansion ($x_2 = x_5 = x_6 = 0$), but does not permit more than one warehouse to be expanded. This type of constraint is often called a *mutually exclusive constraint*.

---

[3]This solution was found using the branch-and-bound solution procedure presented in Section 8.4. (Problem 8 at the end of this chapter asks you to develop the branch-and-bound solution of this problem.)

k Out of n Alternatives Constraint

An extension of the notion of a multiple-choice constraint can be used to model situations in which k out of a set of n projects must be selected. Suppose x_2, x_5, x_6, x_7, and x_8 represent five potential warehouse expansion projects and it is considered necessary to accept two of the five projects. The following constraint ensures satisfaction of this new requirement:

$$x_2 + x_5 + x_6 + x_7 + x_8 = 2$$

If it is required that no more than two of the projects be selected, we would use the following less-than-or-equal-to constraint:

$$x_2 + x_5 + x_6 + x_7 + x_8 \leq 2$$

Once again, each of the above variables must be restricted to *0–1* values.

Conditional and Corequisite Constraints

Sometimes the acceptance of one project is conditional on the acceptance of another. For example, suppose for the Ice-Cold Refrigerator Company that the warehouse expansion project was conditional on the plant expansion project. That is, the company will not consider expanding the warehouse unless the plant is expanded. With x_1 representing plant expansion and x_2 representing warehouse expansion, the following conditional constraint could be introduced to enforce this requirement:

$$x_2 \leq x_1$$

or

$$x_2 - x_1 \leq 0$$

Since both x_1 and x_2 are required to be 0 or 1, we see that whenever x_1 is 0, x_2 will be forced to 0. When x_1 is 1, x_2 is also allowed to be 1; thus, both the plant and the warehouse can be expanded. However, we note that the above constraint does not force the warehouse expansion project (x_2) to be accepted if the plant expansion project (x_1) is.

If it were required that the warehouse expansion project be accepted whenever the plant expansion project was, and vice versa, then we would say that x_1 and x_2 represented *corequisite* projects. To model such a situation we simply write the above constraint as an equality

$$x_2 = x_1$$

or

$$x_2 - x_1 = 0$$

This constraint forces x_1 and x_2 to take on the same value.

Cautionary Note on Sensitivity Analysis

Sensitivity analysis is often more critical for integer linear programming problems than for linear programming problems. A very small change in one of the coefficients in the constraints can cause a relatively large change in the value of the optimal solution. To see why this is so, consider the following integer programming model of a simple capital budgeting problem involving four projects and a budgetary constraint for a single time period:

$$\max \quad 40x_1 + 60x_2 + 70x_3 + 160x_4$$

s.t.

$$16x_1 + 35x_2 + 45x_3 + 85x_4 \le 100$$

$$x_1, x_2, x_3, x_4 = 0, 1$$

The optimal solution to this problem can be quickly found by enumerating the alternatives. It is $x_1 = 1$, $x_2 = 1$, $x_3 = 1$, and $x_4 = 0$, with an objective function value of $170. However, note that if the budget available is increased by $1 (from 100 to 101), the optimal solution changes to $x_1 = 1$, $x_2 = 0$, $x_3 = 0$, and $x_4 = 1$, with an objective function value of $200. That is, one additional dollar in the budget would lead to a $30 increase in the return. Surely management, when faced with such a situation, would increase the budget by $1. Because of the extreme sensitivity of the value of the optimal solution to the constraint coefficients, practitioners usually recommend resolving the integer linear program several times with slight variations in the coefficients before attempting to choose an optimal solution for implementation.

Distribution System Design

In Chapter 7 the following linear programming formulation for the transportation problem was developed:

$$\min \quad \sum_{i=1}^{m} \sum_{j=1}^{n} c_{ij} x_{ij}$$

s.t.

$$\sum_{j=1}^{n} x_{ij} \le s_i \quad i = 1, 2, \ldots, m \quad \text{Supply}$$

$$\sum_{i=1}^{m} x_{ij} = d_j \quad j = 1, 2, \ldots, n \quad \text{Demand}$$

$$x_{ij} \ge 0 \qquad \text{for all } i \text{ and } j$$

where

$i =$ index for origins, $i = 1, 2, \ldots, m$

$j =$ index for destinations, $j = 1, 2, \ldots, n$

$x_{ij} =$ number of units shipped from origin i to destination j

$c_{ij} =$ cost per unit of shipping from origin i to destination j

$s_i =$ supply or capacity in units at origin i

$d_j =$ demand in units at destination j

In the transportation problem it is assumed that the origins and destinations are fixed. Consequently, the problem is to determine how much of the product to ship from each origin to each destination in order to minimize the total transportation cost. However, in more general distribution system design problems, it is necessary to select the best locations for the origins as well as the amounts to ship from each origin to each destination.

Suppose the origins represent m potential locations for plants with capacities s_i and the destinations represent n retail outlets with demand d_j. A more complex distribution system design problem must now be solved. If site i is selected for a plant location, there will be a fixed cost associated with plant construction and then a variable cost associated with the number of units shipped from plant i to the various retail outlets. On the other hand, if site i is not selected, then there is no fixed cost, and no units can be shipped from site i. The introduction of one integer $0-1$ variable for each potential plant location allows us to develop a mixed-integer linear programming model for this distribution system design problem. Let

$$y_i = 1 \text{ if a plant is constructed at site } i; \, 0 \text{ if not}$$

$$f_i = \text{fixed cost of constructing a plant at site } i \text{ with capacity } s_i$$

To represent the constraint that nothing can be shipped from site i if a plant is not constructed, the supply constraints in the transportation model are modified as follows:

$$\sum_{j=1}^{n} x_{ij} \le s_i y_i \qquad i = 1, 2, \ldots, m$$

or

$$\sum_{j=1}^{n} x_{ij} - s_i y_i \le 0 \quad i = 1, 2, \ldots, m$$

Also, another term must be added to the objective function to represent the fixed cost of plant construction at each site selected:

$$\text{Fixed cost of plant construction } = \sum_{i=1}^{m} f_i y_i$$

The complete model for our distribution system design problem can now be written as

$$\min \; \sum_{i=1}^{m} \sum_{j=1}^{n} c_{ij} x_{ij} + \sum_{i=1}^{m} f_i y_i$$

s.t.

$$\sum_{j=1}^{n} x_{ij} - s_i y_i \le 0 \quad i = 1, 2, \ldots, m \quad \text{Plant capacities}$$

$$\sum_{i=1}^{m} x_{ij} = d_j \quad j = 1, 2, \ldots, n \quad \text{Demand at retail outlets}$$

$$x_{ij} \ge 0 \text{ for all } i \text{ and } j$$

$$y_i = 0, 1, \quad i = 1, 2, \ldots, m$$

This basic model[4] can be expanded to accommodate distribution systems involving shipments from plants, to warehouses, to retail outlets, and multiple products.[5] Using the special properties of $0-1$ variables, it can also be expanded to accommodate a variety of configuration constraints on the plant locations. For example, suppose site 1 were in Dallas and site 2 in Fort Worth. A company might not want to locate plants in both Dallas and Fort Worth because the cities are so close together. To prevent this, the following constraint can be added to the model:

$$y_1 + y_2 \leq 1$$

This constraint was called a mutually exclusive constraint in the previous subsection. It allows either y_1 or y_2 to equal 1, but not both. If we had written the constraint as an equality, it would be the same as the multiple-choice constraint we encountered in the capital budgeting problem. Other constraints such as the conditional or corequisite constraint can be introduced to satisfy managerially specified requirements on the configuration of plant locations.

▼ NOTES AND COMMENTS ▼

1. The general linear programming formulation of the assignment problem (see Chapter 7) is really a $0-1$ integer linear program. However, the special structure of the assignment problem allows us to solve the problem as a regular linear program and still obtain integer values for the decision variables.
2. The optimal solution to a transportation or transshipment problem with integer values for the supply and destination nodes will always be integer valued. Thus, these problems can be modeled as general linear programs or as integer programs.

8.4 ▼ BRANCH-AND-BOUND SOLUTION OF INTEGER LINEAR PROGRAMS

As with linear programs, integer linear programs involving three variables are awkward to solve graphically. Moreover, since larger problems are impossible to solve using a graphical approach, other solution procedures must be employed. Branch and bound is currently the most efficient general-purpose solution procedure for integer linear programs. Almost all commercially available integer programming computer codes employ the branch-and-bound approach.

The branch-and-bound procedure divides the set of feasible solutions to an integer programming problem into smaller subsets (branching). Then various rules are used to (1) identify the subsets that are most likely to contain the optimal solution and (2) identify the subsets that need not be explored further because they could not possibly contain the optimal solution.

[4]For computational reasons it is usually preferable to replace the m plant capacity constraints with mn shipping route capacity constraints of the form $x_{ij} \leq \min \{s_i, d_j\} y_i$ for $i = 1, \ldots, m$ and $j = 1, \ldots, n$. The coefficient for y_i in each of these constraints is the smaller of the origin capacity or the destination demand. These additional constraints often cause the solution of the LP Relaxation to be integer.
[5]A model of this type was used by a large food chain and resulted in substantial savings in distribution system costs. See Geoffrion and Graves, ''Distribution System Design by Benders Decomposition,'' *Management Science* (January 1974):

An upper bound on the value of the best solution in each subset is obtained by solving an LP Relaxation. Any time the solution to the LP Relaxation results in an integer solution, the best solution in the subset has been found, and a lower bound for the subset is obtained. The best of the integer feasible solutions (considering all the subsets) is the optimal solution.

In this section we show how the branch-and-bound approach can be used to solve integer programming problems by applying it to the all-integer Security Realty Investors problem. We then comment on how it can be extended to mixed-integer linear programs and present a flowchart summarizing the steps in the procedure.

The branch-and-bound procedure begins by solving the LP Relaxation of the integer linear program. The LP Relaxation of the Security Realty Investors problem is restated below:

$$\max \quad 2x_1 + 3x_2$$

s.t.

$$195x_1 + 273x_2 \leq 1365$$
$$4x_1 + 40x_2 \leq 140$$
$$x_1 \qquad \leq 4$$
$$x_1, x_2 \geq 0$$

The solution is $x_1 = 2.44$ and $x_2 = 3.26$, with an objective function value equal to 14.66. Had the optimal solution to the LP Relaxation satisfied the integer requirements, we would have had the optimal solution to the integer linear program. Since this did not occur, we will continue with the branch-and-bound procedure. As a first step, note that property 1 in Section 8.2 indicates that solving the LP Relaxation of an integer linear program provides an upper bound on the value of the solution to the integer linear programming problem. Thus, we know that the value of the integer optimal solution to the Security Realty problem cannot exceed 14.66.

Since the coefficients of all the variables in the constraints are nonnegative and since the constraints are all of the $\leq$ type, a feasible integer solution can be found by rounding down for each decision variable; that is, rounding down can only reduce the left-hand side of the inequality and hence must always provide a feasible solution. The feasible solution found by rounding down is $x_1 = 2$ and $x_2 = 3$, with an objective function value of 13. The value of this feasible solution provides a lower bound on the value of the optimal solution to the integer linear program since we know that the value of the optimal solution must yield a value greater than or equal to the value of any feasible solution. Thus, a lower bound of 13 can be established. The first node of our branch-and-bound solution tree appears as shown below, where UB refers to upper bound and LB to lower bound.

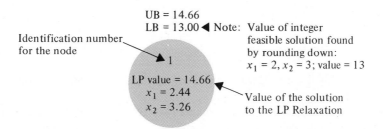

We now know that the value of the optimal solution must be between the upper bound of 14.66 and the lower bound of 13. Although we have already found a feasible solution with a value of 13, we must continue to see if a better solution can be found. This is where the branching part of the branch-and-bound solution procedure comes into play.

The set of feasible solutions to the LP Relaxation is partitioned into two subsets. These subsets are created by choosing the integer variable that is furthest from being integral to branch on; hence, x_1 with a value of 2.44 is selected. In the optimal integer solution, x_1 must be integer, so we see that either x_1 will be less than or equal to 2 or x_1 will be greater than or equal to 3. Thus, two branches and two *descendant nodes* are created for our branch-and-bound solution tree. One descendant node corresponds to the subset of solutions with $x_1 \leq 2$; the other corresponds to the subset of solutions with $x_1 \geq 3$. Since x_1 must be integral, the optimal solution must be contained in one of these two subsets.

The first branch is created by adding the constraint $x_1 \leq 2$ to the Security Realty problem. We will refer to the node created as node 2. Thus, at node 2 the LP Relaxation is solved.

LP Relaxation at node 2:

$$\max \quad 2x_1 + 3x_2$$

$$\text{s.t.}$$

$$195x_1 + 273x_2 \leq 1365$$
$$4x_1 + 40x_2 \leq 140$$
$$x_1 \qquad \leq 4$$
$$x_1 \qquad \leq 2$$
$$x_1, x_2 \geq 0$$

We note that the added constraint ($x_1 \leq 2$) makes the constraint $x_1 \leq 4$ redundant. This is just a coincidence and does not always happen. The solution to this linear program yields $x_1 = 2$ and $x_2 = 3.30$, with value equal to 13.90.

The second branch from node 1 is created by adding the constraint $x_1 \geq 3$ to the LP Relaxation of the Security Realty problem. Thus, at node 3 the following LP Relaxation is solved.

LP Relaxation at node 3:

$$\max \quad 2x_1 + 3x_2$$

$$\text{s.t.}$$

$$195x_1 + 273x_2 \leq 1365$$
$$4x_1 + 40x_2 \leq 140$$
$$x_1 \qquad \leq 4$$
$$x_1 \qquad \geq 3$$
$$x_1, x_2 \geq 0$$

The solution to this linear program yields $x_1 = 3$, and $x_2 = 2.86$, with value equal to 14.58.

From property 1 we know that the value of the LP Relaxation at node 2 is an upper bound on all solutions with $x_1 \leq 2$, and the value of the LP Relaxation at node 3 is an upper bound on all solutions with $x_1 \geq 3$. Since these two subsets include all solutions to the Security Realty problem, we can compute a new upper bound. It is the maximum of the LP Relaxation value for node 2 (13.90) and the LP Relaxation value for node 3 (14.58). Hence, our new upper bound on the value of the integer linear programming solution to the Security Realty problem is 14.58. In general, we will recompute the upper bound each time the two branches from a node have been completed.

At this time the lower bound is also recomputed. The new value for the lower bound is the maximum value of all feasible integer solutions found so far. Since the LP Relaxation solutions at nodes 2 and 3 did not yield a feasible integer solution, the lower bound of 13 established at node 1 is not revised. At this point of the branch-and-bound solution procedure we have UB = 14.58 and LB = 13.00. The current partial branch-and-bound solution tree is shown in Figure 8.3.

We have established (at node 2) that 13.90 is an upper bound on all solutions with $x_1 \leq 2$ and (at node 3) that 14.58 is an upper bound on all solutions with $x_1 \geq 3$. Property 2 below shows how these results can be used in continuing with the branch-and-bound solution procedure.

Property 2.

The LP Relaxation value at each node of a maximization problem is an upper bound on the LP Relaxation value at any descendent node.

Using this property, we see that if we were to branch from node 2, we could not find any solution with a value greater than 13.90. If we were to branch from node 3, no solution with a value greater than 14.58 could be found. Since node 3 could potentially lead to a better solution, we choose to select it (rather than node 2) to branch from. In

FIGURE 8.3
Partial Branch-and-Bound Solution Tree for Security Realty Problem

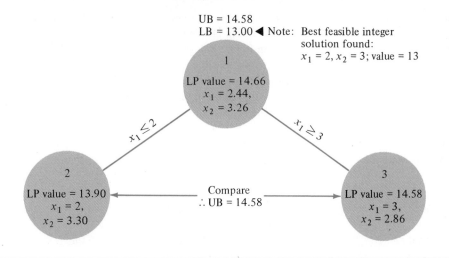

general, we will always select the node with the largest LP Relaxation value to continue branching.

Since x_2 is the only variable with a fractional value at node 3, we choose to branch on it. Thus, two branches are created from node 3: one with $x_2 \leq 2$ and another with $x_2 \geq 3$. Two descendent nodes are then created by solving the following LP Relaxations at nodes 4 and 5.

LP Relaxation at node 4:

$$\max \quad 2x_1 + 3x_2$$

s.t.

$$195x_1 + 273x_2 \leq 1365$$
$$4x_1 + 40x_2 \leq 140$$
$$x_1 \leq 4$$
$$x_1 \geq 3$$
$$x_2 \leq 2$$
$$x_1, x_2 \geq 0$$

LP Relaxation at node 5:

$$\max \quad 2x_1 + 3x_2$$

s.t.

$$195x_1 + 273x_2 \leq 1365$$
$$4x_1 + 40x_2 \leq 140$$
$$x_1 \leq 4$$
$$x_1 \geq 3$$
$$x_2 \geq 3$$
$$x_1, x_2 \geq 0$$

Note that since we are branching from node 3, we require $x_1 \geq 3$ in both LP Relaxations.

After solving these linear programming problems, we can construct the branch-and-bound approach solution tree shown in Figure 8.4. Note that at node 4, which corresponds to adding the constraint $x_2 \leq 2$, we find a feasible integer solution. At node 5, however, we find that after adding the constraint $x_2 \geq 3$, there is no feasible solution.

At this point we have found a feasible solution ($x_1 = 4$, $x_2 = 2$) with a value of 14.00 (see node 4). Thus the lower bound is revised to LB = 14.00. From UB = 14.00 we know that the optimal solution cannot yield a value greater than 14.00. Therefore, the solution $x_1 = 4$, $x_2 = 2$ with a value 14 is optimal for the Security Realty problem. We can now state the stopping rule for the branch-and-bound solution procedure.

Stopping Rule.

When UB = LB, the optimal solution has been found. It is the feasible solution with value equal to LB.

FIGURE 8.4
Complete Branch-and-Bound Solution Tree for Security Realty Problem

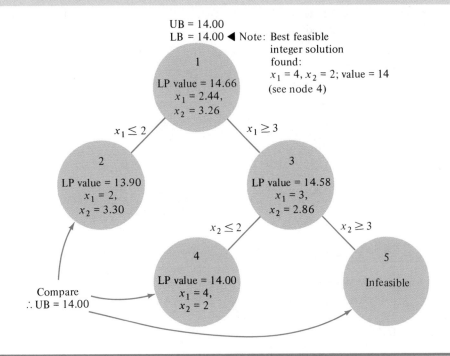

We have seen how the branch-and-bound solution procedure is applied to solve the all-integer Security Realty Investors problem. A summary of the general procedure for the all-integer linear program is presented in flowchart form in Figure 8.5.

Extension to Mixed-Integer Linear Programs

A big advantage of the branch-and-bound solution procedure for integer programming is that it is applicable to both all-integer and mixed-integer linear programs. To see how the branch-and-bound solution approach can be applied to a mixed-integer linear program, let us return to the Security Realty problem and suppose that x_2 was not required to be integer. This would be the case if fractional shares could be purchased in the apartment buildings. In this situation the LP Relaxation solved at node 1 would be exactly the same, yielding a value of 14.66 as an upper bound. But the lower bound would be found by rounding down on x_1 only. Thus, the value of the lower bound at node 1 would be 13.78, given by the feasible mixed integer solution $x_1 = 2$, $x_2 = 3.26$. This is shown below.

UB = 14.66
LB = 13.78 ◀ Note: Best feasible mixed
                    integer solution found:
                    $x_1 = 2$, $x_2 = 3.26$;
                    value = 13.78

1
LP value = 14.66
$x_1 = 2.44$
$x_2 = 3.26$

FIGURE 8.5
Flowchart of Branch-and-Bound Solution Procedure for the All-Integer Linear Program

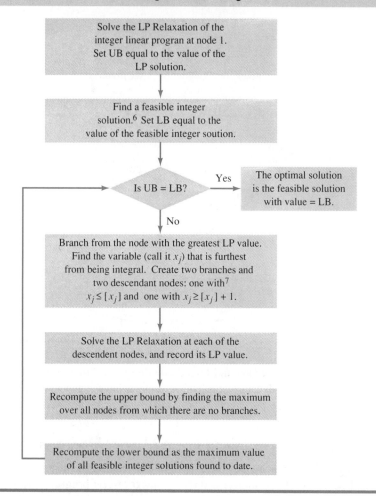

In order to branch, we now restrict consideration to only those variables that are required to be integer. Selecting the integer variable with the largest fractional part leads us to again branch on x_1; we require $x_1 \leq 2$ on one branch and $x_1 \geq 3$ on the other. Thus, the LP Relaxations solved at nodes 2 and 3 would be the same as before (see Figure 8.6). However, note that a feasible mixed integer solution exists whenever the linear programming solution at a node yields x_1 integer. Thus, the solutions at both nodes 2 and 3 are feasible for the mixed-integer linear program. A new lower bound of LB = 14.58 can be established by comparing the values of all the feasible mixed-integer solutions found. A new upper bound of UB = 14.58 can be established by comparing the LP Relaxation values at nodes 2 and 3. Since the upper and lower bounds are equal, the optimal solution

---

[6]In case the constraints are all of the $\leq$ type with nonnegative coefficients, the solution found by rounding down will be feasible. Otherwise, some knowledge of the particular application may provide a feasible integer solution.

[7]The notation $[x_j]$ means the greatest integer less than or equal to x_j—for example, $[2.86] = 2$.

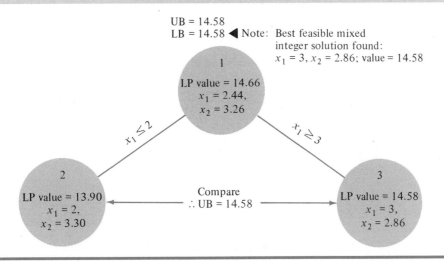

FIGURE 8.6
Branch-and-Bound Tree for Security Realty Mixed-Integer Linear Program
(x_1 Integer, x_2 Not Integer)

to the Security Realty problem with only x_1 required to be integer has been found. It is given by $x_1 = 3$ and $x_2 = 2.86$, with an objective function value of 14.58. The branch-and-bound tree for this mixed-integer linear program is shown in Figure 8.6.

8.5 ▼ COMPUTER SOLUTION

As mentioned in the chapter introduction, computer packages for solving integer linear programs are now widely available. Such codes are generally reliable for problems involving up to 100 or more integer variables and have often been used to solve specially structured problems with a few thousand variables.

Most of the general-purpose codes use a linear-programming-based branch-and-bound solution procedure similar to the one described in the previous section. While the branch-and-bound solution procedure can be used to solve small problems by hand, in practice a computer code is needed to solve integer linear programs. In this section we will show how another application of integer programming can be formulated and solved using LINDO/PC.

A Bank Location Application

The long-range planning department for the Ohio Trust Company is considering expanding its operation into a 20-county region in northeastern Ohio (see Figure 8.7). Currently, Ohio Trust does not have a principal place of business in any of the 20 counties under consideration. According to the banking laws in Ohio, if a banking firm establishes a principal place of business (PPB) in any county, then branch banks can be established in that county and in any adjacent county. However, in order to establish a new principal place of business, Ohio Trust must either obtain approval for a new bank from the state's superintendent of banks or purchase an existing bank.

Table 8.2 provides a listing of the 20 counties n the region together with the adjacent counties. From the table we see that Ashtabula County is adjacent to Lake, Geauga, and

FIGURE 8.7
Map of 20-County Area in Northeastern Ohio

Counties

1. Ashtabula   11. Stark
2. Lake   12. Geauga
3. Cuyahoga   13. Portage
4. Lorain   14. Columbiana
5. Huron   15. Mahoning
6. Richland   16. Trumbull
7. Ashland   17. Knox
8. Wayne   18. Holmes
9. Medina   19. Tuscarawas
10. Summit   20. Carroll

Trumbull counties; Lake County is adjacent to Ashtabula, Cuyahoga, and Geauga counties; and so on.

As an initial step in its planning, Ohio Trust would like to determine the minimum number of PPBs necessary to do business throughout the 20-county region. A $0-1$ integer programming model can be used to solve this problem for Ohio Trust. Let us define the following variables:

$$x_i = 1 \text{ if a PPB is established in county } i; 0 \text{ otherwise}$$

With the goal of minimizing the number of PPBs needed, the objective function can be written as

$$\min \quad x_1 + x_2 + \ldots + x_{20}$$

In order to place branch banks in a county, the county must either contain a PPB or be adjacent to another county with a PPB. Thus, there will be one constraint for

TABLE 8.2
Counties in Region of Expansion for Ohio Trust

Counties Under Consideration	Adjacent Counties (by Number)
1. Ashtabula	2, 12, 16
2. Lake	1, 3, 12
3. Cuyahoga	2, 4, 9, 10, 12, 13
4. Lorain	3, 5, 7, 9
5. Huron	4, 6, 7
6. Richland	5, 7, 17
7. Ashland	4, 5, 6, 8, 9, 17, 18
8. Wayne	7, 9, 10, 11, 18
9. Medina	3, 4, 7, 8, 10
10. Summit	3, 8, 9, 11, 12, 13
11. Stark	8, 10, 13, 14, 15, 18, 19, 20
12. Geauga	1, 2, 3, 10, 13, 16
13. Portage	3, 10, 11, 12, 15, 16
14. Columbiana	11, 15, 20
15. Mahoning	11, 13, 14, 16
16. Trumbull	1, 12, 13, 15
17. Knox	6, 7, 18
18. Holmes	7, 8, 11, 17, 19
19. Tuscarawas	11, 18, 20
20. Carroll	11, 14, 19

each county. For example, the constraint for Ashtabula County would be written as follows:

$$x_1 + x_2 + x_{12} + x_{16} \geq 1 \quad \text{Ashtabula}$$

Note that satisfaction of this constraint ensures that a PPB will be placed in Ashtabula County *or* in one or more of the adjacent counties. Thus, this constraint guarantees that Ohio Trust will be able to place branch banks in Ashtabula County.

The complete statement of the bank location problem is shown below.

$$\min \quad x_1 + x_2 + \quad \cdots \quad + x_{20}$$

s.t.

$$x_1 + x_2 \quad + x_{12} + x_{16} \quad \geq 1 \quad \text{Ashtabula}$$

$$x_1 + x_2 + x_3 + x_{12} \quad \geq 1 \quad \text{Lake}$$

$$\cdot$$
$$\cdot$$
$$\cdot$$

$$x_{11} + x_{14} + x_{19} + x_{20} \geq 1 \quad \text{Carroll}$$

$$x_1 = 0, 1 \qquad i = 1, 2, \ldots, 20$$

Given this 20-variable, 20-constraint problem formulation, we can now solve it using LINDO/PC. The input data are entered in the same manner as for a linear program. Then to make LINDO/PC treat each of the 20 decision variables as *0–1* integer variables, we enter the LINDO/PC command "INTEGER 20." When the "GO" command is given, the LINDO/PC program will determine the optimal integer solution.

In Figure 8.8 we show a portion of the computer output. Note that the variable names used correspond to the first four letters in the name of each county. Using the output, we see that the optimal solution calls for principal places of business in Ashland, Stark, and Geauga counties. With PPBs in these three counties, Ohio Trust can place branch banks in all 20 counties (see Figure 8.9). All other decision variables have an optimal value of zero, indicating that a PPB should not be placed in these counties. Clearly the integer programming model could be enlarged to allow for expansion into a larger area or throughout the entire state.[8]

▼ NOTES AND COMMENTS ▼

1. Most practical applications of integer linear programming involve only *0–1* integer variables. Indeed, some mixed-integer computer codes are only designed to handle integer variables that can take on binary values. However, if a clever mathematical trick is employed, these codes can still be used for problems involving general integer variables. The trick is called *binary expansion* and requires that an upper bound be established for each integer variable. More advanced texts on integer programming show how this can be done.

2. General-purpose mixed-integer linear programming codes can be used for linear programming problems, all-integer problems, and problems involving some

---

FIGURE 8.8
Microcomputer Solution of Bank-Location Problem Using LINDO/PC

```
        OBJECTIVE FUNCTION VALUE

   1)     3.00000000

        VARIABLE         VALUE      REDUCED COST
            ASHT       .000000          .000000
            LAKE       .000000          .000000
            CUYA       .000000          .000000
            LORA       .000000          .000000
            HURO       .000000          .000000
            RICH       .000000         1.000000
            ASHL      1.000000          .000000
            WAYN       .000000          .000000
            MEDI       .000000          .000000
            SUMM       .000000          .000000
            STAR      1.000000          .000000
            GEAU      1.000000          .000000
            PORT       .000000          .000000
            COLU       .000000          .000000
            MAHO       .000000          .000000
            TRUM       .000000          .000000
            KNOX       .000000         1.000000
            HOLM       .000000          .000000
            TUSC       .000000          .000000
            CARR       .000000          .000000
```

---

[8]A model of this type allowing for expansion throughout the state and some other variations is presented in D. J. Sweeney, L. Mairose, and R. Martin, "Strategic Planning in Bank Location," *AIDS Proceedings* (November 1979).

FIGURE 8.9
Principal Place of Business Counties for Ohio Trust

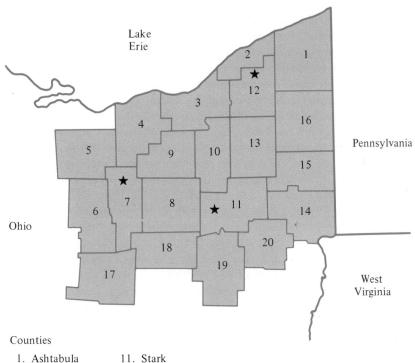

Lake
Erie

Ohio

Pennsylvania

West
Virginia

Counties

1. Ashtabula
2. Lake
3. Cuyahoga
4. Lorain
5. Huron
6. Richland
7. Ashland
8. Wayne
9. Medina
10. Summit

11. Stark
12. Geauga
13. Portage
14. Columbia
15. Mahoning
16. Trumbull
17. Knox
18. Holmes
19. Tuscarawas
20. Carroll

★ A Principal Place of
Business should be
located in these counties

continuous and some integer variables. General-purpose codes are seldom the fastest for solving problems with special structure (such as the transportation, assignment, and transshipment problems); however, unless the problems are very large, speed is usually not a critical issue. Thus, for most practitioners, it is probably better to become familiar with one general-purpose computer package that can be used on a variety of problems than to maintain a variety of computer codes that are designed for special problems.

3. Several computer software packages are used to provide the solution to both general linear programming problems and integer linear programming problems. The output from some of these packages shows sensitivity analysis information for integer linear programs. This sensitivity analysis information does not have the same meaning as it does for linear programming problems and should ordinarily be disregarded.

▼ SUMMARY

We have introduced an important extension of the linear programming model: the integer linear program. The only difference between the integer linear programming problem and the linear programming problem studied in previous chapters is the added restriction on some of the variables. If all of the variables are required to be integer, we have an all-integer linear program; if some, but not necessarily all, of the variables are required to be integer, we have a mixed-integer linear program. Finally, in case the integer variables are only permitted to assume the values 0 or 1, we have a *0–1* (binary) integer linear program. Binary integer linear programs may be either all integer or mixed integer.

There are two primary reasons for studying integer linear programming. First, in many applications, fractional values of the decision variables are not permitted. Since we have seen that rounding the linear programming solution can provide poor results, methods for finding the optimal integer solution are needed. For any two-variable problem a simple extension of the graphical procedure for linear programs can be used to find solutions. The branch-and-bound solution procedure was presented for solving larger integer linear programs. A major advantage of the branch-and-bound solution procedure is its flexibility; it can be used for both all-integer and mixed-integer linear programs. Almost all existing commercial computer codes employ the branch-and-bound approach.

A second reason for studying integer linear programming is that it provides increased modeling flexibility through the use of *0–1* variables. In our discussion of the capital budgeting and distribution system design problems, we saw how a number of important managerial considerations can be incorporated through the use of multiple-choice constraints, conditional constraints, and so on. In addition, the Ohio Trust problem presented in the previous section provided another example of the modeling flexibility available using integer variables.

In recent years, with the availability of commercial integer linear programming computer codes, we have seen a rapid growth in the use of integer linear programming. As researchers develop solution procedures capable of solving integer linear programs with larger numbers of variables, we can expect to see a continuation of this rapid growth and the development of new applications.

▼ GLOSSARY

Integer linear program   A linear program with the additional requirement that some or all of the decision variables must be integer.

All-integer linear program   An integer linear program in which all the decision variables are required to be integer.

LP Relaxation   The linear program that results from dropping the integer requirements for the decision variables. For a maximization problem, the value of the optimal solution to the LP Relaxation is an upper bound on the value of the optimal integer solution.

Mixed-integer linear program   An integer linear program in which some, but not all, of the decision variables are required to be integer.

***0–1* integer linear program**   An all-integer or mixed-integer linear program in which the integer variables are only permitted to assume the values 0 or 1.

Upper bound   A value that is known to be greater than or equal to the value of any feasible solution. The solution to the LP Relaxation of an integer linear program provides an upper bound for a maximization problem.

Multiple-choice constraint   A constraint requiring that the sum of two or more $0-1$ variables equal 1. Thus, any feasible solution makes a choice of one of these variables to set equal to 1.

Mutually exclusive constraint   A constraint requiring that the sum of two or more $0-1$ variables be less than or equal to 1. Thus, if one of the variables equals 1, the others must equal 0. However, all variables could equal 0.

***k* out of *n* alternatives constraint**   An extension of the multiple-choice constraint. This constraint requires that the sum of n $0-1$ variables equal k.

Conditional constraints   Constraints involving $0-1$ variables that do not allow certain variables to equal 1 unless certain other variables are equal to 1.

Corequisite constraint   A constraint requiring that two $0-1$ variables be equal. Thus, they are both in or out of solution together.

Branch and bound   A solution procedure for integer linear programs that sequentially partitions the set of feasible solutions into smaller and smaller subsets until the optimal solution is found.

Lower bound   A value that is less than or equal to the value of the optimal solution. For a maximization problem the value of any feasible integer solution to an integer linear program is a lower bound.

Descendant node   A node created in a branch-and-bound solution tree by branching from another node by adding a constraint to the LP Relaxation solved at the previous node.

▼ PROBLEMS

1. Indicate which of the following are all-integer linear programs, which are mixed-integer linear programs, and which are ordinary linear programs. For each of the all-integer and mixed-integer linear programs, write the LP Relaxation. (Do not attempt to solve.)

a. max $30x_1 + 25x_2$

s.t.

$$3x_1 + 1.5x_2 \leq 400$$
$$1.5x_1 + 2x_2 \leq 250$$
$$1x_1 + 1x_2 \leq 150$$
$$x_1, x_2 \geq 0 \text{ and } x_2 \text{ integer}$$

b. min $3x_1 + 4x_2$

s.t.

$$2x_1 + 4x_2 \geq 8$$
$$2x_1 + 6x_2 \geq 12$$
$$x_1, x_2 \geq 0 \text{ and integer}$$

c. min $30x_1 + 4x_2$

s.t.

$$3x_1 + 2x_2 \geq 50$$
$$0.1x_1 + 0.2x_2 \geq 2$$
$$x_1, x_2 \geq 0 \text{ and } x_1 \text{ integer}$$

d. max $3x_1 + 4x_2$

s.t.

$$-1x_1 + 2x_2 \leq 8$$
$$1x_1 + 2x_2 \leq 12$$
$$2x_1 + 1x_2 \leq 16$$
$$x_1, x_2 \geq 0 \text{ and integer}$$

e. max $20x_1 + 5x_2$

s.t.

$$5x_1 + 1x_2 \leq 15$$
$$6x_1 + 4x_2 \leq 24$$
$$1x_1 + 1x_2 \leq 5$$
$$x_1, x_2 \geq 0$$

2. Consider the all-integer linear program given below.

$$\text{max} \quad 5x_1 + 8x_2$$

s.t.

$$6x_1 + 5x_2 \leq 30$$
$$9x_1 + 4x_2 \leq 36$$
$$1x_1 + 2x_2 \leq 10$$
$$x_1, x_2 \geq 0 \text{ and integer}$$

a. Graph the constraints for this problem. Indicate with heavy dots all the feasible integer solutions.
b. Find the optimal solution to the LP Relaxation. Round down to find a feasible integer solution.
c. Find the optimal integer solution. Is it the same as the solution found in part (b) above by rounding down?

3. Consider the all-integer linear program given below.

$$\text{max} \quad 1x_1 + 1x_2$$

s.t.

$$4x_1 + 6x_2 \leq 22$$
$$1x_1 + 5x_2 \leq 15$$
$$2x_1 + 1x_2 \leq 9$$
$$x_1, x_2 \geq 0 \text{ and integer}$$

a. Graph the constraints for this problem. Indicate with heavy dots all the feasible integer solutions.
b. Solve the LP Relaxation of this problem.
c. Find the optimal integer solution.

4. Consider the integer linear program given below.

$$\text{max} \quad 10x_1 + 3x_2$$

s.t.

$$6x_1 + 7x_2 \leq 40$$
$$3x_1 + 1x_2 \leq 11$$
$$x_1, x_2 \geq 0 \text{ and integer}$$

a. Formulate and solve the LP Relaxation of the problem. Solve it graphically. Round down to find a feasible solution. State upper and lower bounds on the value of the optimal solution.

b. Solve the integer linear program graphically. Compare the value of this solution with the solution found in part (a).

c. Suppose the objective function changes to max $3x_1 + 6x_2$. Repeat parts (a) and (b) above.

5. Consider the mixed-integer linear program given below.

$$\text{max} \quad 2x_1 + 3x_2$$

s.t.

$$4x_1 + 9x_2 \leq 36$$
$$7x_1 + 5x_2 \leq 35$$
$$x_1, x_2 \geq 0 \text{ and } x_1 \text{ integer}$$

a. Graph the constraints for this problem. Indicate on your graph all feasible mixed-integer solutions.

b. Find the optimal solution to the LP Relaxation. Round the value of x_1 down to find a feasible mixed-integer solution. Is this solution optimal? Why or why not?

c. Find the optimal solution for the mixed-integer linear program.

6. Consider the mixed-integer linear program given below.

$$\text{max} \quad 1x_1 + 1x_2$$

s.t.

$$7x_1 + 9x_2 \leq 63$$
$$9x_1 + 5x_2 \leq 45$$
$$3x_1 + 1x_2 \leq 12$$
$$x_1, x_2 \geq 0 \text{ and } x_2 \text{ integer}$$

a. Graph the constraints for this problem. Indicate on your graph all feasible mixed-integer solutions.

b. Find the optimal solution to the LP Relaxation. Round the value of x_2 down to find a feasible mixed-integer solution. Specify upper and lower bounds on the value of the optimal solution to the mixed-integer linear program.

c. Find the optimal solution to the mixed-integer linear program.

7. Consider again the all-integer linear program in problem 4. It is restated below.

$$\text{max} \quad 10x_1 + 3x_2$$

s.t.

$$6x_1 + 7x_2 \leq 40$$
$$3x_1 + 1x_2 \leq 11$$
$$x_1, x_2 \geq 0 \text{ and integer}$$

Solve this problem using the branch-and-bound procedure.

8. The integer programming formulation of the Ice-Cold Refrigerator Company capital budgeting problem is presented below.

$$\max \quad 90x_1 + 40x_2 + 10x_3 + 37x_4$$

s.t.

$$15x_1 + 10x_2 + 10x_3 + 15x_4 \leq 40$$
$$20x_1 + 15x_2 \qquad\quad + 10x_4 \leq 50$$
$$20x_1 + 20x_2 \qquad\quad + 10x_4 \leq 40$$
$$15x_1 + 5x_2 + 4x_3 + 10x_4 \leq 35$$
$$x_1, x_2, x_3, x_4 = 0, 1$$

Solve this problem using the branch-and-bound procedure. Note that in the case of variables restricted to *0 or 1* each branch corresponds to setting one of the variables equal to *0 or 1*. Thus, the branching variable is treated as a constant in the linear programming problem solved at the descendent node.

9. Refer to the Ohio Trust bank location problem introduced in Section 8.5. Table 8.2 shows the counties under consideration and the adjacent counties.
   a. Write the complete integer programming model if Ohio Trust is considering expansion only into the following counties: Lorain, Huron, Richland, Ashland, Wayne, Medina, and Knox.
   b. Solve the problem in part (a) using trial and error.

10. Consider the mixed-integer linear program given below.

$$\max \quad 1x_1 + 2x_2 + 1x_3$$

s.t.

$$7x_1 + 4x_2 + 3x_3 \leq 28$$
$$4x_1 + 7x_2 + 2x_3 \leq 28$$
$$x_1, x_2, x_3 \geq 0 \text{ and } x_1, x_2 \text{ integer}$$

Solve this problem using the branch-and-bound procedure.

11. Grave City is considering the relocation of a number of police substations in order to obtain better enforcement in high-crime areas. The locations being considered together with the areas that can be covered from these locations are given below.

Potential Locations for Substations	Areas Covered
A	1, 5, 7
B	1, 2, 5, 7
C	1, 3, 5
D	2, 4, 5
E	3, 4, 6
F	4, 5, 6
G	1, 5, 6, 7

   a. Formulate an integer programming model that could be solved to find the minimum number of locations necessary to provide coverage to all areas.
   b. Solve the problem in part (a) using any means at your disposal.

12. The Martin-Beck Company is in the process of planning for new production facilities and developing a more efficient distribution system design. At present they have one plant at St. Louis with a capacity of 30,000 units. But because of increased demand, management is considering four potential new plant sites: Detroit, Denver, Toledo, and Kansas City. The transportation tableau below summarizes the projected plant capacities, the cost per unit of shipping from each plant to each destination (upper right-hand corner of each cell), and the demand forecasts over a 1-year planning horizon.

	Boston	Atlanta	Houston	Capacities
Detroit	5	2	3	10,000
Toledo	4	3	4	20,000
Denver	9	7	5	30,000
Kansas City	10	4	2	40,000
St. Louis	8	4	3	30,000
Demand	30,000	20,000	20,000	

Suppose that the fixed costs of constructing the new plants are

Detroit	$175,000
Toledo	$300,000
Denver	$375,000
Kansas City	$500,000

The Martin-Beck Company would like to minimize the total cost of plant construction and distribution of goods.

a. Develop a *0–1* mixed-integer linear programming model of this problem. (Do not attempt to solve.)

b. Modify your formulation in part (a) to account for the policy restriction that one plant, but not two, must be located in Detroit or in Toledo. (Do not attempt to solve.)

c. Modify your formulation in part (a) to account for the policy restriction that at most two plants can be located in Denver, Kansas City, and St. Louis. (Do not attempt to solve.)

d. Suppose that there are two possible sizes for the Denver plant: the one mentioned earlier with a capacity of 30,000 and a cost of $375,000, and another with a capacity of 60,000 and a cost of $550,000. Modify your formulation in part (a) to account for this consideration. (Do not attempt to solve.)

13. Spencer Enterprises is attempting to choose among a series of new investment alternatives. The potential investment alternatives, the net present value of the future stream of returns, the capital requirements, and the available capital funds over the next 3 years are summarized below.

a. Develop an integer programming model for maximizing the net present value. (Do not solve.)

b. Assume that only one of the warehouse expansion projects can be implemented. Modify your model of part (a).

c. Suppose that if the test-marketing of the new product is carried out, then the advertising campaign must also be conducted. Modify your formulation of part (b) to reflect this new situation.

Alternative	Net Present Value ($)	Capital Requirements ($)		
		Year 1	*Year 2*	*Year 3*
Limited warehouse expansion	4,000	3,000	1,000	4,000
Extensive warehouse expansion	6,000	2,500	3,500	3,500
Test marketing of new product	10,500	6,000	4,000	5,000
Advertising campaign	4,000	2,000	1,500	1,800
Basic research	8,000	5,000	1,000	4,000
Purchase of new equipment	3,000	1,000	500	900
Capital funds available		10,500	7,000	8,750

14. The following questions refer to a capital budgeting problem with six projects represented by *0–1* variables x_1, x_2, x_3, x_4, x_5, and x_6.

a. Write a constraint modeling a situation in which two of the projects 1, 3, 5, and 6 must be undertaken.

b. Write a constraint modeling a situation in which projects 3 and 5 must be undertaken simultaneously.

c. Write a constraint modeling a situation in which project 1 or 4 must be undertaken, but not both.

d. Write constraints modeling a situation where project 4 cannot be undertaken unless projects 1 and 3 are also undertaken.

e. Revise the requirement in part (d) to accommodate the case in which, when projects 1 and 3 are undertaken, project 4 must also be undertaken.

15. Consider the following integer linear program:

$$\max \quad 6x_1 + 9x_2 + 11x_3$$

s.t.

$$2x_1 + 1x_2 + 1.5x_3 \le 10$$

$$3x_1 + 2x_2 + 8x_3 \le 18$$

$$x_1, x_2, \text{ and } x_3 \ge 0 \text{ and integer}$$

Determine *integer* upper bounds for each variable. (*Hint:* From constraint 1 we see that when x_2 and x_3 are 0, $x_1 \le 5$. Similarly, from constraint 2, we see that when x_2 and x_3 are 0, $x_1 \le 6$. Thus, the largest integer value x_1 can take on is 5.

16. The Northshore Bank is working to develop an efficient work schedule for full-time and part-time tellers. The schedule must provide for efficient operation of the bank including adequate customer service, employee breaks, and so on. On Fridays the bank is open from 9:00 A.M. to 7:00 P.M. The number of tellers necessary to provide adequate customer service during each hour of operation is summarized below.

Time	9–10	10–11	11–12	12–1	1–2	2–3	3–4	4–5	5–6	6–7
Number of Tellers	6	4	8	10	9	6	4	7	6	6

Each full-time employee starts on the hour and works a 4-hour shift, followed by 1 hour for lunch and then a 3-hour shift. Part-time employees work one 4-hour shift beginning on the hour and extending for 4 consecutive hours. Considering salary and fringe benefits, full-time employees cost the bank $7.50 per hour ($52.50 per day), and part-time employees cost the bank $4 per hour ($16 per day).

a. Formulate an integer programming model that can be used to develop a schedule that will satisfy customer service needs at a minimum employee cost. (*Hint:* Let x_i = number of full-time employees coming on duty at the beginning of hour i and y_i = number of part-time employees coming on duty at the beginning of hour i.)

b. Solve the LP Relaxation of your model in part (a).

c. Solve for the optimal schedule of tellers. Comment on the solution.

d. After reviewing the solution to part (c), the bank manager has realized that some additional requirements must be specified. Specifically, she wants to ensure that one full-time employee is on duty at all times and that there is a staff of at least five full-time employees. Revise your model to incorporate these additional requirements, and solve for the optimal solution.

17. CHB, Inc., is a bank holding company that is evaluating the potential for expanding into a 13-county region in the southwestern part of the state. State law permits establishing branches in any county that is adjacent to a county in which a PPB (principal place of business) is located. Below is a map of the 13-county region; the population of each county also is indicated on the map.

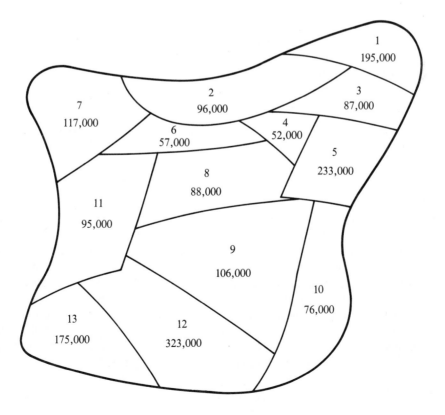

a. Assume that only one PPB can be established in the region. Where should it be located in order to maximize the population served? (*Hint:* Review the Ohio Trust formulation in Section 8.5. Consider minimizing the population not served, and introduce variable $y_i = 1$ if it is not possible to establish a branch in county i and $y_i = 0$ otherwise.)

b. Suppose that two PPBs can be established in the region. Where should they be located to maximize the population served?

c. Management has learned that a bank located in county 5 is considering selling. If CHB, Inc., purchases this bank, it will establish for CHB a PPB in county 5 and provide a base for beginning expansion in the region. What advice would you give the management of CHB?

▼ CASE PROBLEM

Textbook Publishing

ASW Publishing, Inc., a small publisher of college textbooks, must reach a decision regarding which books to publish next year. The books that the company is considering are listed in the following table, along with the projected sales that are expected from each book over the next 3 years if the book is published.

Book Subject	Type of Book	Projected Sales (units)
Business calculus	New	20,000
Finite mathematics	Revision	30,000
General statistics	New	15,000
Mathematical statistics	New	10,000
Business statistics	Revision	25,000
Finance	New	18,000
Financial accounting	New	25,000
Managerial accounting	Revision	50,000
English literature	New	20,000
German	New	30,000

The books that are listed as revisions are texts that ASW already has under contract; these texts are being considered for publication as new editions. The books that are listed as new have been reviewed by the company, but contracts as yet have not been signed.

The company has three individuals who can be assigned to these projects, all of whom have varying amounts of time available; John has 60 days available, Susan has 40 days available, and Monica has 40 days available. The numbers of days required by each person to complete each project are shown below; in this table an "X" indicates that the person will not be used for the project because of a lack of expertise in the area, a personality conflict with the author(s), or some other reason. At least 2 staff members are capable of being assigned to each project except the finance book.

Book Subject	John	Susan	Monica
Business calculus	30	40	X
Finite mathematics	16	24	X
General statistics	24	X	30
Mathematical statistics	20	X	24
Business statistics	10	X	16
Finance	X	X	14
Financial accounting	X	24	26
Managerial accounting	X	28	30
English literature	40	34	30
German	X	50	36

ASW will not publish more than two statistics books or more than one accounting text in a single year. In addition, management has decided that one of the mathematics books (business calculus or finite math) must be published, but not both.

MANAGERIAL REPORT

Prepare a report for the general manager of ASW that describes your findings and recommendations regarding the best publication strategy for ASW to follow next year. In carrying out your analysis, assume that the fixed costs and the per-unit sales revenues are approximately equal for all books; thus, management is primarily interested in maximizing the total sales volume.

The general manager has also asked that you include recommendations regarding the following possible changes:

1. If it would be advantageous to do so, Susan can be moved off another project in order to allow her to work 12 more days.
2. Again, if it would be advantageous to do so, Monica can be made available for another 10 days.
3. If one or more of the revisions could be postponed for another year, should they be? Clearly the company will risk losing market share by postponing a revision.

Include details of your analysis in an appendix to your report.

Ketron*
Arlington, Virginia

Ketron, Inc., is a consulting firm with several branch offices located throughout the United States. An important part of Ketron's business involves national defense and other government applications.

The Management Science Systems division of Ketron is responsible for the maintenance, development, enhancement, and marketing of MPSIII, a proprietary mathematical programming system for use on IBM computers. Members of the Management Science Systems division consult with users of MPSIII and assist them in developing and implementing solutions to their problems. One such mixed-integer programming (MIP) application developed for a major sporting equipment company is outlined below.

A CUSTOMER ORDER ALLOCATION MODEL

A major sporting equipment company satisfies demand for its products by making shipments from its factories and other locations around the country where inventories are maintained. The company markets approximately 300 products and has about 30 sources of supply (factory and warehouse locations). The problem of interest is to determine how best to allocate customer orders to the various sources of supply such that the total manufacturing cost is minimized. Although transportation cost is not directly considered, it can be accounted for indirectly by not including variables corresponding to shipments from distant locations. Figure 8.10 provides a graphical representation of this problem. Note in the figure that each customer can receive shipments from only a few of the various sources of supply. For example, we see that customer 1 may be supplied by source A or B, customer 2 may be supplied only by source A, and so on.

The customer order allocation problem is solved periodically. In a typical period there are between 30 and 40 customers to be supplied. Since most customers require several products, there are usually between 600 and 800 orders that must be assigned to the sources of supply.

The sporting equipment company classifies each customer order as either a "guaranteed" or a "secondary" order. Guaranteed orders are single-source orders in that they must be filled by a single supplier to ensure that the complete order will be delivered to the customer at one time. It is this "single source" requirement that necessitates the use of integer variables in the model. Approximately 80% of the company's orders are guaranteed orders.

Secondary orders can be split between the various sources of supply. These orders are made by customers restocking inventory, and there is no problem in

*The authors are indebted to J.A. Tomlin, Ketron, Inc., San Bruno, Calif., for providing this application.

FIGURE 8.10
Graphical Representation of the Customer Order Allocation Problem

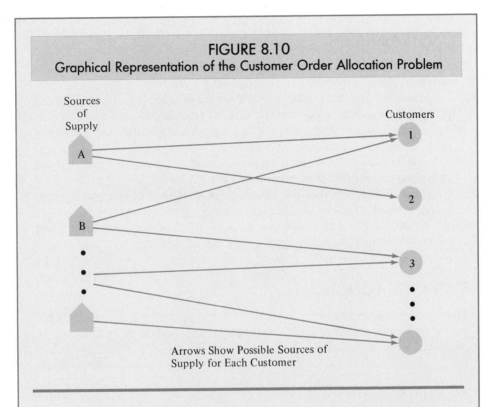

Arrows Show Possible Sources of
Supply for Each Customer

receiving partial shipments from different sources at different times. The total of all secondary orders for a given product is treated as a goal or target in the model formulation. Deviations below the goal are permitted, but a penalty cost is associated with these deviations in the objective function. When deviations occur in the optimal solution, the secondary orders will not be completely satisfied; the "shortfall" is spread among customers in specified proportions.

Manufacturing considerations are such that raw material availability and the type of process used constrain the amount of production. In addition, groups of items that are similar may belong to a "model group" that must be jointly constrained at some factories. There are also several restrictions on international shipping. For various policy reasons, shipments between sources and customers in certain countries may not be made. This reduces the number of variables in the model, but necessitates extensive data checking to ensure that all "guaranteed" orders have a permissible source. If they do not, some means must be found to make the problem feasible before even beginning to solve the mixed-integer programming model.

The primary objective of the model is to minimize the total manufacturing costs, subject to the requirement that the guaranteed orders be met. As indicated previously, the deviations below the secondary demand goals are dealt with by defining "shortfall" variables with an associated cost. This cost represents a penalty for not having the item in inventory when it is required.

A description of the constraints and the objective function for the model is presented below.

CONSTRAINTS

Guaranteed orders: Each customer's order for each product is assigned to a single supplier. (This is a multiple-choice constraint.)

Secondary orders: For each product the total amount of secondary demand assigned plus the shortfall must equal the total demand goal (target).

Raw material capacities: The amount of each type of raw material used at a supply source cannot exceed the amount available.

Manufacturing capacities: At each supply source the capacity for each type of production process cannot be exceeded.

Individual product capacities: The amount of product produced at a site cannot exceed that site's capacity for the product.

Group capacities: The total production for a group of similar products at a site cannot exceed that site's capacity for the group of products.

OBJECTIVE FUNCTION

The objective is to minimize the sum of (1) the manufacturing cost for guaranteed orders, (2) the manufacturing cost for secondary orders, and (3) the penalty cost for unsatisfied secondary demand.

MODEL SOLUTION

It is unreasonable to expect to obtain an optimal solution for a problem of this complexity. Furthermore, the goal programming methodology for handling the secondary demand means that an "optimum" is of questionable interpretation. What is needed is a "good" feasible mixed-integer solution. This is one of the advantages of the branch-and-bound approach. If an integer solution is found whose value is within a few percent of the value of the lower bound, the room for improvement is obviously small.

The solution procedure used is to make a sequence of runs, each beginning where the previous one terminated. Each run allows at most 40 linear programming evaluations (boundings), though many more variables will usually be set to some integer value (branched on). In almost every case the first such run, which includes finding the LP Relaxation solution, produces a solution satisfactory to the user.

A fairly typical problem has about 800 constraints, 2000 *0–1* assignment variables for the guaranteed orders, and 500 continuous variables associated with the secondary orders. This model is solved using Ketron's MPSIII system.

IMPLEMENTATION NOTES

In large-scale applications such as this, considerable systems work is involved in generating the data for the model and the managerial reports. Special data processing languages are often available to ease the programming burden of these phases. The DATAFORM language facility of MPSIII is used to generate the data for this model and to prepare the reports.

In this application it is necessary to make a completely separate preprocessing run to check for internal consistency and errors in the data. Only when the data appear logically error-free is the model generated and solved. Although tedious, this kind of preprocessing effort is critical for mixed-integer models since the cost of solving the wrong model can be significant. Furthermore, in some cases the data preprocessing step permits the size of the model to be reduced. Such a reduction is possible in this application when a demand for a product has only one legitimate source. The computational benefits of such reductions can be substantial.

Questions

1. Discuss the relationship between the method for handling secondary orders and goal programming.
2. It is mentioned that an "optimum" is of questionable interpretation. Discuss what is meant by this statement. Does it mean that any feasible solution is acceptable?

9

Network Models

Many managerial problems in areas such as transportation systems design, information systems design, and project scheduling have been successfully solved with the aid of network models and network analysis techniques. In Chapter 7 we showed how *networks* consisting of nodes and arcs can be used to provide graphical representations of transportation, assignment, and transshipment problems. In this chapter we present three additional network problems: the shortest-route problem, the minimal spanning tree problem, and the maximal flow problem. In each case we will show how a network model can be developed and solved in order to provide an optimal solution to the problem.

9.1 ▼ THE SHORTEST-ROUTE PROBLEM

In this section we consider a network application where the primary objective is to determine the *shortest route* or *shortest path* through the network. Let us demonstrate the shortest-route problem by considering the situation facing the Gorman Construction Company. Gorman has several construction projects located throughout a three-county area. Construction sites are sometimes located as far as 50 miles from Gorman's main office. With multiple daily trips carrying personnel, equipment, and supplies to and from the construction locations, the costs associated with transportation activities are substantial. For any given construction site, the travel alternatives between the site and the office can be described by a network of roads, streets, and highways. The network shown in Figure 9.1 describes the travel alternatives to and from six of Gorman's newest construction sites. The circles or *nodes* of the network correspond to the site locations. The roads, streets, and highways appear as the *arcs* in the network. The distances between the sites are shown above the corresponding arcs. Note that the length of each arc is not necessarily drawn proportional to the travel distance. Gorman would like to determine the routes or paths that will minimize the total travel distance from the office to each site.

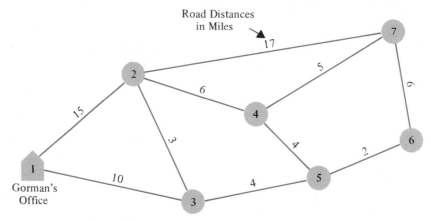

FIGURE 9.1
Road Network for the Gorman Company Shortest-Route Problem

Note: The length of each arc is not necessarily drawn proportional to the distance associated with the arc

A Shortest-Route Algorithm

In order to solve Gorman's problem, we need to determine the shortest route from Gorman's office, node 1, to each of the other nodes in the network. The algorithm we present uses a labeling procedure to find the shortest distance from node 1 to each of the other nodes. As we perform the steps of the labeling procedure, we will identify a *label* for each node consisting of two numbers enclosed in brackets. The first number in the label for a particular node indicates the distance from node 1 to that node, while the second number indicates the preceding node on the route from node 1 to that node. We will show the label for each node directly above or below the node in the network. For example, a label for a particular node might appear as shown in Figure 9.2.

At any step of the labeling procedure a node is said to be either labeled or unlabeled. A labeled node is any node for which we have identified a path from node 1 to that node, and an unlabeled node is any node for which no path has yet been identified. For those nodes that are labeled, the node is said to be either permanently labeled or tentatively labeled. That is, whenever the algorithm has determined the *shortest* distance from node

FIGURE 9.2
An Example of a Node Label

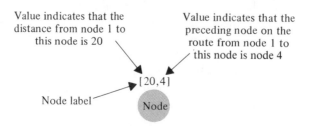

Value indicates that the distance from node 1 to this node is 20

Value indicates that the preceding node on the route from node 1 to this node is node 4

Node label

[20,4]

Node

1 to a particular node, the node is said to have a *permanent* label. If, however, the shortest distance from node 1 to a particular labeled node has not yet been determined, the node is said to have a *tentative* label. Now that we have an idea of what a label is, let us see how labels are computed and how the labeling process can be used to determine the shortest route from node 1 to each of the other nodes in the network.

We begin the labeling process by associating with node 1 the permanent label $[0,S]$. The S simply identifies that node 1 is the starting node, and the 0 indicates that the distance from node 1 to itself is zero. To distinguish between tentatively and permanently labeled nodes, we follow the practice of shading darkly all permanently labeled nodes in the network. In addition, an arrow will be used to point to the permanently labeled node being investigated at each step of the labeling algorithm. The initial identification of Gorman's network is shown in Figure 9.3. Only node 1 is permanently labeled.

To perform the first step or iteration of the labeling procedure, we must consider every node that can be reached directly from node 1; hence, we look at nodes 2 and 3. Consider for the moment node 2. We see that the direct distance from node 1 to node 2 is 15 miles. Thus, node 2 can be tentatively labeled $[15,1]$. The first number in the label indicates that node 2 can be reached in 15 miles, and the second number in the label indicates that the preceding node on the route to node 2 is node 1. Next, considering node 3, we find that the direct distance from node 1 to node 3 is 10 miles. Thus, the tentative label at node 3 is $[10,1]$. Figure 9.4 shows the results thus far. Nodes 2 and 3 are tentatively labeled.

Refer to Figure 9.4. We now consider all tentatively labeled nodes and identify the node with the smallest distance value in its label; thus, node 3 is selected. The tentative label associated with node 3 indicates that we can reach node 3 from node 1 by traveling a distance of 10 miles. Could we get to node 3 following a shorter route? Since any other route to node 3 would require passing through other nodes, and since the distance from node 1 to all other nodes is greater than or equal to 10, a shorter route to node 3 cannot be found by first going to some other node. Thus, we have identified the best or shortest route to node 3, and accordingly node 3 is permanently labeled with a distance of 10 miles. Shading node 3 darkly to indicate it is a permanently labeled node and adding an arrow to indicate that node 3 will be used to start the next step of the labeling process provides the network shown in Figure 9.5.

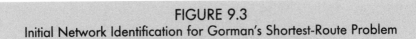

FIGURE 9.3
Initial Network Identification for Gorman's Shortest-Route Problem

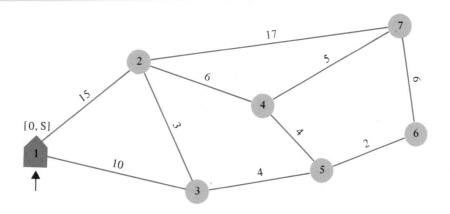

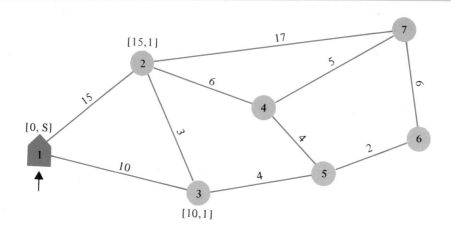

FIGURE 9.4
Gorman's Network with Tentative Labels for Nodes 2 and 3

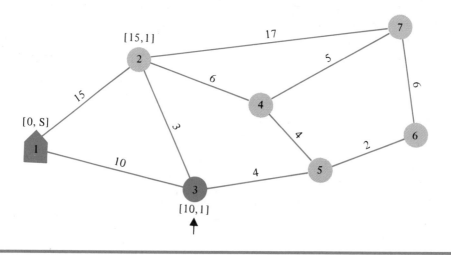

FIGURE 9.5
Gorman's Network with Node 3 Identified as a Permanently Labeled Node

We proceed by considering all nodes that are not permanently labeled and can be reached directly from node 3. Thus, we consider nodes 2 and 5. Note that 3 miles is the direct distance from node 3 to node 2 and 4 miles is the direct distance from node 3 to node 5. Since the permanent label for node 3 indicates that the shortest distance to node 3 is 10 miles, we see that we can reach node 2 in $10 + 3 = 13$ miles and node 5 in $10 + 4 = 14$ miles. Thus, the tentative label at node 2 is revised to [13,3] to indicate that we have now found a route from node 1 to node 2 with a distance of 13 miles and that the preceding node on the route to node 2 is node 3. Similarly, the tentative label for node 5 is [14,3]. Figure 9.6 shows the network computations up to this point.

FIGURE 9.6
Gorman's Network with New Tentative Labels for Nodes 2 and 5

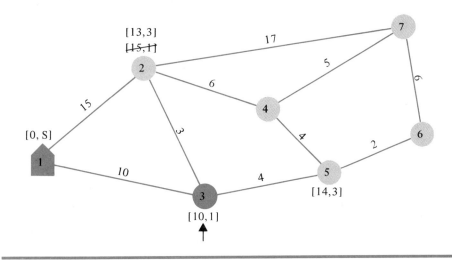

We next consider all tentatively labeled nodes in order to identify the node having the smallest distance value in its label. From Figure 9.6 we see that this is node 2 with a distance value of 13 miles. Node 2 is now declared permanently labeled because we now know that node 2 can be reached from node 1 in the shortest possible distance of 13 miles by going through node 3.

The next step or iteration begins at node 2, the most recently permanently labeled node. As before, we consider every nonpermanently labeled node that can be reached directly from node 2; that is, nodes 4 and 7. Starting with the distance value of 13 in the permanent label at node 2 and adding the direct distance from node 2 to each of nodes 4 and 7, we see that node 4 can be reached in 13 + 6 = 19 miles, while node 7 can be reached in 13 + 17 = 30 miles. Thus, the tentative labels at nodes 4 and 7 are as shown in Figure 9.7.

From among the tentatively labeled nodes (nodes 4, 5, and 7), we select the node with the smallest distance value and declare that node permanently labeled. Thus node 5, with a distance of 14, becomes the new permanently labeled node. From node 5, then, we consider all nonpermanently labeled nodes that can be reached directly from node 5. Thus, the tentative label on node 4 is revised, and node 6 is tentatively labeled. Figure 9.8 depicts these calculations.

Identifying the smallest distance for the remaining tentatively labeled nodes results in node 6 being permanently labeled. From node 6 we can determine a new tentative label for node 7. After this step, the network appears as shown in Figure 9.9.

We now have only two remaining nonpermanently labeled nodes. Since the distance portion of the label at node 4 is smaller than the distance value at node 7, node 4 becomes the new permanently labeled node. Since node 7 is the only nonpermanently labeled node that can be reached directly from node 4, we compare the distance value of 22 in its label with the sum of the distance in the label on node 4 and the direct distance from node 4 to node 7. Note in this case that the [22,6] tentative label already existing at node 7 has the smaller distance value; thus, the tentative label at node 7 remains unchanged. Figure 9.10 shows the network at this point in time.

FIGURE 9.7
Gorman's Network with a Permanent Label at Node 2 and New Tentative Labels for Nodes 4 and 7

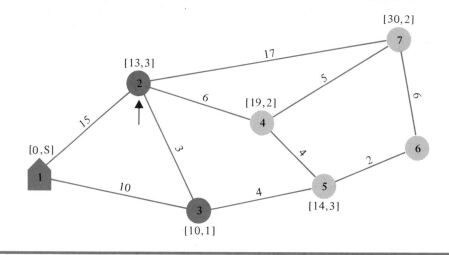

FIGURE 9.8
Gorman's Network with a Permanent Label at Node 5 and New Tentative Labels for Nodes 4 and 6

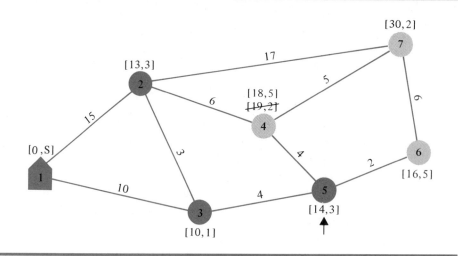

Since node 7 is the only remaining node with a tentative label, it is now permanently labeled. Whenever all nodes have been permanently labeled, we have found the shortest route from node 1 to every node in the network. Figure 9.11 shows the final network with all nodes permanently labeled.

We can now use the information in the permanent labels to find the shortest route from node 1 to each of the nodes in the network. For example, the permanent label at node

FIGURE 9.9
Gorman's Network with a Permanent Label at Node 6 and a New Tentative Label for Node 7

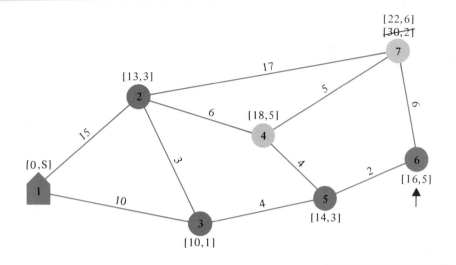

FIGURE 9.10
Gorman's Network with a Permanent Label at Node 4

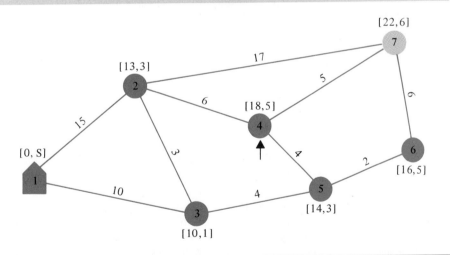

7 tells us the shortest distance from node 1 to node 7 is 22 miles. To find the particular route that enables us to reach node 7 in 22 miles, we note that the label for node 7 tells us that the preceding node on the shortest route from node 1 is node 6. Moving back through the network to node 6, we see from its permanent label that we reach node 6 by coming from node 5. Continuing this process, we note that we reach node 5 from node 3 and finally that we reach node 3 from node 1. Therefore, the shortest route from node

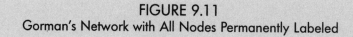

FIGURE 9.11
Gorman's Network with All Nodes Permanently Labeled

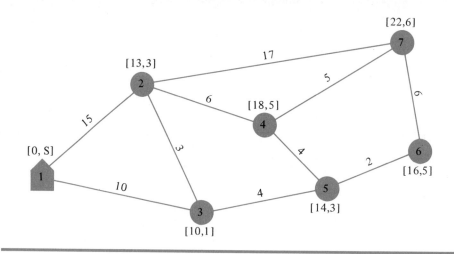

1 to node 7 is 1–3–5–6–7. Using this approach, the following shortest routes are identified for the Gorman transportation network:

Node	Shortest Route from Node 1	Distance in Miles
2	1–3–2	13
3	1–3	10
4	1–3–5–4	18
5	1–3–5	14
6	1–3–5–6	16
7	1–3–5–6–7	22

Perhaps for a problem as small as the Gorman problem you could have found the shortest routes just as fast, if not faster, by inspection. However, when we begin to investigate problems with 15 to 20 or more nodes, it becomes very time consuming to attempt to find the shortest routes by inspection. In fact, because of the increased number of alternate routes in a larger network, it is very easy to miss one or more routes and come up with the wrong answer. Thus, for larger problems a systematic procedure such as the labeling procedure described above is required. Even with the labeling method, we find that as the networks grow in size, it becomes necessary to implement the algorithm on a computer.

To provide a summary of the shortest-route algorithm, let us think of a network consisting of N nodes. The following procedure can be used to find the shortest route from node 1 to each of the other nodes in the network:

Step 1. Assign node 1 the permanent label [0,S]; the S indicates that node 1 is the starting node, and the 0 indicates that the distance from node 1 to itself is zero.

Step 2. Compute tentative labels for the nodes that can be reached directly from node 1. The first number in each label is the direct distance from node 1 to the node in question; we refer to this portion of the label as the distance value. The second number in each label, which we refer to as the preceding node value, indicates the preceding node on the route from node 1 to the node in question; thus, in this step the preceding node value is 1 since we are only considering nodes that can be directly reached from node 1.

Step 3. Identify the tentatively labeled node with the smallest distance value, and declare that node permanently labeled. If all nodes are permanently labeled, go to step 5.

Step 4. Consider all nodes that are not permanently labeled and can be reached directly from the new permanently labeled node identified in step 3. Compute tentative labels for these nodes as follows:

    a. If the nonpermanently labeled node in question has a tentative label, compute the sum of the distance value at the new permanently labeled node and the direct distance from the new permanently labeled node to the node in question. If this sum is less than the distance value for the node in question, set the distance value for this node equal to this sum; in addition, set the preceding node value equal to the new permanently labeled node that provided the smaller distance. Go to step 3.

    b. If the nonpermanently labeled node in question does not have a tentative label, a tentative label is created with a distance value equal to the sum of the distance value at the new permanently labeled node and the direct distance from the new permanently labeled node to the node in question. The preceding node value is set equal to the new permanently labeled node. Go to step 3.

Step 5. The permanent labels identify the shortest distance from node 1 to each node and the preceding node on the shortest route. The shortest route to a given node can be found by starting at the given node and moving to its preceding node. Continuing this backward movement through the network will provide the shortest route from node 1 to the node in question.

The above algorithm will determine the shortest distance from node 1 to each of the other nodes in the network. Note that $N - 1$ iterations of the algorithm are required to find the shortest distance to all other nodes. If the shortest distance is not needed to every node, the algorithm can be stopped when those nodes of interest have been permanently labeled. The algorithm can also be easily modified to find the shortest distance from any node, say node k, to all other nodes in the network. To make such a change, we would merely begin by labeling node k with the permanent label $[0,S]$. Then by applying the steps of the algorithm, we can find the shortest route from node k to each of the other nodes in the network.

The microcomputer package The Management Scientist can be used to solve small shortest-route problems. Input for the program includes the number of nodes, the number of arcs, and the length of each arc. The output shown in Figure 9.12 provides the shortest route from node 1 to node 7.

▼ NOTES AND COMMENTS ▼

1. Many applications of the shortest-route algorithm involve criteria such as time or cost instead of distance. In these cases the shortest-route algorithm provides the minimum-time or minimum-cost solution. However, since the shortest-route

continued on next page

FIGURE 9.12
Computer Solution of the Gorman Shortest-Route
Problem Provided by The Management Scientist

```
****    NETWORK DESCRIPTION    ****

        7 NODES AND 10 ARCS

  ARC    START NODE    END NODE    DISTANCE
  ---    ----------    --------    --------
   1         1            2           15
   2         1            3           10
   3         2            3            3
   4         2            4            6
   5         2            7           17
   6         3            5            4
   7         4            5            4
   8         4            7            5
   9         5            6            2
  10         6            7            6



THE SHORTEST ROUTE FROM NODE 1 TO NODE 7
*****************************************

  START NODE         END NODE         DISTANCE
  ----------         --------         --------
      1                 3                10
      3                 5                 4
      5                 6                 2
      6                 7                 6

         TOTAL DISTANCE               22
```

algorithm always identifies a minimum value solution, it would not make sense to apply the algorithm to problems that involve a profit criterion.

2. In some applications the value associated with an arc may be negative. For example, in situations where cost is the criterion, a negative arc value would denote a negative cost; in other words, a profit would be realized by traversing the arc. The shortest-route algorithm presented in this section can only be applied to networks with nonnegative arc values. More advanced texts discuss algorithms that can be used to solve problems having negative arc values.

9.2 ▼ THE MINIMAL SPANNING TREE PROBLEM

In network terminology, the minimal spanning tree problem involves using the branches (arcs) of the network to reach *all* nodes of the network in such a fashion that the total length of all the branches used is minimized. To better understand this problem, let us consider the communications system design problem encountered by a regional computer center.

The Southwestern Regional Computer Center must have special computer communications lines installed in order to connect five satellite users with a new central computer. The telephone company will install the new communications network. However, the installation is an expensive operation. In order to reduce costs, the center's management group wants the total length of the new communications lines to be as small as possible. While the central computer could be connected directly to each user, it appears to be more economical to install a direct line to some users and let other users tap into the system by linking with the users that are already connected to the system. The determination of this minimal length communications system design is an example of the *minimal spanning tree* problem. The network for this problem with possible connection alternatives and distances is shown in Figure 9.13. An algorithm that can be used to solve this network model is explained below.

A Minimal Spanning Tree Algorithm

The network algorithm that can be used to solve the minimal spanning tree problem is very simple. The steps of the algorithm are as follows:

Step 1. Arbitrarily begin at any node and connect it to the closest node. The two nodes are referred to as *connected* nodes, and the remaining nodes are referred to as *unconnected* nodes.

Step 2. Identify the unconnected node that is closest to one of the connected nodes. Break ties arbitrarily if two or more nodes qualify as the closest node. Add this new node to the set of connected nodes. Repeat this step until all nodes have been connected.

This network algorithm is easily implemented by making the connection decisions directly on the graph of the network.

Referring to the communications network for the regional computer center and arbitrarily beginning at node 1, we find the closest node is node 2 with a distance of 20.

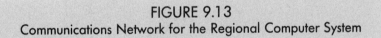

FIGURE 9.13
Communications Network for the Regional Computer System

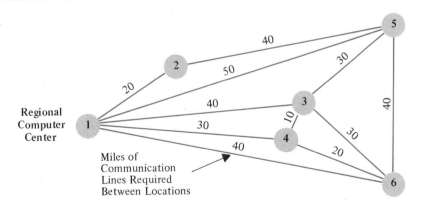

Using a bold line to connect nodes 1 and 2, step 1 of the algorithm provides the following result:

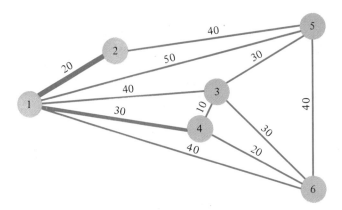

In step 2 of the algorithm we find that the unconnected node that is closest to one of the connected nodes is node 4, with a distance of 30 miles from node 1. Adding node 4 to the set of connected nodes provides the following result:

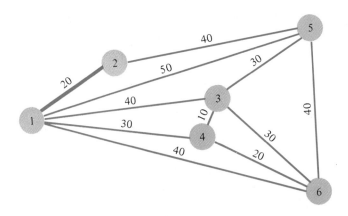

Repeating the step of always adding the closest unconnected node to the connected segment of the network provides the minimal spanning tree solution shown in Figure 9.14. Follow the steps of the algorithm, and see if you obtain this solution. The minimal length of the spanning tree is given by the sum of the distances on the arcs forming the spanning tree. In this case the total distance is 110 miles for the computer center's communications network. Note that while the computer center's network arcs were measured in distance, other network models may measure the arcs in terms of other criteria such as cost, time, and so on. In such cases the minimal spanning tree algorithm will identify the optimal solution (minimal cost, minimal time, and so on) for the criterion being considered.

The computer solution to the regional computer center's problem is shown in Figure 9.15. The Management Scientist was used to obtain the minimal spanning tree solution of 110 miles.

FIGURE 9.14
Minimal Spanning Tree Communications Network for the Regional Computer Center

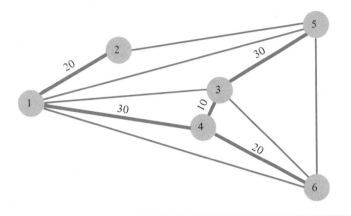

FIGURE 9.15
Computer Solution of the Regional Computer Center Minimal Spanning Tree Problem Provided by The Management Scientist

```
****   NETWORK DESCRIPTION   ****

6 NODES AND 11 ARCS

ARC     START NODE     END NODE     DISTANCE
---     ----------     --------     --------
 1          1             2            20
 2          1             3            40
 3          1             4            30
 4          1             5            50
 5          1             6            40
 6          2             5            40
 7          3             4            10
 8          3             5            30
 9          3             6            30
10          4             6            20
11          5             6            40


       MINIMAL SPANNING TREE
       *********************

START NODE     END NODE     DISTANCE
----------     --------     --------
    1             2            20
    1             4            30
    4             3            10
    4             6            20
    3             5            30

     TOTAL LENGTH          110
```

▼ NOTES AND COMMENTS ▼

The minimal spanning tree algorithm is considered a *greedy algorithm* since at each stage we can be "greedy" and take the best action available at that stage. Following this strategy at all stages will provide the overall optimal solution. Greedy algorithms such as the minimal spanning tree algorithm are rare because there are very few problems where the greedy approach will guarantee an optimal solution.

9.3 ▼ THE MAXIMAL FLOW PROBLEM

Consider a network with one input or *source* node and one output or *sink* node. The maximal flow problem asks, What is the maximum amount of flow (that is, vehicles, messages, fluid, and so on) that can enter and exit from the network system in a given period of time? In this problem we attempt to transmit flow through all branches (arcs) of the network as efficiently as possible. The amount of flow is limited due to capacity restrictions on the various branches of the network. For example, highway types limit vehicle flow in a transportation system, while pipe sizes limit oil flow in an oil distribution system. The maximum or upper limit on the flow in a branch is referred to as the *flow capacity* of the branch. While we do not specify capacities for the nodes, we do assume that the flow out of a node is equal to the flow into the node.

As an example of the maximal flow problem, consider the north–south interstate highway system passing through Cincinnati, Ohio. The north–south vehicle flow reaches a level of 15,000 vehicles per hour at peak times. Due to a planned summer highway maintenance program, calling for the temporary closing of lanes and lower speed limits, a network of alternate routes through Cincinnati has been proposed by a transportation planning committee. The alternate routes include other highways as well as city streets. Because of differences in speed limits and traffic patterns, flow capacities vary depending on the particular streets or roads used. The proposed network with branch flow capacities is shown in Figure 9.16.

The flow capacities are based on the direction of the flow. For example, highway section or branch 1–2 shows a capacity of 5000 vehicles per hour in the 1–2 direction; however, a 0 capacity exists in the 2–1 direction. This means that the highway network planners do not want vehicles flowing from node 2 into node 1. Logically speaking, since node 1 is the input, or source, and a potential traffic jam location, it would be undesirable to permit traffic flow into the node 1 intersection from node 2. The directional capacities on branch 1–2 can also be interpreted as indicating a one-way street leading from the node 1 intersection. In any case this example shows that the flow capacities of branches can be dependent on the direction of the flow. Do you believe the highway system network shown in Figure 9.16 can accommodate the north–south maximum flow of 15,000 vehicles per hour? What is the maximal flow in vehicles per hour for the network? How much flow should go over each branch?

A Maximal Flow Algorithm

As we shall see, the maximal flow algorithm presented in this section uses the following common-sense approach:

1. Find any path from the input (source) node to the output (sink) node that has flow capacities in the direction of the flow greater than zero for all branches on the path.

FIGURE 9.16
Network of Highway System and Flow Capacities (in 1000s/Hour) for Cincinnati

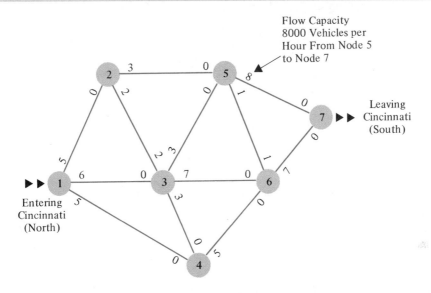

Flow Capacity
8000 Vehicles per
Hour From Node 5
to Node 7

Leaving
Cincinnati
(South)

Entering
Cincinnati
(North)

2. Increase the flow along the path by as much as possible.
3. Continue looking for source-to-sink paths that have remaining flow capacities in the direction of the flow greater than zero for all branches, and increase the flow along these paths as much as possible.
4. Stop when it is no longer possible to find a source-to-sink path with flow capacities in the direction of the flow greater than zero for all branches on the path.

Before presenting the details of the maximal flow algorithm, let us briefly discuss a procedure that will ensure that the above intuitive steps result in an optimal solution to the problem of finding the maximal flow from the source to the sink node.

The procedure permits previously assigned flow to take an alternate route by permitting fictional flows in the reverse direction. For example, consider the 3–6 branch:

Here we see that the initial flow capacity in the 3–6 direction is 7000 vehicles per hour, while no flow is permitted in the 6–3 direction.

If we choose to let 6000 vehicles per hour flow in the 6–3 direction, we will revise the flow capacities as follows:

Note that we have decreased the flow capacity in the 3–6 direction by 6000 vehicles per hour and simultaneously increased the flow capacity in the 6–3 direction by the same amount. The revised flow capacity of 1000 vehicles per hour in the 3–6 direction is readily interpreted as the remaining flow capacity in the branch. However, note that the 6–3 direction that had an initial flow capacity of zero now shows a revised flow capacity of 6000 vehicles per hour. This revised capacity in the 6–3 direction is actually indicating that a fictitious flow of up to 6000 vehicles per hour is permitted in this direction. Fictitious flow would not send vehicles in the 6–3 direction, but rather would simply decrease the amount of flow originally committed to the 3–6 branch direction. In effect, fictitious flow in the 6–3 direction would result in diverting flow originally committed to the 3–6 direction to other branches in the network.

The above process of tracking flow capacities is an important part of the maximal flow algorithm. For example, in an earlier step of the algorithm we might commit flow along a certain branch. Later, due to flows identified in other branches it may be desirable to decrease the flow along the original branch. The procedure we have described above will identify the extent to which our original decision to commit some flow needs to be revised in order to increase the total flow through the network.

Let us look now at the steps of the maximal flow algorithm.

Step 1. Find any path from the source node to the sink node that has flow capacities in the direction of the flow greater than zero for all branches on the path. If no path is available, the optimal solution has been reached.

Step 2. Find the smallest branch capacity, P_f, on the path selected in step 1. Increase the flow through the network by sending an amount P_f over the path selected in step 1.

Step 3. For the path selected in step 1, reduce all branch flow capacities in the direction of flow by P_f and increase all branch flow capacities in the reverse direction by P_f. Go to step 1.

While the procedure will vary depending on the analyst's choice of paths in step 1, the algorithm will eventually provide the maximal flow solution. Our calculations for the highway flow network are as follows:

Iteration 1

The path selected is 1–3–6–7; P_f, determined by branch 1–3, is 6. The revised network is as follows:

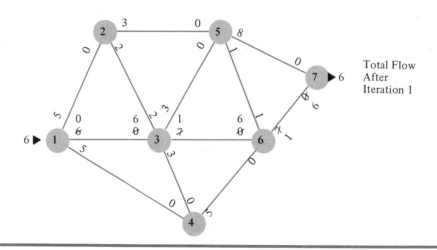

Total Flow
After
Iteration 1

Iteration 2

The path selected is $1-2-5-7$; P_f, determined by branch $2-5$, is 3. The revised network is as follows:

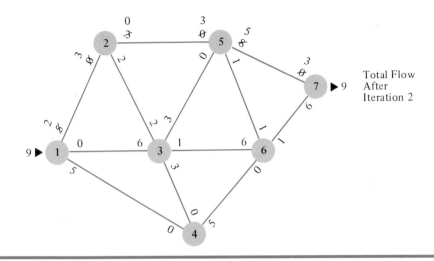

Total Flow After Iteration 2

Note that the total flow through the network can be found by summing the P_f values from each iteration.

While we will not show the revised network after each iteration, you should attempt to update the network flow capacities as you follow the discussion. For example, what will this network look like after the following three iterations?

Iteration 3

The path selected is $1-2-3-5-7$; P_f, determined by branch $1-2$ (or $2-3$), is 2.

Iteration 4

The path selected is $1-4-6-7$; P_f, determined by branch $6-7$, is 1.

Iteration 5

The path selected is $1-4-6-5-7$; P_f, determined by branch $6-5$, is 1.

At this point we have a total flow of 13,000 vehicles per hour, and the revised network capacities are as follows:

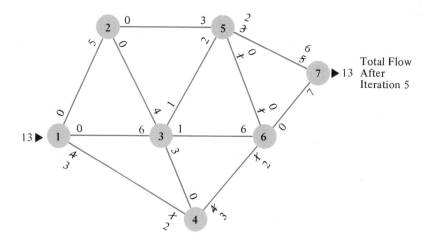

Total Flow
▶ 13 After
Iteration 5

Are there any other paths from node 1 to node 7 that have flow capacities in the direction of the flow greater than 0? Try 1–4–6–3–5–7, with a flow of $P_f = 1$ determined by branch 3–5. This increases the flow to 14,000 vehicles per hour. However, as you can see from the following revised network, there are no more paths from node 1 to node 7 that have flow capacities greater than 0 on all branches of the path; thus, 14,000 vehicles per hour is the maximal flow for this network.

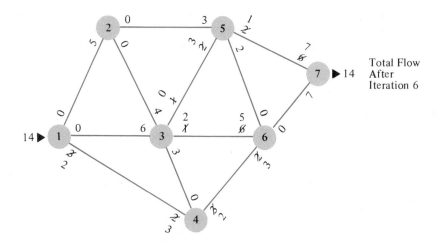

Total Flow
▶ 14 After
Iteration 6

Note that in iteration 6 a flow of 1000 vehicles per hour was permitted in the 6–3 direction. From the initial network, however, we know that the flow capacity in the 6–3 direction is zero; thus, the 1000 units of flow in the 6–3 direction represent a fictitious flow. The real effect of this flow is to divert 1000 units of flow originally committed to the 3–6 branch in iteration 1 along the 3–5 branch in order to enable us to get 1000 units more of flow through the network. Let us now determine the amount and direction of flow in each branch so that the total flow of 14,000 vehicles per hour can be attained.

Branch flows for the maximal flow solution can be found by comparing the final branch flow capacities with the initial branch flow capacities. If the final flow capacity is *less* than the initial flow capacity, flow is occurring in the branch with an amount equal to the difference between the initial and final flow capacities. For example, consider the 3–6 branch with initial flow and final flow capacities shown below.

Initial capacities:

Final capacities:

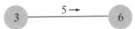

Since the final flow capacity in the 3–6 direction is less than the initial flow capacity, the branch has a flow of $7 - 2 = 5$ in the 3–6 direction. This branch flow is summarized as follows:

Comparing final and initial branch flow capacities for all branches in the network enables us to determine the final flow pattern as shown in Figure 9.17.

FIGURE 9.17
Maximal Flow Pattern for the Highway System Network

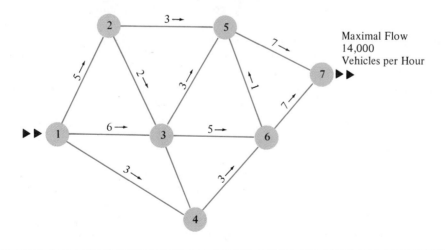

The results of the maximal flow analysis indicate that the planned highway network system will not handle the peak flow of 15,000 vehicles per hour. The transportation planners will have to expand the highway network, increase current branch flow capacities, or be prepared for serious traffic jam problems. If the network is extended or modified, another maximal flow analysis will determine the extent of any improved flow.

▼ NOTES AND COMMENTS ▼

Network models can be used to describe a variety of management science problems. Unfortunately, there is no one network solution algorithm or computer code that can be used to solve every network problem. It is important to recognize the specific type of problem being modeled in order to be able to select the specialized algorithms and computer codes that are available for developing an optimal solution.

▼ SUMMARY

In this chapter we extended the discussion of the use of network models in managerial decision making. We introduced the shortest-route, minimal spanning tree, and maximal flow problems and presented specialized solution algorithms for each. The key to success in network approaches to problem solving is in seeing how the problem can be represented as a network model. While some network formulations are obvious, other problems may require substantial ingenuity to develop the appropriate network representation. In any case, once the network representation has been developed, specialized solution algorithms are available to solve the problem.

▼ GLOSSARY

Shortest route   Shortest path between two nodes in a network.

Spanning tree   A set of branches (arcs) that connect every node in the network with all other nodes.

Minimal spanning tree   The spanning tree with the minimum length.

Maximal flow   The maximum amount of flow that can enter into and exit from a network system during a given period of time.

Arc capacity   The maximum flow for an arc of the network. The arc capacity in one direction may not equal the arc capacity in the reverse direction.

Source   A node that generates flow such that flow can only move away from it and never into it.

Sink   A node that absorbs flow such that flow can only move into it and never away from it.

▼ PROBLEMS

1. Find the shortest route from node 1 to each of the other nodes in the transportation network shown.

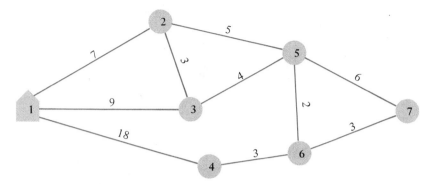

2. For the Gorman Construction Company problem (see Figure 9.1), assume that node 7 is the company's warehouse and supply center. Often several daily trips are made from node 7 to the other nodes or construction sites. Using node 7 as the starting node, find the shortest route from this node to each of the other nodes in the network.

3. In the original Gorman Construction Company problem, we found the shortest distance from the office (node 1) to each of the other nodes or construction sites. Because some of the roads are highways and others are city streets, the shortest-distance routes between the office and the construction sites may not necessarily provide the quickest or shortest-time routes. Shown below is the Gorman road network with travel time values rather than distance values. Find the shortest route from Gorman's office to each of the construction sites if the objective is to minimize travel time rather than distance.

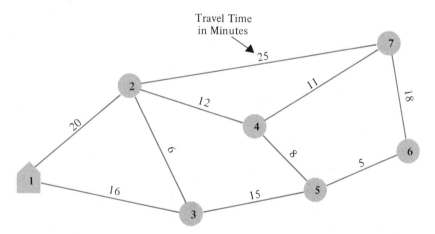

4. Find the shortest route between nodes 1 and 8 in the following network:

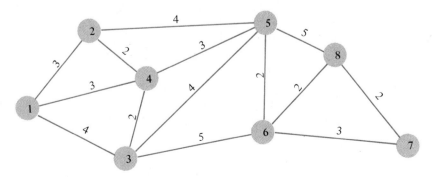

5. Find the shortest route between nodes 1 and 10 in the following network:

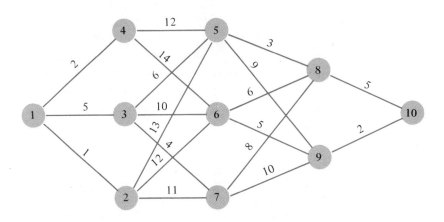

6. Morgan Trucking Company operates a special fast-service pickup and delivery service between Chicago and 10 other cities located in a four-state area. When Morgan receives a request for service, it dispatches a truck from Chicago to the city requesting service as soon as possible. Since both fast service and minimum travel costs are objectives for Morgan, it is important that the dispatched truck take the shortest route from Chicago to the specified city. Assume that the following network (not drawn to scale) with distances given in miles represents the highway network for this problem:

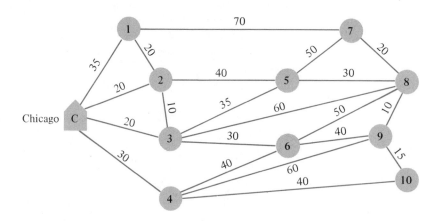

   a. Find the shortest-route distances from Chicago to all 10 cities.
   b. What is the shortest route to city 7? City 9?

7. City Cab Company has identified 10 primary pickup and drop locations for cab riders in New York City. In an effort to minimize travel time, improve customer service, and improve the utilization of the company's fleet of cabs, management would like the cab drivers to take the shortest route between locations whenever possible. Using the network of roads and streets shown below, what is the route a driver beginning at location 1 should take to reach location 10? The travel times in minutes are shown on the arcs of the network.

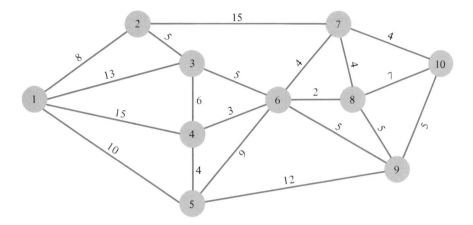

8. The Wisman Candy Company manufactures a variety of candy products. Company trucks are used to deliver local orders directly to retail outlets. When the business was small, the drivers of the trucks were free to take routes of their choice as they made the delivery rounds to the retail outlets. However, as the business has grown, transportation and delivery costs have become significant. In an effort to improve the efficiency of the delivery operation, Wisman's management would like to determine the shortest delivery routes between retail outlets. For example, the network below shows the roads that may be taken between a retail outlet at node 1 and a retail outlet at node 11. Determine the shortest route for a truck that must make deliveries to both outlets.

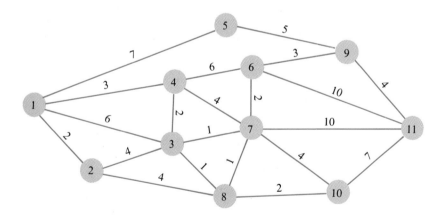

9. The five nodes in the network shown below represent points in time 1 year apart over a 4-year period. Each node indicates a time when a decision is made to keep or to replace a firm's computer equipment. If a decision is made to replace the equipment, a decision must also be made as to how long the new equipment will be used. The arc from node 0 to node 1 represents the decision to keep the current equipment 1 year and replace it at the end of the year. The arc from node 0 to node 2 represents the

decision to keep the current equipment 2 years and replace it at the end of year 2. The numbers above the arcs indicate the total cost associated with the equipment replacement decisions. These costs include discounted purchase price, trade-in value, operating costs, and maintenance costs. Determine the minimum-cost equipment replacement policy for the 4-year period.

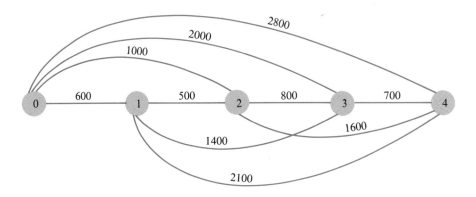

10. Develop the minimal spanning tree solution for the following emergency communications network.

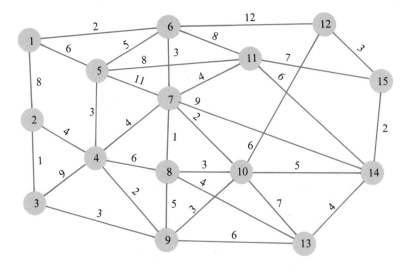

11. The State of Ohio recently purchased land for a new state park. Planners of the park have identified the ideal locations for the lodge, cabins, picnic groves, boat dock, and scenic points of interest. These locations are represented by the nodes of the network below. The branches of the network represent possible road alternatives in the park. If the state park designers want to minimize the total road miles that must be constructed in the park and still permit access to all facilities (nodes), which road alternatives should be constructed?

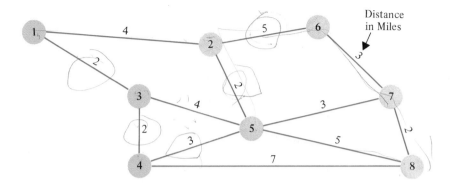

12. In a large soap products plant, quality control inspectors sample various products from the different production areas and then return the samples to the lab for analysis. The inspection process is slow, and the inspectors spend substantial time transporting samples from the production areas to the lab. The company is considering installing a pneumatic tube conveyor system that could be used to transport the samples between the production areas and the lab. The network below shows the locations of the lab and the production areas (nodes) where the samples must be collected. The branches are the alternatives being considered for the conveyor system. What is the minimum total length and layout of the conveyor system that will enable all production areas to send samples to the lab?

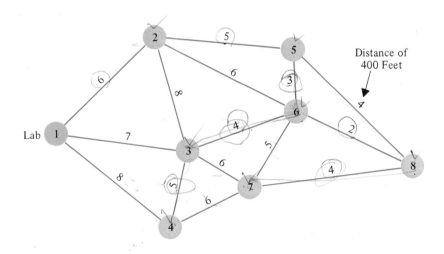

13. Midwest University is installing a computerized electronic mail system that will enable messages to be transmitted instantly among eight college offices. The network with possible electronic connections among the offices is shown below. Distances between offices are shown in thousands of feet. Develop a design for the office communication system that will enable all offices to have access to the electronic mail

service. Provide the design that minimizes the total length of connections among the eight offices.

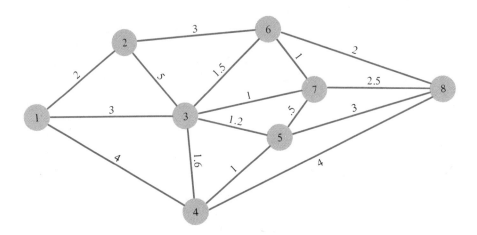

14. The Metrovision Cable Company has just received approval to begin providing cable television service to a suburb of Memphis, Tenn. The nodes of the network below show the distribution points that must be reached by the company's primary cable lines. The arcs of the network show the number of miles between the distribution points. Determine the solution that will enable the company to reach all distribution points with the minimum length of primary cable line.

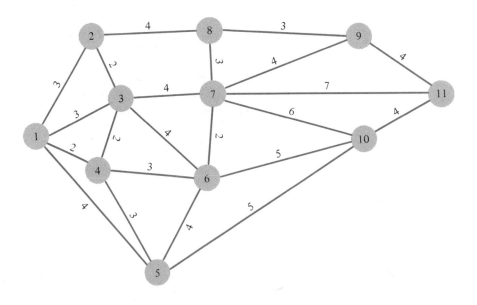

15. The north–south highway system passing through Albany, N.Y., can accommodate the capacities shown.

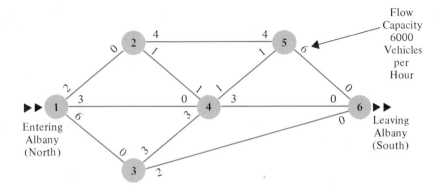

Do you believe the highway system can accommodate a north–south flow of 10,000 vehicles per hour?

16. If the Albany highway system problem has flow capacities revised as shown in the following network, what is the maximal flow in vehicles per hour through the system?

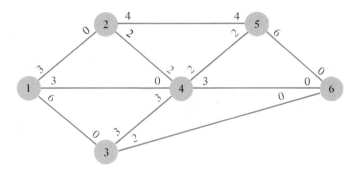

How many vehicles per hour must travel over each road (branch) in order to obtain this maximal flow?

17. A long-distance telephone company uses an underground cable network of communication lines to provide high-quality audio communication between two major cities. Calls are carried through series cable lines and connecting nodes in the network as shown below. Also shown are the number of telephone calls (in thousands) that may occur simultaneously at any point in time. What is the maximum number of telephone calls that can be transmitted simultaneously between the two cities? What are the connecting nodes and cable flows when the system is operating at capacity?

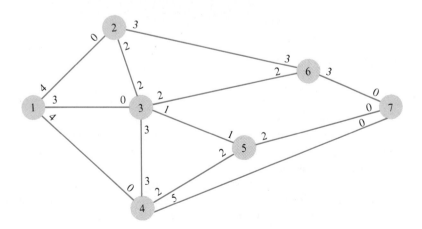

18. The High-Price Oil Company owns a pipeline network that is used to transmit oil from its source to several storage locations. A portion of the network is as follows:

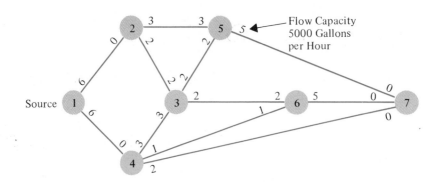

Due to the varying pipe sizes, the flow capacities also vary. By selectively opening and closing sections of the pipeline network, the firm can supply any of the storage locations.

a. If the firm wants to supply storage location 7 and fully utilize the system capacity, how long will it take to satisfy a location 7 demand of 100,000 gallons? What is the maximal flow for this pipeline system?

b. If a break occurs on line 2−3 and it is closed down, what is the maximal flow for the system? How long will it take to transmit 100,000 gallons to location 7?

19. For the highway network system shown below determine the maximal flow in vehicles per hour.

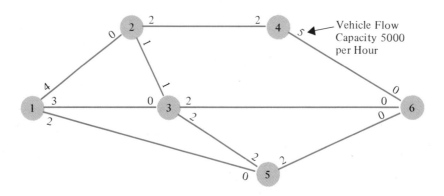

The highway commission is considering expanding highway section 3−4 to permit a flow of 2000 vehicles per hour or, at an additional cost, a flow of 3000 vehicles per hour. What is your recommendation for the 3−4 branch of the network?

20. A chemical processing plant has a network of pipes that are used to transfer liquid chemical products from one part of the plant to another. The pipe network and pipe flow capacities in gallons per minute are shown. What is the maximum flow capacity for the system if the company wishes to transfer as much liquid chemical as possible from location 1 to location 9? How much of the chemical will flow through the section of pipe from node 3 to node 5?

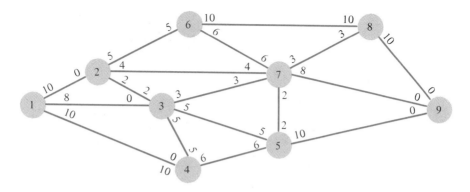

▼ CASE PROBLEM

Ambulance Routing

The city of Binghamton is served by two major hospitals: Western Medical and Binghamton General. Western Medical is located in the southwest part of the city, and Binghamton General is in the northeast.

Bob Jones, the hospital administrator at Western Medical, has been discussing the problem of scheduling and routing ambulances with Margaret Johnson, the hospital administrator at Binghamton General. Both administrators feel that some type of system needs to be developed to better coordinate the use of the ambulance services at the two hospitals so that together they can provide the fastest possible emergency service for the city.

A proposal being considered is for all ambulance service calls to be handled through a central dispatcher, who could assign a call to the hospital capable of providing the fastest service. In studying this proposal, a project team consisting of employees from both hospitals met and decided that the best approach would be to divide the city into 20 service zones. In the proposed configuration, Western Medical would be located in zone 1 and Binghamton General in zone 20. A map showing the placement of the 20 zones and the travel time (in minutes) between adjacent zones is provided in Figure 9.18.

According to the proposed operating procedure, incoming emergency calls would be identified by zone number, and an ambulance from the hospital closest to that zone would be assigned the service call. However, if all ambulances from the closest hospital were occupied with other emergencies, the service call would be assigned to the other hospital. Regardless of which hospital responded to the service call, the individual or individuals requiring the emergency service would be taken to the closest hospital.

To make the coordinated service as efficient as possible, the ambulance drivers must know in advance the quickest route to take to each zone, to which hospital the individual or individuals in that zone should be taken, and the quickest route to that hospital.

MANAGERIAL REPORT

Prepare a report for the two hospital administrators describing your analysis of the problem. Include in your report recommendations regarding the following items:

1. A chart for the dispatcher that identifies the primary hospital ambulance service for every zone in the city.

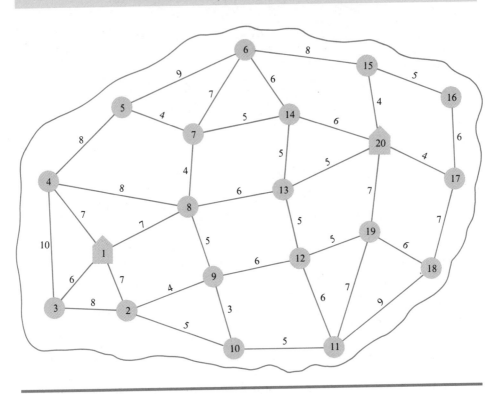

FIGURE 9.18
Network for Proposed Ambulance Service

2. A chart for the Western Medical ambulance drivers that provides the minimum-time routes from Western Medical to every zone in the city, including Binghamton General. Include a chart that tells Western Medical drivers which hospital the individuals should be taken to and the route that should be followed.

3. A chart for the Binghamton General ambulance drivers that provides the minimum-time routes from Binghamton General to every zone in the city, including Western Medical. Include a chart that tells Binghamton General drivers which hospital the individuals should be taken to and the route that should be followed.

4. Include recommendations regarding how the system could be modified to take into account varying traffic conditions that occur throughout the day and/or changes in driving conditions resulting from temporary road construction projects.

Project Management: PERT/CPM

10

In many situations, managers assume the responsibility for planning, scheduling, and controlling projects that consist of numerous separate jobs or tasks performed by a variety of departments, individuals, etc. Often these projects are so large and/or complex that the manager cannot possibly keep all the information pertaining to the plan, schedule, and progress of the project in his/her head. In these situations the techniques of PERT (Program Evaluation and Review Technique) and CPM (Critical Path Method) have proven to be extremely valuable in assisting managers in carrying out their project management responsibilities.

PERT and CPM have been used to plan, schedule, and control a wide variety of projects, such as

1. Research and development of new products and processes
2. Construction of plants, buildings, and highways
3. Maintenance of large and complex equipment
4. Design and installation of new systems

In projects such as these, project managers must schedule and coordinate the various jobs or activities so that the entire project is completed on time. A complicating factor in carrying out this task is the interdependence of the activities; for example, some activities depend on the completion of other activities before they can be started. When we realize that projects can have as many as several thousand activities, we see why project managers look for procedures that will help them answer questions such as the following:

1. What is the total time to complete the project?
2. What are the scheduled start and finish dates for each specific activity?
3. Which activities are "critical" and must be completed *exactly* as scheduled in order to keep the project on schedule?
4. How long can "noncritical" activities be delayed before they cause a delay in the total project?

As you will see, PERT and CPM can be used to help answer the above questions.

While PERT and CPM have the same general purpose and utilize much of the same terminology, the techniques were actually developed independently. PERT was introduced in the late 1950s specifically for planning, scheduling, and controlling the Polaris missile project. Since many jobs or activities associated with the Polaris missile project had never been attempted previously, it was difficult to predict the time to complete the various jobs or activities. Consequently, PERT was developed with an objective of being able to handle uncertainties in activity completion times.

On the other hand, CPM was developed primarily for scheduling and controlling industrial projects where job or activity times were considered known. CPM offered the option of reducing activity times by adding more workers and/or resources, usually at an increased cost. Thus, a distinguishing feature of CPM was that it enabled time and cost trade-offs for the various activities in the project.

In today's usage the distinction between PERT and CPM as two separate techniques has largely disappeared. Computerized versions of the PERT/CPM approach often contain options for considering uncertainty in activity times as well as activity time-cost tradeoffs. In this regard modern project planning, scheduling, and controlling procedures have essentially combined the features of PERT and CPM such that a distinction between the two techniques is no longer necessary.

10.1 ▼ PERT/CPM NETWORKS

The first step in the PERT/CPM project scheduling process is to determine the specific jobs, or activities, that make up the project. As a simple illustration involving the process of buying a small business, consider the list of four activities shown in Table 10.1. The development of an accurate list of activities such as this is a key step in any project. Since we will be planning the entire project and estimating the project completion date based on the list of activities, poor planning and omission of activities can be disastrous and lead to inaccurate schedules. We will assume that careful planning has been completed for the example problem and that Table 10.1 lists all activities for the small business project.

Note that Table 10.1 contains additional information in the column labeled Immediate Predecessor. The *immediate predecessors* for a particular activity are the activities that, when completed, enable the start of the activity in question. For example, the information in Table 10.1 tells us we can start work on activities A and B anytime since neither of these activities depends on the completion of prior activities. However, activity C cannot be started until activity B has been completed, and activity D cannot be started until both activities A and C have been completed. As you will see, immediate predecessor information must be known for each activity in order to describe the interdependencies among the activities in the project.

TABLE 10.1
Activity List for the Example Project of Buying a Small Business

Activity	Description	Immediate Predecessor
A	Develop a list of sources for financing	—
B	Analyze the financial records of the business	—
C	Develop a business plan (e.g., sales projections, cash flow projections, etc.)	B
D	Submit a proposal to a lending institution	A, C

FIGURE 10.1
PERT/CPM Network for the Example Project of Buying a Small Business

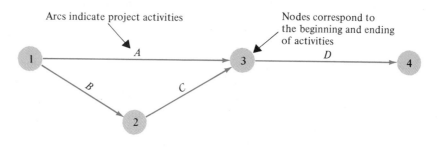

Arcs indicate project activities

Nodes correspond to the beginning and ending of activities

In Figure 10.1 we have drawn a network that not only depicts the activities listed in Table 10.1, but also portrays the predecessor relationships among the activities. This graphical representation is referred to as the PERT/CPM network for the project. The activities are shown on the branches, or arcs, of the network. The circles, or nodes, of the network correspond to the beginning and ending of the activities. The completion of all the activities that lead into a node is referred to as an *event*. For example, node 2 corresponds to the event that activity B has been completed, and node 3 corresponds to the event that both activities A and C have been completed.

Let us now attempt to develop the network for a project having the following activities and immediate predecessors:

Activity	Immediate Predecessor
A	—
B	—
C	B
D	A, C
E	C
F	C
G	D, E, F

A portion of the PERT/CPM network that could be used for the first four activities is as follows:

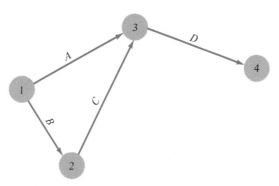

This portion of the network causes no particular problem for activity *D* since it shows activities *A* and *C* as the correct immediate predecessors. However, when we attempt to add activity *E* to the network, we encounter a problem. At first we might attempt to show activity *E* beginning at node 3. However, this indicates that both activities *A* and *C* are the immediate predecessors for activity *E*, which is incorrect. Referring to the original activity schedule for the project, we see that activity *E* only has activity *C* as its immediate predecessor.

We can avoid the above problem by inserting a *dummy activity*, which, as the name implies, is not an actual activity, but rather a fictitious activity used to ensure that the proper precedence relationships among the activities are depicted in the network. For example, we can add node 5 and insert a dummy activity, indicated by a dashed line from node 5 to node 3, forming the network shown below.

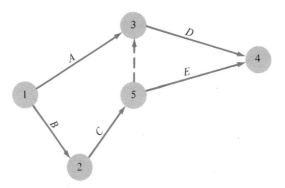

With this change in the network, activity *E* starting at node 5 has the correct predecessor of only activity *C*. The dummy activity does not have a time requirement, but is merely used to maintain the proper precedence relationships in the network. Note that the insertion of the dummy activity also correctly shows activities *A* and *C* as the immediate predecessors for activity *D*.

Completion of the seven-activity network could be shown as follows:

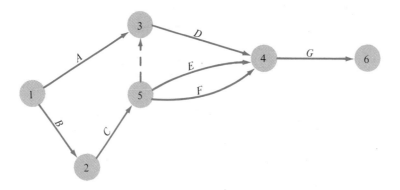

Note how the network correctly identifies activities *D*, *E*, and *F* as the immediate predecessors for activity *G*. However, note that activities *E* and *F* both start at node 5 and end at node 4. This situation causes problems for certain computer programs that use starting and ending nodes to identify the activities in a PERT/CPM network. In these programs the computer procedure would recognize activities E and F as the same activity since they have the same starting and ending nodes. When this condition occurs, dummy activities can be added to a network to make sure that two or more activities do not have the same starting and ending nodes. The use of node 7 and a dummy activity as shown below eliminates this problem for activities E and F.

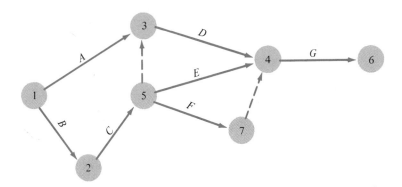

Dummy activities can be used to identify precedence relationships correctly as well as to eliminate the possible confusion of two or more activities having the same starting and ending nodes. Although dummy activities may not be required for all PERT/CPM networks, larger and/or more complex projects may require many dummy activities in order to depict the network properly.

10.2 ▼ PROJECT SCHEDULING WITH PERT/CPM

The owner of the Western Hills Shopping Center is considering modernizing and expanding the current 32-business shopping complex. Financing for the expansion has been arranged through a private investor. If the expansion project is undertaken, the owner hopes to add 8 to 10 new businesses or tenants to the shopping complex.

The specific activities that make up the expansion project are listed in Table 10.2. Note that the list includes the immediate predecessor for each activity as well as the number of weeks required to complete the activity. The PERT/CPM network for the project is shown in Figure 10.2. Check for yourself to see that the network does in fact maintain the immediate predecessor relationships shown in Table 10.2.

Information in Table 10.2 indicates that the total time required to complete all activities in the shopping center expansion project is 51 weeks. However, we can see from the network (Figure 10.2) that several of the activities can be conducted simultaneously (*A* and *B*, for example). Being able to work on two or more activities at the same time will shorten the total project completion time to less than 51 weeks. However, the total time required to complete the project is not directly available from the data in Table 10.2.

In order to facilitate the PERT/CPM computations that we will be making, the project network has been redrawn as shown in Figure 10.3. Note that each activity letter is written above and each activity time is written below the corresponding arc.

TABLE 10.2
Activity List for the Western Hills Shopping Center Expansion Project

Activity	Activity Description	Immediate Predecessor	Completion Time (weeks)
A	Prepare architectural drawings of planned expansion	—	5
B	Identify potential new tenants	—	6
C	Develop prospectus for tenants	A	4
D	Select contractor	A	3
E	Prepare building permits	A	1
F	Obtain approval for building permits	E	4
G	Perform construction	D, F	14
H	Finalize contracts with tenants	B, C	12
I	Have tenants move in	G, H	2
			Total 51

FIGURE 10.2
PERT/CPM Network for the Western Hills Shopping Center Expansion Project

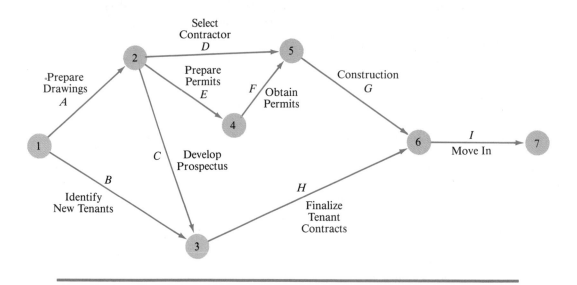

The Critical Path

Once we have the PERT/CPM network and the activity times, we are ready to proceed with the calculations necessary to determine the total time required to complete the project. In addition, we will use the results of the calculations to develop a detailed start and finish schedule for each activity.

FIGURE 10.3
Western Hills Shopping Center Project Network with Activity Times

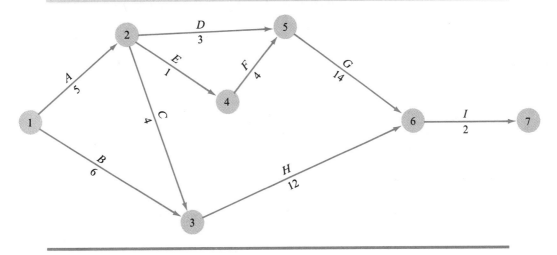

In order to determine the project completion time we will have to analyze the network and identify what is called its *critical path*. A *path* is a sequence of connected activities that leads from the starting node (1) to the completion node (7). The connected activities defined by nodes 1–2–3–6–7 form a path consisting of activities *A, C, H,* and *I*. Nodes 1–2–5–6–7 define the path associated with activities *A, D, G,* and *I*. Since *all* paths must be traversed in order to complete the project, we need to analyze the amount of time the various paths require. In particular, we will be interested in the longest path through the network. Since all other paths are shorter in duration, the longest path determines the total time required to complete the project. If activities on the longest path are delayed, the entire project will be delayed. Thus, the longest-path activities are the *critical path activities* of the project, and the longest path is called the *critical path*. If managers wish to reduce the total project time, they will have to reduce the length of the critical path by shortening the duration of the critical path activities. The following discussion presents a step-by-step procedure or algorithm for finding the critical path of a project network.

Starting at the network's origin (node 1) and using a starting time of 0, compute an *earliest start* and *earliest finish* time for each activity in the network. Let

$$\text{ES} = \text{earliest start time for a particular activity}$$
$$\text{EF} = \text{earliest finish time for a particular activity}$$
$$t = \text{expected activity time for the activity}$$

The following expression can be used to find the earliest finish time for a given activity:

$$\text{EF} = \text{ES} + t \tag{10.1}$$

For example, for activity *A*, ES = 0 and *t* = 5; thus, the earliest finish time for activity *A* is EF = 0 + 5 = 5.

We will write the earliest start and earliest finish times directly on the network in brackets next to the letter of the activity. Using activity *A* as an example, we have

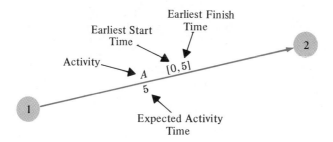

Since activities leaving a node cannot be started until *all* immediately preceding activities have been completed, the following rule can be used to determine the earliest start times for activities:

Earliest Start Time Rule

The earliest start time for an activity leaving a particular node is equal to the *largest* of the earliest finish times for all activities entering the node.

In applying this rule to a portion of the network involving activities *A, B, C,* and *H,* we obtain the following:

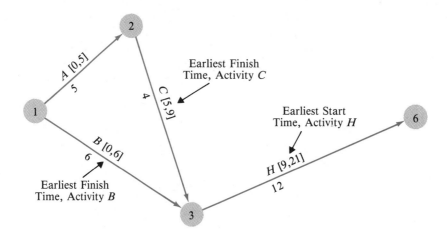

Note that in applying the earliest start time rule for activity *C,* which leaves node 2, we first recognize that activity *A* is the only activity entering node 2. Since the earliest finish time for activity *A* is 5, the earliest start time for activity *C* is 5. Thus, the earliest finish time for activity *C* must be EF = ES + t = 5 + 4 = 9.

The above diagram also shows that the earliest finish time for activity *B* is 6. Applying the earliest start time rule for activity *H,* we see that the earliest start time for this activity must be equal to the largest of the earliest finish times for the two activities that enter node 3, activities *B* and *C.* Thus, the earliest start time for activity *H* is 9, and the earliest finish time is EF = ES + t = 9 + 12 = 21.

Proceeding in a *forward pass* through the network, we can establish the earliest start time and then the earliest finish time for each activity. The Western Hills Shopping Center PERT/CPM network, with the ES and EF values for each activity, is shown in Figure 10.4. Note that the earliest finish time for activity *I*, the last activity, is 26 weeks. Thus, the total time required to complete the project is 26 weeks.

We now continue the algorithm for finding the critical path by making a *backward pass* calculation. Starting at the completion point (node 7) and using a latest finish time of 26 for activity *I*, we trace back through the network, computing a latest start and latest finish time for each activity. Let

$$LS = \text{latest start time for a particular activity}$$
$$LF = \text{latest finish time for a particular activity}$$

The following expression can be used to find the latest start time for a given activity:

$$LS = LF - t \tag{10.2}$$

Given $LF = 26$ and $t = 2$ for activity *I*, the latest start time for this activity can be computed as $LS = 26 - 2 = 24$.

The following rule is necessary in order to determine the latest finish time for any activity in the network:

Latest Finish Time Rule

The latest finish time for an activity entering a particular node is equal to the *smallest* of the latest start times for all activities leaving the node.

Logically the above rule states that the latest time an activity can be finished is equal to the earliest (smallest) value for the latest start time of following activities. The complete network with the LS and LF backward pass calculations is shown in Figure 10.5.

FIGURE 10.4
Western Hills Shopping Center Project with Earliest Start Times and Earliest Finish Times Shown Above the Activity Arcs

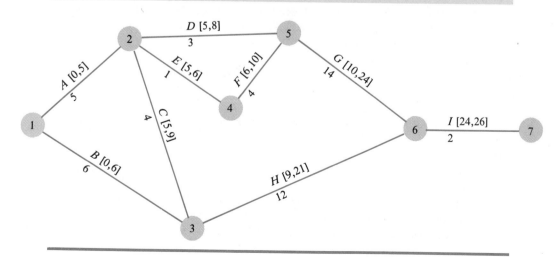

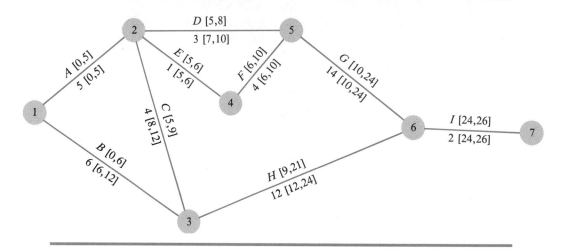

FIGURE 10.5
Western Hills Shopping Center Project with Latest Start Times
and Latest Finish Times Shown Below the Activity Arcs

The latest start and latest finish times for the activities are written in brackets directly under the earliest start and earliest finish times.

Note the application of the latest finish time rule for activity A, which enters node 2. The latest finish time for activity A (LF = 5) is the smallest of the latest start times for the activities that leave node 2; that is, the smallest LS value for activities C (LS = 8), E (LS = 5), and D (LS = 7) is 5.

After obtaining the start and finish activity times as summarized in Figure 10.5, we can find the amount of slack or free time associated with each of the activities. *Slack* is defined as the length of time an activity can be delayed without affecting the total time required to complete the project. The amount of slack for each activity is computed as follows:

$$\text{Slack} = \text{LS} - \text{ES} = \text{LF} - \text{EF} \tag{10.3}$$

For example, we see that the slack associated with activity C is LS − ES = 8 − 5 = 3 weeks. This means that activity C can be delayed up to 3 weeks (start anywhere between weeks 5 and 8) and the entire project can still be completed in 26 weeks. Thus, activity C is not a critical path activity. Using (10.3), we see that the slack associated with activity E is LS − ES = 5 − 5 = 0. Thus, activity E has no slack time and cannot be delayed without affecting the entire project. In general, the critical path activities are the activities with zero slack.

The start and finish times shown on the network in Figure 10.5 provide a detailed schedule for all activities. That is, from Figure 10.5 we know the earliest and latest start and finish times for the activities. Putting this information in tabular form provides the activity schedule shown in Table 10.3. Note that by computing the slack associated with each activity, we see that activities A, E, F, G, and I each have zero slack; hence, these activities form the critical path in the shopping center expansion network. Note that Table 10.3 also shows the slack or delay that can be tolerated for the noncritical activities before these activities will cause a project delay.

TABLE 10.3
Activity Schedule for the Western Hills Shopping Center Expansion Project

Activity	Earliest Start (ES)	Latest Start (LS)	Earliest Finish (EF)	Latest Finish (LF)	Slack (LS − ES)	Critical Path?
A	0	0	5	5	0	Yes
B	0	6	6	12	6	
C	5	8	9	12	3	
D	5	7	8	10	2	
E	5	5	6	6	0	Yes
F	6	6	10	10	0	Yes
G	10	10	24	24	0	Yes
H	9	12	21	24	3	
I	24	24	26	26	0	Yes

Contributions of PERT/CPM

Previously we stated that project managers look for procedures that will help answer many important questions regarding the planning, scheduling, and controlling of projects. Let us reconsider these questions in light of the information the PERT/CPM network and the critical path calculations have provided about the Western Hills Shopping Center expansion project.

1. What is the total time to complete the project?
   Answer: The project can be completed in 26 weeks if the individual activities are completed on schedule.

2. What are the scheduled start and completion times for each activity?
   Answer: The activity schedule (see Table 10.3) shows the earliest start, latest start, earliest finish, and latest finish times for each activity.

3. Which activities are "critical" and must be completed *exactly* as scheduled in order to keep the project on schedule?
   Answer: The five activities—*A, E, F, G,* and *I*—are the critical path activities.

4. How long can "noncritical" activities be delayed before they cause a delay in the completion time for the project?
   Answer: The activity schedule (see Table 10.3) shows the slack time associated with each activity.

   In managing any project the above information is important and valuable. While larger projects may substantially increase the time required to draw the PERT/CPM network and to make the necessary calculations, the procedure and contributions of PERT/CPM to larger projects are identical to those observed in the shopping center expansion project. Furthermore, computer packages exist that carry out the steps of the PERT/CPM procedure. Figure 10.6 shows the activity schedule for the shopping center expansion project developed by The Management Scientist computer software package. Input to the program included the activities, their immediate predecessors, and the expected activity times. Only a few minutes were required to input the information and generate this critical path and activity schedule information.

FIGURE 10.6
Activity Schedule for the Western Hills Shopping Center Expansion Project
Developed Using The Management Scientist

```
    ***     ACTIVITY SCHEDULE    ***


              EARLIEST   LATEST    EARLIEST   LATEST                CRITICAL
  ACTIVITY     START     START      FINISH    FINISH     SLACK      ACTIVITY
  ----------------------------------------------------------------------------
     A           0         0          5          5         0          YES
     B           0         6          6         12         6
     C           5         8          9         12         3
     D           5         7          8         10         2
     E           5         5          6          6         0          YES
     F           6         6         10         10         0          YES
     G          10        10         24         24         0          YES
     H           9        12         21         24         3
     I          24        24         26         26         0          YES
  ----------------------------------------------------------------------------

     CRITICAL PATH:  A-E-F-G-I

     PROJECT COMPLETION TIME = 26
```

Summary of the PERT/CPM Critical Path Procedure

Before leaving this section, let us summarize the PERT/CPM critical path procedure that can be used to plan, schedule, and control projects.

Step 1. Develop a list of activities that make up the project.

Step 2. Determine the immediate predecessor activities for each activity in the project.

Step 3. Estimate the completion time for each activity.

Step 4. Draw a network depicting the activities and immediate predecessors listed in steps 1 and 2.

Step 5. Using the network and the activity time estimates, determine the earliest start time and the earliest finish time for each activity by making a forward pass through the network. The earliest finish time for the last activity in the project identifies the total time required to complete the project.

Step 6. Using the project completion time identified in step 5 as the latest finish time for the last activity, make a backward pass through the network to identify the latest start time and latest finish time for each activity.

Step 7. Use the difference between the latest start time and the earliest start time for each activity to identify the slack time available for the activity.

Step 8. The critical path activities are the activities with zero slack.

Step 9. Use the information from steps 5 and 6 to develop the activity schedule for the project.

▼ NOTES AND COMMENTS ▼

In some applications, even when the activities may be completed according to the PERT/CPM schedule, management may find that the project cannot be completed by a predesignated due date. When this occurs, action designed to shorten the project duration is desired. First, management should review the original PERT/CPM network to see if the immediate predecessor relationships can be modified so that at least some of the critical path activities can be done simultaneously. Second, management should consider adding resources to critical path activities in an attempt to shorten the critical path; this alternative is referred to as *crashing*.

10.3 ▼ PROJECT SCHEDULING WITH UNCERTAIN ACTIVITY TIMES

In this section we consider the details of project scheduling for a problem involving the research and development of a new product. Because many of the activities in this project have never been previously attempted, the project manager wants to identify and account for the uncertainties in the activity times. Let us show how project scheduling can be conducted with uncertain activity times.

The Daugherty Porta-Vac Project

The H. S. Daugherty Company has manufactured industrial vacuum cleaning systems for a number of years. Recently a member of the company's new-product research team submitted a report suggesting that the company consider manufacturing a cordless vacuum cleaner. The vacuum cleaner, referred to as a Porta-Vac, could contribute to Daugherty's expansion into the household market. Management hopes that the new product can be manufactured at a reasonable cost and that its portability and no-cord convenience will make it extremely attractive.

Daugherty's management would like to initiate a project to study the feasibility of manufacturing the Porta-Vac product. The end result of the feasibility study will be a report recommending the action to be taken for the new product. In order to complete the feasibility study, information must be obtained from the firm's research and development (R&D), product testing, manufacturing, cost estimating, and market research groups. How long do you think this feasibility study project will take? When should we tell the product testing group to schedule its work? Obviously, we do not have enough information to answer these questions at this time. In the following discussion we will learn how to answer these questions and provide an activity schedule for the project.

Again, the first step in the project scheduling process is to determine all the activities that make up the project as well as the immediate predecessors for each activity. For the Porta-Vac project, these data are shown in Table 10.4

The PERT/CPM network for the Porta-Vac project is shown in Figure 10.7. Check for yourself to see that the network does in fact maintain the immediate predecessor relationships shown in Table 10.4.

Uncertain Activity Times

Once we have developed a PERT/CPM network for the project, we will need information on the time required to complete each activity. This information will be used in the calculation of the total time required to complete the project and the scheduling of the specific activities. For repeat projects, such as construction and/or maintenance projects, managers may have the experience and historical data necessary to provide accurate activity time estimates. However, for new or unique projects, activity time estimation may

TABLE 10.4
Activity List for the Daugherty Porta-Vac Project

Activity	Description	Immediate Predecessor
A	Prepare R&D product design	—
B	Plan market research	—
C	Prepare routing (manufacturing engineering)	A
D	Build prototype model	A
E	Prepare marketing brochure	A
F	Prepare cost estimates (industrial engineering)	C
G	Do preliminary product testing	D
H	Complete market survey	B, E
I	Prepare pricing and forecast report	H
J	Prepare final report	F, G, I

FIGURE 10.7
Network for the Porta-Vac Project

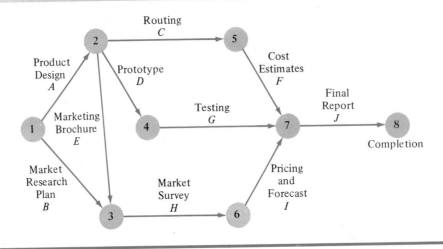

be significantly more difficult. In fact, in many cases activity times are uncertain and are best described by a range of possible values rather than by one specific activity time estimate. In these instances the uncertain activity times are treated as random variables with associated probability distributions. As a result, probability statements will be provided about the ability to meet a specific project completion date.

In order to incorporate uncertain activity times into the network analysis, we will need to obtain three time estimates for each activity. The three estimates are

Optimistic time (a)   The activity time if everything progresses in an ideal manner

Most probable time (m)   The most likely activity time under normal conditions

Pessimistic time (b)   The activity time if significant delays are encountered

The three time estimates enable the manager to develop a best guess of the most likely activity time and then express the uncertainty by providing time estimates ranging from the best possible (optimistic) time to the worst possible (pessimistic) time.

As an illustration of the PERT/CPM procedure with uncertain activity times, let us consider the optimistic, most probable, and pessimistic time estimates for the Porta-Vac activities as presented in Table 10.5.

Using activity A as an example, we see that management estimates that this activity will require from 4 weeks (optimistic) to 12 weeks (pessimistic), with the most likely time 5 weeks. If the activity could be repeated a large number of times, what would be the average time for the activity? This average or *expected time* (*t*) can be determined from the following formula:

$$t = \frac{a + 4m + b}{6} \tag{10.4}$$

For activity A we have an estimated average or expected completion time of

$$t_A = \frac{4 + 4(5) + 12}{6} = \frac{36}{6} = 6 \text{ weeks}$$

With uncertain activity times we can use the common statistical measure of the *variance* to describe the dispersion or variation in the activity time values. The variance of the activity time is given by the following formula:[1]

$$\sigma^2 = \left(\frac{b - a}{6}\right)^2 \tag{10.5}$$

As you can see, the difference between the pessimistic (*b*) and optimistic (*a*) time estimates greatly affects the value of the variance. Large differences in these two values

TABLE 10.5
Optimistic, Most Probable, and Pessimistic Activity Time Estimates (in Weeks) for the Porta-Vac Project

Activity	Optimistic (a)	Most Probable (m)	Pessimistic (b)
A	4	5	12
B	1	1.5	5
C	2	3	4
D	3	4	11
E	2	3	4
F	1.5	2	2.5
G	1.5	3	4.5
H	2.5	3.5	7.5
I	1.5	2	2.5
J	1	2	3

[1]The variance equation is based on the notion that a standard deviation is approximately ⅙ of the difference between the extreme values of the distribution: (*b* − *a*)/6. The variance is simply the square of the standard deviation.

reflect a high degree of uncertainty in the activity time. Accordingly, the variance given by (10.5) will be large. Using (10.5), we see that the measure of uncertainty—that is, the variance—of activity A, denoted σ_A^2, is

$$\sigma_A^2 = \left(\frac{12 - 4}{6}\right)^2 = \left(\frac{8}{6}\right)^2 = 1.78$$

Equations (10.4) and (10.5) are based on the assumption that the uncertainty in activity times can be described by a *beta probability distribution*.[2] With this assumption, the probability distribution for the time to complete activity A is as shown in Figure 10.8. Using equations (10.4) and (10.5) and the data in Table 10.5, the expected times and variances for all of the Porta-Vac activities are as summarized in Table 10.6.

A network depicting the Porta-Vac project and expected activity times is shown in Figure 10.9. Note that above each arc we write the letter of the corresponding activity, and directly under the arc we write the expected time of the activity.

The Critical Path

Once we have the network and the expected activity times, we are ready to proceed with the critical path calculations necessary to determine the expected time required to complete the project and the activity schedule. In the critical path calculations we will treat the expected activity times (Table 10.6) as the *fixed length* or *known duration* of each activity. As a result, we can use the critical path calculation procedure introduced in Section 10.2 to find the critical path for the Porta-Vac project. After the critical activities and the

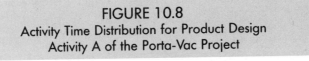

FIGURE 10.8
Activity Time Distribution for Product Design Activity A of the Porta-Vac Project

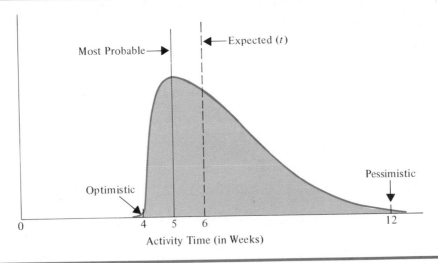

Activity Time (in Weeks)

---

[2]In order for the equations for t and σ^2 to be exact, additional assumptions are required about the parameters of the beta probability distribution. However, even when these additional assumptions are not made, the equations still tend to provide very good and useful approximations of t and σ^2.

TABLE 10.6
Expected Times and Variances for the Porta-Vac Activities

Activity	Expected Time (weeks)	Variance
A	6	1.78
B	2	0.44
C	3	0.11
D	5	1.78
E	3	0.11
F	2	0.03
G	3	0.25
H	4	0.69
I	2	0.03
J	2	0.11
	Total 32	

FIGURE 10.9
Porta-Vac Project Network with Expected Activity Times

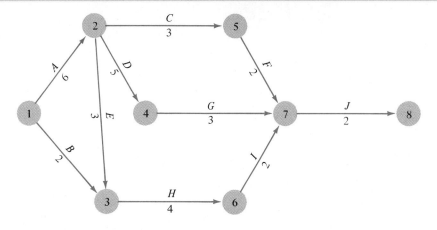

expected time to complete the project have been determined, we will analyze the effect of the activity time variability.

Proceeding with a forward pass through the network shown in Figure 10.9, we can establish the earliest start (ES) and earliest finish (EF) times for each activity. The PERT/CPM network with the ES and EF values is shown in Figure 10.10. Note that the earliest finish time for activity J, the last activity, is 17 weeks. Thus, the expected completion time for the entire project is 17 weeks. Next, we continue with the procedure for finding the critical path by making a backward pass through the network. The backward pass provides the latest start (LS) and latest finish (LF) times shown in Figure 10.11.

The start and finish times shown in Figure 10.11 provide the detailed schedule for all activities. Putting this information in tabular form provides the activity schedule shown in

FIGURE 10.10
Porta-Vac Network with Earliest Start and Earliest Finish Times Shown Above Activities

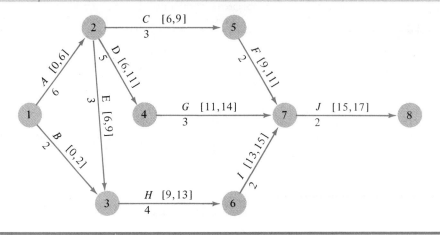

FIGURE 10.11
Porta-Vac Network with Latest Start and Latest Finish Times Shown Below Activities

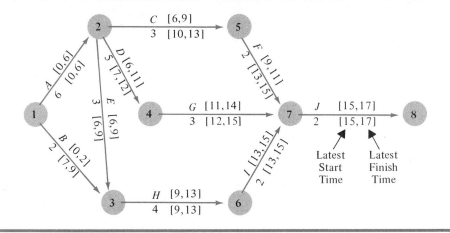

Table 10.7. Note that the slack time (LS − ES) is also shown for each activity. The activities with zero slack (A, E, H, I, and J) form the critical path for the Porta-Vac project network.

Variability in the Project Completion Time

In carrying out the critical path calculations, we treated the activity times as fixed at their expected values; we are now ready to consider the uncertainty in the activity times and

TABLE 10.7
Activity Schedule (in Weeks) for the Porta-Vac Project

Activity	Earliest Start (ES)	Latest Start (LS)	Earliest Finish (EF)	Latest Finish (LF)	Slack (LS − ES)	Critical Path?
A	0	0	6	6	0	Yes
B	0	7	2	9	7	
C	6	10	9	13	4	
D	6	7	11	12	1	
E	6	6	9	9	0	Yes
F	9	13	11	15	4	
G	11	12	14	15	1	
H	9	9	13	13	0	Yes
I	13	13	15	15	0	Yes
J	15	15	17	17	0	Yes

determine the effect this uncertainty or variability has on the total time required to complete the project. Recall that for the Porta-Vac project the critical path of A–E–H–I–J resulted in an expected total project completion time of 17 weeks.

Just as the critical path activities govern the expected total project completion time, variation in the critical path activities can cause variation in the total time required to complete the project. Variation in noncritical path activities will ordinarily have no effect on the total project completion time because of the slack time associated with these activities. However, if a noncritical path activity were delayed long enough to expend all its slack time, then that activity would become part of a new critical path, and further delays would extend the total time required to complete the project. Variability leading to a longer than expected total time for the critical path activities will always extend the project completion time. On the other hand, variability in critical path activities resulting in a shorter critical path will result in a shorter expected completion time, unless the activity times on the other paths become critical. Let us now use the variance in the critical path activities to determine the variance in the project completion time.

If we let T denote the total time required to complete the project, then the expected value of T, which is determined by the critical activities A–E–H–I–J in the Porta-Vac problem, is

$$E(T) = t_A + t_E + t_H + t_I + t_J$$
$$= 6 + 3 + 4 + 2 + 2 = 17 \text{ weeks}$$

where t_A, t_E, t_H, t_I and t_J are the expected completion times for the critical path activities.

Similarly, the variance in the total time required to complete the project is given by the sum of the variance of the critical path activities. Thus, the variance for the Porta-Vac project completion time is given by

$$\sigma^2 = \sigma_A^2 + \sigma_E^2 + \sigma_H^2 + \sigma_I^2 + \sigma_J^2$$
$$= 1.78 + 0.11 + 0.69 + 0.03 + 0.11 = 2.72$$

where σ_A^2, σ_E^2, σ_H^2, σ_I^2, and σ_J^2 are the variances of the critical path activities.

This formula is based on the assumption that all the activity times are independent. If two or more activities are dependent, the formula only provides an approximation to the variance of the project completion time. The closer the activities are to being independent, the better the approximation.

Since we know that the standard deviation is the square root of the variance, we can compute the standard deviation σ for the Porta-Vac project completion time as follows:

$$\sigma = \sqrt{\sigma^2} = \sqrt{2.72} = 1.65$$

A final assumption that the distribution of the project completion time T follows a normal or bell-shaped distribution[3] allows us to draw the distribution shown in Figure 10.12. With this distribution we can compute the probability of meeting a specified project completion date. For example, suppose that management has allotted 20 weeks for the Porta-Vac project. What is the probability that we will meet the 20-week deadline? Using the normal distribution from Figure 10.12, we are asking for the probability that $T \leq 20$. This is shown graphically as the shaded area in Figure 10.13. The z value for the normal distribution at $T = 20$ is given by

$$z = \frac{20 - 17}{1.65} = 1.82$$

Using $z = 1.82$ and the table for the normal distribution (see Appendix A), we see that the probability of the project's meeting the 20-week deadline is $0.4656 + 0.5000 =$

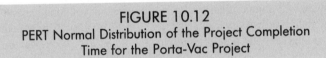

FIGURE 10.12
PERT Normal Distribution of the Project Completion Time for the Porta-Vac Project

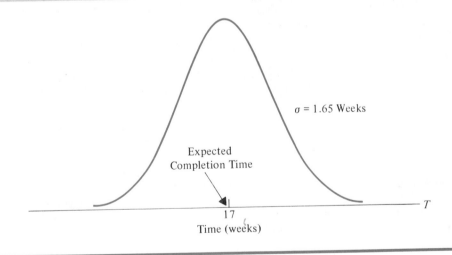

$\sigma = 1.65$ Weeks

Expected Completion Time

17

Time (weeks)

T

---

[3]The use of the normal distribution as an approximation is based on the central limit theorem, which indicates that the sum of independent activity times follows a normal distribution as the number of activities becomes large.

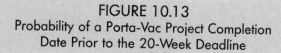

FIGURE 10.13
Probability of a Porta-Vac Project Completion
Date Prior to the 20-Week Deadline

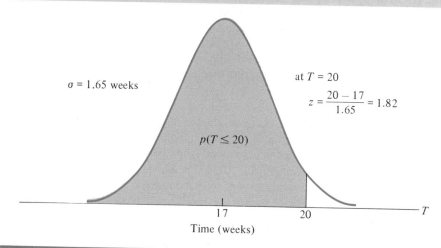

0.9656. Thus, while activity time variability may cause the total time required to complete the project to exceed 17 weeks, there is an excellent chance that the project will be completed before the 20-week deadline. Similar probability calculations can be made for other project deadline alternatives.

Thus, we see that a PERT/CPM project scheduling procedure can be used to schedule projects with uncertain activity times. A three–time estimate procedure for each activity (optimistic time, most likely time, and pessimistic time) enables the computation of an expected time and a variance for each activity. Using the expected time as the fixed time, the critical activities and critical path for the project can be found using the procedure presented in Section 10.2. The sum of the expected times of critical path activities provides the expected project completion time. The sum of the variances of critical path activities provides the variance in the project completion time. Using the normal probability distribution assumption for the completion time, standard procedures from probability can be used to compute the probability of the project's being completed by a specific date.

▼ NOTES AND COMMENTS ▼

For projects involving uncertain activity times, the probability that the project can be completed by a stated due date is helpful managerial information. However, remember that this probability estimate is based *only* on the critical path activities. When uncertain activity times exist, longer than expected completion times for one or more noncritical path activities may cause an original noncritical path to become critical and may increase the time required to complete the project. By frequently monitoring the progress of the project to make sure all activities are on schedule, the project manager will be better prepared to take corrective action if any noncritical activity begins to lengthen the duration of the project.

10.4 ▼ CONSIDERING TIME–COST TRADE-OFFS

The original developers of the CPM approach to project scheduling provided the project manager with the capability of adding resources to selected activities in an attempt to reduce activity—and thus project—completion times. Since added resources such as more workers, overtime, and so on generally increase project costs, the decision to reduce activity times must take into consideration the additional cost involved. In effect, the project manager has to make a decision that involves trading off decreased activity time against increased project cost.

In the Porta-Vac project the 17-week scheduled completion time could be reduced if management were willing to add resources to shorten any of the critical path activities: A, E, H, I, and J. Since the Porta-Vac project has a high probability of meeting the 20-week project deadline, it is doubtful that management would be willing to add costs to reduce activity times for this particular project. Thus, let us consider another project where time–cost trade-offs would most likely need to be considered.

Table 10.8 defines a two-machine maintenance project consisting of five activities. Since management has had substantial experience with similar projects, the times for maintenance activities are considered known; hence, a single time estimate is provided for each activity. The network for this project is shown in Figure 10.14.

Critical path calculations for the maintenance project network are computed following the procedure we used to find the critical path in both the Western Hills Shopping Center Expansion and the Porta-Vac networks. Making the forward pass and backward pass calculations for the network in Figure 10.14, we can obtain the activity schedule shown in Table 10.9. As you can see, the zero slack times, and thus the critical path, are associated with activities A–B–E or nodes 1–2–4–5. The length of the critical path, and thus the total time required to complete the project, is 12 days.

Crashing Activity Times

Now suppose that the current production levels make it imperative for the maintenance project to be completed within 2 weeks, or 10 working days. By looking at the length of the critical path of the network (12 days), we realize that it is impossible to meet the desired project completion time unless we can shorten selected activity times. This shortening of activity times, which usually can be achieved by adding resources such as labor

TABLE 10.8
Activity List for a Two-Machine Maintenance Project

Activity	Description	Immediate Predecessor	Expected Time (days)
A	Overhaul machine I	—	7
B	Adjust machine I	A	3
C	Overhaul machine II	—	6
D	Adjust machine II	C	3
E	Test system	B, D	2

FIGURE 10.14
Network of a Two-Machine Maintenance Project

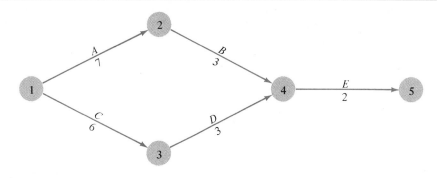

TABLE 10.9
Activity Schedule for the Two-Machine Maintenance Project

Activity	Earliest Start (ES)	Latest Start (LS)	Earliest Finish (EF)	Latest Finish (LF)	Slack (LS − ES)	Critical Path?
A	0	0	7	7	0	Yes
B	7	7	10	10	0	Yes
C	0	1	6	7	1	
D	6	7	9	10	1	
E	10	10	12	12	0	Yes

or overtime, is referred to as *crashing* the activity times. However, since the added resources associated with crashing activity times usually result in added project costs, we will want to identify the activities that cost least to crash and then crash those activities only the amount necessary to meet the desired project completion time.

In order to determine just where and how much to crash activity times, we will need information on how much each activity can be crashed and how much the crashing process costs. To accomplish this we must ask management for the following information on each activity:

1. Estimated activity cost under the normal or expected activity time
2. Activity completion time under maximum crashing (that is, the shortest possible activity time)
3. Estimated activity cost under maximum crashing

Let

$$\tau_j = \text{normal time for activity } j$$

$$\tau_j' = \text{time for activity } j \text{ under maximum crashing}$$

$$M_j = \text{maximum possible reduction in time for activity } j \text{ due to maximum crashing}$$

With both τ_j and τ_j' known, we can compute M_j as follows:

$$M_j = \tau_j - \tau_j' \qquad (10.6)$$

Next, let C_j denote the estimated cost for activity j under the normal or expected activity time and C_j' denote the estimated cost for activity j under maximum crashing. Thus, on a per-unit time basis (for example, per day), the crashing cost K_j for each activity is given by

$$K_j = \frac{C_j' - C_j}{M_j} \qquad (10.7)$$

For example, if the normal or expected time for activity A is 7 days at a cost of $C_A = \$500$ and the time under maximum crashing is 4 days at a cost of $C_A' = \$800$, equations (10.6) and (10.7) show that the maximum possible reduction in time for activity A is

$$M_A = 7 - 4 = 3 \text{ days}$$

with a crashing cost of

$$K_A = \frac{C_A' - C_A}{M_A} = \frac{800 - 500}{3} = \frac{300}{3} = \$100 \text{ per day}$$

We will make the assumption that any portion or fraction of the activity crash time can be achieved for a corresponding portion of the activity crashing cost. For example, if we decided to crash activity A by only 1½ days, we would assume that this could be accomplished with an added cost of 1½($100) = $150, which results in a total activity cost of $500 + $150 = $650. Figure 10.15 shows the graph of the time–cost relationship for activity A.

The complete normal and crash activity data for the two-machine maintenance project are given in Table 10.10.

FIGURE 10.15
Time–Cost Relationship for Activity A

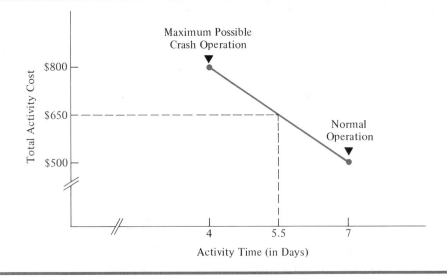

TABLE 10.10
Normal and Crash Activity Data for the Two-Machine Maintenance Project

Activity	Normal Time (days)	Crash Time (days)	Total Normal Cost (C_j)	Total Crash Cost (C_j')	Maximum Reduction in Time (M_j)	Crash Cost per Day $\left(K_j = \dfrac{C_j' - C_j}{M_j}\right)$
A	7	4	$ 500	$ 800	3	$100
B	3	2	200	350	1	150
C	6	4	500	900	2	200
D	3	1	200	500	2	150
E	2	1	300	550	1	250
			$ 1700	$ 3100		

Now the question is, Which activities should be crashed—and by how much—in order to meet the 10-day project completion deadline at minimum cost? Your first reaction to this question may be to consider crashing the critical path activities—A, B, or E. Activity A has the lowest crashing costs of the three, and crashing this activity by 2 days will reduce the A–B–E path to the desired 10 days. While this is correct, keep in mind that as you crash the current critical path activities, other paths may become critical. Thus, you will need to check the critical path in the revised network and perhaps either identify additional activities to crash or modify your initial crashing decision. For a small network this trial-and-error approach can be used to make crashing decisions; in larger networks however, a mathematical procedure is required in order to determine the optimal crashing decisions. The following discussion shows how linear programming can be used to solve the network crashing problem.

A Linear Programming Model for Crashing Decisions

First, recall that an event refers to the completion of all the activities that lead into a node. Since we have five nodes or events in the two-machine maintenance project, we need five decision variables to identify the time of occurrence for each event. In addition, we will need five decision variables to represent the amount of crash time used for each of the five activities. Thus, we define the following decision variables:

x_i = time of occurrence of event i $i = 1, 2, 3, 4, 5$

y_j = amount of crash time used for activity j $j = A, B, C, D, E$

Since the total normal time project cost is fixed at $1700 (see Table 10.10), we can minimize the total project cost (normal cost plus crash cost) by minimizing the total crashing costs. Thus, the linear programming objective function becomes

$$\min \sum_j K_j y_j \tag{10.8}$$

or

$$\min 100y_A + 150y_B + 200y_C + 150y_D + 250y_E \tag{10.9}$$

where K_j is the crash cost for activity j, $j = A, B, C, D, E$, on a per-unit time basis.[4]

The constraints for the model involve describing the network, limiting the activity crash times, and meeting the project completion date. Of these, the constraints used to describe the network are perhaps the most difficult. These constraints are based on the following conditions:

1. The time of occurrence of event i (x_i) must be greater than or equal to the activity completion time for all activities leading into the node or event.
2. An activity start time is equal to the occurrence time of its preceding node or event.
3. An activity time is equal to its normal time less the length of time it is crashed.

Using an event occurrence time of zero at node 1 ($x_1 = 0$), we can create the following set of network description constraints:

Event 2:

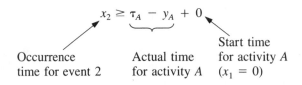

$$x_2 \geq \tau_A - y_A + 0$$

Occurrence time for event 2   Actual time for activity A Start time for activity A ($x_1 = 0$)

or

$$x_2 + y_A \geq 7 \tag{10.10}$$

Event 3:

$$x_3 \geq \tau_C - y_C + 0$$

or

$$x_3 + y_C \geq 6 \tag{10.11}$$

Since two activities enter event or node 4, we have the following two constraints:

Event 4:

$$x_4 \geq \tau_B - y_B + x_2$$
$$x_4 \geq \tau_D - y_D + x_3 \tag{10.12}$$

or

$$-x_2 + x_4 + y_B \geq 3$$
$$-x_3 + x_4 + y_D \geq 3 \tag{10.13}$$

Event 5:

$$x_5 \geq \tau_E - y_E + x_4$$

or

$$-x_4 + x_5 + y_E \geq 2 \tag{10.14}$$

The five constraints [(10.10) to (10.14)] are necessary to describe the network.

---

[4]Note that the x_i variables indicating event occurrences do not result in costs; thus, they have zero coefficients in the objective function.

The maximum allowable crash time constraints are

$$y_A \leq 3 \tag{10.15}$$

$$y_B \leq 1 \tag{10.16}$$

$$y_C \leq 2 \tag{10.17}$$

$$y_D \leq 2 \tag{10.18}$$

$$y_E \leq 1 \tag{10.19}$$

and the desired project completion time provides another constraint:

$$x_5 \leq 10 \tag{10.20}$$

Adding the nonnegativity restrictions and solving the above 9-variable, 11-constraint [(10.10) to (10.20)] linear programming model provides the following solution:

$$
\begin{array}{ll}
x_2 = 5 & y_A = 2 \\
x_3 = 6 & y_B = 0 \\
x_4 = 8 & y_C = 0 \\
x_5 = 10 & y_D = 1 \\
& y_E = 0
\end{array}
$$

Objective function = $350

The solution values of $y_A = 2$ and $y_D = 1$ tell us activity A must be crashed 2 days ($200) and activity D must be crashed 1 day ($150) in order to meet the 10-day project completion deadline. Because of this crashing, the time for activity A will be reduced to $7 - 2 = 5$ days, while the time for activity D will be reduced to $3 - 1 = 2$ days. The total project cost (normal cost plus crashing cost) will be $1700 + $200 + $150 = $2050. To generate the new activity schedule under crashing, we use the crashed activity times and repeat the critical path calculations for the network. Doing this provides the activity schedule shown in Table 10.11. Note that in the final solution all activities are critical. Resolving the linear programming model with alternate desired project completion times [constraint (10.20)] will show the project manager the costs associated with crashing the project to meet alternate deadlines.

TABLE 10.11
New Activity Schedule for the Two-Machine Maintenance Project After Crashing Activities A and D

Activity	Time After Crashing	ES	LS	EF	LF	Slack
A	5	0	0	5	5	0
B	3	5	5	8	8	0
C	6	0	0	6	6	0
D	2	6	6	8	8	0
E	2	8	8	10	10	0

Due to the substantial formulation and computational effort associated with activity crashing, most applications of this technique use specialized computer programs developed to handle crashing and the related network analyses.

10.5 ▼ PERT/COST

As you have seen, PERT/CPM concentrates on the *time* aspect of a project and provides information that can be used to schedule and control individual activities so that the entire project is completed on time. Although project time is a primary consideration for almost every project, there are many situations in which the *cost* associated with the project is just as important as time. In this section we show how the technique referred to as PERT/Cost can be used to help plan, schedule, and control project costs. The ultimate objective of a PERT/Cost system is to provide information that can be used to maintain project costs within a specified budget.

Planning and Scheduling Project Costs

The budgeting process for a project usually involves identifying all costs associated with the project and then developing a schedule or forecast of when the costs are expected to occur. Then at various stages of project completion, the actual project costs incurred can be compared to the scheduled or budgeted costs; if actual costs exceed budgeted costs, corrective action may be taken in order to keep the total project cost within the budget.

The first step in a PERT/Cost control system is to divide the entire project into components that are convenient in terms of measuring and controlling costs. While a PERT/CPM network may already show detailed activities for the project, we may find that these activities are too detailed for conveniently controlling project costs. In such cases, related activities that are under the control of one department, subcontractor, etc., are often grouped together to form what are referred to as *work packages*. By identifying costs of each work package, a project manager can use a PERT/Cost system to help plan, schedule, and control project costs.

Since the projects we discuss in this chapter have a relatively small number of activities, we will find it convenient to define work packages as having only one activity. Thus, in our discussion of the PERT/Cost technique we will treat each activity as a separate work package. Realize, however, that in large and complex projects we would almost always group related activities so that a cost control system could be developed for a more reasonable number of work packages.

In order to illustrate the PERT/Cost technique, let us consider the research and development project network shown in Figure 10.16. We are assuming that each activity is an acceptable work package and that a detailed cost analysis has been made on an activity basis. The activity cost estimates, along with the expected activity times, are shown in Table 10.12. In using the PERT/Cost technique we assume that activities (work packages) are defined such that their costs occur at a constant rate over the duration of the activity. For example, activity B, with an estimated cost of $30,000 and an expected 3-month duration, is assumed to have a cost rate of $30,000/3 = $10,000 per month. The cost rates for all activities are provided in Table 10.12. Note that the total estimated or budgeted cost for the project is $87,000.

Using the expected activity times, we can compute the critical path for the project. A summary of the critical path calculations and the resulting activity schedule is shown in Table 10.13. Activities B, D, and F determine the critical path and provide an expected project completion time of 8 months.

FIGURE 10.16
A Project Network

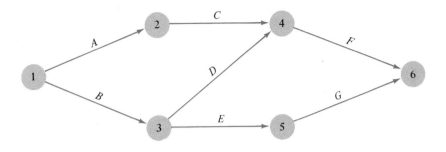

TABLE 10.12
Activity Times and Cost Estimates

Activity	Expected Time (months)	Budgeted or Estimated Cost	Budgeted Cost per Month
A	2	$ 10,000	$ 5,000
B	3	30,000	10,000
C	1	3,000	3,000
D	3	6,000	2,000
E	2	20,000	10,000
F	2	10,000	5,000
G	1	8,000	8,000
		Total project budget = $87,000	

TABLE 10.13
Activity Schedule

Activity	Earliest Start (ES)	Latest Start (LS)	Earliest Finish (EF)	Latest Finish (LF)	Slack	Critical Path?
A	0	3	2	5	3	
B	0	0	3	3	0	Yes
C	2	5	3	6	3	
D	3	3	6	6	0	Yes
E	3	5	5	7	2	
F	6	6	8	8	0	Yes
G	5	7	6	8	2	

We are now ready to develop a budget for the project that will show when costs should occur during the 8 months. First, let us assume that all activities begin at their earliest possible start time. Using the monthly activity cost rates shown in Table 10.12 and the earliest start times, we can prepare the month-by-month cost forecast as shown in Table 10.14. For example, using the earliest start date for activity A as 0, we expect activity A, which has a 2-month duration, to show a cost of $5000 in each of the first 2 months of the project. By similarly using the earliest start time and monthly cost rate for each activity, we are able to complete Table 10.14 as shown. Note that by summing the costs in each column, we obtain the total cost anticipated for each month of the project. Finally, by accumulating the monthly costs, we can show the budgeted total cost schedule, provided all activities are started at the *earliest* starting times. Table 10.15 shows the budgeted total cost schedule when all activities are started at the *latest* starting times.

TABLE 10.14
Budgeted Costs for an Earliest Starting Time Schedule ($1000s)

Activity	Month 1	2	3	4	5	6	7	8
A	5	5						
B	10	10	10					
C			3					
D				2	2	2		
E				10	10			
F							5	5
G						8		
Monthly Cost	15	15	13	12	12	10	5	5
Total project cost	15	30	43	55	67	77	82	87

TABLE 10.15
Budgeted Costs for a Latest Starting Time Schedule ($1000s)

Activity	Month 1	2	3	4	5	6	7	8
A				5	5			
B	10	10	10					
C						3		
D				2	2	2		
E						10	10	
F							5	5
G								8
Monthly cost	10	10	10	7	7	15	15	13
Total project cost	10	20	30	37	44	59	74	87

Provided the project progresses on its PERT/CPM time schedule, each activity will be started somewhere between its earliest and latest starting times. This implies that the total project costs should occur at levels between the earliest start and latest start costs schedules. For example, using the data in Tables 10.14 and 10.15, we see that by month 3, total project costs should be between $30,000 (latest starting time schedule) and $43,000 (earliest starting time schedule). Thus, at month 3 a total project cost between $30,000 and $43,000 would be expected.

In Figure 10.17 we show the forecasted total project costs for both the earliest and the latest starting time schedules. The shaded region between the two cost curves shows the possible budgets for the project. If the project manager is willing to commit activities to specific starting times, a specific project forecast or budget can be prepared. However, based on the above analysis we know that such a budget will have to be in the feasible region shown in Figure 10.17.

Controlling Project Costs

The information that we have developed thus far is helpful in terms of planning and scheduling total project costs. However, if we are going to have an effective cost control system, we will need to identify costs on a much more detailed basis. For example, information that the project's actual total cost is exceeding the budgeted total cost will be of little value unless we can identify the activity or group of activities that are causing the cost overruns.

The PERT/Cost system provides the desired cost control by budgeting and then recording actual costs on an activity (i.e., work package) basis. Periodically throughout

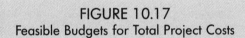

FIGURE 10.17
Feasible Budgets for Total Project Costs

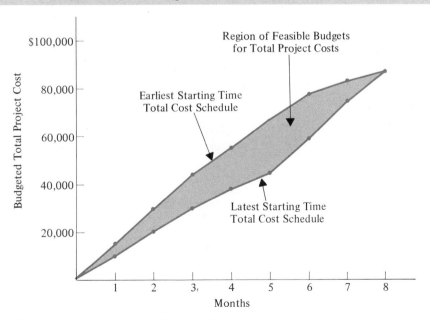

the project's duration, actual costs for all completed and in-process activities are compared with the appropriate budgeted costs. The project manager is then provided with up-to-date information on the cost status of each activity. If at any point in time actual costs exceed budgeted costs, a cost overrun has occurred. On the other hand, if actual costs are less than the budgeted costs, we have a condition referred to as a cost underrun. By identifying the sources of cost overruns and cost underruns, the manager can take corrective action where necessary. Note that the budgeted or estimated activity costs for the R&D project network of Figure 10.16 are shown in Table 10.16.

Now at any point during the project's duration the manager can use a PERT/Cost procedure to obtain an activity cost status report by collecting the following information for *each activity:*

1. Actual cost to date
2. Percent completion to date

A PERT/Cost system will require periodic—perhaps biweekly or monthly— collection of the above information. Let us suppose we are at the end of the fourth month of the project and have the actual cost and percent completion data for each activity, as shown in Table 10.17. This current status information shows that activities A and B have been completed; activities C, D, and E are in process; and activities F and G have not yet been started.

TABLE 10.16
Activity Cost Estimates

Activity	Budgeted Cost	Activity	Budgeted Cost
A	$10,000	E	$20,000
B	30,000	F	10,000
C	3,000	G	8,000
D	6,000		

TABLE 10.17
Activity Cost and Percent Completion Data at the End of Month 4

Activity	Actual Cost	Percent Completion
A	$ 12,000	100
B	30,000	100
C	1,000	50
D	2,000	33
E	10,000	25
F	0	0
G	0	0
Total =	$55,000	

In order to prepare a cost status report we will need to compute the value for all work completed to date. Let

$$V_i = \text{value of work completed for activity } i$$

$$p_i = \text{percent completion for activity } i$$

$$B_i = \text{budget for activity } i$$

The following relationship is used to find the value of work completed for each activity:

$$V_i = (p_i/100)B \qquad (10.21)$$

For example, the values of work completed for activities A and C are as follows:[5]

$$V_A = (100/100)(\$10,000) = \$10,000$$

$$V_C = (50/100)(\$3000) = \$1500$$

Cost overruns and cost underruns can now be found by comparing the actual cost of each activity with its appropriate budget value. Let

$$AC_i = \text{actual cost to date for activity } i$$

$$D_i = \text{difference between actual cost and value of work completed}$$
$$\text{for activity } i$$

We have

$$D_i = AC_i - V_i \qquad (10.22)$$

A positive D_i indicates the activity has a cost *overrun*, while a negative D_i indicates a cost *underrun*. $D_i = 0$ indicates that actual costs are in agreement with the budgeted costs. For example,

$$D_A = AC_A - V_A = \$12,000 - \$10,000 = \$2000$$

shows that activity A, which has already been completed, has a $2000 cost overrun. However, activity C, with $D_C = \$1000 - \$1500 = -\$500$, is currently showing a cost underrun, or savings, of $500. A complete cost status report such as the one shown in Table 10.18 can now be prepared for the project manager.

This cost report shows the project manager that the costs to date are $6500 over the estimated or budgeted costs. On a percentage basis, we would say the project is experiencing a ($6500/$48,500 \times 100 = 13.4\%$ cost overrun, which for most projects is a serious situation. By checking each activity, we see that activities A and E are causing the cost overrun. Since activity A has been completed, its cost overrun cannot be corrected; however, activity E is in process and is only 25% complete. Thus, activity E should be reviewed immediately. Corrective action for activity E can help to bring actual costs closer to the budgeted costs. The manager may also want to consider cost reduction possibilities for activities C, D, F, and G in order to keep the total project cost within the budget.

While the PERT/Cost procedure described above can be an effective cost control system, it is not without possible drawbacks and implementation problems. First, the activity-by-activity cost recording system can require significant clerical effort, especially for firms with large and/or numerous projects. Thus, the personnel and other costs associated with maintaining a PERT/Cost system may offset some of the advantages. Second,

[5]Equation (10.21) and the succeeding calculations are based on the PERT/Cost assumption that activity costs occur at a constant rate over the duration of the activity.

TABLE 10.18
Project Cost Status Report at Month 4

Activity	Actual Cost (AC)	Value of Work Completed (V)	Differences (D)
A	$ 12,000	$ 10,000	$ 2,000
B	30,000	30,000	0
C	1,000	1,500	−500
D	2,000	2,000	0
E	10,000	5,000	5,000
F	0	0	0
G	0	0	0
Totals	$ 55,000	$ 48,500	$ 6,500

Total project cost
overrun to date

questions can arise as to how costs should be allocated to activities or work packages. Overhead, indirect, and even material costs can cause cost allocation and measurement problems. Third, and perhaps most critical, is the fact that PERT/Cost requires a system of cost recording and control that is significantly different from most cost accounting systems. Firms using departments or other organizational units as cost centers will need a substantially revised accounting system to handle the PERT/Cost activity-oriented system. Problems of modifying accounting procedures and/or carrying dual accounting systems are not trivial matters.

▼ SUMMARY

In this chapter we introduced PERT/CPM and PERT/Cost as procedures designed to assist managers in planning, scheduling, and controlling projects. The key to these project management techniques the development of a PERT/CPM network that depicts the activities and their precedence relationships. Given this network and the activity time estimates, the critical path for the network and the associated critical path activities can be identified. In the process an activity schedule showing the earliest start time, the earliest finish time, the latest start time, the latest finish time, and the slack for each activity can be identified.

We showed how we can include capabilities for handling variable or uncertain activity times and how this information can be used to provide a probability statement about the chances the project can be completed in a specified period of time. Crashing was introduced as a procedure for reducing activity times to meet project completion deadlines. A linear programming model can be used to make the crashing decisions that minimize the cost of reducing the project completion time.

In the final section of this chapter we described how the PERT/Cost technique can be used to help plan, schedule, and control project costs. Because of the numerous computations associated with planning, updating, and revising PERT/CPM and PERT/Cost networks, computer programs are frequently used to implement these project management techniques. For modest-sized projects, computerized project management procedures are available on microcomputers.

A summary of some of the key steps in any project management task follows:

1. Clearly state the objectives of the project; focus specifically on identifying what is to be accomplished.
2. Make a list of all activities and their immediate predecessors. Provide estimates of the activity times by either specifying the expected time directly or using the optimistic, most likely, and pessimistic time estimates to compute an expected time.
3. Develop the PERT/CPM network for the project.
4. Perform the critical path computations in order to identify the critical path activities and develop an activity schedule for the project.
5. Make resource allocations and crashing decisions as necessary to achieve the desired project completion time.
6. Be sure someone is responsible for each activity in the project and is working to see that activities are completed as scheduled.
7. Control the project by monitoring actual performance, taking corrective action where necessary.

▼ GLOSSARY

Program evaluation and review technique (PERT)   A network-based project management procedure.

Critical path method (CPM)   A network-based project management procedure.

Activities   Specific jobs or tasks that are components of a project. These are represented by arcs in a PERT/CPM network.

Immediate predecessors   The activities that must immediately precede a given activity.

Event   An event occurs when *all* the activities leading into a node have been completed.

Dummy activity   A fictitious activity with zero activity time used to create a PERT/CPM network.

Optimistic time   An activity time estimate based on the assumption that the activity will progress in an ideal manner.

Most probable time   An activity time estimate for the most likely activity time.

Pessimistic time   An activity time estimate based on the assumption that the most unfavorable conditions occur.

Expected activity time   The average activity time.

Beta distribution   A probability distribution used to describe PERT activity times.

Path   A sequence of branches (activities) connecting the first node and the last node of a network.

Critical path   The longest path in a PERT/CPM network. The time it takes to traverse this path is the total time required to complete the project.

Critical path activities   The activities on the critical path.

Earliest start time   The earliest time at which an activity may begin.

Earliest finish time   The earliest time at which an activity may be completed.

Latest start time   The latest time at which an activity may begin without delaying the complete project.

Latest finish time   The latest time at which an activity may be completed without delaying the complete project.

Forward pass   That part of the PERT/CPM calculation procedure that involves moving forward through the network in order to determine the early start and early finish times for each activity.

Backward pass   That part of the PERT/CPM calculation procedure that involves moving backward through the network in order to determine the latest start and latest finish times for each activity.

Slack   The length of time an activity can be delayed without affecting the project completion time.

Crashing   The process of reducing an activity time by adding resources and hence usually increasing cost.

PERT/Cost   A technique designed to assist in the planning, scheduling, and controlling of project costs.

Work package   A natural grouping of interrelated project activities for purposes of cost control. A work package is a unit of cost control in a PERT/Cost system.

▼ PROBLEMS

1. The Mohawk Discount Store is designing a management training program for individuals at its corporate headquarters. The company would like to design the program so that the trainees can complete it as quickly as possible. There are important precedence relationships that must be maintained between assignments or activities in the program. For example, a trainee cannot serve as an assistant to the store manager until the trainee has obtained experience in the credit department and at least one sales department. The activities shown below are the assignments that must be completed by each trainee in the program:

Activity	Immediate Predecessor
A	—
B	—
C	A
D	A, B
E	A, B
F	C
G	D, F
H	E, G

Construct a PERT/CPM network for this problem. Do not attempt to perform any further analysis.

2. Consider the PERT/CPM network shown below.

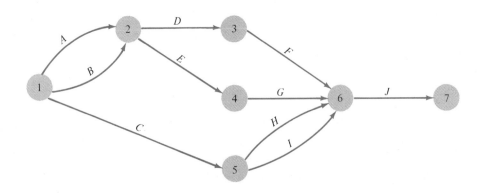

a. Add the dummy activities that will eliminate the problem that activities have the same starting and ending nodes.

b. Add dummy activities that will satisfy the following immediate predecessor requirements:

Activity	Immediate Predecessor
H	B, C
I	B, C
G	D, E

3. Construct a PERT/CPM network for a project having the following activities:

Activity	Immediate Predecessor
A	—
B	—
C	A
D	A
E	C, B
F	C, B
G	D, E

The project is completed when both activities F and G are complete.

4. Assume that the project in problem 3 has the following activity times:

Activity	Time (months)
A	4
B	6
C	2
D	6
E	3
F	3
G	5

a. Find the critical path.

b. The project must be completed in 1½ years. Do you anticipate difficulty in meeting the deadline? Explain.

5. Management Decision Systems (MDS) is a consulting company specializing in the development of decision support systems. MDS has just obtained the contract to develop a computer system to assist the management of a large company in formulating its capital expenditure plan. The project leader has developed the following list of activities and immediate predecessors:

Activity	Immediate Predecessor
A	—
B	—
C	—
D	B
E	A
F	B
G	C, D
H	B, E
I	F, G
J	H

Construct a PERT/CPM network for this problem.

6. Consider the following project network (the times shown are in weeks):

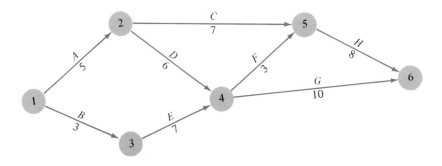

a. Identify the critical path.
b. How long will it take to complete this project?
c. Can activity D be delayed without delaying the entire project? If so, how many weeks?
d. Can activity C be delayed without delaying the entire project? If so, how many weeks?
e. What is the schedule for activity E (that is, start and completion times)?

7. A project involving the installation of a computer system consists of eight activities. The immediate predecessors and activity times in weeks are shown below.

Activity	Immediate Predecessor	Time (weeks)
A	—	3
B	—	6
C	A	2
D	B, C	5
E	D	4
F	E	3
G	B, C	9
H	F, G	3

a. Draw the PERT/CPM network for this project.

b. What are the critical path activities?

c. What is the expected project completion time?

8. Colonial State College is considering building a new multipurpose athletic complex on campus. The complex would provide a new gymnasium for intercollegiate basketball games, expanded office space, classrooms, and intramural facilities. The activities that would have to be undertaken before beginning construction are shown below. Activity times are stated in weeks.

Activity	Description	Immediate Predecessor	Time (weeks)
A	Survey building site	—	6
B	Develop initial design	—	8
C	Obtain board approval	A, B	12
D	Select architect	C	4
E	Establish budget	C	6
F	Finalize design	D, E	15
G	Obtain financing	E	12
H	Hire contractor	F, G	8

a. Develop a PERT/CPM network for this project.

b. Identify the critical path.

c. Develop the activity schedule for the project.

d. Does it appear reasonable that construction of the athletic complex could begin 1 year after the decision to begin the project with the site survey and initial design plans? What is the expected completion time for the project?

9. Hamilton County Parks is planning to develop a new park and recreational area on a recently purchased 100-acre tract. Activities making up the park development project include clearing playground and picnic areas, constructing roads, constructing a shelter house, purchasing picnic equipment, and so on. The PERT/CPM network shown below is being used to assist in the planning, scheduling, and controlling of this project:

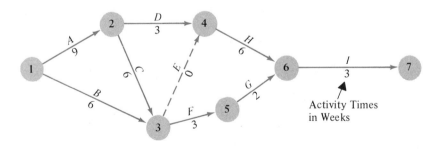

a. What is the critical path for this network?

b. Show the activity schedule for this project.

c. The park commissioner would like to open the park to the public within 6 months from the time the work on the project is started. Does this opening date appear feasible? Explain.

10. The following estimates of activity times (days) are available for a small project:

Activity	Optimistic	Most Probable	Pessimistic
A	4	5	6
B	8	9	10
C	7	7.5	11
D	7	9	10
E	6	7	9
F	5	6	7

    a. Compute the expected activity completion times and the variance for each activity.

    b. The management science staff has found that the critical path consists of activities B–D–F. Compute the expected project completion time and the variance.

11. The project of building a backyard swimming pool consists of nine major activities. The activities and their immediate predecessors are shown below. Develop the PERT/CPM network for this project.

Activity	Immediate Predecessor
A	—
B	—
C	A, B
D	A, B
E	B
F	C
G	D
H	D, F
I	E, G, H

12. Assume that the activity time estimates in days for the swimming pool construction project from problem 11 are as follows:

Activity	Optimistic	Most Probable	Pessimistic
A	3	5	6
B	2	4	6
C	5	6	7
D	7	9	10
E	2	4	6
F	1	2	3
G	5	8	10
H	6	8	10
I	3	4	5

a. What are the critical path activities?
b. What is the expected time to complete the project?
c. What is the probability that the project can be completed in 25 working days or less?

13. Suppose that the following estimates of activity times (weeks) were provided for the network shown in problem 6:

Activity	Optimistic	Most Probable	Pessimistic
A	4	5	6
B	2.5	3	3.5
C	6	7	8
D	5	5.5	9
E	5	7	9
F	2	3	4
G	8	10	12
H	6	7	14

What is the probability that the project will be completed within
a. 21 weeks?
b. 22 weeks?
c. 25 weeks?

14. Consider the project network given below:

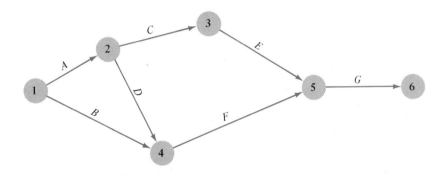

Estimates of the optimistic, most probable, and pessimistic times (in days) for the activities are as follows:

Activity	Optimistic	Most Probable	Pessimistic
A	5	6	7
B	5	12	13
C	6	8	10
D	4	10	10
E	5	6	13
F	7	7	10
G	4	7	10

a. Find the critical path.

b. How much slack time, if any, is there in activity *C?*

c. Determine the expected project completion time and the variance.

d. Find the probability that the project will be completed in 30 days or less.

15. Doug Casey is in charge of planning and coordinating next spring's sales management training program for his company. Doug has listed the following activity information for this project:

Activity	Description	Immediate Predecessor	Times (weeks) Optimistic	Times (weeks) Most Probable	Times (weeks) Pessimistic
A	Plan topic	—	1.5	2	2.5
B	Obtain speakers	A	2	2.5	6
C	List meeting locations	—	1	2	3
D	Select location	C	1.5	2	2.5
E	Finalize speaker travel plans	B, D	0.5	1	1.5
F	Make final check with speakers	E	1	2	3
G	Prepare and mail brochure	B, D	3	3.5	7
H	Take reservations	G	3	4	5
I	Handle last-minute details	F, H	1.5	2	2.5

a. Show the PERT/CPM network for this project.

b. Prepare the activity schedule for this project.

c. What are the critical path activities and the expected project completion time?

d. If Doug wants a 0.99 probability of completing the project on time, how far ahead of the scheduled meeting date should he begin working on the project?

16. The Daugherty Porta-Vac project discussed in section 10.3 had an expected project completion time of 17 weeks. The probability that the project could be completed in 20 weeks or less was found to be 0.9656. Shown below are the noncritical paths in the Porta-Vac project network.

$$A–D–G–J$$
$$A–C–F–J$$
$$B–H–I–J$$

a. Using the information in Table 10.6, compute the expected time and variance for each of the above paths.

b. Compute the probability that each path will be completed in the desired 20-week period.

c. Why is the computation of the probability of completing a project on time based on the analysis of the critical path? In what case, if any, would it be desirable to make the probability computation for a noncritical path?

17. Refer to the Porta-Vac project network shown in Figure 10.7. Suppose Daugherty's management revises the activity time estimates as follows:

Activity	Optimistic	Most Probable	Pessimistic
A	3	7	11
B	2	2.5	6
C	2	3	4
D	6	7	14
E	2	3	4
F	2.5	3	3.5
G	2.5	4	5.5
H	4.5	5.5	9.5
I	1	2	3
J	1	2	3

a. Compute the expected time and variance for each activity.
b. Show the new activity schedule.
c. What are the critical path activities?
d. What is the expected project completion time?
e. What is the new probability that the project will be completed within the 20-week deadline?

18. The manager of the Oak Hills Swimming Club is planning the club's swimming team program. The first team practice is scheduled for May 1. The activities, their immediate predecessors, and the activity time estimates in weeks are as follows:

Activity	Description	Immediate Predecessor	Time (weeks) Optimistic	Most Probable	Pessimistic
A	Meet with board	—	1	1	2
B	Hire coaches	A	4	6	8
C	Reserve pool	A	2	4	6
D	Announce program	B, C	1	2	3
E	Meet with coaches	B	2	3	4
F	Order team suits	A	1	2	3
G	Register swimmers	D	1	2	3
H	Collect fees	G	1	2	3
I	Plan first practice	E, H, F	1	1	1

a. Show the PERT/CPM network for this project.
b. Develop an activity schedule for the project.
c. What are the critical path activities, and what is the expected project completion time?
d. If the club manager plans to start the project on February 1, what is the probability the swimming program will be ready by the scheduled May 1 date (13 weeks)? Should the manager begin planning the swimming program prior to February 1?

19. The product development group at Landon Corporation has been working on a new computer software product that has the potential to capture a large market share. Through outside sources, Landon's management has learned that a competitor is working to bring a similar product to the market. As a result, Landon's top management has increased its pressure on the product development group. The group's leader has turned to PERT/CPM as an aid to the scheduling the activities remaining before the new product can be brought to the market. The PERT/CPM network is shown below.

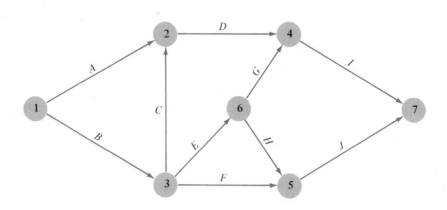

The activity time estimates in weeks are given below:

Activity	Optimistic	Most Probable	Pessimistic
A	3	4	5
B	3	3.5	7
C	4	5	6
D	2	3	4
E	6	10	14
F	7.5	8.5	12.5
G	4.5	6	7.5
H	5	6	13
I	2	2.5	6
J	4	5	6

a. Develop an activity schedule for this project, and identify the critical path activities.

b. What is the probability that the project will be completed so that Landon Corporation may introduce the new product within 25 weeks? 30 weeks?

20. Using the computer installation project referred to in problem 7, assume that the project has to be completed in 16 weeks. Crashing of the project is necessary. Relevant information is shown.

Activity	Normal Time (weeks)	Crash Time (weeks)	Normal Cost ($)	Crash Cost ($)
A	3	1	900	1700
B	6	3	2000	4000
C	2	1	500	1000
D	5	3	1800	2400
E	4	3	1500	1850
F	3	1	3000	3900
G	9	4	8000	9800
H	3	2	1000	2000

a. Formulate a linear programming model that can be used to make the crashing decisions for the above project.

b. Solve the linear programming model, and make the minimum cost crashing decisions. What is the added cost of meeting the 16-week completion time?

c. Develop a complete activity schedule using the crashed activity times.

21. Consider the following network with activity times shown in days:

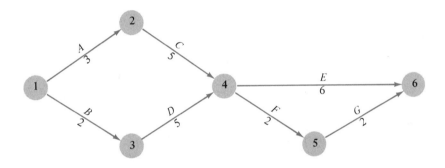

The crash data for this project are as follows:

Activity	Normal Time (days)	Crash Time (days)	Total Normal Cost ($)	Total Crash Cost ($)
A	3	2	800	1400
B	2	1	1200	1900
C	5	3	2000	2800
D	5	3	1500	2300
E	6	4	1800	2800
F	2	1	600	1000
G	2	1	500	1000

a. Find the critical path and the expected project completion time.

b. What is the total project cost using the normal times?

22. Refer to problem 21. Assume that management desires a 12-day project completion time.
    a. Formulate a linear programming model that can be used to assist with the crashing decisions.
    b. What are the activities that should be crashed?
    c. What is the total project cost for the 12-day completion time?
23. Assume that the following crash data are available for the project described in problem 4:

Activity	Normal Time (months)	Crash Time (months)	Total Normal Cost ($1000s)	Total Crash Cost ($1000s)
A	4	2	50	70
B	6	3	40	55
C	2	1	20	24
D	6	4	100	130
E	3	2	50	60
F	3	3	25	25
G	5	3	60	75

    a. Develop a linear programming model that could be used to make the crash decisions if the project has to be completed in T months.
    b. If $T = 12$ months, what activities should be crashed, what is the crashing cost, and what are the critical path activities?
24. Office Automation, Inc., has developed a proposal for introducing a new computerized office system that will improve word processing and interoffice communications for a particular company. Contained in the proposal is a list of activities that must be accomplished in order to complete the new office system project. Information about the activities is shown below. Times are in weeks, and costs are in thousands of dollars.

Activity	Description	Immediate Predecessor	Normal Time (weeks)	Crash Time (weeks)	Normal Cost ($1000s)	Crash Cost ($1000s)
A	Plan needs	—	10	8	30	70
B	Order equipment	A	8	6	120	150
C	Install equipment	B	10	7	100	160
D	Set up training lab	A	7	6	40	50
E	Conduct training course	D	10	8	50	75
F	Test system	C, E	3	3	60	—

    a. Show the network for the project.
    b. Develop an activity schedule for the project.

c. What are the critical path activities, and what is the expected project completion time?

d. Assume that the company wishes to complete the project in 6 months or 26 weeks. What crashing decisions would be recommended in order to meet the desired completion time at the least possible cost? Work through the network, and attempt to make the crashing decisions by inspection.

e. Develop an activity schedule for the crashed project.

f. What is the added project cost to meet the 6-month completion time?

25. Because Landon Corporation (see problem 19) is being pressured to complete the product development project at the earliest possible date, the project leader has requested an evaluation of the possibility of crashing the project.

a. Develop a linear programming model that could be used to help in making the crashing decisions.

b. What information would have to be provided before the linear programming model could be implemented?

26. For the Daugherty Porta-Vac project shown in Figure 10.7, suppose that the expected activity costs are as follows:

Activity	Expected Cost ($1000s)
A	90
B	16
C	3
D	100
E	6
F	2
G	60
H	20
I	4
J	2

Develop a total cost budget based on both an earliest start and a latest start schedule. Show the graph of feasible budgets for the total project cost.

27. Using the Daugherty Porta-Vac project cost data given in problem 26, prepare a PERT/Cost analysis for each of the following three points in time. For each case, show the percent overrun or underrun for the project to date, and indicate any corrective action that should be undertaken. *Note:* If an activity is not listed below, assume that it has not been started.

a. At the end of the 5th week:

Activity	Actual Cost ($1000s)	Percent Completion
A	62	80
B	6	50

b. At the end of the 10th week:

Activity	Actual Cost ($1000s)	Percent Completion
A	85	100
B	16	100
C	1	33
D	100	80
E	4	100
H	10	25

c. At the end of the 15th week:

Activity	Actual Cost ($1000s)	Percent Completion
A	85	
B	16	
C	3	
D	105	
E	4	100
F	3	
G	55	
H	25	
I	4	

28. The two-machine maintenance project discussed in Section 10.4 is shown below:

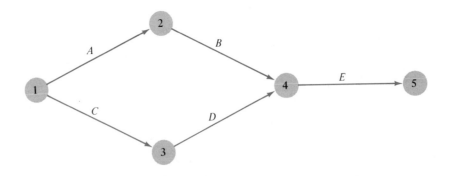

The recommended crashed activity schedule is shown in Table 10.11. Final times and costs for the project are as follows:

Activity	Expected Time (days)	Cost ($)
A	5	700
B	3	200
C	6	500
D	2	350
E	2	300
		Total 2050

a. Show the graph of feasible budgets for the project's total cost. Does this represent an unusual feasible budget region? Explain.

b. Suppose that at the start of day 8 we find the following activity status report:

Activity	Actual Cost ($)	Percent Completion
A	800	100
B	100	67
C	450	100
D	250	50
E	0	0

In terms of both time and cost, is the project on schedule? What action is recommended?

29. A firm is modifying its warehouse operation with the installation of an automated stock handling system. Specific activities include redesigning the warehouse layout, installing the new equipment, testing the new equipment, etc. The project management network is shown below.

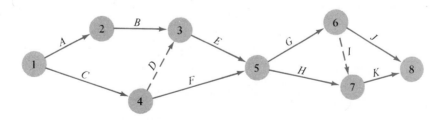

Pertinent time and cost data are as follows:

Activity	Expected Time (weeks)	Variance	Budgeted Cost ($)
A	3	0.3	6,000
B	2	0.5	4,000
C	8	2.0	16,000
D	0	0.0	0
E	6	1.0	18,000
F	4	0.2	20,000
G	5	0.4	15,000
H	1	0.1	2,000
I	0	0.0	0
J	5	1.0	5,000
K	6	0.6	12,000

a. Develop an activity schedule for the project.
   (1) What is the critical path?
   (2) What is the expected completion time?
   (3) What is the probability of meeting a desired 6-month (26-week) completion time?
b. Develop a PERT/Cost budget for total project costs over the project's duration. What should the range be for expenditures after 12 weeks of the project?
30. Refer to the network in problem 29. Suppose that after 12 weeks of operation the following data are available on all completed and in-process activities:

Activity	Actual Cost ($)	Percent Completion
A	5,000	100
B	4,000	100
C	18,000	100
E	9,000	50
F	18,000	75

Is the project in control based on both time and cost considerations? What corrective action, if any, is desirable?

▼ CASE PROBLEM:

Warehouse Expansion

R. C. Coleman distributes a variety of food products that are sold through grocery store and supermarket outlets. The company receives orders directly from the individual outlets, with a typical order requesting the delivery of several cases of anywhere from 20 to 50 different products. Under the company's current warehouse operation, warehouse clerks dispatch order-picking personnel to fill each order and have the goods moved to the warehouse shipping area. Because of the high labor costs and relatively low productivity of hand order-picking, the company has decided to automate the warehouse operation by installing a computer-controlled order-picking system, along with a conveyor system for moving goods from storage to the warehouse shipping area.

R. C. Coleman's director of material management has been named the project manager in charge of the automated warehouse system. After consulting with members of the engineering staff and warehouse management personnel, the director has compiled a list of activities associated with the project. The optimistic, most probable, and pessimistic times in weeks have also been provided for each activity. This information is as follows:

Activity	Description	Immediate Predecessor
A	Determine equipment needs	—
B	Obtain vendor proposals	—
C	Select vendor	A, B
D	Order system	C
E	Design new warehouse layout	C
F	Design warehouse	E
G	Design computer interface	C
H	Interface computer	D, F, G
I	Install system	D, F
J	Train system operators	H
K	Test system	I, J

| Activity | Time (weeks) | | |
	Optimistic	Most Probable	Pessimistic
A	4	6	8
B	6	8	16
C	2	4	6
D	8	10	24
E	7	10	13
F	4	6	8
G	4	6	20
H	4	6	8
I	4	6	14
J	3	4	5
K	2	4	6

MANAGERIAL REPORT

Develop a report that presents the activity schedule and expected project completion time for the warehouse expansion project. Include a PERT/CPM network of the project in the report. In addition, take into consideration the following issues.

a. R. C. Coleman's top management has established a required 40-week completion time for the project. Can this completion time be achieved? Include probability information in your discussion. What recommendations do you have if the 40-week completion time is required?

b. Suppose that management requests that activity times be shortened in order to provide an 80% chance of meeting the 40-week completion time. Assuming the variance in the project completion time is the same as you found in part (a), how much should the expected project completion time be shortened in order to achieve the goal of providing an 80% chance of completion within 40 weeks?

c. Using the expected activity times as the normal times and the following crashing information, determine the activity crashing decisions and revised activity schedule for the warehouse expansion project.

Activity	Normal Cost ($)	Crashed Activity Time (weeks)	Crash Cost ($)
A	1,000	4	1,900
B	1,000	7	1,800
C	1,500	2	2,700
D	2,000	8	3,200
E	5,000	7	8,000
F	3,000	4	4,100
G	8,000	5	10,250
H	5,000	4	6,400
I	10,000	4	12,400
J	4,000	3	4,400
K	5,000	3	5,500

Seasongood & Mayer

Cincinnati, Ohio

Seasongood & Mayer, established in 1887, is an investment securities firm that engages in the following areas of municipal finance:

1. Underwriting new issues of municipal bonds
2. Trading—for example, acting as a market maker for the buying and selling of previously issued bonds
3. Investment banking–that is, the process of obtaining money from the capital markets at the lowest possible cost

The major applications of management science at Seasongood & Mayer are in the investment banking area. One particular application involved the use of PERT/CPM in the introduction of a $31 million hospital revenue bond issue.

SCHEDULING THE INTRODUCTION OF A BOND ISSUE

In any major building project there are certain common steps:

1. Defining the project
2. Determining the cost of the project
3. Financing the project

The role of the investment banker in building projects is to develop a method of financing that will result in the owner's receiving the necessary funds in a timely manner. In a hospital building project, such as the one we will be discussing, the typical method of financing is tax-free hospital revenue bonds.

    The construction cost for the building project is an important factor in determining the best approach to financing. Normally, the construction cost is based on a bid submitted by a contractor or a construction manager. However, this cost is usually guaranteed only for a specified period of time, such as 60 to 90 days. The major function of the hospital's investment banker is to arrange the timing of the financing in such a way that the proceeds of the bond issue can be made available within the time limit of the guaranteed-price construction bid. Since most hospitals must have the proceeds of their permanent long-term financing in hand prior to committing to major construction contracts, the investment banker plays a very significant role.

    To arrange for the financing, the investment banker must coordinate the activities of hospital attorneys, the bond counsel, and so on. The cooperation of all parties and the coordination of project activities are best achieved if everyone recognizes the interdependency of the activities and the necessity of completing individual tasks in a timely manner. Seasongood & Mayer has found PERT/CPM to be useful in scheduling and coordinating such a project.

As managing underwriter for a $31,050,000 issue of Hospital Facilities Revenue Bonds for Providence Hospital in Hamilton County, Ohio Seasongood & Mayer utilized a critical path analysis to coordinate and schedule the project financing activities. Descriptions of the activities, times required, and immediate predecessors are given in Table 10.19. The complete network is shown in Figure 10.17. The critical path activities K–L–M–N–P–Q–R–S–U–W resulted in a scheduled project completion time of 29.14 weeks. Specific schedules showing start and finish times for all activities were used to keep the entire project on schedule. The use of PERT/CPM was instrumental in helping Seasongood & Mayer obtain financing for this project within the time specified in the construction bid.

TABLE 10.19
Activities for the Providence Hospital Project

Activity	Time Required (weeks)	Description of Activity	Immediate Predecessor
A	4	Drafting and distribution of legal documents	—
B	3	Preparation and distribution of unaudited financial statements of hospital	—
C	2	Drafting and distribution of hospital history, description of services, and existing facilities for Preliminary Official Statement (POS)	—
D	8	Drafting and distribution of demand portion of feasibility study	—
E	4	Review (additions/deletions) and approval as to form of legal documents	A
F	1	Review (additions/deletions) and approval of history, etc., for POS	C
G	4	Review (additions/deletions) and approval of demand portion of feasibility study	D
H	2	Drafting and distribution of financial portion (as to form) of feasibility study	E, G
I	2	Drafting and distribution of plan of financing and all pertinent facts relevant to the bond transaction for POS	E
J	0.5	Review and approval of unaudited financial statements	B
K	20	Receipt of firm price for project	—
L	1	Review (additions/deletions), approval, and completion of financial portion of feasibility study	H, K
M	1	Drafting of POS completed	$F, I J, L$
N	0.14	Distribution of all material to bond rating services	M
O	0.28	Printing and distribution of POS to all interested parties	M

TABLE 10.19
Continued

Activity	Time Required (weeks)	Description of Activity	Immediate Predecessor
P	1	Presentation to bond rating services (Standard & Poor's, Moody's)	N
Q	1	Receipt of bond rating	P
R	2	Marketing of bonds	O, Q
S	0*	Execution of purchase Contract	R
T	0.14	Authorization and completion of Final Official Statement, completion of legal documents	S
U	3	Fulfillment of all terms and conditions of Purchase Contract	S
V	0	Bond proceeds available to hospital	T, U
W	0*	Hospital able to sign construction contract	T, U

*Occurs instantaneously.

FIGURE 10.18
Seasongood & Mayer PERT/CPM Network for Providence Hospital Project

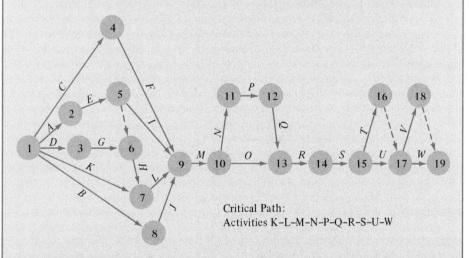

Critical Path:
Activities K–L–M–N–P–Q–R–S–U–W

Questions

1. What is the role of the investment banker in building projects?
2. For the hospital project described, what is the primary objective of the investment banker?
3. Perform the critical path calculations for the network shown in Figure 10.18. Is there more than one critical path? Discuss.

Inventory Models

Inventories are idle goods or materials that are waiting to be used. For most organizations, the expense associated with financing and maintaining inventories is a substantial part of the cost of doing business. In large organizations, especially those with many and/or expensive products, the cost associated with raw material, in-process, and finished goods inventories can run into millions of dollars.

Two important questions that managers must answer in order to effectively manage their inventories are as follows:

1. *How much* should be ordered when the inventory for a given item is replenished?
2. *When* should the inventory for a given item be replenished?

The purpose of this chapter is to show how quantitative models can assist in making the above decisions.

We will first consider *deterministic* inventory models where it is reasonable to assume that the rate of demand for the item is constant or nearly constant. Later we will consider *probabilistic* inventory models where the demand for the item fluctuates and can be described only in probabilistic terms. In addition, we will describe an inventory procedure referred to as *material requirements planning* (MRP); this approach to inventory management is suited for managing inventories of raw materials, subassemblies, and components whose demand is directly dependent on the demand for the final products in the inventory system. Finally, in the last section of the chapter, we discuss a philosophy of material management and control known as *just-in-time* (JIT); the primary objective of JIT is to eliminate all sources of waste, including unnecessary inventory.

11.1 ▼ ECONOMIC ORDER QUANTITY (EOQ) MODEL

The best known and most fundamental inventory model is the *economic order quantity (EOQ) model*. This model is applicable when the demand for an item has a constant, or nearly constant, rate and when the entire quantity ordered arrives in inventory at one point in time. The *constant demand rate* assumption means that the same number of units is taken from inventory each period of time, such as 5 units every day, 25 units every week, 100 units every 4-week period, and so on.

To illustrate how the EOQ model can be applied, let us consider the situation faced by the R & B Beverage Company. R & B Beverage is a distributor of beer, wine, and soft drink products. From a main warehouse located in Columbus, Ohio, R & B supplies nearly 1000 retail stores with beverage products. The beer inventory, which constitutes about 40% of the company's total inventory, averages approximately 50,000 cases. With an average cost per case of approximately $5, R & B estimates the value of its beer inventory to be $250,000.

The warehouse manager has decided to do a detailed study of the inventory costs associated with Bub Beer, the number-one-selling R & B beer. The purpose of the study is to establish the *how-much*-to-order and the *when*-to-order decision rules for Bub Beer that will result in the lowest possible total inventory cost. As the first step in the study, the warehouse manager has obtained the following historical demand data for Bub during the past 10 weeks:

Week	Demand (cases)
1	2,000
2	2,025
3	1,950
4	2,000
5	2,100
6	2,050
7	2,000
8	1,975
9	1,900
10	2,000
Total cases	20,000
Average cases per week	2,000

Strictly speaking, the above weekly demand figures do not show a constant demand rate. However, given the relatively low variability exhibited by the weekly demand, inventory planning with a constant demand rate of 2000 cases per week appears acceptable.

In practice you will find that the real inventory situation seldom, if ever, satisfies the assumptions of the model exactly. Thus, in any particular application it is the job of the manager and the management scientist to determine whether the model assumptions are close enough to reality for the model to be useful. In this situation, since demand varies from a low of 1900 cases to a high of 2100 cases, it appears that the assumption of constant demand of 2000 cases per week is a reasonable approximation.

The how-much-to-order decision involves selecting an order quantity that draws a compromise between (1) keeping small inventories and ordering frequently and (2) keeping large inventories and ordering infrequently. The first alternative can result in undesirably high ordering costs, while the second alternative can result in undesirably high holding costs. In order to find an optimal compromise between these conflicting alternatives, let us develop a mathematical model that will show the total cost[1] as the sum of the holding cost and the ordering cost.

Holding costs are the costs associated with maintaining or carrying a given level of inventory; these costs are dependent on the size of the inventory. First, there is the cost of financing the inventory investment. If money is borrowed, an interest charge is incurred; if the firm's own money is used, there is an opportunity cost associated with not being able to use the money for other investments. In either case a financing charge exists in the form of an interest cost for the capital tied up in inventory. The *cost of capital* is usually expressed as a percentage of the amount invested. Since R & B estimates its cost of capital at an annual rate of 18%, this portion of the total holding cost is 0.18($250,000) = $45,000 per year.

There are a number of other holding costs, such as insurance, taxes, breakage, pilferage, and warehouse overhead, that also depend for the most part on the value of the inventory. R & B estimates these other costs at an annual rate of approximately 7% of the value of its inventory. Thus, the total holding cost for the R & B beer inventory is 25% of its value, or 0.25($250,000) = $62,500 per year. When we consider that the beer inventory constitutes only about 40% of R & B's total inventory, we can begin to see that holding costs are a major expense for the R & B Beverage Company.

Assume that the cost of one case of Bub Beer is $5. Since R & B estimates its annual holding cost to be 25% of the value of its inventory, the cost of holding one case of Bub Beer in inventory for one year is 0.25($5) = $1.25. Note that defining the holding cost as a percentage of the value of the product is convenient because it is easily transferable to other products. For example, a case of Carle's Red Ribbon Beer, which costs $4.20 per case, would have an annual holding cost of 0.25($4.20) = $1.05 per case.

The next step in our inventory analysis is to determine the *ordering cost*. For R & B the largest portion of this cost involves the salaries of the purchasers. An analysis of the purchasing process showed that a purchaser spends approximately 45 minutes preparing and processing an order for Bub Beer. This amount of time is required regardless of the number of cases ordered. With a wage rate and fringe benefit cost for purchasers of $16 per hour, the labor portion of the ordering cost is $12. Making allowances for paper, postage, telephone, transportation, and receiving costs at $8 per order, the manager estimates that the ordering cost is $20 per order. That is, R & B is paying $20 per order regardless of the quantity requested in the order.

The holding cost, the ordering cost, and the demand information are the three data items that must be prepared prior to the use of the EOQ model. Since these data have now been developed for the R & B example, let us see how they are used to develop a total cost model. We begin by defining Q to be the order quantity. Thus, the how-much-to-order decision involves finding the value of Q that will minimize the sum of holding and ordering costs.

The inventory level for Bub will have a maximum value of Q units when the order of size Q is received from the supplier. R & B will then satisfy customer demand from inventory until the inventory is depleted, at which time another shipment of Q units will be received. Suppose that R & B is open five days each week. Thus, assuming a constant demand rate of 2000 cases per week or 400 cases per day, the sketch of the inventory level for Bub Beer is shown in Figure 11.1.

[1]While management scientists typically refer to "total cost" models for inventory systems, often these models describe only the total *variable* or total *relevant* costs for the decision being considered. Costs that are not affected by the how-much-to-order decision are considered fixed or constant and are not included in the model.

FIGURE 11.1
Sketch of the Inventory Level for Bub Beer

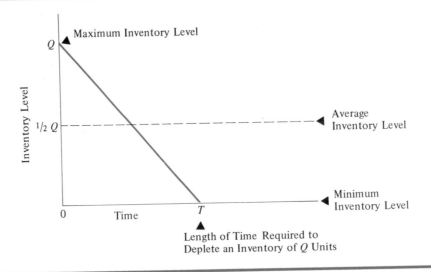

FIGURE 11.2
Inventory Pattern for the EOQ Inventory Decision Model

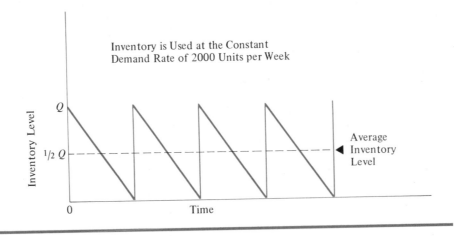

Note that the sketch indicates that the average inventory level for the period in question is $\frac{1}{2} Q$. This should appear reasonable since the maximum inventory level is Q, the minimum is 0, and the inventory level declines at a constant rate over the period.

Figure 11.1 shows the inventory pattern during one order cycle of length T. As time goes on, this pattern will repeat. The complete inventory pattern is shown in Figure 11.2. If the average inventory during each cycle is $\frac{1}{2} Q$, the average inventory level over any number of cycles is also $\frac{1}{2} Q$. Thus, as long as the time period involved contains an integral number of order cycles, the average inventory level for the period will be $\frac{1}{2} Q$.

The holding cost can be calculated using the average inventory level. That is, we can calculate the holding cost by multiplying the average inventory level by the cost of carrying one unit in inventory for the stated period. The period of time selected for the model is up to you; it could be 1 week, 1 month, 1 year, or more. However, since the cost for many industries and businesses expressed as an *annual* percentage or rate, most inventory models are developed on an *annual cost* basis.

Let

$$I = \text{annual holding cost rate (.25 for R \& B)}$$

$$C = \text{unit cost of the inventory item (\$5 for Bub Beer)}$$

The cost of holding one unit in inventory for the year, denoted by C_h, is $C_h = IC$; thus, for Bub Beer $C_h = 0.25(\$5) = \$1.25$. The general equation for the annual holding cost is as follows:

$$\begin{matrix} \text{Annual} \\ \text{holding cost} \end{matrix} = \begin{pmatrix} \text{average} \\ \text{inventory} \\ \text{level} \end{pmatrix} \begin{pmatrix} \text{annual holding} \\ \text{cost} \\ \text{per unit} \end{pmatrix}$$

$$= \frac{1}{2}QC_h \tag{11.1}$$

To complete the total cost model, we must now include the ordering cost. The goal is to express the ordering cost in terms of the order quantity, Q. Since the holding cost was expressed as an annual cost, we need to express the ordering cost on an annual basis. The first question is, How many orders will be placed during the year? Let D denote the annual demand for the product [for R & B, $D = (52 \text{ weeks})(2000 \text{ cases per week}) = 104,000$ cases per year]. We know that by ordering Q units each time we order, we will have to place D/Q orders per year. If C_0 is the cost of placing one order, the general equation for the annual ordering cost is as follows:

$$\begin{matrix} \text{Annual} \\ \text{ordering cost} \end{matrix} = \begin{pmatrix} \text{number of} \\ \text{orders} \\ \text{per year} \end{pmatrix} \begin{pmatrix} \text{cost} \\ \text{per} \\ \text{order} \end{pmatrix}$$

$$= \left(\frac{D}{Q}\right)C_0 \tag{11.2}$$

Thus, the total annual cost, denoted TC, can be expressed as follows:

$$\begin{matrix} \text{Total} & & \text{Annual} & & \text{Annual} \\ \text{Annual} & = & \text{Holding} & + & \text{Ordering} \\ \text{Cost} & & \text{Cost} & & \text{Cost} \end{matrix}$$

or

$$TC = \frac{1}{2}QC_h + \frac{D}{Q}C_0 \tag{11.3}$$

Using the Bub Beer data ($C_h = \$1.25$, $C_0 = \$20$, and $D = 104,000$), the total annual cost model is

$$TC = \frac{1}{2}Q(\$1.25) + \frac{104,000}{Q}(\$20) = 0.625\,Q + \frac{2,080,000}{Q} \tag{11.4}$$

The development of the above total cost model has gone a long way toward helping solve the inventory problem. We now are able to express the total annual cost as a function of *how much* should be ordered. The development of a realistic total cost model is perhaps the most important part of applying quantitative techniques to inventory decision making. Equation (11.3) is the general total cost equation for inventory situations in which the assumptions of the economic order quantity model are valid.

The How-Much-to-Order Decison

The next step is to find the order quantity, Q, that will minimize the total annual cost as stated in equation (11.4). Using a trial-and-error approach, we can compute the total annual cost for several possible order quantities. As a starting point, let us consider $Q = 8000$. The total annual cost is

$$TC = 0.625 \ (8000) + \frac{2,080,000}{8000} = \$5260$$

A trial order quantity of 5000 gives

$$TC = 0.625 \ (5000) + \frac{2,080,000}{5000} = \$3541$$

The results of several other trial order quantities are shown in Table 11.1. As can be seen, the lowest cost solution is around 2000 cases. Graphs of the annual holding, annual ordering, and total annual costs are shown in Figure 11.3.

The advantage of the trial-and-error approach is that it is rather easy to do and provides the total annual cost for a number of possible order quantity decisions. Also, we can see that approximately 2000 cases appears to be the minimum-cost order quantity. The disadvantage of this approach, however, is that it does not provide the exact minimum cost order quantity.

Refer to Figure 11.3. The minimum-total-cost order quantity is denoted by an order size of Q^*. By using differential calculus it can be shown (see Appendix 11.1) that the value of Q^* that minimizes the total annual cost is given by the formula

$$Q^* = \sqrt{\frac{2DC_0}{C_h}} \tag{11.5}$$

This formula is referred to as the *economic order quantity (EOQ) formula*.

Using (11.5), the minimum-total-annual-cost order quantity for Bub Beer is

$$Q^* = \sqrt{\frac{2(104,000)20}{1.25}} = 1824 \text{ cases}$$

TABLE 11.1
Annual Holding, Annual Ordering, and Total Annual Costs for Various Order Quantities of Bub Beer

Order Quantity	Annual Holding Cost	Annual Ordering Cost	Total Annual Cost
5000	$3125	$ 416	$3541
4000	2500	520	3020
3000	1875	693	2568
2000	1250	1040	2290
1000	625	2080	2705

FIGURE 11.3
Graphs of Annual Holding, Ordering, and Total Costs for Bub Beer

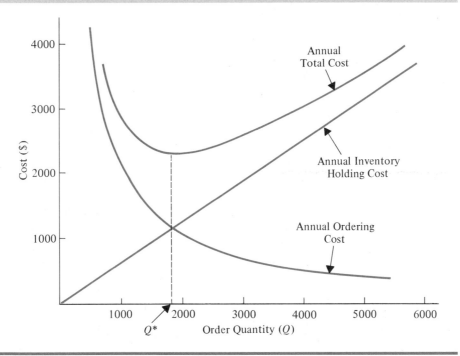

The use of an order quantity of 1824 in equation (11.4) shows that the minimum-cost inventory policy for Bub Beer has a total annual cost of $2280. Note that $Q^* = 1824$ has balanced the holding cost and the ordering cost. Check for yourself to see that these costs are equal.[2] (Problem 2 at the end of the chapter will ask you to show that having equal holding and ordering costs is a property of the EOQ model.)

The When-to-Order Decision

Now that we know how much to order, we want to address the question of *when* to order. To answer this question, we need to introduce the concept of inventory position. The *inventory position* for an item is defined as the amount of inventory on hand plus the amount of inventory on order. The when-to-order decision is expressed in terms of a *reorder point*—the inventory position at which a new order should be placed.

The manufacturer of Bub Beer guarantees a 2-day delivery on any order placed by R & B. Hence, assuming a constant demand rate of 2000 cases per week or 400 cases per day, we expect (2 days) (400 cases/day) = 800 cases of Bub to be sold during the 2 days it takes a new order of Bub to reach the R & B warehouse. In inventory terminology, the 2-day delivery period is referred to as the *lead time* for a new order, and the 800 cases of demand anticipated during this period is referred to as the *lead time demand*. Thus, R &

---

[2]Actually, Q^* from equation (11.5) is 1824.28, but since we cannot order fractional cases of beer, a Q^* of 1824 is shown. This value of Q^* may cause a few cents deviation between the two costs. If Q^* is used at its exact value, the holding and ordering costs will be exactly the same.

B should order a new shipment of Bub Beer from the manufacturer when the inventory level reaches 800 cases. For inventory systems using the constant demand rate assumption and a fixed lead time, the reorder point is the same as the lead time demand. For these systems the general expression for the reorder point is as follows:

$$r = dm \tag{11.6}$$

where

$$r = \text{reorder point}$$
$$d = \text{demand per day}$$
$$m = \text{lead time for a new order in days}$$

The question of how frequently the order will be placed can now be answered. This period between orders is referred to as the *cycle time*. Previously [see equation (11.2)] we defined D/Q as the number of orders that will be placed in a year. Thus, $D/Q^* = 104,000/1824 = 57$ is the number of orders R & B will place for Bub Beer each year. If R & B purchasers place 57 orders over 250 working days, they will order approximately every $250/57 = 4.4$ working days. Thus, the cycle time is computed to be 4.4 working days. The general expression[3] for a cycle time of T days is given by

$$T = \frac{250}{D/Q^*} = \frac{250Q^*}{D} \tag{11.7}$$

Sensitivity Analysis in the EOQ Model

Even though substantial time may have been spent in arriving at the cost per order ($20) and the holding cost (25%), we should realize that these figures are at best good estimates. Thus, we may want to consider how much the recommended order quantity would change if the estimated ordering and holding costs had been different. To determine this, we can calculate the recommended order quantity under several different cost conditions; Table 11.2 shows the minimum-total-cost order quantity for several cost possibilities. As you can see from the table, the value of Q^* appears relatively stable, even with some varia-

TABLE 11.2
Optimal Order Quantities for Several Cost Possibilities

Possible Inventory Holding Cost (%)	Possible Cost per Order	Optimal Order Quantity (Q^*)	Projected Total Annual Cost Using Q^*	Projected Total Annual Cost Using $Q = 1824$
24	$19	1815	$2178	$2178
24	$21	1908	$2289	$2292
26	$19	1744	$2267	$2269
26	$21	1833	$2383	$2383

[3]This general expression for cycle time is based on 250 working days per year. If the firm operated 300 working days per year and wanted to express cycle time in terms of working days, the cycle time would be given by $T = 300Q^*/D$.

tions in the cost estimates. Based on these results it appears that the best order quantity for Bub Beer is somewhere around 1700 to 2000 cases. If operated properly, the total cost for the Bub Beer inventory system should be close to $2200 to $2300 per year. We also note that there is very little risk associated with implementing the calculated order quantity of 1824. In the worst case (when $I = 24\%$, $C_0 = \$21$, and the true optimal order quantity $Q^* = 1908$), there is only a $3 increase in the total annual cost; that is, $\$2292 - \$2289 = \$3$.

From the above analysis we would say that this EOQ model is insensitive to small variations or errors in the cost estimates. This is a property of EOQ models in general, which indicates that if we have at least reasonable estimates of ordering costs and holding costs, we can expect to obtain a good approximation of the true minimum-cost order quantity.

The Manager's Use of the EOQ Model

The EOQ model results in a recommended order quantity of 1824 units. Is this the final decision, or should the manager's judgment enter into the establishment of the final inventory policy? Although the model has provided a good order quantity recommendation, it may not have taken into account all aspects of the inventory situation. As a result, the decision maker may want to modify the final order quantity recommendation to meet the unique circumstances of his or her inventory situation. In this case the warehouse manager felt that it would be desirable to increase the order quantity from 1824 cases to 2000 cases in order to have an order quantity equal to 5 working days' demand. By doing so, R & B can maintain a weekly order cycle.

The warehouse manager also realized that the EOQ model was based on the constant demand rate assumption of 2000 cases per week. While this is a good approximation, we must also recognize that sometimes the demand exceeds 2000 cases per week. If a reorder point of 800 cases is used, we would be expecting an 800-case demand during the lead time and the new order to arrive exactly when the inventory level reached zero. Such close timing would leave little room for error, and the scheduling of arrivals would be very critical if stockouts were to be avoided. To protect against shortages due to higher than expected demands or slightly delayed incoming orders, the warehouse manager recommended a 1200-case reorder point. Thus, under normal conditions R & B will order 2000 cases of Bub whenever the current inventory reaches 1200 cases. During the expected 2-day lead time 800 cases should be demanded, and thus 400 cases should be in inventory when an order arrives. The extra 400 cases serve as a safety precaution against a higher than expected demand or a delayed incoming order. In general the amount by which the reorder point exceeds the expected lead time demand is referred to as *safety stock*.

The decisions to adjust the order quantity and reorder point were purely judgment decisions and were not necessarily made with a minimum-cost objective in mind. However, they are examples of how managerial judgment might interface with the inventory decision model to arrive at a sound inventory policy. The final decision of $Q = 2000$ with a 400-case safety stock resulted in a total annual cost of $2790.[4]

---

[4]A Q of 2000 units resulted in a total cost of $2290 (see Table 11.1). The additional safety stock inventory of 400 units increases the average inventory by 400 units since it is on hand all year long. Thus, the inventory carrying charge is increased by 1.25(400) = $500, and the total cost of the revised policy is $2290 + 500 = $2790.

How Has the EOQ Decision Model Helped?

The EOQ model has objectively included holding costs and ordering costs and, with the aid of some management judgment, has led to a low-cost inventory policy. In addition, the general optimal order quantity model, equation (11.5), is potentially applicable to other R & B products. For example, Red Ribbon Beer ($4.20/case), which has an ordering cost of $20.00, a constant demand rate of 1200 cases per week (62,400 cases/year), and a 2-day lead time period, has a recommended order quantity of

$$Q^* = \sqrt{\frac{2(62,400)(20.00)}{(0.25)(4.20)}} = 1542 \text{ cases}$$

demand

a cycle time of $T = [250(1542)]/62,400 = 6.18$ days, and a reorder point of $r = (240)$ (2) = 480 cases.

We will now investigate additional inventory decision models that are designed to make *how-much-* and *when*-to-order decisions for other types of inventory systems.

▼ NOTES AND COMMENTS ▼

1. With relatively long lead times, the lead time demand and the resulting reorder point, r, determined by (11.6) may exceed Q^*. If this condition occurs, there will be at least one order outstanding when a new order is placed. For example, assume that Bub Beer has a lead time of $m = 6$ days. With a daily demand of $d = 400$ cases, (11.6) shows that the reorder point would be $r = dm = 6 \times 400 = 2400$ cases. Thus, a new order for Bub Beer should be placed whenever the inventory position (the amount of inventory on hand plus the amount of inventory on order) reaches 2400. With a economic order quantity of $Q^* = 1824$ cases, the inventory position of 2400 cases occurs when one order of 1824 cases is outstanding and $2400 - 1824 = 576$ cases are on hand.

2. The EOQ inventory model is based on the assumption that the demand rate is constant; this situation is rarely, if ever, encountered in practice. However, the use of this assumption enables the development of a model that yields a minimum-total-cost order quantity, Q^*. Applying the model to real-world problems where the constant demand rate is a reasonable assumption, managers are able to identify near-minimum-cost order quantity and reorder-point policies for their inventory systems.

11.2 ▼ ECONOMIC PRODUCTION LOT SIZE MODEL

The inventory model presented in this section is similar to the EOQ model in that we are attempting to determine *how much* we should order and *when* the order should be placed. Again we will assume a constant demand rate. However, instead of the goods arriving in a shipment of size Q^*, as assumed in the EOQ model, we will assume that units are supplied to inventory at a constant rate over several days or several weeks. The *constant supply rate* assumption implies that the same number of units is supplied to inventory each period of time (for example, 10 units every day, 50 units every week, and so on). This model is designed for production situations in which, once an order is placed, production begins and a constant number of units is added to inventory each day until the production run has been completed.

If we have a production system that produces 50 units per day and we decide to schedule 10 days of production, we have a 50(10) = 500-unit *production lot size*. In general, if we let Q indicate the production lot size, the approach to the inventory decisions will be similar to the EOQ model; that is, we will attempt to build a holding and ordering cost model that expresses the total cost as a function of the production lot size. Then we will attempt to find the production lot size that minimizes the total cost.

One other condition that should be mentioned at this time is that the model will only apply to situations where the production rate is greater than the demand rate; the production system must be able to satisfy demand. For instance, if the constant demand rate is 2000 units per week, the production rate must be at least 2000 units per week in order to satisfy demand.

During the production run, demand will be reducing the inventory while production will be adding to inventory. Since we have assumed that the production rate exceeds the demand rate, each day during a production run we will be producing more units than are demanded. Thus, the excess production will cause a gradual inventory buildup during the production period. When the production run is completed, the continuing demand will cause the inventory to gradually decline until a new production run is started. The inventory pattern for this system is shown in Figure 11.4

As in the EOQ model, we are now dealing with two costs, the holding cost and the ordering cost. While the holding cost is identical to our definition in the EOQ model, the interpretation of the ordering cost is slightly different. In fact, in a production situation the ordering cost is more correctly referred to as the *production setup cost*. This cost, which includes hours of labor, material, and lost production costs incurred while preparing the production system for operation, is a fixed cost that occurs for every production run regardless of the production lot size.

The Total Cost Model

Let us begin building the production lot size model by writing the holding cost in terms of the production lot size, Q. Again, the approach will be to develop an expression for

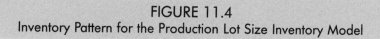

FIGURE 11.4
Inventory Pattern for the Production Lot Size Inventory Model

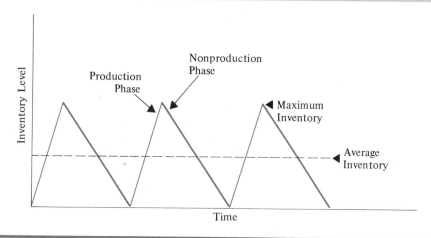

average inventory and then establish the holding costs associated with the average inventory level. We will use a 1-year time period and an annual cost for the model.

We saw in the EOQ model that the average inventory was simply one-half the maximum inventory or $\frac{1}{2} Q$. Since Figure 11.4 shows a constant inventory buildup rate during the production run and a constant inventory depletion rate during the nonproduction period, the average inventory for the production lot size model will also be one-half of the maximum inventory level. However, in this inventory system the production lot size, Q, does not go into inventory at one point in time, and thus the inventory level never reaches a level of Q units.

Let us see how we can compute the maximum inventory level. First, we define the following:

$$d = \text{daily demand rate for the product}$$
$$p = \text{daily production rate for the product}$$
$$t = \text{number of days for a production run}$$

Since we are assuming p will be larger than d, the daily inventory buildup rate during the production phase is $p - d$. If we run production for t days and place $p - d$ units in inventory each day, the inventory level at the end of the production run will be $(p - d)t$. From Figure 11.4 we can see that the inventory level at the end of the production run is also the maximum inventory level. Thus,

$$\text{Maximum inventory level} = (p - d)t \tag{11.8}$$

If we know we are producing a production lot size of Q units at a daily production rate of p units, then $Q = pt$, and the length of the production run t must be

$$t = \frac{Q}{p} \text{ days} \tag{11.9}$$

Thus,

$$\text{Maximum inventory level} = (p - d)t = (p - d)\left(\frac{Q}{p}\right) \tag{11.10}$$

$$= \left(1 - \frac{d}{p}\right)Q$$

The average inventory level, which is one-half of the maximum inventory level, is given by

$$\text{Average inventory level} = \frac{1}{2}\left(1 - \frac{d}{p}\right)Q \tag{11.11}$$

With an annual holding cost of $C_h = IC$ per unit, the general equation for annual holding cost is as follows:

$$\begin{array}{c}\text{Annual} \\ \text{holding cost}\end{array} = \left(\begin{array}{c}\text{average} \\ \text{inventory} \\ \text{level}\end{array}\right)\left(\begin{array}{c}\text{annual holding} \\ \text{cost} \\ \text{per unit}\end{array}\right) \tag{11.12}$$

$$= \frac{1}{2}\left(1 - \frac{d}{p}\right)QC_h$$

If D is the annual demand for the product and C_0 is the setup cost for a production run, then the annual setup cost, which takes the place of the annual ordering cost in the EOQ model, is as follows:

$$\text{Annual setup cost} = \left(\begin{array}{c}\text{number of production}\\ \text{runs per year}\end{array}\right)\left(\begin{array}{c}\text{setup cost}\\ \text{per run}\end{array}\right) \qquad (11.13)$$

$$= \frac{D}{Q}C_0$$

Thus, the total annual cost (TC) model is

$$*\text{TC} = \frac{1}{2}\left(1 - \frac{d}{p}\right)QC_h + \frac{D}{Q}C_0 \qquad (11.14)$$

Suppose that a production facility operates 250 days per year; 115 days are idle due to weekends and holidays. Then we can write daily demand, d, in terms of annual demand, D, as follows:

$$d = \frac{D}{250}$$

Now let P denote the annual production for the product if it were produced every day. Then

$$P = 250p \qquad \text{and} \qquad *p = \frac{P}{250}$$

Thus,[5]

$$\frac{d}{p} = \frac{D/250}{P/250} = \frac{D}{P}$$

Therefore, we can write the total annual cost model as follows:

$$\text{TC} = \frac{1}{2}\left(1 - \frac{D}{P}\right)QC_h + \frac{D}{Q}C_0 \qquad (11.15)$$

Equations (11.14) and (11.15) are equivalent. However, equation (11.15) may be used more frequently since an *annual* cost model tends to make the analyst think in terms of collecting *annual* demand data (D) and *annual* production data (P) rather than daily rate data.

Finding the Economic Production Lot Size

Given the estimates of the holding cost, (C_h), setup cost, (C_0), annual demand rate, (D), and annual production rate, (P), we could use a trial-and-error approach to compute the total annual cost for various production lot sizes (Q). However, this is not necessary; we can use the minimum-cost formula for $Q*$ that has been developed using differential calculus (see Appendix 11.2). The equation is as follows:

$$Q* = \sqrt{\frac{2DC_0}{(1 - D/P)C_h}} \qquad (11.16)$$

[5]The ratio $d/p = D/P$ regardless of the number of days of operation; 250 days was used here merely as an illustration.

An Example. Beauty Bar Soap is produced on a production line that has an annual capacity of 60,000 cases. The annual demand is estimated at 26,000 cases, with the demand rate essentially constant throughout the year. The cleaning, preparation, and setup of the production line cost approximately $135.00. The manufacturing cost per case is $4.50, and the annual holding cost is figured at a 24% rate. Thus, $C_h = IC = 0.24(\$4.50) = \$1.08$. What is the recommended production lot size?

Using equation (11.16), we have

$$Q^* = \sqrt{\frac{2(26,000)(135)}{(1 - 26,000/60,000)(1.08)}} = 3387$$

The total annual cost using equation (11.15) and $Q^* = 3387$ is estimated to be $2073.

Other relevant data include a 1-week lead time to schedule and set up a production run. Thus, the lead time demand of $26,000/52 = 500$ cases is the reorder point. The cycle time between production runs, using equation (11.7), is estimated to be $T = [(250)(3387)]/26,000$, or about 33 working days. Thus, we should plan a production run of 3387 units about every 33 working days.

Certainly the manager will want to review the model recommendations. Adjusting the recommended $Q^* = 3387$ to a slightly more practical figure and/or adding safety stock may be desirable.

11.3 ▼ AN INVENTORY MODEL WITH PLANNED SHORTAGES

A shortage or stockout is a demand that cannot be supplied from inventory or production. In many situations shortages are undesirable and should be avoided if at all possible. However, there are other cases in which it may be desirable—from an economic point of view—to plan for and allow shortages. In practice these types of situations are most commonly found where the value per unit of the inventory is very high and hence the holding cost is high. An example of this type of situation is a new car dealer's inventory. It is not uncommon for a dealer not to have the specific car you want in stock. However, if you are willing to wait a few weeks, the dealer may be able to order a car for you.

The model developed in this section takes into account a type of shortage known as a *backorder*. In a backorder situation we assume that when a customer places an order and discovers that the supplier is out of stock, the customer waits until the next shipment arrives, and then the order is filled. Frequently, the waiting period in backordering situations is relatively short; thus by promising the customer top priority and immediate delivery when the goods become available, companies may be able to convince the customer to wait until the order arrives. In these cases the backorder assumption is valid. In situations where the customer is not willing to wait until the next shipment arrives, the backorder model would not be the appropriate inventory model.

The backorder model that we will develop is an extension of the EOQ model presented in Section 11.1. The EOQ model assumptions of the goods arriving in inventory all at one time and a constant demand rate for the product will be used. If we let S indicate the amount of the shortage or the number of backorders that have accumulated when a new shipment of size Q is received, then the inventory system for the backorder case has the following characteristics:

1. If S backorders exist when a new shipment of size Q arrives, the S backorders are shipped to the appropriate customers and the remaining $Q - S$ units are placed in inventory.
2. $Q - S$ is the maximum inventory level.
3. The inventory cycle of T days is divided into two distinct phases: t_1 days when inventory is on hand and orders are filled as they occur, and t_2 days when there are stockouts and all orders are placed on backorder.

The inventory pattern for the inventory model with backorders, where negative inventory represents the number of backorders, is shown in Figure 11.5.

    With the inventory pattern now defined, we should be able to proceed with the basic step of all inventory models—namely, the development of a total cost model. For the inventory model with backorders we will encounter the usual holding costs and ordering costs. In addition, we will incur a backorder cost in terms of the labor and special delivery costs directly associated with the handling of the backorders. Another portion of the backorder cost accounts for the loss of good will due to the fact that some customers will have to wait for their orders. Since the *goodwill cost* depends on how long the customer has to wait, it is customary to adopt the convention of expressing all backorder costs in terms of how much it costs to have a unit on backorder for a stated period of time. This method of costing backorders on a time basis is similar to the method we have used to compute the inventory holding cost.

    Using this method for costing backorders, we can compute a total annual cost of backorders once the average backorder level and the backorder cost per unit per time period are known.

    Admittedly, the backorder cost rate (especially the goodwill cost) is difficult to determine. However, noting that EOQ models are rather insensitive to the cost estimates (see Table 11.2), we should feel confident that reasonable estimates of the backorder cost will lead to a good approximation of the overall minimum cost inventory policy.

    Let us begin the development of a total cost model by showing how to calculate the inventory holding costs. First, we use a small hypothetical example to suggest a procedure for computing the average inventory level. If we have an average inventory of 2 units for

FIGURE 11.5
Inventory Pattern for an Inventory Model with Backorders

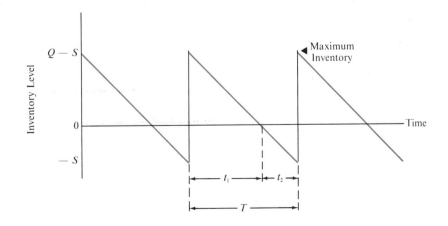

3 days and no inventory on the fourth day, what is the average inventory level over the 4-day period? It is

$$\frac{2 \text{ units } (3 \text{ days}) + 0 \text{ units } (1 \text{ day})}{4 \text{ days}} = \frac{6}{4} = 1.5 \text{ units}$$

Refer to Figure 11.5. You can see that the above situation is what happens in the backorder model. With a maximum inventory of $Q - S$ units, the t_1 days we have inventory on hand will have an average inventory of $(Q - S)/2$. No inventory is carried for the t_2 days in which we experience backorders. Thus, over the total cycle time of $T = t_1 + t_2$ days, we can compute the average inventory level as follows:

$$\text{Average inventory level} = \frac{\frac{1}{2}(Q - S)t_1 + 0t_2}{t_1 + t_2} = \frac{\frac{1}{2}(Q - S)t_1}{T} \qquad (11.17)$$

Can we find other ways of expressing t_1 and T? Since we know that the maximum inventory is $Q - S$ and that d represents the constant daily demand, we have

$$t_1 = \frac{Q - S}{d} \text{ days} \qquad (11.18)$$

That is, the maximum inventory level of $Q - S$ units will be used up in $(Q - S)/d$ days. Since Q units are ordered and shipped each cycle, we know the length of a cycle must be

$$T = \frac{Q}{d} \text{ days} \qquad (11.19)$$

Using equations (11.18) and (11.19) with equation (11.17), we can write the following:

$$\text{Average inventory level} = \frac{\frac{1}{2}(Q - S)[(Q - S)/d]}{Q/d} = \frac{(Q - S)^2}{2Q} \qquad (11.20)$$

Thus, the average inventory level is expressed in terms of two inventory decisions, how much we order (Q) and the maximum number of backorders we will allow (S).

The formula for the annual number of orders placed under this model is identical to that for the EOQ model. With D representing the annual demand, we have

$$\text{Annual number of orders} = \frac{D}{Q} \qquad (11.21)$$

The next step is to develop an expression for the average backorder level. Since there is a maximum of S backorders, we can use the same logic that we used to establish average inventory to find the average number of backorders. We have an average number of backorders during the period t_2 of $\frac{1}{2}$ the maximum number of backorders or $\frac{1}{2} S$. Since we do not have any backorders during the t_1 days we have inventory, we can calculate the average backorder level in a manner similar to equation (11.17). Using this approach, we have

$$\text{Average backorder level} = \frac{0t_1 + (S/2)t_2}{T} = \frac{(S/2)t_2}{T} \qquad (11.22)$$

Since we let the maximum number of backorders reach an amount S at a daily rate of d, the length of the backorder portion of the inventory cycle is

$$t_2 = \frac{S}{d} \qquad (11.23)$$

Using equations (11.23) and (11.19) in equation (11.22), we have

$$\text{Average backorder level} = \frac{(S/2)(S/d)}{Q/d} = \frac{S^2}{2Q} \tag{11.24}$$

Let

C_h = cost to maintain one unit in inventory for 1 year

C_0 = cost per order

C_b = cost to maintain one unit on backorder for 1 year

The total annual cost model (TC) for the inventory model with backorders becomes

$$TC = \frac{(Q-S)^2}{2Q}C_h + \frac{D}{Q}C_0 + \frac{S^2}{2Q}C_b \tag{11.25}$$

Given the cost estimates C_h, C_0, and C_b and the annual demand D, the minimum cost values for the order quantity Q^* and the planned backorders S^* are as follows (see Appendix 11.3):

$$Q^* = \sqrt{\frac{2DC_0}{C_h}\left(\frac{C_h + C_b}{C_b}\right)} \tag{11.26}$$

$$S^* = Q^*\left(\frac{C_h}{C_h + C_b}\right) \tag{11.27}$$

An Example. Suppose the Higley Radio Components Company has a product for which the assumptions of the inventory model with backorders are valid. Information obtained by the company is as follows:

D = 2000 units per year

I = 20% per year

C = \$50 per unit

$C_h = IC$ = \$10 per unit per year

C_0 = \$25 per order

The company is considering the possibility of allowing some backorders to occur for the product. The annual unit backorder cost has been estimated to be \$30 per unit per year. Using equations (11.26) and (11.27), we have

$$Q^* = \sqrt{\frac{2(2000)(25)}{10}\left(\frac{10 + 30}{30}\right)} = 115$$

and

$$S^* = 115\left(\frac{10}{10 + 30}\right) = 29$$

If this solution is implemented, the system will operate with the following properties:

$$\text{Maximum inventory} = Q - S = 115 - 29 = 86$$

$$\text{Cycle time} = T = \frac{Q}{D}(250) = 14.4 \text{ working days}$$

The total annual cost is

$$\text{Holding cost} = \frac{(86)^2}{2(115)}(10) = \$322 \qquad \frac{(Q^*-S)^2}{2Q^*}C_h$$

$$\text{Ordering cost} = \frac{2000}{115}(25) = \$435 \qquad \frac{D}{Q^*}C_o$$

$$\text{Backorder cost} = \frac{(29)^2}{2(115)}(30) = \underline{\$110} \qquad \frac{(S)^2}{2(Q^*}C_b$$

$$\text{Total cost} = \$867$$

If the company had chosen to prohibit backorders and had adopted the regular EOQ model, the recommended inventory decision would have been

$$Q^* = \sqrt{\frac{2(2000)(25)}{10}} = \sqrt{10,000} = 100 \qquad \begin{array}{c} *\,EOQ \\ Q^* = \sqrt{\dfrac{2DC_o}{C_h}} \end{array}$$

This order quantity would have resulted in a holding cost and an ordering cost of \$500 each or a total annual cost of \$1000. Thus, in this example, allowing backorders is projecting a \$1000 - \$867 = \$133 or 13.3% savings in cost from the no-stockout EOQ model. The above comparison and conclusion are based on the assumption that the backorder model (no lost sales) with an annual cost per backordered unit of \$30 is a valid model for the actual inventory situation. If the company has strong fears that stockouts might lead to lost sales, then the above savings might not be enough to warrant switching to an inventory policy that allowed for planned shortages.

▼ NOTES AND COMMENTS ▼

Equation (11.27) shows that the number of planned backorders, S^*, is proportional to the ratio $C_h/(C_h + C_b)$, where C_h is the holding cost per unit and C_b is the backorder cost per unit. Whenever the holding cost, C_h, increases, the above ratio becomes larger, and the number of planned backorders increases. This explains why items that have a high per-unit cost and a correspondingly high holding cost are more economically handled on a backorder basis. On the other hand, whenever the backorder cost, C_b, increases, the above ratio becomes smaller, and the number of planned backorders decreases. Thus, the model provides the intuitive result that items with high backordering costs will be handled with very few backorders. In fact, with high backorder costs, the backorder model and the EOQ model with no backordering allowed provide very similar inventory policies.

11.4 ▼ QUANTITY DISCOUNTS FOR THE EOQ MODEL

Quantity discounts occur in numerous businesses and industries where suppliers provide an incentive for large order quantities by offering a lower purchase cost when items are ordered in larger lots or quantities. In this section we show how the EOQ model can be used when quantity discounts are offered.

Assume that we have a product where the basic EOQ model is applicable, but instead of a fixed unit cost, the supplier quotes the following discount schedule:

Discount Category	Order Size	Discount	Unit Cost
1	0 to 999	0%	$5.00
2	1000 to 2499	3%	$4.85
3	2500 and over	5%	$4.75

The 5% discount for the 2500-unit minimum order quantity looks tempting; however, realizing that higher order quantities result in higher inventory holding costs, we should prepare a thorough cost analysis before making a final ordering and inventory policy recommendation.

Suppose the data and cost analyses show an annual holding cost of 20%, an ordering cost of $49 per order, and an annual demand of 5000 units; what order quantity should we select? The following three-step procedure shows the calculations necessary to make this decision. In our preliminary calculations we will use Q_1 to indicate the order quantity for discount category 1, Q_2 the order quantity for discount category 2, and Q_3 the order quantity for discount category 3.

Step 1. For each discount category, compute a Q^* using the EOQ formula based upon the unit cost associated with the discount category.

Recall that the EOQ model provides $Q^* = \sqrt{2DC_0/C_h}$, where $C_h = IC$. With three discount categories, we obtain

$$Q_1^* = \sqrt{\frac{2(5000)49}{(0.20)(5.00)}} = 700$$

$$Q_2^* = \sqrt{\frac{2(5000)49}{(0.20)(4.85)}} = 711$$

$$Q_3^* = \sqrt{\frac{2(5000)49}{(0.20)(4.75)}} = 718$$

Since the only differences in the EOQ formulas are slight differences in the holding cost, the economic order quantities resulting from this step will be approximately the same. However, these order quantities will usually not all be of the size necessary to qualify for the discount price assumed. In the above case, both Q_2^* and Q_3^* are insufficient order quantities to obtain their assumed discounted costs of $4.85 and $4.75, respectively. For those order quantities for which the assumed price is incorrect, the following procedure must then be used.

Step 2. For those Q^*'s that are too small to qualify for the assumed discount price, adjust the order quantity upward to the nearest order quantity that will allow the product to be purchased at the assumed price.

In our example this causes us to set

$$Q_2^* = 1000$$

and

$$Q_3^* = 2500$$

If a calculated Q^* for a given discount price is large enough to qualify for a bigger discount, that value of Q^* cannot lead to an optimal solution. While the reason may not be obvious, it does turn out to be a property of the EOQ quantity discount model. (Problem 23 at the end of the chapter will ask you to show that this property is true.)

In the previous inventory models considered the annual purchase cost of the item was not included because it was constant and never affected by the inventory-order policy decision. However, in the quantity discount model, annual purchase cost depends on the order quantity decision and the associated unit cost. Thus, annual purchase cost (annual demand D × unit cost C) is included in the total cost model as shown below.

$$TC = \frac{Q}{2}C_h + \frac{D}{Q}C_0 + DC \qquad (11.28)$$

Using this total cost formula, we can determine the optimal order quantity for the EOQ discount model in step 3 below.

Step 3. For each of the order quantities resulting from step 1 and step 2, compute the total annual cost using the unit price from the appropriate discount category and equation (11.28). The order quantity yielding the minimum total annual cost is the optimal order quantity.

The step 3 calculations for the example problem are summarized in Table 11.3. As you can see, a decision to order 1000 units at the 3% discount rate yields the minimum-cost solution. While the 2500-unit order quantity would result in a 5% discount, its excessive holding cost makes it the second best solution. Figure 11.6 shows the total cost curves for the three discount categories. Note that $Q^* = 1000$ provides the minimum-cost order quantity.

11.5 ▼ A SINGLE-PERIOD INVENTORY MODEL WITH PROBABILISTIC DEMAND

The inventory models that we have discussed thus far have been based on the assumption that the demand rate is constant or *deterministic* throughout the year. We developed

TABLE 11.3
Total Annual Cost Calculations for the EOQ Model with Quantity Discounts

Discount Category	Unit Cost	Order Quantity	Annual Holding Cost	Annual Ordering Cost	Annual Purchase Cost	Total Annual Cost
1	$5.00	700	$ 350	$350	$25,000	$25,700
2	$4.85	1000	$ 485	$245	$24,250	$24,980
3	$4.75	2500	$1188	$ 98	$23,750	$25,036

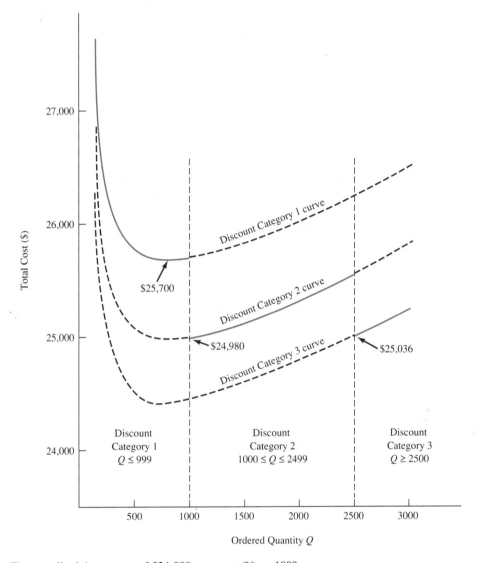

FIGURE 11.6
Total Cost Curves for the Three Discount Categories.

The overall minimum cost of $24,980 occurs at $Q^* = 1000$.

minimum-cost order quantity and reorder point policies based on this assumption. In situations where the demand rate is not deterministic, models have been developed that treat demand as *probabilistic* and best described by a probability distribution. In this section we consider a *single-period* inventory model with probabilistic demand.

The *single-period* inventory model refers to inventory situations in which *one* order is placed for the product; at the end of the period the product has either sold out, or there is a surplus of unsold items that will be sold for a salvage value. The single-period model is applicable in situations involving seasonal or perishable items that cannot be carried in inventory and sold in future periods. Seasonal clothing (such as bathing suits, winter coats) are typically handled in a single-period manner. In these situations a buyer places one preseason order for each item and then experiences a stockout or holds a clearance sale on the surplus stock at the end of the season. No items are carried in inventory and sold the following year. Newspapers are another example of a product that is ordered one time and is either sold or not sold during the single period. While newspapers are ordered daily, they cannot be carried in inventory and sold in later periods. Thus, newspaper orders may be treated as a sequence of single-period models; that is, each day or period is separate, and a single-period inventory decision must be made each period (day). Since we order only once for the period, the only inventory decision we must make is *how much* of the product to order at the start of the period. Because newspaper sales is an excellent example of a single-period situation, the single-period inventory problem is sometimes referred to as the *newsboy problem*.

Obviously, if the demand were known for a single-period inventory situation, the solution would be easy: we would simply order the amount we knew would be demanded. However, in most single-period models the exact demand is not known. In fact, forecasts may show that demand can have a wide variety of values. If we are going to analyze this type of inventory problem in a quantitative manner, we will need information about the probabilities associated with the various demand values. Thus, the single-period model presented in this section is based on probabilistic demand.

The Johnson Shoe Company Example

Let us consider a single-period inventory model that could be used to make a how-much-to-order decision for the Johnson Shoe Company. The buyer for the Johnson Shoe Company has decided to order a shoe for men that has just been shown at a buyers' meeting in New York City. The shoe will be part of the company's spring-summer promotion and will be sold through nine retail stores in the Chicago area. Since the shoe is designed for spring and summer months, it cannot be expected to sell in the fall. Johnson plans to hold a special August clearance sale in an attempt to sell all shoes that have not been sold by July 31. The shoes cost $40 per pair and retail for $60 per pair. At the sale price of $30 per pair, it is expected that all surplus shoes can be sold during the August sale. If you were the buyer for the Johnson Shoe Company, how many pairs of the shoes would you order?

An obvious question at this time is, What are the possible values of demand for the shoe? We will need this information in order to answer the question of how much to order. Let us suppose that the uniform probability distribution shown in Figure 11.7 can be used to describe the demand for the size 10D shoes. In particular, note that the range of demand is from 350 to 650 pairs of shoes, with an average or expected demand of 500 pairs of shoes.

Let us show how the method of *incremental analysis* can be used to determine the optimal order quantity for a single-period inventory model. Incremental analysis addresses the how-much-to-order question by comparing the cost or loss of *ordering one additional unit* with the cost or loss of *not ordering one additional unit*. The costs involved are defined as follows:

c_o = the cost of per unit of *overestimating* demand; this cost represents the loss of ordering one additional unit and finding that it cannot be sold.

c_u = the cost per unit of *underestimating* demand; this cost represents the opportunity loss of not ordering one additional unit and finding that it could have been sold.

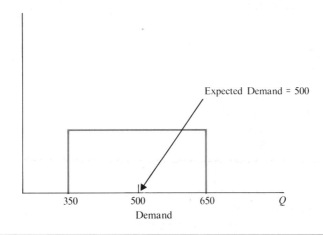

FIGURE 11.7
Uniform Probability Distribution of Demand for the
Johnson Shoe Company Size 10D Shoes

In the Johnson Shoe Company example, the company will incur the cost of over-estimating demand whenever it orders too much and has to sell the extra shoes during the August sale. Thus, the cost per unit of overestimating demand is equal to the purchase cost per unit minus the August sales price per unit; that is, $c_o = \$40 - \$30 = \$10$. Therefore, Johnson will lose $10 for each pair of shoes that it orders over the quantity demanded. The cost of underestimating demand is the lost profit (opportunity loss) due to the fact that a pair of shoes that could have been sold was not available in inventory. Thus, the per-unit cost of underestimating demand is the difference between the regular selling price per unit and the purchase cost per unit; that is, $c_u = \$60 - \$40 = \$20$.

Since the exact level of demand for the size 10D shoes is unknown, we will have to consider the probability of demand and thus the probability of obtaining the above costs or losses. For example, let us assume that the Johnson Shoe Company wished to consider an order quantity equal to the average or expected demand for 500 pairs of shoes. In incremental analysis we will consider the possible losses associated with an order quantity of 501 (ordering one additional unit) and an order quantity of 500 (not ordering one additional unit). The order quantity alternatives and the possible losses are summarized below.

Order Quantity Alternatives	Loss Occurs If	Possible Loss	Probability Loss Occurs
$Q = 501$	Demand overestimated; the additional unit *cannot* be sold.	$c_o = \$10$	$P(\text{demand} \leq 500)$
$Q = 500$	Demand underestimated; an additional unit *could have* been sold.	$c_u = \$20$	$P(\text{demand} > 500)$

By looking at the demand probability distribution in Figure 11.7, we see that $P(\text{demand} \leq 500) = 0.50$ and that $P(\text{demand} > 500) = 0.50$. By multiplying the possible losses, $c_o = \$10$ and $c_u = \$20$, by the probability of obtaining the loss, we can compute the expected value of the loss, or simply the *expected loss* (EL), associated with the order quantity alternatives. Thus,

$$EL(Q = 501) = c_o P(\text{demand} \leq 500) = \$10(0.50) = \$5$$

$$EL(Q = 500) = c_u P(\text{demand} > 500) = \$20(0.50) = \$10$$

Based on the above expected losses, do you prefer an order quantity of 501 or an order quantity of 500 pairs of shoes? Since the expected loss is greater for $Q = 500$, and since we want to avoid this higher cost or loss, we should make $Q = 501$ the preferred decision. We could now consider incrementing the order quantity one additional unit to $Q = 502$ and repeating the above expected loss calculations.

While we could continue this unit-by-unit analysis, it would be very time consuming and cumbersome. We would have to evaluate $Q = 502, Q = 503, Q = 504$, and so on, until we found the value of Q where the expected loss of ordering one incremental unit is equal to the expected loss of not ordering one incremental unit; that is, the optimal order quantity Q^* occurs when the incremental analysis shows that

$$EL(Q^* + 1) = EL(Q^*) \tag{11.29}$$

When the above relationship holds, there is no economic advantage to increasing the order quantity by one additional unit. Using the logic we used to compute the expected losses for the order quantities of 501 and 500, the general expressions for $EL(Q^* + 1)$ and $EL(Q^*)$ can be written

$$EL(Q^* + 1) = c_o P(\text{demand} \leq Q^*) \tag{11.30}$$

$$EL(Q^*) = c_u P(\text{demand} > Q^*) \tag{11.31}$$

Since we know from basic probability that

$$P(\text{demand} \leq Q^*) + P(\text{demand} > Q^*) = 1 \tag{11.32}$$

we can write

$$P(\text{demand} > Q^*) = 1 - P(\text{demand} \leq Q^*) \tag{11.33}$$

Using this expression, (11.31) can be rewritten as

$$EL(Q^*) = c_u[1 - P(\text{demand} \leq Q^*)] \tag{11.34}$$

Expressions (11.30) and (11.34) can be used to show that $EL(Q^* + 1) = EL(Q^*)$ whenever

$$c_o P(\text{demand} \leq Q^*) = c_u[1 - P(\text{demand} \leq Q^*)] \tag{11.35}$$

Solving for $P(\text{demand} \leq Q^*)$, we have

$$P(\text{demand} \leq Q^*) = \frac{c_u}{c_u + c_o} \tag{11.36}$$

The above expression provides the general condition for the optimal order quantity Q^* in any single-period inventory model.

In the Johnson Shoe Company example $c_o = \$10$ and $c_u = \$20$. Thus, (11.36) shows that the optimal order size for Johnson shoes must satisfy the following condition:

$$P(\text{demand} \leq Q^*) = \frac{c_u}{c_u + c_o} = \frac{20}{20 + 10} = \frac{20}{30} = \frac{2}{3}$$

We can find the optimal order quantity, Q^*, by referring to the assumed probability distribution shown in Figure 11.7 and finding the value of Q that will provide $P(\text{demand} \leq Q^*) = \frac{2}{3}$. In order to do this, we note that in the uniform distribution the probability is evenly distributed over the range from 350 to 650 pairs of shoes. Thus, we can satisfy the expression for Q^* by moving two-thirds of the way from 350 to 650. Since this is a range of $650 - 350 = 300$, we move 200 units from 350 toward 650. Doing so provides the optimal order quantity of 550 pairs of size 10D shoes.

In summary, the key to establishing an optimal order quantity for single-period inventory models is to identify the probability distribution that describes the demand for the item and the costs of overestimation and underestimation. Then, using the information for the costs of overestimation and underestimation, equation (11.36) can be used to find the location of Q^* in the probability distribution.

The Kremer Chemical Company Example

As another example of a single-period inventory model with probabilistic demand, consider the situation faced by the Kremer Chemical Company. Kremer has a contract with one of its customers to supply a unique liquid chemical product. Historically the customer places orders approximately every 6 months. Since an aging process of 2 months exists for the product, Kremer will have to make its production quantity decision before the customer places an order. Kremer's inventory problem is to determine the number of pounds of the chemical to produce in anticipation of the customer's order.

Kremer's manufacturing costs for the chemical are $15 per pound, and the product sells at the fixed contract price of $20 per pound. If Kremer "underproduces," it will be unable to satisfy the customer's demand. When this condition occurs, Kremer has agreed to absorb the added cost of filling the order by purchasing a higher-quality substitute product from another chemical firm. The substitute product, including additional transportation expenses, will cost Kremer $24 per pound. If Kremer "overproduces," it will have more product in inventory than the customer requires. Because of the spoilage potential for the product, Kremer cannot store excess production until the customer's next order. As a result, Kremer reprocesses the excess production and sells the surplus for $5 per pound.

Based on previous experience with the customer's orders, Kremer believes that the normal probability distribution shown in Figure 11.8 best describes the possible levels of demand the customer may request. Note that the normal distribution shows an average or expected demand of $\mu = 1000$ pounds with a standard deviation of $\sigma = 100$ pounds. Using Kremer's price and cost data as well as the probability distribution of demand shown in Figure 11.8, how much production should Kremer plan for in anticipation of the customer's order for the liquid chemical?

Let us begin by computing the cost of underestimation, c_u, and the cost of overestimation, c_o, as required for equation (11.36). First, if Kremer underproduces, it will have to purchase a substitute product at a higher cost per unit in order to satisfy the

FIGURE 11.8
Normal Probability Distribution of Demand for Kremer Chemical Company

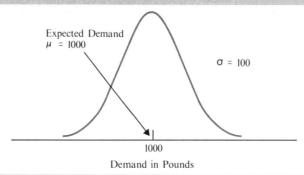

customer's demand for the product. Kremer sells the product to the customer for $20 per pound; however, the substitute product costs $24 per pound. As a result, Kremer incurs a cost of $c_u = \$24 - \$20 = \$4$ for every pound of underestimated demand. If Kremer overestimates demand, the company incurs a cost of $15 per pound to manufacture the product and then sells the reprocessed excess product for $5 per pound. Thus, Kremer has a per-unit cost of $c_o = \$15 - \$5 = \$10$ for overestimating demand.

Applying equation (11.36) indicates that the optimal order quantity must satisfy the following condition:

$$P(\text{demand} \leq Q^*) = \frac{c_u}{c_u + c_o} = \frac{4}{4 + 10} = 0.29$$

We can use the normal probability distribution for demand as shown in Figure 11.9 to find the order quantity that satisfies the condition that $P(\text{demand} \leq Q^*) = 0.29$. From Appendix A we see that 0.29 of the area in the left tail of the curve of the normal

FIGURE 11.9
Probability Distribution of Demand for Kremer Chemical Company
Showing the Location of the Optimal Order Quantity, Q*

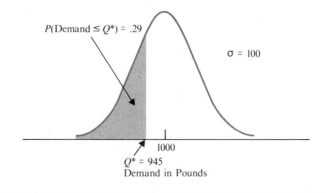

probability distribution occurs at $z = 0.55$ standard deviations *below* the mean. Since the mean or expected demand is given by $\mu = 1000$ and the standard deviation is $\sigma = 100$, we have

$$Q^* = \mu - 0.55\sigma$$
$$= 1000 - 0.55(100) = 945$$

Thus, with the assumed normal probability distribution of demand, the Kremer Chemical Company should produce 945 pounds of the chemical in anticipation of the customer's order. Note that in this case the cost of underestimation is less than the cost of overestimation. Thus, Kremer is willing to risk a higher probability of underestimation and hence a higher probability of a stockout. In fact, Kremer's optimal order quantity has a 0.29 probability of having a surplus and a $1 - 0.29 = 0.71$ probability of a stockout.

▼ NOTES AND COMMENTS ▼

1. In any probabilistic inventory model the assumption about the probability distribution for demand is critical and can affect the recommended inventory decision. In the examples presented in this section we used the uniform and the normal probability distributions to describe demand. In some situations other probability distributions may be more appropriate. In using probabilistic inventory models, we must exercise care in selecting the probability distribution that most realistically describes demand.

2. In the single-period inventory model, the value of $c_u/(c_u + c_o)$ plays a critical role in selecting the order quantity [see equation (11.36)]. Whenever $c_u = c_o$, $c_u/(c_u + c_o)$ equals .50; in this case we should select an order quantity corresponding to the median demand. With this choice it is just as likely to have a stockout as it is to have a surplus; this makes sense because the two costs are equal. However, whenever $c_u < c_o$, a smaller order quantity will be recommended. In this case there will be a higher probability of a stockout; however, the more expensive cost of overestimating demand and having a surplus will tend to be avoided. Finally, whenever $c_u > c_o$, a larger order quantity will be recommended. In this case the larger order quantity provides a lower probability of a stockout in an attempt to avoid the more expensive cost of underestimating demand and experiencing a stockout.

11.6 ▼ AN ORDER-QUANTITY, REORDER-POINT MODEL WITH PROBABILISTIC DEMAND

In the previous section we considered a single-period inventory model with probabilistic demand. In this section, we extend our discussion to a multiperiod order-quantity, reorder-point inventory model with probabilistic demand. In the multiperiod model, the inventory system operates continuously with many repeating periods or cycles; inventory can be carried from one period to the next. Whenever the inventory position reaches the reorder point, an order for Q units is placed. Since demand is probabilistic, the time the reorder point will be reached, the time between orders, and the time the order of Q units will arrive in inventory cannot be determined in advance.

The inventory pattern for the order-quantity, reorder-point model with probabilistic demand will have the general appearance shown in Figure 11.10. Note that the increases or jumps in the inventory level occur whenever an order of Q units arrives. The inventory level decreases at a nonconstant rate based on the probabilistic demand. A new order is placed whenever the reorder point is reached. At times, the order quantity of Q units will arrive before inventory reaches zero. However, at other times, higher demand will cause a stockout before a new order is received. As with other order-quantity, reorder-point models, the manager must determine the order quantity, Q, and the reorder point, r, for the inventory system.

The mathematical sophistication required for an exact formulation of an order-quantity, reorder-point inventory model with probabilistic demand is beyond the scope of this text. However, we will present a procedure that can be used to obtain good, workable order-quantity and reorder-point inventory policies. While the solution procedure can be expected to provide only an approximation of the optimal solution, it has been found to yield very good solutions in many practical situations.

Let us consider the inventory problem of Dabco Industrial Lighting Distributors. Dabco purchases a special high-intensity light bulb for industrial lighting systems from a well-known light bulb manufacturer. Dabco would like a recommendation on how much to order and when to order so that a low-cost inventory policy can be maintained. Pertinent facts are that ordering costs are $12 per order, one bulb cost $6, and Dabco uses a 20% annual holding cost for its inventory ($C_h = IC = 0.20 \times \$6 = \$1.20$). Dabco, which has over 1000 different customers, experiences a probabilistic demand; the number of units demanded varies considerably from day to day and from week to week. The lead time for a new order of light bulbs is 1 week. Demand is not at a constant rate, but historical sales data indicate that demand during a 1-week lead time can be described by a normal probability distribution with a mean of 154 light bulbs and a standard deviation of 25 light bulbs. The normal distribution of demand during the lead time is shown in Figure 11.11. Since the mean demand during 1-week is 154 units, Dabco can anticipate a mean or expected annual demand of 154 units/week $\times$ 52 weeks/year $=$ 8008 units/year.

FIGURE 11.10
Inventory Pattern for an Order-Quantity, Reorder-Point Model with Probabilistic Demand

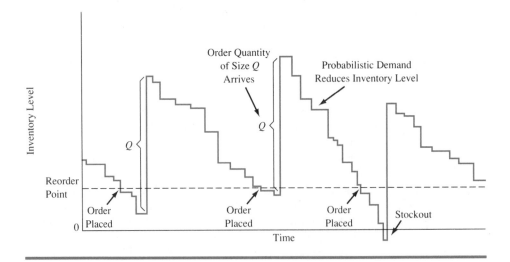

FIGURE 11.11
Distribution of Demand During the Lead Time for Dabco

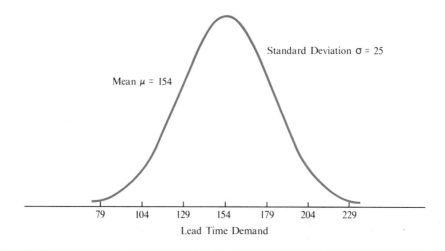

Mean $\mu = 154$

Standard Deviation $\sigma = 25$

Lead Time Demand

79   104   129   154   179   204   229

The How-Much-to-Order Decision

Although we are in a probabilistic demand situation, we have an estimate of the expected annual volume of 8008 units. As an approximation of the best order quantity we can apply the EOQ model from Section 11.1, with the expected annual volume substituted for the annual demand, D. In Dabco's case

$$Q^* = \sqrt{\frac{2DC_0}{C_h}} = \sqrt{\frac{2(8008)(12)}{(1.20)}} = 400 \text{ units}$$

When we studied the sensitivity of the EOQ model, we learned that the total cost of operating an inventory system was relatively insensitive to order quantities that were in the neighborhood of Q^*. Using this knowledge, we expect 400 units per order to be a good approximation of the optimal order quantity. Even if annual demand were as low as 7000 units or as high as 9000 units, an order quantity of 400 units should be a relatively good low-cost order size. Thus, given our best estimate of annual demand at 8008 units, we will use $Q^* = 400$.

We have established the 400-unit order quantity by ignoring the fact that demand is probabilistic. Using $Q^* = 400$, Dabco can anticipate placing approximately $D/Q^* = 8008/400 = 20$ orders per year with an average of approximately $250/20 = 12.5$ working days between orders.

The When-to-Order Decision

We now want to establish a when-to-order decision rule or reorder point that will trigger the ordering process. With a mean lead time demand of 154 units, you might first suggest a 154-unit reorder point. However, it now becomes extremely important to consider the probability of demand. If 154 is the mean lead time demand, and if demand is symmetrically distributed about 154, then the lead time demand will be more than 154 units roughly 50% of the time. When the demand during the 1-week lead time exceeds 154 units, Dabco will experience a shortage or stockout. Thus, using a reorder point of 154 units, approximately 50% of the time (10 of the 20 orders a year) Dabco will be short of bulbs before the new supply arrives. This shortage rate would most likely be viewed as unacceptable.

Refer again to the distribution of demand during the lead time as shown in Figure 11.11. Given the lead time demand probability distribution, we can now determine how the reorder point, r, affects the probability of a stockout. Since stockouts occur whenever the demand during the lead time exceeds the reorder point, we can find the probability of a stockout by using the lead time demand distribution to compute the probability that demand will exceed r.

We could now approach the when-to-order problem by defining a cost per stockout and then attempting to include this cost in a total cost equation. Possibly a more practical approach is to ask management to define an acceptable *service level*, where the service level refers to the average number of stockouts management is willing to tolerate per year. If demand for a product is probabilistic, a manager who will never tolerate a stockout is being somewhat unrealistic because attempting to avoid stockouts completely will require high reorder points, high inventory levels, and an associated high holding cost.

Suppose in this case that Dabco management is willing to tolerate an average of one stockout per year. Since Dabco places 20 restocking orders per year, this implies management is willing to allow demand during lead time to exceed the reorder point 1 time in 20, or 5% of the time. This suggests that the reorder point, r, can be found by using the lead time demand distribution to find the value of r for which there is only a 5% chance of having a lead time demand that will exceed it. This situation is shown graphically in Figure 11.12.

From the normal distribution tables in Appendix A, we see that an r value that is 1.645 standard deviations above the mean will result in stockouts during lead time 5% of the time. Therefore, for the assumed normal distribution for lead time demand with $\mu = 154$ and $\sigma = 25$, the reorder point, r, is determined by

$$r = 154 + 1.645(25) = 195$$

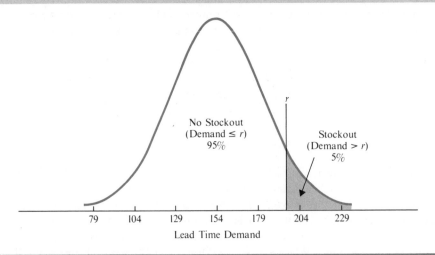

FIGURE 11.12
Reorder Point, r, that Allows a 5% Chance of Stockout for Dabco Light Bulbs

If a normal distribution is used for lead time demand, the general equation for r is

$$r = \mu + z\sigma \qquad (11.37)$$

where z is the number of standard deviations necessary to obtain the acceptable stockout probability.

Thus, the recommended inventory decision is to order 400 units whenever the inventory level reaches the reorder point of 195. Since the mean or expected demand during the lead time is 154 units, the $195 - 154 = 41$ units serve as a safety stock, which absorbs higher than usual demand during the lead time. Roughly 95% of the time the 195 units will be able to satisfy demand during the lead time. The anticipated annual cost for this system is as follows:

Ordering cost	$(D/Q)C_0 = (8000/400)12 = \$240.00$
Holding cost—normal inventory	$(Q/2)C_h = (400/2)(1.20) = \$240.00$
Holding cost—safety stock	$(41)C_h = 41(1.20) = \$\ 49.20$
	$\$529.20$

If Dabco could have assumed that a known, constant demand rate of 8008 units per year existed for the light bulbs, then $Q^* = 400$, $r = 154$, and a total annual cost of $\$240 + \$240 = \$480$ would have been optimal. When demand is uncertain and can only be expressed in probabilistic terms, a larger total cost can be expected. The larger cost occurs in the form of larger holding costs due to the fact that more inventory must be maintained in order to limit stockouts. For Dabco this additional inventory or safety stock was 41 units, with an additional annual holding cost of $\$49.20$.

11.7 ▼ A PERIODIC-REVIEW MODEL WITH PROBABILISTIC DEMAND

The order-quantity, reorder-point inventory models discussed in the previous sections of this chapter require a *continuous-review* inventory system. In a continuous-review inventory system the inventory is monitored continuously so that an order can be placed whenever the reorder point is reached. Computerized inventory systems can easily provide the continuous review required by the order-quantity, reorder-point models.

An alternative to the continuous-review system is the *periodic-review* system. With a periodic-review system the inventory level is checked and reordering is done only at specific periodic points in time. For example, in a periodic-review system, inventory levels may be checked and necessary orders placed on a weekly, biweekly, monthly, or some other periodic basis. When a firm or business handles multiple products, the periodic-review system has the advantage of requiring that the orders for several items be placed at the same preset periodic review time. With this type of inventory system the shipping and receiving of orders for multiple products are easily coordinated. Under the previously discussed order-quantity, reorder-point systems, the reorder points for various products can be encountered at substantially different points in time, making the coordination of orders for multiple products more difficult.

In this section we consider a periodic-review inventory model with probabilistic demand. The firm in the example, Dollar Discounts, has several retail stores that carry a wide variety of products for household use. Dollar Discounts operates its inventory system with a two-week periodic review. Under this system a retail store manager may order any number of units of any product from the Dollar Discounts central warehouse every two weeks. The orders for all products going to a particular store are combined into one shipment. When making the order-quantity decision for each product at a given review period, the store manager knows that a reorder for the product cannot be made until the next review period.

Assuming that the lead time is less than the length of the review period, an order placed at a review period will be received prior to the next review period. In this case the how-much-to-order decision at any review period is determined using the following:

$$Q = M - I \tag{11.38}$$

where

$$Q = \text{the order quantity}$$
$$M = \text{the replenishment level}$$
$$I = \text{the inventory on hand at the review period}$$

Since the demand is probabilistic, the inventory on hand at the review period, I, will vary. Thus, the order quantity that must be sufficient to bring the inventory position back to its maximum or replenishment level, M, can be expected to vary each period. For example, if the replenishment level for a particular product is 50 units, and the inventory on hand at the review period is $I = 12$ units, an order of $Q = M - I = 50 - 12 = 38$ units should be made. Thus, under the periodic-review model enough units are ordered each review period to bring the inventory position back up to the replenishment level.

A typical inventory pattern for a periodic-review system with probabilistic demand is shown in Figure 11.13. Note that the time between periodic reviews is predetermined and fixed. The order quantity Q at each review period can vary and is shown to be the

FIGURE 11.13
Inventory Pattern for a Periodic Review Model with Probabilistic Demand

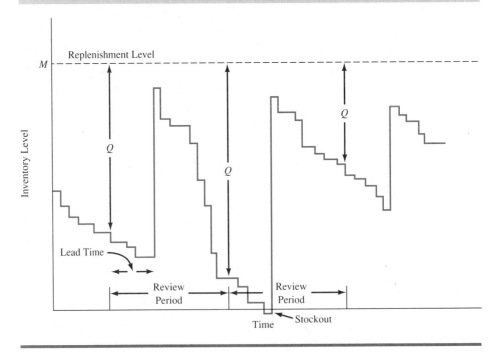

difference between the replenishment level and the inventory on hand. Finally, as with other probabilistic models, an unusually high demand can result in an occasional stockout.

The decision variable in the periodic-review model is the replenishment level, M. To determine M we could begin by developing a total cost model, including holding, ordering, and stockout costs. Instead, we will describe an approach to the periodic-review model with probabilistic demand that is often used in practice. In this alternate approach the objective is to identify or determine a replenishment level that will meet a desired performance level, such as a reasonably low probability of stockout or a reasonably low number of stockouts per year.

In the Dollar Discounts example we will assume that management's objective is to determine the replenishment level for which there is only a 1% chance of a stockout. In the periodic-review model, the order quantity at each review period must be sufficient to cover demand for the *review period plus the demand for the following lead time*. That is, the order quantity that brings the inventory position up to the replenishment level, M, must last until the order made at the next review period is received in inventory. The length of this time is equal to the review period plus the lead time. Figure 11.14 shows the normal probability distribution of demand during the review period plus the lead time period for one of the Dollar Discounts products. The mean demand is 250 units, and the standard deviation of demand is 45 units. Given this situation, the logic used to establish M is similar to the logic used to establish the reorder point in Section 11.7. Figure 11.15 shows the replenishment level, M, for which there is a 1% chance that demand will exceed that replenishment level. In other words, Figure 11.15 shows the replenishment level that allows a 1% chance of a stockout associated with the replenishment decision. Using the normal probability distribution table in Appendix A, we see that a value of M that is 2.33 standard deviations above the mean will allow stockouts with a 1% probability. Therefore, for the assumed normal probability distribution with $\mu = 250$ and $\sigma = 45$, the replenishment level is determined by

$$M = 250 + 2.33(45) = 355$$

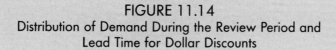

FIGURE 11.14
Distribution of Demand During the Review Period and Lead Time for Dollar Discounts

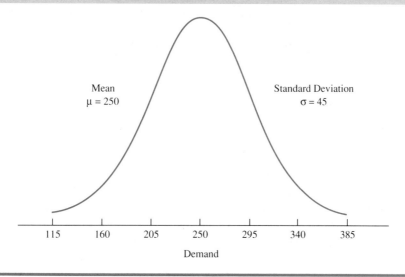

Mean
$\mu = 250$

Standard Deviation
$\sigma = 45$

115   160   205   250   295   340   385

Demand

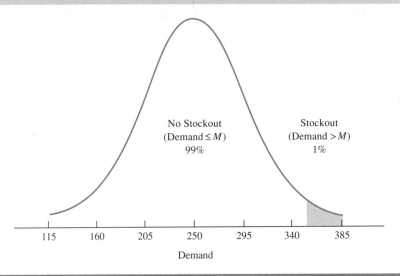

FIGURE 11.15
Replenishment Level M that Allows a 1% Chance of Stockout for Dollar Discounts

While other probability distributions can be used to express the demand during the review period plus the lead time period, if the normal probability distribution is used, the general expression for M is

$$M = \mu + z\sigma \qquad (11.39)$$

where z is the number of standard deviations necessary to obtain the acceptable stockout probability.

If demand had been deterministic rather than probabilistic, the replenishment level would have been the mean or expected demand during the review period plus the expected demand during the lead time period. In this case the replenishment level would have been 250 units, and no stockout would have occurred. However, with the probabilistic demand, we have seen that higher inventory levels are necessary to allow for the uncertain demand and to control the probability of a stockout. In the Dollar Discounts example, $355 - 250 = 105$ is the safety stock that is necessary to absorb any higher than usual demand during the review period plus the demand during lead time period. It is this safety stock that limits the probability of a stockout to 1%.

More Complex Periodic-Review Models

The periodic-review model that we have just discussed is one approach to determining a replenishment level for the periodic-review inventory system with probabilistic demand. More complex versions of the periodic-review model incorporate a reorder point as another decision variable. That is, instead of ordering at every periodic review, a reorder point is established. If the inventory on hand at the periodic review is at or below the reorder point, an order-up-to-the-replenishment-level decision is made. However, if the inventory on hand at the periodic review is greater than the reorder level, an order is not placed, and the system continues until the next periodic review. In this case the cost of ordering is a relevant cost and can be included in a cost model along with holding and stockout costs. Optimal policies can be reached based on minimizing the expected total cost. Situations with lead times longer than the review period add to the complexity of the model. The mathematical level required to treat these more extensive periodic-review models is beyond the scope of this text.

▼ NOTES AND COMMENTS ▼

1. The periodic-review model presented in this section is based on the assumption that the lead time for an order is less than the periodic-review period. Most periodic-review systems operate under this condition. However, the case in which the lead time is longer than the review period can be handled by defining I in equation (11.38) as the inventory position, where I includes the inventory on hand plus the inventory on order. In this case the order quantity at any review period is the amount needed for the inventory on hand plus *all* outstanding orders to reach the replenishment level.

2. In the order-quantity, reorder-point model discussed in Section 11.6, a continuous review was used to initiate an order whenever the reorder point was reached. The safety stock for this model was based on the probabilistic demand during the lead time. The periodic-review model presented in this section also determined a recommended safety stock. However, since the inventory review was only periodic, the safety stock was based on the probabilistic demand during the *review period plus the lead time period*. This longer period for the safety stock computation means that periodic-review systems tend to require larger safety stocks than do continuous review systems.

11.8 ▼ MATERIAL REQUIREMENTS PLANNING

The inventory models we have discussed thus far have been found to be most appropriate for managing the inventories of finished goods. Finished goods are characterized as having *independent* demands that may be forecast. In this section we focus on the planning and controlling of manufacturing inventories such as raw materials, components, and subassemblies. The demand for these types of items is *dependent* on the amounts of finished goods that are scheduled to be produced and can be *calculated* from the forecasts and scheduled production of finished goods. A technique that can be used to manage dependent-demand inventories is called *material requirements planning* (MRP).

Dependent Demand and the MRP Concept

Let us consider a finished product with one component part in order to illustrate dependent demand and the MRP concept. The demand for the finished product consists of many independent demands from many customers. Since these demands occur somewhat randomly, the demand rate is often fairly constant, and the assumptions of the production lot size model are reasonable. The inventory level for the finished product is shown at the top of Figure 11.16. Assume that the single component is purchased from an outside supplier. When production of the finished product is initiated (point A on the time axis), the component parts are withdrawn from inventory in order to meet the manufacturing needs. The inventory level of the component part is shown at the bottom of Figure 11.16. When

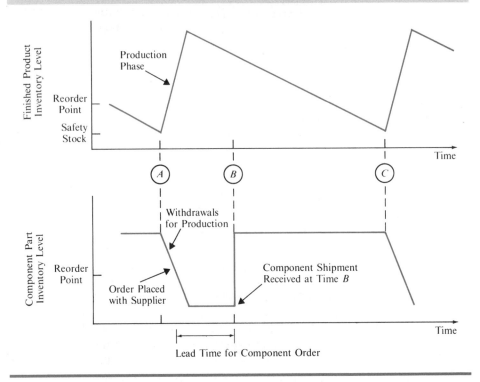

FIGURE 11.16
Finished Product and Component Part Inventory
Levels Without an MRP System

the component inventory level falls below its reorder point, an order for the component is placed with the supplier. The shipment is received at point *B,* and the component inventory is replenished. However, note that the component is not needed again until the next production run for the finished product, which is scheduled to occur at point *C.* Clearly, the investment in the component inventory from points *B* to *C* is unnecessary. We can eliminate this unnecessary component inventory by "backing up" from point *C* according to the purchase lead time so that the components will arrive just at time *C.* This situation is illustrated in Figure 11.17. Note that the component inventory level and corresponding inventory investment are less in Figure 11.17 than in Figure 11.16.

The philosophy of ordering component inventory depending on the demand and production needs of other items is the approach followed by MRP. When operating properly, the MRP system will reduce inventory investment, improve work flow, reduce the shortage of materials and components, and help achieve more reliable delivery schedules.

Information System for MRP

What makes the MRP process difficult to implement is that many finished products consist of dozens or hundreds of parts, many of which are in turn dependent on other parts. Therefore, there must be accurate data and a reliable computer information system to perform the many calculations that will be required for MRP.

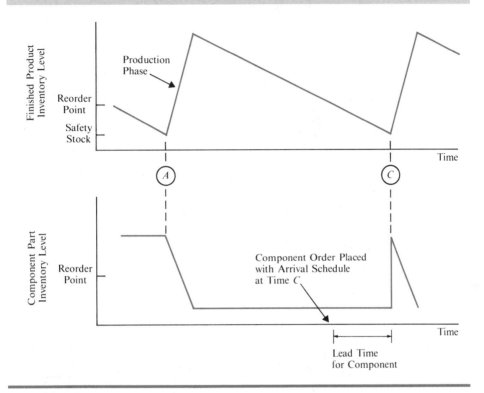

FIGURE 11.17
Finished Product and Component Part Inventory Levels with an MRP System

Material requirements planning calculations begin with the *master production schedule,* which states the number of units of each finished product to be produced each time period. With the information in the master production schedule, we can begin to determine when the various components that make up the final products must be available. Thus, the next step will be to identify the list of components that are required by the products. This information is available from the *bill of materials* (BOM).

The BOM is a structured parts list; however, it differs from an ordinary parts list in that it shows the hierarchical relationship between the finished product and its various components. An example of a BOM for the Spiecker Company is shown in Figure 11.18. This figure shows the bill of materials for a 14-inch snowblower. The finished product is shown at the top of the hierarchy (called level 0). It consists of one main housing assembly, one wheel assembly, one engine assembly, and one handle assembly. If we consider the BOM as a "family tree," then the 14-inch snowblower is the "parent" item for each of these assemblies. These assemblies, in turn, are parent items for all the components included in them. Thus, the wheel assembly is the parent item of one blade assembly and two wheels. In general, items at level k are parent items for components at level $k + 1$. From the BOM we can determine exactly how many components are needed in order to produce the quantity of finished products stated in the master production schedule.

A schematic diagram of an MRP information system is given in Figure 11.19. Forecasts and orders are used to develop the master production schedule. The master production schedule, BOM, and current inventory files are the inputs needed to begin the

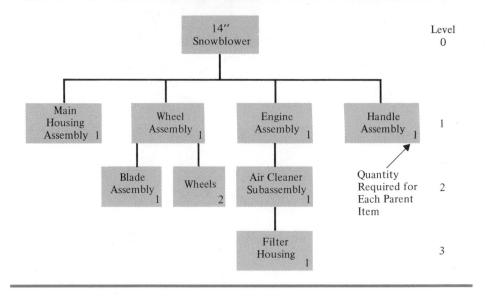

FIGURE 11.18
Bill of Materials for the Spiecker 14-inch Snowblower

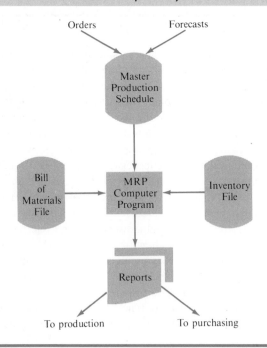

FIGURE 11.19
An MRP Computer System

MRP computations. The outputs from the MRP system are the requirements for each item in the BOM along with the dates each item is needed. This information is used to plan order releases for production and purchasing. In order to illustrate how these calculations are performed, let us consider an MRP system for the Spiecker snowblower example.

MRP Calculations

In MRP terminology, the time periods are called *buckets* and are usually 1 week in length. Small buckets, such as 1 week, are good for scheduling production over a short time horizon, but may be too precise for long-range planning. Often, larger buckets are used as the planning horizon gets larger. However, for the Spiecker Manufacturing problem, we assume that all buckets are 1 week in length.

The master production schedule calls for the final assembly of 1250 units of the 14-inch snowblower during week 21 of the current planning period. The assembly lead time is 1 week; thus, to meet this schedule, the four main assemblies in the bill of materials must be completed no later than the end of week 20. We now examine the production and inventory control aspects for the engine assembly in detail, concentrating on how the MRP approach can be applied. Relevant data regarding the number of units in inventory and lead time are given in Table 11.4.

Before the advent of MRP, the net requirement for each component was often found using the following formula:

$$
\text{Net component requirement} = \begin{pmatrix} \text{number of components} \\ \text{required to meet} \\ \text{demand for} \\ \text{finished good} \end{pmatrix} - \begin{pmatrix} \text{number of} \\ \text{components} \\ \text{in inventory} \end{pmatrix}
$$

Thus, the net requirements based on 1250 snowblowers are calculated as follows:

Components	Number of Components Required to Meet Demand for 1250 Snowblowers	−	Number in Inventory	=	Net Requirement
Engines	1250	−	450	=	800
Air cleaners	1250	−	250	=	1000
Filter housings	1250	−	500	=	750

TABLE 11.4
Inventory on Hand and Lead Time for the Spiecker Manufacturing Example

Component	Units in Inventory	Lead Time (weeks)
Engine assembly	450	4
Air cleaner subassembly	250	1
Filter housing	500	2

However, note that this approach does not recognize the nature of dependent demand; for example, the number of filter housings required is dependent on the number of air cleaners produced, and so on.

The approach to determining net requirements whenever a dependent demand situation exists is

$$\begin{pmatrix} \text{Net component} \\ \text{requirement} \end{pmatrix} = \begin{pmatrix} \text{gross component} \\ \text{requirement} \end{pmatrix} - \begin{pmatrix} \text{scheduled} \\ \text{receipts} \end{pmatrix} - \begin{pmatrix} \text{number of} \\ \text{components} \\ \text{in inventory} \end{pmatrix}$$

where the gross component requirement is the quantity of the component needed to support production at the next higher level of assembly. For example, the gross component requirement for the filter housing is the number of filter housings required to meet the net requirement for the air cleaner subassembly; the gross component requirement for the air cleaner subassembly is the number of air cleaners needed to meet the net requirement for the engine assembly; and so on. Let us see how these requirements can be computed for Spiecker Manufacturing. (We assume, for simplicity, that scheduled receipts are zero.)

Quantity of snowblowers to be produced:	1250
Gross requirements, engines:	1250
Less engines in inventory:	450
Net requirements, engines:	800 ← Engines
Gross requirements, air cleaners:	800
Less air cleaners in inventory:	250
Net requirements, air cleaners:	550 ← Air cleaners
Gross requirements, filter housings:	550
Less filter housings in inventory:	500
Net requirements, filter housings:	50 ← Filter housings

While the net requirement for engines under the MRP approach is still 800 units, note how MRP has used the dependent-demand information to show that fewer air cleaners and filter housings will be needed. In addition to considering dependent demand in the determination of net requirements for components, an MRP system also determines when the net requirements are needed. MRP handles this aspect of production and inventory control using the *time-phasing* concept. By starting with the time that the finished product must be completed, we can work backward in order to determine when an order for each component must be placed. For example, the time-phasing calculations for the Spiecker snowblower problem might appear as follows:

	Week
Complete order for engines:	20
Minus lead time for engines:	4
Place an order for engines:	16 ← Order engines
Complete order for air cleaners:	16
Minus lead time for air cleaners:	1
Place an order for air cleaners:	15 ← Order air cleaners
Complete order for filter housings:	15
Minus lead time for filter housings:	2
Place an order for filter housings:	13 ← Order filter housings

The components are scheduled so that they are made available only when required for the next higher level of assembly. Similar calculations can be made for all the other components of the snowblower, and if the bill of materials is exploded into detailed part requirements, a complete schedule for shop orders and purchase requisitions is available.

Until the development of large-scale computers, the sheer volume of calculations prohibited the implementation of an MRP system. For example, even in our small illustration, you can begin to appreciate the complexity involved in keeping track of the production and inventory status for every component.

11.9 ▼ THE JUST-IN-TIME APPROACH TO INVENTORY MANAGEMENT

The Japanese have captured a sizable share of world markets for many products because of the progress they have made in manufacturing. Among the reasons for this success are the Japanese style of management, the development of new technologies, and the use of new methods of material management and control. One new method that has received much attention in recent years is known as *just-in-time* (JIT). JIT represents a philosophy whose objective is to eliminate all sources of waste including unnecessary inventory.

The fundamental principle of JIT is to produce the right units in the right quantity at the right time. With JIT, units are produced only when they are required. Ideally, the number of parts produced or purchased at any one time should be just enough to produce one unit of the finished product. Inventories are not needed, or at least are minimized. In order for JIT to function effectively, fundamental changes in traditional production systems must take place. These changes require modification of the design of the production layout and the material flow process; in addition, setup times must be reduced.

Poor equipment layout is one of the major causes of inefficiencies in manufacturing. In a typical U.S. manufacturing environment, material is transported from the supplier to the warehouse and then to the plant. Within the plant, material may be transported from department to department. When production is completed, the finished goods may be returned to the warehouse, where they are stored until later distribution to the customer. Even with optimal inventory models, inventory and material handling costs can be substantial. The JIT approach helps reduce inventory and material handling costs by providing a flow of raw materials and finished goods in which material introduced at one end of the manufacturing process moves without delays into the finished products.

The driving force behind JIT production is the coordination of successive production activities. A key component of this coordination is an information system called a *Kanban*—the Japanese word for *card*. The type and number of units required by the production process are written on Kanbans, which are used to initiate the withdrawal and the production of units through the production process. By beginning at the final assembly, the Kanban ''pulls'' parts and components from preceding work stations. Thus, the entire manufacturing operation is synchronized to the final assembly stage. In this fashion, JIT prohibits earlier sources of supply and production from ''pushing'' units forward and building unnecessary and excessive inventories.

It is important to realize that the total quality concept is critical in the implementation of the JIT philosophy. Since lot sizes are small and inventory levels are minimal, there is no safety stock to replace nonconforming or defective units. Any quality problems disrupt the flow of materials throughout the plant and can be disastrous to the JIT system.

Finally, the coordination of the materials flow from suppliers to the manufacturer is another critical component of JIT. The JIT philosophy does not permit the shipment of large lots from suppliers that would build unnecessarily high inventory levels and costs. To maintain the smooth flow required by JIT, suppliers must make just-in-time deliveries. Instead of the large shipments that must be counted, inspected, and stored, suppliers make smaller deliveries on a daily basis or even more frequently in order to accommodate the manufacturer's daily production schedule. JIT requires a trusting partnership between the suppliers and the manufacturer in order to obtain materials on time and with zero defects.

The benefits of JIT are improved profits, resulting from reduced inventory costs, and improved quality. In the area of inventory management, the more obvious benefits of JIT are the reduced inventory levels, the increased inventory turnover, and the overall lower holding costs. While these benefits are significant, the behavioral and cultural differences between the Japanese and American people at both the management and the labor force levels make it unclear whether the Japanese success with JIT can be duplicated in American production systems. A few American companies are attempting the JIT philosophy, but most are still employing their traditional systems of inventory management.

▼ SUMMARY

In this chapter we presented some of the approaches management scientists use when developing inventory models that will assist managers in establishing low-cost operating policies. We first considered cases where the demand rate for the product is constant. In analyzing these inventory systems, total cost models were developed, which include ordering costs, holding costs, and, in some cases, backordering costs. Then minimum cost formulas for the order quantity, Q, were presented. A reorder point, r, can be established by considering the lead time demand for the item.

In addition, we discussed inventory decision models where a deterministic or constant rate could not be assumed, and, thus, demand was described by a probability distribution. A critical issue with these probabilistic demand models is obtaining a probability distribution that most realistically approximates the demand distribution for the item. We first described a single-period model where only one order is placed for the product and at the end of the period either the product has sold out or there is a surplus of unsold products that will be sold for a salvage value. Solution procedures were then presented for multi-period models based on either an order-quantity, reorder-point, continuous-review system or a replenishment-level, periodic-review system.

We pointed out that the models presented in the earlier sections of the chapter are for independent-demand situations and are most applicable for managing finished goods inventory. For manufacturing inventories of subassemblies and component parts, where dependent demand exists, methods such as material requirements planning (MRP) offer significant advantages. Finally, we discussed the just-in-time philosophy that has evolved from the Japanese approach to material management and control. In inventory management, JIT is directed at reducing inventory levels and increasing inventory turnover.

In closing this chapter we reemphasize that inventory and inventory systems can be an expensive phase of a firm's operation. It is of utmost economic importance for managers to be aware of the cost of inventory systems and to make the best possible operating policy decisions for the inventory system. Inventory decision models, as presented in this chapter, can help managers to develop good inventory policies.

▼ GLOSSARY

Holding cost The cost associated with maintaining an inventory investment: holding cost includes the cost of the capital investment in the inventory, insurance, taxes, warehouse overhead, and so on. This cost may be stated as a percentage of the inventory investment or a cost per unit.

Cost of capital   The cost a firm incurs, usually interest payments on borrowed funds or dividend payments on stocks, in order to obtain capital for investment. The cost of capital, which may be stated as an annual percentage rate, is part of the holding cost associated with maintaining inventory levels.

Ordering cost   The fixed cost (salaries, paper, transportation, and so on) associated with placing an order for an item.

Constant demand rate   An assumption of many inventory models that states that the same number of units are taken from inventory in each period of time.

Economic order quantity (EOQ)   The order quantity that minimizes the annual holding cost plus the annual ordering cost in the most fundamental inventory model.

Inventory position   The inventory on hand plus the inventory on order.

Reorder point   The inventory position at which a new order should be placed.

Lead time   The time between the placing of an order and its receipt in the inventory system.

Lead time demand   The number of units demanded during the lead time period.

Cycle time   The length of time between the placing of two consecutive orders.

Safety stock   Inventory maintained in order to reduce the number of stockouts resulting from higher than expected demand.

Constant supply rate   The situation in which the inventory is built up at a constant rate over a period of time.

Backorder   The receipt of an order for a product when there are no units on hand in inventory. These backorders become shortages, which are eventually satisfied when a new supply of the product becomes available.

Quantity discounts   Discounts or lower unit costs offered by the manufacturer when a customer purchases larger quantities of the product.

Goodwill cost   A cost associated with a backorder, a lost sale, or any form of stockout or unsatisfied demand. This cost may be used to reflect the loss of future profits due to the fact a customer experienced an unsatisfied demand.

Deterministic demand rate   Another term for *constant demand rate*—that is, the rate of demand for an inventory item that is considered known and not subject to uncertainty.

Probabilistic demand rate   When the demand rate for the inventory item is not known exactly, probabilities must be used to describe the possible values for demand.

Single-period inventory models   Inventory models in which it is assumed that only one order is placed for the product, and at the end of the period either the item has sold out, or there is a surplus of unsold items that will be sold for a salvage value.

Lead time demand distribution   In probabilistic inventory models, this is the distribution of demand that occurs during the lead time period.

Continuous review   When the inventory position is monitored or reviewed on a continuous basis so that reorders can be placed as soon as the reorder point is reached.

Periodic review   When the inventory position is checked or reviewed at predetermined periodic points in time. If reorders are necessary, they are placed only at the periodic review points in time.

Independent demand   Demand for a product or an item that is independent of the demand for other products or items.

Dependent demand   Demand for a product, component, subassembly, or item that is dependent on the demand for another product or item.

Material requirements planning (MRP)   A computerized inventory management system whose functions are to schedule production and to control the level of inventory for components with dependent demand.

Master production schedule   A statement of how many finished items are to be produced and when.

Bill of materials   A structured parts list that shows the manner in which the product is actually put together.

Time phasing   Adding the dimension of time to inventory status data in an MRP environment.

Just-in-time   A philosophy that encourages the elimination of waste in time and resources. In inventory management, JIT works to reduce inventory levels and increase inventory turnover.

Kanban   The Japanese word for *card*, which refers to the information system used for implementing JIT.

▼ PROBLEMS

1. Suppose that R & B Beverage Company has a soft-drink product that has a constant annual demand rate of 3600 cases. A case of the soft drink costs R & B $3. Ordering costs are $20 per order and holding costs are charged at 25% of the cost per unit. There are 250 working days per year and the lead time is 5 days. Identify the following aspects of the inventory policy.
   a. Economic order quantity
   b. Reorder point
   c. Cycle time
   d. Total annual cost

2. A general property of the EOQ inventory model is that total inventory holding and total ordering costs are equal or balanced at the optimal solution. Use the data in problem 1 to show that this result is observed for this problem. Use equations (11.1), (11.2), and (11.3) to show in general that total holding costs and total ordering costs are equal whenever Q^* is used.

3. The reorder point [see equation (11.6)] is defined as the lead time demand for the item. In cases of long lead times, the lead time demand and thus the reorder point may exceed the economic order quantity Q^*. In such cases the inventory position will not equal the inventory on hand when an order is placed and the reorder point may either be expressed in terms of the inventory position or the inventory on hand. Consider the economic order quantity model with $D = 5000$, $C_o = \$32$, $C_h = \$2$, and 250 working days per year. Identify the reorder point in terms of the inventory position and in terms of the inventory on hand for each of the following lead times.
   a. 5 days
   b. 15 days
   c. 25 days
   d. 45 days

4. The XYZ Company purchases a component used in the manufacture of automobile generators directly from the supplier. XYZ's generator production operation, which is operated at a constant rate, will require 1000 components per month throughout the year (12,000 units annually). Assume that the ordering costs are $25 per order, the unit cost is $2.50 per component, and that annual holding costs are charged at 20%. There are 250 working days per year and the lead time is 5 days. Answer the following inventory policy questions for XYZ.
   a. What is the EOQ for this component?
   b. What is the reorder point?
   c. What is the cycle time?

d. What are the total annual holding and ordering costs associated with your recommended EOQ?

5. Suppose that XYZ's management in problem 4 likes the operational efficiency of ordering in quantities of 1000 units and ordering once each month. How much more expensive would this policy be than your EOQ recommendation? Would you recommend in favor of the 1000-unit order quantity? Explain. What would the reorder point be if the 1000-unit quantity were acceptable?

6. Tele-Reco is a new specialty store that sells television sets, videotape recorders, video games, and other television-related products. A new Japanese-manufactured videotape recorder costs Tele-Reco $600 per unit. Tele-Reco's holding cost is figured at an annual rate of 22%. Ordering costs are estimated to be $70 per order.

   a. If demand for the new videotape recorder is expected to be constant with a rate of 20 units per month, what is the recommended order quantity for the videotape recorder?

   b. What are the estimated annual inventory holding and ordering costs associated with this product?

   c. How many orders will be placed per year?

   d. With 250 working days per year, what is the cycle time for this product?

7. A large distributor of oil-well drilling equipment has operated over the past 2 years with EOQ policies based on an annual holding cost rate of 22%. Under the EOQ policy, a particular product has been ordered with a $Q^* = 80$. A recent evaluation of holding costs shows that because of an increase in the interest rate associated with bank loans, the annual holding cost rate should be 27%.

   a. What is the new economic order quantity for the product?

   b. Develop a general expression showing how the economic order quantity changes when the holding cost rate is changed from I to I'.

8. Nation-Wide Bus Lines is proud of its 6-week bus driver training program that it conducts for all new Nation-Wide drivers. As long as the class size remains less than or equal to 35, a 6-week training program costs Nation-Wide $22,000 for instructors, equipment, and so on. The Nation-Wide training program must provide the company with approximately five new drivers per month. After completing the training program, new drivers are paid $1600 per month but do not work until a full-time driver position is open. Nation-Wide views the $1600 per month paid to each idle new driver as a holding cost necessary to maintain a supply of newly trained drivers available for immediate service. Viewing new drivers as inventory-type units, how large should the training classes be in order to minimize Nation-Wide's total annual training and new driver idle-time costs? How many training classes should the company hold each year? What is the total annual cost associated with your recommendation?

9. Cress Electronic Products manufactures components used in the automotive industry. Cress purchases parts for use in its manufacturing operation from a variety of different suppliers. One particular supplier provides a part where the assumptions of the EOQ model are realistic. The annual demand is 5000 units, ordering costs are $80 per order, and holding costs are figured at an annual rate of 25%.

   a. If the cost of the part is $20 per unit, what is the economic order quantity?

   b. Assume 250 days of operation per year. If the lead time for an order is 12 days, what is the reorder point?

   c. If the lead time for the part is 7 weeks (35 days), what is the reorder point?

   d. What is the reorder point for part (c) if the reorder point is expressed in terms of the inventory on hand rather than the inventory position?

10. All-Star Bat Manufacturing, Inc. supplies baseball bats to major and minor league baseball teams. After an initial order in January, demand over the 6-month baseball season is approximately constant at 1000 bats per month. Assuming that the bat production process can handle up to 4000 bats per month, the bat production setup costs are $150 per setup, the production cost is $10 per bat, and that holding costs are figured at a monthly rate of 2%, what production lot size would you recommend to meet the demand during the baseball season? If All-Star operates 20 days per month, how often will the production process operate, and what is the length of a production run?

11. Assume that a production line operates such that the production lot size model of Section 11.2 is applicable. Given $D = 6400$ units per year, $C_0 = \$100$, and $C_h = \$2$ per unit per year, compute the minimum-cost production lot size for each of the following production rates:
   a. 8000 units per year
   b. 10,000 units per year
   c. 32,000 units per year
   d. 100,000 units per year
   Compute the EOQ recommended lot size using equation (11.5). What two observations can you make about the relationship between the EOQ model and the production lot size model?

12. Assume that you are reviewing the production lot size decision associated with a production operation where $P = 8000$ units per year, $D = 2000$ units per year, $C_0 = \$300$, and $C_h = \$1.60$ per unit per year. Also assume that current practice calls for production runs of 500 units every 3 months. Would you recommend changing the current production lot size? Why or why not? How much could be saved by converting to your production lot size recommendation?

13. Wilson Publishing Company produces books for the retail market. Demand for a current book is expected to occur at a constant annual rate of 7200 copies. The cost of one copy of the book is $14.50. The holding cost is based on an 18% annual rate, and production setup costs are $150 per setup. The equipment the book is produced on has an annual production volume of 25,000 copies. There are 250 working days per year and the lead time for a production run is 15 days. Use the production lot size model to compute the following values:
   a. Minimum-cost production lot size
   b. Number of production runs per year
   c. Cycle time
   d. Length of a production run
   e. Maximum inventory level
   f. Total annual cost
   g. Reorder point

14. A well-known manufacturer of several brands of toothpaste uses the production lot size model to determine production quantities for its various products. The product known as Extra White is currently being produced in production lot sizes of 5000 units. The length of the production run for this quantity is 10 days. Because of a recent shortage of a particular raw material, the supplier of the material has announced a cost increase that will be passed along to the manufacturer of Extra White. Current estimates are that the new raw material cost will increase the manufacturing cost of the toothpaste products by 23% per unit. What will be the effect of this price increase on the production lot sizes for Extra White?

15. Suppose that the XYZ Company of problem 4, with $D = 12,000$ units per year, $C_h = (2.50)(0.20) = \$0.50$, and $C_0 = \$25$, decided to operate with a backorder

inventory policy. Backorder costs are estimated to be $5 per unit per year. Identify the following:

a. Minimum-cost order quantity
b. Maximum number of backorders
c. Maximum inventory level
d. Cycle time
e. Total annual cost

16. Assuming 250 days of operation per year and a lead time of 5 days, what is the reorder point for the XYZ Company in problem 15? Show the general formula for the reorder point for the EOQ model with backorders. In general, is the reorder point when backorders are allowed greater than or less than the reorder point when backorders are not allowed? Explain.

17. A manager of an inventory system believes that inventory models are important decision-making aids. While often using an EOQ policy, the manager has never considered a backorder model because of the assumption that backorders were "bad" and should be avoided. However, with upper management's continued pressure for cost reduction, you have been asked to analyze the economics of a backordering policy for some products that can possibly be backordered. For a specific product with $D = 800$ units per year, $C_0 = \$150$, $C_h = \$3$, and $C_b = \$20$, what is the difference in total annual cost between the EOQ model and the planned shortage or backorder model? If the manager adds constraints that no more than 25% of the units can be backordered and that no customer will have to wait more than 15 days for an order, should the backorder inventory policy be adopted? Assume 250 working days per year.

18. If the lead time for new orders is 20 days for the inventory system discussed in problem 17, find the reorder point for both the EOQ and the backorder models.

19. The A&M Hobby Shop carries a line of radio-controlled model racing cars. Demand for the cars is assumed to be constant at a rate of 40 cars per month. The cars cost $60 each, and ordering costs are approximately $15 per order, regardless of the order size. The annual holding cost rate is 20%.

a. Determine the economic order quantity and total annual cost under the assumption that no backorders are permitted.
b. Using a $45 per unit per year backorder cost, determine the minimum-cost inventory policy and total annual cost for the model racing cars.
c. What is the maximum number of days a customer would have to wait for a backorder under the policy in part (b)? Assume that the Hobby Shop is open for business 300 days per year.
d. Would you recommend a no-backorder or a backorder inventory policy for this product? Explain.
e. If the lead time is 6 days, what is the reorder point for both the no-backorder and backorder inventory policies?

20. Assume that the following quantity discount schedule is appropriate:

Order Size	Discount	Unit Cost
0 to 49	0%	$30.00
50 to 99	5%	$28.50
100 or more	10%	$27.00

If annual demand is 120 units, ordering costs are $20 per order, and the annual holding cost rate is 25%, what order quantity would you recommend?

21. Apply the EOQ model to the following quantity discount situation:

Discount Category	Order Size	Discount	Unit Cost
1	0 to 99	0%	$10.00
2	100 or more	3%	$ 9.70

$D = 500$ units per year, $C_0 = \$40$, and an annual holding cost rate of 20% are given. What order quantity do you recommend?

22. Keith Shoe Stores carries a basic black dress shoe for men that sells at an approximate constant rate of 500 pairs of shoes every 3 months. Keith's current buying policy is to order 500 pairs each time an order is placed. It costs Keith $30 to place an order. The annual holding cost rate is 20%. With the order quantity of 500, Keith obtains the shoes at the lowest possible unit cost of $28 per pair. Other quantity discounts offered by the manufacturer are as follows:

Order Quantity	Price per Pair
0–99	$36
100–199	$32
200–299	$30
300 or more	$28

What is the minimum cost order quantity for the shoes? What are the annual savings of your inventory policy over the policy currently being used by Keith?

23. In the EOQ model with quantity discounts we stated that if the Q^* for a price category is larger than necessary to qualify for the category price, the category cannot be optimal. Use the two discount categories in problem 21 to show that this is true. That is, plot the total cost curves for the two categories and show that if the category 2 minimum cost Q is an acceptable solution, we do not have to consider category 1.

24. The J&B Card Shop sells calendars with different Colonial pictures shown for each month. The once-a-year order for each year's calendar arrives in September. From past experience the September-to-July demand for the calendars can be approximated by a normal distribution with $\mu = 500$ and $\sigma = 120$. The calendars cost $1.50 each, and J&B sells them for $3 each.

   a. If J&B throws out all unsold calendars at the end of July (that is, salvage value is zero), how many calendars should be ordered?

   b. If J&B reduces the calendar price to $1 at the end of July and can sell all surplus calendars at this price, how many calendars should be ordered?

25. The Gilbert Air-Conditioning Company is considering the purchase of a special shipment of portable air conditioners manufactured in Japan. Each unit will cost Gilbert $80 and it will be sold for $125. Gilbert does not want to carry surplus air conditioners over until the following year. Thus all surplus air conditioners will be

sold to a wholesaler for $50 per unit. Assume that the air conditioner demand follows a normal probability distribution with $\mu = 20$ and $\sigma = 8$.

a. What is the recommended order quantity?

b. What is the probability that Gilbert will sell all units it orders?

26. A popular newsstand in a large metropolitan area is attempting to determine how many copies of the Sunday paper it should purchase each week. Demand for the newspaper on Sundays can be approximated by a normal probability distribution with $\mu = 450$ and $\sigma = 100$. The newspaper costs the newsstand 35¢ a copy and sells for 50¢ a copy. The newsstand does not receive any value from surplus papers and thus absorbs a 100% loss on all unsold papers.

a. How many copies of the Sunday paper should be purchased each week?

b. What is the probability that the newsstand will have a stockout?

c. The manager of the newsstand is concerned about the newsstand's image if the probability of stockout is high. The customers often purchase other items after coming to the newsstand for the Sunday paper. Frequent stockouts would cause customers to go to another newsstand. The manager agrees that a 50¢ goodwill cost should be assigned to any stockout. What is the new recommended order quantity and the new probability of a stockout?

27. A perishable dairy product is ordered daily at a particular supermarket. The product, which costs $1.19 per unit, sells for $1.65 per unit. If units are unsold at the end of the day, the supplier takes them back at a rebate of $1 per unit. Assume that daily demand is approximately normally distributed with $\mu = 150$ and $\sigma = 30$.

a. What is your recommended daily order quantity for the supermarket?

b. What is the probability that the supermarket will sell all the units it orders?

c. In problems such as these, why would the supplier offer a rebate as high as $1? For example, why not offer a nominal rebate of, say, 25¢ per unit? What happens to the supermarket order quantity as the rebate is reduced?

28. A retail outlet sells a seasonal product for $10 per unit. The cost of the product is $8 per unit. All units not sold during the regular season are sold for half the retail price in an end-of-season clearance sale. Assume that demand for the product is uniformly distributed between 200 and 800.

a. What is the recommended order quantity?

b. What is the probability that at least some customers will ask to purchase the product after the outlet is sold out? That is, what is the probability of a stockout using your order quantity in part (a)?

c. In order to keep customers happy and returning to the store later, the owner feels that stockouts should be avoided if at all possible. What is your recommended order quantity if the owner is willing to tolerate a 0.15 probability of a stockout?

d. Using your answer to part (c), what is the goodwill cost you are assigning to a stockout?

29. Floyd Distributors, Inc. provides a variety of auto parts to small local garages. Floyd purchases parts from manufacturers according to the EOQ model and then ships the parts from a regional warehouse direct to its customers. For a particular type of muffler, Floyd's EOQ analysis recommends orders with $Q^* = 25$ to satisfy an annual demand of 200 mufflers. There are 250 working days per year and the lead time averages 15 days.

a. What is the reorder point if Floyd assumes a constant demand rate?

b. Suppose that an analysis of Floyd's muffler demand shows that the lead time demand follows a normal probability distribution with $\mu = 12$ and $\sigma = 2.5$. If Floyd's management can tolerate one stockout per year, what is the revised reorder point?

c. What is the safety stock for part (b)? If C_h = $5/unit/year, what is the extra cost due to the uncertainty of demand?

30. For Floyd Distributors in problem 29, we were given Q^* = 25, D = 200, C_h = $5, and a normal lead time demand distribution with μ = 12 and σ = 2.5.
    a. What is Floyd's reorder point if the firm is willing to tolerate two stockouts during the year?
    b. What is Floyd's reorder point if the firm wants to restrict the probability of a stockout on any one cycle to at most 1%?
    c. What are the safety stock levels and the annual safety stock costs for the reorder points found in parts (a) and (b)?

31. A product with an annual demand of 1000 units has C_0 = $25.50 and C_h = $8. The demand exhibits some variability such that the lead time demand follows a normal probability distribution with μ = 25 and σ = 5.
    a. What is the recommended order quantity?
    b. What are the reorder point and safety stock if the firm desires at most a 2% probability of stockout on any given order cycle?
    c. If a manager sets the reorder point at 30, what is the probability of a stockout on any given order cycle? How many times would you expect to stockout during the year if this reorder point were used?

32. The B&S Novelty and Craft Shop in Bennington, Vermont, sells a variety of quality handmade items to tourists. B&S will sell 300 hand-carved miniature replicas of a Colonial soldier each year, but the demand pattern during the year is uncertain. The replicas sell for $20 each, and B&S uses a 15% annual inventory holding cost rate. Ordering costs are $5 per order, and demand during the lead time follows a normal probability distribution with μ = 15 and σ = 6.
    a. What is the recommended order quantity?
    b. If B&S is willing to accept a stockout roughly twice a year, what reorder point would you recommend? What is the probability that B&S will have a stockout in any one order cycle?
    c. What are the safety stock and annual safety stock costs for this product?

33. A firm uses a one-week periodic review inventory system. There is a two-day lead time for any order, and the firm's service guideline indicates a willingness to tolerate an average of 1 stockout per year.
    a. Using the firm's service guideline, what is the probability of a stockout associated with each replenishment decision?
    b. What is the replenishment level if demand during the review period plus lead time period is normally distributed with a mean of 60 units and a standard deviation of 12 units?
    c. What is the replenishment level if demand during the review period plus lead time period is uniformly distributed between 35 and 85 units?

34. Foster Drugs, Inc. handles a variety of health and beauty aid products. A particular hair conditioner product costs Foster Drugs $2.95 per unit. The annual holding cost rate 20%. An order-quantity, reorder-point inventory model recommends and order quantity of 300 units per order.
    a. Lead time is one week and the lead time demand is normally distributed with a mean of 150 units and a standard deviation of 40 units. What is the reorder point if the firm is willing to tolerate a 1% chance of stockout on any one cycle?
    b. What safety stock and annual safety stock cost is associated with your recommendation in part (a)?
    c. The order-quantity, reorder-point model requires a continuous review system. Foster is considering making a transition to a periodic review system in an at-

tempting to coordinate ordering for many of its products. The demand during the proposed two-week review period and the one-week lead time period is normally distributed with a mean of 450 units and a standard deviation of 70 units. What is the recommended replenishment level for this period review system if the firm is willing to tolerate the same 1% chance of stockout associated with any replenishment decision?

   d. What safety stock and annual safety stock cost is associated with your recommendation in part (c)?

   e. Compare your answers to parts (b) and (d). The company is seriously considering the periodic review system. Would you support this decision? Explain.

   f. Would you tend to favor the continuous review system for more expensive items? For example, assume that the product in the above example sold for $295 per unit. Explain.

35. Statewide Auto Parts uses a four-week periodic review system to reorder parts for its inventory stock. A one-week lead time is required to fill the order. Demand for one particular part during the five-week replenishment period is normally distributed with a mean of 18 units and a standard deviation of 6 units.

   a. At a particular periodic review, 8 units are in inventory. The parts manager places an order for 16 units. What is the probability that this part will have a stockout before an order that is placed at the next four-week review period arrives?

   b. Assume that the company is willing to tolerate a 2.5% chance of a stockout associated with a replenishment decision. How many parts should the manager have ordered in part (a)? What is the replenishment level for the four-week periodic review system?

36. Rose Office Supplies, Inc., which is open six days a week, uses a two-week periodic review for its store inventory. On alternating Monday mornings the store manager fills out an order sheet requesting a shipment of various items from the company's warehouse. A particular three-ring notebook sells at an average rate of 16 notebooks per week. The standard deviation in sales is 5 notebooks per week. The lead time for a new shipment is 3 days. The mean lead time demand is 8 notebooks with a standard deviation of 3.5.

   a. What is the mean or expected demand during the review period plus the lead time period?

   b. Under the assumption of independent demands from week to week, the variances in demands are additive. Thus, the variance of the demand during the review period plus the lead time period is equal to the variance of demand during the first week plus the variance of demand during the second week plus the variance of demand during the lead time period. What is the variance of demand during the review period plus the lead period? What is the standard deviation of demand during the review period plus the lead time period?

   c. Assuming that demand has a normal probability distribution, what is the replenishment level that will provide an expected stockout rate of one per year?

   d. On Monday, March 22, 18 notebooks remain in inventory at the store. How many notebooks should the store manager order?

37. Consider the Spiecker Manufacturing example of Section 11.8. Determine the net requirements for the engine assembly, the air cleaner subassembly, and the filter housing if the number of units in inventory were 2000, 1500, and 1000, respectively. Assume that 5000 units of the 14-inch snowblower are required in week 21.

38. For the Spiecker Manufacturing example of Section 11.8, determine the effect on time phasing if lead times were 10 for the engine assembly, 3 for the air cleaner subassembly, and 5 for the filter housing.

39. C & D Lawn Products manufactures a rotary spreader for applying fertilizer. A portion of the bill of materials is shown below:

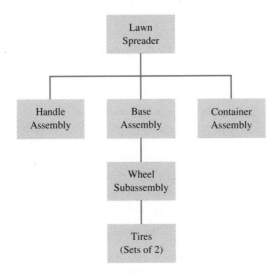

If 3000 lawn spreaders are needed to satisfy a customer's order, determine the net requirements for the base assembly, wheel subassembly, and tires (sets of two). Assume that 1000 base assemblies, 1500 wheel subassemblies, and 800 tires (sets of two) are currently in inventory.

40. In problem 39, assume that the lead time for the base assembly, wheel subassembly, and tires are 2 weeks, 4 weeks, and 5 weeks, respectively. If all components must be completed no later than week 15 of the current production period, determine when orders must be placed to meet the production schedule.

▼ CASE PROBLEM

A Make or Buy Analysis

Wagner Fabricating Company is reviewing the economic feasibility of manufacturing a part that it currently purchases from a supplier. Forecasted annual demand for the part is 3200 units. Wagner operates 250 days per year.

Wagner's financial analysts have established a cost of capital of 14% for the use of funds for investments within the company. In addition, over the past year $600,000 has been the average investment in the company's inventory. Accounting information shows that a total of $24,000 was spent on taxes and insurance related to the company's inventory. In addition, it has been estimated that $9000 was lost due to inventory shrinkage, which included damaged goods as well as pilferage. A remaining $15,000 was spent on warehouse overhead, including utility expenses for heating and lighting.

An analysis of the purchasing operation shows that approximately 2 hours are required to process and coordinate an order for the part regardless of the quantity ordered. Purchasing salaries average $28 per hour, including employee benefits. In addition, a detailed analysis of 125 orders showed that $2375 was spent on telephone, paper, and postage directly related to the ordering process.

A 1-week lead time is required to obtain the part from the supplier. An analysis of demand during the lead time shows that lead time demand is approximately normally distributed with a mean of 64 units and a standard deviation of 10 units. Service level guidelines indicate that one stockout per year is acceptable.

Currently the company has a contract to purchase the part from a supplier at a cost of $18 per unit. However, over the past few months, the company's production capacity has been expanded. As a result, excess capacity is now available in certain production departments and the company is considering the alternative of producing the parts itself.

Forecasted utilization of equipment shows that production capacity will be available for the part being considered. The production capacity is available at the rate of 1000 units per month, with up to 5 months of production time available. It is felt that with a 2-week lead time, schedules can be arranged so that the part can be produced whenever needed. The demand during the 2-week lead time is approximately normally distributed, with a mean of 128 units and a standard deviation of 20 units. Production costs are expected to be $17 per part.

A concern of management is that setup costs will be significant. The total cost of labor and lost production time is estimated to be $50 per hour, and it will take a full 8-hour shift to set up the equipment for producing the part.

MANAGERIAL REPORT

Develop a report for management of Wagner Fabricating that will address the question of whether the company should continue to purchase the part from the supplier or should begin to produce the part itself. Include the following factors in your report:

1. An analysis of the holding costs, including the appropriate annual holding cost rate.
2. An analysis of ordering costs, including the appropriate cost per order from the supplier.
3. An analysis of setup costs for the production operation.
4. A development of the inventory policy for the following two alternatives:
   a. Ordering a fixed quantity, Q, from the supplier
   b. Ordering a fixed quantity, Q, from in-plant production
5. Include the following in the policies of 4(a) and 4(b) above:
   a. The optimal quantity Q^*
   b. The number of order or production runs per year
   c. The cycle time
   d. The reorder point
   e. The amount of safety stock
   f. The expected maximum inventory level
   g. The average inventory level
   h. The annual holding cost
   i. The annual ordering cost
   j. The annual cost of the units purchased or manufactured
   k. The total annual cost of the purchase policy and the total annual cost of the production policy
6. Make a recommendation as to whether the company should purchase or manufacture the part. What is the saving associated with your recommendation as compared with the other alternative?

APPENDIX

11.1

Development of the Optimal Order Quantity (Q*) Formula for the EOQ Model

Given equation (11.3) as the general total annual cost formula for the EOQ model,

$$TC = \frac{1}{2}QC_h + \frac{D}{Q}C_0 \tag{11.3}$$

we can find the order quantity, Q, that minimizes the total cost by setting the derivative, dTC/dQ, equal to zero and solving for Q^*.

$$\frac{d\,TC}{dQ} = \frac{1}{2}C_h - \frac{D}{Q^2}C_0 = 0$$

$$\frac{1}{2}C_h = \frac{D}{Q^2}C_0$$

$$C_hQ^2 = 2DC_0$$

$$Q^2 = \frac{2DC_0}{C_h}$$

Hence,

$$Q^* = \sqrt{\frac{2DC_0}{C_h}} \tag{11.5}$$

The second derivative is

$$\frac{d^2TC}{dQ^2} = \frac{2D}{Q^3}C_0$$

Since the value of the second derivative is greater than zero for D, C_0, and Q greater than zero, Q^* from equation (11.5) is in fact the minimum-cost solution.

APPENDIX
11.2

Development of the Optimal Lot Size (Q*) Formula for the Production Lot Size Model

Given equation (11.15) as the total annual cost formula for the production lot size model,

$$\text{TC} = \frac{1}{2}\left(1 - \frac{D}{P}\right)QC_h + \frac{D}{Q}C_0 \qquad (11.15)$$

we can find the order quantity, Q, that minimizes the total cost by setting the derivative, $d\,\text{TC}/dQ$, equal to zero and solving for Q^*.

$$\frac{d\,\text{TC}}{dQ} = \frac{1}{2}\left(1 - \frac{D}{P}\right)C_h - \frac{D}{Q^2}C_0 = 0$$

Solving for Q^*, we have

$$\frac{1}{2}\left(1 - \frac{D}{P}\right)C_h = \frac{D}{Q^2}C_0$$

$$\left(1 - \frac{D}{P}\right)C_h Q^2 = 2DC_0$$

$$Q^2 = \frac{2DC_0}{(1 - D/P)C_h}$$

Hence,

$$Q^* = \sqrt{\frac{2DC_0}{(1 - D/P)C_h}} \qquad (11.16)$$

The second derivative is

$$\frac{d^2\text{TC}}{dQ^2} = \frac{2DC_0}{Q^3}$$

Since the value of the second derivative is greater than zero for D, C_0, and Q greater than zero, Q^* from equation (11.16) is a minimum-cost solution.

APPENDIX
11.3

Development of the Optimal Order Quantity (Q*) and Optimal Backorder (S*) Formulas for the Planned Shortage Model

Given equation (11.25) as the total annual cost model for the planned shortage case,

$$TC = \frac{(Q - S)^2}{2Q}C_h + \frac{D}{Q}C_0 + \frac{S^2}{2Q}C_b \tag{11.25}$$

we have two inventory decision variables, Q and S. To find the Q and S values that minimize equation (11.25), we must set the two partial derivatives, $\partial TC/\partial Q$ and $\partial TC/\partial S$, equal to zero.

First, let us rewrite equation (11.25) as follows:

$$TC = \left(\frac{Q^2 - 2QS + S^2}{2Q}\right)C_h + \frac{D}{Q}C_0 + \frac{S^2}{2Q}C_b$$

$$= \frac{Q}{2}C_h - SC_h + \frac{C_h}{2Q}S^2 + \frac{DC_0}{Q} + \frac{C_b}{2Q}S^2$$

$$= \left(\frac{C_h + C_b}{2Q}\right)S^2 - SC_h + \frac{QC_h}{2} + \frac{DC_0}{Q}$$

Then, setting $\partial TC/\partial S = 0$, we get

$$\frac{\partial TC}{\partial S} = \left(\frac{C_h + C_b}{Q}\right)S - C_h = 0$$

Solving for $S*$, we have

$$\left(\frac{C_h + C_b}{Q}\right)S = C_h$$

Thus,

$$S* = Q\left(\frac{C_h}{C_h + C_b}\right) \tag{11.27}$$

Setting $\partial TC/\partial Q = 0$, we get

$$\frac{\partial TC}{\partial Q} = \frac{-(C_h + C_b)S^2}{2Q^2} + \frac{C_h}{2} - \frac{DC_0}{Q^2} = 0$$

Substituting S^* of equation (11.27), we have

$$\frac{\partial TC}{\partial Q} = \frac{-(C_h + C_b)Q^2(C_h)^2/(C_h + C_b)^2}{2Q^2} + \frac{C_h}{2} - \frac{DC_0}{Q^2} = 0$$

We can solve for Q^* as follows:

$$\frac{-(C_h)^2}{2(C_h + C_b)} + \frac{C_h}{2} = \frac{DC_0}{Q_2}$$

$$\frac{-(C_h)^2 + C_h(C_h + C_b)}{2(C_h + C_b)} = \frac{DC_0}{Q^2}$$

$$Q^2 = \frac{2(C_h + C_b)DC_0}{C_h C_b}$$

$$Q^2 = \frac{2C_h DC_0}{C_h C_b} + \frac{2C_b DC_0}{C_h C_b}$$

$$Q^2 = \frac{2DC_0}{C_h}\left(\frac{C_h}{C_b} + \frac{C_b}{C_b}\right)$$

Hence,

$$Q^* = \sqrt{\frac{2DC_0}{C_h}\left(\frac{C_h + C_b}{C_b}\right)} \qquad (11.26)$$

The second-order conditions will show that equations (11.26) and (11.27) are the minimum-cost solutions.

MANAGEMENT SCIENCE IN PRACTICE

SupeRx Inc.*
Cincinnati, Ohio

SupeRx is a chain of conventional-size drug stores with locations in 15 states. The company operates a total of 345 stores that are part of Hook-SupeRx, Inc., which operates over 1100 stores, primarily in the Midwest and Northeast. As in any retail business, the primary functions and concerns revolve around sales growth, profit margins, expense control, and inventory management.

Inventory management is undergoing a rapid transformation from an art to a science. No longer can any retail business continue to operate profitably without a sound inventory-management program. A key consideration is product movement information that in turn determines reorder quantities both at the store and the warehouse levels. Seasonal fluctuations and advertising can affect product movement, and their effects must be measured using past history rather than seat-of-the-pants guesswork.

General inventory management involves several product categories: basic products carried on an everyday basis, seasonal products carried only during certain times of the year (such as fruitcakes during Christmas), and special items bought on an in-and-out basis throughout the year.

By far the most critical inventory issue is the replenishment of basic products. In most retail drug chains, including SupeRx, this type of product is ordered under a periodic-review inventory system, with the review period being 1 week. The weekly review uses electronic ordering equipment that scans an order label affixed to the shelf. Such a label is located on the shelf directly below each item. Among other information on this label is the ''order-to quantity.'' (*Note:* This is the replenishment level referred in the periodic-review inventory model of Section 11.7.) The store employee placing the order determines the quantity to order by subtracting the number of units of product on the shelf from the order-to quantity (OTQ). For example, if the OTQ is 6 and there are 2 units of product on the shelf, the quantity ordered would be 4. The OTQ is the key factor in inventory control for basic products.

There are several factors to consider in determining individual item OTQs. The most obvious is average weekly demand or movement. SupeRx uses movement figures from the warehouse to the stores. Suppose, for example, an item averages 2 units per week per store in warehouse deliveries. Setting the OTQ equal to 2 would not allow for sales fluctuations that went into the average of 2. To compensate for this and avoid stockouts, SupeRx sets the OTQ equal to a 3-week demand or movement. Thus, in our example, the OTQ would become 6.

Another factor to consider is whether an item can be ordered in units or cases. In some instances it is not feasible for the warehouse to deliver to stores in anything less than case quantities. An example would be candy bars. Stores must order a minimum of 1 case (36 units) no matter what the movement indicates. Thus, the OTQ is 36 or a multiple of 36 to accommodate the case order restriction. Merchan

*The authors are indebted to Bob Carver of SupeRx, Inc., for providing this application.

dising esthetics must also be considered when determining an OTQ. If an item has 4 facings on the shelf, but the optimum OTQ determined by movement is 3, there would be one space without product. This would create an out-of-stock impression to the customer, and, thus, the OTQ would be increased to at least 4. Seasonal fluctuations in movement must be considered when OTQs are determined. For example, the OTQ for a cough and cold item would be significantly higher in January than it would be in July. Adhesive bandages would be just the opposite, with higher usage in the summer than in the winter.

SupeRx, like many other drug chains, is in the process of taking advantage of new technological breakthroughs in inventory management. Today, its OTQs are based on average company warehouse movement into the stores. Soon SupeRx will have a program in place to produce OTQs by item by individual store, based on that store's movement, rather than on the company movement. Once that is in place, SupeRx will be able to accommodate seasonal fluctuations by individual store as well.

The chain drug industry is well behind other retail industries (most notably the grocery industry) in the ability to capture point-of-sale information with the use of scanning registers. Once these are in place, SupeRx will be able to use actual point-of-sale product information instead of warehouse movement. Taking this one step farther, these scanning registers actually have the ability to place an order to the warehouse automatically, based on what is actually sold that week.

One final subject needs to be discussed in order to bring inventory management into perspective. Good inventory management does not occur in a vacuum, but must be interrelated with sales, gross margin, and expense control objectives. SupeRx is fortunate in that it has had an electronic planogramming software and hardware system in place for some time. In addition to producing superior-quality planograms for the stores, this system allows SupeRx merchandisers to act out ''what if'' scenarios relating to OTQs, product costs, retail sales prices, inventory carrying costs, sales, and other factors. As an example, optimum order-to quantities will normally result in some percentage of missed sales due to individual item movement fluctuations. On the other hand, increasing the OTQs to maximize sales will increase inventory, decrease inventory turnover, and thus tie up capital that could otherwise be used for building new stores, remodeling existing locations, etc. By working with the numbers, the merchandiser can maximize both sales and inventory turnover. The use of this modern technology is rapidly becoming a necessity rather than a luxury in developing and operating models to ensure the maximization of sales, profits, and inventory turnovers that will ultimately determine the success or failure of a drug chain.

12

Waiting Line Models

Recall the last time that you had to wait at a supermarket checkout counter, wait for a teller at your local bank, or wait to be served at a restaurant. In these and many other waiting line situations, the time spent waiting is undesirable. Since adding more checkout clerks, more bank tellers, or more waiters is not always the most economical strategy for improving service, businesses are trying harder to understand their waiting line characteristics and find ways to keep waiting times within tolerable limits.

Quantitative models have been developed to help managers understand and make better decisions concerning the operation of waiting lines. In management science terminology a waiting line is referred to as a *queue,* and the body of knowledge dealing with waiting lines is known as *queuing theory.* In the early 1900s A. K. Erlang, a Danish telephone engineer, began a study of the congestion and waiting times occurring in the completion of telephone calls. Since then, queuing theory has grown far more sophisticated and has been applied to a wide variety of waiting line situations.

Waiting line models consist of mathematical formulas and relationships which can be used to determine the *operating characteristics* (performance measures) for a waiting line. Some of the operating characteristics that are of interest are the following:

1. The probability that there are no units in the system
2. The average number of units in the waiting line
3. The average number of units in the system (the number of units in the waiting line plus the number of units being served)
4. The average time a unit spends in the waiting line
5. The average time a unit spends in the system (the waiting time plus the service time)
6. The probability that an arriving unit has to wait for service
7. The probability of *n* units in the system

Managers who are provided with the above information will be better equipped to make decisions that balance desirable service levels against the cost of providing the service.

12.1 ▼ THE STRUCTURE OF A WAITING LINE SYSTEM

To illustrate the basic features of a waiting line model we will consider the waiting line situation at the Burger Dome fast-food restaurant. Burger Dome sells hamburgers, cheeseburgers, french fries, soft drinks, and milk shakes, as well as a limited number of specialty items and dessert selections. Although the management of Burger Dome would like to provide immediate service to each customer, at times more customers arrive than can be handled by the Burger Dome food-service staff. Thus, customers wait in line to place and receive their orders.

The management of Burger Dome is concerned that the methods they are currently using to serve customers are resulting in excessive waiting times. They have asked that a waiting line study be performed in order to help determine the best approach for improving service.

The Single-Channel Waiting line

In the current Burger Dome operation with one cash register, a server takes the customer's order, determines the total cost of the order, takes the money from the customer, and then fills the order. Once the first customer's order is filled, the server takes the order of the next customer waiting for service. This operation is an example of a *single-channel* waiting line. By this, we mean that each customer entering the Burger Dome restaurant must pass through the *one* channel—one cash-register, order-taking, and order-filling station—in order to place the order, pay the bill, and receive the food. When more customers arrive than can be served immediately, the customers form a waiting line and wait for the order-taking, order-filling station to become available. A diagram of the Burger Dome single-channel waiting line is shown in Figure 12.1.

The Process of Arrivals

Defining the arrival process for a waiting line involves determining the probability distribution for the number of arrivals in a given period of time. For many waiting line situations, the arrivals occur in a *random fashion;* that is, each arrival is independent of

FIGURE 12.1
Diagram of the Burger Dome Single-Channel Waiting Line

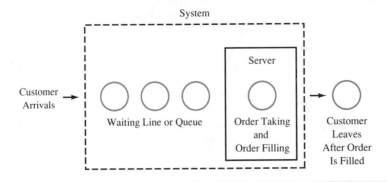

other arrivals, and we cannot predict when an arrival will occur. In such cases, management scientists have found that the *Poisson probability distribution* provides a good description of the arrival pattern.

Using the Poisson probability function,[1] the probability of x arrivals in a specific time period is defined as follows:

$$P(x) = \frac{\lambda^x e^{-\lambda}}{x!} \text{ for } x = 0, 1, 2 \ldots \tag{12.1}$$

where

x = the number of arrivals in the time period

λ = the average or mean number of arrivals per time period

e = 2.71828

Values of $e^{-\lambda}$ are provided in Table 12.1.

Suppose that Burger Dome has analyzed data on customer arrivals and has concluded that the mean arrival rate is 45 customers per hour. For a 1-minute period of time, the mean number of arrivals would be $\lambda = 45/60 = 0.75$ arrivals per minute. Thus, we can use the following Poisson probability function to compute the probability of x arrivals during a 1-minute time period:

$$P(x) = \frac{\lambda^x e^{-\lambda}}{x!} = \frac{0.75^x e^{-0.75}}{x!} \tag{12.2}$$

Table 12.1 shows that $e^{-0.75} = 0.4724$. Thus, the probabilities of 0, 1, and 2 arrivals during a 1-minute period are as follows:

$$P(0) = \frac{(0.75)^0 e^{-0.75}}{0!} = e^{-0.75} = 0.4724$$

$$P(1) = \frac{(0.75)^1 e^{-0.75}}{1!} = 0.75 e^{-0.75} = 0.75(0.4724) = 0.3543$$

$$P(2) = \frac{(0.75)^2 e^{-0.75}}{2!} = \frac{0.75^2 e^{-0.75}}{2!} = \frac{(0.5625)(0.4724)}{2} = 0.1329$$

Thus, we see that the probability of no arrivals in a 1-minute period is 0.4724, the probability of exactly 1 arrival in a 1-minute period is 0.3543, and the probability of exactly 2 arrivals in a 1-minute period is 0.1329. The Poisson probability distribution of arrivals during a 1-minute period is shown in Table 12.2.

In the waiting line models we present in Sections 12.2 and 12.3, we will use the Poisson distribution to describe the customer arrivals at Burger Dome. In practice you will want to record the actual number of arrivals per time period for several days or weeks and compare the frequency distribution of the observed number of arrivals to the Poisson distribution in order to determine if the Poisson distribution provides a reasonable approximation of the arrival distribution.

[1]The term $x!$, x *factorial*, is defined as $x! = x(x-1)(x-2) \ldots (2)(1)$. For example, $4! = (4)(3)(2)(1) = 24$. For the special case of $x = 0$, $0! = 1$ by definition.

TABLE 12.1
Values of $e^{-\lambda}$

λ	$e^{-\lambda}$	λ	$e^{-\lambda}$	λ	$e^{-\lambda}$
0.05	0.9512	2.05	0.1287	4.05	0.0174
0.10	0.9048	2.10	0.1225	4.10	0.0166
0.15	0.8607	2.15	0.1165	4.15	0.0158
0.20	0.8187	2.20	0.1108	4.20	0.0150
0.25	0.7788	2.25	0.1054	4.25	0.0143
0.30	0.7408	2.30	0.1003	4.30	0.0136
0.35	0.7047	2.35	0.0954	4.35	0.0129
0.40	0.6703	2.40	0.0907	4.40	0.0123
0.45	0.6376	2.45	0.0863	4.45	0.0117
0.50	0.6065	2.50	0.0821	4.50	0.0111
0.55	0.5769	2.55	0.0781	4.55	0.0106
0.60	0.5488	2.60	0.0743	4.60	0.0101
0.65	0.5220	2.65	0.0707	4.65	0.0096
0.70	0.4966	2.70	0.0672	4.70	0.0091
0.75	0.4724	2.75	0.0639	4.75	0.0087
0.80	0.4493	2.80	0.0608	4.80	0.0082
0.85	0.4274	2.85	0.0578	4.85	0.0078
0.90	0.4066	2.90	0.0550	4.90	0.0074
0.95	0.3867	2.95	0.0523	4.95	0.0071
1.00	0.3679	3.00	0.0498	5.00	0.0067
1.05	0.3499	3.05	0.0474	5.05	0.0064
1.10	0.3329	3.10	0.0450	5.10	0.0061
1.15	0.3166	3.15	0.0429	5.15	0.0058
1.20	0.3012	3.20	0.0408	5.20	0.0055
1.25	0.2865	3.25	0.0388	5.25	0.0052
1.30	0.2725	3.30	0.0369	5.30	0.0050
1.35	0.2592	3.35	0.0351	5.35	0.0047
1.40	0.2466	3.40	0.0334	5.40	0.0045
1.45	0.2346	3.45	0.0317	5.45	0.0043
1.50	0.2231	3.50	0.0302	5.50	0.0041
1.55	0.2122	3.55	0.0287	5.55	0.0039
1.60	0.2019	3.60	0.0273	5.60	0.0037
1.65	0.1920	3.65	0.0260	5.65	0.0035
1.70	0.1827	3.70	0.0247	5.70	0.0033
1.75	0.1738	3.75	0.0235	5.75	0.0032
1.80	0.1653	3.80	0.0224	5.80	0.0030
1.85	0.1572	3.85	0.0213	5.85	0.0029
1.90	0.1496	3.90	0.0202	5.90	0.0027
1.95	0.1423	3.95	0.0193	5.95	0.0026
2.00	0.1353	4.00	0.0183	6.00	0.0025
				7.00	0.0009
				8.00	0.000335
				9.00	0.000123
				10.00	0.000045

TABLE 12.2
Poisson Probabilities for the Number of Arrivals at a Burger Dome Restaurant During a 1-Minute Period ($\lambda = 0.75$)

Number of Arrivals	Probability
0	0.4724
1	0.3543
2	0.1329
3	0.0332
4	0.0062
5 or more	0.0010

The Distribution of Service Times

The service time is the time the customer or unit spends at the service facility once the service has started. At Burger Dome, the service time starts when the customer begins to place the order with the food server and continues until the customer has received the order. Service times are rarely constant. At Burger Dome, the number of items ordered and the mix of items ordered vary considerably from one customer to the next. Small orders can be handled in a matter of seconds, while larger orders may require more than 2 minutes to process.

Management scientists have determined that the *exponential probability distribution* often provides a good approximation of service times in waiting line situations. If the probability distribution for the service times follows an exponential probability distribution, the probability that the service time will be less than or equal to a time of length t is given by

$$P(\text{service time} \leq t) = 1 - e^{-\mu t} \tag{12.3}$$

where

$$\mu = \text{the average or mean number of units that}$$
$$\text{can be served per time period}$$

Suppose that Burger Dome has studied the order-taking and order-filling process and has found that the single food server can process an average of 60 customer orders per hour. On a 1-minute time period basis, the average or mean service rate would be $\mu = 60/60 = 1$ customer per minute. For example, using $\mu = 1$, equation (12.3) can be used to compute probabilities such as the probability a order can be processed in ½ minute or less, 1 minute or less, and 2 minutes or less. These computations are as follows:

$$P(\text{service time} \leq 0.5 \text{ min.}) = 1 - e^{-1(0.5)} = 1 - 0.6065 = 0.3935$$
$$P(\text{service time} \leq 1.0 \text{ min.}) = 1 - e^{-1(1.0)} = 1 - 0.3679 = 0.6321$$
$$P(\text{service time} \leq 2.0 \text{ min.}) = 1 - e^{-1(2.0)} = 1 - 0.1353 = 0.8647$$

Thus, we would conclude that there is a 0.3935 probability an order can be processed in ½ minute (30 seconds) or less, a 0.6321 probability an order can be processed in 1 minute or less, and a 0.8647 probability an order can be processed in 2 minutes or less.

In several of the waiting line models presented in this chapter we will assume that the probability distribution for the service times follows an exponential probability distribution. In practice you will want to collect data on actual service times to see if the exponential probability distribution is a reasonable approximation of the service times for your application.

Queue Discipline

In describing a waiting line system, we must define the manner in which the waiting units are arranged for service. For the Burger Dome waiting line, and in general for most customer-oriented waiting lines, the units waiting for service are arranged on a *first-come, first-served* basis; serving units in this manner is referred to as an FCFS queue discipline. However, some situations call for different queue disciplines. For example, when people wait for an elevator, the last one on the elevator is usually the first one to complete service (that is, the first to leave the elevator). Other types of queue disciplines assign priorities to the waiting units and then service the unit with the highest priority first. In this chapter we restrict our attention to waiting lines that use a first-come, first-served queue discipline.

✳ Steady-State Operation

When the Burger Dome restaurant opens in the morning, no customers are in the restaurant. Gradually the business activity builds up to a normal or steady state. The beginning or start-up period is referred to as the *transient period*. The transient period ends when the system reaches the normal or *steady-state* operation. Waiting line models provide results describing the steady-state operating characteristics of the waiting line.

12.2. ▼ THE SINGLE-CHANNEL WAITING LINE MODEL WITH POISSON ARRIVALS AND EXPONENTIAL SERVICE TIMES

In this section we will present formulas that can be used to determine the steady-state operating characteristics for a single-channel waiting line. The formulas can be used if the following assumptions regarding the waiting line are applicable:

1. The waiting line has a single channel.
2. The pattern of arrivals follows a Poisson probability distribution.
3. The service times follow an exponential probability distribution.
4. The queue discipline is first-come, first-served (FCFS).

Since these assumptions apply to the Burger Dome waiting line problem introduced in Section 12.1, we will show how the formulas can be used to determine Burger Dome's operating characteristics and thus provide management with helpful decision-making information.

The mathematical methodology used to derive the formulas for the operating characteristics of waiting lines is rather complex. However, our purpose in this chapter is not to provide the theoretical development of waiting line models, but rather to show how the formulas based on waiting line models can provide information about the operating characteristics of the waiting line. Readers interested in the mathematical development of the formulas can consult any of the specialized texts listed in the References and Bibliography section at the end of the text.

The Operating Characteristics

The formulas that can be used to develop the steady-state operating characteristics for a single-channel waiting line with Poisson arrivals and exponential service times use the following notation:

λ = the mean or average number of arrivals per time period (the mean arrival rate)

μ = the mean or average number of services per time period (the mean service rate)

1. The probability that there are no units in the system

$$P_0 = 1 - \frac{\lambda}{\mu} \tag{12.4}$$

2. The average number of units in the waiting line

$$L_q = \frac{\lambda^2}{\mu(\mu - \lambda)} \tag{12.5}$$

3. The average number of units in the system

$$L = L_q + \frac{\lambda}{\mu} \tag{12.6}$$

4. The average time a unit spends in the waiting line

$$W_q = \frac{L_q}{\lambda} \tag{12.7}$$

5. The average time a unit spends in the system

$$W = W_q + \frac{1}{\mu} \tag{12.8}$$

6. The probability that an arriving unit has to wait for service

$$P_w = \frac{\lambda}{\mu} \tag{12.9}$$

7. The probability of n units in the system

$$P_n = \left(\frac{\lambda}{\mu}\right)^n P_0 \tag{12.10}$$

The values of the mean arrival rate λ and the mean service rate μ are clearly important components in determining the operating characteristics of the waiting line. From equation (12.9) we see that the ratio of the mean arrival rate to the mean service rate, λ/μ, provides the probability that an arriving unit has to wait because the service facility is busy. Since λ/μ provides the probability the service facility is busy, it is often referred to as the *utilization factor* for the service facility.

The operating characteristics presented in equations (12.4) to (12.10) are applicable only when the mean service rate, μ, is *greater than* the mean arrival rate, λ—in other words, when $\lambda/\mu < 1$. If this condition does not exist, the waiting line will continue to grow without limit since the service facility does not have sufficient capacity to handle the arriving units. Thus, in using equations (12.4) to (12.10), we must have $\mu > \lambda$.

Characteristics for The Burger Dome Problem

Recall that for the Burger Dome problem we had a mean arrival rate of $\lambda = 0.75$ customer per minute and a mean service rate of $\mu = 1$ customer per minute. Thus, since $\mu > \lambda$, equations (12.4) to (12.10) can be used to provide the following operating characteristics for the Burger Dome single-channel waiting line:

$$P_0 = 1 - \frac{\lambda}{\mu} = 1 - \frac{0.75}{1} = 0.25$$

$$L_q = \frac{\lambda^2}{\mu(\mu - \lambda)} = \frac{0.75^2}{1(1 - 0.75)} = 2.25 \text{ customers}$$

$$L = L_q + \frac{\lambda}{\mu} = 2.25 + \frac{0.75}{1} = 3 \text{ customers}$$

$$W_q = \frac{L_q}{\lambda} = \frac{2.25}{0.75} = 3 \text{ minutes}$$

$$W = W_q + \frac{1}{\mu} = 3 + \frac{1}{1} = 4 \text{ minutes}$$

$$P_w = \frac{\lambda}{\mu} = \frac{0.75}{1} = 0.75$$

Equation (12.10) can be used to determine the probability of any number of customers in the system. Applying (12.10) provides the probability information summarized in Table 12.3.

The Manager's Use of Waiting Line Models

Looking at the results of the single-channel waiting line for Burger Dome, we can learn several important things about the operation of the waiting line. In particular, customers

TABLE 12.3
The Probability of n Customers in the System for the Burger Dome Waiting Line Problem

Number of Customers	Probability
0	0.2500
1	0.1875
2	0.1406
3	0.1055
4	0.0791
5	0.0593
6	0.0445
7 or more	0.1335

wait an average of 3 minutes before beginning to place an order, and this appears some-what long for a business based on fast service. In addition, the facts that the average number of customers waiting in line is 2.25 and that 75% of the arriving customers have to wait for service are indicators that something should be done to improve the efficiency of the waiting line operation. Table 12.3 shows that there is a .1335 probability that 7 or more customers are in the Burger Dome system at one time. This indicates a fairly large probability that Burger Dome will periodically experience some very long waiting lines if it continues to use the single-channel operation.

If the operating characteristics are unsatisfactory in terms of meeting company stan-dards for service, Burger Dome's management should consider alternative designs or plans for improving the waiting line operation.

Improving the Waiting Line Operation

After reviewing the operating characteristics provided by the waiting line model, Burger Dome's management concluded that improvements in the system are desirable. Improve-ments in the waiting line operation most often focus on ways to improve the service rate. Generally, service improvements are made along the following lines:

1. Increase the mean service rate, μ, by making a creative design change or by employing new technology.
2. Add parallel service channels so that more units can be serviced at a time.

Assume that in considering alternative (1), Burger Dome's management decides to employ an order filler who will assist the order taker at the cash register. The customer begins the service process by placing the order with the order taker. As the order is placed, the order taker announces the order over an intercom system, and the order filler imme-diately begins filling the order. When the order is completed, the order taker handles the money, while the order filler continues to fill the order. With this design, Burger Dome's management estimates the mean service rate can be increased from the current service rate of 60 customers per hour to 75 customers per hour. On a per-minute basis, the mean service rate for the revised system is $\mu = 75/60 = 1.25$ customers per minute. Using $\lambda = 0.75$ and $\mu = 1.25$, equations (12.4) to (12.10) provide the operating characteristics summarized in Table 12.4.

As can be seen in Table 12.4, the operating characteristics or performance measures have all improved due to the increased service rate provided by the order-filler assistant. Are other alternatives possible for increasing the service rate in the future? If other

TABLE 12.4
Operating Characteristics for the Burger Dome System with the Mean Service Rate Increased to $\mu = 1.25$ Customers per Minute

Probability the system is empty	0.400
Average number of units in the waiting line	0.900
Average number of units in the system	1.500
Average time in the waiting line	1.200 min
Average time in the system	2.000 min
Probability an arriving unit has to wait	0.600
Probability 7 or more are in system	0.028

alternatives can be identified, and if the mean service rate μ can be identified for these alternatives, equations (12.4) to (12.10) will provide the information needed to assess the amount of improvement from the proposed alternatives. The added cost of any proposed change can be compared with the corresponding service improvements to help the manager determine whether or not the proposed service improvements are worthwhile.

As mentioned previously, another option that is usually available is to provide one or more additional service channels so that more than one customer may be served at the same time. The extension of the single-channel waiting line model to the multiple-channel waiting line model is the topic of the next section.

▼ NOTES AND COMMENTS ▼

1. The assumption that arrivals follow a Poisson probability distribution is equivalent to the assumption that the time between arrivals has an exponential probability distribution. For example, if the arrivals for a waiting line follow a Poisson probability distribution with a mean of 20 arrivals per hour, the time between arrivals will follow an exponential probability distribution, with a mean time between arrivals of 1/20 or .05 hour.
2. Many individuals believe that whenever the mean service rate μ is greater than the mean arrival rate λ, the system should be able to handle or service all arrivals. However, as the Burger Dome example shows, the variability of arrival times and service times may result in long waiting times even when the mean service rate exceeds the mean arrival rate. A contribution of waiting line models is that they can point out undesirable waiting line operating characteristics even when the $\mu > \lambda$ condition appears satisfactory.

12.3 ▼ THE MULTIPLE-CHANNEL WAITING LINE MODEL WITH POISSON ARRIVALS AND EXPONENTIAL SERVICE TIMES

A multiple-channel waiting line consists of two or more channels or service locations that are assumed to be identical in terms of service capability. In the multiple-channel system, arriving units wait in a single waiting line and then move to the first available channel to be served.

The single-channel Burger Dome operation could be expanded to a two-channel system by opening a second cash register and employing a second order taker, order filler to operate the second service channel. A diagram of the Burger Dome two-channel waiting line is shown in Figure 12.2.

In this section we present formulas that can be used to determine the steady-state operating characteristics for a multiple-channel waiting line. These formulas are applicable if the following assumptions for the waiting line are reasonable:

1. The waiting line has two or more channels.
2. The pattern of arrivals follows a Poisson probability distribution.
3. The service time for each channel follows an exponential probability distribution.
4. The mean service rate, μ, is the same for each channel.

FIGURE 12.2
Diagram of the Burger Dome Two-Channel Waiting Line

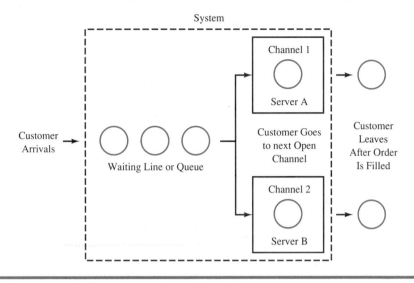

5. The arrivals wait in a single waiting line and then move to the first open channel for service.
6. The queue discipline is first-come, first-served (FCFS).

The Operating Characteristics

The formulas used to compute the steady-state operating characteristics for multiple-channel waiting lines use the following notation:

$$\lambda = \text{the mean arrival rate for the system}$$

$$\mu = \text{the mean service rate for } each \text{ channel}$$

$$k = \text{the number of channels}$$

Since μ is the mean service rate for each channel, $k\mu$ is the mean service rate for the multiple-channel system. As was true for the single-channel waiting line model, the formulas for the operating characteristics of multiple-channel waiting lines can be applied only in situations where the mean service rate for the system is greater than the mean arrival rate for the system; in other words, the formulas are applicable only if $k\mu$ is greater than λ.

1. The probability that there are no units in the system

$$P_0 = \frac{1}{\displaystyle\sum_{n=0}^{k-1}\frac{(\lambda/\mu)^n}{n!} + \frac{(\lambda/\mu)^k}{k!}\left(\frac{k\mu}{k\mu-\lambda}\right)} \qquad (12.11)$$

2. The average number of units in the waiting line

$$L_q = \frac{(\lambda/\mu)^k \lambda\mu}{(k-1)!(k\mu - \lambda)^2} P_0 \qquad (12.12)$$

3. The average number of units in the system

$$L = L_q + \frac{\lambda}{\mu} \tag{12.13}$$

4. The average time a unit spends in the waiting line

$$W_q = \frac{L_q}{\lambda} \tag{12.14}$$

5. The average time a unit spends in the system

$$W = W_q + \frac{1}{\mu} \tag{12.15}$$

6. The probability that an arriving unit has to wait

$$P_w = \frac{1}{k!}\left(\frac{\lambda}{\mu}\right)^k \left(\frac{k\mu}{k\mu - \lambda}\right) P_0 \tag{12.16}$$

7. The probability of n units in the system

$$P_n = \frac{(\lambda/\mu)^n}{n!} P_0 \text{ for } n \le k \tag{12.17}$$

$$P_n = \frac{(\lambda/\mu)^n}{k!k^{(n-k)}} P_0 \text{ for } n > k \tag{12.18}$$

While some of the above expressions for the operating characteristics of multiple-channel waiting lines are more complex than their single-channel counterparts, the expressions provide the same operating characteristics information. This information is used by managers in the same way as that for the single-channel model. To help simplify the use of the multiple-channel equations, we have provided Table 12.5, which contains values of P_0 for selected values of λ/μ and k. The values provided in the table correspond to cases where $k\mu > \lambda$, and hence the service rate is sufficient to process all arrivals.

Operating Characteristics for the Burger Dome Problem

As an illustration of the multiple-channel waiting line model, let us return to the Burger Dome fast-food restaurant waiting line problem. Suppose management wishes to evaluate the desirability of opening a second cash register and order-processing station so that two customers can be served simultaneously. Assume there will be a single waiting line with the next customer in line moving to the first available server. If this were done, Burger Dome would have a two-channel waiting line. Let us evaluate the operating characteristics for this two-channel system.

We will use equations (12.11) to (12.18) for the $k = 2$ channel system. Recalling the mean arrival rate is $\lambda = 0.75$ customer per minute and the mean service rate is $\mu = 1$ customer per minute for each channel, we have the following operating characteristics:

$$P_0 = 0.4545 \text{ (from Table 12.5 with } \lambda/\mu = 0.75)$$

$$L_q = \frac{(0.75/1)^2(0.75)(1)}{(2 - 1)![2(1) - 0.75]^2}(0.4545) = 0.1227 \text{ customer}$$

$$L = L_q + \frac{\lambda}{\mu} = 0.1227 + \frac{0.75}{1} = 0.8727 \text{ customer}$$

TABLE 12.5
Values of P_0 for Multiple-Channel Waiting Lines with Poisson Arrivals and Exponential Service Times

Ratio λ/μ	Number of Channels (k)			
	2	3	4	5
0.15	0.8605	0.8607	0.8607	0.8607
0.20	0.8182	0.8187	0.8187	0.8187
0.25	0.7778	0.7788	0.7788	0.7788
0.30	0.7391	0.7407	0.7408	0.7408
0.35	0.7021	0.7046	0.7047	0.7047
0.40	0.6667	0.6701	0.6703	0.6703
0.45	0.6327	0.6373	0.6376	0.6376
0.50	0.6000	0.6061	0.6065	0.6065
0.55	0.5686	0.5763	0.5769	0.5769
0.60	0.5385	0.5479	0.5487	0.5488
0.65	0.5094	0.5209	0.5219	0.5220
0.70	0.4815	0.4952	0.4965	0.4966
0.75	0.4545	0.4706	0.4722	0.4724
0.80	0.4286	0.4472	0.4491	0.4493
0.85	0.4035	0.4248	0.4271	0.4274
0.90	0.3793	0.4035	0.4062	0.4065
0.95	0.3559	0.3831	0.3863	0.3867
1.00	0.3333	0.3636	0.3673	0.3678
1.20	0.2500	0.2941	0.3002	0.3011
1.40	0.1765	0.2360	0.2449	0.2463
1.60	0.1111	0.1872	0.1993	0.2014
1.80	0.0526	0.1460	0.1616	0.1646
2.00		0.1111	0.1304	0.1343
2.20		0.0815	0.1046	0.1094
2.40		0.0562	0.0831	0.0889
2.60		0.0345	0.0651	0.0721
2.80		0.0160	0.0521	0.0581
3.00			0.0377	0.0466
3.20			0.0273	0.0372
3.40			0.0186	0.0293
3.60			0.0113	0.0228
3.80			0.0051	0.0174
4.00				0.0130
4.20				0.0093
4.40				0.0063
4.60				0.0038
4.80				0.0017

$$W_q = \frac{L_q}{\lambda} = \frac{0.1227}{0.75} = 0.16 \text{ minute}$$

$$W = W_q + \frac{1}{\mu} = 0.16 + \frac{1}{1} = 1.16 \text{ minutes}$$

$$P_w = \frac{1}{2!}\left(\frac{0.75}{1}\right)^2\left(\frac{2(1)}{(2-0.75)}\right)(0.4545) = 0.2045$$

TABLE 12.6
The Probability of *n* Customers in the System for the Burger Dome Two-Channel Waiting Line

Number of Customers	Probability
0	0.4545
1	0.3409
2	0.1278
3	0.0479
4	0.0180
5 or more	0.0109

By using equations (12.17) and (12.18), the probabilities of *n* customers in the system can be computed. The results from these computations are summarized in Table 12.6.

We can now compare the steady-state operating characteristics of the two-channel service operation to the operating characteristics of the original single-channel system discussed in Section 12.2.

1. The average time required between when a customer enters the waiting line and when the customer receives the order (waiting time plus service time) is reduced from $W = 4$ minutes to $W = 1.16$ minutes.
2. The average length of the waiting line is reduced from $L_q = 2.25$ customers to $L_q = 0.1227$ customer.
3. The average time a customer waits for service to begin is reduced from $W_q = 3$ minutes to $W_q = 0.16$ minute.
4. The percentage of customers having to wait for service is reduced from $P_w = 0.75$ or 75% to $P_w = 0.2045$ or 20.45%.

It is clear that the two-channel system will greatly improve the operating characteristics of the waiting line. However, we saw in the previous section that adding a separate order filler at each service station would increase the mean service rate and also improve the operating characteristics of the system. The final decision regarding the staffing policy at Burger Dome rests with the Burger Dome management. The waiting line study has simply provided the operating characteristics that can be anticipated under three configurations: a single-channel system with one or two employees and a two-channel system with a server for each channel. After considering these results, what action would you recommend? In this case, Burger Dome adopted the following policy statement: for periods when customer arrivals are expected to average 45 customers per hour, Burger Dome will open 2 cash-register, order-processing stations, with 1 employee assigned to each station.

By changing the mean arrival rate, λ, to reflect arrival rates at different times of the day, and then computing the operating characteristics, Burger Dome's management can establish guidelines and policies that tell the store managers when they should schedule service operations with a single channel, two channels, and perhaps even three or more channels.

▼ NOTES AND COMMENTS ▼

1. The multiple-channel waiting line model assumes a single waiting line. You may have also encountered situations where each of the k channels has its own waiting line. Management scientists have shown that the operating characteristics of multiple-channel systems are better if a single waiting line is used. People like them better also; no one who comes in after you can be served ahead of you. Thus, in practice, banks, airline reservation counters, food-service establishments, and other businesses typically use the single waiting line for a multiple-channel system.

2. The formulas given here will provide approximate results for multiple-channel systems with a line for each channel. The approximation will be best when service times are short. In this case the FCFS queue discipline is usually a reasonable assumption.

12.4 ▼ SOME GENERAL RELATIONSHIP FOR WAITING LINE MODELS

In Sections 12.2 and 12.3 we presented formulas for computing the operating characteristics for single-channel and multiple-channel waiting lines with Poisson arrivals and exponential service times. The primary operating characteristics of interest were

L_q = the average number of units in the waiting line

L = the average number of units in the system

W_q = the average time a unit spends in the waiting line

W = the average time a unit spends in the system

John D.C. Little showed that these four characteristics are related by some very general relationships, which apply to a variety of different waiting line models. Two of the general relationships, referred to as *Little's flow equations*, are as follows:

$$L = \lambda W \qquad (12.19)$$

$$L_q = \lambda W_q \qquad (12.20)$$

Equation (12.19) shows that the average number of units in the system, L, can be found by multiplying the mean arrival rate, λ, by the average time a unit spends in the system, W. Equation (12.20) shows that the same general relationship holds between the average number of units in the waiting line, L_q, and the average time a unit spends in the waiting line, W_q.

Using (12.20) and solving for W_q, we obtain

$$W_q = \frac{L_q}{\lambda} \qquad (12.21)$$

This equation, which follows directly from Little's flow equation [equation (12.20)], was used for the single-channel waiting line model in Section 12.2 and the multiple-channel waiting line model in Section 12.3 [see equations (12.7) and (12.14)]. Once L_q is computed for either of these models, equation (12.21) can then be used to compute W_q.

Another general expression that applies to waiting line models is that the average time in the system, W, is equal to the average time in the waiting line, W_q, plus the average service time. For a system with a mean service rate, μ, the average or mean service time is $1/\mu$. Thus, we have the following general relationship:

$$W = W_q + \frac{1}{\mu} \qquad (12.22)$$

Recall that this equation was used to provide the average time in the system for both the single-channel and the multiple-channel waiting line models [See equations (12.8) and (12.15)].

The importance of Little's flow equations is that they apply to *any waiting line model* regardless of whether or not arrivals follow the Poisson probability distribution and regardless of whether or not service times follow the exponential probability distribution. For example, in a study of the grocery checkout counters at Murphy's Foodliner, an analyst concluded that arrivals follow the Poisson probability distribution with the mean arrival rate of 24 customers per hour or $\lambda = 24/60 = 0.40$ customer per minute. However, the analyst found that service times follow a normal probability distribution rather than an exponential probability distribution. The mean service rate was found to be 30 customers per hour or $\mu = 30/60 = 0.50$ customer per minute. A time study of actual customer waiting times showed that, on average, a customer spends 4.5 minutes in the system (waiting time plus checkout time); that is, $W = 4.5$. Using the general waiting line relationships in this section, we can now compute the other operating characteristics for this waiting line situation.

First, using (12.22) and solving for W_q, we have

$$W_q = W - \frac{1}{\mu} = 4.5 - \frac{1}{0.50} = 2.5 \text{ minutes}$$

With both W and W_q known, we can use the flow equations [(12.19) and (12.20)] to compute

$$L = \lambda W = 0.40(4.5) = 1.8 \text{ customers}$$
$$L_q = \lambda W_q = 0.40(2.5) = 1 \text{ customer}$$

Murphy's manager can now review these operating characteristics to see if action should be taken to improve the service and to reduce the waiting time and the length of the waiting line.

▼ NOTES AND COMMENTS ▼

1. The advantage of the general relationships presented in this section is that W, L, W_q and L_q can be determined for any waiting line regardless of the arrival distribution, service time distribution, and number of channels. In fact, as soon as *any one* of the four operating characteristics—W, L, W_q, and L_q—has been determined, the other three can be computed. Thus, management scientists first compute the operating characteristic that is easiest to estimate. With the value of this operating characteristic and the basic relationships of this section, the other operating characteristics can be easily determined.

2. In waiting line systems where the length of the waiting line is limited (e.g., a small waiting area), some of the arriving units will be blocked from joining the waiting line and will be lost. In this case the blocked or lost arrivals will make the arrival rate in terms of units entering the system something less than the overall mean arrival rate. By defining λ as the mean rate for units *joining the system*, rather than the overall mean arrival rate, the relationships used in this section can be used to determine W, L, W_q, and L_q.

12.5 ▼ ECONOMIC ANALYSIS OF WAITING LINES

Frequently the decisions involving the design of waiting lines, such as determining the number of channels, will be based on a subjective evaluation of the waiting line characteristics. For example, a manager may decide that an average waiting time of 1 minute or less and an average of 2 customers or less in the system are reasonable goals for the system. The waiting line models presented in the preceding sections can be used to determine the number of channels to be used to meet the manager's waiting line performance goals.

In some instances it may be desirable to attempt to identify the cost of operating the waiting line system and then to make the decisions regarding the design of the system based on a minimum hourly or minimum daily operating cost criterion. In order to conduct an economic analysis of a waiting line system, a total cost model, which includes the cost of waiting and the cost of service, must be developed.

To develop a total cost model for a waiting line system, we begin by defining the following notation:

c_w = the waiting cost per time period for each unit

L = the average number of units in the system

c_s = the service cost per time period for each channel

k = the number of channels

TC = the total cost per time period

The total cost is the sum of the total waiting cost and the total service cost; that is,

$$TC = c_w L + c_s k \qquad (12.23)$$

A critical issue in conducting an economic analysis of a waiting line system is to be able to obtain reasonable estimates of the waiting cost per time period and the service cost per time period. Of these two costs, the waiting cost per time period is usually the more difficult to evaluate. In the Burger Dome restaurant example, the waiting cost per time period would be the cost per minute of a customer waiting for service. This cost is not a direct cost to Burger Dome. However, if Burger Dome ignores this cost and allows long waiting lines, customers will ultimately take their business elsewhere. Thus, Burger Dome will experience lost sales and in effect will incur a cost when the customer waits for service.

The service cost per time period is generally easier to determine. This cost is the variable or relevant cost associated with operating each service channel. In the Burger Dome example, this cost would include the server's wages, benefits, and any other direct

costs associated with operating the service channel. At Burger Dome, this cost is estimated to be $7 per hour.

In order to use (12.23), let us assume that Burger Dome is willing to assign an
opportunity cost of $10 per hour for customer waiting time. Using the average number of
units in the system, L, as computed in Sections 12.2 and 12.3, the total hourly cost for
the single-channel and two-channel systems would be as follows:

Single-channel system ($L = 3$ customers):

$$TC = c_w L + c_s k$$
$$TC = \$10(3) + \$7(1) = \$37.00 \text{ per hour}$$

Two-channel system ($L = 0.8727$ customers):

$$TC = c_w L + c_s k$$
$$= \$10(0.8727) + \$7(2) = \$22.73 \text{ per hour}$$

Thus, given the cost data provided by Burger Dome, the two-channel system provides the
most economical operation.

The general shapes of the cost curves in the economic analysis of waiting lines are
shown in Figure 12.3. The service cost increases as the number of channels is increased.
However, with more channels, the service is better. As a result, the waiting time, as well
as the waiting cost, decreases as the number of channels is increased. The number of

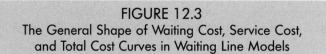

FIGURE 12.3
The General Shape of Waiting Cost, Service Cost,
and Total Cost Curves in Waiting Line Models

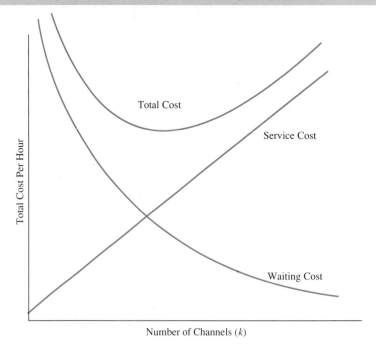

channels that will provide a good approximation of the minimum total cost design can be found by evaluating the total cost for several design alternatives.

▼ NOTES AND COMMENTS ▼

1. In dealing with many government agencies and utilities, customers cannot take their business elsewhere. In these situations no lost business occurs when long waiting times are encountered. This is one of the reasons why such organizations may tend to provide poor service and why customers in such situations experience long waiting times.

2. In some instances the organization providing the service also employs the units or customers waiting for the service. For example, consider the case of a company that owns and operates the trucks used to deliver goods to and from its manufacturing plant. In addition to the costs associated with the trucks waiting to be loaded or unloaded, the firm also pays the wages of the truck loaders and unloaders who operate the service channel. In this case, the cost of having the trucks wait and the cost of operating the service channel are direct expenses to the firm. An economic analysis of the waiting line system is highly recommended in these types of situations.

12.6 ▼ OTHER WAITING LINE MODELS

D. G. Kendall suggested a notation that is helpful in classifying the wide variety of different waiting line models that have been developed. The three-symbol Kendall notation is as follows:

$$A/B/s$$

where

A denotes the probability distribution for the number of arrivals

B denotes the probability distribution for the service time

s denotes the number of channels

Depending on the value of the letter appearing in the A or B position, a wide variety of waiting line systems can be simply described. The values for A and B that are commonly used are as follows:

M Designates a Poisson probability distribution for the number of arrivals or an exponential probability distribution for the service time

D Designates that the number of arrivals or the service time is deterministic or constant

G Designates a general distribution with a known mean and variance for the number of arrivals or the service time

Using the Kendall notation, the single-channel waiting line model with Poisson arrivals and exponential service times is classified as an $M/M/1$ model. The 2-channel waiting line model with Poisson arrivals and exponential service times, which we presented Section 12.3 for the Burger Dome problem, would be classified as an $M/M/2$ model.

▼ NOTES AND COMMENTS ▼

In some cases the Kendall notation is extended to five symbols. The fourth symbol indicates the largest number of units that can be in the system, and the fifth symbol indicates the size of the input or calling population. The fourth symbol is used in situations where the waiting line can hold a finite or maximum number of units, and the fifth symbol is necessary when the population of arriving units or customers is finite. When the fourth and fifth symbols of the Kendall notation are omitted, the waiting line system is assumed to have unlimited or infinite capacity, and the calling population is assumed to be infinite.

12.7 ▼ THE SINGLE-CHANNEL WAITING LINE MODEL WITH POISSON ARRIVALS AND ARBITRARY SERVICE TIMES

Let us return to the single-channel waiting line model where arrivals are described by a Poisson probability distribution. However, let us now assume that the probability distribution for the service times is not necessarily an exponential probability distribution. Thus, using the Kendall notation, the waiting line model that is appropriate is an $M/G/1$ model, where G denotes a general or unspecified probability distribution. Let us show how operating characteristics can be developed for the $M/G/1$ waiting line model.

Operating Characteristics for the M/G/1 Model

The following notation is used to describe the operating characteristics for the $M/G/1$ model:

$$\lambda = \text{the average or mean arrival rate}$$

$$\mu = \text{the average or mean service rate}$$

$$\frac{1}{\mu} = \text{the average or mean service time}$$

$$\sigma = \text{the standard deviation of the service time}$$

Using this notation, some of the steady-state operating characteristics of the $M/G/1$ waiting line model are as follows:

1. The probability that there are no units in the system

$$P_0 = 1 - \frac{\lambda}{\mu} \tag{12.24}$$

2. The average number of units in the waiting line

$$L_q = \frac{\lambda^2\sigma^2 + (\lambda/\mu)^2}{2(1 - \lambda/\mu)} \tag{12.25}$$

3. The average number of units in the system

$$L = L_q + \frac{\lambda}{\mu} \tag{12.26}$$

4. The average time a unit spends in the waiting line

$$W_q = \frac{L_q}{\lambda} \qquad (12.27)$$

5. The average time a unit spends in the system

$$W = W_q + \frac{1}{\mu} \qquad (12.28)$$

6. The probability that an arriving unit has to wait

$$P_w = \frac{\lambda}{\mu} \qquad (12.29)$$

Note that the relationships for L, W_q, and W are the same as the relationships used for the waiting line models of Sections 12.2 and 12.3. They are based on Little's flow equations.

An Example: Hartledge's Nut and Candy Shop is a specialty store located in a shopping mall. During the afternoon hours the store is staffed by one clerk. Customer arrivals are random, and the average arrival rate is 21 customers per hour or $\lambda = 21/60 = 0.35$ customer per minute. A study of the service process shows that the average or mean service time is 2 minutes per customer, with a standard deviation of $\sigma = 1.2$ minutes. The mean time of 2 minutes per customer shows that the clerk has a mean service rate of $\mu = \frac{1}{2} = 0.50$ customer per minute. The following calculations provide the operating characteristics of this $M/G/1$ waiting line system:

$$P_0 = 1 - \frac{\lambda}{\mu} = 1 - \frac{0.35}{0.50} = 0.30$$

$$L_q = \frac{(0.35)^2(1.2)^2 + (0.35/0.50)^2}{2(1 - 0.35/0.50)} = 1.11 \text{ customers}$$

$$L = L_q + \frac{\lambda}{\mu} = 1.11 + \frac{0.35}{0.50} = 1.81 \text{ customers}$$

$$W_q = \frac{L_q}{\lambda} = \frac{1.1107}{0.35} = 3.17 \text{ minutes}$$

$$W = W_q + \frac{1}{\mu} = 3.17 + \frac{1}{0.50} = 5.17 \text{ minutes}$$

$$P_w = \frac{\lambda}{\mu} = \frac{0.35}{0.50} = 0.70$$

Hartledge's manager can review these operating characteristics to determine if scheduling a second clerk appears worthwhile.

Constant Service Times

Let us comment briefly on the single-channel waiting line model that assumes arrivals are random, but service times are constant. Such a waiting line can occur in production and manufacturing environments where machine-controlled service times are constant. This waiting line situation is described by the $M/D/1$ model, with the D referring to the deterministic service times. With the $M/D/1$ model, the average number of units in the waiting line, L_q, can be found by using (12.25) with the condition that the standard deviation of the constant service time is $\sigma = 0$. Thus, the expression for the average number of units in the waiting line for the $M/D/1$ waiting line becomes

$$L_q = \frac{(\lambda/\mu)^2}{2(1 - \lambda/\mu)} \qquad (12.30)$$

The other expressions presented in this section can be used to determine the other operating characteristics of the $M/D/1$ system.

▼ NOTES AND COMMENTS ▼

Whenever the operating characteristics of a waiting line are unacceptable, managers often try to improve service by increasing the mean service rate, μ. While this is a good idea, equation (12.25) shows that the variation in the service times also affects the operating characteristics of the waiting line. Since the standard deviation of service times, σ, appears in the numerator of (12.25), we see that a larger variation in service times results in a larger average number of units in the waiting line. This fact suggests that a second alternative for improving the service capabilities of a waiting line is to reduce the variation in the service times. Thus, even when the mean service rate of the service facility cannot be increased, a reduction in σ will reduce the average number of units in the waiting line and, in general, improve the other operating characteristics of the system.

12.8 ▼ A MULTIPLE-CHANNEL MODEL WITH POISSON ARRIVALS, ARBITRARY SERVICE TIMES, AND NO WAITING LINE

An interesting variation of the waiting line models discussed thus far involves a system in which no waiting is allowed. Arriving units or customers seek service from one of several service channels. If all the channels are busy, any units that arrive are denied access to the system. In waiting line terminology, the arrivals occurring when the system is full are *blocked* and cleared from the system. Such customers may be lost or may attempt a return to the system at a later point in time.

The specific model considered in this section is based on the following assumptions:

1. The system has k channels.
2. The pattern of arrivals follows a Poisson probability distribution, with mean arrival rate, λ.
3. The service times for each channel may have any probability distribution.
4. The mean service rate, μ, is the same for each channel.
5. The arrivals enter the system only if at least one of the k channels is available. Arrivals occurring when all channels are busy are blocked, denied service, and not allowed to enter the system.

With G denoting a general or unspecified probability distribution for service times, the appropriate model for this type of situation is referred to as an $M/G/k$ model with "blocked customers cleared." The most common question addressed in this type of situation is, How many channels or servers should be employed?

One of the primary applications of this model involves the design of telephone and other communication systems where the arrivals are the calls and the channels are the number of telephone or communication lines available. In this system the calls are made to one telephone number, with each call automatically switched to an open channel if possible. When all channels are busy, additional calls receive a busy signal and are denied access to the system.

The Operating Characteristics for the *M/G/k* Model with Blocked Customers Cleared

The problem of selecting the best number of channels is approached by computing the steady-state probabilities that exactly *j* of the *k* channels will be busy. These probabilities are computed as follows:

$$P_j = \frac{(\lambda/\mu)^j/j!}{\displaystyle\sum_{i=0}^{k} (\lambda/\mu)^i/i!} \qquad (12.31)$$

where

λ = the mean arrival rate

μ = the mean service rate of each channel

k = the number of channels in the system

P_j = the probability that exactly *j* of the *k* channels are busy

for $j = 0, 1, 2, \ldots k$

Perhaps the most important probability calculation is P_k, which is the probability that all *k* channels are busy. On a percentage basis, P_k indicates the percentage of arrivals that are blocked and denied access to the system.

Another operating characteristic of interest for the above model is the average number of units in the system; note that this is equivalent to the average number of channels in use. Letting *L* denote the average number of units in the system, we have

$$L = \frac{\lambda}{\mu}(1 - P_k) \qquad (12.32)$$

An Example: Microdata Software, Inc., uses a telephone ordering system for its computer software products. Callers place orders with Microdata by using the company's 800 telephone number. Assume that calls to this telephone number arrive at the average rate of 12 per hour. The time required to process a telephone order varies considerably from order to order. However, each Microdata sales representative can be expected to handle an average of 6 calls per hour. Currently, the Microdata 800 telephone number has three internal lines or channels, each operated by a separate sales representative. Calls received on the 800 number are automatically transferred to one of the open lines or channels if available.

Whenever all three lines are busy, callers receive a busy signal. In the past, Microdata has assumed that callers receiving a busy signal will call back later. However, recent research on telephone ordering has shown that a substantial portion of callers who are denied access do not call back later. Since these lost calls represent lost revenues for the firm, Microdata's management has requested an analysis of the telephone ordering system. Specifically, the management would like to know the percentage of callers who are experiencing busy signals and are being blocked from the system. If management's goal is to provide sufficient capacity to handle 90% of the callers, how many telephone lines and sales representatives should Microdata use?

Let us demonstrate the use of (12.31) by computing P_3, the probability that all three of the currently available telephone lines will be in use and that the caller will be blocked.

$$P_3 = \frac{(12/6)^3/6}{(12/6)^0/1 + (12/6)^1/1 + (12/6)^2/2 + (12/6)^3/6} = \frac{1.3333}{6.3333} = 0.2105$$

With $P_3 = 0.2105$, we see that approximately 21% of the calls, or slightly more than one in five calls, are being blocked. Only 79% of the calls are being handled immediately by the three-telephone-line system.

Let us assume Microdata expands to a four-channel (or 4-line) system. The following calculation shows the probability that all four channels will be in use and that callers will be blocked.

$$P_4 = \frac{(12/6)^4/24}{(12/6)^0/1 + (12/6)^1/1 + (12/6)^2/2 + (12/6)^3/6 + (12/6)^4/24} = \frac{0.6667}{7} = 0.0952$$

With only 9.52% of the callers blocked, 90.48% of the callers will reach the Microdata sales representatives. Thus, Microdata should expand its order-processing operation to four lines in order to meet management's goal of providing sufficient capacity to handle at least 90% of the callers. The following calculation shows the average number of calls in the four-channel system and thus the average number of lines and sales representatives that will be busy.

$$L = \lambda/\mu(1 - P_4) = 12/6(1 - .0952) = 1.81$$

Although an average of less than 2 lines will be busy, the 4-line system is necessary to provide the capacity to handle at least 90% of the callers. By using equation (12.31), the probability that exactly j of the four channels will be busy can be computed. These probabilities are summarized in Table 12.7.

As we discussed in Section 12.5, economic analysis of waiting lines can be used to guide the system design decisions. In the Microdata system the cost of the additional line and additional sales representative should be relatively easy to establish. This cost can be balanced against the cost of the blocked calls. With 9.52% of the calls blocked and $\lambda = 12$ calls per hour, an 8-hour day will have an average of $8(12)(.0952) = 9.1$ blocked calls. If Microdata can estimate the cost of possible lost sales, the cost of these blocked calls can

TABLE 12.7
The Probability of the Number of Busy Lines for the Microdata 4-Line System

Number of Busy Lines	Probability
0	0.1429
1	0.2857
2	0.2857
3	0.1905
4	0.0952

be established. The economic analysis based on the service cost and the blocked-call cost can assist in determining the best number of lines for the system.

▼ NOTES AND COMMENTS ▼

Many of the operating characteristics we have considered in previous sections are not applicable for the *M/G/k* model with blocked customers cleared. In particular, the average time in the waiting line W_q, and the average number of units in the waiting line, L_q, are no longer considered because waiting is not permitted in this type of system.

12.9 ▼ WAITING LINE MODELS WITH FINITE CALLING POPULATIONS

For the waiting line models we have introduced thus far the population of units or customers arriving for service was considered unlimited. In technical terms, when there is no limit placed on how many units may seek service, the model is said to have an *infinite calling population*. Under this assumption, the mean arrival rate, λ, remains constant regardless of how many units are in the waiting line system. The assumption of an infinite calling population is made in most waiting line models.

In some cases the maximum number of units or customers that may seek service is fixed at a finite value. In this situation the mean arrival rate for the system changes depending on the number of units in the waiting line. Whenever a finite population is assumed, the waiting line model is said to have an *finite calling population*. The formulas for the operating characteristics of the previous waiting line models must be modified to account for the effect of the finite calling population.

The finite calling population model discussed in this section is based on the following assumptions:

1. The waiting line has a single channel.
2. The population of units that may seek service is finite.
3. The pattern of arrivals for *each unit* follows a Poisson probability distribution, with mean arrival rate, λ.
4. The service times follow an exponential probability distribution, with mean service rate, μ.
5. The queue discipline is first-come, first-served (FCFS).

The waiting line model that is appropriate in such cases is referred to as an *M/M/*1 model with a finite calling population.

Note that the mean arrival rate for the *M/M/*1 model with a finite calling population is defined in terms of how often *each unit* arrives or seeks service. This differs from previous waiting line models, which used λ to denote the mean arrival rate for the system. The difference in the definition of λ is due to the fact that with a finite calling population, the mean arrival rate for the system varies depending on how many units are in the system. Instead of trying to adjust for the changing system arrival rate, the finite calling population model uses λ to indicate the mean arrival on an individual unit basis. Each unit will be assumed to have the same arrival rate.

The Operating Characteristics for the M/M/1
Model with a Finite Calling Population

The formulas used to determine the steady-state operating characteristics for an $M/M/1$ model with a finite calling population use the following notation:

$$\lambda = \text{the mean arrival rate for each unit}$$
$$\mu = \text{the mean service rate}$$
$$N = \text{the size of the population}$$

1. The probability that there are no units in the system

$$P_0 = \frac{1}{\displaystyle\sum_{n=0}^{N} \frac{N!}{(N-n)!} \left(\frac{\lambda}{\mu}\right)^n} \tag{12.33}$$

2. The average number of units in the waiting line

$$L_q = N - \frac{\lambda + \mu}{\lambda}(1 - P_0) \tag{12.34}$$

3. The average number of units in the system

$$L = L_q + (1 - P_0) \tag{12.35}$$

4. The average waiting time in the waiting line

$$W_q = \frac{L_q}{(N - L)\lambda} \tag{12.36}$$

5. The average waiting time in the system

$$W = W_q + \frac{1}{\mu} \tag{12.37}$$

6. The probability of n units in the system

$$P_n = \frac{N!}{(N - n)!}\left(\frac{\lambda}{\mu}\right)^n P_0 \quad \text{for } n = 0, 1, \ldots N \tag{12.38}$$

One of the primary applications of the $M/M/1$ model with a finite calling population is referred to as the *machine repair problem*. In this problem a group of machines is considered the finite population of "customers" that may request repair service. Whenever a machine breaks down, an arrival occurs in the sense that a new repair request is initiated. If another machine breaks down before the repair work has been completed on the first machine, the second machine begins to form a "waiting line" as it waits for the repair service. Additional breakdowns by other machines will add to the length of the waiting line. The assumption of first-come, first-served indicates that machines are repaired in the order they break down. The $M/M/1$ model shows that one person or one channel is available to perform the repair service. In order to return the machine to operation, each machine with a breakdown must be handled by the single-channel repair operation.

An Example: The Kolkmeyer Manufacturing Company has a group of 6 identical machines; each machine operates an average of 20 hours between breakdowns. Thus, the mean arrival rate or request for repair service for each individual machine is $\lambda = \frac{1}{20} = 0.05$ machines per hour. With randomly occurring breakdowns, the Poisson probability distribution is used to describe the machine breakdown arrival process. One person from the maintenance department provides the single-channel repair service for the 6 machines. The exponentially distributed service times have a mean of 2 hours per machine or a mean service rate of $\mu = \frac{1}{2} = 0.50$ machines per hour.

With $\lambda = 0.05$ and $\mu = 0.50$, let us use equations (12.33) to (12.37) to compute the operating characteristics of the machine repair waiting line system. In using (12.33), you will note that the computations involved with the finite calling population model are somewhat cumbersome. Check for yourself to confirm that (12.30) provides the value $P_0 = 0.4845$. The computations for the other operating characteristics are shown below.

$$L_q = 6 - \left(\frac{0.05 + 0.50}{0.05}\right)(1 - 0.4845) = 0.3295 \text{ machine}$$

$$L = 0.3295 + (1 - 0.4845) = 0.845 \text{ machine}$$

$$W_q = \frac{0.3295}{(6 - 0.845)0.05} = 1.28 \text{ hours}$$

$$W = 1.28 + \frac{1}{0.50} = 3.28 \text{ hours}$$

Finally, (12.38) can be used to compute the probabilities of any number of machines being in the repair system.

FIGURE 12.4
Computer Printout of the Operating Characteristics for the Kolkmeyer Two-Channel Machine Repair Problem

```
WAITING LINE MODELS
*******************
    NUMBER OF CHANNELS = 2
    POISSON ARRIVALS WITH MEAN RATE = .05
    EXPONENTIAL SERVICE TIMES WITH MEAN RATE = .5 PER CHANNEL
    FINITE CALLING POPULATION OF SIZE = 6


OPERATING CHARACTERISTICS
-------------------------
THE PROBABILITY OF NO UNITS IN THE SYSTEM             0.5602
THE AVERAGE NUMBER OF UNITS IN THE WAITING LINE      0.0227
THE AVERAGE NUMBER OF UNITS IN THE SYSTEM            0.5661
THE AVERAGE TIME A UNIT SPENDS IN THE WAITING LINE   0.0834
THE AVERAGE TIME A UNIT SPENDS IN THE SYSTEM         2.0834
THE PROBABILITY THAT AN ARRIVING UNIT HAS TO WAIT    0.1036


Number of Units in the System            Probability
-----------------------------            -----------
              0                             0.5602
              1                             0.3361
              2                             0.0840
              3                             0.0168
              4                             0.0025
              5                             0.0003
              6                             0.0000
```

As with other waiting line models, the operating characteristics provide the manager with information about the waiting line operation. Whether or not these operating characteristics suggest that better repair service is needed depends on the cost of the idle machine waiting time compared to the cost of assigning an additional person in order to make the repair operation a two-channel system or a faster one-channel system.

Computations for the multiple-channel finite calling population model are more complex than those for the single-channel model. A computer solution is virtually mandatory in this case. The Management Scientist software package that accompanies this text has the capability of analyzing the finite calling population model. The computer output for the Kolkmeyer machine repair problem with a 2-person, 2-channel, repair system is shown in Figure 12.4.

▼ SUMMARY

In this chapter we have presented a variety of waiting line models that have been developed to help managers understand and make better decisions concerning the operation of waiting lines. For each model introduced, formulas were presented that could be used to develop operating characteristics for the waiting line system being studied. Some of the operating characteristics that were presented included the following:

1. The probability that there are no units in the system
2. The average number of units in the waiting line
3. The average number of units in the system
4. The average time a unit spends in the waiting line
5. The average time a unit spends in the system
6. The probability that arriving units will have to wait for service
7. The probability that the service facility is in use

We also showed how an economic analysis of the waiting line situation could be conducted by developing a total cost model that includes the cost associated with units waiting for service and the cost required to operate the service facility.

The complexity and diversity of waiting line systems found in practice often prevents an analyst from finding an existing waiting line model that fits the specific application being studied. Computer simulation, the topic discussed in the next chapter, provides another approach to determining the operating characteristics of waiting line systems. With computer simulation, a computer program is written that describes the logic of the waiting line system being studied. Then, by running the computer simulation program, data are collected on the usual waiting line operating characteristics, such as average waiting time, average number of units in the waiting line, average number of units in the system, and so on.

In general, waiting line models can be applied whenever arriving units seek service and are willing to or are required to wait for the service if it is not immediately available. As many of the examples in this chapter showed, the most obvious applications of waiting line models are when people or customers arrive for service, such as at a grocery checkout counter, bank, restaurant, and so on. However, with a little creativity, waiting line models can be applied to many different situations—for instance, telephone calls waiting for connections, mail orders waiting for processing, machines waiting for repairs, manufacturing jobs waiting to be processed, money waiting to be spent or invested, and so on.

▼ GLOSSARY

Queuing theory The body of knowledge dealing with waiting lines.

Queue A waiting line.

Single-channel A waiting line with only one service facility.

Multiple-channel A waiting line with two or more parallel service facilities.

Mean arrival rate The average number of customers or units arriving in a given period of time.

Mean service rate The average number of customers or units that can be serviced by one service facility in a given period of time.

Poisson probability distribution The probability distribution used to describe the random arrival pattern for some waiting line models.

Exponential probability distribution The probability distribution used to describe the pattern of service times for some waiting line models.

FCFS The queue discipline that orders service of the waiting units on a first-come, first-served basis.

Transient period The start-up period for a waiting line, occurring before the waiting line reaches a normal or steady-state period.

Steady-state period The normal operation of the waiting line after it has gone through a start-up or transient period. General operating characteristics of waiting lines are computed for steady-state conditions.

Blocking The condition that exists when arriving units cannot enter the waiting line system because the system is full. Blocking can occur when waiting lines are not allowed or when waiting lines have a finite capacity.

Infinite calling population The assumption made when the population of customers or units who may seek service does not have a specified upper limit.

Finite calling population The assumption made when the population of customers or units who may seek service has a fixed and finite value.

▼ PROBLEMS

1. Willow Brook National Bank operates a drive-in teller window, which allows customers to complete bank transactions without getting out of their cars. On weekday mornings, arrivals to the drive-in teller window occur at random, with a mean arrival rate of 24 customers per hour or 0.4 customer per minute.
   a. What is the mean or expected number of customers that will arrive in a 5-minute period?
   b. Since the arrival of customers is random, the Poisson probability distribution can be used to describe the arrival process. Using the mean in part (a), compute the probabilities that exactly 0, 1, 2, and 3 customers will arrive during a 5-minute period.
   c. Delay problems are expected if more than 3 customers arrive during any 5-minute period. What is the probability that delay problems will occur?

2. In the Willow Brook National Bank waiting line system (see problem 1), assume that the service times for the drive-in teller follow an exponential probability distribution with a mean service rate of 36 customers per hour or 0.6 customer per minute. Use the exponential probability distribution to answer the following questions:
   a. What is the probability that the service time is 1 minute or less?
   b. What is the probability that the service time is 2 minutes or less?
   c. What is the probability that the service time is more than 2 minutes?

3. Using the single-channel bank teller window operation referred to in problems 1 and 2, determine the following operating characteristics for the drive-in waiting line system:
   a. The probability that there are no customers in the system
   b. The average number of customers waiting
   c. The average number of customers in the system
   d. The average time a customer spends waiting
   e. The average time a customer spends in the system
   f. The probability that arriving customers will have to wait for service

4. Using the single-channel bank teller window operation referred to in problems 1, 2, and 3, find the probabilities of 0, 1, 2, and 3 customers in the system. What is the probability that more than 3 customers will be in the drive-in teller window system?

5. The reference desk of a university library receives requests for assistance. Assume that a Poisson probability distribution with a mean rate of 10 requests per hour can be used to describe the arrival pattern and that service times follow the exponential probability distribution, with a mean service rate of 12 requests per hour.
   a. What is the probability that there are no requests for assistance in the system?
   b. What is the average number of requests that will be waiting for service?
   c. What is the average waiting time in minutes before service begins?
   d. What is the average time at the reference desk in minutes (waiting time plus service time)?
   e. What is the probability that a new arrival has to wait for service?

6. Trucks using a single-channel loading dock arrive according to the Poisson probability distribution. The time required to load/unload follows the exponential probability distribution. The mean arrival rate is 12 trucks per day, and the mean service rate is 18 trucks per day.
   a. What is the probability that there are no trucks in the system?
   b. What is the average number of trucks waiting for service?
   c. What is the average time a truck waits for the loading/unloading service to begin?
   d. What is that probability that a new arrival will have to wait?

7. A mail-order nursery specializes in European beech trees. New orders, which are processed by a single shipping clerk, have a mean arrival rate of 6 per day and a mean service rate of 8 per day. Assume that arrivals follow a Poisson probability distribution and that service times follow an exponential probability distribution.
   a. What is the average number of orders in the system?
   b. What is the average time that an order spends waiting before the clerk is available to begin service?
   c. What is the average time an order spends in the system?

8. For the Burger Dome single-channel waiting line in Section 12.2, assume that the arrival rate is increased to 1 customer per minute and the mean service rate is increased to 1.25 customers per minute. Compute the following operating characteristics for the new system: P_0, L_q, L, W_q, W and P_w. Does this system provide better or poorer service as compared to the original system? Discuss any differences and the reason for these differences.

9. Marty's Barber Shop has one barber. Customers arrive at the rate of 2.2 customers per hour, and haircuts are given at the average rate of 5 per hour. Use the Poisson arrivals and exponential service times model to answer the following questions:
   a. What is the probability that there are no units in the system?
   b. What is the probability the 1 customer is receiving a haircut and no one is waiting?

c. What is the probability that 1 customer is receiving a haircut and 1 customer is waiting?

d. What is the probability that 1 customer is receiving a haircut and 2 customers are waiting?

e. What is the probability that more than 2 customers are waiting?

f. What is the average time a customer waits for service?

10. Trosper Tire Company has decided to hire a new mechanic to handle all tire changes for customers ordering a new set of tires. Two mechanics have applied for the job. One mechanic has limited experience and can be hired for $7 per hour. It is expected that this mechanic can service an average of 3 customers per hour. The other mechanic has several years of experience. This mechanic can service an average of 4 customers per hour, but must be paid $10 per hour. Assume that customers arrive at the Trosper garage at the rate of 2 customers per hour.

   a. Compute the waiting line characteristics for each mechanic, assuming Poisson arrivals and exponential service times.

   b. If the company assigns a customer waiting cost of $15 per hour, which mechanic provides the lower operating cost?

11. Agan Interior Design provides home and office decorating assistance for its customers. In normal operation an average of 2.5 customers arrive each hour. One design consultant is available to answer customer questions and make product recommendations. The consultant averages 10 minutes with each customer.

   a. Compute the operating characteristics of the customer waiting line, assuming Poisson arrivals and exponential service times.

   b. Service goals dictate that an arriving customer should not wait for service more than an average of 5 minutes. Is this goal being met? What action do you recommend?

   c. If the consultant can reduce the average time spent per customer to 8 minutes, what is the mean service rate? Will the service goal be met?

12. Pete's Market is a small local grocery store with only 1 checkout counter. Assume that shoppers arrive at the checkout lane according to the Poisson probability distribution, with a mean arrival rate of 15 customers per hour. The checkout service times follow an exponential probability distribution, with a mean service rate of 20 customers per hour.

   a. Compute the operating characteristics for this waiting line.

   b. If the manager's service goal is to limit the waiting time prior to beginning the checkout process to at most 5 minutes, what recommendations would you provide regarding the current checkout system?

13. After reviewing the waiting line analysis of problem 12, the manager of Pete's Market felt it would be desirable to improve service by considering one of the following alternatives:

   a. Hire a second person to bag the groceries while the cash-register operator is entering the cost data and collecting money from the customer. With this improved single-channel operation, the mean service rate could be increased to 30 customers per hour.

   b. Hire a second person to operate a second checkout counter. The two-channel operation would have a mean service rate of 20 customers per hour for each channel.

   What alternative would you recommend? Justify your recommendation.

14. Keuka Park Savings and Loan currently has one drive-in teller window. The arrivals follow a Poisson probability distribution, with a mean arrival rate of 10 cars per hour. The service times follow an exponential probability distribution, with a mean service rate of 12 cars per hour.

a. What is the probability there are no customers in the system?

b. If you were to drive up to the facility, how many cars would you expect to see waiting and being serviced?

c. What is the probability that at least one car will be waiting to be serviced?

d. What is the average time in the queue waiting for service?

e. As a potential customer of the system, would you be satisfied with the above waiting line characteristics?

15. In order to improve the service to the customer, Keuka Park Savings and Loan (see problem 14) wants to investigate the effect of a second drive-in teller window. Assume a mean arrival rate of 10 cars per hour. In addition, assume a mean service rate of 12 cars per hour for each drive-in window. What effect would the addition of a new teller window have on the system? Does this system appear acceptable?

16. Fore and Aft Marina is a newly planned marina that will be located on the Ohio River near Madison, Ind. Assume that Fore and Aft has decided to build a docking facility where one boat at a time can stop for gas and servicing. Assume that arrivals follow a Poisson probability distribution, with a mean of 5 boats per hour, and that service times follow an exponential probability distribution, with a mean of 10 boats per hour. Consider the following questions:

a. What is the probability that there are no boats in the system?

b. What is the average number of boats that will be waiting for service?

c. What is the average time a boat will spend waiting for service?

d. What is the average time a boat will spend at the dock?

e. If you were the management of Fore and Aft Marina, would you be satisfied with the service level your system would be providing?

17. The management of the Fore and Aft Marina in problem 16 wants to investigate the possibility of enlarging the docking facility so that two boats can stop for gas and servicing simultaneously. Assume that the mean arrival rate is 5 boats per hour and that the mean service rate for each of the channels is 10 boats per hour.

a. What is the probability that the boat dock will be idle?

b. What is the average number of boats that will be waiting for service?

c. What is the average time a boat will spend waiting for service?

d. What is the average time a boat will spend at the dock?

e. If you were the manager of Fore and Aft Marina, would you be satisfied with the service level your system will be providing?

18. The City Beverage Drive-Thru is considering a two-channel service system. Cars arrive according to the Poisson probability distribution, with a mean arrival rate of 6 cars per hour. The service times have an exponential probability distribution, with a mean service rate of 10 cars per hour for each channel.

a. What is the probability there are no cars in the system?

b. What is the average number of cars waiting for service?

c. What is the average time waiting for service?

d. What is the average time in the system?

e. What is the probability that an arrival will have to wait for service?

19. Consider a two-channel waiting line with Poisson arrivals and exponential service times. The mean arrival rate is 14 units per hour, and the mean service rate is 10 units per hour for each channel.

a. What is the probability that there are no units in the system?

b. What is the average number of units in the system?

c. What is the average time a unit waits for service?

d. What is the average time a unit is in the system?

e. What is the probability of having to wait for service?

20. Refer to problem 19. Assume that the system is expanded to a three-channel operation.

   a. Compute the operating characteristics for this waiting line system.

   b. If the service goal is to provide sufficient capacity so that at most 25% of the customers have to wait for service, is the two-channel or the three-channel system preferred?

21. Refer to the Agan Interior Design situation in problem 11. Agan would like to evaluate two alternatives:

   (1) Use one consultant with an average service time of 8 minutes per customer.

   (2) Expand to two consultants, each of whom has an average service time of 10 minutes per customer.

   If the consultants are paid $16 per hour and the customer waiting time is valued at $25 per hour for waiting time prior to service, should Agan expand to the two–design consultant system? Explain.

22. A fast-food franchise is considering operating a drive-up window food service operation. Assume that customer arrivals follow a Poisson probability distribution, with a mean arrival rate of 24 cars per hour, and that service times follow an exponential probability distribution. Arriving customers place orders at an intercom station at the back of the parking lot and then drive up to the service window to pay for and receive their order. The following three service alternatives are being considered:

   (1) A single-channel operation where one employee fills the order and takes the money from the customer. The average service time for this alternative is 2 minutes.

   (2) A single-channel operation where one employee fills the order while a second employee takes the money from the customer. The average service time for this alternative is 1.25 minutes.

   (3) A two-channel operation with two service windows and two employees. The employee stationed at each window fills the order and takes the money for customers arriving at the window. The average service time for this alternative is 2 minutes for each channel.

   Compute the following operating characteristics for each alternative, and recommend an alternative design for the fast-food franchise:

   a. What is the probability that there are no customers in the system?

   b. What is the average number of cars waiting for service?

   c. What is the average time a car waits for service?

   d. What is the average time in the system?

   e. What is the average number of cars in the system?

   f. What is the probability an arriving car will have to wait for service?

23. The following cost information is available for the fast-food franchise in problem 22.

   ● Customer waiting time is valued at $25.00 per hour to reflect the fact that waiting time is costly to the fast-food business.

   ● The cost of each employee is $6.50 per hour.

   ● To account for equipment and space, an additional cost of $20.00 per hour is attributable to each channel.

   What is the lowest-cost design for the fast-food business?

24. Patients arrive at a dentist's office at the mean rate of 2.8 patients per hour. The dentist can service patients at the mean rate of 3 patients per hour. A study of patient waiting times shows that, on average, a patient waits 30 minutes before seeing the dentist.

   a. What are the mean arrival rate and the mean service rate in terms of patients per minute?

b. What is the average number of patients in the waiting room?

c. If a patient arrives at 10:10 A.M., what is the expected time the patient will leave the office?

25. A study of the multichannel food-service operation at the Red Birds' baseball park shows that the average time between the arrival of a customer at the food-service counter and his or her departure with a filled order is 10 minutes. During the game, customers arrive at the average rate of 4 per minute. The food service operation requires an average of 2 minutes per customer order.

    a. What is the mean service rate per channel in terms of customers per minute?

    b. What is average waiting time in the line prior to placing an order?

    c. On average, how many customers are in the food-service system?

26. Tri-County Autos operates an automotive service counter. While completing the repair work, Tri-County mechanics arrive at the company's parts department counter at the mean rate of 4 per hour. The parts coordinator spends an average of 6 minutes with each mechanic, discussing what parts the mechanic needs and retrieving the parts from inventory.

    a. Currently there is one parts coordinator. On average, each mechanic waits 4 minutes before the parts coordinator is available to answer questions and/or retrieve parts from inventory. Find L_q, W, and L for this single-channel parts operation.

    b. A trial period with a second parts coordinator showed that, on average, each mechanic waited only 1 minute before a parts coordinator was available. Find L_q, W, and L for this two-channel parts operation.

    c. If the cost of each mechanic is $20 per hour and the cost of each parts coordinator is $12 per hour, is the one-channel or the two-channel system the more economical?

27. Gubser Welding, Inc., operates a welding service for construction and automotive repair jobs. Assume that the arrival of jobs at the company's office can be described by a Poisson probability distribution with a mean arrival rate of 2 jobs per eight-hour day. The time required to complete the jobs follows a normal probability distribution with a mean time of 3.2 hours and a standard deviation of 2 hours. Answer the following questions assuming Gubser uses one welder to complete all jobs.

    a. What is the mean arrival rate in jobs per hour?

    b. What is the mean service rate in jobs per hour?

    c. What is the average number of jobs waiting for service?

    d. What is the average time a job waits before the welder can begin working on it?

    e. What is the average number of hours between when a job is received and when it is completed?

    f. What percentage of the time is the Gubser welder busy?

28. Jobs arrive randomly at a particular assembly plant; assume that the mean arrival rate is 5 jobs per hour. Service times do not follow the exponential probability distribution. Two proposed designs for the plant's assembly operation are shown below.

| Design | Service Times (in minutes per job) | |
	Mean	Standard Deviation
A	6.0	3.0
B	6.25	0.6

a. What is the mean service rate in jobs per hour for each of the designs?

b. Using the mean service rates in part (a), what design appears to provide the best or fastest service rate?

c. What are the standard deviations of the service times expressed in hours?

d. Use the $M/G/1$ model in Section 12.7 to compute the operating characteristics for each of the designs.

e. Which design provides the best operating characteristics? Why?

29. The Burger Dome single-channel waiting line model discussed in Section 12.2 has a mean arrival rate of 0.75 customer per minute and a mean service rate of 1 customer per minute. The model was based on the assumption of Poisson arrivals and exponential service times. The mean service rate of 1 customer per minute implies that the standard deviation of service times is 1 minute. Burger Dome is considering a new computerized cash-register, order-taking system that will maintain the current mean service mean rate of 1 customer per minute. However, the standard deviation of service times for the new system will be reduced to 0.50 minute. Use the $M/G/1$ waiting line model to determine if the proposed system is worthwhile. In what ways, if any, will the proposed system improve the operating characteristics of the waiting line?

30. A large insurance company has a central computing system which contains a variety of information about customer accounts. Insurance agents, located throughout a 6-state area use telephone lines to access the customer information database. Currently the company's central computer system allows 3 simultaneous users to access the central computer. Agents who attempt to use the system when it is full are denied access; no waiting is allowed. The company realizes that with its expanding business, more requests will be made to the central information system. Being denied access to the system is inefficient as well as annoying for the agents. Access requests follow a Poisson probability distribution, with a mean of 42 calls per hour. The mean service rate per line is 20 calls per hour.

a. What is the probability that 0, 1, 2, and 3 access lines will be in use?

b. What is the probability that an agent will be denied access to the system?

c. What is the average number of access lines in use?

d. In planning for the future, the company would like to be able to handle a mean of 50 calls per hour; in addition, the probability that an agent will be denied access to the system should be no greater than your answer to part (b). How many access lines should this system have?

31. Mid-West Publishing Company publishes college textbooks. The company operates an 800 telephone number where potential adopters can ask questions about forthcoming texts, request examination copies of texts, and place orders. Currently, two extension lines are used, with two representatives handling the telephone inquiries. Calls occurring when both extension lines are being used receive a busy signal; no waiting is allowed. Each representative can accommodate an average of 12 calls per hour.

a. If the mean arrival rate is 20 calls per hour, what percentage of the calls receive a busy signal?

b. How many extensions should be used if the company would like to handle 90% of the calls immediately?

c. What is the average number of extensions that will be busy if your recommendation in part (b) is used?

32. City Cab, Inc., uses two dispatchers to handle requests for service and dispatch the cabs. The telephone calls that are made to City Cab use a common telephone number. When both dispatchers are busy, the caller hears a busy signal; no waiting is allowed.

Callers who receive a busy signal can call back later or call another cab service. Assume that the arrival of calls follows a Poisson probability distribution, with mean of 40 calls per hour, and that each dispatcher can handle a mean of 30 calls per hour.

a. What percentage of the time are both dispatchers idle?

b. What percentage of the time are both dispatchers busy?

c. What is the probability callers will receive a busy signal if 2, 3, or 4 dispatchers are used?

d. If the company wants at most 12% of the callers to receive a busy signal, how many dispatchers should be used?

33. Kolkmeyer Manufacturing Company (see Section 12.9) is considering adding 2 machines to its manufacturing operations; this will bring the number of machines to 8. Mr. Andrew, the president of Kolkmeyer, has asked for a study of the need to add a second employee to the repair process. The mean arrival rate is 0.05 machines per hour for each machine, and the mean service rate for each individual assigned to the repair operation is 0.50 machines per hour.

a. Compute the following operating characteristics if the company retains the single-employee repair service:
   - The probability that all machines are in operation and the repair person is idle
   - The average number of machines waiting for repair
   - The average number of machines down (those waiting plus those being serviced)
   - The averaging waiting time before repair can begin
   - The average down time (waiting time plus servicing time)

b. Use The Management Scientist software package to compute the above characteristics if a second employee is added to the machine repair operation.

c. Each employee assigned to the service operation is paid $20 per hour. Machine down time is valued at $80 per hour. From an economic point of view, should 1 or 2 employees handle the machine repair operation?

34. Five secretaries use an office copier. The average time between arrivals for each secretary is 40 minutes, which is equivalent to a mean arrival rate of $1/40 = 0.025$ arrivals per minute. The mean time each secretary spends at the copier is 5 minutes, which is equivalent to a mean service rate of $1/5 = 0.20$ users per minute. Use the $M/M/1$ model with a finite calling population to determine the following:

a. The probability that the copier is idle

b. The average number of secretaries in the waiting line

c. The average number of secretaries at the copier

d. The average time a secretary spends waiting for the copier

e. The average time a secretary spends at the copier

f. During an 8-hour day, how many minutes does a secretary spend at the copier? How much of this time is waiting time?

g. Should the company consider purchasing a second copier? Explain.

35. Schips Department Store operates a fleet of 10 trucks. The trucks arrive at random times throughout the day at the store's truck dock to be loaded with new deliveries or to have incoming shipments from the regional warehouse unloaded. Each truck returns to the truck dock for service 2 times per 8-hour day. Thus, the mean arrival rate per truck is 0.25 trucks per hour. The mean service rate is 4 trucks per hour. Using the Poisson arrivals and exponential service times model with a finite calling population of 10 trucks, determine the following operating characteristics:

a. The probability no trucks are at the truck dock

b. The average number of trucks waiting for loading/unloading

c. The average number of trucks in the truck dock area
d. The average waiting time before loading/unloading begins
e. The average waiting time in the system
f. What is the hourly cost of operation if the cost is $50 per hour for each truck and $30 per hour for the truck dock?
g. In considering a two-channel truck dock operation where the second channel could be operated for an additional $30 per hour, what would be the average number of trucks waiting for loading/unloading have to be reduced to with the two-channel operation to make the two-channel truck dock economically feasible?
h. Should the company consider expanding to the two-channel truck dock? Explain.

▼ CASE PROBLEM

Airline Reservations

Regional Airlines is establishing a new telephone system for handling flight reservations. During the 10:00 A.M. to 11:00 A.M. time period, calls to the reservation agent occur randomly at an average of 1 call every 3.75 minutes. Historical service time data show that a reservation agent spends an average of 3 minutes with each customer. The waiting line model assumptions of Poisson arrivals and exponential service times appear reasonable for the telephone reservation system.

Regional Airlines' management feels that offering an efficient telephone reservation system is an important part of establishing an image as a service-oriented airline. If the system is properly implemented, Regional Airlines will establish good customer relations, which in the long run will increase business. However, if the telephone reservation system is frequently overloaded and customers have difficulty contacting an agent, a negative customer reaction may lead to an eventual loss of business. The cost of a ticket reservation agent is $20 per hour. Thus, management wants to provide good service, but does not want to incur the cost of overstaffing the telephone reservation operation by using more agents than necessary.

At a planning meeting, Regional's management team agreed that an acceptable customer service goal is to answer at least 85% of the incoming calls immediately. During the planning meeting, Regional's vice president of administration pointed out that the data show that the average service rate for an agent is faster than the average arrival rate of the telephone calls. His conclusion was that the personnel costs could be minimized by using 1 agent and that the 1 agent should be able to handle the telephone reservations and still have some idle time. The vice president of marketing restated the importance of customer service and expressed support for at least two reservation agents.

The current telephone reservation system design does not allow callers to wait. Callers who attempt to reach a reservation agent when all agents are occupied receive a busy signal and are blocked from the system. A representative from the telephone company suggested that Regional Airlines consider an expanded system that will accommodate waiting. In this case, if a customer calls and all agents are busy, a recorded message tells the customer that the call is being held in the order received and that an agent will be available shortly. The customer can stay on the line and listen to background music while waiting for an agent. Regional's management will need more information before switching to the system that permits waiting.

MANAGERIAL REPORT

Prepare a managerial report for Regional Airlines analyzing the telephone reservation system. Evaluate both the system that does not allow waiting and the system that allows waiting. Include the following information in your report:

1. A detailed analysis of the operating characteristics of the reservation system with 1 agent as proposed by the vice president of administration. What is your recommendation concerning a 1-agent system?
2. A detailed analysis of the operating characteristics of the reservation system based on your recommendation regarding the number of agents Regional should use and whether or not the system should allow customers to wait.
3. What appear to be the advantages or disadvantages of the system that allows waiting? If the system that allows waiting were to be used, discuss the number of waiting callers the system will need to accommodate.
4. The telephone arrival data presented above are for the 10:00 A.M. to 11:00 A.M. time period; however, the arrival rate of incoming calls is expected to change from hour to hour. Describe how your waiting line analysis could be used to develop a ticket agent staffing plan that would enable the company to provide different levels of staffing for the ticket reservation system at different times during the day. Indicate the information that you would need to develop this staffing plan.

Goodyear Tire & Rubber Company*

Akron, Ohio

The Goodyear Tire & Rubber Company* had its beginning in an old converted strawboard factory in 1898. Its first product was bicycle tires. Since 1926 it has been the world's largest rubber company and one of the nation's leading industrial corporations.

Although tires are Goodyear's biggest single product line, the company has become a highly diversified corporate enterprise. The company's product line has changed from the original bicycle tires, carriage tires, and horseshoe pads to tires of all types, chemicals, industrial rubber products, defense products, packaging films, foam cushioning, shoe soles and heels, flooring and counter tops, metal rims and wheels, aircraft brakes and wheels, aerospace products, and atomic energy.

Goodyear has more than 129 production facilities—about half in the United States and half overseas—and approximately 155,000 employees. Its sales and distribution operations cover virtually all areas of the free world. Corporate headquarters are in Akron, Ohio.

Familiar to millions of people are the company airships, named the *Enterprise, Columbia,* and *America,* which are stationed in the United States, and the *Europa,* which is stationed in Europe. These airships are made by Goodyear Aerospace Corporation, a subsidiary of The Goodyear Tire & Rubber Company.

MANAGEMENT SCIENCE AT GOODYEAR

Goodyear has many departments that make use of management science applications. Most analyses are performed by one of the computer programming departments under the guidance of a user (client) department. These computer programming departments are involved in a variety of applications from routine data collection and systems maintenance to queuing analysis. For example, one department is responsible for maintaining a system that gathers records of orders and sales, another department is responsible for forecasting and assisting production schedulers, and a third department is responsible for quality control. The waiting line (queuing) application discussed in the remainder of this presentation is the responsibility of yet another department. Many of the applications performed by the departments are interrelated, and one department will often use data generated by another department.

A WAITING LINE APPLICATION

The application discussed involves a system for dispatching maintenance personnel to fix machines. Under the manual system, whenever a machine needed repair, a

*The authors are indebted to Dr. Walt Fenske of The Goodyear Tire & Rubber Company for providing this application.

production supervisor used a phone intercom system to call an individual referred to as a dispatcher. The dispatcher recorded the information provided by the production supervisor on cards. Then, whenever maintenance personnel called the dispatcher to request a new assignment, the information on these cards was used by the dispatcher to tell the maintenance personnel which machine should be repaired.

Due primarily to a need to develop a computerized database that could be analyzed to improve the maintenance function, Goodyear decided to replace the manual system with a computer-controlled system. In the computer-controlled system the dispatcher function is performed by a person called a coordinator. The function of the coordinator is to enter service information when received into the computer, using a remote computer terminal. The need for more information to be entered causes the coordinator's task to be more time consuming than the dispatcher's function in the old system. However, the computer-controlled system offers many potential advantages in other areas because of the wide variety of information entered by the coordinator.

A waiting line model was used in designing the computer-controlled system. The problem to be solved was to determine how many coordinators (and, consequently, remote computer terminals) were needed. If there are not enough coordinators, production supervisors and maintenance personnel will have difficulty reaching a coordinator. If the computer system is to be a success, people trying to reach the coordinator should not have long waits. However, if there are too many coordinators, excessive coordinator and computer terminal expenses will be incurred. Some of the questions that had to be answered were the following:

1. What percentage of the time will the coordinator be busy?
2. What is the maximum number of people waiting to reach the coordinator?
3. What is the average time spent waiting to reach the coordinator?
4. How many calls does the coordinator receive?
5. How many callers have to wait longer than 4 minutes to reach the coordinator?
6. How many callers do not have to wait to reach the coordinator?

These questions suggest that the design of the new system may be aided through the use of a waiting line model. In a waiting line model of this situation the coordinators are the servers, and the people waiting to talk to the coordinators constitute the units in the waiting line. Thus, if 1 coordinator is used, the model is a single-channel waiting line model. Otherwise, it is a multiple-channel waiting line model.

The complexity of the proposed computer system can best be understood by considering the four types of arrivals that must be handled. The first type of arrival is a call received from a production supervisor stating that a machine needs repair. At this time a *work order is initiated*. The second type of arrival is a call from a maintenance person stating that the repair work is being started; this is referred to as *placing the work order in process*. The third type of arrival, referred to as *completing a work order*, is a call from a maintenance person stating that the repair work has been completed. The fourth type of arrival is any other type of call. Note that each work order generates three calls to the coordinator.

For this problem the arrivals were known to differ from the Poisson probability distribution. In addition, there were a number of other complicating factors that precluded the use of the waiting line models introduced in this chapter. However, a simulation model of the system, built on many of the basic waiting line principles in this chapter, was implemented. The General Purpose Simulation System (GPSS) was the programming language used for the simulation model.

Computer simulation runs were performed for a system with 1 coordinator and a system with 2 coordinators. In the 1-coordinator system the simulation runs showed that the coordinator would be busy about 69% of the time and that the average waiting time to reach the coordinator would be 4.9 minutes. The average waiting time for the 1-coordinator system was considered to be much too high.

For the 2-coordinator system the simulation results indicated that each coordinator would be busy approximately 35% of the time. However, the average waiting time to reach a coordinator dropped to 42 seconds. In fact, it was found that a call would get through immediately about 90% of the time. Since management believed that these times were reasonable, the system was designed to have 2 coordinators and 2 remote computer terminals.

Questions

1. What is the primary reason that Goodyear decided to replace the manual system with a computer-controlled system?
2. What factors in this application led to the use of a simulation model rather than an analytical model of the waiting line?

13

Computer Simulation

Computer simulation is a method that can be used to study the performance of a real-world system. First, a computer simulation model that "behaves likes" or simulates the real system is developed; at this stage, great care is taken to ensure that the computer simulation model is descriptive of the real system. Then through a series of computer runs, or experiments, we learn about the behavior of the simulation model. The characteristics that are observed in the model are then used to make inferences about the real system.

The surveys of current uses of management science referred to in Chapter 1 indicate that computer simulation is one of the most frequently used management science tools. For example, computer simulation models have been developed for each of the following situations:

1. Simulating traffic flow through a busy intersection. The objective is to determine whether or not putting in a left turn signal will improve traffic flow.
2. Simulating the behavior of an inventory system. The objective is to determine the best order quantity and reorder point.
3. Simulating earthquake behavior. The objective is to improve the capability to respond to natural disasters.
4. Simulating airplane flight conditions. The objective is to train future pilots.
5. Simulating the operation of an integrated pulp and paper mill facility. The objective is to determine the benefits of expanding the production operation.

Computer simulation should not be viewed as an optimization technique. For instance, examples 3 and 4 above (simulating earthquake behavior and simulating airplane flight conditions) have nothing to do with optimizing. On the other hand, the simulation models in examples 1, 2, and 5 above were developed with an objective of improving the behavior of a system. In many applications where a simulation model has been developed, it is natural to think in terms of adjusting the parameters of the model in order to improve the performance of the system. When good parameter settings have been found for the model, these settings can be used to improve the performance of the real system.

Computer simulation can also be used to model the performance of a waiting line system. In Chapter 12 we showed how analytic procedures based on the use of mathematical formulas could be used to evaluate waiting line systems. The mathematics involved for simple waiting line systems are difficult enough; for more complex systems, analytic procedures are more difficult and may not be available. Thus, computer simulation is often used to evaluate and improve the operation of complex waiting line systems.

In the material that follows, we introduce the concepts and procedures of computer simulation by studying how computer simulation can be applied to waiting line systems and to inventory systems. Analytical techniques for these systems have been presented in Chapters 11 and 12. These analytical techniques should be used whenever the assumptions underlying the techniques are adequate approximations of the real-world system. If this is not the case, the computer simulation approach described in this chapter is a viable alternative to modeling the real-world system.

13.1 ▼ COUNTY BEVERAGE DRIVE-THRU

County Beverage Drive-Thru, Inc., is a company that is building a chain of beverage supply stores throughout an area in northern Illinois. The stores are designed to enable customers to pick up beverages, snacks, and party supplies without getting out of their cars. A typical store design is shown in Figure 13.1. A service lane runs through the middle of the store, and soft drinks, beer, and other supplies are stored at various locations along both sides of the service lane. When a customer drives into the store, the store clerk takes the order, fills the order, and collects the money. The customer remains in the car while receiving service. When additional customers arrive at the store, they wait in a line outside the store until the preceding customer's order is complete. Then the next customer in line drives into the store for service.

The County Beverage Drive-Thru operation is a *waiting line* or *queuing system*. This particular waiting line configuration has one service lane and is therefore a *single-channel waiting line* with a first-come, first-served (FCFS) queue discipline. If we are willing to assume that the number of cars arriving at the store has a Poisson probability distribution and that the length of time that the customer is actually in the store (service time) has an exponential probability distribution, the mathematical models presented in the previous chapter can be used to study this waiting line system. However, for the County Beverage Drive-Thru we are not willing to make these assumptions; thus, we will be using computer simulation to study the operation of the store.

FIGURE 13.1
Layout of County Beverage Drive-Thru

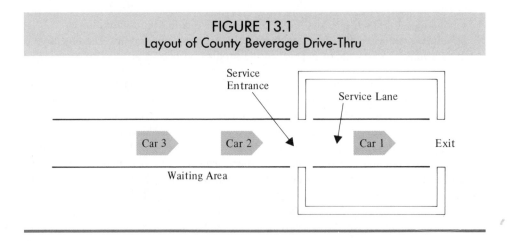

The specific situation we will simulate is a new store that will be located near a major shopping center. Construction of the store will not begin for approximately 3 months. County Beverage's president has requested planning information on the projected operation of the store, including estimates of the number of customers served, the profitability of the store, and the number of lost sales due to long waiting lines.

In modeling the system we will study the store's operation in terms of what happens during time periods of 3 minutes each. That is, we will count the number of customer arrivals, count the number of customers lost, and determine whether or not a customer is being serviced during each 3-minute interval. A simulation model, such as this, that increments time in fixed intervals is referred to as a *fixed-time simulation model*. Simulation models that increment time based on the occurrence of the next event (time of next arrival, time of next service, and so on) are referred to as *next-event simulation models*.

Based on a study of traffic flow, the company has estimated that the probability distribution of customer arrivals is as shown in Table 13.1. This probability distribution is believed to be representative of the number of arrivals during the peak business period occurring in the late afternoon and early evening. As the data show, there is a 0.19 probability of no customers arriving during a given 3-minute period, a 0.39 probability of 1 customer arriving during the same 3-minute period, and so on.

Sales records from the company's other stores show customer variability in terms of the size of the order placed. For three classes of order size (small, medium, and large), the probability for the various order sizes, the average time to fill the orders, and the average profit per order are shown in Table 13.2.

As an additional operating condition, experience with other company stores indicates that customers will wait for service only if there are less than 4 cars in the waiting line. If a customer arrives and there are already 4 cars in the waiting area, the customer will drive off. This failure to enter the waiting line is referred to as *balking* and results in a lost customer and thus an opportunity loss corresponding to the lost profit.

Simulation of Customer Arrivals and Order Sizes

Before developing the complete simulation model, let us concentrate on simulating the number of customers that arrive at the store during any 3-minute period. In simulating the customer arrival process for County Beverage we will also be demonstrating how the probabilistic component of a real-world system is modeled.

TABLE 13.1
Probability Distribution for the Number of Customers Arriving at the County Beverage Drive-Thru During a 3-Minute Period

Number of Customers Arriving	Probability
0	0.19
1	0.39
2	0.19
3	0.15
4	0.08
	1.00

TABLE 13.2
Order Size Data for the County Beverage Drive-Thru

Order Size	Probability	Average Time to Fill Order	Average Profit
Small	0.39	3 minutes	$0.75
Medium	0.50	6 minutes	$1.50
Large	0.11	9 minutes	$3.00
	1.00		

The technique used to simulate customer arrivals is based on the use of random numbers. Almost everyone who has been exposed to simple random sampling and basic statistics is familiar with tables of random digits or random numbers.[1] We have included a table of random numbers in Appendix B. Twenty random numbers from the first line of this table are as follows:

$$63271 \qquad 59986 \qquad 71744 \qquad 51102$$

The digit appearing in a given position is a random selection of the digits 0, 1, 2, . . . , 9, with each digit having an equal chance of appearing. The grouping of the numbers in sets of five is simply for the convenience of making the table easier to read.

Suppose we select random numbers from the table in sets of 2 digits. There are 100 2-digit random numbers from 00 to 99, with each 2-digit random number having a $1/100 = 0.01$ chance of occurring. While we could select 2-digit random numbers from any part of the random number table, suppose we start by using the first row of random numbers from Appendix B. The first 10 2-digit random numbers are

$$63 \quad 27 \quad 15 \quad 99 \quad 86 \quad 71 \quad 74 \quad 45 \quad 11 \quad 02$$

Now let us see how we can simulate the number of customers arriving in a 3-minute period by associating a given number of arrivals with each of the 100 2-digit random numbers. For example, let us consider the possibility of no customers arriving during a 3-minute interval. The probability distribution in Table 13.1 shows this event to have a 0.19 probability. Since each 2-digit random number has a 0.01 probability of occurrence, we can let 19 of the 100 possible 2-digit random numbers correspond to no customers arriving. Any 19 numbers from 00 to 99 will do, but for convenience we associate the arrival of 0 customers with the first 19 2-digit numbers: 00, 01, 02, 03, . . . , 18. Thus, any time one of these 2-digit numbers is observed in a random selection, we will say that no customers arrived. Since the numbers 00 to 18 include 19% of the possible 2-digit random numbers, we expect the arrival of no customers for any given 3-minute interval to have a probability of 0.19.

Now consider the possibility of 1 customer arriving during a 3-minute period, an event that has a 0.39 probability of occurring (see Table 13.1). Letting 39 of the 100 2-digit numbers (such as 19, 20, 21, 22, . . . , 57) correspond to a simulated arrival of 1 customer will provide a 0.39 probability for 1 customer arrival. Continuing to assign the number of customers arriving to sets of 2-digit numbers according to the probability

[1]See, for example, *A Million Random Digits with 100,000 Normal Deviates,* (Rand Corporation, 1983).

distribution shown in Table 13.1 results in the sets of random numbers and customer arrival assignments shown in Table 13.3.

Using Table 13.3 and the 2-digit random numbers in the first row of Appendix B (63, 27, 15, 99, 86, . . .), we can simulate the number of customers arriving during the 3-minute periods. The results for 10 such 3-minute periods, or 1/2 hour of store operation, are shown in Table 13.4. The first 2-digit random number, 63, is in the interval 58 to 76; thus, according to Table 13.3 this corresponds to 2 customers arriving during the first 3-minute period. The second random number, 27, is in the interval 19 to 57; thus, the number of simulated customer arrivals during the second period is 1, and so on.

By selecting a 2-digit random number for each 3-minute period, we can simulate the number of customer arrivals for as many 3-minute periods as desired. In doing so, the simulated probability distribution for customer arrivals will be the same as the actual probability distribution shown in Table 13.1. A simulation model that involves generating probabilistic inputs such as the number of customer arrivals is referred to as a *Monte Carlo simulation*.

TABLE 13.3
Random Number Assignments for the Number of Customers Arriving at the County Beverage Drive-Thru During a 3-Minute Time Period

Number of Customers	Associated 2-Digit Random Numbers	Interval Description	Probability
0	00, 01, . . . , 18	00 but less than 19	0.19
1	19, 20, . . . , 57	19 but less than 58	0.39
2	58, 59, . . . , 76	58 but less than 77	0.19
3	77, 78, . . . , 91	77 but less than 92	0.15
4	92, 93, . . . , 99	92 but less than 100	0.08

TABLE 13.4
Simulated Customer Arrivals for 10 3-Minute Periods at the County Beverage Drive-Thru

Period	Random Number	Simulated Customer Arrivals
1	63	2
2	27	1
3	15	0
4	99	4
5	86	3
6	71	2
7	74	2
8	45	1
9	11	0
10	02	0
	Total	15

TABLE 13.5
Random Number Assignments for the Order Size of Customers at the County Beverage Drive-Thru

Order Size	Associated 2-Digit Random Numbers	Interval Description	Probability
Small	00, 01, . . . , 38	00 but less than 39	0.39
Medium	39, 40, . . . , 88	39 but less than 89	0.50
Large	89, 90, . . . , 99	89 but less than 100	0.11

It is relatively easy to apply the above procedure to simulate values of a random variable for any simulation model. First, develop a table similar to Table 13.3 by associating an interval of random numbers with each possible value of the random variable. In doing so, make the probability of selecting a random number from each interval the same as the actual probability associated with the value of the random variable. Then each time a value of the random variable is needed, we simply select a new random number and use the corresponding interval of random numbers to find the value of the random variable.

Associating random number intervals with order sizes, we see that the random number intervals given in Table 13.5 can be used to simulate order sizes for customers stopping at the County Beverage Drive-Thru. Thus, the simulation model for the County Beverage Drive-Thru has two probabilistic components: arrivals and order size.

Logic of the Simulation Model for County Beverage Drive-Thru

Now that we know how to simulate the number of customers arriving and the customer order size, let us proceed with the development of the logic for the sequence of operations in the County Beverage simulation model. We will develop the model in a step-by-step manner. In doing so, we will carry out the necessary calculations to demonstrate how the simulation process works.

Whenever we need to generate a value for the number of customers arriving and/or the order size, we will use the random numbers from row 10 of Appendix B. Tables 13.3 and 13.5 will be used to determine the corresponding number of customer arrivals and the order sizes. For convenience, the first 5 2-digit random numbers from row 10 are reproduced here:

$$81 \quad 62 \quad 83 \quad 61 \quad 00$$

In developing the logic for the simulation model, we follow the logic of the actual operation as closely as possible. Suppose we begin with an idle or empty store and simulate what happens for each of the first three periods. Try to follow the logic of the model and see if you agree with the statements under the column labeled ''Things That Happen.''

The flowchart containing the logic of the simulation model we have been using is shown in Figure 13.5. Continue to use the random numbers from row 10 of Appendix B

Period 1 (see Figure 13.2)

Random Number	Things That Happen
81	Three cars arrive for service; thus, the first car, identified as car 1, gets immediate service.
62	Car 1 places a medium order and hence will not finish service until the end of period 2 (6 minutes).
	Cars 2 and 3 join the waiting line.

Period 2 (see Figure 13.3)

Random Number	Things That Happen
83	Three more cars, identified as cars 4, 5, and 6, arrive for service.
	The drive-thru is still busy serving the customer from period 1; hence, no order size is generated.
	Five cars (2 waiting plus 3 new customers) are wanting service this period, but only 4 cars will wait; hence, 1 customer (car 6) will be lost.
	Car 1 completes service at the end of this period; a profit of $1.50 is recorded.

Period 3 (see Figure 13.4)

Random Number	Things That Happen
61	Two more cars, identified as cars 7 and 8, arrive for service.
	The service area is free at the beginning of the period since the customer from period 1 (car 1) has completed service and left the drive-thru.
	One car from the waiting line (car 2) begins service, leaving 5 cars still wanting service; hence, 1 customer (car 8) will be lost and 4 cars will remain in the waiting line.
00	The customer in car 2 places a small order; thus, car 2 will finish service at the end of this period. Total profit as of the end of this period will be $1.50 (car 1) + $0.75 (car 2) = $2.25.

and see if you can conduct the simulation calculations for the first 10 periods of operation. Your simulation results should agree with those shown in Table 13.6.

At this point we have succeeded in simulating 10 periods, or a total of 30 minutes of operation. Although the results in Table 13.6 show evidence of long waiting lines and high lost customer rates (8 in the first 1/2 hour), a 30-minute simulation period is too short a time frame from which to draw general conclusions about the operation of the store. In order to take full advantage of the simulation model, we must continue to simulate the store's operation for many more time periods. But even for this relatively small simulation problem, continuing the hand simulation computations as we have been doing is unrealistic. Thus, we will look to the computer to provide the computational assistance necessary.

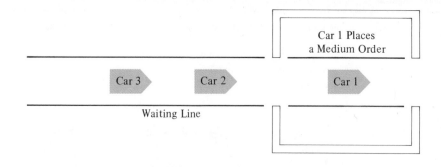

FIGURE 13.2
Status of the Operation for the First 3-Minute Simulation Period

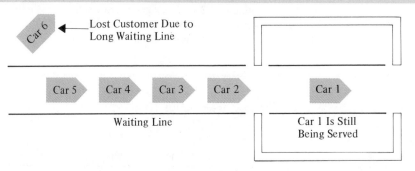

FIGURE 13.3
Status of the Operation for the Second 3-Minute Simulation Period

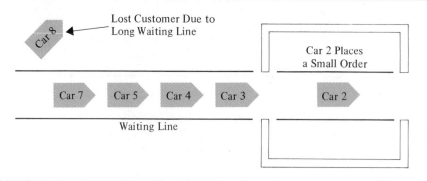

FIGURE 13.4
Status of the Operation for the Third 3-Minute Simulation Period

Generating Pseudorandom Numbers

If a computer procedure is going to be used to perform the simulation calculations, we will need a way for the computer to generate random numbers and values for the probabilistic components of the model. While the computer could be programmed to store random number tables and then follow the procedure outlined previously, the computer storage

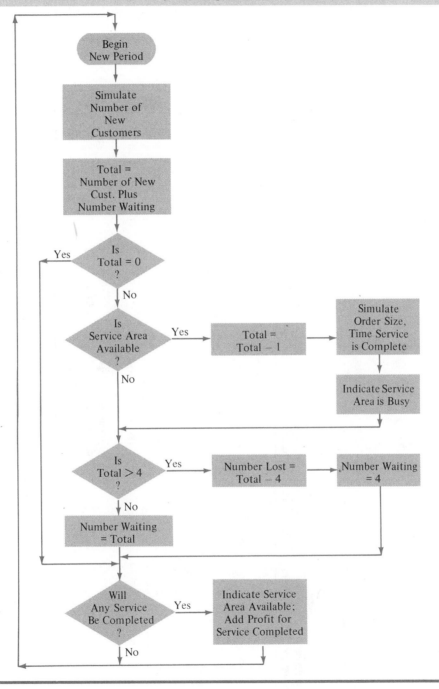

FIGURE 13.5
Flowchart of the County Beverage Drive-Thru Simulation Model

TABLE 13.6
Simulation Results from 10 3-Minute Periods of Operation for the County Beverage Drive-Thru

Period	Random Numbers	Number of New Customers	Is Service Area Available?	Random Number	Order Size	Service Periods	Number of Lost Customers	Number Waiting	Was Service Completed This Period?	Profit
1	81	3	Yes	62	Medium	2	0	2	No	—
2	83	3	No	—	—	—	1	4	Yes	$1.50
3	61	2	Yes	00	Small	1	1	4	Yes	0.75
4	39	1	Yes	25	Small	1	0	4	Yes	0.75
5	45	1	Yes	68	Medium	2	0	4	No	—
6	35	1	No	—	—	—	1	4	Yes	1.50
7	37	1	Yes	63	Medium	2	0	4	No	—
8	60	2	No	—	—	—	2	4	Yes	1.50
9	24	1	Yes	21	Small	1	0	4	Yes	0.75
10	98	4	Yes	06	Small	1	3	4	Yes	0.75

Total customers served   7
Total profit $7.50
Total lost customers   8

space required would result in an inefficient use of computer resources. For this reason, computer simulations make use of mathematical formulas that generate numbers which, for all practical purposes, have the same properties as the numbers selected from random number tables. These numbers are called *pseudorandom numbers*. In computer simulations, pseudorandom numbers are used in the same way as the random numbers selected from random number tables in our hand simulation. We associate an interval of pseudorandom numbers with each value of the random variable.

Most mathematical formulas designed to generate pseudorandom numbers produce numbers from 0 up to but not including 1. Thus to use the computer to generate arrivals for the County Beverage simulation model, we must now associate an interval of pseudorandom numbers with each number of arrivals so that the probability of generating a pseudorandom number in the interval will be equal to the probability of the corresponding number of arrivals. Table 13.7 shows how this would be done for the number of cars arriving at the County Beverage Drive-Thru. Note that Table 13.7 shows that a pseudorandom number less than 0.19 corresponds to no arrivals, a pseudorandom number greater than or equal to 0.19 but less than 0.58 corresponds to 1 arrival, and so on. Table 13.8 provides the pseudorandom number intervals that can be used to simulate the order sizes for County Beverage customers.

TABLE 13.7
Pseudorandom Number Intervals and the Associated Number of Customers Arriving at the County Beverage Drive-Thru

Interval of Pseudorandom Numbers	Simulated Customer Arrivals	Probability
0.00 but less than 0.19	0	0.19
0.19 but less than 0.58	1	0.39
0.58 but less than 0.77	2	0.19
0.77 but less than 0.92	3	0.15
0.92 but less than 1.00	4	0.08
		1.00

TABLE 13.8
Pseudorandom Number Intervals and the Associated Order Sizes for County Beverage Customers

Interval of Pseudorandom Numbers	Simulated Order Size	Probability
0.00 but less than 0.39	Small	0.39
0.39 but less than 0.89	Medium	0.50
0.89 but less than 1.00	Large	0.11
		1.00

Computer Program and Results

A computer *simulator* is a computer program written to conduct simulation computations. In order to simulate the operation of the County Beverage Drive-Thru, we need to develop a computer program containing the logic shown in Figure 13.5. Such a program would perform the calculations and keep track of the simulation results in a form similar to that shown in Table 13.6. Figure 13.6 shows a computer program written in the BASIC language that will simulate the County Beverage operation. This particular program was developed for and run on an IBM Personal Computer. For relatively small simulation models, the use of the BASIC language and a microcomputer is a realistic approach to conducting a simulation of a particular system.

Results from the computer simulation are shown in Table 13.9. The store's operation was simulated for a total of 30 hours (600 time periods). Based on the simulation results, we are able to make the following observations about the behavior of the system:

1. 365 customers were serviced during the 30 hours of simulated operation. However, 575 customers (61.2%) were lost because of long waiting lines.
2. The average profit was \$16.28 per hour or \$1.34 per car serviced (\$488.25/365 = \$1.34).
3. The biggest problem with the store's operation appears to be the number of lost customers (an average of 19.17 per hour). An estimate of the average dollar loss per hour due to lost customers is 19.17 (\$1.34 per car) = \$25.69.

Recall for a moment that a primary objective of simulation is to describe the behavior of a real system. In the County Beverage Drive-Thru simulation this is exactly what we have done. We have not determined an optimal solution or decision for the store; we have

FIGURE 13.6
BASIC Program for Simulation of the County Beverage Drive-Thru

```
 10 RANDOMIZE
 20 REM
 30 REM   THIS PROGRAM SIMULATES THE OPERATION OF THE
 40 REM   COUNTY BEVERAGE DRIVE-THRU
 50 REM
 60 WORKING$ = "NO"
 70 HOUR = 0
 80 NUMBER.WAITING = 0
 90 FINISH = 0
100 TOTAL.SERVED = 0
110 TOTAL.PROFIT = 0
120 TOTAL.LOST = 0
130 HOUR = HOUR + 1
135 TIME = 0
140 IF FINISH > = 20 THEN FINISH = FINISH - 20
150 REM
160 REM   SIMULATE THE NUMBER OF CARS ARRIVING IN A TIME PERIOD
170 REM
180 TIME = TIME + 1
190 X = RND(1)
200 IF X < .19 THEN NEW.CARS = 0
210 IF X > = .19 AND X < .58 THEN NEW.CARS = 1
220 IF X > = .58 AND X < .77 THEN NEW.CARS = 2
230 IF X > = .77 AND X < .92 THEN NEW.CARS = 3
240 IF X > = .92 THEN NEW.CARS = 4
250 TOTAL.IN.LINE = NUMBER.WAITING + NEW.CARS
260 IF TOTAL.IN.LINE = 0 THEN GOTO 500
```

FIGURE 13.6
continued

```
270 IF WORKING$ = "YES" THEN GOTO 400
280 TOTAL.IN.LINE = TOTAL.IN.LINE - 1
290 REM
300 REM   SIMULATE THE ORDER SIZE FOR THEN NEXT CAR TO BE SERVICED
310 REM
320 X = RND(1)
330 IF X < .39 THEN LENGTH = 1
340 IF X > = .39 AND X < .89 THEN LENGTH = 2
350 IF X > = .89 THEN LENGTH = 3
360 FINISH = TIME + LENGTH - 1
370 WORKING$ = "YES"
380 REM
390 REM   CALCULATE THE NUMBER OF LOST CUSTOMERS AND THE NUMBER WAITING
400 REM
410 IF TOTAL.IN.LINE > 4 THEN GOTO 440
420 NUMBER.WAITING = TOTAL.IN.LINE
430 GOTO 500
440 LOST.CUSTOMERS = TOTAL.IN.LINE - 4
450 NUMBER.WAITING = 4
460 TOTAL.LOST = TOTAL.LOST + LOST.CUSTOMERS
470 REM
480 REM   RELEASE A CAR COMPLETING SERVICE AND RECORD THE PROFIT
490 REM
500 IF FINISH > TIME THEN GOTO 180
510 IF LENGTH = 1 THEN PROFIT = .75
520 IF LENGTH = 2 THEN PROFIT = 1.5
530 IF LENGTH = 3 THEN PROFIT = 3
540 TOTAL.PROFIT = TOTAL.PROFIT + PROFIT
550 TOTAL.SERVED = TOTAL.SERVED + 1
560 WORKING$ = "NO"
570 REM
580 REM   SIMULATION RUN OF 20 TIME PERIODS PER HOUR
590 REM
600 IF TIME < 20 THEN GOTO 180
620 IF HOUR < 30 THEN GOTO 130
630 REM
640 REM   WRITE THE SUMMARY RESULTS FOR THE SIMULATION RUN
650 REM
670 AVERAGE.SERVED = TOTAL.SERVED / 30
680 PERCENT.SERVED = TOTAL.SERVED / (TOTAL.SERVED + TOTAL.LOST) = 100
682 TS = TOTAL.SERVED
684 AV = AVERAGE.SERVED
686 PS = PERCENT.SERVED
690 AVERAGE.LOST = TOTAL.LOST / 30
700 PERCENT.LOST = 100 - PERCENT.SERVED
702 TL = TOTAL.LOST
704 AL = AVERAGE.LOST
706 PL = PERCENT.LOST
710 AVERAGE.PROFIT = TOTAL.PROFIT / 30
712 TP = TOTAL.PROFIT
714 AP = AVERAGE.PROFIT
718 CLS
720 PRINT
730 PRINT
740 PRINT TAB(8): "ITEM OF INTEREST"; TAB(29); "TOTAL"; TAB(41); "PERCENT";
745 PRINT TAB(55); "AVERAGE"
750 PRINT
755 PRINT
760 PRINT TAB(10); "NUMBER SERVED";
770 PRINT USING "     ######        ###.#     ######.##"; TS, PS, AV
780 PRINT
790 PRINT TAB(10); "NUMBER LOST    ";
800 PRINT USING "       ####        ###.#      ####.##"; TL, PL, AL
810 PRINT
820 PRINT TAB(10); "PROFIT          ";
830 PRINT USING "  ######.##                  #####.##"; TP, AP
840 END
```

TABLE 13.9
Computer Simulation Results for 30 Hours of Operation

Item of Interest	Total	Percent	Hourly Average
Number served	365	38.8	12.17
Number lost	575	61.2	19.17
Profit	$488.25	—	$16.28

simply simulated what could happen in 30 hours of actual operation of the drive-thru. If the actual operation behaves as the simulation model indicates, County Beverage will have a significant waiting line problem with a sizable lost profit. In the next section we shall see how the simulation model can be used to investigate ways to improve the operation of the County Beverage Drive-Thru.

▼ NOTES AND COMMENTS ▼

1. Most applications of computer simulation involve probabilistic components. When the computer simulation involves generating values from probability distributions, it is called Monte Carlo simulation. However, computer simulation can also be used when there are no probabilistic components in the model. For instance, computer simulation can be used as a heuristic procedure to find a good solution to a complex optimization problem (such as a nonlinear integer program). In this case simulation is a trial-and-error procedure; a variety of values is generated for the decision variables, and the best of the feasible solutions is chosen.

2. There are essentially two approaches to the logic and record keeping of a simulation model: fixed time period and next event. We have employed the fixed time period approach for the County Beverage Drive-Thru problem. Each time period is of equal length, and the state of the system is updated at either the beginning or the end of each time period. The next event approach would be to randomly generate the time between arrivals and the time to complete service for a customer. The state of the system would be updated each time there was either a customer arriving or a customer completing service. Thus, the time between system updates is variable. Either approach is acceptable; we have chosen to demonstrate the fixed time period approach because, for an introductory treatment, it is easier to understand.

3. We have shown how to generate values of a random variable from a discrete probability distribution. With continuous random variables the random number generation is the same, but there is only one (not an interval) random number corresponding to each value of the random variable. The value of the pseudo-random number (between 0 and 1) is taken to be the value of the cumulative distribution function, from which the corresponding value of the random variable is generated.

13.2 ▼ COUNTY BEVERAGE DRIVE-THRU: IMPROVING THE SYSTEM DESIGN

The primary conclusion from the simulation results presented in Section 13.1 for the County Beverage operation is that the current store design cannot handle the amount of business that is anticipated. Undoubtedly, County Beverage management would like to explore alternative operating policies and designs that might improve service and enhance company profits. Certainly, the addition of a second store clerk should help the performance of the system. In addition, since construction of the building has not begun, management could consider a possible redesign of the store.

We are now ready to see how simulation can be used to improve system design. Once a model that is descriptive of the real system has been developed, we can think in terms of modifying the system design and using the simulation model to see if the modifications improve system performance. The modifications explored are often called *"what if"* questions. The capability to ask "what if" questions is one of the biggest advantages of computer simulation. The model serves as an experimental laboratory for answering such questions as "What if a second clerk is added?" and "What if the store is redesigned?" The two "what if" questions we want to address deal with the performance of systems *A* and *B*.

System A (see Figure 13.7)

Two clerks will operate the store during the peak business period. Two cars will be permitted into the store area for servicing at the same time. Bottlenecks may still occur because both cars must use the same lane. If the second car completes service before the first car, it will have to wait for the first car to complete service before it can leave the store. Also, if the first car finishes service first, it can leave the store, but a new customer cannot enter the store until the car in the second position has its order filled.

System B (see Figure 13.8)

Two clerks will operate the store during the peak period. The service lane of the store will be widened to permit 2 cars to be serviced simultaneously, with each car being permitted to leave the store as soon as it is finished. Waiting cars move into the store as soon as either lane opens up.

FIGURE 13.7
Proposed Design, System A, for the County Beverage Drive-Thru

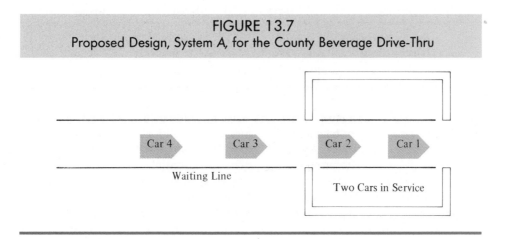

FIGURE 13.8
Proposed Design, System B, for the County Beverage Drive-Thru

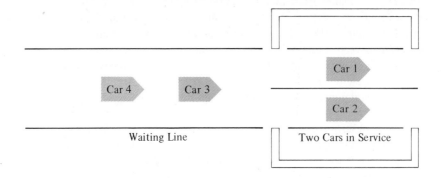

Car 4   Car 3

Car 1

Car 2

Waiting Line   Two Cars in Service

TABLE 13.10
Computer Simulation Results for 30 Hours of Operation
at the County Beverage Drive-Thru Under System A

Item of Interest	Total	Percent	Hourly Average
Number served	618	67.2	20.60
Number lost	302	32.8	10.07
Profit	$836.25	—	$27.88

TABLE 13.11
Computer Simulation Results for 30 Hours of Operation
at the County Beverage Drive-Thru Under System B

Item of Interest	Total	Percent	Hourly Average
Number served	785	84.1	26.17
Number lost	148	15.9	4.93
Profit	$1034.25	—	$34.48

In order to help the company determine which system should be adopted, simulation models were developed for both systems. Tables 13.10 and 13.11 show the results of 30 hours of simulation for each system. These simulation results provide answers to our what if questions and useful information to the individual responsible for the final design.

System A shows an average profit of $27.88 per hour, an increase of $11.60 per hour over the original 1-lane, 1-server system. However, 302 customers (32.8%) were lost because of long waiting lines. Although system B shows a higher average profit ($34.48 per hour) and a lower lost customer rate (15.9%), the advantage of system B may be offset by the added construction cost required to widen the service lane. The final decision may still take more study, but the simulation results provide important information for the decision maker. Perhaps a creative person could come up with an idea for modifying the single-service-lane operation to increase the number of cars served and still avoid the costly 2-lane construction. If such an idea occurs, the simulation model could be modified to evaluate its effectiveness.

▼ NOTES AND COMMENTS ▼

With the County Beverage Drive-Thru problem we have seen how "what if" questions can play an important role in improving system design. If the original model is representative of the real system, the behavior of the model in response tothe "what if" questions will be representative of how the real system will respond to the proposed modifications. Thus, the simulation model will help by predicting what can be expected in practice.

13.3 ▼ MODELING, VALIDATION, AND STATISTICAL CONSIDERATIONS

The value of a computer simulation model depends on its being descriptive of the real system and on the proper use of statistical experimental design concepts in using and evaluating the simulation results. In this section we discuss some of the issues to consider in developing, validating, and using the results of simulations.

Selecting a Simulation Language

In developing the computer program or simulator, a decision must be made as to the computer language that will be used. General-purpose programming languages such as BASIC, FORTRAN, PASCAL, and PL/1 can be used to develop the computer programs. However, as simulation applications and interest have increased, users as well as computer manufacturers have recognized that most computer simulations have many common features: values of random variables must be generated from probability distributions, tables are needed to keep track of simulation results, and so on. Thus, special programming languages have been developed to enable analysts and programmers to describe simulation models more easily.

Some of the more common simulation languages in use today are GPSS, SIMSCRIPT, and SLAM. These special simulation languages frequently have automatic or built-in time indicators, simplified procedures for generating probabilistic components, and provide automatic collection and printout of statistical results. One programming statement of a simulation language often performs the computation and record keeping that would require several BASIC, FORTRAN, PASCAL, or PL/1 statements to duplicate. Complete textbooks are devoted to a discussion of the use of computer languages in simulation, and the interested reader can refer to one of the references listed at the end of this text.

Validation

An important step in any simulation study is the validation of the simulation model. Validation involves verifying that the simulation model accurately represents (describes) the real-world system it is designed to simulate. Models that do not adequately reflect the behavior of the real system cannot be expected to provide worthwhile information. Thus, before implementing any simulation results, the analyst must be sure that a thorough job of model validation has been done.

If the simulation model applies to a system currently in operation, the simulation results can be compared with the current and past behavior of the real system in order to determine the validity of the model. The procedure usually followed is to run the simulation model using an actual set of past observations. In this way the output of the simulation model can be compared directly with the behavior of the actual system. Any major difference in the results is indicative of problems in the model.

Another approach to model validation is to have the overall model reviewed by experts who are most familiar with the operation of the real system. This review is subjective in nature, with the appropriate individuals evaluating the reasonableness of the simulation model and the simulation results.

In addition, careful attention should also be paid to the programming of the simulation model. Even if the model is formulated correctly, improper programming of the model can lead to inaccurate results. Standard quality control steps and good programming practice can be the best safeguards against this type of error.

A further check in the validation procedure is to compare the simulated distributions for the probabilistic components with the corresponding probability distributions in the real system. For example, in the County Beverage study the probability distribution for the number of cars arriving in a 3-minute period was considered known and was an important input for the simulation model. Recall that the simulation results shown in Table 13.9 were based on 30 hours of simulated operation. Since each hour has 20 3-minute periods, the total simulation contained 30(20) = 600 3-minute periods. Thus, if the simulation model is correctly simulating the number of customers arriving at the store, the relative frequencies of the number of cars arriving should approximate the probability distribution for the real system as shown in Table 13.1.

Table 13.12 shows the relative frequencies for the number of customers that arrived during the 600 3-minute periods in the simulation run. A comparison of the simulated distribution and the actual probability distribution from Table 13.1 shows no major differences. Thus, we conclude that the number of customer arrivals is being simulated

TABLE 13.12
Model Validation Step Showing a Comparison of the Simulated Relative Frequencies and the Actual Probability Distribution for the Number of Customer Arrivals at the County Beverage Drive-Thru

Number of Customer Arrivals	Number of Simulated Periods Having This Number of Arrivals	Simulated Relative Frequencies	Actual Probabilities (See Table 13.1)
0	124	0.207	0.19
1	229	0.382	0.39
2	104	0.173	0.19
3	86	0.143	0.15
4	57	0.095	0.08
Totals	600	1.000	1.00

correctly.[2] A similar comparison of the actual and simulated distributions for the size of the customer orders resulted in the conclusion that the model was valid in terms of its simulation of this probabilistic component.

Start-Up Problems

Most simulation studies are concerned with the operation of a system during its normal, or *steady-state,* condition. Recall from Chapter 12 that steady state for a system refers to the system behavior after it has been running long enough for the effect of any start-up conditions to have dissipated. In the County Beverage example the firm is interested in what happens during a "normal" hour of operation. Recall, however, that when we started the simulation calculations, we assumed that no cars were waiting and that no cars were being served. Therefore, data collected during the first part of the simulation run can be expected to differ from data collected during time intervals later in the simulation. The usual way to avoid start-up difficulties is to run the simulation model for a specified time period without collecting any data. The length of this start-up period must be sufficient for the system to have stabilized. Data are then collected on the system after it has reached a stable, or steady-state, condition. For the County Beverage simulation, the first hour of operation was considered a start-up period. The data for the 30 hours of simulation reported in Table 13.9 are the simulation results for hours 2 through 31.

Statistical Considerations

The results of any simulation run actually represent a sample. For example, the simulation results in Table 13.9 can be viewed as a sample of 30 hours of operation. Thus, $16.28 is an estimate of the average hourly profit for the County Beverage operation. The important thing to keep in mind is that different values for average hourly profit would be observed if the simulation was run again using a different sequence of random numbers. To ullustrate this, we ran two additional simulations each for 30 hours of operation. The results are as follows:

	Simulation 1	Simulation 2	Simulation 3
Number served	365	361	356
Number lost	575	558	622
Average hourly profit	$16.28	$16.13	$16.10

Although different results are obtained in each case, by running the simulation for a long period of time, most analysts are willing to use the values obtained from a single simulation run to estimate the true mean value of interest.

Determining the best statistical approach to estimating the statistical significance of differences due to design modifications is not a simple problem. A complete study of this issue would require a background in the area of statistics referred to as experimental

[2]Standard statistical procedures, such as the chi-square goodness-of-fit test, can be performed to test whether or not the results observed are representative of those expected. The use of such tests is described in most standard statistics texts. For example, see D. R. Anderson, D. J. Sweeney, and T. A. Williams, *Statistics for Business and Economics,*4th ed. (St. Paul, Minn.: West Publishing Company, 1990).

design. Consequently, the interested reader is referred to one of the more advanced texts in simulation listed at the end of the text.

13.4 ▼ AN INVENTORY SIMULATION MODEL

In this section we present another illustration of computer simulation by modeling an inventory system being operated by an auto supply company. While we are interested in accurately describing how the inventory system operates, we are also interested in making decisions concerning the reorder point and order quantity for a particular inventory item. By designing a set of experiments, we will simulate the operation of the inventory system for a variety of "what if" questions concerning reorder point and order quantity alternatives. Upon completion of the experiments with the simulation model, we should be able to select a good reorder point and order quantity for the item.

Art's Auto Supplies, Inc., is a specialty auto supplies store that carries over 1000 items in inventory. Although the store's manager has used inventory models to determine how much to order and when to order for most of the products, the manager has become especially concerned about the inventory problem for a deluxe tool cabinet. Demand for the cabinets has been relatively low, but subject to some variability. On approximately one-half of the days the store is open for business no one orders a cabinet, but on about 1 day per month 3 or 4 orders occur. If variable demand were the only source of uncertainty, the store manager believes that the order quantity and reorder point decisions could be based on an inventory model, perhaps similar to the inventory model discussed in Section 11.1. However, the tool cabinet inventory problem is further complicated by the fact that the lead time—the time between order placement and order arrival—also varies. Historically the length of the lead time has been between 1 and 5 days. The variable lead times have caused the store to run out of inventory on several occasions and orders received during the out-of-stock period have caused lost sales. Given this situation, the store manager would like to establish order quantity and reorder point decisions that minimize total relevant inventory costs—that is, ordering, holding, and stockout or shortage costs.

After an analysis of delivery charges and other costs associated with each order, the store manager was able to estimate the order cost at $20 per order. An analysis of interest, insurance, and other inventory carrying costs led to an estimate for the holding cost of $0.10 per unit per day. Finally, the shortage cost was estimated to be $50 per unit. The total relevant cost of the inventory system is given by the sum of the ordering cost, the holding cost, and the shortage cost. The objective is to find the order quantity and reorder point combination that will result in the lowest possible total cost.

A first step in the simulation approach to this problem is to develop a model that can be used to simulate the total relevant costs corresponding to a specific order size and reorder point. Then, using this model, "what if" questions can be posed by varying the two decision variables systematically in order to determine what appears to be the lowest-cost combination. Let us begin by developing such a model to carry out a 1-day simulation of the inventory process.

Assume that a specific reorder point and order quantity have already been selected. We begin each day of the simulation by checking whether any inventory that had previously been ordered has arrived. If so, the current inventory on hand is increased by the quantity of goods received. This assumes that orders are received and inventory on hand is updated at the start of each day. If such an assumption is not appropriate, a different

model, perhaps calling for goods to be received at the end of the day, would have to be developed.

Next, our simulator must randomly generate a value for the daily demand from the appropriate probability distribution. If there is sufficient inventory on hand to meet the daily demand, the inventory on hand will be decreased by the amount of the daily demand. If, however, inventory on hand is not sufficient to satisfy all the demand, as much as possible will be satisfied. The inventory will be reduced to zero, and a shortage cost will be computed for all unsatisfied demand. Updating the process in this fashion, we are assuming that if a customer orders more cabinets than the store has in inventory, the customer will take what is available and shop elsewhere for the remainder of the order. With another auto supply store only two blocks away, the store manager is sure that unsatisfied demand will result in lost sales, and a $50 per unit shortage cost is appropriate.

After the daily demand has been processed, the next step is to determine if the ending inventory has reached the reorder point and a new order should be placed. However, prior to placing a new order, we must check to see if the most recent order is outstanding. If so, we do not place another order.[3] Otherwise, an order is placed, and the company incurs an ordering cost. When an order is placed, a lead time must be randomly generated to reflect the time between the placement of the order and the receipt of the goods.

Finally, holding cost, which is $0.10 for each unit in the daily ending inventory, is computed. The sum of the shortage costs, ordering costs, and holding costs becomes the total daily cost for the simulation. Performing the above sequence of operations would complete 1 day of simulation. Figure 13.9 depicts this daily simulation process for the deluxe tool cabinet inventory operation.

The daily simulation process should be repeated for as many days as are necessary to reach steady state and obtain meaningful results. The output from the simulation will show the total cost involved in using one particular order quantity and reorder point combination. By simulating the inventory operation with different order quantity–reorder point combinations, we can compare total operating costs and select the apparent "best" order quantity and reorder point decisions for the deluxe tool cabinets.

Suppose that the store has a complete set of records showing the demand for the deluxe tool cabinets for the past year (300 days). Furthermore, suppose that the records also show the number of days between placement and receipt of each order over the same period. Table 13.13 shows the frequency and relative frequency distributions for demand, and Table 13.14 shows the frequency and relative frequency distributions for lead time.

In order to carry out the simulation steps depicted in Figure 13.9, we must develop the procedure for generating values from the demand and lead time distributions. As before, we will associate with each value of the random variable an interval of pseudorandom numbers such that the probability of generating a pseudorandom number in that interval is the same as the relative frequency of the associated demand and lead time. The intervals of pseudorandom numbers are shown in Tables 13.15 and 13.16.

To appreciate how the simulation method works for this problem, we will first follow a 10-day simulation of the process. Let us assume that the store manager wants to determine the effect of using an order quantity of 5 units with a reorder point of 3 units. For purposes of starting the simulation, let us assume that we have a beginning inventory of 5 units at the start of day 1 of our 10-day simulation.

Refer to the flowchart in Figure 13.9. The first step is to check to see if any shipments have arrived. Since this is the first day of the simulation, we assume no arrivals and

---

[3]We are assuming that it will never be necessary to have two orders outstanding simultaneously. However, in other simulation models, having several orders outstanding may be an entirely appropriate assumption.

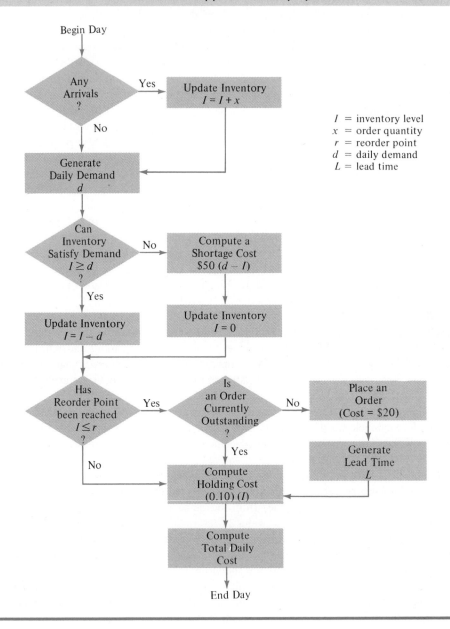

FIGURE 13.9
Flowchart of the Simulation of 1 Day of Operation for the Art's Auto Supplies Inventory System

I = inventory level
x = order quantity
r = reorder point
d = daily demand
L = lead time

generate the daily demand for day 1. Let us assume that we use a computer to generate pseudorandom numbers between 0 and 0.999 . . . and that the first number generated is 0.093. From Table 13.15 we see that this pseudorandom number corresponds to a demand of 0 units. There are no shortage costs to compute since the inventory on hand (5 units) is greater than the reorder point (3 units), and we do not place an order. The holding cost for day 1 is computed to be ($0.10)5, or $0.50. With no shortages and no ordering, the

TABLE 13.13
Frequency and Relative Frequency Distributions for Demand in Art's Auto Supplies Problem

Demand (units)	Frequency (days)	Relative Frequency
0	150	0.50
1	75	0.25
2	45	0.15
3	15	0.05
4	15	0.05
	300	1.00

TABLE 13.14
Frequency and Relative Frequency Distributions for Lead Time in Art's Auto Supplies Problem

Lead Time (days)	Frequency (days)	Relative Frequency
1	6	0.20
2	3	0.10
3	12	0.40
4	6	0.20
5	3	0.10
	30	1.00

TABLE 13.15
Pseudorandom Numbers and Associated Daily Demands for Art's Auto Supplies Problem

Daily Demand	Relative Frequency	Interval of Pseudorandom Numbers	Probability of Selecting a Pseudorandom Number in Interval
0	0.50	0.00 but less than 0.50	0.50
1	0.25	0.50 but less than 0.75	0.25
2	0.15	0.75 but less than 0.90	0.15
3	0.05	0.90 but less than 0.95	0.05
4	0.05	0.95 but less than 1.00	0.05
	1.00		1.00

TABLE 13.16
Pseudorandom Number Intervals and Associated Lead Times for Art's Auto Supplies Problem

Lead Time (days)	Relative Frequency	Interval of Pseudorandom Numbers	Probability of Selecting a Pseudorandom Number in Interval
1	0.20	0.00 but less than 0.20	0.20
2	0.10	0.20 but less than 0.30	0.10
3	0.40	0.30 but less than 0.70	0.40
4	0.20	0.70 but less than 0.90	0.20
5	0.10	0.90 but less than 1.00	0.10
	1.00		1.00

TABLE 13.17
Computer Simulation Results for 10 Days of Operation of Art's Auto Supplies with an Order Quantity of 5 and a Reorder Point of 3

Day	Beg Inv	Units Rec'd	Rndm Num	Units Demd	End Inv	Rndm Num	Lead Time	Holding Cost ($)	Order Cost ($)	Short Cost ($)	Total Cost ($)
1	5	0	0.093	0	5			0.50	0.00	0.00	0.50
2	5	0	0.681	1	4			0.40	0.00	0.00	0.40
3	4	0	0.292	0	4			0.40	0.00	0.00	0.40
4	4	0	0.528	1	3	0.620	3	0.30	20.00	0.00	20.30
5	3	0	0.866	2	1			0.10	0.00	0.00	0.10
6	1	0	0.975	4	0			0.00	0.00	150.00	150.00
7	0	5	0.622	1	4			0.40	0.00	0.00	0.40
8	4	0	0.819	2	2	0.939	5	0.20	20.00	0.00	20.20
9	2	0	0.373	0	2			0.20	0.00	0.00	0.20
10	2	0	0.353	0	2			0.20	0.00	0.00	0.20
			Average cost for 10 simulated days					0.27	4.00	15.00	19.27

total cost for day 1 is just the holding cost of $0.50. Continuing the simulation in this manner, we obtained the computer-generated results shown in Table 13.17.

At the start of day 4 the beginning inventory was 4 units. The random number selected to generate daily demand was 0.528; thus, a daily demand of 1 unit was generated. As a result, the ending inventory dropped to 3 units, and an order for 5 units was placed. Generating another random number—in this case, 0.620—indicates (see Table 13.16) a lead time of 3 days, which means that the new order will be available on day 7. The day 4 costs thus far are ($0.10)3 = $0.30 for the holding cost and $20.00 for the ordering cost. Since there is no shortage cost, the total cost for the day is $20.30. The figures at the bottom of Table 13.17 provide the average holding cost, average ordering cost, average shortage cost, and average total cost for the 10-day simulation. Prior to drawing any firm conclusions based on these limited simulation results, we should run the simulation for many more days. Also we will want to test many other order quantity–reorder point combinations.

A computer programmer could develop a computer simulation program or simulator that would enable the store to explore a variety of order quantities and reorder points for a large number of simulated days. In Table 13.18 we present output from a simulator that was developed to solve inventory problems such as the auto supplies problem. In this simulator the decision maker has the option of selecting a variety of order quantities and reorder points. For purposes of illustration, the computer simulation output is shown for simulations with order quantities of from 5 to 50 units in increments of 5 and for reorder points of from 1 to 10 units in increments of 1. A total of 1000 days is represented in the simulation of each order quantity-reorder point combination.

We see that the results of this computer simulation indicate that the lowest-cost solution occurs at an order quantity of 25 units and a reorder point of 6 units; in this case the resulting average total cost is $2.39 per day. After studying these results, the store manager might wish to explore other order quantities near the apparent ''best'' order quantity of 25. In Table 13.19 the results of varying the order quantity from 21 to 30 (in increments of 1) and the reorder point from 4 to 8 are shown. The smallest simulated average total cost of $2.33 now occurs when the order quantity is 22 units and the reorder point is 6 units. Note, however, that in this second set of simulation experiments the previously best order quantity of 25 units and reorder point of 6 units has a total cost of $2.75 per day. Since different random numbers were used in the two simulations, different total costs are to be expected. The selection of the ''best'' order quantity and reorder point is now up to the analyst. What decisions would you make? While you might want to run more or longer simulations, the simulation data of Tables 13.18 and 13.19 indicate that good solutions apparently exist with order quantities around 20 to 25 units and reorder points around 6 or 7 units. Thus, while simulation has not guaranteed an optimal solution, it has enabled us to identify apparent low-cost or ''near-optimal'' decisions for the inventory problem. The final decision for an order quantity and reorder point will be based on the store manager's preference from among the good or ''near-optimal'' solutions.

TABLE 13.18
Simulated Average Daily Cost for 1000 Days of Art's Auto Supplies Inventory Problem

Reorder Point	Order Quantity									
	5	*10*	*15*	*20*	*25*	*30*	*35*	*40*	*45*	*50*
1	14.35	8.30	6.58	5.20	5.35	4.16	3.30	4.42	3.98	5.22
2	11.51	5.93	5.46	3.92	3.91	3.44	2.96	3.69	3.62	3.71
3	9.34	5.64	3.37	3.01	3.03	2.84	3.96	3.29	2.90	3.07
4	6.90	4.12	3.47	2.78	3.14	2.79	3.29	3.25	3.37	3.42
5	5.41	3.31	2.85	2.42	2.61	3.24	3.25	2.93	3.18	3.22
6	4.72	2.75	2.69	2.60	2.39	2.74	2.93	3.06	3.13	3.34
7	4.72	2.85	2.52	2.60	2.76	2.71	3.06	2.99	3.02	3.28
8	5.50	2.89	2.66	2.50	2.62	2.75	2.99	3.05	3.33	3.56
9	4.36	3.11	2.62	2.62	2.66	2.77	3.05	3.18	3.34	3.49
10	4.68	3.05	2.75	2.72	2.80	2.85	3.18	3.28	3.31	3.72

TABLE 13.19
Simulated Average Daily Cost for 1000 Days of
Art's Auto Supplies Inventory Problem

Reorder Point	Order Quantity									
	21	22	23	24	25	26	27	28	29	30
4	2.94	3.02	3.13	2.74	2.89	2.56	2.74	3.07	2.67	3.24
5	2.59	2.58	2.84	2.70	2.66	2.59	2.88	2.57	2.48	2.75
6	2.55	2.33	2.87	2.35	2.75	2.45	2.81	2.79	2.61	2.60
7	2.52	2.45	2.47	2.51	2.57	2.62	2.61	2.63	2.62	2.67
8	2.50	2.69	2.48	2.49	2.63	2.57	2.63	2.69	2.69	2.71

13.5 ▼ ADVANTAGES AND DISADVANTAGES OF COMPUTER SIMULATION

A primary advantage of computer simulation is that it is applicable in complex cases where analytical procedures cannot be employed. For example, the County Beverage waiting line system and the Art's Auto Supplies inventory system were sufficiently complex that the analytical approaches discussed in other chapters of this text do not apply. That is, the forms of the probability distributions involved do not satisfy the assumptions of the analytical models. In general, the larger the number of probabilistic components in the system becomes, the more likely it is that simulation will be the best approach.

Another advantage of the simulation approach is that the simulation model and simulator provide a convenient experimental laboratory. Once the computer program has been developed, it is usually relatively easy to experiment with the model by asking ''what if'' questions. For example, if we wanted to know the effect of an increase in shortage cost on the recommended solution to our inventory problem, we could have simply changed the shortage cost input value and rerun the simulation. The effect of experimental changes in other inputs, such as the probability distributions of customer arrivals, lead time, and so on, could also be investigated.

Simulation is not without its disadvantages. One obvious disadvantage is that someone must develop the computer program. For large simulation projects this is usually a substantial undertaking. Hence, one should certainly not attempt to develop a simulation model unless the potential gains promise to outweigh the costs of model development. This disadvantage has been reduced with the development of computer simulation languages such as GPSS, SIMSCRIPT, and SLAM (available on microcomputers). The use of these languages often leads to considerable savings in time and money as the computer program or simulator is developed.

Another disadvantage of simulation is that it does not guarantee an optimal solution to a problem. One usually selects those values of the decision variables to test in the model that have a good chance of being near the optimal solution. However, since it is usually too costly to try all values of the decision variables, and since different simulation runs may provide different results, there is no guarantee that the best simulation solution found is the overall optimal solution. Nonetheless, the danger of obtaining bad solutions is slight if good judgment is exercised in developing and running the simulation model. The decision maker usually has a good idea of reasonable values to try for the decision variables, and it is usually possible to run the simulation long enough to reach steady state and identify the apparent best decisions.

▼ SUMMARY

Computer simulation is used extensively for a wide variety of applications. Some of the reasons why computer simulation is so widely used are the following:

1. It can be used for a large number of practical problems.
2. It can be used to obtain good solutions to problems that are too complex to be solved with procedures such as linear programming, waiting line models, or inventory models.
3. The simulation approach is straightforward and hence is relatively easy to explain and understand. As a result, management confidence is increased, and, consequently, acceptance of the model is more easily obtained.
4. Computer manufacturers have developed extensive software packages consisting of specialized simulation programming languages, thus facilitating use of simulation in practice.

In this chapter we have developed simulation models for a waiting line system and an inventory system. In both cases we saw how a series of experiments with key design parameters of the simulation model could be conducted to identify good values for these parameters of the real system. In the County Beverage problem, simulation experiments helped to identify the 2-lane design as the one yielding the highest average hourly profit. In the simulation of Art's Auto Supplies, the simulation experiments helped identify an order quantity of 22 and a reorder level of 6 as a good low-cost inventory policy.

A primary objective of simulation is to develop a model that is descriptive of the real system; the purpose of validation is to make sure that it is. Once validation has shown that a simulation model is descriptive, the model can be used to address "what if" questions and conduct experiments concerning system performance. We have stressed that proper experimental designs must be developed and appropriate statistical methodology must be employed in analyzing the experimental results.

▼ GLOSSARY

Simulation   A technique used to describe the behavior of a real-world system over time. Most often this technique employs a computer program to perform the simulation computations.

Monte Carlo simulations   Simulations that use a random number procedure to generate values for the probabilistic components.

Pseudorandom numbers   Computer-generated numbers developed from mathematical expressions that have the properties of random numbers.

Simulator   The computer program written to perform the simulation calculations.

"What if" questions   Modifications made to model parameters to explore the effect on simulation output.

▼ PROBLEMS

Most of the problems in this section are designed to enable you to perform simulations with hand calculations. To keep the calculations reasonable, we will ask you to consider only a few decision alternatives and relatively short periods of simulation. While this should give you a good understanding of the simulation process, the simulation results will not be sufficient for you to make final conclusions or decisions about the problem situation. If you have access to a computer, we suggest that you develop a computer simulation model for some of the problems. Then, by using the model to test several decision alternatives over a much longer simulated period of time, you will be able to obtain the desired decision-making information.

1. A retail store has experienced the following historical daily demand for a particular product:

Sales (units)	Frequency (days)
0	4
1	6
2	14
3	12
4	7
5	5
6	2
Total	50

a. Develop a relative frequency distribution for the above data.

b. Use the random numbers from row 4 of Appendix B to simulate daily sales for a 10-day period. This row begins with the random numbers   46276   87453   44790.

2. A study was conducted in order to investigate the number of cars arriving at the drive-in window of Community Savings Bank. The following data were collected for 100 randomly selected 5-minute intervals:

Number of Arrivals	Number of Occurrences
0	12
1	24
2	37
3	19
4	8
Total	100

a. Develop a relative frequency distribution for the above data.

b. Use random numbers 08, 61, and 22 to simulate the number of customers that arrive between 9:00 A.M. and 9:15 A.M. on a given day.

3. A car rental agency has collected data on the demand for luxury-class automobiles over the past 25 days. The data are shown below.

Rental Demand	Number of Days
7	2
8	5
9	8
10	7
11	3
	25

Because customers drop cars at another location, the agency only has 9 cars available currently.

a. Use the following 5 random numbers to generate 5 days of demand for the rental agency: 15   48   71   56   90.

b. What is the average number of cars rented for the 5 days?

c. How many rentals will be lost over the 5 days in part (a)?

d. What is the expected daily demand for luxury cars? Use the probability distribution to compute expected demand.

e. What is the average daily demand for the 5 days simulated in part (a)? How does this differ from the expected daily demand in part (d)? Why does it differ?

4. Refer again to the data in problem 2 concerning arrivals at the Community Savings Bank.

a. Use the following random numbers to generate arrivals for the next 6 5-minute intervals: 01   09   26   05   33   14.

b. Compute the average number of arrivals for the 6 periods in part (a).

c. Would you feel comfortable estimating the average number of arrivals using the arrivals generated in part (a)? Why or why not?

d. Compute the expected number of arrivals in a 5-minute period using the relative frequencies in problem 2 as the appropriate probabilities. Compare this with the average computed in part (b).

5. Decca Industries has experienced the following weekly absenteeism frequency over the past 20 weeks:

Number of Employees Absent	Frequency
1	2
2	4
3	7
4	3
5	2
6	2
Total	20

a. Develop a relative frequency distribution for the above data.

b. Use random numbers to simulate weekly absenteeism for a 15-week period.

6. Given below are 50 weeks of historical sales data for cars sold by Domoy Motors, Inc., a new-car dealer in Newton, Ohio.

Number of Sales	Number of Weeks
0	2
1	5
2	8
3	22
4	10
5	3
Total	50

   a. Develop the relative frequency distribution for these data.
   b. Use a random number procedure to simulate weekly automobile sales for a 12-week period.

7. Charlestown Electric Company is building a new generator for its Mount Washington plant. Even with good maintenance procedures, the generator will have periodic failures or breakdowns. Historical figures for similar generators indicate that the relative frequency of failures during a year is as follows:

Number of Failures	Relative Frequency
0	0.80
1	0.15
2	0.04
3	0.01

Assume that the useful lifetime of the generator is 25 years. Use simulation to estimate the number of breakdowns that will occur in the 25 years of operation. Is it common to have 5 or more consecutive years of operation without a failure?

8. Use row 15 of Appendix B beginning with 20711 and 55609 to simulate 15 minutes of operation for the County Beverage Drive-Thru application presented in Section 13.1. Show your simulation results in the format of Table 13.6.

9. A service technician for a major photocopier company is trained to service two models of copier: the X100 and the Y200. Approximately 60% of the technician's service calls are for the X100, and 40% are for the Y200. The service time distributions for the two models are as follows:

X100		Y200	
Time (minutes)	Relative Frequency	Time (minutes)	Relative Frequency
25	0.50	20	0.40
30	0.25	25	0.40
35	0.15	30	0.10
40	0.10	35	0.10

a. Show the random number intervals that can be used to simulate the type of machine to be serviced and the length of the service time for each model.

b. Simulate 20 service calls. What is the total service time the technician spends on the 20 calls?

10. Bushnell's Sand and Gravel (BSG) is a small firm that supplies sand, gravel, and topsoil to contractors and landscaping firms. BSG maintains an inventory of high-quality screened topsoil that is used to supply the weekly orders for two companies: Bath Landscaping Service and Pittsford Lawn Care, Inc. The problem BSG has is to determine how many cubic yards of screened topsoil to have in inventory at the beginning of each week in order to satisfy the needs of both its customers. BSG would like to select the lowest possible inventory level that would have a 0.95 probability of satisfying the combined weekly orders from both customers. The demand distributions for the two customers are as follows:

	Weekly Demand (cubic yards)	Relative Frequency
Bath Landscaping	10	0.20
	15	0.35
	20	0.30
	25	0.10
	30	0.05
Pittsford Lawn Care	30	0.20
	40	0.40
	50	0.30
	60	0.10

Simulate 20 weeks of operation for beginning inventories of 70 and of 80 cubic yards. Based on your limited simulation results, how many cubic yards should BSG maintain in inventory? Discuss what you would want to do in a full-scale simulation of this problem.

11. Three discount pharmacies (Super Z, Devco, and Floorgreen) compete for business in a suburban area. Customers often make a purchase at one of the stores and then make the next purchase at another store. The matrix below shows the probability that a customer will switch stores from one purchase to the next.

Current Purchase	Next Purchase Super Z	Devco	Floorgreen
Super Z	0.7	0.1	0.2
Devco	0.3	0.5	0.2
Floorgreen	0.1	0.1	0.8

a. Show the probability distribution and the intervals of random numbers that could be used to generate the next purchase for a customer who last made a purchase at Super Z.

b. Repeat part (a) for a customer who last made a purchase at Devco.

c. Repeat part (a) for a customer who last made a purchase at Floorgreen.

d. Gary Hatcher made his last purchase at Super Z. Use the following 4 random numbers to simulate the store at which he makes his next 4 purchases: 04   23   74   68.

e. Suppose Gary Hatcher's last purchase in part (d) had been mistakenly recorded and it had actually been made at Devco. Use the same 4 random numbers to generate his next 4 purchases.

f. If the simulation were run for a large number of purchases (say, 1000), the fraction of Hatcher's purchases from each store would be about the same regardless of which store he made his last purchase from. This is what it means to reach steady state. Use your results from parts (d) and (e) to comment on whether or not simulating 4 purchases is enough to reach steady state.

12. A door-to-door magazine salesperson has the historical sales record shown below. If the salesperson talks to the woman of the house, there is a 15% chance of making a sale. Furthermore, if the salesperson convinces the woman of the house to purchase some magazines, the relative frequency distribution for the number of the subscriptions ordered is as follows:

Number of Subscriptions	Relative Frequency
1	0.60
2	0.30
3	0.10

On the other hand, if the man of the house answers the door, the salesperson's chances of making a sale are 25%. In addition, the relative frequency distribution for the number of subscriptions ordered is as follows:

Number of Subscriptions	Relative Frequency
1	0.10
2	0.40
3	0.30
4	0.20

The salesperson has found that no one answers the door at about 30% of the houses contacted. However, of the people who do answer the door, 80% are women, and 20% are men. The salesperson's profit is $2 for each subscription sold.

a. Simulate this problem, and show the house-by-house results for 25 calls.

b. What is the total profit projected for the 25 calls?

c. Based on your results from part (b), how many subscriptions should the salesperson expect to sell by calling on 100 houses per day? What is the salesperson's expected daily profit?

13. A project has four activities (A, B, C, and D) that must be completed sequentially in order to complete the project. The probability distribution for the time required to complete each of the activities is as follows:

Activity	Activity Time (weeks)	Probability
A	5	0.25
	6	0.30
	7	0.30
	8	0.15
B	3	0.20
	5	0.55
	7	0.25
C	10	0.10
	12	0.25
	14	0.40
	16	0.20
	18	0.05
D	8	0.60
	10	0.40

    a. Use a random number procedure to simulate the completion time for each activity. Sum the activity times to establish a completion time for the entire project.

    b. Use the simulation procedure developed in part (a) to simulate 20 completions of this project. Show the distribution of completion times, and estimate the probability that the project can be completed in 35 weeks or less.

14. A New York City corner newsstand orders 250 copies of *The New York Times* daily. Primarily due to weather conditions, the demand for newspapers varies from day to day. The probability distribution of the demand for newspapers is as follows:

Number of Newspapers	Probability
150	0.10
175	0.30
200	0.30
225	0.20
250	0.10

The newsstand makes a 15-cent profit on every paper sold, but it loses 10 cents on every paper unsold by the end of the day. Use 10 days of simulated results to determine whether the newsstand should order 200, 225, or 250 papers per day. What is the average daily profit that the newsstand can anticipate based on your recommendation?

15. For the Art's Auto Supplies problem in Section 13.4, develop a 10-day simulation when the following demand distribution is assumed:

Demand	Relative Frequency
0	0.25
1	0.50
2	0.15
3	0.05
4	0.05

Using an order quantity of 5 and a reorder point of 3, show your results in the format of Table 13.17.

16. Bristol Bikes, Inc., would like to develop an order quantity and reorder point policy that would minimize the total costs associated with the company's inventory of exercise bikes. The relative frequency distribution for retail demand on a weekly basis is as follows:

Demand	Probability
0	0.20
1	0.50
2	0.10
3	0.10
4	0.05
5	0.05

The relative frequency distribution for lead time is as follows:

Lead Time (weeks)	Relative Frequency
1	0.10
2	0.25
3	0.60
4	0.05

The holding cost is $1 per unit per week, the ordering cost is $20 per order, the shortage cost is $25 per unit, and the beginning inventory is 7 units. Using an order quantity of 12 and a reorder point of 5, simulate 10 weeks of operation of this inventory system.

17. Stollar's Bakery Shop would like to determine how many 10-inch white cakes should be produced each day in order to maximize profits. The production cost is $2.50 per cake, and the selling price is $4.50. Any cakes that are not sold at the end of the day are sold for $1.50 to a local store that specializes in day-old goods. Assume that the

bakery has available the following data showing the daily demand during the past month (20 days of operation):

Daily Demand	Frequency (number of days observed)
0	1
1	2
2	1
3	2
4	3
5	6
6	3
7	1
8	1
Total	20

Develop a 10-day simulation for production sizes ranging from 1 to 8 cakes per day. Use the following random numbers to generate daily demand:

48   12   77   24   32   43   96   03   62   77

What appears to be the best production size?

18. Domoy Motors, Inc., purchases a certain model automobile for $5778. In order to finance the purchase of cars of this model, Domoy must pay an 18% annual interest rate on borrowed capital. This interest rate amounts to approximately $20 per car per week. Orders for additional cars can be placed each week, but a minimum order size of 5 cars is required on any given order. It currently takes 3 weeks to receive a new shipment of cars after the order is placed. The cost of placing an order is $50. If Domoy runs out of cars in inventory, a shortage cost of $300 per car is incurred. Currently Domoy has 20 cars of this model in inventory. Historical data showing the weekly demand were given in problem 6.

a. Assuming an order quantity of 15 cars and a reorder point of 10 cars, perform a 12-week simulation of Domoy's operation. Use the first 12 2-digit random numbers from row 2 of Appendix B beginning with the number 88547. Show your simulation results in the format of Table 13.17.

b. Write a computer program to simulate weekly sales at Domoy Motors. Use the program to determine the order policy that appears to minimize Domoy's overall costs.

19. A firm with a national chain of hotels and motels is interested in learning where individuals prefer to stay when on business trips. Three competing hotel and motel chains are included in the study. They are the Marimont Inn, the Harrison Inn, and the Hinton Hotel. The study found that where an individual stays on one trip is a good predictor of where the individual will stay the next trip. However, the study showed that sometimes individuals switch from one chain to another. The probabilities of staying at each chain are shown below. For example, if an individual stayed at the Marimont Inn on one trip, there is a 0.70 probability of staying at the Marimont Inn the next trip, a 0.10 probability of staying at the Harrison Inn the next trip, and a 0.20 probability of staying at the Hinton Hotel the next trip. Similar probability values are

shown for individuals staying at the Harrison Inn and the Hinton Hotel on a particular trip.

Currently Staying at	Probability of Staying the Next Trip at		
	Marimont	*Harrison*	*Hinton*
Marimont	0.70	0.10	0.20
Harrison	0.20	0.60	0.20
Hinton	0.15	0.05	0.80

a. Show the random number assignments that can be used to simulate the next visit for an individual currently staying at the Marimont, Harrison, and Hinton chains.

b. Develop a flowchart that describes the simulation process for simulating where an individual will stay during a series of business trips.

c. Assume that an individual most recently stayed at the Marimont Inn. Simulate where the individual would stay on the next 50 business trips. What percentage of time will the person select each chain? Which appears to be the most popular chain?

d. Repeat the simulation in part (c) starting with an individual most recently staying at the Harrison Inn. Repeat part (c) again with the individual most recently staying at the Hinton Inn. Which is the most popular chain based on these simulation results?

20. Shown below is the probability distribution for the number of pins a bowler obtains on a first ball.

Number of Pins	Probability
6	0.02
7	0.08
8	0.20
9	0.30
10	0.40

The probability table showing the number of pins obtained on a second ball is as follows:

If Number of Pins on First Ball Is	Number of Pins on Second Ball Is				
	0	*1*	*2*	*3*	*4*
6	0.01	0.03	0.20	0.26	0.50
7	0.04	0.10	0.36	0.50	
8	0.05	0.25	0.70		
9	0.15	0.85			

a. Using the above information, simulate a game of bowling. What is the bowler's score?

b. Develop a simulation program for this problem, and simulate several games of bowling. What is an estimate of the bowler's average score?

21. Mount Washington Garage sells regular and unleaded gasoline. Pump 1, a self-service facility, is used by customers who want to pump their own gas. Pump 2, a full-service facility, is used by customers who are willing to pay a higher cost per gallon in order to have an attendant pump the gas, check the oil, and so on. Both pumps can service 1 car at a time. Based on past data, the owner of the garage estimates that 70% of the customers select the self-service pump and 30% want full service. The arrival rate of cars for each minute of operation is given by the following probability distribution:

Number of Arrivals in 1 Minute of Operation	Probability
0	0.10
1	0.20
2	0.35
3	0.30
4	0.05
	1.00

The time to service a car, which depends on whether the self-service or the full-service facility is used, is given by the following probability distribution:

| Self-Service Pump | | Full-Service Pump | |
Service Time (minutes)	Probability	Service Time (minutes)	Probability
2	0.10	3	0.20
3	0.20	4	0.30
4	0.60	5	0.35
5	0.10	6	0.10
	1.00	7	0.05
			1.00

Study the operation of the system for 10 minutes using simulation. As part of your analysis, consider the following types of questions: What is the average number of cars waiting for service per minute at both facilities? What is the average amount of time a car must wait for service? Prepare a brief report for Mount Washington Garage that describes your analysis and any conclusions.

22. A medical consulting firm has been asked to determine the facilities required in the x-ray laboratory of a new hospital. In particular, the firm should provide recommendations on the number of x-ray units for the laboratory. How could computer simulation assist in reaching a good decision? What factors would you consider in a simulation model of this problem?

23. Consider a medium-sized community that currently has only one fire station. You have been hired by the city manager to assist in the determination of the best location for a second fire station. What would be your objective for this problem? Explain how computer simulation might be used to evaluate alternative locations and help identify the best location.

24. A bus company is considering adding a new 10-stop route to its operation. The bus will be scheduled to complete the route once each hour. If the company has determined the approximate demand distribution for each location, discuss how simulation might be used to project the hourly profit associated with the new route. If the company can assign a regular bus or a more economical minibus to this route, discuss how simulation might help make this decision. Note that with the minibus the company's management is concerned about being unable to pick up customers if the bus is already carrying its maximum number of riders.

▼ CASE PROBLEM

Machine Repair

Jerry Masters, president of Pacific Plastics, Inc. (PPI), has become concerned with reports that down time for PPI's plastic injection-molding machines has been increasing. The down time for a machine includes the time the machine must wait for a repair service technician to arrive after a breakdown plus the actual repair time. Currently PPI has 3 plastic injection-molding machines, which are repaired by 1 service technician. However, because of an increase in business, PPI is considering the purchase of 3 additional machines. Jerry is concerned that with the additional machines the down time problem will increase.

An analysis of historical data shows that the probability of each machine breaking down during 1 hour of operation is 0.10. In addition, the distribution of the repair time for a machine that breaks down is as follows:

Repair Time (hours)	Probability
1	0.20
2	0.35
3	0.25
4	0.15
5	0.05

The loss in revenue associated with a machine being down for 1 hour is $100. PPI pays its service technician $22 per hour, and it is believed that additional service technicians can be hired at the same wage rate.

In reviewing the breakdown problem, Jerry decided that the best way to learn about the machine repair operation would be to simulate the performance of the system. In considering the potential use of simulation, Jerry indicated that PPI must deal with the two conflicting sources of cost: the cost of the service technician(s) and the cost of machine down time. He indicated that PPI could minimize salaries by employing only 1 service technician. On the other hand, PPI could minimize the cost of machine down time by hiring so many service technicians that a machine could be serviced immediately after a breakdown.

Jerry would like you to develop a simulation model of the machine repair operation and use it to determine how many service technicians PPI should employ in order to minimize its total cost. When developing the simulation model, you can assume that if a machine has a breakdown, the breakdown can be treated as occurring at the beginning of the hour of operation. Thus, if a machine were to break down in hour 4, it would be considered to break down at the beginning of the hour. If 1 hour was spent waiting for a service technician and the length of time required to service the machine was 2 hours, the machine would be down during hours 4, 5, and 6 and then ready for operation at the beginning of hour 7. You can also assume that the probability of any machine breakdown is independent of the breakdown of any other machine and that each service time is also independent of other service times.

MANAGERIAL REPORT

Prepare a report that discusses the general development of the simulation model, the conclusions that you plan to draw by using the model, and any recommendations that you have regarding the best decision for PPI. Include the following:

1. List the information the simulation model should generate so that the decision can be made about the desired number of service technicians.
2. Set up a flowchart of the machine repair operation for 1 machine and 1 service technician.
3. Use a random number table and hand computations to demonstrate the simulation of the machine repair operation with 3 machines and 1 service technician. Use a table similar to Table 13.6 to summarize 10 hours of simulation results.
4. Develop a computer simulation model for the machine repair operation when PPI expands to 6 machines. Use your simulation results to make a recommendation about the number of service technicians that PPI should employ.

Champion International Corporation*
New York, New York

Champion International Corporation is one of the largest forest products companies in the world, employing over 41,000 people in the United States, Canada, and Brazil. Champion manages over 3 million acres of timberlands in the United States. The company's objective is to maximize the return of this timber base by converting trees into three basic product groups: (1) building materials, such as lumber and plywood; (2) white paper products, including printing and writing grades of white paper; and (3) brown paper products, such as linerboard and corrugated containers. Given the highly competitive markets within the forest products industry, survival dictates that Champion maintain its position as a low-cost producer of quality products. This requires an ambitious capital program to improve the timber base and to build additional modern, cost-effective timber-conversion facilities.

MANAGEMENT SCIENCE FUNCTION

The management science function at Champion International Corporation is organizationally structured within the corporate planning department and operates as an internal consulting service within the company. Approximately 40% of the project activity is involved with facility and production planning, 30% with physical distribution, 20% with process improvement, and 10% with capital budgeting. The primary techniques used are mathematical programming (e.g., linear programming), simulation, and statistical analyses.

A SIMULATION APPLICATION

An integrated pulp and paper mill is a facility in which wood chips and chemicals are processed in order to produce paper products or dried pulp. To begin with, wood chips are cooked and bleached in the pulp mill; the resulting pulp is piped directly into storage tanks, as shown in Figure 13.10. From the storage tanks the pulp is sent to either the paper mill or a dryer. In the paper mill the pulp is routed to one or more paper machines, which produce the finished paper products. Alternatively, the pulp is sent to a dryer, and the dried pulp is then sold to other paper mills that do not have the capability of producing their own pulp. The total system, referred to as an integrated pulp and paper mill, is a large facility costing several hundred million dollars.

One of Champion's major pulp and paper facilities consists of a pulp mill, three paper machines, and a dryer. As the facility developed, it was found that the pulp mill could produce more pulp than the combination of the paper machines and the

*The authors are indebted to Bill Griggs and Walter Foody of Champion International for providing this application.

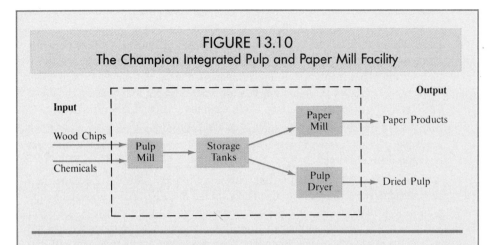

FIGURE 13.10
The Champion Integrated Pulp and Paper Mill Facility

dryer could use. A study was undertaken to determine whether it would be worthwhile to invest in improvements that would increase the capacity of the dryer. One of the first questions to be answered in the study was this: How much additional pulp could be produced and dried, given each possible capacity increase for the dryer?

A simple approach to this question is to look at average flows. For example, the pulp mill has a capacity of 940 tons† per day (TPD), the three paper machines together average 650 TPD of pulp use, and the dryer can handle 200 TPD. Based on average flows for each ton of increased dryer capacity, we can produce 1 more ton of pulp in the pulp mill. Note, however, that this is true only until the capacity of the dryer reaches 290 TPD, after which further improvements to the dryer will have no benefit.

The average flow analysis is inadequate because it ignores the day-to-day deviations from the average. That is, all of the equipment in the mill is subject to down time and to variations in efficiency. For example, suppose on one day the pulp mill is inoperable for more than the average length of time and on the same day the paper machines are experiencing less than the usual down time. In this case there will be very little pulp available for the dryer, regardless of its capacity. This lack of pulp will not "average out" on days when the opposite conditions occur since there will be far more pulp available than the pulp dryer can handle. Consequently, the pulp storage tanks will become full, and the pulp mill will have to shut down.

Based on the above analysis, we can conclude that in order not to reduce the production of the paper machines, the ratio of additional pulp production to the increase in dryer capacity will be less than 1. Since the benefits of any investment in the dryer are directly proportional to this ratio, a simulation was undertaken in order to estimate this ratio as precisely as possible. The simulation model that was developed had the following components:

Pulp mill   The pulp mill was assumed to have an average production rate of 1044 TPD when it is operating, with an average of 10% down time. The actual down time used in the model in each time period simulated was drawn randomly from a sample of actual down times experienced by the pulp mill over several months. Thus, one day the pulp mill might be down 2% of the time, the next day 20%, etc.

†All numerical values have been modified to protect proprietary information.

Paper machine   The rate of pulp flow to the paper machines in a time period is a function of the particular type of paper being made and the amount of down time on the paper machines. In the simulation, the rate of pulp flow was input to the model based on a typical schedule of types of paper to be made. The down time for each machine was drawn from a sample of actual down times.

Pulp dryer   In each run of the model, down time on the dryer was drawn from a sample of actual down times. The capacity of the dryer was set at different levels in different runs.

Storage tanks   The connecting link between the pulp mill and the paper machines and dryer is the pulp storage tanks. In the model all pulp produced by the pulp mill is added to the inventory in these tanks. All pulp drawn by the dryer and paper machines is subtracted from this inventory. If the storage tanks are empty, the model must shut down the paper machines. If the tanks are full, the pulp mill must be shut down. The actual rate at which the dryer is operated at any moment must be set by the model (as it is in reality) to try to keep the storage tanks from becoming "too empty or too full."

RESULTS

A PL/1 computer program was developed to simulate the above process. The simulation program was run at various levels of dryer capacity. The simulation results showed that for every TPD of additional pulp capacity, approximately 0.8 TPD of additional pulp could actually be dried without reducing the production of the paper machines. This number was then used by management in comparing the costs and benefits of the capital investment necessary to increase the pulp dryer capacity. Note that if the "average basis" analysis had been used, the benefits of the project would have been overstated by 25%.

Questions

1. Briefly describe the function of an integrated pulp and paper facility.
2. What is the primary reason why Champion conducted a study of its integrated pulp and paper facility?
3. Why is an analysis of average flows inadequate in studying the current operation?
4. Describe how you might use a sample of actual down times for the pulp mill in order to simulate its operation.
5. What were the advantages of using a simulation model of the pulp and paper mill facility?

▽ 14

Decision Analysis

Decision analysis can be used to determine optimal strategies when a decision maker is faced with several decision alternatives and an uncertain or risk-filled pattern of future events. For example, a manufacturer of a new style or line of seasonal clothing would like to manufacture large quantities of the product if consumer acceptance and consequently demand for the product are going to be high. However, the manufacturer would like to produce much smaller quantities if consumer acceptance and demand for the product are going to be low. Unfortunately, seasonal clothing items require the manufacturer to make a production quantity decision before the demand is known. Actual consumer acceptance of the new product will not be determined until the items have been placed in the stores and buyers have had the opportunity to purchase them. Selection of the best production volume decision from among several production volume alternatives when the decision maker is faced with the uncertainty of future demand is a problem suited for decision analysis.

We begin the study of decision analysis by considering problems in which there are reasonably few decision alternatives and possible future events. The concepts of a payoff table and a decision tree are introduced to provide a structure for this type of decision situation and to illustrate the fundamentals involved in decision analysis and the expected value approach to decision making. The discussion is then extended to show how additional information obtained through experimentation can be combined with the decision maker's preliminary information in order to develop an optimal decision strategy.

The last section of the chapter introduces the concepts of utility and the expected utility criterion. Utility takes into account the decision maker's attitude toward the profit, loss, and risk associated with an outcome. In situations where the decision maker feels that monetary values do not adequately reflect the preferences for the payoffs, a utility analysis of the problem should be considered.

14.1 ▼ STRUCTURING THE DECISION PROBLEM

In order to illustrate the decision analysis approach, let us consider the case of Political Systems, Inc. (PSI), a newly formed computer service firm specializing in information services such as surveys and data analysis for individuals running for political office. PSI is in the final stages of selecting a computer system for its Midwest branch, located in Chicago. While the firm has decided on a computer manufacturer, it is currently attempting to determine the size of the computer system that would be the most economical to lease. We will use decision analysis to help PSI make its computer leasing decision.

The first step in the decision analysis approach is to identify the alternatives considered by the decision maker. For PSI, the final decision will be to lease one of three computer systems, which differ in size and capacity. The three *decision alternatives,* denoted by d_1, d_2, and d_3, are as follows:

$$d_1 = \text{lease the large computer system}$$

$$d_2 = \text{lease the medium-sized computer system}$$

$$d_3 = \text{lease the small computer system}$$

Obviously, the selection of the *best* decision alternative will depend on what PSI management foresees as the possible market acceptance of the service and consequently the possible demand or load on the PSI computer system. Often the future events associated with a decision situation are uncertain. That is, while a decision maker may have an idea of the variety of possible future events, the decision maker will often be unsure as to which particular event will occur. Thus, the second step in a decision analysis approach is to identify the future events that might occur. These future events, which are not under the control of the decision maker, are referred to as the *states of nature*. It is assumed that the list of possible states of nature includes everything that can happen, and that the individual states of nature do not overlap; that is, the states of nature are defined so that one and only one of the listed states of nature will occur.

When asked about the states of nature for the PSI decision problem, management viewed the possible acceptance of the PSI service as an either-or situation. That is, management believed that the firm's overall level of acceptance in the marketplace would be one of two possibilities: high acceptance and low acceptance. Thus, the PSI states of nature, denoted s_1 and s_2, are as follows:

$$s_1 = \text{high customer acceptance of PSI services}$$

$$s_2 = \text{low customer acceptance of PSI services}$$

Given the three decision alternatives and the two states of nature, which computer system should PSI lease? In order to answer this question, we will need information on the profit associated with each combination of a decision alternative and a state of nature. For example, what profit would PSI experience if the firm decided to lease the large computer system (d_1) and market acceptance was high (s_1)? What profit would PSI experience if the firm decided to lease the large computer system (d_1) and market acceptance was low (s_2)?

Payoff Tables

In decision analysis terminology, we refer to the outcome resulting from making a certain decision and the occurrence of a particular state of nature as the *payoff*. Using the best information available, management has estimated the payoffs or profits for the PSI computer leasing problem. These estimates are presented in Table 14.1. A table of this form is referred to as a *payoff table*. In general, entries in a payoff table can be stated in terms of profits, costs, or any other measure of output that may be appropriate for the particular

*

TABLE 14.1
Payoff Table for the PSI Computer Leasing Problem

| | | States of Nature | |
| | | High Acceptance | Low Acceptance |
Decision Alternatives		s_1	s_2
Lease a large system	d_1	$200,000	$-20,000
Lease a medium system	d_2	$150,000	$20,000
Lease a small system	d_3	$100,000	$60,000

situation being analyzed. The notation we will use for the entries in the payoff table is $V(d_i, s_j)$, which denotes the payoff associated with decision alternative d_i and state of nature s_j. Using this notation we see that $V(d_3, s_1) = \$100,000$.

Decision Trees

A *decision tree* provides a graphical representation of the decision-making process. Figure 14.1 shows a decision tree for the PSI computer leasing problem. Note that the tree shows the natural or logical progression that will occur over time. First, the firm must make its decision (d_1, d_2, or d_3); then, once the decision is implemented, the state of nature (s_1 or s_2) will occur. The number at each end point of the tree represents the payoff associated with a particular chain of events. For example, the topmost payoff of 200,000 arises whenever management makes the decision to purchase a large system (d_1) and customer acceptance turns out to be high (s_1). The next-lower terminal point of $-20,000$ is reached when management has made the decision to lease the large system (d_1) and the state of nature turns out to be a low degree of customer acceptance (s_2). Thus, we see that each possible sequence of events for the PSI problem is represented in the decision tree.

Using the general terminology associated with decision trees, we refer to the intersection or junction points of the tree as *nodes* and the arcs or connectors between the nodes

FIGURE 14.1
Decision Tree for the PSI Computer Leasing Problem

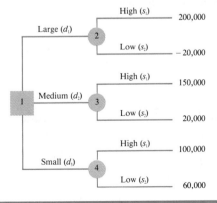

as *branches*. Figure 14.1 shows the PSI decision tree with the nodes numbered 1 to 4. When the branches *leaving* a given node are decision branches, we refer to the node as a *decision node*. Decision nodes are denoted by squares. Similarly, when the branches leaving a given node are state-of-nature branches, we refer to the node as a *state-of-nature node*. State-of-nature nodes are denoted by circles. Using this node-labeling procedure, node 1 is a decision node, whereas nodes 2, 3, and 4 are state-of-nature nodes.

The identification of the decision alternatives, the identification of the states of nature, and the determination of the payoff associated with each decision alternative and state of nature combination are the first three steps in the decision analysis process. The question we now turn to is the following: How can the decision maker best utilize the information presented in the payoff table or the decision tree to arrive at a decision? As we will see, several approaches may be used.

▼ NOTES AND COMMENTS ▼

1. Experts in problem-solving approaches generally agree that the first step in solving a complex problem is to decompose the overall problem into a series of smaller subproblems. Decision trees provide a useful method for showing how the overall problem can be decomposed, as well as showing the sequential nature of the decision process.
2. Different decision makers often view the same problem from different perspectives. Thus, there is no one correct way to develop a decision tree for a specific problem. Oftentimes the discussion regarding what is the ''best'' decision tree provides additional insight regarding the problem.

14.2 ▼ DECISION MAKING WITHOUT PROBABILITIES

In this section we consider approaches to decision making that do not require knowledge of the probabilities of the states of nature. These approaches are appropriate in situations where the decision maker has very little confidence in his or her ability to assess the probabilities of the various states of nature, or where it is desirable to consider best- and worst-case analyses that are independent of state-of-nature probabilities. Because different approaches sometimes lead to different decision recommendations, it is important for the decision maker to understand the approaches available and then select the specific approach that, according to the decision maker's judgment, is the most appropriate.

Optimistic Approach

The *optimistic approach* evaluates each decision alternative in terms of the *best* payoff that can occur. The decision alternative that is recommended is the one that provides the best possible payoff. For a problem in which it is desired to maximize profit, as it is in the PSI leasing problem, the optimistic approach would lead the decision maker to choose the alternative corresponding to the largest profit. For problems involving minimization, this approach leads to choosing the alternative with the smallest payoff.

To illustrate the use of the optimistic approach we will show how it can be used to develop a recommendation for the PSI leasing problem. First, we determine the maximum.

payoff possible for each of the decision alternatives; then we select the decision alternative that provides the overall maximum profit. This is just a systematic way of identifying the decision alternative that provides the largest possible profit. Table 14.2 illustrates this calculation for the PSI problem.

Since $200,000, corresponding to d_1, yields the maximum of the maximum payoffs, the decision to lease a large system is the recommended decision alternative using the optimistic approach. It is easy to see why this is called an optimistic approach. It simply recommends the decision alternative that provides the best of all payoffs, $200,000.

Conservative Approach

The *conservative approach* evaluates each decision alternative in terms of the *worst* payoff that can occur. The decision alternative recommended is the one that provides the best of the worst possible payoffs. For a problem in which the output measure is profit, as it is in the PSI leasing problem, the conservative approach would lead the decision maker to choose the alternative that maximizes the minimum possible profit that could be obtained. For problems involving minimization, this approach identifies the alternative that will minimize the maximum payoff.

To illustrate the use of the conservative approach, we will show how it can be used to develop a recommendation for the PSI leasing problem. First, the decision maker would identify the minimum payoff for each of the decision alternatives; then the decision maker would select the alternative that maximizes the minimum payoff. Table 14.3 illustrates this approach for the PSI problem.

Since $60,000, corresponding to d_3, yields the maximum of the minimum payoffs, the decision alternative to lease a small system is recommended. This decision approach is considered conservative because it concentrates on the worst possible payoffs and then recommends the decision alternative that avoids the possibility of extremely "bad" payoffs. In using the conservative approach, PSI is guaranteed a profit of at least $60,000. While PSI may still make more, it *cannot* make less than $60,000.

TABLE 14.2
PSI Maximum Payoff for Each Decision Alternative

Decision Alternatives		Maximum Payoff ($)	
Large system	(d_1)	200,000 ←	Maximum of the
Medium system	(d_2)	150,000	maximum payoff values
Small system	(d_3)	100,000	

TABLE 14.3
PSI Minimum Payoff for Each Decision Alternative

Decision Alternatives		Minimum Payoff ($)	
Large system	(d_1)	−20,000	
Medium system	(d_2)	20,000	Maximum of the
Small system	(d_3)	60,000 ←	minimum payoff values

✳ Minimax Regret Approach

Minimax regret is another approach to decision making without probabilities. This approach is neither purely optimistic nor purely conservative. Let us illustrate the minimax regret approach by showing how it can be used to select a decision alternative for the PSI leasing problem.

Suppose we make the decision to lease the small system (d_3) and afterwards learn that customer acceptance of the PSI service is high (s_1). Table 14.1 shows the resulting profit to be $100,000. However, now that we know that state of nature s_1 has occurred, we see that the large system decision (d_1), yielding a profit of $200,000, would have been the optimal decision. The difference between the optimal payoff ($200,000) and the payoff experienced ($100,000) is referred to as the *opportunity loss* or *regret* associated with the d_3 decision when state of nature s_1 occurs ($200,000 − $100,000 = $100,000). If we had made decision d_2 and state of nature s_1 had occurred, the opportunity loss or regret would have been $200,000 − $150,000 = $50,000.

In maximization problems, the general expression for opportunity loss or regret is given by

$$✳\quad R(d_i,s_j) = V^*(s_j) - V(d_i,s_j) \tag{14.1}$$

where

$R(d_i,s_j)$ = regret associated with decision alternative d_i and state of nature s_j

$V^*(s_j)$ = best payoff value[1] under state of nature s_j

$V(d_i,s_j)$ = payoff associated with decision alternative d_i and state of nature s_j

Using equation (14.1) and the payoffs in Table 14.1, we can compute the regret associated with all combinations of decision alternatives d_i and states of nature s_j. We simply replace each entry in the payoff table with the value found by subtracting the entry from the largest entry in its column. Table 14.4 shows the regret, or opportunity loss, table for the PSI problem.

The next step in applying the minimax regret approach requires the decision maker to identify the maximum regret for each decision alternative. These data are shown in Table 14.5. The choice of a best decision is made by selecting the alternative correspond-

TABLE 14.4
Regret or Opportunity Loss for the PSI Computer Leasing Problem

Decision Alternatives		States of Nature	
		High Acceptance s_1	Low Acceptance s_2
Large system	d_1 (200,000 −200,000) 0		$80,000 (−20,000 −60,000)
Medium system	d_2	$ 50,000	$40,000
Small system	d_3	$100,000	0

[1]In cost minimization problems, $V^*(s_j)$ will be the smallest entry in column j. Thus, for minimization problems, equation (14.1) must be changed to $R(d_i,s_j) = V(d_i, s_j) - V^*(s_j)$.

TABLE 14.5
PSI Maximum Regret or Opportunity Loss for Each Decision Alternative

Decision Alternatives		Maximum Regret or Opportunity Loss ($)	
Large system	(d_1)	80,000	
Medium system	(d_2)	50,000 ◄———————	Minimum of the
Small system	(d_3)	100,000	maximum regret

ing to the *mini*mum of the *max*imum *regret* values—hence the name *minimax regret*. For the PSI problem the decision to lease a medium-sized computer system, with a corresponding regret of $50,000, is the recommended minimax regret decision.

Note that the three approaches discussed in this section have provided different recommendations. This is not in itself bad. It simply reflects the difference in decision-making philosophies that underlie the various approaches. Ultimately, the decision maker will have to choose the most appropriate approach and then make the final decision accordingly. The major criticism of the approaches discussed in this section is that they do not consider any information about the probabilities of the various states of nature. In the next section we discuss an approach that utilizes probability information in selecting a decision alternative.

14.3 ▼ DECISION MAKING WITH PROBABILITIES

In many decision-making situations it is possible to obtain probability estimates for each of the possible states of nature. When such probabilities are available, the *expected value approach* can be used to identify the best decision alternative. The expected value approach evaluates each decision alternative in terms of its expected value. The decision alternative that is recommended is the one that provides the best expected value. Let us first define the expected value of a decision alternative and then show how it can be used for the PSI decision problem.

Let

$$N = \text{the number of possible states of nature}$$

$$P(s_j) = \text{the probability of state of nature } s_j$$

Since one and only one of the N states of nature can occur, the associated probabilities must satisfy the following two conditions:

$$P(s_j) \geq 0 \text{ for all states of nature} \tag{14.2}$$

$$\sum_{j=1}^{N} P(s_j) = P(s_1) + P(s_2) + \ldots + P(s_N) = 1 \tag{14.3}$$

The expected value (EV) of decision alternative d_i is defined as follows:

$$EV(d_i) = \sum_{j=1}^{N} P(s_j)V(d_i,s_j) \tag{14.4}$$

In words, the expected value of a decision alternative is the sum of weighted payoffs for the alternative. The weight for a payoff is the probability of the associated state of nature and therefore the probability that the payoff occurs. Let us now return to the PSI problem to see how the expected value approach can be applied.

Suppose PSI management believes that s_1, the high-acceptance state of nature, has a .3 probability of occurrence and that s_2, the low-acceptance state of nature, has a .7 probability. Thus, $P(s_1) = .3$ and $P(s_2) = .7$. Using the payoff values $V(d_i, s_j)$ shown in Table 14.1 and equation (14.4), expected values for the three decision alternatives can be calculated:

$$
\begin{aligned}
EV(d_1) &= .3(\$200,000) + .7(-\$20,000) = \$46,000 \\
EV(d_2) &= .3(\$150,000) + .7(\$20,000) \quad = \$59,000 \\
EV(d_3) &= .3(\$100,000) + .7(\$60,000) \quad = \$72,000
\end{aligned}
$$

Thus, according to the expected value approach, since d_3 has the highest expected value ($72,000), d_3 is the recommended decision.

The calculations required to identify the decision alternative with the best expected value can be conveniently carried out on a decision tree. Figure 14.2 shows the decision tree for the PSI problem with state-of-nature branch probabilities. We will now use the branch probabilities and the expected value approach to arrive at the optimal decision for PSI.

Working backward through the decision tree, we first compute the expected value at each state-of-nature node. That is, at each state-of-nature node we weigh each possible payoff by its chance of occurrence. By doing this, we obtain the expected values for nodes 2, 3, and 4 as shown in Figure 14.3.

Since the decision maker controls the branch leaving decision node 1, and since we are trying to maximize expected profits, the best decision branch at node 1 is d_3. Thus, the decision tree analysis leads us to recommend d_3, with an expected value of $72,000. Note that this is the same recommendation that was obtained using the expected value approach in conjunction with the payoff table.

We have seen how decision trees can be used to analyze decisions with state-of-nature probabilities. While other decision problems may be substantially more complex than the

FIGURE 14.2
PSI Decision Tree with State-of-Nature Branch Probabilities

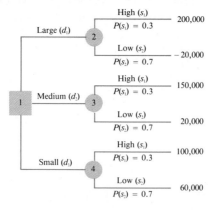

FIGURE 14.3
Applying the Expected Value Approach Using Decision Trees

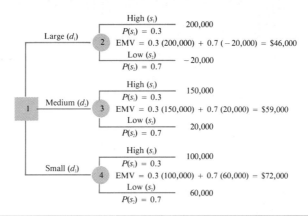

PSI problem, if there are a reasonable number of decision alternatives and states of nature, the decision tree approach outlined in this section can be used. First, the analyst must draw a decision tree consisting of decision and state-of-nature nodes and branches that describe the sequential nature of the problem. Assuming that the expected value approach is to be used, the next step is to determine the probabilities for each of the state-of-nature branches and compute the expected value at each state-of-nature node. The decision branch leading to the state-of-nature node with the best expected value is then selected. The decision alternative associated with this branch is the decision recommended.

14.4 ▼ SENSITIVITY ANALYSIS

For the PSI problem, management provided a .3 probability for s_1, the high-acceptance state of nature, and a .7 probability for s_2, the low-acceptance state of nature. Using these probabilities we found that decision alternative d_3 had the highest expected value and was the recommended decision. In this section we consider how changes in the probability estimates for the states of nature affect or alter the recommended decision. The study of the effect of such changes is referred to as *sensitivity analysis*.

One approach to sensitivity analysis is to consider different probabilities for the states of nature and then recompute the expected value for each of the decision alternatives. Repeating this several times, we can begin to learn how changes in the probabilities for the states of nature affect the recommended decision. For example, suppose that we consider a change in the probabilities for the states of nature such that $P(s_1) = .6$ and $P(s_2) = .4$. Using these probabilities and repeating the expected value computations, we find the following:

$$EV(d_1) = .6(\$200,000) + .4(-\$20,000) = \$112,000$$

$$EV(d_2) = .6(\$150,000) + .4(\$20,000) = \$98,000$$

$$EV(d_3) = .6(\$100,000) + .4(\$60,000) = \$84,000$$

Thus, with these probabilities, the recommended decision alternative is d_1, with an expected value of $112,000.

Obviously, we could continue to modify the probabilities of the states of nature and begin to learn more about how such changes affect the recommended decision. The only drawback to this approach is that there will be numerous calculations required to evaluate the effect of several possible changes in the state of nature probabilities.

For the special case of decision analysis with two states of nature, the sensitivity analysis computations can be eased substantially through the use of a graphical procedure. Let us demonstrate this procedure by further analyzing the PSI problem. We begin by denoting the probability of state of nature s_1 by p. That is,

$$P(s_1) = p$$

and, thus,

$$P(s_2) = 1 - P(s_1) = 1 - p$$

The expected value for decision alternative d_1 can then be written as a function of p.

$$
\begin{aligned}
EV(d_1) &= P(s_1)(200,000) + P(s_2)(-20,000) \\
&= p(200,000) + (1 - p)(-20,000) \\
&= 220,000p - 20,000
\end{aligned}
\tag{14.5}
$$

Repeating the expected value computation for decision alternatives d_2 and d_3, we obtain the following expressions for expected value as a function of p:

$$EV(d_2) = 130,000p + 20,000 \tag{14.6}$$

$$EV(d_3) = 40,000p + 60,000 \tag{14.7}$$

Thus, we have developed three linear equations that express the expected value of the three decision alternatives as a function of the probability of state of nature s_1.

Let us continue by developing a graph with the values of p on the horizontal axis and the associated expected values on the vertical axis. Since expressions (14.5), (14.6), and (14.7) are all linear equations, we can graph each equation, or line, by finding any two points on the line and drawing the line through the points. Using $EV(d_1)$ in (14.5) as an example, we first let $p = 0$ and find that $EV(d_1) = -20,000$. Then, letting $p = 1$, we find that $EV(d_1) = 200,000$. Connecting these two points, $(0, -20,000)$ and $(1,200,000)$, provides the line labeled $EV(d_1)$ in Figure 14.4. This figure also shows a line labeled $EV(d_2)$ and a line labeled $EV(d_3)$; these are the graphs of (14.6) and (14.7), respectively.

Figure 14.4 can now be used for sensitivity analysis. Recall that PSI is seeking to maximize profit. Note that for small values of p, decision alternative d_3 provides the largest expected value and is thus the recommended decision. Similarly, for large values of p, we see that decision alternative d_1 provides the largest expected value and is thus the recommended decision. Further, note that there is no section of the graph for which decision alternative d_2 provides the largest expected value. Thus, with the exception of the point where the three expected value lines intersect and all three expected values are equal, decision alternative d_2 can never be the decision alternative recommended by the expected value approach.

Referring to Figure 14.4 again, we see that the three lines intersect at a value of p between .4 and .5. In other words, at some point between .4 and .5, all three decision alternatives provide the same expected value.

FIGURE 14.4
Expected Value as a Function of *p*

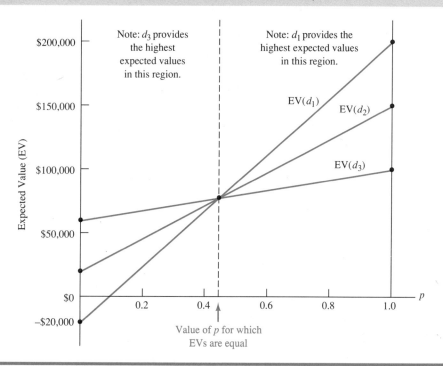

Whenever two or more lines intersect on a sensitivity analysis graph, we can set the equations for two of the intersecting lines equal to each other and solve for the value of *p*. Using the equations for decision alternatives d_1 and d_3, we obtain

$$220,000p - 20,000 = 40,000p + 60,000$$

Thus,

$$180,000p = 80,000$$

$$p = \frac{80,000}{180,000} = .44$$

Hence, whenever $p = .44$, each decision alternative will provide the same expected value. Using this value of *p* in Figure 14.4, we can now conclude that for $p < .44$, decision alternative d_3 provides the largest expected value, and that for $p > .44$, decision alternative d_1 provides the largest expected value. Since *p* is simply the probability of state of nature s_1 and $(1 - p)$ is the probability of state of nature s_2, we now have the sensitivity analysis information that tells us how changes in the state-of-nature probabilities affect the recommended decision alternative.

The benefit of performing sensitivity analysis is that it can provide a better perspective on management's original judgment regarding the state-of-nature probabilities. Management originally estimated the probability of high customer acceptance as $P(s_1) = .3$. As a result, decision alternative d_3 was recommended. After carrying out the sensitivity analysis, we can now tell management that the original estimate of $P(s_1)$ is not extremely critical in order for d_3 to be the recommended decision. In fact, as long as $P(s_1) < .44$, the d_3 decision alternative remains optimal.

Note that in the PSI problem the three lines for the three decision alternatives graphed in Figure 14.4 intersect at the same point ($p = .44$). Similar sensitivity analysis computations for other decision analysis problems with two states of nature and three decision alternatives should not be expected to result in the same type of graph. With a different sensitivity analysis graph, d_1 could be the best decision alternative for certain values of p, d_2 the best decision alternative for other values of p, and d_3 the best decision alternative for the remaining values of p. (This situation is demonstrated in the sensitivity analysis computation for problem 8.)

The graphical sensitivity analysis procedure we have described for the PSI problem applies only to decision analysis problems with two states of nature. However, sensitivity analysis is important in problems with more than two states of nature. In these cases a computer software package can be used to assist with the computations. Basically, we use the approach of testing a variety of likely changes for the state-of-nature probabilities. The software package is helpful in making the necessary expected value computations and providing the decision alternative recommendations with a minimum of time and effort on the part of the analyst.

*14.5 ▼ EXPECTED VALUE OF PERFECT INFORMATION

Suppose that PSI had the opportunity to conduct a market research study that would evaluate consumer needs for the PSI service. Such a study could help by improving the current probability assessments for the states of nature. However, if the cost of obtaining the market research information exceeds its value, PSI should not conduct the market research study.

To determine the maximum possible value that PSI should pay for additional information, let us suppose that PSI could obtain perfect information regarding the states of nature; that is, we will assume that PSI could determine with certainty which state of nature will occur. To make use of perfect information we need to develop a decision strategy for PSI to follow. As we will show, a decision strategy is simply a policy or decision rule that is to be followed by the decision maker. In computing the *expected value of perfect information* (EVPI), the decision strategy is a rule that specifies which decision alternative should be selected, given each state of nature.

To help determine the optimal decision strategy for PSI we have reproduced PSI's payoff table as Table 14.6. We see that if state of nature s_1 occurs, then the best decision alternative is d_1, with a profit of $200,000. Similarly, if state of nature s_2 occurs, then the best decision alternative is d_3, with a profit of $60,000. Thus, the optimal decision strategy PSI should follow if perfect information is available can be stated as follows:

If s_1 occurs, then select d_1.

If s_2 occurs, then select d_3.

What is the expected value for this decision strategy? Since $P(s_1) = .3$ and $P(s_2) = .7$, we see that there is a .3 probability that PSI will make $200,000 and a .7 probability PSI will make $60,000. Thus, the expected value of the decision strategy that uses perfect information is

$$(.3)(\$200,000) + (.7)(\$60,000) = \$102,000$$

TABLE 14.6
Payoff Table for the PSI Computer Leasing Problem

Decision Alternatives		States of Nature	
		High Acceptance s_1	Low Acceptance s_2
Large system	d_1	$200,000	-$20,000
Medium system	d_2	$150,000	$20,000
Small system	d_3	$100,000	$60,000

Recall that when perfect information was not available, the expected value approach resulted in recommending decision alternative d_3, with an expected value of $72,000. Since $72,000 is the expected value without perfect information and $102,000 is the expected value with perfect information, $102,000 − $72,000 = $30,000 represents the expected value of perfect information (EVPI); that is,

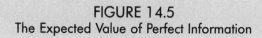

$$\text{EVPI} = \$102,000 - \$72,000 = \$30,000$$

In other words, $30,000 represents the additional expected value that can be obtained if perfect information is available about the states of nature. Figure 14.5 provides a summary of the computation of the EVPI for the PSI problem.

Generally speaking, a market research study will not provide "perfect" information; however, the information provided might be worth a good portion of the $30,000. In any case, PSI's management knows it should never pay more than $30,000 for any information, no matter how good. Provided the market survey cost is reasonably small—say,

FIGURE 14.5
The Expected Value of Perfect Information

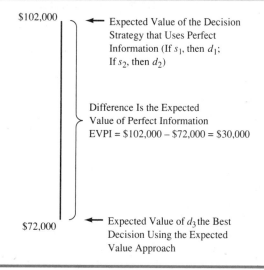

$102,000 — Expected Value of the Decision Strategy that Uses Perfect Information (If s_1, then d_1; If s_2, then d_2)

Difference Is the Expected Value of Perfect Information EVPI = $102,000 – $72,000 = $30,000

$72,000 — Expected Value of d_3 the Best Decision Using the Expected Value Approach

$5000 to $10,000—it appears economically desirable for PSI to consider the market research study.

14.6 ▼ DECISION ANALYSIS WITH SAMPLE INFORMATION

In applying the expected value approach, we have seen how probability information about the states of nature affects the expected value calculations and thus the decision recommendation. Frequently decision makers have preliminary or prior probability estimates for the states of nature that are initially the best probability estimates available. However, in order to make the best possible decision, the decision maker may want to seek additional information about the states of nature. This new information can be used to revise or update the prior probabilities so that the final decision is based on more accurate probability estimates for the states of nature.

The seeking of additional information is most often accomplished through experiments designed to provide sample information or more current data about the states of nature. Raw material sampling, product testing, and test market research are examples of experiments that may enable a revision or updating of the state-of-nature probabilities. In the following discussion we will reconsider the PSI computer leasing problem and show how sample information can be used to revise the state-of-nature probabilities. We will then show how the revised probabilities can be used to develop an optimal decision strategy for PSI.

Recall that management had assigned a probability of $P(s_1) = .3$ to state of nature s_1 and a probability of $P(s_2) = .7$ to state of nature s_2. At this point we will refer to these initial probability estimates, $P(s_1)$ and $P(s_2)$, as the *prior probabilities* for the states of nature. Using these prior probabilities we found that d_3, the decision to lease the small system, was optimal, yielding an expected value of $72,000. Recall also that we showed that the expected value of new information about the states of nature could potentially be worth as much as EVPI = $30,000.

Suppose PSI decides to consider hiring a market research firm to study the potential acceptance of the PSI service. The market research study will provide new information that can be combined with the prior probabilities through a Bayesian procedure to obtain updated or revised probability estimates for the states of nature. These *revised* probabilities are called *posterior probabilities*. The process of revising probabilities is depicted in Figure 14.6.

We will refer to the new information obtained through research or experimentation as an *indicator*. Since in many cases the experiment conducted to obtain the additional information will consist of taking a statistical sample, the new information is also often referred to as *sample information*.

Using the indicator terminology, we can denote the outcomes of the PSI marketing research study as follows:

I_1 = favorable market research report (i.e., in the market research study the individuals contacted generally expressed interest in PSI's services)

I_2 = unfavorable market research report (i.e., in the market research study the individuals contacted generally expressed little interest in PSI's services)

Given one of these possible indicators, our objective is to provide improved estimates of the probabilities of the two states of nature. The end result of the *Bayesian revision* process depicted in Figure 14.6 is a set of posterior probabilities of the form $P(s_j|I_k)$,

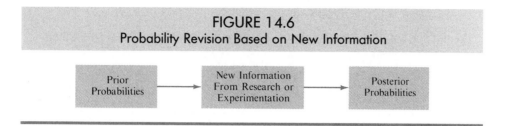

FIGURE 14.6
Probability Revision Based on New Information

Prior Probabilities → New Information From Research or Experimentation → Posterior Probabilities

where $P(s_j|I_k)$ represents the conditional probability that state of nature s_j will occur, given that the outcome of the market research study was indicator I_k.

To make effective use of this indicator information, we must know something about the probability relationships between the indicators and the states of nature. For example, in the PSI problem, given that the state of nature ultimately turns out to be high customer acceptance, what is the probability that the market research study will result in a favorable report? In this case we are asking about the conditional probability of indicator I_1, given state of nature s_1—written $P(I_1|s_1)$. In order to carry out the analysis, we will need conditional probabilities for all indicators, given all states of nature—that is, $P(I_1|s_1)$, $P(I_1|s_2)$, $P(I_2|s_1)$, and $P(I_2|s_2)$.

In the PSI example the past record of the marketing research company on similar studies has led to the following estimates of the relevant conditional probabilities:

States of Nature	Market Research Report Favorable (I_1)	Unfavorable (I_2)
High acceptance (s_1)	$P(I_1\|s_1) = .8$	$P(I_2\|s_1) = .2$
Low acceptance (s_2)	$P(I_1\|s_2) = .1$	$P(I_2\|s_2) = .9$

Note that these probability estimates indicate that a good degree of confidence can be placed in the market research report. When the true state of nature is s_1, the market research report will be favorable 80% of the time and unfavorable only 20%. When the true state of nature is s_2, the report will make the correct indication 90% of the time. Now let us see how this additional information can be incorporated into the decision-making process.

14.7 ▼ DEVELOPING A DECISION STRATEGY

A decision strategy is a policy or decision rule that is to be followed by the decision maker. In the PSI case, with the market research study, a decision strategy is a rule that recommends a particular decision based on whether the market research report is favorable or unfavorable. We will employ a decision tree analysis to find the optimal decision strategy for PSI.

Figure 14.7 shows the decision tree for the PSI computer leasing problem provided that a market research study is conducted. Note that as you move from left to right, the tree shows the natural or logical order of the decision-making process. First, the firm will obtain the market research report indicator (I_1 or I_2); then a decision (d_1, d_2, or d_3) will be made; finally, the state of nature (s_1 or s_2) will occur. The decision and the state of nature combine to provide the final profit or payoff.

FIGURE 14.7
The PSI Decision Tree Incorporating the Results of the Market Research Study

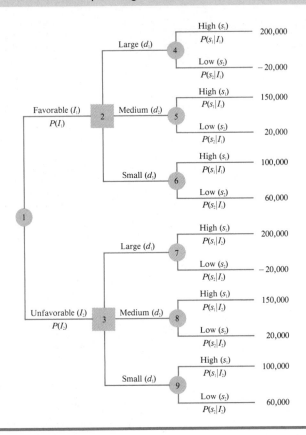

Using decision tree terminology, we have now introduced an *indicator node,* node 1, and *indicator branches, I_1* and I_2. Since the branches emanating from indicator nodes are not under the control of the decision maker, but are determined by chance, these nodes are depicted by a circle (just like the state-of-nature nodes). We see that nodes 2 and 3 are decision nodes, while nodes 4, 5, 6, 7, 8, and 9 are state-of-nature nodes. For decision nodes the decision maker must select the specific branch, d_1, d_2, or d_3, that will be taken. Selecting the best decision branch is equivalent to making the best decision. However, since the indicator and state-of-nature branches are not controlled by the decision maker, the specific branch leaving an indicator or a state-of-nature node will depend on the probability associated with the branch. Thus, before we can carry out an analysis of the decision tree and develop a decision strategy, we must compute the probability of each indicator branch and the probability of each state-of-nature branch. Note from the decision tree that the state-of-nature branches occur *after* the indicator branches. Thus, when we attempt to compute state-of-nature branch probabilities, we will need to consider which indicator was previously observed. That is, we will express state-of-nature probabilities in terms of the probability of state of nature s_j, *given* indicator I_k was observed. Thus, all state-of-nature probabilities will be expressed in a $P(s_j|I_k)$ form.

Computing Branch Probabilities

The prior probabilities for the states of nature in the PSI problem were given as $P(s_1) = .3$ and $P(s_2) = .7$. In section 14.6 we identified the relationships between the market research indicators and states of nature with the conditional probabilities

$$P(I_1|s_1) = .8 \qquad P(I_2|s_1) = .2$$
$$P(I_1|s_2) = .1 \qquad P(I_2|s_2) = .9$$

In order to develop a decision strategy utilizing the decision tree in Figure 14.7, we need indicator branch probabilities $P(I_k)$ and state-of-nature branch probabilities $P(s_j|I_k)$. The problem now facing us is determining how to use the given prior probability estimates $P(s_j)$ and conditional probability estimates $P(I_k|s_j)$ to calculate the branch probabilities $P(I_k)$ and $P(s_j|I_k)$. In this section we will show how the Bayesian revision process referred to in Figure 14.6 can be used to calculate the branch probabilities $P(I_k)$ and $P(s_j|I_k)$.

In order to see how this Bayesian procedure is applied and at the same time understand how the procedure works, let us look closely at the calculation of the indicator branch probability $P(I_1)$ for the PSI market research study. First, note that there are only two ways in which the outcome I_1 can occur:

1. The market research report is favorable (I_1) *and* and the state of nature turns out to be high acceptance (s_1), written ($I_1 \cap s_1$).
2. The market research report is favorable (I_1) *and* the state of nature turns out to be low acceptance (s_2), written ($I_1 \cap s_2$).

The probabilities of these two outcomes are written $P(I_1 \cap s_1)$ and $P(I_1 \cap s_2)$, respectively. We can now add these two probabilities to obtain the following branch probability:

$$P(I_1) = P(I_1 \cap s_1) + P(I_1 \cap s_2) \tag{14.8}$$

The multiplication law of probability provides the following formulas for $P(I_1 \cap s_1)$ and $P(I_1 \cap s_2)$:

$$P(I_1 \cap s_1) = P(I_1|s_1)P(s_1) \tag{14.9}$$
$$P(I_1 \cap s_2) = P(I_1|s_2)P(s_2) \tag{14.10}$$

Finally, substituting the above expressions for $P(I_1 \cap s_1)$ and $P(I_1 \cap s_2)$ in equation (14.8), we obtain

$$P(I_1) = P(I_1|s_1)P(s_1) + P(I_1|s_2)P(s_2) \tag{14.11}$$

Generalizing the above expression for any indicator branch probability, $P(I_k)$, and N states of nature, $s_1, s_2, \ldots, s_N$, we have

$$P(I_k) = P(I_k|s_1)P(s_1) + P(I_k|s_2)P(s_2) + \cdots + P(I_k|s_N)P(s_N) \tag{14.12}$$

or

$$P(I_k) = \sum_{j=1}^{N} P(I_k|s_j)P(s_j) \tag{14.13}$$

Returning to the PSI problem with the two prior probabilities $P(s_1) = .3$ and $P(s_2) = .7$ and the conditional probabilities $P(I_1|s_1) = .8$, $P(I_1|s_2) = .1$,

$P(I_2|s_1) = .2$, and $P(I_2|s_2) = .9$, we can use equation (14.13) to compute the two indicator branch probabilities. These calculations are as follows:

$$P(I_1) = P(I_1|s_1)P(s_1) + P(I_1|s_2)P(s_2)$$
$$= (.8)(.3) + (.1)(.7) = .31$$

and

$$P(I_2) = P(I_2|s_1)P(s_1) + P(I_2|s_2)P(s_2)$$
$$= (.2)(.3) + (.9)(.7) = .69$$

The above probabilities indicate that the probability of I_1, a favorable market research report, is .31 and the probability of I_2, an unfavorable market research report, is .69.

Now that we know the indicator branch probabilities, let us show how the Bayesian process enables us to compute the revised, or posterior, state-of-nature branch probabilities $P(s_j|I_k)$. We will illustrate this procedure by considering the state-of-nature branch probability $P(s_1|I_1)$, the probability the market acceptance is high (s_1) given that the market research report is favorable (I_1). The fundamental conditional probability relationship as presented in texts dealing with probability and statistics can be written

$$P(s_1|I_1) = \frac{P(I_1 \cap s_1)}{P(I_1)} \tag{14.14}$$

Using equation (14.9) for $P(I_1 \cap s_1)$, we have

$$P(s_1|I_1) = \frac{P(I_1|s_1)P(s_1)}{P(I_1)} \tag{14.15}$$

With known probabilities $P(I_1|s_1) = .8$, $P(s_1) = .3$, and $P(I_1) = .31$, the revised state-of-nature probability, $P(s_1|I_1)$, becomes

$$P(s_1|I_1) = \frac{(.8)(.3)}{0.31} = \frac{.24}{.31} = .7742$$

Recall that the prior probability of a high market acceptance was $P(s_1) = .3$. The preceding probability information now tells us that if the market research indicator is favorable, the probability of a high market acceptance should be revised to $P(s_1|I_1) = .7742$.

Generalizing (14.15) for any state of nature s_j and any indicator I_k provides

$$P(s_j|I_k) = \frac{P(I_k|s_j)P(s_j)}{P(I_k)} \tag{14.16}$$

Thus, we can use (14.16) to compute the revised or posterior state-of-nature branch probabilities. For example, the revised probability of low market acceptance, s_2, given that the market research indicator is favorable, I_1, becomes

$$P(s_2|I_1) = \frac{P(I_1|s_2)P(s_2)}{P(I_1)} = \frac{(.1)(.7)}{.31} = \frac{.07}{.31} = .2258$$

Similar calculations for an unfavorable market research indicator, I_2, will provide the revised state-of-nature branch probabilities $P(s_1|I_2) = .0870$ and $P(s_2|I_2) = .9130$. Fig-

FIGURE 14.8
The PSI Decision Tree with Branch Probabilities

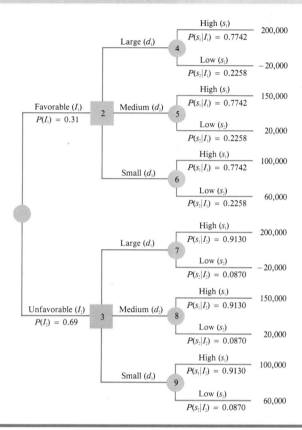

ure 14.8 shows the PSI decision tree after all indicator and all revised state-of-nature branch probabilities have been computed.

Although the above procedure can be used to compute branch probabilities, the calculations can become quite cumbersome as the problem size grows larger. Thus, in order to assist in applying Bayes' theorem to compute branch probabilities, we present the following tabular procedure that will make it easier to carry out the computations, especially for large decision analysis problems.

Computing Branch Probabilities: A Tabular Procedure

The procedure used for computing the probabilities of the indicator and state-of-nature branches can be carried out by utilizing a tabular approach. First, for each indicator I_k we form a table consisting of the following five column headings:

Column 1 States of nature s_j
Column 2 Prior probabilities $P(s_j)$
Column 3 Conditional probabilities $P(I_k | s_j)$
Column 4 Joint probabilities $P(I_k \cap s_j)$
Column 5 Posterior probabilities $P(s_j | I_k)$

Then, given any indicator I_k, the following procedure can be used to calculate $P(I_k)$ and the $P(s_j|I_k)$ values:

Step 1 In column 1 list the states of nature appropriate to the problem being analyzed.

Step 2 In column 2 enter the prior probability corresponding to each state of nature listed in column 1.

Step 3 In column 3 enter the appropriate value of $P(I_k|s_j)$ for each state of nature specified in column 1.

Step 4 To compute each entry in column 4, multiply each entry in column 2 by the corresponding entry in column 3.

Step 5 To compute the value of $P(I_k)$ sum the entries in column 4. For convenience, write the sum below column 4.

Step 6 To compute each entry in column 5 divide the corresponding entry in column 4 by $P(I_k)$.

We will now use this procedure to compute $P(I_1)$ and the revised state-of-nature probabilities $P(s_j|I_1)$ for the PSI problem.

Steps 1, 2, and 3:

s_j	$P(s_j)$	$P(I_1|s_j)$	$P(I_1 \cap s_j)$	$P(s_j|I_1)$
s_1	.3	.8		
s_2	.7	.1		

Steps 4 and 5:

s_j	$P(s_j)$	$P(I_1|s_j)$	$P(I_1 \cap s_j)$	$P(s_j|I_1)$
s_1	.3	.8	.24	
s_2	.7	.1	.07	
			$P(I_1) = .31$	

Step 6:

s_j	$P(s_j)$	$P(I_1|s_j)$	$P(I_1 \cap s_j)$	$P(s_j|I_1)$
s_1	.3	.8	.24	.24/.31 = .7742
s_2	.7	.1	.07	.07/.31 = .2258
			$P(I_1) = .31$	

Note that $P(I_1)$, $P(s_1|I_1)$, and $P(s_2|I_1)$ are exactly the same as we calculated by applying equations (14.13) and (14.16) directly. The preceding tabular computations could be repeated in order to compute $P(I_2)$ and the revised state-of-nature probabilities $P(s_j|I_2)$.

An Optimal Decision Strategy

Regardless of the method used to compute the branch probabilities, we can now use the branch probabilities and the expected value approach to arrive at the optimal decision for PSI. Working *backward* through the decision tree, we first compute the expected value at each state-of-nature node. That is, at each state-of-nature node the possible payoffs are weighted by their chance of occurrence. Thus, the expected values for nodes 4 through 9 are computed as follows:

$$EV(\text{node } 4) = (.7742)(200,000) + (.2258)(-20,000) = 150,324$$
$$EV(\text{node } 5) = (.7742)(150,000) + (.2258)(20,000) \quad = 120,646$$
$$EV(\text{node } 6) = (.7742)(100,000) + (.2258)(60,000) \quad = \quad 90,968$$
$$EV(\text{node } 7) = (.0870)(200,000) + (.9130)(-20,000) = \quad -860$$
$$EV(\text{node } 8) = (.0870)(150,000) + (.9130)(20,000) \quad = \quad 31,310$$
$$EV(\text{node } 9) = (.0870)(100,000) + (.9130)(60,000) \quad = \quad 63,480$$

Figure 14.9 shows the above calculations directly on the decision tree. Since the decision maker controls the branch leaving a decision node, and since we are trying to maximize expected profits, the optimal decision at node 2 is d_1. Thus, since d_1 leads to an expected value of $150,324, we say that $EV(\text{node } 2) = \$150,324$.

A similar analysis of decision node 3 shows that the optimal decision branch at this node is d_3. Thus, $EV(\text{node } 3)$ becomes $63,480, provided that the optimal decision of d_3 is made.

As a final step, we can continue working backward to the indicator node and establish its expected value. We see that since node 1 has probability branches, we cannot select the best branch. Rather, we must compute the expected value over all possible branches. Thus, we have

$$EV(\text{node } 1) = (.31)EV(\text{node } 2) + (.69)EV(\text{node } 3)$$
$$= (.31)(\$150,324) + (.69)(\$63,480) = \$90,402$$

The value of $90,402 is viewed as the expected value of the optimal decision strategy when the market research study is used. In other words, it is the expected value using the sample information provided by the market research report.

Note that the final decision has not yet been determined. We will need to know the results of the market research study before deciding to lease a large system (d_1) or a small system (d_3). The results of the decision theory analysis at this point, however, have provided us with the following optimal *decision strategy* if the market research study is conducted:

If	Then
Report favorable (I_1)	Lease large system (d_1)
Report unfavorable (I_2)	Lease small system (d_3)

Thus, we have seen how the decision tree approach can be used to develop optimal decision strategies when sample information is available. While other decision analysis

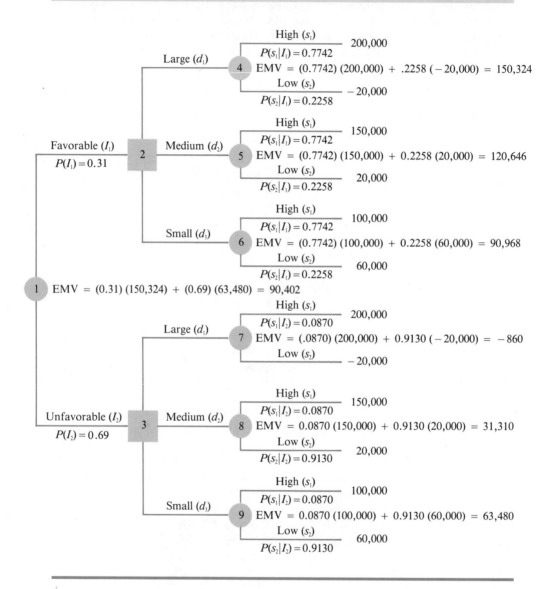

FIGURE 14.9
Developing a Decision Strategy for the PSI Computer Leasing Problem

problems may not be as simple as the PSI problem, the approach we have outlined is still applicable. First, draw a decision tree consisting of indicator, decision, and state-of-nature nodes and branches such that the tree describes the specific sequence of decisions and chance outcomes. Posterior probability calculations must be made in order to establish indicator and state-of-nature branch probabilities. Then, by working backward through the tree, computing expected values at state-of-nature and indicator nodes, and selecting the best decision branch at decision nodes, the analyst can determine an optimal decision strategy and its associated expected value.

14.8 ▼ EXPECTED VALUE OF SAMPLE INFORMATION

In the PSI problem, management now has a decision strategy of leasing the large computer system if the market research report is favorable and leasing the small computer system if the market research report is unfavorable. Since the additional information provided by the market research firm will result in an added cost for PSI in terms of the fee paid to the research firm, PSI management may question the value of this market research information.

The value of sample information is often measured by calculating what is referred to as the *expected value of sample information* (EVSI). For maximization problems,[2]

$$\text{EVSI} = \begin{bmatrix} \text{expected value of the} \\ \text{optimal decision } with \\ \text{sample information} \end{bmatrix} - \begin{bmatrix} \text{expected value of the} \\ \text{optimal decision } without \\ \text{sample information} \end{bmatrix} \quad (14.17)$$

For PSI the market research information is considered the "sample" information. The decision tree calculations indicated that the expected value of the optimal decision with the market research information was $90,402, while the expected value of the optimal decision without the market research information was $72,000. Using equation (14.17), the expected value of the market research report is

$$EVSI = \$90,402 - \$72,000 = \$18,402$$

Thus, PSI should be willing to pay up to $18,402 for the market research information.

Efficiency of Sample Information

In Section 14.5 we saw that the expected value of perfect information (EVPI) for the PSI problem was $30,000. While we never expected the market research report to obtain perfect information, we can use an *efficiency* measure to express the value of the report. With perfect information having an efficiency rating of 100%, the efficiency rating E for sample information is computed as follows:

$$E = \frac{\text{EVSI}}{\text{EVPI}} \times 100 \quad (14.18)$$

For the PSI example

$$E = \frac{18,402}{30,000} \times 100 = 61.3\%$$

In other words, the information from the market research firm is 61.3% as "efficient" as perfect information.

Low efficiency ratings for sample information might lead the decision maker to look for other types of information. On the other hand, high efficiency ratings indicate that the

---

[2]In minimization problems, the expected value of the optimal decision with sample information will be less than or equal to the expected value of the optimal decision without sample information. Thus, in minimization problems,

$$EVSI = \begin{bmatrix} \text{expected value of the} \\ \text{optimal decision } without \\ \text{sample information} \end{bmatrix} - \begin{bmatrix} \text{expected value of the} \\ \text{optimal decision } with \\ \text{sample information} \end{bmatrix}$$

sample information is almost as good as perfect information, and additional sources of information should not be worthwhile.

▼ NOTES AND COMMENTS ▼

1. The use of microcomputer software packages for decision analysis is becoming commonplace. The ARBORIST, a software package available from Texas Instruments, allows the user to develop a graph of the decision tree on the screen; the package will then perform all the decision analysis calculations. SUPER-TREE, a product of SDG Decision Systems, requires the user to specify the tree in a manner similar to that used in PERT/CPM problems; that is, the user provides the system with the nodes and their immediate predecessors, and the software package develops the resulting decision tree. Although packages such as the ARBORIST and SUPERTREE are not needed for problems as small as those introduced in this chapter, computer support is necessary for larger decision problems.

2. In discussing decision analysis we have considered only situations where there are a finite number of states of nature. The next step would be to consider situations where the states of nature are so numerous that it would be impractical, if not impossible, to treat the states of nature as a discrete random variable. The solution procedure that is used in such circumstances is to treat the state of nature as a continuous random variable. More advanced texts on decision analysis present techniques that have been developed to handle such situations.

14.9 ▼ UTILITY AND DECISION MAKING

In the previous sections of this chapter we expressed the payoffs in terms of monetary values. When probability information was available about the states of nature, we recommended selecting the decision alternative with the best expected monetary value. However, there are situations in which the decision alternative with the best expected monetary value is not the most desirable decision.

By the most desirable decision we mean the one that is preferred by the decision maker, taking into account not only monetary value but also many other factors, such as the possibility of making a very large profit and/or incurring a very large loss. Examples of situations in which selecting the decision alternative with the best expected monetary value may not lead to the selection of the most preferred alternative are numerous. One such example is the decision made by most people to buy insurance. Clearly, the decision to buy insurance for a house does not provide a higher expected monetary value than not buying such insurance. Otherwise, insurance companies could not pay expenses and make a profit. Similarly, many people buy tickets for state lotteries even though the expected monetary value of such a decision is negative.

Should we conclude that persons or businesses that buy insurance or participate in lotteries do so because they are unable to determine which decision alternative leads to the best expected monetary value? On the contrary, we take the view that in these cases monetary value is not the sole measure of the true worth of the outcome to the decision maker.

We will see that in cases where expected monetary value does not lead to the most preferred decision alternative, expressing the value (or worth) of an outcome in terms of its *utility* will permit the use of *expected utility* to identify the most desirable decision.

The Meaning of Utility

Utility is a measure of the total worth of a particular outcome; it reflects the decision maker's attitude toward a collection of factors such as profit, loss, and risk. As an example of a case where utility can help in selecting the best decision alternative, let us consider the problem faced by Swofford, Inc., a relatively small real estate investment firm located in Atlanta, Ga. Swofford currently has two investment opportunities, which require approximately the same cash outlay. The cash requirements necessary prohibit Swofford from making more than one investment at this time. Consequently, there are three possible decision alternatives that may be considered.

The three decision alternatives, denoted by d_1, d_2, and d_3, are as follows:

$$d_1 = \text{make investment } A$$
$$d_2 = \text{make investment } B$$
$$d_3 = \text{do not invest}$$

The monetary payoffs associated with the investment opportunities depend largely on what happens to the real estate market during the next 6 months. Real estate prices will go up, remain stable, or go down. Thus, the Swofford states of nature, denoted by s_1, s_2, and s_3, are as follows:

$$s_1 = \text{real estate prices go up}$$
$$s_2 = \text{real estate prices remain stable}$$
$$s_3 = \text{real estate prices go down}$$

Using the best information available, Swofford has estimated the profits or payoffs associated with each decision alternative and state-of-nature combination. The resulting payoff table is shown in Table 14.7.

The best estimate of the probability that prices will go up is .3, the best estimate of the probability that prices will remain stable is .5, and the best estimate of the probability that real estate prices will go down is .2. Thus, the expected values for the three decision alternatives are

$$\text{EV}(d_1) = .3(\$30,000) + .5(\$20,000) + .2(-\$50,000) = \$9,000$$
$$\text{EV}(d_2) = .3(\$50,000) + .5(-\$20,000) + .2(-\$30,000) = -\$1,000$$
$$\text{EV}(d_3) = .3(\$0) + .5(\$0) + .2(\$0) = \$0$$

TABLE 14.7
Payoff Table for Swofford, Inc.

Decision Alternatives		Prices Up s_1	States of Nature Prices Stable s_2	Prices Down s_3
Investment A	d_1	$30,000	$20,000	− $50,000
Investment B	d_2	$50,000	− $20,000	− $30,000
Do not invest	d_3	0	0	0

Using the expected value approach, the optimal decision is to select investment A, with an expected monetary value of $9000. Is this really the best decision alternative? Let us consider some other relevant factors that relate to Swofford's capability for absorbing the loss of $50,000 if investment A is made and prices actually go down.

It turns out that Swofford's current financial position is very weak. This was partly reflected in Swofford's ability to undertake, at most, one investment at the current time. More important, however, the firm's president feels that if the next investment results in substantial losses, Swofford's future will be in jeopardy. Although the expected value approach leads to a recommendation for d_1, do you think this is the decision the firm's president would prefer? We suspect that d_2 or d_3 would be selected in order to avoid the possibility of incurring a $50,000 loss. In fact, it is reasonable to believe that if a loss as great as even $30,000 could drive Swofford out of business, the president would select d_3, feeling that both investment A and investment B are too risky for Swofford's current financial position.

The way we can resolve Swofford's dilemma is first to determine Swofford's utility for the various monetary outcomes. Recall that the utility of any outcome is the total worth of that outcome, taking into account the risks and payoffs involved. If the utilities for the various outcomes are assessed correctly, then the decision alternative with the highest expected utility is the most preferred or best alternative.

Developing Utilities for Payoffs

The procedure we will use to establish utility values for the payoffs requires that we first assign a utility value to the best and worst possible payoffs in the decision situation. Any values will work as long as the utility assigned to the best payoff is greater than the utility assigned to the worst payoff. In Swofford's case, $50,000 is the best payoff and–$50,000 is the worst. Suppose, then, that we arbitrarily make the following assignments to these two payoffs:

$$\text{Utility of} -\$50,000 = U(-\$50,000) = 0$$
$$\text{Utility of} \quad \$50,000 = U(\$50,000) \quad = 10$$

Now let us see how we can determine the utility associated with every other payoff.

Consider the process of establishing the utility of a payoff of $30,000. First, we ask Swofford's president to state a preference between a guaranteed $30,000 payoff and the opportunity to engage in the following *lottery,* or bet:

Lottery: Swofford's obtains a payoff of $50,000 with probability p
and a payoff of $-\$50,000$ with probability $(1 - p)$.

If p is very close to 1, Swofford's president would prefer the lottery to the certain payoff of $30,000 since the firm would virtually guarantee itself a payoff of $50,000. On the other hand, if p is very close to 0, Swofford's president would clearly prefer the guarantee of $30,000. In any event, as p changes continuously from 0 to 1, the preference for the guaranteed payoff of $30,000 will change at some point into a preference for the lottery. At this value of p, Swofford's president would have no greater preference for the guaranteed payoff of $30,000 than for the lottery. For example, let us assume that when $p =$

0.95, Swofford's president is indifferent between the certain payoff of $30,000 and the lottery. Given this value of p, we can compute the utility of a $30,000 payoff as follows:

$$U(\$30,000) = pU(\$50,000) + (1 - p)U(-\$50,000)$$
$$= 0.95(10) + (0.05)(0)$$
$$= 9.5$$

Obviously, if we had started with a different assignment of utilities for payoffs of $50,000 and $-$50,000, we would have ended up with a different utility for $30,000. Hence, we must conclude that the utility assigned to each payoff is not unique, but merely depends on the initial choice of utilities for the best and worst payoffs. We will discuss this further at the end of this section. For now, however, we will continue to use a value of 10 for the utility of $50,000 and a value of 0 for the utility of $-$50,000.

Before computing the utility for the other payoffs, let us consider the significance of Swofford's president assigning a utility of 9.5 to a payoff of $30,000. Clearly, when $p = 0.95$, the expected value of the lottery is

$$EV(\text{lottery}) = 0.95(\$50,000) + 0.05(-\$50,000)$$
$$= \$47,500 - \$2,500$$
$$= \$45,000$$

We see that although the expected value of the lottery when $p = 0.95$ is $45,000, Swofford's president would just as soon take a guaranteed payoff of $30,000. Thus, Swofford's president is taking a conservative, or risk-avoiding, viewpoint. The president would rather have $30,000 for certain than risk anything greater than a 5% chance of incurring a loss of $50,000. One can view the difference between the EV of $45,000 and the $30,000 amount for certain as the risk premium that Swofford's president would be willing to pay to avoid the 5% chance of losing $50,000.

To compute the utility associated with a payoff of $-$20,000, we must ask Swofford's president to state a preference between a guaranteed $-$20,000 payoff and the opportunity to engage in the following lottery.

Lottery: Swofford's obtains a payoff of $50,000 with probability p
and a payoff of $-$50,000 with probability $(1 - p)$.

Note that this is exactly the same lottery we used to establish the utility of a payoff of $30,000. In fact, this will be the lottery used to establish the utility for any monetary value in the Swofford payoff table. Using this lottery, then, we must ask Swofford's president to state the value of p that would make the president indifferent between a guaranteed payoff of $-$20,000 and the lottery. For example, we might begin by asking the president to choose between a certain loss of $20,000 and the lottery with a payoff of $50,000 with probability $p = 0.90$ and a payoff of $-$50,000 with probability $(1 - p) = 0.10$. What answer do you think we would get? Surely, with this high probability of obtaining a payoff of $50,000, the president would elect the lottery. Next, we might ask if $p = 0.85$ would result in indifference between the loss of $20,000 for certain and the lottery. Again, the president might tell us that the lottery would be preferred. Suppose that we continue in this fashion until we get to $p = 0.55$, where we find that with this value of p, the president is indifferent between the payoff of $-$20,000 and the lottery. That is, for any value of p less than 0.55, the president would rather take a loss of

$20,000 for certain than risk the potential loss of $50,000 with the lottery; and for any value of p above 0.55, the president would elect the lottery. Thus, the utility assigned to a payoff of $-\$20,000$ is

$$
\begin{aligned}
U(-\$20,000) &= pU(\$50,000) + (1 - p)U(-\$50,000) \\
&= 0.55(10) + 0.45(0) \\
&= 5.5
\end{aligned}
$$

Again, let us examine the significance of this assignment as compared with the expected value approach. When $p = 0.55$, the expected value of the lottery is

$$
\begin{aligned}
EV(\text{lottery}) &= 0.55(\$50,000) + 0.45(-\$50,000) \\
&= \$27,500 - \$22,500 \\
&= \$5,000
\end{aligned}
$$

Thus, Swofford's president would just as soon absorb a loss of $20,000 for certain as take the lottery, even though the expected value of the lottery is $5000. Once again we see the conservative, or risk-avoiding, point of view of Swofford's president.

In the above two examples where we computed the utility for a specific monetary payoff, M, we first found the probability p where the decision maker was indifferent between a guaranteed payoff of M and a lottery with a payoff of $50,000 with probability p and $-\$50,000$ with probability $(1 - p)$. The utility of M was then computed as

$$
\begin{aligned}
U(M) &= pU(\$50,000) + (1 - p)U(-\$50,000) \\
&= p(10) + (1 - p)0 \\
&= 10p
\end{aligned}
$$

Using the above procedure, utility values for the rest of the payoffs in Swofford's problem were developed. The results are presented in Table 14.8.

Now that we have determined the utility value of each of the possible monetary values, we can write the original payoff table in terms of utility values. Table 14.9 shows the utility for the various outcomes in the Swofford problem. The notation we will use for the entries in the utility table is $U(d_i,s_j)$, which denotes the utility associated with decision alternative d_i and state of nature s_j. Using this notation, we see that $U(d_2,s_3) = 4.0$.

TABLE 14.8
Utility of Monetary Payoffs for the Swofford, Inc., Problem

Monetary Value ($)	Indifference Value of p	Utility Value
50,000	Does not apply	10.0
30,000	0.95	9.5
20,000	0.90	9.0
0	0.75	7.5
−20,000	0.55	5.5
−30,000	0.40	4.0
−50,000	Does not apply	0

TABLE 14.9
Utility Table for Swofford, Inc., Problem

Decision Alternatives		States of Nature		
		Prices Up s_1	Prices Stable s_2	Prices Down s_3
Investment A	d_1	9.5	9.0	0
Investment B	d_2	10.0	5.5	4.0
Do not invest	d_3	7.5	7.5	7.5

The Expected Utility Approach

We can now apply the expected value computations introduced in Section 14.3 to the payoffs in Table 14.9 in order to select an optimal decision alternative for Swofford, Inc. However, since utility values represent such a special case of expected value, we will refer to the expected value when applied to utility values as the *expected utility* (EU). In this way we will avoid any possible confusion between the expected value for the original payoff table and the expected value for the payoff table consisting of *utility values*. Thus, the expected utility approach requires the analyst to compute the expected utility for each decision alternative and then select the alternative yielding the best expected utility. If there are N possible states of nature, the expected utility of a decision alternative d_i is given by

$$EU(d_i) = \sum_{j=1}^{N} P(s_j) U(d_i, s_j) \tag{14.19}$$

The expected utility for each of the decision alternatives in the Swofford problem is computed as follows:

$$EU(d_1) = .3(9.5) + .5(9.0) + .2(0) = 7.35$$
$$EU(d_2) = .3(10) + .5(5.5) + .2(4.0) = 6.55$$
$$EU(d_3) = .3(7.5) + .5(7.5) + .2(7.5) = 7.50$$

We see that the optimal decision using the expected utility approach is d_3, do not invest. The ranking of alternatives according to the president's utility assignments and the associated monetary values is as follows:

Ranking of Decision Alternatives	Expected Utility	Expected Monetary Value
Do not invest	7.50	$ 0
Investment A	7.35	$9000
Investment B	6.55	−$1000

Note that whereas investment A had the highest expected monetary value of $9000, the analysis indicates that Swofford should decline this investment. The rationale behind not selecting investment A is that the .2 probability of a $50,000 loss was considered by Swofford's president to involve a very serious risk. The seriousness of this risk and its associated impact on the company were not adequately reflected by the expected monetary value of investment A. It was necessary to assess the utility for each payoff in order to adequately take this risk into account.

Unfortunately, the determination of the appropriate utilities is not a trivial task. As we have seen, measuring utility requires a degree of subjectivity on the part of the decision maker, and different decision makers will have different utility functions. This aspect of utility often causes decision makers to feel uncomfortable about using the expected utility approach in decision making. However, if we encounter a decision situation in which we are convinced monetary value is not necessarily the primary measure of performance, and if we agree that a quantitative analysis of the decision problem is desirable, then some form of utility analysis should be performed.

▼ NOTES AND COMMENTS ▼

1. In the Swofford problem we used a utility of 10 for the largest possible payoff and 0 for the smallest. Had we chosen 1 for the utility of the largest payoff and 0 for the utility of the smallest, the utility for any monetary value M would have been the value of p at which the decision maker was indifferent between a payoff of M for certain and a lottery in which the best payoff is obtained with probability p and the worst payoff is obtained with probability $(1 - p)$. Thus, the utility for any monetary value would have been equal to the probability of earning the highest payoff. Often this choice is made because of the ease in computation. We chose not to do so to emphasize the distinction between the utility values and the indifference probabilities for the lottery.

2. It is generally agreed that when the payoffs for a particular decision-making problem fall into a reasonable range—the best is not too good and the worst is not too bad—decision makers tend to express preferences in agreement with the expected value approach. Thus, as a general guideline we suggest asking the decision maker to consider the best and worst possible payoffs for a problem and assess their reasonableness. If the decision maker believes they are in the reasonable range, the expected monetary value criterion can be used. However, if the payoffs appear unreasonably large or unreasonably small (for example, a huge loss), and if the decision maker feels monetary values do not adequately reflect her or his true preferences for the payoffs, a utility analysis of the problem should be considered.

▼ SUMMARY

In this chapter we have emphasized how decision analysis can be used to solve problems with a limited number of decision alternatives and a limited number of possible states of nature. The goal of decision analysis is to identify the best decision alternative given an uncertain or risk-filled pattern of future events (that is, states of nature).

We presented three approaches to decision making without probabilities and discussed the use of the expected value approach for solving problems with probabilities. Then we showed how additional information about the states of nature can be used to revise or update the probability estimates and develop an optimal decision strategy for the problem. The concepts of expected value of sample information, expected value of perfect information, and efficiency of information were used to evaluate the contribution of the sample information.

We suggested that the expected utility approach should be used in situations in which the expected monetary value approach would lead to unacceptable decisions. Unlike monetary value, utility is a measure of the total worth of an outcome resulting from the choice of a decision alternative and the occurrence of a state of nature. As such, utility takes into account the decision maker's attitude toward the profit, loss, and risk associated with an outcome. In our examples we have seen how the use of utility analysis can lead to decision recommendations that differ from those that would be selected under the expected value approach.

▼ GLOSSARY

States of nature   The uncontrollable future events that can affect the payoff associated with a decision.

Payoff   The outcome measure, such as profit, cost, time, and so on. Each combination of a decision alternative and a state of nature has an associated payoff.

Payoff table   A tabular representation of the payoffs for a decision problem.

Optimistic approach   An approach to choosing a decision alternative without using probabilities. For a maximization problem, it leads to choosing the alternative corresponding to the largest payoff; for a minimization problem, it leads to choosing the alternative corresponding to the smallest payoff.

Conservative approach   An approach to choosing a decision alternative without using probabilities. For a maximization problem, it leads to choosing the alternative that maximizes the minimum payoff; for a minimization problem, it leads to choosing the alternative that minimizes the maximum payoff.

Minimax regret   An approach to choosing a decision alternative without using probabilities. For each alternative, the maximum regret is computed. This approach leads to choosing the alternative that minimizes the maximum regret.

Opportunity loss or regret   The amount of loss (lower profit or higher cost) due to not making the best decision for each state of nature.

Decision tree   A graphical representation of the decision problem which shows the sequential nature of the decision-making situation.

Nodes   The intersection or junction points of the decision tree.

Branches   Lines or arcs connecting nodes of the decision tree.

Expected value   For a decision alternative, it is the weighted average of the payoffs. The weights are the state-of-nature probabilities.

Expected value of perfect information (EVPI)   The expected value of information that would tell the decision maker exactly which state of nature was going to occur (that is, perfect information).

Prior probabilities   The probabilities of the states of nature prior to obtaining sample information.

Posterior (revised) probabilities   The probabilities of the states of nature after using Bayes' theorem to adjust the prior probabilities based on given indicator information.

Indicators   Information about the states of nature. An indicator may be the result of a sample.

Bayesian revision   The process of revising prior probabilities to create the posterior probabilities based on sample information.

Expected value of sample information (EVSI)   The difference between the expected value of an optimal strategy based on sample information and the "best" expected value without any sample information.

Efficiency   The ratio of EVSI to EVPI; perfect information is 100% efficient.

Utility   A measure of the total worth of an outcome reflecting a decision maker's attitude toward considerations such as profit, loss, and intangibles such as risk.

Lottery   A hypothetical investment alternative with a probability p of obtaining the best possible payoff and a probability of $(1 - p)$ of obtaining the worst possible payoff.

Expected utility approach   An approach that requires the analyst to compute the expected utility for each decision alternative and then select the alternative yielding the highest expected utility.

▼ PROBLEMS

1. Suppose that a decision maker faced with four decision alternatives and four states of nature develops the following profit payoff table:

		States of Nature			
		s_1	s_2	s_3	s_4
	d_1	14	9	10	5
Decision	d_2	11	10	8	7
Alternatives	d_3	9	10	10	11
	d_4	8	10	11	13

   a. If the decision maker knows nothing about the probabilities of the four states of nature, what is the recommended decision using the optimistic, conservative, and minimax regret approaches?

   b. Which approach do you prefer? Explain. Is it important for the decision maker to establish the most appropriate approach before analyzing the problem? Explain.

   c. Assume that the payoff table provides *cost* rather than profit payoffs. What is the recommended decision using the optimistic, conservative, and minimax regret approaches?

2. Southland Corporation's decision to produce a new line of recreational products has resulted in the need to construct either a small plant or a large plant. The decision as to which plant size to select depends on how the marketplace reacts to the new product line. In order to conduct an analysis, marketing management has decided to view the possible long-run demand as low, medium, or high. The following payoff table shows the projected profit in millions of dollars.

		Long-Run Demand		
		Low	Medium	High
Decision	Small plant	150	200	200
Alternatives	Large plant	50	200	500

a. Construct a decision tree for this problem.

b. Determine the recommended decision using the optimistic, conservative, and minimax regret approaches.

3. McHuffter Condominiums, Inc., of Pensacola, Fla., recently purchased land near the Gulf of Mexico and is attempting to determine the size of the condominium development it should build. Three sizes of developments are being considered: small, d_1; medium, d_2; and large, d_3. At the same time an uncertain economy makes it difficult to ascertain the demand for the new condominiums. McHuffter's management realizes that a large development followed by a low demand could be very costly to the company. However, if McHuffter makes a conservative small development decision and then finds a high demand, the firm's profits will be lower than they might have been. With the three levels of demand—low, medium, and high—McHuffter's management has prepared the following payoff table:

		Demand		
		Low S_1	Medium S_2	High S_3
Decision	Small	400	400	400
Alternatives	Medium	100	600	600
	Large	−300	300	900

Profit in $1000s

a. Construct a decision tree for this problem.

b. If nothing is known about the demand probabilities, what are the decision recommendations using the optimistic, conservative, and minimax regret approaches?

4. The payoff table presented in problem 1 is repeated here:

		States of Nature			
		s_1	s_2	s_3	s_4
Decision	d_1	14	9	10	5
Alternatives	d_2	11	10	8	7
	d_3	9	10	10	11
	d_4	8	10	11	13

Suppose that the decision maker obtains information that enables the following probability estimates to be made: $P(s_1) = .5$, $P(s_2) = .2$, $P(s_3) = .2$, $P(s_4) = .1$.

a. Use the expected value approach to determine the optimal decision.

b. Now assume that the entries in the payoff table are costs; use the expected value approach to determine the optimal decision.

5. Hale's TV Productions is considering producing a pilot for a comedy series for a major television network. While the network may reject the pilot and the series, it may also purchase the program for 1 or 2 years. Hale may decide to produce the pilot

or transfer the rights for the series to a competitor for $100,000. Hale's profits are summarized in the following payoff table:

		States of Nature		
		Reject	1 Year	2 Years
Produce pilot	d_1	− 100	50	150 ◄——— Profit in
Sell to competitor	d_2	100	100	100 $1000s

If the probability estimates for the states of nature are $P(\text{reject}) = .2$, $P(1 \text{ year}) = .3$, and $P(2 \text{ years}) = .5$, what should the company do?

6. Consider the McHuffter Condominium scenario presented in problem 3. If $P(\text{low}) = .20$, $P(\text{medium}) = .35$, and $P(\text{high}) = .45$, what is the decision recommended using the expected value approach?

7. Martin's Service Station is considering investing in a heavy-duty snowplow this fall. Martin has analyzed the situation carefully and feels that this would be a very profitable investment if the snowfall is heavy. A small profit could still be made if the snowfall is moderate, but Martin would lose money if the snowfall is light. Specifically, Martin forecasts a profit of $7000 if the snowfall is heavy and $2000 if it is moderate, and a $9000 loss if it is light. Based on the weather bureau's long-range forecast, Martin estimates that $P(\text{heavy snowfall}) = .4$, $P(\text{moderate snowfall}) = .3$, and $P(\text{light snowfall}) = .3$.

   a. Prepare a decision tree for Martin's problem.
   b. What is the expected value at each state-of-nature node?
   c. Using the expected value approach, would you recommend that Martin invest in the snowplow?

8. The payoff table showing profit for a decision problem with two states of nature and three decision alternatives is presented below:

		States of Nature	
		s_1	s_2
Decision	d_1	80	50
Alternatives	d_2	65	85
	d_3	30	100

Use graphical sensitivity analysis to determine the values of the probability of state of nature s_1 for which each of the decision alternatives has the largest expected value.

9. Milford Trucking, located in Chicago, has requests to haul two shipments, one to St. Louis and one to Detroit. Because of a scheduling problem, Milford will be able to accept only one of these assignments. The St. Louis customer has guaranteed a return shipment, but the Detroit customer has not. Thus, if Milford accepts the Detroit shipment and cannot find a Detroit-to-Chicago return shipment, the truck will return to Chicago empty. The payoff table showing profit is as follows:

Shipment		Return Shipment from Detroit s_1	No Return Shipment from Detroit s_2
St. Louis	d_1	2000	2000
Detroit	d_2	2500	1000

a. If the probability of a Detroit return shipment is .4, what should Milford do?

b. Use graphical sensitivity analysis to determine the values of the probability of state of nature s_1, for which d_1 has the largest expected value.

10. Consider the Hale's TV Productions situation (problem 5). What is the maximum that Hale should be willing to pay for inside information on what the network will do?

11. Consider the McHuffter Condominium scenario (problem 6). What is the expected value of perfect information?

12. Refer again to the investment problem faced by Martin's Service Station (problem 7). Martin can purchase a blade to attach to his service truck that can also be used to plow driveways and parking lots. Since this truck must also be available to start cars, etc., Martin will not be able to generate as much revenue plowing snow if he elects this alternative. But he will keep his loss smaller if the snowfall is light. Under this alternative Martin forecasts a profit of $3500 if the snowfall is heavy and $1000 if it is moderate and a $1500 loss if the snowfall is light.

a. Prepare a new decision tree showing all three alternatives.

b. Using the expected value approach, what is the optimal decision?

c. What is the expected value of perfect information?

13. Consider the Milford Trucking situation (problem 9). What is the expected value of perfect information that would tell Milford Trucking whether or not Detroit has a return shipment?

14. Suppose that you are given a decision situation with three possible states of nature: s_1, s_2, and s_3. The prior probabilities are $P(s_1) = .2$, $P(s_2) = .5$, and $P(s_3) = .3$. Indicator information I is obtained, and it is known that $P(I|s_1) = .1$, $P(I|s_2) = .05$, and $P(I|s_3) = .2$. Compute the revised or posterior probabilities: $P(s_1|I)$, $P(s_2|I)$, and $P(s_3|I)$.

15. The payoff table showing profit for a decision problem with two states of nature and three decision alternatives is presented below:

	s_1	s_2
d_1	15	10
d_2	10	12
d_3	8	20

The prior probabilities for s_1 and s_2 are $P(s_1) = .8$ and $P(s_2) = .2$.

a. Using only the prior probabilities and the expected value approach, find the optimal decision.

b. Use graphical sensitivity analysis to determine the values of the probability of state of nature s_1 for which each of the decision alternatives has the largest expected value.

c. Find the EVPI.
d. Suppose that some indicator information I is obtained with $P(I|s_1) = .2$ and $P(I|s_2) = .75$. Find the posterior probabilities $P(s_1|I)$ and $P(s_2|I)$. Recommend a decision alternative based on these probabilities.

16. Consider the following decision tree representation of a decision analysis problem with two indicators, two decision alternatives, and two states of nature:

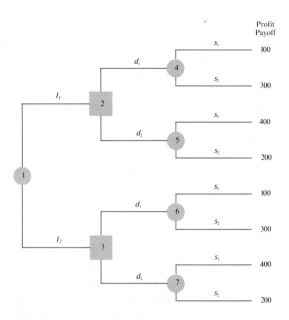

Assume that the following probability information is given:

$$P(s_1) = .4 \qquad P(I_1|s_1) = .8 \qquad P(I_2|s_1) = .2$$
$$P(s_2) = .6 \qquad P(I_1|s_2) = .4 \qquad P(I_2|s_2) = .6$$

a. What are the values for $P(I_1)$ and $P(I_2)$?
b. What are the values of $P(s_1|I_1)$, $P(s_2|I_1)$, $P(s_1|I_2)$, and $P(s_2|I_2)$?
c. Use the decision tree approach, and determine the optimal decision strategy. What is the expected value of your solution?

17. The payoff table for Problem 16 is as follows:

	s_1	s_2
d_1	100	300
d_2	400	200

a. What is your decision without the indicator information?
b. What is the expected value of the indicator or sample information, EVSI?
c. What is the expected value of perfect information, EVPI?
d. What is the efficiency of the indicator information?

18. The payoff table for Hale's TV Productions (problem 5) is as follows:

Decision Alternatives		States of Nature		
		s_1	s_2	s_3
Produce pilot	d_1	-100	50	150
Sell to competitor	d_2	100	100	100
Probability of states of nature		.2	.3	.5

For a consulting fee of $2500, an agency will review the plans for the comedy series and indicate the overall chances of a favorable network reaction to the series. If the special agency review results in a favorable (I_1) or an unfavorable (I_2) evaluation, what should Hale's decision strategy be? Assume that Hale believes that the following conditional probabilities are realistic appraisals of the agency's evaluation accuracy:

$$P(I_1|s_1) = .3 \qquad P(I_2|s_1) = .7$$
$$P(I_1|s_2) = .6 \qquad P(I_2|s_2) = .4$$
$$P(I_1|s_3) = .9 \qquad P(I_2|s_3) = .1$$

a. Show the decision tree for this problem.
b. What are the recommended decision strategy and the expected value, assuming that the agency information is obtained?
c. What is the EVSI? Is the $2500 consulting fee worth the information? What is the maximum that Hale should be willing to pay for the consulting information?

19. McHuffter Condominiums (problem 3) is conducting a survey that will help evaluate the demand for the new condominium development. McHuffter's payoff table (profit) is as follows:

Decision Alternatives			States of Nature		
			Low	Medium	High
			s_1	s_2	s_3
Decision Alternatives	Small	d_1	400	400	400
	Medium	d_2	100	600	600
	Large	d_3	-300	300	900
Probability of states of nature			.20	.35	.45

The survey will result in three indicators of demand [weak (I_1), average (I_2), or strong (I_3)], where the conditional probabilities are as follows:

	$P(I_k|s_k)$		
	I_1	I_2	I_3
s_1	.6	.3	.1
s_2	.4	.4	.2
s_3	.1	.4	.5

a. What is McHuffter's optimal strategy?
b. What is the value of the survey information?
c. What are the EVPI and the efficiency of the survey information?
20. The payoff table for Martin's Service Station (problems 7 and 12) is as follows:

Decision Alternatives		Snowfall Heavy s_1	Moderate s_2	Light s_3
Purchase snowplow	d_1	7000	2000	−9000
Do not invest	d_2	0	0	0
Purchase snowplow blade	d_3	3500	1000	−1500
Probabilities of states of nature		.4	.3	.3

Suppose that Martin decides to wait to check the September temperature pattern before making a final decision. Estimates of the probabilities associated with an unseasonably cold September (I_1) are as follows: $P(I_1|s_1) = .3$, $P(I_1|s_2) = .2$, $P(I_1|s_3) = .05$. If Martin observes an unseasonably cold September, what is the recommended decision? If Martin does not observe an unseasonably cold September (I_2), what is the recommended decision?

21. Milford Trucking Co. (problem 9) has the following payoff table:

Shipment		Return Shipment from Detroit s_1	No Return Shipment from Detroit s_2
St. Louis	d_1	2000	2000
Detroit	d_2	2500	1000
Probabilities		.40	.60

a. Milford can phone a Detroit truck dispatch center and determine if the general Detroit shipping activity is busy (I_1) or slow (I_2). If the report is busy, the chances of obtaining a return shipment will increase. Suppose the following conditional probabilities are given:

$$P(I_1|s_1) = .6 \qquad P(I_2|s_1) = .4$$
$$P(I_1|s_2) = .3 \qquad P(I_2|s_2) = .7$$

What should Milford do?
b. If the Detroit report is busy (I_1), what is the probability that Milford will obtain a return shipment if it makes the trip to Detroit?
c. What is the efficiency of the phone information?

22. In order to save on gasoline expenses, Rona and Jerry agreed to form a carpool for traveling to and from work. After limiting the travel routes to two alternatives, Rona and Jerry could not agree on the best way to travel to work. Jerry preferred the expressway since it was usually the fastest; however, Rona pointed out that traffic jams on the expressway sometimes led to long delays. Rona preferred the somewhat longer but more consistent Queen City Avenue. While Jerry still preferred the ex-

pressway, he agreed with Rona that they should take Queen City Avenue if the expressway had a traffic jam. Unfortunately, they do not know the state of the expressway ahead of time. The following payoff table provides the one-way time estimates for traveling to or from work:

| Route | | States of Nature | |
		Expressway Open s_1	Expressway Jammed s_2
Expressway	d_1	25	45
Queen City Avenue	d_2	30	30

Travel time in minutes

a. After driving to work on the expressway for 1 month (20 days), they found the expressway jammed three times. Assuming that these days are representative of future days, should they continue to use the expressway for traveling to work? Explain.

b. Use graphical sensitivity analysis to determine the values of the probability of state of nature s_1 for which d_1 has the best expected value.

c. Would it make sense not to adopt the expected value approach for this particular problem? Explain.

After a period of time Rona and Jerry noted that the weather seemed to affect the traffic conditions on the expressway. They identified three weather conditions (indicators) with the following conditional probabilities:

$$I_1 = \text{clear}$$
$$I_2 = \text{overcast}$$
$$I_3 = \text{rain}$$

$P(I_1|s_1) = .8$	$P(I_2|s_1) = .2$	$P(I_3|s_1) = 0$
$P(I_1|s_2) = .1$	$P(I_2|s_2) = .3$	$P(I_3|s_2) = .6$

d. Show the decision tree for the problem of traveling to work.

e. What are the optimal decision strategy and the expected travel time?

f. What is the efficiency of the weather information?

23. The Gorman Manufacturing Company must decide whether it should purchase a component part from a supplier or manufacture the component at its Milan, Michigan, plant. If demand is high, it would be to Gorman's advantage to manufacture the component. However, if demand is low, Gorman's unit manufacturing cost will be high due to underutilization of equipment. The projected profit in thousands of dollars for Gorman's make-or-buy decision is shown below.

| Decision Alternatives | Demand | | |
	Low	Medium	High
Manufacture component	−20	40	100
Purchase component	10	45	70

The states of nature have the following probabilities: P(low demand) $= .35$, P(medium demand) $= .35$, and P(high demand) $= .30$.

a. Use a decision tree to recommend a decision.

b. Use EVPI to determine whether Gorman should attempt to obtain a better estimate of demand.

A test market study of the potential demand for the product is expected to report either a favorable (I_1) or an unfavorable (I_2) condition. The relevant conditional probabilities are as follows:

$$P(I_1|s_1) = .10 \qquad P(I_2|s_1) = .90$$
$$P(I_1|s_2) = .40 \qquad P(I_2|s_2) = .60$$
$$P(I_1|s_3) = .60 \qquad P(I_2|s_3) = .40$$

c. What is the probability that the market research report will be favorable?

d. What is Gorman's optimal decision strategy?

e. What is the expected value of the market research information?

f. What is the efficiency of the information?

24. Sealcoat, Inc., has a contract with one of its customers to supply a unique liquid chemical product that will be used by the customer in the manufacture of a lubricant for airplane engines. Because of the chemical process used by Sealcoat, batch sizes for the liquid chemical product must be 1000 pounds. The customer has agreed to adjust manufacturing to the full batch quantities and will order 1, 2, or 3 batches every 3 months. Since an aging process of 1 month exists for the product, Sealcoat will have to make its production (how much to make) decision before the customer places an order. Thus, Sealcoat can list the product demand alternatives of 1000, 2000, or 3000 pounds, but the exact demand is unknown.

Sealcoat's manufacturing costs are $150 per pound, and the product sells at the fixed contract price of $200 per pound. If the customer orders more than Sealcoat has produced, Sealcoat has agreed to absorb the added cost of filling the order by purchasing a higher-quality substitute product from another chemical firm. The substitute product, including transportation expenses, will cost Sealcoat $240 per pound. Since the product cannot be stored more than 2 months without spoilage, Sealcoat cannot inventory excess production until the customer's next 3-month order. Therefore, if the customer's current order is less than Sealcoat has produced, the excess production will be reprocessed and is valued at $50 per pound.

The inventory decision in this problem is, How much should Sealcoat produce given the above costs and the possible demands of 1000, 2000, or 3000 pounds? Based on historical data and an analysis of the customer's future demands, Sealcoat has assessed the following probability distribution for demand:

Demand	Probability
1000	0.3
2000	0.5
3000	0.2

a. Develop a payoff table for the Sealcoat problem.

b. How many batches should Sealcoat produce every 3 months?

c. How much of a discount should Sealcoat be willing to allow the customer for specifying in advance exactly how many batches will be purchased?

Sealcoat has identified a pattern in the demand for the product based on the customer's previous order quantity. Let

$$I_1 = \text{customer's last order was 1000 pounds}$$

$$I_2 = \text{customer's last order was 2000 pounds}$$

$$I_3 = \text{customer's last order was 3000 pounds}$$

The conditional probabilities are as follows:

$$P(I_1|s_1) = .10 \qquad P(I_2|s_1) = .40 \qquad P(I_3|s_1) = .50$$

$$P(I_1|s_2) = .22 \qquad P(I_2|s_2) = .68 \qquad P(I_3|s_2) = .10$$

$$P(I_1|s_3) = .80 \qquad P(I_2|s_3) = .20 \qquad P(I_3|s_3) = 0$$

d. Develop an optimal decision strategy for Sealcoat.
e. What is the EVSI?
f. What is the efficiency of the information for the most recent order?

25. A quality-control procedure involves 100% inspection of parts received from a supplier. Historical records show that the following defective rates have been observed:

Percent Defective	Probability
0	.15
1	.25
2	.40
3	.20

The cost to inspect 100% of the parts received is $250 for each shipment of 500 parts. If the shipment is not 100% inspected, defective parts will cause rework problems later in the production process. The rework cost is $25 for each defective part.

a. Complete the following payoff table, where the entries represent the total cost of inspection and reworking:

| Inspection | Percent Defective | | | |
	0	1	2	3
100% inspection	$250	$250	$250	$250
No inspection				

b. The plant manager is considering eliminating the inspection process in order to save the $250 inspection cost per shipment. Do you support this action? Use expected value to justify your answer.
c. Show the decision tree for this problem.

Suppose that a sample of 5 parts is selected from the shipment and 1 defect is found.

d. Let $I = 1$ defect in a sample of 5. Use the binomial probability distribution to compute $P(I|s_1)$, $P(I|s_2)$, $P(I|s_3)$, and $P(I|s_4)$ where the state of nature identifies the value for p. The binomial probability function is as follows:

$$f(x) = \frac{n!}{x!(n-x)!} p^x (1-p)^{n-x}$$

where

$$n = \text{the sample size}$$
$$x = \text{the number of defects}$$
$$p = \text{the proportion defective}$$

In this problem, $n = 5$, $x = 1$, and $p = 0$, .01, .02 and .03.

e. If I occurs, what are the revised probabilities for the states of nature?

f. Should the entire shipment be 100% inspected whenever 1 defect is found in a sample of size 5?

g. What is the cost saving associated with the sample information?

26. A food processor considers daily production runs of 100, 200, and 300 cases. Possible demands for the product are 100, 200, and 300 cases. The payoff table is as follows:

			Demand		
			100	200	300
			s_1	s_2	s_3
Production	100	d_1	500	200	−100
	200	d_2	−400	800	700
	300	d_3	−1000	−200	1600

a. If $P(s_1) = 0.2$, $P(s_2) = 0.2$, and $P(s_3) = 0.6$, what is your recommended production quantity?

b. On some days the firm receives phone calls for advance orders, and on some days it does not. Let I_1 = advance orders are received and I_2 = no advance orders are received. If $P(I_2|s_1) = .8$, $P(I_2|s_2) = .4$, and $P(I_2|s_3) = .1$, what is your recommended production quantity for days the company does not receive any advance orders?

27. The research and development manager for Beck Company is trying to decide whether or not to fund a project to develop a new lubricant. It is assumed that the project will be a major technical success, a minor technical success, or a failure. The company has estimated that the value of a major technical success is $150,000 since the lubricant can be used in a number of products the company is making. If the project is a minor technical success, its value is $10,000 since Beck feels that the knowledge gained will benefit some other ongoing projects. If the project is a failure, it will cost the company $100,000.

Based on the opinion of the scientists involved and the manager's own subjective assessment, the assigned prior probabilities are as follows:

$$P(\text{major success}) = .15$$
$$P(\text{minor success}) = .45$$
$$P(\text{failure}) = .40$$

a. Using the expected value approach, should the project be funded?

b. Suppose that a group of expert scientists from a research institute could be hired as consultants to study the project and make a recommendation. If this study will cost $30,000, should the Beck Company consider hiring the consultants?

Suppose an experiment can be conducted to shed some light on the technical feasibility of the project. There are three possible outcomes for the experiment:

I_1 = prototype lubricant works well at all temperatures

I_2 = prototype lubricant works well only at temperatures above 10°F

I_3 = prototype lubricant does not work well at any temperature

Suppose we can determine the following conditional probabilities:

$$P(I_1 \mid \text{major success}) = .70$$
$$P(I_1 \mid \text{minor success}) = .10$$
$$P(I_1 \mid \text{failure}) = .10$$
$$P(I_2 \mid \text{major success}) = .25$$
$$P(I_2 \mid \text{minor success}) = .70$$
$$P(I_2 \mid \text{failure}) = .30$$
$$P(I_3 \mid \text{major success}) = .05$$
$$P(I_3 \mid \text{minor success}) = .20$$
$$P(I_3 \mid \text{failure}) = .60$$

c. Assuming that the experiment is conducted and the prototype lubricant works well at all temperatures, should the project be funded?

d. Assuming that the experiment is conducted and the prototype lubricant works well only at temperatures above 10°F, should the project be funded?

e. Develop a decision strategy that Beck's R&D manager can use to recommend a funding decision based on the outcome of the experiment.

f. Find the EVSI for the experiment. How efficient is the information in the experiment?

28. A firm has three investment alternatives. The payoff table and associated probabilities are as follows:

		Economic Conditions		
		Up	Stable	Down
Investments	d_1	100	25	0
	d_2	75	50	25 ← $1000s
	d_3	50	50	50
Probabilities		.40	.30	.30

a. Using the expected value approach, which decision is preferred?

b. For the lottery having a payoff of $100,000 with probability p and $0 with probability $(1 - p)$, two decision makers expressed the following indifference probabilities:

| | Indifference Probability (p) | |
Profit	Decision Maker A	Decision Maker B
$75,000	.80	.60
$50,000	.60	.30
$25,000	.30	.15

Find the most preferred decision for each decision maker using the expected utility approach.

c. Why don't decision makers A and B select the same decision alternative?

29. Alexander Industries is considering purchasing an insurance policy for its new office building in St. Louis. The policy has an annual cost of $10,000. If Alexander Industries does not purchase the insurance and minor fire damage occurs to the office building, a cost of $100,000 is anticipated; the cost if major or total destruction occurs is $200,000. The payoff table, including the state-of-nature probabilities, is as follows:

| | | | | Damage | |
| | | | None | Minor | Major |
			s_1	s_2	s_3
	Purchase	d_1	$10,000	$10,000	$10,000
Decision	insurance				
Alternatives	Do not purchase	d_2	$0	$100,000	$200,000
	insurance				
	Probabilities		.96	.03	.01

a. Using the expected value approach, what decision do you recommend?

b. What lottery would you use to assess utilities? (Note that since the data are costs, the best payoff is $0.)

c. Assume we found the following indifference probabilities for the lottery defined in part (b):

Cost	Indifference Probability (p)
$ 10,000	.99
$100,000	.60

What decision would you recommend?

d. Do you favor using expected value or expected utility for this decision problem? Why?

30. In a certain state lottery, a lottery ticket costs $2. In terms of the decision to purchase or not to purchase a lottery ticket, suppose the following payoff table applies:

			States of Nature	
			Win s_1	Lose s_2
Decision	Purchase lottery ticket	d_1	$300,000	-$2
Alternatives	Do not purchase lottery ticket	d_2	$0	$0

a. If a realistic estimate of the chances of winning are 1 in 250,000, use the expected value approach to recommend a decision.

b. If a particular decision maker assigns an indifference probability of 0.000001 to the $0 payoff, would this individual purchase a lottery ticket? Use expected utility to justify your answer.

31. There are two different routes for traveling between two cities. Route A normally takes 60 minutes, while route B normally takes 45 minutes. If traffic problems are encountered on route A, the travel time increases to 70 minutes; traffic problems on route B increase travel time to 90 minutes. The probability of the delay is .2 for route A and .3 for route B.

a. Using the expected value approach, what is the recommended route?

b. If utilities are to be assigned to the travel times, what is the appropriate lottery? Note that the smaller times should reflect higher utilities.

c. Using the lottery of part (b), assume the decision maker expresses indifference probabilities of

$$p = .8 \quad \text{for 60 minutes}$$
$$p = .6 \quad \text{for 70 minutes}$$

What route should this decision maker select?

32. Suppose that the point spread for a particular sporting event is 10 points and that with this spread you are convinced you would have a .6 probability of winning a bet on your team. However, the local bookie will accept only a $1000 bet. Assuming that such bets are legal, would you bet on your team? (Disregard any commission charged by the bookie.) Remember that *you* must pay losses out of your own pocket. Your payoff table is as follows:

			States of Nature	
			You Win s_1	You Lose s_2
Decision	Bet	d_1	$1,000	-$1,000
Alternatives	Don't bet	d_2	$0	$0

a. What decision does the expected value approach recommend?

b. What is *your* indifference probability for the $0 payoff? (While this is not easy, be as realistic as possible. Remember, this is required if we are to do an analysis that reflects your attitude toward risk.)

   c. What decision would you make based on the expected utility approach?

   d. Would other individuals assess the same utility values you do? Explain.

   e. If your decision in part (c) was to place the bet, repeat the analysis, assuming a minimum bet of $10,000.

33. A Las Vegas roulette wheel has 38 different numerical values. If an individual bets on 1 number and wins, the payoff is 35 to 1.

   a. Show a payoff table for a $10 bet on 1 number using decision alternatives of bet and do not bet.

   b. What is the recommended decision using the expected value approach?

   c. What range of utility values would a decision maker have to assign to the $0 payoff in order to have expected utility justify his or her decision to place the $10 bet?

34. A new product has the following profit projections and associated probabilities:

Profit	Probability
$150,000	.10
$100,000	.25
$ 50,000	.20
0	.15
−$ 50,000	.20
−$100,000	.10

   a. Use the expected value approach to make the decision of whether to market the new product.

   b. Because of the high dollar values involved, especially the possibility of a $100,000 loss, the marketing vice-president has expressed some concern about the use of the expected value approach. As a consequence, if a utility analysis is performed, what is the appropriate lottery? Assume the following indifference probabilities are assigned:

Profit	Indifference Probability (p)
$100,000	.95
$ 50,000	.70
0	.50
−$ 50,000	.25

   c. Use expected utility to make a recommended decision.

   d. Should the decision maker feel comfortable with the final decision recommended by the analysis?

35. A television network has been receiving low ratings for its programs. Currently, management is considering two alternatives for the Monday night 8:00 P.M.–9:00 P.M. time slot: a Western program with a well-known star and a musical variety program with a relatively unknown husband-and-wife team. The percentages of viewing audience estimates depend on the degree of program acceptance. The relevant data are as follows:

Program Acceptance	Percentage of Viewing Audience	
	Western	Musical Variety
High	30%	40%
Moderate	25%	20%
Poor	20%	15%

The probabilities associated with the program acceptance levels are as follows:

Program Acceptance	Probability	
	Western	Musical Variety
High	.30	.30
Moderate	.60	.40
Poor	.10	.30

a. Using the expected value approach, which program should the network choose?
b. Assuming a utility analysis is desired, what is the appropriate lottery?
c. Using the appropriate lottery in part (b), assume that the network's program manager has assigned the following indifference probabilities:

Percentage of Audience	Indifference Probability (p)
30%	.40
25%	.30
20%	.10

Using utility measures, which program would you recommend?

▼ CASE PROBLEM

Property Purchase Strategy

Glenn Foreman, president of Oceanview Development Corporation, is considering submitting a bid to purchase property that will be sold by sealed bid at a county tax foreclosure. Glenn's initial judgment is to submit a bid of $5 million. From past experience Glenn estimates that a bid of $5 million will have a .2 probability of being the highest bid and securing the property for Oceanview. The current date is June 1. Sealed bids for the property must be submitted by August 15. The winning bid will be announced on September 1.

If Oceanview submits the highest bid and obtains the property, the firm plans to build and sell a complex of luxury condominiums. However, a complicating factor is that the property is currently zoned for single-family residences only. Glenn feels that a referendum could be placed on the voting ballot in time for the November election. Passage of the referendum would change the zoning of the property and permit construction of the condominiums.

The sealed-bid procedure requires the bid to be submitted with a certified check for 10% of the amount bid. If the bid is rejected, the deposit is refunded. If the bid is accepted, the deposit is the down payment for the property. However, if the bid is accepted and the bidder does not follow through with the purchase and meet the remainder of the financial obligation within 6 months, the deposit will be forfeited. In this case the county will offer the property to the next highest bidder.

In order to determine whether or not to submit the $5 million bid, Glenn has done some preliminary analysis. This preliminary work provided an estimate of 0.3 for the probability that the referendum for a zoning change will be approved and resulted in estimates of the costs and revenues that will be incurred if the condominiums are built. The data obtained are shown below.

Cost and Revenue Estimates	
Revenue from condominium sales	$15,000,000
Cost	
Property	$ 5,000,000
Construction expenses	$ 8,000,000

If Oceanview obtains the property and the zoning change is not approved in November, Glenn feels that the best option would be for the firm not to complete the purchase of the property. In this case Oceanview would forfeit the 10% deposit that accompanied the bid.

Because the likelihood that the zoning referendum will be approved is such an important factor in the decision process, Glenn has suggested that the firm hire a market research service to conduct a survey of voters. The survey would provide a better estimate of the likelihood that the referendum for a zoning change would be approved. The market research firm that Oceanview Development has worked with in the past has agreed to do the study for $15,000. The results of the study will be available August 1, so that Oceanview will have this information before the August 15 bid deadline. The results of the survey will be either a prediction that the zoning change will be approved or a prediction that the zoning change will not be approved. After considering the record of the market research service in previous studies conducted for Oceanview, Glenn has developed the following probability estimates concerning the accuracy of the market research information:

$$P(I_1|s_1) = .9 \qquad P(I_2|s_1) = .1$$
$$P(I_1|s_2) = .2 \qquad P(I_2|s_2) = .8$$

where

I_1 = prediction that the zoning change will be approved

I_2 = prediction that the zoning change will not be approved

s_1 = the zoning change is approved by the voters

s_2 = the zoning change is not approved by the voters

▼ MANAGERIAL REPORT

Perform an analysis of the problem facing the Oceanview Development Corporation, and prepare a report that summarizes your findings and recommendations. Include information on an analysis of the following:

1. A decision tree that shows the logical sequence of the decision problem.
2. A recommendation regarding what Oceanview should do if the market research information is not available.
3. A decision strategy that Oceanview should follow if the market research is conducted.
4. A recommendation as to whether Oceanview should employ the market research firm. What is the value of the information provided by the market research firm?

Include a copy of the details of your analysis in the appendix to your report.

Ohio Edison Company*
Akron, Ohio

Ohio Edison Company is an investor-owned electric utility headquartered in northeastern Ohio. Ohio Edison and a Pennsylvania subsidiary provide electrical service to over 2 million people. Most of this electricity is generated by coal-fired power plants. In order to meet evolving air-quality standards, Ohio Edison has embarked on a program to replace existing pollution control equipment on most of its generating plants with more efficient equipment. The combination of this program to upgrade air-quality control equipment with the continuing need to construct new generating plants to meet future power requirements has resulted in a large capital investment program.

Management science activities at Ohio Edison are distributed throughout the company rather than centralized in a specific department. This activity is more or less evenly divided among the following areas: fossil and nuclear fuel planning, environmental studies, capacity planning, large equipment evaluation, and corporate planning. Applications include decision analysis, optimal ordering strategies, computer modeling, and simulation.

A DECISION ANALYSIS APPLICATION

The flue gas emitted by coal-fired power plants contains small ash particles and sulfur dioxide (SO_2). Federal and state regulatory agencies have established emission limits for both particulates and sulfur dioxide. Recently, Ohio Edison developed a plan to comply with new air-quality standards at one of its largest power plants. This plant consists of seven coal-fired units and constitutes about one-third of the generating capacity of Ohio Edison and the subsidiary company. Most of these units had been constructed in the 1960s. Although all the units had initially been constructed with equipment to control particulate emissions, that equipment was not capable of meeting new particulate emission requirements.

A decision had already been made to burn low-sulfur coal in four of the smaller units (units 1 to 4) at the plant in order to meet SO_2 emission standards. Fabric filters were to be installed on these units to control particulate emissions. Fabric filters, also known as baghouses, use thousands of fabric bags to filter out the particulates; they function in much the same way as a household vacuum cleaner.

It was considered likely, although not certain, that the three larger units (units 5 to 7) at this plant would burn medium- to high-sulfur coal. A method of controlling particulate emissions at these units had not yet been selected. Preliminary studies had narrowed the particulate control equipment choice to a decision between fabric filters and electrostatic precipitators (which remove particulates suspended in the flue gas as charged particles by passing the flue gas through a strong electric

*The authors are indebted to Thomas J. Madden and M.S. Hyrnick of Ohio Edison Company, Akron, Ohio, for providing this application.

field). This decision was affected by a number of uncertainties, including the following:

Uncertainty exists in the way some air-quality laws and regulations might be interpreted.

Certain interpretations could require that either low-sulfur coal or high-sulfur Ohio coal (or neither) be burned in units 5 to 7.

Future changes could be made to air quality laws and regulations.

An overall plant reliability improvement program was under way at this plant.

The outcome of this program would affect the operating costs of whichever pollution control technology was installed in these units.

Construction costs of the equipment were uncertain, particularly since limited space at the plant site made it necessary to install the equipment on a massive bridge deck over a four-lane highway immediately adjacent to the power plant.

The costs associated with replacing the electrical power required to operate the particulate control equipment were uncertain.

Various uncertain factors, including potential accidents and chronic operating problems that could increase the costs of operating the generating units, were identified. The degree to which each of these factors affected operating costs varied with the choice of technology and with the sulfur content of the coal.

DECISION ANALYSIS

The decision to be made involved a choice between two types of particulate control equipment (fabric filters and electrostatic precipitators) for units 5 to 7. Because of the complexity of the problem, the high degree of uncertainty associated with factors affecting the decision, and the importance (because of potential reliability and cost impact on Ohio Edison) of the choice, decision analysis was used in the selection process.

The decision measure used to evaluate the outcomes of the particulate technology decision analysis was the annual revenue requirements for the three large units over their remaining lifetime. Revenue requirements are the monies that would have to be collected from the utility customers in order to recover costs resulting from the decision. They include not only direct costs, but also the cost of capital and return on investment.

A decision tree was constructed to represent the particulate control decision and its uncertainties and costs. A simplified version of this decision tree is shown in Figure 14.10. The decision and state-of-nature nodes are indicated. Note that to conserve space, a type of shorthand notation is used. The coal sulfur content state-of-nature node should actually be located at the end of each branch of the capital cost state-of-nature node, as the dotted lines indicate. Each of the indicated state-of-nature nodes actually represents several probabilistic cost models or submodels. The total revenue requirements calculated are the sum of the revenue requirements for capital and operating costs. Costs associated with these models

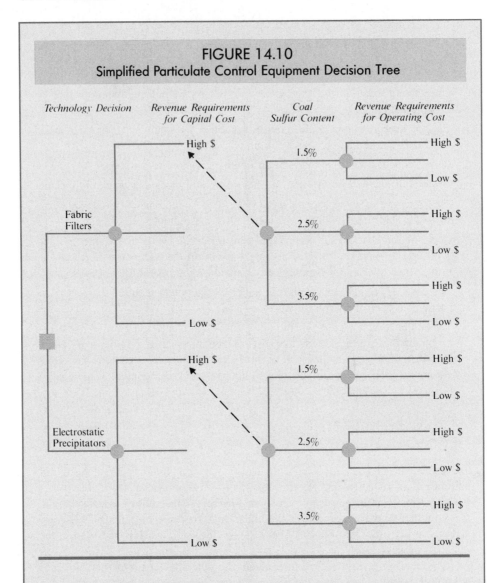

FIGURE 14.10
Simplified Particulate Control Equipment Decision Tree

were obtained from engineering calculations or estimates. Probabilities were obtained from existing data or the subjective assessments of knowledgeable persons.

RESULTS

A decision tree similar to that shown in Figure 14.10 was used to generate cumulative probability distributions for the annual revenue requirements outcomes calculated for each of the two particulate control alternatives. Careful study of these results led to the following conclusions:

> The expected value of annual revenue requirements for the electrostatic precipitator technology was approximately $1 million lower than that for the fabric filters.

The fabric filter alternative had a higher "upside risk"—that is, a higher probability of high revenue requirements—than did the precipitator alternative.

The precipitator technology had nearly an 80% probability of having lower annual revenue requirements than the fabric filters.

Although the capital cost of the fabric filter equipment (the cost of installing the equipment) was lower than for the precipitator, this was more than offset by the higher operating costs associated with the fabric filter.

These results led Ohio Edison to select the electrostatic precipitator technology for the generating units in question. Had the decision analysis not been performed, the particulate control decision might have been based chiefly on capital cost, a decision measure that would have favored the fabric filter equipment. Decision analysis offers a means for effectively analyzing the uncertainties involved in a decision. Because of this, it is felt that the use of decision analysis methodology in this application resulted in a decision that yielded both lower expected revenue requirements and lower risk.

Questions

1. Why was decision analysis used in the selection of particulate control equipment for units 5, 6, and 7?
2. List the decision alternatives for the decision analysis problem developed by Ohio Edison.
3. What were the benefits of using decision analysis in this application?

Multicriteria Decision Problems

In previous chapters we have seen how management science can help managers make better decisions. Whenever it was desired to find an optimal solution, we employed a single criterion (e.g.; maximize profit, minimize cost, minimize expected cost). In this chapter we present management science approaches that are appropriate for situations in which the decision maker desires to consider multiple criteria in arriving at the overall best decision. For example, consider a company that is involved in selecting a location for a new manufacturing plant. Since the cost of land and construction may vary from location to location, one criterion in selecting the best site would be the total cost involved in building the plant; if this were the sole criterion of interest, management would simply select the location where the land cost plus the construction cost is minimized. Before making any decision, however, management might also want to consider additional criteria such as the availability of transportation from the plant to the firm's distribution centers, the attractiveness of the proposed location in terms of hiring and retaining employees, energy costs at the proposed site, and state and local taxes. In situations such as this, the complexity of the problem increases since one location can be more desirable from the perspective of one criterion and less desirable from the perspective of one or more of the other criteria.

To introduce the topic of multicriteria decision making we will first consider a technique referred to as *goal programming*. This technique was developed to handle multicriteria situations within the general framework of linear programming. The other approach we will consider, referred to as the *analytic hierarchy process,* permits the inclusion of subjective factors in arriving at a recommended decision. In this approach the decision maker must provide judgments about the relative importance of each of the decision criteria and then specify a preference for each decision alternative relative to each criterion; the output is a prioritized ranking indicating the overall preference for each of the decision alternatives.

15.1 ▼ GOAL PROGRAMMING: FORMULATION AND GRAPHICAL SOLUTION

To illustrate the goal programming approach to multicriteria decision problems let us consider a problem facing Nicolo Investment Advisors. A particular client has up to $80,000 to invest and, as an initial investment strategy, would like the portfolio restricted to a mix of the following two stocks:

Stock	Price/Share	Estimated Annual Return/Share	Risk Index/Share
U.S. Oil	$25	$3	.50
Hub Properties	$50	$5	.25

U.S. Oil, which has a return of $3 on a $25 share price, provides an annual rate of return of 12% and Hub Properties provides an annual rate of return of 10%. The risk index per share, .50 for U.S. Oil and .25 for Hub Properties, is a rating Nicolo has assigned to measure the relative risk of the two investment alternatives. Higher values imply greater risk; hence, we see that Nicolo has judged U.S. Oil to be the riskier investment. By specifying a maximum portfolio risk, Nicolo is able to avoid placing too much of the portfolio in high-risk investments.

To illustrate how the risk index per share can be used to measure the total portfolio risk, suppose Nicolo chooses a portfolio which invests all $80,000 in U.S. Oil, the highest-risk, but highest-return investment. We could purchase $80,000/$25 = 3200 shares of U.S. Oil, and the portfolio would have a risk index of 3200(.50) = 1600. On the other hand, if no shares of either stock are purchased, there will be no risk, but no return. Thus, the portfolio risk index will vary from 0 (least risk) to 1600 (most risk).

In this case, the client would like to avoid a high-risk portfolio; thus investing all funds in U.S. Oil (the highest-risk investment) would not be desirable. After consulting with Nicolo, the client agreed that an acceptable level of risk would correspond to portfolios with a total risk index of at most 700. Thus, considering only risk, the objective or *goal* is to find a portfolio with a risk index of 700 or less.

Another goal of the client is to receive an annual return of at least $9,000. This goal can be achieved with a portfolio consisting of 2000 shares of U.S. Oil [at a cost of 2000($25) = $50,000] and 600 shares of Hub Properties [at a cost of 600($50) = $30,000]; the annual return in this case would be 2000($3) + 600($5) = $9,000. Note, however, that the portfolio risk for this investment strategy would be 2000(.50) + 600(.25) = 1150; thus, this portfolio achieves the annual return goal but does not satisfy the portfolio risk goal.

It is now clear that the portfolio selection problem is a multicriteria decision problem involving two conflicting goals: one dealing with risk and one dealing with annual return. This is the kind of problem for which the goal programming approach was developed. Goal programming can be used to identify a portfolio that comes closest to achieving both of the goals. Before applying the methodology, the client must determine which, if either, of the goals is the most important.

Suppose the top-priority goal is restricting the risk; that is, keeping the portfolio risk index at 700 or less is so important the client is not willing to trade off the achievement of this goal for any amount of an increase in annual return. On the other hand, as long as the portfolio risk does not exceed 700, the client seeks the best possible return. Given this statement of priorities, the goals for the problem can be written as follows:

Primary Goal (Priority Level 1)

Goal 1: Find a portfolio that has a risk index of 700 or less.

Secondary Goal (Priority Level 2)

Goal 2: Find a portfolio that will provide an annual return of at least $9000.

We have noted, in parentheses above, that the primary goal is called a priority level 1 goal and the secondary goal is called a priority level 2 goal. In goal programming terminology, these are called *preemptive priorities* because the decision maker is not willing to sacrifice any amount of achievement of the priority level 1 goal for the lower priority goal. The portfolio risk index of 700 is the *target value* for the priority level 1 (primary) goal, and the annual return of $9000 is the target value for the priority level 2 (secondary) goal. The difficulty in finding a solution (a portfolio) that will achieve these goals is that there is only $80,000 available for investment.

Developing the Constraints and the Goal Equations

To see how a goal programming model can be developed for the portfolio selection problem, we begin by defining the following decision variables:

$$x_1 = \text{number of shares of U.S. Oil purchased}$$

$$x_2 = \text{number of shares of Hub Properties purchased}$$

Constraints for goal programming problems are handled in the same way as in an ordinary linear programming problem. Using the decision variables, we write a constraint corresponding to the funds available. Since each share of U.S. Oil costs $25 and each share of Hub Properties costs $50, the constraint representing the funds available is

$$25x_1 + 50x_2 \le 80,000$$

This is the only constraint for the problem.

In order to complete the formulation of the goal programming model, we must develop a *goal equation* for each goal. Let us begin by writing the goal equation for the primary goal. Since each share of U.S. Oil has a risk index of .50 and each share of Hub Properties has a risk index of .25, the portfolio risk index is $.50x_1 + .25x_2$. Depending on the values of x_1 and x_2, the portfolio risk may be less than or greater than the target value of 700. To represent these two possibilities mathematically, we create the following *goal equation:*

$$.50x_1 + .25x_2 = 700 + d_1^+ - d_1^-$$

where

d_1^+ = the amount by which the portfolio risk exceeds the target value of 700

d_1^- = the amount by which the portfolio risk is less than the target value of 700

In goal programming, d_1^+ and d_1^- are called *deviation variables*. The purpose of the deviation variables is to allow for the possibility of not meeting the target value for the goal exactly. Consider, for example, a portfolio that consists of $x_1 = 2000$ shares of U.S. Oil and $x_2 = 0$ shares of Hub Properties. The portfolio risk is $.50(2000) + .25(0) =$

1000, and $d_1^+ = 300$ reflects the fact that the portfolio risk exceeds the target value by 300 units; note also that since d_1^+ is greater than zero, the value of d_1^- must be zero. For a portfolio consisting of $x_1 = 0$ shares of U.S. Oil and $x_2 = 2000$ shares of Hub Properties, the portfolio risk would be $.50(0) + .25(1000) = 250$. In this case $d_1^- = 450$ (and $d_1^+ = 0$), indicating that the solution provides a portfolio risk of 450 less than the target value of 700.

In general, the letter d is used for deviation variables in a goal programming model. A superscript of plus $(+)$ or minus $(-)$ is used to indicate whether the variable corresponds to a positive or negative deviation from the target value for the goal. If we bring the deviation variables to the left-hand side, we can rewrite the goal equation for the primary goal as

$$.50x_1 + .25x_2 - d_1^+ + d_1^- = 700$$

In general, the value on the right-hand side of the goal equation is the target value for the goal. The left-hand side of the goal equation consists of two parts:

1. A function that defines the amount of goal achievement in terms of the decision variables (e.g., $.50x_1 + .25x_2$).
2. The difference between the target value for the goal and the amount of achievement, represented by the two deviation variables.

To develop a goal equation for the secondary goal, we begin by writing a function representing the annual return for the investment.

$$\text{Annual return} = 3x_1 + 5x_2$$

Then we define two deviation variables that represent the amount of over- or underachievement of the goal. Doing so, we obtain

d_2^+ = the amount by which the annual return for the portfolio is greater than the target value of $9000

d_2^- = the amount by which the annual return for the portfolio is less than the target value of $9000

Using these two deviation variables, we can write the goal equation for goal 2 as

$$3x_1 + 5x_2 = 9000 + d_2^+ - d_2^-$$

or

$$3x_1 + 5x_2 - d_2^+ + d_2^- = 9,000$$

This completes the development of the goal equations and the constraints for the Nicolo portfolio problem. We are now ready to develop an appropriate objective function for the problem.

Developing an Objective Function with Preemptive Priorities

The objective function in a goal programming model calls for minimizing a function of the deviation variables. In the portfolio problem, the most important goal is to find a portfolio with a total risk of 700 or less. Since this is the most important goal, it is assigned the highest-priority level, which we will denote as P_1. There are only two goals in the problem, and the client is unwilling to incur a risk greater than 700 in order to achieve the secondary goal. Therefore, the annual return goal is assigned the priority level P_2. These priorities are referred to as *preemptive priorities* in goal programming terminology because the satisfaction of a higher-level goal cannot be traded off for the satisfaction of a lower-level goal.

Goal programming problems with preemptive priorities are solved by treating priority level 1 goals (P_1) first in an objective function. The idea is to start with a solution that comes closest to satisfying the priority level 1 goals. The solution found is then modified by solving a problem with an objective function involving only priority level 2 goals (P_2); however, revisions in the solution minimizing deviations from the P_1 goals are permitted only if they do not cause a reduction in the achievement of the P_1 goals. In general, when we solve a goal programming problem with preemptive priorities, a sequence of linear programs with different objective functions is solved; P_1 goals are considered first, P_2 goals second, P_3 goals third, and so on. At each stage of the solution procedure a revision in the solution is permitted only if it causes no reduction in the achievement of a higher-priority goal.

The number of linear programs we must solve in sequence to develop the solution to a goal programming problem is determined by the number of priority levels. One linear program must be solved for each priority level. We will call the first linear program solved the priority level 1 problem, the second the priority level 2 problem, and so on. Each of the linear programs is obtained from the one at the next higher level by changing the objective function and adding a constraint. Let us formulate the priority level 1 problem.

We first formulate the objective function. The client has stated a desire for portfolio risk not to exceed 700. Is underachieving the target value of 700 a concern? Clearly, the answer is no since values less than 700 correspond to less risk. Is overachieving the target value of 700 a concern? The answer is yes since portfolios with a risk greater than 700 correspond to levels of risk higher than the client is willing to accept. Thus, the objective function corresponding to the priority level 1 goal should minimize the value of d_1^+.

The goal equations and the funds available constraint have already been developed. Thus, the priority level 1 linear program can now be stated.

P_1 *Problem*

$$\min \quad d_1^+$$

s.t.

$$
\begin{array}{llll}
25x_1 + 50x_2 & & \leq 80{,}000 & \text{Funds available} \\
.50x_1 + .25x_2 - d_1^+ + d_1^- & & = 700 & P_1 \text{ goal} \\
3x_1 + 5x_2 & - d_2^+ + d_2^- & = 9{,}000 & P_2 \text{ goal} \\
\end{array}
$$

$$x_1, x_2, d_1^+, d_1^-, d_2^+, d_2^- \geq 0$$

The Graphical Solution Procedure

The goal programming graphical solution procedure is similar to the linear programming graphical solution procedure presented in Chapter 2, but it involves a stage for each priority level. Recall that the linear programming graphical solution procedure used a graph to display the possible solution values for the decision variables. Since the decision variables are nonnegative, we only consider that portion of the graph where $x_1 \geq 0$ and $x_2 \geq 0$. Recall also that every point on the graph is called a *solution point*.

For the portfolio problem, the available funds constraint is

$$25x_1 + 50x_2 \leq 80{,}000$$

The region in color in part A of Figure 15.1, Feasible Portfolios, consists of all points that satisfy the above constraint—that is, values of x_1 and x_2 for which $25x_1 + 50x_2 \leq 80{,}000$.

Now we are ready to consider positive deviations from the P_1 level goal. Recall that the goal equation is

$$.50x_1 + .25x_2 - d_1^+ + d_1^- = 700$$

When the goal is met exactly, $d_1^+ = 0$, and $d_1^- = 0$; the goal equation then reduces to $.50x_1 + .25x_2 = 700$. In part B of Figure 15.1 we show the graph of this equation. It is a straight line. The area shown in color in part B identifies all solution points that satisfy the available funds constraint and also result in the value of $d_1^+ = 0$. Since any solution for which $d_1^+ = 0$ will achieve the priority level 1 goal, the area in color contains all the solutions that will enable us to achieve the goal of establishing a portfolio with a total risk of at most 700.

At this point we have found the optimal solution to the priority level 1 problem. Note that there are alternative optimal solutions; in fact, all solution points in the color-shaded region in part B of Figure 15.1 maintain portfolio risk ≤ 700, and, hence, $d_1^+ = 0$. We are now ready to consider the priority level 2 problem. The priority level 2 problem is one of minimizing negative deviations from the annual return goal subject to one extra constraint. There can be no degradation of the optimal solution to the priority level 1 problem. The priority level 2 problem is as follows.

FIGURE 15.1
The Goal Programming Graphical Solution Procedure
A: Portfolios That Satisfy the Available Funds Constraint

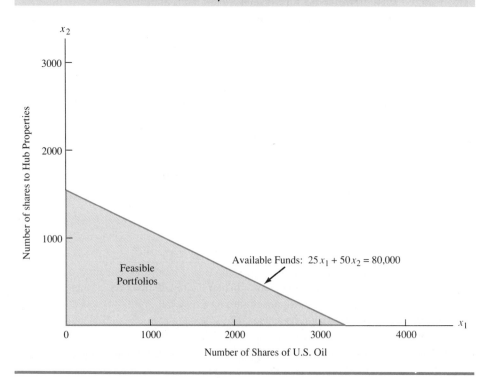

FIGURE 15.1
B: Portfolios That Satisfy the P_1 Goal

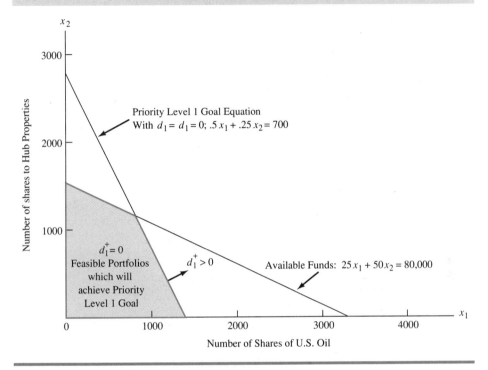

P_2 Problem

min d_2^-

s.t.

$$25x_1 + 50x_2 \qquad\qquad\qquad\qquad\qquad \leq 80{,}000 \quad \text{Funds available}$$

$$.50x_1 + .25x_2 - d_1^+ + d_1^- \qquad\qquad = \quad 700 \quad P_1 \text{ goal}$$

$$3x_1 + 5x_2 \qquad\qquad - d_2^+ + d_2^- = 9{,}000 \quad P_2 \text{ goal}$$

$$d_1^+ \qquad\qquad\qquad\qquad = \quad 0 \quad \text{Maintain achievement of } P_1 \text{ goal}$$

$$x_1, x_2, d_1^+, d_1^-, d_2^+, d_2^-, \geq 0$$

We note that the priority level 2 problem differs from the priority level 1 problem in two ways. The objective function involves minimizing the negative deviations from the priority level 2 goal, and another constraint has been added to ensure that no amount of achievement of the priority level 1 goal is sacrificed.

Let us now continue the graphical solution. The goal equation for the priority level 2 goal is

$$3x_1 + 5x_2 - d_2^+ + d_2^- = 9{,}000$$

When both d_2^+ and d_2^- equal zero, this equation reduces to $3x_1 + 5x_2 = 9000$; in part C of Figure 15.1 we show the graph of this equation.

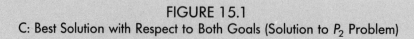

FIGURE 15.1
C: Best Solution with Respect to Both Goals (Solution to P_2 Problem)

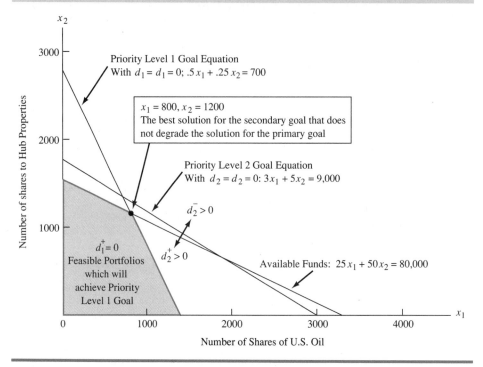

At this stage we cannot consider any solutions that will degrade the achievement of the priority level 1 goal. Viewing part C, we see that there are no solution points that will achieve the priority level 2 goal and maintain the level we were able to achieve for the priority level 1 goal. In fact, the best solution that can be obtained when considering the priority level 2 goal is given by the point (x_1 = 800, x_2 = 1200); in other words, this point comes the closest to satisfying the priority level 2 goal from among those solutions satisfying the priority level 1 goal. Since the annual return corresponding to this solution is 3($800) + 5($1200) = $8400, we see that it is not possible to identify a portfolio that will satisfy both the priority level 1 and the priority level 2 goals; in fact, the best solution underachieves goal 2 by d_2^- = $600.

In summary, the graphical solution procedure for goal programming is as follows:

1. Identify the feasible solutions; these are the ones that satisfy the problem constraints.
2. Identify all feasible solutions that achieve the highest-priority goal; if there are no feasible solutions that will achieve the highest-priority goal, identify the solution(s) that comes closest to achieving the highest-priority goal.
3. Move down one priority level, and determine the "best" solution possible without sacrificing any achievement of higher-priority goals.
4. Repeat step 3 until all priority levels have been considered.

Although the goal programming graphical solution procedure is a convenient method for solving goal programming problems involving two decision variables, larger problems require a computer-based approach. In the next section we will illustrate how to use a computer software package to solve more complex goal programming problems.

The Goal Programming Model

As we have stated, goal programming problems are solved as a sequence of linear programs; there is one for each priority level. However, it is helpful to have a notation that permits writing a goal programming problem in one concise statement. We show how this is done for the portfolio problem.

In writing the overall objective for the problem, we must write the objective function in a way that reminds us of the preemptive priorities inherent in the problem. We can do this by writing the objective function as follows:

$$\min \quad P_1(d_1^+) + P_2(d_2^-)$$

The priority levels P_1 and P_2 are not numerical weights on the deviation variables, but simply labels that remind us of the priority levels for the goals.

We now write, in one statement, the complete goal programming model as follows:

$$\min \quad P_1(d_1^+) + P_2(d_2^-)$$

s.t.

$$
\begin{aligned}
25x_1 + 50x_2 && \le 80{,}000 && \text{Funds available} \\
.50x_1 + .25x_2 - d_1^+ + d_1^- && = 700 && P_1 \text{ goal} \\
3x_1 + 5x_2 \quad - d_2^+ + d_2^- &= 9000 && P_2 \text{ goal} \\
x_1, x_2, d_1^+, d_1^-, d_2^+, d_2^- \ge 0
\end{aligned}
$$

With the exception of the P_1 and P_2 priority levels in the objective function, the goal programming model we have developed is really just a linear programming model. It is understood that to solve such a problem a sequence of linear programs involving goals at decreasing priority levels is solved.

We now summarize the procedure used to develop a goal programming model.

1. Identify the goals and any constraints that reflect resource capacities or other restrictions that may prevent achievement of the goals.
2. Determine the priority level of each goal; goals with priority level P_1 are most important, those with priority level P_2 are next most important, and so on.
3. Define the decision variables.
4. Formulate the constraints in the usual linear programming fashion.
5. For each goal, develop a goal equation, with the right-hand side specifying the target value for the goal. Deviation variables d_i^+ and d_i^- are included in each goal equation in order to reflect the possible deviations above or below the target value for the goal.
6. Write the objective function in terms of minimizing a prioritized function of the deviation variables.

▼ NOTES AND COMMENTS ▼

1. The constraints in the general goal programming model are of two types: goal equations and ordinary linear programming constraints. Some management scientists call the goal equations *goal constraints* and the ordinary linear programming constraints *system constraints*.

continued on next page

2. One can think of the general goal programming model as having "hard" and "soft" constraints. The hard constraints are the ordinary linear programming constraints that cannot be violated. The soft constraints are the ones resulting from the goal equations. Soft constraints can be violated, but there is a penalty paid for doing so. The penalty paid is reflected by the coefficient of the deviation variable in the objective function.

3. Note that the constraint added when moving from the linear programming problem at one priority level to the linear programming problem at the next lower priority level becomes a hard constraint. No amount of achievement of a higher priority goal may be sacrificed to achieve a lower priority goal.

15.2 ▼ GOAL PROGRAMMING: SOLVING MORE COMPLEX PROBLEMS

In Section 15.1 we formulated and solved a goal programming model that involved one priority level 1 goal and one priority level 2 goal. In this section we show how to formulate and solve goal programming models that involve multiple goals within the same priority level. Although computer packages have been specially developed to solve goal programming models, these packages are not as readily available as general purpose linear programming packages are. Thus, the computer solution procedure outlined in this section develops a solution to a goal programming model by solving a sequence of linear programming models using a general purpose linear programming package.

The Suncoast Office Supplies Problem

Management of Suncoast Office Supplies establishes monthly goals, or quotas, for the types of customers contacted. For the next 4 weeks, Suncoast's customer contact strategy calls for the sales force, which consists of 4 salespeople, to make 200 contacts with customers who have previously purchased supplies from the firm. In addition, the strategy calls for 120 contacts of new customers. The purpose of this latter goal is to ensure that the sales force is continuing to investigate new sources of sales.

Making allowances for travel and waiting time, as well as for demonstration and direct sales time, Suncoast has allocated 2 hours of sales force effort to each contact of a previous customer. New customer contacts tend to take longer and require 3 hours per contact. Normally, each salesperson works 40 hours per week, or 160 hours over the 4-week planning horizon; under a normal work schedule, the 4 salespeople will have $4(160) = 640$ hours of sales force time available for customer contacts.

Management is willing to use some overtime, if needed, or to accept a solution that uses less than the scheduled 640 hours available. However, management desires a solution that will limit both overtime and underutilization of the work force to at most 40 hours over the 4-week period. Thus, from an overtime perspective, management's goal is to use no more than $640 + 40 = 680$ hours of sales force time, and from a labor utilization perspective, management's goal is to use at least $640 - 40 = 600$ hours of sales force time.

In addition to the customer contact goals, Suncoast has established a goal regarding sales volume. Based on past experience, Suncoast estimates that each previous customer contacted will generate $250 of sales and each new customer contacted will generate $125 of sales. Management would like to generate sales of at least $70,000 for the next month.

After further consideration of these goals, management has concluded that the most important goals are the labor utilization goals. That is, given Suncoast's small sales force and the short time frame involved, management has decided that the overtime goal and the labor utilization goal are both priority level 1 goals. Management also concluded that the $70,000 sales goal should be a priority level 2 goal and that the two customer contact goals should be priority level 3 goals. Given these priorities, we can now summarize the goals as follows:

Priority Level 1 Goals

Goal 1:   Do not use any more than 680 hours of sales force time.

Goal 2:   Do not use any less than 600 hours of sales force time.

Priority Level 2 Goal

Goal 3:   Generate sales revenues of at least $70,000.

Priority Level 3 Goals

Goal 4:   Call on at least 200 previous customers.

Goal 5:   Call on at least 120 new customers.

Formulating the Goal Equations

First, we must define the decision variables whose values will be used to determine whether or not we are able to achieve the goals. Let

$$x_1 = \text{the number of previous customers contacted}$$

$$x_2 = \text{the number of new customers contacted}$$

Using these decision variables and appropriate deviation variables, a goal equation can be developed for each goal. The procedure used parallels the approach used in the previous section. A summary of the results obtained is shown for each goal.

Goal 1

$$2x_1 + 3x_2 - d_1^+ + d_1^- = 680$$

where

$d_1^+ = $ the amount by which the number of hours used by the sales force is greater than the target value of 680 hours

$d_1^- = $ the amount by which the number of hours used by the sales force is less than the target value of 680 hours

Goal 2

$$2x_1 + 3x_2 - d_2^+ + d_2^- = 600$$

where

$d_2^+ = $ the amount by which the number of hours used by the sales force is greater than the target value of 600 hours

d_2^- = the amount by which the number of hours used by the sales force is less than the target value of 600 hours

Goal 3

$$250x_1 + 125x_2 - d_3^+ + d_3^- = 70,000$$

where

d_3^+ = the amount by which the sales revenue is greater than the target value of $70,000

d_3^- = the amount by which the sales revenue is less than the target value of $70,000

Goal 4

$$x_1 - d_4^+ + d_4^- = 200$$

where

d_4^+ = the amount by which the number of previous customer contacts exceeds the target value of 200 previous customer contacts

d_4^- = the amount by which the number of previous customer contacts falls short of the target value of 200 previous customer contacts

Goal 5

$$x_1 - d_5^+ + d_5^- = 120$$

where

d_5^+ = the amount by which the number of new customer contacts exceeds the target value of 120 new customer contacts

d_5^- = the amount by which the number of new customer contacts falls short of the target value of 120 new customer contacts

Formulating the Objective Function

To develop the objective function for the Suncoast Office Supplies problem we begin by considering the priority level 1 goals. When considering goal 1, note that if $d_1^+ = 0$, we will have found a solution that uses no more than 680 hours of sales force time. Since solutions for which d_1^+ is greater than zero represent overtime beyond the desired level, the objective function should minimize the value of d_1^+. When considering goal 2, if $d_2^- = 0$, we will have found a solution that uses *at least* 600 hours of sales force time. If d_2^- is greater than zero, however, labor utilization will not have reached the acceptable level. Thus, the objective function for the priority level 1 goals should also minimize the value of d_2^-. Assuming that both of these priority level 1 goals are equally important, the objective function for the priority level 1 problem would be written as

$$\min \quad d_1^+ + d_2^-$$

In considering the priority level 2 goal, we note that management's objective is to achieve sales revenues of at least \$70,000. Note that if $d_3^- = 0$, Suncoast will achieve revenues of *at least* \$70,000, and if $d_3^- > 0$, revenues of less than \$70,000 will be obtained. Thus, the objective function for the priority level 2 problem is to minimize d_3^-. Next, let us consider what the objective function must be for the priority level 3 problem.

When considering goal 4, note that if $d_4^- = 0$, we will have found a solution with *at least* 200 previous customer contacts; however, if $d_4^- > 0$, we will have underachieved the goal of contacting at least 200 previous customers. Thus, for goal 4 the objective is to minimize d_4^-. When considering goal 5, if $d_5^- = 0$, we will have found a solution with *at least* 120 new customer contacts; however, if $d_5^- > 0$, we will have underachieved the goal of contacting at least 120 new customers. Thus, for goal 5 the objective is to minimize d_5^-.

If both goals 4 and 5 are equal in importance, the objective function for the priority level 3 problem would be

$$\min \quad d_4^- + d_5^-$$

However, suppose management believes that generating new customers is so vital to the long-run success of the firm that goal 5 should be weighted more than goal 4. Assuming management believes that goal 5 is 2 times as important as goal 4, we would write the objective function for the priority level 3 problem as

$$\min \quad d_4^- + 2d_5^-$$

Combining the objective functions for all three priority levels, we obtain the following objective function for the Suncoast Office Supplies problem:

$$\min \quad P_1(d_1^+) + P_1(d_2^-) + P_2(d_3^-) + P_3(d_4^-) + P_3(2d_5^-)$$

As we indicated previously, P_1, P_2, and P_3 are simply labels that remind us that goals 1 and 2 are the first-priority goals, goal 3 is the second-priority goal, and goals 4 and 5 are the third-priority level goals. Since this completes the formulation of the goal programming model, we can now write the complete goal programming model for the Suncoast Office Supplies problem as follows:

$$\min \quad P_1(d_1^+) + P_1(d_2^-) + P_2(d_3^-) + P_3(d_4^-) + P_3(2d_5^-)$$

s.t.

$$
\begin{array}{llll}
2x_1 + 3x_2 - d_1^+ + d_1^- & & = & 680 \text{ Goal 1} \\
2x_1 + 3x_2 \quad\; - d_2^+ + d_2^- & & = & 600 \text{ Goal 2} \\
250x_1 + 125x_2 \quad\; - d_3^+ + d_3^- & & = & 70{,}000 \text{ Goal 3} \\
x_1 \quad\quad\quad\quad\quad\;\; - d_4^+ + d_4^- & & = & 200 \text{ Goal 4} \\
x_2 \quad\quad\quad\quad\quad\quad\quad\;\; - d_5^+ + d_5^- & & = & 120 \text{ Goal 5}
\end{array}
$$

$$x_1, x_2, d_1^+, d_1^-, d_2^+, d_2^-, d_3^+, d_3^-, d_4^+, d_4^-, d_5^+, d_5^- \geq 0$$

Computer Solution

The computer solution procedure illustrated in this subsection develops a solution to a goal programming model by solving a sequence of linear programming problems. The first problem consists of all the constraints and all the goal equations for the complete goal programming model; however, the objective function for this problem involves only the P_1 priority level goals. We refer to this problem as the P_1 problem.

Whatever the solution is to the P_1 problem, a P_2 problem is formed by adding a constraint to the P_1 model that ensures that subsequent problems will not degrade the solution obtained for the P_1 problem. The objective function for this second-stage problem takes into consideration only the P_2 priority level goals. The process continues until all priority levels have been considered. We will illustrate the procedure for the Suncoast Office Supplies problem using the LINDO/PC microcomputer package.

To solve the Suncoast Office Supplies problem we begin by solving the following P_1 problem:

$$\min \quad d_1^+ + d_2^-$$

s.t.

$$
\begin{array}{llll}
2x_1 + 3x_2 - d_1^+ + d_1^- & & = & 680 \text{ Goal 1} \\
2x_1 + 3x_2 \quad\;\; - d_2^+ + d_2^- & & = & 600 \text{ Goal 2} \\
250x_1 + 125x_2 \quad\;\; - d_3^+ + d_3^- & & = & 70,000 \text{ Goal 3} \\
x_1 \quad\quad\quad\quad\quad - d_4^+ + d_4^- & & = & 200 \text{ Goal 4} \\
x_2 \quad\quad\quad\quad\quad - d_5^+ + d_5^- & = & 120 \text{ Goal 5}
\end{array}
$$

$$x_1, x_2, d_1^+, d_1^-, d_2^+, d_2^-, d_3^+, d_3^-, d_4^+, d_4^-, d_5^+, d_5^- \geq 0$$

In Figure 15.2 we show the LINDO/PC solution for this P_1 problem. Note that D1MINUS refers to d_1^-, D1PLUS refers to d_1^+, D2MINUS refers to d_2^-, and so on. We see that the solution consisting of $x_1 = 200$ previous customer contacts and $x_2 = 66.66$ new customer contacts does achieve both goals 1 and 2 since D1PLUS and D2MINUS are equal to zero; alternatively, the objective function value of D1PLUS + D2MINUS = 0 also confirms that both priority level 1 goals have been achieved. Note that this solution underachieves

---

FIGURE 15.2
Solution of the P_1 Problem Using LINDO/PC

```
                    OBJECTIVE FUNCTION VALUE

        1)              .00000000

           VARIABLE          VALUE          REDUCED COST
             D1PLUS          .000000           1.000000
            D2MINUS          .000000           1.000000
                 X1       200.000000            .000000
                 X2        66.666660            .000000
            D1MINUS        80.000000            .000000
             D2PLUS          .000000            .000000
             D3PLUS          .000000            .000000
            D3MINUS     11666.670000            .000000
             D4PLUS          .000000            .000000
            D4MINUS          .000000            .000000
             D5PLUS          .000000            .000000
            D5MINUS        53.333330            .000000
```

the sales revenue goal by D3MINUS = \$11,666.67, achieves goal 4, and underachieves goal 5 by D5MINUS = 53.33 new customers. Most important, however, we now know that a solution exists that achieves the priority level 1 goals.

The model for the P_2 problem is formed by adding a constraint to the P_1 problem that ensures that subsequent solutions will not degrade the solution already obtained for the priority level 1 goals. We can do this by requiring that all future solutions satisfy the constraint $d_1^+ + d_2^- = 0$. Adding this constraint to the model and writing the objective function in terms of the priority level 2 goal, we obtain the problem and LINDO/PC solution shown in Figure 15.3.

The optimal solution to the P_2 problem is to contact $x_1 = 270$ previous customers and $x_2 = 20$ new customers. Since D3MINUS = 0, we now know that it is possible to achieve both the P_1 and the P_2 level goals. In other words, we now know that a solution can be found that will achieve the labor utilization goals and also generate sales revenues of at least \$70,000. Note, however, that this solution overachieves the previous customer contact goal by D4PLUS = 70 previous customers and falls short of the new customer contact goal by D5MINUS = 100 new customers.

The third linear programming problem requires adding a constraint to the P_2 problem that will ensure that the P_2 sales revenue goal will continue to be achieved. Note that this can be done by adding the constraint $d_3^- = 0$. With the addition of this constraint and the objective function corresponding to the P_3 priority level goals, we obtain the priority level 3 problem and LINDO/PC solution shown in Figure 15.4. We see that the optimal solution consisting of $x_1 = 250$ previous customer contacts and $x_2 = 60$ customer contacts overachieves goal 4 by D4PLUS = 50 previous customers; however, this solution underachieves goal 5 by D5MINUS = 60 new customers.

FIGURE 15.3
Solution of the P_2 Problem Using LINDO/PC

```
MIN     D3MINUS
SUBJECT TO
        2)  - D1PLUS + 2 X1 + 3 X2 + D1MINUS =      680
        3)    D2MINUS + 2 X1 + 3 X2 - D2PLUS =      600
        4)    250 X1 + 125 X2 - D3PLUS + D3MINUS =      70000
        5)    X1 - D4PLUS + D4MINUS =      200
        6)    X2 - D5PLUS = D5MINUS =      120
        7)    D1PLUS + D2MINUS =      0
END


        OBJECTIVE FUNCTION VALUE

  1)          .00000000

    VARIABLE            VALUE          REDUCED COST
      D1PLUS          .000000            .000000
     D2MINUS          .000000            .000000
          X1       270.000000            .000000
          X2        20.000000            .000000
     D1MINUS        80.000000            .000000
      D2PLUS          .000000            .000000
      D3PLUS          .000000            .000000
     D3MINUS          .000000           1.000000
      D4PLUS        70.000000            .000000
     D4MINUS          .000000            .000000
      D5PLUS          .000000            .000000
     D5MINUS       100.000000            .000000
```

FIGURE 15.4
Solution of the P_3 Problem Using LINDO/PC

```
MIN     D4MINUS + 2 D5MINUS
SUBJECT TO
        2) - D1PLUS + 2 X1 + 3 X2 + D1MINUS =      680
        3)   D2MINUS + 2 X1 + 3 X2 - D2PLUS =      600
        4)   250 X1 + 125 X2 - D3PLUS + D3MINUS =      70000
        5)   X1 - D4PLUS + D4MINUS =    200
        6)   X2 - D5PLUS + D5MINUS =    120
        7)   D1PLUS + D2MINUS =    0
        8)   D3MINUS =    0
END


              OBJECTIVE FUNCTION VALUE

1)              120.000000

    VARIABLE           VALUE          REDUCED COST
     D1PLUS          .000000            .000000
    D2MINUS          .000000           1.000000
         X1       250.000000            .000000
         X2        60.000000            .000000
    D1MINUS          .000000           1.000000
     D2PLUS        80.000000            .000000
     D3PLUS          .000000            .008000
    D3MINUS          .000000            .000000
     D4PLUS        50.000000            .000000
    D4MINUS          .000000           1.000000
     D5PLUS          .000000           2.000000
    D5MINUS        60.000000            .000000
```

Since all the priority levels have been considered, the solution procedure is finished. The optimal solution to the goal programming model is to call on 250 previous customers and 60 new customers. Although this solution will not achieve management's goal of contacting at least 120 new customers, it does achieve each of the other goals specified. If management is still not happy with this solution, a different set of priorities could be considered. Management must keep in mind, however, that in any problem situation involving multiple goals at different priority levels, rarely will we be able to achieve all the goals given the existing resources.

▼ NOTES AND COMMENTS ▼

1. All goal programming problems do not have multiple priority levels. For problems with one priority level, only one linear program need be solved to obtain the goal programming solution. One simply minimizes the weighted deviations

from the goals. Trade-offs are permitted among the goals since they are all at the same priority level.

2. The goal programming approach can be employed when one is confronted with an infeasible solution to an ordinary linear program. By reformulating some of the constraints as goal equations with deviation variables, a solution can be found that minimizes the weighted sum of the deviation variables. Often this approach will suggest a reasonable solution to management.

3. The approach we have utilized to solve goal programming problems with multiple priority levels is to solve a sequence of linear programs. These linear programs are closely related so that complete reformulation and solution are not necessary. One simply changes the objective function and adds a constraint to go from one problem to the next.

15.3 ▼ THE ANALYTIC HIERARCHY PROCESS

The analytic hierarchy process (AHP), developed by Thomas L. Saaty,[1] is designed to solve complex problems involving multiple criteria. The process requires the decision maker to provide judgments about the relative importance of each of the criteria and then to specify a preference for each decision alternative on each criterion. The output of the AHP is a prioritized ranking indicating the overall preference for each of the decision alternatives.

In order to introduce the AHP, we consider the problem faced by Dave Payne. Dave is planning to purchase a new car. After a preliminary analysis of the makes and models available, Dave has narrowed the list of decision alternatives to three cars, which we will refer to as car A, car B, and car C. Table 15.1 provides a summary of the information Dave has collected regarding these cars.

Based on the information in Table 15.1—as well as his own personal feelings resulting from driving each car—Dave decided that there were several criteria that he needed to consider in making the purchase decision. After some thought, he selected purchase price, miles per gallon (MPG), comfort, and style as the four criteria to be considered. Quantitative data regarding the purchase price and MPG criteria are provided directly in Table 15.1. However, measures of comfort and style cannot be specified so

TABLE 15.1
Information for the Car-Selection Example

	Car A	Car B	Car C
Price	$13,100	$11,200	$9500
MPG	18	23	29
Interior	Deluxe	Above average	Standard
Body	4-door midsize	2-door sport	2-door compact
Radio	AM/FM, tape	AM/FM	AM
Engine	6-cylinder	4-cylinder turbo	4-cylinder

[1]Thomas L. Saaty, *The Analytic Hierarchy Process* (New York: McGraw-Hill 1980).

easily. Dave will need to consider factors such as car interior, type of radio, ease of entry and exit, seat-adjustment features, etc., in order to determine the comfort level for each car. The style criterion will need to be measured in terms of Dave's subjective evaluation of each car.

Even when we deal with a criterion as easily measured as purchase price, however, subjectivity becomes an issue whenever a particular decision maker indicates his or her personal preferences. For instance, car A costs \$3600 more than car C; this difference might represent a great deal of money to one person, but not very much money to another person. Thus, whether car A is considered extremely more expensive than car C or only moderately more expensive than car C is a subjective judgment that will depend primarily on the financial status of the person making the comparison. An advantage of the AHP is that it is designed to handle situations such as this, in which the subjective judgments of individuals constitute an important part of the decision process.

Developing the Hierarchy

The first step in the AHP is to develop a graphical representation of the problem in terms of the *overall goal*, the *criteria*, and the *decision alternatives*. Such a graph depicts the *hierarchy* for the problem. Figure 15.5 shows the hierarchy for the car-selection problem. Note that the first level of the hierarchy shows that the overall goal is to select the best car. At the second level, we see that the four criteria (purchase price, MPG, comfort, and style) will contribute to the achievement of the overall goal. Finally, at the third level, we see that each decision alternative (car A, car B, and car C) can contribute to each criterion in a unique way.

The approach AHP takes is to have the decision maker specify his or her judgments about the relative importance of each criterion in terms of its contribution to the achievement of the overall goal. At the next level, the AHP asks the decision maker to indicate a preference or priority for each decision alternative in terms of how it contributes to each criterion. For example, in the car-selection problem, Dave will need to specify his judgment about the relative importance of each of the four criteria. He will also need to indicate his preference for each of the three cars relative to each criterion. Given the

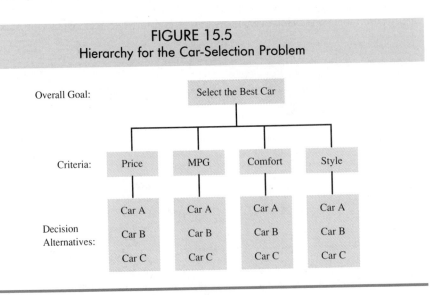

FIGURE 15.5
Hierarchy for the Car-Selection Problem

information on relative importance and preferences, a mathematical process is used to synthesize the information and provide a priority ranking of the three cars in terms of their overall preference.

15.4 ▼ ESTABLISHING PRIORITIES USING THE AHP

In this section we will show how the AHP utilizes pairwise comparisons to establish priority measures for both the criteria and the decision alternatives. The sets of priorities that need to be determined in the car-selection problem are as follows:

1. The priorities of the four criteria in terms of the overall goal
2. The priorities of the three cars in terms of the purchase-price criterion
3. The priorities of the three cars in terms of the MPG criterion
4. The priorities of the three cars in terms of the comfort criterion
5. The priorities of the three cars in terms of the style criterion

In the following discussion we will demonstrate how to establish priorities for the three cars in terms of the *comfort* criterion. The other sets of priorities can be determined in a similar fashion.

Pairwise Comparisons

Pairwise comparisons are fundamental building blocks of the AHP. In establishing the priorities for the three cars in terms of comfort, we will ask Dave to state a preference for the comfort of the cars when the cars are considered two at a time (pairwise). That is, Dave will be asked to compare the comfort of car *A* to car *B*, car *A* to car *C*, and car *B* to car *C* in three separate comparisons.

The AHP employs an underlying scale with values from 1 to 9 to rate the relative preferences for two items. Table 15.2 provides the numerical ratings recommended for the verbal preferences expressed by the decision maker. Research and experience have confirmed the 9-unit scale as a reasonable basis for discriminating between the preferences for two items.

TABLE 15.2
Pairwise Comparison Scale for the AHP Preferences

Verbal Judgment of Preference	Numerical Rating
Extremely preferred	9
Very strongly to extremely	8
Very strongly preferred	7
Strongly to very strongly	6
Strongly preferred	5
Moderately to strongly	4
Moderately preferred	3
Equally to moderately	2
Equally preferred	1

In the car-selection example, suppose that Dave has compared the comforts of car A with those of car B and is convinced that car A is more comfortable. Dave is then asked to state his preference for the comfort of car A compared to that of car B using one of the verbal descriptions shown in Table 15.2. If he believes that car A is *moderately* preferred to car B, a value of 3 is utilized in the AHP; if he believes that car A is *strongly* preferred, a value of 5 is utilized; if he believes that car A is *very strongly* preferred, a value of 7 is utilized; if he believes that car A is *extremely* preferred, a value of 9 is utilized. Values of 2, 4, 6, and 8 are the intermediate values for the scale. A value of 1 is reserved for the case where the two items are judged to be *equally* preferred.

Suppose that when asked his preference between cars A and B with respect to the comfort criterion, Dave states that car A is between equally and moderately more preferred than car B; the numerical measure that reflects this judgment is 2. Dave is then asked to provide his preference between car A and car C. Suppose in this case he states that car A is very strongly to extremely more preferred than car C; this corresponds to a numerical rating of 8. Finally, Dave is asked to state his preference for car B compared to car C. Suppose in this case he indicates that car B is strongly to very strongly preferred to car C; the AHP would assign a numerical rating of 6.

The Pairwise Comparison Matrix

In order to develop the priorities for the three cars in terms of the comfort criterion, we need to develop a matrix of the pairwise comparison ratings. Since three cars are being considered, the pairwise comparison matrix will consist of three rows and three columns. Shown below is a portion of the *pairwise comparison matrix* based on the preferences Dave has specified.

Comfort	Car A	Car B	Car C
Car A		2	8
Car B			6
Car C			

Note: In the pairwise comparison matrix, the value in row i and column j is the measure of preference of the car in row i when compared to the car in column j.

We see that the value in the matrix that corresponds to comparing car A with car B is 2, the value that corresponds to comparing car A with car C is 8, and the value that corresponds to comparing car B with car C is 6.

In order to determine the remaining entries in the pairwise comparison matrix, first note that when we compare any car against itself, the judgment must be that they are equally preferred. Thus, using the scale shown in Table 15.2, the rating of car A compared to car A, car B compared to car B, and car C compared to car C must be 1. Hence, the AHP assigns a 1 to all elements on the diagonal of the pairwise comparison matrix.

Given these entries, all that remains is to determine the rating for car B compared to car A, car C compared to car A, and car C compared to car B. Obviously, we could follow the same procedure and ask Dave to provide his preferences for these pairwise comparisons. However, since we already know that Dave has rated his preference for car A compared to car B as 2, there is no need for him to make another pairwise comparison with these two cars. In fact, we will conclude that the preference rating for car *B* when compared to car *A* is simply the reciprocal of the preference rating for car *A* when compared to car *B*: ½. To see intuitively why the reciprocal can be used, note that the preference value of 2 is interpreted as indicating that car *A* is twice as preferable as car *B*. Thus, it follows that car *B* must be one-half as preferable as car *A*. Using this logic, the AHP obtains the preference rating of car *B* compared to car *A* by computing the reciprocal of the rating of car *A* compared to car *B*. Using this inverse, or reciprocal, relationship, we find that the rating of car *C* compared to car *A* is ⅛ and the rating of car *C* compared to car *B* is ⅙. Using these numerical values of preference, the complete pairwise comparison matrix for the comfort criterion is shown in Table 15.3.

Synthesis

Once the matrix of pairwise comparisons has been developed, we can calculate what is called the *priority* of each of the elements being compared. For example, we would now like to use the pairwise comparison information in Table 15.3 to estimate the relative priority for each of the cars in terms of the comfort criterion. This part of the AHP is referred to as *synthesization*.

The exact mathematical procedure required to perform this synthesization involves the computation of eigenvalues and eigenvectors and is beyond the scope of this text. However, the following three-step procedure provides a good approximation of the synthesized priorities.

Procedure for Synthesizing Judgments

Step 1 Sum the values in each column of the pairwise comparison matrix.

Step 2 Divide each element in the pairwise comparison matrix by its column total; the resulting matrix is referred to as the *normalized pairwise comparison matrix*.

Step 3 Compute the average of the elements in each row of the normalized matrix; these averages provide an estimate of the relative priorities of the elements being compared.

To see how the synthesization process works for our example problem, we carry out the procedure using the pairwise comparison matrix shown in Table 15.3. The three steps are as follows.

TABLE 15.3
Pairwise Comparison Matrix Showing Preferences for the Three Cars in Terms of Comfort

Comfort	Car *A*	Car *B*	Car *C*
Car *A*	1	2	8
Car *B*	1/2	1	6
Car *C*	1/8	1/6	1

Step 1 Sum the values in each column.

Comfort	Car *A*	Car *B*	Car *C*
Car *A*	1	2	8
Car *B*	1/2	1	6
Car *C*	1/8	1/6	1
Column totals	13/8	19/6	15

Step 2 Divide each element of the matrix by its column total.

Comfort	Car *A*	Car *B*	Car *C*
Car *A*	8/13	12/19	8/15
Car *B*	4/13	6/19	6/15
Car *C*	1/13	1/19	1/15

Note that all columns in the normalized pairwise comparison matrix now have a sum of 1.

Step 3 Average the elements in each row. (The values in the normalized pairwise comparison matrix have been converted to decimal form.)

Comfort	Car *A*	Car *B*	Car *C*	Row Avg.
Car *A*	0.615	0.632	0.533	0.593
Car *B*	0.308	0.316	0.400	0.341
Car *C*	0.077	0.053	0.067	0.066
			Total	1.000

This synthesis provides the relative priorities for the three cars with respect to the comfort criterion. Thus, we see that, considering comfort, the most preferred car is car *A* (with a priority of 0.593). Car *B* (with a priority of 0.341) is second, followed by car *C* (with a priority of 0.066). The priority vector showing the relative priorities of car *A*, car *B*, and car *C* with respect to the comfort criterion is written as follows:

$$\begin{bmatrix} 0.593 \\ 0.341 \\ 0.066 \end{bmatrix}$$

Consistency

A key step in the AHP is the establishment of priorities through the use of the pairwise comparison procedure just described. An important consideration in terms of the quality of the ultimate decision relates to the *consistency* of judgments that the decision maker demonstrated during the series of pairwise comparisons. For example, consider a situation involving the comparison of three job offers with respect to the salary criterion. Suppose that the following pairwise comparison matrix was developed:

Salary	Job 1	Job 2	Job 3
Job 1	1	2	8
Job 2	1/2	1	3
Job 3	1/8	1/3	1

The interpretation of the preference scores is that the preference for job 1 is twice the preference for job 2, and the preference for job 2 is three times the preference for job 3. Using these two pieces of information, we would logically conclude that the preference for job 1 should be $2 \times 3 = 6$ times the preference for job 3. The fact that the pairwise comparison matrix showed a preference of 8 instead of 6 indicates that some lack of consistency exists in the pairwise comparisons.

However, before we become too concerned about a lack of consistency in the pairwise comparisons, realize that perfect consistency is very difficult to achieve and that some lack of consistency is expected to exist in almost any set of pairwise comparisons. To handle the consistency question, the AHP provides a method for measuring the degree of consistency among the pairwise judgments provided by the decision maker. If the degree of consistency is acceptable, the decision process can continue. However, if the degree of consistency is unacceptable, the decision maker should reconsider and possibly revise the pairwise comparison judgments before proceeding with the analysis.

The AHP provides a measure of the consistency of pairwise comparison judgments by computing a *consistency ratio*. This ratio is designed in such a way that values of the ratio exceeding 0.10 are indicative of inconsistent judgments; in such cases the decision maker would probably want to reconsider and revise the original values in the pairwise comparison matrix. Values of the consistently ratio of 0.10 or less are considered to indicate a reasonable level of consistency in the pairwise comparisons.

Although the exact mathematical computation of the consistency ratio is beyond the scope of this text, an approximation of the ratio can be obtained. We will illustrate this computational procedure for the car-selection problem by considering Dave's pairwise comparisons for the comfort criterion. The steps of the computational procedure are described and demonstrated next.

Estimating the Consistency Ratio

Step 1 Multiply each value in the first column of the pairwise comparison matrix by the relative priority of the first item considered; multiply each value in the second column of the matrix by the relative priority of the second item considered; multiply each value in the third column of the matrix by the relative priority of the third item considered. Sum the values across the rows to obtain a vector of values labeled "weighted sum." This computation for the car-selection example is

$$
0.593 \begin{bmatrix} 1 \\ 1/2 \\ 1/8 \end{bmatrix} + 0.341 \begin{bmatrix} 2 \\ 1 \\ 1/6 \end{bmatrix} + 0.066 \begin{bmatrix} 8 \\ 6 \\ 1 \end{bmatrix} = \begin{bmatrix} 0.593 \\ 0.297 \\ 0.074 \end{bmatrix} + \begin{bmatrix} 0.682 \\ 0.341 \\ 0.057 \end{bmatrix} + \begin{bmatrix} 0.528 \\ 0.396 \\ 0.066 \end{bmatrix} = \overset{\substack{\text{Weighted} \\ \text{Sum Vector}}}{\begin{bmatrix} 1.803 \\ 1.034 \\ 0.197 \end{bmatrix}}
$$

Step 2 Divide the elements of the vector of weighted sums obtained in step 1 by the corresponding priority value. For the car-selection example, we obtain

$$
\frac{1.803}{0.593} = 3.040
$$

$$
\frac{1.034}{0.341} = 3.032
$$

$$
\frac{0.197}{0.066} = 2.985
$$

Step 3 Compute the average of the values computed in step 2; this average is denoted by λ_{max}. For the car-selection example, we obtain

$$\lambda_{max} = \frac{3.040 + 3.032 + 2.985}{3} = 3.019$$

Step 4 Compute the consistency index (CI), which is defined as follows:

$$CI = \frac{\lambda_{max} - n}{n - 1}$$

where

$$n = \text{the number of items being compared}$$

For the car-selection example with $n = 3$, we obtain

$$CI = \frac{3.019 - 3}{2} = 0.010$$

Step 5 Compute the consistency ratio (CR), which is defined as follows:

$$CR = \frac{CI}{RI}$$

where RI, the random index, is the consistency index of a randomly generated pairwise comparison matrix. It can be shown that RI depends on the number of elements being compared and takes on the following values:

n	RI
3	0.58
4	0.90
5	1.12
6	1.24
7	1.32
8	1.41

Thus, for our car-selection example with $n = 3$ and $RI = 0.58$, we obtain the following consistency ratio:

$$CR = \frac{0.01}{0.58} = 0.017$$

As mentioned previously, a consistency ratio of 0.10 or less is considered acceptable. Since our example shows a consistency ratio of 0.017, the degree of consistency exhibited in the pairwise comparison matrix for comfort is acceptable.

Other Pairwise Comparisons for the Car-Selection Example

In continuing with the AHP analysis of the car-selection problem, we need to use the pairwise comparison procedure to determine the priorities of the three cars in terms of the purchase price, MPG, and style criteria. This requires that Dave express pairwise comparison preferences for the cars, considering each of these criteria one at a time. Assume that this has been done and that Dave's preferences are summarized in the pairwise comparison matrices shown in Table 15.4.

The interpretation of the numerical values in the Table 15.4 is the same as the interpretation of the preference values we observed for the comfort criterion. For example, consider the comparison of car A and car B in terms of the purchase price criterion. Car B ($11,200) is considered more preferable than car A ($13,100). In fact, the pairwise comparison matrix shows Dave's preference for car B is three times greater than his preference for car A in terms of purchase price. Similarly, car A is only ⅓ as preferred as car B. Recall that the pairwise comparison matrix is set up to show the preference of the item in row i when compared to the item in column j.

Following the same synthesis procedure that we used for the comfort criterion, the priority vectors for these criteria can be computed. The result of this synthesis is shown in Table 15.5.

In interpreting these priorities we see that car C is the most preferable in terms of purchase price (0.557) and miles per gallon (0.639). Car B is the most preferable in terms of style (0.655). No car is the most preferred with respect to all criteria. Thus, before a final decision can be made, we must assess the relative importance of the criteria.

TABLE 15.4
Pairwise Comparison Matrices for Price, MPG, and Style for the Car-Selection Example

Price	Car A	Car B	Car C
Car A	1	1/3	1/4
Car B	3	1	1/2
Car C	4	2	1

MPG	Car A	Car B	Car C
Car A	1	1/4	1/6
Car B	4	1	1/3
Car C	6	3	1

Style	Car A	Car B	Car C
Car A	1	1/3	4
Car B	3	1	7
Car C	1/4	1/7	1

TABLE 15.5
Priority Vectors for Price, MPG, and Style

Price	MPG	Style
$\begin{bmatrix} 0.123 \\ 0.320 \\ 0.557 \end{bmatrix}$	$\begin{bmatrix} 0.087 \\ 0.274 \\ 0.639 \end{bmatrix}$	$\begin{bmatrix} 0.265 \\ 0.655 \\ 0.080 \end{bmatrix}$

TABLE 15.6
Pairwise Comparison Matrix for the Four Criteria in the Car-Selection Problem

Criterion	Price	MPG	Comfort	Style
Price	1	3	2	2
MPG	1/3	1	1/4	1/4
Comfort	1/2	4	1	1/2
Style	1/2	4	2	1

In addition to the pairwise comparisons for the decision alternatives, we must use the same pairwise comparison procedure to set priorities for all four criteria in terms of the importance of each in contributing toward the overall goal of selecting the best car. To develop this final pairwise comparison matrix, Dave would have to specify how important he thought each criterion was compared to each of the other criteria. In order to do this, six pairwise judgments have to be made: purchase price compared to MPG; purchase price compared to comfort; purchase price compared to style; MPG compared to comfort; MPG compared to style; and comfort compared to style. For example, in the pairwise comparison of the purchase price and MPG criteria, Dave indicated that purchase price was *moderately* more important than MPG. Using the AHP 9-point numerical rating scale (see Table 15.2), a value of 3 was recorded to show the higher importance of the purchase-price criterion. The summary of the pairwise comparison matrix preferences for the four criteria is shown in Table 15.6.

The synthesization process described earlier in this section can now be used to convert the pairwise comparison information into the priorities for the four criteria. The results obtained are as follows:

Priorities for the Four Criteria	
Price	0.398
MPG	0.085
Comfort	0.218
Style	0.299

We see that the purchase price (0.398) has been identified as the highest-priority or most important criterion in the car-selection decision. Style (0.299) and comfort (0.218) rank next in importance. Miles per gallon (0.085) is a relatively unimportant criterion in terms of the overall goal of selecting the best car. In the next section we show how the AHP uses the priority information generated in this section to develop an overall priority ranking for the three cars.

15.5 ▼ USING THE AHP TO DEVELOP AN OVERALL PRIORITY RANKING

In the previous section we showed how a pairwise comparison matrix can be used to develop a prioritized ranking of the items being compared. In this section we show how the criterion priorities and the priorities of each decision alternative relative to each criterion can be combined to develop an overall priority ranking of the decision alternatives. Table 15.7 contains a matrix that summarizes the priorities for each car in terms of each criterion as computed in Section 15.4. We will refer to this matrix as the *priority matrix*.

The procedure used to compute the overall priorities for each decision alternative can be best understood if we think of the priority for each criterion as a weight that reflects its importance. The overall priority for each decision alternative is obtained by summing the product of the criterion priority times the priority of the decision alternative with respect to that criterion. Recall that the criterion priorities were found to be 0.398 for purchase price, 0.085 for MPG, 0.218 for comfort, and 0.299 for style. Thus, the computation of the overall priority for car A is as follows:

$$\text{Overall car } A \text{ priority} = 0.398(0.123) + 0.085(0.087) + 0.218(0.593) + 0.299(0.265)$$
$$= 0.265$$

Repeating this calculation for cars B and C provides their overall priorities as follows:

$$\text{Overall car } B \text{ priority} = 0.398(0.320) + 0.085(0.274) + 0.218(0.341) + 0.299(0.655)$$
$$= 0.421$$

$$\text{Overall car } C \text{ priority} = 0.398(0.557) + 0.085(0.639) + 0.218(0.066) + 0.299(0.080)$$
$$= 0.314$$

Ranking these priority values, we have the following AHP ranking of the decision alternatives:

Alternative	Priority
Car B	0.421
Car C	0.314
Car A	0.265
Total	1.000

These results provide a basis for Dave to make a decision regarding the purchase of a car. Based on the AHP priorities, Dave should select car B. Whether or not Dave actually decides to purchase car B based on the AHP analysis is still his decision to make. If Dave believes that the judgments that he has made regarding the importance of the criteria and his preferences for the cars in terms of the criteria are valid, then the AHP priorities show

TABLE 15.7
The Priority Matrix for the Car-Selection Problem

	Price	MPG	Comfort	Style
Car A	0.123	0.087	0.593	0.265
Car B	0.320	0.274	0.341	0.655
Car C	0.557	0.639	0.066	0.080

that car *B* is the preferred car. Whether or not Dave actually decides to purchase car *B* may not be as important as the additional understanding of the problem that he has obtained as a result of performing the analysis required by the AHP. This in itself may be as helpful to Dave as the actual decision recommendation that has been obtained.

15.6 ▼ USING EXPERT CHOICE TO IMPLEMENT THE AHP

Expert Choice (EC), a software package marketed by Decision Support Software, provides a user-friendly procedure for implementing the AHP on a microcomputer. In this section we provide an introduction to this software package by showing how it can be used to compute the priorities for the car-selection problem.

Expert Choice enables the user to simply construct a graphical representation of the hierarchy. For example, to create the hierarchy for the car-selection example, the user selects the option to develop a new application; what appears on the computer's monitor is a request to define the overall goal. After the user defines the overall goal, a rectangular box, or node, appears on the screen, with the goal description written directly above it. The user selects the EDIT command and then the INSERT option; another rectangular box or node appears below the goal node, and the user now types the name of a criterion, which will be entered inside the box. This process continues until all four criterion nodes have been specified. Figure 15.6 shows the partial hierarchy appearing on the computer screen after the four criteria have been specified.

In Figure 15.6 we see that in addition to the names of each criterion, the criterion nodes also contain the decimal value of 0.250. This value represents the initial weight, or priority, given to each criterion at the start of the EC session. The user can now continue the process of using the EDIT command with the INSERT option to define the decision alternative nodes associated with each of the criterion nodes. In Figure 15.7 we show the result of defining the decision alternative nodes for the price criterion; note that since there are three alternatives, the initial priorities are set at 0.333. A similar set of decision alternatives is then identified for each of the other three criteria.

Once the user has developed the complete hierarchy for the problem, he or she can focus on any particular part of the hierarchy through the use of the REDRAW command.

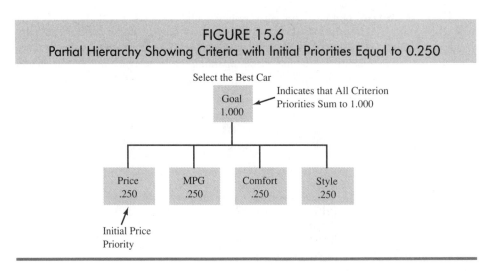

FIGURE 15.6
Partial Hierarchy Showing Criteria with Initial Priorities Equal to 0.250

FIGURE 15.7
Partial Hierarchy Showing the Price Criterion with Initial Priorities for Cars A, B, and C Equal to 0.333

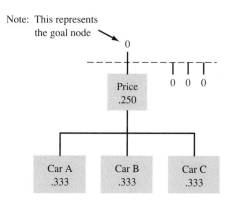

In fact, to show the detail displayed in Figure 15.7, all we did was to point to the price node (using the arrows on the keyboard's numeric key pad) and then type R for redraw. Our intent here is not to attempt to show you how to use EC, but merely to let you develop some appreciation for the ease with which the analysis can be performed using this software package.

Now that the hierarchy has been input to EC, we are ready to begin developing the pairwise comparisons needed to establish priorities for the decision alternatives. In order to illustrate the type of approach used, we moved back to the goal node with EC and then selected the COMPARE command by typing C. After selecting the option to make comparisons based on the importance of the decision criteria, the EC system begins to go through the pairwise comparison analysis.

One portion of this analysis, which shows the approach used by EC to establish the comparative importance between the purchase price and MPG criteria, is shown in Figure 15.8. Note that this figure indicates to the EC system that price is moderately more important than MPG. This process continues until all the entries in the pairwise comparison matrix for criteria have been developed. The synthesization process is then performed to compute the priorities for the criteria; Figure 15.9 shows the priorities that were obtained after synthesization.

The process of entering pairwise preferences for the cars relative to each of the criteria was then performed in a similar manner. The overall decision was then arrived at by entering the command S, which is an abbreviation for synthesizing; this command is used only when we have entered all the data for the pairwise comparison matrices and want to obtain an overall prioritization of the decision alternatives. Figure 15.10 shows the results obtained. Note that the results indicate that the final priority for car B, the most preferable, is 0.422.

The EC system is much more powerful and comprehensive than our brief introduction can begin to show. It is a very helpful software package in performing the multiple-criteria decision analysis of the AHP. In addition to providing the overall priorities for the decision alternatives, EC has the capability of doing "what if" types of analyses, where the decision maker can begin to learn how the overall priorities for the decision alternative are affected by changes in the preference input data.

FIGURE 15.8
Determining the Rating for the Price and MPG Pairwise Comparison

```
              GOAL: SELECT THE BEST CAR

With respect to

                      GOAL

    Are PRICE and MILEAGE Equally IMPORTANT? (Y/N) N ◄─── [User Response]

    Is PRICE more IMPORTANT than MILEAGE? (Y/N) Y ◄─── [User Response]

              With respect to
                    GOAL

        PRICE
            is EQUAL to MODERATELY MORE IMPORTANT THAN
        MILEAGE

        EXTREME------------

        VERY STRONG--------

        STRONG-------------

        MODERATE-----------                    ┌─────────────────────────┐
                                               │ System initially positions
                            <-- ◄──────────────│ pointer here because we
        EQUAL-------------                      │ said price and mileage are
                                               │ not equally important.
              With respect to                  └─────────────────────────┘
                    GOAL

        PRICE
            is MODERATELY MORE IMPORTANT THAN
        MILEAGE

        EXTREME------------

        VERY STRONG--------

        STRONG-------------                     ┌─────────────────────────┐
                                                │ User moves the arrow to
        MODERATE----------- <-- ◄───────────────│ the position that best
                                                │ describes the relationship.
        EQUAL-------------                      └─────────────────────────┘
```

FIGURE 15.9
The Hierarchy Showing Priorities After Synthesization for the Criteria

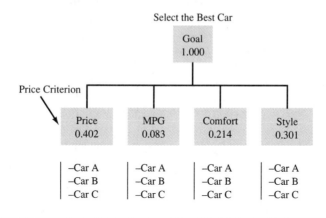

FIGURE 15.10
Final Results of Using the AHP for the Car-Selection Example

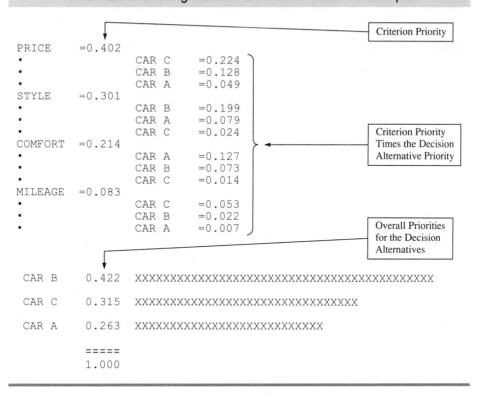

▼ SUMMARY

In this chapter we have shown how goal programming can be used to solve problems with multiple objectives or goals within the linear programming framework. We have shown that the goal programming model contains one or more goal equations and an objective function that is designed to minimize the deviations from the goals. In situations where resource capacities or other restrictions affect the achievement of the goals, the model will contain constraints that are formulated and treated in the same manner as constraints in an ordinary linear programming model.

In goal programming problems with preemptive priorities, first-priority goals are treated first in an objective function in order to identify a solution that will best satisfy the first-priority goals. This solution is then revised by considering an objective function involving only the second-priority goals; solution modifications are considered only if they do not degrade the solution obtained for the first-priority goals. This process continues until all priority levels have been considered.

We have also shown a variation of the linear programming graphical solution procedure can be used to solve goal programming problems with two decision variables. Specialized goal programming computer packages are available for solving the general goal programming problem, but such computer codes are not as readily available as are general purpose linear programming computer packages. As a result, we have shown how a general linear programming package such as LINDO/PC can be used in an iterative manner to provide a solution for a goal programming problem.

We have also presented an approach to multiple-criteria decision making known as the analytic hierarchy process (AHP). We showed that a key part of the AHP is the development of judgments concerning the relative importance of, or preference for, the elements being compared. A consistency ratio is computed to determine the degree of consistency exhibited by the decision maker in making the pairwise comparisons. Values of the consistency ratio less than or equal to 0.10 are considered acceptable.

Once the set of all pairwise comparisons has been developed, a process referred to as synthesization is used to determine the priorities for the elements being compared. The final step of the AHP process is a further synthesization, in which the priority levels established for the decision alternatives relative to each criterion are multiplied by the priority levels reflecting the importance of the criteria themselves; the sum of these products over all the criteria is the overall priority level for the decision alternative. The chapter concluded with a brief introduction to Expert Choice, a software package designed to perform the computational steps of the AHP.

▼ GLOSSARY

Goal programming   A linear programming–based approach developed for problems involving multiple criteria. The objective function for goal programming models is designed to minimize deviations from goals.

Target value   A value referred to in the statement of the goal. Based on the context of the problem, management will want the solution to the goal programming problem to result in a value for the goal that is less than, equal to, or greater than the target value.

Deviation variables   Variables that are added to the goal equation in order to allow the solution to deviate from the target value for the goal.

Goal equation An equation whose right-hand side is the target value for the goal; the left-hand side of the goal equation consists of a function representing the level of achievement and deviation variables representing the difference between the target value for the goal and the level achieved.

Analytic hierarchy process (AHP) An approach to multiple-criteria decision making based in part on pairwise comparisons of preference for elements in a hierarchy.

Hierarchy A figure that shows the levels of a problem in terms of the overall goal, the criteria, and the decision alternatives.

Pairwise comparison matrix A matrix that consists of the preference, or relative importance, ratings provided during a series of pairwise comparisons.

Synthesization A mathematical process that uses the preference values in the pairwise comparison matrix to develop priorities.

Normalized pairwise comparison matrix The matrix obtained by dividing each element of the pairwise comparison matrix by its column total. This matrix is computed as an intermediate step in the synthesization of priorities.

Consistency A concept developed to assess the quality of preference judgments made during a series of pairwise comparisons. It is a measure of the internal consistency of these comparisons.

Consistency ratio A numerical measure of the degree of consistency in a series of pairwise comparisons. Values less than or equal to 0.10 are considered acceptable.

Expert Choice (EC) A computer software package used to perform the computations required by the analytic hierarchy process.

▼ PROBLEMS

1. The RMC Corporation blends three raw materials in order to produce two products: a fuel additive and a solvent base. Each ton of fuel additive is a mixture of $2/5$ ton of material 1 and $3/5$ ton of material 3. A ton of solvent base is a mixture of $1/2$ ton of material 1, $1/5$ ton of material 2, and $3/10$ ton of material 3. RMC's production is constrained by a limited availability of the three raw materials. For the current production period RMC has the following quantities of each raw material: material 1, 20 tons; material 2, 5 tons; material 3, 21 tons. Management would like to achieve the following P_1 priority level goals:

   Goal 1: Produce at least 30 tons of fuel additive.

   Goal 2: Produce at least 15 tons of solvent base.

   Assume there are no other goals in the problem.
   a. Is it possible for management to achieve both P_1 level goals, given the constraints on the amounts of each material available? Explain.
   b. Treating the amounts of each material available as constraints, formulate a goal programming model to determine the optimal product mix. Assume both of the P_1 priority level goals are equally important to management.
   c. Use the graphical goal programming procedure to solve the model formulated in part (b).
   d. If goal 1 is twice as important as goal 2, what is the optimal product mix?

2. DJS Investment Services must develop an investment portfolio for a new client. As an initial investment strategy the new client would like to restrict the portfolio to a mix of the following two stocks:

Stock	Price/Share	Estimated Annual Return
AGA Products	$ 50	6%
Key Oil	$100	10%

The client has $50,000 available to invest and has established the following two investment goals:

Priority Level 1 Goal

Goal 1: Obtain an annual return of at least 9%.

Priority Level 2 Goal

Goal 2: Limit the investment in Key Oil, the riskier investment, to at most 60% of the total investment.

a. Formulate a goal programming model for the DJS Investment problem.
b. Use the graphical goal programming procedure to obtain a solution.

3. The L. Young & Sons Manufacturing Company produces two products, which have the following profit and resource requirement characteristics:

	Product 1	Product 2
Profit/unit	$4	$2
Dept. *A* hours/unit	1	1
Dept *B* hours/unit	2	5

Last month's production schedule used 350 hours of labor in department *A* and 1000 hours of labor in department *B*.

Young's management has been experiencing work force morale and labor union problems during the past 6 months because of monthly departmental workload fluctuations. New hiring, layoffs, and interdepartmental transfers have been common because the firm has not attempted to stabilize workload requirements.

Management would like to develop a production schedule for the coming month that will achieve the following goals:

Goal 1: Use 350 hours of labor in department *A*.

Goal 2: Use 1000 hours of labor in department *B*.

Goal 3: Earn a profit of at least $1300.

a. Formulate a goal programming model for this problem assuming goals 1 and 2 are P_1 priority level goals and goal 3 is a P_2 priority level goal; assume goals 1 and 2 are equally important.
b. Solve the model formulated in part (a) using the graphical goal programming procedure.

c. Suppose the firm ignores the workload fluctuations and considers the 350 hours in department A and the 1000 hours in department B as the maximum available. Formulate and solve a linear programming problem to maximize profit subject to these constraints.

d. Compare the solutions obtained in parts (b) and (c). Discuss which approach you favor, and tell why.

e. Reconsider part (a), assuming the priority level 1 goal is goal 3 and the priority level 2 goals are goals 1 and 2; as before, assume goals 1 and 2 are equally important. Solve this revised problem using the graphical goal programming procedure, and compare your solution to the one obtained for the original problem.

4. Industrial Chemicals produces two adhesives that are used in the manufacturing process for airplanes. The two adhesives, which have different bonding strengths, require different amounts of production time: the IC–100 adhesive requires 20 minutes of production time per gallon of finished product, and the IC–200 adhesive uses 30 minutes of production time per gallon. Both products use 1 pound of a highly perishable resin for each gallon of finished product. There are 300 pounds of the resin in inventory, and more can be obtained if necessary. However, because of the shelf life of the material, any amount not used in the next 2 weeks will be discarded.

The firm has existing orders for 100 gallons of IC–100 and 120 gallons of IC–200. Under normal conditions, the production process operates 8 hours per day, 5 days per week. Management would like to schedule production for the next 2 weeks in order to achieve the following goals:

Priority Level 1 Goals

Goal 1: Avoid underutilization of the production process.

Goal 2: Avoid overtime in excess of 20 hours for the 2 weeks.

Priority Level 2 Goals

Goal 3: Satisfy existing orders for the IC–100 adhesive; that is, produce at least 100 gallons of IC–100.

Goal 4: Satisfy existing orders for the IC–200 adhesive; that is, produce at least 120 gallons of IC–200.

Priority Level 3 Goal

Goal 5: Use up all the available resin.

a. Formulate a goal programming model for the Industrial Chemicals problem. Assume both of the priority level 1 goals and both of the priority level 2 goals are equally important.

b. Use the graphical goal programming procedure to develop a solution for the model formulated in part (a).

5. Reconsider the RMC data presented in problem 1. Assume the two P_1 priority level goals remain the same and both goals are equally important to management. Suppose management has learned that additional amounts of material 3 can be obtained from another RMC plant. Although management would like to obtain a solution that satisfies their production goals using the 21 tons of material 3 currently available, they are willing to consider using additional amounts of material 3 from the other

plant. Introducing this new objective or goal as a P_2 priority level goal, the problem goals can now be restated as follows:

Priority Level 1 Goals

Goal 1: Produce at least 30 tons of fuel additive.

Goal 2: Produce at least 15 tons of solvent base.

Priority Level 2 Goals

Goal 3: Use at most 21 tons of material 3.

a. Treating the amounts of materials 1 and 2 available as problem constraints, formulate a goal programming model for this problem.

b. Use the goal programming computer procedure illustrated in Section 15.2 to solve the model formulated in part (a).

c. How many tons of material 3 need to be obtained from RMC's other plant?

6. Michigan Motors Corporation (MMC) has just introduced a new luxury touring sedan. As part of its promotional campaign the marketing department has decided to send personalized invitations to test drive the new sedan to two target groups: (1) current owners of an MMC luxury automobile and (2) owners of luxury cars manufactured by one of MMC's competitors. The cost to send a personalized invitation to each customer is estimated to be $1 per letter. Based on previous experience with this type of advertising, MMC estimates that 25% of the customers contacted from group 1 and 10% of the customers contacted from group 2 will test drive the new sedan. As part of this campaign, MMC has set the following goals:

Goal 1: Get at least 10,000 customers from group 1 to test drive the new sedan.

Goal 2: Get at least 5,000 customers from group 2 to test drive the new sedan.

Goal 3: Limit the expenses for sending out the invitations to at most $70,000.

Assume goals 1 and 2 are P_1 priority level goals and goal 3 is a P_2 priority level goal.

a. Suppose goals 1 and 2 are equally important; formulate a goal programming model of the MMC problem.

b. Use the goal programming computer procedure illustrated in Section 15.2 to solve the model formulated in part (a).

c. If management believes that contacting customers from group 2 is twice as important as contacting customers from group 1, what should MMC do?

7. A committee in charge of promoting a Ladies Professional Golf Association tournament is trying to determine how to best advertise the event over the 2 weeks prior to the tournament. The following table shows the information the committee obtained for the three advertising media they are considering using:

	Audience Reached per Advertisement	Cost per Advertisement	Maximum Number of Advertisements
TV	200,000	$2500	10
Radio	50,000	$ 400	15
Newspaper	100,000	$ 500	20

The last column in this table shows the maximum number of advertisements that can be run over the next 2 weeks and should be treated as a constraint in the problem. The committee has established the following goals for the campaign:

Priority Level 1 Goal

Goal 1: Reach at least 4,000,000 people.

Priority Level 2 Goal

Goal 2: The number of television advertisements should be at least 30% of the total number of advertisements.

Priority Level 3 Goal

Goal 3: The number of radio advertisements should not exceed 20% of the total number of advertisements.

Priority Level 4 Goal

Goal 4: Limit the total amount spent for advertising to at most $20,000.

a. Formulate a goal programming model for this problem.
b. Use the goal programming computer procedure illustrated in Section 15.2 to solve the model formulated in part (a).

8. Morley Company is attempting to determine the best location for a new machine in an existing layout of three machines. The existing machines are located at the following x_1, x_2 coordinates on the shop floor:

$$\text{Machine 1:} \quad x_1 = 1, x_2 = 7$$
$$\text{Machine 2:} \quad x_1 = 5, x_2 = 9$$
$$\text{Machine 3:} \quad x_1 = 6, x_2 = 2$$

a. Develop a goal programming model that can be solved to minimize the total distance of the new machine from the three existing machines. The distance is to be measured rectangularly. For example (see below), if the location of the new machine is ($x_1 = 3$, $x_2 = 5$), it is considered to be a distance of 4 units from machine 1. *Hint:* In the goal programming formulation, let

x_1 = first coordinate of the new machine location

x_2 = second coordinate of the new machine location

d_i^+ = amount by which the x_1 coordinate of the new machine exceeds the x_1 coordinate of machine i ($i = 1, 2, 3$)

d_i^- = amount by which the x_1 coordinate of machine i exceeds the x_1 coordinate of the new machine ($i = 1, 2, 3$)

e_i^+ = amount by which the x_2 coordinate of the new machine exceeds the x_2 coordinate of machine i ($i = 1, 2, 3$)

e_1^- = amount by which the x_2 coordinate of machine i exceeds the x_2 coordinate of the new machine ($i = 1, 2, 3$)

b. What is the optimal location for the new machine?

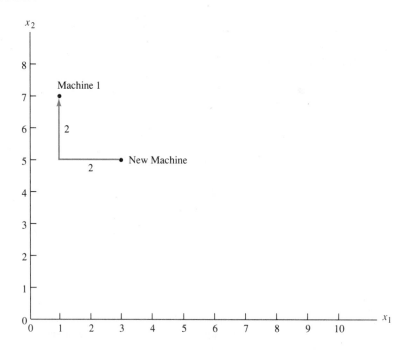

9. A fast-food chain is attempting to determine the best location of a new outlet. Management would like to determine the best location for drawing customers from three population centers. Letting (x_1, x_2) represent the map coordinates of the three population centers, we can show their locations as follows:

Population center 1: $x_1 = 2, x_2 = 8$

Population center 2: $x_1 = 6, x_2 = 6$

Population center 3: $x_1 = 1, x_2 = 1$

If the new outlet is located at coordinates $(x_1 = 3, x_2 = 2)$, then it is a distance of $(3 - 1) + (2 - 1) = 3$ miles from population center 3 (distance is measured as the sum of the east–west and north–south differences in coordinates).

a. Formulate and solve a goal programming model to determine what location for the new outlet will minimize the total distance from the three population centers. (*Hint:* Let x_1, x_2 represent the coordinates of the new location.)

b. Population center 1 is four times as large as center 3, and center 2 is twice as large as center 3. The firm feels that the importance of locating near a population center is proportional to its population. Develop and solve a new goal programming model where the weights on the deviations reflect this importance.

10. Using the pairwise comparison matrix for the price criterion as shown in Table 15.4, verify that the priorities after synthesization are 0.123, 0.320, and 0.557. Compute the consistency ratio, and comment on its acceptability.

11. Using the pairwise comparison matrix for the MPG criterion as shown in Table 15.4, verify that the priorities after synthesization are 0.087, 0.274, and 0.639. Compute the consistency ratio and comment on its acceptability.

12. Using the pairwise comparison matrix for the style criterion as shown in Table 15.4, verify that the priorities after synthesization are 0.265, 0.655 and 0.080. Compute the consistency ratio and comment on its acceptability.

13. Dan Joseph was considering entering one of two graduate schools of business to pursue studies for an MBA degree. When asked how he compared the two schools with respect to reputation, he responded that school A was strongly to very strongly preferred over school B.

   a. Set up the pairwise comparison matrix for this problem.
   b. Determine the priorities for the two schools relative to this criterion.

14. An organization was considering relocating its corporate headquarters to one of three possible cities. The following pairwise comparison matrix shows the president's judgments regarding the desirability for the three cities:

	City 1	City 2	City 3
City 1	1	5	7
City 2	1/5	1	3
City 3	1/7	1/3	1

   a. Determine the priorities for the three cities.
   b. Is the president consistent in terms of the judgments provided? Explain.

15. The following pairwise comparison matrix contains the judgments of an individual regarding the fairness of two proposed tax programs, A and B:

	A	B
A	1	3
B	1/3	1

   a. Determine the priorities for the two programs.
   b. Are the individual's judgments consistent? Explain.

16. An individual was asked to compare three soft drinks with respect to flavor. The following judgments were obtained:

   A is moderately more preferable than B.

   A is equally to moderately more preferable than C.

   B is strongly more preferable than C.

   a. Set up the pairwise comparison matrix for this problem.
   b. Determine the priorities for soft drinks with respect to the flavor criterion.
   c. Compute the consistency ratio. Are the individual's judgments consistent? Explain.

17. Refer to problem 16. Suppose that the individual had provided the following judgments instead of those given in problem 16:

   A is strongly more preferable than C.

   B is equally to moderately more preferable than A.

   B is strongly more preferable than C.

   Answer parts (a), (b), and (c) as stated in problem 16.

18. The national sales director for Jones Office Supplies needs to determine the best location for the next national sales meeting. Three locations have been proposed: Dallas, San Francisco, and New York. One criterion considered important in the decision is the desirability of the location in terms of restaurants, entertainment, and

so on. The national sales manager provided the following judgments with regard to this criterion:

New York is very strongly more preferred than Dallas.

New York is moderately more preferred than San Francisco.

San Francisco is moderately to strongly more preferred than Dallas.

a. Set up the pairwise comparison matrix for this problem.

b. Determine the priorities for the desirability criterion.

c. Compute the consistency ratio. Are the sales manager's judgments consistent? Explain.

19. A study comparing four personal computers resulted in the following pairwise comparison matrix for the performance criterion:

		Computer			
		1	2	3	4
Computer	1	1	3	7	1/3
	2	1/3	1	4	1/4
	3	1/7	1/4	1	1/6
	4	3	4	6	1

a. Determine the priorities for the four computers relative to the performance criterion.

b. Compute the consistency ratio. Are the judgments regarding performance consistent? Explain.

20. An individual was interested in determining in which of two stocks, Central Computing Company (CCC) or Software Research, Inc. (SRI), to invest. The criteria thought to be most relevant in making the decision are the potential yield of the stock and the risk associated with the investment. The pairwise comparison matrices for this problem are as follows:

Criterion	Yield	Risk
Yield	1	2
Risk	1/2	1

Yield	CCI	SRI
CCI	1	3
SRI	1/3	1

Risk	CCI	SRI
CCI	1	1/2
SRI	2	1

a. Draw the hierarchy for this problem.

b. Compute the priorities for each of the pairwise comparison matrices.

c. Determine the overall priority for the two investments.

21. The vice-president of Harling Equipment needs to select a new director of marketing. The two possible candidates are Bill Jacobs and Sue Martin, and the criteria thought to be most relevant in the selection are leadership ability (L), personal skills (P), and administrative skills (A). The following pairwise comparison matrices were obtained:

Criterion	L	P	A
L	1	1/3	1/4
P	3	1	2
A	4	1/2	1

Leadership	Jacobs	Martin
Jacobs	1	4
Martin	1/4	1

Personal	Jacobs	Martin
Jacobs	1	1/3
Martin	3	1

Administrative	Jacobs	Martin
Jacobs	1	2
Martin	1/2	1

a. Draw the hierarchy for this decision problem.
b. Compute the priorities for each of the pairwise comparison matrices.
c. Determine an overall priority for each of the candidates.

22. A woman considering the purchase of a custom sound stereo system for her car looked at three different systems that varied in terms of price (P), sound quality (Q), and FM reception (FM). The following pairwise consistency matrices were developed:

Criterion	P	Q	FM
P	1	3	4
Q	1/3	1	3
FM	1/4	1/3	1

Price	A	B	C
A	1	4	2
B	1/4	1	1/3
C	1/2	3	1

Quality	A	B	C
A	1	1/2	1/4
B	2	1	1/3
C	4	3	1

FM Reception	A	B	C
A	1	4	2
B	1/4	1	1
C	1/2	1	1

a. Draw the hierarchy for this decision problem.
b. Compute the priorities for each of the pairwise comparison matrices.
c. Determine an overall priority for each of the systems.

▼ CASE PROBLEM

Production Scheduling

EZ Trailers, Inc., manufactures a variety of general purpose trailers, including a complete line of boat trailers. Two of their best-selling boat trailers are the EZ–190 and the EZ–250; the EZ–190 is designed for boats up to 19 feet in length, and the EZ–250 can be used for boats up to 25 feet in length.

EZ Trailers would like to schedule production for the next 2 months for these two models. Each unit of the EZ–190 requires 4 hours of production time, and each unit of the EZ–250 uses 6 hours of production time. The following orders have been received for March and April:

Model	March	April
EZ–190	800	600
EZ–250	1100	1200

The ending inventory from February was 200 units of the EZ–190 and 300 units of the EZ–250. The total number of hours of production time used in February was 6300 hours.

The management of EZ Trailers is very much concerned about being able to satisfy existing orders for the EZ–250 for both March and April. In fact, they feel that this is the most important goal they would like to achieve in developing a production schedule. Next in importance is satisfying existing orders for the EZ–190. In addition, management does not want to implement any production schedule that would involve significant labor fluctuations from month to month. In this regard, their goal is to find a production schedule that would limit fluctuations in labor hours used to a maximum of 1000 hours from one month to the next.

▼ MANAGERIAL REPORT

Perform an analysis of EZ Trailers' production scheduling problem, and prepare a report for EZ's president that summarizes your findings. Include a discussion and analysis of the following in your report:

1. The production schedule that best achieves the goals as specified by management.
2. Suppose EZ Trailers' storage facilities would only accommodate up to 300 trailers in any one month. What effect would this have on the production schedule?
3. Suppose EZ Trailers can only store up to 300 trailers in any one month. In addition, suppose management would like to have an ending inventory in April of at least 100 units of each model. What effect would both of these changes have on the production schedule?
4. What changes would occur in the production schedule if the labor fluctuation goal was the highest-priority goal?

Forecasting

A critical aspect of managing any organization is planning for the future. Indeed, the long-run success of an organization is closely related to how well management is able to foresee the future and develop appropriate strategies. Good judgment, intuition, and an awareness of the state of the economy may give a manager a rough idea or "feeling" of what is likely to happen in the future. However, it is often difficult to convert this feeling into a number that can be used as next quarter's sales volume or next year's raw material cost per unit. The purpose of this chapter is to introduce several methods that can help predict many future aspects of a business operation.

Suppose we have been asked to provide quarterly estimates of the sales volume for a particular product during the coming 1-year period. Production schedules, raw material purchasing plans, inventory policies, and sales quotas will all be affected by the quarterly estimates we provide. Consequently, poor estimates may result in poor planning and hence result in increased costs for the firm. How should we go about providing the quarterly sales volume estimates?

We will certainly want to review the actual sales data for the product in past periods. Suppose we have actual sales data for each quarter over the past 3 years. Using these historical data we can identify the general level of sales and determine whether or not there is any trend, such as an increase or decrease in sales volume over time. A further review of the data might reveal a seasonal pattern, such as peak sales occurring in the third quarter of each year and sales volume bottoming out during the first quarter. By reviewing historical data over time we can often develop a better understanding of the pattern of past sales; often this can lead to better predictions of future sales for the product.

The historical sales data form what is called a *time series*. Specifically, a time series is a set of observations measured at successive points in time or over successive periods of time. In this chapter we will introduce several procedures that can be used to analyze time series data. The objective of this analysis will be to provide good *forecasts* or predictions of future values of the time series.

Forecasting methods can be classified as quantitative or qualitative. Quantitative forecasting methods are based on an analysis of historical data concerning a time series and possibly other related time series. If the historical data used are restricted to past values of the series that we are trying to forecast, the forecasting procedure is called a time series method. In this chapter we discuss three time series methods: smoothing (moving averages and exponential smoothing), trend projection, and trend projection adjusted for seasonal influence. If the historical data used in a quantitative forecasting method involve other time series that are believed to be related to the time series that we are trying to forecast, we say that we are using a causal method. We discuss the use of multiple regression analysis as a causal forecasting method.

Qualitative forecasting methods generally utilize the judgment of experts to make forecasts. An advantage of these procedures is that they can be applied in situations where no historical data are available. We discuss some of these approaches in Section 16.6. Figure 16.1 provides an overview of the different types of forecasting methods.

16.1 ▼ THE COMPONENTS OF A TIME SERIES

In order to explain the pattern or behavior of the data in a time series, it is often helpful to think of the time series as consisting of several components. The usual assumption is that four separate components—trend, cyclical, seasonal, and irregular—combine to make the time series take on specific values. Let us look more closely at each of these components of a time series.

Trend Component

In time series analysis the measurements may be taken every hour, day, week, month, or year, or at any other regular interval.[1] Although time series data generally exhibit random fluctuations, the time series may still show gradual shifts or movements to relatively higher or lower values over a longer period of time. The gradual shifting of the time

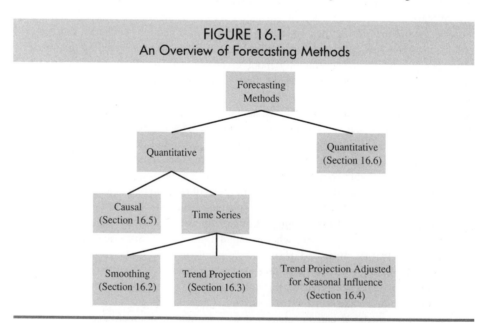

FIGURE 16.1
An Overview of Forecasting Methods

---

[1]We restrict our attention here to time series where the values of the series are recorded at equal intervals. Treatment of cases where the observations are not made at equal intervals is beyond the scope of this text.

series, which is usually due to long-term factors such as changes in the population, changes in demographic characteristics of the population, changes in technology, and changes in consumer preferences, is referred to as the *trend* in the time series.

For example, a manufacturer of photographic equipment may see substantial month-to-month variability in the number of cameras sold. However, in reviewing the sales over the past 10 to 15 years this manufacturer may find a gradual increase in the annual sales volume. Suppose the sales volume was approximately 1800 cameras per month in 1980, 2200 cameras per month in 1985, and 2600 cameras per month in 1990. While actual month-to-month sales volumes may vary substantially, this gradual growth in sales over time shows an upward trend for the time series. Figure 16.2 shows a straight line that may be a good approximation of the trend in the sales data. While the trend for camera sales appears to be linear and increasing over time, sometimes the trend in a time series is better described by other patterns.

Figure 16.3 shows some other possible time series trend patterns. In part A of this figure we see a nonlinear trend. The curve shown describes a time series showing very little growth initially, followed by a period of rapid growth, and then a leveling off. This might be a good approximation of sales for a product from introduction through a growth period and into a period of market saturation. The linear decreasing trend in part B of Figure 16.3 is useful for time series displaying a steady decrease over time. The horizontal line in part C of Figure 16.3 is used for a time series that does not show any consistent increase or decrease over time. It is actually the case of no trend.

Cyclical Component

Although a time series may exhibit a gradual shifting or trend pattern over long periods of time, we cannot expect all future values of the time series to be exactly on the trend line. In fact, time series often show alternating sequences of points below and above the

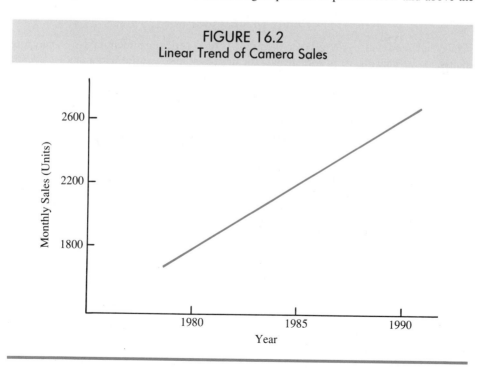

FIGURE 16.2
Linear Trend of Camera Sales

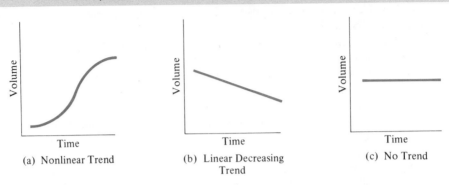

FIGURE 16.3
Examples of Some Possible Time Series Trend Patterns

(a) Nonlinear Trend

(b) Linear Decreasing Trend

(c) No Trend

trend line. Any regular pattern of sequences of points above and below the trend line lasting more than 1 year is attributable to the *cyclical component* of the time series. Figure 16.4 shows the graph of a time series with an obvious cyclical component. The observations are taken at intervals 1 year apart.

Many time series exhibit cyclical behavior with regular runs of observations below and above the trend line. The general belief is that this component of the time series represents multiyear cyclical movements in the economy. For example, periods of moderate inflation followed by periods of rapid inflation can lead to many time series that alternate below and above a generally increasing trend line (e.g., a time series for housing costs). Many time series in the late 1970s and early 1980s displayed this type of behavior.

Seasonal Component

While the trend and cyclical components of a time series are identified by analyzing multiyear movements in historical data, many time series show a regular pattern of

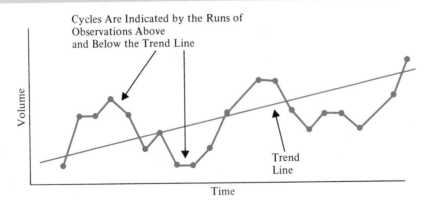

FIGURE 16.4
Trend and Cyclical Components of a Time Series (Data Points Are 1 Year Apart)

Cycles Are Indicated by the Runs of Observations Above and Below the Trend Line

Trend Line

variability within 1-year periods. For example, a manufacturer of swimming pools expects low sales activity in the fall and winter months, with peak sales occurring in the spring and summer months. Manufacturers of snow removal equipment and heavy clothing, however, expect just the opposite yearly pattern. It should not be surprising that the component of the time series that represents the variability in the data due to seasonal influences is called the *seasonal component*. Although we generally think of seasonal movement in a time series as occurring within 1 year, the seasonal component can also be used to represent any regularly repeating pattern that is less than 1 year in duration. For example, daily traffic volume data show within-the-day "seasonal" behavior, with peak levels during rush hours, moderate flow during the rest of the day and early evening, and light flow from midnight to early morning.

Irregular Component

The *irregular component* of the time series is the residual, or "catchall," factor that accounts for the deviations of the actual time series values from what we would expect given the effects of the trend, cyclical, and seasonal components. It accounts for the random variability in the time series. The irregular component is caused by the short-term, unanticipated, and nonrecurring factors that affect the time series. Since this component accounts for the random variability in the time series, it is unpredictable. We cannot attempt to predict its impact on the time series in advance.

16.2 ▼ FORECASTING USING SMOOTHING METHODS

In this section we discuss forecasting techniques that are appropriate for a fairly stable time series—that is, one that exhibits no significant trend, cyclical, or seasonal effects. In such situations the objective of the forecasting method is to "smooth out" the irregular component of the time series through an averaging process. We begin with a consideration of the method known as moving averages.

Moving Averages

The *moving averages* method uses the average of the *most recent n* data values in the time series as the forecast for the next period. Mathematically, the moving average calculation is made as follows:

$$\text{Moving average} = \frac{\Sigma(\text{most recent } n \text{ data values})}{n} \qquad (16.1)$$

The term *moving* average is based on the fact that as a new observation becomes available for the time series, it replaces the oldest observation in (16.1), and a new average is computed. As a result, the average will change, or move, as new observations become available.

To illustrate the moving averages method, consider the 12 weeks of data presented in Table 16.1 and Figure 16.5. These data show the number of gallons of gasoline sold by a gasoline distributor in Bennington, Vt., over the past 12 weeks.

In order to use moving averages to forecast gasoline sales, we must first select the number of data values to be included in the moving average. As an example, let us

TABLE 16.1
Gasoline Sales Time Series

Week	Sales (1000s of gallons)
1	17
2	21
3	19
4	23
5	18
6	16
7	20
8	18
9	22
10	20
11	15
12	22

FIGURE 16.5
Graph of Gasoline Sales Time Series

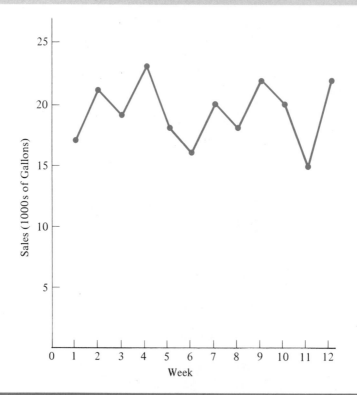

compute forecasts using a 3-week moving average. The moving average calculation for the first 3 weeks of the gasoline sales time series is as follows:

$$\text{Moving average (weeks 1–3)} = \frac{17 + 21 + 19}{3} = 19$$

This moving average value is then used as the forecast for week 4. Since the actual value observed in week 4 is 23, we see that the forecast error in week 4 is $23 - 19 = 4$. In general, the error associated with any forecast is the difference between the observed value of the time series and the forecast.

The calculation for the second 3-week moving average is shown below.

$$\text{Moving average (weeks 2–4)} = \frac{21 + 19 + 23}{3} = 21$$

Hence, the forecast for week 5 is 21. The error associated with this forecast is $18 - 21 = -3$. Thus, we see that the forecast error can be positive or negative depending on whether the forecast is too low or too high. A complete summary of the 3-week moving average calculations for the gasoline sales time series is shown in Table 16.2 and Figure 16.6.

An important consideration in using any forecasting method is the accuracy of the forecast. Clearly, we would like the forecast errors to be small. The last two columns of Table 16.2, which contain the forecast errors and the forecast errors squared, can be used to develop measures of accuracy.

One measure of forecast accuracy you might think of using would be to simply sum the forecast errors over time. The problem with this measure is that if the errors are random (as they should be if the forecasting method selected is appropriate), some errors will be positive and some errors will be negative, resulting in a sum near zero regardless of the size of the individual errors. Indeed, we see from Table 16.2 that the sum of forecast errors for the gasoline sales time series is zero. This difficulty can be avoided by squaring each of the individual forecast errors.

TABLE 16.2
Summary of 3-Week Moving Average Calculations

Week	Time Series Value	Moving Average Forecast	Forecast Error	Squared Forecast Error
1	17			
2	21			
3	19			
4	23	19	4	16
5	18	21	-3	9
6	16	20	-4	16
7	20	19	1	1
8	18	18	0	0
9	22	18	4	16
10	20	20	0	0
11	15	20	-5	25
12	22	19	3	9
		Totals	0	92

FIGURE 16.6
Graph of Gasoline Sales Time Series and 3-Week Moving Average Forecasts

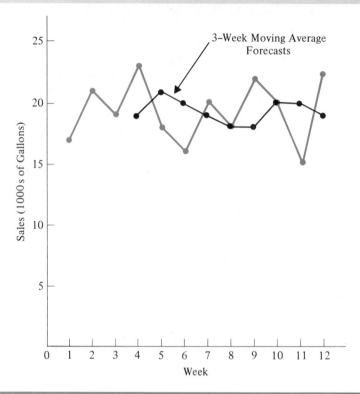

For the gasoline sales time series we can use the last column of Table 16.2 to compute the average of the sum of the squared errors. Doing so we obtain

$$\text{Average of the sum of squared errors} = \frac{92}{9} = 10.22$$

This average of the sum of squared errors is commonly referred to as the *mean squared error* (MSE). The mean squared error is an often used measure of the accuracy of a forecasting method and is the one we use in this chapter.

As we indicated previously, in order to use the moving averages method we must first select the number of data values to be included in the moving average. It should not be too surprising that for a particular time series, different length moving averages will differ in their ability to accurately forecast the time series. One possible approach to choosing the number of values to be included is to use trial and error to identify the length that minimizes the MSE. Then, if we are willing to assume that the length that is best for the past will also be best for the future, we would forecast the next value in the time series using the number of data values that minimized the MSE for the historical time series. (Problem 2 at the end of the chapter will ask you to consider 4-week and 5-week moving averages for the gasoline sales data. A comparison of the mean squared error for each will indicate the number of weeks of data you may want to include in the moving average calculation.)

Weighted Moving Averages

In the moving averages method each observation in the moving averages calculation receives the same weight. One possible variation, known as *weighted moving averages,* involves selecting different weights for each data value and then computing a weighted mean as the forecast. In most cases the most recent observation receives the most weight, and the weight decreases for older data values. For example, using the gasoline sales time series, let us illustrate the computation of a weighted 3-week moving average, where the most recent observation receives a weight 3 times as great as that given the oldest observation, and the next oldest observation receives a weight twice as great as the oldest. The weighted moving averages forecast for week 4 would be computed as follows:

Weighted moving averages forecast for week 4 $= \frac{3}{6}(19) + \frac{2}{6}(21) + \frac{1}{6}(17) = 19.33$

Note that for the weighted moving average the sum of the weights is equal to 1. This was also true for the simple moving average, where each weight was $\frac{1}{3}$. However, recall that the simple or unweighted moving average provided a forecast of 19. (Problem 3 at the end of the chapter asks you to calculate the remaining values for the 3-week weighted moving average and compare the forecast accuracy with what we have obtained for the unweighted moving average.)

Exponential Smoothing

Exponential smoothing is a forecasting technique that uses a weighted average of past time series values to forecast the value of the time series in the next period. The basic exponential smoothing model is as follows:

$$F_{t+1} = \alpha Y_t + (1 - \alpha)F_t \qquad (16.2)$$

where

$$F_{t+1} = \text{forecast of the time series for period } t + 1$$
$$Y_t = \text{actual value of the time series in period } t$$
$$F_t = \text{forecast of the time series for period } t$$
$$\alpha = \textit{smoothing constant } (1 \leq \alpha \leq 1)$$

To see that the forecast for any period is a weighted average of *all the previous actual values* for the time series, suppose we have a time series consisting of three periods of data, Y_1, Y_2, and Y_3. To get the exponential smoothing calculations started, we let F_1 equal the actual value of the time series in period 1; that is, $F_1 = Y_1$. Hence, the forecast for period 2 is written as follows:

$$F_2 = \alpha Y_1 + (1 - \alpha)F_1$$
$$= \alpha Y_1 + (1 - \alpha)Y_1$$
$$= Y_1$$

In general, then, the exponential smoothing forecast for period 2 is equal to the actual value of the time series in period 1.

To obtain the forecast for period 3, we substitute $F_2 = Y_1$ in the expression for F_3; the result is

$$F_3 = \alpha Y_2 + (1 - \alpha)Y_1$$

Finally, substituting this expression for F_3 in the expression for F_4, we obtain

$$F_4 = \alpha Y_3 + (1 - \alpha)[\alpha Y_2 + (1 - \alpha)Y_1]$$
$$= \alpha Y_3 + \alpha(1 - \alpha)Y_2 + (1 - \alpha)^2 Y_1$$

Hence, we see that F_4 is a weighted average of the first three time series values. The sum of the coefficients or weights for Y_1, Y_2, and Y_3 equals 1. A similar argument can be made to show that any forecast F_{t+1} is a weighted average of the previous t time series values.

An advantage of exponential smoothing is that it is a simple procedure and requires very little historical data for its use. Once the smoothing constant α has been selected, only two pieces of information are required in order to compute the forecast for the next period. Referring to (16.2), we see that with a given α we can compute the forecast for period $t + 1$ simply by knowing the actual and forecast time series values for period t—that is, Y_t and F_t.

To illustrate the exponential smoothing approach to forecasting, consider the gasoline sales time series presented previously in Table 16.1 and Figure 16.5. As we indicated in the discussion above, the exponential smoothing forecast for period 2 is equal to the actual value of the time series in period 1. Thus, with $Y_1 = 17$, we will set $F_2 = 17$ to get the exponential smoothing computations started. Referring to the time series data in Table 16.1, we find an actual time series value in period 2 of $Y_2 = 21$. Thus, period 2 has a forecast error of $21 - 17 = 4$.

Continuing with the exponential smoothing computations provides the following forecast for period 3:

$$F_3 = 0.2Y_2 + 0.8F_2 = 0.2(21) + 0.8(17) = 17.8$$

Once the actual time series value in period 3, $Y_3 = 19$, is known, we can generate a forecast for period 4 as follows:

$$F_4 = 0.2Y_3 + 0.8F_3 = 0.2(19) + 0.8(17.8) = 18.04$$

By continuing the exponential smoothing calculations we are able to determine the weekly forecast values and the corresponding weekly forecast errors, as shown in Table 16.3. Note that we have not shown an exponential smoothing forecast or the forecast error for period 1 because F_1 was set equal to Y_1 in order to begin the smoothing computations. For week 12, we have $Y_{12} = 22$ and $F_{12} = 18.48$. Can you use this information to generate a forecast for week 13 before the actual value of week 13 becomes known? Using the exponential smoothing model, we have

$$F_{13} = 0.2Y_{12} + 0.8F_{12} = 0.2(22) + 0.8(18.48) = 19.18$$

Thus, the exponential smoothing forecast of the amount sold in week 13 is 19.18, or 19,180 gallons of gasoline. With this forecast the firm can make plans and decisions accordingly. The accuracy of the forecast will not be known until the firm conducts its business through week 13. Figure 16.7 shows the plot of the actual and the forecast time series values. Note in particular how the forecasts "smooth out" the irregular fluctuations in the time series.

In the preceding exponential smoothing calculations we used a smoothing constant of $\alpha = 0.2$. Although any value of α between 0 and 1 is acceptable, some values will yield

TABLE 16.3
Summary of the Exponential Smoothing Forecasts and Forecast Errors for
Gasoline Sales with Smoothing Constant $\alpha = 0.2$

Week (t)	Time Series Value (Y_t)	Exponential Smoothing Forecast (F_t)	Forecast Error $(Y_t - F_t)$
1	17		
2	21	17.00	4.00
3	19	17.80	1.20
4	23	18.04	4.96
5	18	19.03	−1.03
6	16	18.83	−2.83
7	20	18.26	1.74
8	18	18.61	−0.61
9	22	18.49	3.51
10	20	19.19	0.81
11	15	19.35	−4.35
12	22	18.48	3.52

FIGURE 16.7
Graph of Actual and Forecast Gasoline Sales Time Series with
Smoothing Constant $\alpha = 0.2$

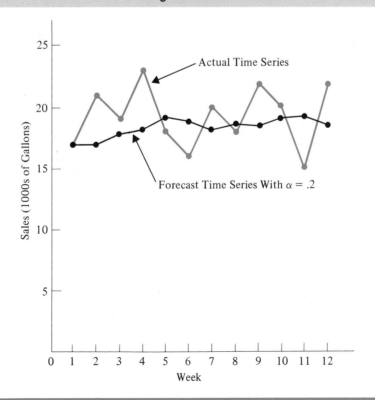

better forecasts than others. Insight into choosing a good value for α can be obtained by rewriting the basic exponential smoothing model as follows:

$$F_{t+1} = \alpha Y_t + (1 - \alpha)F_t$$
$$F_{t+1} = \alpha Y_t + F_t - \alpha F_t \tag{16.3}$$
$$F_{t+1} = F_t + \alpha(Y_t - F_t)$$

Forecast in Period t Forecast Error in Period t

Thus, we see that the new forecast, F_{t+1}, is equal to the previous forecast, F_t, plus an adjustment, which is α times the most recent forecast error, $Y_t - F_t$. That is, the forecast in period $t + 1$ is obtained by adjusting the forecast in period t by a fraction of the forecast error. If the time series contains substantial random variability, a small value of the smoothing constant is preferred. The reason for this choice is that since much of the forecast error is due to random variability, we do not want to overreact and adjust the forecasts too quickly. For a time series with relatively little random variability, larger values of the smoothing constant have the advantage of quickly adjusting the forecasts when forecasting errors occur and therefore allowing the forecast to react faster to changing conditions.

The criterion we will use to determine a desirable value for the smoothing constant α is the same as the criterion we proposed earlier for determining the number of periods of data to include in the moving averages calculation. That is, we choose the value of α that minimizes the mean squared error (MSE). A summary of the MSE calculations for the exponential smoothing forecast of gasoline sales with $\alpha = 0.2$ is shown in Table 16.4. Note that there is one less squared error term than the number of time periods because we had no past values with which to make a forecast for period 1. Would a different value of α have provided better results in terms of a lower MSE value? Perhaps the most straightforward way to answer this question is simply to try another value for α. We will then

TABLE 16.4
Mean Squared Error Computations for Forecasting Gasoline Sales with $\alpha = 0.2$

Week (t)	Time Series Value (Y_t)	Forecast (F_t)	Forecast Error ($Y_t - F_t$)	Squared Forecast Error ($Y_t - F_t)^2$
1	17			
2	21	17.00	4.00	16.00
3	19	17.80	1.20	1.44
4	23	18.04	4.96	24.60
5	18	19.03	-1.03	1.06
6	16	18.83	-2.83	8.01
7	20	18.26	1.74	3.03
8	18	18.61	-0.61	0.37
9	22	18.49	3.51	12.32
10	20	19.19	0.81	0.66
11	15	19.35	-4.35	18.92
12	22	18.48	3.52	12.39
			Total	98.80

$$\text{Mean squared error (MSE)} = \frac{98.80}{11} = 8.98$$

compare its mean squared error with the MSE value of 8.98, obtained using a smoothing constant of 0.2.

The exponential smoothing results with $\alpha = 0.3$ are shown in Table 16.5. With MSE = 9.35, we see that for the current data set a smoothing constant of $\alpha = 0.3$ results in less forecast accuracy than a smoothing constant of $\alpha = 0.2$. Thus, we would be inclined to prefer the original smoothing constant of 0.2. With a trial-and-error calculation with other values of α, a "good" value for the smoothing constant can be found. This value can be used in the exponential smoothing model to provide forecasts for the future. At a later date, after a number of new time series observations have been obtained, it is good practice to analyze the newly collected time series data to see if the smoothing constant should be revised to provide better forecasting results.

▼ NOTES AND COMMENTS ▼

Another commonly used measure of forecast accuracy is the *mean absolute deviation* (MAD). This measure is simply the average of the sum of the absolute values of all the forecast errors. Using the errors given in Table 16.2, we obtain

$$\text{Mean absolute deviation (MAD)} = \frac{4 + 3 + 4 + 1 + 0 + 4 + 0 + 5 + 3}{9}$$

$$= 2.67$$

One major difference between the MSE and the MAD is that the MSE measure is influenced much more by large forecast errors than by small errors (since for the MSE measure the errors are squared). The selection of the best measure of forecasting accuracy is not a simple matter. Indeed, forecasting experts often disagree as to which measure should be used. In this chapter we will use the MSE measure.

TABLE 16.5
Mean Squared Error Computations for Forecasting Gasoline Sales with $\alpha = 0.3$

Week (t)	Time Series Value (Y_t)	Forecast (F_t)	Forecast Error ($Y_t - F_t$)	Squared Forecast Error ($Y_t - F_t$)^2
1	17			
2	21	17.00	4.00	16.00
3	19	18.20	0.80	0.64
4	23	18.44	4.56	20.79
5	18	19.81	−1.81	3.28
6	16	19.27	−3.27	10.69
7	20	18.29	1.71	2.92
8	18	18.80	−0.80	0.64
9	22	18.56	3.44	11.83
10	20	19.59	0.41	0.17
11	15	19.71	−4.71	22.18
12	22	18.30	3.70	13.69
			Total	102.83

$$\text{Mean Squared Error (MSE)} = \frac{102.83}{11} = 9.35$$

16.3 ▼ FORECASTING A TIME SERIES USING TREND PROJECTION

In this section we will see how to forecast the values of a time series that exhibits a long-term linear trend. Specifically, let us consider the time series data for bicycle sales of a particular manufacturer over the past 10 years, as shown in Table 16.6 and Figure 16.8. Note that 21,600 bicycles were sold in year 1, 22,900 were sold in year 2, and so on; in year 10, the most recent year, 31,400 bicycles were sold. Although the graph in Figure 16.8 shows some up-and-down movement over the past 10 years, the time series seems to have an overall increasing or upward trend in the number of bicycles sold.

We do not want the trend component of a time series to follow each and every "up" and "down" movement. Rather, the trend component should reflect the gradual shifting—in our case, growth—of the time series values. After we view the time series data in Table 16.6 and the graph in Figure 16.8, we might agree that a linear trend as shown in Figure 16.9 has the potential of providing a reasonable description of the long-run movement in the series. Thus, we can now concentrate on finding the linear function that best approximates the trend.

Using the bicycle sales data to illustrate the calculations involved, we will now describe how regression analysis can be used to identify a linear trend for a time series. For a linear trend the estimated sales volume expressed as a function of time can be written as follows:

$$T_t = b_0 + b_1 t \qquad (16.4)$$

where

T_t = forecast value (based on trend) of the time series in period t

b_0 = intercept of the trend line

b_1 = slope of the trend line

t = point in time

In (16.4), we will let $t = 1$ for the time of the first observation on the time series data, $t = 2$ for the time of the second observation, and so on. Note that for the time series on

TABLE 16.6
Bicycle Sales Data

Year (t)	Sales (1000s) (Y_t)
1	21.6
2	22.9
3	25.5
4	21.9
5	23.9
6	27.5
7	31.5
8	29.7
9	28.6
10	31.4

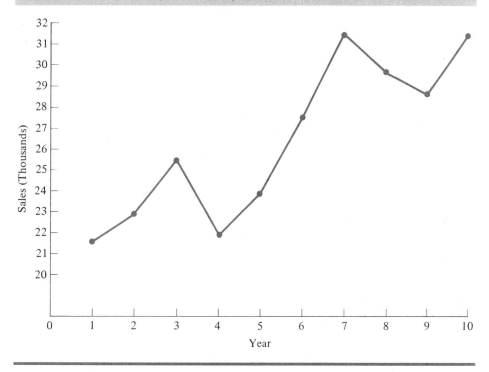

FIGURE 16.8
Graph of the Bicycle Sales Time Series

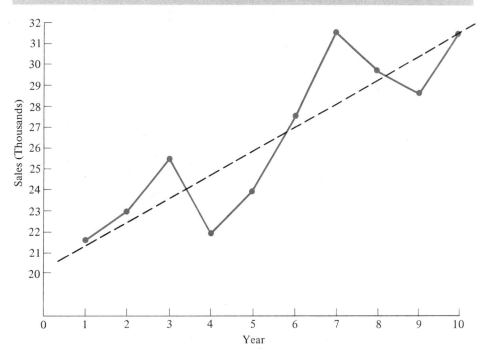

FIGURE 16.9
Trend Represented by a Linear Function for Bicycle Sales

bicycle sales $t = 1$ corresponds to the oldest time series value and $t = 10$ corresponds to the most recent year's data. Formulas for computing b_1 and b_0 are shown below:

$$b_1 = \frac{\Sigma t Y_t - (\Sigma t \Sigma Y_t)/n}{\Sigma t^2 - (\Sigma t)^2/n} \tag{16.5}$$

$$b_0 = \bar{Y} - b_1 \bar{t} \tag{16.6}$$

where

Y_t = actual value of the time series in period t

n = number of periods

$\bar{Y}$ = average value of the time series; that is, $\bar{Y} = \Sigma Y_t/n$

$\bar{t}$ = average value of t; that is, $\bar{t} = \Sigma t/n$

Using these relationships for b_0 and b_1 and the bicycle sales data of Table 16.6, we have the following calculations:

t	Y_t	tY_t	t^2
1	21.6	21.6	1
2	22.9	45.8	4
3	25.5	76.5	9
4	21.9	87.6	16
5	23.9	119.5	25
6	27.5	165.0	36
7	31.5	220.5	49
8	29.7	237.6	64
9	28.6	257.4	81
10	31.4	314.0	100
Totals 55	264.5	1545.5	385

$$\bar{t} = \frac{55}{10} = 5.5 \text{ years}$$

$$\bar{Y} = \frac{264.5}{10} = 26.45 \text{ thousands}$$

$$b_1 = \frac{1545.5 - (55)(264.5)/10}{385 - (55)^2/10} = \frac{90.75}{82.50} = 1.10$$

$$b_0 = 26.45 - 1.10(5.5) = 20.4$$

Therefore,

$$T_t = 20.4 + 1.1t \tag{16.7}$$

is the expression for the linear trend component for the bicycle sales time series.

Trend Projections

The slope of 1.1 in the trend equation indicates that over the past 10 years the firm has experienced an average growth in sales of around 1100 units per year. If we assume that the past 10-year trend in sales is a good indicator of the future, then (16.7) can be used to project the trend component of the time series. For example, substituting $t = 11$ into (16.7) yields next year's trend projection, T_{11}:

$$T_{11} = 20.4 + 1.1(11) = 32.5$$

Thus, using the trend component only, we would forecast sales of 32,500 bicycles next year.

The use of a linear function to model the trend is common. However, as we discussed earlier, sometimes time series exhibit a curvilinear, or nonlinear, trend similar to those shown in Figure 16.10. More advanced texts discuss in detail how to develop models for these more complex relationships.

16.4 ▼ FORECASTING A TIME SERIES WITH TREND AND SEASONAL COMPONENTS

In the previous section we showed how to forecast a time series that had a trend component. In this section we expand the discussion by showing how to forecast a time series that has both trend and seasonal components. The approach we will take is first to remove the seasonal effect or seasonal component from the time series. This step is referred to as *deseasonalizing* the time series. After deseasonalizing, the time series will have only a trend component. As a result, we can use the method described in the previous section to identify the trend component of the time series. Then, using a trend projection calculation, we will be able to forecast the trend component of the time series in future periods. The final step in developing the forecast will be to incorporate the seasonal component by using a seasonal index to adjust the trend projection. In this manner we will be able to identify the trend and seasonal components and consider both in forecasting the time series.

In addition to a trend component (T) and a seasonal component (S), we will assume that the time series also has an irregular component (I). The irregular component accounts

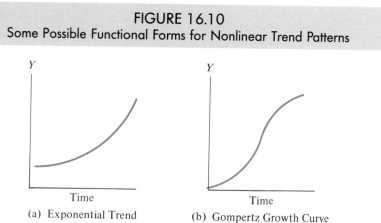

FIGURE 16.10
Some Possible Functional Forms for Nonlinear Trend Patterns

(a) Exponential Trend   (b) Gompertz Growth Curve

for any random effects in the time series that cannot be explained by the trend and seasonal components. Using T_t, S_t, and I_t to identify the trend, seasonal, and irregular components at time t, we will assume that the actual time series value, denoted by Y_t, can be described by the following *multiplicative time series model:*

$$Y_t = T_t \times S_t \times I_t \qquad (16.8)$$

In this model T_t is the trend measured in units of the item being forecast. However, the S_t and I_t components are measured in relative terms, with values above 1.00 indicating effects above the normal or average level. Values below 1.00 indicate below-average levels for each component. In order to illustrate the use of (16.8) to model a time series, suppose we have a trend projection of 540 units. In addition, suppose $S_t = 1.10$ shows a seasonal effect 10% above average and $I_t = 0.98$ shows an irregular effect 2% below average. Using these values in (16.8), the time series value would be $Y_t = 540(1.10)(0.98) = 582$.

In this section we will illustrate the use of the multiplicative model with trend, seasonal, and irregular components by working with the quarterly data presented in Table 16.7 and Figure 16.11. These data show the television set sales (in thousands of units) for a particular manufacturer over the past 4 years. We begin by showing how to identify the seasonal component of the time series.

Calculating the Seasonal Indexes

Looking at Figure 16.11 we observe that sales are lowest in the second quarter of each year, followed by higher sales levels in quarters 3 and 4. Thus, we conclude that a seasonal pattern exists for the television set sales. The computational procedure used to

TABLE 16.7
Quarterly Data for Television Set Sales

Year	Quarter	Sales (1000s)
1	1	4.8
	2	4.1
	3	6.0
	4	6.5
2	1	5.8
	2	5.2
	3	6.8
	4	7.4
3	1	6.0
	2	5.6
	3	7.5
	4	7.8
4	1	6.3
	2	5.9
	3	8.0
	4	8.4

FIGURE 16.11
Graph of Quarterly Television Set Sales Time Series

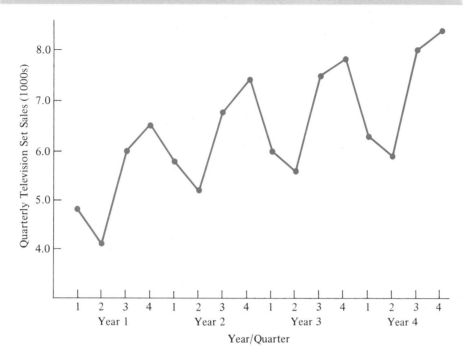

identify each quarter's seasonal influence begins by computing a moving average to isolate the combined seasonal and irregular components, S_t and I_t.

In using moving averages to do this, we use 1 year of data in each calculation. Since we are working with a quarterly series, we will use 4 data values in each moving average. The moving average calculation for the first 4 quarters of the television set sales data is as follows:

$$\text{First moving average} = \frac{4.8 + 4.1 + 6.0 + 6.5}{4} = \frac{21.4}{4} = 5.35$$

Note that the moving average calculation for the first 4 quarters yields the average quarterly sales over the first year of the time series. Continuing the moving average calculation, we next add the 5.8 value for the first quarter of year 2 and drop the 4.8 for the first quarter of year 1. Thus, the second moving average is

$$\text{Second moving average} = \frac{4.1 + 6.0 + 6.5 + 5.8}{4} = \frac{22.4}{4} = 5.6$$

Similarly, the third moving average calculation is $(6.0 + 6.5 + 5.8 + 5.2)/4 = 5.875$.

Before we proceed with the moving average calculations for the entire time series, let us return to the first moving average calculation, which resulted in a value of 5.35. The 5.35 value represents an average quarterly sales volume (across all seasons) for year 1. As we look back at the calculation of the 5.35 value, perhaps it makes sense to associate 5.35 with the "middle" quarter of the moving average group. However, note that some difficulty in identifying the middle quarter is encountered; with 4 quarters in the moving average, there is no middle quarter. The 5.35 value corresponds to the last half of quarter 2 and the first half of quarter 3. Similarly, if we go to the next moving average value of 5.60, the middle corresponds to the last half of quarter 3 and the first half of quarter 4.

Recall that the reason we are computing moving averages is to isolate the combined seasonal and irregular components. However, the moving average values we have computed do not correspond directly to the original quarters of the time series. We can resolve this difficulty by using the midpoints between successive moving average values. For example, since 5.35 corresponds to the first half of quarter 3 and 5.60 corresponds to the last half of quarter 3, we will use $(5.35 + 5.60)/2 = 5.475$ as the moving average value for quarter 3. Similarly, we associate a moving average value of $(5.60 + 5.875)/2 = 5.738$ with quarter 4. What results is called a *centered moving average*. A complete summary of the moving average calculations for the television set sales data is shown in Table 16.8.

TABLE 16.8
Moving Average Calculations for the Television Set Sales Time Series

Year	Quarter	Sales (1000s)	Four-Quarter Moving Average	Centered Moving Average
1	1	4.8		
	2	4.1		
			5.350	
	3	6.0		5.475
			5.600	
	4	6.5		5.738
			5.875	
2	1	5.8		5.975
			6.075	
	2	5.2		6.188
			6.300	
	3	6.8		6.325
			6.350	
	4	7.4		6.400
			6.450	
3	1	6.0		6.538
			6.625	
	2	5.6		6.675
			6.725	
	3	7.5		6.763
			6.800	
	4	7.8		6.838
			6.875	
4	1	6.3		6.938
			7.000	
	2	5.9		7.075
			7.150	
	3	8.0		
	4	8.4		

Note that if the number of data points in a moving average calculation is an odd number, the middle point will correspond to one of the periods in the time series. In such cases, we would not have to center the moving average values to correspond to a particular time period, as we did in the calculations in Table 16.8.

Let us pause for a moment to consider what the moving averages in Table 16.8 tell us about this time series. Plots of the actual time series values and the corresponding centered moving average are shown in Figure 16.12. Note particularly how the centered moving average values tend to "smooth out" the fluctuations in the time series. Since the moving average values were computed for 4 quarters of data, they do not include the fluctuations due to seasonal influences. Each point in the centered moving average represents what the value of the time series would be if there were no seasonal or irregular influence.

By dividing each time series observation by the corresponding centered moving average value we can identify the seasonal-irregular effect in the time series. For example, the third quarter of year 1 shows $6.0/5.475 = 1.096$ as the combined seasonal-irregular component. The resulting seasonal-irregular values for the entire time series are summarized in Table 16.9.

Consider the third quarter. The results from years 1, 2, and 3 show third-quarter values of 1.096, 1.075, and 1.109, respectively. Thus, in all cases the seasonal-irregular component appears to have an above average influence in the third quarter. Since the year-to-year fluctuations in the seasonal-irregular component can be attributed primarily

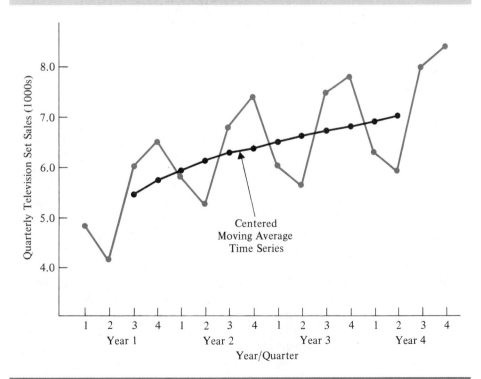

FIGURE 16.12
Graph of Quarterly Television Set Sales Time Series and Centered Moving Average

TABLE 16.9
Seasonal-Irregular Factors for the Television Set Sales Time Series

Year	Quarter	Sales (1000s)	Centered Moving Average	Seasonal-Irregular Component
1	1	4.8		
	2	4.1		
	3	6.0	5.475	1.096
	4	6.5	5.738	1.133
2	1	5.8	5.975	.971
	2	5.2	6.188	.840
	3	6.8	6.325	1.075
	4	7.4	6.400	1.156
3	1	6.0	6.538	.918
	2	5.6	6.675	.839
	3	7.5	6.763	1.109
	4	7.8	6.838	1.141
4	1	6.3	6.938	.908
	2	5.9	7.075	.834
	3	8.0		
	4	8.4		

to the irregular component, we can average the computed values to eliminate the irregular influence and obtain an estimate of the third-quarter seasonal influence:

$$\text{Seasonal effect of third quarter} = \frac{1.096 + 1.075 + 1.109}{3} = 1.09$$

We refer to 1.09 as the *seasonal index* for the third quarter. In Table 16.10 we summarize the calculations involved in computing the seasonal indexes for the television set sales time series. Thus, we see that the seasonal indexes for all 4 quarters are as follows: quarter 1, .93; quarter 2, .84; quarter 3, 1.09; and quarter 4, 1.14.

Interpretation of the values in Table 16.10 provides some observations about the "seasonal" component in television set sales. The best sales quarter is the fourth quarter, with sales averaging 14% above the average quarterly value. The worst, or slowest, sales quarter is the second quarter, with its seasonal index at .84, showing the sales average 16% below the average quarterly sales. The seasonal component corresponds nicely to the intuitive expectation that television viewing interest and thus television purchase patterns tend to peak in the fourth quarter, with its coming winter season and fewer outdoor activities. The low second-quarter sales reflect the reduced television interest resulting from the spring and presummer activities of the potential customers.

One final adjustment is sometimes necessary in obtaining the seasonal indexes. The multiplicative model requires that the average seasonal index equal 1.00; that is, the sum of the four seasonal indexes in Table 16.10 must equal 4.00. This is necessary if the seasonal effects are to even out over the year, as they must. The average of the seasonal indexes in our example is equal to 1.00, and hence this type of adjustment is not necessary. In other cases a slight adjustment may be necessary. The adjustment can be made by simply multiplying each seasonal index by the number of seasons divided by the sum of the unadjusted seasonal indexes. For example, for quarterly data we would multiply each

TABLE 16.10
Seasonal Index Calculations for the Television Set Sales Time Series

Quarter	Seasonal-Irregular Component Values $(S_t I_t)$	Seasonal Index (S_t)
1	.971, .918, .908	.93
2	.840, .839, .834	.84
3	1.096, 1.075, 1.109	1.09
4	1.133, 1.156, 1.141	1.14

seasonal index by 4/(sum of the unadjusted seasonal indexes). (Some of the problems at the end of the chapter will require this adjustment in order to obtain the appropriate seasonal indexes.)

Deseasonalizing the Time Series

Often the purpose of finding seasonal indexes is to remove the seasonal effects from a time series. This process is referred to as *deseasonalizing* the time series. Economic time series adjusted for seasonal variations (deseasonalized time series) are often reported in publications such as the *Survey of Current Business* and *The Wall Street Journal*. Using the notation of the multiplicative model, we have

$$Y_t = T_t \times S_t \times I_t$$

By dividing each time series observation by the corresponding seasonal index, we have removed the effect of season from the time series. The deseasonalized time series for television set sales is summarized in Table 16.11. A graph of the deseasonalized television set sales time series is shown in Figure 16.13.

Using the Deseasonalized Time Series to Identify Trend

Looking at Figure 16.13, we see that while the graph shows some up-and-down movement over the past 16 quarters, the time series seems to have an upward linear trend. To identify this trend, we will use the same procedure we introduced for identifying trend when forecasting with annual data; in this case, since we have deseasonalized the data, quarterly sales values can be used. Thus, for a linear trend the estimated sales volume expressed as a function of time can be written

$$T_t = b_0 + b_1 t$$

where

T_t = trend value for television set sales in period t

b_0 = intercept of the trend line

b_1 = slope of the trend line

As we did before, we will let $t = 1$ for the time of the first observation on the time series data, $t = 2$ for the time of the second observation, and so on. Thus, for the deseason-

TABLE 16.11
Deseasonalized Values for the Television Set Sales Time Series

Year	Quarter	Sales (1000s) (Y_t)	Seasonal Index (S_t)	Deseasonalized Sales $(Y_t/S_t = T_tI_t)$
1	1	4.8	.93	5.16
	2	4.1	.84	4.88
	3	6.0	1.09	5.50
	4	6.5	1.14	5.70
2	1	5.8	.93	6.24
	2	5.2	.84	6.19
	3	6.8	1.09	6.24
	4	7.4	1.14	6.49
3	1	6.0	.93	6.45
	2	5.6	.84	6.67
	3	7.5	1.09	6.88
	4	7.8	1.14	6.84
4	1	6.3	.93	6.77
	2	5.9	.84	7.02
	3	8.0	1.09	7.34
	4	8.4	1.14	7.37

FIGURE 16.13
Deseasonalized Television Set Sales Time Series

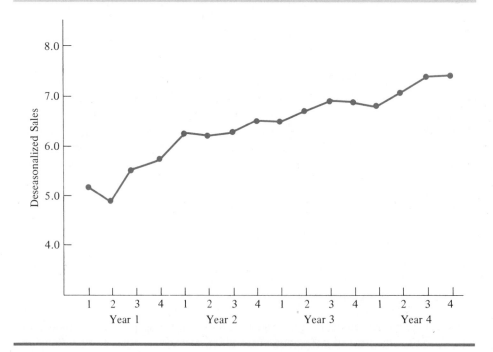

alized television set sales time series, $t = 1$ corresponds to the first deseasonalized quarterly sales value, and $t = 16$ corresponds to the most recent deseasonalized quarterly sales value. The formulas for computing the values of b_0 and b_1 are shown again

$$b_1 = \frac{\Sigma t Y_t - (\Sigma t \Sigma Y_t)/n}{\Sigma t^2 - (\Sigma t)^2/n}$$

$$b_0 = \bar{Y} - b_1 \bar{t}$$

Note, however, that Y_t now refers to the deseasonalized time series value at time t and not the actual value of the time series. Using the given relationships for b_0 and b_1 and the deseasonalized sales data of Table 16.11, we have the following calculations:

t	Y_t (deseasonalized)	tY_t	t^2
1	5.16	5.16	1
2	4.88	9.76	4
3	5.50	16.50	9
4	5.70	22.80	16
5	6.24	31.20	25
6	6.19	37.14	36
7	6.24	43.68	49
8	6.49	51.92	64
9	6.45	58.05	81
10	6.67	66.70	100
11	6.88	75.68	121
12	6.84	82.08	144
13	6.77	88.01	169
14	7.02	98.28	196
15	7.34	110.10	225
16	7.37	117.92	256
Totals 136	101.74	914.98	1496

$$\bar{t} = \frac{136}{16} = 8.5$$

$$\bar{Y} = \frac{101.74}{16} = 6.359$$

$$b_1 = \frac{914.98 - (136)(101.74)/16}{1496 - (136)^2/16} = \frac{50.19}{340} = .148$$

$$b_0 = 6.359 - .148(8.5) = 5.101$$

Therefore,

$$T_t = 5.101 + .148t$$

is the expression for the linear trend component of the time series.

The slope of .148 indicates that over the past 16 quarters the firm has experienced an average deseasonalized growth in sales of around 148 sets per quarter. If we assume that the past 16-quarter trend in sales data is a reasonably good indicator of the future, then this equation can be used to project the trend component of the time series for future quarters. For example, substituting $t = 17$ into the equation yields next quarter's trend projection, T_{17}:

$$T_{17} = 5.101 + .148(17) = 7.617$$

Using the trend component only, we would forecast sales of 7617 television sets for the next quarter. In a similar fashion, if we use the trend component only, we would forecast sales of 7765, 7913, and 8061 televisions sets in quarters 18, 19, and 20, respectively.

Seasonal Adjustments

Now that we have a forecast of sales for each of the next 4 quarters based on trend, we must adjust these forecasts to account for the effect of season. For example, since the seasonal index for the first quarter of year $5(t = 17)$ is .93, the quarterly forecast can be obtained by multiplying the forecast based on trend ($T_{17} = 7617$) times the seasonal index (.93). Thus, the forecast for the next quarter is 7617(.93) = 7084. Table 16.12 shows the quarterly forecast for quarters 17, 18, 19, and 20. The quarterly forecasts show the high-volume fourth quarter with a 9190-unit forecast, while the low-volume second quarter has a 6523-unit forecast.

Models Based on Monthly Data

The television-set sales example provided in this section used quarterly data to illustrate the computation of seasonal indexes with relatively few computations. Many businesses use monthly rather than quarterly forecasts. In such cases the procedures introduced in this section can be applied with minor modifications. First, a 12-month moving average replaces the 4-quarter moving average; second, 12 monthly seasonal indexes, rather than 4 quarterly seasonal indexes, will need to be computed. Other than these changes, the computational and forecasting procedures are identical. Exercise 17 at the end of this section asks you to develop monthly seasonal indexes for a situation requiring monthly forecasts.

TABLE 16.12
Quarterly Forecasts for the Television Set Sales Time Series

Year	Quarter	Trend Forecast	Seasonal Index (see Table 16.10)	Quarterly Forecast
5	1	7617	.93	(7617)(.93) = 7084
	2	7765	.84	(7765)(.84) = 6523
	3	7913	1.09	(7913)(1.09) = 8625
	4	8061	1.14	(8061)(1.14) = 9190

Cyclical Component

Mathematically the multiplicative model of (16.8) can be expanded to include a cyclical component as follows:

$$Y_t = T_t \times C_t \times S_t \times I_t \qquad (16.9)$$

Just as with the seasonal component, the cyclical component is expressed as a percentage of trend. As mentioned in Section 16.1, this component is attributable to multiyear cycles in the time series. It is analogous to the seasonal component, but over a longer period of time. However, because of the length of time involved, it is often difficult to obtain enough relevant data to estimate the cyclical component. Another difficulty is that the length of cycles usually varies. We leave further discussion of the cyclical component to texts on forecasting methods.

16.5 ▼ FORECASTING USING REGRESSION MODELS

Looking at regression analysis as a forecasting tool, the time series value that we would like to forecast can be viewed as the dependent variable. Thus, if we can identify a good set of related independent, or predictor, variables, we may be able to develop an estimated regression equation for predicting or forecasting the time series.

The approach we used in Section 16.3 to fit a linear trend line to the bicycle sales time series is a special case of regression analysis. In that example two variables—bicycle sales and time—were shown to be linearly related.[2] The inherent complexity of most real-world problems necessitates the consideration of more than one independent variable to predict the dependent variable. The statistical technique known as multiple regression analysis can be used in such situations.

In order to develop an estimated regression equation we need a sample of observations for the dependent variable and all independent variables. In time series analysis the n periods of time series data provide a sample of n observations on each variable that can be used in the analysis. For a function involving k independent variables we use the following notation:

$$Y_t = \text{actual value of the time series in period } t$$

$$x_{1t} = \text{value of independent variable 1 in period } t$$

$$x_{2t} = \text{value of independent variable 2 in period } t$$

.

.

.

$$x_{kt} = \text{value of independent variable } k \text{ in period } t$$

[2] In a purely technical sense the number of bicycles sold is not thought of as being related to time; instead, time is used as a surrogate for variables that the number of bicycles sold is actually related to but that are unknown or too difficult or too costly to measure.

The n periods of data necessary to develop the estimated regression equation would appear as follows:

Period	Time Series Value (Y_t)	Value of Independent Variables						
		x_{1t}	x_{2t}	x_{3t}	.	.	.	x_{kt}
1	Y_1	x_{11}	x_{21}	x_{31}	.	.	.	x_{k1}
2	Y_2	x_{12}	x_{22}	x_{32}	.	.	.	k_{k2}
.	.	.	.	.	.	.	.	.
.	.	.	.	.	.	.	.	.
.	.	.	.	.	.	.	.	.
n	Y_n	x_{1n}	x_{2n}	x_{3n}	.	.	.	x_{kn}

As you might imagine, there are a number of possible choices for the independent variables in a forecasting model. One possible choice for an independent variable is simply time. This is the choice we made in Section 16.3 when we estimated the trend of the time series using a linear function of the independent variable time. Letting

$$x_{1t} = t$$

we obtain an estimated regression equation of the form

$$\hat{Y}_t = b_0 + b_1 t$$

where $\hat{Y}_t$ is the estimate of the time series value Y_t and where b_0 and b_1 are the estimated regression coefficients. In a more complex model, additional terms could be added corresponding to time raised to other powers. For example, if

$$x_{2t} = t^2$$

and

$$x_{3t} = t^3$$

the estimated regression equation would then become

$$\hat{Y}_t = b_0 + b_1 x_{1t} + b_2 x_{2t} + b_3 x_{3t}$$
$$= b_0 + b_1 t + b_2 t^2 + b_3 t^3$$

Note that this model provides a forecast of a time series with curvilinear characteristics over time.

Other regression-based forecasting models employ a mixture of economic and demographic independent variables. For example, in forecasting the sale of refrigerators we might select independent variables such as the following:

x_{1t} = price in period t

x_{2t} = total industry sales in period $t - 1$

x_{3t} = number of building permits for new houses in period $t - 1$

x_{4t} = population forecast for period t

x_{5t} = advertising budget for period t

According to the usual multiple regression procedure, an estimated regression equation with 5 independent variables would be used to develop forecasts.

Whether or not a regression approach provides a good forecast depends largely on how well we are able to identify and obtain data for independent variables that are closely related to the time series. Generally, during the development of an estimated regression equation we will want to consider many possible sets of independent variables. Thus, part of the regression analysis procedure should focus on the selection of the set of independent variables that provides the best forecasting model.

In the chapter introduction we stated that *causal forecasting models* utilized time series related to the one being forecast in an effort to better explain the cause of a time series' behavior. Regression analysis is the tool most often used in developing these causal models. The related time series become the independent variables, and the time series being forecast is the dependent variable.

Another type of regression-based forecasting model occurs whenever the independent variables are all previous values of the same time series. For example, if the time series values are denoted by $Y_1, Y_2, \ldots, Y_n$, then with a dependent variable Y_t we might try to find an estimated regression equation relating Y_t to the most recent time series values, Y_{t-1}, Y_{t-2}, and so on. With the 3 most recent periods as independent variables, the estimated regression equation would be

$$\hat{Y}_t = b_0 + b_1 Y_{t-1} + b_2 Y_{t-2} + b_3 Y_{t-3}$$

Regression models where the independent variables are previous values of the time series are referred to as *autoregressive models*.

Finally, another regression-based forecasting approach is one that incorporates a mixture of the independent variables previously discussed. For example, we might select a combination of time variables, some economic/demographic variables, and some previous values of the time series variable itself.

16.6 ▼ QUALITATIVE APPROACHES TO FORECASTING

In the previous sections we discussed several types of quantitative forecasting methods. Since each of these techniques requires historical data on the variable of interest, in situations where no historical data are available these techniques cannot be applied. Furthermore, even when historical data are available, a significant change in environmental conditions affecting the time series may make the use of past data questionable in predicting future values of the time series. For example, a government-imposed gasoline rationing program would cause one to question the validity of a gasoline sales forecast based on past data. Qualitative forecasting techniques offer an alternative in these and other cases.

One of the most commonly used qualitative forecasting methods is the *Delphi approach*. This technique, originally developed by a research group at the Rand Corporation, attempts to obtain forecasts through "group consensus." In the usual application of this technique the members of a panel of experts—all of whom are physically separated from and unknown to each other—are asked to respond to a series of questionnaires. The responses from the first questionnaire are tabulated and used to prepare a second questionnaire that contains information and opinions of the whole group. Each respondent is then asked to reconsider and possibly revise his or her previous response in light of the group information that has been provided. This basic process continues until the coordinator feels that some degree of consensus has been reached. Note that the goal of the Delphi approach is not to produce a single answer as output, but to produce instead a relatively narrow spread of opinions within which the "majority" of experts concur.

The qualitative procedure referred to as *scenario writing* consists of developing a conceptual scenario of the future based on a well-defined set of assumptions. Thus, by starting with a different set of assumptions, many different future scenarios can be presented. The job of the decision maker is to decide which scenario is most likely to occur in the future and then to make decisions accordingly.

Subjective or *intuitive qualitative approaches* are based on the ability of the human mind to process a variety of information that is, in most cases, difficult to quantify. These techniques are often used in group work, wherein a committee or panel seeks to develop new ideas or solve complex problems through a series of "brainstorming sessions." In such sessions individuals are freed from the usual group restrictions of peer pressure and criticism since any idea or opinion can be presented without regard to its relevancy and, even more importantly, without fear of criticism.

▼ SUMMARY

The purpose of this chapter has been to provide an introduction to the basic methods of time series analysis and forecasting. First, we showed that in order to explain the behavior of a time series, it is often helpful to think of the time series as consisting of four separate components: trend, cyclical, seasonal, and irregular. By isolating these components and measuring their apparent effect, it is possible to forecast future values of the time series.

We discussed how smoothing methods can be used to forecast a time series that exhibits no significant trend, seasonal, or cyclical effect. The moving averages approach consists of computing an average of past data values and then using this average as the forecast for the next period. The exponential smoothing method is a more preferred technique; it uses a weighted average of past time series values to compute a forecast.

When the time series exhibits only a long-term trend, we showed how regression analysis could be used to make trend projections. When both trend and seasonal influences are significant, we showed how to isolate the effects of the two factors and prepare better forecasts. Finally, regression analysis was described as a procedure for developing so-called causal forecasting models. A causal forecasting model is one that relates the time series value (dependent variable) to other independent variables that are believed to explain (cause) the time series behavior.

Qualitative forecasting methods were discussed as approaches that could be used when little or no historical data were available. These methods are also considered most appropriate when the past pattern of the time series is not expected to continue into the future.

It is important to realize that time series analysis and forecasting is a major field in its own right. In this chapter we have just scratched the surface of the field of time series and forecasting methodology.

▼ GLOSSARY

Time series A set of observations measured at successive points in time or over successive periods of time.

Forecast   A projection or prediction of future values of a time series.

Trend   The long-run shift or movement in the time series observable over several periods of data.

Cyclical component   The component of the time series model that results in periodic above-trend and below-trend behavior of the time series lasting more than 1 year.

Seasonal component   The component of the time series model that shows a periodic pattern over 1 year or less.

Irregular component   The component of the time series model that reflects the random variation of the actual time series values beyond what can be explained by the trend, cyclical, and seasonal components.

Moving averages   A method of forecasting or smoothing a time series by averaging each successive group of data points. The moving averages method can be used to isolate the seasonal component of the time series.

Mean squared error (MSE)   One approach to measuring the accuracy of a forecasting model. This measure is the average of the sum of the squared differences between the forecasted values and the actual time series values.

Weighted moving averages   A method of forecasting or smoothing a time series by computing a weighted average of past data values. The sum of the weights must equal 1.

Exponential smoothing   A forecasting technique that uses a weighted average of past time series values in order to arrive at smoothed time series values that can be used as forecasts.

Smoothing constant   A parameter of the exponential smoothing model that provides the weight given to the most recent time series value in the calculation of the forecast.

Multiplicative time series model   A model that assumes that the separate components of the time series can be multiplied together to identify the actual time series value. When the 4 components of trend, cyclical, seasonal, and irregular are assumed present, we obtain $Y_t = T_t \times C_t \times S_t \times I_t$. When cyclical effects are not modeled, we obtain $Y_t = T_t \times S_t \times I_t$.

Deseasonalized time series   A time series that has had the effect of season removed by dividing each original time series observation by the corresponding seasonal index.

Causal forecasting methods   Forecasting methods that relate a time series to other variables that are believed to explain or cause its behavior.

Autoregressive model   A time series model that uses a regression relationship based on past time series values to predict the future time series values.

Delphi approach   A qualitative forecasting method that obtains forecasts through "group consensus."

Scenario writing   A qualitative forecasting method that consists of developing a conceptual scenario of the future based on a well-defined set of assumptions.

▼ PROBLEMS

1. Corporate Triple A Bond interest rates for 12 consecutive months are shown below.

    9.5   9.3   9.4   9.6   9.8   9.7   9.8   10.5   9.9   9.7   9.6   9.6

   a. Develop 3-month and 4-month moving averages for this time series. Does the 3-month or 4-month moving average provide the better forecasts? Explain.
   b. What is the moving average forecast for the next month?

2. Refer to the gasoline sales time series data in Table 16.1.
   a. Compute 4-week and 5-week moving averages for the time series.
   b. Compute the MSE for the 4-week and 5-week moving average forecasts.
   c. What appears to be the best number of weeks of past data to use in the moving average computation? Remember that the MSE for the 3-week moving average is 10.22.

3. Refer again to the gasoline sales time series data in Table 16.1.
   a. Using a weight of $\frac{1}{2}$ for the most recent observation, $\frac{1}{3}$ for the second most recent, and $\frac{1}{6}$ for third most recent, compute a 3-week weighted moving average for the time series.
   b. Compute the MSE for the weighted moving average in part (a). Do you prefer this weighted moving average to the unweighted moving average? Remember that the MSE for the unweighted moving average is 10.22.
   c. Suppose you are allowed to choose any weights as long as they sum to 1. Could you always find a set of weights that would make the MSE smaller for a weighted moving average than for an unweighted moving average? Why or why not?

4. Use the gasoline time series data from Table 16.1 to show the exponential smoothing forecasts using $\alpha = 0.1$. Using the mean squared error criterion, would you prefer a smoothing constant of $\alpha = 0.1$ or $\alpha = 0.2$ for the gasoline sales time series?

5. Data below show the monthly percentages of all shipments that were received on time over the past 12 months.

   80   82   84   83   83   84   85   84   82   83   84   83

   a. Compare a 3-month moving average forecast with an exponential smoothing forecast using $\alpha = 0.2$. Which provides the better forecasts?
   b. What is the forecast for next month?

6. Using a smoothing constant of $\alpha = 0.2$, equation (16.2) shows that the forecast for the 13th week of the gasoline sales data from Table 16.1 is given by $F_{13} = 0.2Y_{12} + 0.8F_{12}$. However, the forecast for week 12 is given by $F_{12} = 0.2Y_{11} + 0.8F_{11}$. Thus, we could combine these two results to show that the forecast for the 13th week can be written

   $$F_{13} = 0.2Y_{12} + 0.8(0.2Y_{11} + 0.8F_{11}) = 0.2Y_{12} + 0.16Y_{11} + 0.64F_{11}$$

   a. Making use of the fact that $F_{11} = 0.2Y_{10} + 0.8F_{10}$ (and similarly for F_{10} and F_9), continue to expand the expression for F_{13} until it is written in terms of the past data values Y_{12}, Y_{11}, Y_{10}, Y_9, and Y_8, and the forecast for period 8.
   b. Refer to the coefficients or weights for the past data values Y_{12}, Y_{11}, Y_{10}, Y_9, and Y_8; what observation do you make about how exponential smoothing weights past data values in arriving at new forecasts? Compare this weighting pattern with the weighting pattern of the moving averages method.

7. Alabama building contracts for a 12-month period are shown below. Data are in millions of dollars.

   240   350   230   260   280   320   220   310   240   310   240   230

   a. Compare a 3-month moving average forecast with an exponential smoothing forecast using $\alpha = 0.2$. Which provides the better forecasts?
   b. What is the forecast for the next month?

8. The following time series shows the sales of a particular product over the past 12 months:

Month	Sales
1	105
2	135
3	120
4	105
5	90
6	120
7	145
8	140
9	100
10	80
11	100
12	110

a. Use $\alpha = 0.3$ to compute the exponential smoothing values for the time series.

b. Use a smoothing constant of 0.5 to compute the exponential smoothing values. Does a smoothing constant of 0.3 or 0.5 appear to provide the better forecasts?

9. The Dow Jones Industrial Average is based on common stock prices of 30 industrial stocks. This average is used to describe what is happening in the stock market. The weekly closing levels of the Dow Jones average for 12 weeks during 1989 are shown below.

Week	Dow Jones	Week	Dow Jones
1	2480	7	2520
2	2470	8	2470
3	2475	9	2440
4	2510	10	2480
5	2500	11	2530
6	2480	12	2550

a. Compute the exponential smoothing forecasts using $\alpha = 0.2$.

b. Compute the exponential smoothing forecasts using $\alpha = 0.3$.

c. Which exponential smoothing model provides the better forecasts? What is the forecast of the Dow Jones Industrial Average for week 13?

10. The number of component parts used in a production process during the last 10 weeks are shown below.

Week	Parts	Week	Parts
1	200	6	210
2	350	7	280
3	250	8	350
4	360	9	290
5	250	10	320

Using a smoothing constant of 0.25, develop the exponential smoothing values for this time series. Indicate your forecast for week 11.

11. A chain of grocery stores experienced the following weekly demand (cases) for a particular brand of automatic-dishwasher detergent:

Week	Demand	Week	Demand
1	22	6	24
2	18	7	20
3	23	8	19
4	21	9	18
5	17	10	21

Use exponential smoothing with $\alpha = 0.2$ in order to develop a forecast for week 11.

12. United Dairies, Inc., supplies milk to several independent grocers throughout Dade County, Fla. The management of United Dairies would like to develop a forecast of the number of half-gallons of milk sold per week. Sales data for the past 12 weeks are as follows:

Week	Sales (Units)	Week	Sales (Units)
1	2750	7	3300
2	3100	8	3100
3	3250	9	2950
4	2800	10	3000
5	2900	11	3200
6	3050	12	3150

Using exponential smoothing with $\alpha = 0.4$, develop a forecast of demand for week 13.

13. Ten weeks of data on the Commodity Futures Index are shown below.

   7.35   7.40   7.55   7.56   7.60   7.52   7.52   7.70   7.62   7.55

   a. Compute the exponential smoothing forecasts using $\alpha = 0.2$.
   b. Compute the exponential smoothing forecasts using $\alpha = 0.3$.
   c. Which exponential smoothing model provides the better forecasts? What is the forecast for week 11?

14. The enrollment data for a state college for the past 6 years are shown below.

Year	Enrollment
1	20,500
2	20,200
3	19,500
4	19,000
5	19,100
6	18,800

Develop the equation for the linear trend component for this time series. Comment on what is happening to enrollment at this institution.

15. The time series for the retail price index of consumer goods and services over a nine-year period is shown below.

Year	Price Index
1	66.9
2	74.8
3	81.2
4	85.0
5	89.2
6	94.6
7	97.8
8	101.9
9	106.9

Use trend projection to forecast the retail price index for years 10 and 11.

16. Average attendance figures at home football games for a major university show the following pattern for the past 7 years:

Year	Attendance
1	28,000
2	30,000
3	31,500
4	30,400
5	30,500
6	32,200
7	30,800

Develop the equation for the linear trend component [equation (16.4)] for this time series.

17. Automobile sales at B. J. Scott Motors, Inc., provided the following 10-year time series:

Year	Sales
1	400
2	390
3	320
4	340
5	270
6	260
7	300
8	320
9	340
10	370

Plot the time series, and comment on the appropriateness of a linear trend. What type of functional form do you believe would be most appropriate for the trend pattern of this time series?

18. The president of a small manufacturing firm has been concerned about the continual growth in manufacturing costs over the past several years. Shown below is a time series of the cost per unit for the firm's leading product over the past 8 years.

Year	Cost/Unit ($)
1	20.00
2	24.50
3	28.20
4	27.50
5	26.60
6	30.00
7	31.00
8	36.00

a. Show a graph of this time series. Does a linear trend appear to exist?
b. Develop the equation for the linear trend component for the above time series. What is the average cost increase that the firm has been realizing per year?

19. Earnings per share for the Walgreen Company for a 10-year period are as follows:

.84   .73   .94   1.14   1.33   1.53   1.67   1.68   2.10   2.50

a. Use a linear trend projection to forecast this time series for the coming year.
b. What does this time series analysis tell you about the Walgreen Company? Do the historical data indicate the Walgreen Company is a good investment?

20. The gross revenue data for Delta Airlines for a ten-year period are shown below. Data are in millions of dollars.

Year	Revenue
1	2428
2	2951
3	3533
4	3618
5	3616
6	4264
7	4738
8	4460
9	5318
10	6915

a. Develop a linear trend expression for this time series. Comment on what the expression tells about the gross revenue for Delta Airlines for the 10-year period.
b. Provide the forecasts of gross revenue for years 11 and 12.

21. The vacancy rate for office rentals is reported in terms of the percentage of available offices that are not rented. Office vacancy rates for downtown Philadelphia over an eight-year period are shown below.

Year	Vacancy Rate
1	5.9
2	4.6
3	6.4
4	9.5
5	9.2
6	9.5
7	10.8
8	11.0

   a. Develop a linear trend for this time series.

   b. Provide forecasts of the vacancy rate for years 9, 10, and 11.

   c. Should city planners be concerned with the forecasts of office vacancy? What conclusion should be reached, and what possible actions should the city planners consider?

22. Canton Supplies, Inc., is a service firm that employs approximately 100 individuals. Because of the necessity of meeting monthly cash obligations, the management of Canton Supplies would like to develop a forecast of monthly cash requirements. Because of a recent change in operating policy, only the past 7 months of data were considered to be relevant. Use the historical data shown below to develop a forecast of cash requirements for each of the next 2 months using trend projection.

Month	1	2	3	4	5	6	7
Cash Required ($1000s)	205	212	218	224	230	240	246

23. Data below show the time series of the most recent quarterly capital expenditures in billions of dollars for the 1000 largest manufacturing firms.

    24   25   23   24   22   26   28   31   29   32   37   42

   a. Develop a linear trend expression for the above time series.

   b. Show a graph of the time series and the linear trend expression.

   c. Using the time series, what appears to be happening to the capital expenditures? What is the forecast 1 year or 4 quarters into the future?

24. The Costello Music Company has been in business for 5 years. During this time the sale of electric organs has grown from 12 units in the first year to 76 units in the most recent year. Fred Costello, the firm's owner, would like to develop a forecast of organ sales for the coming year. The historical data are shown below.

Year	1	2	3	4	5
Sales	12	28	34	50	76

a. Show a graph of this time series. Does a linear trend appear to exist?

b. Develop the equation for the linear trend component for the above time series. What is the average increase in sales that the firm has been realizing per year?

25. Hudson Marine has been an authorized dealer for C&D marine radios for the past 7 years. The number of radios sold each year is shown below.

Year	1	2	3	4	5	6	7
Number Sold	35	50	75	90	105	110	130

a. Show a graph of this time series. Does a linear trend appear to exist?

b. Develop the equation for the linear trend component for the above time series.

c. Use the linear trend developed in part (b) to prepare a forecast for annual sales in year 8.

26. Aggregate personal income data by month are as follows:

January	3.92	July	4.05
February	3.96	August	4.08
March	4.00	September	4.10
April	4.01	October	4.12
May	4.02	November	4.18
June	4.04	December	4.22

a. Develop a linear trend expression for the above time series. What was happening to aggregate personal income during the year?

b. Provide estimates of aggregate personal income for the first 6 months of the coming year.

c. Assume in June of the coming year, the actual level of aggregate personal income turned out to be 4.41. Comment on the forecasting error based on your trend projection.

27. The quarterly sales data (number of copies sold) for a college textbook over the past 3 years are as follows:

Quarter	Year 1	Year 2	Year 3
1	1690	1800	1850
2	940	900	1100
3	2625	2900	2930
4	2500	2360	2615

a. Show the 4-quarter moving average values for this time series. Plot both the original time series and the moving averages on the same graph.

b. Compute seasonal indexes for the 4 quarters.

c. When does the textbook publisher experience the largest seasonal index? Does this appear reasonable? Explain.

28. Identify the monthly seasonal indexes for the following 3 years of expenses for a 6-unit apartment house in southern Florida. Use a 12-month moving average calculation.

Month	Year 1	Year 2	Year 3
January	170	180	195
February	180	205	210
March	205	215	230
April	230	245	280
May	240	265	290
June	315	330	390
July	360	400	420
August	290	335	330
September	240	260	290
October	240	270	295
November	230	255	280
December	195	220	250

29. Air pollution control specialists in southern California monitor the amount of ozone, carbon dioxide, and nitrogen dioxide in the air on an hourly basis. The hourly time series data exhibit seasonality, with the levels of pollutants showing similar patterns over the hours in the day. On July 15, 16, and 17 the observed levels of nitrogen dioxide in a city's downtown area for the 12 hours from 6:00 A.M. to 6:00 P.M. were as follows:

July 15:	25	28	35	50	60	60	40	35	30	25	25	20
July 16:	28	30	35	48	60	65	50	40	35	25	20	20
July 17:	35	42	45	70	72	75	60	45	40	25	25	25

a. Identify the hourly seasonal factors for the 12-hour daily readings.

b. Using the seasonal factors from part (a), the data were deseasonalized; the trend equation developed for the deseasonalized data was $T_t = 32.983 + 0.3922t$. Using the trend component only, develop forecasts for the 12 hours for July 18.

c. Use the seasonal factors from part (a) to adjust the trend forecasts developed in part (b).

30. Refer to problem 25. Suppose the quarterly sales values for the 7 years of historical data are as follows:

Year	Quarter 1	Quarter 2	Quarter 3	Quarter 4	Total Sales
1	6	15	10	4	35
2	10	18	15	7	50
3	14	26	23	12	75
4	19	28	25	18	90
5	22	34	28	21	105
6	24	36	30	20	110
7	28	40	35	27	130

a. Show the 4-quarter moving average values for this time series. Plot both the original time series and the moving averages on the same graph.

b. Compute the seasonal indexes for the 4 quarters.

c. When does Hudson Marine experience the largest seasonal effect? Does this seem reasonable? Explain.

31. Consider the Costello Music Company scenario presented in problem 24. The quarterly sales data are shown below.

Year	Quarter 1	Quarter 2	Quarter 3	Quarter 4	Total Yearly Sales
1	4	2	1	5	12
2	6	4	4	14	28
3	10	3	5	16	34
4	12	9	7	22	50
5	18	10	13	35	76

a. Compute the seasonal indexes for the 4 quarters.

b. When does Costello Music experience the largest seasonal effect? Does this appear reasonable? Explain.

32. Refer to the Hudson Marine data presented in problem 30.

a. Deseasonalize the data, and use the deseasonalized time series to identify the trend.

b. Use the results of part (a) to develop a quarterly forecast for next year based on trend.

c. Use the seasonal indexes developed in problem 30 to adjust the forecasts developed in part (b) to account for the effect of season.

33. Consider the Costello Music Company time series presented in problem 31.

a. Deseasonalize the data, and use the deseasonalized time series to identify the trend.

b. Use the results of part (a) to develop a quarterly forecast for next year based on trend.

c. Use the seasonal indexes developed in problem 31 to adjust the forecasts developed in part (b) to account for the effect of season.

▼ CASE PROBLEM

Forecasting Sales

The Vintage Restaurant is located on Captiva Island, a resort community located near Fort Meyers, Fla. The restaurant, which is owned and operated by Karen Payne, has just completed its third year of operation. During this period of time, Karen has sought to establish a reputation for the restaurant as a high-quality dining establishment that specializes in fresh seafood. The efforts made by Karen and her staff have proved successful, and her restaurant has become one of the best and fastest-growing restaurants on the island.

Karen has concluded that in order to plan better for the growth of the restaurant in the future, it is necessary to develop a system that will enable her to forecast food and beverage sales by month for up to 1 year in advance. Karen has available data on the total food and beverage sales that were realized during the previous 3 years of operation. These data are provided below.

Food and Beverage Sales for the Vintage Restaurant ($1000s)

Month	First Year	Second Year	Third Year
January	242	263	282
February	235	238	255
March	232	247	265
April	178	193	205
May	184	193	210
June	140	149	160
July	145	157	166
August	152	161	174
September	110	122	126
October	130	130	148
November	152	167	173
December	206	230	235

MANAGERIAL REPORT

Perform an analysis of the sales data for the Vintage Restaurant. Prepare a report for Karen that summarizes your findings, forecasts, and recommendations. Include information on the following:

1. A graph of the time series.
2. An analysis of the seasonality of the data. Include the seasonal indexes for each month, and comment on the high seasonal and low seasonal sales months. Do the seasonal indexes make intuitive sense? Discuss.
3. Forecast sales for January through December of the fourth year.
4. Assume that January sales for the fourth year turned out to be $295,000. What was your forecast error? If this is a large error, Karen may be puzzled as to why there is such a difference between your forecast and the actual sales value. What can you do to resolve her uncertainty in the forecasting procedure?
5. Develop recommendations as to when the system that you have developed should be updated to account for new sales data that will occur.
6. Include any detailed calculations of your analysis in the appendix of your report.

The Cincinnati Gas & Electric Company*

Cincinnati, Ohio

The Cincinnati Gas Light and Coke Company was chartered by the state of Ohio on April 3, 1837. Under this charter the company manufactured gas by distillation of coal and sold it for lighting purposes. During the last quarter of the 19th century the company successfully marketed gas for lighting, heating, and cooking and as fuel for gas engines.

In 1901 the Cincinnati Gas Light and Coke Company and the Cincinnati Electric Light Company merged to form The Cincinnati Gas & Electric Company (CG&E). This new company was able to shift from manufactured gas to natural gas and adopt the rapidly emerging technologies in generating and distributing electricity. CG&E operated as a subsidiary of the Columbia Gas Electric Company from 1909 until 1944.

Today CG&E is a privately owned public utility serving approximately 370,000 gas customers and 600,000 electric customers. The company's service area covers approximately 3000 square miles in and around the Greater Cincinnati area.

FORECASTING AT CG&E

As in any modern company, forecasting at CG&E is an integral part of operating and managing the business. Depending on the decision to be made, the forecasting techniques used range from judgment and graphical trend projections to sophisticated multiple regression models.

Forecasting in the utility industry offers some unique perspectives as compared to other industries. Since there are no finished-goods or in-process inventories of electricity, this product must be generated to meet the instantaneous requirements of the customers. Electrical shortages are not just lost sales, but ''brownouts'' or ''blackouts.'' This situation places an unusual burden on the utility forecaster. On the positive side, the demand for energy and the sale of energy are more predictable than for many other products. Also, unlike the situation in a multiproduct firm, a great amount of forecasting effort and expertise can be concentrated on the two products: gas and electricity.

FORECASTING ELECTRIC ENERGY AND PEAK LOADS

The two types of forecasts discussed in this section are the long-range forecasts of electric peak load and electric energy. The largest observed electric demand for any

*The authors are indebted to Dr. Richard Evans, The Cincinnati Gas & Electric Company, Cincinnati, Ohio, for providing this application.

given period, such as an hour, a day, a month, or a year, is defined as the peak load. The cumulative amount of energy generated and used over the period of an hour is referred to as electric energy.

Until the mid-1970s the seasonal patterns of both electric energy and electric peak load were very regular; the time series for both of these exhibited a fairly steady exponential growth. Business cycles had little noticeable effect on either. Perhaps the most serious shift in the behavior of these time series came from the increasing installation of air conditioning units in the Greater Cincinnati area. This fact caused an accelerated growth in the trend component and also in the relative magnitude of the summer peaks. Nevertheless, the two time series were very regular and generally quite predictable.

Trend projection was the most popular method used to forecast electric energy and electric peak load. The forecast accuracy was quite acceptable and even enviable when compared to forecast errors experienced in other industries.

A NEW ERA IN FORECASTING

In the mid-1970s a variety of actions by the government, the off-and-on energy shortages, and price signals to the consumer began to affect the consumption of electric energy. As a result the behavior of the peak load and electric energy time series became more and more unpredictable. Hence, a simple trend projection forecasting model was no longer adequate. As a result, a special forecasting model—referred to as an econometric model—was developed by CG&E to better account for the behavior of these time series.

The purpose of the econometric model is to forecast the annual energy consumption by residential, commercial, and industrial classes of service. These forecasts are then used to develop forecasts of summer and winter peak loads. First, energy consumption in the industrial and commercial classes is forecast. For an assumed level of economic activity, the projection of electric energy is made along with a forecast of employment in the area. The employment forecast is converted to a forecast of adult population through the use of unemployment rates and labor force participation rates. Household forecasts are then developed through the use of demographic statistics on the average number of persons per household. The resulting forecast of households is used as an indicator of residential customers.

At this point a comparison is made with the demographic projections for the area population. The differences between the residential customers forecast and the population forecast are reconciled to produce the final forecast of residential customers. This forecast becomes the principal independent variable in forecasting residential electric energy.

Summer and winter peak loads are then forecast by applying class peak contribution factors to the energy forecasts. The contributions that each class makes toward the peak are summed to establish the peak forecast.

A number of economic and demographic time series are used in the construction of the above econometric model. Simply speaking, the entire forecasting system is a compilation of several statistically verified multiple regression equations.

IMPACT AND VALUE OF THE FORECASTS

The forecast of the annual electric peak load guides the timing decisions for constructing future generating units. The financial impact of these decisions is great. For example, the last generating unit built by the company cost nearly $600 million, and the interest rate on a recent first mortgage bond was 16%. At this rate, annual interest costs would be nearly $100 million. Obviously, a timing decision that leads to having the unit available no sooner than necessary is crucial.

The energy forecasts are important in other ways also. For example, purchases of coal and nuclear fuel for the generating units are based on the forecast levels of energy needed. The revenue from the electric operations of the company is determined from forecasted sales, which in turn enters into the planning of rate changes and external financing. These planning and decision-making processes are among the most important management activities in the company. It is imperative that the decision makers have the best forecast information available to assist them in arriving at these decisions.

Questions

1. Describe some of the unique perspectives associated with forecasting in the utility industry as compared with other industries.
2. Until the mid-1970s what type of forecasting procedure was used by CG&E? What necessitated a change?
3. Briefly describe CG&E's current approach to forecasting.
4. What are the benefits of accurate forecasts for CG&E?

Markov Processes

Markov process models are useful in studying the evolution of certain systems over repeated trials. The repeated trials are often successive time periods where the state or outcome of the system in any particular time period cannot be determined with certainty. Rather, transition probabilities are used to describe the manner in which the system makes transitions from one period to the next. Hence, we talk about the probability of the system being in a particular state at a given time period.

Markov processes have been used to describe the probability that a machine that is functioning in one period will continue to function or will break down in the next period. They have also been used to describe the probability that a consumer purchasing brand *A* in one period will purchase brand *B* in the next period. In this chapter we will study a marketing application that involves an analysis of the store-switching behavior of supermarket customers. As a second illustration we will consider an accounting application that is concerned with the transitioning of accounts receivable dollars to different aging categories.

Since an in-depth treatment of Markov processes is beyond the scope of this text, the analysis in both illustrations will be restricted to situations in which there are a finite number of states, the transition probabilities remain constant over time, and the probability of being in a particular state at any one time period depends only on the state of the process in the immediately preceding period. Such Markov processes are referred to as Markov chains with stationary transition probabilities.

17.1 ▼ MARKET SHARE ANALYSIS

Suppose that we are interested in analyzing the market share and customer loyalty for Murphy's Foodliner and Ashley's Supermarket, the only two grocery stores in a small town. We focus on the sequence of shopping trips of one customer. We assume that the customer makes one shopping trip each week to either Murphy's Foodliner or Ashley's Supermarket, but not both.

Using the terminology of Markov processes, we refer to the weekly time periods or shopping trips as the *trials of the process*. Thus, at each trial the customer will shop at

737

either Murphy's Foodliner or Ashley's Supermarket. The particular store selected in a given week is referred to as the *state of the system* in that time period. Since the customer has two shopping alternatives at each trial, we say the system has two states. Since the number of states is finite, we can list and identify each state in detail. The two possible states are:

State 1 The customer shops at Murphy's Foodliner
State 2 The customer shops at Ashley's Supermarket

If we say the system is in state 1 at trial 3, we are simply saying that the customer shops at Murphy's during the third weekly shopping period.

As we continue the shopping trip process into the future, we cannot say for certain where the customer will shop during a given week or trial. In fact, we realize that during any given week, the customer may be either a Murphy's customer or an Ashley's customer. However, using a Markov process model we will be able to compute the probability that the customer shops at each store during any time period. For example, we may find there is a 0.6 probability that the customer will shop at Ashley's during a particular week and a 0.4 probability that the customer will shop at Murphy's.

In order to determine the probabilities of the various states occurring at successive trials of the Markov process, we need information on the probability that a customer remains with the same store or switches to the competing store as the process continues from trial to trial or week to week.

Suppose as part of a market research study we collect data from 100 shoppers over a 10-week period. Suppose further that these data show each customer's weekly shopping-trip pattern in terms of the sequence of visits to Murphy's and Ashley's. In order to develop a Markov process model for the sequence of weekly shopping trips, we need to express the probability of selecting each store (state) in a given time period solely in terms of the store (state) that was selected during the previous time period. In reviewing the data, suppose we find that out of all customers who shopped at Murphy's in a given week, 90% shopped at Murphy's the following week while 10% switched to Ashley's. Suppose that similar data for the customers who shopped at Ashley's in a given week show that 80% shopped at Ashley's the following week while 20% switched to Murphy's. Probabilities based on these data are shown in Table 17.1. Since these are the probabilities that a customer moves, or makes a transition, from a state in a given period to a state in the following period, these probabilities are called *transition probabilities*.

An important property of the table of transition probabilities is that the sum of the entries in each row is 1; this indicates that each row of the table provides a probability distribution. For example, a customer who shops at Murphy's one week must shop at either Murphy's or Ashley's the next week. The entries in row 1 give the probabilities associated with each of these events. The 0.9 and 0.8 probabilities in Table 17.1 can be

TABLE 17.1
Transition Probabilities for Murphy's and Ashley's Grocery Stores

		Next Weekly Shopping Period	
		Murphy's Foodliner	*Ashley's Supermarket*
Current Weekly	*Murphy's Foodliner*	0.9	0.1
Shopping Period	*Ashley's Supermarket*	0.2	0.8

interpreted as measures of store loyalty in that they indicate the probability of a repeat visit to the same store. Similarly, the 0.1 and 0.2 probabilities are measures of the store-switching characteristics of the customers.

It is important to realize that in developing a Markov process model for the problem, we are assuming that the transition probabilities will be the same for any customer and that the transition probabilities will not change over time.

Note that the table of transition probabilities, Table 17.1, has one row and one column for each state of the system. We will use the symbol p_{ij} to represent the individual transition probabilities and the symbol P to represent the matrix of transition probabilities; that is,

$$p_{ij} = \text{probability of making a transition from state } i \text{ in a given time}$$
$$\text{period to state } j \text{ in the next time period}$$

For the supermarket problem we have

$$P = \begin{bmatrix} p_{11} & p_{12} \\ p_{21} & p_{22} \end{bmatrix} = \begin{bmatrix} 0.9 & 0.1 \\ 0.2 & 0.8 \end{bmatrix}$$

Using the matrix of transition probabilities, we can now determine the probability that a customer will be a Murphy's or an Ashley's customer at some time period in the future. Let us begin by assuming that we have a customer whose last weekly shopping trip was to Murphy's. What is the probability that this customer will shop at Murphy's on the next weekly shopping trip, time period 1? In other words, what is the probability that the system will be in state 1 after the first transition? The matrix of transition probabilities indicates that this probability is $p_{11} = 0.9$.

Now let us consider the state of the system in period 2. A useful way of depicting what can happen on the second weekly shopping trip is to draw a tree diagram of the possible outcomes (see Figure 17.1). Using this tree diagram, we see that the probability that the customer shops at Murphy's during both the first and the second weeks is $(0.9)(0.9) = 0.81$. Also, note that the probability of the customer switching to Ashley's on the first trip and then switching back to Murphy's on the second trip is $(0.1)(0.2) = 0.02$. Since these are the only two ways that the customer can be in state 1 (shopping at Murphy's) during the second period, the probability of the system being in state 1 during the second period is $0.81 + 0.02 = 0.83$. Similarly, the probability of the system being in state 2 during the second period is $0.09 + 0.08 = 0.17$.

As desirable as the tree diagram approach may be from an intuitive point of view, this approach becomes very cumbersome when we want to extend the analysis to three, four, or more periods into the future. Fortunately, there is an easier way to calculate the probabilities of the system being in state 1 or state 2 for any subsequent period. First, we introduce notation that will allow us to represent the probability of the system being in state 1 or state 2 for any given period of time. Let

$$\pi_i(n) = \text{probability that the system is in state } i \text{ in period n}$$

Index denotes the state

Denotes the time period or number of transitions

For example, $\pi_1(1)$ would represent the probability of the system being in state 1 in period 1 (that is, after 1 transition), while $\pi_2(1)$ denotes the probability of the system being in state 2 after one transition. Since $\pi_i(n)$ is the probability that the system is in state i in period n, this probability is referred to as a *state probability*.

FIGURE 17.1
Tree Diagram Depicting Two Weekly Shopping Trips of a Customer Who Shopped Last at Murphy's

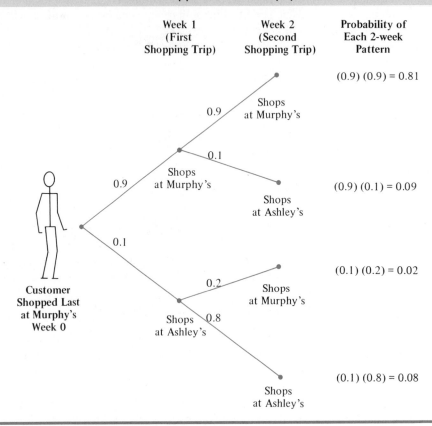

| Week 1 (First Shopping Trip) | Week 2 (Second Shopping Trip) | Probability of Each 2-week Pattern |

$(0.9)(0.9) = 0.81$

$(0.9)(0.1) = 0.09$

$(0.1)(0.2) = 0.02$

$(0.1)(0.8) = 0.08$

$\pi_1(0)$ and $\pi_2(0)$ will denote the probability of the system being in state 1 or state 2 at some initial or starting time period. Period or week 0 represents the most recent time period, when we are beginning the analysis of a Markov process. If we set $\pi_1(0) = 1$ and $\pi_2(0) = 0$, we are saying that as an initial condition the customer shopped last week at Murphy's; alternatively, if we set $\pi_1(0) = 0$ and $\pi_2(0) = 1$, we would be starting the system with a customer who shopped last week at Ashley's. In the tree diagram of Figure 17.1 we considered the situation where the customer shopped last at Murphy's. Thus,

$$[\pi_1(0) \quad \pi_2(0)] = [1 \quad 0]$$

is a vector that represents the initial state probabilities of the system. In general, we use the notation

$$\Pi(n) = [\pi_1(n) \quad \pi_2(n)]$$

to denote the vector of state probabilities for the system in period n. In our example, $\Pi(1)$ is a vector representing the state probabilities for the first week, $\Pi(2)$ is a vector representing the state probabilities for the second week, and so on.

Using this notation, we can find the state probabilities for period $n + 1$ by simply multiplying the known state probabilities for period n by the transition probability matrix. Using the vector of state probabilities and the matrix of transition probabilities, the multiplication[1] can be expressed as follows:

$$\Pi(\text{next period}) = \Pi(\text{current period})P$$

or

$$\Pi(n + 1) = \Pi(n)P \tag{17.1}$$

Beginning with the system in state 1 at period 0, we have $\Pi(0) = [1 \ 0]$. We can compute the state probabilities for period 1 as follows:

$$\Pi(1) = \Pi(0)P$$

or

$$[\pi_1(1) \quad \pi_2(1)] = [\pi_1(0) \quad \pi_2(0)] \begin{bmatrix} p_{11} & p_{12} \\ p_{21} & p_{22} \end{bmatrix}$$

$$= [1 \quad 0] \begin{bmatrix} 0.9 & 0.1 \\ 0.2 & 0.8 \end{bmatrix}$$

$$= [0.9 \quad 0.1]$$

The state probabilities $\pi_1(1) = 0.9$ and $\pi_2(1) = 0.1$ are the probabilities that a customer who shopped at Murphy's during week 0 will shop at Murphy's or Ashley's during week 1.

Using equation (17.1), we can compute the state probabilities for the second week as follows:

$$\Pi(2) = \Pi(1)P$$

or

$$[\pi_1(2) \ \pi_2(2)] = [\pi_1(1) \ \pi_2(1)] \begin{bmatrix} p_{11} \ p_{12} \\ p_{21} \ p_{22} \end{bmatrix}$$

$$= [0.9 \quad 0.1] \begin{bmatrix} 0.9 & 0.1 \\ 0.2 & 0.8 \end{bmatrix}$$

$$= [0.83 \quad 0.17]$$

We see that the probability of shopping at Murphy's during the second week is 0.83, while the probability of shopping at Ashley's during the second week is 0.17. These same results were previously obtained using the tree diagram of Figure 17.1. By continuing to apply equation (17.1), we can compute the state probabilities for any future time period; that is,

$$\Pi(3) = \Pi(2)P$$
$$\Pi(4) = \Pi(3)P$$
$$\vdots \qquad \vdots$$
$$\Pi(n + 1) = \Pi(n)P$$

---

[1]Appendix E provides the step-by-step procedure for vector and matrix multiplication.

Table 17.2 shows the result of carrying out these calculations for a number of periods in the future.

The vectors $\Pi(1)$, $\Pi(2)$, $\Pi(3)$, . . . contain the probabilities that a customer who started out as a Murphy customer will be in state 1 or state 2 in the first period, the second period, the third period, and so on. In Table 17.2 we see that after a large number of periods these probabilities do not change much from one period to the next. In fact, the probability of the system being in state 1 or state 2 is approaching $2/3$ and $1/3$ after a large number of shopping periods.

If we had started with 1000 Murphy customers—that is, 1000 consumers who last shopped at Murphy's—our analysis indicates that during the fifth subsequent weekly shopping period, 723 would be customers of Murphy's and 277 would be customers of Ashley's. Moreover, after a large number of shopping periods, approximately 667 would be customers of Murphy's and 333 customers of Ashley's.

Now let us repeat the analysis, but this time we will begin the process with a customer who shopped last at Ashley's. Thus,

$$\Pi(0) = [\pi_1(0) \quad \pi_2(0)] = [0 \quad 1]$$

Using equation (17.1), the probability of the system being in state 1 or state 2 in period 1 is given by

$$\Pi(1) = \Pi(0)P$$

or

$$[\pi_1(1) \quad \pi_2(1)] = [\pi_1(0) \quad \pi_2(0)] \begin{bmatrix} p_{11} & p_{12} \\ p_{12} & p_{22} \end{bmatrix}$$

$$= [0 \quad 1] \begin{bmatrix} 0.9 & 0.1 \\ 0.2 & 0.8 \end{bmatrix}$$

$$= [0.2 \quad 0.8]$$

Proceeding as before, we can calculate subsequent state probabilities. Doing so, we obtain the results shown in Table 17.3.

In the fifth shopping period the probability that the customer will be shopping at Murphy's is 0.555, and the probability that the customer will be shopping at Ashley's is 0.445. After a large number of shopping periods the probability of the system being in state 1 approaches $2/3$, and the probability of it being in state 2 approaches $1/3$. These are the same as the probabilities obtained after a large number of transitions when the system started in state 1. Thus, we see that the probability of the system being in a particular state after a large number of periods is independent of the beginning state of the system. The probabilities that we approach after a large number of transitions are referred to as the

TABLE 17.2
State Probabilities for Future Periods Beginning Initially with a Murphy's Customer

State Probability	0	1	2	3	4	5	6	7	8	9	10
$\pi_1(n)$	1	0.9	0.83	0.781	0.747	0.723	0.706	0.694	0.686	0.680	0.676
$\pi_2(n)$	0	0.1	0.17	0.219	0.253	0.277	0.294	0.306	0.314	0.320	0.324

TABLE 17.3
State Probabilities for Future Periods Beginning Initially with an Ashley's Customer

State Probability	Period (n)										
	0	1	2	3	4	5	6	7	8	9	10
$\pi_1(n)$	0	0.2	0.34	0.438	0.507	0.555	0.589	0.612	0.628	0.640	0.648
$\pi_2(n)$	1	0.8	0.66	0.562	0.493	0.445	0.411	0.388	0.372	0.360	0.352

steady-state probabilities. We shall denote the steady-state probability for state 1 with the symbol π_1 and the steady-state probability for state 2 with the symbol π_2. In otherwords, in the steady-state case we simply omit the period designation from $\pi_i(n)$ since it is no longer necessary.

Thus, if we have 1000 customers in the system, the Markov process model tells us that in the long run, with steady-state probabilities $\pi_1 = \frac{2}{3}$ and $\pi_2 = \frac{1}{3}$, $\frac{2}{3}(1000) = 667$ customers would be Murphy's and $\frac{1}{3}(1000) = 333$ customers would be Ashley's. The steady-state probabilities can be interpreted as the market shares for the two stores.

The analysis of Tables 17.2 and 17.3 indicates that as n gets larger, the difference between the state probabilities for the nth shopping period and the $(n + 1)$th period becomes increasingly smaller. This leads us to the conclusion that as n gets extremely large, the state probabilities at the $(n + 1)$th period are very close to those at the nth period. This observation provides the basis for a simple method for computing the steady-state probabilities without having to actually carry out a large number of calculations.

In general, we know from equation (17.1) that

$$[\pi_1(n + 1) \quad \pi_2(n + 1)] = [\pi_1(n) \quad \pi_2(n)] \begin{bmatrix} p_{11} & p_{12} \\ p_{21} & p_{22} \end{bmatrix}$$

Since for sufficiently large n the difference between $\Pi(n + 1)$ and $\Pi(n)$ is negligible, we see that in the steady state $\pi_1(n + 1) = \pi_1(n) = \pi_1$ and $\pi_2(n + 1) = \pi_2(n) = \pi_2$. Thus, we have

$$[\pi_1 \quad \pi_2] = [\pi_1 \quad \pi_2] \begin{bmatrix} p_{11} & p_{12} \\ p_{21} & p_{22} \end{bmatrix}$$

$$= [\pi_1 \quad \pi_2] \begin{bmatrix} 0.9 & 0.1 \\ 0.2 & 0.8 \end{bmatrix}$$

After carrying out the above multiplications we obtain

$$\pi_1 = 0.9\pi_1 + 0.2\pi_2 \qquad (17.2)$$

and

$$\pi_2 = 0.1\pi_1 + 0.8\pi_2 \qquad (17.3)$$

However, we also know that

$$\pi_1 + \pi_2 = 1 \qquad (17.4)$$

since the sum of the probabilities must equal 1.

Using equation (17.4) to solve for π_2 and substituting the result in equation(17.2), we obtain

$$\pi_1 = 0.9\pi_1 + 0.2(1 - \pi_1)$$
$$\pi_1 = 0.9\pi_1 + 0.2 - 0.2\pi_1$$
$$\pi_1 - 0.7\pi_1 = 0.2$$
$$0.3\pi_1 = 0.2$$
$$\pi_1 = \tfrac{2}{3}$$

Then using equation (17.4), we can conclude that $\pi_2 = 1 - \pi_1 = \tfrac{1}{3}$.

Thus, using equations (17.2) and (17.4) we can solve for the steady-state probabilities directly. You can check for yourself that we could have obtained the same result using equations (17.3) and (17.4).[2]

The market share information is often quite valuable in decision-making situations. For example, suppose Ashley's Supermarket is contemplating an advertising campaign to attract more of Murphy's customers to its store. Let us suppose further that Ashley's believes this promotional strategy will increase the probability of a Murphy's customer switching to Ashley's from 0.10 to 0.15. The new transition probabilities that would result are given in Table 17.4.

Given the new transition probabilities, we can use equations (17.2) and (17.4) to solve for the new steady-state probabilities or market shares. Thus, we obtain

$$\pi_1 = 0.85\pi_1 + 0.20\pi_2$$

Substituting $\pi_2 = 1 - \pi_1$ from equation (17.4), we have

$$\pi_1 = 0.85\pi_1 + 0.20(1 - \pi_1)$$
$$\pi_1 = 0.85\pi_1 + 0.20 - 0.20\pi_1$$
$$\pi_1 - 0.65\pi_1 = 0.20$$
$$0.35\pi_1 = 0.20$$
$$\pi_1 = 0.57$$

and

$$\pi_2 = 1 - 0.57 = 0.43$$

TABLE 17.4
New Transition Probabilities for Murphy's and Ashley's Grocery Stores

| | | Next Weekly Shopping Period | |
		Murphy's Foodliner	Ashley's Supermarket
Current Weekly	*Murphy's Foodliner*	0.85	0.15
Shopping Period	*Ashley's Supermarket*	0.20	0.80

[2]Even though equations (17.2) and (17.3) provide two equations and two unknowns, we must include equation (17.4) when solving for π_1 and π_2 to ensure that the sum of steady-state probabilities will equal 1.

Thus, we see that the proposed promotional strategy will increase Ashley's market share from $\pi_2 = 0.33$ to $\pi_2 = 0.43$. Suppose that the total market consists of 6000 customers per week. The new promotional strategy will increase the number of customers doing their weekly shopping at Ashley's from 2000 to 2580. If the average weekly profit per customer is $10, the proposed promotional strategy can be expected to increase Ashley's profits by $5800 per week. Clearly, then, if the cost of the promotional campaign is less than $5800 per week, Ashley should consider such a strategy.

This is one illustration of how a Markov analysis of a firm's market share can be useful in a decision-making situation. Suppose that instead of trying to attract customers from Murphy's Foodliner, Ashley's directed a promotional effort at increasing the loyalty of its own customers. In this case p_{22} would increase, and p_{21} would decrease. Once we knew the amount of the change, we could calculate new steady-state probabilities and compute the impact on profits.

▼ NOTES AND COMMENTS ▼

1. The Markov processes presented in this section have what is called the *memoryless* property: the current state of the system together with the transition probabilities contains all the information necessary to predict the future behavior of the system. The prior states of the system do not have to be considered. Such Markov processes are considered first-order Markov processes. Higher-order Markov processes are ones in which future states of the system depend on two or more previous states.

2. Analysis of a Markov process model is not intended to optimize any particular aspect of a system. Rather, the analysis predicts or describes the future and steady-state behavior of the system. For instance, in the grocery store example, the analysis of the steady-state behavior provided a forecast or prediction of the market shares for the two competitors. In other applications, management scientists have extended the study of Markov processes to what are called *Markov decision processes*. In these models, decisions can be made at each period that affect the transition probabilities and hence influence the future behavior of the system. Markov decision processes have been used in analyzing machine breakdown and maintenance operations, planning the movement of patients in hospitals, developing inspection strategies, determining newspaper subscription duration, and analyzing equipment replacement.

17.2 ▼ ACCOUNTS RECEIVABLE ANALYSIS

Another area in which Markov processes have produced useful results involves the estimation of the allowance for doubtful accounts. This allowance is an estimate of the amount of accounts receivable that will ultimately prove to be uncollectible (that is, bad debts).

Let us consider the accounts receivable situation for Heidman's Department Store. Heidman's has two aging categories for its accounts receivable: (1) accounts that are classified as 0 to 30 days old and (2) accounts that are classified as 31 to 90 days old. If any portion of an account balance exceeds 90 days, that portion is written off as a bad debt. Heidman's follows the procedure of aging the total balance in any customer's account according to the oldest unpaid bill. For example, suppose one customer's account balance on September 30 is as follows:

Date of Purchase		Amount Charged
August 15		$25
September 18		10
September 28		50
	Total	$85

An aging of accounts receivable on September 30 would assign the total balance of $85 to the 31–90-day-old category because the oldest unpaid bill of August 15 is 46 days old. Let us assume that one week later, October 7, the customer pays the August 15 bill of $25. The remaining total balance of $60 would now be placed in the 0–30-day age category since the oldest unpaid amount, corresponding to the September 18 purchase, is less than 31 days old. This method of aging accounts receivable is called the *total balance method* since the total account balance is placed in the age category corresponding to the oldest unpaid amount.

Note that under the total balance method of aging accounts receivable, dollars appearing in a 31–90-day age category at one point in time may appear in a 0–30-day age category at a later point in time. In the above example this was true for $60 of September billings, which shifted from a 31–90-day to a 0–30-day age category after the August bill had been paid.

Let us assume that on December 31 Heidman's shows a total of $3000 in its accounts receivable and that the firm's management would like an estimate of how much of the $3000 will eventually be collected and how much will eventually result in bad debts. The estimated amount of bad debts will appear as an allowance for doubtful accounts in the year-ending financial statements.

Let us see how we can view the accounts receivable operation as a Markov process. First, concentrate on what happens to *one* dollar currently in accounts receivable. As the firm continues to operate into the future, we can consider each week as a trial of a Markov process with a dollar existing in one of the following states of the system:

State 1   Paid category
State 2   Bad debt category
State 3   0–30-day age category
State 4   31–90-day age category

Thus, we can track the week-by-week status of one dollar by using a Markov analysis to identify the state of the system at a particular week or time period in the future.

Using a Markov process model with the above states, we define the transition probabilities as follows:

p_{ij} = probability of a dollar in state i in one week moving to state j in the next week

Based on historical transitions of accounts receivable dollars, the following matrix of transition probabilities, P, has been developed for Heidman's Department Store:

$$P = \begin{bmatrix} p_{11} & p_{12} & p_{13} & p_{14} \\ p_{21} & p_{22} & p_{23} & p_{24} \\ p_{31} & p_{32} & p_{33} & p_{34} \\ p_{41} & p_{42} & p_{43} & p_{44} \end{bmatrix} = \begin{bmatrix} 1 & 0 & 0 & 0 \\ 0 & 1 & 0 & 0 \\ 0.4 & 0 & 0.3 & 0.3 \\ 0.4 & 0.2 & 0.3 & 0.1 \end{bmatrix}$$

Note that the probability of a dollar in the 0–30-day age category (state 3) moving to the paid category (state 1) in the next period is 0.4. Also, there is a 0.3 probability that this dollar will remain in the 0–30-day category (state 3) one week later, while there is a 0.3 probability that it will be in the 31–90-day category (state 4) one week later. Note also that a dollar in a 0–30-day account cannot make the transition to a bad debt (state 2) in one week.

An important property of the Markov process model for Hiedman's accounts receivable situation is the presence of *absorbing states*. For example, once a dollar makes a transition to state 1, the paid state, the probability of making a transition to any other state is zero. Similarly, once a dollar is in state 2, the bad debt state, the probability of a transition to any other state is zero. Thus, once a dollar reaches state 1 or state 2, the system will remain in this state indefinitely. This leads us to conclude that all accounts receivable dollars will eventually be absorbed into either the paid or the bad debt state, and hence the name *absorbing state*.

When a Markov process has absorbing states present, we do not compute steady-state probabilities in the context of the previous section because the process will eventually end up in one of the absorbing states. However, we may be interested in knowing the probability that the dollar will end up in each of the absorbing states. To determine these probabilities, we need to develop the notion of a fundamental matrix.

The Fundamental Matrix and Associated Calculations

In the following discussion we present the appropriate formulas for determining the probability that a dollar starting in state 3 or 4 will end up in each of the absorbing states. The underlying concept in the analysis involves the notion of a *fundamental matrix*. We begin the development of this concept by partitioning the matrix of transition probabilities into four parts; that is, we let

$$P = \begin{bmatrix} 1 & 0 & 0 & 0 \\ 0 & 1 & 0 & 0 \\ \hline 0.4 & 0 & 0.3 & 0.3 \\ 0.4 & 0.2 & 0.3 & 0.1 \end{bmatrix} = \begin{bmatrix} I & O \\ \hline R & Q \end{bmatrix}$$

where

$$I = \begin{bmatrix} 1 & 0 \\ 0 & 1 \end{bmatrix} \qquad O = \begin{bmatrix} 0 & 0 \\ 0 & 0 \end{bmatrix}$$

$$R = \begin{bmatrix} 0.4 & 0 \\ 0.4 & 0.2 \end{bmatrix} \qquad Q = \begin{bmatrix} 0.3 & 0.3 \\ 0.3 & 0.1 \end{bmatrix}$$

A matrix N, called a *fundamental matrix,* can be calculated using the following formula:

$$N = (I - Q)^{-1} \qquad\qquad (17.5)$$

The superscript -1 is used to indicate the inverse of the matrix $(I - Q)$. In Appendix E we present formulas for finding the inverse of a matrix with two rows and two columns. In the current problem,

$$I - Q = \begin{bmatrix} 1 & 0 \\ 0 & 1 \end{bmatrix} - \begin{bmatrix} 0.3 & 0.3 \\ 0.3 & 0.1 \end{bmatrix}$$

$$= \begin{bmatrix} 0.7 & -0.3 \\ -0.3 & 0.9 \end{bmatrix}$$

and (see Appendix E)

$$N = (I - Q)^{-1} = \begin{bmatrix} 1.67 & 0.56 \\ 0.56 & 1.30 \end{bmatrix}$$

If we multiply the fundamental matrix N times the R portion of the P matrix, we obtain the probabilities that accounts receivable dollars initially in states 3 or 4 will eventually reach each of the absorbing states. The multiplication of N times R for the Heidman's Department Store problem is shown below (see Appendix E for the steps of this matrix multiplication):

$$NR = \begin{bmatrix} 1.67 & 0.56 \\ 0.56 & 1.30 \end{bmatrix} \begin{bmatrix} 0.4 & 0 \\ 0.4 & 0.2 \end{bmatrix} = \begin{bmatrix} 0.89 & 0.11 \\ 0.74 & 0.26 \end{bmatrix}$$

The first row of the product NR is the probability that a dollar in the 0–30 age category will end up in each of the absorbing states. Thus, we see that there is a 0.89 probability that a dollar in the 0–30-day-old category will eventually be paid and a 0.11 probability that it will become a bad debt. Similarly, the second row shows the probabilities associated with a dollar in the 31–90-day category; that is, a dollar in the 31–90-day category has a 0.74 probability of eventually being paid and a 0.26 probability of proving to be uncollectible. Using this information we can predict the amount of money that will be paid and the amount that will be lost as bad debts.

Establishing the Allowance for Doubtful Accounts

Let B represent a two-element vector that contains the current accounts receivable balances in the 0–30-day and the 31–90-day age categories; that is,

$$B = [b_1 \quad b_2]$$

| Total dollars in the 0–30-day category | Total dollars in the 31–90-day category |

Suppose that the December 31 balance of accounts receivable for Heidman's shows $1000 in the 0–30-day category (state 3) and $2000 in the 31–90-day category (state 4).

$$B = [1000 \quad 2000]$$

We can multiply B times NR to determine how much of the $3000 will be collected and how much will be lost. For example

$$BNR = [1000 \quad 2000] \begin{bmatrix} 0.89 & 0.11 \\ 0.74 & 0.26 \end{bmatrix}$$

$$= [2370 \quad 630]$$

Thus, we see that $2370 of the accounts receivable balances will be collected and $630 will have to be written off as a bad debt expense. Based on this analysis, the accounting department of the company would set up an allowance for doubtful accounts of $630.

The matrix multiplication of BNR is simply a convenient way of computing the eventual collections and bad debts of the accounts receivable. Recall that the NR matrix showed a 0.89 probability of collecting dollars in the 0–30-day category and a 0.74 probability of collecting dollars in the 31–90-day category. Thus, as was shown by the BNR calculation, we expect to collect a total of $0.89(1000) + 0.74(2000) = 890 + 1480 = \$2370$.

Suppose that on the basis of the previous analysis Heidman's would like to investigate the possibility of reducing the amount of bad debts. Recall that our analysis indicated that a 0.11 probability or 11% of the dollars in the 0–30-day age category and 26% of the amount in the 31–90-day age category will prove to be uncollectible. Let us assume that Heidman's is considering instituting a new credit policy involving a discount for prompt payment.

Management believes that the policy under consideration will increase the probability of a transition from the 0–30-day age category to the paid category and decrease the probability of a transition from the 0–30-day to the 31–90-day age category. Let us assume that a careful study of the effects of this new policy leads management to conclude that the following transition matrix would be applicable:

$$P = \begin{bmatrix} 1 & 0 & | & 0 & 0 \\ 0 & 1 & | & 0 & 0 \\ - & - & - & - & - \\ 0.6 & 0 & | & 0.3 & 0.1 \\ 0.4 & 0.2 & | & 0.3 & 0.1 \end{bmatrix}$$

We see that the probability of a dollar in the 0–30-day age category making a transition to the paid category in the next period has increased to 0.6 and that the probability of a dollar in the 0–30-day age category making a transition to the 31–90-day category has decreased to 0.1. To determine the effect of these changes on bad debt expense we must calculate N, NR, and BNR. We begin by using equation (17.5) to calculate the fundamental matrix N:

$$N = (I - Q)^{-1} = \left\{ \begin{bmatrix} 1 & 0 \\ 0 & 1 \end{bmatrix} - \begin{bmatrix} 0.3 & 0.1 \\ 0.3 & 0.1 \end{bmatrix} \right\}^{-1}$$

$$= \begin{bmatrix} 0.7 & -0.1 \\ -0.3 & 0.9 \end{bmatrix}^{-1}$$

$$= \begin{bmatrix} 1.5 & 0.17 \\ 0.5 & 1.17 \end{bmatrix}$$

By multiplying N times R we obtain the new probabilities that the dollars in each age category will end up in the two absorbing states:

$$NR = \begin{bmatrix} 1.5 & 0.17 \\ 0.5 & 1.17 \end{bmatrix} \begin{bmatrix} 0.6 & 0 \\ 0.4 & 0.2 \end{bmatrix}$$

$$= \begin{bmatrix} 0.97 & 0.03 \\ 0.77 & 0.23 \end{bmatrix}$$

We see that with the new credit policy we would expect only 3% of the funds in the 0–30-day age category and 23% of the funds in the 31–90-day age category to prove to be uncollectible. If, as before, we assume that there is a current balance of $1000 in the 0–30-day age category and $2000 in the 31–90-day age category, we can calculate the total amount of accounts receivable that will end up in the two absorbing states by multiplying B times NR. We obtain

$$BNR = \begin{bmatrix} 1000 & 2000 \end{bmatrix} \begin{bmatrix} 0.97 & 0.03 \\ 0.77 & 0.23 \end{bmatrix}$$

$$= \begin{bmatrix} 2510 & 490 \end{bmatrix}$$

Under the previous credit policy we found the bad debt expense to be $630. Thus, a savings of $630 − 490 = $140 could be expected as a result of the new credit policy. Given our total accounts receivable balance of $3000, this is a 4.7% reduction in bad debt expense. After considering the costs involved, management can evaluate the economics of adopting the new credit policy. If the cost, including discounts, is less than 4.7% of the accounts receivable balance, we would expect the new policy to lead to increased profits for Heidman's Department Store.

▼ SUMMARY

In this chapter we have presented Markov process models as well as examples of their application. We saw that a Markov analysis could provide helpful decision-making information about a process or situation that involved a sequence of repeated trials with a number of possible outcomes or states on each trial. A primary objective was obtaining information about the probability of each state occurring a certain number of transitions or time periods in the future.

A market share application showed the computational procedure for determining the steady-state probabilities that could be interpreted as market shares for two competing supermarkets. In an accounts receivable application of Markov processes we introduced the notion of absorbing states; the two absorbing states were the bad debt and paid categories, and we showed how to determine the percentage of accounts receivable balances that would be absorbed in each of these states.

▼ GLOSSARY

Trials of the process The events that trigger transitions of the system from one state to another. In many applications, successive time periods represent the trials of the process.

State of the system The condition of the system at any particular trial or time period.

Transition probability Given the system is in state i during one period, the transition probability p_{ij} is the probability that the system will be in state j during the next period.

State probability The probability that the system will be in any particular state. [$\pi_i(n)$ is the probability of the system being in state i in period n.]

Steady-state probability The probability that the system will be in any particular state after a large number of transitions. Once steady state has been reached, the state probabilities do not change from period to period.

Absorbing state A state is said to be absorbing if the probability of making a transition out of that state is zero. Thus, once the system has made a transition into an absorbing state, it will remain there forever.

Fundamental matrix A matrix necessary for the computation of probabilities associated with absorbing states of a Markov process.

▼ PROBLEMS

1. In the market share analysis of Section 17.1 suppose that we are considering the Markov process associated with the shopping trips of one customer, but we do not know where the customer shopped during the last week. Thus, we might make the assumption that there is a 0.5 probability that the customer shopped at Murphy's and a 0.5 probability that the customer shopped at Ashley's at time period 0; that is, $\pi_1(0) = 0.5$ and $\pi_2(0) = 0.5$. Given these initial state probabilities, develop a table similar to Table 17.2 showing the probability of each state in future periods. What do you observe about the long-run probabilities of each state?

2. Management of the New Fangled Softdrink Company believes that the probability of a customer purchasing Red-Rot Pop or the company's major competition, Super Cola, is based on the customer's most recent purchase. Suppose the following transition probabilities are appropriate:

		To	
		Red-Rot Pop	Super Cola
From	Red-Rot Pop	0.9	0.1
	Super Cola	0.1	0.9

a. Show the 2-period tree diagram for a customer who last purchased Red-Rot Pop. What is the probability that this customer purchases Red-Rot Pop on the second purchase?

b. What is the long-run market share for each of these two products?

c. A major advertising campaign is being planned to increase the probability of attracting Super Cola customers. Management believes that the new campaign will increase the probability of a customer switching from Super Cola to Red-Rot Pop to 0.15. What is the projected effect of the advertising campaign on the market shares?

3. The computer center at Rockbottom University has been experiencing substantial periods of computer down time. Let us assume that the trials of an associated Markov process are defined to be 1-hour periods and that the probability of the system being

in a running state or a down state is based on the state of the system in the previous period. Historical data show the following transition probabilities:

		To	
		Running	Down
From	Running	0.90	0.10
	Down	0.30	0.70

a. If the system is initially running, what is the probability of the system being down in the next hour of operation?

b. What are the steady-state probabilities of the system being in the running state and in the down state?

4. In problem 3 one cause of the down time problem was traced to a specific piece of computer hardware. Management believes that switching to a different hardware component will result in the following transition probability matrix:

		To	
		Running	Down
From	Running	0.95	0.05
	Down	0.60	0.40

a. What are the steady-state probabilities of the system being in the running and down states?

b. If the cost of the system being down for any period is estimated to be $500 (including lost profits for time down and maintenance), what is the breakeven cost for the new hardware component on a time-period basis?

5. A major traffic problem in the greater Cincinnati area involves traffic attempting to cross the Ohio River from Cincinnati to Kentucky using Interstate I-75. Let us assume that the probability of no traffic delay in one period, given no traffic delay in the preceding period, is 0.85 and that the probability of finding a traffic delay in one period, given a delay in the preceding period, is 0.75. Traffic will be classified as having either a delay or a no-delay state, and the time period will be considered to be 30 minutes.

a. Assuming you are a motorist entering the traffic system and receive a radio report of a traffic delay, what is the probability that for the next 60 minutes (2 time periods) the system will be in the delay state? Note that this is the probability of being in the delay state for 2 consecutive periods.

b. What is the probability that in the long run the traffic will not be in the delay state?

c. An important assumption of the Markov process models presented in this chapter has been the constant or stationary transition probabilities as the system operates in the future. Do you believe this assumption is appropriate in the above traffic problem? Explain.

6. The purchase patterns of two brands of toothpaste can be expressed as a Markov process with the following transition probabilities:

		To	
		Special B	MDA
From	Special B	0.90	0.10
	MDA	0.05	0.95

a. Which brand appears to have the most loyal customers? Explain.

b. What are the projected market shares for the two brands?

7. Suppose that in problem 6 a new toothpaste brand enters the market such that the following transition probabilities exist:

		To		
		Special B	MDA	T-White
From	Special B	0.80	0.10	0.10
	MDA	0.05	0.75	0.20
	T-White	0.40	0.30	0.30

What are the new long-run market shares? Which brand will suffer most from the introduction of the new brand of toothpaste? Note that solving for the steady-state probabilities for this problem requires the solution of three equations and three unknowns.

8. Given the following transition matrix with states 1 and 2 as absorbing states, what is the probability that units in state 3 and state 4 end up in each of the absorbing states?

$$P = \begin{bmatrix} 1 & 0 & 0 & 0 \\ 0 & 1 & 0 & 0 \\ 0.2 & 0.1 & 0.4 & 0.3 \\ 0.2 & 0.2 & 0.1 & 0.5 \end{bmatrix}$$

9. In the Heidman's Department Store problem of Section 17.2, suppose the following transition matrix is appropriate:

$$P = \begin{bmatrix} 1 & 0 & 0 & 0 \\ 0 & 1 & 0 & 0 \\ 0.5 & 0 & 0.25 & 0.25 \\ 0.5 & 0.2 & 0.05 & 0.25 \end{bmatrix}$$

If Heidman's has $4000 in the 0–30-day age category and $5000 in the 31–90-day age category, what is your estimate of the amount of bad debts the company will experience?

10. The KLM Christmas Tree Farm owns a plot of land with 5000 evergreen trees. Each year KLM allows retailers of Christmas trees to select and cut trees for sale to individual customers. KLM protects small trees (usually less than 4 feet tall) so that they will grow and be available for sale in future years. Currently 1500 trees are classified as protected trees, while the remaining 3500 are available for cutting. However, even though a tree is available for cutting in a given year, it may not be selected for cutting until future years. While most trees not cut in a given year live until the next year, some trees die during the year and are lost.

In viewing the KLM Christmas tree operation as a Markov process with yearly time periods, we define the following four states:

State 1 Cut and sold

State 2 Lost to disease

State 3 Too small for cutting

State 4 Available for cutting but not cut and sold

The following transition matrix is appropriate:

$$P = \begin{bmatrix} 1 & 0 & 0 & 0 \\ 0 & 1 & 0 & 0 \\ 0.1 & 0.2 & 0.5 & 0.2 \\ 0.4 & 0.1 & 0 & 0.5 \end{bmatrix}$$

How many of the farm's 5000 trees will be sold eventually, and how many will be lost?

U.S. General Accounting Office*
Washington, D.C.

The U.S. General Accounting Office (GAO) is an independent, nonpolitical audit organization in the legislative branch of the federal government. The GAO was created by the Budget and Accounting Act of 1921 and has three basic purposes:

1. To assist Congress, its committees, and its members in carrying out their legislative and oversight responsibilities, consistent with its role as an independent, nonpolitical agency.
2. To audit and evaluate the programs, activities, and financial operations of federal departments and agencies and to make recommendations toward more efficient and effective operations.
3. To carry out financial control and other functions with respect to federal government programs and operations including accounting, legal, and claims settlement work.

GAO evaluators, the main occupation in the GAO, determine the effectiveness of existing or proposed federal programs and the efficiency, economy, legality, and effectiveness with which federal agencies carry out their responsibilities. These evaluations culminate in reports to the Congress and to the heads of federal departments and agencies. Such reports typically include recommendations to Congress concerning the need for enabling or remedial legislation and suggestions to agencies concerning the need for changes in programs or operations to improve their economy, efficiency, and effectiveness.

GAO evaluators analyze policies and practices and the use of resources within and among federal programs, identify problem areas and deficiencies in meeting program goals, develop and analyze alternative solutions to problems of program execution, and develop and recommend changes to enable the programs to better conform to congressional goals and legislative intent. To effectively carry out their duties, evaluators must be proficient in interviewing, data processing, records review, legislative research, management science, and statistical analysis techniques.

IMPACT OF SERVICES ON THE WELL-BEING OF OLDER PEOPLE

GAO evaluators obtained data from a random sample of noninstitutionalized persons aged 65 and older living in Cleveland, Ohio. The health conditions of the sampled individuals in the 65- to 69-year-old groups were defined by the following three states:

*The authors are indebted to Bill Ammann, U.S. General Accounting Office, Washington, D.C., for providing this application.

Best. Individual able to perform 13 identified activities of daily living without help.
Next best. Individual able to perform the same 13 activities, but required help for at least one activity.
Worst. Individual unable to perform the same 13 activities even with help.

Using a 2-year period of time, GAO evaluators developed estimates of the year-to-year transition probabilities for individuals in the 65- to 69-year-old group. These estimates were then used to develop a transition probability matrix such as that shown in Table 17.5. Note that a death state has been added as an absorbing state.

TABLE 17.5
Transition Probability Matrix for the Health Condition of Individuals 65 to 69 Years Old

		Following Year Condition			
		Best	Next Best	Worst	Death
Current	Best	p_{11}	p_{12}	p_{13}	p_{14}
Year	Next Best	p_{21}	p_{22}	p_{23}	p_{24}
Condition	Worst	p_{31}	p_{32}	p_{33}	p_{34}
	Death	0	0	0	1

Using the transition probabilities, a Markov process analysis can be used to determine the state probabilities for any number of periods (years) into the future. To verify the appropriateness of the Markov process model, GAO evaluators used the transition probabilities to determine the state probabilities for the 65- to 69-year-old age group 5 years into the future. The resulting state probabilities were compared with the health states of individuals in a known 70- to 74-year-old age group. There was no statistically significant difference between the probabilities provided by the model and the actual state probabilities of the 70- to 74-year-old group.

ESTIMATING THE LIKELY EFFECTS OF HEALTH CARE PROGRAMS

The individuals in the original study were subdivided into two groups: those receiving all appropriate health care and those not receiving all appropriate health care. For the purpose of the study, a person was classified as receiving all appropriate health care if the person was taking medication and/or treatment for each illness present and if the person was receiving the help necessary to perform each of the 13 specific activities of daily living that could not be performed without help. As a result, GAO evaluators developed two matrices of transition probabilities: one for individuals receiving all appropriate health care and one for individuals not receiving all appropriate health care.

For any individuals not receiving all appropriate help, the kind of additional help needed was determined, and the cost of that help was estimated. Then those persons were artificially aged over time using the transition probabilities in order to establish the likely benefits in terms of improved health states for the individuals. Over a 20-year period of time, there was shown to be a net savings for the health care program provided all other factors remained equal. That is, the increased cost to provide sufficient appropriate help to all persons was eventually offset by individuals either improving their health state or by not spending as much time in a worse state. Although benefits of health care are often proclaimed theoretically, the Markov process model provided evidence that indicated benefits would be achieved with the health care program.

This type of Markov analysis was also conducted for economic, social, and life view status as well as for the health status. In some instances the Markov model showed that additional help and/or programs did not result in net savings over time.

Questions

1. Suppose the transition probabilities in Table 17.5 were as follows:

$$
\begin{bmatrix}
0.80 & 0.10 & 0.06 & 0.04 \\
0.05 & 0.75 & 0.15 & 0.05 \\
0.00 & 0.05 & 0.75 & 0.20 \\
0 & 0 & 0 & 1
\end{bmatrix}
$$

Assume a particular city has 1000 individuals in the best state, 2000 in the next best state, and 500 in the worst state. Estimate how many of each of these individuals will be in each state 2 years from now.

2. How might health care programs affect the matrix of transition probabilities in (1) above? What effect would you expect to see in the distribution of individuals across the 4 states 2 years from now?

Dynamic Programming

Dynamic programming is an approach to problem solving that permits decomposing one large mathematical model that may be very difficult to solve into a number of smaller problems that are usually much easier to solve. Moreover, the dynamic programming approach allows us to break up a large problem in such a fashion that once all the smaller problems have been solved, we are left with an optimal solution to the large problem. We shall see that each of the smaller problems created is identified with a *stage* of the dynamic programming solution procedure. As a consequence, the technique has been applied to many decision problems that are multistage in nature. Often the multiple stages are created by the fact that a sequence of decisions must be made over time. For example, a problem of determining an optimal decision over a 1-year time horizon might be broken into 12 smaller stages, where each stage requires an optimal decision over a 1-month time horizon. In most cases each of these smaller problems cannot be considered to be completely independent of the others, and this is where the dynamic programming approach is helpful. Let us begin by discovering how to solve a shortest-route problem using a dynamic programming approach.

18.1 ▼ A SHORTEST-ROUTE PROBLEM

In Chapter 9 we studied a labeling algorithm for solving the shortest-route problem. Let us now illustrate the dynamic programming approach by using it to solve a shortest-route problem. Consider the network presented in Figure 18.1. Assuming that the numbers above each arc denote the direct distance in miles between two nodes, find the shortest route from node 1 to node 10.

Before attempting to solve this problem, let us note an important characteristic of shortest-route problems. This characteristic is actually a restatement of Richard Bellman's famous *principle of optimality* as it applies to the shortest-route problem:[1]

---

[1]See S. Dreyfus, *Dynamic Programming and the Calculus of Variations* (New York: Academic Press, 1965).

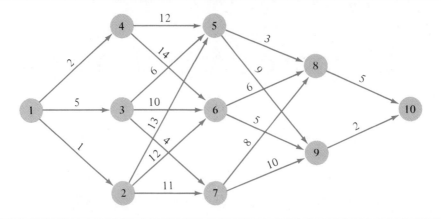

FIGURE 18.1
Network for the Shortest-Route Problem

The Principle of Optimality
If a particular node is on the optimal route, then the shortest path from that node to the end is also on the optimal route.

The dynamic programming approach to this problem essentially involves treating each node as if it were on the optimal route and making calculations accordingly. In doing so, we work backward; that is, we start at the terminal node, node 10, and work backward, calculating the shortest route from each node to node 10 until we reach the origin, node 1. Then we will have solved the original problem of finding the shortest route from node 1 to node 10.

As we stated in the introduction to this chapter, the dynamic programming approach decomposes the original problem into a number of smaller problems that are much easier to solve. In the shortest-route problem for the network in Figure 18.1 the smaller problems that we will create define a four-stage dynamic programming problem. The first stage begins with nodes that are exactly one arc away from the destination and ends at the destination node. Note from Figure 18.1 that only nodes 8 and 9 are exactly one arc away from node 10. The second stage begins with all nodes that are exactly two arcs away from the destination and ends with all nodes that are exactly one arc away. Hence, in dynamic programming terminology nodes 5, 6, and 7 would be considered the input nodes for stage 2 and nodes 8 and 9 would be considered the output nodes for stage 2. The output nodes for stage 2 are the input nodes for stage 1. The input nodes for the third-stage problem are those that are exactly three arcs away from the destination—that is, nodes 2, 3, and 4. The output nodes, all of which are one arc closer to the destination, are nodes 5, 6, and 7. Finally, the input to stage 4 is node 1, and the output nodes are 2, 3, and 4. The decision problem we shall want to solve at each stage is to determine which arc it is best to travel over in moving from each particular input node to an output node. Let us consider the stage 1 problem.

We arbitrarily begin the stage 1 calculations with node 9. Since there is only one way to travel from node 9 to node 10, this is obviously the shortest route and requires us to travel a distance of 2 miles. Similarly, there is only one path from node 8 to node 10. The shortest route from node 8 to the end is thus the length of that route, or 5 miles. The stage 1 decision problem is solved. For each input node we have identified an optimal decision—that is, the best arc to travel over to reach the output node. The stage 1 results are summarized below.

	Stage 1	
Input Node	Arc Decision	Shortest Distance to Node 10 (miles)
8	8–10	5
9	9–10	2

To begin the solution to the stage 2 problem, we move to node 7. (We could have selected node 5 or 6; the order of the nodes selected at any stage is arbitrary.) There are two arcs that leave node 7 and are connected to input nodes for stage 1. These are arc 7–8, which has a length of 8, and arc 7–9, which has a length of 10. If we select arc 7–8, we will have a distance from node 7 to node 10 that is 8 (that is, the length of arc 7–8) plus the shortest distance to node 10 from node 8. Thus, the decision to select arc 7–8 has a total associated distance of $8 + 5 = 13$. With a distance of 10 for arc 7–9 and stage 1 results showing a distance of 2 from node 9 to node 10, the decision to select arc 7–9 has an associated distance of $10 + 2 = 12$. Thus, given we are at node 7, we should select arc 7–9 since it is on the path that will reach node 10 in the shortest distance (12 miles). By performing similar calculations for nodes 5 and 6, we can generate the following stage 2 results:

	Stage 2		
Input Node	Arc Decision	Output Node	Shortest Distance to Node 10 (miles)
5	5–8	8	8
6	6–9	9	7
7	7–9	9	12

In Figure 18.2 the number in the square by each node considered so far indicates the length of the shortest route from that node to the end. We have completed the solution to the first two subproblems (stages 1 and 2). We now know the shortest route from nodes 5, 6, and 7 to node 10.

To begin the third stage, let us start with node 2. To find the shortest route from node 2 to node 10, we must make three calculations because we have three arcs that connect node 2 to stage 2 input nodes. If we select arc 2–7 and then follow the shortest route to the end, we will travel $11 + 12 = 23$ miles. Similarly, selecting arc 2–6 requires $12 + 7 = 19$ miles, and selecting arc 2–5 requires $13 + 8 = 21$ miles. Thus, the shortest route from node 2 to node 10 is 19 miles, which indicates that arc 2–6 is the best decision, given that we are at node 2. Similarly, we find that the shortest route from node 3 to node 10 is given by min $\{4 + 12, 10 + 7, 6 + 8\} = 14$; the shortest route from node 4 to node

FIGURE 18.2
Intermediate Solution to the Shortest-Route Problem Using Dynamic Programming

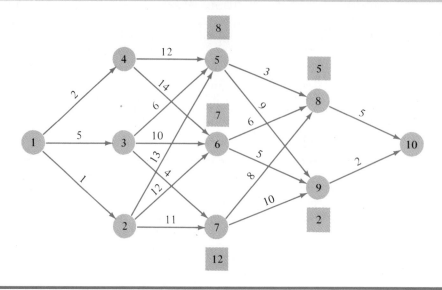

10 is given by min {14 + 7, 12 + 8} = 20. This completes the stage 3 calculations. The results are summarized below.

Stage 3

Input Node	Arc Decision	Output Node	Shortest Distance to Node 10 (miles)
2	2–6	6	19
3	3–5	5	14
4	4–5	5	20

In solving the stage 4 subproblem we find that the shortest route from node 1 to node 10 is given by min {1 + 19, 5 + 14, 2 + 20} = 19. Thus, the optimal decision at stage 4 is to select arc 1–3. By moving through the network from stage 4 to stage 3 to stage 2 to stage 1, we can identify the best decision at each stage and therefore the shortest route from node 1 to node 10. This is as follows:

Stage	Arc Decision
4	1– 3
3	3– 5
2	5– 8
1	8–10

Thus, the shortest route is through nodes $1-3-5-8-10$ with a distance of $5 + 6 + 3 + 5 = 19$ miles.

Note how the calculations at each successive stage made use of the calculations at prior stages. This characteristic is an important part of the dynamic programming procedure. Figure 18.3 illustrates the final network calculations. Note that we have now determined the shortest route from every node to node 10.

The dynamic programming approach, while enumerating or evaluating several paths at each stage, did not require us to enumerate all possible paths from node 1 to node 10. Returning to the stage 4 calculations, we considered three alternatives for leaving node 1. The complete route associated with each of these alternatives is presented below.

Arc Alternatives at Node 1	Complete Path to Node 10	Distance (miles)	
1–2	1–2–6–9–10	20	
1–3	1–3–5–8–10	19	◄————— Selected as best
1–4	1–4–5–8–10	22	

However, when you realize that there are a total of 16 alternate routes from node 1 to node 10, you can see that dynamic programming has provided substantial computational savings over a total enumeration of all possible solutions.

The fact that we did not have to evaluate all the paths at each stage as we moved backward from node 10 to node 1 is illustrative of the power of dynamic programming. Using dynamic programming, we need only make a small fraction of the number of calculations that would be required using total enumeration. If our example network had been larger, the computational savings provided by dynamic programming would have been even greater.

FIGURE 18.3
Final Solution to the Shortest-Route Problem Using Dynamic Programming

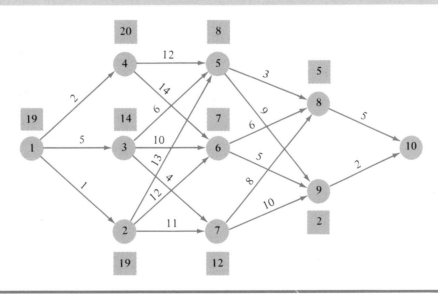

18.2 ▼ DYNAMIC PROGRAMMING NOTATION

Perhaps one of the most difficult aspects of learning how to apply dynamic programming involves understanding the notation used to develop the approach. The notation we will use is the same as that used by Nemhauser[2] and is fairly standard.

The *stages* of a dynamic programming solution procedure are formed by decomposing the original problem into a number of subproblems. Associated with each subproblem is a stage in the dynamic programming solution procedure. For example, the shortest-route problem introduced in the preceding section was solved using a four-stage dynamic programming solution procedure. We had four stages because we decomposed the original problem into the following four subproblems:

1. **Stage 1 Problem:** Where should we go from nodes 8 and 9 so that we will reach node 10 along the shortest route?
2. **Stage 2 Problem:** Using the results of stage 1, where should we go from nodes 5, 6, and 7 so that we will reach node 10 along the shortest route?
3. **Stage 3 Problem:** Using the results of stage 2, where should we go from nodes 2, 3, and 4 so that we will reach node 10 along the shortest route?
4. **Stage 4 Problem:** Using the results of stage 3, where should we go from node 1 so that we will reach node 10 along the shortest route?

Let us look closely at what occurs at the stage 2 problem. Consider the following representation of this stage:

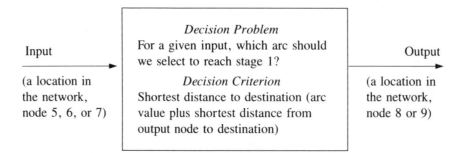

Using dynamic programming notation, we define

x_2 = input to stage 2. x_2 represents the location in the network at the beginning of stage 2 (node 5, 6, or 7). Note that the input to stage 2 is the output of stage 3.

d_2 = decision variable at stage 2. This represents the arc selected to move to stage 1.

x_1 = output for stage 2. This will be the node we reach (node 8 or 9) after considering the input x_2 and the decision d_2. This will also be the input to stage 1.

Using this notation the stage 2 problem can be partially represented as follows:

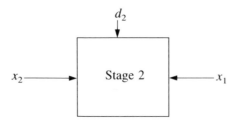

[2]See G. L. Nemhauser, *Introduction to Dynamic Programming* (New York: Wiley, 1966).

Recall that in the dynamic programming approach to the shortest-route problem we worked backward through the stages, beginning at node 10. When we reached stage 2 we did not know x_2 because the stage 3 problem had not yet been solved. The approach used was to consider *all* alternatives for the input x_2. Then we determined the best decision d_2 for each of the inputs x_2. Later, when we moved forward through the system to recover the optimal sequence of decisions, we saw that the stage 3 decision provided a specific x_2, node 5, and from our previous analysis we knew the best decision (d_2) to make as we continued on to stage 1.

Let us consider a general dynamic programming problem with N stages and adopt the following general notation:

$$x_n = \text{input to stage } n \text{ (output from stage } n + 1)$$
$$d_n = \text{decision at stage } n$$

The general N-stage problem is decomposed as follows:

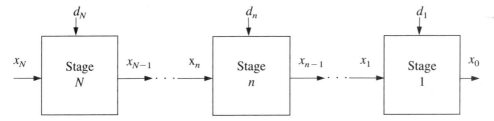

The four-stage shortest-route problem can be represented as follows:

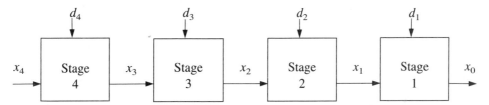

The values of the input and output variables x_4, x_3, x_2, x_1, and x_0 are important because they couple the four subproblems together. At any stage we will ultimately need to know the input x_n in order to make the best decision d_n. These x_n variables can be thought of as defining the *state* or condition of the system as we move from stage to stage. Accordingly, these variables are referred to as the *state variables* of the problem. In the shortest-route problem, the state variables represented the location in the network at each stage (that is, a particular node).

At stage 2 of the shortest-route problem we considered the input x_2 and made the decision d_2 that would provide the shortest distance to the destination. The output x_1 was based on a combination of the input and the decision; that is, x_1 was a function of x_2 and d_2. In dynamic programming notation we could write

$$x_1 = t_2(x_2, d_2)$$

where $t_2(x_2, d_2)$ is the function at stage 2 that determines the stage 2 output.

Since $t_2(x_2, d_2)$ is the function that "transforms" the input to the stage into the output, this function is referred to as the *stage transformation function*. The general expression for this function is

$$x_{n-1} = t_n(x_n, d_n) \qquad\qquad (18.1)$$

The mathematical form of the stage transformation function is dependent on the particular dynamic programming problem. In the shortest-route problem, the transformation function was based on a tabular type of calculation. For example, Table 18.1 shows the stage transformation function $t_2(x_2, d_2)$ for stage 2. The possible values of d_2 are the arcs selected in the body of the table.

Each stage also has a return associated with it. In the shortest-route problem the return was the arc distance traveled in moving from an input node to an output node. For example, if node 7 were the input state for stage 2 and we selected arc 7–9 as d_2, the return for that stage would be the arc length, 10 miles. The return at a stage, which may be thought of as the payoff or value for a stage, is represented by the general notation $r_n(x_n, d_n)$.

Using the stage transformation function and the *return function,* our shortest-route problem can be shown as follows.

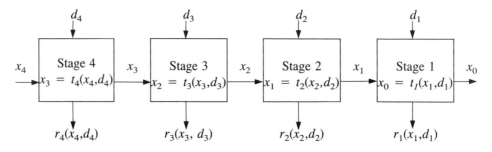

If we view a system or a process as consisting of N stages, we can represent a dynamic programming formulation schematically as follows:

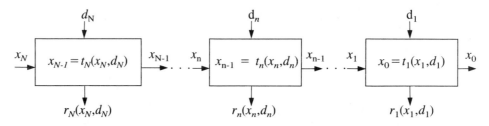

Each of the squares in the diagram represents a stage in the process. As indicated, there are two inputs to each stage: the state variable and the decision variable. There are also two outputs: a new value for the state variable and a return for the stage. The new value

TABLE 18.1
Table Showing Output Node Corresponding to Each Input Node and Decision, $x_1 = t_2(x_2, d_2)$

	x_1	Output State	
x_2		8	9
Input State	5	5–8	5–9
	6	6–8	6–9
	7	7–8	7–9

for the state variable is determined as a function of the inputs using $t_n(x_n, d_n)$. The value of the return for a stage is also determined as a function of the inputs using $r_n(x_n, d_n)$.

In addition we will use the notation $f_n(x_n)$ to represent the optimal total return from stage n and all remaining stages, given an input of x_n to stage n. For example, in the shortest-route problem $f_2(x_2)$ represents the optimal total return (that is, the minimum distance) from stage 2 and all remaining stages, given an input of x_2 to stage 2. Thus, we see from Figure 18.3 that $f_2(x_2 = \text{node } 5) = 8$, $f_2(x_2 = \text{node } 6) = 7$, and $f_2(x_2 = \text{node } 7) = 12$. These are just the values in the squares at nodes 5, 6, and 7.

▼ NOTES AND COMMENTS ▼

1. The primary advantage of dynamic programming is its "divide and conquer" solution strategy. Using dynamic programming, a large, complex problem can be divided into a sequence of smaller interrelated problems. By solving the smaller problems sequentially, the optimal solution to the larger problem is found. Dynamic programming is a general approach to problem solving; it is not a specific technique such as linear programming which can be applied in the same fashion to a variety of problems. Although there are some common characteristics of all dynamic programming problems, each application requires some degree of creativity, insight, and expertise to recognize how the larger problems can be broken into a sequence of interrelated smaller problems.
2. Dynamic programming has been applied to a wide variety of problems including inventory control, production scheduling, capital budgeting, resource allocation, equipment replacement, and maintenance. In many of these applications, time periods such as days, weeks, months, and so on provide the sequence of interrelated stages for the larger multiperiod problem.

18.3 ▼ THE KNAPSACK PROBLEM

The knapsack problem is often encountered in dynamic programming applications. The basic idea is that there are N different types of items that can be put into a knapsack. Each item has a certain weight associated with it as well as a value. The problem is to determine how many units of each item to place in the knapsack in order to maximize the total value. A constraint is placed on the maximum weight permissible.

Consider a manager of a manufacturing operation who must make a biweekly selection of jobs to process during the following 2-week period. A list of the jobs waiting to be processed at the beginning of the current week is presented in Table 18.2. The estimated time required for completion and the value rating associated with each category of job are also shown in the table.

The value rating assigned to each job is a subjective score assigned by the supervisor. A scale from 1 to 20 is used to measure the value of each job, where 1 represents jobs of the least value, and 20 represents jobs of most value. The value of a job depends on such things as expected profit, length of time the job has been waiting to be processed, priority, and so on. In this situation we would like to make a selection of jobs to process during the next 2 weeks such that all the jobs selected can be processed within 10 days and that the total value of the jobs selected is maximized. In knapsack problem terminology we are in essence selecting the best jobs for our 2-week knapsack, where the knapsack has a

TABLE 18.2
Job Data for the Manufacturing Operation

Job	Number of Jobs to Be Processed	Estimated Completion Time per Job (days)	Value Rating
Category 1	4	1	2
Category 2	3	3	8
Category 3	2	4	11
Category 4	2	7	20

capacity equal to the 10-day production capacity. Let us formulate and solve this problem using a dynamic programming solution procedure.

This problem can be formulated as a dynamic programming problem involving four stages. At stage 1 we must decide how many jobs from category 1 to process, at stage 2 we must decide how many jobs from category 2 to process, and so on. Thus, we let d_n denote the number of jobs in category n selected (that is, the decision variable at stage n). The state variable x_n is defined as the number of days of processing time remaining when we reach stage n.

Thus, with a 2-week production period, $x_4 = 10$ represents the total number of days that are available for processing jobs. The stage transformation functions are then defined so that

$$Stage\ 4:\quad x_3 = t_4(x_4,d_4) = x_4 - 7d_4$$
$$Stage\ 3:\quad x_2 = t_3(x_3,d_3) = x_3 - 4d_3$$
$$Stage\ 2:\quad x_1 = t_2(x_2,d_2) = x_2 - 3d_2$$
$$Stage\ 1:\quad x_0 = t_1(x_1,d_1) = x_1 - 1d_1$$

The return at each stage is based on the value rating of the jobs and the number of jobs selected at each stage. The return functions are as follows:

$$Stage\ 4:\quad r_4(x_4,d_4) = 20d_4$$
$$Stage\ 3:\quad r_3(x_3,d_3) = 11d_3$$
$$Stage\ 2:\quad r_2(x_2,d_2) = 8d_2$$
$$Stage\ 1:\quad r_1(x_1,d_1) = 2d_1$$

Figure 18.4 shows a schematic representation of the problem.

As with the shortest-route problem in Section 18.1, we will apply a backward solution procedure; that is, we will begin by considering the stage 1 decision. A restatement of the principle of optimality can be made in terms of this problem. That is, regardless of whatever decisions have been made at previous stages, if the decision at stage n is to be part of an optimal overall strategy, the decision made at stage n must necessarily be optimal for all remaining stages.

Let us set up a table that will help us calculate the optimal decisions for stage 1.

Stage 1   Note that the input to stage 1, x_1, which is the number of days of processing time available at stage 1, is unknown because we have not yet identified the decisions

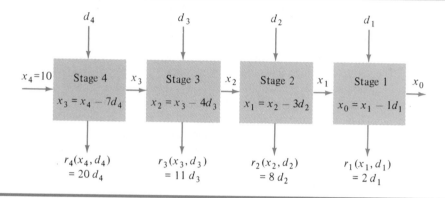

FIGURE 18.4
Schematic Presentation of the Dynamic Programming Formulation of the
Manufacturing Problem

at the previous stages. Therefore, in our analysis at stage 1 we will have to consider all possible values of x_1 and identify the best decision d_1 for each case; $f_1(x_1)$ will be the total return after decision d_1 is made. The possible values of x_1 and the associated d_1 and $f_1(x_1)$ values are as follows:

x_1	d_1^*	$f_1(x_1)$
0	0	0
1	1	2
2	2	4
3	3	6
4	4	8
5	4	8
6	4	8
7	4	8
8	4	8
9	4	8
10	4	8

The d_1^* column gives the optimal values of d_1 corresponding to a particular value of x_1, where x_1 can range from 0 to 10. The specific value of x_1 will depend on how much processing time has been used by the jobs in the other categories selected in stages 2, 3, and 4. Since each stage 1 job requires 1 day of processing time and has a positive return of 2 per job, we always select as many jobs at this stage as possible. The number of category 1 jobs selected will depend on the processing time available, but cannot exceed 4.

Recall that $f_1(x_1)$ represents the value of the optimal total return from stage 1 and all remaining stages, given an input of x_1 to stage 1. Therefore, $f_1(x_1) = 2x_1$ for values of $x_1 \le 4$. Thus, the optimization of stage 1 is accomplished. Let us now move on to stage 2 and carry out the optimization at that stage.

Stage 2 Again we will use a table to help identify the optimal decision. Since the input to stage 2, x_2, is unknown, we have to consider all possible values from 0 to 10. Also we have to consider all possible values of d_2 (that is, 0, 1, 2, or 3). The entries under the heading $r_2(x_2, d_2) + f_1(x_1)$ represent the total return that will be forthcoming from the final two stages, given the input of x_2 and the decision of d_2. For example, if stage 2 were entered with $x_2 = 7$ days of processing time remaining, and if a decision were made to select two jobs from category 2 (that is, $d_2 = 2$), the total return for stages 1 and 2 would be 18.

The return for stage 2 would be $r_2(x_2, d_2) = 8d_2 = 8(2) = 16$, and with $x_2 = 7$ and $d_2 = 2$, we would have $x_1 = x_2 - 3d_2 = 7 - 6 = 1$. From the previous table we see that the optimal return from stage 1 with $x_1 = 1$ is $f_1(1) = 2$. Thus, the total return corresponding to $x_2 = 7$, $d_2 = 2$ is given by $r_2(7, 2) + f_1(1) = 16 + 2 = 18$. Similarly, with $x_2 = 5$, and $d_2 = 1$, we get $r_2(5, 1) + f_1(2) = 8 + 4 = 12$. Note that some combinations of x_2 and d_2 are not

x_2 \ d_2	0	1	2	3	d_2^*	$f_2(x_2)$	$x_1 = t_2(x_2, d_2^*)$ $= x_2 - 3d_2^*$
			$r_2(x_2,d_2) + f_1(x_1)$				
0	⓪	—	—	—	0	0	0
1	②	—	—	—	0	2	1
2	④	—	—	—	0	4	2
3	6	⑧	—	—	1	8	0
4	8	⑩	—	—	1	10	1
5	8	⑫	—	—	1	12	2
6	8	14	⑯	—	2	16	0
7	8	16	⑱	—	2	18	1
8	8	16	⑳	—	2	20	2
9	8	16	22	㉔	3	24	0
10	8	16	24	㉖	3	26	1

feasible. For example, with $x_2 = 2$ days, $d_2 = 1$ is infeasible because category 2 jobs each require 3 days to process. The infeasible solutions are indicated by a dash.

After all the total returns in the rectangle have been calculated, we can determine an optimal decision at this stage for each possible value of the input or state variable x_2. For example, if $x_2 = 9$ there are four possible values we can select for d_2: 0, 1, 2, or 3. Clearly $d_3 = 3$ with a value of 24 yields the maximum total return for the last two stages. Therefore, we record this value in the d_2^* column. For additional emphasis we circle the element inside the rectangle corresponding to the optimal return. The optimal total return, given that we are in state $x_2 = 9$ and must pass through two more stages, is thus 24, and we record this value in the $f_2(x_2)$ column. Given that we enter stage 2 with $x_2 = 9$ and make the optimal decision $d_2^* = 3$, we will enter stage 1 with $x_1 = t_2(9, 3) = x_2 - 3d_2 = 9 - 3(3) = 0$. This value is recorded in the last column in our table. We can now go on to stage 3.

Stage 3 The table we construct here is much the same as for stage 2. The entries under the heading $r_2(x_3, d_3) + f_2(x_2)$ represent the total return over stages 3, 2, and 1 for all possible inputs x_3 and all possible decisions d_3.

x_3 \ d_3	$r_3(x_3, d_3) + f_2(x_2)$			d_3^*	$f_3(x_3)$	$x_2 = t_3(x_3, d_3^*)$ $= x_3 - 4d_3^*$
	0	1	2			
0	⓪	—	—	0	0	0
1	②	—	—	0	2	1
2	④	—	—	0	4	2
3	⑧	—	—	0	8	3
4	10	⑪	—	1	11	0
5	12	⑬	—	1	13	1
6	⑯	15	—	0	16	6
7	18	⑲	—	1	19	3
8	20	21	㉒	2	22	0
9	㉔	23	㉔	0,2	24	9,1
10	26	㉗	26	1	27	6

There are some features of interest in this table that were not present at stage 2. We note that if the state variable $x_3 = 9$, then there are two decisions that will lead to an optimal total return from stages 1, 2, and 3; that is, we may elect to process no jobs from category 3, in which case we will obtain no return from stage 3, but will enter stage 2 with $x_2 = 9$. Since $f_2(9) = 24$, the selection of $d_3 = 0$ would result in a total return of 24. However, a selection of $d_3 = 2$ also leads to a total return of 24. We obtain a return of $11(d_3) = 11(2) = 22$ for stage 3 and a return of 2 for the remaining two stages since $x_2 = 1$. To show that there are alternate optimal solutions at this stage we have placed two entries in the d_3^* and $x_2 = t_3(x_3, d_3^*)$ columns. The other entries in this table are calculated in the same manner as at stage 2. Let us now move on to the last stage.

Stage 4 Since we know that there are 10 days available in the planning period, the input to stage 4 is $x_4 = 10$. Thus, we have to consider only one row in the table, corresponding to stage 4.

x_4 \ d_4	$r_4(x_4, d_4) + f_3(x_3)$		d_4^*	$f_4(x_4)$	$x_3 = t_4(x_4, d_4^*)$ $= 10 - 7d_4^*$
	0	1			
10	27	㉘	1	28	3

The optimal decision, given $x_4 = 10$, is $d_4^* = 1$.

We have completed the dynamic programming solution of this problem. In order to identify the overall optimal solution, we must now trace back through the tables, beginning at stage 4. The optimal decision at stage 4 is $d_4^* = 1$. Thus, $x_3 = 10 - 7d_4^* = 3$, and we enter stage 3 with 3 days available for processing. With $x_3 = 3$ we see that the best decision at stage 3 is $d_3^* = 0$. Thus, we enter stage 2 with $x_2 = 3$. The optimal decision at stage 2 with $x_2 = 3$ is $d_2^* = 1$, resulting in $x_1 = 0$. Finally, the decision at stage 1 must be $d_1^* = 0$. The optimal strategy for our manufacturing operation is then as follows:

Decision	Return
$d_1^* = 0$	0
$d_2^* = 1$	8
$d_3^* = 0$	0
$d_4^* = 1$	20
Total return	28

We should schedule one job from category 2 and one job from category 4 for processing over the next 10-day planning period.

Another advantage of the dynamic programming approach can now be illustrated. Suppose we wanted to schedule the jobs to be processed over an 8-day period only. We can solve this new problem simply by making a recalculation at stage 4. The new stage 4 table would appear as follows:

x_4 $\diagdown$ d_4	$r_4(x_4,d_4) + f_3(x_3)$ 0	1	d_4^*	$f_4(x_4)$	$x_3 = t_4(x_4, d_4^*)$ $= 8 - 7d_4^*$
8	㉒	㉒	0,1	22	8,1

Actually, we are testing the sensitivity of our optimal solution to a small change in the total number of days available for processing. We have here the case of alternate optimal solutions. One solution can be found by setting $d_4^* = 0$ and tracing through the tables. Doing so, we obtain the following:

Decision	Return
$d_1^* = 0$	0
$d_2^* = 0$	0
$d_3^* = 2$	22
$d_4^* = 0$	0
Total return	22

A second optimal solution can be found by setting $d_4^* = 1$ and tracing back through the tables. Doing so, we obtain another solution (which has exactly the same total return):

Decision	Return
$d_1^* = 1$	2
$d_2^* = 0$	0
$d_3^* = 0$	0
$d_4^* = 1$	20
Total return	22

From the shortest-route and the knapsack examples you should start to become familiar with the basic stage-by-stage solution procedure of dynamic programming. In the next section we see how dynamic programming can be used to solve a production and inventory control problem.

18.4 ▼ A PRODUCTION AND INVENTORY CONTROL PROBLEM

Suppose we have developed forecasts of the demand for a particular product over a certain number of periods and we would like to decide on a production quantity for each of the periods so that demand can be satisfied at a minimum cost. There are two costs to be considered: production costs and holding costs. We will assume that one production setup will be made each period; thus, setup costs will be constant. As a result, setup costs are not considered in the analysis.

We will allow the production and holding costs to vary across periods. This makes the model more flexible since it also allows for the possibility of using different facilities for production and storage in different periods. Production and storage capacity constraints, which may vary across periods, will be included in the model. Let us adopt the following notation:

N = number of periods (stages in the dynamic programming formulation)

D_n = demand during stage n; n = 1, 2, . . ., N

x_n = a state variable representing the amount of inventory on hand at the beginning of stage n; n = 1, 2, . . ., N

d_n = decision variable for stage n; the production quantity for the corresponding period; n = 1, 2, . . ., N

P_n = production capacity in stage n; n = 1, 2, . . ., N

W_n = storage capacity at the end of stage n; n = 1, 2, . . ., N

C_n = production cost per unit in stage n; n = 1, 2, . . ., N

H_n = holding cost per unit of ending inventory for stage n; n = 1, 2, . ., N

We will develop the dynamic programming solution for a problem covering 3 months of operation. The data for our problem are presented in Table 18.3.

We can think of each month in our problem as a stage in a dynamic programming formulation. Figure 18.5 shows a schematic representation of such a formulation. Note that the beginning inventory in January is one unit.

In Figure 18.5 we have numbered the periods backward; that is, stage 1 corresponds to March, stage 2 corresponds to February, and stage 3 corresponds to January. The stage transformation functions take the form of ending inventory = beginning inventory + production − demand. Thus, we have

$$x_3 = 1$$
$$x_2 = x_3 + d_3 - D_3 = x_3 + d_3 - 2$$
$$x_1 = x_2 + d_2 - D_2 = x_2 + d_2 - 3$$
$$x_0 = x_1 + d_1 - D_1 = x_1 + d_1 - 3$$

TABLE 18.3
Data for the Production and Inventory Control Problem

Month	Demand	Production Capacity	Storage Capacity	Production Cost per Unit	Holding Cost per Unit
January	2	3	2	$175	$30
February	3	2	3	150	30
March	3	3	2	200	40

The beginning inventory for January is one unit.

FIGURE 18.5
Schematic Representation of the Production and Inventory Control Problem as a Three-Stage Dynamic Programming Problem

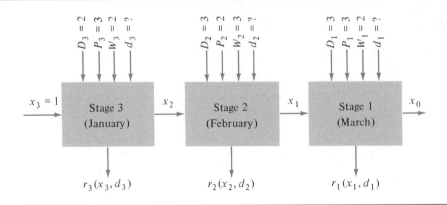

The return functions for each stage represent the sum of production and holding costs for the month. For example, in stage 1 (March), $r_1(x_1, d_1) = 200d_1 + 40(x_1 + d_1 - 3)$ represents the total production and holding costs for the period. The productions costs are $200 per unit, and the holding costs are $40 per unit of ending inventory. The other return functions are

$$r_2(x_2, d_2) = 150d_2 + 30(x_2 + d_2 - 3) \quad \text{Stage 2—February}$$
$$r_3(x_3, d_3) = 175d_3 + 30(x_3 + d_3 - 2) \quad \text{Stage 3—January}$$

This problem is particularly interesting because there are three constraints that must be satisfied at each stage as we perform the optimization procedure. Two are fairly straightforward, while the third is a little tricky. The first constraint is that the ending inventory must be less than or equal to the warehouse capacity. Mathematically we have

$$x_n + d_n - D_n \le W_n$$

or

$$x_n + d_n \le W_n + D_n \tag{18.2}$$

The second constraint is that the production level in each period may not exceed the production capacity. Mathematically we have

$$d_n \le P_n \tag{18.3}$$

The most difficult constraint to handle is the requirement that beginning inventory plus production must exceed demand for each period. The difficulty with this constraint becomes clear if we study stage 2. The demand for this period is 3, but the production capacity is 2. Therefore, we must require that the beginning inventory, x_2, be greater than or equal to 1. In general, for each stage this means we must have a constraint that requires beginning inventory plus production to be greater than or equal to demand. Mathematically this constraint can be written as

$$x_n + d_n \ge D_n \tag{18.4}$$

Let us now begin the stagewise solution procedure. At each stage we want to minimize $r_n(x_n, d_n) + f_{n-1}(x_{n-1})$ subject to the constraints given by equations (18.2), (18.3), and (18.4).

Stage 1 The stage 1 problem is as follows:

$$\min \quad r_1(x_1, d_1) = 200d_1 + 40(x_1 + d_1 - 3)$$

s.t.

$$x_1 + d_1 \leq 5 \quad \text{Warehouse constraint}$$
$$d_1 \leq 3 \quad \text{Production constraint}$$
$$x_1 + d_1 \geq 3 \quad \text{Satisfy demand constraint}$$

Combining terms in the objective function, we can rewrite the problem:

$$\min \quad r_1(x_1, d_1) = 240d_1 + 40x_1 - 120$$

s.t.

$$x_1 + d_1 \leq 5$$
$$d_1 \leq 3$$
$$x_1 + d_1 \geq 3$$

Following the tabular approach we adopted in Section 18.3, we will consider all possible inputs to stage 1 (x_1) and make the corresponding minimum cost decision. Since we are attempting to minimize cost, we will want the decision variable d_1 to be as small as possible and still satisfy the demand constraint. Thus, the table for stage 1 is as follows:

x_1	d_1^*		$f_1(x_1) = r_1(x_1, d_1^*)$ $240d_1 + 40x_1 - 120$
0	3		600
1	2		400
2	1	Production	200
3	0	capacity of 3 for stage 1 limits d_1	0

Warehouse capacity of 3 from stage 2 limits value of x_1

Demand constraint: $x_1 + d_1 \geq 3$

Now let us proceed to stage 2.

Stage 2

$$\min \quad r_2(x_2, d_2) + f_1(x_1) = 150d_2 + 30(x_2 + d_2 - 3) + f_1(x_1)$$
$$= 180d_2 + 30x_2 - 90 + f_1(x_1)$$

s.t.

$$x_2 + d_2 \leq 6$$
$$d_2 \geq 2$$
$$x_2 + d_2 \geq 3$$

The stage 2 calculations are summarized in the table below:

x_2 \ d_2	$r_2(x_2, d_2) + f_1(x_1)$ 0	1	2	d_2^*	Production capacity of 2 for stage 2 $f_2(x_2)$	$x_1 = x_2 + d_2^* - 3$
0	—	—	—	—	M	—
1	—	—	900	2	900	0
2	—	750	730	2	730	1

Warehouse capacity of 2 from stage 3

Check demand constraint $x_2 + d_2 \geq 3$ for each x_2, d_2 combination (– indicates an infeasible solution)

The detailed calculations for $r_2(x_2, d_2) + f_1(x_1)$ when $x_2 = 1$ and $d_2 = 2$ are as follows:

$$r_2(1, 2) + f_1(0) = 180(2) + 30(1) - 90 + 600 = 900$$

For $r_2(x_2, d_2) + f_1(x_1)$ when $x_2 = 2$ and $d_2 = 1$, we have

$$r_2(2,1) + f_1(0) = 180(1) + 30(2) - 90 + 600 = 750$$

For $x_2 = 2$ and $d_2 = 2$, we have

$$r_2(2, 2) + f_1(1) = 180(2) + 30(2) - 90 + 400 = 730$$

Note that an arbitrarily high cost M is assigned to the $f_2(x_2)$ column for $x_2 = 0$. Since an input of 0 to stage 2 does not provide a feasible solution, the M cost associated with the $x_2 = 0$ input will prevent $x_2 = 0$ from occurring in the optimal solution.

Stage 3

$$\min \quad r_3(x_3,d_3) + f_2(x_2) = 175d_3 + 30(x_3 + d_3 - 2) + f_2(x_2)$$
$$= 205d_3 + 30x_3 - 60 + f_2(x_2)$$

s.t.

$$x_3 + d_3 \leq 4$$
$$d_3 \leq 3$$
$$x_3 + d_3 \geq 2$$

With $x_3 = 1$ already defined by the beginning inventory level, the table for stage 3 becomes

x_3 \ d_3	$r_3(x_3, d_3) + f_2(x_2)$ 0	1	2	3	d_3^*	Production capacity of 3 at stage 3 $f_3(x_3)$	$x_2 = x_3 + d_3^* - 2$
1	—	M	1280	1315	2	1280	1

Thus, we find that the total cost associated with the optimal production and inventory policy is $1280. To find the optimal decisions and inventory levels for each period, we may trace back through each stage and identify x_n and d_n^* as we go. Table 18.4 summarizes the optimal production and inventory policy.

TABLE 18.4
Optimal Production and Inventory Control Policy

Month	Beginning Inventory	Production	Production Cost	Ending Inventory	Holding Cost	Total Monthly Cost
January	1	2	$ 350	1	$ 30	$ 380
February	1	2	300	0	0	300
March	0	3	600	0	0	600
Totals			$ 1250		$ 30	$ 1280

▼ NOTES AND COMMENTS ▼

1. With dynamic programming, as with other management science techniques, the computer can be a valuable computational aid. However, since dynamic programming is a general approach with stage decision problems differing substantially from application to application, no one algorithm or computer software package is available for solving dynamic programs. Some software packages exist for specific types of dynamic programs. However, most new applications of dynamic programming will require specially designed software if a computer solution is to be obtained.

2. The introductory illustrations of dynamic programming presented in this chapter are deterministic and involve a finite number of decision alternatives and a finite number of stages. For problems such as these, computations can be organized and carried out in a tabular form. With this structure, the optimization problem at each stage can usually be solved by total enumeration of all possible outcomes. More complex dynamic programming models may include probabilistic components, continuous decision variables, and/or an infinite number of stages. In cases where the optimization problem at each stage involves continuous decision variables, linear programming or the calculus-based procedures presented in the next chapter may be needed to obtain an optimal solution.

▼ SUMMARY

Dynamic programming is an attractive approach to problem solving when it is possible to break a large problem up into smaller multiple stages. The solution procedure then proceeds recursively, solving one of the smaller problems at each stage. Dynamic programming is not a specific algorithm, but rather an approach to problem solving. Thus, the recursive optimization may be carried out differently for different problems. In any case it is almost always easier to solve a series of smaller problems than one large one. This is how the dynamic programming approach obtains its power.

▼ GLOSSARY

Dynamic programming   An approach to problem solving that permits decomposing a large problem that may be very difficult to solve into a number of smaller problems that are usually easier to solve.

Principle of optimality   Regardless of the decisions that have been made at the previous stages, if the decision made at stage n is to be part of an overall optimal solution, the decision made at stage n must be optimal for all remaining stages.

Stages   When a large problem is decomposed into a number of smaller problems, the dynamic programming solution approach creates a stage to correspond to each of the subproblems.

State variables x_n and x_{n-1}   An input state variable x_n and an output state variable x_{n-1} together define the condition of the process at the beginning and end of stage n.

Decision variable d_n   A variable representing the possible decisions that can be made at stage n.

Stage transformation function $t_n(x_n, d_n)$ The rule or equation that relates the output state variable x_{n-1} for stage n to the input state variable x_n and the decision variable d_n.

Return function $r_n(x_n, d_n)$ A value (such as profit or loss) associated with making decision d_n at stage n for a specific value of the input state variable x_n.

Knapsack problem N items, each of which has a different weight and value, are to be placed into a knapsack with limited weight capacity so as to maximize the total value of the items placed in the knapsack.

▼ PROBLEMS

1. In Section 18.1 we solved a shortest-route problem using dynamic programming. Find the optimal solution to this problem by total enumeration; that is, list all possible routes from the origin, node 1, to the destination, node 10, and pick the one with the smallest value. Explain why the dynamic programming approach results in fewer computations for this problem.

2. Consider the following network. The numbers above each arc represent the distance between the connected nodes.

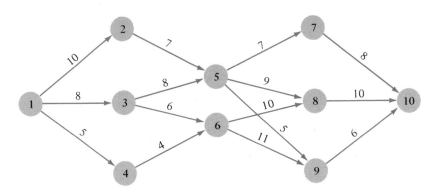

   a. Find the shortest route from node 1 to node 10 using dynamic programming.
   b. What is the shortest route from node 4 to node 10?
   c. Enumerate all possible routes from node 1 to node 10. Explain how dynamic programming has reduced the number of computations to fewer than the number required by total enumeration.

3. A firm has just hired eight new employees and would like to determine how to allocate the new employees to four activities. The firm has prepared the table below, which gives the estimated profit for each activity as a function of the number of new employees allocated to it:

Activities	Number of New Employees								
	0	1	2	3	4	5	6	7	8
1	22	30	37	44	49	54	58	60	61
2	30	40	48	55	59	62	64	66	67
3	46	52	56	59	62	65	67	68	69
4	5	22	36	48	52	55	58	60	61

a. Use dynamic programming to determine the optimal allocation of new employees to the activities.

b. Suppose there were only 6 new employees hired. Which activities would you assign to these 6 employees?

4. A sawmill receives logs in 20-foot lengths, cuts them to smaller lengths, and then sells these smaller lengths to a number of manufacturing companies. The lengths the company has orders for are

$$l_1 = 3 \text{ ft}$$
$$l_2 = 7 \text{ ft}$$
$$l_3 = 11 \text{ ft}$$
$$l_4 = 16 \text{ ft}$$

The sawmill currently has an inventory of 2000 logs in 20-foot lengths and would like to select a cutting pattern that will maximize the profit made on this inventory. Assuming the sawmill has sufficient orders available, its problem becomes one of determining the cutting pattern that will maximize profits. The per-unit profit for each of the smaller lengths is as follows:

Length (feet)	Profit ($)
3	1
7	3
11	5
16	8

Any cutting pattern is permissible as long as

$$3d_1 + 7d_2 + 11d_3 + 16d_4 \leq 20$$

where d_i is the number of pieces of length l_i cut, $i = 1, 2, 3, 4$.

a. Set up a dynamic programming model of this problem, and solve it. What are your decision variables? What is your state variable?

b. Explain briefly how this model can be extended to find the best cutting pattern in cases where the overall length l can be cut into N lengths, $l_1, l_2, \ldots, l_N$.

5. A large manufacturing company has a very well developed management training program. Each trainee is expected to complete a four-phase program, but there are a number of different assignments each trainee can be given at each phase of the

training program. The assignments available and the estimated completion times in 0months at each phase of the program are shown below:

Phase I	Phase II	Phase III	Phase IV
A–13	E–3	H–12	L–10
B–10	F–6	I–6	M–5
C–20	G–5	J–7	N–13
D–17		K–10	

Assignments made at subsequent phases depend on the previous assignment. For example, a trainee who completes assignment A at phase I may only go on to assignment F or G at phase II. That is, there is a precedence relationship for each assignment as shown below.

Assignment	Feasible Succeeding Assignments
A	F, G
B	F
C	G
D	E, G
E	H, I, J, K
F	H, K
G	J, K
H	L, M
I	L, M
J	M, N
K	N
L	Finish
M	Finish
N	Finish

a. The company would like to determine the sequence of assignments that will minimize the time in the training program. Formulate and solve this as a dynamic programming problem. (*Hint*: Develop a network representation of the problem where each node represents completion of an activity.)

b. If a trainee has just completed assignment F and would like to complete the remainder of the training program in the shortest possible time, which assignment should be chosen next?

6. Crazy Robin, the owner of a small chain of Robin Hood Sporting Goods stores in Des Moines and Cedar Rapids, Iowa, has just purchased a new supply of 500 dozen top-line golf balls. Because she was willing to purchase the entire amount of a production overrun, Robin was able to buy the golf balls at one-half the usual price.

Three of Robin's stores do a good business in the sale of golf equipment and supplies, and, as a result, Robin has decided to retail the balls at these three stores. Thus, Robin is faced with the problem of determining how many dozen balls to allocate to each store. The following estimates show the expected profit from allocating 100, 200, 300, 400, or 500 dozen to each store:

	Number of Dozens of Golf Balls				
	100	*200*	*300*	*400*	*500*
Store 1	$600	$1100	$1550	$1700	$1800
Store 2	500	1200	1700	2000	2100
Store 3	550	1100	1500	1850	1950

Assuming the lots cannot be broken into any sizes smaller than 100 dozen each, how many dozen golf balls should Crazy Robin send to each store?

7. The Max X. Posure Advertising Agency is conducting a 10-day advertising campaign for a local department store. The agency has determined that the most effective campaign would possibly include placing ads in four media: daily newspaper, Sunday newspaper, radio, and television. A total of $8000 has been made available for this campaign, and the agency would like to distribute this in $1000 increments across the media in such a fashion that an advertising exposure index is maximized. Research that has been conducted by the agency permits the following estimates to be made of the exposure per each $1000 expenditure in each of the media.

Media	Thousands of Dollars Spent							
	1	*2*	*3*	*4*	*5*	*6*	*7*	*8*
Daily newspaper	24	37	46	59	72	80	82	82
Sunday newspaper	15	55	70	75	90	95	95	95
Radio	20	30	45	55	60	62	63	63
Television	20	40	55	65	70	70	70	70

a. How much should the agency spend on each medium in order to maximize the department store's exposure?

b. How would your answer change if only $6000 were budgeted?

c. How would your answers in parts (a) and (b) change if television were not considered as one of the media?

8. Suppose we have a three-stage process where the yield for each stage is a function of the decision made. In mathematical notation we may state our problem as follows:

$$\text{max} \quad r_1(d_1) + r_2(d_2) + r_3(d_3)$$

s.t.

$$d_1 + d_2 + d_3 \leq 1000$$

The possible values the decision variables may take on at each stage and the corresponding returns are presented in tabular form below.

Stage 1		Stage 2		Stage 3	
d_1	$r_1(d_1)$	d_2	$r_2(d_2)$	d_3	$r_3(d_3)$
0	0	100	120	100	175
100	110	300	400	500	700
200	300	500	650		
300	400	600	700		
400	425	800	975		

a. Use total enumeration to list all feasible sequences of decisions for this problem. Which one is optimal [that is, maximizes $r_1(d_1) + r_2(d_2) + r_3(d_3)$]?

b. Use dynamic programming to solve this problem.

9. Recall the production and inventory control problem of Section 18.4. Mills Manufacturing Company has just such a production and inventory control problem for an armature the company manufactures as a component for a generator. The available data for the next 3-month planning period are presented below.

Month	Demand	Production Capacity	Warehouse Capacity	Production Cost per Unit	Holding Cost per Unit
1	20	30	40	$2.00	$0.30
2	30	20	30	1.50	0.30
3	30	30	20	2.00	0.20

Using the dynamic programming approach outlined in Section 18.4 find the optimal production quantities and inventory levels in each period for the Mills Manufacturing Company. Assume there is a beginning inventory of 10 units on hand at the beginning of month 1 and production runs are completed in multiples of 10 units (that is, 10, 20, or 30 units).

10. A chemical processing plant is considering introducing a new product on the market. However, before making a final decision, management has requested you to provide estimates of profits associated with different process designs. The general flow process is represented below.

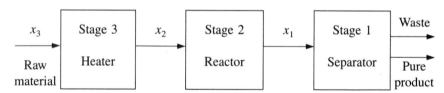

Raw material is fed into a heater at the rate of 4500 pounds per week. The heated material is then routed to a reactor where a portion of the raw material is converted to pure product. A separator then withdraws the finished product for sale. The unconverted material is discarded as waste.

Profit considerations are to be based on a 2-year payback period on investments; that is, all capital expenditures must be recovered in 2 years (100 weeks). All calculations will be based on weekly operations. Raw material costs are expected to stay fixed at $1 per pound, and it has been forecast that the finished product will sell for $6 per pound.

It is your responsibility to determine the process design that will yield maximum profit per week. You and your co-workers have collected the following preliminary data.

At stage 3 one heater with an initial cost of $12,000 is being considered. Two temperatures, 700°F and 800°F, are feasible. The operating costs for the heater depend directly on the temperature to be attained. These costs are as follows:

Operating Costs at Stage 3			
		Decisions at Stage 3	
		700°F	*800°F*
Input x_3	*4500 lb*	$280/week	$380/week

The output from stage 3, x_2, which is also the input to stage 2, may be expressed as 4500 pounds of raw material heated to either 700°F or 800°F. One of the decisions you must make is to what temperature the raw material should be heated.

For Stage 2, a reactor, which can operate with either of two catalysts, C1 or C2, is to be used. The initial cost of this reactor is $50,000. The operating costs of this reactor are independent of the input, x_2, and depend only on the catalyst selected. The costs of the catalysts are included in the operating costs. The output will be expressed in pounds of converted (or pure) material. The percentage of material converted depends on the incoming temperature and the catalyst used. The tables below summarize the pertinent information. Thus, a second decision you must make is to specify which catalyst should be used.

Percent Conversion			
		Decisions at Stage 2	
		C1	*C2*
x_2	*(4500 lb, 700°F)*	20%	40%
	(4500 lb, 800°F)	40%	60%

Operating Costs Decision at Stage 2	
C1	*C2*
$450/week	$650/week

One of two separators, S1 or S2, will be purchased for stage 1. S1 has an initial cost of $20,000 and a weekly operating cost of $0.10 per pound of pure product to be separated. Comparatively, S2 has an initial cost of $5000 and a weekly operating cost of $0.20 per pound of pure product to be separated. Included in these operating costs is the expense of discarding the unconverted raw material as waste.

Develop a dynamic programming model for this problem. What is your recommendation for best temperature for the heater? Best catalyst to use with the reactor? Best separator to purchase? What is the maximum weekly profit?

The United States Environmental Protection Agency*
Washington, D.C.

The United States Environmental Protection Agency (EPA) is an independent agency of the executive branch of the federal government. Fifteen components of five executive departments and independent agencies were consolidated to form the EPA on December 2, 1970, under Reorganization Plan No. 3 by then President Richard M. Nixon. Today, the EPA administers comprehensive environmental protection laws related to

Water pollution control, water quality, and drinking water
Air pollution and radiation
Pesticides and toxic substances
Solid and hazardous waste including emergency spill response and Superfund site remediation

Program offices for each of these media support the EPA administrator through policy development, standards and criteria development, and support and evaluation or regional activities. The 10 regional offices implement and enforce standards, conduct monitoring and surveillance programs, and provide technical and financial assistance to state and local governments.

Functional activities at EPA headquarters, which transcend all media, include planning and management, enforcement, and research and development. Quantitative analysis techniques are used extensively in the experimental design of research studies, providing quality assurance of monitoring surveys and enforcement actions, as well as environmental modeling and simulation studies to evaluate the cost effectiveness of alternative environmental policies, regulations, and control technologies.

The EPA's Office of Research and Development serves as the primary source of scientific and technical support to the agency's operating programs and regional offices by conducting in-house and extramural research at 14 locations throughout the country. Research activities focus on analytical methods development and quality assurance, environmental processes and effects research, health effects research, and environmental engineering. Environmental modeling is conducted for all media at many of these research locations. ORD maintains a Center for Water Quality Modeling at its laboratory in Athens, Ga. The following dynamic programming application was developed by the Municipal Environmental Research Laboratory in Cincinnati, Ohio, as part of an effort to evaluate the usefulness of seasonal discharge permits in reducing the cost of wastewater treatment while maintaining water quality.

---

*The authors are indebted to John Convery, Environmental Protection Agency, for providing this application.

WATER QUALITY MANAGEMENT PROGRAM

The Environmental Protection Agency administers programs designed to maintain acceptable water quality conditions for rivers and streams throughout the United States. In order to guard against polluted rivers and streams, the government requires companies to obtain a discharge permit from federal or state authorities before any form of pollutants can be discharged into a body of water. These permits specifically notify each discharger as to the amount of legally dischargeable waste that can be placed in the river or stream. The discharge limits are determined by ensuring that water quality criteria are met even in unusually dry seasons when the river or stream has a critically low flow condition. Most often this low-flow condition is based on the lowest flow recorded over the past 10 years. By ensuring that water quality is maintained under the low-flow conditions, there is a high degree of reliability that the water quality criteria can be maintained throughout the year.

At different seasons of the year, water will flow at different rates in the various rivers and streams. With these seasonal flow variations, seasonal discharge permits can be issued which allow different discharge limits at the different times of the year. As a result, companies can take advantage of higher stream flow rates to reduce treatment requirements and to lower the discharge treatment costs. A goal of the EPA is to establish seasonal discharge limits that enable lower treatment costs while maintaining water quality standards at a prescribed level of reliability.

A DYNAMIC PROGRAMMING MODEL FOR SEASONAL DISCHARGE LIMITS

A dynamic programming model has been formulated for establishing the allowable waste discharge load during the various seasons of the year. The periods or stages of the model correspond to different seasons considered during the year; there is a separate stage for each season. The return function at each stage is the cost of the waste treatment for waste discharged during the stage, or season. The decision variable at each stage is the design streamflow for the body of water receiving the waste. Once the design streamflow has been established, an allowable waste discharge and its associated treatment cost can be determined. The design streamflow decisions at each stage interact to determine the overall reliability that the annual water quality conditions will be maintained. In this regard, the decision variable choice at any one stage, or period, is affected by the decision variable choices at the other stages.

The probability that there will be no water quality violations over the entire year is the product of the seasonal probabilities of no violations. To maintain reliability standards the probability of no violation during the year must exceed a certain value. Suppose we let $P_j(q_j)$ represent the probability of no violation during season j when the design streamflow is q_j. Then the probability of no water quality violation over the entire year is given by

$$\prod_{j=1}^{N} P_j(q_j) = \text{probability of no violation}$$

where N is the number of seasons during the year.

The reliability requirement is satisfied when this probability is sufficiently high. Suppose α is the minimal acceptable probability. The water quality constraint is then

$$\prod_{j=1}^{N} P_j(q_j) \geq \alpha$$

By taking the logarithm of both sides, this constraint can be written as

$$\sum_{j=1}^{N} \log P_j(q_j) \geq \log \alpha$$

The state variable at stage j is then defined to be

$$s_j = \sum_{k=1}^{j} P_k(q_k)$$

The design streamflows (the decision variables) are chosen to minimize treatment cost subject to requirements that the allowable waste discharge be within given limits and that the state variable ensure sufficient reliability of no water quality violations.

The solution to the model provides the design streamflows for each seasonal period. These streamflows combine with the water quality criterion to estabish the seasonal waste discharge load. With the return function measuring treatment cost, the model obtains the minimum treatment cost solution that will maintain the EPA water quality standards.

Questions

1. Suppose there are four seasons and the probabilities of a water quality violation in each season are 0.01, 0.05, 0.02, and 0.01, respectively. What is the probability that there will be no water quality violation over the entire year?
2. Let P_j = the probability of no water quality violation in season j. Suppose there are three seasons. Write a constraint specifying that the minimal acceptable probability of no violation over the three seasons is 0.90.

Calculus-Based Solution Procedures

In this chapter we consider mathematical models where the functions or mathematical relationships involved are not all linear. For example, in formulating a profit or cost function for a specific problem we may find that a linear function is inappropriate and that a curve or a nonlinear function is necessary. Recall that in the analysis of inventory models (see Section 11.1) we developed the following nonlinear function to show how total relevant cost could be expressed in terms of the order quantity Q:

$$\text{TC} = \frac{Q}{2} C_h + \frac{D}{Q} C_0$$

The graph of the total cost curve for an economic order quantity inventory model is shown in Figure 19.1.

In determining the optimal values of the decision variables in nonlinear models, we will find calculus-based solution procedures quite valuable. In this chapter we show how differential calculus can be used to find maximum and minimum values for such models. We begin by using differential calculus to analyze nonlinear objective functions having only one decision variable. Then we discuss the procedures for handling nonlinear functions with two or more decision variables. Finally, we show how calculus-based solution procedures can be used to solve nonlinear models that have constraints.

This is the only chapter in this book where a working knowledge of calculus, specifically differential calculus, is a prerequisite. However, the reader with no calculus background may still find this chapter useful in terms of learning about nonlinear models and the role that calculus-based solution procedures play in analyzing these models.

19.1 ▼ MODELS WITH ONE DECISION VARIABLE

The Macon Psychiatric Institute, a nonprofit organization, is interested in redesigning its mental health care delivery system in order to maximize the number of people who can benefit from its services. Based on some recent studies, the institute has learned that the

FIGURE 19.1
Total Cost Curve for the Economic Order Quantity Inventory Model

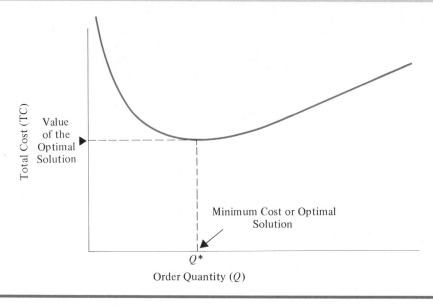

average treatment time per patient is a function of the number of patients the clinic is treating simultaneously. With more patients receiving treatment, the patients remain in residence longer; that is, with more patients in the system, the clinic's staff becomes overloaded, and the patient's time in residence at the clinic increases. If the institute reduces the number of patients being treated, the patients can receive more personal attention, and thus the treatment time can be shortened. The institute's problem can be stated in terms of how many active or in-residence patients should be maintained by the clinic so that the total number of patients treated per year is maximized.

Based on patient records and recovery time estimates by the clinic's staff members, the following mathematical relationship can be used to describe how the number of in-residence patients affects the patient treatment or recovery time:

$$T = \frac{45}{180 - P} \qquad (19.1)$$

where

$$T = \text{average patient treatment time in years}$$
$$P = \text{number of in-residence patients}$$

This relationship is believed to be valid as long as the number of in-residence patients, P, remains between 45 and 135.

Using equation (19.1), we see that if the clinic operates with $P = 135$ patients, then $T = 45/(180 - 135) = 1$ year (that is, on the average a patient receives 1 year of treatment before being released). However, if the clinic reduces its number of in-residence patients to 60, then the average recovery period can be shortened to $T = 45/(180 - 60) = 0.375$ year, or 4.5 months. The relationship between the number of in-residence patients and the average treatment time is shown in Figure 19.2.

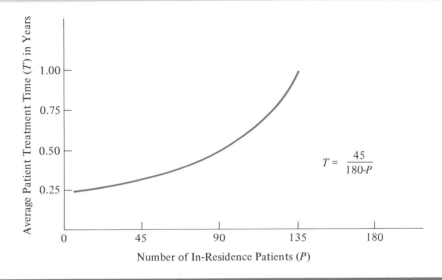

FIGURE 19.2
Average Treatment Time, T, as a Function of the Number of In-Residence Patients, P

$$T = \frac{45}{180 - P}$$

The institute wants to maximize the total number of people treated per year. Since T is the average treatment time per patient and since the clinic treats P patients *simultaneously,* the total number of patients treated per year is given by

$$N = \frac{1}{T}P = \frac{P}{T} \tag{19.2}$$

For $P = 135$ we saw earlier that $T = 1$ year; thus, $N = P/T = 135/1 = 135$ patients per year. However, for $P = 60$, $T = 0.375$ and $N = 60/0.375 = 160$ patients per year. Therefore, reducing the number of active patients to 60 does improve the effectiveness of the clinic; more patients can be treated over a specified time period. However, the question of what the optimal number of in-residence patients is still needs to be answered.

Since T is a function of P [equation (19.1)], we can substitute into equation (19.2) and write the mathematical model for the problem as a function of the one variable, P:

$$N = \frac{P}{T} = \frac{P}{45/(180 - P)} = \frac{(180 - P)P}{45} = 4P - \frac{1}{45}P^2 \tag{19.3}$$

We are interested in maximizing the number of patients treated per year N. Thus, the above model provides a nonlinear objective function for a maximization problem with one decision variable, P, and our problem becomes

$$\max N = 4P - \frac{1}{45}P^2 \tag{19.4}$$

With only one decision variable we can observe how the number of patients treated per year varies for different P values by drawing a graph of the relationship. This graph, shown in Figure 19.3, indicates that the maximum value of the objective function is 180, corresponding to an in-residence patient volume of 90. Since sketching the graph of a function may be time consuming, and since the determination of the optimal solution is

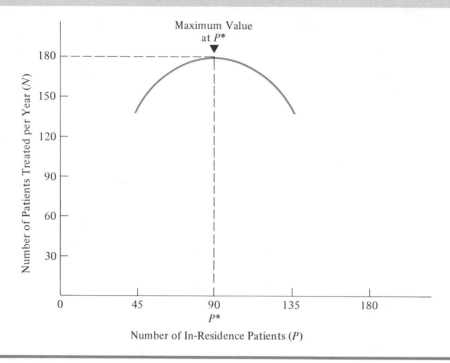

FIGURE 19.3
Number of Patients Treated per Year as a Function of the
Number of Patients in Residence

dependent on the accuracy of the graph, we will usually want to use a differential calculus procedure for solving such a problem.

Recall from calculus that the first derivative of an unconstrained function must be equal to zero at a *local maximum* or *local minimum*. The reason for this is that the first derivative is the slope of the line tangent to the curve, and the slope of the tangent line is zero at any local maximum or local minimum value of the function. In the Macon Psychiatric Institute problem we see that the function relating the number of patients treated per year to the number of in-residence patients has one local maximum (Figure 19.3). Many functions, however, possess a number of local maxima and/or minima. For example, consider the graph of the function depicted in Figure 19.4, which has two local maxima and one local minimum. At each of the local maxima and at the local minimum the first derivatives, and hence the slope of the tangent lines, are equal to zero. Rule 1 below summarizes the above discussion in the form of a *necessary condition* for determining all the local maxima or minima of an unconstrained function of one variable:

Rule 1 (Necessary Condition)
The first derivative of an unconstrained function of one variable must equal zero at its local maximum or local minimum points.

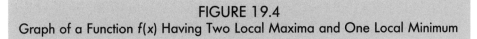

FIGURE 19.4
Graph of a Function f(x) Having Two Local Maxima and One Local Minimum

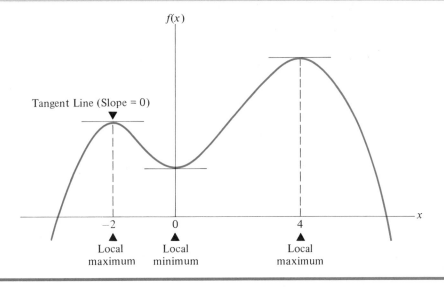

Let us now calculate the first derivative for the institute's problem:[1]

$$\text{First derivative} = \frac{dN}{dP} = 4 - \frac{2}{45}P$$

Setting the first derivative equal to zero and solving, we obtain

$$\frac{dN}{dP} = 4 - \frac{2}{45}P = 0$$

$$\frac{2}{45}P = 4$$

$$P^* = \frac{(4)(45)}{2} = 90$$

Thus, we see that $P^* = 90$ is the value of P that sets the first derivative equal to zero. Figure 19.5 shows that the slope of the line tangent to the curve at this local maximum point is in fact zero.

Unfortunately, while it is a necessary condition that the first derivative equal zero at a local maximum point, this is not sufficient to guarantee that we have in fact located a local maximum. Actually, a point where the first derivative equals zero could be a local maximum, a local minimum, or an inflection point. Thus, a second derivative test is needed to determine whether or not we have a local maximum. Rule 2 provides such a test and establishes a *sufficient condition* that guarantees that we have reached a local maximum (or a local minimum) solution.

---

[1] A short table of derivative formulas is provided in Appendix D.

FIGURE 19.5
Maximum Is at Value of P Where Derivative = 0

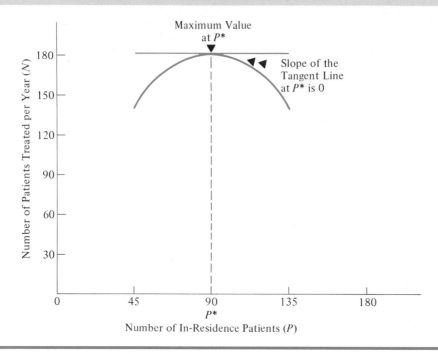

Rule 2 (Sufficient Condition)

If rule 1 is satisfied at a point, and
a. If the second derivative[2] *is greater than* zero, then the point is a local *minimum*.
b. If the second derivative *is less than* zero, then the point is a local *maximum*.

Let us apply this second derivative test to the Macon Psychiatric Institute problem. The second derivative is given by

$$\text{Second derivative} = \frac{d^2N}{dP^2} = -\tfrac{2}{45} < 0$$

Since the second derivative is less than zero, rule 2 tells us that $P^* = 90$ does indeed yield a local maximum of the objective function for our problem.

We call a point a *global maximum* if it yields the highest value for the function. Similarly, we call a point a *global minimum* if it yields the lowest value. In this case it is easy to verify that the local maximum, $P^* = 90$, is also a global maximum. Since the function has only one point at which rule 1 is satisfied, and since rule 2 says that this point is a local maximum, this local maximum must be the global maximum.

---

[2]The second derivative is found simply by applying the differentiation rule to the first derivative function.

Assuming that the relationships we used in developing the mathematical model are accurate reflections of reality, the institute should admit 90 patients and maintain this many patients in residence all the time. This will maximize the number of patients the institute can treat per year at 180.

The problem we have just described illustrates how calculus can assist in finding the optimum for an unconstrained function of one variable. However, in some situations we will find that it is of interest to consider finding the optimal value for a function over a specified interval. This situation may come about because of constraints placed on the decision maker or because the function of interest is defined only over a specified interval, and as a result we choose to limit ourselves to finding the best value for the function over that interval. In problems of this type the optimal solution could occur at the endpoints of the interval as well as at points where rules 1 and 2 hold.

As an illustration of this type of situation, suppose we are trying to find the maximum of the function $f(x) = x^3 - 3x^2$ over the interval $-1 \leq x \leq 4$. A graph of the function over this interval is shown in Figure 19.6.

Clearly, the global maximum of the function over this interval occurs at $x = 4$. However, rule 1 is not satisfied at this point because the first derivative (the slope of the tangent line) is not equal to zero. When we are constrained to a specific interval in the search for the optimum of a function of one variable, we must extend the solution procedure beyond just checking points that satisfy rules 1 and 2. The general procedure for finding the global maximum or minimum of a function of one variable is as follows:

Step 1 Find all the points that satisfy rules 1 and 2. These are candidates for yielding the optimal solution to the problem.

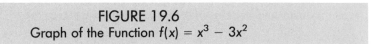

FIGURE 19.6
Graph of the Function $f(x) = x^3 - 3x^2$

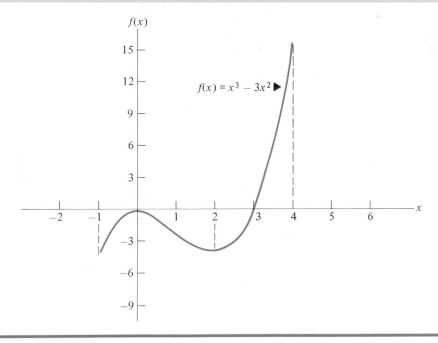

Step 2 If the solution is restricted to a specified interval, evaluate the function at the endpoints of the interval.

Step 3 Compare the values of the function at all the points found in steps 1 and 2. The largest of these is the global maximum solution; the smallest is the global minimum solution.

Let us apply this procedure to the function in Figure 19.6. Following step 1 we first find all the points at which the first derivative equals zero:

$$\frac{df(x)}{dx} = 3x^2 - 6x = 0$$

Therefore,

$$x(3x - 6) = 0$$

and we see that both $x = 0$ and $x = 2$ satisfy rule 1. Checking rule 2, we find

$$\frac{d^2f(x)}{dx^2} = 6x - 6$$

At $x = 0$,

$$\frac{d^2f(0)}{dx^2} = -6 < 0$$

and we have a local maximum of the function at $x = 0$. The value of the function at $x = 0$ is $f(0) = 0^3 - 3(0)^2 = 0$. Looking back to Figure 19.6 we see that this is indeed a local maximum and the slope of the tangent line is equal to zero at this point. At $x = 2$,

$$\frac{d^2f(2)}{dx^2} = 6(2) - 6 = 6 > 0$$

Therefore, by rule 2 we have a local minimum at $x = 2$. The value of the function at $x = 2$ is $f(2) = (2)^3 - 3(2)^2 = -4$.

Proceeding to step 2 we evaluate the function at both of its endpoints:

$$f(-1) = (-1)^3 - 3(-1)^2 = -4$$
$$f(4) = (4)^3 - 3(4)^2 = 16$$

At step 3 we compare the values at the points found in steps 1 and 2. The largest value occurs at $x = 4$ and yields a global maximum value of 16 over the specified interval. The smallest value occurs at both $x = -1$ and $x = 2$; that is, there is a tie for global minimum, and we say that both $x = -1$ and $x = 2$ are global minima. The minimum value is -4. Note that one of these candidates was found in step 1 and the other in step 2 of our solution procedure. Figure 19.6 illustrates graphically the conclusions we have reached.

Let us return for a moment to the Macon Psychiatric Institute problem. The objective function for this problem was believed to be applicable only over the interval $45 \leq P \leq 135$. It may be reasonable to assume that this means the institute will not consider letting the number of in-residence patients fall below 45 or exceed 135. If this were the case then, why did we not need to check the endpoints of this interval in our search for a maximum? The reason is that there was only one point ($P^* = 90$) that satisfied rule 1, and it was a local maximum. Since P^* is a local maximum, the value of the function decreases as we move away from it, and since no other points satisfy rule 1, we know that the function does not turn up again anywhere. Therefore, no other point could yield a higher value than $P^* = 90$. Nevertheless, the three-step procedure we have specified for maximizing or minimizing a function of one variable would have led to the same conclusion. The value of the function is smaller at $P = 45$ and $P = 135$ than at the maximum, $P^* = 90$.

Before concluding this section, let us consider another numerical example to make sure that we know how to apply steps 1, 2, and 3.

Example. Suppose we want to minimize the function

$$f(x) = x^3 - 6x^2 + 50 \tag{19.5}$$

over the interval $0 \le x \le 5$.

Step 1 Setting the first derivative equal to zero, we find

$$\frac{df(x)}{dx} = 3x^2 - 12x = 0$$

or

$$x(3x - 12) = 0$$

This provides two possible values for x: either $x = 0$ or $3x - 12 = 0$ and $x = 4$. That is, $x = 0$ and $x = 4$ both set the first derivative equal to zero, satisfying rule 1. To see if either of these yields a local minimum, we must calculate the second derivative:

$$\frac{d^2f(x)}{dx^2} = 6x - 12$$

At $x = 0$ we have

$$\frac{d^2f(0)}{dx^2} = 6(0) - 12 = -12 < 0$$

Therefore, by rule 2, $x = 0$ yields a local maximum for $f(x)$. At $x = 4$ we have

$$\frac{d^2f(4)}{dx^2} = 6(4) - 12 = 12 > 0$$

Therefore, by rule 2, $x = 4$ yields a local minimum for $f(x)$. The graph of $f(x)$ [equation (19.5)] is shown in Figure 19.7. Again note that the slopes of the lines tangent to the curve at these local minimum and local maximum points are both zero.

Step 2 Evaluating the function at the endpoints, we obtain

$$f(0) = 50$$

$$f(5) = 25$$

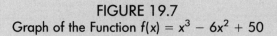

FIGURE 19.7
Graph of the Function $f(x) = x^3 - 6x^2 + 50$

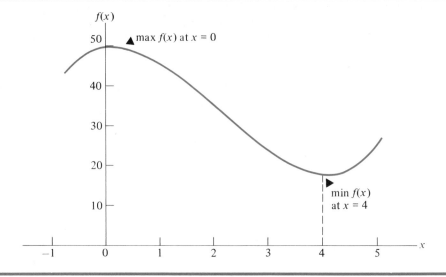

Step 3 Since we are searching for a minimum and $f(4) = 18 < f(5) = 25$, we conclude that $x^* = 4$ is the global minimum solution. We note also in this example that the local maximum found in step 1 corresponded to one of the endpoints. This is purely a coincidence where the first derivative of the function happens to be zero at an endpoint of the interval.

▼ NOTES AND COMMENTS ▼

1. The material in this chapter illustrates the development of models based on nonlinear relationships. When one realizes that many real-world relationships are nonlinear, the appeal of developing nonlinear models becomes apparent. However, nonlinear models are much more difficult to solve than linear models. For this reason, we recommend that a linear model be considered first. If a linear model is judged to be a reasonable approximation, solution procedures such as linear programming computer software are readily available. If a linear model does not provide an acceptable approximation, a nonlinear model should be used. Even if only an approximate solution can be found to the correct nonlinear model, this is better than having an optimal solution to an inappropriate linear model.

2. The difference between a local and a global optimal solution is a critical issue in solving calculus-based optimization models. The calculus-based necessary and sufficient conditions only permit us to identify local optimal solutions. Once all the local optimal solutions have been found, we can choose the best as the global optimal solution. Computer codes are available for helping identify local optimal solutions. Searching for the global optimal solution usually requires some experimentation and trial-and-error with different starting solutions. The expertise of a management scientist is often critical in arriving at the global optimal solution to a nonlinear model.

19.2 ▼ UNCONSTRAINED MODELS WITH MORE THAN ONE DECISION VARIABLE

As we have seen in the previous section and elsewhere in the text, there are a number of problem situations for which we can develop mathematical models involving only one decision variable. However, there are perhaps even more decision-making situations in which the decision maker must select the best values for two or more decision variables. In this section we discuss a problem that leads to the formulation of a nonlinear mathematical model involving two decision variables. Then we show how first and second derivative tests similar to rules 1 and 2 can be developed for finding the local maximum and local minimum values of unconstrained functions of two variables. We do not attempt to extend the analysis to the case where each of the variables is restricted to an interval. This case is inherently more difficult than the situation for one variable, and its analysis would take us too far afield for an introductory text of this nature.[3] For completeness, we will discuss the extension to unconstrained models involving several decision variables.

In order to see how a mathematical model involving two decision variables might arise, let us suppose that Lawn King, Inc., manufactures two styles of lawn mower. One is a riding mower, and the other is a standard walking power mower. Lawn King is interested in establishing a pricing policy for the two mowers that will maximize the total profit for the product line. Sales for these two products are not independent. Over time, Lawn King has observed that an increase in the price of the riding mower is usually accompanied by a decrease in the number of riding mowers sold and an increase in the number of walking mowers sold. Similarly, increases in the price of the walking mower have been accompanied by a decrease in sales of the walking mower and an increase in sales of the riding mower. Economists would say that the two types of lawn mower are *substitutable products*. Because these two products are substitutable, we should expect that an appropriate mathematical model for maximizing total profit would involve the simultaneous consideration of prices for both products.

Suppose that after a study of the relationships between sales prices and quantities sold, Lawn King has established the following expressions:

$$q_1 = 95 - 2p_1 + 0.7p_2 \tag{19.6}$$

$$q_2 = 188 + 0.3p_1 - 0.5p_2 \tag{19.7}$$

where

$q_1 = $ number of walking mowers sold in thousands

$q_2 = $ number of riding mowers sold in thousands

$p_1 = $ price of walking mower in dollars

$p_2 = $ price of riding mower in dollars

Further information, prepared by the accounting department, is available on the total cost of producing each type of mower:

$$c_1 = 100 + 90q_1 \tag{19.8}$$

$$c_2 = 50 + 250q_2 \tag{19.9}$$

---

[3]The analysis of this case essentially involves treating each endpoint as a separate constraint. For a discussion, see B. S. Gottfried and J. Weisman, *Introduction to Optimization Theory* (Englewood Cliffs, N.J.: Prentice-Hall, 1973).

where

c_1 = total cost of producing q_1 walking mowers in thousands of dollars

c_2 = total cost of producing q_2 riding mowers in thousands of dollars

Note that the production costs are in thousands of dollars and the number of lawn mowers are being measured in thousands of units. The fixed cost of producing walking mowers (the part that is independent of the number of units produced) is thus $100,000, and the variable cost is $90,000 per 1000 walking mowers, or $90 per mower. Similarly, the fixed cost of production for riding mowers is $50,000, and the variable cost is $250,000 per 1000 mowers, or $250 per mower.

We would like to develop a mathematical model of the relationship between the controllable inputs, p_1 and p_2, and the output we would like to maximize, gross profit (GP). The appropriate relationship is established as follows:

$$GP = \text{total revenue} - \text{total cost}$$
$$= (p_1 q_1 + p_2 q_2) - (c_1 + c_2) \tag{19.10}$$

We can use equations (19.6) through (19.9) to eliminate q_1 and q_2 from the model, permitting us to write a mathematical model that is a function of only the two decision variables p_1 and p_2. Using equations (19.6) and (19.7) to substitute into equations (19.8) and (19.9), we obtain (in thousands of dollars)

$$c_1 = 100 + 90(95 - 2p_1 + 0.7p_2)$$
$$= 8650 - 180p_1 + 63p_2$$

and

$$c_2 = 50 + 250(188 + 0.3p_1 - 0.5p_2)$$
$$= 47,050 + 75p_1 - 125p_2$$

Substituting these two expressions along with equations (19.6) and (19.7) into the gross profit expression [equation (19.10)] allows us to write the gross profit model as a function of p_1 and p_2 only:

$$GP = p_1(95 - 2p_1 + 0.7p_2) + p_2(188 + 0.3p_1 - 0.5p_2)$$
$$- (8650 - 180p_1 + 63p_2) - (47,050 + 75p_1 - 125p_2)$$

After multiplying and collecting terms we obtain

$$GP = -2p_1^2 - 0.5p_2^2 + p_1 p_2 + 200p_1 + 250p_2 - 55,700 \tag{19.11}$$

This is the function we would like to maximize. The gross profit in this model is represented by an unconstrained nonlinear function of two variables. The rules for finding the local maximum and/or local minimum of functions of two variables are similar to the ones we developed in the previous section for functions of one variable. There is a first derivative test that serves as a necessary condition that must be satisfied by any local maximum or local minimum point. In addition, there is a second derivative test that can be applied to determine whether a point satisfying the necessary condition is a local maximum, a local minimum, or neither. This second derivative test is referred to as a sufficient condition. The first derivative test is stated as rule 3:

Rule 3 (Necessary Condition)

Both partial derivatives of an unconstrained function of two variables must equal zero at any local maximum or local minimum point.

Let us apply the first derivative test to the gross profit function [equation (19.11)] in our Lawn King problem. Recall from calculus that when taking the partial derivative of a function of more than one variable, we treat all the variables except the one we are taking the partial derivative with respect to as if they were constants. Taking the two partial derivatives of the gross profit function yields

$$\frac{\partial GP}{\partial p_1} = -4p_1 + p_2 + 200 \tag{19.12}$$

and

$$\frac{\partial GP}{\partial p_2} = -p_2 + p_1 + 250 \tag{19.13}$$

Following rule 3 and setting both partial derivatives equal to zero, we obtain a system of two simultaneous equations in the two variables p_1 and p_2:

$$-4p_1 + p_2 + 200 = 0 \tag{19.14}$$
$$p_1 - p_2 + 250 = 0 \tag{19.15}$$

Adding equations (19.14) and (19.15) yields

$$-3p_1 + 450 = 0$$

Thus, we have

$$3p_1 = 450$$

or

$$p_1 = 150$$

Substituting $p_1 = 150$ into equation (19.15) yields

$$p_2 = 400$$

Hence, the point $p_1 = 150$ and $p_2 = 400$ satisfies the necessary condition given by rule 3. Since $p_1 = 150$ and $p_2 = 400$ are the only values of p_1 and p_2 satisfying the necessary condition, we know that if this point is a local maximum, it must also be the global maximum. Just as in the single-variable case, when there is only one point satisfying the necessary condition, the function cannot have more than one local maximum or local minimum. In order to ensure that we have found a local maximum, and not perhaps a local minimum, a second derivative test is necessary.

The second derivative test requires that we know the values of all the second partial derivatives of the function. There are four second partial derivatives for a function of two variables; each of the two first partial derivatives has two partial derivatives itself. Let us calculate the second partial derivatives for our Lawn King problem.

In order to calculate the partial derivative of GP, first with respect to p_1 and then again with respect to p_1, we simply take the partial derivative of equation (19.12) with respect to p_1. Thus,

$$\frac{\partial^2 \text{GP}}{\partial p_1^2} = -4$$

The notation $\partial^2 \text{GP}/\partial p_1^2$ is used to indicate that the partial derivative of GP was taken first with respect to p_1 and then again with respect to p_1.

To calculate the second partial derivative denoted by $\partial^2 \text{GP}/\partial p_2 \partial p_1$ we first take the partial derivative of GP with respect to p_1 and then again with respect to p_2. Thus, we can compute this partial derivative by taking the partial derivative of equation (19.12) with respect to p_2. Doing so, we obtain

$$\frac{\partial^2 \text{GP}}{\partial p_2 \partial p_1} = 1$$

Similarly, the notation $\partial^2 \text{GP}/\partial p_1 \partial p_2$ is used to indicate that the partial derivative of GP was taken first with respect to p_2 and then with respect to p_1. Taking the partial derivative of equation (19.13) with respect to p_1, we obtain this second partial derivative:

$$\frac{\partial^2 \text{GP}}{\partial p_1 \partial p_2} = 1$$

Finally, the notation $\partial^2 \text{GP}/\partial p_2^2$ is used to indicate that the partial derivative of GP was taken first with respect to p_2 and then again with respect to p_2. Hence, we obtain this second partial derivative by taking the partial derivative of equation (19.13) with respect to p_2:

$$\frac{\partial^2 \text{GP}}{\partial p_2^2} = -1$$

We can make one observation as a result of calculating these second partial derivatives. In our Lawn King problem the *mixed partials* (that is, with respect to one variable, then the other) are equal. This is true except for certain rare cases. We shall not be interested in such cases and thus will assume that the second mixed partials are always equal. Rule 4 can now be stated as supplying sufficient conditions for a point (x_1, x_2) to give a local maximum, a local minimum, or a saddle point of an unconstrained function $f(x_1, x_2)$ of two variables:

Rule 4 (Sufficient Condition)

If rule 3 is satisfied at the point (x_1, x_2) and
  a. If

$$\frac{\partial^2 f}{\partial x_1^2} > 0$$

  and

$$\left(\frac{\partial^2 f}{\partial x_1^2}\right)\left(\frac{\partial^2 f}{\partial x_2^2}\right) - \left(\frac{\partial^2 f}{\partial x_1 \partial x_2}\right)^2 > 0$$

then the point is a local *minimum*.

b. If

$$\frac{\partial^2 f}{\partial x_1^2} < 0$$

and

$$\left(\frac{\partial^2 f}{\partial x_1^2}\right)\left(\frac{\partial^2 f}{\partial x_2^2}\right) - \left(\frac{\partial^2 f}{\partial x_1 \partial x_2}\right)^2 > 0$$

then the point is a local *maximum*.

c. If

$$\left(\frac{\partial^2 f}{\partial x_1^2}\right)\left(\frac{\partial^2 f}{\partial x_2^2}\right) - \left(\frac{\partial^2 f}{\partial x_1 \partial x_2}\right)^2 < 0$$

then the point is a *saddle point,* which is neither a local maximum nor a local minimum.

Condition (c) of rule 4 referring to a saddle point means that the point we have found attains a maximum with respect to one of the variables, but a minimum with respect to the other. Hence, the function indeed looks like a saddle at that point, and the solution is neither a local maximum nor a local minimum value of the function.

Cases in which

$$\left(\frac{\partial^2 f}{\partial x_1^2}\right)\left(\frac{\partial^2 f}{\partial x_2^2}\right) - \left(\frac{\partial^2 f}{\partial x_1 \partial x_2}\right)^2 = 0$$

have not been mentioned. In this situation the point could actually be a local minimum or a local maximum, but further analysis would be necessary to establish that fact. However, that further analysis is beyond the scope of this text.

Let us now apply rule 4 to the Lawn King problem to see if we have found a local maximum. We have

$$\frac{\partial^2 GP}{\partial p_1^2} = -4 < 0$$

and

$$\left(\frac{\partial^2 GP}{\partial p_1^2}\right)\left(\frac{\partial^2 GP}{\partial p_2^2}\right) - \left(\frac{\partial^2 GP}{\partial p_1 \partial p_2}\right)^2 = (-4)(-1) - (1)^2 = 3 > 0$$

Therefore, case (b) of rule 4 applies, and we have indeed found a local maximum, which from our previous discussion we know to be a global maximum.

Our analysis of the Lawn King problem is now complete. We have determined that a pricing policy of $150 for the walking mower and $400 for the riding mower will maximize the company's gross profit. Using equation (19.11), the gross profit the company can anticipate if it employs this pricing policy is

$$GP = -2(150)^2 - 0.5(400)^2 + (150)(400) + 200(150)$$
$$+ 250(400) - 55,700 = 9300$$

Since the model measures gross profit in thousands of dollars, Lawn King can anticipate a gross profit of $9,300,000 with this pricing policy. Of course, there are a number of other expenses that must yet be subtracted before we can determine the company's net profit.

At a price of $150 for the walking mower and $400 for the riding mower, we can now determine the number of mowers that will be sold by using equations (19.6) and (19.7). The number of walking mowers sold, q_1, is

$$q_1 = 95 - 2p_1 + 0.7p_2$$
$$= 95 - 2(150) + 0.7(400)$$
$$= 75 \text{ (thousand)}$$

The number of riding mowers sold, q_2, is

$$q_2 = 188 + 0.3p_1 - 0.5p_2$$
$$= 188 + 0.3(150) - 0.5(400)$$
$$= 33 \text{ (thousand)}$$

Thus, if Lawn King produces 75,000 walking mowers at a price of $150 each and 33,000 riding mowers at a price of $400 each, the company will maximize gross profit at an anticipated level of $9,300,000. Note that the applicability of these results depends critically on the confidence management has in the relationships established between sales prices and quantities sold and costs and quantities sold. That is, if management believes equations (19.6) to (19.9) are accurate representations of the true relationships between these factors, then the information developed using our calculus-based solution procedures can be valuable input to the decision-making process.

In our discussion of the Lawn King problem we concluded that the local maximum point $p_1 = 150$ and $p_2 = 400$ was also the global maximum since $p_1 = 150$ and $p_2 = 400$ were the only values satisfying the necessary condition given by rule 3. Let us now discuss in general how we can determine the global optimal solution for any unconstrained function of two variables. We will state the procedure for a maximization problem in order to simplify the exposition. The modifications necessary to solve minimization problems should be apparent.

Step 1 Find all local maxima by applying rules 3 and 4.
Step 2 Select the largest of the local maxima as the global maximum (maxima).[4]

Note that a function can have more than one global maximum. Such situations are analogous to the case of alternate optima in a linear program.

To make sure that we understand the concepts involved in optimizing unconstrained mathematical models with two decision variables, let us consider the following numerical example.

Example. Suppose we want to find all the minimum and maximum points of the function below.

$$f(x_1, x_2) = 5x_1^2 + 10x_2^2 + 10x_1x_2 - 22x_1 - 26x_2 + 25 \qquad (19.16)$$

---

[4] For those unconstrained functions that go to infinity, a global maximum does not exist. Hence, in such cases steps 1 and 2 will not yield a global maximum. However, such functions could never be realistic models of real-world optimization problems, and consequently we avoid a digression into such considerations in this text.

Applying rule 3, we must set the partial derivatives with respect to x_1 and x_2 equal to zero and then solve the resulting equations for x_1 and x_2:

$$\frac{\partial f}{\partial x_1} = 10x_1 + 10x_2 - 22 = 0$$

$$\frac{\partial f}{\partial x_2} = 20x_2 + 10x_1 - 26 = 0$$

Solving these equations, we obtain the solution $x_1 = \frac{9}{5}, x_2 = \frac{2}{5}$. To see if this is a local maximum or a local minimum, we must calculate the second partial derivatives and apply rule 4. Calculating the second partial derivatives, we get

$$\frac{\partial^2 f}{\partial x_1^2} = 10 \qquad \frac{\partial^2 f}{\partial x_2^2} = 20 \qquad \frac{\partial^2 f}{\partial x_1 \partial x_2} = 10$$

Since

$$\frac{\partial^2 f}{\partial x_1^2} = 10 > 0$$

and

$$\left(\frac{\partial^2 f}{\partial x_1^2}\right)\left(\frac{\partial^2 f}{\partial x_2^2}\right) - \left(\frac{\partial^2 f}{\partial x_1 \partial x_2}\right)^2 = (10)(20) - (10)^2 = 100 > 0$$

case (a) of rule 4 applies, and the point $x_1 = \frac{9}{5}, x_2 = \frac{2}{5}$ yields a local minimum value for the function. Since this is the only point at which rule 3 applies, we can further conclude that this local minimum is the global minimum.

Let us pause for a moment to reflect on what we have learned in this section. Just as for unconstrained functions of a single variable, there is a first and second derivative test that must be applied in order to determine if a point is a local maximum or a local minimum. The first derivative test, which must be satisfied by both local maximum and local minimum points, is called a necessary condition and is stated in rule 3. The second derivative test, just as with functions of a single variable, allows us to distinguish among a local maximum point, a local minimum point, and a point that may be neither a local maximum nor a local minimum. This is called a sufficient condition and is stated in rule 4.

We would like to comment, before closing this section, that for unconstrained functions of more than two variables, the first and second derivative tests are given by extensions of rules 3 and 4. For an unconstrained function of n variables, $f(x_1, x_2, \ldots, x_n)$, the first derivative test for a local maximum or a local minimum requires that all n of the partial derivatives equal zero. Since it is a simple extension of rule 3, we state it here as rule 5:

Rule 5 (Necessary Condition)

All n partial derivatives of an unconstrained function of n variables, $f(x_1, x_2, \ldots, x_n)$, must equal zero at any local maximum or local minimum point.

For an unconstrained function of n variables, the second derivative test requires that all the second partial derivatives be calculated. Although this test is similar to rule 4, a simple statement of the test requires that we construct a matrix of second partial derivatives and perform some tests on the matrix. The tests require a knowledge of determinants of matrices, which is not a prerequisite for the text. Thus, we omit an extension of rule 4 to a second derivative test for functions of n variables. This extension is discussed in a number of more advanced texts on mathematical programming.[5]

19.3 ▼ MODELS WITH EQUALITY CONSTRAINTS: LAGRANGE MULTIPLIERS

In this section we discuss a problem that leads to the formulation of a nonlinear mathematical model involving two decision variables and one constraint. After we have seen how such a problem might arise, we present a solution procedure which once again involves a calculus-based first and second derivative test.

Green Lawns, Inc., provides a lawn fertilizer and weed control service. The company provides four treatments of fertilizer and weed control chemical to its subscribers each year. Green Lawns is adding a special aeration treatment as a low-cost extra service option, which it hopes will help attract new customers. Management is planning to promote this new service in two media: radio and direct-mail advertising. A budget of $2000 is to be used on this promotional campaign over the next quarter. Based on past experience in promoting its other services, Green Lawns has been able to obtain an estimate of the relationship between sales and the amount spent on promotion in these two media:

$$s = -2x_1^2 - 10x_2^2 - 8x_1x_2 + 18x_1 + 34x_2 \qquad (19.17)$$

where

$$s = \text{total sales in thousands of dollars}$$

$$x_1 = \text{thousands of dollars spent on radio advertising}$$

$$x_2 = \text{thousands of dollars spent on direct-mail promotion}$$

Green Lawns would like to develop a promotional strategy that will lead to maximum sales subject to the restriction provided by the promotional budget. Recognizing that the promotional budget is $2000, we may state Green Lawn's problem as the following constrained optimization problem:

$$\max \quad -2x_1^2 - 10x_2^2 - 8x_1x_2 + 18x_1 + 34x_2$$

$$\text{s.t.} \qquad\qquad\qquad\qquad\qquad\qquad\qquad (19.18)$$

$$x_1 + x_2 = 2$$

We note that the constraint is written as $x_1 + x_2 = 2$ because x_1 and x_2 are being measured in thousands of dollars. Also, the objective function calls for the maximization of sales in thousands of dollars.

In general, all problems involving the minimization or maximization of a function of two variables subject to an equality constraint can be written as follows:

---

[5] A good discussion of these tests is contained in D.G. Luenberger, *Introduction to Linear and Nonlinear Programming* (Reading, Mass.: Addison-Wesley, 1973).

$$\text{min or max} \quad f(x_1, x_2)$$

$$\text{s.t.} \tag{19.19}$$

$$g(x_1, x_2) = b$$

The approach we shall follow to solve the above class of problems is first to introduce a new variable, called a *Lagrange multiplier,* and use this new variable to combine the constraint and objective function together into a single function. The new single function we shall form is called a *Lagrangian function* and is written below, where λ denotes the Lagrange multiplier.

$$\text{Lagrangian function} = L(x_1, x_2, \lambda) = f(x_1, x_2) + \lambda[g(x_1, x_2) - b] \tag{19.20}$$

The first derivative test that every local minimum or local maximum point of a constrained problem must satisfy[6] is stated in rule 6:

Rule 6 (Necessary Condition)

For a function of two variables, x_1 and x_2, subject to one constraint to have a local minimum or a local maximum at a point, the partial derivatives of the Lagrangian function with respect to x_1, x_2, and λ must all equal zero at that point.

Thus, once we have set up the Lagrangian function, this first derivative test for a constrained problem turns out to be very similar to the first derivative test for unconstrained functions. Let us now apply this test to the problem faced by Green Lawns, Inc.

Introducing a Lagrange muliplier as indicated by equations (19.19) and (19.20), we obtain the following Lagrangian function:

$$L(x_1, x_2, \lambda) = -2x_1^2 - 10x_2^2 - 8x_1x_2 + 18x_1 + 34x_2$$
$$+ \lambda(x_1 + x_2 - 2) \tag{19.21}$$

Following rule 6, we first determine the partial derivatives with respect to x_1, x_2, and λ, and then set them equal to zero:

$$\frac{\partial L}{\partial x_1} = -4x_1 - 8x_2 + 18 + \lambda = 0 \tag{19.22}$$

$$\frac{\partial L}{\partial x_2} = -20x_2 - 8x_1 + 34 + \lambda = 0 \tag{19.23}$$

$$\frac{\partial L}{\partial \lambda} = x_1 + x_2 - 2 = 0 \tag{19.24}$$

We are left with three equations in three unknowns: x_1, x_2, and λ. Solving these will give us a point satisfying rule 6 and thus a candidate for a maximum solution of the Green

---

[6]There are certain examples that can be constructed for which the maximum or minimum does not satisfy rule 6, but these are exceptions that rarely occur in practice. Thus, we shall not be concerned with them.

Lawns problem. Subtracting equation (19.22) from equation (19.23) allows us to form a new equation not including λ:

$$-4x_1 - 12x_2 + 16 = 0 \tag{19.25}$$

Multiplying equation (19.24) by 4 and adding the result to equation (19.25) yields

$$-8x_2 + 8 = 0$$

Hence,

$$x_2 = 1$$

Substituting $x_2 = 1$ into equation (19.24), we find that $x_1 = 1$. As a consequence, from equations (19.22) and (19.23) we find that $\lambda = -6$. Thus, the necessary condition of rule 1 is satisfied with

$$x_1^* = 1$$
$$x_2^* = 1$$
$$\lambda^* = -6$$

Since there is only one solution satisfying rule 6, we know that if it is a local maximum, it is also a global maximum. It remains to be seen if this point truly yields a local maximum solution for the Green Lawns problem. We must develop a second derivative rule in order to make that determination. Rule 7 provides such a test and thus gives sufficient conditions for a local maximum or local minimum point.

Rule 7 (Sufficient Condition)

If rule 6 is satisfied at a point $(x_1^*, x_2^*, \lambda^*)$, apply conditions (a) and (b) of rule 4 to the Lagrangian function with λ fixed at a value of λ^* in order to determine if the point (x_1^*, x_2^*) is a local maximum or a local minimum.

Rule 7 says first to fix λ at the value necessary to satisfy rule 6. Then the Lagrangian function is expressed as a function of the two variables x_1 and x_2, with λ fixed at the value λ^*. Conditions (a) and (b) of rule 4 may be applied to this new function in order to determine if we have a local maximum or a local minimum.[7]

Let us apply rule 7 to the Green Lawns problem to see if the solution we have found is a local maximum.

The Lagrangian function [equation (19.21)] with λ fixed at $\lambda^* = -6$ is

$$L(x_1, x_2, \lambda = -6) = -2x_1^2 - 10x_2^2 - 8x_1x_2 + 18x_1 + 34x_2$$
$$- 6(x_1 + x_2 - 2)$$

We need to find the second partial derivatives of this function with respect to x_1 and x_2 to determine if the $x_1^* = 1$ and $x_2^* = 1$ solution yields a maximum. Taking the first partial

---

[7]Condition (c) of rule 4 is not used for equality constrained problems since a saddle point of the Lagrangian function need not correspond to a saddle point of the equality constrained problem we want to solve.

derivatives with respect to x_1 and x_2, we obtain the same result we could have obtained by substituting $\lambda = -6$ into equations (19.22) and (19.23):

$$\frac{\partial L}{\partial x_1} = -4x_1 - 8x_2 + 18 - 6 = -4x_1 - 8x_2 + 12$$

$$\frac{\partial L}{\partial x_2} = -20x_2 - 8x_1 + 34 - 6 = -20x_2 - 8x_1 + 28$$

The second partial derivatives of this function with respect to x_1 and x_2 are

$$\frac{\partial^2 L}{\partial x_1^2} = -4 \qquad \frac{\partial^2 L}{\partial x_2^2} = -20 \qquad \frac{\partial^2 L}{\partial x_1 \partial x_2} = -8$$

To see if the Lagrangian function with λ fixed at $\lambda^* = -6$ has an unconstrained minimum at $x_1^* = 1$ and $x_2^* = 1$, we apply the second derivative test developed in rule 4 for unconstrained functions of two variables:

$$\frac{\partial^2 L}{\partial x_1^2} = -4 < 0$$

$$\left(\frac{\partial^2 L}{\partial x_1^2}\right) \left(\frac{\partial^2 L}{\partial x_2^2}\right) - \left(\frac{\partial^2 L}{\partial x_1 \partial x_2}\right)^2 = (-4)(-20) - (-8)^2 = 16 > 0$$

Case (b) of rule 4 applies, and the point $x_1^* = 1$, $x_2^* = 1$ is an unconstrained maximum of the Lagrangian function with $\lambda = -6$. Thus, we see that $x_1^* = 1$ and $x_2^* = 1$ is the optimal solution to the Green Lawns problem. The company should invest $1000 in radio advertising and $1000 in direct-mail promotion. To determine the expected sales volume from this strategy we must evaluate the objective function [equation (19.17)] with $x_1 = 1$ and $x_2 = 1$. Doing so, we obtain

$$\text{Sales} = -2(1)^2 - 10(1)^2 - 8(1)(1) + 18(1) + 34(1) = 32$$

Thus, the expected sales volume resulting from this promotional strategy is $32,000.

The following numerical example provides another illustration of the use of the Lagrange multiplier method for solving equality constrained optimization problems.

Example. Suppose we have the following constrained optimization problem:

$$\min \quad x_1^2 + 2x_2^2 - 8x_1 - 12x_2 + 34$$

$$\text{s.t.}$$

$$x_1 + 2x_2 = 4$$

Setting up the Lagrangian function for this problem, we obtain

$$L(x_1, x_2, \lambda) = x_1^2 + 2x_2^2 - 8x_1 - 12x_2 + 34 + \lambda(x_1 + 2x_2 - 4) \quad (19.26)$$

Applying rule 6 we set the partial derivatives of this Lagrangian function with respect to x_1, x_2, and λ equal to zero:

$$\frac{\partial L}{\partial x_1} = 2x_1 - 8 + \lambda = 0$$

$$\frac{\partial L}{\partial x_2} = 4x_2 - 12 + 2\lambda = 0$$

$$\frac{\partial L}{\partial \lambda} = x_1 + 2x_2 - 4 = 0$$

Solving the resulting three equations for the three unknowns, we obtain

$$x_1^* = 2 \quad x_2^* = 1 \quad \lambda^* = 4$$

Once again, there is only one solution satisfying rule 6. Thus, if it is a local maximum or minimum, it must also be a global maximum or minimum.

We must now apply rule 7 to see if this is a local maximum or a local minimum point. Setting $\lambda^* = 4$ in equation (19.26), the second partial derivatives of the Lagrangian function with respect to x_1 and x_2 are

$$\frac{\partial^2 L}{\partial x_1^2} = 2 \quad \frac{\partial^2 L}{\partial x_2^2} = 4 \quad \frac{\partial^2 L}{\partial x_1 \partial x_2} = 0$$

Checking conditions (a) and (b) of the test procedures for rule 4, we have

$$\frac{\partial^2 L}{\partial x_1^2} = 2 > 0$$

and

$$\left(\frac{\partial^2 L}{\partial x_1^2}\right)\left(\frac{\partial^2 L}{\partial x_2^2}\right) - \left(\frac{\partial^2 L}{\partial x_1 \partial x_2}\right)^2 = (2)(4) - (0)^2 = 8 > 0$$

Thus, we have a local minimum of the Lagrangian function with λ fixed at 4, and in light of the previous discussion we have found a global minimum at $x_1 = 2$ and $x_2 = 1$.

The Green Lawns, Inc., problem and the above problem are examples of models having a nonlinear objective function and a linear equality constraint. In applying rules 6 and 7, we were able to develop the necessary and sufficient condition test relatively easily. However, for problems where the equality constraint is also nonlinear, you will find that the solution computations become somewhat more difficult. (Problems 12 and 14 at the end of this chapter ask you to use rules 6 and 7 to solve a problem with a nonlinear objective function and a nonlinear equality constraint.)

To complete our discussion, we mention briefly how rule 6 can be extended to supply a necessary condition for minimizing or maximizing a function of n variables subject to m equality constraints. This extended problem may be stated in the following form:

$$\text{min or max} \quad f(x_1, x_2, \ldots, x_n)$$

s.t.

$$g_1(x_1, x_2, \ldots, x_n) = b_1$$
$$g_2(x_1, x_2, \ldots, x_n) = b_2$$
$$\vdots \qquad\qquad \vdots \tag{19.27}$$
$$g_m(x_1, x_2, \ldots, x_n) = b_m$$

A Lagrangian function, combining the objective function and all the constraints into one function, can be formulated by introducing a separate Lagrange multiplier for each constraint:

$$
\begin{aligned}
L(x_1, x_2, &\ldots, x_n, \lambda_1, \lambda_2, \ldots, \lambda_m) \\
&= f(x_1, x_2, \ldots, x_n) + \lambda_1[g_1(x_1, x_2, \ldots, x_n) - b_1] \\
&\quad + \lambda_2[g_2(x_1, x_2, \ldots, x_n) - b_2] + \ldots \quad (19.28) \\
&\quad + \lambda_m[g_m(x_1, x_2, \ldots, x_n) - b_m]
\end{aligned}
$$

The extension of rule 6 to this problem can now be stated in terms of this new Lagrangian function:

Rule 8 (Necessary Condition)

For a function of n variables, $f(x_1, x_2, \ldots, x_n)$, subject to m constraints to have a local minimum or a local maximum at a point, the partial derivatives of the Lagrangian function with respect to $x_1, x_2, \ldots, x_n$ and $\lambda_1, \lambda_2, \ldots, \lambda_m$ must all equal zero at that point.

The second derivative test for this problem is a natural extension to rule 7; that is, we would check for a local maximum or a local minimum of the Lagrangian function with $\lambda_1, \lambda_2, \ldots, \lambda_m$ fixed at the values found when applying rule 8. This would require that we have a second derivative test for an unconstrained function of n variables. A matrix of second partial derivatives provides the basis for this test; however, as we stated earlier, the methodology is beyond the scope of this text.

Before concluding this section, we comment briefly on its similarity to the previous two sections. Once again we had a first derivative test that any local maximum or local minimum point had to satisfy. Then we had a second derivative test that could be used to determine if a point satisfying the first derivative test was indeed a local maximum or a local minimum. The only conceptual difference in solving these constrained problems was that we had to formulate a Lagrangian function and then perform the first and second derivative tests on that function. Only conditions (a) and (b) of the second derivative test were applicable for constrained problems.

19.4 ▼ INTERPRETATION OF THE LAGRANGE MULTIPLIER

In the previous section we saw that it was necessary to introduce an additional variable called a Lagrange multiplier in order to solve constrained problems. This variable was used in setting up the Lagrangian function. In meeting the necessary condition (rule 6), we actually found a value for the Lagrange multiplier. The value of this Lagrange multiplier can often be used to provide valuable managerial information about the sensitivity of an optimal solution to changes in resource levels.

In order to be more specific, let us reconsider the Green Lawns problem, which is restated below:

$$\text{max} \quad -2x_1^2 - 10x_2^2 - 8x_1x_2 + 18x_1 + 34x_2$$

s.t.

$$x_1 + x_2 = 2$$

Here, x_1 represents the amount spent on radio advertising and x_2 the amount spent on direct-mail promotion. The constraint indicates that $2000 is to be used for the promotional campaign and that it is to be divided between the two media, x_1 and x_2. In the previous section we saw that the optimal allocation was to divide the budget equally between the two media: $x_1 = 1$ and $x_2 = 1$. Management might wonder what the effect on sales would be if a different amount—say, $1000 or $3000—were budgeted for the promotional campaign. The value of the Lagrange multiplier provides an estimate of that effect. Let us see how.

Recall that the general model with two decision variables and one equality constraint was written as

$$\text{min or max} \quad f(x_1, x_2)$$

s.t.

$$g(x_1, x_2) = b$$

The interpretation of the Lagrange multiplier for this problem is stated as property 1.

Property 1 (Interpretation of the Lagrange Multiplier)

The value of the Lagrange multiplier associated with the general model above is the negative of the rate of change of the objective function with respect to a change in b. More formally, it is the negative of the partial derivative of $f(x_1, x_2)$ with respect to b; that is, $\lambda = -\partial f/\partial b$ or

$$\frac{\partial f}{\partial b} = -\lambda \qquad (19.29)$$

The optimal solution to the Green Lawns problem has

$$x_1^* = 1 \qquad x_2^* = 1 \qquad \lambda^* = -6$$

Since $\lambda^* = -6$, property 1 indicates that with $\partial f/\partial b = -\lambda = -(-6) = 6$, the objective function should increase by approximately 6 if b is increased by 1. For example, if the budget is increased from $2000 to $3000 in the Green Lawns problem, the objective function should increase by approximately $6000. Let us change the budget to $3000 and see what happens.

After increasing the budget to $3000 the Green Lawns problem can be written as follows:

$$\text{max} \quad -2x_1^2 - 10x_2^2 - 8x_1x_2 + 18x_1 + 34x_2 \qquad (19.30)$$

s.t.

$$x_1 + x_2 = 3$$

Formulating the Lagrangian function and setting the partial derivatives equal to zero yield

$$L(x_1, x_2, \lambda) = -2x_1^2 - 10x_2^2 - 8x_1x_2 + 18x_1 + 34x_2 \qquad (19.31)$$
$$+ \lambda(x_1 + x_2 - 3)$$

and

$$\frac{\partial L}{\partial x_1} = -4x_1 - 8x_2 + 18 + \lambda = 0$$

$$\frac{\partial L}{\partial x_2} = -20x_2 - 8x_1 + 34 + \lambda = 0$$

$$\frac{\partial L}{\partial \lambda} = x_1 + x_2 - 3 = 0$$

Solving these three equations simultaneously for x_1, x_2, and λ yields

$$x_1^* = 2.5 \qquad x_2^* = 0.5 \qquad \lambda^* = -4$$

To check to see if we have a maximum we must determine the second partial derivatives of the Lagrangian with λ fixed at $\lambda^* = -4$. Using equation (19.31) with $\lambda = -4$, these second partial derivatives are

$$\frac{\partial^2 L}{\partial x_1^2} = -4 \qquad \frac{\partial^2 L}{\partial x_2^2} = -20 \qquad \frac{\partial^2 L}{\partial x_1 \partial x_2} = -8$$

Applying rule 4, we see that $x_1^* = 2.5$ and $x_2^* = 0.5$ does indeed yield an unconstrained maximum of the Lagrangian with λ fixed at $\lambda^* = -4$. According to rule 7 we have found the maximum for this new problem.

Now we would like to see how close the $6000 increase in the objective function predicted by $\lambda^* = -6$ comes to the true increase. The value of the objective function for $x_1^* = 2.5$ and $x_2^* = 0.5$ is

$$f(x_1, x_2) = \text{sales} = -2(2.5)^2 - 10(0.5)^2 - 8(2.5)(0.5)$$
$$+ 18(2.5) + 34(0.5) = 37$$

The maximum value of sales, given a budget of $3000, is thus $37,000. Since the maximum value for a budget of $2000 was found previously to be $32,000, the increase in sales is $5000 and not the $6000 the value of the Lagrange multiplier predicted. We should not be too surprised at this. What we are observing is the law of diminishing returns in action. As the amount of resources available increases (advertising budget in this case), the per-unit increase in the objective function decreases. Note that the value we obtained for the Lagrange multiplier when the budget was increased to $3000 was $\lambda^* = -4$. This would lead us to predict that sales would increase by another $4000 if the budget were further increased to $4000. The rate of return per unit increase in the budget has decreased from 6 to 4 as the budget has increased from 2 to 3.

Also, we should note that the Lagrange multiplier value associated with a budget of $3000, $\lambda^* = -4$, would lead us to predict that sales would decrease by $4000 if the budget were decreased to $2000. The actual change, as we now know, is $5000. Thus, if we used the Lagrange multiplier associated with $b = 2000$, $\lambda^* = -6$, to predict the change in sales associated with a $1000 change in the budget, we would overestimate the change. On the other hand, if we used the Lagrange multiplier associated with $b = 3000$,

$\lambda^* = -4$, to predict the change in sales associated with changing the budget from $3000 to $2000, we would underestimate the change. The actual change, $5000, is halfway between.

In Table 19.1 we show the maximum sales levels for budget amounts varying between $1000 and $3000 in increments of $200 together with the maximum sales levels we would have predicted by using the property of the Lagrange multiplier.

Table 19.1 verifies that the estimates based on the Lagrange multiplier are good as long as the change in b is not large. For a $200 change in the budget, the estimate based on the Lagrange multiplier is pretty good. There is only a $40 error in the sales estimate. Of course, as we get farther away from a budget of $2000, the predictions continue to get worse. We can also see the effect of diminishing returns with respect to the advertising budget from studying the table. When the budget is set at $1000, a $200 increase causes an increase in sales of $1560. When the budget is set at $2800, a $200 increase causes an increase in sales of only $840.

From a managerial point of view we see that the value of the Lagrange multiplier can provide important information. It is an indication of the sensitivity of the optimal solution to changes in resource levels. In most real-world problems these resource levels are not some sacred number that cannot be changed. For example, in the Green Lawns situation, management has initially budgeted $2000 for an advertising campaign. If the quantitative analyst can show the manager that an increase in the advertising budget of $1 can be expected to increase sales by $6, then the manager may want to consider expanding the budget. Of course, whether or not the manager chooses to expand it will depend on a number of other considerations as well. Can funds be freed from other uses for the campaign? How much confidence do we have that our model is representative of the real relationship between advertising in the two media and sales? Also, since the $6 increase in sales will cost us $1 of advertising, is the remaining $5 enough to offset all the other costs associated with the increased sales? Regardless of how this sensitivity information is eventually used by the manager, it is important to know what it means and that it can be made available as a by-product of the model solution.

TABLE 19.1
Maximum Sales Levels for Varying Budgets Compared with Estimates Based on the Lagrange Multiplier of $\lambda = -6$ for the Green Lawns Problem

Budget	Actual Maximum Sales $f(x_1^*, x_2^*)$	Estimated Maximum Sales $\lambda^* = -6$	Difference
$1000	$25,000	$26,000	-1000
1200	26,560	27,200	$-\ 640$
1400	28,040	28,400	$-\ 360$
1600	29,440	29,600	$-\ 160$
1800	30,760	30,800	$-\ \ 40$
2000	32,000	32,000	0
2200	33,160	33,200	$-\ \ 40$
2400	34,240	34,400	$-\ 160$
2600	35,240	35,600	$-\ 360$
2800	36,160	36,800	$-\ 640$
3000	37,000	38,000	-1000

The Lagrange multiplier analysis can be extended to problems with more variables and more constraints. However, because of the additional complexity involved, we leave a discussion of this extension to more advanced texts on mathematical programming.

▼ NOTES AND COMMENTS ▼

The managerial interpretation of the Lagrange multiplier in a constrained optimization model parallels the interpretation of shadow prices or dual prices in a linear programming model. The value of a Lagrange multiplier provides the marginal value of making a change in the right-hand side of a constraint. In applications where the right-hand side of a constraint represents the amount of a scarce resource, the multiplier identifies the marginal value of obtaining additional quantities of the resource. However, since nonlinear relationships are involved, the value of the multiplier can change as soon as any change is made in the value of the right-hand side. There is no ''range of feasibility'' over which the value of the Lagrange multiplier does not change. A manager should keep this in mind and recognize that using the Lagrange multiplier can only be interpreted as an approximation of the value of additional resources in a nonlinear model.

19.5 ▼ MODELS INVOLVING INEQUALITY CONSTRAINTS

In this section we study problems that lead to nonlinear mathematical models involving two decision variables and one inequality constraint. We will find that this type of problem can be solved using the approaches we have already learned in the previous sections of this chapter.

Suppose that instead of stating that a budget of $2000 had to be spent on an advertising campaign for the aeration service, the management of Green Lawns, Inc., had stated that the amount spent had to be less than or equal to the $2000 budget. This is actually a more realistic interpretation of the budget constraint. Certainly if more sales could be realized by spending less on advertising, the company would be willing to do so. Given this less-than-or-equal-to interpretation of the constraint, the Green Lawns model would involve two decision variables and one inequality constraint as shown below.

$$\max \quad -2x_1^2 - 10x_2^2 - 8x_1x_2 + 18x_1 + 34x_2$$

s.t.

$$x_1 + x_2 \leq 2$$

In solving this problem we recognize that there are actually two possibilities with respect to the constraint. The first is that the constraint $x_1 + x_2 \leq 2$ will be binding at the optimal solution. In this case we could assume that the constraint has the form $x_1 + x_2 = 2$ and solve just as we did in Section 19.3 for problems with equality constraints. The second possibility is that at the optimal solution the constraint is not binding; that is, $x_1^* + x_2^* < 2$. In this case we could simply ignore the constraint and solve as we did in Section 19.2 for unconstrained problems. The recognition that these are the only two possibilities is what motivates the solution procedure we are about to present.

We state the solution procedure for a maximization problem in order to simplify the exposition. The modifications necessary to solve minimization problems should be apparent.

Step 1 Assume the constraint is not binding, and apply the procedures of Section 19.2 to find the global maximum of the function, if it exists. (Functions that go to infinity do not have a global maximum.) If this global maximum satisfies the constraint, stop. This is the global maximum for the inequality constrained problem. If not, the constraint may be binding at the optimum. Record the value of any local maximum that satisfies the inequality constraint, and go on to step 2.

Step 2 Assume the constraint is binding and apply the procedures of Section 19.3 to find all the local maxima of the resulting equality constrained problem. Compare these values with any feasible local maxima found in step 1. The largest of these is the global maximum.

Let us apply this solution procedure to our new version of the Green Lawns problem. Applying step 1 and ignoring the constraint $x_1 + x_2 \le 2$ would lead us to solve the unconstrained problem

$$\max \quad -2x_1^2 - 10x_2^2 - 8x_1x_2 + 18x_1 + 34x_2$$

Applying rule 3, we set the partial derivatives of the objective function equal to zero:

$$\frac{\partial f}{\partial x_1} = -4x_1 - 8x_2 + 18 = 0$$

$$\frac{\partial f}{\partial x_2} = -20x_2 - 8x_1 + 34 = 0$$

Solving these two equations simultaneously, we obtain $x_1^* = 5\frac{1}{2}$ and $x_2^* = -\frac{1}{2}$. Before checking the second derivatives for a local maximum or minimum, however, let us see if these values for x_1 and x_2 satisfy our constraint. Clearly, $x_1^* + x_2^* = 5\frac{1}{2} - \frac{1}{2} = 5$ is not less than or equal to 2, and, therefore, even if this solution did yield the global maximum to our unconstrained problem (which it does, by the way), it could not be optimal since it does not satisfy the inequality constraint. There are no other local maxima to record the values of; therefore, we go on to step 2 and solve the following equality constrained optimization problem:

$$\max \quad -2x_1^2 - 10x_2^2 - 8x_1x_2 + 18x_1 + 34x_2$$

s.t.

$$x_1 + x_2 = 2$$

The global maximum for this problem was found in Section 19.3 and is given by $x_1 = 1$ and $x_2 = 1$. Since there are no feasible local maxima from step 1, the optimal solution to our constrained optimization problem is also $x_1 = 1$, $x_2 = 1$, with an expected sales volume of $32,000.

Let us now look at another example involving a minimization problem.

Example. Suppose we want to solve the following problem:

$$\min \quad f(x_1, x_2) = x_1^2 - 10x_1 + x_2^2 - 10x_2$$

s.t.

$$x_1 + 2x_2 \le 20$$

Step 1 of the solution procedure says to ignore the constraint and solve the resulting unconstrained optimization problem. Applying rule 3, we set the partial derivatives of the objective function equal to zero:

$$\frac{\partial f}{\partial x_1} = 2x_1 - 10 = 0$$

$$\frac{\partial f}{\partial x_2} = 2x_2 - 10 = 0$$

Solving these two equations, we obtain $x_1^* = 5$ and $x_2^* = 5$. Since this point satisfies the constraint, we must check to see if it is a local minimum. Applying the second derivative test of rule 4, we obtain

$$\frac{\partial^2 f}{\partial x_1^2} = 2 > 0$$

and

$$\left(\frac{\partial^2 f}{\partial x_1^2}\right)\left(\frac{\partial^2 f}{\partial x_2^2}\right) - \left(\frac{\partial^2 f}{\partial x_2 \partial x_1}\right)^2 = (2)(2) - 0^2 = 4 > 0$$

Therefore, the point $x_1 = 5$, $x_2 = 5$ yields a local minimum for our function. Further, since no other values of x_1, x_2 satisfy rule 3, we can conclude that $x_1 = 5, x_2 = 5$ yields a global minimum for our unconstrained function. Thus, it is unnecessary to go on to step 2 since no point on the constraint boundary could possibly be better than the global minimum. We can therefore conclude that $x_1 = 5, x_2 = 5$ is the global minimum for our inequality constrained problem.

We have seen how the solution procedure of this section can be applied both when the constraint is satisfied as an equality at the optimum and when it is satisfied as a strict inequality. Unfortunately, the solution procedure we have outlined here cannot be extended to problems with more than one inequality constraint or to problems with both equality and inequality constraints. We will comment briefly on what to do in such cases.

In some applications the appropriate mathematical model may have a mixture of equality and inequality constraints. In these kinds of mathematical models, the solution approach invariably requires a computerized mathematical programming algorithm. There are many research papers and a number of mathematical programming textbooks devoted to these computerized algorithms. The approach taken by all these algorithms is iterative in nature. Initially a starting point, which is a guess at the optimal solution, is picked, and then an improved solution is determined by the computer algorithm. Another improvement is made, and so on, until eventually the optimal solution is reached. The details of these solution algorithms are beyond the scope of this text.

▼ NOTES AND COMMENTS ▼

With linear programming models, we have shown how the computer plays an important role in determining the optimal solution to a particular problem. A number of computer codes are readily available for solving linear programming models. Computer codes are also helpful in solving nonlinear models. However, such codes are not as readily available and not as easy to use. This situation is

continued on next page

complicated by the fact that many codes are especially designed to solve a particular type of nonlinear model. Thus, more mathematical expertise is required to understand the special characteristics of the given nonlinear model and then select a computer code that will solve the problem.

▼ SUMMARY

The kinds of problems discussed in this chapter have been examples of decision-making situations in which the appropriate mathematical model of the problem involved nonlinear relationships. When these decision-making situations arise, the linear programming procedures of Chapters 2 through 6 are not applicable, and calculus-based procedures must be employed.

For both unconstrained and constrained problems we saw that first and second derivative tests were required. In the unconstrained single-variable case these tests were made on the first and second derivatives of the objective function. In the unconstrained two-variable case these tests were made on the first and second partial derivatives of the objective function. Equality constrained problems with two decision variables and one constraint were solved by first introducing a new variable called a Lagrange multiplier. A Lagrangian function was then formed by combining the objective function and constraint into one function. Tests on the first and second partial derivatives of the Lagrangian function were then developed to find the optimal solution. The Lagrange multiplier was found to provide valuable managerial information about the sensitivity of the optimal solution to changes in the value of the right-hand side of the constraint (the resource level).

▼ GLOSSARY

Necessary conditions   Conditions, usually requiring first derivatives to be equal to zero, that must be satisfied at an optimal solution. They do not guarantee an optimal solution.

Sufficient conditions   Conditions, usually involving the sign of second derivatives, that determine whether a solution meeting the necessary conditions is a maximum solution, a minimum solution, or no solution.

Saddle point   A condition that occurs in models with more than one decision variable when one variable reaches its maximum value and another reaches its minimum value at the same point.

Lagrange multiplier   A new variable added to a constrained nonlinear model in order to obtain a solution. In sensitivity analysis this variable tells us what effect a change in the level of resources will have on the objective function.

Lagrangian function   The function formed by using the Lagrange multiplier to combine the objective function and the constraint(s) into one function. For example, the constrained problem

$$\min \quad f(x_1, x_2)$$

s.t.

$$g(x_1, x_2) = b$$

has the following Lagrangian function:

$$L(x_1, x_2, \lambda) = f(x_1, x_2) + \lambda[g(x_1, x_2) - b]$$

where λ is the Lagrange multiplier.

Local maximum (minimum)   A point that gives at least as high (low) a value of the objective function as any nearby point.

Global maximum (minimum)   The point, or points, at which a function takes on its greatest (lowest) value.

▼ PROBLEMS

1. **a.** Maximize the function

$$f(x) = 12x - 6x^2 - 30$$

   b. Maximize the above function over the interval

$$0 \le x \le 10$$

   c. Maximize the above function over the interval

$$2 \le x \le 10$$

2. **a.** Find the minimum of the function

$$f(x) = 3x^3 - 20x^2 + 60$$

   b. Find the minimum of the above function over the interval

$$0 \le x \le 4$$

3. A large grocery chain is interested in determining the best size for a new store that is being built at a particular site. The chain has made an extensive study of the sector in which the new store will be located. Based on such factors as sector population, weekly per capita food expenditures, and competition, the grocery chain has developed the following model that relates sales (in thousands of dollars) to the size of the store x (in units of 10,000 square feet):

$$\text{Sales} = 100x - 10x^2 - 150$$

Determine the size of the store that will maximize sales. What are the maximum sales corresponding to the store size?

4. The manufacturer of King's Chunk Style Peanut Butter has determined that sales in any particular store are related to the amount of shelf space devoted to the peanut butter and the amount of traffic through the store. A detailed analysis led to the following equation relating the square feet on shelves and the number of store customers per week to the total weekly sales in dollars:

$$\text{Sales} = -20x^2 - 50C^2 - 60Cx + 220x - 340C + 610$$

where

$$x = \text{square feet of shelf space}$$
$$C = \text{thousands of customers}$$

King uses the above formula to determine the optimal amount of shelf space for its product in any particular store. Suppose a particular store averages a thousand customers per week. How many square feet of shelf space would be required to maximize sales?

5. Suppose the total cost (TC) of producing x pounds of a certain cleaning fluid is given by

$$TC = \tfrac{1}{3}x^4 - 3x^3 + 2x^2 + 5x$$

Write the mathematical expression for the cost per pound. If x must be at least 0.3, what batch size will lead to the minimum cost per pound?

6. A certain product sells for $5 per unit. The total cost C of producing and selling this product is given by

$$C(x) = x^2 - 15x + 20$$

   a. What is the fixed cost of production? That is, what portion of the cost is independent of the number of units produced?
   b. Develop a mathematical model that shows total profit as a function of the number of units produced.
   c. What level of production will maximize profit?

7. The cost per batch of a certain production process is related to the setting of two control instruments. Suppose the total cost per batch is given by

$$f(x_1, x_2) = 4x_1^2 + 2x_2^2 + 4x_1x_2 - 8x_1 - 6x_2 + 35$$

Determine the settings for the two instruments that will minimize this cost.

8. Consider the function $f(x_1, x_2) = 2x_1^4 - 12x_1^2 + 2x_1^2x_2 + x_2^2 - 4x_2 + 20$. Determine whether the points below yield local minima, local maxima, saddle points, or none of these.

$$\begin{pmatrix} x_1 = 0 \\ x_2 = 2 \end{pmatrix} \quad \begin{pmatrix} x_1 = +2 \\ x_2 = -2 \end{pmatrix} \quad \begin{pmatrix} x_1 = -2 \\ x_2 = -2 \end{pmatrix}$$

9. The prices for two products, denoted by p_1 and p_2, are related to the quantities sold of the two products, x_1 and x_2, by the expressions

$$x_1 = 32 - 2p_1$$
$$x_2 = 22 - p_2$$

Further, the total cost (TC) of producing and selling the product is related to the quantitites sold by the function

$$TC(x_1, x_2) = \tfrac{1}{2}x_1^2 + 2x_1x_2 + x_2^2 + 73$$

   a. Develop a mathematical model that shows profit as a function of the quantities produced.
   b. Determine the prices and quantities that maximize profit.

10. A shoe store has determined that its earnings $E(x_1, x_2)$, in thousands of dollars, can be approximated by a function of x_1, its investment in inventory in thousands of dollars, and x_2, its expenditure on advertising in thousands of dollars:

$$E(x_1, x_2) = -3x_1^2 + 2x_1x_2 - 6x_2^2 + 30x_1 + 24x_2 - 86$$

Find the maximum earnings, along with the amount of advertising expenditure and inventory investment, that yields this maximum.

11. Consider the problem

$$\min \quad x_1^2 - 14x_1 + x_2^2 - 16x_2 + 113$$

s.t.

$$2x_1 + 3x_2 = 12$$

a. Find the minimum solution to this problem.

b. How much would you expect the value of the solution to change if the right-hand side of the constraint were increased from 12 to 13?

12. Consider the problem

$$\max \quad -x_1^2 - 4x_1x_2 + 20x_1 - 5x_2^2 + 82x_2 - 397$$

s.t.

$$2x_1^2 - 16x_1 + 9x_2^2 - 18x_2 + 5 = 0$$

Determine whether or not the point $x_1 = 4$, $x_2 = 3$ provides an optimal solution.

13. Heller Manufacturing has two production facilities that manufacture baseball gloves. Production costs at the two facilities differ because of varying labor rates, local property taxes, type of equipment, capacity, and so on. The Dayton plant has weekly production costs that can be expressed as a function of the number of gloves produced:

$$TC_1(x_1) = x_1^2 - x_1 + 5$$

where x_1 is the weekly production volume in thousands of units and $TC_1(x_1)$ is the cost in thousands of dollars. The Hamilton plant's weekly production costs are given by

$$TC_2(x_2) = x_2^2 + 2x_2 + 3$$

where x_2 is the weekly production volume in thousands of units and $TC_2(x_2)$ is the cost, in thousands of dollars. Heller Manufacturing would like to produce 8000 gloves per week at the lowest possible cost.

a. Formulate a mathematical model that can be used to determine the number of gloves to produce each week at each facility.

b. Find the solution to your mathematical model to determine the optimal number of gloves to produce at each facility.

14. Solve the problem

$$\min \quad x_1^2 + 2x_2^2 - 8x_1 - 12x_2 + 34$$

s.t.

$$x_1^2 + 2x_2^2 = 5$$

15. Consider the problem

$$\min \quad 2x_1^2 - 20x_1 + 2x_1x_2 + x_2^2 - 14x_2 + 58$$

s.t.

$$x_1 + 4x_2 \le 8$$

a. Find the minimum solution to this problem.

b. If the right-hand side of the constraint is increased from 8 to 9, how much do you expect the objective function to change?

16. Jingle Bells, Inc., has received a rush order for as many of two types of Christmas bells as can be produced and shipped during a 2-week period. Preliminary analysis by Jingle Bells indicates that the profit on this order is related to the number of each type of bell manufactured by the following function:

$$P = -x_1^2 - x_2^2 + 12x_1 + 10x_2 + 61$$

where

P = profit in thousands of dollars

x_1 = number of units of type 1 bells in thousands

x_2 = number of units of type 2 bells in thousands

Because of other commitments over the next 2 weeks, Jingle Bells has available only 60 hours in the shipping and packaging department to get the order out. It is estimated that every 1000 units of type 1 bells will require 20 hours in the shipping and packaging department and every 1000 units of type 2 bells will require 30 hours. Given the above information, how many of each type of bell should Jingle Bells produce in order to maximize profit?

17. Through regression analysis a firm has learned that total profit P as a function of the number of units of two products manufactured is given by the following function:

$$P = -x_1^2 - 4x_2^2 + 6x_1 + 16x_2 + 500$$

where

x_1 = thousands of units of product 1

x_2 = thousands of units of product 2

The number of units of each product that can be produced in the next planning period is constrained by the fact that only 12,000 pounds of an ingredient used in the production of both products are available. Both products require 2 pounds of the ingredient per unit produced.

a. Develop a mathematical model that can be used to determine how many units of each product to manufacture in the next planning period.

b. Solve the mathematical model to determine how many units of x_1 and x_2 should be produced in order to maximize profit.

c. How much would you expect profit to increase if 1 extra pound of the scarce ingredient became available?

U.S. Department of Agriculture Forest Service*

Washington, D.C.

The U.S. Department of Agriculture Forest Service is responsible for the management of the nation's forest resources. The Forest Engineering group at the Intermountain Forest and Range Experiment Station located in Montana is concerned with the application of engineering and management science principles to the harvesting of timberlands. This group conducts and contracts for studies related to the utilization of harvesting equipment, the modeling of cable yarding (timber collection) systems, the modeling of helicopter or other aerial yarding systems, the designing of statistically valid models for experimental forests, and the developing of a variety of forest harvesting methods. Among the concerns of many of these studies are the productivity and cost of the harvesting method. Ultimately, the primary objective of all these studies is to determine the "best" methods for harvesting timber under a variety of conditions.

A HELICOPTER YARDING APPLICATION

Over the years the best and most accessible timber has tended to be harvested first. As a result, much of the currently available timber lies in relatively inaccessible regions of the forests where traditional harvesting methods cannot be used. This has created a need for new harvesting techniques. One development has been to use helicopters to remove felled trees from inaccessible regions.

A major problem with using helicopters in the harvesting process is the high cost of the helicopter operation. When helicopters are used, the usual harvesting procedure is to mark felled trees where they lie for inclusion in a helicopter load (called a turn). This approach has proved somewhat unsatisfactory due to the added cost of helicopter time to collect and prepare the load for removal. Also, problems with helicopter underloading (wasted capacity) and overloading (aborted loads) have occurred too often. If helicopters are to be used, high utilization of helicopter capacity is essential to maintain the highest possible levels of productivity and the lowest possible costs.

A study was proposed for exploring the feasibility and cost effectiveness of harvesting methods that would prebunch felled trees into unit loads for helicopter transport. Preliminary tests indicated that unit loads could be assembled with the aid of a radio-controlled winch. The winch is anchored to a tree in the "bunching" area. In order to collect the felled trees for the unit loads, a cable from the winch is hooked to the felled trees. The winch then pulls the trees onto a deck where the unit loads can be assembled. Once the feasibility of this method was established, it

*The authors are indebted to Dr. William R. Taylor and Dr. Christopher B. Lofgren, consultants to the USDA Forest Service, for providing this application.

became important to develop strategies that would provide the best productivity and cost advantages. A mathematical model was developed to identify the optimal movement and locations of the radio-controlled winch so that the total costs associated with preparing the loads in a given cutting area could be minimized.

Once a section of the forest, called a cutting unit, is identified for harvesting, the problem is to subdivide the cutting unit into smaller sections called bunching units. Figure 19.8 shows a cutting unit that has been subdivided into nine bunching units. The numerical sequence shows how the winch is moved from one bunching unit to the next.

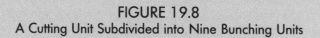

FIGURE 19.8
A Cutting Unit Subdivided into Nine Bunching Units

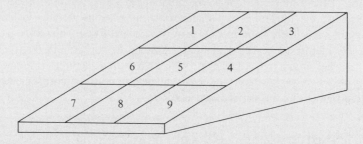

The total time to harvest a cutting unit is dependent on specification of the bunching units. As the size of the bunching unit is increased, the idle time due to the setup of the winch is reduced because fewer bunching units and fewer winch setups are necessary. However, as the size of the bunching unit is increased, the production time per tree increases because the average distance from the felled trees to the winch is greater. Thus, optimal sizing of the bunching units requires a balance of the setup time for the winch with the production time for the trees. The effect of larger bunching areas (greater distance between anchor trees for the winch) on setup, production, and total time is shown in Figure 19.9. Ideally, we would like to find the bunching unit configuration that minimizes the total time to harvest the cutting unit.

The mathematical formulation of the problem involved two decision variables and seven constraints. The decision variables are as follows:

$$x_1 = \text{length of the bunching unit}$$
$$x_2 = \text{width of the bunching unit}$$

The objective function expresses the total time of production (bunching the trees) and the total time of the winch moves and setups in terms of the two decision variables. Four of the seven constraints represent upper and lower bounds on the acceptable length and width of the bunching units. A fifth constraint restricts the size of the bunching unit so that the winch cable can reach all areas of the unit. The sixth and seventh constraints place upper and lower bounds on the load weight.

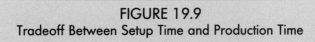

FIGURE 19.9
Tradeoff Between Setup Time and Production Time

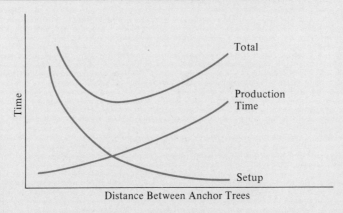

Because of the complex nature of the objective function and constraints, it is not possible to simply form the Lagrangian function and take the derivatives in order to solve for the optimal values of x_1 and x_2. The solution procedure used is a computer algorithm that systematically identifies all the local optimal solutions to the problem. The local optimal solution that requires the minimum total time is selected as the optimal solution. The model provided excellent guidelines for increasing the productivity of the prebunching operation.

Questions

1. What factor necessitated the consideration of using helicopters in the harvesting process?
2. What was the objective of the mathematical model developed in this application?
3. What type of solution procedure was used? Why?

APPENDIXES

APPENDIX A ▼ AREAS FOR
THE STANDARD NORMAL DISTRIBUTION

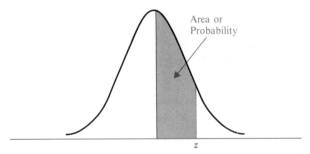

Entries in the table give the area under the curve between the mean and z standard deviations above the mean. For example, for $z = 1.25$ the area under the curve between the mean and z is 0.3944.

z	0.00	0.01	0.02	0.03	0.04	0.05	0.06	0.07	0.08	0.09
0.0	0.0000	0.0040	0.0080	0.0120	0.0160	0.0199	0.0239	0.0279	0.0319	0.0359
0.1	0.0398	0.0438	0.0478	0.0517	0.0557	0.0596	0.0636	0.0675	0.0714	0.0753
0.2	0.0793	0.0832	0.0871	0.0910	0.0948	0.0987	0.1026	0.1064	0.1103	0.1141
0.3	0.1179	0.1217	0.1255	0.1293	0.1331	0.1368	0.1406	0.1443	0.1480	0.1517
0.4	0.1554	0.1591	0.1628	0.1664	0.1700	0.1736	0.1772	0.1808	0.1844	0.1879
0.5	0.1915	0.1950	0.1985	0.2019	0.2054	0.2088	0.2123	0.2157	0.2190	0.2224
0.6	0.2257	0.2291	0.2324	0.2357	0.2389	0.2422	0.2454	0.2486	0.2518	0.2549
0.7	0.2580	0.2612	0.2642	0.2673	0.2704	0.2734	0.2764	0.2794	0.2823	0.2852
0.8	0.2881	0.2910	0.2939	0.2967	0.2995	0.3023	0.3051	0.3078	0.3106	0.3133
0.9	0.3159	0.3186	0.3212	0.3238	0.3264	0.3289	0.3315	0.3340	0.3365	0.3389
1.0	0.3413	0.3438	0.3461	0.3485	0.3508	0.3531	0.3554	0.3577	0.3599	0.3621
1.1	0.3643	0.3665	0.3686	0.3708	0.3729	0.3749	0.3770	0.3790	0.3810	0.3830
1.2	0.3849	0.3869	0.3888	0.3907	0.3925	0.3944	0.3962	0.3980	0.3997	0.4015
1.3	0.4032	0.4049	0.4066	0.4082	0.4099	0.4115	0.4131	0.4147	0.4162	0.4177
1.4	0.4192	0.4207	0.4222	0.4236	0.4251	0.4265	0.4279	0.4292	0.4306	0.4319
1.5	0.4332	0.4345	0.4357	0.4370	0.4382	0.4394	0.4406	0.4418	0.4429	0.4441
1.6	0.4452	0.4463	0.4474	0.4484	0.4495	0.4505	0.4515	0.4525	0.4535	0.4545
1.7	0.4554	0.4564	0.4573	0.4582	0.4591	0.4599	0.4608	0.4616	0.4625	0.4633
1.8	0.4641	0.4649	0.4656	0.4664	0.4671	0.4678	0.4686	0.4693	0.4699	0.4706
1.9	0.4713	0.4719	0.4726	0.4732	0.4738	0.4744	0.4750	0.4756	0.4761	0.4767
2.0	0.4772	0.4778	0.4783	0.4788	0.4793	0.4798	0.4803	0.4808	0.4812	0.4817
2.1	0.4821	0.4826	0.4830	0.4834	0.4838	0.4842	0.4846	0.4850	0.4854	0.4857
2.2	0.4861	0.4864	0.4868	0.4871	0.4875	0.4878	0.4881	0.4884	0.4887	0.4890
2.3	0.4893	0.4896	0.4898	0.4901	0.4904	0.4906	0.4909	0.4911	0.4913	0.4916
2.4	0.4918	0.4920	0.4922	0.4925	0.4927	0.4929	0.4931	0.4932	0.4934	0.4936
2.5	0.4938	0.4940	0.4941	0.4943	0.4945	0.4946	0.4948	0.4949	0.4951	0.4952
2.6	0.4953	0.4955	0.4956	0.4957	0.4959	0.4960	0.4961	0.4962	0.4963	0.4964
2.7	0.4965	0.4966	0.4967	0.4968	0.4969	0.4970	0.4971	0.4972	0.4973	0.4974
2.8	0.4974	0.4975	0.4976	0.4977	0.4977	0.4978	0.4979	0.4979	0.4980	0.4981
2.9	0.4981	0.4982	0.4982	0.4983	0.4984	0.4984	0.4985	0.4985	0.4986	0.4986
3.0	0.4986	0.4987	0.4987	0.4988	0.4988	0.4989	0.4989	0.4989	0.4990	0.4990

63271	59986	71744	51102	15141	80714	58683	93108	13554	79945
88547	09896	95436	79115	08303	01041	20030	63754	08459	28364
55957	57243	83865	09911	19761	66535	40102	26646	60147	15702
46276	87453	44790	67122	45573	84358	21625	16999	13385	22782
55363	07449	34835	15290	76616	67191	12777	21861	68689	03263
69393	92785	49902	58447	42048	30378	87618	26933	40640	16281
13186	29431	88190	04588	38733	81290	89541	70290	40113	08243
17726	28652	56836	78351	47327	18518	92222	55201	27340	10493
36520	64465	05550	30157	82242	29520	69753	72602	23756	54935
81628	36100	39254	56835	37636	02421	98063	89641	64953	99337
84649	38968	75215	75498	49539	74240	03466	49292	36401	45525
63291	11618	12613	75055	43915	26488	41116	64531	56827	30825
70502	53225	03655	05915	37140	57051	48393	91322	25653	06543
06426	24771	59935	49801	11082	66762	94477	02494	88215	27191
20711	55609	29430	70165	45406	78484	31639	52009	18873	96927
41990	70538	77191	25860	55204	73417	83920	69468	74972	38712
72452	36618	76298	26678	89334	33938	95567	29380	75906	91807
37042	40318	57099	10528	09925	89773	41335	96244	29002	46453
53766	52875	15987	46962	67342	77592	57651	95508	80033	69828
90585	58955	53122	16025	84299	53310	67380	84249	25348	04332
32001	96293	37203	64516	51530	37069	40261	61374	05815	06714
62606	64324	46354	72157	67248	20135	49804	09226	64419	29457
10078	28073	85389	50324	14500	15562	64165	06125	71353	77669
91561	46145	24177	15294	10061	98124	75732	00815	83452	97355
13091	98112	53959	79607	52244	63303	10413	63839	74762	50289
73864	83014	72457	22682	03033	61714	88173	90835	00634	85169
66668	25467	48894	51043	02365	91726	09365	63167	95264	45643
84745	41042	29493	01836	09044	51926	43630	63470	76508	14194
48068	26805	94595	47907	13357	38412	33318	26098	82782	42851
54310	96175	97594	88616	42035	38093	36745	56702	40644	83514
14877	33095	10924	58013	61439	21882	42059	24177	58739	60170
78295	23179	02771	43464	59061	71411	05697	67194	30495	21157
67524	02865	39593	54278	04237	92441	26602	63835	38032	94770
58268	57219	68124	73455	83236	08710	04284	55005	84171	42596
97158	28672	50685	01181	24262	19427	52106	34308	73685	74246
04230	16831	69085	30802	65559	09205	71829	06489	85650	38707
94879	56606	30401	02602	57658	70091	54986	41394	60437	03195
71446	15232	66715	26385	91518	70566	02888	79941	39684	54315
32886	05644	79316	09819	00813	88407	17461	73925	53037	91904
62048	33711	25290	21526	02223	75947	66466	06232	10913	75336

This table is reproduced with permission from The Rand Corporation, *A Million Random Digits,* The Free Press, New York, 1955 and 1983.

APPENDIX C ▼ VALUES OF $e^{-\lambda}$

λ	$e^{-\lambda}$	λ	$e^{-\lambda}$	λ	$e^{-\lambda}$
0.05	0.9512	2.05	0.1287	4.05	0.0174
0.10	0.9048	2.10	0.1225	4.10	0.0166
0.15	0.8607	2.15	0.1165	4.15	0.0158
0.20	0.8187	2.20	0.1108	4.20	0.0150
0.25	0.7788	2.25	0.1054	4.25	0.0143
0.30	0.7408	2.30	0.1003	4.30	0.0136
0.35	0.7047	2.35	0.0954	4.35	0.0129
0.40	0.6703	2.40	0.0907	4.40	0.0123
0.45	0.6376	2.45	0.0863	4.45	0.0117
0.50	0.6065	2.50	0.0821	4.50	0.0111
0.55	0.5769	2.55	0.0781	4.55	0.0106
0.60	0.5488	2.60	0.0743	4.60	0.0101
0.65	0.5220	2.65	0.0707	4.65	0.0096
0.70	0.4966	2.70	0.0672	4.70	0.0091
0.75	0.4724	2.75	0.0639	4.75	0.0087
0.80	0.4493	2.80	0.0608	4.80	0.0082
0.85	0.4274	2.85	0.0578	4.85	0.0078
0.90	0.4066	2.90	0.0550	4.90	0.0074
0.95	0.3867	2.95	0.0523	4.95	0.0071
1.00	0.3679	3.00	0.0498	5.00	0.0067
1.05	0.3499	3.05	0.0474	5.05	0.0064
1.10	0.3329	3.10	0.0450	5.10	0.0061
1.15	0.3166	3.15	0.0429	5.15	0.0058
1.20	0.3012	3.20	0.0408	5.20	0.0055
1.25	0.2865	3.25	0.0388	5.25	0.0052
1.30	0.2725	3.30	0.0369	5.30	0.0050
1.35	0.2592	3.35	0.0351	5.35	0.0047
1.40	0.2466	3.40	0.0334	5.40	0.0045
1.45	0.2346	3.45	0.0317	5.45	0.0043
1.50	0.2231	3.50	0.0302	5.50	0.0041
1.55	0.2122	3.55	0.0287	5.55	0.0039
1.60	0.2019	3.60	0.0273	5.60	0.0037
1.65	0.1920	3.65	0.0260	5.65	0.0035
1.70	0.1827	3.70	0.0247	5.70	0.0033
1.75	0.1738	3.75	0.0235	5.75	0.0032
1.80	0.1653	3.80	0.0224	5.80	0.0030
1.85	0.1572	3.85	0.0213	5.85	0.0029
1.90	0.1496	3.90	0.0202	5.90	0.0027
1.95	0.1423	3.95	0.0193	5.95	0.0026
2.00	0.1353	4.00	0.0183	6.00	0.0025
				7.00	0.0009
				8.00	0.000335
				9.00	0.000123
				10.00	0.000045

APPENDIX D ▼ A SHORT TABLE OF DERIVATIVES

1. $\dfrac{d(c)}{dx} = 0$ (where c is a constant)

2. $\dfrac{d(xn)}{dx} = nx^{n-1}$

3. $\dfrac{d(cu)}{dx} = c\dfrac{du}{dx}$

4. $\dfrac{d(u + v)}{dx} = \dfrac{du}{dx} + \dfrac{dv}{dx}$

5. $\dfrac{d(uv)}{dx} = u\dfrac{dv}{dx} + v\dfrac{du}{dx}$

6. $\dfrac{d(u^n)}{dx} = nu^{n-1}\dfrac{du}{dx}$

7. $\dfrac{d\left(\dfrac{u}{v}\right)}{dx} = \dfrac{v\dfrac{du}{dx} - u\dfrac{dv}{dx}}{v^2}$

8. $\dfrac{d(\ln x)}{dx} = \dfrac{1}{x}$

9. $\dfrac{d(e^x)}{dx} = e^x$

10. $\dfrac{d(\ln u)}{dx} = \left(\dfrac{1}{u}\right)\dfrac{du}{dx}$

11. $\dfrac{d(e^u)}{dx} = e^u\dfrac{du}{dx}$

APPENDIX E ▼ MATRIX NOTATION AND OPERATIONS

Matrix Notation

We define a matrix to be a rectangular array of numbers. For example, the following array of numbers is a matrix D:

$$D = \begin{bmatrix} 1 & 3 & 2 \\ 0 & 4 & 5 \end{bmatrix}$$

The matrix D is said to consist of six elements, where each element of D is a number. In order to identify a particular element of a matrix, we have to specify its precise location. To do this, we introduce the notion of rows and columns.

All elements across some horizontal line in a matrix are said to be in a row of the matrix. For example, elements 1, 3, and 2 in the matrix D are in the first row of D, and elements 0, 4, and 5 are in the second row of D. Thus we see that D is a matrix that has two rows. By convention, we always refer to the top row as row 1, the second row from the top as row 2, and so on.

All elements along some vertical line are said to belong to a column of the matrix. Elements 1 and 0 in the matrix D are elements in the first column of D, elements 3 and 4 are elements of the second column, and elements 2 and 5 are elements of the third column. Thus we see that the matrix D has three columns. By convention, we always refer to the leftmost column as column 1, the next column to the right as column 2, and so on.

An easy way to identify a particular element in a matrix is to specify its row and column position. For example, the element in row 1 and column 2 of the matrix D is the number 3. This is written as

$$d_{12} = 3$$

In general we use the following notation to refer to specific elements of the matrix D:

$$d_{ij} = \text{element located in the } i\text{th row and } j\text{th column of } D$$

We always use capital letters for the names of matrices and the corresponding lowercase versions of the same letter with two subscripts to denote the elements.

The *size* of a matrix is defined to be the number of rows and columns in the matrix and is written as the number of rows $\times$ the number of columns. Thus the size of the matrix D above is 2×3.

Frequently we will encounter matrices that have only one row or one column. For example,

$$G = \begin{bmatrix} 6 \\ 4 \\ 2 \\ 3 \end{bmatrix}$$

is a matrix that has only one column. Whenever we have a matrix that has only one column like G, we call the matrix a column vector. In a similar manner, any matrix that has only one row is called a row vector. Using our previous notation for elements of a matrix, we could refer to specific elements in G by writing g_{ij}. However, since G has only one column, the column position is unimportant, and we need only specify the row the element of interest is in. That is, instead of referring to elements in a vector using g_{ij}, we specify only one subscript, which denotes the position of the element in the vector. For example,

$$g_1 = 6 \quad g_2 = 4 \quad g_3 = 2 \quad g_4 = 3$$

Matrix Operations

Matrix Transpose Given any matrix, we can form the transpose of the matrix by making the rows in the original matrix the columns in the transpose matrix, and by making the columns in the original matrix the rows in the transpose matrix. For example, if we take the transpose of the matrix

$$D = \begin{bmatrix} 1 & 3 & 2 \\ 0 & 4 & 5 \end{bmatrix}$$

we get

$$D^t = \begin{bmatrix} 1 & 0 \\ 3 & 4 \\ 2 & 5 \end{bmatrix}$$

Note that we use the superscript t to denote the transpose of a matrix.

Matrix Multiplication We will demonstrate how to perform two types of matrix multiplication: (1) how to multiply two vectors, and (2) how to multiply a matrix times a matrix.

The product of a row vector of size $1 \times n$ times a column vector of size $n \times 1$ is the number obtained by multiplying the first element in the row vector times the first element in the column vector, the second element in the row vector times the second element in the column vector, and continuing on through the last element in the row vector times the last element in the column vector, and then summing the products. Suppose, for example, that we wanted to multiply the row vector H times the column vector G, where

$$H = \begin{bmatrix} 2 & 1 & 5 & 0 \end{bmatrix} \text{ and } G = \begin{bmatrix} 6 \\ 4 \\ 2 \\ 3 \end{bmatrix}$$

The product HG is given by

$$HG = 2(6) + 1(4) + 5(2) + 0(3) = 26$$

The product of a matrix of size $p \times n$ and a matrix of size $n \times m$ is a new matrix of size $p \times m$. The element in the ith row and jth column of the new matrix is given by the vector product of the ith row of the $p \times n$ matrix times the jth column of the $n \times m$ matrix. Suppose, for example, that we want to multiply D times A, where

$$D = \begin{bmatrix} 1 & 3 & 2 \\ 0 & 4 & 5 \end{bmatrix} \quad A = \begin{bmatrix} 1 & 3 & 5 \\ 2 & 0 & 4 \\ 1 & 5 & 2 \end{bmatrix}$$

Let us denote by $C = DA$ the product of D times A. The element in row 1 and column 1 of C is given by the vector product of the first row of D times the first column of A. Thus we get

$$c_{11} = \begin{bmatrix} 1 & 3 & 2 \end{bmatrix} \begin{bmatrix} 1 \\ 2 \\ 1 \end{bmatrix} = 1(1) + 3(2) + 2(1) = 9$$

The element in row 2 and column 1 of C is given by the vector product of the second row of D times the first column of A. Thus we get

$$c_{21} = \begin{bmatrix} 0 & 4 & 5 \end{bmatrix} \begin{bmatrix} 1 \\ 2 \\ 1 \end{bmatrix} = 0(1) + 4(2) + 5(1) = 13$$

Calculating the remaining elements of C in a similar fashion, we obtain

$$C = \begin{bmatrix} 9 & 13 & 21 \\ 13 & 25 & 26 \end{bmatrix}$$

Clearly the product of a matrix and a vector is just a special case of multiplying a matrix times a matrix. For example, the product of a matrix of size $m \times n$ and a vector of size $n \times 1$ is a new vector of size $m \times 1$. The element in the ith position of the new vector is given by the vector product of the ith row of the $m \times n$ matrix times the $n \times 1$ column vector. Suppose, for example, that we want to multiply D times K, where

$$D = \begin{bmatrix} 1 & 3 & 2 \\ 0 & 4 & 5 \end{bmatrix} \quad K = \begin{bmatrix} 1 \\ 4 \\ 2 \end{bmatrix}$$

The first element of DK is given by the vector product of the first row of D times K. Thus we get

$$\begin{bmatrix} 1 & 3 & 2 \end{bmatrix} \begin{bmatrix} 1 \\ 4 \\ 2 \end{bmatrix} = 1(1) + 3(4) + 2(2) = 17$$

The second element of DK is given by the vector product of the second row of D and K. Thus we get

$$\begin{bmatrix} 0 & 4 & 5 \end{bmatrix} \begin{bmatrix} 1 \\ 4 \\ 2 \end{bmatrix} = 0(1) + 4(4) + 5(2) = 26$$

Hence we see that the product of the matrix D times the vector K is given by

$$DK = \begin{bmatrix} 1 & 3 & 2 \\ 0 & 4 & 5 \end{bmatrix} \begin{bmatrix} 1 \\ 4 \\ 2 \end{bmatrix} = \begin{bmatrix} 17 \\ 26 \end{bmatrix}$$

Can any two matrices be multiplied? The answer is no. In order to multiply two matrices, the number of the columns in the first matrix must equal the number of rows in the second. If this property is satisfied, the matrices are said to conform for multiplication. Thus in our example D and K could be multiplied because D had three columns and K had three rows.

Matrix Inverse   The inverse, denoted by A^{-1}, of any square matrix A consisting of two rows and two columns is computed as follows:

$$A = \begin{bmatrix} a_{11} & a_{12} \\ a_{21} & a_{22} \end{bmatrix}$$

$$A^{-1} = \begin{bmatrix} a_{22}/d & -a_{12}/d \\ -a_{21}/d & a_{11}/d \end{bmatrix}$$

where $d = a_{11}a_{22} - a_{21}a_{12}$ is the determinant of the 2×2 matrix A. For example, if

$$A = \begin{bmatrix} 0.7 & -0.3 \\ -0.3 & 0.9 \end{bmatrix}$$

then

$$d = (0.7)(0.9) - (-0.3)(-0.3) = 0.54$$

and

$$A^{-1} = \begin{bmatrix} 0.9/0.54 & 0.3/0.54 \\ 0.3/0.54 & 0.7/0.54 \end{bmatrix} = \begin{bmatrix} 1.67 & 0.56 \\ 0.56 & 1.30 \end{bmatrix}$$

REFERENCES AND BIBLIOGRAPHY

THE ROLE AND NATURE OF MANAGEMENT SCIENCE (CHAPTER 1)

Churchman, C. W., R. L. Ackoff, and E. L. Arnoff, *Introduction to Operations Research.* New York, John Wiley & Sons, 1957.

Forgionne, G. A., "Corporate Management Science Activities: An Update." *Interfaces*, Vol. 13, No. 3, pp. 20–23, 1983.

Gaither, N., "The Adoption of Operations Research Techniques by Manufacturing Organizations." *Decision Sciences,* Vol. 6, No. 4, 1975, pp. 797–813.

Grayson, C. J., Jr., "Management Science and Business Practice," *Harvard Business Review.* Vol. 51, 1973, pp. 41–48.

Hillier, F., and G. J. Lieberman, *Introduction to Operations Research.* 4th ed., San Francisco, Holden-Day, 1986.

Ledbetter, W. and J. Cox, "Are OR Techniques Being Used?" *Industrial Engineering,* Vol. 9, 1977, pp. 19–21.

Radnor, M., and R. D. Neal, "The Progress of Management Science Activities in Large U.S. Industrial Corporations."*Operations Research* 21 (1973): 427–450.

Shannon, R. E., S. S. Long, and B. P. Buckles, "Operations Research Methodologies in Industrial Engineering: A Survey." *AIIE Transactions,* Vol. 12, No. 4, 1980, pp. 364–367.

Thomas, G., and J. DaCosta, "A Sample Survey of Corporate Operations Research." *Interfaces,* August 1979.

Thomas G., and M. Mitchell, "OR in the U.S. Marine Corps: A Characterization." *Interfaces,* June 1983.

LINEAR PROGRAMMING, TRANSPORTATION, ASSIGNMENT AND TRANSSHIPMENT PROBLEMS (CHAPTERS 2 TO 7)

Anderson, D. R., D. J. Sweeney, and T. A. Williams, *Linear Programming for Decision Making.* St. Paul, West Publishing, 1974.

Bazarra, M. S., and J. J. Jarvis, *Linear Programming and Network Flows.* 2nd ed. New York, John Wiley & Sons, 1990.

Bradley, S. P., A. C. Hax, and T. L. Magnanti, *Applied Mathematical Programming.* Reading, Mass., Addison-Wesley, 1977.

Charnes, A., and W. W. Cooper, *Management Models and Industrial Applications of Linear Programming*. New York, John Wiley & Sons, 1961.

Charnes, A., W. W. Cooper, and E. Rhodes, "Measuring Efficiency of Decision Making Units", *European Journal of Operations Research,* Vol. 2, 1978, pp. 429–449.

Daellenbach, Hans G., and J. Bell, *User's Guide to Linear Programming*. Englewood Cliffs, N.J., Prentice-Hall, 1970.

Dantzig, G. B., *Linear Programming and Extensions*. Princeton University Press, 1963.

Gass, S., *Linear Programming,* 4th ed. New York, McGraw-Hill, 1975.

Hillier, F., and G. J. Lieberman, *Introduction to Operations Research,* 4th ed. San Francisco, Holden-Day, 1986.

Hooker, J. N., "Karmarkar's Linear Programming Algorithm." *Interfaces,* Vol. 16, No. 4, pp. 75–90, 1986.

Lewin, A. Y., and R. C. Morey, "Measuring the Relative Efficiency and Output Potential of Public Sector Organizations: An Application of Data Envelopment Analysis", *International Journal of Policy Analysis and Information Systems,* Vol. 5, No. 4, 1981, pp. 267–285.

Phillips, D. T., A. Ravindran, and J. J. Solberg, *Operations Research: Principles and Practice,* 2nd ed. New York, John Wiley & Sons, 1987.

Schrage, L., *Linear, Integer, and Quadratic Programming with LINDO*. Palo Alto, Calif., Scientific Press, 1986.

Schrage, L., *User's Manual for Linear, Integer, and Quadratic Programming with LINDO*. Redwood City, Calif., Scientific Press, 1987.

Sherman, H. D., "Hospital Efficiency Measurement and Evaluation", *Medical Care,* Vol. 22, No. 10, October 1984, pp. 922–938.

Wagner, H., *Principles of Operations Research,* 2nd ed. Englewood Cliffs, N.J., Prentice-Hall, 1975.

INTEGER LINEAR PROGRAMMING (CHAPTER 8)

Garfinkel, R. S., and G. L. Nemhauser, *Integer Programming*. New York, John Wiley & Sons, 1972.

Plane, D. R., and C. McMillan, *Discrete Optimization*. Englewood Cliffs, N.J., Prentice-Hall, 1971.

Salkin, H. M., *Integer Programming*. Reading, Mass., Addison-Wesley, 1975.

Zionts, Stanley, *Linear and Integer Programming*. Englewood Cliffs, N.J., Prentice-Hall, 1974.

NETWORK MODELS (CHAPTER 9)

Bazarra, M. S., and J. J. Jarvis, *Linear Programming and Network Flows*. New York, John Wiley & Sons, 1977.

Glover, F., and D. Klingman, "Network Application in Industry and Government." *AIIE Transactions,* December 1977.

Ford, L. R., and D. R. Fulkerson, *Flows and Networks*. Princeton, N.J., Princeton University Press, 1962.

Jensen, P., and J. W. Barnes, *Network Flow Programming*. New York, John Wiley & Sons, 1980.

Minieka, Edward, *Optimization Algorithms for Networks and Graphs*. New York, Marcel Dekker, 1978.

PERT/CPM (CHAPTER 10)

Evarts, H. F., *Introduction to PERT*. Boston, Allyn & Bacon, 1964.

Moder, J. J., and C. R. Phillips, *Project Management with CPM and PERT,* 2nd ed. New York, Van Nostrand, 1970.

Wagner, H., *Principles of Operations Research with Applications to Managerial Decisions,* 2nd ed. Englewood Cliffs, N.J., Prentice-Hall, 1975.

Wiest, J., and F. Levy, *Management Guide to PERT-CPM,* 2nd ed. Englewood Cliffs, N.J., Prentice-Hall, 1977.

INVENTORY MODELS (CHAPTER 11)

Buffa, E. S., and W. Taubert, *Production-Inventory Systems: Planning and Control,* 3rd ed. Homewood, Ill., Richard D. Irwin, 1979.

Davis, E. W., *Case Studies in Material Requirements Planning.* Washington, D. C., APICS, 1978.

Greene, J. H., *Production and Inventory Control Handbook.* New York, McGraw-Hill, 1970.

Hadley, G., and T. M. Whitin, *Analysis of Inventory Systems.* Englewood Cliffs, N.J., Prentice-Hall, 1963.

Hillier, F., and G. J. Lieberman, *Introduction to Operations Research,* 4th ed. San Francisco, Holden-Day, 1986.

Naddor, E., *Inventory Systems.* New York, John Wiley & Sons, 1966.

Orlicky, J., *Material Requirements Planning.* New York, McGraw-Hill, 1975.

Plossl, G. W., *Manufacturing Control: The Last Frontier for Profits.* Reston, Va., Reston, 1973.

Starr, M., and D. Miller, *Inventory Control: Theory and Practice.* Englewood Cliffs, N.J., Prentice-Hall, 1962.

Stockton, R. S., *Basic Inventory Systems: Concepts and Analysis.* Boston, Allyn & Bacon , 1965.

Wagner, H., *Principles of Operations Research with Applications to Managerial Decisions,* 2nd ed. Englewood Cliffs, N.J., Prentice-Hall, 1975.

Wight, O. W., *Production and Inventory Management in the Computer Age.* Boston, Cahners Books, 1974.

WAITING LINES (CHAPTER 13)

Bhat, U. N., *Elements of Applied Stochastic Processes.* New York, John Wiley & Sons, 1972.

Cooper, R. B., *Introduction to Queueing Theory.* New York, Macmillan, 1972.

Cox, D. R., and W. L. Smith, *Queues.* New York, John Wiley & Sons, 1965.

Gross, D., and C. M. Harris, *Fundamentals of Queueing Theory.* New York, John Wiley & Sons, 1974.

Hillier, F. and G. J. Lieberman, *Introduction to Operations Research,* 4th ed. San Francisco, Holden-Day, 1986.

Newell, G. F., *Applications of Queueing Theory.* London, Chapman & Hall, Ltd., 1971.

COMPUTER SIMULATION (CHAPTER 12)

Christy, D. P., and H. J. Watson, ''The Application of Simulation: A Survey of Industry Practice.'' *Interfaces,* October 1983.

Emshoff, J. R., and R. L. Sisson, *Design and Use of Computer Simulation Models.* New York, Macmillan, 1970.

Fishman, George S., *Principles of Discrete Event Simulation.* New York, John Wiley & Sons, 1978.

Greenberg, S., *GPSS Primer.* New York, John Wiley & Sons, 1972.

Maisel, H., and G. Gnugnoli, *Simulation of Discrete Stochastic Systems.* Chicago, SRA, 1972.

Naylor, T. H., *Computer Simulation Experiments with Models of Economic Systems.* New York, John Wiley & Sons, 1971.

Naylor, T. H., J. L. Balintfy, D. S. Burdick, and K. Chu, *Computer Simulation Techniques.* New York, John Wiley & Sons, 1968.

Schmidt, J. W., and R. E. Taylor, *Simulation and Analysis of Industrial Systems*. Homewood, Ill., Richard D. Irwin, 1970.

Schriber, T. J., *Simulation Using GPSS*. New York, John Wiley & Sons, 1974.

DECISION ANALYSIS (CHAPTER 14)

Bunn, D., *Applied Decision Analysis*. New York, McGraw-Hill, 1984.

Chernoff, H., and L. E. Moses, *Elementary Decision Theory*. New York, John Wiley & Sons, 1959.

Fishburn, P. C., "Foundations of Decision Analysis: Along the Way", *Management Science*, Vol. 35, No. 4, April 1989, pp. 387–405.

Keeney, R. L., and H. Raiffa, *Decisions with Multiple Objectives: Preferences and Value Trade Offs*, New York, John Wiley & Sons, Inc., 1976.

Raiffa, H., *Decision Analysis*. Reading, Mass., Addison-Wesley, 1968.

Samson, D., *Managerial Decision Analysis*, Homewood, Illinois, Irwin, 1988.

Schlaifer, R., *Analysis of Decisions under Uncertainty*. New York, McGraw-Hill, 1969.

Winkler, R. L., *An Introduction to Bayesian Inference and Decision*. New York, Holt, Rinehart & Winston, 1972.

Winkler, R. L., and W. L. Hays, *Statistics: Probability, Inference and Decision*, 2nd ed. New York, Holt, Rinehart & Winston, 1975.

MULTICRITERIA DECISION PROBLEMS (CHAPTER 15)

Baird, B. F., *Managerial Decisions Under Uncertainty*, New York, John Wiley & Sons, 1989.

Bunn, D. W., *Analysis for Optimal Decisions*, New York, John Wiley & Sons, 1982.

Dyer, J. S., "Remarks on the Analytic Hierarchy Process", *Management Science*, Vol. 36, No. 3, March 1990, pp. 249–258.

Dyer, J. S., "A Clarification of Remarks on the Analytic Hierarchy Process", *Management Science*, Vol. 36, No. 3, March 1990, pp. 274–275.

Harker, P. T., and L. G. Vargas, "The Theory of Ratio Scale Estimation: Saaty's Analytic Hierarchy Process", *Management Science*, Vol. 33, No. 11, November, 1987, pp. 1383–1403.

Harker, P. T., and L. G. Vargas, "Reply to Remarks on the Analytic Hierarchy Process by J. S. Dyer" *Management Science*, Vol. 36, No. 3, March 1990, pp. 269–273.

Ignizio, J. P., *Goal Programming and Extensions*, Lexington, Massachusetts, D. C. Heath and Company, 1976.

Keeney, R. L., and H. Raiffa, *Decisions with Multiple Objectives: Preferences and Value Tradeoffs*, New York, John Wiley & Sons, 1976.

Lee, S. M., *Goal Programming for Decision Analysis*, Philadelphia, Auerbach Publishers Inc., 1972.

Saaty, T. L., "Rank Generation, Preservation, and Reversal in the Analytic Hierarchy Decision Process", *Decision Sciences*, Vol. 18, 1987, pp. 157–177.

Saaty, T. L., "An Exposition of the AHP in Reply to the Paper Remarks on the Analytic Hierarchy Process", *Management Science*, Vol. 36, No. 3, March 1990, pp. 259–268.

Weiss, E. N., and V. R. Rao, "AHP Design Issues for Large-Scale Systems", *Decision Sciences*, Vol. 18, 1987, pp. 43–61.

Winkler, R. L., "Decision Modeling and Rational Choice: AHP and Utility Theory", *Management Science*, Vol. 36. No. 3, March 1990, pp. 247–248.

Zahedi, F., "Analytic Hierarchy Process—A Survey of the Method and its Applications", *Interfaces*, Vol. 16, No. 4, August 1986, pp. 96–108.

FORECASTING (CHAPTER 16)

Bowerman, B. L., and R. T. O'Connell, *Forecasting and Time Series.* North Scituate, Mass., Duxbury Press, 1979.

Box, G. E. P., and G. M. Jenkins, *Time Series Analysis: Forecasting and Control,* rev. ed. San Francisco, Holden-Day, 1976.

Gilchrist, W. G., *Statistical Forecasting.* New York, John Wiley & Sons, 1976.

Hanke, J. E., and A. G. Reitsch, *Business Forecasting,* 2nd ed. Boston, Allyn & Bacon, 1986.

Makridakis, S., S. C. Wheelwright, and Victor E. McGee, *Forecasting: Methods and Applications,* 2nd ed. New York, John Wiley & Sons, 1983.

Nelson, C. R., *Applied Time Series Analysis.* San Francisco, Holden-Day, 1973.

Thomopoulos, N. T., *Applied Forecasting Methods.* Englewood Cliffs, N.J., Prentice-Hall, 1980.

Wheelwright, S. C., and S. Makridakis, *Forecasting Models for Management,* 4th ed. New York, John Wiley & Sons, 1985.

MARKOV PROCESSES (CHAPTER 17)

Derman, C., *Finite State Markovian Decision Processes.* New York, Academic Press, 1970.

Howard, R. A., *Dynamic Programming and Markov Processes.* Cambridge, Mass., M.I.T. Press, 1960.

Kemeny, J. G., and J. L. Snell, *Finite Markov Chains.* Englewood Cliffs, N.J., Prentice-Hall, 1960.

Phillips, D. T., A. Ravindran, and J. J. Solberg, *Operations Research: Principles and Practice.* New York, John Wiley & Sons, 1976.

Ross, S. M., *Applied Probability Models with Optimization Applications.* San Francisco, Holden-Day, 1970.

DYNAMIC PROGRAMMING (CHAPTER 18)

Bellman, R., *Dynamic Programming.* Princeton, N.J., Princeton University Press, 1957.

Dreyfus, S., *Dynamic Programming and the Calculus of Variations.* New York, Academic Press, 1965.

Dreyfus, S., and A. M. Law, *The Art and Theory of Dynamic Programming.* New York, Academic Press, 1977.

Hillier, F., and G. J. Lieberman, *Introduction to Operations Research, 4th ed. San Francisco, Holden-Day, 1986.*

Nemhauser, G. L., *Introduction to Dynamic Programming.* New York, John Wiley & Sons, 1967.

CALCULUS-BASED SOLUTION PROCEDURE (CHAPTER 19)

Beightler, C. S., D. T. Phillips, and D. Wilde, *Foundations of Optimization,* 2nd ed. Englewood Cliffs, N.J., Prentice-Hall, 1979.

Cooper, L., and D. Steinberg, *Introduction to Methods of Optimization.* Philadelphia, W. B. Saunders, 1970.

Gottfried, B. S., and J. Weisman, *Introduction to Optimization Theory.* Englewood Cliffs, N.J., Prentice-Hall, 1973.

Himmelblau, D. M., *Applied Nonlinear Programming.* New York, McGraw-Hill, 1972.

Luenberger, D. G., *Introduction to Linear and Nonlinear Programming.* Reading, Mass., Addison-Wesley, 1973.

Answers to Even-Numbered Problems

Chapter 1

2. Methodological developments based on research advances in computer technology
4. The problem is large, complex, important, new, and repetitive
6. Iconic—scale model of a new building
   Analog—barometer
   Mathematical—inventory cost equation
8. **a.** max $10x + 5y$
   s.t.
   $$5x + 2y \geq 40$$
   $$x \geq 0, y \geq 0$$
   b. Controllable inputs: x and y
   Uncontrollable inputs: profit, labor hours per units, and total labor hours available
   d. $x = 0, y = 20$, profit $= \$100$
10. For $a = 3, x = 13\frac{1}{3}$ and profit $= \$133$
    for $a = 4, x = 10$ and profit $= \$100$
    For $a = 5, x = 8$ and profit $= \$80$
    For $a = 6, x = 6\frac{2}{3}$ and a profit $= \$67$
12. A deterministic model with $d =$ distance, $m =$ miles per gallon, and $c =$ cost per gallon, where Total Cost $= (2d/m)c$
14. Quicker to formulate, easier to solve and/or more easily understood
16. **a.** max $6x + 4y$
    b. $50x + 30y \leq 80,000$
    $$50x \qquad \leq 50,000$$
    $$30y \leq 45,000$$

Chapter 2

6. $x_1 = 100, x_2 = 50, z = 750$
10. $x_1 = 12/7, x_2 = 15/7, z = 69/7$
12. **a.** $x_1 = 2, x_2 = 2, z = 10$
    b. Yes, constraint 2
14. Cutting and dyeing; inspection and packaging
16. **a.** One possibility is $3x_1 + 9x_2$
    b. $x_1 = 0$ and $x_2 = 540$
    c. 90, 150, 348, 0

18. a. max $25x_1 + 30x_2$

　　　s.t.

$$1.5x_1 +\ \ 3x_2 \le 450$$
$$2x_1 +\ \ 1x_2 \le 350$$
$$0.25x_1 + 0.25x_2 \le 50$$
$$x_1, x_2 \ge 0$$

b. $x_1 = 100, x_2 = 100; z = 5500$

c.

Department	Usage	Slack
A	450	0
B	300	50
C	50	0

20. $x_1 = 800, x_2 = 1200; z = 8400$

22.

Extreme Point	z	Slack or Surplus
$x_1 = 250, x_2 = 100$	800	$s_1 = 125, s_2 = 0,\ \ s_3 = 0$
$x_1 = 125, x_2 = 225$	925	$s_1 = 0,\ \ s_2 = 0,\ \ s_3 = 125$
$x_1 = 125, x_2 = 350$	1300	$s_1 = 0,\ \ s_2 = 125, s_3 = 0$

24. $x_1 = 12, x_2 = 3$; cost = \$63
26. $x_1 = 6, x_2 = 10$; cost = \$0.54 per can
28. a. max $x_1 + 1.5x_2 + 0s_1 + 0s_2 + 0s_3 + 0s_4$

　　　s.t.

$$x_1 +\ \ x_2 + s_1 \qquad\qquad\qquad = 150$$
$$\tfrac{1}{4}x_1 + \tfrac{1}{2}x_2 \qquad + s_2 \qquad\qquad = 50$$
$$x_1 \qquad\qquad\qquad - s_3 \qquad = 50$$
$$x_2 \qquad\qquad\quad - s_4 = 25$$
$$x_1, x_2, s_1, s_2, s_3, s_4 \ge 0$$

b. $s_1 = 0, s_2 = 0, s_3 = 50, s_4 = 25$
c. Dough and Topping are the binding constraints
30. a. max $100x_1 + 200x_2$

　　　s.t.

$$x_1 +\ \ x_2 \le\ \ 500$$
$$x_1 \qquad\ \ \le\ \ 200$$
$$2x_1 +\ \ 6x_2 \le 1200$$
$$x_1, x_2 \ge 0$$

b. Add a slack variable to each constraint
c. $x_1 = 200, x_2 = 133\tfrac{1}{3}, z = 46,666$
d. $(x_1 = 0, x_2 = 0), (x_1 = 200, x_2 = 0), (x_1 = 200, x_2 = 133\tfrac{1}{3}),$
　　$(x_1 = 0, x_2 = 200)$
e. Labor hours
32. a. $x_1 = 0, x_2 = 0$
　　$x_1 = 35, x_2 = 0$
　　$x_1 = 25, x_2 = 20$
　　$x_1 = 18.75, x_2 = 25$
　　$x_1 = 0, x_2 = 25$
b. Yes; $x_1 = 18.75, x_2 = 25, z = 2250$
c. Alternate optimal solutions: $x_1 = 25, x_2 = 20$ and $x_1 = 18.75, x_2 = 25$
34. b. $(x_1 = 2, x_2 = 4), (x_1 = 5, x_2 = 1)$
c. $x_1 = 2, x_2 = 4; z = 10$
36. Add a slack variable to each constraint
38. b. $x_1 = \tfrac{20}{3}, x_2 = \tfrac{8}{3}, z = 30\tfrac{2}{3}$
c. $s_1 = \tfrac{28}{3}, s_2 = 0, s_3 = 0$

40. Infeasible

42. a. $x_1 = \frac{30}{16}$, $x_2 = \frac{30}{16}$, $z = \frac{60}{16}$
   b. $x_1 = 0$, $x_2 = 3$, $z = 6$
   c. $1x_1 + \frac{5}{3}x_2$

44. Alternate optimal solutions: $x_1 = 125$, $x_2 = 225$ and $x_1 = 250$, $x_2 = 100$

46. a. Infeasibility
   b. Alternate optimal solutions: $x_1 = 500$, $x_2 = 150$ and $x_1 = 0$, $x_2 = 400$
   c. All three constraints removed

Chapter 3

2. Shadow price $= 44.44$

4. a. Constraint 1: 1.5, Constraint 2: 0
   b. Same as shadow prices

6. a. Constraint 1: .333, Constraint 2: .333, Constraint 3: 0
   b. Constraint 1: $-.333$, Constraint 2: $-.333$, Constraint 3: 0

8. a. Optimal solution: $x_1 = 9$, $x_2 = 4$
   b. Constraint 2: 0, Constraint 3: .0769

10. a. $x_1 = 0$, $x_2 = 10$
   b. Same as for problem 7: $x_1 = 7$, $x_2 = 7$

12. a. $4 \le c_1 \le 12$ $3.33 \le c_2 \le 10$

   c.

Min RHS	Max RHS
725	No Upper Limit
133.33	400
75	135

   d. 560

14. a. more than $7.00
   b. more than $3.50
   c. None

16. a. $x_1 = 4000$, $x_2 = 10,000$; total risk $= 62,000$
   b. $3.75 \le c_1 \le$ No Upper Limit
      No Lower Limit $\le c_2 \le 6.4$
   c. $60,000
   d. 5%
   e. approximately 6 cents
   f. 5.7%

18. a. $x_1 = 0$, $x_2 = 25$, $x_3 = 125$, $x_4 = 0$; $z = 525$
   b. A and C
   c. B; 425 hours
   d. Yes

20. a. $x_1 = 7.30$, $x_2 = 0$, $x_3 = 1.89$; $z = 139.73$
   b. two and three
   c. 0, -3.41, and -4.43
   d. 0, 3.41, and 4.43
   e. decrease the right-hand side of constraint 3 from 20 to 19

22. a. All Pro: 1000, College: 200, High School: 0
   b. Sewing and minimum All-Pro production requirement
   c. 4000 min. of unused cutting and dyeing time; all the sewing time is being used; 5200 min. of unused inspection and packaging time; only the minimum number of All-Pro models is being produced
   d. No Lower Limit $\le c_1 \le 5$
      $5 \le c_2 \le$ No Upper Limit
      No Lower Limit $\le c_3 \le 4$

24. **a.** $x_1 = 600$, $x_2 = 700$, $x_3 = 200$
   b. No Lower Limit $\leq c_1 \leq 9$
   $5.33 \leq c_2 \leq 9$
   $6 \leq c_3 \leq$ No Upper Limit

   c.

Constraint	Min RHS	Max RHS
1	4400	7440
2	6300	No Upper Limit
3	100	900
4	600	No Upper Limit
5	700	No Upper Limit
6	514.29	1000

   d. Nothing
   e. No

Chapter 4

2. **a.**

Advertisement	Number	Budget Allocation
television	4	$ 8,000
radio	14	4,200
newspaper	10	6,000
		$18,200

   Audience = 1,052,000

   b. Approximately 5130
4. **a.** $x_1 = 77.89$, $x_2 = 63.16$, $z = \$3,284.21$
   b. Dept. A $15.79, Dept. B $47.37
   c. $x_1 = 87.21$, $x_2 = 65.12$, $z = \$3,341.34$
   Dept. A 10 hours, Dept. B 3.2 hours
6. **a.** $x_1 = 500$, $x_2 = 300$, $x_3 = 200$, $z = \$550$
   b. $0.55
   c. Aroma 75, Taste 84.4
   d. $0.60
8. 50 units of product 1
   0 units of product 2
   300 hours dept. A, 600 hours dept. B
10. Schedule 19 officers as follows:
   3 begin at 8:00 a.m.
   3 begin at noon
   7 begin at 4:00 p.m.
   4 begin at midnight
   2 begin at 4:00 a.m.

12.

	Modern Line	Old Line	
1	500	0	
2	300	400	Cost = $3850

14.

	Mfr.	Purchase	
Base	3750	1250	
Cartridge	5000	0	
Handle	3750	1250	Cost = $11,875

   b. Depts. A and B; add only to A
   c. Only 25 hours can be used

16. x_1 = number of 10-inch rolls processed by cutting alternative i
  a. $x_1 = 0$, $x_2 = 125$, $x_3 = 500$, $x_4 = 1500$, $x_5 = 0$, $x_6 = 0$, $x_7 = 0$;
     2125 rolls with waste of 750 inches
  b. 2500 rolls with no waste; however, 1½ inch size is overproduced by 3000 units
18. a. 5 super, 2 regular, and 3 econotankers
     Total cost $583,000; monthly operating cost $4650
20. $x_1 = 48$, $x_2 = 96$, $z = 456$
    Assembler times: 480, 480 and 456
22. Investment Strategy: 45.8% of A and 100% of B.
    Objective Function = $4340.40
    Savings/Loan Schedule:

	Period 1	Period 2	Period 3	Period 4
Savings	242.11	—	—	341.04
Funds from Loan	—	200.00	127.58	—

24. a. Marginal = 0.6; average = .079; diminishing marginal returns have set in
26. b. $E = 0.924$
       $wa = 0.074$
       $wc = 0.436$
       $we = 0.489$
       All other weights are zero.
    c. E is relatively inefficient
       Composite requires 92.4% of E's resources.
    d. 34.37 patient days (65 or older)
       41.99 patient days (under 65)
    e. Hospitals A, C and E
28. b. $E = 0.9595$
       $wb = 0.175$
       $wc = 0.000$
       $wj = 0.575$
       $wn = 0.250$
       $ws = 0.000$
    c. Clarksville is relatively inefficient
       Composite requires 95.95% of Clarksville's resources.
    d. Output: $220 more profit
       Input: 4.4 less hours of operation
              2.6 less employees
              $186.25 less supplies expenses
    e. Bardstown, Jeffersonville and New Albany

Chapter 5

2. $x_1 = 5$, $x_2 = 1$, $x_3 = 4$
4. c. basic variables s_1, s_2, s_3;
      nonbasic variables x_1, x_2, x_3; yes
   d. 0
   e. x_3 enters and s_2 leaves
   f. 30; 750
   g. $x_1 = 10$, $x_3 = 30$, $s_1 = 20$, $z = 800$
8. a. $x_1 = 540$, $x_2 = 252$
   b. $7668
   c. 630, 480, 708, 117
   d. $s_1 = 0$, $s_2 = 120$, $s_3 = 0$, $s_4 = 18$

10. $x_2 = 650, s_1 = 690, s_3 = 310, z = 3250$
12. 35
14. **b.** No, any $c_j - z_j > 0$ will work
16. $x_1 =$ number of units of product A; $x_2 =$ number of units of product B; x_3 number of units of product C; $x_1 = 0, x_2 = 0, x_3 = 33\frac{1}{3}, z = 500$
18. $x_1 =$ Gal. Heid. Sweet, $x_2 =$ Gal. Heid. Reg, $x_3 =$ Gal Deut.
   a. $x_1 = 0, x_2 = 50, x_3 = 75, z = 210$
   c. Grade B grapes and hours
22. $x_1 = 9, x_2 = 2, x_3 = \frac{1}{2}, z = 41.5$
24. $x_1 = 20$ Gal., $x_2 = 30$ Gal., $x_3 = 33$ Gal;
   $x_1 = 0, x_2 = 0, x_3 = 2400, z = 480$

26.

	Incentive	Temptation	
John	480	0	
Brenda	0	480	
Red	0	800	$z = 46{,}400$

28. $x_1 = 203.5, x_2 = 285.2, x_3 = 20, z = 4{,}269{,}565$
30. Alternate optimal solutions
   $x_1 = 4, x_2 = 4$ and $x_1 = 8, x_2 = 0; z = 24$
32. Alternate optimal solutions
   $x_1 = 4, x_2 = 0, x_3 = 0$ and $x_1 = 0, x_2 = 0, x_3 = 8; z = 8$
34. Infeasible

Chapter 6

2. **a.** $12 \le b_2 \, \infty$
   b. $233\frac{1}{3} \le b_3 \le 400$
   c. 104
4. **a.** $0 \le b_1 \le 12$ $2 \le b_2 \le 6$ $4.5 \le b_3 < \infty$
   b. $1\frac{7}{8}$
   c. $7\frac{1}{2}$
   d. 0
6. **a.** $495.6 \le b_1 \le 682.36$
   b. $480 \le b_2 < \infty$
   c. $580 \le b_3 \le 900$
   d. $117 \le b_4 < \infty$
   e. Cutting and dyeing, Finishing
8. **a.** 131.25
   b. No decrease
   c. 262.5
10. **a.** $24 \le c_1 \le 60$ $20 \le c_2 \le 50$
   b. No change in solution. Profit reduced to $1350
   c. 33.33
   d. Pay up to $44.44 per ton for material 3
12. **a.** $x_3 = 15$ $x_4 = 8\frac{1}{3}$
   b. $2 \le c_3 < \infty$
   c. New solution $x_1 = 10, x_4 = 8\frac{1}{3}$
   d. $-\infty < c_2 \le 4\frac{1}{2}$
   e. No effect
14. **b.** $u_1 = \frac{3}{10}$ $u_2 = 0$ $u_3 = \frac{54}{30}$
   c. Machines A and C at capacity. Machine C has priority
16. Dual because of fewer constraints
20. **c.** $u_1 = \frac{1}{2}$ $u_2 = 0$ $u_3 = \frac{1}{2}$
   d. Reduce cost by $.50

24. a. Extreme point 1 : $x_1 = 0$, $x_2 = 6$ value = 0 .
Extreme point 2 : $x_1 = 5$, $x_2 = 0$ value = 15
Extreme point 3 : $x_1 = 4$, $x_2 = 2$ value = 16
b. $u_1 = \frac{1}{3}$, $u_2 = \frac{4}{3}$
c. $u_1 = 3$, $u_2 = 0$ value = 24
$u_1 = \frac{1}{3}$, $u_2 = \frac{4}{3}$ value = 16
$u_1 = 0$, $u_2 = 2$ value = 20
d. Values of dual extreme points $\geq$ values of primal extreme points
e. No

Chapter 7

2. c. Change to maximize
4. b. Seattle–Denver : 4000, Seattle–Los Angeles : 5000,
Columbus–Mobile : 4000, New York–Pittsburgh : 3000,
New York–Mobile : 1000, New York–Los Angeles : 1000,
New York–Washington : 3000   Cost = $150,000
c. Seattle–Denver : 4000, Seattle–Los Angeles : 5000,
Columbus–Mobile : 5000, New York–Pittsburgh : 4000,
New York–Los Angeles : 1000, New York–Washington : 3000
Cost = $141,000
6. $P_1 - W_2 : 300$, $P_2 - W_1 : 100$, $P_2 - W_2 : 100$, $P_2 - W_3 : 300$
$P_3 - W_1 : 100$
8. a. $O_1 - D_1 : 150$ $O_1 - D_2 : 100$ $O_2 - D_2 : 100$
$O_2 - D_3 : 50$ $O_3 - D_3 : 100$ Cost = $4600
b. $O_1 - D_1 : 150$ $O_1 - D_2 : 50$ $O_1 - D_3 : 50$
$O_2 - D_2 : 150$ $O_3 - D_3 : 100$ Cost = $4500
c. $O_1 - D_1 : 50$ $O_1 - D_2 : 50$ $O_1 - D_3 : 150$
$O_2 - D_2 : 150$ $O_3 - D_1 : 100$ Cost = $4500
10. Clifton Springs—D_2 4000
Clifton Springs—D_4 1000
Danville—D_1 2000
Danville—D_4 1000
Customer 2 is 1000 short
Customer 3 is 3000 short
12. a. Product A: 300 on I, 1200 on II, 500 on III
Product B: 500 on III
Product C: 1200 on I
b. Yes   Product A: 1500 on I, 500 on III
Product B: 500 on III
Product C: 1200 on II
Recommend second solution—only one changeover

14. a.

Changes	Effect on Cost
Add 1 unit Bed.–Chi.	+5
Reduce 1 unit Cleve.–Chi.	−2
Add 1 unit Cleve.–Bost.	+3
Reduce 1 unit Bed.–Bost.	−7
Net Effect	−1

b. Net effect = +7
16. b. Pd. 1 Production : 600, Pd. 2 Production : 300
Pd. 3 Production : 400, Pd. 4 Production : 400

18. Jackson–2, Ellis–1, Smith–3; Total Time is 64 days.
20. **b.** Bostock–Southwest
    Miller–Northwest
22. Terry–Client 2, Carle–Client 3, McClymonds–Client 1
24. Toy–2   Auto Parts–4
    Housewares–3   Record–1
26. Toy–4   Auto Parts–1
    Housewares–3   Record–2
28. Washington–B   Benson–D
    Fredricks–C   Hodson–A
30. 1 to D   2 to C   3 to B   4 to A
32. **a.** Cost Matrix ($1,000s)

		Supplier					
		1	2	3	4	5	6
	1	614	660	534	680	590	630
	2	603	639	702	693	693	630
Division	3	865	830	775	850	900	930
	4	532	553	511	581	595	553
	5	720	648	684	693	657	747

   b. S1–D2, S2–D5, S3–D3, S5–D1, S6–D4
34. **c.** Augusta–Albany 50, Augusta–Portsmouth 250
    Tupper Lake–Albany 100, Albany–Philadelphia 150
    Portsmouth–Boston 150, Prtsmouth–New York 100
36. Muncie–Cinti 1, Cinti–Concord 3
    Brazil–Lville. 6, Lville.–Macon 2
    Lville.–Greenwood 4, Xenia–Cinti 5
    Cinti–Chatham 3
            2 rail cars held at Muncie

Chapter 8

2. **b.** $x_1 = 1.43$, $x_2 = 4.29$; its value is 41.47
    $x_1 = 1$, $x_2 = 4$; its value is 37
   c. $x_1 = 0$, $x_2 = 5$; its value is 40
4. **a.** LP Solution: $x_1 = 3.67$, $x_2 = 0.00$; its value is 36.7
    Rounded solution: $x_1 = 3.00$, $x_2 = 0.00$; its value is 30.0
    Lower bound = 30, upper bound is 36.7 (actually an upper bound of 36)
   b. $x_1 = 3$, $x_2 = 2$; its value is 36
   c. LP relaxation: $x_1 = 0$, $x_2 = 5.71$; its value is 34.26
    Rounding down: $x_1 = 0$, $x_2 = 5$ with value 30
    Upper bound = 34.26, lower bound = 30
    Optimal integer: $x_1 = 0$, $x_2 = 5$; its value is 30 or $x_1 = 2$, $x_2 = 4$
6. **b.** $x_1 = 1.96$, $x_2 = 5.48$; its value is 7.44
    Upper bound = 7.44, lower bound = 6.96
   c. $x_1 = 1.29$, $x_2 = 6$; its value is 7.29
8. $x_1 = x_2 = x_3 = 1$ and $x_4 = 0$ with a value of $140,000
10. $x_1 = 0$, $x_2 = 2$, $x_3 = 6\frac{2}{3}$; its value is $10\frac{2}{3}$
14. **a.** $x_1 + x_3 + x_5 + x_6 = 2$
   b. $x_3 - x_5 = 0$
   c. $x_1 + x_4 = 1$

d. $x_4 \le x_1$ $x_4 \le x_3$

e. $x_4 \le x_1$ $x_4 \le x_3$ $x_4 \ge x_1 + x_3 - 1$

16. **b. & c.** $y_9 = 6$, $y_{10} = 2$, $y_{12} = 6$, $y_1 = 1$, and $y_3 = 6$; all other variables are 0

d. $x_9 = 1$, $x_{11} = 4$, $y_9 = 5$, $y_{12} = 5$, $y_3 = 2$; all other variables equal zero

Chapter 9

2.

Node	Shortest Route from Node 7
1	7–6–5–3–1
2	7–4–2
3	7–6–5–3
4	7–4
5	7–6–5
6	7–6

4. 1–4–5–6–8

6.

Node	Shortest Route from Node C
1	C–1
2	C–2
3	C–3
4	C–4
5	C–3–5
6	C–3–6
7	C–3–8–7
8	C–3–8
9	C–4–10–9
10	C–4–10

8. 1–2–8–10–11 or

1–4–3–7–6–9–11;

value = 15

10. length = 38

12. 1–2, 2–5, 5–6, 6–3, 6–8, 3–4, 8–7; length = 29

14. 28 miles

16. 11,000 vehicles per hour

18. a. 10 hours; 10,000 gallons per hour

20. 23; 5

Chapter 10

2. **b.**

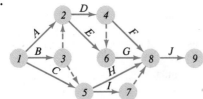

4. **a.** A–D–G

b. No; Time = 15 months

6. **a.** A–D–F–H
    b. 22 weeks
    c. No, it is a critical activity
    d. Yes, 2 weeks
    e. ES = 3, LS = 4, EF = 10, LF = 11
8. **b.** B–C–E–F–H
    d. Yes; Time = 49 weeks

10. **a.**

Activity	Time	Variance
A	5.00	0.11
B	9.00	0.11
C	8.00	0.44
D	8.83	0.25
E	7.17	0.25
F	6.00	0.11

    b. 23.83, 0.47
12. **a.** A–D–H–I
    b. 25.66 days
    c. 0.2578
14. **a.** A–D–F–G
    b. 1.5 days
    c. 29.5, 2.36
    d. 0.6293

16. **a.**

E(T)	Variance
16	3.92
13	2.03
10	1.27

    b. 0.9783, approximately 1.00, approximately 1.00
18. **c.** A–B–D–G–H–I, 14.17 weeks
    d. Yes, P(13 weeks completion) = 0.0951
20. **b.** Crash B(1 week), D(2 weeks), E(1 week), F(1 week), G(1 week)
    Total Cost = $2427
    c. All activities are critical
22. **b.** Crash C(1 day) and E(1 day)
    c. $9300
24. **c.** A–B–C–F, 31 weeks
    d. Crash A(2 weeks), B(2 weeks), C(1 week), D(1 week), E(1 week)
    e. All activities are critical
    f. $112,500

26.

Activity	Cost/Week
A	15
B	8
C	1
D	20
E	2
F	1
G	20
H	5
I	2
J	1

28. **b.** 6% overrun; followup on activity D

30. Corrective action desired
    Activity E—one week behind
    Activity F—$3000 cost overrun

Chapter 11

2. $164.32 for each; Total Cost = $328.64
4. a. 1095.45
  b. 240
  c. 22.82 days
  d. $273.86 for each; Total Cost = $547.72
6. a. 15.95
  b. $2106
  c. 15.04
  d. 16.62 days
8. $Q^* = 11.73$, use 12 classes
  5 classes per year
  $225,200 for 12 classes
10. $Q^* = 1414.21$
  $T = 28.28$ days
  Production runs of 7.07 days
12. $Q^* = 1000$ Total Cost = $1200
  Yes, the change saves $300 per year
14. New $Q^* = 4509$
16. 135.55; $r = dm - S$; less than
18. 64, 24.44
20. $Q^* = 100$; Total Cost = $3,601.50
22. $Q^* = 300$; Savings = $480
24. a. 500
  b. 580.4
26. a. 397
  b. 0.70
  c. 489, 0.35
28. a. 440
  b. 0.60
  c. 7.10
  d. $c_u = 17; Goodwill Cost = $15
30. a. 13.68 (14)
  b. 17.83 (18)
  c. 2, $10; 6, $30
32. a. 31.62
  b. 19.86 (20); .2108
  c. 5, $15
34. a. 243
  b. 93, $54.87
  c. 613
  d. 163, $96.17
  e. Yes; added cost only $41.30 per year
  f. Yes; added cost would be $4,130 per year
36. a. 40
  b. 62.25; 7.9
  c. 54
  d. 36

38. Order 10 engines
Order 7 air cleaners
Order 2 filter housings
40. Order 13 bases
Order 9 wheels
Order 4 tires

Chapter 12

2. a. 0.4512
  b. 0.6988
  c. 0.3012
4. 0.3333, 0.2222, 0.1481, 0.0988, 0.1976
6. a. 0.3333
  b. 1.3333
  c. 0.1111 hours
  d. 0.6667
8. 0.20, 3.2, 4, 3.2, 4, 0.80
  slightly poorer service
10. a. New: 1.3333, 2, 0.6667, 1, 0.6667
    Experience: 0.50, 1, 0.25, 0.50, 0.50
  b. New \$37; Experience \$25; Hire experienced.
12. a. 0.25, 2.25, 3, 0.15 hrs., 0.20 hrs, 0.75
  b. The service needs improvement.
14. a. 0.1667
  b. 5
  c. 0.4167 hours
  d. 0.8333
  e. No
16. a. 0.50
  b. 0.50
  c. 0.10 hours
  d. 0.20 hours
18. a. 0.5385
  b. 0.0593
  c. 0.0099 hours
  d. 0.1099 hours
  2. 0.1384
20. a. 0.2360, 0.1771, 1.5771, 0.0127 hrs., 0.1127 hrs.
  b. P(wait) = 0.2023; prefer 3-channel system

22.

Characteristic	A	B	C
P_o	0.2000	0.5000	0.4286
L_q	3.2000	0.5000	0.1524
L	4.0000	1.0000	0.9524
W_q	0.1333	0.0200	0.0063
W	0.1667	0.0417	0.0397
P_w	0.8000	0.5000	0.2286

(System C provides the best service)

24. a. 0.0466, 0.05
  b. 1.4
  c. 11:00 A.M.

26. **a.** 0.2668, 10 minutes, 0.6667
    b. 0.0667, 7 minutes, 0.4669
    c. $25.33; $33.34; one-channel
28. **a.** 10, 9.6
    b. Design A with $\mu = 10$
    c. .05, .01
    d. A: 0.5, 0.3125, 0.8125, 0.0625, 0.1625, 0.5
       B: 0.4792, 0.2857, 0.8065, 0.0571, 0.1613, 0.5208
    e. Design B is slightly better
30. **a.** 0.1460, 0.3066, 0.3220, 0.2254
    b. 0.2254
    c. 1.6267
    d. 4; 0.1499
32. **a.** 31.04%
    b. 27.58%
    c. 0.2758, 0.1092, 0.0351
    d. 3, 10.92%
34. **a.** 0.4790
    b. 0.3110
    c. 0.8320
    d. 2.9846
    e. 7.9846
    f. 95.8 min; 35.8 min
    g. Yes

Chapter 13

2. **a.**

Number of Arrivals	Relative Frequency
0	.12
1	.24
2	.37
3	.19
4	.08
	1.00

4. **a.** 0, 0, 1, 0, 1, 1
   b. Ave. No. of Arrivals = .5
   c. No, sample is too small
   d. 1.87

6. **a.**

Cars sold	Relative Frequency
0	.04
1	.10
2	.16
3	.44
4	.20
5	.06
	1.00

8. Number served = 3, total profit = $3.75, average profit = $1.25, number lost = 0
14. Preferred order size is 200
18. Average costs: holding − 190.00, order − 12.50, shortage − 0, total − 202.50

Chapter 14

2. b. Optimistic: d_2, conservative: d_1, minimax: d_2

4. a. d_1

  b. d_4

6. d_2 (medium)

8.

Value(s) of p	Best Decision(s)
$0 \le p < 0.3$	d_3
0.3	d_2 or d_3
$0.3 < p < 0.7$	d_2
0.7	d_2 or d_1
$0.7 < p \le 1.0$	d_1

10. $25,000

12. b. d_3

  c. $2150

14. $P(s_1|I) = .1905$, $P(s_2|I) = .2381$, $P(s_3|I) = .5714$

16. a. $P(I_1) = .56$ $P(I_2) = .44$

  b. .57143, .42857, .18182, .81818

18. b. If I_1, then d_1. If I_2, then d_2.
    EV (node 1) = $101.50

  c. EVSI = $1500

20. If unseasonably cold, then purchase snowplow.
   If not unseasonably cold, then purchase blade.

22. a. Yes

  b. p = 0.75

  c. Expected value approach may not be the best approach

  e. If I, then d_1
    If I_2 then d_1
    If I_3 then d_2
    Expected travel time is 26.65 minutes

  f. 60%

24. a.

		Demand (lbs)		
		1000	2000	3000
Amount	1000	50,000	10,000	-30,000
Produced	2000	-50,000	100,000	60,000
(lbs)	3000	-150,000	0	150,000

  b. 2000 lbs

  c. Up to $48,000

  d. If I_1, then d_1
    If I_2, then d_2

  e. EVSI = $3650

  f. 40.6%

26. a. 300 cases

  b. 100 cases

28. a. d_2

  b. A: d_3, B: d_1

  c. Difference in attitude toward risk.

30. a. Do not purchase lottery ticket

  b. Yes

32. a. d_1
   b. Will use $p = 0.90$ as an example
   c. d_2
   d. No
34. a. Market the product
   b. $p =$ probability of $150,000
      $(1-p) =$ probability of - $100,000
   c. Market the product
   d. Yes

Chapter 15

2. a. min $P_1(d_1^-) + P_2(d_2^+)$
   s.t.

$$
\begin{aligned}
50x_1 + 100x_2 &\leq 50{,}000 \\
3x_1 + 10x_2 - d_1^+ + d_1^- &= 4500 \\
x_2 - d_2^+ + d_2^- &= 300 \\
x_1, x_2, d_1^+, d_1^-, d_2^+, d_2^-, &\geq 0
\end{aligned}
$$

   b. $x_1 = 250, x_2 = 375$

4. a. min $P_1(d_1^-) + P_1(d_2^+) + P_2(d_3^-) + P_2(d_4^-) + P_5(d_5^-)$
   s.t.

$$
\begin{aligned}
20x_1 + 30x_2 - d_1^+ + d_1^- &= 1800 \\
20x_1 + 30x_2 - d_2^+ + d_2^- &= 6000 \\
x_1 \qquad - d_3^+ + d_3^- &= 100 \\
x_2 - d_4^+ + d_4^- &= 120 \\
x_1 + x_2 - d_5^+ + d_5^- &= 300 \\
x_1, x_2, \text{ all deviation variables} &\geq 0
\end{aligned}
$$

   b. $x_1 = 120, x_2 = 120$

6. a. Let

   $x_1 =$ number of letters mailed to group 1 customers
   $x_2 =$ number of letters mailed to group 2 customers

   min $P_1(d_1^-) + P_1(d_2^-) + P_2(d_3^+)$
   s.t.

$$
\begin{aligned}
x_1 \qquad - d_1^+ + d_1^- &= 40{,}000 \\
x_2 - d_2^+ + d_2^- &= 50{,}000 \\
x_1 + x_2 - d_3^+ + d_3^- &= 70{,}000 \\
x_1, x_2, \text{ all deviation variables} &\geq 0
\end{aligned}
$$

   b. $x_1 = 40{,}000, x_2 = 50{,}000$
   c. Optimal solution does not change

8. a. min $d_1^- + d_1^+ + e_1^- + e_1^+ + d_2^- + d_2^+ + e_2^- + e_2^+ + d_3^- + d_3^+ + e_3^- + e_3^+$
   s.t.

$$
\begin{aligned}
x_1 \qquad + d_1^- - d_1^+ &= 1 \\
x_2 + e_1^- - e_1^+ &= 7 \\
x_1 \qquad + d_2^- - d_2^+ &= 5 \\
x_2 + e_2^- - e_2^+ &= 9 \\
x_1 \qquad + d_3^- - d_3^+ &= 6 \\
x_2 + e_3^- - e_3^+ &= 2
\end{aligned}
$$

   all variables ≥ 0
   b. $x_1 = 5, x_2 = 7$

10. Since CR $= 0.017$ is less than .10, the degree of consistency exhibited in the pairwise comparison matrix is acceptable.
12. Since CR $= 0.029$ is less than .10, the degree of consistency exhibited in the pairwise comparison matrix is acceptable.

14. a. .723, .193, .083

b. Since CR = 0.055 is less than .10, the degree of consistency exhibited in the pairwise comparison matrix is acceptable.

16. a. .503, .348, .149

b. Since CR = 0.417 is greater than .10, the individual's judgments are not consistent.

18. a.

	D	S	N
D	1	$1/4$	$1/7$
S	4	1	$1/3$
N	7	3	1

b. .080, .265, .655

c. Since CR = .029 is less than .10, the manager's judgments are consistent.

20. b. Criterion: .667, .333
Yield: .75, .25
Risk: .333, .667

c. CCI: .611; SRI: .389

22. b. Criterion: .608, .272, .120
Price: .557, .123, .320
Quality: .137, .240, .623
FM Reception: .579, .187, .234

c. A: .445, B: .163, C: .392

Chapter 16

2. a.

Week	4-Week	5-Week
10	19.00	18.80
11	20.00	19.20
12	18.75	19.00

b. 9.65, 7.41

c. 5-week

4. Weeks 10, 11 and 12: 18.48, 18.63, 18.27
MSE = 9.25; α = .2 is better.

6. b. The more recent data receives the greater weight or importance in determining the forecast

8. a. Month 13: 106.4; MSE = 510.29

b. Month 13: 104.62; MSE = 540.55
Conclusion: a smoothing constant of .3 is better.

10. Forecast for weeks 8, 9, 10 and 11: 258.64, 281.48, 283.61 and 292.71.

12. 3117

14. $T_t = 20{,}746.67 - 351.429t$
Enrollment appears to be decreasing by an average of 351 students per year

16. $T_t = 28{,}800 + 421.429t$

18. a. Linear trend appears to be reasonable.

b. $T_t = 19.993 + 1.774t$
Average cost increase of $1.77 per unit per year

20. a. $T_t = 1997.6 + 397.545t$

b. 6371; 6768

22. $T_8 = 252.28; T_9 = 259.10$

24. a. A linear trend appears to exist.

b. $T_t = -5 + 15t$
Average increase in sales is 15 units per year.

26. **a.** $T_t = 3.9041 + .0236t$
    Personal income increasing at an average of .0236 per month
    b. 4.21, 4.23, 4.26, 4.28, 4.31, 4.33
    c. Actual 4.41 is above the forecast 4.33.
28. .707, .777, .827, .966, 1.016, 1.305, 1.494, 1.225, 0.976, 0.986, 0.936, 0.787
30. **a.** Selected centered moving averages for
    $t = 5, 10, 15$ and 20 are 11.125, 18.125, 22.875 and 27.000.
    b. 0.899, 1.362, 1.118, 0.621
    c. Quarter 2, prior to summer boating season.
32. **a.** $T_t = 6.329 + 1.055t$
    b. 36.92, 37.98, 39.03, 40.09
    c. 33.23, 51.65, 43.71, 24.86

Chapter 17

2. **b.** $\pi_1 = 0.5, \pi_2 = 0.5$
   c. $\pi_1 = 0.6, \pi_2 = 0.4$
4. **a.** $\pi_1 = 0.92, \pi_2 = 0.08$
   b. $85
6. **a.** MDA
   b. $\pi_1 = \frac{1}{3}, \pi_2 = \frac{2}{3}$
8. $3 - 1 (0.59), 4 - 1 (0.52)$
10. 1420 will be lost

Chapter 18

2. **a.** $1 - 4 - 6 - 9 - 10$
   b. $4 - 6 - 9 - 10$
4. **a.** Set up a stage for each possible length of the log
   b. Create a stage for every lenegth
6. $200 - 3,200 - 2,100 - 1 (\$2900)$
8. **a.** $d_1 = 200, d_2 = 300, d_3 = 500$
   b. Same as part a
10. 800°F catalyst C_2, separator S_1, weekly profit = $4470

Chapter 19

2. **a.** $\frac{40}{9}$
   b. 4
4. 4 ($540)
6. **a.** $20
   b. $-x^2 + 20x - 20$
   c. 10
8. $x_1 = 0, x_2 = 2$ is a saddle point
   $x_1 = 2, x_2 = -2$ is a local minimum
   $x_1 = -2, x_2 = -2$ is a local minimum
10. $x_1 = 6, x_2 = 3$ ($40,000 earnings)
12. Provides maximum solution
14. $x_1 = \frac{4}{\sqrt{34/5}}, x_2 = \frac{3}{\sqrt{34/5}}$ (minimum)

    $x_1 = \frac{-4}{\sqrt{34/5}}, x_2 = \frac{-3}{\sqrt{34/5}}$ (maximum)
16. $x_1 = \frac{36}{13}, x_2 = \frac{2}{13}$

Index